Birnbaum's 95
Italy

A BIRNBAUM TRAVEL GUIDE

Alexandra Mayes Birnbaum
EDITORIAL CONSULTANT

Lois Spritzer
Editorial Director

Laura L. Brengelman
Managing Editor

Mary Callahan
Senior Editor

David Appell
Patricia Canole
Gene Gold
Jill Kadetsky
Susan McClung
Associate Editors

HarperPerennial
A Division of HarperCollins*Publishers*

For Giovanna and Luca Salvadore, who are responsible for so many of our most memorable moments in Italy.

BIRNBAUM'S ITALY 95. Copyright © 1995 by HarperCollins Publishers.
All rights reserved. Printed in the United States of America. No part of this book may be used or reproduced in any manner whatsoever without written permission except in the case of brief quotations embodied in critical articles and reviews. For information address HarperCollins*Publishers*, 10 East 53rd Street, New York, NY 10022.

FIRST EDITION

ISSN 0749-2561 (Birnbaum Travel Guides)
ISSN 0890-1139 (Italy)
ISBN 0-06-278194-4 (pbk.)

95 96 97 ❖/CW 5 4 3 2 1

Cover design © Drenttel Doyle Partners
Cover photograph © Art Wolfe/AllStock
Entry, Verrazano Castle, Chianti Region of Tuscany

BIRNBAUM TRAVEL GUIDES

Bahamas, and Turks & Caicos
Berlin
Bermuda
Boston
Canada
Cancun, Cozumel & Isla Mujeres
Caribbean
Chicago
Country Inns and Back Roads
Disneyland
Eastern Europe
Europe
Europe for Business Travelers
France
Germany
Great Britain
Hawaii
Ireland
Italy
London
Los Angeles
Mexico
Miami & Ft. Lauderdale
Montreal & Quebec City
New Orleans
New York
Paris
Portugal
Rome
San Francisco
Santa Fe & Taos
South America
Spain
United States
USA for Business Travelers
Walt Disney World
Walt Disney World for Kids, By Kids
Washington, DC

Contributing Editors

Burton Anderson
Maria Grazia Asselle
Frederick H. Brengelman
Stephanie Curtis
Karen Marie Ebersold
Sari Gilbert
Marilyn Green
Judith Harris
Anthony Iannacci
Theordora Lurie
Diane Melville
Michael Mewshaw
Roderick Conway Morris
Linda Parseghian
Clare Pedrick
Peter Rosenwald
Patricia Schultz
Phoebe Tait
Robert Tine
David Wickers
Faith Heller Willinger
Nancy Wolfson
Anne Marshall Zwack

Maps

B. Andrew Mudryk

Contents

Getting Ready to Go

Practical information for planning your trip.

The Cities

Thorough, qualitative guides to each of the 13 cities most often visited by vacationers and businesspeople. Each section offers a comprehensive report on the city's most compelling attractions and amenities—highlighting our top choices in every category.

Diversions

*A selective guide to active and/or cerebral vacation
themes, pinpointing the best places to pursue them.*

Unexpected Pleasures and Treasures

For the Experience

For the Mind

For the Body

Directions

The most spectacular routes and roads; most arresting natural wonders; and most magnificent palazzos, villas, and gardens—all organized into 20 specific driving tours.

Glossary

Foreword

In the course of our roamings around Italy to collect data for this guide, it became increasingly obvious that "Italians" are a rare species. Oh, we found lots of folks who were enthusiastic about describing themselves as Venetian, Milanese, Roman, or Neapolitan, but almost no one who would characterize himself or herself as an Italian. This is hardly inexplicable in a nation that became unified only as recently as 1870, and where regional distinctions are such a source of local pride and delight, and occasionally, divisiveness.

Our guidebook contradicts the fiction that Italy is any sort of homogeneous country, a nation with a single face and similar sensitivities stretching from Sicily to the Swiss border. As anyone who has traveled widely in Italy soon discovers, nothing could be further from the truth. The atmosphere and ambience that thrive across the length of the Italian peninsula are spectacularly varied, and in trying to provide an accurate guide to each distinct region, the travel editor often feels as though at least a dozen distinct countries are demanding attention—not entirely incomprehensible, since about that number of sovereign city-states once occupied the boundaries of what modern maps now cavalierly call Italy.

That's why we've tried to create a guide to Italy that's specifically organized, written, and edited for today's demanding traveler, one for whom qualitative information is infinitely more desirable than mere quantities of unappraised data. We realize that it's impossible for any single travel writer to visit thousands of restaurants (and nearly as many hotels) in any given year and provide accurate appraisals of each. And even if it were physically possible for one human being to survive such an itinerary, it would of necessity have to be done at a dead sprint, and the perceptions derived therefrom would probably be less valid than those of any other intelligent individual visiting the same establishments. It is, therefore, both impractical and undesirable (especially in a large, annually revised and updated guidebook *series* such as we offer) to have only one person provide all the data on the entire world. Instead, we have chosen what we like to describe as the "thee and me" approach to restaurant and hotel evaluation and, to a somewhat more limited degree, to the sites and sights we have included in the other sections of our text. What this really reflects is a personal sampling tempered by intelligent counsel from informed local sources.

This guidebook is directed to the "visitor," and such elements as restaurants have been specifically picked to provide the visitor with a representative, enlightening, and, above all, pleasant experience. Since so many extraneous considerations can affect the reception and service accorded a regular restaurant patron, our choices can in no way be construed as an exhaustive guide to resident dining. We think we've listed all the best places, in various price ranges, but they were chosen with a visitor's enjoyment in mind.

Other evidence of how we've tried to tailor our text to reflect changing travel habits is apparent in the section we call DIVERSIONS. Where once it was common for travelers to spend a foreign visit seeing only the obvious sights, today's traveler is more likely to want to pursue a special interest or to venture off the beaten path. In response to this trend, we have collected a series of special experiences so that it is no longer necessary to wade through a pound or two of superfluous prose just to find exceptional pleasures and treasures.

Finally, I also should point out that every good travel guide is a living enterprise; that is, no part of this text is carved in stone. In our annual revisions, we refine, expand, and further hone all our material to serve your travel needs better. To this end, no contribution is of greater value to us than your personal reaction to what we have written, as well as information reflecting your own experiences while using the book. Please write to us at 10 E. 53rd St., New York, NY 10022.

We sincerely hope to hear from you.

Alexandra Mayes Birnbaum

ALEXANDRA MAYES BIRNBAUM, editorial consultant to the *Birnbaum Travel Guides*, worked with her late husband, Stephen Birnbaum, as co-editor of the series. She has been a world traveler since childhood and is known for her travel reports on radio on what's hot and what's not.

Italy

ITALY

Sicily

Tyrrhenian Sea

Lipari Islands

Stromboli I.
Ustica I.
Panarea I.
Salina I.
Aliculi I.
Filicudi
Lipari I.
Vulcano I.

CALABRIA
Crotone
Catanzaro
Tropea
Pizzo
Vibo
Valentia
Nicotera
Gioia
Tauro
Palmi
Bagnara
Gerace
Scilla
Villa S.
Giovanni
Locri
Bova

S. Vito
lo Capo
Capo
d'Orlando
S. Stefano di
Camastro
Milazzo
Messina
Reggio
di
Calabria

Palermo
Solunto
Bagheria
Naso
Erice
Monreale
Alcamo
Cefalù
Mistretta
Taormina
Egadi
Is.
Trapani
Segesta
Termini
Imerese
Marsala
Castelvetrano
Selinunte
Sciacca
Enna
Calascibetta
Mt. Etna
Acireale
Catania
Caltanissetta
Agrigento
Favara
Naro
Piazza
Armerina
Morgantina
Caltagirone
Gela
Palazzolo
Acreide
Augusta
Syracuse
Floridia
Noto
Ragusa
Modica
Ispica

SICILY
Ionian
Sea

Pantelleria

Miles 50
km 50

Elba

Miles 10
km 10
Piombino

Ligurian Sea
Cavo
Marciana
Bidola
Portoferraio
Rio
Marina
Porto Azzurro
Marina
di Campo
Capoliveri
Tyrrhenian Sea

Ischia

Tyrrhenian Sea
Lacco
Ameno
Ischia
Porto
Forio
Mt.
Epomeo
Ischia
Ponte
Sant'
Angelo
Bay
of Naples
Miles 3
km

BOSNIA
AND
HERZEGOVINA

CROATIA

Adriatic Sea

Pescara
Chieti
Tremiti Is.
Vico del
Gargano
Casseroli
ABRUZZO
NAT. PARK
Agnone
Termoli
GARGANO
MTS.
Vieste
S. Giovanni
Rotondo
Mattinata
Monte
Sant'Angelo
Manfredonia
ernia
Campobasso
Foggia
serta
oles
Benevento
Herculaneum
Pompei
Avellino
Trani
Barletta
Molfetta
Andria
Bari
Castel
del Monte
Terlizzi
Mola di Bari
Salerno
Eboli
Amalfi
Coast
Potenza
Polignano
Monopoli
Alberobello
Matera
Ostuni
Paestum
Agropoli
Ferrandina
Castellaneta
Martina
Franca
Ceglie
Brindisi
Stigliano
Pisticci
Taranto
Lecce
BASILICATA
Chiaromonte
Scanzano
Metaponto
Porto
Cesareo
Otranto
Camerota
Scario
Sapri
Lauria
Gallipoli
Maglie
Palinuro
Maratea
Praia a Mare
Scalea
Maratea
Porto
Gulf of Taranto
Diamante
Belvedere
Terme
Luigiane
Camigliatello
Longobucco
Lor ca
S. Giovanni
in Fiore
Paola
Cosenza
CALABRIA
Crotone
Ionian
Sea

Capri

Bay of Naples
Blue
Grotto
Anacapri
Marina
Grande
Mt.
Solaro
Capri
Marina
Piccola
Pta Tragara
Gulf
of Salerno
Miles 2
km 2

Continuation of the main map

Map continues on the inset above

How to Use This Guide

A great deal of care has gone into the organization of this guidebook, and we believe it represents a real breakthrough in the presentation of travel material. Our goal is to create a more modern generation of travel books, and to make this guide the most useful and practical travel tool available today.

Our text is divided into five basic sections in order to present information in the best way on every possible aspect of a vacation to Italy. Our aim is to highlight what's where and to provide basic information—how, when, where, how much, and what's best—to assist you in making the most intelligent choices possible.

Here is a brief summary of what you can expect to find in each section. We believe that you will find both your travel planning and en-route enjoyment enhanced by having this book at your side.

GETTING READY TO GO

A mini-encyclopedia of practical travel facts with all the precise data necessary to create a successful trip to Italy. Here you will find how to get where you're going, currency information and exchange rates, plus selected resources—including pertinent publications, and companies and organizations specializing in discount and special-interest travel—providing a wealth of information and assistance useful both before and during your trip.

THE CITIES

Individual reports on the 13 cities in Italy most visited by travelers and businesspeople offer a short-stay guide, including an essay introducing the city as a historic entity and a contemporary place to visit; *At-a-Glance* contains a site-by-site survey of the most important, interesting, and unique sights to see and things to do; *Sources and Resources* is a concise listing of pertinent tourist information, such as the address of the local tourism office, which sightseeing tours to take, where to find the best nightspot, to play golf, or to get a taxi. *Best in Town* lists our cost-and-quality choices of the best places to eat and sleep on a variety of budgets.

DIVERSIONS

This section is designed to help travelers find the best places in which to engage in a variety of exceptional experiences for the mind and body without having to wade through endless pages of unrelated text. In every case, our particular suggestions are intended to guide you to that special place where the quality of experience is likely to be the highest.

DIRECTIONS

Here are 28 itineraries that range all across Italy, along the most beautiful routes and roads, past the most spectacular natural wonders, and through the most historic cities and countryside. DIRECTIONS is the only section of this book that is organized geographically, and its itineraries cover the touring highlights of Italy in short, independent journeys of five to seven days' duration. Itineraries can be "connected" for longer sojourns or used individually for short, intensive explorations.

GLOSSARY

This compendium of helpful travel information includes a climate chart, a weights and measures table, and *Useful Words and Phrases,* a brief introduction to the Italian language that will help you to make a hotel or dinner reservation, order a meal, mail a letter, and even buy toothpaste in Italy. Though most large hotels, restaurants, and attractions in major Italian cities have English-speaking staff, at smaller establishments and in rural, out-of-the-way towns and villages, a little knowledge of Italian will go a long way.

To use this book to full advantage, take a few minutes to read the table of contents and random entries in each section to get a firsthand feel for how it all fits together. You will find that the sections of this book are building blocks designed to help you put together the best possible trip. Use them selectively as a tool, a source of ideas, a reference work for accurate facts, and a guidebook to the best buys, the most exciting sights, the most pleasant accommodations, the tastiest foods—*the best travel experience* that you can possibly have.

Getting
Ready to Go

Getting Ready to Go

When to Go

Much of Italy is blessed with a Mediterranean climate, with dry, warm summers and mild winters. In the north—particularly near the Alps and the Apennines—the weather is more typically continental, with colder winters. With the exception of mountainous regions, snow is rare, although there is plenty of rain, especially from October through December.

The period from mid-May to mid-September has long been—and remains—the peak travel period, traditionally the most popular vacation time. Travel during the off-season (roughly November to *Easter*) and shoulder seasons (the months immediately before and after the peak months) offers relatively fair weather and smaller crowds. During these periods, travel also can be less expensive.

If you have a touch-tone phone, you can call *The Weather Channel Connection* (phone: 900-WEATHER) for current worldwide weather forecasts. This service, available from *The Weather Channel* (2600 Cumberland Pkwy., Atlanta, GA 30339; phone: 404-434-6800), costs 95¢ per minute; the charge will appear on your phone bill.

Traveling by Plane

SCHEDULED FLIGHTS

Leading airlines offering flights between the US and Italy include *Air France, Alitalia, American, Austrian Airlines, British Airways, Delta, Iberia, KLM, Lufthansa, Sabena, SAS, SwissAir, TAP Air Portugal, TWA,* and *United.*

FARES The great variety of airfares can be reduced to the following basic categories: first class, business class, coach (also called economy or tourist class), excursion or discount, and standby, as well as various promotional fares. For information on applicable fares and restrictions, contact the airlines listed above or ask your travel agent. Most airfares are offered for a limited time. Once you've found the lowest fare for which you can qualify, purchase your ticket as soon as possible.

RESERVATIONS Reconfirmation is strongly recommended for all international flights. It is essential that you confirm your round-trip reservations—*especially the return leg*—as well as any flights within Europe.

SEATING Airline seats usually are assigned on a first-come, first-served basis at check-in, although you may be able to reserve a seat when purchasing your ticket. Seating charts sometimes are available from airlines and also are included in the *Airline Seating Guide* (Carlson Publishing Co., 11132 Los Alamitos Blvd., Los Alamitos, CA 90720; phone: 310-493-4877).

SMOKING US law prohibits smoking on flights scheduled for six hours or less within the US and its territories on both domestic and international carriers. These restrictions do not apply to nonstop flights between the US and international destinations, and at press time, major carriers allowed smoking on all flights to Italy. If the flight includes European connections, however, smoking may not be permitted on the intra-European leg of the trip. A free wallet-size guide that describes the rights of nonsmokers under current regulations is available from *ASH* (*Action on Smoking and Health;* DOT Card, 2013 H St. NW, Washington, DC 20006; phone: 202-659-4310).

SPECIAL MEALS When making your reservation, you can request one of the airline's alternate menu choices for no additional charge. Though not always required, it's a good idea to reconfirm your request the day before departure.

BAGGAGE On major international airlines, passengers usually are allowed to carry on board one bag that will fit under a seat or in an overhead bin and to check two bags in the cargo hold. Specific regulations regarding dimensions and weight restrictions vary among airlines, but a checked bag usually cannot exceed 62 inches in combined dimensions (length, width, and depth), or weigh more than 70 pounds. There may be charges for additional, oversize, or overweight luggage, and for special equipment or sporting gear. Note that baggage allowances may be more limited on domestic flights abroad. Check that the tags the airline attaches are correctly coded for your destination.

CHARTER FLIGHTS

By booking a block of seats on a specially arranged flight, charter operators frequently can offer travelers bargain airfares. If you do fly on a charter, however, read the contract's fine print carefully. Federal regulations permit charter operators to cancel a flight or assess surcharges of as much as 10% of the airfare up to 10 days before departure. You usually must book in advance, and once booked, no changes are permitted, so buy trip cancellation insurance. Also, make your check out to the company's escrow account, which provides some protection for your investment in the event that the charter operator fails. For further information, consult the publication *Jax Fax* (397 Post Rd., Darien, CT 06820; phone: 203-655-8746; fax: 203-655-6257).

DISCOUNTS ON SCHEDULED FLIGHTS

COURIER TRAVEL In return for arranging to accompany some kind of freight, a traveler pays only a portion of the total airfare (and sometimes a small registration fee). One agency that matches up would-be couriers with courier companies is *Now Voyager* (74 Varick St., Suite 307, New York, NY 10013; phone: 212-431-1616; fax: 212-334-5243).

Courier Companies

Discount Travel International (169 W. 81st St., New York, NY 10024; phone: 212-362-3636; fax: 212-362-3236; and 801 Alton Rd., Suite 1, Miami Beach, FL 33139; phone: 305-538-1616; fax: 305-673-9376).

F.B. On Board Courier Club (10225 Ryan Ave., Suite 103, Dorval, Quebec H9P 1A2, Canada; phone: 514-633-0740; fax: 514-633-0735).

Halbart Express (147-05 176th St., Jamaica, NY 11434; phone: 718-656-8279; fax: 718-244-0559).

Midnite Express (925 W. Hyde Park Blvd., Inglewood, CA 90302; phone: 310-672-1100; fax: 310-671-0107).

Way to Go Travel (6679 Sunset Blvd., Hollywood, CA 90028; phone: 213-466-1126; fax: 213-466-8994).

Publications

Insiders Guide to Air Courier Bargains, by Kelly Monaghan (The Intrepid Traveler, PO Box 438, New York, NY 10034; phone: 212-569-1081 for information; 800-356-9315 for orders; fax: 212-942-6687).

Travel Unlimited (PO Box 1058, Allston, MA 02134-1058; no phone).

CONSOLIDATORS AND BUCKET SHOPS These companies buy blocks of tickets from airlines and sell them at a discount to travel agents or directly to consumers. Since many bucket shops operate on a thin margin, be sure to check a company's record with the *Better Business Bureau*—before parting with any money.

Council Charter (205 E. 42nd St., New York, NY 10017; phone: 800-800-8222 or 212-661-0311; fax: 212-972-0194).

International Adventures (60 E. 42nd St., Room 763, New York, NY 10165; phone: 212-599-0577; fax: 212-599-3288).

Travac Tours and Charters (989 Ave. of the Americas, New York, NY 10018; phone: 800-872-8800 or 212-563-3303; fax: 212-563-3631).

Unitravel (1177 N. Warson Rd., St. Louis, MO 63132; phone: 800-325-2222 or 314-569-0900; fax: 314-569-2503).

LAST-MINUTE TRAVEL CLUBS Members of such clubs receive information on imminent trips and other bargain travel opportunities. There usually is an annual fee, although a few clubs offer free membership. Despite the names of some of the clubs listed below, you don't have to wait until literally the last minute to make travel plans.

Discount Travel International (114 Forrest Ave., Suite 203, Narberth, PA 19072; phone: 215-668-7184; fax: 215-668-9182).

FLY ASAP (PO Box 9808, Scottsdale, AZ 85252-3808; phone: 800-FLY-ASAP or 602-956-1987; fax: 602-956-6414).

Last Minute Travel (1249 Boylston St., Boston, MA 02215; phone: 800-LAST-MIN or 617-267-9800; fax: 617-424-1943).

Moment's Notice (425 Madison Ave., New York, NY 10017; phone: 212-486-0500/1/2/3; fax: 212-486-0783).

Spur of the Moment Cruises (411 N. Harbor Blvd., Suite 302, San Pedro, CA 90731; phone: 800-4-CRUISES or 310-521-1070 in California; 800-343-1991 elsewhere in the US; 24-hour hotline: 310-521-1060; fax: 310-521-1061).

Traveler's Advantage (3033 S. Parker Rd., Suite 900, Aurora, CO 80014; phone: 800-548-1116 or 800-835-8747; fax: 303-368-3985).

Vacations to Go (1502 Augusta Dr., Suite 415, Houston, TX 77057; phone: 713-974-2121 in Texas; 800-338-4962 elsewhere in the US; fax: 713-974-0445).

Worldwide Discount Travel Club (1674 Meridian Ave., Miami Beach, FL 33139; phone: 305-534-2082; fax: 305-534-2070).

GENERIC AIR TRAVEL These organizations operate much like an ordinary airline standby service, except that they offer seats on not one but several scheduled and charter airlines. One pioneer of generic flights is *Airhitch* (2790 Broadway, Suite 100, New York, NY 10025; phone: 212-864-2000).

BARTERED TRAVEL SOURCES Barter—the exchange of commodities or services in lieu of cash payment—is a common practice among travel suppliers. Companies that have obtained travel services through barter may sell these services at substantial discounts to travel clubs, who pass along the savings to members. One organization offering bartered travel opportunities is *Travel World Leisure Club* (225 W. 34th St., Suite 909, New York, NY 10122; phone: 800-444-TWLC or 212-239-4855; fax: 212-564-5158).

CONSUMER PROTECTION

Passengers whose complaints have not been satisfactorily addressed by the airline can contact the *US Department of Transportation* (*DOT;* Consumer Affairs Division, 400 Seventh St. SW, Room 10405, Washington, DC 20590; phone: 202-366-2220). Also see *Fly Rights* (Publication #050-000-00513-5; *US Government Printing Office,* PO Box 371954, Pittsburgh, PA 15250-7954; phone: 202-783-3238; fax: 202-512-2250). If you have safety-related questions or concerns, write to the *Federal Aviation Administration* (*FAA;* 800 Independence Ave. SW, Washington, DC 20591) or call the *FAA Consumer Hotline* (phone: 800-322-7873). If you have a complaint against a local travel service in Italy, contact the Italian tourist authorities.

Traveling by Ship

Your cruise fare usually includes all meals, recreational activities, and entertainment. Shore excursions are available at extra cost, and can be booked in advance or once you're on board. An important factor in the price of a cruise is the location (and sometimes the size) of your cabin. Charts issued by the *Cruise Lines International Association* (*CLIA;* 500 Fifth Ave., Suite 1407, New York, NY 10110; phone: 212-921-0066; fax: 212-921-0549) provide information on ship layouts and facilities and are available at some *CLIA*-affiliated travel agencies.

The *US Public Health Service (PHS)* inspects all passenger vessels calling at US ports; for the most recent summary or a particular inspection report, write to Chief, Vessel Sanitation Program, *National Center for Environmental Health* (1015 N. America Way, Room 107, Miami, FL 33132; phone: 305-536-4307). Most cruise ships have a doctor on board, plus medical facilities.

For further information on cruises and cruise lines, consult *Ocean and Cruise News* (PO Box 92, Stamford, CT 06904; phone/fax: 203-329-2787). And for a free list of travel agencies specializing in cruises, contact the *National Association of Cruise Only Agencies* (*NACOA;* 3191 Coral Way, Suite 630, Miami, FL 33145; phone: 305-446-7732; fax: 305-446-9732).

A potentially less expensive alternative to cruise ships is travel by freighter—cargo ships that also transport a limited number of passengers. For information, consult the *Freighter Travel Club of America* (3524 Harts Lake Rd., Roy, WA 98580; no phone), *Freighter World Cruises* (180 S. Lake Ave., Suite 335, Pasadena, CA 91101; phone: 818-449-3106; fax: 818-449-9573), *Pearl's Travel Tips* (9903 Oaks La., Seminole, FL 34642; phone: 813-393-2919; fax: 813-392-2580), and *TravLtips Cruise and Freighter Travel Association* (PO Box 188, 163-07 Depot Rd., Flushing, NY 11358; phone: 800-872-8584 or 718-939-2400; fax: 718-939-2047).

Numerous ferries connect the mainland and Italy's two major islands, Sicily and Sardinia, as well as several smaller islands, including Lipari, Stromboli, Panarea, Vulcano, Ustica, Favignana, and Pantelleria. Nearly all of them carry both passengers and cars and most routes are in service year-round.

International Cruise Lines

Chandris Celebrity and *Chandris Fantasy Cruises* (5200 Blue Lagoon Dr., Miami, FL 33126; phone: 800-437-3111 or 305-262-6677; fax: 305-262-2677).

Classical Cruises (132 E. 70th St., New York, NY 10021; phone: 800-252-7745 or 212-794-3200; fax: 212-517-4735).

Club Med (3 E. 54th St., New York, NY 10022; phone: 800-CLUB-MED or 212-750-1687; fax: 212-750-1697).

Costa Cruises (80 SW Eighth St., Miami, FL 33130; phone: 800-462-6782 or 305-358-7325; fax: 305-375-0676).

Crystal Cruises (2121 Ave. of the Stars, Los Angeles, CA 90067; phone: 800-446-6620 or 310-785-9300; fax: 310-785-0011).

Cunard (555 Fifth Ave., New York, NY 10017; phone: 800-5-CUNARD or 800-221-4770; fax: 718-786-0038).

Epirotiki Lines (901 South America Way, Miami, FL 33132; phone: 800-221-2470 or 305-358-1910; fax: 305-358-4807).

EuroCruises (303 W. 13th St., New York, NY 10014; phone: 800-688-3876 or 212-691-2099; fax: 212-366-4747).

Holland America Line (300 Elliot Ave. W., Seattle, WA 98119; phone: 800-426-0327; fax: 800-628-4855).

P&O Cruises (c/o *Golden Bear Travel,* 16 Digital Dr., Suite 100, Novato, CA 94948; phone: 800-551-1000 or 415-382-8900; fax: 415-382-9086).

Princess Cruises (10100 Santa Monica Blvd., Los Angeles, CA 90067; phone: 800-421-0522; fax: 310-284-2844).

Raymond & Whitcomb (400 Madison Ave., New York, NY 10017; phone: 212-759-3960 in New York State; 800-245-9005 elsewhere in the US; fax: 212-935-1644).

Regency Cruises (260 Madison Ave., New York, NY 10016; phone: 212-972-4774 in New York State; 800-388-5500 elsewhere in the US; fax: 800-388-8833).

Renaissance Cruises (1800 Eller Dr., Suite 300, Ft. Lauderdale, FL 33316; phone: 800-525-2450; fax: 800-243-2987 or 305-463-8125).

Royal Caribbean Cruise Lines (1050 Caribbean Way, Miami, FL 33132; phone: 800-432-6559 in Florida; 800-327-6700 elsewhere in the US; fax: 800-722-5329).

Royal Cruise Line (1 Maritime Plaza, Suite 1400, San Francisco, CA 94111; phone: 800-792-2992 in California; 800-227-4534 elsewhere in the US; fax: 415-956-1656).

Royal Viking Line (95 Merrick Way, Coral Gables, FL 33134; phone: 800-422-8000; fax: 305-448-1398).

Seabourn Cruise Line (55 Francisco St., Suite 710, San Francisco, CA 94133; phone: 800-929-9595 or 415-391-7444; fax: 415-391-8518).

SSC Radisson Diamond Cruise (11340 Blondo St., Omaha, NE 68164; phone: 800-333-3333; fax: 402-498-5055).

Sun Line (1 Rockefeller Plaza, Suite 315, New York, NY 10020; phone: 800-872-6400 or 212-397-6400; fax: 212-765-9685).

Swan Hellenic Cruises (c/o *Esplanade Tours,* 581 Boylston St., Boston, MA 02116; phone: 800-426-5492 or 617-266-7465; fax: 617-262-9829).

Windstar Cruises (300 Elliott Ave. W., Seattle, WA 98119; phone: 800-258-7245; fax: 206-281-0627).

Freighter Companies

Lykes Lines (Lykes Center, 300 Poydras, New Orleans, LA 70130; phone: 504-528-1400 in Louisiana; 800-535-1861 elsewhere in the US; fax: 504-528-1420).

Mediterranean Great Lakes Line (c/o *Freighter World Cruises;* address above).

Mineral Shipping (c/o *Freighter World Cruises;* address above).

Ferry Companies

Adriatica (c/o *Extra Value Travel,* 683 S. Collier Blvd., Marco Island, FL 33937; phone: 813-394-3384; fax: 813-394-4848).

Aliscafi SNAV (10 Via Francesca Caracciolo, Naples 80122, Italy; phone: 39-81-761-2348; fax: 39-81-761-2141).

Caremar (Molo Beverello, Naples 80133, Italy; phone: 39-81-551-3882; fax: 39-81-551-4551).

Corsica-Sardinia-Elba Ferries (Porta Andrea Doria, Genoa 16100, Italy; phone: 39-10-593301; fax: 39-10-593774).

Grimaldi Siosa Compagnia di Navigazione e Crociere (13 Via Campo d'Isola, Naples 80127, Italy; phone: 39-81-469111; fax: 39-81-551-7716, 39-81-551-7401, or 39-81-551-7323).

Navarma (4 Viale Elba, Portoferraio 57037, Italy; phone: 39-565-914133; fax: 39-565-917758).

Samer Shipping (3 Via Luigi Einaudi, Trieste 34121, Italy; phone: 39-40-7354).

Siremar (118 Via Francesco Crispi, Palermo 90139, Italy; phone: 39-91-582403; fax: 39-91-327147).

Tirrenia (c/o *Extra Value Travel,* address above).

Toremar (8 Via Calafate, Livorno 57100, Italy; phone: 39-586-825511; fax: 39-586-025624).

Traveling by Train

The government-owned and -operated *Ferrovie Italiane dello Stato (FS)*— also known as *Italian State Railways*—is among the least expensive railway systems in Europe. *Italian State Railways* trains include *EuroCity (EC)*, *InterCity (IC*—such as the high-speed *Pendolino*), express, local, and car-carrying trains (called *Trasporto a Bagaglio di Auto al Seguito del Viaggiatore*).

Most trains have both first and second class cars. Food service ranges from traditional dining cars to vendors dispensing sandwiches, snacks, and beverages aboard trains or on station platforms. Overnight accommodations include *couchettes* (coach seats of a compartment converted to sleeping berths) and *vetture-letti,* or sleepers (bedroom compartments providing one to three beds). Luggage often can be placed just inside the doors; otherwise, you can use the overhead racks. It is best to travel light, as most domestic Italian trains do not have baggage cars, and you usually cannot send your luggage ahead as registered baggage. (Some *EuroCity* trains crossing the Italian border do have baggage cars—check in advance.) Also, porters and self-service luggage carts are both in short supply at most stations.

Reservations are required for some trains (such as the *Pendolino*) and advisable on all trains during the summer months and holidays, as well as on popular routes. Note that seats for some types of local service cannot be reserved, and no reservations are accepted for trains departing a few days before *Christmas* and *Easter*—with the exception of those for which reservations are mandatory.

Seat purchases for most *EuroCity* and *InterCity* trains require payment of an additional fee, called a "supplement." Children under four travel free if not occupying a seat, and children ages four through 11 travel at half price. Various discount excursion tickets and rail passes are available, including the Eurailpass (which covers train travel throughout much of Europe) and the Europass (a more limited version of the Eurailpass), as well as the Italian Tourist Ticket (*Biglietto Turistico di Libera Circolazione* or *BTLC*) and other domestic Italian rail passes. Note that most rail passes must be purchased before you leave the US.

You can reserve and purchase tickets or passes in the US through travel agents, through the US offices of *Compagnia Italiana Turismo* (*CIT;* 6033 W. Century Blvd., Suite 980, Los Angeles, CA 90045; phone: 800-CIT-RAIL or 310-338-8620; fax: 310-670-4269; and 342 Madison Ave., Suite 207, New York, NY 10173; phone: 800-CIT-RAIL, 800-248-8687, or 212-697-2100; fax: 212-697-1394), or through *Rail Europe* (phone: 800-4-EURAIL; fax: 800-432-1329), which represents various European rail lines. In Italy, tickets can be purchased at train stations, *CIT* offices, and other travel agencies displaying the *FS* sign, as well as aboard trains—usually for a surcharge.

For travelers seeking a truly luxurious train trip, the *Venice Simplon–Orient Express,* which features sumptuously restored 1920s carriages, runs between Venice and London twice weekly from mid-February to mid-November. For more information, contact the *Venice Simplon–Orient Express* (c/o *Abercrombie & Kent,* 1520 Kensington Rd., Oak Brook, IL 60521; phone: 800-524-2420 or 708-954-2944; fax: 708-954-3324). Packaged rail tours in Italy are offered by other companies, including *Accent on Travel* (112 N. Fifth St., Klamath Falls, OR 97601; phone: 503-885-7330), which also sells Eurailpasses, domestic Italian rail passes, and individual tickets.

FURTHER INFORMATION

Useful information about European rail travel, including rail passes, is provided in *Europe on Track* and other publications available from *Rail Europe* (phone above). The *Thomas Cook European Timetable,* a compendium of European rail services, is available in bookstores and from the *Forsyth Travel*

Library (9154 W. 57th St., PO Box 2975, Shawnee Mission, KS 66201-1375; phone: 800-367-7984 or 913-384-3440; fax: 913-384-3553). Other useful resources include the *Eurail Guide,* by Kathryn Turpin and Marvin Saltzman (Eurail Guide Annual, 27540 Pacific Coast Hwy., Malibu, CA 90265; no phone) and *Europe by Eurail,* by George and LaVerne Ferguson (Globe Pequot Press, 6 Business Park Rd., PO Box 833, Old Saybrook, CT 06475; phone: 203-395-0440; fax: 203-395-0312).

In major Italian train stations, a large timetable display, called an *"orario ferroviario,"* indicates arrivals *(arrivi)* and departures *(partenze).* Train schedules also are posted near the tracks in most stations, and there are racks with printed timetables. In addition, some stations have computer terminals which provide scheduling information when the user types in the point of departure and destination. Signs displaying standardized pictorial codes indicate the various amenities (telephones, restrooms, and so on) available at each station.

Traveling by Car

If you plan to visit only larger Italian cities, a car is not a good idea because of the many pedestrians, one-way streets, and frequently heavy traffic. However, driving is the most flexible way to explore the Italian countryside.

To drive in Italy, a US citizen needs a US driver's license and an International Driver's Permit (IDP). The IDP—essentially a translation of your license into nine languages—can be obtained from US branches or the main office of the *American Automobile Association (AAA;* for locations, check the yellow pages or contact the main office: 1000 AAA Dr., Heathrow, FL 32746-5080; phone: 407-444-7000; fax: 407-444-7380).

Proof of liability insurance also is necessary and is a standard part of any car rental contract. To be sure of having the appropriate coverage, let the rental staff know in advance about the national borders you plan to cross. If buying a car and using it abroad, you must carry an International Insurance Certificate, known as a Green Card (*Carta Verde* in Italy), which can be obtained from your insurance agent or through the *AAA.*

Driving in Italy is on the right side of the road. In most cases (and this is strictly enforced) passing is on the left; passing on the right is allowed only if the car ahead of you has signaled a left-hand turn or if you are on a three-lane highway. Unless otherwise indicated, those coming from the right at intersections have the right of way, but streetcars have priority over other vehicles. Pedestrians, provided they are on the marked crosswalks, take precedence over all vehicles. On mountain passes, traffic going up has priority over traffic coming down. Pictorial direction signs are standardized under the International Roadsign System and their meanings are indicated by their shapes: Triangular signs indicate danger, circular signs give instructions, and rectangular signs provide information.

Distances are measured in kilometers rather than miles (1 mile = approximately 1.6 kilometers; 1 kilometer equals approximately .62 mile), and speed limits are in kilometers per hour (designated km/h in Italy). In cities and towns, the speed limit usually is 50 km/h (about 31 mph). On main and secondary roads outside towns, the speed limit usually is 90 km/h (56 mph). On superhighways *(autostrade)* the speed limit ranges from 110 to 130 km/h (69 to 81 mph).

The use of seat belts is compulsory for front- and back-seat passengers; children too small for seat belts must travel in child safety seats. Use the horn sparingly—only in emergencies and when approaching blind curves on country roads. In many municipalities, honking is discouraged during the day and forbidden at night; flash your headlights instead. If you park in a restricted zone, you may return to find a wheel "clamped," which renders the car inoperable and involves a tedious—and costly—procedure to get it freed. For more information, consult *Euroad: The Complete Guide to Motoring in Europe* (VLE Ltd., PO Box 444, Ft. Lee, NJ 07024; phone: 201-585-5080; fax: 201-585-5110)

MAPS

Road maps are sold at some gas stations, newsstands, and tobacconists in Italy. Some free regional and city maps can be obtained from US branches of the *Italian Government Travel Office (ENIT)*. Excellent road maps of Italy are published by the *Automobil Club Italiano (ACI;* 8 Via Marsala, Rome 00185, Italy; phone: 39-6-499-8183; and 83 Via Sapori, Rome 00143, Italy; phone: 39-6-501-3530) and the *Istituto Geografico De Agostini (IGDA;* 62 Via Montefeltro, Milan 20156, Italy; phone: 39-238-086416; fax: 39-238-086453).

Among the best maps for touring are those available from Michelin Travel Publications (PO Box 19008, Greenville, SC 29602-9008; phone: 803-458-5000 in South Carolina; 800-423-0485 elsewhere in the US; fax: 803-458-5665). *The Hallwag Road Map of Italy* (Rand McNally, 8255 N. Central Park, Skokie, IL 60076; phone: 800-627-2897; fax: 800-673-0280) is another good resource. *Freytag & Berndt* maps cover most destinations in Europe (including Italy), and can be ordered—along with the maps of many other publishers—from *Map Link* (25 E. Mason St., Suite 201, Santa Barbara, CA 93101; phone: 805-965-4402; fax: 800-MAP-SPOT or 805-962-0884). The *American Automobile Association (AAA;* address above) also provides some useful reference sources, including a map of Italy and an overall planning map of Europe, as well as the *Travel Guide to Europe* and *Motoring in Europe.*

AUTOMOBILE CLUBS AND BREAKDOWNS

To protect yourself in case of breakdowns while driving to and through Italy, and for travel information and other benefits, consider joining a reputable automobile club. The largest of these is the *American Automobile*

Association (*AAA;* address above). Before joining this or any other automobile club, check whether it has reciprocity with Italian clubs such as the *Automobil Club Italiano* (address above).

GASOLINE

Gasoline is sold in liters (approximately 3.8 liters = 1 gallon). Leaded, unleaded, and diesel fuel are available.

RENTING A CAR

You can rent a car through a travel agent or international rental firm before leaving home, or from a regional or local company once in Italy. Reserve in advance.

Most car rental companies require a credit card, although some will accept a substantial cash deposit. The minimum age to rent a car is set by the company; some also may impose special conditions on drivers above a certain age. Electing to pay for collision damage waiver (CDW) protection will add to the cost of renting a car, but releases you from financial liability for the vehicle. Additional costs include drop-off charges or one-way service fees.

Car Rental Companies

Auto Europe (phone: 800-223-5555).

Auto Maggiore (phone: 39-6-229351; in the US, call *Central Holiday Tours;* phone: 800-935-5000 or 201-798-5777).

Avis (phone: 800-331-1084).

Budget (phone: 800-472-3325).

Dollar Rent A Car (known in Europe as *EuroDollar Rent A Car;* phone: 800-800-6000).

Europe by Car (phone: 212-581-3040 in New York State; 800-223-1516 elsewhere in the US).

European Car Reservations (phone: 800-535-3303).

Foremost Euro-Car (phone: 800-272-3299).

Hertz (phone: 800-654-3001).

Kemwel Group (phone: 800-678-0678).

Meier's International (phone: 800-937-0700).

National (known in Europe as *Europcar;* phone: 800-CAR-EUROPE).

Town and Country/ITS (phone: 800-248-4350 in Florida; 800-521-0643 elsewhere in the US).

Tropea (phone: 39-6-488-1189).

Package Tours

A package is a collection of travel services that can be purchased in a single transaction. Its principal advantages are convenience and economy—the cost usually is lower than that of the same services purchased separately. Tour programs generally can be divided into two categories: escorted or locally hosted (with a set itinerary) and independent (usually more flexible).

When considering a package tour, read the brochure *carefully* to determine exactly what is included and any conditions that may apply, and check the company's record with the *Better Business Bureau*. The *United States Tour Operators Association* (*USTOA;* 211 E. 51st St., Suite 12B, New York, NY 10022; phone: 212-750-7371; fax: 212-421-1285) also can be helpful in determining a package tour operator's reliability. As with charter flights, to safeguard your funds, always make your check out to the company's escrow account.

Many tour operators offer packages focused on special interests such as the arts, nature study, sports, and other recreations. *All Adventure Travel* (5589 Arapahoe St., Suite 208, Boulder, CO 80303; phone: 800-537-4025 or 303-440-7924; fax: 303-440-4160) represents such specialized packagers. Many also are listed in the *Specialty Travel Index* (305 San Anselmo Ave., Suite 313, San Anselmo, CA 94960; phone: 415-459-4900 in California; 800-442-4922 elsewhere in the US; fax: 415-459-4974).

Package Tour Operators

Abercrombie & Kent (1520 Kensington Rd., Oak Brook, IL 60521; phone: 800-323-7308 or 708-954-2944; fax: 708-954-3324).

Adventure Center (1311 63rd St., Suite 200, Emeryville, CA 94608; phone: 510-654-1879 in northern California; 800-227-8747 elsewhere in the US; fax: 510-654-4200).

Adventure Golf Holidays/Adventures on Skis (815 North Rd., Westfield, MA 01085; phone: 800-628-9655 or 413-568-2855; fax: 413-562-3621).

AESU (2 Hamill Rd., Suite 248, Baltimore, MD 21210; phone: 800-638-7640 or 410-323-4416; fax: 410-323-4498).

AHI International (701 Lee St., Des Plaines, IL 60016; phone: 800-323-7373 or 312-694-9330; fax: 708-699-7108).

Alitalia Tours (666 Fifth Ave., New York, NY 10103; phone: 800-237-0517, 800-845-3365, or 212-765-2183; fax: 800-848-6286).

Alternative Travel Groups (69-71 Banbury Rd., Oxford 0X2 6PE, England; phone: 800-527-5997 in the US; 44-1865-310255 in Great Britain; fax: 44-1865-310299).

Amelia Tours (280 Old Country Rd., Hicksville, NY 11801; phone: 800-742-4591 or 516-433-0696; fax: 516-579-1562).

American Airlines FlyAAway Vacations (offices throughout the US; phone: 800-321-2121).

American Express Vacations (offices throughout the US; phone: 800-YES-AMEX).

American Jewish Congress (15 E. 84th St., New York, NY 10028; phone: 212-879-4588 in New York State; 800-221-4694 elsewhere in the US; fax: 212-717-1932).

American Museum of Natural History Discovery Tours (Central Park W. at 79th St., New York, NY 10024; phone: 212-769-5700).

Archaeological Tours (271 Madison Ave., Suite 904, New York, NY 10016; phone: 212-986-3054; fax: 212-370-1561).

AutoVenture (425 Pike St., Suite 502, Seattle, WA 98101; phone: 800-426-7502 or 206-624-6033; fax: 206-340-8891).

Bacchants' Pilgrimages (475 Sansome St., Suite 840, San Francisco, CA 94111; phone: 800-952-0226 or 415-981-8518; fax: 415-291-9419).

Backroads (1516 Fifth St., Berkeley, CA 94710-1740; phone: 800-462-2848 or 510-527-1555; fax: 510-527-1444).

Bombard European Balloon Adventures (855 Donald Ross Rd., Juno Beach, FL 33408; phone: 407-775-0039; fax: 407-775-7008).

Blue Marble Travel (2 Rue Dussoubs, Paris 75002, France; phone: 33-1-42-36-02-34; fax: 33-1-42-21-14-77; in the US, contact *Odyssey Adventures,* 305 Commercial St., Suite 505, Portland, ME 04101; phone: 800-544-3216 or 207-773-0905; fax: 207-773-0943).

Brendan Tours (15137 Califa St., Van Nuys, CA 91411; phone: 800-421-8446 or 818-785-9696; fax: 818-902-9876).

British Airways Holidays (75-20 Astoria Blvd., Jackson Heights, NY 11370; phone: 800-AIRWAYS).

British Coastal Trails (California Plaza, 1001 B Ave., Suite 302, Coronado, CA 92118; phone: 800-473-1210 or 619-437-1211; fax: 619-437-8394).

Brooks Country Cycling (140 W. 83rd St., New York, NY 10024; phone: 212-874-5151 in New York, New Jersey, and Connecticut; 800-284-8954 elsewhere in the US; fax: 212-874-5286).

Butterfield & Robinson (70 Bond St., Suite 300, Toronto, Ontario M5B 1X3, Canada; phone: 800-387-1147 or 416-864-1354; fax: 416-864-0541).

Caravan Tours (401 N. Michigan Ave., Chicago, IL 60611; phone: 800-CARAVAN or 312-321-9800; fax: 312-321-9810).

Catholic Travel (10018 Cedar Lane, Kensington, MD 20895; phone: 301-530-8963 or 301-530-7682; fax: 301-530-6614).

Central Holiday Tours (206 Central Ave., Jersey City, NJ 07307; phone: 800-935-5000 or 201-798-5777; fax: 201-963-0966).

Certified Vacations (110 E. Broward Blvd., Ft. Lauderdale, FL 33302; phone: 800-233-7260 or 305-522-1440; fax: 305-468-4781).

Club Europa (802 W. Oregon St., Urbana, IL 61801; phone: 800-331-1882 or 217-344-5863; fax: 217-344-4072).

Collette Tours (162 Middle St., Pawtucket, RI 02860; phone: 800-752-2655 in New England; 800-832-4656 elsewhere in the US; fax: 401-727-4745).

Contiki Holidays (300 Plaza Alicante, Suite 900, Garden Grove, CA 92640; phone: 800-266-8454 or 714-740-0808; fax: 714-740-0818).

Coopersmith's England (6441 Valley View Rd., Oakland, CA 94611; phone: 510-339-3977; fax: 510-339-7135).

Dailey-Thorp (330 W. 58th St., New York, NY 10019-1817; phone: 212-307-1555; fax: 212-974-1420).

Delta's Dream Vacations (PO Box 1525, Ft. Lauderdale, FL 33302; phone: 800-872-7786).

DER Tours (11933 Wilshire Blvd., Los Angeles, CA 90025; phone: 800-782-2424 or 310-479-4411; fax: 310-479-2239; and 9501 W. Devon Ave., Rosemont, IL 60018; phone: 800-782-2424 or 708-692-6300; fax: 708-692-4506).

Distant Journeys (PO Box 1211, Camden, ME 04843; phone/fax: 207-236-9788).

Donna Franca Tours (470 Commonwealth Ave., Boston, MA 02215; phone: 617-227-3111 in Massachusetts; 800-225-6290 elsewhere in the US; fax: 617-266-1062).

Earthwatch (680 Mt. Auburn St., PO Box 403, Watertown, MA 02272; phone: 800-776-0188 or 617-926-8200; fax: 617-926-8532).

Educational Adventures (c/o *Adventure Golf Holidays/Adventures on Skis,* address above).

Esplanade Tours (581 Boylston St., Boston, MA 02116; phone: 800-426-5492 or 617-266-7465; fax: 617-262-9829).

Equitour (PO Box 807, Dubois, WY 82513; phone: 307-455-3363 in Wyoming; 800-545-0019 elsewhere in the US; fax: 307-455-2354).

EuroConnection (2004 196th St. SW, Suite 4, Lynnwood, WA 98036; phone: 800-645-3876 or 206-670-1140; fax: 206-775-7561).

Europe Express (4040 Lake Washington Blvd. NE, Kirkland, WA 98072; phone: 800-927-3876 or 206-822-1950; fax: 206-822-6051).

Europe Through the Back Door (PO Box 2009, Edmonds, WA 98020; phone: 206-771-8303; fax: 206-771-0833).

European Tours Limited (5725 77th St., Lubbock, TX 79424; phone: 800-722-3679 or 806-794-4991; fax: 806-794-8550).

Exodus (9 Weir Rd., London SW12 OLT, England; phone: 44-181-675-5550; fax: 44-181-673-0779; represented in the US by *Safaricenter,* 3201 N. Sepulveda Blvd., Manhattan Beach, CA 90266; phone: 800-223-6046 or 310-546-4411; fax: 310-546-3188).

Extra Value Travel (683 S. Collier Blvd., Marco Island, FL 33937; phone: 813-394-3384; fax: 813-394-4848).

Fishing International (PO Box 2132, Santa Rosa, CA 95405; phone: 800-950-4242 or 707-539-3366; fax: 707-539-1320).

FITS Equestrian (685 Lateen Rd., Solvang, CA 93463; phone: 800-666-3487 or 805-688-9494; fax: 805-688-2493).

Forum Travel International (91 Gregory La., Suite 21, Pleasant Hill, CA 94523; phone: 510-671-2900; fax: 510-671-2993 or 510-946-1500).

4th Dimension Tours (1150 NW 72nd Ave., Suite 333, Miami, FL 33126; phone: 800-343-0020 or 305-477-1525; fax: 305-477-0731).

Funway Holidays Funjet (PO Box 1460, Milwaukee, WI 53201-1460; phone: 800-558-3050 for reservations; 800-558-3060 for customer service).

Gadabout Tours (700 E. Tahquitz Canyon Way, Palm Springs, CA 92262-6767; phone: 800-952-5068 or 619-325-5556; fax: 619-325-5127).

Globus/Cosmos (5301 S. Federal Circle, Littleton, CO 80123; phone: 800-221-0090, 800-556-5454, or 303-797-2800; fax: 303-347-2080).

GOGO Tours (69 Spring St., Ramsey, NJ 07446-0507; phone: 201-934-3759).

Golfing Holidays (231 E. Millbrae Ave., Millbrae, CA 94030; phone: 800-652-7847 or 415-697-0230; fax: 415-697-8687).

HF Holidays, Ltd. (Imperial House, Edgware Rd., London NW9 5AL, England; phone: 44-181-905-9558; fax: 44-181-905-9558).

Himalayan Travel (112 Prospect St., Stamford, CT 06901; phone: 800-225-2380 or 203-359-3711; fax: 203-359-3669).

In Quest of the Classics (PO Box 890745, Temecula, CA 92589-0745; phone: 800-227-1393 or 909-694-5866 in California; 800-221-5246 elsewhere in the US; fax: 909-694-5873).

Insight International Tours (745 Atlantic Ave., Suite 720, Boston, MA 02111; phone: 800-582-8380 or 617-482-2000; fax: 617-482-2425).

INTRAV (7711 Bonhomme Ave., St. Louis, MO 63105-1961; phone: 800-456-8100; fax: 314-727-6198).

ITC Golf Tours (4134 Atlantic Ave., Suite 205, Long Beach, CA 90807; phone: 800-257-4981 or 310-595-6905; fax: 310-424-6683).

KLM/Northwest Vacations Europe (c/o *MLT,* 5130 Hwy. 101, Minnetonka, MN 55345; phone: 800-727-1111; fax: 800-655-7890).

Liberty Travel (for the nearest location, contact the central office: 69 Spring St., Ramsey, NJ 07446; phone: 201-934-3500; fax: 201-934-3888).

Marathon Tours (108 Main St., Charlestown, MA 02129; phone: 800-444-4097 or 617-242-7845; fax: 617-242-7686).

Matterhorn Travel Service (2450 Riva Rd., Annapolis, MD 21401; phone: 410-224-2230 in Maryland; 800-638-9150 elsewhere in the US; fax: 410-266-3868).

Maupintour (PO Box 807, Lawrence, KS 66044; phone: 800-255-4266 or 913-843-1211; fax: 913-843-8351).

Mercator Travel (122 E. 42nd St., New York, NY 10168; phone: 800-514-9880 or 212-682-6979; fax: 212-682-7379).

Mountain Travel-Sobek (6420 Fairmount Ave., El Cerrito, CA 94530; phone: 510-527-8100 in California; 800-227-2384 elsewhere in the US; fax: 510-525-7710).

Odyssey Adventures (305 Commercial St., Suite 505, Portland, ME 04101; phone: 800-544-3216 or 207-773-1156; fax: 207-773-0943).

Olson Travelworld (970 W. 190th St., Suite 425, Torrance, CA 90502; phone: 800-421-2255 or 310-354-2600; fax: 310-768-0050).

Perillo Tours (577 Chestnut Ridge Rd., Woodcliff Lake, NJ 07675; phone: 800-431-1515 or 201-307-1234; fax: 201-307-1808).

Petrabax Tours (97-45 Queens Blvd., Suite 600, Rego Park, NY 11374; phone: 800-367-6611 or 718-897-7272; fax: 718-275-3943).

Pleasure Break (3701 Algonquin Rd., Suite 900, Rolling Meadows, IL 60008; phone: 708-670-6300 in Illinois; 800-777-1885 elsewhere in the US; fax: 708-670-7689).

Progressive Travels (224 W. Galer Ave., Suite C, Seattle, WA 98119; phone: 800-245-2229 or 206-285-1987; fax: 206-285-1988).

Prospect Music and Art Tours (454-458 Chiswick High Rd., London W4 5TT, England; phone: 44-181-995-2151 or 44-181-995-2163; fax: 44-181-742-1969).

Regina Tours (401 South St., Room 4B, Chardon, OH 44024; phone: 800-228-4654 or 216-286-9166; fax: 216-286-4231).

Saga International Holidays (222 Berkeley St., Boston, MA 02116; phone: 800-343-0273 or 617-262-2262).

Select Travel Service (main office: Bridgefoot House, 159 High St., Huntington, Cambridgeshire PE18 7TF, England; phone: 44-181-480-433783; fax: 44-181-480-433514; US office: 795 Franklin Ave., Franklin Lakes, NJ 07417; phone: 800-752-6787 or 201-891-4143; fax: 201-847-0053).

Sierra Club Outings (730 Polk St., San Francisco, CA 94109; phone: 415-923-5630).

Smithsonian Study Tours and Seminars (1100 Jefferson Dr. SW, Room 3045, Washington, DC 20560; phone: 202-357-4700; fax: 202-786-2315).

Steve Lohr's Holidays (206 Central Ave., Jersey City, NJ, 07307; phone: 201-798-3900 in New Jersey; 800-929-5647 elsewhere in the US; fax: 201-693-0966).

Take-A-Guide (main office: 11 Uxbridge St., London W8 7TQ, England; phone: 44-181-960-0459; fax: 44-181-964-0990; US office: 954 Lexington Ave., New York, NY 10021; phone: 800-825-4946; fax: 800-635-7177).

Tauck Tours (PO Box 5027, Westport, CT 06881; phone: 800-468-2825 or 203-226-6911; fax: 203-221-6828).

Thomas Cook (headquarters: 45 Berkeley St., Piccadilly, London W1A 1EB, England; phone: 44-171-499-4000; fax: 44-171-408-4299; main US office: 100 Cambridge Park Dr., Cambridge, MA 02140; phone: 800-846-6272; fax: 617-349-1094).

Tourlite International (551 Fifth Ave., New York, NY 10176; phone: 212-599-2727 in New York State; 800-272-7600 elsewhere in the US; fax: 212-370-0913).

Trafalgar Tours (11 E. 26th St., Suite 1300, New York, NY 10010-1402; phone: 800-854-0103 or 212-689-8977; fax: 212-725-7776).

TRAVCOA (PO Box 2630, Newport Beach, CA 92658; phone: 800-992-2004 or 714-476-2800 in California; 800-992-2003 elsewhere in the US; fax: 714-476-2538).

Travel Bound (599 Broadway, Penthouse, New York, NY 10012; phone: 212-334-1350 in New York State; 800-456-8656 elsewhere in the US; fax: 800-208-7080).

Travel Concepts (62 Commonwealth Ave., Suite 3, Boston, MA 02116; phone: 617-266-8450; fax: 617-267-2477).

Travent International (PO Box 800, Bristol, VT 05443-0800; phone: 800-325-3009 or 802-453-5710; fax: 802-453-4806).

TWA Getaway Vacations (Getaway Vacation Center, 10 E. Stow Rd., Marlton, NJ 08053; phone: 800-GETAWAY; fax: 609-985-4125).

United Airlines Vacations (PO Box 24580, Milwaukee, WI 53224-0580; phone: 800-328-6877).

Value Holidays (10224 N. Port Washington Rd., Mequon, WI 53092; phone: 800-558-6850 or 414-241-6373; fax: 414-241-6379).

Vermont Bicycle Touring (PO Box 711, Bristol, VT 05443-0711; phone: 802-453-4811; fax: 802-453-4806).

Voyagers International (PO Box 915, Ithaca, NY 14851; phone: 800-633-0299 or 607-257-3091; fax: 607-257-3699).

Wander Tours (PO Box 8607, Somerville, NJ 08876; phone: 800-282-1808 or 908-707-8420).

The Wayfarers (172 Bellevue Ave., Newport, RI 02840; phone: 800-249-4620 or 401-849-5087; fax: 410-849-5878).

Wide World of Golf (PO Box 5217, Carmel, CA 93921; phone: 800-214-4653 or 408-624-6667; fax: 408-625-9671).

Wilderness Travel (801 Allston Way, Berkeley, CA 94710; phone: 800-368-2794 or 510-548-0420; fax: 510-548-0347).

Worldwide Rocky Mountain Cycle Tours (PO Box 1978, Canmore, Alberta T0L 0M0, Canada; phone: 800-661-2453 or 403-678-6770; fax: 403-678-4451).

X.O. Travel Consultants (38 W. 32nd St., Suite 1009, New York, NY 10001; phone: 212-947-5530 in New York State; 800-262-9682 elsewhere in the US; fax: 212-971-0924).

Insurance

The first person with whom you should discuss travel insurance is your own insurance broker. You may discover that the insurance you already carry protects you adequately while traveling and that you need little additional coverage. If you charge travel services, the credit card company also may provide some insurance coverage (and other safeguards).

Types of Travel Insurance

Automobile insurance: Provides collision, theft, property damage, and personal liability protection while driving.

Baggage and personal effects insurance: Protects your bags and their contents in case of damage or theft at any point during your travels.

Default and/or bankruptcy insurance: Provides coverage in the event of default and/or bankruptcy on the part of the tour operator, airline, or other travel supplier.

Flight insurance: Covers accidental injury or death while flying.

Personal accident and sickness insurance: Covers cases of illness, injury, or death in an accident while traveling.

Trip cancellation and interruption insurance: Guarantees a refund if you must cancel a trip; may reimburse you for additional travel costs incurred in catching up with a tour or traveling home early.

Combination policies: Include any or all of the above.

Disabled Travelers

Make travel arrangements well in advance. Specify to all services involved the nature of your disability to determine if there are accommodations and facilities that meet your needs.

The *Consorzio Cooperative Integrate* (*CO.IN;* 54A Via E. Giglioli, Rome 00169, Italy; phone: 39-6-232-67504 or 39-6-232-67505) publishes *guide di accessibilità* (accessibility guides) for various Italian cities; the guides cover hotels, museums, and other facilities. In addition, the *Italian Government Travel Office*'s *Italia* guide includes lists of associations for the disabled in cities throughout Italy. These publications are available from branches of the *Italian Government Travel Office (ENIT)* in the US (see *For Further Information* for addresses), and at local tourist offices in Italy.

Regularly revised hotel and restaurant guides, such as the *Michelin Red Guide to Italy* (Michelin Travel Publications, PO Box 19008, Greenville, SC 29602-9008; phone: 803-458-5000 in South Carolina; 800-423-0485 elsewhere in the US; fax: 803-458-5665), use a standard symbol of access (person in a wheelchair) to point out accommodations suitable for wheelchair-bound guests.

Italian State Railways personnel can assist disabled visitors with travel arrangements and ticket purchases, as well as with boarding and exiting trains. For information, contact *Compagnia Italiana Turismo* (*CIT;* 6033 W. Century Blvd., Suite 980, Los Angeles, CA 90045; phone: 800-CIT-RAIL or 310-338-8620; fax: 310-670-4269; and 342 Madison Ave., Suite 207, New York, NY 10173; phone: 800-CIT-RAIL, 800-248-8687, or 212-697-2100; fax: 212-697-1394).

Organizations

ACCENT on Living (PO Box 700, Bloomington, IL 61702; phone: 800-787-8444 or 309-378-2961; fax: 309-378-4420).

Access: The Foundation for Accessibility by the Disabled (PO Box 356, Malverne, NY 11565; phone/fax: 516-887-5798).

Associazione a Difesa dei Diritti degli Handicap (57 Via della Republica, Praia-a-Mare 87028, Italy; phone: 39-985-72075; fax: 39-985-72613).

Associazione Italiana Assistenza allo Spastico (*AIAS;* 4-H Via Cipro, Rome 00135, Italy; phone: 39-6-397-31704 or 39-6-397-31829).

American Foundation for the Blind (15 W. 16th St., New York, NY 10011; phone: 800-232-5463 or 212-620-2147; fax: 212-727-7418).

Holiday Care Service (2 Old Bank Chambers, Station Rd., Horley, Surrey RH6 9HW, England; phone: 44-1293-774535; fax: 44-1293-784647).

Information Center for Individuals with Disabilities (Ft. Point Pl., 27-43 Wormwood St., Boston, MA 02210; phone: 800-462-5015 in Massachusetts; 617-727-5540 elsewhere in the US; TDD: 617-345-9743; fax: 617-345-5318).

Lega del Filo d'Oro (1 Via Montecerno, Ocimo 60027, Italy; phone: 39-71-713-1202; fax: 39-71-717102).

Mobility International (main office: 228 Borough High St., London SE1 1JX, England; phone: 44-171-403-5688; fax: 44-171-378-1292; US office: *MIUSA,* PO Box 10767, Eugene, OR 97440; phone/TDD: 503-343-1284; fax: 503-343-6812).

Moss Rehabilitation Hospital Travel Information Service (telephone referrals only; phone: 215-456-9600; TDD: 215-456-9602).

National Rehabilitation Information Center (8455 Colesville Rd., Suite 935, Silver Spring, MD 20910; phone: 301-588-9284; fax: 301-587-1967).

Paralyzed Veterans of America (*PVA;* PVA/ATTS Program, 801 18th St. NW, Washington, DC 20006; phone: 202-872-1300 in Washington, DC; 800-424-8200 elsewhere in the US; fax: 202-785-4452).

Royal Association for Disability and Rehabilitation (*RADAR;* 12 City Forum, 250 City Rd., London EC1V 8AF, England; phone: 44-171-250-3222; fax: 44-171-250-0212).

Society for the Advancement of Travel for the·Handicapped (*SATH;* 347 Fifth Ave., Suite 610, New York, NY 10016; phone: 212-447-7284; fax: 212-725-8253).

Travel Industry and Disabled Exchange (*TIDE;* 5435 Donna Ave., Tarzana, CA 91356; phone: 818-368-5648).

Tripscope (The Courtyard, Evelyn Rd., London W4 5JL, England; phone: 44-181-994-9294; fax: 44-181-994-3618).

GETTING READY TO GO

27

Publications

Access Travel: A Guide to the Accessibility of Airport Terminals (Consumer Information Center, Dept. 578Z, Pueblo, CO 81009; phone: 719-948-3334).

Air Transportation of Handicapped Persons (Publication #AC-120-32; *US Department of Transportation,* Distribution Unit, Publications Section, M-443-2, 400 Seventh St. SW, Washington, DC 20590; phone: 202-366-0039).

The Diabetic Traveler (PO Box 8223 RW, Stamford, CT 06905; phone: 203-327-5832; fax: 203-975-1748).

Directory of Travel Agencies for the Disabled and Travel for the Disabled, both by Helen Hecker (Twin Peaks Press, PO Box 129, Vancouver, WA 98666; phone: 800-637-CALM or 206-694-2462; fax: 206-696-3210).

Guide to Traveling with Arthritis (Upjohn Company, PO Box 989, Dearborn, MI 48121; phone: 800-253-9860).

The Handicapped Driver's Mobility Guide (*American Automobile Association,* 1000 AAA Dr., Heathrow, FL 32746-5080; phone: 407-444-7000; fax: 407-444-7380).

Handicapped Travel Newsletter (PO Box 269, Athens, TX 75751; phone/fax: 903-677-1260).

Handi-Travel: A Resource Book for Disabled and Elderly Travellers, by Cinnie Noble (*Canadian Rehabilitation Council for the Disabled,* 45 Sheppard Ave. E., Suite 801, Toronto, Ontario M2N 5W9, Canada; phone/TDD: 416-250-7490; fax: 416-229-1371).

Holidays and Travel Abroad, edited by John Stanford (*Royal Association for Disability and Rehabilitation,* address above).

Incapacitated Passengers Air Travel Guide (*International Air Transport Association,* Publications Sales Department, 2000 Peel St., Montreal, Quebec H3A 2R4, Canada; phone: 514-844-6311; fax: 514-844-5286).

Ticket to Safe Travel (*American Diabetes Association,* 1660 Duke St., Alexandria, VA 22314; phone: 800-232-3472 or 703-549-1500; fax: 703-836-7439).

Travel for the Patient with Chronic Obstructive Pulmonary Disease (Dr. Harold Silver, 1601 18th St. NW, Washington, DC 20009; phone: 202-667-0134; fax: 202-667-0148).

Travel Tips for Hearing-Impaired People (*American Academy of Otolaryngology,* 1 Prince St., Alexandria, VA 22314; phone: 703-836-4444; fax: 703-683-5100).

Travel Tips for People with Arthritis (*Arthritis Foundation,* 1314 Spring St. NW, Atlanta, GA 30309; phone: 800-283-7800 or 404-872-7100; fax: 404-872-0457).

Traveling Like Everybody Else: A Practical Guide for Disabled Travelers, by Jacqueline Freedman and Susan Gersten (Modan Publishing, PO

Box 1202, Bellmore, NY 11710; phone: 516-679-1380; fax: 516-679-1448).

Package Tour Operators

Accessible Journeys (35 W. Sellers Ave., Ridley Park, PA 19078; phone: 800-846-4537 or 215-521-0339; fax: 215-521-6959).

Accessible Tours/Directions Unlimited (Attn.: Lois Bonnani, 720 N. Bedford Rd., Bedford Hills, NY 10507; phone: 800-533-5343 or 914-241-1700; fax: 914-241-0243).

Beehive Business and Leisure Travel (1130 W. Center St., N. Salt Lake, UT 84054; phone: 800-777-5727 or 801-292-4445; fax: 801-298-9460).

Classic Travel Service (8 W. 40th St., New York, NY 10018; phone: 212-869-2560 in New York State; 800-247-0909 elsewhere in the US; fax: 212-944-4493).

Dialysis at Sea Cruises (611 Barry Pl., Indian Rocks Beach, FL 34635; phone: 800-775-1333 or 813-596-4614; fax: 813-596-0203).

Evergreen Travel Service (4114 198th St. SW, Suite 13, Lynnwood, WA 98036-6742; phone: 800-435-2288 or 206-776-1184; fax: 206-775-0728).

Flying Wheels Travel (143 W. Bridge St., PO Box 382, Owatonna, MN 55060; phone: 800-535-6790 or 507-451-5005; fax: 507-451-1685).

Good Neighbor Travel Service (124 S. Main St., Viroqua, WI 54665; phone: 800-338-3245 or 608-637-2128; fax: 608-637-3030).

The Guided Tour (7900 Old York Rd., Suite 114B, Elkins Park, PA 19117-2339; phone: 800-783-5841 or 215-782-1370; fax: 215-635-2637).

Hinsdale Travel (201 E. Ogden Ave., Hinsdale, IL 60521; phone: 708-325-1335 or 708-469-7349; fax: 708-325-1342).

MedEscort International (*ABE International Airport*, PO Box 8766, Allentown, PA 18105-8766; phone: 800-255-7182 or 215-791-3111; fax: 215-791-9189).

Prestige World Travel (5710-X High Point Rd., Greensboro, NC 27407; phone: 800-476-7737 or 910-292-6690; fax: 910-632-9404).

Sprout (893 Amsterdam Ave., New York, NY 10025; phone: 212-222-9575; fax: 212-222-9768).

Weston Travel Agency (134 N. Cass Ave., Westmont, IL 60559; phone: 708-968-2513 in Illinois; 800-633-3725 elsewhere in the US; fax: 708-968-2539).

Single Travelers

The travel industry is not very fair to people who vacation by themselves— they often end up paying more than those traveling in pairs. There are services catering to single travelers, however, that match travel companions, offer travel arrangements with shared accommodations, and provide information and discounts. Useful publications include *Going Solo* (Doerfer Communications, PO Box 123, Apalachicola, FL 32329; phone/fax: 904-653-8848) and *Traveling on Your Own*, by Eleanor Berman (Random House, Order Dept., 400 Hahn Rd., Westminster, MD 21157; phone: 800-733-3000; fax: 800-659-2436).

Organizations and Companies

Club Europa (802 W. Oregon St., Urbana, IL 61801; phone: 800-331-1882 or 217-344-5863; fax: 217-344-4072).

Contiki Holidays (300 Plaza Alicante, Suite 900, Garden Grove, CA 92640; phone: 800-466-0610 or 714-740-0808; fax: 714-740-0818).

Gallivanting (515 E. 79th St., Suite 20F, New York, NY 10021; phone: 800-933-9699 or 212-988-0617; fax: 212-988-0144).

Globus/Cosmos (5301 S. Federal Circle, Littleton, CO 80123; phone: 800-221-0090, 800-556-5454, or 303-797-2800; fax: 303-347-2080).

Insight International Tours (745 Atlantic Ave., Boston, MA 02111; phone: 800-582-8380 or 617-482-2000; fax: 617-482-2425).

Jane's International and Sophisticated Women Travelers (2603 Bath Ave., Brooklyn, NY 11214; phone: 718-266-2045; fax: 718-266-4062).

Marion Smith Singles (611 Prescott Pl., N. Woodmere, NY 11581; phone: 516-791-4852, 516-791-4865, or 212-944-2112; fax: 516-791-4879).

Partners-in-Travel (11660 Chenault St., Suite 119, Los Angeles, CA 90049; phone: 310-476-4869).

Singles in Motion (545 W. 236th St., Riverdale, NY 10463; phone/fax: 718-884-4464).

Singleworld (401 Theodore Fremd Ave., Rye, NY 10580; phone: 800-223-6490 or 914-967-3334; fax: 914-967-7395).

Solo Flights (63 High Noon Rd., Weston, CT 06883; phone: 800-266-1566 or 203-226-9993).

Suddenly Singles Tours (161 Dreiser Loop, Bronx, NY 10475; phone: 718-379-8800 in New York City; 800-859-8396 elsewhere in the US; fax: 718-379-8858).

Travel Companion Exchange (PO Box 833, Amityville, NY 11701; phone: 516-454-0880; fax: 516-454-0170).

Travel Companions (Atrium Financial Center, 1515 N. Federal Hwy., Suite 300, Boca Raton, FL 33432; phone: 800-383-7211 or 407-393-6448; fax: 407-451-8560).

Travel in Two's (239 N. Broadway, Suite 3, N. Tarrytown, NY 10591; phone: 914-631-8301 in New York State; 800-692-5252 elsewhere in the US).

Umbrella Singles (PO Box 157, Woodbourne, NY 12788; phone: 800-537-2797 or 914-434-6871; fax: 914-434-3532).

Older Travelers

Special discounts and more free time are just two factors that have given older travelers a chance to see the world at affordable prices. Many travel suppliers offer senior discounts—sometimes only to members of certain senior citizens organizations (which provide benefits of their own). When considering a particular package, make sure the facilities—and the pace of the tour—match your needs and physical condition.

Publications

Going Abroad: 101 Tips for Mature Travelers (Grand Circle Travel, 347 Congress St., Boston, MA 02210; phone: 800-221-2610 or 617-350-7500; fax: 617-423-0445).

The Mature Traveler (PO Box 50820, Reno, NV 89513-0820; phone: 702-786-7419).

Take a Camel to Lunch and Other Adventures for Mature Travelers, by Nancy O'Connell (Bristol Publishing Enterprises, PO Box 1737, San Leandro, CA 94577; phone: 510-895-4461 in California; 800-346-4889 elsewhere in the US; fax: 510-895-4459).

Unbelievably Good Deals & Great Adventures That You Absolutely Can't Get Unless You're Over 50, by Joan Rattner Heilman (Contemporary Books, 1200 Stetson Ave., Chicago, IL 60601; phone: 312-782-9181; fax: 312-540-4687).

Organizations

American Association of Retired Persons (AARP; 601 E St. NW, Washington, DC 20049; phone: 202-434-2277).

Golden Companions (PO Box 754, Pullman, WA 99163-0754; phone: 208-858-2183).

Mature Outlook (Customer Service Center, 6001 N. Clark St., Chicago, IL 60660; phone: 800-336-6330).

National Council of Senior Citizens (1331 F St. NW, Washington, DC 20004; phone: 202-347-8800; fax: 202-624-9595).

Package Tour Operators

Elderhostel (75 Federal St., Boston, MA 02110-1941; phone: 617-426-7788; fax: 617-426-8351).

Evergreen Travel Service (4114 198th St. SW, Suite 13, Lynnwood, WA 98036-6742; phone: 800-435-2288 or 206-776-1184; fax: 206-775-0728).

Gadabout Tours (700 E. Tahquitz Canyon Way, Palm Springs, CA 92262; phone: 800-952-5068 or 619-325-5556; fax: 619-325-5127).

Grand Circle Travel (347 Congress St., Boston, MA 02210; phone: 800-221-2610 or 617-350-7500; fax: 617-423-0445).

Grandtravel (6900 Wisconsin Ave., Suite 706, Chevy Chase, MD 20815; phone: 800-247-7651 or 301-986-0790; fax: 301-913-0166).

Insight International Tours (745 Atlantic Ave., Suite 720, Boston, MA 02111; phone: 800-582-8380 or 617-482-2000; fax: 617-482-2425).

Interhostel (*University of New Hampshire,* Division of Continuing Education, 6 Garrison Ave., Durham, NH 03824; phone: 800-733-9753 or 603-862-1147; fax: 603-862-1113).

Mature Tours (c/o *Solo Flights,* 63 High Noon Rd., Weston, CT 06883; phone: 800-266-1566 or 203-226-9993).

OmniTours (104 Wilmot Rd., Deerfield, IL 60015; phone: 800-962-0060 or 708-374-0088; fax: 708-374-9515).

Saga International Holidays (222 Berkeley St., Boston, MA 02116; phone: 800-343-0273 or 617-262-2262; fax: 617-375-5950).

Money Matters

The basic unit of currency in Italy is the **lira** (plural, **lire**). Italian currency is distributed in coin denominations of 5, 10, 20, 50, 100, 200, and 500 lire, and in bills of 1,000, 2,000, 5,000, 10,000, 20,000, 50,000, and 100,000 lire. At the time of this writing, the exchange rate for Italian currency was 1600 lire to $1 US.

Exchange rates are published in international newspapers such as the *International Herald Tribune.* Foreign currency information and related services are provided by banks and companies such as *Thomas Cook Foreign Exchange* (for the nearest location, call 800-621-0666 or 312-236-0042; fax: 312-807-4895); *Harold Reuter and Company* (200 Park Ave., Suite 332E, New York, NY 10166; phone: 800-258-0456 or 212-661-0826; fax: 212-557-6622); and *Ruesch International* (for the nearest location, call 800-424-2923 or 202-408-1200; fax: 202-408-1211). In Italy, you will find the official rate of exchange posted in banks, airports, money exchange houses, hotels, and some shops. Since you will get more lire for your US dollar at banks and money exchanges, don't change more than $10 for foreign currency at other commercial establishments. Ask how much commission you're being charged and the exchange rate, and don't buy money on the black market (it may be counterfeit). Estimate your needs carefully; if you overbuy, you lose twice—buying and selling back.

CREDIT CARDS AND TRAVELER'S CHECKS

Most major credit cards enjoy wide domestic and international acceptance; however, not every hotel, restaurant, or shop in Italy accepts all (or in some cases any) credit cards. (Some cards may be issued under different names in Europe; for example, *MasterCard* may go under the name *Access* or *Eurocard,* and *Visa* sometimes is called *Carte Bleue.*) When making purchases with a credit card, note that the rate of exchange depends on when the charge is processed; most credit card companies charge a 1% fee for converting foreign currency charges.

It's also wise to carry traveler's checks while on the road, since they are widely accepted and replaceable if stolen or lost. You can buy traveler's checks at banks and some are available by mail or phone. Keep a separate list of all traveler's checks (noting those that you have cashed) and the names and numbers of your credit cards. Both traveler's check and credit card companies have international numbers to call for information or in the event of loss or theft.

CASH MACHINES

Automated teller machines (ATMs) are increasingly common worldwide, and most banks participate in international ATM networks such as *CIR-RUS* (phone: 800-4-CIRRUS) and *PLUS* (phone: 800-THE-PLUS). Cardholders can withdraw cash from any machine in the same network using either a "bank" card or, in some cases, a credit card. For instance, in Italy, ATMs that accept *MasterCard* or *Visa* are quite common. Additional information on ATMs and networks can be obtained from your bank or credit card company.

SENDING MONEY ABROAD

Should the need arise, you can have money sent to you in most major Italian cities via the services provided by *American Express MoneyGram* (phone: 800-926-9400 for information; 800-866-8800 for money transfers) or *Western Union Financial Services* (phone: 800-325-6000 or 800-325-4176). If you are down to your last cent and have no other way to obtain cash, the nearest *US Consulate* will let you call home to set these matters in motion.

Accommodations

For specific information on hotels, resorts, *pensioni,* and other selected accommodations see *Checking In* in THE CITIES, *Best en Route* in DIRECTIONS, and sections throughout DIVERSIONS. The *Italian Government Travel Office (ENIT)* provides lists of hotels officially rated by the government, with addresses, phone numbers, and prices. An annual catalogue of private farms, cottages, and villas that accept paying guests (with meals sometimes included) is published by the *Associazione Nazionale per l'Agriturismo* (101 Corso Vittorio Emanuele, Rome 00186, Italy; phone: 6-685-2342; fax: 6-685-2424).

RELAIS & CHÂTEAUX

Founded in France, the *Relais & Châteaux* association has grown to include establishments in numerous countries. At press time, there were 31 members in Italy. All maintain very high standards in order to retain their memberships, as they are reviewed annually. An illustrated catalogue of properties is available from *Relais & Châteaux* (11 E. 44th St., Suite 707, New York, NY 10017; phone: 212-856-0115; fax: 212-856-0193).

RENTAL OPTIONS

An attractive accommodations alternative for the visitor content to stay in one spot is a vacation rental. For a family or group, the per-person cost can be reasonable. To have your pick of the properties available throughout Italy, make inquiries at least six months in advance. The *Worldwide Home Rental Guide* (3501 Indian School Rd. NE, Albuquerque, NM 87106; phone/fax: 505-255-4271) lists rental properties and managing agencies.

Rental Property Agents

At Home Abroad (405 E. 56th St., Suite 6H, New York, NY 10022-2466; phone: 212-421-9165; fax: 212-752-1591).

B & V Associates (140 E. 56th St., Suite 4C, New York, NY 10022; phone: 800-546-4777 or 212-688-9538; fax: 212-688-9467).

British Travel Associates (PO Box 299, Elkton, VA 22827; phone: 800-327-6097 or 703-298-2232; fax: 703-298-2347).

Castles, Cottages and Flats (7 Faneuil Hall Marketplace, Boston, MA 02109; phone: 800-742-6030 or 617-742-6030; fax: 617-367-4521).

Cuendet (Il Cerreto, Monteriggioni 53035, Italy; phone: 39-577-301012; fax: 39-577-301149; in the US, contact *Suzanne Pidduck Rentals in Italy,* 1742 Calle Corva, Camarillo, CA 93010; phone: 800-726-6702 or 805-987-5278; fax: 805-482-7976).

Europa-Let (92 N. Main St., Ashland, OR 97520; phone: 800-462-4486 or 503-482-5806; fax: 503-482-0660).

Grandluxe International (165 Chestnut St., Allendale, NJ 07401; phone: 201-327-2333; fax: 201-825-2664).

Hideaways International (767 Islington St., Portsmouth, NH 03801; phone: 800-843-4433 or 603-430-4433; fax: 603-430-4444).

Hometours International (PO Box 11503, Knoxville, TN 37939; phone: 800-367-4668).

Interhome (124 Little Falls Rd., Fairfield, NJ 07004; phone: 201-882-6864; fax: 201-808-1742).

Keith Prowse & Co. (USA) Ltd. (234 W. 44th St., Suite 1000, New York, NY 10036; phone: 800-669-8687 or 212-398-1430; fax: 212-302-4251).

La Cure Villas (11661 San Vicente Blvd., Suite 1010, Los Angeles, CA 90049; phone: 800-387-2726 or 416-968-2374; fax: 416-968-9435).

Orion (c/o *B & V Associates,* 140 E. 56th St., Suite 4C, New York, NY 10022; phone: 800-755-8266 or 212-688-9526; fax: 212-688-9467).

Property Rentals International (1 Park W. Circle, Suite 108, Midlothian, VA 23113; phone: 800-220-3332 or 804-378-6054; fax: 804-379-2073).

Rent a Home International (7200 34th Ave. NW, Seattle, WA 98117; phone: 206-789-9377; fax: 206-789-9379).

Rent a Vacation Everywhere (*RAVE;* 383 Park Ave., Rochester, NY 14607; phone: 716-256-0760; fax: 716-256-2676).

Sterling Tours (2707 Congress St., Suite 2G, San Diego, CA 92110; phone: 800-727-4359 or 619-299-3010; fax: 619-299-5728).

Vacanze in Italia (22 Railroad St., Great Barrington, MA 10230; phone: 800-533-5405 or 413-528-6610; fax: 413-528-6222).

VHR Worldwide (235 Kensington Ave., Norwood, NJ 07648; phone: 201-767-9393 in New Jersey; 800-633-3284 elsewhere in the US; fax: 201-767-5510).

Villas and Apartments Abroad (420 Madison Ave., Suite 1105, New York, NY 10017; phone: 212-759-1025 in New York State; 800-433-3020 elsewhere in the US; fax: 212-755-8316).

Villas International (605 Market St., Suite 510, San Francisco, CA 94105; phone: 800-221-2260 or 415-281-0910; fax: 415-281-0919).

HOME EXCHANGES

For comfortable, reasonable living quarters with amenities that no hotel could possibly offer, consider trading homes with someone abroad. The following companies provide information on exchanges:

Home Base Holidays (7 Park Ave., London N13 5PG, England; phone/fax: 44-181-886-8752).

Intervac US/International Home Exchange (PO Box 590504, San Francisco, CA 94159; phone: 800-756-HOME or 415-435-3497; fax: 415-386-6853).

Loan-A-Home (2 Park La., Apt. 6E, Mt. Vernon, NY 10552-3443; phone: 914-664-7640).

Vacation Exchange Club (PO Box 650, Key West, FL 33041; phone: 800-638-3841 or 305-294-3720; fax: 305-294-1448).

Worldwide Home Exchange Club (main office: 50 Hans Crescent, London SW1X 0NA, England; phone: 44-171-589-6055; US office: 806 Brantford Ave., Silver Spring, MD 20904; phone: 301-680-8950).

HOME STAYS

United States Servas (11 John St., Room 407, New York, NY 10038; phone: 212-267-0252; fax: 212-267-0292) maintains a list of hosts worldwide willing to accommodate visitors free of charge. The aim of this nonprofit cultural program is to promote international understanding and peace, and *Servas* emphasizes that member travelers should be interested mainly in their hosts, not in sightseeing, during their stays.

CONVENTS, MONASTERIES, AND SEMINARIES

Travelers to Italy also have the option of staying in a convent, monastery, or other religious institution. Some provide accommodations for men or women only, and many observe curfews, closing their doors promptly at 10 or 11 PM. The *Italian Government Travel Office (ENIT)* can supply a list of institutions; you also can write directly to the archdiocese of the city or town you plan to visit.

Time Zones

Italy falls into the Greenwich plus 1 time zone, which means that the time is six hours later than in East Coast US cities. Italy moves its clocks ahead an hour in the spring and back an hour in the fall, corresponding to daylight saving time, although the exact dates of the changes are different from those observed in the US. Italian timetables use a 24-hour clock to denote arrival and departure times, which means that hours are expressed sequentially from 1 AM—for example, 1:30 PM would be "13:30" or "13h30."

Business and Shopping Hours

Most businesses and shops are open weekdays from 8:30 AM to 1 PM, and from 3 or 3:30 PM until 6 or 7 PM, although an increasing number are staying open through midday and closing at 5 PM. Shops also often are open on Saturdays (usually from around 10 AM to 1 PM, and from 3 PM to 6 or 7 PM). Major department stores and shopping centers are open Mondays through Saturdays from 9:30 AM to 6:30 PM and usually skip the midday break.

Most shops are closed on Sundays, and smaller establishments may be closed for a half or full day on Mondays as well. Department stores (and some shops), however, may open on Sundays, and also may stay open late (until around 8 PM) at least one day a week.

Banks typically are open weekdays from 8:30 AM to 1:30 PM; some also reopen between 3:00 and 5:30 PM. Money exchanges in international airports may be open 24 hours daily.

Holidays

Below is a list of public holidays in Italy and the dates they will be observed this year. (Note that the dates of some holidays vary from year to year; others occur on the same day every year.) In addition to the national holidays listed below, the feast day of a city's patron saint—such as the *Feast Day of St. Mark* in Venice (April 25)—is a local public holiday.

New Year's Day (January 1)
Epiphany (January 6)
Good Friday (April 14)
Easter Sunday (April 16)
Easter Monday (April 17)
Liberation Day (April 25)
Labor Day (May 1)

Ferragosto or *The Assumption of the Virgin* (August 15)
All Saints' Day (November 1)
Immaculate Conception (December 8)
Christmas Day (December 25)
Feast Day of St. Stephen (December 26)

San Marino celebrates most of the Italian public holidays, as well as a few of its own. Many businesses stay open on these days.

Feast of St. Agatha (February 5)
Investiture of the Captains Regent (April 1 and October 1)
San Marino's Day (September 3)

Mail

The *Italian Postal Service,* or *Ufficio Postale,* has branches in every city, town, and village, as well as at train stations, airports, and other transportation centers. Most post offices are open weekdays from 8 or 8:30 AM to 1 or 1:30 PM, and Saturdays until noon. Branches at international airports and main post offices in major cities provide telegram, telex, and fax services 24 hours daily. Stamps *(francobolli)* also are sold at some hotels, authorized tobacconists, and shops. Letters can be mailed in the red letter boxes found on the street, but it is better to mail letters (and certainly packages) directly from post offices.

Mail service to and from Italy can be slow; allow at least 10 days for delivery in either direction. Send mail *posta aerea* (airmail) if it's going any distance, and to ensure or further speed delivery, send it *raccomandata* (registered mail) or *espresso* (special delivery). Always use postal codes; delivery of your letter or parcel may depend on it. If your correspondence is especially important, you may want to send it via an international courier service, such as *Federal Express* (phone: 800-238-5355 in the US; 167-833040, toll-free, in Italy) or *DHL Worldwide Express* (phone: 800-225-5345 in the US; 39-6-790821 for the Rome office).

You can have mail sent to you care of your hotel or the main post office *(Ufficio Postale Centrale)* in any Italian city or town. The address should include *"Fermo Posta"*—the Italian equivalent of "General Delivery." Most *American Express* offices in Italy also will hold mail for customers ("c/o Client Letter Service"); information is provided in their pamphlet *Travelers' Companion.* Note that *US Embassies* and *Consulates* abroad will hold mail for US citizens *only* in emergency situations.

Telephone

Direct dialing and other familiar services all are available in Italy. The number of digits in Italian phone numbers varies throughout the country. Italian telephone directories and other sources often include the 0 (used for dialing within Italy) as part of the city code; when dialing from the US, follow the procedure described below, *leaving off the 0.* Also note that the city code may be included in the digits quoted as the "local" number.

The standard procedures for making calls to, from, and within Italy are as follows:

> **To call a number in Italy from the US:** Dial 011 (the international access code) + 39 (the country code for Italy) + the city code + the local number.
>
> **To call a number in the US from Italy:** Dial 00 (the international access code) + 1 (the US country code) + the area code + the local number.
>
> **To make a call between Italian cities:** Dial 0 + the city code + the local number.
>
> **To call a number within the same Italian city code coverage area:** Dial the local number.

Public telephones are found in cafés, restaurants, and, less commonly, in booths on the street. Although many public phones in Italy used to take special tokens *(gettoni),* these are being phased out, and most phones now accept lire coins or phone debit cards *(carte telefoniche).* Phone debit cards (as well as the old *gettoni*) can be purchased at offices of the *Società Italiana per l'Esercizio Telefonico (SIP),* the Italian national telephone company, and at train stations, tobacconists, newsstands, cafés, and bars. They also are sold at *Posto Telefonico Pubblico (PTP)* telephone centers in cities and towns throughout Italy, where long-distance and international calls can be made.

You can use a telephone company calling card number on any phone, and some pay phones take major credit cards *(American Express, MasterCard, Visa,* and so on). Also available are combined telephone calling/bank credit cards, such as the *AT&T Universal Card* (PO Box 44167, Jacksonville, FL 32231-4167; phone: 800-423-4343). Similarly, *Sprint* (8140 Ward Pkwy., Kansas City, MO 64114; phone: 800-THE-MOST or 800-800-USAA) offers the *VisaPhone* program, through which you can add phone card privileges to your existing *Visa* card. Companies offering long-distance phone cards without additional credit card privileges include *AT&T* (phone: 800-CALL-ATT), *Executive Telecard International* (4260 E. Evans Ave., Suite 6, Denver, CO 80222; phone: 800-950-3800), *MCI* (323 Third St. SE, Cedar Rapids, IA 52401; phone: 800-444-4444; and 12790 Merit Dr., Dallas, TX 75251; phone: 800-444-3333), *Metromedia Communications* (1 International Center, 100 NE Loop 410, San Antonio, TX 78216; phone: 800-275-0200), and *Sprint* (address above).

Hotels routinely add surcharges to the cost of phone calls made from their rooms. Long-distance telephone services that may help you avoid this added expense are provided by a number of companies, including *AT&T*

(International Information Service, 635 Grant St., Pittsburgh, PA 15219; phone: 800-874-4000), *MCI* (address above), *Metromedia Communications* (address above), and *Sprint* (address above). Note that even when you use such long-distance services, some hotels still may charge a fee for line usage.

AT&T's Language Line Service (phone: 800-752-6096) provides interpretive services for telephone communications in Italian. Additional resources for travelers include the *AT&T 800 Travel Directory* (phone: 800-426-8686 for orders), the *Toll-Free Travel & Vacation Information Directory* (Pilot Books, 103 Cooper St., Babylon, NY 11702; phone: 516-422-2225; fax: 516-422-2227), and *The Phone Booklet* (Scott American Corporation, PO Box 88, W. Redding, CT 06896; no phone).

Important Phone Numbers

Emergency assistance: 113.
Local and countrywide information: 1412.
Local and long-distance operator (for calls within Italy): 156
International operator: 15 for intra-European calls; 170 for other international calls.

Electricity

Italy uses 220-volt, 50-cycle alternating current, although 125-volt current still exists in some areas. Travelers from the US will need electrical converters to operate the appliances they use at home, or dual-voltage appliances, which can be switched from one voltage standard to another. (Some large tourist hotels may offer 110-volt current or may have converters available.) You also will need a plug adapter set to deal with the different plug configurations found in Italy.

Staying Healthy

For up-to-date information on current health conditions, call the Centers for Disease Control's *International Travelers' Hotline*: 404-332-4559.

Travelers to Italy face few serious health risks. Tap water generally is clean and potable throughout the country. Ask if the water is meant for drinking, but if you're at all unsure, bottled water is readily available in stores. Milk is pasteurized (although it may not be homogenized), and dairy products are safe to eat, as are fruit, vegetables, meat, poultry, and fish. Because of Mediterranean pollution, however, all seafood should be eaten cooked, and make sure it is *fresh,* particularly in the heat of the summer, when inadequate refrigeration is an additional concern.

When swimming in the ocean, be careful of the undertow (the water running back down the beach after a wave has washed ashore), which can knock you off your feet, and riptides (currents running against the tide), which can pull you out to sea. Sharks are found in coastal waters, but rarely come close to shore. Jellyfish—including the Portuguese man-of-war—as well as eels and sea urchins also are found, although these creatures are relatively uncommon.

Italy has socialized medicine, and low-cost medical care is provided to Italian citizens. However, visitors from the US and other countries that are not members of the European Economic Community (which provides reciprocal health coverage) will have to pay full fees.

There are both public and private hospitals in Italy. Italian law specifies that seriously injured, ill, or unconscious persons be taken directly to a public hospital *(ospedale)*. After treatment in the emergency room *(pronto soccorso)*, a patient in stable condition may transfer to the hospital of his or her choice. The private hospitals are called *case di cura* (houses of care or cure), villas, or clinics. In cases of extreme medical emergency, US military hospitals on bases in Catania (Sicily), Livorno, Naples, and Vicenza may treat travelers who are seriously ill or injured until their conditions are stabilized and they can be moved to another facility. Public hospitals often have walk-in clinics; visits to clinics at private hospitals usually require appointments.

Italian drugstores, *(farmacie;* singular, *farmacia)* are identified by a red cross or a caduceus in front. Night duty rotates among pharmacies, and those that are closed display the address of the nearest drugstore on duty that evening *(la farmacia di torno)*. This information also may be published in local newspapers or may be available from telephone operators or the police. Note that a pharmacy on night duty will not necessarily stay open all night. In larger cities, however, the pharmacist remains "on call" once the store has closed, and there always is someone you can contact should you need a prescription filled in an emergency. In smaller towns, you may have to go to the nearest hospital emergency room to have a prescription filled after hours.

Should you need non-emergency medical attention, ask at your hotel for the house physician or for help in reaching a doctor. Referrals also are available from the *US Embassy* or a *US Consulate.* **In an emergency: Go to the emergency room of the nearest hospital, dial the emergency number provided in *Telephone*, above, or call an operator for assistance. If possible, someone who can translate into Italian should make the call.**

Additional Resources

InterContinental Medical (2720 Enterprise Pkwy., Suite 106, Richmond, VA 23294; phone: 804-527-1094; fax: 804-527-1941).

International Association for Medical Assistance to Travelers (*IAMAT;* 417 Center St., Lewiston, NY 14092; phone: 716-754-4883; and 40 Regal Rd., Guelph, Ontario N1K 1B5, Canada; phone: 519-836-0102; fax: 519-836-3412).

International Health Care Service (440 E. 69th St., New York, NY 10021; phone: 212-746-1601).

International SOS Assistance (PO Box 11568, Philadelphia, PA 19116; phone: 800-523-8930 or 215-244-1500; fax: 215-244-2227).

Medic Alert Foundation (2323 Colorado Ave., Turlock, CA 95382; phone: 800-ID-ALERT or 209-668-3333; fax: 209-669-2495).

Travel Care International (*Eagle River Airport*, PO Box 846, Eagle River, WI 54521; phone: 800-5-AIR-MED or 715-479-8881; fax: 715-479-8178).

TravMed (PO Box 10623, Baltimore, MD 21285-0623; phone: 800-732-5309 or 410-296-5225; fax: 410-825-7523).

Consular Services

The American Services section of the *US Consulate* is a vital source of assistance and advice for US citizens abroad. If you are injured or become seriously ill, the consulate can direct you to sources of medical attention and notify your relatives. If you become involved in a dispute that could lead to legal action, the consulate can provide a list of English-speaking attorneys. In cases of natural disasters or civil unrest, consulates handle the evacuation of US citizens if necessary.

The *US State Department* operates an automated 24-hour *Citizens' Emergency Center* travel advisory hotline (phone: 202-647-5225). You also can reach a duty officer at this number from 8:15 AM to 10 PM, eastern standard time on weekdays, and from 9 AM to 3 PM on Saturdays. At all other times, call 202-647-4000. For faxed travel warnings and other consular information, call 202-647-3000 using the handset on your fax machine; instructions will be provided. With a PC and a modem, you can access the consular affairs electronic bulletin board (phone: 202-647-9225).

The US Embassy and Consulates in Italy

Embassy

Rome: 119/A Via Veneto, Rome 00187, Italy (phone: 39-6-46741; fax: 39-6-467-42217); *Consular section:* 121 Via Veneto, Rome 00187, Italy (phone: same as *Embassy;* fax: 39-6-488-2672).

Consulates

Florence: 38 Lungarno Amerigo Vespucci, Florence 50123, Italy (phone: 39-55-239-8276; fax: 39-55-284088).

Milan: 2-10 Via Principe Amedeo, Milan 20121, Italy (phone: 39-2-290351; fax: 39-2-290-01165).

Naples: Piazza della Repubblica, Naples 80122, Italy (phone: 39-81-583-8111; fax: 39-81-761-1869).

Entry Requirements and Customs Regulations

ENTERING ITALY

A valid US passport is the only document a US citizen needs to enter Italy. As a general rule, a passport entitles the bearer to remain in Italy for up to 90 days as a tourist. A traveler wishing to stay for an additional 90-day period can apply at any police station *(questura)*. Visitors are required to register with the local police within three days of arrival at each separate destination in Italy. (If you are staying at a hotel, the staff can do this for you.)

A visa is required for study, residency, work, or stays of more than six months. Proof of means of independent financial support is pertinent to the acceptance of any long-term–stay application. US citizens should contact the *Italian Embassy* or the nearest *Italian Consulate* well in advance of their trip.

You are allowed to enter Italy with the following items duty-free: 400 cigarettes and 500 grams (1.1 pounds) of cigars or pipe tobacco; 2 bottles of wine and 1 bottle of hard liquor; 2 still cameras and 10 rolls of film for each camera; 1 movie camera or camcorder and 10 reels of film or videocassettes; and personal effects and sports equipment appropriate to a pleasure trip.

DUTY-FREE SHOPS

Located in international airports, duty-free shops provide bargains on the purchase of goods imported to Italy from other countries. But beware: Not all foreign goods are automatically less expensive. You *can* get a good deal on some items, but know what they cost elsewhere. Also note that although these goods are free of the duty that *Italian Customs* normally would assess, they will be subject to US import duty upon your return to the US (see below).

VALUE ADDED TAX (VAT)

Called *imposta sul valore aggiunto (IVA)* in Italy, this sales tax (typically 19%) is applicable to most goods and services. Although everyone must pay the tax, foreigners often can obtain a partial refund if their purchases in a single store total at least 300,000 lire (about $188 at press time). Note that a refund is *not* applicable to purchases of certain goods, such as food, medicine, books, and records.

Many stores participate in the *Europe Tax-Free Shopping (ETFS)* program, which enables visitors to obtain cash refunds at the airport upon departure. The procedure is as follows: Request a tax-free shopping voucher at the store when you make your purchase. Keep the store receipt with the voucher as proof of purchase. At the airport, have the voucher stamped by

Italian Customs officials, and then take it to the cash refund desk or agent (customs officials can direct you) for your refund.

If you purchase goods at a store that does not participate in the *ETFS* program, you still may be able to obtain a refund, although the procedure is somewhat more complicated and, unfortunately, subject to long delays. Request special refund forms for this purpose when making your purchase. These must be stamped by *Italian Customs* officials at the airport upon departure, and then mailed back to the *store,* which processes the refund. The refund will arrive—eventually—in the form of a check (usually in lire) mailed to your home or, if the purchase was made with a credit card, as a credit to your account.

Note that stores are under no obligation to participate in either of the VAT refund programs, so ask if you will be able to get a refund *before* making any major purchases. For additional information, contact the Italian office of *Europe Tax-Free Shopping* (3 Via C. Battisti, Gazzada 21045, Italy; phone: 39-332-870770; fax: 39-332-870771) or the Italian tourist authorities.

RETURNING TO THE US

You must declare to the *US Customs* official at the point of entry everything you have acquired in Italy. The standard duty-free allowance for US citizens is $400. If your trip is shorter than 48 continuous hours, or if you have been outside the US within 30 days of your current trip, the duty-free allowance is reduced to $25. Families traveling together may make a joint customs declaration. To avoid paying duty unnecessarily on expensive items (such as computer equipment) that you plan to take with you on your trip, register these items with *US Customs* before you depart.

A flat 10% duty is assessed on the next $1,000 worth of merchandise; additional items are taxed at a variety of rates (see *Tariff Schedules of the United States* in a library or any *US Customs Service* office). Some articles are duty-free only up to certain limits. The $400 allowance includes one carton of (200) cigarettes, 100 cigars (not Cuban), and one liter of liquor or wine (for those over 21); the $25 allowance includes 10 cigars, 50 cigarettes, and four ounces of perfume. With the exception of gifts valued at $50 or less sent directly to the recipient, *all* items shipped home are dutiable.

Antiques (at least 100 years old) and paintings or drawings done entirely by hand are duty-free. However, you must obtain a permit from the local office of the *Ufficio Esportazione d'Oggetti d'Arte* (1 Via Cernaia, Rome 00185, Italy; phone: 39-6-488-1457) to take works of art, archaeological finds, or other artifacts out of Italy. If items are purchased in a gallery, the gallery often will obtain the permit for you.

FORBIDDEN IMPORTS

Note that US regulations prohibit the import of some goods sold abroad, such as fresh fruits and vegetables, most meat products (except certain canned goods), and dairy products (except for fully cured cheeses). Also prohibited are articles made from plants or animals on the endangered species list.

FOR ADDITIONAL INFORMATION Consult one of the following publications, available from the *US Customs Service* (PO Box 7407, Washington, DC 20044): *Currency Reporting; GSP and the Traveler; Importing a Car; International Mail Imports; Know Before You Go; Pets, Wildlife, US Customs;* and *Pocket Hints. Travelers' Tips on Bringing Food, Plant, and Animal Products into the United States* is available from the *United States Department of Agriculture, Animal and Plant Health Inspection Service (USDA-APHIS;* 6505 Belcrest Rd., Room 613-FB, Hyattsville, MD 20782; phone: 301-436-7799; fax: 301-436-5221). For tape-recorded information on customs-related topics, call 202-927-2095 from any touch-tone phone.

For Further Information

Branches of the *Italian Government Travel Office (ENIT)* in the US are the best sources of travel information. Offices generally are open on weekdays, during normal business hours. For information on entry requirements and customs regulations, contact the *Italian Embassy* or an *Italian Consulate.*

Italian Government Travel Offices

Chicago: 500 N. Michigan Ave., Suite 1046, Chicago, IL 60611 (phone: 312-644-0990).

Los Angeles: 12400 Wilshire Blvd., Suite 550, Los Angeles, CA 90025 (phone: 310-820-0098; fax: 310-820-6357).

New York: 630 Fifth Ave., Suite 1565, New York, NY 10111 (phone: 212-245-4822; fax: 212-586-9249).

The Italian Embassy and Consulates in the US

Embassy

Washington, DC: 1601 Fuller St. NW, Washington, DC 20009 (phone: 202-328-4760; fax: 202-462-3605).

Consulates

California: *Consulate General,* 12400 Wilshire Blvd., Suite 300, Los Angeles, CA 90025 (phone: 310-820-0622; fax: 310-820-0727); *Consulate General,* 2590 Webster St., San Francisco, CA 94115 (phone: 415-931-4924; fax: 415-931-7205).

Florida: *Consulate General,* 1200 Brickell Ave., Eighth floor, Miami, FL 33131 (phone: 305-374-6322; fax: 305-374-7945).

Illinois: *Consulate General,* 500 N. Michigan Ave., Suite 1850, Chicago, IL 60611 (phone: 312-467-1550/1/2/3; fax: 312-467-1335).

Louisiana: *Consulate,* 630 Camp St., New Orleans, LA 70130 (phone: 504-524-1557; fax: 504-581-4590).

Massachusetts: *Consulate General,* 100 Boylston St., Suite 900, Boston, MA 02116 (phone: 617-542-0483/4; fax: 617-542-3998).

Michigan: *Consulate,* 535 Griswold St., Suite 1840, Detroit, MI 48226 (phone: 313-963-8560; fax: 313-963-8180).

New York: *Consulate General,* 690 Park Ave., New York, NY 10021 (phone: 212-737-9100; fax: 212-249-4945).

Pennsylvania: *Consulate General,* 1026 Public Ledger Building, 100 S. Sixth St., Philadelphia, PA 19106 (phone: 215-592-7329; fax: 215-592-9808).

Texas: *Consulate General,* 1300 Post Oak Blvd., Suite 660, Houston, TX 77056 (phone: 713-850-7520; fax: 713-850-9113).

The Cities

Bologna

The principal city of the Emilia-Romagna region, Bologna is known to Italians by a variety of nicknames: *Bologna la Dotta* (the Learned), *Bologna la Turrita* (the Turreted), and *Bologna la Grassa* (the Fat). The first sobriquet refers to the city's university, believed to be Europe's oldest, founded in the 11th century; the second recalls the few remaining, spectacular medieval towers that once gave Bologna an astonishing skyline; and the third attests to the city's reputation as the country's gastronomic center.

Human settlement first appeared on the site of the present city sometime in the 9th century BC, followed by the Etruscans. The Etruscans named their city Felsina, and the settlement grew rapidly until it became the Etruscan capital of the entire Po Valley. For about 200 years (600–400 BC), the city enjoyed great prosperity as a result of the fertility of the surrounding plain. In fact, the extraordinarily productive farmland of Emilia-Romagna was to prove as much a curse as a blessing, since everybody wanted it.

The first marauders were the Gauls, who took Felsina and—some say—called the city Bononia, after the name of their Gaulish tribe, the Boia. Others claim that the modern name of the city originated some two centuries later with the arrival of the Romans, who already had a flourishing seaport not far away at Rimini. In 189 BC, the Romans evicted the Gauls and immediately set about building a new city, whose name eventually became Bologna. The Romans gave the city a single, extremely important reason to be: They built the consular road that joins Milan to Rimini, the Via Emilia, directly through the middle of it—and the road still slices through the heart of the city today.

Bologna's Roman period seems to have been tranquil except for a devastating fire in AD 53. In an odd twist of history, Nero, the Roman emperor at the time, insisted that Bologna be rebuilt; not long afterward he was to burn his hometown, Rome, to the ground.

With the decline of Roman influence, Bologna alternated between masters, a period that was to last, with few interruptions, until World War II. In 476, the city was taken by the Goths, who held it for less than a century. Then it came under the Byzantine rule of the Eastern Roman Empire. By the beginning of the 8th century, the Lombards had taken over the city; by the end of that century, Charlemagne had taken it for the Franks—and promptly gave it to the pope.

A rebellion of the Bolognese in 1116 loosened the papal grip on the city, but it wasn't long before Frederick Barbarossa swept down from the north and conquered the entire area, Bologna included. By 1176 Barbarossa had been defeated at Legnano by the Lombard League, and the Bolognese immediately began a lengthy struggle to remain independent, this time successfully resisting one of Frederick II's sons, Enzo, King of Sardinia. They succeeded, capturing Enzo and imprisoning him (in luxury) until the day he died.

During the next few centuries, the turmoil that afflicted the city was primarily homegrown: Three noble families—the Viscontis, the Pepolis, and the Bentivoglios—battled for control, with the last finally winning out. The Bentivoglios held Bologna until 1506, when Julius II, the Warrior Pope, wrested it from their control and set out to make it the Rome of the north. In 1582 Pope Gregory XIII, one of Bologna's more illustrious native sons (and one of the three popes born in Bologna), gave the world its present calendar. Meanwhile, over the next several decades, the Bentivoglios tried in vain to reconquer the city many times. Bologna was in papal hands until 1796, when it was lost again, this time to the French, who had invaded Italy under the command of Napoleon. From 1796 to 1816, the city passed back and forth between the French and their Austrian enemies three times.

By 1816, the Austrians had taken charge and, despite being evicted often by the Bolognese themselves, held effective sway until 1860, when the city passed by plebiscite to the kingdom of Savoy and thus to the kingdom of Italy. Bologna had little role in World War I, but in World War II, as the center of German resistance in the Po Valley (which the Germans used as a breadbasket for the fatherland), it was severely damaged.

Despite all this martial to-and-fro, Bologna had time to build a city of great beauty and charm, remarkably intact, considering its warlike past. (Its *centro storico*—historic center—is considered to be one of Italy's first and best urban conservation projects.) And as the great buildings and the arcaded streets that are Bologna's signature were going up, some magnificent meals were being served. Bolognese history—not to mention its civic pride—is inextricably bound up with its food. The fertility of the surrounding land made the city a target, and its culinary traditions marked it a worthy prize.

Ask any Italian where the best food in Italy is served, and the answer is sure to be "my hometown." But that is just regional chauvinism—all Italians agree that the *second*-best food in Italy comes from Bologna. Food—its preparation, presentation, and consumption—is particularly serious business in Bologna. The city has given its name to the international classic *spaghetti alla bolognese* and, less notably, to "baloney" (although a Bolognese would probably be hard-pressed to find any connection between American delicatessen baloney and its noble Italian ancestor, mortadella, that has been made hereabouts since Roman times). Once you've had the real thing, it will be hard to settle for a pale imitation.

The dish for which *la cucina bolognese* is most famous is a pasta called tortellini, tiny sachets stuffed with lean pork, grated cheese, eggs, and nutmeg. Bologna's ancient and more recent history is filled with references to the quality of tortellini—it has been featured in plays, songs, and poems.

Another aspect of everyday life in Bologna is its university. Believed to be the oldest in Europe (and possibly the world), it celebrated its 900-year anniversary in 1988. At its beginnings, this institution of higher education was the first to make learning a secular activity. Bologna's *Alma Mater Studiorum* (as it was originally known) explored the concept of society, teaching the basics of what would later come to be regarded as European law. Because Bologna was a free commune in the *Studiorum*'s early days, new ideas flourished and were liberally exchanged. The *Palazzo dell'Archiginnasio* was built in 1562 (when students accounted for one-third of the city's population) as the seat of the university in order to bring together all the faculties that were scattered around Bologna. In 1803, the university moved into the *Palazzo Poggi,* where it remains today. For centuries, the life of the city and university were inextricable, and today the school still plays a major role in Bologna—the average age of everyone you see appears to be twentysomething, and the most prevalent profession is long-term student.

Bologna has never really caught on as a prime stop for foreign visitors, which is both good and bad. Hotel rooms are easy to find (except during one of the frequent major trade fairs or conventions), prices are comparatively moderate, and hotel workers and waiters are cordial. But Bologna deserves to be more widely appreciated, and much awaits the lucky visitor: beautiful buildings, fabulous shops, an unhurried pace, charming and courteous people, and, best of all, the food that made Bologna *la Grassa.*

Bologna At-a-Glance

SEEING THE CITY

Pisa is by no means the only city in Italy that boasts a leaning tower. In the heart of Bologna, in Piazza di Porta Ravegnana, are its two famous leaning towers, *Le Due Torri,* side by side. The taller of the two, the *Torre degli Asinelli,* was built between 1109 and 1119; it is said to have been used as a prison in the 14th century. It soars 320 feet above the busy streets and leans four feet from the perpendicular. Steep stairs—486 of them—lead to the top, and the vista from the viewing platform is nothing short of spectacular. On a clear day, all of Bologna is visible, and most of the surrounding province as well. It's open daily; admission charge. The shorter of the twin towers is the *Torre Garisenda,* which dates from about the same time as its partner. A mere 160 feet high, it's closed to visitors—just as well, perhaps, since it has a noticeable 10-foot list. The *Garisenda* is thought to have once been as tall as its neighbor but was shortened for (understandable) reasons of safety in the 14th century. Taken together, the two towers provide a good sense of the historic *Bologna la Turrita.* It is thought that there were once 180 such towers in the city, and some 20 truncated stumps still mark the skyline.

SPECIAL PLACES

The heart of Bologna is made up of two adjoining squares, the huge Piazza Maggiore and the smaller Piazza del Nettuno, which takes its name from the robust statue of Neptune that dominates it. A major restoration of Piazza Maggiore's ancient pavement was scheduled to begin at press time, funds permitting. Clustered around these two majestic spaces are some of the major sights of the city. Together with the nearby Piazza di Porta Ravegnana, they create a blend of rare architectural beauty. Note that some sites of interest in Bologna close for a midday break, usually from noon or 12:30 PM to 3 or 3:30 PM; we suggest calling ahead to check exact hours.

CENTER

BASILICA DI SAN PETRONIO (BASILICA OF ST. PETRONIUS) This huge church on one side of Piazza Maggiore is dedicated to St. Petronius, a 5th-century Bishop of Bologna and one of the town's patron saints, who was well known both for his political interests and civic-mindedness and for his devoutness. Although it would seem an obvious choice (given its size and location), *San Petronio* is not the city's cathedral. That distinction belongs to *San Pietro* (also known as *La Metropolitana*), an impressive structure begun in 1605, close by on Via dell'Indipendenza. *San Petronio* was begun in 1390 based on plans by the Bolognese maestro Antonio di Vincenzo, and although work went on for the next three centuries or so, it was never finished, as is immediately evident in the only partly decorated façade. The bottom half is faced in marble and graced with exceptional carvings over and around the three doorways. Particularly noteworthy is the center door, capped with a lovely Madonna and Child flanked by Saints Petronius and Ambrose, an early-15th-century work by the Sienese sculptor Jacopo della Quercia. The rest of the façade is unadorned, affording a good look at an Italian Gothic cathedral "under the skin," so to speak—this is considered a fine example of Gothic brickwork.

The first impression on entering the basilica is one of vast, unadulterated space. While grand, the dimensions—433 feet long, 190 feet wide, and 144 feet high—shrink somewhat with the realization that the building was designed to be some *300 feet longer* and was meant to be surmounted by a dome soaring 500 feet from the floor. A depleted treasury and Bologna's unsettled history account for this more "modest" structure. (Outside, beyond the apse, is a row of columns erected as part of the unfinished plan.) The interior is notable not only for its size but also for some highly original works of art in the 22 side chapels, the most peculiar of which is the *Inferno* of Giovanni da Modena in the *Chapel of the Magi*. This large painting is a particularly gruesome, but finely executed, fantasy vision of hell: A black beast single-mindedly devouring the damned through two mouths (one rather unconventionally placed) dominates a very busy group of devils as they fry, puncture, and flay hordes of sinners. The picture was meant to scare the living onto the straight and narrow path—and probably succeeded.

Set in the floor, and running the length of the nave at a slight angle to the left of the main altar, is the meridian line of the astronomer Gian Domenico Cassini. Laid down in 1655, the line in effect turned the entire church into a giant timepiece. A tiny hole in the roof admits a ray of the sun that works its way along the line, showing local time. Although adjusted several times over the centuries, it is now seriously out of whack. Open daily. The on-site museum details the church's history; it's open Mondays, Wednesdays, and Fridays through Sundays from 10 AM to 12:30 PM. No admission charge. Piazza Maggiore (phone: 220637, museum).

PALAZZO DEL PODESTÀ (MAYOR'S PALACE) Directly across Piazza Maggiore from the basilica, this older building dates from the 13th century, although it was considerably remodeled in 1470 by Aristotle Fioravanti, who also designed the *Basilica of Our Lady of the Assumption* in the Kremlin in Moscow. The *Torre dell'Arengo,* the tower surmounting it, dates from the original structure and contains a massive bell that was rung in times of celebration or distress. Nestled in the corners of the vaults of the archway are four sculpted figures representing the four patrons of the city: St. Petronius, St. Florian, St. Eligius, and St. Francis. The interior of the palazzo is open sporadically for exhibits on its upper floors, or with a private guide. Admission charge. Piazza Maggiore (no phone).

PALAZZO COMUNALE (TOWN HALL) Also facing Piazza Maggiore is this restored massive edifice, actually two buildings joined together. The extreme difference in façade marks where one ends and the other begins. Also known as the *Palazzo d'Accursio,* the structure has been the seat of the Bolognese city government since the 14th century. Over the entrance is a heavy bronze statue of Pope Gregory XIII, a native of Bologna who gave his name in 1582 to the calendar still in use today. The 15th-century terra cotta statue of the Virgin and Child, to the left of the pope, is by Nicolò dell'Arca, a Pugliese artist who worked extensively in Bologna. In the courtyard of the palace is a wide and gently sloping staircase said to be by Bramante; the width of the steps and their easy grade were designed to be climbed by men on horseback, since fully armed and mounted riders were always a feature of ceremonial occasions. On the first floor of the building is the *Sala di Ercole* (Chamber of Hercules), taking its name from the giant statue of the mythical strong man that dominates the room. There is more sculpture on the second floor in the *Sala* and *Cappella Farnese.* About 20 rooms usually are open to the public (although at press time a number were closed for restoration) on this upper floor of the palazzo, all lavishly decorated and displaying paintings of the Bolognese school and works of other Italian masters of the 13th to 19th centuries that make up the Municipal Art Collections. The large windows afford excellent views of the piazza and the city. In 1993, the building became home to the *Museo Giorgio Morandi* (see below). Piazza Maggiore (phone: 203040; 203526, Municipal Art Collections).

MUSEO GIORGIO MORANDI (GIORGIO MORANDI MUSEUM) Ensconced in reconstructed rooms on the second floor of the *Palazzo Comunale* (see above), this is the world's richest collection of work by Bologna's favorite son, who died in 1964. In the museum are 216 works (paintings, etchings, watercolors, and drawings), as well as the artist's own collection of antique art, his private library of more than 500 volumes, and his reconstructed bedroom and studio. Closed Mondays. Admission charge. Piazza Maggiore (phone: 203464).

FONTANA DEL NETTUNO (NEPTUNE FOUNTAIN) Whether viewed from above, from the windows of the *Palazzo Comunale,* or head on at street level, the proportions and grace of this famous fountain are readily apparent. However viewed, Neptune's pose was designed to encourage a desire to walk around him. One of the best examples of a Renaissance fountain in this part of Italy, it was designed by Tomaso Lareti, but actually was constructed and sculpted (1564) by a Flemish artist. His name, however, has been Italianized: No longer Jean de Boulogne, he is now known as Giambologna. The fountain has been painstakingly restored twice, most recently in 1992. Piazza del Nettuno.

PALAZZO DI RE ENZO (KING ENZO'S PALACE) Built in 1200 and last restored in 1905, this somber building next to the *Palazzo del Podestà* (see above) has much within it to recall Bologna's violent past. From 1249 to 1272, it was the prison of the hapless son of the emperor Federico Barbarossa, King Enzo (who died here; he's buried at *San Domenico)*, and other unfortunates. In the courtyard of the building is a small church, *Santa Maria dei Carcerati* (St. Mary of the Incarcerated), built to offer last rites to prisoners as they were taken from the palazzo to their execution in Piazza Maggiore just outside. The *Carroccio,* the medieval battle symbol of the warlike Bolognese, is usually kept inside the palace, although it has been removed for restoration. Consisting of an ox cart carrying an altar, a bell, and the sacred and secular banners of Bologna, the *Carroccio* was hauled into battle and defended to the death by an elite corps of soldiers drawn from the first families of the city. Open only when there are exhibits, or with a private guide. Admission charge. Piazza del Nettuno (no phone).

PALAZZO DELL'ARCHIGINNASIO Originally the seat of the university, this palazzo was built in the 16th century to bring the university's scattered campuses under one roof. Today, it serves as the town library, with approximately half a million volumes on its top floors. The courtyard, corridors, and staircases are covered with the coats of arms of early professors and students, and upstairs in the *Teatro Anatomico* (which the custodian will open on request) are models of the human anatomy set on pedestals. Built in 1637 and completely rebuilt following damage in World War II, it's paneled in wood and contains two interesting anatomical figures dating from 1735. Some parts of the palazzo are open only with a private guide. Library closed

Saturday afternoons and Sundays; *Teatro Anatomico* closed afternoons and Sundays. No admission charge. 1 Piazza Galvani (phone: 236488).

BASILICA DI SAN DOMENICO (CHURCH OF ST. DOMINIC) Both this church and the site it occupies are rich in associations with St. Dominic, who founded a convent on the spot in 1219 and died here in 1221. In the building itself (construction was begun immediately after his death), the sacristan will show, on request, the cell where he lived. An 18th-century renovation totally ruined the medieval character of the interior, but it still contains an exceptional work of art, the *Arca di San Domenico,* or tomb of the saint. Many artists contributed to this masterpiece, but the one who had the greatest hand in it was Nicolò da Bari, who became so famous for this work that he was ever after known as Nicolò dell'Arca. (*Arca* is an archaic term for a chest or tomb; it does not refer to an arch over the tomb.) The kneeling angel on the right of the tomb and the figures of St. Petronius (holding a model of Bologna in his arms) and St. Proculus are some of the earliest known works of Michelangelo. Be sure also to see the inlaid wooden choir stalls, made by a monk, Damiano of Bergamo, in the 15th century. There are works by Filippino Lippi, Guercino, and Guido Reni (who also is buried here). A museum chronicles the church's founding, its history, and the story of St. Dominic. Closed Mondays and for a midday break. No admission charge. Outside the church in the piazza are two curious aboveground tombs, for Rolandino de' Passeggeri and Egidio Foscherari, Bologna jurists in the 13th and 14th centuries who adapted ancient Roman law to the needs of the day. Open daily, with a midday closing. 13 Piazza San Domenico (phone: 237017).

CHIESA DI SANTA MARIA DELLA VITA (ST. MARY OF LIFE CHURCH) This 17th-century church is surmounted by a beautiful 18th-century copper dome. Inside is a wonderful terra cotta *Pietà,* another masterpiece by Nicolò dell'Arca, done after 1460. Also known as the *Crying Marys,* the group is full of movement, especially in the figure of Mary Magdalene, who is almost frantic in her grief. 10 Via Clavature (phone: 236245).

CHIESA DI SANTO STEFANO (ST. STEPHEN'S CHURCH) The complex of churches that makes up this ancient house of worship is one of the most interesting sights in Bologna. There is not one church here but four; once there were seven. The four churches that remain—*Trinità, San Sepolcro* or *Calvario, Crocifisso,* and *Santi Vitale e Agricola,* the latter dating from the 5th century and said to be the oldest ecclesiastical building in Bologna—are united in a patchwork of adjoining cloisters and passages, making the complex an extremely quiet and restful place in a very busy city. The warren of rooms contains some odd and affecting devotional objects. The *San Sepolcro* (Holy Sepulcher), for example, contains what the 12th-century Bolognese imagined a replica of the tomb of Christ would look like; it also houses relics of the 5th-century St. Petronius. Beyond *San Sepolcro* is the Cortile di Pilato

(Courtyard of Pilate). Legend has it that the deep basin in the center of this beautiful courtyard is the actual bowl in which Pontius Pilate washed his hands after the condemnation of Christ. The inscription on the rim, however, dates it to the 8th century. Beyond the courtyard is an ancient, rather rustic *presepio,* a nativity scene that becomes a shrine of particular importance for the children of Bologna at *Christmas.* The remaining courtyard is given over to a memorial to the Bersaglieri, the mountain troops of the Italian army, who achieved immortality in 1870 by seizing Rome from the pope on behalf of the new Italian nation. In the back of the church is a museum that displays photographs of archaeological digs. The church and museum are open daily, with a midday closing. No admission charge. Piazza Santo Stefano (phone: 223256, museum).

PINACOTECA NAZIONALE (NATIONAL PICTURE GALLERY) Established in 1797, just after the arrival of Napoleon, this important gallery near the university contains one of the most noted collections of paintings in northern Italy. Here are first-rate examples by the immortals of Italian art—celebrated Bolognese painters of the 14th through the 19th century in particular—as well as by distinguished outsiders: Giotto, Titian, Tintoretto, and El Greco. Raphael's *Santa Cecilia* is the most famous picture displayed here. The huge exhibition space is housed in a beautifully restored former Jesuit monastery, the paintings expertly placed and perfectly lighted. Open Tuesdays through Saturdays from 9 AM to 2 PM; Sundays to 1 PM; closed Mondays. Admission charge. 56 Via delle Belle Arti (phone: 243222).

ENVIRONS

SANTUARIO DELLA MADONNA DI SAN LUCA (SANCTUARY OF THE MADONNA OF ST. LUKE) On the way into town is one of Bologna's most distinctive landmarks—an 18th-century church perched atop a hill and approached by what appears to be an attenuated version of the *Great Wall of China.* The church's main point of interest is an heirloom inherited from a previous church built on the same spot, an image of the Madonna said to have been painted by St. Luke but more likely executed much later, in the 12th century, probably by a Byzantine artist. Visitors may not be moved to come all the way to Monte della Guardia to see the Madonna (it's on view once a year in the *Cattedrale di San Pietro* on Via dell'Indipendenza; see *Special Events*), but for those who like to climb to the tops of cupolas and bell towers, the wall presents a challenge. Actually, it's a portico, the most remarkable of many such walkways in Bologna (see *Extra Special,* below) and the longest in the world. Built in the 17th and 18th centuries (it took 65 years to erect), it connects one of the old gates of the city, *Porta Saragozza,* and the church via a series of 666 covered and connected arches that climb uphill for a total distance of more than 2 miles. The view from the church is well worth the ascent, but most people take public transportation up and save the portico for a leisurely descent. Open daily, with a midday closing (phone: 412460).

EXTRA SPECIAL

Virtually all of Bologna's central streets are lined with gracefully arched and vaulted-covered passages (*portici*) leading for miles, so that it is possible to walk from one end of town to the other in the rain without getting wet—except when crossing streets. They also provide relief from Bologna's hot summer sun. There are just under 30 miles of *portici*, and they have been around a long time. They were born sometime in the 11th or 12th century, when the old wooden city of the Dark Ages was being rebuilt in stone; porticoes went up in front of each building, and gradually they were joined to make the continuous complex seen today. By 1400 their existence had been codified—uniform heights and widths were established—and laws stated that new buildings had to join the arcades, whether their owners wanted to or not. The *portici* have become as much a part of Bolognese life as tortellini and mortadella—they are always crowded with strollers, gossips, and students studying the manifestoes pasted on the inner walls. Not everybody has appreciated them, however: Goethe thought they were dark, ugly, and impractical. The local newspapers criticized him savagely for this heretical opinion and suggested that he might be happier elsewhere. Goethe left.

Sources and Resources

TOURIST INFORMATION

Two information offices in downtown Bologna offer advice and assistance in English. One, in the center of the city (6 Piazza Maggiore; phone: 239660), is closed Sunday afternoons; the other, at the main railway station (Piazza delle Medaglie d'Oro; phone: 246541), is closed Sundays and for a midday break. A third office is located at the international arrivals area at the airport (phone: 381732); it is closed Sundays and afternoons. All three offices can recommend English-language guides and make arrangements for visitors (guides can gain access to many palazzi otherwise closed to the public). One knowledgeable, multilingual guide is Herta Mulazzini (46 Via Venezia, San Lazzaro di Savena; phone: 463441). Less expensive alternatives are the guided tours offered by the city, which leave daily from 6 Piazza Maggiore; contact the tourist office at that location (see above).

LOCAL COVERAGE The bimonthly, bilingual *A Guest in Bologna* is distributed free at hotels and the tourist office. Bologna's film, music, and gallery listings can be found in *Mongolfiera,* a biweekly magazine in Italian that is available at newsstands. The newspaper that serves Bologna and the rest of the province is *Il Resto del Carlino,* one of Italy's oldest dailies. The Italian-language national newspaper, *L'Unità,* has a special insert on Fridays that lists the following week's special events. The *International Herald Tribune* can be purchased on the day of publication at the larger newsstands around Piazza Maggiore and at the train station. A colorful local guidebook published in English, *Bologna: A City to Discover,* can be bought at newsstands, bookshops, and souvenir stands.

TELEPHONE The city code for Bologna is 51. When calling from within Italy, dial 051 before the local number.

GETTING AROUND

Bologna is best seen on foot. Almost all sights of note are near the city center, and the porticoes make pedestrian traffic easy in any weather. A good part of the *centro storico* (historic center) is closed to traffic, and there are many traffic police checkpoints. Even if you don't speak Italian, merely mentioning the name of your hotel to an officer will assure you a clear passage. Once at the hotel, it's best to leave your car in a safe spot—parking in the city is nearly impossibile.

AIRPORT *Aeroporto Civile Guglielmo Marconi* (also known as *Borgo Pinigale*; 38 Via Aeroporto, 4 miles/6 km northwest of the city center; phone: 311578; 312259, information; 312297, reservations; 311810, baggage problems) serves domestic and international flights. Bus No. 91 leaves every half hour from the airport for downtown; the fare is very reasonable. With heavy traffic, the trip can take a half hour or more. A taxi to the airport is considerably more expensive.

BUS Service is excellent, comprehensive, fast, and inexpensive. Most lines run 24 hours a day, although frequency drops off considerably after midnight. You must purchase a ticket at tobacco shops or newsstands before boarding. Passengers cancel their own tickets once on board. For information, call 248374 or 247005.

CAR RENTAL All major firms are represented.

TAXI Hail cabs as they cruise, or reserve them in advance by calling 534141 or 372727. There are major taxi stands in Piazza Nettuno, Piazza Galvani, at the main train station, and at many other locations. Fares are expensive; there is a supplement at night and on Sundays and a charge for each piece of luggage that goes in the trunk.

TRAIN The main train station, *Bologna Centrale* (phone: 246490), is an important rail hub for central Italy. It's at Piazza delle Medaglie d'Oro, along Viale Pietro Pietramellara, at the head of Via dell'Indipendenza.

SPECIAL EVENTS

At any given time of the year, Bologna is probably playing host to some industrial fair or convention; the city's more than 30 annual fairs are among the most important in Europe. For information, contact *BolognaFiere* (phone: 282111; fax: 282332). The important international

Fiera del Libro per Ragazzi (Children's Book Fair), in April, and the *Bologna Motor and Bike Show*, in December, are perhaps the best known. More traditional events are definitely subordinate to such shows, but they do exist. For instance, every year, on the Sunday before *L'Ascensione* (Ascension Thursday) in May, the 12th-century Madonna that's usually in the *Santuario della Madonna di San Luca* is carried down to the city amid great fanfare to be displayed in the *Cattedrale di San Pietro* on Via dell'Indipendenza. While there, she receives the homage of the faithful, attended by men in tuxedos, and then returns home the following Sunday at the head of a procession, an event first carried out in the early 15th century. Funds permitting, every July through August the city hosts *Bologna Sogna*, when piazzas, museums, and courtyards throughout the city are backdrops for concerts, cabaret, ballets, and film revivals; contact the tourist office for details. This year marks the hundred-year anniversary of the discovery of the radio by Bologna native Marconi. Special exhibits were under way at press time; contact the tourist office for more information.

MUSEUMS

Besides those mentioned in *Special Places,* a number of other museums in Bologna may be of interest. All museums listed below charge admission unless otherwise indicated.

GALLERIA COMUNALE D'ARTE MODERNA (MODERN ART MUSEUM) An impressive exhibition of 20th-century art includes works by the surrealists, the *scuola romana,* Pollock, and Sutherland. Near the *Fiera di Bologna,* the convention center at the edge of town. Closed Mondays and for a midday break. 3 Piazza della Costituzione (phone: 502859).

MUSEO CIVICO ARCHEOLOGICO (CIVIC ARCHAEOLOGICAL MUSEUM) Housed here are Egyptian and Greco-Roman antiquities, plus a notable collection of local proto-Etruscan and Etruscan finds. Open Tuesdays through Fridays from 9 AM to 2 PM; weekends to 7 PM, with a midday closing; closed Mondays. 2 Via dell'Archiginnasio (phone: 233849).

MUSEO CIVICO MEDIOEVALE (CIVIC MEDIEVAL MUSEUM) A number of medieval sculptures, marble sepulchral monuments, applied art, armor, and weapons—mostly from Bologna and the surrounding region—are all impressively housed in a noble 15th-century palazzo. Open weekdays to 2 PM; weekends to 7 PM, with a midday closing; closed Tuesdays. No admission charge. 4 Via Manzoni (phone: 228912).

MUSEO CIVICO DEL RISORGIMENTO (CIVIC MUSEUM OF THE RISORGIMENTO) A collection of historical artifacts from the mid-19th century, housed in the home of the great poet Carducci (the wing with his memorabilia has been closed indefinitely because of a lack of funds). Closed Mondays and afternoons. 5 Piazza Carducci (phone: 347592).

SHOPPING

Bologna is one of the richest cities in Italy, and the quality and quantity of the merchandise sold here reflect its taste for *la dolce vita*. The main shopping streets are Via Rizzoli, Via Ugo Bassi, Via dell'Indipendenza, the Portico Paviglione, Via d'Azeglio, and Via Farini. Virtually all the side streets running off these are lined with shops stocking everything from puppets to high-fashion wear.

Bologna is Italy's culinary center, and much of the city is devoted to the pursuit of gastronomic pleasures. East of Piazza Maggiore is the Quadrilatero—one of the most authentic and oldest areas of Bologna. Predominantly a food district, the Quadrilatero is a medieval labyrinth of narrow streets filled with small, family-run shops that display fresh produce and handmade pasta. Street names recall the bygone era of medieval guild associations—Via Caprarie (goat and mutton butchers), Via Pescherie Vecchie (fishmongers), Via Orefici (goldsmiths), Via Mercanzie (merchants), and Via Drapperie (fabrics and tailors). Also within the Quadrilatero is the *Mercato di Via Clavature,* a produce market on the street of the same name. West of Piazza Maggiore is the larger *Mercato delle Erbe* (25 Via Ugo Bassi), where all kinds of edibles are sold at over a hundred stalls in a turn-of-the-century building.

There also are markets that sell non-food items. On Fridays and Saturdays, from dawn to dusk, the popular *Mercato della Piazzola* (Piazza VIII Agosto off Via dell'Indipendenza) offers new and secondhand goods. Here you might discover some great finds—everything from unnoticeably imperfect Richard Ginori china to closeouts on fashionable, rugged outerwear. At the *Mercato di Santo Stefano,* an antiques fair held the second weekend of every month in Piazza Santo Stefano, you won't find many bargains, but there's interesting browsing. And it wouldn't be *Christmas* in Bologna without the December fair held under the portico of *Santa Maria dei Servi.* Items for sale include local candies and endless additions for the crèche back home.

Just off the Piazza Maggiore is *Galleria Cavour,* a modern arcade of over 40 stores and boutiques. Most of the shops sell men's and women's clothing, with an emphasis on Italian designers. It also has become a popular place for a pre-dinner stroll. Enter from the Paviglione portico at Via Ferrini.

Most shops are open from 9 or 9:30 AM to 1 PM and 3:30 or 4 to 7 or 7:30 PM; closed Sundays and Thursday afternoons, with an occasional shop in the center opting to close on Saturday afternoons as well. Food stores are closed Thursday and Saturday afternoons.

Arti Decorativi A beautiful collection of Art Deco and Liberty glass, furniture, and objets d'art. 12/A Via Santo Stefano (phone: 222758).

Atti Since 1880, this has been the city's premier source for pasta, bread, and pastry. The rich and delicious fruitcake-like *certosino* is popular as a (heavy) souvenir that travels well. Two locations: 7 Via Caprarie (phone: 220425) and 6 Via Drapperie (phone: 220405).

Bongiovanni The best place in town for classical music since 1905, featuring rare operatic recordings, tapes, and disks. 28/E Via Rizzoli (phone: 225722).

Bordoli (SAIA) Fine, rare art objects; very expensive, but high quality. 1 Piazza Galvani (phone: 222603).

Bruno Magli Born in Bologna in 1908, Magli opened his first shoe factory in 1934 and went on to become an Italian ambassador of men's and women's footwear. Three central locations: 9 *Galleria Cavour* (phone: 266915); 1 Piazza della Mercanzia (phone: 231126); and 5 Via Ugo Bassi (phone: 231849).

Demitrio Presini A famous puppeteer, one of the last to make *burratini*—delightful wooden puppets with handmade costumes. 12 Via Vittorio Veneto (phone: 649-1837).

Draganczuk Top-of-the-line womenswear from Italian designers. 2/E *Galleria Cavour* (phone: 269965).

Galleria Marescalchi Bologna's finest art gallery, featuring important paintings by modern Italian masters such as De Chirico and Bologna's own Morandi. 116/B Via Marescalchi (phone: 240368).

Majani Dating from 1796, this Old World chocolate store is said to be Italy's oldest sweets source. 5 Via Carbonesi (phone: 234302).

Marisell Clothes for women, including some of the best-known Italian designers. 4 Via Farini (phone: 234670). Men shop next door at 3 Via Farini (phone: 239353).

Paris, Texas Men's and women's designer closeouts, from Armani to Moschino. 11 Via Altabella (phone: 225741) and 67/2 Via dell'Indipendenza (phone: 241994).

Piero Men's Italian-made footwear up to American size 20! 56 Via Lame (phone: 558680).

Scaramagli Bologna's answer to *Fauchon* in Paris, this wonderfully stocked and centrally located wine and food shop has flourished since 1912. 31 Strada Maggiore (phone: 227131).

Schiavina A wide selection of Italian and imported cookware and utensils in a city that's kitchen-crazy. 16 Via Clavature (phone: 223438).

Stefano Fazzini Italian and Austrian design from the early 1900s through the 1950s, including works by Gio Ponti and signed Murano glass from Venini and Seguso. 91 Via Galliera (phone: 251855).

Tamburini Always busy, Italy's most lavish food shop stocks an unbelievable assortment of prepared meat, salads, vegetables, fish, soups, and sweets. 1 Via Caprarie (phone: 234726).

Veronesi This local family name has been synonymous with excellent jewelry for centuries. Three locations: *Arrigo Veronesi* (4/F Via dell'Archiginnasio; phone: 235790) sells watches and jewelry from the 1920s as well as new items; *F. Veronesi & Figli* (4 Piazza Maggiore; phone: 224835) also has watches; and *Giulio Veronesi* (1 Piazza di Re Enzo; phone: 234237) specializes in the finest precious set stones.

SPORTS AND FITNESS

BICYCLING Rent wheels at *Tandem* (90/C Strada Maggiore; phone: 308830; or at the train station; phone: 630-2015).

GOLF *Golf Club Bologna* is an 18-hole course about 10 miles (16 km) west of town (*Calderino di Monte San Pietro,* 69 Via Sabattini; phone: 969100). It's closed Mondays.

HORSE RACING Trotting races take place year-round at the *Ippodromo Arcoveggio* (37/2 Via Arcoveggio; phone: 371505). There also is a good restaurant here (same phone number as racetrack).

HORSEBACK RIDING For a lazy afternoon canter through the hills near the city, contact the riding school and stable *Gruppo Emiliano Sport Equestre* (126 Via Jussi, San Lazzaro; phone: 625-1452).

SOCCER The Bolognese are passionate supporters of their home team (*Bologna*), which plays September through May at the *Stadio Comunale* (174 Via Andrea Costa; phone: 411651 or 411818).

SWIMMING Try *Record* (8 Via Pilastro; phone: 503311), open year-round, or the covered *Sterlino* (113 Via Murri; phone: 623-7034), closed Tuesdays and Thursdays.

TENNIS The *Federazione Tennis* (174 Via A. Costa; phone: 617-9044) can provide information about clubs and courts around Bologna that are open to the public.

THEATER

The major theater in town, *Teatro Duse* (42 Via Cartoleria; phone: 231836), stages a repertoire of modern and classical plays by Italian and foreign playwrights. Avant-garde and experimental productions are presented at *Teatro Testoni* (2 Via Tiarini; phone: 368708) and *Teatro Dehon* (59 Via Libia; phone: 344772). The *Dehon* also stages modern drama, as does the tiny *Teatro Moline* (1 Via delle Moline; phone: 235288) inside the *Palazzo Bentivoglia*.

MUSIC

Bologna's opera season runs from late November through March at the magnificent restored 18th-century *Teatro Comunale* (Piazza Verdi; phone: 529011; 1 Largo Respighi for tickets; phone: 529999). From October through June, a season of symphonic concerts takes place; among the highlights are the inexpensive Sunday-morning concerts held January through March in the *Chiesa di Santa Lucia* (36 Via Castiglione), which also is the venue for concerts (November through April) by *I Filarmonici di Bologna* (phone: 533430, tickets).

Also check the programs of the *Sala Bossi* at the *Conservatorio* (2 Piazza Rossini; phone: 221483) and the *Sala Mozart, Accademia Filarmonica* (13 Via Guerrazzi; phone: 235346); the former was closed for restoration at press time. Classical music concerts occasionally are held in the *Sala Europa* at the *Palazzo dei Congressi* (Fairgrounds; phone: 637-5165).

NIGHTCLUBS AND NIGHTLIFE

Bologna's active nighttime scene tends to be crowded with university students. Some of the better discos for the young crowd are *Living* (218 Via di Corticella; phone: 321043); *Flamengo* (50 Via Toscana; phone: 471951); and *La Capannina* (Via di Barbiano; phone: 581115), which has dancing outdoors in the summer. Good contemporary music can be heard at *Desiree Club* (1/D Via Paradiso; phone: 261648); *Club Hobby One* (2/A Via Mascarella; phone: 221003); *Vertigo* (35 Via San Luca; phone: 614-0888); and *Les Bains Douches* (3 Via Ravone; phone: 411912). A typical night out consists of dinner at one of the city's fine restaurants or neighborhood trattorie, followed by animated conversation over grappa and coffee, or a bottle of wine in one of the many *osterie* and *enoteche* (wine bars that usually serve food). *Osteria dell'Orsa* (1/F Via Mentana; phone: 231576) has jazz on Wednesdays and Fridays from October through April (closed Sundays); *Cantina Bentivoglio* (4/B Via Mascarella; phone: 265416) offers a wide selection of wines and nightly jazz (closed Mondays); and the *Osteria de' Poeti* (see *Eating Out*), revered poet Giosuè Carducci's hangout, features informal musicians and other performers. In summer, cabaret and vintage movies occasionally can be seen at the *Palazzo dell'Archiginnasio* (see *Special Places*), the *Museo Civico Archeologico,* the *Museo Civico Medioevale* (see *Museums* for both), and other places. Ticket prices include museum admission. Contact the tourist office (see *Tourist Information,* above) for a schedule of events.

Best in Town

CHECKING IN

Bologna's hotels fall into two distinct categories. The larger, commercial properties are oriented to the needs of businesspeople and conventioneers; the smaller, more intimate hostelries cater to visitors at leisure. Most hotels in the first category are in the newer part of town, where streets are wider, traffic is heavier, and access to and from the train station, airport, and convention center is easy. The smaller hotels are mostly on quieter, narrower streets in the historic center. The top hotel in town, listed as very expensive, costs about $300 for a double room; expensive is $175 to $275; moderate means $100 to $150; and inexpensive is $100 or less. All hotels feature private baths unless otherwise indicated. All telephone numbers are in the 51 city code unless otherwise indicated.

VERY EXPENSIVE

Baglioni The grande dame of Bologna hotels, this 17th-century palace–turned-hotel has 117 simply and tastefully decorated rooms. Of special note are the traces of an ancient Roman consular road, visible on the way to the lovely breakfast room downstairs. The service is impeccable, and *I Carracci* restaurant (see *Eating Out*) is one of the city's finest. 8 Via dell'Indipendenza (phone: 225445; 800-346-5358; fax: 234840).

EXPENSIVE

Al Cappello Rosso Near Piazza Maggiore, this is one of Bologna's most sophisticated and intimate hotels. The building itself is a 16th-century palazzo, but the tasteful, ultramodern interiors seem closer to the 21st century. Each of the 35 rooms has a TV set, mini-bar, and radio, and some have small kitchenettes; most are grouped around an interior courtyard that has a small garden. Service is excellent. No restaurant. 9 Via dei Fusari (phone: 261891; fax: 227179).

Corona d'Oro This special hotel has a 14th-century portico, palm trees, and masses of carefully arranged flowers in the public areas. Wooden beams from the original building adorn the ceilings of four of the 35 rooms (No. 105 is the most handsome), and all feature exceptional paintings and decor from various periods. There is a meeting room with a medieval coffered ceiling. No restaurant. Nearby parking available. In the center of town, at 12 Via Oberdan (phone: 236456; fax: 262679).

Elite Just beyond the city gates on the road to the airport, this sophisticated hotel—popular with business travelers and fairgoers—has 86 tastefully furnished rooms; mini-apartments; a splendid restaurant, the *Cordon Bleu* (see *Eating Out*); a piano bar; and parking. 36 Via Aurelio Saffi (phone: 649-1432; fax: 424968).

Internazionale First-rate, with a convenient location, it has 140 modern rooms with all the amenities the business traveler expects, except a restaurant. The service is efficient, and parking is available. 60 Via dell'Indipendenza (phone: 245544; fax: 249544).

Royal Hotel Carlton Geared primarily to international businesspeople, this modern establishment offers 250 rooms—most with terraces and all with mini-bars, color TV sets, and air conditioning—and the well-known *Royal Grill* restaurant. The staff is attentive and there is ample parking, but the decor is bland. The location, in the newer section of town near the busy Piazza dei Martiri and the train station, is acceptable, though not ideal. 8 Via Montebello (phone: 249361; fax: 249724).

MODERATE

Dei Commercianti This modern hotel is housed in a converted medieval building, just off Piazza Maggiore and right next to *St. Petronius.* The quiet property has 31 rooms and side views of the Gothic basilica. No restaurant, but parking is available. 11 Via de' Pignattari (phone: 233052; fax: 224733).

Orologio Small and pleasant in decor, it offers basic, clean accommodations. This restored hotel is perfectly located in the Piazza Maggiore, facing the *Palazzo Comunale,* and some of the 29 rooms afford excellent views of the piazza or the clock tower that stands just in front and gives this establishment its name. It is well run (owned by the *Corona d'Oro*) and has a private garage, but no restaurant. 10 Via IV Novembre (phone: 231253; fax: 260552).

Roma One of the rarest birds around—a first-rate hotel at a reasonable price— it's on an elegant pedestrian street only a block away from Piazza Maggiore. This best buy for the leisure traveler has 84 comfortable rooms (most of them recently refurbished), plus a fine dining room and a small indoor bar. There is good English-speaking service and ample—but not free—parking. 9 Via d'Azeglio (phone: 226322; fax: 239909).

Touring This hostelry offers a color TV set and telephone in each of the 38 guestrooms, plus an elevator, a rooftop terrace, and a private garage—amenities usually found only in higher-priced places. The slightly distant location keeps the rate low, yet it's only a pleasant 10-minute walk to Piazza Maggiore. No restaurant. 1/2 Via dei Mattuiani (phone: 584305; fax: 334763).

INEXPENSIVE

Accademia In the heart of the busy university area, this modest and clean hostelry (28 rooms) is well placed for sightseeing, dining, and shopping. There's no restaurant, but parking is available. 6 Via delle Belle Arti (phone: 232318; fax: 248174).

Centrale Many of the 20 rooms in this restored hotel overlook the two leaning towers and characteristic roofscape of the *centro storico.* Its fourth-floor location (there's an elevator) makes it comfortably removed and tranquil, even though it is indeed *centrale.* Pleasant management, modern and simple furnishings, and a great location keep this place full at all times. No restaurant. 2 Via della Zecca (phone: 225114).

Rossini Two steps from the *Teatro Comunale* and in the university district, this 20-room hotel keeps costs down by forsaking an elevator and breakfast (there's no restaurant). But the furnishings are clean, the bathrooms are modern, and it's just a five-minute walk to the leaning towers. 11 Via dei Bibiena (phone: 237716; fax: 268035).

EATING OUT

Bologna's celebrity as the home of some of the best food in Italy gives its restaurateurs a big responsibility. Most live up to the challenge, and others surpass expectations. Tortellini, mortadella, and dishes prepared *alla bolognese* (with the traditional *ragù* of onions, carrots, chopped pork, and tomatoes) are the items most closely associated with the city, but other culinary inventions are worth sampling as well. It is said that lasagna was born here, and most dining spots are sure to have *lasagne al forno* (oven-baked lasagna) on their menus. Another pasta the Bolognese are credited with inventing is *tagliatelle*, ribbons of golden noodles usually served *alla bolognese*. Favorite second courses are *cotolette alla bolognese*, breaded veal cutlets baked with a dressing of ham, white wine, and white truffles; *maiale al latte alla bolognese*, pork roast simmered in milk with mushrooms; and *involtini alla bolognese*, veal slices wrapped around a stuffing of chopped pork and served in a sauce of onions, tomatoes, and butter. The best-known wine of the region is lambrusco, a sparkling red that comes semisweet and dry. Lambrusco reggiano is particularly good. Also consider pagadebit, a dry white, and trebbiano di Romagna, a characteristic white. In the list below, an expensive meal for two will cost $100 or more; a moderate one, $50 to $100; and an inexpensive one, $50 or less. Prices include service and a carafe of house wine. All restaurants are open for lunch and dinner unless otherwise noted. All telephone numbers are in the 51 city code unless otherwise indicated.

EXPENSIVE

I Carracci One of the city's best, in the deluxe *Baglioni* hotel, this place features fine traditional cooking, excellent national specialties, and a topnotch wine cellar. Its 15th-century frescoed ceilings, Empire decor, and Ginori china create an elegant and formal ambience. Open daily. Reservations necessary. Major credit cards accepted. 2 Via Manzoni (phone: 222049).

Cordon Bleu In the *Elite* hotel, this well-known restaurant has a reputation for serving *piatti antichissimi,* or very old traditional dishes that still tantalize the palate. Favorites include filet of beef flambéed with a sauce of puréed strawberries, a bit of ricotta, and cognac that comes from an old Estense recipe, and a thousand-year-old Pugliese dish, *purea di fave con la cicoria* (puréed beans with chicory). It also has an excellent wine list. Closed Sundays and late July to late August. Reservations necessary. Major credit cards accepted. 36 Via Aurelio Saffi (phone: 649-8222).

Notai Big and beautiful, this turn-of-the-century restaurant near the main square is thought by many to be the best and most elegant dining place in the city, if not the country. Sample traditional Bolognese dishes such as *tagliatelle ai Notai* and scaloppine of veal with *porcini* mushrooms. Trebbiano and sangiovese are the best of an excellent collection of local wines. Closed Sundays (except during trade fairs). Reservations necessary. Major credit cards accepted. 1 Via de' Pignattari (phone: 228694; fax: 265872).

Al Pappagallo The vaulted dining room of this famous dining spot, dramatically decorated à la Belle Epoque, is extremely elegant and boasts excellent service, with black-tied waiters hovering about to refill your glass the moment it is empty. Try the *tagliatelle* with basil and mushrooms, the breast of turkey, or the braised chicken in white wine sauce. The wine cellar is excellent. Closed Sunday dinner, Monday lunch, and the first half of August. Reservations necessary. Major credit cards accepted. 3/C Piazza della Mercanzia (phone/fax: 232807).

Sandro al Naviglio The perfect choice for an evening of country ambience in a charming farmhouse/inn-turned-restaurant has been in the same family for over 125 years. It is informal and friendly, but the service is professional, and the food, excellent. The homemade pasta dishes will make it hard to keep going, but save room for an order of heavenly *parmigiano* cheese and one of Sandro's homemade gelati or desserts. There's alfresco dining in warm weather. Closed Sundays, the first three weeks of August, and December 29 through January 6. Reservations advised. Major credit cards accepted. 15 Via Sostegno (phone: 634-3100; fax: 634-7592).

MODERATE

Antica Osteria Romagnola It took the arrival of Neapolitan Antonio Amura to bring mouth-watering dishes of the south to this eating sanctuary in the north. Eggplant lovers will be thrilled with its appearance in many dishes—assuming they still have room for a main course after sampling the vast assortment of vegetable antipasti that highlights the season's best offerings. The wine selection is good. Closed Mondays, Tuesday lunch, most of August, and *Christmas Eve* through January 6. Reservations advised. Major credit cards accepted. 13 Via Rialto (phone: 263699).

Da Bertino One of the last of a dying breed—the reliable neighborhood trattoria—serves good, old-fashioned cooking to regular customers who know exactly what to expect: nothing exotic, but good value for the money, with excellent fresh pasta and roast meat dishes. Closed Sundays, Monday lunch, *Christmas* through *Epiphany* (January 6), and three weeks in August. Reservations unnecessary. Major credit cards accepted. 55 Via delle Lame (phone: 522230).

Cantina Bentivoglio This delightful, cavernous *enoteca* is filled with the *ambiente* and effervescent clientele that give an idea of what Bologna really is like—casual yet sophisticated. Choose from the thousands of wine bottles around you and the many soups, cheeses, and meat while listening to live jazz until

2 AM. Closed Mondays and one week in mid-August. Reservations advised. Major credit cards accepted. Close to the university, at 4/B Via Mascarella (phone: 265416).

Da Carlo A wonderful place for a modestly priced dinner or lunch—particularly in summer, when meals are served outdoors under a delightful medieval loggia. The sausages, minestrone, *piccione brasato* (braised pigeon), guinea hen with artichokes, and desserts are all good, as is the service. Closed Tuesdays, three weeks in January, and one week in late August. Reservations advised. Major credit cards accepted. 6 Via Marchesana (phone: 233227).

Da Cesari An informal, relaxed atmosphere as well as fine pasta dishes, superlative *rognoncini con aceto balsamico* (veal kidneys in balsamic vinegar), and good grilled meat make this a favorite among the Bolognese literati. After a dessert of delicate half-moon pastries filled with fresh fruit, try a smooth *grappa mirtilli* (made from bilberries) as a special "digestive" drink. Closed Thursdays. Reservations advised. Major credit cards accepted. 8 Via Carbonesi (phone: 237710).

Osteria de' Poeti Of the dozens of *osterie* where the kitchens stay open well after midnight, this is the most celebrated. The food served on the 15th-century premises is good enough to inspire diners at times to break into song. If that is too tall an order, then there's always entertainment in the in-house cabaret. Open to 4 AM; closed Mondays. Reservations advised. Major credit cards accepted. Near Piazza Cavour, at 1/B Via de' Poeti (phone: 236166).

Al Portichetto A delightful hillside trattoria, with terrace dining in warm weather, it's just a few miles from town. The regional country cooking emphasizes wild truffles and mushrooms. Closed Mondays and January. Reservations advised. Visa accepted. 21 Via dei Colli, beyond the town's favorite park, *Giardini Margherita* (phone: 581110).

Rosteria da Luciano This is a genuine anomaly—a high-quality restaurant that doesn't make diners pay an arm and a leg. As the name suggests, roast and baked meat are the specialty in this small, always crowded place, the centerpiece being *maialino di latte al forno,* a tender pork dish. Also try the "royal" salad of mushrooms and truffles, if it's on the menu. Closed Wednesdays, August, and *Christmas.* Reservations necessary. Major credit cards accepted. 19 Via Nazario Sauro (phone: 231249).

Sale e Peppe Despite its name, you won't need to add any salt and pepper to what graces your table. Regulars ask for the house specialty, an *assagio di primi,* a delicious sampling of pasta dishes with sauces that change with the seasons (there's a good chance you won't make it to the main course). It's informal, forever popular, and near the *Chiesa di Santo Stefano.* Closed Mondays and Tuesdays. Reservations advised. No credit cards accepted. 9/2 Via dei Coltelli (phone: 228532).

Birreria Lamme A Bolognese institution, it once kept students fed and active and now attracts businesspeople and locals in the know. There are good pasta dishes (it's known for its fresh lasagna), chops, steaks, sausages, and roasts. It's a great place for lunch (but come before or after the 1 to 2:30 PM rush). There is counter service, too, and a wide selection of beer. It's open continuously from 11:30 AM to 11:30 PM—almost unheard of in Italy. Closed Sundays and August. No reservations. Major credit cards accepted. A few steps from the twin towers, at 4 Via dei Giudei (phone: 268362).

C'Entro Right on Via dell'Indipendenza and with a covered area for dining outside, this eatery is a rare find for its first class, self-service lunch. Come early or late to avoid the crush of highly fashionable habitués who gravitate to sample its trendy ambience. The place also is open for dinner for a slightly more expensive waiter service. Closed Sundays. No reservations. Major credit cards accepted. 45 Via dell'Indipendenza (phone: 223216).

Pino Pizza is not native to Bologna, but there's little that the Bolognese make that does not approach perfection. This place is one of the best and most popular of the centrally located *pizzerie.* Closed Mondays. No reservations. Major credit cards accepted. 2 Via Goito (phone: 227291). A second location, which is closed Wednesdays, is at 172 Via Santo Stefano (phone: 301974).

Zelig Stop by for the social scene at this sophisticated, postmodern interpretation of the traditional *osteria* that serves interesting cocktails and has a great selection of bottled and draft foreign beers. Meals are simple, and there's a reliably delicious choice of pasta dishes. Closed Sundays. No reservations. No credit cards accepted. 9 Via Porta Nuova (phone: 236737).

BARS AND CAFFÈS

In Bologna *la Grassa*, an eating experience lies around every corner. So save your appetite and lire for a memorable dinner, but spend your mornings and afternoons indulging in the wide variety of historical *caffès,* pastry shops, and *gelaterie* that have been sustaining the Bolognese for centuries. The following places are a few of our favorites (all are inexpensive, and none accept credit cards):

Bricco d'Oro This busy, handsome, old-fashioned *caffè* is known for its wood-and-polished-brass ambience and rich hot chocolate topped with fresh cream. Counter service only. Closed Sundays. 6 Via Farini (phone: 236231).

Caffè della Galleria Both Bologna's monied matrons and young managerial types who can pass as Armani models stop here for aperitifs. Closed Sundays. 2 *Galleria Cavour* (phone: 260489).

Calderoni A wide selection of homemade pizza, sandwiches, pastries, and ice cream is available at this large, always crowded institution. The tearoom upstairs becomes a piano bar from 9:30 PM to 1:30 AM. It's a good place to start the day with a delicious fresh brioche. Closed Tuesdays. 60 Via dell'Indipendenza (phone: 248208).

Gelateria Regina This centrally located, modern ice-cream place is a favorite with children and their families. Fresh pastries are made on the premises. Closed Mondays. 51 Via dell'Indipendenza (phone: 248853).

Lagana Few will dispute that this is Bologna's best *pasticceria*. It's a good place to linger over a cappuccino while savoring one of its famous meringue specialties. Closed Mondays. 112 Via Santo Stefano (phone: 347869).

Roberto This nonsmoking *caffè/pasticceria* near the market area is always filled with shoppers and shopkeepers who come for the fresh, delicious sandwiches and small puff pastries—either sweet or stuffed with meat. Closed Sundays. 9/A Via Orefici (phone: 232256).

La Torinese In the historical setting of the *Palazzo di Re Enzo,* this popular *caffè* serves fresh sandwiches, pastries, and its famous hot chocolate. Closed Thursdays. 1/C Piazza di Re Enzo (phone: 236743).

Zanarini Bologna's young and elegant invariably end their stroll along the Portico Paviglione with an *aperitivo* or light snack at this large Old World *caffè*. In the cold months, sit upstairs in the tearoom; in warmer weather, try to get a table outside (although you will have lots of competition from university students). Closed Mondays. Next to the *Palazzo dell'Archiginnasio* in the Portico Paviglione, 1 Piazza Galvani (phone: 222717).

Florence

City of the arts, jewel of the Renaissance, symbol of the Tuscan pride in grace and refinement, Florence nonetheless can be an acquired taste for many. Next to the mellow tangerine hues of Rome, the pinks of Venice, and the orgy of color that is Naples, Florence is a study in neutral and often harsh shades: blacks and whites, beiges and browns, a splattering of dark green. And its people are reserved, with a sort of innate sense of dignity and pride.

At first glance, Florentine palazzi are more like fortresses. But step inside and you will be awed by the beauty of fine details, as well as by some of the world's greatest art treasures. Look at the fine Florentine crafts in gold and leather and exquisite fabrics in the elegant but classically serious shops. It won't take long before you will understand why the culture and art of Florence have attracted people from around the world through the centuries, and why it is as much a favorite of artists, students, and expatriates today as it was at its apogee under the Medicis in the 15th century.

Florence was the home of Cimabue and Giotto, the fathers of Italian painting; of Brunelleschi, Donatello, and Masaccio, who paved the way for the Renaissance; of the Della Robbias, Botticelli, Leonardo, and Michelangelo; of writers and poets Dante Alighieri, Petrarch, and Boccaccio; and of philosopher Machiavelli and scientist Galileo. Art, science, and life found their finest, most powerful expression in Florence, and records of this splendid past fill the city's many galleries, museums, churches, and palaces.

Florence (*Firenze* in Italian) originated as an Etruscan center, but it was only under the Romans in the 1st century BC that it became a true city. Like so many other cities of its time, Roman Florence grew up along the fertile banks of a river, in this case the Arno, amid the rolling green hills of Tuscany. Its Latin name, *Florentia* ("flowering"), probably referred to the city's florid growth, although some ancient historians attributed it to Florinus, the Roman general who besieged the nearby Etruscan hilltown of Fiesole in 63 BC.

During Roman rule, Florence became a flourishing military and trading center, with its share of temples, baths, a town hall, and an amphitheater, but few architectural monuments of that epoch have survived. After the fall of the Roman Empire, Florence sank into the decadence of the Dark Ages, and despite a temporary reprieve during Charlemagne's 8th- and 9th-century European empire, it did not really flourish again until the late 11th century. It was then that the great trade guilds developed and the florin-based currency appeared, and Florence became a powerful, self-governing republic.

In the 12th century, interfamily feuds were widespread, and over 150 square stone towers—built for defense by influential families right next to their houses—dominated the city's skyline. But during that century and the next, Florentines were busily engaged in trade with the rest of the Mediterranean. The amazing building boom that followed, bringing about the demolition of the fortified houses in favor of more gracious public and private palazzi and magnificent churches, reflected the great prosperity of the city's trading and banking families, its wool and silk industries, and the enormous strength of the florin.

As a free city-state or *comune,* Florence maintained a balance between the authority of the emperors and that of the popes, overcoming the difficulties of internal struggles between the burgher Guelphs (who supported the pope) and the aristocratic Ghibellines (who were behind the Holy Roman Emperor). Eventually, by the late 13th century, the Guelphs won power, and a democratic government was inaugurated by the famous Ordinances of Justice. So began Florence's ascent, which spanned three centuries and reached its height and greatest splendor under the Medici family.

Owing in large measure to the patronage of the Medicis, Florence became the liveliest and most creative city in Europe. First there was Giovanni di Bicci de' Medici (1360–1429) and his illustrious dynasty of merchants, bankers, and art patrons, followed by his son Cosimo the Elder (1389–1464), who continued to gather artists around him. However, it was Cosimo's grandson, Lorenzo the Magnificent (1449–92), who put Florence in the forefront of the Italian Renaissance.

Today, the Medicis might be thought of as something of a political machine, since they controlled—through their wealth and personal power— a city that was governed by members of the trade guilds. Their de facto rule was not uncontested, however. They suffered reversals, such as the Pazzi Conspiracy in 1478, and twice they were expelled—from 1494 to 1512, when a revolution brought the religious reformer Savonarola briefly to power (and an attempt was made to reestablish democracy), and again from 1527 to 1530, when another republic was set up, only to fall to the troops of Emperor Charles V and lead to the Medici restoration.

Finally, in the late 16th century, their glory days behind them, the Medici gained an official title. They became grand dukes (Cosimo I was the first), and Florence became the capital of the grand duchy of Tuscany. In the 18th century, the grand duchy of the Medici was succeeded by that of the house of Lorraine, until Tuscany became part of the kingdom of Italy in 1860. From 1865 to 1871, Florence reigned as temporary capital of the kingdom, but with the capital's transfer to Rome, the history of Florence merges with that of the rest of Italy.

Several catastrophes in this century have caused inestimable damage to Florence's art treasures. In 1944, all the beloved bridges crossing the Arno— except for the Ponte Vecchio—and the historical buildings that surrounded them were blown up by the retreating Nazis. Reconstruction began as soon as the Germans were gone. Then, two decades later, in 1966, the Arno burst its banks, submerging the city and covering the historic center with a muddy slime. Over 1,400 works of art, two million valuable books, and countless homes were damaged by floodwaters that reached heights of 23 feet. With help from all over the world, the people of Florence rose to the challenge. Even before the floodwaters had receded, they began the painstaking chore of rescuing their treasures from 600,000 tons of mud, oil, and debris. And in 1993, a car bomb exploded in a small side street between the Piazza della Signoria and the Arno. Seemingly aimed at the cultural wealth of the nearby *Galleria degli Uffizi*, the act damaged a small number of works of secondary importance. Restorers still working on the paintings damaged in the 1966 flood were immediately called in; the government allocated an unprecedented $20 million to proceed with the necessary restoration. The museum opened almost immediately, with its artistic patrimony practically unscathed.

Today, the city of Florence—with a population of slightly less than half a million—still is a vital force in the arts, culture, and science, as well as an industrial, commercial, and university center and a leader in handicrafts and fashion. Note how the Florentines dress, their fine attention to detail, and the remarkable sense of style that turns an ordinary outfit into something personal and special. Perhaps it's the almost arrogant swagger. Then realize that these are people who wake up every morning to the marvels of Michelangelo, who literally live in a 15th-century Renaissance textbook. Their artistic and cultural heritage is unsurpassed. No doubt you'll agree that they have every reason to be proud.

Florence At-a-Glance

SEEING THE CITY

The best picture-postcard view of Florence is from Piazzale Michelangelo, on the far side of the Arno. From here, more than 300 feet above sea level, the eye embraces the entire city and neighboring hilltowns as far as Pistoia, but it is the foreground that rivets the attention. The Arno, with all its bridges, from Ponte San Niccolò to Ponte della Vittoria; the *Palazzo Vecchio*, with its bell tower and crenelations; the *Galleria degli Uffizi*; the flank of the *Basilica di Santa Croce*; and numerous spires and domes—all are in the picture. Looming in the center of it all is the massive *Duomo*, with Giotto's bell tower and giant red cupola. The *piazzale* is reached by the splendid, tree-lined Viale dei Colli, which begins at Ponte San Niccolò and winds up to the enormous square under the name of Viale Michelangelo. It then proceeds beyond the square and back down to the Porta Romana under the names Viale Galileo and Viale Machiavelli. From the bridge up to the *piazzale* and down to the Roman Gate is a scenic 4-mile walk, but it's also possible to trace the same route aboard bus No. 13 from the station. An extraordinary view of Florence and the entire Arno Valley from the opposite (north) side of town can be enjoyed from the lookout terrace just before the *Chiesa di San Francesco* (Church of St. Francis), perched on a hill studded with cypress trees and sumptuous villas in neighboring Fiesole (see *Special Places*). For a more convenient and equally breathtaking 360-degree panorama, climb the 400-odd steps up the *Campanile di Giotto* (see *Special Places,* below).

SPECIAL PLACES

The Arno is a good orientation point for first-time visitors to Florence. Most of the city sits on the north, or right, bank of the river, including its principal squares: Piazza del Duomo, the religious heart of Florence; Piazza della Repubblica, the city's bustling commercial center and a favorite meeting place because of its outdoor *caffès;* and Piazza della Signoria, the ancient political center. The most elegant shopping street, Via Tornabuoni, runs from the Arno to Piazza Antinori. The other side of the river is known as the Oltrarno, literally "beyond the Arno." Sights here include the *Palazzo Pitti* and *Giardini di Boboli*, the churches of *Santo Spirito* and *Santa Maria del Carmine,* and Piazzale Michelangelo. Note that some sites of interest in Florence close for a midday break, which can begin anytime between 11 AM and 1 PM and end at 3 or 4 PM; we suggest calling ahead to check exact hours.

THE DUOMO (CATHEDRAL) COMPLEX

DUOMO (CATHEDRAL) The cathedral of *Santa Maria del Fiore* was begun in 1296 by the Sienese architect Arnolfo di Cambio, and it took 173 years to complete. Dominating a large double square, it is the fourth-longest church in the world (after the *Duomo* of Milan, *St. Peter's* in Rome, and *St. Paul's* in London) and can hold over 20,000 people. The gigantic project was financed by the Florentine republic and the Clothmakers Guild, in an age of faith when every city-state and its prosperous mercantile unions aspired to claim the biggest and most important cathedral as its own.

The original façade, never completed, was destroyed in the 16th century and replaced in the late 19th century (an extensive restoration is scheduled to be completed this year). Whereas the exterior walls are encased in colorful marble (white from Carrara, green from Prato, and pink from Siena), the interior seems plain and cold by comparison, a brownish-gray sandstone called *pietra forte* and soberly decorated in keeping with the Florentine character. Most of the original statuary that adorned the *Duomo,* including Michelangelo's unfinished *Pietà,* has been moved to the *Museo dell'Opera del Duomo* (see below). The remains of the ancient *Chiesa di Santa Reparata* (Church of Saint Reparata), the original cathedral of Florence, which came to light under the *Duomo* during the extensive excavation after the 1966 flood, are interesting; the crypt is particularly haunting. To get there, take the staircase near the entrance on the right side of the nave.

The public competition for the design of the cathedral's dome was won by a Florentine, Filippo Brunelleschi, who had marveled at the great engineering feat of ancient Rome, the dome of the *Pantheon*. The Renaissance architect's mighty cupola, built between 1420 and 1438, the first since antiquity, subsequently inspired Michelangelo as he designed the dome of *St. Peter's* in Rome.

Brunelleschi's dome surpasses both the *Pantheon* and *St. Peter's,* although today it is seriously cracked and monitored by computer. Over 371 feet high and 148 feet across, it has double walls between which a 463-step staircase leads to a lantern at the top (also a Brunelleschi design). Restorations have been under way for more than a decade, together with a five-year, $5.8 million restoration of the cupola's 16th-century frescoes by Federico Zuccari and Giorgio Vassari, completed last year. The 40-minute climb up and down (there's no elevator) is well worth the effort for the breathtaking panorama of the city from the top and for a true sense of the awesome size of this artistic and technical masterpiece that Henry James rhapsodized was "the image of some mighty hillside enameled with blooming flowers." To view the restored frescoes, a small elevator will take six people at a time up to 165 feet, the lowest scaffolding level. The complex is open daily. Separate admission charges to the crypt and dome. Piazza del Duomo (phone: 294514).

CAMPANILE DI GIOTTO (GIOTTO'S BELL TOWER) The graceful freestanding belfry of the *Duomo,* one of the most intricate and unusual in Italy, was begun by Giotto in 1334 and completed by Francesco Talenti. The bas-reliefs adorning the base are copies of originals by Giotto and Luca della Robbia that are in the *Museo dell'Opera del Duomo* (see below), as are the statues of the Prophets (done by various artists, including Donatello) that stood in the niches. The 414-step climb to the top leads to a terrace with a breathtaking bird's-eye view of Florence. There's no elevator. Closed Sundays. Admission charge. Piazza del Duomo (phone: 230-2885).

BATTISTERO (BAPTISTRY) Dedicated to St. John the Baptist, the patron saint of Florence, the *Battistero* is a unique treasure whose origins are lost in time. The small octagonal building in front of the cathedral's main entrance may date to the 4th century, contemporary with the *Chiesa di Santa Reparata,* while the exterior of green-and-white marble dates to the 12th century and is typical of the Tuscan Romanesque style, with an Asian influence. It was Florence's cathedral from the time it was built until the construction of *Santa Maria del Fiore.* To this day, the *Battistero* is still occasionally used for baptisms, and many a famous Florentine (including Dante Alighieri) has been baptized here. On the *Festa di San Giovanni Battista* (June 24), the relics of the saint are displayed in the building, and candles are lit in his honor (see *Special Events*).

The interior is covered with magnificent Byzantine mosaics by 13th- and 14th-century Florentine and Venetian masters, but the three gilded bronze doorways are the main attraction. The south door (used as the entrance to the *Battistero*), by Andrea Pisano, is the oldest, dating from the early 14th century. In the Gothic style, it has 28 panels with reliefs of the life of St. John the Baptist and the cardinal and theological virtues. The north door (1403–24), in late Gothic style, was the result of a competition in which the unanimous winner was Lorenzo Ghiberti. It, too, is divided into 28 panels, this time depicting scenes from the life of Christ, the Evangelists, and the Doctors of the Church. Ghiberti's east door, facing the cathedral, is his masterpiece. In full Renaissance style, it was defined by Michelangelo as worthy of being the "gate of paradise." Begun in 1425 and completed in 1452, it has 10 panels illustrating Old Testament stories and medallions containing self-portraits of Ghiberti and his adopted son, Vittorio (who designed the frame), as well as portraits of their principal contemporaries. The originals of four of these panels are in the *Museo dell'Opera del Duomo* (see below); some are still on the door, and at press time others were being restored. Closed Monday through Saturday mornings and Sunday afternoons. No admission charge. Piazza del Duomo (phone: 230-2885).

MUSEO DELL'OPERA DEL DUOMO (DUOMO MUSEUM) Masterpieces from the *Duomo*, the *Battistero,* and the *Campanile* are here, especially sculpture: Michelangelo's unfinished *Pietà* (third of his four; the hooded figure is believed to be the 80-year-old sculptor's self-portrait), Donatello's wooden *Mary Magdalene,* the famous marble *cantorie* (choir lofts) by Luca della Robbia and Donatello, the precious silver altar frontal from the *Battistero,* fragments from the original cathedral façade, and the original wooden scale model of Brunelleschi's dome. Closed Sundays. Admission charge. 29 Piazza del Duomo (phone: 230-2885).

ELSEWHERE DOWNTOWN

GALLERIA DEGLI UFFIZI (UFFIZI MUSEUM AND GALLERY) Italy's—and one of the world's—most important art museums is in a Renaissance palace built on the site of an 11th-century church (*San Piero Scheraggio*), whose remains are incorporated in the palazzo and may still be seen. The splendor of this museum derives not only from the great works it contains (reflect on the fact that over 90% of Italy's artistic patrimony is in storage here, and what is on display represents the *crema della crema* of the major Italian artists) but also from the 16th-century building itself, which was commissioned by Cosimo I and designed by Vasari (completed by Buontalenti) to house the Medicis' *uffizi* (administrative offices). In 1581, Francesco I began converting the top floor into an art museum destined to become one of the world's greatest. The three corridors, with light streaming through their great windows, are a spectacle in themselves, and the collection they contain is so vast—the most important Italian and European paintings of the 13th through the 18th centuries, arranged chronologically—that we suggest taking along a good guide or guidebook (Luciano Berti's is excellent).

And allow more time for a visit here than you think you'll need. It's also a good idea to go early in the morning or in the late afternoon in high season, as the lines can otherwise be quite long. At the top of the monumental staircase (there also is an elevator) on the second floor is the *Prints and Drawings Collection;* the museum proper (painting and sculpture) is on the third floor. Particularly beautiful, and often overlooked, are the 13th- and 14th-century religious paintings on wood panels. Fifteen rooms are devoted to Florentine and Tuscan masterpieces, including the work of Cimabue, Giotto, Fra Filippo Lippi, Paolo Uccello, Fra Angelico, Leonardo, and Michelangelo, not to mention such other non-Florentine masters as Raphael, Titian, Tintoretto, Caravaggio, Rubens, Van Dyck, and Rembrandt. The *Botticelli Room* contains the master's *Birth of Venus* and his restored *Allegoria della Primavera* (Allegory of Spring), as well as other allegorical and mythological works that make this the most important Botticelli collection in the world. Although none of these masterpieces were touched by the car bomb in 1993, two lesser-known paintings were destroyed, and several others were damaged.

An important collection of self-portraits lines the *Corridoio Vasariano* (Vasari Corridor); at press time, the hall was temporarily closed due to extensive damage from the 1993 bombing. Among the portraits are those of Raphael, Rubens, Van Dyck, Velázquez, Bernini, Canova, Corot, Fattori, and Chagall. Even without the portraits, the half-mile walk would be fascinating. The corridor is a raised passageway built in the 1560s to allow members of the Medici court to move from their old palace and offices (*Palazzo Vecchio* and *Uffizi)* to their new palace (*Palazzo Pitti)*. It crosses the river on the tops of shops on the Ponte Vecchio and affords splendid views of the Arno, the *Chiesa di Santa Felicità,* and the *Giardini di Boboli.* The rooms are decorated with frescoes that span the 17th, 18th, and 19th centuries. The bomb blast partially collapsed its ceiling, and its reopening remained undetermined as we went to press. To check on its opening status and to visit the *Corridoio Vasariano,* write to the *Uffizi* (*Galleria degli Uffizi,* Firenze 50100) well in advance of your arrival (there's no extra fee). The museum is closed Mondays, holidays, and late afternoons on Sundays. Admission charge. Piazza della Signoria (phone: 23885).

PALAZZO DELLA SIGNORIA OR PALAZZO VECCHIO (OLD PALACE) This fortress-like palace, built by Arnolfo di Cambio between 1298 and 1314 as the seat of Florence's new democratic government of *priori* (guild leaders), began as (and still is) Florence's *Town Hall.* From 1540 to 1550, it was temporarily the residence of the Medicis as they progressed from their ancestral home, the *Palazzo Medici-Riccardi,* to their new home in the *Palazzo Pitti.* Designed in a rather severe Gothic style, the palace is at once powerful and graceful, with a lofty tower 308 feet high. Beyond its rusticated façade is an elaborately ornate courtyard highlighted by Verrocchio's delightful fountain of a bronze cherub holding a dolphin (1476).

The medieval austerity of the exterior also contrasts with the sumptuous apartments inside. The massive *Salone dei Cinquecento* (Salon of the Five Hundred) on the first floor, built in 1496 for Savonarola's short-lived republican Council of Five Hundred, is decorated with frescoes by Vasari. Don't miss Vasari's *studiolo,* Francesco de' Medici's gem of a study, with magnificent *armadio* doors painted by artists of the schools of Bronzino and Vasari. On the third floor is an exhibition of 140 works of art removed from Italy by the Nazis and recovered by Rodolfo Siviero, the famed Italian art sleuth. Closed Thursdays, holidays, and Sunday afternoons. Admission charge. Piazza della Signoria (phone: 276-8465).

PIAZZA DELLA SIGNORIA Punctuated with the giant, needle-like tower of the *Palazzo Vecchio,* this is a noteworthy spot, not least because of the towering, weathered copy of Michelangelo's *David* (currently under restoration), the emblem of the city, that stands at its portal. It has also been the heart of Florence for a millennium. Over the troubled centuries of the Renaissance, the square was gradually expanded as powerful families razed the houses of the rivals they expelled. The equestrian statue of Cosimo I is by Giambologna, as are the bronze figures at the base of Ammannati's fountain of Neptune. It was in this piazza that the puritanical priest Savonarola organized his 1497 "Burning of the Vanities," a bonfire fed with purportedly lewd drawings, books, and other trinkets of worldly corruption, such as mirrors and jewelry. And it was also here that Savonarola himself was later hanged and burned, on a spot now marked by an etched inscription. Now that the violence has given way to the peaceful ringing of the bells every quarter hour, the piazza is shiningly beautiful.

LOGGIA DEI LANZI OR LOGGIA DELLA SIGNORIA Built between 1376 and 1382 for the election and proclamation of public officials and other ceremonies, the loggia took its name in the 16th century from Cosimo I's Germano-Swiss mercenary soldiers (known in Italian as *lanzichenecchi*), who were stationed here. Today the loggia is a delightful open-air museum (extensive structural renovations were under way at press time), with masterpieces of sculpture from various periods under its arches. Particularly noteworthy are Cellini's *Perseus* and Giambologna's *Rape of the Sabines.* Piazza della Signoria.

PONTE VECCHIO The "Old Bridge" is indeed Florence's oldest (and the only one to survive the Nazi destruction in 1944), although the houses at either end were bombed by the Germans. Built on the site of a Roman crossing at the Arno's narrowest point, the first stone version was swept away in a flood in 1333 and rebuilt in 1345 as it is now, with rows of shops lining both sides (whose backs, supported on brackets, overhang the Arno). They were occupied by butchers and blacksmiths until Cosimo I assigned them to the more genteel gold- and silversmiths in the late 16th century because he wanted to create a more aesthetic passage linking the two sides of town.

PALAZZO PITTI E GALLERIA PALATINA (PITTI PALACE AND PALATINE GALLERY)

Across the Arno from the *Galleria degli Uffizi* and a few blocks from the riverbank is a rugged, austere, 15th-century palace built for Luca Pitti from Brunelleschi's designs. It is believed that Pitti had the palazzo constructed because he wanted to outdo his political rival, Cosimo de' Medici. Ironically, it was later bought by Cosimo I and his wife, Eleonora of Toledo, in 1549, and expanded by Ammannati, becoming the seat of the Medici grand dukes and later of the Savoy royal family until 1871. Three dynasties—Medici, Lorraine, and Savoy—resided in this palace, which now houses several museums. The *Galleria Palatina,* upstairs on the first floor and the most important of the must-sees, is devoted to 16th- and 17th-century art—works by Raphael, Rubens, Murillo, Andrea del Sarto, Fra Filippo Lippi, Titian, Veronese, and Tintoretto, to name a few (there are over 650)—arranged in no apparent order. The gallery, in fact, still resembles a sumptuous palace apartment more than it does a museum, with elaborately decorated rooms filled with tapestries, frescoes, and gilded stuccoes. The *Appartamenti Monumentali* (Royal Apartments), in another wing of the same floor, were inhabited in turn by the Medici, Lorraine, and Savoy families. The apartments are often closed but occasionally can be visited by appointment.

The *Museo degli Argenti* (Silver Museum), occupying 16 rooms on the ground floor and another must-see, is filled with silverware, gold, jewels, cameos, Oriental tapestries, furniture, crystal, and ivory of the Medicis. Still another museum, the *Galleria d'Arte Moderna,* on the second floor, houses mainly 19th-century Tuscan works, including a lovely selection from the local impressionist Macchiaioli School. An entrance on the left side of the palace leads to the *Giardini di Boboli* (see below). The *Galleria del Costume* (Costume Gallery) in the *Palazzina della Meridiana* contains an impressive collection of 18th- to 20th-century costumes. Attention is paid to every detail, with careful documentation and an impressive sense of display and lighting. The *Museo delle Porcellane* (Porcelain Museum), at the top of the *Giardini di Boboli,* consists of three rooms filled with Austrian, French, German, and Italian porcelain objects (it was closed at press time because of a lack of funds).

The *Galleria Palatina* (phone: 238-8611); *Gallery d'Arte Moderna* (phone: 287096); the *Museo degli Argenti* (phone: 294279); and the *Galleria del Costume* (phone: 294279) are closed Mondays and late afternoons. Separate admission charge to each. Piazza Pitti (phone: 238-8611, main number).

GIARDINI DI BOBOLI (BOBOLI GARDENS)

Designed in 1550 by Il Tribolo (Niccolò Pericolo) for the Medicis when they moved into the *Palazzo Pitti,* these exquisite cypress tree–studded gardens encompass lanes, fountains, unusual statuary, an amphitheater, a pond with enormous goldfish, a tiny garden with lemon trees, and even a grotto with a statue of Venus by Giambologna. Extending for acres, the gardens are the best place in town for a picnic; they offer marvelous views of Florence. Gazing at the scene today, it is hard to imagine the difficulty the architect encountered when he was commissioned to create such bucolic bliss from what was once a stone quarry. Closed the first and last Monday of each month. Admission charge. Piazza Pitti (phone: 213440).

CHIESA DI SANTO SPIRITO (CHURCH OF THE HOLY SPIRIT) One of Brunelleschi's last works, this is a gem, though you'll notice the church's stark façade is very different from its interior. Brunelleschi died before he could complete what is generally acknowledged as one of the finest examples of a Renaissance church, so a team of architects finished it. Inside are 40 semicircular chapels, with masterpieces by Donatello, Ghirlandaio, Filippino Lippi, Sansovino, and others. Piazza Santo Spirito itself is a charming quiet spot, surrounded by 16th-century buildings and the site of a morning market (as well as an antiques market the second Sunday of every month)— the perfect place to escape from the bustle on the other side of the Arno. Closed Wednesdays and for a long midday break. Admission charge. Piazza Santo Spirito (phone: 210030).

SANTA MARIA DEL CARMINE Dating from the second half of the 13th century, this Carmelite church was mostly destroyed in a fire in 1771, but the *Cappelle Corsini* and *Brancacci* (Corsini and Brancacci Chapels) were spared. The latter contains the recently restored 15th-century Masaccio frescoes that inspired Renaissance masters from Fra Angelico to Raphael and are said to have revolutionized Western art. Church open daily; *Cappella Brancacci* closed Tuesdays and Sunday mornings. Admission charge to the chapel. Piazza del Carmine (phone: 238-2195).

PALAZZO DEL BARGELLO E MUSEO NAZIONALE (BARGELLO PALACE AND NATIONAL MUSEUM) The impressively fortified exterior is an apt reminder of its earlier functions—first as a prison, then as the heavily guarded residence of the city's podesta, or chief magistrate. But within the severe 13th- and 14th-century ramparts is a gracious courtyard, a loggia, and a staircase—the most interesting parts of the building—and a cornucopia of Florentine and Tuscan Renaissance sculpture. Its most noteworthy piece just might be Florence's second-most famous *David*—the bronze by Donatello—sculpted in 1530. Here, David sports a helmet that looks like a flowered *Easter* hat that balances with ballerina-like grace on Goliath's severed head. Another must-see is Giambologna's *Mercury,* who, poised precariously on one foot, looks as if he is about to launch himself into 16th-century space. Major Florentine and Tuscan sculptors are represented here: Donatello, Verrocchio, Cellini, Michelangelo, the Della Robbias, and others. Closed Mondays and late afternoons. Admission charge. 4 Via del Proconsolo (phone: 23885).

BASILICA DI SANTA CROCE (BASILICA OF THE HOLY CROSS) Italy's largest and best-known Franciscan church was begun late in the 13th century. It was enriched over the centuries with numerous works of art, as well as tombs of many famous Italians, including Michelangelo, Machiavelli, Rossini, and Galileo (there is a funeral monument to Dante, born here but buried while in exile in Ravenna), making it a kind of pantheon of Italian genius. Under *Santa Croce* are the remains of an earlier chapel founded by St. Francis of Assisi in 1228. The church is particularly noteworthy for a wooden crucifix by Donatello, for its chapels with frescoes by Taddeo and Agnolo Gaddi, and above all for its fresco cycles by Giotto in the *Cappelle Bardi* and *Peruzzi* (Bardi and Peruzzi Chapels).

Outside the church are the 14th-century cloister and the 15th-century *Cappella di Pazzi,* a Renaissance gem of a chapel by Brunelleschi, designed at the height of his career. During the 1966 flood, the waters reached the top of the cloister's arches, and damage here was particularly severe. Open daily, with a midday closing. Piazza Santa Croce (phone: 244619).

GALLERIA DELL'ACCADEMIA (ACADEMY GALLERY) Michelangelo's original *David* (1501–04) was brought here from the Piazza della Signoria (where a first-rate copy currently under restoration has taken its place) in 1873. Since then, millions of visitors have come just to see this monumental sculpture carved from a single block of Carrara marble when the artist was 26 years old. No matter how many postcards and reproductions you may have seen of this gigantic man, relaxed and self-confident in the moment before dispatching Goliath, the first in-person vision of him is always intensely dramatic. A protective six-foot plexiglass screen now surrounds the sculpture's base to avoid further instances of vandalism—a deranged devotee smashed David's toe in 1991 (it was almost immediately restored). Don't ignore the rest of the rich collection. Retrace your steps through the hall to enter the tortured world of *The Slaves.* Originally intended for the tomb of Pope Julius II, these figures try desperately to wrench themselves out of the rough stone blocks that Michelangelo never finished sculpting. In the next room is the splendid *Cassone Adimari,* a 15th-century Tuscan wedding chest. Also displayed is one of Michelangelo's four *Pietà*—attributed to him only since the late 18th century (an uncharacteristic heaviness in the Christ figure had skeptics wondering until then). In the summer, lines form down the street, and the doors often close when it gets too crowded.

Unfortunately, many visitors ignore the rich collection of Florentine paintings—from 13th-century primitives to 16th-century Mannerists—and the extraordinary collection of Russian icons brought to Florence by the Lorraines in the first half of the 18th century, when they succeeded the Medicis. Closed Mondays and late afternoons. Admission charge. 60 Via Ricasoli (phone: 23885).

MUSEO DI SAN MARCO (MUSEUM OF ST. MARK) Vasari described this structure as a perfect example of monastic architecture. It was built in the 15th century by the Medici architect Michelozzo (who actually rebuilt a more ancient Dominican monastery); its walls—as well as more than 40 cells on the second floor—were frescoed by Fra Angelico (and his assistants), who lived here as a monk from 1438 to 1445. Now primarily a Fra Angelico museum, it contains panel paintings brought from various churches and galleries, in addition to the painter's wonderful *Crucifixion* (in the chapter house across the cloister) and his exquisite *Annunciation* (at the top of the stairs leading to the dormitory). Stand in solitary silence in the courtyard—it is not hard to imagine the monastic life of centuries past. Don't miss the cell used by the fanatical Savonarola, the prior of *San Marco* hanged in Piazza della Signoria in 1498 for heresy. There also are paintings by Fra Bartolomeo (see his portrait of Savonarola), Ghirlandaio, Paolo Uccello, and others. Closed Mondays and late afternoons. Admission charge. 1 Piazza San Marco (phone: 23885).

PIAZZA DELLA SANTISSIMA ANNUNZIATA (SQUARE OF THE MOST HOLY ANNUNCIATION) This square best preserves the essence of the Florentine Renaissance spirit. It has porticoes on three sides, a 16th-century palazzo (by Ammannati) on the fourth, and an early-17th-century equestrian statue of Ferdinando I de' Medici by Giambologna in the middle. Most interesting is the portico on the east side, that of the *Ospedale degli Innocenti* (Hospital of the Innocents), which was built in the early 15th century by Brunelleschi as a home for orphans and abandoned children. It is one of Florence's oldest charity institutions and the world's first foundling hospital. Except for the two imitations at either end, the ceramic tondos of swaddled babies are by Andrea della Robbia. Inside, the *Galleria dello Spedale degli Innocenti* contains works by Ghirlandaio and others. Closed late afternoons and Wednesdays. Admission charge (phone: 247-7952).

The *Chiesa della Santissima Annunziata* (Church of the Most Holy Annunciation), on the north side of the square, is much loved by Florentine brides, who traditionally leave their bouquets at one of its altars after the wedding ceremony. The church was founded in the 13th century but rebuilt in the 15th century by Michelozzo. The left door of the church portico leads into the *Chiostro dei Morti* (Cloister of the Dead), which contains the *Madonna del Sacco,* a famous fresco by Andrea del Sarto. The middle door leads into the church via the *Chiostrino dei Voti* (Little Cloister of the Vows), with frescoes by several famous artists of the 16th century, including Del Sarto, Pontormo, and Rosso Fiorentino. Of the numerous artworks in the church itself, Andrea del Castagno's fresco of the Trinity, over the altar of the second chapel on the left, is one of the most prized. Open Mondays through Saturdays from 7 AM to 12:30 PM and 4:30 to 5 PM; Sundays from 4 to 5 PM. Admission charge.

BASILICA DI SAN LORENZO (BASILICA OF ST. LAWRENCE) This 15th-century Renaissance building was designed by Brunelleschi as the Medici parish church (the *Palazzo Medici-Ricciardi* is across the street). A later façade by Michelangelo was never completed. Make your way to the *Sagrestia Vecchia* (Old Sacristy), the earliest part of the church and one of Brunelleschi's most notable early creations, remarkable for the purity and harmony of the overall conception. Besides decorations by Donatello, it contains the tombs of several Medicis, including Giovanni di Bicci. Go outside and through a doorway to the left of the façade to the *Chiostro di San Lorenzo* (Cloister of St. Lawrence) and to the *Biblioteca Laurenziana* (Laurentian Library), a Michelangelo masterpiece designed to hold the Medici collection of manuscripts—10,000 precious volumes. The church is open daily, with a long midday closing; the library is closed afternoons and Sundays. No admission charge. Piazza San Lorenzo (phone: 216634, church; 210760, library).

MERCATO DI SAN LORENZO This colorful open-air market has stalls where everything—from a wooden rolling pin for making ravioli to a handmade mohair sweater—is sold. Some of the leather goods can be a good buy, especially belts, jackets, and handbags. It is closed Sundays (note that in winter, few vendors show up Mondays). At its center is the *Mercato Centrale,* a two-story, cast-iron covered building from the 19th century with a lovely glass dome, where all kinds of food products are on sale, including local meat, cheese, and produce, and fresh eggs and homemade wine brought in by farmers from the countryside. It's closed Sundays and for a long midday break. Piazza San Lorenzo.

CAPPELLE MEDICEE (MEDICI CHAPELS) Once part of *San Lorenzo,* these famous Medici funerary chapels now have a separate entrance (behind the church). The first of the chapels, the *Cappella dei Principi* (Chapel of the Princes), where Cosimo I and the other grand dukes of Tuscany lie, is the later of the two, and a family burial vault supreme: The elaborate Baroque interior took two centuries to complete. Note the fine examples of Florentine mosaic—fine inlay done with semi-precious stones. But the real attraction here is the other chapel, the *Sagrestia Nuova* (New Sacristy), a companion piece to the *Sagrestia Vecchia* in the adjoining basilica. This magnificent show is by Michelangelo, who was commissioned by Cardinal Giulio de' Medici (later Pope Clement VII) and Pope Leo X (another Medici) to design both the interior—Michelangelo's first architectural job—and the statuary as a fitting resting place for members of their family. Michelangelo worked on it from 1521 to 1533 and left two of the projected tombs incomplete, but those he finished—the tomb of Lorenzo II, Duke of Urbino, with the figures of Dawn and Dusk, and the tomb of Giuliano, Duke of Nemours, with the figures of Night and Day—are extraordinary. (Lorenzo il Magnifico and his brother Giuliano, the latter murdered in the *Duomo,* are buried in the tomb opposite the altar, which bears a splendid *Madonna with Child* by Michelangelo.)

Don't miss the feeling of the *Sagrestia Nuova* as a whole; taking in its square plan and imposing dome (especially its unusual trapezoidal windows), one almost has a sensation of soaring upward. Closed Mondays and late afternoons. Admission charge. Piazza Madonna degli Aldobrandini (phone: 23885).

PALAZZO MEDICI-RICCARDI (MEDICI-RICCARDI PALACE) Not far from the *Chiesa di San Lorenzo* is the palace where the Medici family lived until 1540, when they moved to the *Palazzo Vecchio*. When Cosimo the Elder decided to build a palace for the family, he first asked Brunelleschi to design it, but rejected the architect's plans as too luxurious and likely to create excessive envy. So Michelozzo was responsible for what was to be the first authentic Renaissance mansion—as well as a barometer of the proper lifestyle for a prosperous Florentine banker. Don't miss the tiny *Cappella dei Magi* (Chapel of the Three Kings) and Benozzo Gozzoli's wonderful fresco of the Three Kings on their way to Bethlehem—the real reason to visit this palazzo. Closed Wednesdays, Sunday afternoons, and for a midday break. No admission charge. 1 Via Cavour (phone: 276-0340).

SANTA MARIA NOVELLA Designed by two Dominican monks in the late 13th century and largely completed by the mid-14th century (except for the façade, which was designed by Leon Battista Alberti and finished in the late 15th century), this church figures in Boccaccio's *Decameron* as the place where his protagonists discuss the plague of 1348, the Black Death. At the age of 13, Michelangelo was sent here to study painting under Ghirlandaio, whose exquisite frescoes adorn the wall behind the main altar. Others include Masaccio (note his *Trinity* halfway down the left wall), Filippino Lippi, and followers of Giotto, Bronzino, and Vasari. See the *Cappelle Gondi* and *Strozzi* (Gondi and Strozzi Chapels), with frescoes by Filippino Lippi in the latter; the great *Chiostro Verde* (Green Cloister), so called for the predominance of green in the decoration by Paolo Uccello and his school; the *Cappella del Crocifisso* (Chapel of the Crucifix) by Brunelleschi to the left of the main altar; and Giovanni della Robbia's ceramic fountain in the sacristy. The church is open Mondays through Saturdays from 7 to 11 AM and 3:30 to 6 PM; Sundays and holidays from 3:30 to 6 PM. The cloister is closed Fridays, late afternoons, and Sunday afternoons. Admission charge. Piazza Santa Maria Novella (phone: 210113).

CHIESA DI ORSANMICHELE (CHURCH OF ORSANMICHELE) This solid, square, 14th-century, Gothic-Renaissance structure once housed wheat for emergency use on its upper floors, while the ground floor was a church. The whole was adopted by the city's artisans and guilds as a trading center and oratory—an unusual combination. Outside, the 14 statues in the niches (most are copies) represent patron saints of the different guilds and were sculpted by the best Florentine artists of the 14th to 16th centuries, including Giambologna and Donatello. The interior is dominated by a huge 14th-century tabernacle of colored marble by Andrea Orcagna, housing a beautiful Madonna by Bernardo Daddi. On July 26, *Festa di Sant'Anna,* the building is decorated with flags of the guilds to commemorate the expulsion of the tyrannical Duke of Athens from Florence in 1343. Open daily, with a long midday closing. Via dei Calzaiuoli (phone: 284715).

SINAGOGA (SYNAGOGUE) Built in the late 19th century by Florence's Jewish community in the Sephardic-Moorish style, this is one of the world's most beautiful temples. It was severely damaged during the 1966 floods but was lovingly and accurately restored. If you ring the bell at the smaller of the two gates, an English-speaking woman will take you around. Inside the grounds is a small museum of memorabilia from throughout the ages. Open Mondays through Thursdays from 11 AM to 1 PM and 2 to 5 PM; Fridays and Sundays from 10 AM to 1 PM. Admission charge to museum. 4 Via Farini (phone: 245252).

MERCATO NUOVO (STRAW MARKET) This covered market near the Piazza della Signoria dates from the 16th century. It holds an amazing assortment of handbags, placemats in traditional Florentine straw and raffia, pretty embroidery work (most made in Hong Kong), typical gilt-pattern wooden articles, and other souvenirs. It is also known as the *Mercato del Porcellino,* after the market's symbol—an imposing and slightly daunting bronze statue of a wild boar. Rub its shiny nose and toss a coin into the fountain to ensure a return visit. Closed Sundays, Mondays in winter, and holidays. Piazza del Mercato Nuovo.

ENVIRONS

SAN MINIATO AL MONTE Near Piazzale Michelangelo, this jewel-like church (beloved by the Florentines) dominates the city's highest point and looks out over a broad panorama of Florence and the surrounding hills—a romantic setting that makes it a particular favorite for weddings. One of the best examples of Tuscan Romanesque architecture and design in the city, it was built from the 11th to the 13th century on the spot where St. Miniato, martyred in the 3rd century, is reputed to have placed his severed head after carrying it up from Florence. The façade is in the typical green-and-white marble of the Florentine Romanesque style, as is the carved-animal pulpit inside. Art treasures include Michelozzo's 15th-century *Cappella del Crocifisso* (Crucifix Chapel), with terra cotta decorations by Luca della Robbia; Spinello Aretino's frescoes in the sacristy; and the *Cappella del Cardinale di Portugale* (Chapel of the Cardinal of Portugal), a Renaissance addition that contains works by Baldovinetti, Antonio and Piero del Pollaiolo, and Luca della Robbia. Dating from 1207 and said to have been inspired by Sicilian tapestries, the pavement is considered one of the prettiest of its kind. The small community of Benedictine monks of *San Miniato* sing vespers in Gregorian chants daily at 4:30 PM. Tourists are welcome if they plan to attend the mass that follows (before the service, a monk may ask visitors to leave if their time is short). Stop by the adjoining cemetery (closed Sundays), a wonderful collection of Italian funerary art (the English painter Henry Savage Landor and Carlo Lorenzini, a.k.a. Carlo Collodi, author of *Pinocchio,* are buried here). A small shop to the left of the church sells "medicinal" elixirs and liquors made by the monks from centuries-old formulas. The fortifications surrounding the church were designed by Michelangelo against the imperial troops of Charles V. Open daily, with a midday closing (except Sundays). Viale Galileo (phone: 234-2768).

FORTE BELVEDERE This imposing star-shaped, 16th-century fort—built by the Florentine architect Buontalenti for the Grand Duke Ferdinand I—forms part of the Old City walls. The fortress commands splendid views of the city below and often has exhibitions of painting and sculpture inside. On summer evenings, the grounds become a makeshift open-air movie theater for films dubbed in Italian. It's a pleasant walk either up through the *Giardini di Boboli* or up the steep Costa San Giorgio from the Ponte Vecchio, or take bus No. 13 from the center. Open daily. No admission charge. Costa San Giorgio (phone: 234-2822).

FIESOLE On a hill overlooking Florence and the Arno, this delightful town was an Etruscan settlement and, later, a Roman city. The *Duomo,* begun in the 11th century and radically restored in the 19th, is on the main square, Piazza Mino da Fiesole; just off the square is the *Teatro Romano,* built about 80 BC, where classical plays are sometimes performed, especially during the summer festival (*L'Estate Fiesolana*), which is devoted primarily to music. Take the picturesque, steep Via San Francesco leading out of the square and walk up to the *Chiesa di San Francesco,* passing the public gardens along the way and stopping at the terrace to enjoy the splendid view of Florence. The church, built during the 14th and 15th centuries, contains some charming cloisters, especially the tiny *Choistrino di San Bernardino* (named for the saint who once lived here). Nearby is the monastery, with an altarpiece by Fra Angelico, and monks' cells, which are furnished as they were in the 15th century. *Badia Fiesolana,* a 15th-century abbey, is also located in the vicinity.

Gelato fans can make a pilgrimage to *Villani* (8 Via S. Domenico) for a cup of custard-like *crema Villani.* Fiesole's tourist office is at 37 Piazza Mino (phone: 598720). Five miles (8 km) north of Florence, Fiesole can be reached by bus No. 7 from the railway station, *Santa Maria Novella,* or Piazza San Marco (be careful, as this bus—always full of foreign visitors—is a notorious venue for pickpockets).

CERTOSA DEL GALLUZZO (MONASTERY OF GALLUZZO) Seven miles (11 km) southwest of downtown is this monastery whose monks have been growing herbs (and making liqueurs from them) for centuries. Though the community was once large and powerful, only a dozen or so monks remain today. Visitors can tour this splendid monastery, set in a magnificent countryside of rolling Tuscan hills, and buy products from a charming *farmacia* (pharmacy). There also is a small museum with some beautiful frescoes, most notably those by Pontormo, from the 16th century. The No. 37 bus from the center goes directly to the *certosa;* by car, it is a 15-minute trip. Follow the signs for *Galluzzo,* and you'll see the monastery loom in front of you.

Closed Mondays and for a long midday break. No admission charge. Galluzzo (phone: 204-9226).

CASA DI MACHIAVELLI (MACHIAVELLI'S HOUSE) In the small village of Sant'Andrea in Percussina, 12 miles (20 km) and a half-hour drive from the city, is this house (known as *Albergaccio*) where Niccolò Machiavelli lived after being exiled from Florence by the Medicis. He wrote his masterpiece *Il Principe* (The Prince) here. The house is furnished as it was when Machiavelli was in residence. Open Tuesdays through Fridays from 9 AM to 2 PM and 7 to 10 PM; Saturdays from 11 AM to 7 PM; and Sundays from 9 to 11 AM and 4:30 to 10 PM. Admission charge (phone: 828471). Across the road is a small trattoria where the writer apparently repaired for a jug of wine between chapters. It still serves an excellent dish of Tuscan beans and very good peasant bread. A private bus company, *SITA* (phone: 483651), runs from Via Santa Caterina da Siena off Piazza Santa Maria Novella to the village; by car, take S2 heading toward Siena and turn off at San Casciano Val di Pesa. The village is signposted from there. Sant'Andrea in Percussina (no phone).

EXTRA SPECIAL

Scattered about the Florentine countryside are a number of stately villas of the historic aristocracy of Florence, three of which are associated with the Medici family. On the road to Sesto Fiorentino, about 5 miles (8 km) north of the city, is the 16th-century *Villa della Petraia* (originally a castle of the Brunelleschi family, rebuilt in 1575 for a Medici cardinal by Buontalenti); just down the hill is the 15th-century *Villa di Castello,* which was taken over by the Medicis in 1477. Both have lovely gardens and fountains by Il Tribolo. The *Villa Medici* at Poggio a Caiano, at the foot of Monte Albano about 10 miles (16 km) northwest of Florence, was rebuilt for Lorenzo the Magnificent by Giuliano da Sangallo from 1480 to 1485. The gardens of all three villas usually are closed Mondays; the interiors of the *Petraia* and *Medici* villas may be visited (hours change often; call 451208 for information regarding the former, 877012 for the latter). Bus service and escorted tours are available from Florence through *SITA* and other companies.

Sources and Resources

TOURIST INFORMATION

The *Azienda Provinciale per il Turismo* (*APT*; 16 Via Alessandro Manzoni, Firenze 50121; phone: 23320) will provide general information, brochures, and maps of the city and the surrounding area if you write in advance. There's also a tourist information booth just outside the train station (Piazza

Stazione; phone: 212245), which is closed Sundays and late afternoons; one immediately behind Piazza Signoria (17-19r Chiasso Baroncelli; phone: 230-2124 or 230-2033), which is closed Sundays and late afternoons; and another at 1r Via Cavour (phone: 290832), which is open daily in summer; closed Sundays and late afternoons in winter. For information on Tuscany, contact the *Regione Toscana/Promozione Turistica* (Regional Tourist Office; 26 Via di Novoli; phone: 438-2111), which is closed afternoons and weekends.

LOCAL COVERAGE Check the very helpful brochure *Florence Concierge Information,* available at most better hotels, or pick up a copy of *Florence Today* at the tourist information office (also distributed in some hotels). *Vista* is an English-language magazine published every two or three months that lists activities of interest to visitors. It is found at major hotels and tourist offices. Florence's daily newspaper is *La Nazione.* A national newspaper, *La Repubblica,* has a section on Florence in which there is a daily calendar of events in English.

Numerous maps and pocket-size guidebooks to Florence, such as the *Storti Guides,* are published in Italy and are available at newsstands throughout the city. Excellent guides in English available in bookstores are by Luciano Berti and by Rolando and Piero Fusi. Background reading before your trip might include Mary McCarthy's classic *The Stones of Florence* (Harcourt Brace Jovanovich; $7.95), a discussion of the history and character of the city as seen through its art, and Christopher Hibbert's *The House of Medici: Its Rise and Fall* (Morrow; $12.95), a study of the city's most influential family.

TELEPHONE The city code for Florence is 55. When calling from within Italy, dial 055 before the local number.

GETTING AROUND

Most visitors find Florence one of the easiest European cities to navigate. Although it is fairly large, the scale of the *centro storico* is rather intimate, and you can get just about anywhere on foot. Almost all major sites are on the north side, or right bank, of the river, while those on the Oltrarno side ("beyond the Arno") are within close walking distance of the center. A large part of the city's center is closed to traffic, except for those with permits, making it pleasant for pedestrians. Florentine buildings are numbered according to a double system. Black (*nero*) numbers indicate dwellings, while red (*rosso*) numbers—indicated by an "r" after the number in street addresses—are commercial buildings (shops and such). The black and the red often have little relationship to each other, so you may find a black 68 next to a red 5.

AIRPORT Florence has no international airport; the closest one is Pisa's *Galileo Galilei Airport* (phone: 50-28088), a one-hour train ride from the city. Travelers destined for flights from Pisa's airport can conveniently check bags through to their final destination from Florence's train station, where there's a Pisa airport check-in counter on Track 5. It's far safer, though, to take the train to Rome and fly out of Italy from there. A special train runs from Rome's *Fiumicino Airport* to Florence's *Stazione Centrale*, so travelers can avoid going into downtown Rome to catch the train to Florence (for more information, see *Train,* below).

Florence does have an expanding airport, *Vespucci Airport,* also referred to as *Peretola,* the area where it is located (11 Via del Termine; phone: 333498); it offers flights to Milan, Rome, Venice, Turin, and Trieste, among other destinations. *Peretola* also receives scheduled international flights from such major European cities as Brussels, Frankfurt, and London, among others. The airport is a 10-minute drive from downtown; an inexpensive bus departs frequently from the *SITA* bus terminal (15r Via Santa Caterina da Siena, off Piazza Santa Maria Novella; phone: 483651 or 211487) to the airport and vice-versa.

BUSES *ATAF* (phone: 580528) is the city bus company, running about 40 city and suburban routes. Bus routes are listed in the yellow pages of the telephone directory. Tickets—which must be purchased before boarding—can be bought at tobacco counters, in bars, and at some newsstands; they can be used more than once, within a 70-minute time limit. Children under one meter (39 inches) tall ride free. As there are no ticket collectors (only automatic stamping machines), many passengers do not buy tickets, but anybody caught without one by the occasional controller is fined $25 and way up on the spot—no excuses. The back door of the bus is for boarding, the middle for disembarking; the front door is only for season ticket holders. At rush hour, buses are impossibly crowded, making it at times difficult to get off at the desired stop. Watch out for pickpockets on crowded buses. Walking often is faster and more enjoyable, but pedestrians are cautioned to watch out for buses and taxis in special lanes permitting them to travel on many streets otherwise closed to traffic.

SITA (15r Via Santa Caterina da Siena; phone: 483651) and *Lazzi* (4-6 Piazza Stazione; phone: 215154) are two private bus companies that serve the surrounding region; they offer a good way to take day trips to some of Tuscany's towns. Their depots are on opposite sides of the train station.

CAR RENTAL All international firms are represented. Be aware that parking is difficult in the center, and the one-way system can be maddening. An alternative is to leave your car at one of the attended parking lots in or outside the center (discounted weekly rates are often available) or at your hotel, and walk or take a taxi. Two new parking facilities—both very central though expensive—are located in Piazza Stazione and Piazza della Libertà.

TAXI You can occasionally hail a cruising taxi (only if the light on top is lit); it's more likely you'll pick one up at one of the numerous cabstands around the city. Call for a taxi by dialing 4798, 4242, or 4390. Cabs are metered, and there are extra charges for Sunday and night rides, luggage, and the like. It is customary to give a small tip; a general rule is to round off the fare to the nearest thousand lire. Daily from 8 AM to 9 PM, *Autoalberghi* (phone: 238-1624) runs a blue-and-white van from in front of the train station to all hotels around the city—if the van's not there, it's out making the rounds. They also have an office near the taxi stand at the station. Because their fares are similar to those of a taxi, the vans are most convenient for groups of five or more (a taxi can fit only four).

TOURS *APT* (see above) has a list of qualified multilingual tourist guides who will lead half- or full-day tours for small or large groups. *SITA* (see above) organizes guided excursions to destinations outside of town, as well as half-day tours of Florence. Guides also are recommended by the *Associazione di Guide Turistiche* (9/A Viale Gramsci; phone: 247-8188; fax: 234-5490).

TRAIN *Stazione Centrale Santa Maria Novella* (phone: 288785), the city's main railway station, is near the church of the same name, at Piazza Stazione. The *Pendolino,* or *ETR 450,* Italy's answer to France's *TGV* or Japan's *Bullet Train,* travels the Rome/Florence/Bologna/Milan route (and back) at high speed and makes very few stops. The drawback is that it doesn't go into Florence's central station, but to Rifredi, outside the city center. There usually are taxis, however, to meet arriving trains.

Travelers flying into Rome's *Fiumicino Airport* from the US can now take *Alitalia*'s twice-daily *Airport Train* (the name is the same in Italian) directly from the airport nonstop to Florence's *Stazione Centrale* (and to return as well). Tickets for the train can be bought at the same time as those for the *Alitalia* travel, and baggage can be checked straight through to Florence from the departure point. For those flying with other airlines, the one-way cost is approximately $80. The train leaves twice daily, and the trip takes two and a half hours.

SPECIAL EVENTS

Florence is bathed in medieval splendor each year during the *Festa di San Giovanni Battista* (Feast of St. John the Baptist) on June 24. Part of the tradition for the past several hundred years has been the *Calcio in Costume.* The first part of this spectacle is a colorful parade of more than 500 Florentines wearing colorful 16th-century costumes—with modern T-shirts and sneakers—followed by an extremely rough game of soccer. Four teams of 27 people play, each representing the old rival neighborhoods of San Giovanni, Santo Spirito, Santa Croce, and Santa Maria Novella (distinguishable by their green, white, blue, and red costumes, respectively). Three games are played—two preliminaries and a final. One is always scheduled on June 24 and the other two within a week or two before (or sometimes after) that date. The game, which resembles wrestling, rugby, and soccer, with the round leather ball thrown (hands are allowed) more often than kicked, originated as the Roman *arpasto,* played on sandy ground by soldiers training for war. It evolved through the Middle Ages and the Renaissance (in 1530 there was a famous match played by the Florentines in defiance of the imperial troops of Charles V, who were besieging the city), lapsed for about a century and a half, and then was revived in 1930. Also reinstated was the preliminary parade of Florentine guild officials, followed by the four teams led by their resident noblemen on horseback. Because the game and its 8,000 or so spectators constitute some danger to the fountains and statuary of Florence's historic piazze, it was moved at one point to the *Giardini di Boboli,* only to be banned there, too. It is now held at its original site, Piazza Santa Croce, covered with dirt for the occasion.

Among the other folkloric events is the centuries-old ceremony called the *Scoppio del Carro,* literally "bursting the cart," which takes place traditionally on *Easter Sunday* in celebration of a Christian victory in one of the Crusades and culminates in a great fireworks display. A large cart drawn by white oxen is brought to Piazza del Duomo and connected to the main altar of the cathedral by a metal wire. At the midday mass, when the bells announce the Resurrection of Christ, the Cardinal Archbishop of Florence sets off a dove-shaped rocket, with flints said to have been brought back from Jerusalem during the Crusades, that runs along the wire to the cart filled with firecrackers. When the cart explodes, the Florentine spectators cheer with joy, taking the event and the flight of the "dove" as a good omen for the future. Occasionally the dove doesn't make it and sighs fill the square, as this is considered a bad omen indeed. On *Ascension Day* each May, Florentine children celebrate the *Festa del Grillo* by going to the *Cascine,* a park along the Arno at the edge of the center, and buying crickets in cages, only to set them free. The *Festa delle Rificolone,* September 7, is celebrated with a procession along the Arno and across the Ponte San Niccolò with colorful paper lanterns and torches.

At the *Fortezza del Basso* in May or June in even-numbered years is the *Mostra Mercato degli Antiquari Toscani,* where regional Tuscan antiques dealers sell everything from Etruscan relics to 19th-century antiques. Far more established and much more prestigious is the *Mostra dell'Antiquariato,* an important international antiques fair, held in odd-numbered years in September and October at the *Palazzo Strozzi.*

MUSEUMS

In addition to those described in *Special Places,* the following museums—along with churches and palaces whose artwork makes them, in effect, museums—may be of interest. Contact the tourist office for information about hours, which often change without notice.

BADIA FIORENTINA The church of a former Benedictine *badia* (abbey), with a part-Romanesque, part-Gothic campanile, it was founded in the 10th century, enlarged in the 13th, and rebuilt in the 17th. It was here during mass that Dante first saw and fell in love with Beatrice. At press time, it was closed for renovations. Open Mondays through Saturdays from 9 AM to noon and 4 to 6 PM; Sundays from 4 to 6 PM. Via del Proconsolo at Via Dante Alighieri (phone: 287389).

CASA BUONARROTI Michelangelo bought this small house for his next of kin. It contains some of the master's early works, such as his important *Madonna della Scala* (1490–92), as well as works done in his honor by some of the foremost artists of the 16th and 17th centuries. Closed Tuesdays and late afternoons. Admission charge. 70 Via Ghibellina (phone: 241752).

CASA DI DANTE A small museum in what is believed to have been Dante's house, it documents his life, times, and work. The museum was closed at press time because of a lack of funds. No admission charge. 1 Via Santa Margherita (phone: 283343).

CASA GUIDI Robert and Elizabeth Barrett Browning lived on the first floor of this 15th-century palazzo near the *Palazzo Pitti* from shortly after their secret marriage in 1846 until Elizabeth's death in 1861. Now called the *Browning Institute,* it is an unfinished museum and a memorial to both poets. Open Tuesdays through Thursdays by appointment only. Admission charge. 8 Piazza San Felice (phone: 284393).

CENACOLO DI SANT'APOLLONIA The refectory of this former convent contains Andrea del Castagno's masterwork, his fresco of the Last Supper (ca. 1450), second only to Leonardo's in Milan. Closed Mondays and late afternoons. No admission charge. 1 Via XXVII Aprile (phone: 23885).

CHIESA DI OGNISSANTI (ALL SAINTS' CHURCH) Built in the 13th century and rebuilt in the 17th, it contains extraordinary frescoes by Ghirlandaio and Botticelli and is the burial place of the latter as well as of the family of Amerigo Vespucci. Next door in the refectory is Ghirlandaio's *Cenacolo* (Last Supper). The church is closed daily from noon to 4 PM; the refectory is closed Sundays, Wednesdays through Fridays, and afternoons. No admission charge. 42 Piazza Ognissanti (phone: 239-8700).

MUSEO DI ANTROPOLOGIA ED ETNOLOGIA (MUSEUM OF ANTHROPOLOGY AND ETHNOLOGY) First of its genre in Italy and continually enlarged, it now comprises more than 30 rooms and a vast collection grouped by race, continent, and culture. Open Thursdays through Saturdays from 9 AM to 1 PM and the third Sunday of the month. No admission charge. 12 Via del Proconsolo (phone: 239-6449).

MUSEO ARCHEOLOGICO (ARCHAEOLOGICAL MUSEUM) This fascinating museum contains a permanent exhibit of gold jewelry and gems from the Medicis. An outstanding collection of Etruscan, Greek, and Roman art is housed in six halls. A topographical section features objects from ancient Etruria, and an Egyptian area has mummies, statues, and a well-preserved chariot found in Thebes. Closed Mondays and late afternoons. Admission charge. 36 Via Colonna (phone: 23575).

MUSEO ARCHEOLOGICO DI FIESOLE A fine selection of treasures from the Etruscan and Roman periods of Fiesolan history, including an especially rich collection of Etruscan pottery. Open daily in summer; closed Tuesdays in winter. Admission charge. Piazza Mino, Fiesole (phone: 59477).

MUSEO FIRENZE COM'ERA (FLORENCE "AS IT WAS" MUSEUM) Here are prints, maps, paintings, photos, and other documents illustrating Florence's urban development from the 15th century to the present. There also is a permanent exhibition of works by the 20th-century artist Ottone Rosai. Closed Thursdays and late afternoons. Admission charge. 24 Via dell'Oriuolo (phone: 239-8483).

MUSEO DELLA FONDAZIONE HORNE (HORNE MUSEUM) In this jewel of a museum are paintings, drawings, sculptures, furniture, ceramics, coins, and unusual old household utensils. The former collection of an Englishman, Herbert Percy Horne, it was bequeathed to the city in 1916 and set up after his death in his handsome 15th-century *palazzetto*. Closed Sundays, holidays, and afternoons. Admission charge. 6 Via dei Benci (phone: 244661).

MUSEO STIBBERT A vast (about 50,000 pieces) medieval collection of art objects, antiques, arms from all over the world, and other curiosities left by the Scottish-Italian collector Stibbert, with his villa and gardens. Closed Thursdays and afternoons. Admission charge. 26 Via Federico Stibbert (phone: 486049).

MUSEO DI STORIA DELLE FOTOGRAFIA (HISTORY OF PHOTOGRAPHY MUSEUM) Also called the *Museo Alinari*, this impressive collection of 19th- and early-20th-century daguerreotypes and photographs of quotidian Italian life is housed in a 15th-century palace designed by Alberti. Closed Wednesdays. Admission charge. 16r Via della Vigna Nuova (phone: 213370).

MUSEO DI STORIA DELLA SCIENZA (HISTORY OF SCIENCE MUSEUM) Scientific instruments, including Galileo's telescopes, and several odd items document the development of modern science from the Renaissance to the 20th century. Closed for an hour at lunch Mondays, Wednesdays, and Fridays; closed Tuesday, Thursday, and Saturday afternoons; and Sundays. Admission charge. 1 Piazza dei Giudici (phone: 293493).

PALAZZO DAVANZATI A perfectly preserved 14th-century palazzo with 15th-century furniture, tapestries, ceramics, and everyday objects in the domestic life of a well-heeled Florentine merchant, also known as the *Museo della Casa Fiorentina Antica* (Florentine House Museum). A visit is recommended just to see some of the first indoor bathrooms, next to the bedrooms. Closed Mondays and late afternoons. Admission charge. 13 Via Porta Rossa (phone: 216518).

SANTA TRINITA (CHURCH OF THE HOLY TRINITY) One of the oldest churches in Florence, it was built in the 11th century with a 16th-century façade. See the Ghirlandaio frescoes in the *Cappella Sassetti*—one shows the church with its original Romanesque façade. Open daily, with a long midday closing. Piazza Santa Trinita (phone: 216912).

SHOPPING

Shopping is wonderful in Florence, arguably Italy's most fashionable city. For clothing, the smartest streets are Via Tornabuoni, Via della Vigna Nuova, Via Calzaiuoli, and Via Roma. The shops lining the Ponte Vecchio have been selling beautiful gold and silver jewelry since 1593. The concentration of antiques shops is highest along Via dei Fossi, Via Maggio, and Borgo Ognissanti. Leather goods and handmade lingerie are other Florentine specialties. Winter store hours are Tuesdays through Saturdays from 9 AM to 1 PM and 3:30 to 7:30 PM; Mondays from 3:30 to 7:30 PM. The summer finds these stores closed on Saturday afternoons rather than Monday mornings, and the evening hours are 4 to 8 PM. Some shops that are geared to tourists (fashion, leather, souvenirs, and so on) stay open all day. Food shops traditionally close on Wednesday afternoons.

There are antiques and flea markets in Piazza dei Ciompi (daily) and Piazza Tasso (Saturdays and the last Sunday of every month). Occasional bargains are there for the finding, and haggling is the rule. The same can be said for the *Mercato di San Lorenzo* and the *Mercato Nuovo* (see *Special Places,* above). The *Mercato delle Cascine* (Tuesday mornings) is a mile-long market offering everything from secondhand clothing to live rabbits.

A. Ugolini Classic Italian menswear and womenswear, including Brioni suits. 65r Via Calzaiuoli (phone: 214439).

After Dark Bookstore Hard-to-find English books, comics, and magazines. 86r Via del Moro (phone: 294203).

Alex The best in designer clothes for women—Gianni Versace, Yamamoto, Byblos, Claude Montana, Basile, and Thierry Mugler. 19r and 5r Via della Vigna Nuova (phone: 214952).

Alinari Housed in *Palazzo Ruccelai,* this shop sells evocative photographs of Italy from the turn of this century and photography books. 46-48r Via della Vigna Nuova (phone: 218975).

Alivar Reproductions of modern design classics—van der Rohe, Breuer, Le Corbusier, Mackintosh, and more—in this stylish showroom. Two locations: 38 Via Cavour (phone: 230-2265) and 104r Via Cavour (phone: 230-2266).

Allegri Known throughout Italy for the finest in fashionable men's and women's rainwear and some overcoats. 27r Via Tornabuoni (phone: 213737).

Armani The famous designer's top-of-the-line wear for men and women: simple, classic, and modern. 51 Via della Vigna Nuova (phone: 219041).

Befani & Tai Quality gold craftsmanship at good prices. Two steps from the Piazza della Signoria, at 13r Via Vacchereccia (phone: 287825).

Beltrami A chain of elegant, expensive leatherwear shops: shoes, bags, sportswear, outerwear, and other items. 31r and 44r Via Calzaiuoli (phone: 212418); 1 Via dei Pecori (phone: 216321); and 48r Via Tornabuoni (phone: 216321).

Berto Berti Furniture, tapestries, majolica, paintings, and sculpture from the 11th to 19th centuries. 29r Via dei Fossi (phone: 294549).

Bijoux Cascio Well-priced, high quality costume jewelry; the designs are the shop's own. Their forte is ersatz stones and pearls set in "gold." 1r Via Por Santa Maria (phone: 294378).

BM A well-stocked English-language bookstore. 4r Borgo Ognissanti (phone: 294575).

Bojola Leather and canvas bags, luggage, and umbrellas and canes with a sporty look crowd this shop, which has become a Florentine institution. 25r Via Rondinelli (phone: 21155).

Bottega Veneta One of the largest selections of leather goods in the signature buttery soft, basket-weave leather. 3-4r Piazza Ognissanti (phone: 294265).

C. O. I. Florence's largest selection of gold jewelry is sold by weight at competitive prices. Upstairs, at 8 Via Por Santa Maria (phone: 283970 or 293424).

Calzoleria di Stefano Bemer Custom-made shoes for men and women in a wide range of materials. Off the beaten path, but well worth the effort—prices start at just $60. 136r Borgo San Frediano (phone: 211356).

Carlo Carnevali Furniture, majolica, paintings, and sculpture from the Alta Epoca (17th century). Antique costumes are also featured. 64r Borgo San Jacopo (phone: 295064).

Casa dei Tessuti *The* place for wonderful Italian wool, silk, and linen. 20-24r Via dei Pecori (phone: 215961).

Cellerini High-quality bags and suitcases handmade from top-of-the-line skins in a workshop above the store. 37r Via del Sole (phone: 282533).

Cirri Lovely hand-embroidered bed and bath linen and lingerie. 38-40r Via Por Santa Maria (phone: 239-6593).

Dino Bartolini An elegant housewares store, it offers a variety of the functional and whimsical for the kitchen. 30r Via dei Servi (phone: 211895).

Emilio Paoli A straw market with class—locally produced gift articles and imports. 26r Via della Vigna Nuova (phone: 214596).

Emilio Pucci A small boutique featuring fashionable womenswear in vibrant hues from the late marchese. 97r Via della Vigna Nuova (phone: 294028).

Emporio Armani Casual, upscale, ready-to-wear clothing for men and women by the well-known designer. 34r Via Pellicceria (phone: 212081).

Enrico Coveri The trademarks of Florence's late native son are bright colors and irreverent men's and women's fashions for the young at heart. 27r Via della Vigna Nuova (phone: 238-1769) and 81r Via Tornabuoni (phone: 211263).

Erboristeria Palazzo Vecchio Small, but stocked to the ceiling with ancient remedies, essences, oils, panaceas, and creams to treat everything from wrinkles to the blues. 9r Via Vacchereccia (phone: 239-6055).

Falai Florence is known for its jewelry shops, but this one will copy much-loved items or help you design new ones from drawings or descriptions. 28r Via Por Santa Maria (phone: 238-1688).

Feltrinelli The original store is extensively stocked and centrally located. It's filled with art books; on the second floor are English-language tomes. 12-20r Via Cavour (phone: 219524). The new superstore (30r Via Ceretani; phone: 238-2652) is the largest in Tuscany.

Ferragamo Run by the offspring of the famous Neapolitan-born shoemaker, this flagship store in an imposing palazzo produces Italy's largest selection of wonderfully crafted shoes, leather goods, and clothing. 16r Via Tornabuoni (phone: 239123).

Frette Luxurious bed, bath, and table linen, plain or decorated with delicate embroidery. 8-10 Lungarno Amerigo Vespucci (phone: 292367).

Gianni Versace The place to buy attention-getting, even outrageous outfits for men and women. 13-15r Via Tornabuoni (phone: 239-6167).

Gino Menicucci A well-stocked toy store, with Pinocchios in all sizes, miniature Ferraris, and some handmade wooden made-in-Italy items. Near the *Palazzo Pitti*. 51r Via Guicciardini (phone: 294934).

Giulio Giannini e Figlio This father-and-son store is one of the oldest selling the famous hand-crafted Florentine paper products, and its selection is one of the best in town. 37r Piazza Pitti (phone: 212621).

Guardaroba Erratic pickings of men's and women's clothing from haute couture Milanese designers, all at discount prices. Two central locations: 85r Via degli Albizi (phone: 234-0271) and 28r Via Verdi (phone: 247-8250).

Gucci Another Florentine name known the world over for chic leather goods and men's and women's clothing. 73r Via Tornabuoni (phone: 264011).

Guido Bartolozzi Antique furniture, tapestries, majolica, and works of art. 18r Via Maggio (phone: 215602).

H. Neuber Classic British and Italian wools. 32r Via Strozzi (phone: 215763).

Libreria Seeber Florence's oldest, this Old World, international bookstore has a good selection of English-language books on Italian themes. 70 Via Tornabuoni (phone: 294311).

Lisio Tessuti d'Arte Housed in a medieval tower, this shop sells an incredible selection of beautiful silks, damasks, and brocades for upholstery and clothing, all handwoven on 17th-century looms. 45r Via dei Fossi (phone: 212430).

Loretta Caponi Exquisite handmade lingerie and linen by this second-generation shop that designs for Nina Ricci and Dior. 12r Borgo Ognissanti (phone: 213-9668).

Lori Clara e Lorenzo Not very central, but a good selection of men's and women's designer clothing at discount prices. 15 Viale Enrico de Nicola (phone: 650-3204).

Luigi Bellini The doyen of local antiques dealers, Bellini is a generalist. 5 Lungarno Soderini (phone: 214031).

Luisa Spagnoli Known for generations for its reliable, conservative, and high-quality women's clothing at moderate prices. 20 Via Strozzi (phone: 211978).

Luisa Via Roma The most fashion-forward of Florence's clothing stores for men and women. 19r Via Roma (phone: 217826).

Madova Italy's most competent and incomparable glovemaker, who will custommake and ship. 1r Via Guicciardini (phone: 239-6526).

Mario Buccellati Exquisite jewelry and silverware in traditional Florentine designs. 71r Via Tornabuoni (phone: 287393).

Maschereri Master mask makers, both traditional and modern. Worth a visit if you don't make it to Venice. 13r Via dei Tavolini (phone: 213823).

MaxMara Classic and contemporary women's clothing in fine fabrics. 89r Via Tornabuoni (phone: 214133) and 23 Via dei Pecori (phone: 287761).

Melli Exquisite antique jewelry, ivory, silver, and clocks. 44-46 Ponte Vecchio (phone: 211413).

Officina Profumo-Farmaceutica di Santa Maria Novella First opened to the public in 1612, this unique pharmacy and perfume shop carries fine cosmetics and unusual products from centuries-old recipes, such as anti-hysteria salts, all beautifully packaged. 16 Via della Scala (phone: 216276).

Paperback Exchange New and used books in English, plus a wide selection of travel guides. Trade in tomes that you don't want to take with you. 31r Via Fiesolana (phone: 247-8154).

Papiro *Papier à cuve,* or marbleized paper, a method of hand-decoration invented in the 17th century; lovely stationery and myriad gift items. 24r Via Cavour (phone: 215262) and other locations.

Passamaneria Toscana Heaven for seasoned and aspiring interior designers, with a wealth of decorative cords, fringes, tassels, buttons, and pillows to swathe, transform, and gussy up your home. 12r Piazza San Lorenzo (phone: 214670) and Via della Vigna Nuova and Via dei Federighi (phone: 239-8047).

Pineider Italy's most famous and prestigious stationers. 13r Piazza della Signoria (phone: 284655).

Pitti Libri Beautiful illustrated books on a wide range of subjects, as well as small antique objects and lovely mementos. 16 Piazza Pitti (phone: 212704).

Prada The merchandise: clothing, handbags, shoes, and accessories. The watchwords: luxurious, classic, minimalist, and chic. 26-28r Via Vacchereccia (phone: 213901).

Quaglia & Forte Intricately hand-carved cameos and reproductions of Etruscan gold jewelry are sold here. 12r Via Guicciardini (phone: 294534).

Raspini One of the city's best sources of quality leather goods, particularly men's and women's shoes and outerwear. 25r Via Roma (phone: 213077) and two other locations.

Richard Ginori The flagship store of Italy's most famous porcelain manufacturer offers exquisite china, as well as fine crystal and silver from its Florentine founder. 17r Via Rondinelli (phone: 210041).

Santa Croce Leather School Quality leather goods (boxes, gloves, handbags, wallets, clothing, and shoes) from the school and shop inside the monastery of *Santa Croce,* through the church. 16 Piazza Santa Croce or (through the garden) 5r Via San Giuseppe (phone: 244533).

Sbigoli Attractive, rustic earthenware ceramics, mostly from Tuscany; shipping can be arranged. 4r Via Sant'Egidio (phone: 2479713).

Schwicker Quality gifts by Florentine artisans. 40r Piazza Pitti (phone: 211851).

Sylvia Seymour Housed in a lovely 16th-century palazzo, this shop offers the late Piero Fornasetti's whimsical designs on everything from trays to ties. 70r Borgo degli Albizi (phone: 234-7398).

Taddei Three generations have carried on the Florentine art of exquisitely handcrafting small leather gift items, including boxes, frames, desk sets, and jewelry boxes. 11 Via Santa Margherita (phone: 239-8960).

Tanino Crisci The most classic shoe shop (for men and women) in town. 43-45r Via Tornabuoni (phone: 214692).

Il Torchio Well-priced, handmade Florentine marbleized paper, books, pencils, desk sets, and more. 17 Via dei Bardi (phone: 234-2862).

Torrini A centuries-old institution, offering exquisite jewelry. 10r Piazza Duomo (phone: 284457).

U. Gherardi The best selection of coral jewelry in town (most of it traditionally produced in Naples), as well as cultured pearls and cameos. 5r Ponte Vecchio (phone: 211809).

Valentino This Roman couturier offers the ultimate in elegant and sophisticated women's fashion. 47r Via della Vigna Nuova (phone: 293142).

Viceversa New-wave, high-tech, and classic designer tableware and gift items of the sort more typically found in Milan. 53r Via Ricasoli (phone: 239-8281).

FAST FORWARD

Can't close your suitcase? *Fracassi International Forwarders* (11 Via Santo Spirito; phone: 289340) will estimate the least expensive and most efficient way to ship home anything from fragile china to a Renaissance armoire. This well-known company with an English-speaking staff is not inexpensive, but it offers reliable, professional service; they will pick up the goods at the store or your hotel. *Oli-Ca* (27r Borgo SS Apostoli; phone: 239-6917) has a wrapping service two blocks from the main post office so visitors can avoid the complexities of the Italian postal system.

SPORTS AND FITNESS

Check with your concierge to find out which sports facilities currently are open to the public. Most are private clubs, but a day visit often can be arranged for a fee.

BICYCLES, MOPEDS, AND MOTORBIKES *Alinari* (85r Via Guelfa; phone: 211748) offers reasonably priced bicycle rentals. Motorbikes are available from *Program* (135r Borgo Ognissanti; phone: 282916); *Motorent* (9r Via San Zanobi; phone: 490113); and *Sabra* (8 Via Artisti; phone: 576256 or 579609), which also rents mopeds. Both bicycles and motorbikes usually can be rented by the hour, day, or week. Ride carefully!

FITNESS CENTERS Try *Gymnasium* (49r Via Palazzuolo; phone: 293308); *Meeting Club* (6 Via Ponte Sospeso; phone: 714069); or *Palestra Savasana* (26 Via J. da Diaccetto; phone: 333230).

GOLF Nestled in the Chianti hills is our favorite Florentine fairway:

TOP TEE-OFF SPOT

Circolo Golf dell'Ugolino Although this 18-hole layout is not very long, its many trees and bushes, bunkers, and out-of-bounds areas require concentration and accuracy. The fourth hole is a long, downhill par 3, the fifth a long par 4 through an olive grove. Wine tasting before a round is not advised. Closed Mondays. 3 Strada Chiantigiana, Grassina (phone: 230-1009; fax: 230-1141).

HORSEBACK RIDING For information, call *Piazzale Cascine* (*Parco delle Cascine;* phone: 360056) or *Agriturist* (3 Piazza San Firenze; phone: 287838). Just outside the city is *Badia Montescalari* (129 Via Montescalari at La Panca; phone: 959596).

JOGGING The best place to run is the *Parco delle Cascine* (Cascine Park). To get there, follow the river to Ponte della Vittoria.

ROWING Florence's most prestigious rowing club (watch them from the Ponte Vecchio) offers a temporary one-month membership to visitors. Contact the *Società Canottieri Firenze* (8 Lungarno dei Medici; phone: 282130).

SOCCER See the *Fiorentina* in action from September through May at the *Stadio Comunale* (4 Viale Manfredo Fanti; phone: 57625), designed by Pier Luigi Nervi.

SWIMMING Swimmers will do best to stay at one of the following hotels: *Jolly Carlton, Kraft, Park Palace,* or *Villa Medici* (see *Checking In* for all), or *Croce di Malta* (although the pool is very small; 7 Via della Scala; phone: 218351); outside the city, at the *Sheraton,* the *Torre di Bellosguardo,* the *Villa Cora,* the *Villa San Michele,* or the *Villa Villoresi* (see *Checking In* for all), or the *Villa La Massa* (6 Villa La Massa; phone: 666141). There also are a few outdoor public pools, including *Piscina Costoli* (Viale Paoli; phone: 669744); *Piscina Le Pavoniere,* in pleasant *Parco delle Cascine* (Viale degli Olmi; phone: 367506); and *Zodiac Sport* (2 Via A. Grandi; phone: 202-2847), which has indoor and outdoor pools.

TENNIS Play at the semi-public *Assi-Giglio-Rosso* (58 Viale Michelangelo; phone: 687858); *Circolo Tennis alle Cascine* (1 Viale Visarno; phone: 332651); *Circolo Tennis Torrigiani* (144 Via dei Serragli; phone: 224409); *Il Poggetto* (24/B Via Michele Mercati; phone: 488964); or *Tennis Pattinaggio Piazzale Michelangelo* (61 Viale Michelangelo; phone: 681-1880).

THEATER

The principal venues in Florence for drama and dance are the *Teatro della Pergola* (32 Via della Pergola; phone: 247-9652); the *Teatro Niccolini* (3 Via Ricasoli; phone: 213282); the *Teatro Tenda* (Lungarno Aldo Moro; phone: 650-4112); and the *Teatro Verdi* (101 Via Ghibellina; phone: 212320). *Teatro Nuovo Variety* (47 Via del Madonnone; phone: 676942) offers singers and humorous contemporary pieces.

Old films in English are shown erratically at the *Cinema Astro* (Piazza San Simone near Santa Croce; no phone), while new arrivals from America are shown Mondays at the *Cinema Goldoni* (Via degli Serragli; phone: 222437).

MUSIC

Although concert performances take a back seat to opera in Florence, one happening stands out.

HIGH NOTES

Maggio Musicale Fiorentino Founded in 1933 and currently under the leadership of Zubin Mehta, this prestigious event, Italy's answer to the king of European music festivals at Salzburg, offers programs that are so diverse that they seem a deliberate attempt to avoid musical chauvinism. This means you're as likely to hear Berg and Stravinsky as Italian composers like Rossini and Puccini. While most of the events are held at the *Teatro Comunale,* some concerts take place in outdoor locations, such as in the lovely courtyard of the *Palazzo Pitti.* Despite a name that translates "Florentine Musical May," the goings-on continue right through June and include some ballet and modern dance. 12 Corso Italia (phone: 27791; 277-9236, ticket office, mornings only).

Opera begins earlier in Florence than in most Italian cities. The season at the *Teatro Comunale* (see above), the principal opera house and concert hall, offers concerts year-round, principally in October and November, with opera in December and January, and ballet in July. The *Teatro della Pergola* (see *Theater*) is often the scene of Saturday-afternoon concerts from autumn through spring. *Amici della Musica* (49 Via Sirtori; phone: 608420) and the *Orchestra da Camera Fiorentina* (Florentine Chamber Orchestra; 6 Via E. Poggi; phone: 470027) regularly stage classical concerts year-round. Open-air concerts are held in the cloisters of the *Badia Fiesolana* (in Fiesole) and of the *Ospedale degli Innocenti* on summer evenings, and occasionally in other historic monuments such as the restored *Chiesa di Santo Stefano al Ponte Vecchio,* once the seat of the *Regional Tuscan Orchestra* (20 Via dei Benci; phone: 242767), still closed at press time due to extensive damage from the 1993 bombing of the nearby *Galleria degli Uffizi.* The orchestra now performs at the *Teatro della Compagnia* (50r Via Cavour; call the orchestra—see above—for information). From June through August, the open-air Roman amphitheater in Fiesole also has cultural events (see *Special Places,* above).

NIGHTCLUBS AND NIGHTLIFE

A Florentine evening usually begins with an *aperitivo* at Piazza della Signoria's elegant *Rivoire* (see *Caffès,* below), or any of the other historical landmark *caffès* on Piazza della Repubblica. An English-speaking clientele favors the cocktails at *Harry's Bar* (22r Lungarno Amerigo Vespucci; phone: 239-6700) or at *Bar Donatello,* on the main floor of the *Excelsior* hotel (see *Checking In*), the pre-dinner gathering place for Florence's smart set.

Discos and piano bars are among the most popular forms of evening entertainment, and tops among the former are *Tenax* (47 Via Pratese; phone: 308160) and *Jackie O'* (24r Via dell'Erta Canina; phone: 234-2442).

Other discos include *Yab* (5r Via Sassetti; phone: 282018) and *Full-Up* (21r Via della Vigna Vecchia; phone: 293006). *Andromeda* (13r Via dei Cimatori; phone: 292002) is a small disco near Piazza della Signoria; *Meccanò Meccanò* (1 Viale degli Olmi; phone: 352743) is a hip disco located in *Parco delle Cascine* that features outdoor dancing in the summer. For the very young crowd, dancing happens at *Space Electronic* (37 Via Palazzuolo; phone: 293082). The *Domino Club* (23r Borgo Santa Croce; phone: 217933) provides après-disco entertainment for young Florentines, with video clips, dancing, gelato, snacks, and breakfast at dawn. One singles spot that attracts an international crowd is *Maramao* (79r Via dei Macci; phone: 244341).

For a quieter evening, there are numerous lovely historical bar/*caffès* from which to choose (see *Caffès,* below). Modern venues include the *Caffè* (9 Piazza Pitti; phone: 239-6241); *Petit Bois* (51 Via Ferrucci, Fiesole; phone: 59578); and *Prezzemolo* (5r Via delle Caldaie; phone: 211530), a champagne bar for night owls. The elegant *Oliviero* (51r Via della Terme; phone: 287643) is a restaurant with piano bar, the place for a romantic evening, as is *Caffè Tornabuoni* (12-14r Lungarno Corsini; phone: 210751). There also are piano bars at most of the deluxe hotels, such as the *Savoy* (see *Checking In*).

Popular watering holes are the *Cotton Club* (15 Via Porta Rossa; phone: 264140); *Caffè Doney* (18 Piazza Strozzi; phone: 239-8206), with outdoor tables for people watching; and the newer *Caffè Cibreo* (5r Via Verrochio; phone: 234-5853). Three other local favorites are *Gilli,* a beautiful Belle Epoque *caffè* with a lively outdoor terrace; *Giacosa,* where the yuppie elite meet over truffle-paste sandwiches (see *Caffès* for both); *Procacci* (64r Via Tornabuoni; phone: 211656), a *caffè*/bar serving white truffle-paste sandwiches and other elegant snacks to a chic local crowd; and *Dolce Vita* (Piazza del Carmine; phone: 284595), *the* hangout for beautiful young folks in Florence. Convivial chatter rarely ceases here, and the bar stays open until 2 AM.

Best in Town

CHECKING IN

Florence is well organized for visitors, with more than 500 hotels to accommodate a year-round stream of travelers. Still, it's hard to find a room in high season (*Easter* through June; September through October; and the *Christmas* holidays) or during the many fashion or trade shows. The hotel count above and the list below include former *pensioni,* something like boardinghouses but now officially designated "hotels." A rare few still require that some meals be taken, a feature we specify. (Half board means you must take breakfast and either lunch or dinner at the establishment.) Although presented as if included, breakfast is often optional; by skipping it, you can save as much as $40 (for two). Expect to pay more than $225 a night for a double room at those places listed as very expensive; from $150 to $225 at an expensive hotel; from $100 to $150 in a moderate establishment; and $90 or less for inexpensive lodgings. Most of Florence's major hotels have complete facilities for the business traveler. Those hotels listed below as having "business services" usually offer such conveniences as an English-speaking concierge, meeting rooms, photocopiers, computers, translation services, and express checkout, among others. Call the hotel for additional information. All hotels feature private baths unless otherwise indicated. All telephone numbers are in the 55 city code unless otherwise noted.

An alternative to conventional hotel accommodations (particularly for long-term stays) is renting or subletting an apartment or villa in the *centro storico,* the environs of the city, or the Tuscan countryside. *Suzanne Pitcher* (2 Via Pietro Thouar; phone: 234-3354; fax: 234-7240) is an independent real estate agent with apartments of all sizes, converted farmhouses, and villas. Prices range from moderate to very expensive.

For an unforgettable Florentine experience, we begin with our favorite hostelry, followed by our cost and quality choices, listed by price category.

A SPECIAL HAVEN

Villa San Michele Originally a monastery built by the Davanzati family in the late 15th century, with a façade believed to have been designed by Michelangelo, it became a private villa during Napoleon's day and was transformed into one of Tuscany's most romantic hotels in the 1950s. Restored to its former glory, this member of the prestigious Orient-Express hotel group now has 28 exquisitely appointed rooms with canopied beds and 16 suites (most with Jacuzzis and many with sweeping views), intimate dining indoors or in the open-air loggia, 24-hour room service, fragrant gardens with splendid views, a pool, and limousine service into the city during the summer. Half board in the elegant restaurant, which serves wonderful Tuscan fare, is heavily encouraged. Business services. Open from about mid-March through November. Dramatically set on the slopes below Fiesole, about 5 miles (8 km) from the town center, at 4 Via Doccia, Fiesole (phone: 59451; 800-237-1236; fax: 598734).

VERY EXPENSIVE

Brunelleschi With its own tiny terra cotta piazza off a quiet back street two steps from the *Duomo,* this elegant 94-room hostelry has been restored with great style. A 6th-century Byzantine tower (once a women's prison) has been incorporated into this complex, originally three hotels; there's a rooftop terrace with exceptional views of the city, a first class restaurant, and an

English-speaking concierge. 3 Piazza S. Elisabetta (phone: 562068; 800-44-UTELL; fax: 219653).

Continental In an ideal, albeit sometimes noisy, spot overlooking the Ponte Vecchio, this contemporary 61-room hotel is as efficient as its two sisters, the *Augustus* (phone: 283054; fax: 268557), which is tucked away behind it, and the *Lungarno* (see below), across the river. All three offer excellent service, have an English-speaking concierge, and are very centrally located. Built after World War II bombardments leveled this part of town, these hotels are neither ultramodern nor charmingly historical. No restaurant. 2 Lungarno Acciaioli (phone: 282392; 800-44-UTELL; fax: 283139).

Excelsior A short walk from the city center, this hostelry is traditional in both style and service. It is part of the reliably luxurious and efficient CIGA chain. Many of its 177 elegantly appointed rooms overlook the Arno, the marble and gilt lobby is reminiscent of bygone days, and the excellent terrace restaurant, *Il Cestello,* affords a splendid river view. Business services are available. 3 Piazza Ognissanti (phone: 264201; 800-221-2340; fax: 210278).

Grand Brunelleschi is said to have designed the 15th-century palazzo as a residence for one of Florence's noble families; today, the Renaissance decor and canopied beds of this 109-room hostelry still evoke royal images. Ask for a room with a river view. Part of the CIGA chain and slightly more expensive than its sister hotel, the *Excelsior,* just across the plaza (see above), it has a restaurant, banquet rooms, 24-hour room service, and business services. 1 Piazza Ognissanti (phone: 288781; 800-221-2340; fax: 217400).

Helvetia & Bristol Considered one of Florence's best in the early 19th century, this very centrally located hotel (a member of the prestigious Relais & Châteaux group) has been restored to its former glory, with antique furniture, velvet drapes, and original oil paintings. The 52 rooms and suites are decorated in different styles, ranging from chinoiserie to Art Nouveau, and the marble bathrooms have Jacuzzis. Ideally located on a tranquil street between the Piazza della Repubblica and Via Tornabuoni, it has a restaurant, 24-hour room service, and business services. 2 Via dei Pescioni (phone: 287814; 800-223-5852; fax: 288353).

Lungarno Set between the Ponte Vecchio and the Ponte Santa Trinita on the Oltrarno side of town are 70 modern rooms, the best of which have terraces and balconies overlooking the Arno (be sure to book one of these in advance), and a well-known collection of contemporary art in the public areas. There is a garage but no restaurant. Business services. 14 Borgo San Jacopo (phone: 264211; 800-44-UTELL; fax: 268437).

Regency Within walking distance of the center of town in a quiet residential area on a tree-lined piazza is this 35-room, exquisitely decorated, late 19th-century patrician villa. Like its sister in Rome (the *Lord Byron*), it offers calm and privacy, discreetly displaying its Relais & Châteaux crest at the entrance. There is a charming garden, an excellent restaurant, *Relais le Jardin* (see *Eating Out*), 24-hour room service, and business services. 3 Piazza Massimo d'Azeglio (phone: 245247; 800-223-6800; fax: 234-2938).

Savoy In the heart of Florence, this classic gem has a hundred rooms decorated in Venetian, Florentine, or contemporary style, and a restaurant. It also has a popular, beautifully frescoed piano bar, an elegant fin de siècle lobby, 24-hour room service, and business services. 7 Piazza della Repubblica (phone: 283313; 800-223-6800; fax: 284840).

Villa Cora This sumptuous neoclassical villa built when Florence was the capital of Italy is particularly enjoyable for a summertime stay. It offers 56 spacious rooms and suites decorated in the original style, grand public rooms, a magnificent garden with a heated pool, and 24-hour room service. Its well-known (but very expensive and formal) restaurant, *Taverna Machiavella*, opens onto the pool in warm weather. Business services are available. Two miles (3 km) from the chaotic city center, at 18 Viale Machiavelli (phone: 229-8451; fax: 229086).

Villa Medici Between the railroad station and the Arno and the least conveniently situated of the hotels in this price category, this reconstruction of an 18th-century palace has 110 charming, spacious rooms (some have balconies affording panoramic views). The restaurant, grand public rooms, tranquil gardens, small pool, 24-hour room service, business services, and all around elegance attract a loyal clientele of international businessfolk. 42 Via il Prato (phone: 238-1331; 800-223-6800; fax: 238-1336).

EXPENSIVE

Beacci Tornabuoni On Florence's most elegant shopping street, this old-fashioned, 30-room former pensione occupies the top three floors of a 15th-century palace. Its devoted clientele returns for the traditional ambience and excellent service. A drink at sunset on the charming terrace overlooking a sea of Florentine tile roofs is a true delight. Guests are heavily encouraged to take half board during high season. No credit cards accepted. 3 Via Tornabuoni (phone: 212645; fax: 283594).

Fenice Palace A good value, it occupies four floors of a restored 19th-century palazzo one block from the *Duomo*. Some of the 72 comfortable guestrooms (all with contemporary decor) offer views of the city's major monuments. No restaurant. Business services. 10 Via Martelli (phone: 289942; 800-44-UTELL; fax: 210087).

Jolly Carlton On the edge of *Parco delle Cascine* near the *Teatro Comunale,* this modern, 167-room member of the efficient chain has a restaurant, 24-hour room service, a pool, business services, and a wonderful view from the terrace. It's popular with group tours. 4/A Piazza Vittorio Veneto (phone:

2770; 800-247-1277 in New York State; 800-221-2626 elsewhere in the US; fax: 292794).

Kraft Near the *Teatro Comunale,* this modern 78-room hotel has a roof-garden restaurant sporting umbrella pines and a cypress tree, as well as a splendid panorama, 24-hour room service, business services, and a small rooftop pool. 2 Via Solferino (phone: 284273; 800-44-UTELL; fax: 239-8267).

Monna Lisa On a narrow side street, this small hostelry in a renovated 14th-century building offers Old World charm and style with modern comforts. All 20 guestrooms are beautifully furnished, though some are on the small side; some have Jacuzzis. Ask for one overlooking the quiet magnolia garden in the back. There is private parking at no extra charge in the low season. No restaurant. 27 Borgo Pinti (phone: 247-9751; fax: 247-9755).

Park Palace Best for a summertime visit, with its lovely garden and pool and a knockout view overlooking the city from the south, this charming, 26-room hotel with a restaurant was a private villa built in the 1920s. Parking is available. 5 Piazzale Galileo (phone: 222431; fax: 220517).

Roma This historical 16th-century palazzo with modern comforts has 51 contemporary rooms. Stained glass windows, frescoed ceilings, and inlaid marble floors grace the public areas. Right outside the door is one of Florence's most important squares. There is a restaurant. Business services. 8 Piazza Santa Maria Novella (phone: 210366; fax: 215306).

Sheraton Three miles (5 km) south of Florence and catering mostly to large groups and conferences, this 300-room member of the chain has a restaurant, 24-hour room service, tennis courts, business services, and an outdoor pool. A shuttle transports guests into the city. Just off the Firenze Sud autostrada exit, at 33 Via G. Agnelli (phone: 64901; 800-325-3535; fax: 680747).

Sofitel Although housed in a 17th-century palazzo, this 84-room hotel is modern and furnished in contemporary style. Its central location, soundproofing, and doting service make this a contender for one of Florence's best hostelries. The restaurant serves very good fare; an American-style buffet breakfast is included in the room rate; there's also 24-hour room service and business services. 10 Via Cerretani (phone: 238-1301; 800-221-4542; fax: 238-1312).

Torre di Bellosguardo A cypress-framed, 15th-century villa on a hill with an unforgettable view of Florence's terra cotta roofs, this handsome hostelry is a special place to stay. A dramatic lobby, lush gardens, and a pool overlooking the city—plus 16 spacious rooms whose ceilings are punctuated by rough hewn beams and each of which is individually decorated with antiques—add to its charm. No restaurant. There is an English-speaking concierge and 24-hour room service. 2 Via Roti Michelozzi (phone: 229-8145; fax: 229008).

Villa Carlotta On a quiet residential street in a lovely country setting minutes away from Porta Romana is this restored 19th-century villa with Oriental rugs, antique reproductions, and 27 charmingly decorated rooms. Breakfast on the lovely terrace is a treat. The dining room is for hotel guests only. Business services. 3 Via Michele di Lando (phone: 233-6134; fax: 233-6147).

MODERATE

Annalena Just past the *Palazzo Pitti,* this seignorial 15th-century palazzo was said to have been a gift from Cosimo de' Medici to a Florentine woman named Annalena. For those who appreciate vaulted ceilings, original frescoes, and period pieces, this 20-room hotel is the place to stay. Ask for a guestroom that opens onto a communal terrace overlooking the adjacent garden. Single rooms can be quite small. No restaurant. 34 Via Romana (phone: 222402; fax: 222403).

Balestri A clean, no-frills hotel overlooking the Arno, it has been in the Balestri-Wittum family for over a century. Thirty simply furnished rooms face the river, but the trade-off is the traffic noise from the ever-busy street below. The other 20 rooms overlook a quiet courtyard. An easy walk to all *centro storico* sites. There is a garage but no restaurant. 7 Piazza Mentana (phone: 214743; fax: 239-8042).

Calzaiuoli The location of this hotel is ideal—midway between the *Duomo* and Piazza Signoria on store-lined Via Calzaiuoli, Florence's largest pedestrian-only street. All 44 guestrooms are decorated in contemporary and functional, yet rather nondescript, furnishings. No restaurant. 6 Via Calzaiuoli (phone: 212456; fax: 268310).

Cavour Just two blocks from the *Duomo,* this tastefully restored palazzo has 89 rooms, many with original brick archways, beamed ceilings, and views of the city's monuments. A real treat is having evening drinks on the top-floor terrace—the vistas are the most breathtaking of any *centro storico* hotel. The *Beatrice* restaurant next door (see *Eating Out*) is impressive not only for the food but for the 16th-century setting. Business services are available. 3 Via del Proconsolo (phone: 282461; fax: 218955).

Hermitage Occupying three floors of a medieval tower literally two steps from the Ponte Vecchio, this recently restored 29-room hotel is one of the most pleasant lodging possibilities in Florence. Six less expensive rooms located on the second floor make up the *Archibusieri Hotel,* all under the same management and sharing the same rooftop terrace, where breakfast can be enjoyed under a lush pergola with million-dollar views of the Arno and historic Florence—reason enough to stay here. No restaurant. 1 Piazza del Pesce (phone: 287216; fax: 212208).

Loggiato dei Serviti Well located on the beautiful Piazza SS Annunziata—thought by many to be one of Italy's most perfectly proportioned squares—and equidistant from the *Duomo* and the *Accademia,* this tastefully restored hotel takes its name from the Serviti religious fraternal order for which it was built in 1527. Half of the 29 rooms overlook the elegant piazza; all are furnished simply but handsomely with antique wrought-iron beds, terra cotta floors, and all the modern comforts (including spacious tiled baths). No restaurant. Book well in advance. 3 Piazza SS Annunziata (phone: 289592; fax: 289595).

Morandi alla Crocetta This small but charming 15-room establishment is run by an Englishwoman and her Italian-born son. Situated in a section of what used to be a 16th-century Dominican convent, it's a 10-minute walk from the *Duomo.* Rooms are furnished with Tuscan antiques. No restaurant. 50 Via Laura (phone: 234-4747; fax: 248-0954).

Pendini An old-style, family-run place, it's been in operation for over a hundred years in a renovated 19th-century building. There are 42 fairly spacious rooms; 10 overlook the *caffè*-ringed Piazza della Repubblica (which can be both charming and irksome in the summer, when live orchestras perform beneath your window well into the night). No restaurant. 2 Via Strozzi (phone: 211170; fax: 210156).

La Residenza On Florence's best shopping street is this small, renovated hotel, with a lovely terrace. Its 24 rooms, on the top floors of a Renaissance palazzo, are attractive (some have balconies overlooking Via Tornabuoni). The staff is unusually helpful. Half board is strongly encouraged, particularly during high season. 8 Via Tornabuoni (phone/fax: 218648).

Silla A charming, friendly place in a 16th-century palazzo, with a quiet courtyard. Its large flowered breakfast terrace overlooks the river and a small park on the Oltrarno side of town (it's a 10-minute walk along the Arno to the Ponte Vecchio). At press time, 40 of the 50 rooms had been renovated, though their Old World charm remains (the 10 guestrooms without private bath are less expensive). No restaurant. Usually closed in December. 5 Via dei Renai (phone: 234-2888; fax: 234-1437).

Villa Villoresi About 5 miles (8 km) from the center of Florence, it's another noble home away from home; the foundations date from the 12th century. For over 200 years it's been in the Villoresi family (they turned it into a hotel in the 1960s), who impart a sense of family as well as history. It has 28 rooms. Bedroom walls have frescoes, the restaurant is good, and there is a pool in the garden among the olive trees. 58 Via delle Torri, Località Colonnata, Sesto Fiorentino (phone: 443692; fax: 442063).

INEXPENSIVE

Bellettini The competent and friendly service, central location, amenities (newly tiled private baths, telephones, optional air conditioning, and an elevator), and tasteful furnishings of a much higher-priced hotel make this one of the best bets in town. All 28 rooms are lovely, but ask for spacious No. 28, which sits above Florence's terra cotta roofs, or No. 45 on the top floor, which overlooks the cupola of the nearby *Duomo.* And you can even sunbathe from the small balcony in room No. 44. No restaurant; parking available. No credit cards accepted. 7 Via dei Conti (phone: 213561; fax: 283551).

Casci In a 15th-century palazzo that was initially a convent, this delightful, 25-room hotel run by the Lombardi family retains some of the original frescoes. Although it is on a centrally located thoroughfare, the rooms in the back are quiet and overlook an enormous magnolia tree and charming rooftops. A recent restoration has added tiled baths to all rooms and color TVs to most. No restaurant. No credit cards accepted. 13 Via Cavour (phone: 211686; fax: 239-6461).

Fiorino A regular international clientele returns time and again to this small hotel, despite its need for a facelift. But the attentive staff, 21 clean rooms, and an excellent location three blocks from the Piazza della Signoria (on a quiet street off the pedestrians-only Via dei Neri) has kept this place popular with generations of visiting Italophiles. No restaurant. 6 Via Osteria del Guanto (phone/fax: 210579).

Sorelle Bandini This simple 10-room pensione is located in the *Palazzo Guadagni,* an august 15th-century landmark. Only five of the large, but unimaginatively furnished, guestrooms have baths, but common areas are clean, and having tea on the flowery open loggia, which looks out onto one of Florence's loveliest piazze, will make you feel like Renaissance royalty. No restaurant. No credit cards accepted. 9 Piazza Santo Spirito (phone: 215308).

EATING OUT

Florentine cooking, while today simpler and more straightforward than during the Renaissance, is still at the top of the list of Italy's many varied regional dishes. No small contributing factor to this culinary art is the quality of the ingredients. Tuscany boasts excellent olive oil and wine, locally grown fruits and vegetables, good game in season, fresh fish from its coast, salami, sausages, and every other kind of meat. A *bistecca alla fiorentina,* thick and juicy on the bone and traditionally accompanied by new potatoes or white beans drenched in pure golden olive oil, is a meal fit for the most exigent of kings. A typical meal can begin with salami, frequently flavored with fennel, and rounds of bread spread with chicken liver sauce. *Fettunta,* toasted bread rubbed with garlic and drizzled with freshly pressed, extra virgin olive oil, is another glorious Florentine appetizer. Meat is simply prepared; it is either grilled, deep-fried, or subjected to long *stracotto* (extra cooked) braising. Beans are a staple in the Florentine diet, flavored with sage and dressed with olive oil. Raw vegetables are served with a small bowl of salt and olive oil for dipping (the technique is known as *pinzimonio*). A plate of hard almond cookies, *biscotti* or *cantucci,* is served with a squat glass of *vin santo*, into which the cookies are dipped. Diners can roughly gauge the price of a restaurant before entering by the cost per kilo (2.2 pounds) of its Florentine steaks on the menu displayed outside. Fortunately, one steak is usually more than enough for two people, and it is commonplace to order one steak for two or more.

Lunch in Florence begins by 12:30 or 1 PM, and dinner by 8 PM. Many of the typical *mamma e papà* restaurants are small, popular, and crowded. If you don't book (and note that many of these places don't accept reservations), be prepared to wait and eventually share a table (both single guests and couples are often seated at a communal table—a respectable way of meeting residents and fellow travelers). And you won't be encouraged to linger too long over your dessert wine if there are people waiting for your table. A full meal for two, including the house wine or the excellent local chianti, will cost from $75 to $150 at an expensive restaurant; from $40 to $75 at a moderate restaurant; and $40 or less at an inexpensive one. All restaurants are open for lunch and dinner unless otherwise noted. All telephone numbers are in the 55 city code unless otherwise indicated.

For an unforgettable dining experience, we begin with our culinary favorite, followed by our cost and quality choices, listed by price category.

DELIGHTFUL DINING

Enoteca Pinchiorri Michelangelo, Botticelli, and this place that has been awarded three Michelin stars make a perfect Florentine day. The edible art, which changes with the market's offerings, often exhibits such masterworks as foie gras with pomegranate salad, sole with onion-and-parsley purée, tiny gnocchi (potato dumplings) with basil, veal with caper-and-lime sauce, and duck in red wine. The charming 15th-century-palace setting and the flawlessly appointed tables complete the picture. An *enoteca* is a wine merchant's showroom—that's how the restaurant got its start—and red, white, and rosé are still its flying colors. Service is impeccable, but the $200 check for two does make one think about opting for more rustic Tuscan fare elsewhere in one of the city's colorful trattorie. Closed Sundays, Monday lunch, and August. Reservations necessary. Major credit cards accepted. 87 Via Ghibellina (phone: 242777; fax: 244983).

EXPENSIVE

Bibe In a bucolic setting on the Bagnese River, this establishment specializes in simple trattoria fare. Homemade pasta and soup, grilled meat and poultry, Florentine fried foods, and tasty desserts grace the menu. Closed

Wednesdays and Thursday lunch. Reservations advised. Major credit cards accepted. 1r Via delle Bagnese (phone: 204-9085).

Al Campidoglio White tablecloths and elegant service set this attractive place apart from most Florentine trattorie, and the excellent Italian fare makes it worth the tab. Closed Tuesdays and most of August. Reservations advised. Major credit cards accepted. 8r Via del Campidoglio (phone: 287770).

Cantinetta Antinori Not quite a restaurant, but a typically rustic (yet fashionably chic) *cantina,* with food designed to accompany an impressive list of Antinori wines. Perfect for a light lunch of *finocchiona* (salami) with bread, *crostini* (chicken liver canapés), soup, or a modest hot dish such as tripe or *bollito misto* (mixed boiled meat). Closed weekends and August. Reservations unnecessary. Major credit cards accepted. 3 Piazza Antinori (phone: 292234).

Cibreò It's named after a historic Florentine dish, one so good it is said to have given Catherine de' Medici near fatal indigestion from overeating. Besides the traditional Florentine fare it does so well, the kitchen offers Genoese minestrone, eggplant parmesan from the south, polenta from the Veneto, savory appetizers such as walnut and pecorino cheese salad, soups, seafood with an unusual twist (mussel terrine, squid stew), and homemade desserts. There's a wide variety of very good wines. In summer, alfresco dining is possible. Closed Sundays, Mondays, and late July to mid-September. Reservations necessary. Major credit cards accepted. 118r Via de' Macci (phone: 234-1100).

Ottorino This stylish establishment in the shadow of the *Duomo*, with its welcoming ambience on the ground floor of a medieval tower, offers beautifully prepared, classic Italian specialties—mostly fresh pasta and fish—served with fine wines. Closed Sundays and August. Reservations advised. Major credit cards accepted. 12r Via delle Oche (phone: 218747).

Quattro Stagioni Perfectly executed, simple Italian dishes are served to regulars for lunch; tourists join the crowd in the evening. Fresh pasta, homemade spinach gnocchi, and wonderful fish and meat dishes are served with flair. Closed Sundays, Saturdays in summer, and August. Reservations advised. Major credit cards accepted. 61r Via Maggio (phone: 218906).

Relais le Jardin Well-heeled Florentines like to dine here, especially in summer, when the tables are moved into the garden. The tone is one of understated elegance, with first class service and faultless Florentine and regional Italian cooking. The menu changes frequently, and the chef turns out some interesting pasta variations. Closed Sundays. Reservations advised. Major credit cards accepted. In the *Regency Hotel*, 3 Piazza Massimo d'Azeglio (phone: 245247).

Taverna del Bronzino Rustic yet elegant, it's set in a 16th-century palazzo furnished with antiques and a garden for alfresco dining in season. *Crostini ai funghi* *porcini* (wild mushroom canapés), *tortelloni al cedro* (large vegetable tortellini in a butter and cider sauce), and renowned Florentine beef with green peppers are specialties. Closed Sundays and most of August. Reservations advised. Major credit cards accepted. 25-27r Via delle Ruote (phone: 495220).

Acqua a Due This place offers a wide selection of possibilities, but most diners come here for the delicious *assaggi* (tasting) menu of pasta and desserts, which changes daily. Closed Mondays and for lunch. Reservations necessary. No credit cards accepted. 40r Via della Vigna Vecchia (phone: 284170).

Angiolino This very good, economical trattoria on the Oltrarno serves traditional Tuscan classics in a cozy ambience. Closed Sundays and Mondays. Reservations unnecessary. No credit cards accepted. 36r Via di Santo Spirito (phone: 239-8976).

La Baraonda Hearty Tuscan dishes, as well as a delicate *risolata* (risotto cooked with lettuce), home-style meat loaf, vegetable timbale, and Baraonda apple pie, are expertly prepared here. The name means "chaos," the antithesis of what you'll find in this rustic dining spot. Closed Sundays, Monday lunch, and August. Reservations advised. Major credit cards accepted. 67r Via Ghibellina (phone/fax: 234-1171).

Beatrice Come here for century-old ceiling frescoes and stained glass windows that evoke a bygone era. The menu includes both classic Florentine dishes and a few "creative" choices. Try the *uovo alla fornaia* (fresh ravioli filled with ricotta and spinach with a truffle butter sauce) and the *filet carpaccio alla Caterina de' Medici* (thinly sliced raw filet with a dash of lemon juice and slivers of parmesan and greens on top). There is an ample wine list. Closed Sundays and Monday lunch. Reservations advised, especially on weekend evenings. Major credit cards accepted. 31r Via del Proconsolo (phone: 239-8762).

Belle Donne This trendy establishment is so small that it's easy to miss from the street (it's west of the Via Tornabuoni). The communal marble tables with butcher-paper placemats are perfect for a quick lunch or complete meal. The desserts are delicious. Closed weekends. Reservations advised. No credit cards accepted. 16r Via delle Belle Donne (phone: 238-2609).

Buzzino The perfect place for lunch or dinner after a cultural feast at the *Uffizi*, just a block away. Although the waiters aren't always friendly, the setting is warm and the food good enough to put tired museumgoers back on their feet. The bill is sweetened by the arrival of the free *vin santo* (a sweet dessert wine). Closed Mondays. Reservations advised. Major credit cards accepted. 8r Via dei Leoni (phone: 239-8013).

Cammillo An appealing, bustling long-time favorite with vaulted brick ceilings near the Ponte Santa Trinita, this restaurant offers authentic dishes such as tripe *alla fiorentina* and, in season, pasta with white truffles. Closed Wednesdays and Thursdays. Reservations advised. Major credit cards accepted. 57r Borgo San Jacopo (phone: 212427).

Cantina Barbagianni An interesting, original menu is the draw at this Tuscan eatery. From the vegetable terrine to the wonderful soup to the delicious grilled meat and fish, each dish here is a completely satisfying experience. The desserts are delicious, and the wine list is quite good. Closed Sundays, Monday lunch, and August. Reservations advised. Most major credit cards accepted. 13r Via Sant'Egidio (phone: 248-0508).

Le Cave di Maiano A delightful stop in Fiesole, it's a great place to dine under the linden trees and gaze out over the splendid valley. Indoors is warm, cozy, and rustic, as is the country-style cooking, beginning with excellent prosciutto, *finocchiona* and other local salami, chicken and truffle croquettes, canapés of mozzarella and mushrooms, *crespelle* or ravioli, or an *assaggio di primi* (a sampling of five different pasta dishes), and the house specialty, *gallina al mattone* (grilled spring chicken seasoned with black pepper and virgin olive oil). Closed Thursdays, Sunday dinner, and August. Reservations necessary. Major credit cards accepted. 16 Via delle Cave, Località Maiano, Fiesole (phone: 59133).

Cinghiale Bianco Cozy and hospitable, this popular trattoria in a medieval tower with whitewashed walls and contrasting dark wood decor is near the Ponte Vecchio. The name, which means "white boar," refers to Tuscans' favorite game, which appears in a number of variations on the menu. This eatery serves great pasta and tasty Florentine specialties such as spinach and ricotta dumplings called *strozzapreti* (priest stranglers), veal scallops, cured beef with arugula, and simple desserts. Closed Tuesdays, Wednesdays, and the last two weeks of July. Reservations advised. Major credit cards accepted. 43r Borgo San Jacopo (phone: 215706).

Coco Lezzone Classic Florentine fare, simple white-tile trattoria decor, and attentive service are the major pluses of this small, popular establishment, whose name in Tuscan dialect means "Big, Smelly Cook." Don't miss the *pappa al pomodoro* or *ribollita* (hearty, bread-thickened soups). It's often crowded, so don't expect to linger over a meal. Closed Sundays, holidays, August, and late December to early January. Reservations advised. Major credit cards accepted. 26r Via del Parioncino (phone: 287178).

Del Fagioli A cheery, rustic ambience and a full bar distinguish this place. Although *fagioli* means beans, the restaurant is named for a famous buffoon from the Medici court. Enjoy the *passato di fagioli con pasta* (thick soup of white beans and pasta). Closed weekends in summer, Sundays in winter, and

August. No reservations. No credit cards accepted. 47r Corso Tintori (phone: 244285).

Le Fonticine Kind and helpful service and hearty portions of down-home yet surprisingly sophisticated *cucina genuina* are the pluses at this large but cozy dining spot. It is a family's labor of love, from the welcome given to both first-time visitors and regulars to the pasta that is made fresh daily. Close to the *Mercato di San Lorenzo* and the train station. Closed Mondays and most of August. Reservations unnecessary. Major credit cards accepted. 79r Via Nazionale (phone: 282106).

Da Ganino Long a Florentine favorite, this typically tiny and plain Tuscan trattoria is family-run. There are just seven communal tables inside and alfresco dining on the tiny square in fine weather. Here is some of the best Florentine *cucina genuina,* including fresh mushrooms and truffles in season and a justifiably famous cheesecake. Closed Sundays, three weeks in August, and *Christmas.* Reservations advised. Major credit cards accepted. 4r Piazza dei Cimatori (phone: 214125).

Garga The unusual specialties of this eatery include *zuppa di cavoli neri* (soup of a bitter green local vegetable), risotto of leeks and bacon, and *gnocchetti verdi* (pasta of spinach and ricotta)—all exquisitely prepared and absolutely terrific. Closed Sundays and Monday lunch. Reservations necessary. No credit cards accepted. 48-52 Via del Moro (phone: 239-8898).

Il Latini Popular yet noisy, this Tuscan trattoria in the former stables of the historic *Palazzo Rucellai* serves solid and abundant fare such as hearty Tuscan soup, unpretentious grilled and roast meat platters, grilled fish, fresh vegetables, and traditional desserts. It's good for a congenial, if not romantic, evening—diners sit at long communal tables, and the food keeps coming. Closed Mondays and mid-July to mid-August. Reservations advised. No credit cards accepted. 6r Via dei Palchetti (phone: 210916).

La Loggia A Florentine favorite, not only for its spectacular view of the entire city but for the traditional Tuscan fare and the efficient service despite the crowds. Drinks are served on the terrace during the summer. Closed Wednesdays and two weeks in August. Reservations advised. Major credit cards accepted. 1 Piazzale Michelangelo (phone: 234-2832; fax: 234-5288).

Omero The menu hasn't changed in decades at this dining spot in the hills. The restaurant affords beautiful views of the Tuscan landscape, and the small garden downstairs is wonderful for summer dining, although the service tends to be slow and the sound of the insect zapper may be distracting. Still, the exceptional *fettunta* (Tuscan garlic bread), ravioli, grilled chicken, ubiquitous *bistecca alla fiorentina,* fried artichokes or zucchini blossoms (in season), and meringue dessert are worth the wait. Closed Tuesdays and August. Reservations advised. Major credit cards accepted. 11r Via Pian dei Giullari (phone: 220053).

Osteria da Quinto A longtime favorite with Florentines, mostly because owner Leo Codacci is a great music lover and often treats customers to bursts of song when the mood strikes him. The *bistecca alla fiorentina* is among the biggest and best in town. Closed Mondays. It's always packed, so be sure to reserve ahead. Major credit cards accepted. 5r Piazza dei Peruzzi (phone: 213323).

Il Pallottino A good selection of Tuscan food, including many hard-to-find dishes, is offered at this popular dining spot. Specialties such as spaghetti with fresh tomatoes and arugula, stuffed chicken neck (tastes much better than it sounds), and *bistecca alla fiorentina* are not to be missed. Closed Mondays and Tuesday lunch. Reservations necessary. Major credit cards accepted. 1r Via Isola delle Stinche (phone: 289573).

Pennello The exciting antipasto table (you're charged for how much you eat) features a wide array of salads, marinated fish, olives, and vegetables. While the pasta and other entrées are good, they are anticlimactic after the splendid appetizers. The ambience is pure trattoria, with a tiny dining terrace in back for outdoor dining in summer. Closed Sunday dinner, Mondays, and August. Reservations advised. Major credit cards accepted. 4r Via Dante Alighieri (phone: 294881).

La Sostanza Popularly called *La Troia*, literally a hog (also a woman of easy virtue), this is one of Florence's oldest and most cherished trattorie, serving some of the best steaks in town. If you haven't had a *bistecca alla fiorentina* with Tuscan beans, enjoy the ritual here. The place is plain and tiny, the turnover as fast as the service (which can be politely rude if you try to linger), and the tables communal. Closed Saturday dinner, Sundays, and August. Reservations necessary. No credit cards accepted. 25r Via del Porcellana (phone: 212691).

Trattoria del Cibreo Commonly referred to as *Cibreino*, the no-frills backroom of the well-known and pricey *Cibreo* serves food from the same kitchen at a fraction of the cost, and in a less formal atmosphere. Closed Sundays, Mondays, and July 15 through August. No reservations. Major credit cards accepted. 35r Piazza Ghiberti (phone: 234-1100).

Alla Vecchia Bettola Quality home-style Tuscan cooking in a typical trattoria, with communal marble-top tables and butcher-paper placemats. Chicken liver canapés, soups and pasta, hearty meat dishes, and some unexpectedly good wines fill the menu. Closed Sundays and Mondays. Reservations advised. No credit cards accepted. 34r Viale Ariosto (phone: 224158).

INEXPENSIVE

Cantinetta dei Verrazano The Cappellini family runs this new and always crowded wine bar, where light and delicious *focaccia* sandwiches are made with a variety of combinations. Most ingredients come from the family's generations-old agricultural estate in Chianti, particularly the extensive wine selection available for tasting and the excellent virgin olive oil. Conveniently located on a cobblestone side street off the main pedestrian-only Via Calzaiuoli, which links the *Duomo* with the Piazza della Signoria. Closed Sundays. No reservations. No credit cards accepted. 18-20r Via dei Tavolini (phone: 268590).

La Casalinga Neighborhood workers, artisans, and shop-owners congregate daily at this simple trattoria to eat on white paper tablecloths and discuss everything from international affairs to philosophy. Closed Sundays and August. No reservations. No credit cards accepted. Near the Piazza Santo Spirito, at 9r Via Michelozzi (phone: 218624).

Centro Vegetariano Before eating at this vegetarian restaurant, you will first need to pay a nominal lifetime membership fee. Select from a blackboard that lists the specials, pay at the cash register, and then bring your receipt to the kitchen. It's worth it for the vegetarian fare, Italian-style. Closed Mondays and dinner on weekends. No reservations. No credit cards accepted. 30r Via delle Ruote (phone: 475030).

Le Mossacce Largely frequented by habitués, this small spot is filled with long paper-covered tables and serves good country cooking. Try the *ribollita* (thick and hearty vegetable soup). Closed weekends and August. No reservations. No credit cards accepted. 55r Via del Proconsolo (phone: 294361).

Nerbone This eatery is perfect for a quick midday bite and a glass of wine while taking in the market's color and bustle. The ambience may be less than elegant, but it is quite cheerful, and the prices are extraordinarily low. Across the aisle from the Nerbone family's food stall are a half-dozen communal marble-topped tables. Closed Sundays and for dinner. No reservations. No credit cards accepted. On the ground floor of the *Mercato di San Lorenzo,* closest to the Via dell'Ariento entrance (Stand No. 292; phone: 219949).

Trattoria da Graziella When you tire of Florentine fare, head to this eatery, where Sardinian-born Ugo Salis offers well-cooked island dishes such as the spectacular and mouth-watering suckling pig. Good Sardinian wines wash down the meal, though chianti fans also will be satisfied. There is a large terrace for alfresco dining. Closed Wednesdays. Reservations advised. Major credit cards accepted. 20 Via Cave di Maiano, Fiesole (phone: 599963).

Zà-Zà The regular clientele of marketgoers and bankers sit elbow-to-elbow at communal tables with faded posters of John Wayne and Greta Garbo on the walls. Basic Tuscan classics such as *ribollita* and a roster of reliably delicious pasta dishes are served here, and you won't raise any eyebrows if you order only a pasta and salad (unlike many places in town). Closed Sundays. No reservations. No credit cards accepted. 26r Piazza Mercato Centrale (phone: 215411).

PIZZA

Although pizza isn't a traditional Florentine dish, when it emerges fresh from a wood-burning oven, it is still one of the glories of Italy. Variations on the simple pie can range from a minimalist *marinara* (tomato, garlic, and oregano) to the classic *margherita* (mozzarella, tomato, and basil) to more ornate creations such as the *capricciosa,* whose ingredients are based on the whims of the pizza maker. In restaurants, pizza is generally the size of a dinner plate and has a thinner, crisper crust than most American pies. *Borgo Antico* (6r Piazza Santo Spirito; phone: 210437) and the centrally located *Yellow Bar* (39r Via Proconsolo; phone: 211766) serve up tasty creations with flair.

CAFFÈS

Just as Parisians religiously congregate in little outdoor *caffès* to read a newspaper or discuss politics with friends, the Italians regard the *caffè* as a home away from home. Here life slows to a romantic standstill as patrons leisurely sip cappuccino or Campari. The following is our favorite, followed by our quality choices (they are all inexpensive, and none accept credit cards):

A CLASSIC CAFFÈ

Rivoire An inspiring view of the *Palazzo Vecchio* combined with a cup of rich hot chocolate is the antidote for even the most exhausted sightseer. Although its prices are rather steep, its location in Florence's loveliest piazza more than compensates for the inflated tab. It was in this piazza that the charming Lucy in Forster's *A Room with a View* fell in love. It is famous for the small red box of its own chocolate—a solid block—a great gift or self-indulgence. Closed Mondays. 5r Piazza della Signoria (phone: 214412).

Giacosa Located on the store-lined Via Tornabuoni, this tony *caffè* is the perfect place for a tasty snack at the bar or for a light lunch while seated with the local well-heeled crowd. Try a Negroni, which was invented here in the 1920s by Count Negroni; a combination of Campari, vermouth, and gin, it is a potent potable. Closed Sundays. 83r Via Tornabuoni (phone: 239-6226).

Gilli The most beautiful Old World *caffè* situated in the wide expanse of Piazza della Repubblica is especially charming in summer, when an orchestra plays music next door at *Paszkowski* (see below) and all seems right with the world. Order a *caffè normale* if you need a shot of energizing espresso, or sample a *caffè corretto,* into which a generous dash of brandy is added. Closed Tuesdays. 39r Piazza della Repubblica (phone: 213896).

Paszkowski Another recommended spot in the piazza for people watching and lively action, whose decor, like that of *Gilli,* is redolent of its Belle Epoque days. If you arrive early enough and are longing for some home cooking, try the filling American breakfast. In the warm-weather months, a live orchestra plays old favorites. Closed Mondays. 6r Piazza della Repubblica (phone: 210236).

Il Rifrullo Just by the old San Niccolò entrance to the city, on the *Palazzo Pitti* side of the river, this bar attracts a young, international crowd. Aside from its extensive menu of aperitifs, it also offers delectable crêpes and some sandwiches. Don't forget to visit its gelateria around the corner, one of the best places in the city to satisfy your sweet tooth. Closed Wednesdays. 55r Via San Niccolò (phone: 234-2621).

GELATO

No one should leave Italy without at least a taste of this delicious treat. Far lighter than ice cream (it's made without cream), it has a creamy consistency. Fruit flavors are composed of fresh fruit, sugar, and water, and other flavors—such as chocolate, coffee, hazelnut, and vanilla—have a milk or custard base. *Semifreddo* is a milk-based gelato that has whipped cream folded in; the chocolate flavor is known as mousse. Ice-cream places are a dime a dozen in Florence, but the best known to gelato connoisseurs are the following:

Frilli A tiny *latteria* (milk shop), it's known for its family's fine *semifreddo,* especially the chocolate mousse and *amarena* (sour cherry). A perfect stop on a hike up to or from *Forte Belvedere.* Closed Wednesdays. 5r Via San Miniato (phone: 234-5014).

Gelateria dei Neri This pretty, relatively new *gelateria* has won the hearts of many Florentines, and no wonder: The ambience is elegant, and the tasty ice cream is served in fancy cones. Closed Wednesdays. 22r Via dei Neri (phone: 210034).

Perchè No? Located on a side street near Piazza della Signoria, this well-known establishment offers a wide variety of fruit flavors; they are a bit less sweet than most Florentine gelati. Closed Tuesdays. 19r Via dei Tavolini (phone: 239-8969).

Pomposi Right on the corner of Piazza della Signoria, this place is considered by many Florentines to have the finest gelato in the land. Try the chocolate or coffee—they're true standouts. Closed Sundays. 9r Via Calzaiuoli (phone: 216651).

Vivoli A venerable and adored institution close to Piazza Santa Croce, this is regarded as the best *gelateria* in town and should be part of every visitor's Florentine experience. The more than two dozen flavors include the knockout rice pudding–like *riso*. Closed Mondays. 7r Via Isola delle Stinche (phone: 292334).

A TASTE OF HOME

If for some reason your tastebuds get homesick, head for *CarLie's* (12r Via delle Brache; phone: 215137). Started by two Smith College graduates, these Yankees offer brownies, cupcakes, strawberry shortcake, and, at *Thanksgiving,* pumpkin or apple pie. Once-skeptical Florentines now stand patiently in line.

Genoa

Unlike two centuries ago, when Genoa occupied a prime position on the itinerary of the European Grand Tour, the modern-day city is often entirely bypassed by visitors to Italy, who little realize that behind the sprawling port lies one of the country's most elegant, interesting, and sophisticated cities. The evidence of past wealth and power is still visible in its many monuments, great churches, countless palaces, and rich art treasures.

Genoa—*La Superba* (The Proud), as it was first described by the poet Petrarch during his visit in 1358—was a flourishing port several hundred years before Christ. With a natural harbor on its southern flank and a semicircle of mountains as a landside frontier, its location has always been ripe for occupation and development. Since its steep terrain was unsuitable for cultivation, the Genoese turned naturally to the sea—but not in the half-hearted style of a modest fishing community. For centuries the Genoese navy, along with the Venetian fleet on the far side of the peninsula, ruled the waves, while its merchants traded with, and established outposts in, far-flung countries (the ruins of a Genoese fort have even been found in the Ukraine, on the banks of the Dniester River).

The capital of Liguria, Genoa has a population of around 815,000. It stretches 25 miles along the coast and spreads up the hills that rise around the bay—the only flat place in town is the sea. Shipping is still its major industry, with related business—in communications, electronics, banking, insurance, and general commerce—also highly developed, making the city one of the most prosperous in Italy. But, remarkably, Genoa has managed to retain its historical legacy. The medieval city center is one of the largest in Europe (surpassed only by that of its archrival, Venice), and it is maintained not as a tourist attraction but as an active, thriving part of contemporary life. The vivid contrasts between the *caruggi*—the ancient winding streets, most so narrow that you can touch opposite walls with outstretched arms—and the orderly planning of the more modern town, with elegant Piazza de Ferrari at its center, somehow seem entirely harmonious.

The word *Genoa* probably derives from the Latin *janua,* meaning "door" or "gate." This explanation is satisfactory at least in a figurative sense, since Genoa forms a natural inlet along the rocky and sometimes inaccessible Riviera coastline and for centuries served as a gateway to the exotic horizons of the Orient. Long before the Romans, the Greeks and the Etruscans used this place as a harbor and penetrated inland. Pre-Roman Ligurians, the original Genoese inhabitants, had a settlement on the hill now called Santa Maria di Castello. By the 5th century BC the city was already an important port and trading center and an ally of Rome. Although Genoa was sacked and its inhabitants massacred in 205 BC by Magone, Hannibal's son, it soon reasserted itself, as it would each time it was plundered in the following centuries. With strong Byzantine and Christian connections, Genoa became a bishopric as early as AD 381. An invasion by barbarians in about AD 640, during which the original city walls were destroyed, roughly marked the end of the Roman era and the beginning of the Middle Ages. From the 7th century, when the Arabs conquered Spain, Genoese shipping—and all Mediterranean trading—was continually under attack by Saracen pirates. Ironically, it was the city's constant struggle to survive Saracen attacks that led to the gradual rise of its powerful fleet. By the middle of the 11th century many Genoese were selling their landholdings and switching over to shipping. By the 12th century the proud Genoese felt protected enough to refuse to pay tribute to Emperor Frederick Barbarossa.

Between the 11th and 13th centuries Genoa's rivals for sea power were Pisa, Venice, and Amalfi, the other three ancient maritime republics. But with the defeat of Pisa in 1284, Genoa ensured its mastery over the Tyrrhenian Sea. The city had also begun a campaign to conquer the two Rivieras lying to its west and east, an undertaking not fully achieved until the 14th century.

Genoa's prosperity was at its peak from the middle of the 13th to the 15th century, when its settlements stretched all over the Middle East (in Constantinople, Beirut, Syria, and Armenia, as well as in Egypt), but politically it was continually threatened by external forces. After 1529, when the great leader Andrea Doria drew up a constitution that was to work effectively for the next 200 years, the city achieved relative peace under the protection of Spain. Its merchants dealt in such profitable commodities as wheat, fish, fur, silk, wool, oil, wine, spices, and slaves. The Genoese were unusually tolerant of foreigners and their religions. In the 16th century they built a mosque in the port for galley slaves. A large Jewish community existed in the city from the 5th century, and was treated with comparative tolerance.

The restored family house of Genoa's most famous citizen, Christopher Columbus, still stands at the bottom of the Vico Diritto di Ponticello, below the impressive medieval *Porta Soprana*. Columbus came from a family of humble weavers but earned a place for himself in world history when, on behalf of the Spanish queen, he "discovered" the New World in 1492. He also changed the fortunes of his native city, which up to that time had been a maritime power. After the "discovery" of the Americas, Genoa increasingly was cut off from what became the most important trade routes, and the city subsequently lost much of its political power. Nevertheless, cordial relations with Spain, which had begun between Andrea Doria and Charles V, continued. For another two centuries Genoa provided Spain with outstanding military and naval leaders and handled much trade between the mother country and the colonies. Genoese banks also financed many Spanish ventures in the New World. Foremost among them was the *Banco San Giorgio,* which the Genoese hold as the world's first bank and which still stands today, recently restored, near the Porto Vecchio (Old Port).

Genoa retained its own government until the beginning of the 19th century, when Napoleon defeated the Austrians and annexed the Genoese Republic to France, effectively ending its independent history. But even after Napoleon's final defeat in 1815, when Genoa was united with the Kingdom of Sardinia, the city's nationalistic fervor remained strong. Genoa, in fact, had been a center for the radical new politics of Jacobinism since 1796, and from then on played a leading part in the Young Italy Movement. Founded in Genoa by Mazzini, the movement led to the unity and independence of the whole of Italy. On September 20, 1870, Rome was finally liberated by Italian troops, thus completing the last stage of the unification.

Today Genoa continues to be Italy's most active port and the second largest in the Mediterranean after Marseilles. Perched in curious layers, it is a complex of steps, tunnels, overpasses, and public elevators, and by night it becomes a study in neon. Here are monuments of all kinds, ranging from the once bombarded, today beautifully restored opera house to the medieval lighthouse said to have been modeled on that of Alexandria. The overriding impression of Genoa is of a city that works hard and then flocks to its outlying flower-strewn coastline whenever possible.

Genoa At-a-Glance

SEEING THE CITY

Access by road or rail is via a series of tunnels carved through the rocks and under the houses; within the city the hills that form a natural amphitheater entail plenty of slopes, steps, and underground passageways, as well as a number of elevators and funicular railways that transport visitors to the city's best vantage points. A funicular runs every 15 minutes from Largo della Zecca up Monte Righi, where, at nearly a thousand feet above sea level, the panorama spans several miles of the Riviera. This is also the best place from which to view the old city fortifications. From Via San Benedetto another funicular climbs to Granarolo for an equally stunning view of the city, while a third goes from Piazza Portello to Sant'Anna. All three run daily from 7 AM to midnight.

SPECIAL PLACES

Although Genoa proper is vast, the city center, which includes the historic section, is exceptionally concentrated, crisscrossed with steep, narrow, winding passages. It is therefore possible to see most of the interesting features of the town on foot, with occasional recourse to funiculars. In fact, some sights are located in pedestrians-only areas and cannot be reached by car. Note that some sites of interest in Genoa close for a midday break, usually from 11:30 AM or noon to around 3 PM; we suggest calling ahead to check exact hours.

CATTEDRALE DI SAN LORENZO (CATHEDRAL OF ST. LAWRENCE) Although not the oldest church in Genoa, *San Lorenzo* is the heart of the medieval city. For many centuries it was the scene of the principal acts of both church and state: ceremonies, celebrations, investitures, negotiations, judgments, and elections. Construction of the church began in 1099; consecration was in 1118. St. Lawrence, to whom it was dedicated, is said to have passed through the city in the 3rd century on his way to Rome. An earthquake in 1222 damaged the building, and some years later a Gothic façade was built to replace the Romanesque original. The alternating bands of black slate and white marble (typical of this region) create an imposing and monumental effect.

Entering the cathedral, the visitor is immediately impressed by the size of the interior and the richness of its design. The eye is led by the black-and-white pattern down the nave toward the spacious apse. Renaissance frescoes depict moments in the life of St. Lawrence. Also of interest is the *Cappella di San Giovanni* (Chapel of St. John the Baptist), which houses sculptures by Sansovino and Guglielmo della Porta, among others. It formerly held a silver casket containing the saint's ashes, brought from Jerusalem by Genoese crusaders; this is now in the treasury. The treasury also contains the salver, made of precious chalcedony, said to have held the head of St. John the Baptist, and the chalice that was believed to have been used at the Last Supper.

The cathedral is open Mondays through Saturdays, with a long midday closing, and Sundays from 3 to 4 PM; the chapel is closed Sundays, Mondays, and for a long midday break. Piazza San Lorenzo (phone: 296695).

CHIESA DI SAN DONATO (CHURCH OF ST. DONATO) This 11th-century church, a few minutes' walk from the cathedral, also exemplifies the transition from Romanesque to Gothic architecture. Its octagonal tower, rising above the conical roof, is formed by a central nave and flanking aisles. At the front of the church are heavy Roman columns; at the back, black and white medieval columns with imitation classical capitals. A splendid triptych hangs on the wall in the apse, making up for the lack of other ornamentation. Depicting the Adoration of the Magi, its panels are attributed to the Flemish artist Joos van Cleve, who probably painted the work on a visit to Genoa in the early 16th century. The simplicity of this church inspires quiet reverence. It's closed Sunday afternoons and for a long midday break. Piazza San Donato (phone: 292869).

ORATORIO DI SAN FILIPPO NERI (ORATORY OF ST. PHILIP NERI) Located in the northwest part of the Old City, this church and its adjoining oratory are exceptional examples of Genoese Baroque art. San Filippo founded the order known as the Oratorians in Rome in the mid-16th century. Another of the founding fathers left a sum of money to the order to establish an oratory in his native Genoa. Construction of the church proper was completed in 1700. The chief features of the exterior are the *Virgin of the Immaculate Conception* marble group and a medallion with a portrait of San Filippo by Carlo Cacciatori of Carrara. The interior of the church is formed by a single nave with highly ornamental walls and vault. Next to the church is the oratory, built in 1750 by Giovanni Battista Montaldo. This elaborate, impressive building is the home of a remarkable sculpture of the Virgin by Pierre Puget. With its swirling draperies and delicate execution, it is one of the artist's finest works. An outstanding mural by Giuseppe Davolio that continues from the wall onto the ceiling creates an impressive illusionistic vision. Open daily; call for hours. Piazza San Filippo Neri (phone: 206740).

PALAZZO DUCALE (DUCAL PALACE) Enlarged in 1590 on 11th-century foundations, this recently restored palace was the seat of Genoa's maritime republic. The elegant neoclassical façade visible today was added after a major fire in 1777; the colorful yellow-and-pink trompe l'oeil covering the east wing that borders Piazza Matteotti is typically Genoese. The palace was destroyed and rebuilt many times, and its penultimate restoration was in honor of Mussolini's visit to Genoa in 1936, when it was used as a courthouse. At press time there were plans to use this imposing site as a *palazzo della cultura*—its main floor will house a major library of city archives, and the second floor already is being used for special exhibitions. There also are *caffès,* restaurants, shops, and a bookstore. Piazza Matteotti (phone: 562440, exhibition information).

PORTO VECCHIO (OLD PORT) This 15-acre waterfront site was elaborately restored in 1992 from the design of the esteemed local architect Renzo Piano, whose *Beaubourg* success in Paris established his prominence worldwide. It includes an enormous aquarium, an open-air theater, a reception area and convention center in a former cotton warehouse, and many colorful outdoor *caffès* and restaurants. The *Bigo,* a steel-and-rigging structure 190 feet high, is another highlight—visitors can ascend it in a slow glass elevator for a spectacular view of the city. At press time the future of the port as a tourist attraction was in doubt; it will remain open to the public only if a private concern is found to manage the site. Aquarium closed Mondays (phone: 273-4515). Admission charge to the aquarium. Porto Vecchio (phone: 20981).

VIA GARIBALDI Originally known as Strada Nuova (New Street), this is the only street in Europe composed entirely of palazzi. In the early 16th century Genoa's wealthy patrician families expanded their living quarters beyond the severely cramped medieval city. The street plan, said to have been devised by the Perugian architect Alessi, eventually included 14 palaces. Some are still owned and inhabited by descendants of the original powerful families, several are now used for local government and commercial functions, and one or two are important museums. Of these, the following are the most interesting and accessible; all charge admission unless otherwise indicated.

Palazzo Tursi Now the *Town Hall,* this is the largest and perhaps the most beautiful of all the palaces. Its façade is of the lovely roseate stone quarried in Finale Ligure. Among the many treasures housed within are a violin of Paganini's that is played every year on the *Festa di Colombo* (October 12), and what are said to be Columbus's ashes. Apply to the director of public relations inside the building to see the violin. Closed weekends, except to groups who arrange visits in advance through the public relations director. 9 Via Garibaldi (phone: 20981).

Palazzo Carrega-Cataldi One of the greatest Genoese financiers, Tobia Pallavicino, commissioned this building. Its exterior is severe, its interior very richly decorated. Among its most dazzling features is the *Sala degli Specchi* (Room of Mirrors), designed by Lorenzo de Ferrari. The glitter and sparkle of this wonderful room provide the setting, ironically, for the sober decisions of the Genoa *Chamber of Commerce,* which now owns the building. Open weekdays on request from 9 AM to 6 PM; Saturdays from 9 AM to noon. The *Sala degli Specchi* is closed to visitors when meetings are in progress. 4 Via Garibaldi (phone: 20941).

Palazzo Bianco This sumptuous 18th-century palace contains a fine collection of paintings from the Genoese and Flemish schools, among them *Venus and Mars* by Rubens and *The Tribute Money* by Van Dyck. At press time many of the works were being restored. Open Tuesdays through Saturdays, with alternating morning (9 AM to 1 PM) and afternoon (2 to 7 PM) hours every other week; open every other Sunday from 9 AM to 12:30 PM. 11 Via Garibaldi (phone: 291803; 282641, group visits).

Palazzo Rosso Anthony Van Dyck, who lived in Genoa for a time, was one of the city's most sought-after portrait painters. Many of his full-length portraits of Genoese citizens are housed here, along with some fine examples of Venetian works, including masterpieces by Titian and Veronese. Hours are the same as for the *Palazzo Bianco,* above. 18 Via Garibaldi (phone: 282641).

Palazzo Spinola Bequeathed to the state as a national gallery by the Spinola family in 1958, the building contains mainly 17th-century Genoese works plus some important ones by non-Italian artists. *Ecce Homo* by Antonello da Messina, one of the many hauntingly beautiful works, is historically interesting as an example of painting techniques. It was Messina who introduced oil painting to Italy after his travels in the north. The first two floors house these works; the third and fourth contain a collection of works by Ligurian painters. Closed Sunday and Monday afternoons. No admission charge. 1 Piazza Pellicceria (phone: 294661).

EXTRA SPECIAL

To the east of the medieval city are ancient fishing villages that seem virtually untouched by time. Boccadasse is noteworthy not only for its historical significance, but also for its many fine trattorie and lively bars. Nervi offers a delightful mile-long promenade along the sea to the left of the harbor with a view of the nearby Portofino promontory. It borders the lush *Parco Nervi,* where visitors can enjoy open-air theater and ballet in the summer. Other easily accessible coastal towns include San Remo, Camogli, Rapallo, Santa Margherita Ligure, Portofino, Chiavari, and Sestri Levante, all of which can be reached in less than an hour by car or by train from the *Stazione Brignole* on Piazza Verdi (also see *The Italian Riviera* in DIRECTIONS). In summer many of the towns are accessible by boat. Some destinations involve an easy bus connection from their inland stations to the coast.

Sources and Resources

TOURIST INFORMATION

The *Azienda Promozione Turistica* (*APT;* 11 Via Roma; phone: 541541) offers information about Genoa and the surrounding region. It's closed Saturday afternoons and Sundays. There also are tourist information offices at the *Stazione Brignole* (18r Piazza Verdi; phone: 562056), which is closed Sundays and for a long midday break, and at the *Stazione Porta Principe* (Piazza Acquaverde; phone: 262633), which is closed Sundays. These offices provide various pamphlets on museum exhibits and hours, tours of the city and the surrounding area, and hotel accommodations.

LOCAL COVERAGE *Il Secolo XIX* (The 19th Century) is the most popular Genoese newspaper and also the most useful to visitors, as it has a good section on local events. Like many Italian newspapers, it is not published on Mondays; an alternative is *La Gazzetta del Lunedì.* Another daily, Genoa's oldest, is *Il Lavoro Nuovo.* There are newsstands with English-language newspapers all over the city. For general guidebooks or other reading material, try the English bookstore *Bozzi* (2 Via Cairoli; phone: 298742), which is closed the first half of August, or the *Libreria di Stefano* (40r Via Ceccardi; phone: 593821). *Un Ospite in Liguria* (A Guest in Liguria), which is a free multilingual booklet, is available at better hotels and sometimes at the tourist offices.

TELEPHONE The city code for Genoa is 10. When calling from within Italy, dial 010 before the local number.

GETTING AROUND

In the center of the city, walking is best, since many places of interest are in pedestrian zones or on very narrow streets. Street numbering can be confusing: According to the importance of an entrance, numbers may be black (for palazzi, residential buildings, office blocks, and banks) or red (for *caffès,* trattorie, and hotels). Black and red numbers do not run consecutively; for example, No. 3 black may be followed by 14 red.

AIRPORT The *Aeroporto Internazionale di Genova Cristoforo Colombo* (Sestri Ponente; phone: 241-5410) is a 20-minute taxi ride from the city center. Hourly *AMT* bus service (phone: 599-7414) is available to the airport as well. The city terminal is at the *Stazione Brignole* (18r Piazza Verdi).

BOAT Tickets for hour-long boat tours around the harbor, organized by the *Cooperativa Battelieri* (Sailors' Cooperative; phone: 265712), are available at the landing stage to the right of the main marine station in Calata Zingari, not far from the *Stazione Porta Principe.* It organizes roughly a half-dozen trips a day on an ad hoc basis and also offers daily mini-cruises along the Riviera in the summer. Ferries run daily year-round to Sardinia, and boats sail to Corsica, Sicily, and Tunisia. For information on service to Sardinia, Sicily, and Tunisia, contact *Tirrenia* (phone: 26981); for Corsica, *Corsica Ferries* (phone: 593301) or *Navarma* (phone: 588753).

BUS AND TRAM Service is frequent and reliable. Purchase tickets (which also cover the funicular and elevators) at tobacconists and newsstands displaying the *AMT* sign. They are valid for any number of journeys within a one-and-a-half-hour period (misuse can result in an on-the-spot fine). A day-long *biglietto turistico* (tourist bus ticket), valid until midnight, cost 4,000 lire ($2.75) at press time. For schedule information, contact *AMT* (phone: 599-7213). *Viaggi Universali* (4r Via Nizza; phone: 302142) offers a number of three-hour bus tours of the city; they leave daily at 9 AM from Piazza della Vittoria.

CAR RENTAL Most major international firms are represented.

TAXI For 24-hour service, call 2696. There is a surcharge at night and on Sundays and holidays.

TRAIN Genoa has two main stations—the *Stazione Porta Principe* (Piazza Acquaverde; phone: 284081) and the newer *Stazione Brignole* (Piazza Verdi; phone: 284081). Connecting bus and train service between them is fast and frequent, so this is a good way to hop from one side of town to the other. Both stations offer frequent service to Milan (90 minutes on a fast train) and to towns along the Riviera.

SPECIAL EVENTS

The *Fiera Internazionale di Genova* (1 Piazzale Kennedy; phone: 53911; fax: 539-1270), a vast exposition center on the sea, usually has an interesting fair or show. *Euroflora,* held there in the spring every five years (the next is scheduled for 1996), transforms the vast *Fiera* into an immense field of flowers. Every four years in late spring the city hosts the *Regata Storica delle Repubbliche Marinare,* a race and procession of historic boats and costumes that hark back to the 11th century, when Genoa was one of the ancient maritime republics (the others were Venice, Pisa, and Amalfi). It will be Genoa's turn next year. The *Festivale Internazionale di Balleto* usually is held in the beautiful *Parco Nervi* (see *Music*) in July (phone: 284091, information). The *Salone Nautico* (International Boat Show), the largest of its kind in Europe, is held for two weeks at the *Fiera* in mid-October. The *Niccolò Paganini* violin contest, another annual international event, is held in October.

MUSEUMS

In addition to those mentioned in *Special Places,* Genoa has many fine museums. The following are among the best; all charge admission (except on Sundays) unless otherwise indicated.

LUNARDI MUSEUM OF AMERICAN STUDIES Displays on life in America illuminate the European view of contemporary American culture. Housed in the 17th-century *Villa Grüber,* the museum has a fine collection of pre-Columbian art. Closed Mondays and for a long midday break; open Sundays from 3 to 5:30 PM. Villa de Mari-Grüber, 39 Corso Solferino (phone: 814737).

MUSEO D'ARTE ORIENTALE (MUSEUM OF ORIENTAL ART) Here is one of Europe's largest collections of Asian art, and undoubtedly the best in Italy. The original Japanese, Chinese, and Thai collections were donated by the painter Edoardo Chiossone. Open Tuesdays through Saturdays, with alternating morning (9 AM to 1 PM) and afternoon (2 to 7 PM) hours every other week; open every other Sunday from 9 AM to 12:30 PM. Villetta di Negro, Via Piaggio (phone: 542285).

MUSEO DEL RISORGIMENTO (MUSEUM OF THE RISORGIMENTO) Visitors will have a better understanding of recent Italian history after visiting this museum, situated in the house where Mazzini was born. The 17th-century building has original frescoes. Open Tuesdays through Saturdays, with alternating morning (9 AM to 1 PM) and afternoon (2 to 7 PM) hours every other week; open every other Sunday from 9 AM to 12:30 PM. 11 Via Lomellini (phone: 207533).

SHOPPING

Many of the smaller, more exclusive stores in Genoa are on Via XX Settembre, Via Roma, and pedestrians-only Via Luccoli, while others are tucked away on the narrow streets of the medieval city. Food, clothing, and the crafts for which the region is famous—ceramics from Sestri Levante, fine lace, and silver and gold filigree—are all found here. Between Piazza Fontane Marose and Largo della Zecca are a number of antiques shops that sell, among other things, curious objects relating to Genoa's seafaring past. Like most Italians, the Genoese are great snackers, and it is not unusual to munch and shop at the same time. Look especially for shops bearing the sign *Torte e Farinate,* which feature local specialties.

Don't miss the colorful *Mercato Orientale* (Via XX Settembre near Via Galata), a covered market with hundreds of stands selling everything from exotic spices to local olive oil. Piazzetta Lavagna is the venue for a small flea market that's worth a visit, even if you are not looking for a bargain. There also is a daily flea market in the small Piazzetta Şant'Elena in front of Porto Genova, where browsing is fun and you even might come across an occasional find. On Monday and Thursday mornings Piazza Palermo becomes an open-air market where locals flock for everything from kitchen utensils to new and used clothing and shoes. A small antiques market is held the first and third Saturday of every month in Piazza della Erbe. Most shops are closed Sundays and Monday mornings; food stores are closed Sundays and Wednesday afternoons.

Antica Erboristeria San Giorgio This old, well-known herbal shop is stocked with everything from old-recipe panaceas to natural cosmetics, health foods, and teas. 47r Via Luccoli (phone: 206888).

Berti Here is the classic English look the Genoese so love, including high-quality clothes by English and Italian manufacturers for both sexes. 94r Via Ottobre (phone: 540026).

Chiarella Amusing, moderate-price Italian and European clothing for men and women. 224r Via XX Settembre (phone: 562868).

Dallai Libreria Antiquaria A large selection of antique books, unusual or first editions, and interesting old prints are in this small store in the *centro storico* (historic center). 11r Piazza de Marini (phone: 298338).

Il Fornaio di Sattanino The perfect place to sample the local staple, *focaccia,* in all its glory—simple or filled with any of a myriad of ingredients. Other breads, rolls, and baked sweets are made around the clock. 18r Via Fiasella (phone: 580972).

Galleria Imperiale Antiques and collectibles from estates fill this beautifully frescoed, deconsecrated chapel located in a 16th-century palazzo in the *centro storico.* 8 Piazza Campetto (phone: 299290).

Lucarda Exceptional nautical clothing and accessories for both men and women. 61 Via Sottoripa (phone: 297963).

Le Mimose A small, delightful store full of exquisite women's lingerie. 58r Via XXV Aprile (phone: 292615).

Pecchioli Ceramics, crystal, and other fine gift items. 126 Via XX Settembre (phone: 564914).

Prini Shoes, bags, other accessories, and quality clothing, since 1860, for both men and women. 17r Via XX Settembre (phone: 561984).

SPORTS AND FITNESS

BOATING For sailboat rentals, contact *Club Vela Pegli* (40 Via Lungomare di Pegli; phone: 696-9354) or the *Federazione Italiana Vela* (2 Viale Brigate Bisagno; phone: 565083; fax: 592864). Experienced sailors can hire yachts for one to two weeks from the *Sailor's Center* (19-26 Via C. Barabino; phone: 592089; fax: 553-3177).

BOCCE One of the most popular ball games in Italy, a bit like French *boules,* it is played in parks and squares all over the city. Contact the *Associazione Bocciofila Genovese* (2 Piazza Zerbino; phone: 810770).

SOCCER Matches take place from September through May at *Luigi Ferraris Stadium* (Via Clavarezza). The Genoese root for two teams: *Genoa* (phone: 540547) and *Sampdoria,* or *"La Samp"* (phone: 585343).

SQUASH You'll find courts at the *Squash Club Genova* (7/A Corso Italia; phone: 362-3718).

SWIMMING Indoor pools are located at the *Stadio del Nuoto* (39 Via de Gaspari; phone: 362-8409) and *Sportiva Sturla* (2 Via V Maggio; phone: 389325). In summer only there's the saltwater *Gropallo* (Passeggiata Anita Garibaldi, Nervi; phone: 321311). The most popular (and crowded) beach for swimming is the Bagni Nuovo Lido (13 Corso Italia; phone: 312398); take bus No. 31 from the city center. The nearby Ligurian resorts offer more attractive, if somewhat rocky, beaches.

TENNIS Courts are at *Valletta Cambiaso* (74 Via Albaro; phone: 317604); *Campo Tennis* (4 Via Campanella; phone: 313056); and the *Tennis Club Genova* (5 Salita Misericordia; phone: 586662).

THEATER

The theatrical tradition remains strong in Italy. One Genoese company stands out:

CENTER STAGE

Teatro di Genova One of Italy's municipally sponsored repertory companies, this group offers contemporary Italian plays as well as foreign works in two theaters: The *Teatro Genovese* (4 Via Piaggio; phone: 839-3589) is the principal building, but productions also take place at the larger and newer *Teatro della Corte* (Corso Buenos Aires, Torre A; phone: 570-2472), in the *Corte Lambruschini.*

In addition, various experimental works, as well as traditional Italian and international productions, can be seen in the small, well-established *Teatro della Tosse* (4 Piazza Negri; phone: 247-0793) and the *Teatro Sala Carignano* (8/canc. Viale Villa Glori; phone: 593533), which also shows English-language films. The tiny *Teatro dell'Archivolto* (1 Piazzetta Chighizola; phone: 281409) often presents avant-garde works by traveling companies. During the summer the *Comune di Genova* stages open-air programs under the title *Acquasola* in the public park near Piazza Corvetto. Detailed information about specific performances can be obtained from the theaters (box offices open at 3 PM) or from the tourist offices.

MUSIC

The Genoese love music, and although their early-19th-century opera house, the *Teatro Carlo Felice* (Piazza de Ferrari; phone: 53811), was bombed during World War II, the mere shell that remained was rebuilt in 1992. In addition to opera (the season runs from December through June), the theater also hosts classical concerts and the occasional rock show. In late June and July concerts and international music and ballet festivals often are held in the public gardens at Nervi, funds permitting. Genoa is also something of a hothouse of a particular brand of folk music, typified by present-day singer Fabrizio De Andrè's laconic, *cantastoria* style. The city still has something of a medieval madrigal tradition. Concerts by *I Madrigalisti*, under the direction of Nevio Zanardi, can be heard at the *Oratorio di San Filippo Neri* (10 Via Lomellini; phone: 292241).

NIGHTCLUBS AND NIGHTLIFE

The best bet is to find a congenial restaurant. There are, however, two established nightclubs in Genoa: *Orchidea* (28 Via Casaregis; phone: 591559) and the *Astoria Club* (7 Via Quarnaro; phone: 361195). Discos come and go; inquire at your hotel about popular places. The *Louisiana Jazz Club* (1 Corso Aurelio Saffi; phone: 585067) swings on Thursday nights in winter only. For a late-night drink or a lullaby, try the piano bars, perhaps the seaside *American Bar La Marinetta* (19 Corso Italia; phone: 310093), nightly except Tuesdays. At the popular *Britannia Pub* (76r Vico Casana; phone: 294878), the atmosphere is British, but the crowd is young Genoese. It also serves a simple light dinner until midnight. On summer evenings head for the terrace of Nervi's *Senhor do Bonfim* (Passeggiata Garibaldi; phone: 372-6312), which has Latin and African music.

Best in Town

CHECKING IN

There are fewer hotels in Genoa than might be expected of a large, busy city. This is perhaps because most visitors stay nearby in the smaller resort towns, which are connected to the city by frequent train service and by two main roads. Nevertheless, Genoa has more than adequate facilities. Hotels listed here as very expensive charge $225 to $300 for a double room per night; expensive, between $125 and $175; moderate, from $75 to $125; and inexpensive, $75 or less. All hotels feature private baths unless otherwise indicated. All telephone numbers are in the 10 city code unless otherwise noted.

VERY EXPENSIVE

Bristol Palace Although lacking the convenience of an in-house restaurant, it is understandably one of the most popular hotels in Genoa because of its fashionable location, Old World charm, and stately atmosphere. Ensconced in a handsome 19th-century palazzo are 133 rooms; the five floors are linked by a grand marble staircase. 35 Via XX Settembre (phone: 592541; fax: 561756).

Jolly Hotel Plaza Two renovated hotels next door to each other operate in tandem as the best of Genoa's hostelries. Modern, quiet, and well located, all 150 rooms have air conditioning, television sets, and mini-bars (a few also have terraces and Jacuzzis). There is a restaurant. 11 Via Martin Piaggio (phone: 839-3641; 800-247-1277 in New York State; 800-221-2626 elsewhere in the US; fax: 839-1850).

Savoia Majestic Facing the *Stazione Porta Principe* and near the historic center, this place offers Old World comfort, with 120 air conditioned rooms and a good restaurant, as well as a grillroom and an American bar. 5 Via Arsenale di Terra (phone: 261641; fax: 261883).

Starhotel President With 200 rooms, this is Genoa's largest, most modern, and most expensive hotel. Part of the *Corte Lambruschini* complex and centrally located, it is especially popular with European businesspeople and conventiongoers. There is a restaurant and parking. Special weekend rates make it more accessible to vacationers. 4 *Corte Lambruschini* (phone: 5727; fax: 553-1820).

EXPENSIVE

Astor In a small, lovely park, this modern, comfortable, and air conditioned hotel has 41 rooms, a restaurant, and a bar. It's a brief stroll from the sea, the public gardens, and an open-air theater. 16 Viale delle Palme, Nervi (phone: 372-8325; fax: 372-8486).

City A member of the Best Western chain, this hotel has 70 tastefully decorated rooms that promise a quiet and pleasant stay on the edge of downtown's historic center. No restaurant. 6 Via San Sebastiano (phone: 5545; 800-528-1234; fax: 586301).

Metropoli This homey, friendly 50-room establishment has a sweet, pervasive fragrance of fresh polish and a central, though noisy, location (ask for a room at the back). No restaurant. 8 Vico Migliorini (phone: 284141; fax: 281816).

La Pagoda There are 21 tastefully furnished, modern rooms (although not all are air conditioned) in this ornate building that seems more like a private home than a hotel. A real pagoda, it was built in the early 19th century by an eccentric sea captain after his return from the Orient. There is a large lounge decorated with Baroque mirrors from Venice, as well as a restaurant and an attractive garden. It's a 10-minute walk from the Nervi train station, which has frequent service to the *Stazione Brignole,* in the center of Genoa, and 10 to 15 minutes by car from the city center. 15 Via Capolungo, Nervi (phone: 372-6161; fax: 321218).

MODERATE

Agnello d'Oro The "Golden Lamb" is one of the better hotels in its price category. All 38 rooms have air conditioning and telephones. Its restaurant (closed October through February) is for guests only. 6 Vico delle Monachette (phone: 262084; fax: 262327).

Bel Soggiorno There are 18 rooms in this rare find on the city's main palazzo-lined street—be sure to ask for a quiet one. No restaurant. Open mid-January to mid-December. 19 Via XX Settembre (phone: 542880; fax: 581418).

Rio For those who wish to sleep in the medieval section of town, this 47-room place is just off the port, very near the ancient *Chiesa di San Siro.* No restaurant. Open February through December. No credit cards accepted. 5 Via al Ponte Calvi (phone: 290551; fax: 290554).

Vittoria e Orlandini Simple and comfortable though not luxurious, it has 60 rooms and a restaurant. Air conditioning is extra. Near Genoa's historic center, just minutes away from magnificent Via Garibaldi, at 33-45 Via Balbi (phone: 261923; fax: 262656).

INEXPENSIVE

Assarotti Twenty-five clean rooms, an accommodating staff, and parking make this a good value. No restaurant. No credit cards accepted. 40/C Via Assarotti (phone: 885822; fax: 839-1207).

EATING OUT

Ligurian cuisine features many dishes normally found only within the region; Genoese restaurants offer these either exclusively or combined with better-known national dishes. Some can be a little heavy, but because they are so well prepared, they may not seem so. One such specialty is pesto, made from a variety of basil native only to Liguria, along with pine nuts, garlic, olive oil, and often pecorino cheese. It is served on gnocchi, locally made *trofie* noodles, or flat spaghetti known as *trenette. Focaccia,* a simple version of pizza as we know it (there is no sauce), is topped—or more often filled—with local delicacies ranging from vegetables to cheese, served as an appetizer, first course, or snack. Whereas other Italian towns have *pizzerie,* Genoa abounds with *focaccerie.* Other Ligurian treats are *pansotti alla salsa di noce,* plump tortellini-like pasta with a creamy walnut sauce; *polpettone,* a meat and vegetable loaf; and *torta pasqualina,* an *Easter* pie (though it's eaten year-round) traditionally made with Swiss chard or artichokes. There are 33 flaky layers of dough—one for each year of Christ's life. Another local favorite, *farinata,* is made from ground chick-peas; baked in the oven, it is flat and served in slices. Veal is the most popular meat. Naturally, the sea provides fresh fish and shellfish in abundance—but be forewarned, fresh fish is not inexpensive. The local wines are excellent although limited in production and variety. The best whites are cinqueterre, vermentino, and the pigato of Albenga. Among the red wines, a favorite is the rossese of Dolceacqua. The Genoese take great pride in their desserts, so most are homemade.

Like other Italians, the Genoese eat out a lot, often with large family groups. As a consequence, there are many restaurants in Genoa and nearby Boccadasse and Nervi, and prices are competitive. A meal for two at a restaurant categorized as very expensive costs $150 or more; expensive, $100 to $150; moderate, from $50 to $100; and inexpensive, $50 or less. The price usually includes wine but not liquor, at least three courses and side dishes, and a tip. All restaurants are open for lunch and dinner unless otherwise noted. All telephone numbers are in the 10 city code unless otherwise indicated.

VERY EXPENSIVE

Antica Osteria del Bai From the outside, you may not want to go in; from the inside, you will never want to leave. Within this crumbling building on the sea, which was a port of call for Garibaldi more than 125 years ago before he set sail for Sicily, the decor is warm and attractively redone in wood, with windows facing the sea. Gianni Malagoli's excellent Genoese fare includes ravioli stuffed with fish, *zuppa di pesce* (a hearty fish soup), and many other delectables, including fine desserts. Closed Mondays and the first three weeks of August. Reservations advised. Major credit cards accepted. On the way to Nervi, at 12 Via Quarto (phone: 387478).

Da Giacomo In a deluxe, modern environment, with spacious seating arrangements and first class service, this is an unusually formal restaurant by Genoese standards. It's popular with businesspeople and the cognoscenti. Dishes tend toward international favorites, though there are also many Ligurian specialties, especially seafood. The wine selection is excellent, and the waiters will gladly offer advice. The menu changes daily but always includes both fish and meat. Closed Sundays in winter, Mondays in summer, and most of August. Reservations necessary. Major credit cards accepted. 1 Corso Italia (phone: 362-9647; fax: 313326).

Gran Gotto The exceptional kitchen in this small, elegantly appointed place specializes in seasonal regional dishes. The pesto and the *ripieni* (stuffed) dishes are especially good. Try the fresh *pesce* (fish) *ripieno*. Homemade desserts such as cinnamon sorbet and *antica torta di mele* (old-fashioned apple pie) are a fitting end to a sublime meal. Closed Saturdays for lunch, Sundays, public holidays, and the last three weeks in August. Reservations advised. Major credit cards accepted. 69r Viale Brigata Bisagno (phone/fax: 564344).

Zeffirino The pasta at this family-run place is made in the *stirata,* or pulled, fashion—by hand with long rollers. Try the *passutelli* (ravioli stuffed with ricotta and fruit), a recipe known only to the owners. The *lasagne al pesto* is another longtime favorite. Other specialties are added daily to the ample menu, which includes a good regional wine list. Both the large upstairs room and the more intimate downstairs one are decorated in traditional style, all in wood. Closed Wednesdays. Reservations advised. Major credit cards accepted. 20 Via XX Settembre (phone: 591990; fax: 586464).

EXPENSIVE

Aladino The central location, warm atmosphere, and chef Vincenzo's fine artistry make this an ideal stopover for a meal. Try the *trenette al pesto,* any of the superbly presented seafood dishes, and the desserts. Closed Sundays. Reservations necessary. Major credit cards accepted. 8 Via E. Vernazza (phone: 566788).

Il Cucciolo It's spacious and modern, specializing in Tuscan dishes such as *pasta e fagioli* (pasta with beans) and *fritto alla livornese* (fish fried with lots of garlic). Closed Sundays and August 1 to 27. Reservations advised. Major credit cards accepted. 33 Viale Sauli (phone: 561321).

Le Fate Originally a wine-and-oil shop, this restaurant serves some of the best food in Genoa, especially fish cooked with herbs, homemade pasta, and desserts. Closed Saturdays for lunch, and Sundays. Reservations necessary. Major credit cards accepted. 31 Via Ruspoli (phone: 588402).

Gheise The name of this quaint dining spot derives from the chants of the washerwomen at a once nearby laundry. Genoese specialties and some excellent meat dishes, particularly Florentine steaks, are served. Closed Mondays and two weeks in August. Reservations advised. Major credit cards accepted. 29 Via Boccadasse, Boccadasse (phone: 377-0086).

Manuelina For travelers along the coastal road to the east of the city, this is an ideal place to stop for a meal. (There also are a few moderately priced guest-rooms upstairs.) It is one of the region's best seafood restaurants, specializing in dishes grilled over an open fire and mushroom dishes in season. Closed Wednesdays, mid-January to mid-February, and the latter half of July. Reservations advised. Major credit cards accepted. 278 Via Roma, Recco (phone: 185-74128; fax: 185-721677).

Il Primo Piano In the center of the modern city, this well-established and pleasant place serves Genoese specialties, particularly fish. The *lasagne al pesto, risotto di scampi,* and other rice dishes are very good. Also try the delicate fish tartare and the unusual *gelato di riso* (rice ice cream). Closed Saturdays for lunch, Sundays, and most of August. Reservations necessary. Major credit cards accepted. 36 Via XX Settembre (phone/fax: 540284).

St. Cyr Elegant, modern, but not spacious, this friendly, lively restaurant is particularly popular for lunch. Innovative selections include *timballo arlecchino* (a casserole with spinach, fontina cheese, and tomato), *risotto ai funghi* (with mushrooms), and *filetto al barolo* (steak smothered in a delicious red wine sauce). Light desserts include fresh fruit terrine and orange mousse.

Closed Saturdays for lunch, Sundays, one week in August, and one week at *Christmastime*. Reservations advised. Major credit cards accepted. 8 Piazza Marsala (phone: 886897; fax: 815039).

La Santa Dining in this 12th-century palace that once housed St. Catherine of Genoa, it's easy to feel transported to a bygone time—the ambience is intimate, with soft lighting and traditional Ligurian furnishings. The food is outstanding: Various *aragosta* (lobster) and *gamberi* (shrimp) dishes, ravioli stuffed with fish, and *tagliatelle* (noodle-like pasta) smothered in walnut sauce are superior possibilities. Don't miss *tiramisù* (a chocolate confection with liberal splashings of Marsala). Closed Mondays. Reservations advised. Major credit cards accepted. 1-3r Vico degli Indoratori (phone: 293613).

Santa Chiara Dine outdoors at this wonderfully located fish restaurant on the coast. The crêpes and seafood risotto are especially good, the pasta homemade. Closed Sundays, three weeks in August, and December 20 to January 6. Reservations necessary on weekends. Major credit cards accepted. 69 Via al Capo di Santa Chiara, just beyond Boccadasse (phone: 377-0081).

MODERATE

Europa People come here not only for the relaxed atmosphere, but because it is open until 2:30 AM. Everything from pizza to Genoese specialties—such as grilled local seafood and *pasta al pesto*—are available. Closed Sundays and most of August. Reservations unnecessary. Major credit cards accepted. 53r *Galleria Mazzini* (phone: 581259).

Del Mario Housed in the loggia of a 13th-century building that is now a national monument, this place has a traditional and seasonal menu, with many mushroom and truffle dishes. Very good *cima* (veal joint stuffed with vegetables and eggs), *stoccafisso* (fish soup), and other Ligurian specialties are served in a courteous and relaxed atmosphere. Closed Saturdays and August. Reservations unnecessary. Major credit cards accepted. 35r Via Conservatori del Mare (phone: 298467; fax: 297788).

Napoleon Always bustling, this modern eatery is two steps from Piazza de Ferrari. Intimate it's not, but an extensive stock of vintage olive oil and wines and a number of traditional local specialties keep everyone coming back. The *menù degustazione* (tasting menu) is more expensive, but is a crash course in fine *cucina genovese*. Closed Sundays and three weeks in summer. Reservations advised. Major credit cards accepted. 35r Via XXV Aprile (phone: 541888).

Sette Nasi Enrico Nasi is one of seven children—hence the name of his eatery, which literally means "Seven Noses." It's a friendly place on the beach offering its own pool and terrace, fresh fish daily, and very good homemade desserts. Closed Tuesdays, two weeks in August, and two weeks in November. Reservations advised. Major credit cards accepted. 16 Via Quarto (phone: 337357; fax: 337210).

Mario Rivaro A few charming rooms decorated with light wood paneling, traditional Genoese fare, and a devoted clientele make this centrally located eatery a favorite. Closed Sundays and holidays. No reservations or credit cards accepted. 16r Via del Portello (phone: 277-0054).

BARS AND CAFFÈS

For lighter meals or snacks or to satisfy a sweet tooth, Genoa's many *caffès* and *gelaterie* are worth trying. All those below are inexpensive; only *Tonitto* accepts credit cards. The following are a few of our favorites:

Antica Gelateria Balilla The handsome *ambiente* of old-fashioned mirrors and cushioned chairs goes unnoticed when the gelato arrives. The specialty is the many varieties of *semifreddo* (soft ice cream). There also are dozens of flavors of freshly made ice cream and hard-to-find authentic Sicilian *granita* (refreshing shaved-ice drinks served in a glass or cone). Closed Mondays. 84r Via Macaggi (phone: 542161).

Bar Romanengo Founded in 1805, this landmark is the oldest bar in the city and now has two branches. All have old-fashioned, wood-trimmed display counters loaded with homemade candies, hand-dipped chocolates, glazed chestnuts, and candied fruits. All are closed Sundays and Monday mornings. 13r Corso Buenos Aires (phone: 591994); 51r Via Roma (phone: 580257); and 74r Piazza Soziglia (phone: 297869).

Cremeria Augusto All the traditional and in-season fruit varieties of gelato are served here, but the custardy *crema* and cappuccino-flavored *panera* are the best. Closed Saturdays and the last three weeks of August. 5r Via Nino Bixio (phone: 591884).

Grattacielo Situated below the *Porta Soprana,* this smart *caffè* serves coffee, snacks, and ice cream (with photographs of various concoctions featured in an album-menu on each table) and occasionally features a pianist. Closed Saturdays. 26 Piazza Dante (phone: 590402).

Klainguti The homemade ice creams and cakes here rival the perfection of *Bar Romanengo*'s chocolates (see above). There also is a pleasant tearoom, open since 1828. Closed Sundays. 100 Piazza Soziglia (phone: 296502).

Mangini Served in a handsome Old World *ambiente, Mangini*'s sweets, pastries, and candies will make your mouth water. Closed Mondays. 91r Via Roma (phone: 564013).

Tonitto A popular coffeehouse and *gelateria*, it sells a host of tempting flavors all made on the spot (and supplied to several restaurants in town). Closed Thursdays in winter. 184r Via XX Settembre (phone: 553-0371).

Milan

With nearly 1.6 million people, Milan—Italy's financial and commercial hub—is about half the size of Rome, but many residents think of their city as Italy's real capital. It boasts 400 banks and a silk market that rivals the one in Lyons. Each spring its *Fiera di Milano* (International Trade Fair) draws hundreds of thousands of businesspeople from all over the world, as do its autumn and spring showings of luxury fashions. Graduates of the city's prestigious *Università Commerciale Luigi Bocconi* (Luigi Bocconi Commercial University) include successful international economists, bankers, and company presidents. Milan also is the center of Italian publishing and furniture design and home of the world-famous *La Scala* opera house.

The heart of Milan is its rose-tinted white marble Gothic *Duomo;* the spires of the city's cathedral soar in defiance of the less ethereal buildings around it, though many of them boast lovely fin de siècle architectural details and delightful, secret courtyard gardens. Milan is also gateway to the Lombardy lake region, to ski resorts along the Swiss border to the north, and to the mist-veiled charm of the broad Po River to the south.

Throughout the city are symbols of its illustrious past: the 16 Corinthian-style columns from the early Roman settlement, placed outside the 4th-century *Basilica di San Lorenzo;* the remains of the 16th-century Spanish ramparts; and the traces of *navigli* (canals) that once crisscrossed the city, linking it to the rivers and thus to other regions of Italy.

Milan has had a tumultuous history. Invading armies continually descended upon it from the time it was a Celtic settlement. The Romans subdued the city they called "Mediolanum" in 222 BC, and it was the capital of the Roman Empire from AD 286 to 402. In AD 313, Constantine the Great officially recognized Christianity in the famous Edict of Milan, and, with the coming of Christianity, Milan found a spiritual father in Bishop Ambrose (later proclaimed a saint), who accomplished the seemingly impossible task of conciliating church and state. After a series of invasions by Huns and Goths, the Lombards (Lungobardi), who had originated in northwest Germany, pushed their way southward to cross the Alps and invade the Po Valley towns, including Milan, in 568. They ruled for more than two centuries, giving their name to the region and leaving their imprint on the art and architecture, language, and laws. Tyrranical Frankish rulers followed, but around the year 1000 the Milanese bishops wrested temporal power from them, and Milan became one of the first Italian city-states to be ruled by the church. Constant wars followed, and after a nine-month siege Milan fell to Frederick Barbarossa. In 1176, all the cities in the area united in the Lombard League to defeat the German invader and win recognition of its independence.

This ushered in a century of prosperity and power, as local family dynasties, beginning with the Torriani, assumed power in 1260. The Visconti then seized power from them in 1277. Under the Visconti, particularly Gian Galeazzo (1345–1402), Milan grew in wealth and splendor. When the Visconti died out in 1447, Milan experienced three years of Republican government before Francesco Sforza proclaimed himself duke. The most famous of the Sforzas was Ludovico il Moro (1451–1508), who brought Leonardo da Vinci, Donato Bramante, and other artists to Milan to enhance the city with new buildings, piazze, and church frescoes. Milan fell to the invading French after Ludovico's death, to the Spanish in 1535, and then to the Austrian Empire in 1713. At the beginning of the 19th century, Napoleon made Milan the capital of the Cisalpine Republic, but the tyrannic Austrian rulers returned when Napoleon fell. The succession of foreign rulers began to ebb in 1848, when the Milanese staged a glorious five-day revolution, known as the Cinque Giornate. But it was nearly 10 years before Milan was liberated and could throw its support to the Piedmontese King Victor Emmanuel of Savoy, who would become king of a unified Italy in 1860.

During World War II, Milan was the site of bitter partisan fighting; it was bombed 15 times, and many of its historic buildings were damaged extensively. But restoration work and new construction began immediately after the war. Bomb damage required the complete rebuilding of about half the region's factories, which proved a blessing in disguise, since the new plants were extremely modern manufacturing entities, making them especially competitive and spawning the boom of the 1950s and 1960s.

Twenty years of Socialist control over City Hall ended in 1993 with the arrests of hundreds of politicians of every stripe for influence peddling. The populist party Lega Lombarda (Lombard League) elbowed its way into the forefront when its candidate, Marco Formentini, was elected mayor of Milan. The Lega, which seeks greater autonomy for Italy's industrial north, wants to turn the country into a federation of states (as in pre-unification days). Milan is something of a melting pot, mainly because of its myriad factories, and the Lega opposes foreign immigrants coming to Italy's north in search of work (one out of every 10 workers in Lombardy is a non-European immigrant). But lately the Lombard League has shown signs of running out of steam. And so, in the 1994 national general elections, the Lega allied itself with a new political movement: TV magnate Silvio Berlusconi's pro-business Forza Italia (it translates roughly as "Go Italy," with a pun on "Italy Strength"). This Milan-based pole garnered about 28% of the vote in the city.

Among modern-day Milan's problems are industrial smog and polluted waterways. However, some steps have been taken recently to reduce the pollution level. Automobile driving, except for cars with catalytic converters, is occasionally banned, and a downtown stretch of shopping area is now traffic-free. Away from the center, Milan is a maze of four-lane highways connecting it to the other northern cities, Genoa, Turin, Venice, and Brescia; to the Lake District and Alpine valleys; and, by the Autostrada del Sole, to Rome and southern Italy.

Milan specializes in innovative industrial design and avant-garde graphics. In textile design and fashions it rivals Paris. The city itself is prosperous and elegant; its people enjoy a high standard of living and a stimulating cultural and intellectual life. Whether you come on business, to attend the opera, to patronize the pace-setting Milanese fashion houses, or to admire the city's art treasures, you will find Milan's sophistication equal to that of London or Paris or New York, but always uncompromisingly Italian.

Milan At-a-Glance

SEEING THE CITY

For a grand view of Milan, the surrounding Lombard plain, the Alps, and the Apennines, climb the 166 steps, or take an elevator, to the roof of the *Duomo* (see *Special Places,* below). From here, more stairs take you to the topmost gallery at the base of the cathedral's central spire, 354 feet from the ground. Enter the stairway to the roof from the south transept near the Medici tomb, or enter the elevator from outside the church, on the north side (toward the *Rinascente* department store); an elevator on the south side is sometimes also in operation. Both elevators are open daily and charge admission. A seventh-floor addition to *Rinascente* boasts a *caffè* whose vast windows bring the *Duomo*'s gargoyles within, it would seem, sipping distance of your *aperitivo.* Here your admission charge for a unique view is the price of a cup of coffee. There also is a 350-foot viewing tower in *Parco Sempione* (Sempione Park), just beyond the *Castello Sforzesco* (see *Special Places*).

SPECIAL PLACES

The huge Piazza del Duomo (Cathedral Square), with its perennial pigeons (note that it is forbidden to feed them) and ever-present pensioners, is one of the city's few pedestrian oases and the heart of this bustling metropolis. North of the piazza toward Piazza della Scala is the elegant glass-domed *Galleria Vittorio Emanuele II.* Built between 1865 and 1877 under the direction of architect Giuseppe Mengoni, the arcade has for decades been considered the *salotto* (salon) for Milan's exclusive shops, bookstores, *caffès,* and fashionable restaurants.

Some of the city's tourist attractions are too far from the center to reach comfortably on foot, but *ATM,* the local bus and tram system, connects these sites efficiently, as does the clean subway system (see *Getting Around,* below).

Note that many sites of interest in Milan close for a midday break, usually from noon or 12:30 PM to 2:30 or 3 PM; we suggest calling ahead to check exact hours.

DUOMO (CATHEDRAL) The most magnificent Milanese monument is its rose-tinged marble cathedral, with 135 spires and more than 2,200 sculptures decorating the exterior. From the roof, reached by an elevator or a 166-step climb, you can study the details of its pinnacles and flying buttresses. The interior, divided into five main aisles by an imposing stand of 58 columns, contains another 2,000 sculptures. Seen from the inside, the stained glass windows depicting Old and New Testament scenes are so huge that the roof seems supported by shafts of colored light. On the site of an early Christian church located in the center of the then Roman city of Mediolanum, the cathedral is considered the finest example of Gothic architecture in northern Italy, although its architectural peculiarities—it was begun in 1386 but not completed until 1813—prevent it from being pure Gothic. Only *San Pietro* in Rome is larger. Next to the cathedral is the modern *Museo del Duomo,* which beautifully displays Milanese artifacts from the early Middle Ages, including illuminated manuscripts, parchments, statuary, architectural plans, and tapestries. A plus is the air conditioned *ambiente.* The *Duomo* is open daily; the museum is closed Mondays and for a midday break. Admission charge to the museum. Piazza del Duomo (phone: 860358).

TEATRO ALLA SCALA (LA SCALA) Built between 1776 and 1778 on the site of the *Chiesa di Santa Maria della Scala* and then restored to rococo glory in 1948 after Allied bombing damaged it during World War II, *La Scala* has always been a queen among opera houses. Works by Donizetti, Rossini, Bellini, and Verdi were first acclaimed here, and it was here that Arturo Toscanini, conductor and artistic director for years, reintroduced the works of Verdi. The house has never lost its aristocratic aura, and its opening night on *Festa di Sant'Ambrogio* (Feast of St. Ambrose; December 7) is a glittering, celebrity-studded gala, with special dinners offered by the tony Milanese restaurants that publish opera soirée menus in the newspapers. With legendarily perfect acoustics, a performance here is truly exhilarating—and also expensive. Tickets for each season's performances, presented December through May, are passionately pursued and hard to come by. They can be purchased—with difficulty—from the box office in advance; at the last minute, concierges at the city's deluxe hotels often can get positive results for a consideration. There also are ballet performances from September through November and concerts featuring the *Filarmonica della Scala,* perhaps Italy's finest orchestra. The box office (phone: 807041/2/3/4) is open from 10 AM to 1 PM and 3:30 to 5:30 PM (to 9:30 PM on the day of a performance); closed Mondays. For information, call 809120 or 720-03744; for credit card purchases, call 809126. The theater can be visited by appointment (phone: 887-9377). The adjacent *Museo della Scala* (La Scala Museum) houses a rich collection of manuscripts, costumes, and other *La Scala* memorabilia. It's closed for a midday break, and Sundays from November through March. Admission charge. The theater and museum are north of Piazza del Duomo, through the *Galleria Vittorio Emanuele II,* at 2 Piazza della Scala (phone: 805-3418).

MUSEO POLDI-PEZZOLI (POLDI-PEZZOLI MUSEUM) A Milanese nobleman bequeathed his home and exquisite private art collection to the city in 1879. The works include some prime examples of Renaissance to 17th-century paintings and sculpture, Oriental porcelain, Persian carpets, and tapestries. There also are a Botticelli portrait of the Madonna, paintings by Giovanni Battista Tiepolo, Pollaiolo, and Fra Bartolomeo, as well as Giovanni Bellini's *Pietà.* Closed Mondays and for a midday break. Admission charge. A short walk from *La Scala,* at 12 Via Manzoni (phone: 794889).

PALAZZO E PINACOTECA DI BRERA (BRERA PALACE AND ART GALLERY) One of the most important state-owned galleries in Italy, and Milan's finest, is housed in this 17th-century palace. Its 38 rooms contain a broad representation of Italian painting, with particularly good examples from the Venetian and Lombard Schools, including such masterpieces as Andrea Mantegna's *Dead Christ,* Raphael's *Wedding Feast of the Virgin,* and Caravaggio's *Dinner at Emmaus.* The palace also has an important library (founded in 1770) of incunabula and manuscripts, plus a collection of all books printed in the Milanese province since 1788. In the courtyard is a monumental statue of Napoleon I, depicted as a conquering Caesar. The art gallery is closed Mondays and Sunday afternoons. Admission charge. The library is closed Sundays. A few blocks north of *La Scala,* at 28 Via Brera (phone: 722631).

CASTELLO SFORZESCO E CIVICI MUSEI (SFORZA CASTLE AND CIVIC MUSEUMS) In the mid-15th century, Duke Francesco Sforza built this large, square brick castle on the site of a castle of the Visconti that had been destroyed. It became a fortress after the fall of the Sforzas and was damaged repeatedly in sieges before restoration began in the 19th century. Further damaged during World War II, it has been repaired and today houses a museum complex that includes the *Museo d'Arte Antica.* One of its treasures is the unfinished *Rondanini Pietà,* Michelangelo's last work. Enter the museum from the courtyard of the residential part of the castle, the *Corte Ducale.* The castle also houses important collections of art, musical instruments, and manuscripts and, occasionally, well-publicized temporary exhibitions. Beyond the castle is the beautiful 116-acre *Parco Sempione,* with an aquarium, sports arena, and neoclassical Arco della Pace (Arch of Peace), a triumphal arch with statues and bas-relief. Inspired by Rome's *Septimius Severus,* the arch marks the beginning of the historic Corso Sempione through the Alps to France, which was built by order of Napoleon. Closed Mondays. No admission charge. West of the *Palazzo e Pinacoteca di Brera,* on Piazza Castello (phone: 6236, ext. 3940).

BASILICA E MUSEO DI SANT'AMBROGIO (ST. AMBROSE'S BASILICA AND MUSEUM) The basilica was founded in the 4th century by Bishop Ambrose (later St. Ambrose), who baptized St. Augustine here. The bas-relief on the doorway dates from the time of Sant'Ambrogio, and the two bronze doors are from the 9th century. The basilica was enlarged in the 11th century, and its superb atrium was added in the 12th century. Two other early Christian saints—Gervase and Protasius—are buried with Sant'Ambrogio in the crypt. The ceiling of the apse is decorated with 10th-century mosaics. Above the portico is the *Museo di Sant'Ambrogio,* where you can see a 12th-century cross, a missal of Gian Galeazzo Visconti, and other religious treasures. The museum is open Mondays and Wednesdays through Fridays, with a long midday break; weekends from 3 to 5 PM; closed Tuesdays. Admission charge. South of the *Castello Sforzesco,* at 15 Piazza Sant'Ambrogio (phone: 872059).

SANTA MARIA DELLE GRAZIE (CHURCH OF ST. MARY OF GRACE) The interior of this restored brick and terra cotta church, representing a period of transition from Gothic to Renaissance, is decorated with some fine 15th-century frescoes. But the church, though beautiful in itself, usually is visited because Leonardo's *The Last Supper* (known as the *Cenacolo Vinciano*) is on a wall of the refectory of the former Dominican convent next to it. Commissioned in 1495 by Ludovico il Moro, Duke of Milan, *The Last Supper* took two years to paint. Leonardo chose the relatively slow-drying (and less durable) tempera instead of fresco technique (paint onto wet plaster) to gain time. The result was a meditative but fragile work of art. Although restoration was begun not long after its completion and has continued through the years, the painting has suffered considerable deterioration. The current restoration is well past the midway point, and, despite the problems, the pale colors seem to glow (visitors can see quite a bit of the masterpiece, notwithstanding the presence of some scaffolding). Open Tuesdays through Sundays from 9 AM to 1:45 PM. Admission charge. A few blocks northwest of the *Basilica e Museo di Sant'Ambrogio,* on Piazza Santa Maria delle Grazie (phone: 498-7588).

ENVIRONS

CERTOSA DI PAVIA (CHARTERHOUSE OF PAVIA) Gian Galeazzo Visconti founded this monastery in 1396 as a family mausoleum. With its façade of multicolored marble sculpture and its interior heavily decorated with frescoes, Baroque grillwork, and other ornamentation, the monastery is one of the most remarkable buildings in Italy. Closed Sundays, Mondays, and late afternoons. No admission charge, but donations are welcome. Sixteen miles (26 km) from Milan, just off the Milan-Pavia Road (phone: 925613, guided tours).

PAVIA On the banks of the Ticino, this gracious city (5 miles/8 km south of the *Certosa di Pavia*) was the capital of the Lombard kingdom and later a free commune, until it fell to the Visconti in 1359. The famous *Università di Pavia* (University of Pavia) was officially founded in the same century, although its origins go back to the 9th century. The 15th-century *Duomo*

(Piazza del Duomo), with a 19th-century façade, is flanked by an 11th-century tower and backed by the 16th-century *Broletto* (Town Hall). Don't miss the house of Renaissance master painter Andrea Mantegna. Pavia's main street, the Strada Nuova, is lined with elegant shops and ends at the river, which is crossed by a postwar reconstruction of a 14th-century covered bridge. The *APT* tourist bureau is at 1 Corso Garibaldi (phone: 382-27238).

MONZA The world-famous Monza *Autodromo* is the scene of the Italian *Grand Prix Formula One* race early in September each year. Except during race-preparation times, visitors can drive around the course, with its well-known "seven corners" (admission charge). The *Autodromo* is in a splendid, 2,500-acre park that was once part of the *Villa Reale* (Royal Villa, open to the public only during special events), and now has golf courses, a racecourse, and a pool, besides the auto track. The historic cathedral here (Piazza del Duomo), built during the 13th and 14th centuries, has a notable façade. The *Museo Serpero* (Piazza del Duomo; phone: 393-23404) houses an interesting collection of precious medieval works in gold from the cathedral, including the famed *corona ferea* (iron crown) of Theodolinda, which Napoleon used to crown himself emperor. It is open Tuesdays through Saturdays, with a long midday break; Sundays from 10:30 AM to noon; closed Mondays. Admission charge. Monza is easily reached by bus or *Metropolitana;* by road, it is 7 miles (11 km) northeast of Milan on S36.

EXTRA SPECIAL

Until the early part of this century, Milan was crisscrossed by *navigli* (canals). Today, only two—the Grande Naviglio and the Pavese Naviglio—remain, and their environs are perhaps the most picturesque in Milan. A stroll through this romantic quarter of art galleries, colorful shops, charming restaurants, *caffès,* and jazz spots is not to be missed. It provides a marked contrast to the rest of this modern, bustling city. On the last Sunday of every month, a fascinating antiques market, the *Mercatone del Naviglio,* takes place along the *navigli.* It's a fair walk: From the Piazza del Duomo, follow Via Torino and Corso di Porta Ticinese, or take a taxi.

Sources and Resources

TOURIST INFORMATION

General tourist information is available at the extremely helpful *Azienda Provinciale per il Turismo (APT)*, conveniently located at the corner of Piazza del Duomo (1 Via Marconi; phone: 861287; fax: 720-22432) and at the *Stazione Central* (Piazzale Duca d'Aosta; phone: 669-0432 or 669-0532). Both offices are closed from 1 to 3 PM. The *APT* will provide information on hotels, current exhibits, and events. A good introduction to the city is the free video presentation offered at the *APT* office by the *Duomo*.

A welcome convenience to travelers low on lire are automatic foreign exchange machines where you can change US dollar bills (as well as many other currencies) into local tender. The exchange rate is usually about what banks offer, and there is a fixed commission fee comparable to what financial institutions charge. A few of the many locations for these ATMs are at the airports; the tourist office (2 Via Marconi); the Banca Cesare Ponti (19 Piazza del Duomo); and the 24-hour ATM for credit card advances at the Banca Commerciale (Piazza della Scala). Another place to get a good exchange rate for US bills is at the main post office (4 Piazza Cordusio).

LOCAL COVERAGE The tourist board can provide copies of *Milan Is,* a useful guide in English, which includes activities, facts, phone numbers, and listings of restaurants and discos. The monthly English-language *A Guest in Milan,* distributed by many hotels, has bulletins on special events, and *Viva Milano,* a weekly entertainment newspaper in Italian, provides up-to-date information on shops, fairs, restaurants, and discos.

Several books in Italian provide listings of restaurants and food and wine shops throughout Italy. Some of the better annually published guides are *La Guida d'Italia* (published annually by *L'Espresso*); *I Ristoranti di Bell'Italia* (published annually by Mondadori); *Gambero Rosso* (published by *Il Manifesto*); and *Osterie d'Italia* (published by Arcigola/Slow Food). They all are sold on newsstands and are available only in Italian.

TELEPHONE The city code for Milan is 2. When calling from within Italy, dial 02 before the local number.

GETTING AROUND

Much of the center of Milan is closed to traffic, so it is most convenient for visitors to use public transportation. Inexpensive day tickets that allow unlimited travel on the bus and tram system can be purchased at the *ATM Ufficio Abbonamenti* at the *Piazza del Duomo* and *Cadorna* subway stations; the *Stazione Centrale;* and the *APT* on Via Marconi.

AIRPORTS *Malpensa Airport* (phone: 268-00606, national flights; 268-00627, international flights; 748-54215, lost luggage) is about 28 miles (45 km) and less than an hour's drive from the center of Milan; a taxi ride into town can be prohibitively expensive. Far less expensive buses to *Malpensa* leave from *Stazione Centrale,* on the east side of the *Galleria delle Carrozze,* every half hour (phone: 868008 or 331-797480). They also stop at the east entrance of *Porta Garibaldi* station en route.

Linate Airport (phone: 281-06300, national flights; 281-06324, international flights; 701-24551; lost luggage) handles domestic traffic, as well as some international—but not intercontinental—flights. *Linate* is 5 miles (8 km) and 15 minutes (longer if traffic is heavy) from downtown; taxi fare into the center of the city is reasonable. The less expensive *ATM* bus No. 73 leaves for the airport from Corso Europa (near Piazza San Babila) and *Porta Garibaldi* station every 15 minutes between 5:40 AM and midnight (phone: 875495). *Doria Agenzia* (phone: 664-0836) has inexpensive buses that leave from *Stazione Centrale* every 20 minutes from 5:40 AM to 8:30 PM.

Although there is no regular transportation between *Malpensa* and *Linate Airports, Alitalia* occasionally provides group transfers when two connecting *Alitalia* flights are involved. For information on all flights, call 26853; for fog information, call 701-25959.

BUS AND TRAM The local bus and tram service, *ATM* (phone: 875495), efficiently connects various points of this sprawling city. Tickets, which must be purchased in advance, are sold at tobacconists and newsstands throughout the city. They are valid for 75 minutes, thus permitting transfer to other lines, and can be used for the subway (see below) as well.

CAR RENTAL Most international firms are represented.

SUBWAY The efficient, clean *Metropolitana Milanese* (*MM*) has three lines. The most useful for tourists is line *M3,* which directly links the main railway station, through Piazza del Duomo, and the Porta Romana. Tickets are sold at coin-operated machines in each station and at many tobacconists.

TAXI Cabs can be hailed while cruising, picked up at a taxi stand, or called (phone: 8388, 8585, 6767, or 5251). Expect a surcharge after 10 PM, on Sundays and holidays, and for baggage.

TOURS *Agenzia Autostradale* (phone: 801161) conducts a three-hour bus tour in English of the city that leaves daily from the Piazzetta Reale. Tickets are available from most hotels and travel agencies, or directly on board. From April through October, the company also offers an all-day tour of the Lombardy lakes. Pick-up points are at Piazza Castello and the *Stazione Centrale*. The *Gestione Governative Navigazione Laghi* (21 Via Ariosto; phone: 481-6230 or 481-2086) arranges boat trips on the lakes.

TRAIN Milan's main train station is *Stazione Centrale* (Piazzale Duca d'Aosta; phone: 675001 or 67711). Several smaller stations serve local commuter lines. The largest of these is *Porta Garibaldi,* the departure point for trains to Turin, Pavia, Monza, Bergamo, and other points (phone: 655-2078). The northern line is *Ferrovie Nord Milano* (phone: 851-1608).

SPECIAL EVENTS

On *Epiphany* (January 6), a parade of the Three Kings proceeds from the *Duomo* to the *Chiesa di Sant'Eustorgio*. The annual *Fiera di Milano*, held in late April since the 1920s, has put Milan squarely on the international business map. Although this is the city's biggest, there are various other trade fairs and exhibitions (including the showings of designer collections, the twice yearly fashion fair, and the September furniture fair) almost every month except July and August. Obtain information, a copy of the useful bilingual periodical *In Fiera,* and a year-round calendar of events from the main *Trade Fair* office (1 Largo Domodossola; phone: 49971). On the first Sunday in June, the *Festa dei Navigli* (Canal Festival) takes place on Milan's two *navigli* and in Darsena—Milan's port—with music, food, and folklore. In July and August, the city sponsors a variety of outdoor cultural events; sometimes restaurants join in by serving regional specialties in the parks. Via Ripamonti is the site of a truffle festival the last Sunday in October. The city's most important antiques fair, the annual *Fiera di Sant'Ambrogio,* takes place in Piazza Sant'Ambrogio and adjoining streets for 15 days beginning on December 7.

MUSEUMS

In addition to those listed in *Special Places,* several other museums and churches in Milan are worth a visit. All except the *Basilica di San Lorenzo Maggiore* charge admission.

BASILICA DI SAN LORENZO MAGGIORE Built in the 4th century, this church is the oldest in the West. Open daily, with a long midday closing. 39 Corso di Porta Ticinese (no phone).

GALLERIA D'ARTE MODERNA (MODERN ART GALLERY) Italian and international contemporary art. At press time, the gallery was closed for restoration after it was severely damaged by a bomb in 1993; call for information on reopening. 16 Via Palestro (phone: 760-02819).

MUSEO E CASA DI MANZONI (MANZONI MUSEUM AND HOUSE) The former home of Alessandro Manzoni, author of the 19th-century classic *I Promessi Sposi* (The Betrothed). Closed Saturdays through Mondays, and for a midday break. 1 Via Morone (phone: 864-60403).

MUSEO DI MILANO (MUSEUM OF MILAN) This collection of artworks and artifacts traces the city's development, from the Roman era through the Renaissance. Closed Mondays. 6 Via Sant'Andrea (phone: 760-6245).

MUSEO DEL RISORGIMENTO NAZIONALE (NATIONAL MUSEUM OF THE RISORGIMENTO) Here are archives and memorabilia dating from Napoleon's first Italian campaign in 1756 through Italy's unification. Closed weekends. 23 Via Borgonuovo (phone: 869-3549).

MUSEO DELLA SCIENZA E DELLA TECNICA LEONARDO DA VINCI (LEONARDO DA VINCI MUSEUM OF SCIENCE AND TECHNOLOGY) Some of these exhibits on inventions and ideas for scientific machines date back centuries. Closed Mondays. 21 Via San Vittore (phone: 480-10040).

PALAZZO REALE (ROYAL PALACE) A beautiful 18th-century building, it houses the *Civico Museo dell'Arte Contemporaneo* (Civic Museum of Contemporary Art) and prestigious temporary exhibitions. Closed Mondays. 12 Piazza del Duomo (phone: 620-83943).

GALLERIES

Milan's scores of art galleries feature interesting shows. They generally are open from 10:30 AM to 1 PM and 4 to 8 PM; closed Mondays. The following offer an excellent selection of contemporary and early-20th-century Italian art:

ANGOLARE 4 Via Urbana III (phone: 837-6239).

ANNUNCIATA GALLERIA 44 Via Manzoni (phone: 796026).

ARTE CENTRO 11 Via Brera (phone: 864-62213).

CAFISO 1 Piazza San Marco (phone: 654864).

CHRISTIE'S 3 Via Manin (phone: 290-01374).

GIAN FERRARI 19 Via Gesù (phone: 760-05250).

HARRY SALAMON 2 Via Damiano (phone: 760-13142).

SOTHEBY'S 19 Via Broggi (phone: 295001).

STUDIO MARCONI 15-17 Via Tadino (no phone).

SHOPPING

With the explosion of Italian design and fashion, Milan is an international style center full of enticing, if expensive, shops, including showrooms and boutiques of many of Italy's major contemporary clothing designers. It also is a center for antiques and home furnishings. The main shopping area comprises the streets near Piazza del Duomo and *La Scala,* particularly the elegant Vias Montenapoleone, della Spiga, and Sant'Andrea. The *Galleria Vittorio Emanuele II* (between the Piazza del Duomo and the Piazza della Scala) is a good place to window shop, dine, or people watch at a *caffè*. Boutiques offering modern fashions and antique clothes also are scattered throughout the old Brera quarter—Milan's Left Bank—and around the *Basilica di Sant'Ambrogio*. *Caffè Moda Durini* (14 Via Durini), the only mini-shopping mall in the city, is filled with fashions by designers such as Valentino (for men). Most shops are open from 9 or 9:30 AM to 12:30 PM and 3:30 to 7:30 PM; closed Sundays and Monday mornings.

Milan also has several outdoor markets. Tuesday mornings and Saturdays, there are clothing stalls on Viale Papiniano and Via V. Marcello in the Naviglio area—go early for the bargains. On the third Saturday of every month, the *Mercato di Brera* sells antiques, real and otherwise, from 10 AM to 11 PM in and around Piazza Formentini. A pre-*Christmas* flea market and fair near the *Basilica e Museo di Sant'Ambrogio* is a beloved tradition.

Algani Newspapers from all over the world. 11 *Galleria Vittorio Emanuele II* (phone: 864-60652).

Beltrami Shoes, handbags, and beautifully styled women's ready-to-wear. 4 Piazza San Babila (phone: 760-00546) and 16 Via Montenapoleone (phone: 760-02975).

Blumarine Women's sportswear with a difference. 42 Via Spiga (phone: 795081).

Borsalino Hats for her and him, with a dash. 92 *Galleria Vittorio Emanuele II* (phone: 874244).

Brigatti Milan's finest men's sportswear shop also has a ski boutique for the entire family. 15 Corso Venezia (phone: 760-00273) and 67 *Galleria Vittorio Emanuele II* (phone: 878346).

Bulgari High-style jewelry made from gold, silver, platinum, and precious stones. 6 Via della Spiga (phone: 760-05406).

Byblos The fashionable women who shop here don't mind paying high prices. 35 Via Senato (phone: 760-02109).

Calderoni Exquisite jewelry and silver. 8 Via Montenapoleone (phone: 760-01293).

Centenari Fine old prints and paintings. 92 *Galleria Vittorio Emanuele II* (no phone).

Cignarelli Wonderful homemade herbal liqueurs. 65 Corso Buenos Aires (phone: 204-3564).

Dolce e Gabbana Women's clothing and funky shoes. 10/A Via Sant'Andrea (phone: 799988).

Drogheria Solferino A converted 1930s spice-and-perfume shop that now sells moderate-priced contemporary clothes for men and women. 1 Via Solferino (phone: 878740).

Emporio Armani The designer's less expensive boutique line. For men and women: 9 Via Sant'Andrea (phone: 760-22757); for kids: 24 Via Durini (phone: 794248).

Enrico Coveri Sophisticated clothing for the whole family by one of Italy's top designers. Boutique at 12 Corso Matteotti (phone: 760-01624).

Ermenegildo Zegna Designer menswear. 3 Via Verri (phone: 760-06437).

Fendi High-fashion silk shirts, purses, and furs designed by Karl Lagerfeld. 9 Via della Spiga (phone: 760-21617).

Franco Maria Ricci Beautifully printed and illustrated art books. 19 Via Durini (phone: 798444).

Frette Luxurious linen for bed and bath, as well as silk negligees. 21 Via Montenapoleone (phone: 760-03791) and 11 Via Manzoni (phone: 864339).

Galtrucco Shimmering silks from Como, by the meter or ready-to-wear. 27 Via Montenapoleone (phone: 760-02978).

Gianfranco Ferré The Italian who designs haute couture for Dior sells his own luxurious clothing here. 11 Via della Spiga (phone: 760-09999).

Gianni Versace Vibrant, sometimes outrageous high fashion clothing. For men: 11 Via Montenapoleone (phone: 760-08528); for women: 4 Via della Spiga (phone: 760-05451).

Gioelleria Buccellati Jewelry famed for its finely chased, engraved gold. Inside the courtyard at 12 Via Montenapoleone (phone: 760-02153).

La Gravure An impressive selection of engravings from the 16th through the 20th centuries. 7 Via Laghetto (phone: 760-23500).

Gucci Leatherwear, clothing, and shoes for men and women from the famous maker. 5 Via Montenapoleone (phone: 760-13050).

Immaginazione Surrealist Fornasetti's famed designs are crafted into all manner of articles—from silk scarves to furniture and housewares. 16 Via Brera (phone: 864-62271).

Krizia High-fashion ready-to-wear. Women's boutique at 23 Via della Spiga (phone: 760-08429); menswear at 17 Via Manin (phone: 655-9629).

Legatoria Artistica Cleverly crafted gifts, including hand-bound books and notebooks. 5 Via Palermo (phone: 720-03632).

Mastro Geppetto Dolls, toys, models, and a life-size Pinocchio. 14 Corso Matteotti (no phone).

Max Mara Women's sportswear—look for the terrific jackets. Several locations include Corso Vittorio Emanuele and *Galleria de Cristoforis* (phone: 760-08849) and 6 Via Simpliciano (phone: 875426).

Mila Schön Women's fashions from Milan's own contemporary clothing designer; her store for men is a few steps away. 2 Via Montenapoleone (phone: 760-01803).

Missoni Sumptuous knitwear for men and women. 2 Via Sant'Andrea (phone: 760-03555) and 14 Via Durini (phone: 760-20941).

Moschino High-fashion ready-to-wear for women. 12 Via Sant'Andrea (phone: 760-00832).

Officina Alessi The ultimate in wooden and stainless steel household objects, in a tiny shop designed by Sottsass, Italy's most famous architect. 9 Corso Matteotti (phone: 390-39145).

Prada The place for shoes with the shape of things to come. 1 Via della Spiga (phone: 760-08636) and 21 Via Sant'Andrea (phone: 760-01426).

Pratesi Luxurious linen. 21 Via Montenapoleone (phone: 760-12755).

Provera Fine northern Italian wines are sold by the bottle or the glass in a 1920s shop that also has a few tables for tasting. 7 Corso Magenta (phone: 864-53518).

Roxy Pure silk ties for gents and scarves for women at realistic prices, with a great selection. 10 Via Tommasi Grossi (phone: 874322).

Salvatore Ferragamo Shoes for women, and accessories, including silk ties for men. 3 Via Montenapoleone (phone: 760-00054); for men: 20 Via Montenapoleone (phone: 760-06660).

Salviati Exquisite hand-blown Venetian glass in decorator bottles, designer desk lamps, and vases. 29 Via Montenapoleone (phone: 783926).

Lo Scarabattolo Fine antiques. 14 Via Solferino (phone: 659-0253).

Shara Pagano The bijoux are not the real thing, but are gems nonetheless. 7 Via della Spiga (no phone).

T & J Vestor For Missoni's carpets and wall hangings, and tablecloth and napkin sets. 38 Via Manzoni (phone: 760-03530).

Tanino Crisci The best in finely crafted men's and women's footwear. 3 Via Montenapoleone (phone: 760-21264).

Trussardi High-fashion leatherwear for men and women. 5 Via Sant'Andrea (phone: 760-20380).

Valentino Donna Women's clothing by the famous designer (3 Via Santo Spirito; phone: 760-06478). Men's fashions sold at *Valentino Uomo* (3 Via Montenapoleone; phone: 760-20285).

Venini Hand-blown glass from perfume bottles to chandeliers, made by one of Venice's foremost artisans. 9 Via Montenapoleone (phone: 760-00539).

Vittorio Siniscalchi One of Milan's best custom shirtmakers for men. 1 Via C. Porta (phone: 290-03365).

DISCOUNT SHOPS

The following are select outlets where fine Italian goods and fashions are often found at far less than the prices in fancier shops. And for indefatigable bargain hunters, a good guide is *Bargain Hunting in Milan, Le Occasioni di Milano,* available at bookstores and some newsstands.

Diecidecimi Men's and women's fashions, all discounted 50%, including a large selection of leather jackets and sheepskin coats. 34 Via Plino (phone: 204-6782).

Emporio Discounted classic, spirited clothing from previous and current seasons; *not* part of *Emporio Armani.* 11 Via Prina, near Corso Sempione (phone: 349-1040).

Mimosa Samples from the salons of name designers. 1 Via Pi da Cannobio (phone: 860581).

Il Salvagente Armani, Valentino, and other famous designer clothes in two warehouse-like stores. Men's and women's labels at 16 Via Fratelli Bronzetti (phone: 761-10328); children's attire at 28 Via Balzaretti (phone: 266-80764).

SPORTS AND FITNESS

Downtown Milan is small and has little green space, few gyms, and a scarcity of public parks. But it has an efficient municipal sports organization. For information on what sports are offered and where, contact the *Ufficio Sport e Ricreazione* (1/A Piazza Diaz; phone: 801466). The staff (some English-speaking) will explain how you can arrange to participate in many sports, including tennis (or ask your hotel concierge to do it for you). The closest and largest green space for jogging, paddling a boat, swimming in a large public pool, picnicking, sunbathing, and *caffè* sitting with Milanese families is the *Idroscalo Parco Azzurro* (Azzurro Park and Boat Landing) near Linate. Its waters are filtered and reportedly not polluted. The city bus No. ID leaves daily from Piazza Fontana for the park at frequent intervals.

BICYCLING Rentals by the hour, day, or month are available at *Cooperativa Il Picchio* (49 Corso San Gottardo; phone: 837-7926 or 837-2757).

FITNESS CENTERS *American Health Fitness Center* (various locations include 10 Via Montenapoleone; phone: 760-05290; and 1/A Piazza Reppublica; phone: 655-2728) and *Skorpion Center* (24 Corso Vittorio Emanuele; phone: 799449).

GOLF There are several golf courses in the Milan area; our favorite is the largest and most accessible.

A TOP TEE-OFF SPOT

Golf Club Milano These 27 holes are in the heart of the *Parco di Monza,* 7 miles (11 km) northeast of Milan, on the former estate of Umberto I (who was assassinated here in 1900). The site of several major tournaments, it also has pros who rank among Italy's best, and the physical facilities are first-rate. Closed Mondays. *Parco di Monza* (phone: 39-303112).

Call the *Federazione Italiana Golf* (44/B Via Piranesi; phone: 701-07410) for information on other courses. Most are closed Mondays, and some do not allow guests on weekends.

HORSE RACING Thoroughbred (March through October) and trotting (year-round) races are run at the internationally famous *Ippodromo San Siro* (phone: 482161), on the eastern outskirts of Milan.

HORSEBACK RIDING There are two riding stables in Milan: the *Centro Ippico Amrosiano* (106 Via Verro; phone: 569-5394) and the *Centro Ippico Milanese* (20 Via Macconago; phone: 539-2013).

JOGGING Try *Parco Sempione* (behind the *Castello Sforzesco*); the *Giardini Pubblici* (Public Gardens; Bastioni di Porta Venezia); or the *Idroscalo Parco Azzurro* (see above).

SOCCER From September through May, both *Inter* and *Milan* play at *Stadio Comunale Giuseppe Meazza* (5 Via Piccolomini; phone: 487-07123).

SWIMMING Indoor public pools include *Cozzi* (35 Viale Tunisia); *Mincio* (13 Via Mincio); and *Solari* (11 Via Montevideo). Open-air pools include *Lido* (15 Piazzale Lotto, near the *Stadio San Siro;* phone: 7398). *Argelati* (6 Via Segantini; phone: 581-00012) is a beach establishment with showers.

TENNIS Book public courts well ahead of time. There are courts at *Bonacossa* (74 Via Mecenate; phone: 506-1277); *Centro Polisportivo* (48 Via Valvassori Peroni; phone: 236-1066); the private *Country Sporting Club* (about 5 miles/8 km from town, at 68 Via G. Pepe Paderno Dugnano; phone: 918-0789); *Lido di Milano* (15 Piazzale Lotto; phone: 392-66100); and *Ripamonti* (4 Via Iseo; phone: 645-9253).

THEATER

Although you can take in classical Italian theater productions in various venues throughout the city, we give the following rave reviews, beginning with our favorite.

CENTER STAGE

Piccolo Teatro Since its creation just after World War II, the so-called *Little Theater* has been the most vital force of the Italian stage. The mission of its ever-active founder and godfather, and arguably Europe's finest stage director, Giorgio Strehler, was to make the theater a medium of popular culture; to that end, the repertory is eclectic and international, the staging vigorous and imaginative, and its public the same patrician group glimpsed the evening before at *La Scala*. After more than a decade of debate, a larger and brand-new theater is being built at a different location; the new quarters are expected to be finished in 1996. 2 Via Rovello, *Palazzo del Broletto* (phone: 877663).

Other places to enjoy classic Italian theater include the *Manzoni* (40 Via Manzoni; phone: 760-00231) and the *Teatro Lirico* (14 Via Larga; phone: 866418). Purchase tickets at the box offices or at the following agencies (for a 10% fee): *La Biglietteria* (61 Corso Garibaldi; phone: 659-8472; and 58 Corso Lodi; phone: 573-01358) or *Virgin Megastore* (Piazza del Duomo;

phone: 720-03354). Three theaters offer English-language films: *Anteo* (9 Via Milazzo; phone: 659-7773) on Mondays; *Arcobaleno* (11 Viale Tunisia; phone: 294-06054) on Wednesdays; and *Mexico* (57 Via Savona; phone: 489-51802) on Thursdays. And don't miss a chance to see the splendid marionettes of the Colla family at the *Teatro delle Marionette* (3/B Via Olivetani; phone: 469-4440), which has afternoon performances.

MUSIC

The renowned *La Scala* is an obvious must for an opera fan lucky enough to have tickets in hand (or to have made the acquaintance of a sharp concierge who knows the ropes), but ballet and concerts also are held here from September through November (for more details, see *Special Places*). Concerts also are held at the *Auditorium Angelicum* (2 Piazza Sant'Angelo; phone: 632748) and the *Conservatorio di Musica* (12 Via Conservatorio; phone: 760-01755). Tickets to the *Angelicum* are sold at 4 Via Gustavo Favo or at *Ricordi Music Shop* (2 Via Berchet).

NIGHTCLUBS AND NIGHTLIFE

Milan has a variety of nightclubs offering both dinner and dancing. For impromptu jazz spots, music with a sandwich, or just people watching, stroll through the Naviglio or Brera quarters. Popular nightclubs include *Charley Max* (2 Via Marconi; phone: 871416); *L'Angelo Azzuro* (11 Ripa di Porta Ticinese; phone: 581-00992), a favorite with jazz and R&B fans; *Budineria* (53 Via Chiesa Rossa; phone: 846-7268), a piano bar; and the funky *Nepentha* (1 Piazza Diaz; phone: 804837), open to 3 AM. Top discos include *American Disaster* (48 Via Boscovich; phone: 225728); *Amnesia* (2 Via Callini; phone: 540-0958), where the "look-makers" hang out; the trendy and crowded *Holliwood* (2 Corso Como; phone: 659-8996); *Lizard* (Largo la Fappa; phone: 659-00890), where fashion models cavort; *Al Vascello* (Piazza Greco; phone: 670-4353); and *Calipso Club* (120 Viale Umbria; phone: 256-0553). Live music, including jazz, can be heard regularly at numerous clubs, among them *Capolinea* (119 Via Ludovico il Moro; phone: 891-22024), the city's oldest jazz spot, where internationally acclaimed musicians perform, and *Ca'Bianca* (117 Via Ludovico il Moro; phone: 891-25777), an excellent music and cabaret spot near the Naviglio Grande. Milanese folk tunes and ballads are performed at *Osteria Amici Miei* (14 Via Nicola d'Apulia; phone: 261-45001). *Zelig* (140 Via Monza; phone: 255-1774) is very popular with the fashion-model set (closed Mondays; reservations necessary). *El Brellin* (14 Alzaia Naviglio Grande; phone: 581-01351) features a social scene in the evenings with snacks and a piano bar.

Milan has many cozy piano bars that are ideal for a late drink and snack. Try *Golden Memory* (22 Via Lazzaro Papi; phone: 548-4209); *Gershwin's* (10 Via Corrado il Salico; phone: 849-7722); or the elegant *Momus* (8 Via Fiori Chiari; phone: 805-6227).

Best in Town

CHECKING IN

An international business center, Milan offers a wide range of accommodations, from traditional, old-fashioned hotels to efficient, modern, and commercial ones. Because of the many fairs and fashion showings, some hotels are fully booked in peak periods a year ahead; summer reservations are sometimes easier to obtain. Milan's hotel prices are very high. In high season (summer and *Easter*), very expensive hotels here will cost $575 or more a night for a double room; expensive hotels will cost from $350 to $550; moderate places charge $200 to $350; and inexpensive ones charge between $100 and $200. Off-season rates are about 10% lower. Those hotels listed below as having "business services" usually offer such conveniences as an English-speaking concierge, meeting rooms, photocopiers, computers, translation services, and express checkout, among others. Call the hotel for additional information. All hotels feature air conditioning, private baths, TV sets, and telephones unless otherwise indicated. All telephone numbers are in the 2 city code unless otherwise noted.

For an unforgettable Milanese experience, we begin with our favorite *alberghi*, followed by our cost and quality choices, listed by price category.

SPECIAL HAVENS

Four Seasons Milan Opened in 1992, this member of the Canada-based chain has zoomed to Milan's top spot, so reserve early. It was constructed on the site of a 15th-century monastery, *Santa Maria del Gesù*, and some of the building's original architecture has been preserved—there are four columns in the hall, and a large, beautiful cloister sheds light into the main floor drawing rooms. (Some rooms overlook the cloister.) Although the 98 rooms and a vast presidential suite are decorated in contemporary Italian design, some 15th-century accents have been incorporated into the decor. Northern Italian fare is served in the fine *Il Teatro* restaurant and in a second eatery, *La Veranda*. There's 24-hour room service and business services. 8 Via Gesù (phone: 77708; 800-332-3442; fax: 770-85000).

Grand Hotel Duomo If modern industrial Italy has a heart, you can watch it beating in this hotel right next to the cathedral. It's here that the country's *pezzi grossi* (big businesspeople) meet to make the country's most important deals. The 156 guestrooms are arranged on two levels—a lower living room section furnished with contemporary pieces and elegant touches of marble, Oriental carpeting, and burnished wood, and a bedroom above. It's in the center of town, just off Piazza del Duomo, but on a pedestrian street that ensures quiet. The restaurant's food is quite good, and there's 24-hour room service and business services. 1 Via San Raffaele (phone: 8833; fax: 864-62027).

VERY EXPENSIVE

Pierre Milano Slightly off the beaten track, this luxurious 47-room hotel is nevertheless a favorite of the VIP business crowd. On the premises is an American bar and a restaurant. Business services. 32 Via de Amicis (phone: 805-6221; fax: 805-2157).

EXPENSIVE

Diana Majestic A lovely Art Nouveau building is the site of this charming, intimate hostelry near the *Giardini Pubblici.* Some of the 94 rooms and the bar overlook a private beautiful garden. No restaurant. A member of the CIGA hotel chain, it usually makes a limited number of tickets to *La Scala* available to guests booking from the US. Business services. 42 Viale Piave (phone: 295-13404; 800-221-2340; fax: 201072).

Doria Baglioni Near the *Stazione Centrale,* this luxurious establishment has 116 soundproof rooms and two suites, all elegantly furnished. No restaurant, but there is a nice bar, business services, and covered parking. 22 Viale Andrea Doria (phone: 290-06363 or 669-6694; fax: 669-6669).

Excelsior Gallia Built by the Gallia family in the early 1930s, this luxury place with 242 spacious rooms and 10 suites has an Art Nouveau façade and is decorated in the grand style. Its service is efficient and friendly; its restaurant, quite good. Another plus is the health club with a sauna, a gym, and massage. Business services. Near the central train station at 9 Piazza Duca d'Aosta (phone: 6785; 800-225-5843 or 800-44-UTELL; fax: 656306).

Hilton International This attractive 321-room hotel in the commercial center facing the *Stazione Centrale* is tastefully decorated in a mixture of Italian provincial and modern styles. There is also a colorful, moderately priced Italian restaurant, 24-hour room service, a discotheque, and business services. The service is first-rate. 12 Via Galvani (phone: 69831; 800-HILTONS; fax: 667-10810).

Jolly President A superb location downtown, a handsome lobby, top-flight services, 235 comfortable rooms, a good restaurant, and full business services make this a reliable favorite of Milan's executive set. 10 Largo Augusto (phone: 7746; fax: 783449).

Palace Part of the reliably luxurious and efficient CIGA chain, each floor of this hostelry has a different color scheme; the 193 rooms and 13 suites are decorated in ultramodern style, while some suites come with a Laura

Ashley–decorated children's room. The smaller new wing is more conventional than the renovated older section. Dining is on the roof garden or in the attractive *Casanova Grill,* and there's 24-hour room service. A limited number of tickets to *La Scala* can be booked (well ahead) through CIGA's US office. Business services. Underground parking available. 20 Piazza della Repubblica (phone: 6336; 800-221-2340; fax: 654485).

Principe di Savoia Just north of the *Duomo* and within walking distance of the train station and boutique-lined Via Montenapoleone, this classic deluxe hotel, a member of the CIGA chain, has a lovely renovated façade, lobby, and reception area. The 294 guestrooms and four suites boast antiques, thick rugs, and marble baths. There are also 40 apartments with kitchenettes and balconies. Two floors house a fitness club with a pool, gym, and sauna. The well-recommended *Galleria* restaurant serves regional fare. A limited number of *La Scala* tickets are offered to guests who reserve in advance through their US office. Business services. 17 Piazza della Repubblica (phone: 6230; 800-221-2340; fax: 659-5838).

MODERATE

Blaise & Francis Fifteen minutes from the center of Milan, it has 110 well-maintained and efficient rooms, business services, and a garage, but no restaurant. 9 Via Butti (phone: 668-02366; fax: 668-02909).

Bonaparte Formerly a residential hotel (now fully refurbished), this 56-room hostelry with a restaurant is luxuriously appointed. Business services. 13 Via Cusani (phone: 8560; fax: 869-3601).

Century Tower Near the train station, this very comfortable, 148-room hotel has a garden, a restaurant, a bar, 24-hour room service, and business services. 25/B Via Fabio Filzi (phone: 67504; fax: 669-80602).

Fieramilano Across the street from the fairgrounds, it has 238 rooms, a dining room, private parking, and business services. 20 Viale Boezio (phone: 336221; fax: 314119).

Manin The newer rooms in this 119-room hostelry have a modern decor; the older guestrooms are not impressive but are spacious and comfortable. A few seventh-floor rooms overlook gardens. There's also a very good restaurant and bar. Business services are available. About a half mile from *La Scala* at 7 Via Manin (phone: 659-6511; fax: 655-2160).

Spadari al Duomo Chic, sleek, and small (38 rooms), this recently renovated hostelry has a tiny *caffè* for guests only. Its contemporary art collection adds to the tony ambience. 11 Via Spadari (phone: 20123; fax: 861184).

Starhotel Ritz Efficient and comfortable, this 205-room hotel aims to please the business traveler. There are a restaurant, a bar, parking, and business services. 40 Via Spallanzani (phone: 2055; fax: 295-18679).

Antica Locanda Solferino This delightful hostelry with only 11 rooms (no TV sets) is in the old Brera quarter a few blocks north of *La Scala*. Once a tavern, the place retains much Old World fin de siècle charm in its furniture and decor. No restaurant. 2 Via Castelfidardo (phone: 290-05205; fax: 657-1361).

Manzoni Small, pleasant, and quiet, it's right in the city's center, and boasts a garage. The 52 rooms have no TV sets, and there's no restaurant, but room service provides snacks. There's an English-speaking concierge, and a shopping mall nearby. 20 Via Santo Spirito (phone: 760-05700; fax: 754212).

Napoleon This small hotel in a nearby suburb offers good value. On the metro line just southeast of the train station, it has 41 soundproof rooms, friendly service, and a pleasant decor, but no restaurant. 12 Via Ozanam (phone: 295-20366; fax: 295-20388).

EATING OUT

Milan's restaurants are among the world's finest. Like much northern fare, *la cucina milanese* differs from other Italian food in that butter is used more often than olive oil. Look for special dishes made with the fabulous *tartufi bianchi* (white truffles) from the neighboring Piedmont region, in season between September and *Christmas*. Rice from the region's plantations is used as a food base, with saffron-perfumed *risotto alla milanese* the favorite provender—best eaten with a steaming osso buco (veal shank). The Milanese also love fresh fish. In September, try delicious white peaches; in December, panettone, a classic sweet brioche filled with candied fruits, is a must. Expect to pay $300 or more for dinner for two at very expensive restaurants—among the priciest in Italy; from $190 to $300 at an expensive place; from $100 to $180 at a moderately priced restaurant; and from $50 to $100 at an inexpensive one. Prices don't include drinks, wine, or tips. It is a good idea to check whether the restaurant you select accepts credit cards. All telephone numbers are in the 2 city code unless otherwise indicated. All restaurants are open for lunch and dinner unless otherwise noted.

For an unforgettable dining experience, we begin with our culinary favorites, followed by our cost and quality choices, listed by price category.

DELIGHTFUL DINING

Aimo and Nadia Gastronomes in search of light, full-flavored food with a Tuscan accent travel from far and wide to this refined and much-praised spot on the outskirts of the city. The menu, which varies with the season, features specialties such as risotto with zucchini blossoms and truffles, ricotta-stuffed zucchini flowers, super-fresh raw tomato soup, spaghetti with a sauce of baby onions and tomatoes, stuffed swordfish, and pheasant with wild mushrooms. Exceptional cheeses and luscious desserts provide the grand finale. Closed Saturday lunch, Sundays, and August. Reservations necessary. Major credit cards accepted. 6 Via Montecuccoli (phone: 416886).

Antica Osteria del Ponte In an old-fashioned inn by a bridge along a picturesque *naviglio* (canal) is one of Italy's few restaurants to be awarded three Michelin stars, plus kudos from all major Italian culinary guides; indeed, it may be Italy's best. Look for creative presentations of classic risotto, as with zucchini blossoms laced with saffron or drenched under precious truffles (in season); ravioli (try the ravioli stuffed with lobster and covered with a lobster sauce); and new and interesting preparations of fresh fish. The wine list and desserts are outstanding. The intimate, antiques-furnished dining room is warmed by a fireplace. Closed Sundays, Mondays, *Christmas* to January 12, and August. Reservations necessary. Major credit cards accepted. Near Abbiategrasso, 15 miles (24 km) from Milan, at 9 Piazza Castello, Cassinetta di Lugagnano (phone: 942-0034).

VERY EXPENSIVE

Biffi Scala Since 1931, this restaurant has been a favorite for late-night suppers, particularly after the opera. The decor is sumptuous, the fare Lombard and international. Closed Sundays, two weeks in August, and *Christmas* week. Reservations necessary. Major credit cards accepted. Piazza della Scala (phone: 866651).

Savini La Callas used to dine here with Arturo Toscanini, and this place still hits the high notes. Today's diners can enjoy some of the style at easier prices by ordering the *menu degustazione*. Otherwise, go for Milanese specialties like an impeccable risotto with saffron or the *cotoletta milanese,* a breaded veal cutlet that is to that traditional dish what La Callas was to *Tosca:* perfection. Vegetables, salads, and desserts off a cart also merit applause. Closed Sundays, 10 days in mid-August, and 10 days at *Christmas*. Reservations advised. Major credit cards accepted. *Galleria Vittorio Emanuele II* (phone: 720-03433; fax: 864-61060).

EXPENSIVE

Bice Years ago, Tuscan-bred Bice Mungai opened a tiny shop in which she served staples from home, such as *ribollita* (vegetable soup made with purple cabbage). From such beginnings evolved one of Milan's most chic restaurants, now run by her children, with branches in Paris, New York, and Washington, DC. Today's wide menu features both meat and fish specialties, including *risotto al pesce* (with fish). In season, wild mushrooms, stuffed pheasant, and truffle toppings are served. Closed Mondays, Tuesday lunch, and part of August. Reservations advised. Major credit cards accepted. 12 Via Borgospesso (phone: 760-02572).

Boeucc Artists dine next to financiers in this traditional and very elegant downtown restaurant. In the local dialect, *boeucc* means "hole-in-the-wall," but the clientele, service, traditional menu (here's the place for the real Milanese, saffron-perfumed risotto), and vast wine list belie the name. Closed Saturdays and Sunday lunch. Reservations advised. Major credit cards accepted. 2 Piazza Belgioioso (phone: 760-20224).

Don Lisander On summer evenings, downtown diners can enjoy the courtyard garden at this reliable old favorite. It offers a sampler menu of impeccably prepared traditional Italian dishes. Closed Sundays and two weeks at *Christmas*. Reservations advised. Major credit cards accepted. 12/A Via Manzoni (phone: 760-20130).

Al Garibaldi This relatively unpretentious eatery caters to Milan's chic young businessfolk. The kitchen dispenses topnotch inventive food with great professionalism. Open until 1 AM. Closed Fridays, Saturday lunch, August, and *Christmas*. Reservations advised. Major credit cards accepted. 7 Viale Montegrappa (phone: 659-8006).

Giannino So famous that some people reserve six months in advance, this bastion of traditional Italian fare includes fish, homemade pasta, and pastries, though it's not as good as it used to be. Elegant private dining rooms are available. Closed Sundays and August. Reservations necessary. Major credit cards accepted. 8 Via Amatore Sciesa (phone: 551-95582).

Gli Orti di Leonardo In this smart, brick-vaulted eatery, specialties include fish hors d'oeuvres and "little risotti," made with surprising ingredients. A rich choice of wines is available. Closed Sundays and most of August. Reservations advised. Major credit cards accepted. 6-8 Via Aristide de Togni (phone: 498-3476).

Peck Around the corner from the *Duomo,* this is an offshoot of the eponymous, elegant food emporium. With its masterful blend of the classics and the creative, it is taking over the block, with an adjacent delicatessen, a pricey takeout, and separate (and reasonably priced) counter service also worth trying. Closed Sundays, holidays, early January, and the first three weeks of July. Reservations advised. Major credit cards accepted. 4 Via Victor Hugo (phone: 876774).

Sadler-Osteria di Porta Cicca In one of the oldest parts of the city, this eatery with only 11 tables serves truly innovative fare. Favorites in season are *tagliolini* with zucchini blossoms and chunks of salmon, and ravioli with mixed wild mushrooms. Closed Sundays, alternate Mondays (when the restaurant offers cooking classes), the first half of January, and August. Reservations advised. Major credit cards accepted. 51 Ripa di Porta Ticinese (phone: 581-04451).

La Scaletta The *nuova cucina* at this outstanding, elegantly appointed two-room restaurant with seating for only 30 diners is so popular among the Milanese that reservations are necessary. Closed Sundays, Mondays, August, *Christmas,* and *New Year's.* No credit cards accepted. 3 Piazza Stazione Porta Genova (phone: 581-00290).

Solferino Milanese tradition holds sway in this pleasant eatery in La Brera, the artists' quarter. The menu, which varies with the season and the inspiration of the kitchen, includes intriguing potato soup with wild mushrooms; the house specialty, *risotto alla milanese*; and the real thing when it comes to the Milanese cutlet. Closed Saturday lunch, Sundays, and in mid-August. Reservations advised. Major credit cards accepted. 2 Via Castelfidardo (phone: 659-9886).

L'Ulmet Milanese adore this place for its successful combination of traditional and creative Italian fare. It was built on ancient Roman foundations, and its roof incorporates a 1,600-year-old plinth. Wild game is served in season. For dessert, try the crêpes with honey and pine nuts. Closed Sundays, Monday lunch, and August. Reservations advised. Major credit cards accepted. 21 Via Olmetto (phone: 864-52712).

MODERATE

Antica Trattoria della Pesa Founded in 1881, this old favorite retains a gaslit atmosphere. Offered are Lombard favorites such as saffron-hued risotto and garlic-flavored lamb shanks. Closed Sundays. Reservations advised. Major credit cards accepted. 10 Viale Pasubio (phone: 655-5741).

Bagutta A big and cheery Tuscan *osteria*, it serves good food, although the waiters can be brusque at times. Under the massive chestnut beams the walls are crammed with paintings from the artists who made this their hangout. Today it's always chockablock with businesspeople dining on polenta with *porcini* mushrooms, the classic *risotto alla parmigiana* with a dusting of truffles in season, or brains with artichokes. The dessert tray is laden with the restaurant's homemade *dolci.* Good chianti wines wash it all down. A patch of garden courtyard is open in the summer. Closed Sundays. Reservations unnecessary. Major credit cards accepted. 14 Via Bagutta (phone: 760-02767).

Bistrot di Gualtiero Marchesi The lacy marble fretwork of the *Duomo* roof seems close enough to touch from this eatery on the seventh floor of *La Rinascente* department store. Italy's most famous chef presides over a place that is simple, chic, and a good value. The prix fixe menu offers traditional Milanese dishes that vary according to season. Valuable modern art adorns the walls. Adjacent is a pleasant but sometimes noisy coffee shop with the same magnificent view. Closed Sundays, Monday lunch, and August. Reservations advised. Major credit cards accepted. During store hours take the escalator; in the evening, enter from 2 Via San Raffaele (phone: 877120).

La Briciola High-fashion models, journalists, and young Milanese-about-town enjoy the light touch of host Giorgio Valveri's homemade pasta, salads, and fresh fish. Good value for the money. Closed Sundays and Monday lunch. Reservations necessary. Most credit cards accepted. 25 Via Solferino (phone: 655-1012).

Alla Clausura Swiss-Italian fare is served in this extremely popular establishment. Specialties of the intimate dining room include *penne alle melanzane* (pasta with eggplant) and *filetto al midollo e rosti* (steak with marrow and Swiss potatoes). The desserts, such as *pinolata* (cream cake topped with pine nuts), are excellent. Closed Sundays and one week in August. Reservations advised. Major credit cards accepted. 13 Via Navarra (phone: 837-8366).

Le Colline Pisane A spot for Tuscan fare, this lively trattoria serves fine food in pleasant surroundings. Closed Sundays and August. Reservations advised. Major credit cards accepted. 5 Largo la Foppa (phone: 659-9136).

Giardino Near the banks of the Naviglio River, this restaurant serves simple but delicious food in an atmosphere reminiscent of a 19th-century Milanese tavern or *osteria.* There is alfresco dining in summer. Closed Tuesdays. Reservations unnecessary. No credit cards accepted. 36 Alzaia Naviglio Grande (phone: 894-09321).

Alle Langhe This popular family-style trattoria serves Piedmontese fare that makes visitors feel welcome. Closed Sundays and most of August. Reservations advised. Major credit cards accepted. 6 Corso Como (phone: 655-4279).

Osteria del Binari Elegant, with an impressive choice of traditional dishes from several Italian regions. The hot soup is topped with an incredibly light puff pastry. Closed for lunch, Sundays, and three weeks in August. Reservations advised. Major credit cards accepted. 1 Via Tortona (phone: 894-06753).

INEXPENSIVE

Al Materel It's rustic Lombardy at its best, with old family recipes, homemade pasta, polenta, and wild game and wild mushrooms in season. Closed Tuesdays, Wednesday lunch, and July. Reservations advised. No credit cards accepted. Corner of Via Laura Solera Montegazza and Corso Garibaldi (phone: 654204).

Montenero This former trattoria is now gussied up and trendy, but it still offers bargains. There are two tasting menus, one expensive and the other less so. The desserts are worth the calories. Closed Sundays and August. Reservations advised. Most credit cards accepted. 34 Via Montenero (phone: 550-19104).

Il Mozzo Pizza is made the right way here, in a wood-burning oven. Brave the evening crowds to try the *pizza alla romana* (tomato, mozzarella, ricotta, and fresh basil in season) or *alla fiamma* (onions, rosemary, and hot red pepper). Closed Wednesdays. Reservations advised. No credit cards accepted. 22 Via Marghera (phone: 498-4676).

Al Pont de Ferr This wine shop/food emporium is hard by an iron bridge (hence its name) crossing the Naviglio Grande, a colorful grand canal. House specialties include pasta, gnocchi, and a few meat dishes. Let the sommelier guide you through the excellent wine list. Closed lunch, Sundays, August, and *Christmas*. Reservations advised. Most credit cards accepted. 55 Ripa di Porta Ticinese (phone: 890-46277).

Rigolo Large and friendly, it's a favorite of local journalists and businesspeople. Tuscan specialties (such as thick, grilled steaks) and a superb selection of homemade desserts are the chief draws. Closed Mondays and August. Reservations advised. Major credit cards accepted. 11 Via Solferino (phone: 804589).

La Risotteria Here's the spot—small, friendly, and always crowded—to test Milan's all-time favorite dish, risotto, in its myriad forms, from the classic Milanese version bright with saffron to trendy fruit-laced concoctions. The variety of salads is interesting, and the desserts are homemade. Closed Saturday dinner, Sundays, and August. Reservations advised. Some credit cards accepted. 2 Via Dandolo (phone: 551-81694).

La Topaia This restaurant features specialties from Liguria, the former Yugoslavia, and the French countryside. With a new verandah for alfresco dining, it is a summertime favorite. Closed Sundays and for lunch. Reservations advised. Major credit cards accepted. In the Naviglio canals quarter, at 46 Via Argelati (phone: 837-3469).

Trattoria Milanese Founded in 1919, it's still a repository of genuine gastronomic tradition, including *risotto alla milanese* and mixed boiled meats. Closed Tuesdays, August, and *Christmas*. Reservations advised. Most credit cards accepted. 11 Via Santa Marta (phone: 864-51991).

Trattoria Toscana Pagni Traditional Tuscan cuisine is served in this family eatery. Try a platter of salami as a starter and then the homemade *pappardelle ai carciofi* (flat noodles with artichoke sauce), or make a single dish of the wild boar with polenta (winter only). Closed Saturday dinner, Sundays, and August. Reservations advised. Some credit cards accepted. 7 Via Orti (phone: 550-11267).

BARS AND CAFFÈS

After a full day of gallery-hopping or nonstop shopping, Milan's many *caffès* and pastry shops are good places to stop for lighter meals and to satisfy those with a sweet tooth. The following is our favorite, followed by a selection of recommended snack spots. Most bars and *caffès* described below are in the inexpensive price range.

A CLASSIC CAFFÈ

Cucchi Sip your Bellini (fresh peach juice and champagne) outdoors in the summer and eye Armani-clad executives. Or nurse a Negroni (red vermouth and gin) indoors in the winter amid the pink velvet and chandeliers preserved from the 1930s, when *tutto* Milano came here to dance. It's renowned for its pastries (the Sacher torte is a wonder); you might want to time your visit for 7:45 AM to sample brioche fresh from the oven. Closed Mondays. 1 Corso Genova (phone: 839-9793).

Milan boasts some of Italy's best *paninerie* (sandwich shops), which offer a variety of hot and cold sandwiches. Try *Montanelli American Bar* (inside the courtyard by *Buccellati* at 12 Via Montenapoleone; no phone); *Bar Magenta* (13 Via Carducci; phone: 805-3808); or *Paninomania* (12 Corso Porta Romana; phone: 576827). Most frequented by local office and fashion industry workers are the tiny coffee bars inside some of downtown Milan's charming courtyards. Some also offer inexpensive, pleasant lunches—a plate of pasta, a cooked vegetable, and a glass of wine.

For Milan's best coffee, visit *Marches* (Via Meravigli); customers must stand at the bar, but they linger over hand-dipped chocolates and the Milanese *Christmas* specialty, the panettone. For tea and chocolates, the *Sant'Ambroeus* (7 Corso Matteotti) is the place to go—big, old-fashioned, and charming, with immense Venetian chandeliers and matrons in furs. The 166-year-old *Cova* (near *La Scala* at 8 Via Montenapoleone; phone: 760-00578) has pink damask tablecloths and waiters in black tie; try the hand-dipped *kikingerli*-filled (sour cherry) chocolates, and take home some candied violets. Conveniently located in the shopping district off a courtyard is *Babington's* (8 Via Sant'Andrea), a sister in spirit to the English tearoom in Rome, with Victorian decor. At the *Café Radetzky* (105 Corso Garibaldi), a 15-minute walk from downtown, the atmosphere of Milan 150 years ago, when the Austrians ruled, has been lovingly re-created in a stylish coffee shop. And sundowners say "cheers" at *Caffè Milano* (1 Piazza Mirabello; phone: 290-03300).

Wheat germ, honey, and pine nuts are only a few of the tempting ice-cream flavors offered at *Gelateria Ecologica Artigiana* (40 Porto Ticinese; phone: 581018), whose name roughly translates as "Craftsman's Environmental Ice Creamery." It stays open until well after midnight.

Naples

Naples, Gothic and Baroque under an azure sky, intellectual capital of the Mezzogiorno, and Italy's third-most-populated city, with nearly 1.7 million inhabitants, has often been described as one of the world's most beautiful seaports. Indeed, the magnificent Bay of Naples has long been lauded by its many illustrious visitors for its gently curving shoreline and palm-lined seaside avenues, mild climate, and romantic islands.

But Naples has always had a darker side. Brooding Mt. Vesuvius, ever hovering over the city, buried neighboring Pompeii and Herculaneum when it erupted in AD 79. And the eerie Campi Flegrei (Phlegrean Fields), a steaming volcanic area just to the north, whose violent beauty inspired both Homer and Virgil, was regarded by the ancients as the entrance to the underworld. More recently the earthquake that devastated southern Italy in 1980 took a tragic toll in Naples, adding yet another major problem to the city's permanent ills of unemployment, crime, and traffic congestion.

The city's Old Quarter is among the most densely populated areas in the world; infant mortality and unemployment rates here are among the highest in Italy. Almost a fifth of Naples's labor force is unemployed, and another estimated 40,000 persons derive their livelihood from smuggling. The crime rate here is one of the highest in Italy, principally because of the stranglehold of the Camorra—the Neapolitan version of the Mafia—on the city and surrounding areas. (Visitors should watch out for their personal belongings, especially purses.) When a cholera outbreak in 1973 revealed that Naples had no sewers and was living on a beautiful but poisoned bay, "See Naples and Die," once a popular saying beckoning visitors to the seductive charms of the city, suddenly acquired a morbid significance. And it is here that the Mussolini name has risen again in Italian politics: Alessandra Mussolini, the granddaughter of Il Duce, won a seat in Parliament in 1992 as a member of the country's neo-Fascist party from her district in Naples, and has shown that she has continued his legacy.

But the poor of Naples continue to survive with a surprising stoicism, and the people themselves are one of the city's attractions, laughing off their many problems, helping each other with an extraordinary sense of warmth and humanity—they are a strongly emotional and sensitive people.

Naples is a theater of life. Stroll along Via Caracciolo and see the fishermen pulling in their nets, oblivious to the traffic behind them; buy lemons and oranges or sulfur water from men and women who transact their business across 17th-century marble tabletops; give in to the importuning of pizza vendors hawking their pies; or, when the jostling of the small, crowded streets becomes too much to bear, retire to a table in the elegant *Galleria Umberto I* or to the old *Caffè Gambrinus* on Via Chiaia and watch well-dressed Neapolitans socialize over an afternoon coffee or *aperitivo*.

Naples also is famous for its music, its festivals, and its colorful arts. Neapolitan popular songs are, short of operatic arias, the best-known tunes to have come out of Italy. In the 17th and 18th centuries the works of a Neapolitan school of composers—Alessandro Scarlatti was its leader—were just as well known; Pergolesi, Paisiello, and Cimarosa drew capacity crowds. The city's opera house, *Teatro San Carlo,* built in 1737, remains one of the world's finest (for details, see *Music*). A Neapolitan school of painting, characterized by realism and warm colors, flourished in the 18th and 19th centuries. In the 18th century, too, the famous Capodimonte porcelain factory was turning out highly elaborate pieces for members of the royal court, while less exalted folk artists were raising the making of nativity scenes into an art form. The shepherds and angels of many an *ignoto Napoletano* (unknown Neapolitan) live on in museums, and at *Christmastime,* an entire street—Via San Gregorio Armeno—is taken over by artisans selling their hand-crafted *presepi,* or crèche scenes. If you are in Naples then, don't miss the giant crèche in the *Galleria Umberto I,* which depicts scenes from Neapolitan life, complete with fishmongers, tavern keepers serving jugs brimming with wine, and peasants tilling the fields. There are also permanent crèches on display in the cloister of the *Chiesa di Santa Chiara* and in the *Certosa di San Martino* (Carthusian Monastery of St. Martin), now a museum.

The city that was to spawn so much natural talent was founded as a Greek colony, probably in the 7th century BC, and was first called Parthenope, later Neapolis. Little remains of its earliest period. Then, along with the rest of the Italian peninsula, it became part of the great Roman Empire, and its intensely green countryside and sunny shores were soon studded with palatial villas of wealthy Romans who chose to spend the winters in Naples's milder climate.

But the tranquillity of the Roman period came to an end with the fall of the empire, and Naples sank into the abyss of the Dark Ages. The city came into its own again under the French rulers of the House of Anjou, who made it the capital of their Angevin kingdom of southern Italy in the 13th century, and continued its progress under the Catalonian rulers of the House of Aragon, who took over in 1442. Then, in 1503, Naples (with Sicily) became a part of Spain, ruled for more than two centuries by viceroys who exploited the Italian provinces for the benefit of the Spanish treasury. So heavily taxed were the commoners (nobles and clergy were exempt) that in 1647 they rose up, led by Masaniello, but the revolution was crushed. After a short period under Austrian rule, it was the turn of the Bourbons, who arrived in 1734 and established the Kingdom of the Two Sicilies, with Naples as the capital. Its ancient dignity restored, Naples became one of Europe's major cities, attracting leaders in art, music, and literature until the unification of Italy in 1870. Economic and political problems gradually diminished its prestige, however, and damage from World War II dealt a severe blow to an already sick economy.

Today, thanks to a busy port, Naples is an important industrial and commercial center. It is a city both wise and violent, religious and pagan, magical and dirty, old and new. It attracts thieves, tourists, artists, and lovers of beauty with a contagious gaiety and exuberant, if chaotic, vitality. Its wealth of historical monuments; proximity to the Amalfi Coast, Capri, and the archaeological treasures of Pompeii and Herculaneum; and the magnificent—if somewhat tarnished—splendors of the romantic Bay of Naples make it one of the world's great cities and a perennial tourist attraction.

Naples At-a-Glance

SEEING THE CITY

Panoramic views of Naples and the bay can be found at every turn. In the city the outstanding view is from Room 25 of the *Certosa di San Martino* (Via Tito Angelini), now a museum. Depending on the weather and the visibility, however, the most spectacular view is from Mt. Vesuvius, some 15 miles (24 km) southeast of Naples. For more information on both these vantage points, see *Special Places*, below.

SPECIAL PLACES

To facilitate sightseeing, think of Naples as divided into sections. In the area roughly between Piazza Municipio and Piazza del Plebiscito are monumental buildings. The Old Quarter is near narrow Via Spacca-Napoli (the classic photos of streets strung with washing are taken here), and the historic center is to the northeast. Farther inland is Naples on the hills, the Vomero being the principal hill and an elegant residential and shopping district. To the west of the Piazza del Plebiscito area is Naples by the bay. Where the working port ends, a lovely promenade begins along the shore before the port of Santa Lucia and extends as far as another port area, Mergellina. Unless otherwise noted, museums in Naples are closed Mondays; Tuesdays through Saturdays after 2 PM; and Sundays and holidays after 1 PM.

DOWNTOWN

CASTEL NUOVO (NEW CASTLE) More often called *Castel Angioino* (Angevin Castle) or *Maschio Angioino,* this waterfront landmark was built in the late 13th century by Charles I of Anjou, who modeled it after the castle at Angers, France. In the mid-15th century Alphonse I of Aragon made substantial alterations. The restored triumphal arch sandwiched between two towers at the entry celebrates his entrance into Naples in 1443 and is an early example of Renaissance art in Naples. Inside the courtyard the doorway to the *Cappella di Santa Barbara* (Chapel of St. Barbara), the only part of the castle remaining from Angevin times, is noteworthy, but most of the castle is closed to visitors. Open to the public are a small museum in the chapel, with 14th- and 15th-century frescoes and sculptures, and the south wing of the castle, where paintings and silver and bronze objects from the 15th through the 20th century are displayed. Both are closed Sundays; weekdays after 2 PM; and Saturdays after 1:30 PM. Admission charge. Piazza Municipio (phone: 551-9662).

PALAZZO REALE (ROYAL PALACE) Built in the early 17th century by Domenico Fontana for the Spanish viceroys, and later enlarged and restored, this became the home of the Bourbon Kings of Naples; it also was inhabited from time to time by the Kings of Italy. The niches on the façade contain statues of eight famous kings of the various dynasties that ruled Naples, including Charles I of Anjou, Alphonse I of Aragon, and Victor Emmanuel II of Italy. The palace is now a museum whose rooms contain original Bourbon furnishings, paintings, statues, and porcelain. Closed Mondays and for a long midday break. Admission charge. Piazza del Plebiscito (phone: 413888).

PIAZZA DEL PLEBISCITO This vast semicircle cut off on one side by the *Palazzo Reale* is the center of public life in Naples. Directly opposite the palace is the *Chiesa di San Francesco di Paola* (Church of St. Francis of Paola), a copy of the *Pantheon* in Rome, built by order of Ferdinand I of Bourbon in the late 18th century. Equestrian statues in the center of the square are of Ferdinand (by Canova) and Charles III of Bourbon.

GALLERIA UMBERTO I Across the street from the *Teatro San Carlo,* this is the perfect place to sit down for a *caffè* or an ice cream. The Victorian arcade of glass and steel, topped with a cupola, was built from 1887 to 1890.

CHIESA DI SANT'ANNA DEI LOMBARDI (CHURCH OF ST. ANNE OF THE LOMBARDS) This church was constructed in the 15th century and rebuilt in the 17th century. It is best known for its Renaissance sculptures, particularly the eight life-size terra cotta figures of the *Pietà* (1492) by Guido Mazzoni— extremely realistic and rather eerie when seen from the main part of the church (it's in a chapel to the right at the far end). Via Monteoliveto (no phone).

CHIESA DI SANTA CHIARA (CHURCH OF ST. CLARE) The church of the Order of Poor Clares was built for Sancia of Majorca, wife of Robert I of Anjou, in the early 14th century. From the beginning it was the church of the Neapolitan nobility. By the 18th century it was covered with Baroque decoration; following serious damage in World War II, it was rebuilt in its original Provençal Gothic style. Be sure to see the 14th-century tomb of Robert of Anjou behind the altar. Then go out to see the adjoining *Chiostro delle Clarisse* (Cloister of the Poor Clares), a unique 18th-century bower of greenery and flowers studded with columns and lined with seats entirely covered with majolica tiles—a colorful surprise. Via Benedetto Croce (phone: 552-6209).

CHIESA DEL GESÙ NUOVO Across the square from *Santa Chiara* on land surrounding the *Palazzo Sanseverino,* the interior of this late-16th-century church is full of Baroque marblework and painting. The unusual façade originally was built in the 15th century for the palace. Piazza del Gesù Nuovo (phone: 551-8613).

CHIESA DI SAN LORENZO MAGGIORE (CHURCH OF ST. LAWRENCE MAJOR) One of the most important medieval churches in Naples, it was begun in the late 13th century by French architects, who did the polygonal Gothic apse, and was finished in the next century by local architects. Boccaccio fell in love with Fiammetta in this church in 1334, and Petrarch, who was living in the adjoining monastery, came here to pray during a terrible storm in 1345. Excavations at this site uncovered some Greek and Roman ruins. Piazza San Gaetano (phone: 290580).

DUOMO (CATHEDRAL) Naples's cathedral is dedicated to the city's patron saint, San Gennaro. It was built by the Angevins (in the late 13th and early 14th centuries) on the site of a previous basilica dedicated to Santa Stefania, which in its turn had been built on the foundations of a Roman temple dedicated to Apollo. It also incorporates a smaller basilica dating from the 5th century and dedicated to Santa Restituta. Rebuilt several times, the *Duomo*'s 19th-century façade still sports 15th-century doorways. It contains the famous *Cappella di San Gennaro* (third chapel on the right), a triumph of 17th-century Baroque art built in fulfillment of a vow made by Neapolitans for the passing of a plague. (The Latin inscription notes that the chapel is consecrated to the saint for his having saved the city not only from plague but also from hunger, war, and the fires of Vesuvius, by virtue of his miraculous blood.) Two vials of San Gennaro's dried blood are stored in a reliquary in the chapel; twice a year people gather at the church to await the miracle of the liquefaction of the blood (see *Special Events*). Via del Duomo (phone: 449097).

MUSEO ARCHEOLOGICO NAZIONALE (NATIONAL ARCHAEOLOGICAL MUSEUM) One of the world's most important museums dedicated to Greco-Roman antiquity is located in this 16th-century palace; it was first a barracks and then the seat of the university until 1777, when the Bourbon King of Naples turned it into a museum. Among its precious holdings are sculptures collected by Pope Paul III of the Farnese family during 16th-century excavations of the ruins of Rome, including two huge statues found at the *Baths of Caracalla:* the *Farnese Hercules,* a Greek copy of a bronze original by Lysippus, and the *Farnese Bull,* a Roman copy of a Hellenistic bronze, carved from a single block of marble. The museum also is the repository of art and artifacts removed from Pompeii and Herculaneum since the 18th century. Most impressive of these are the exquisite mosaics from Pompeii and the bronzes from the *Villa dei Papiri* at Herculaneum, especially the water carriers (or dancers) and the two athletes. Other items from these cities include silver- and glassware; combs, mirrors, and other toiletry articles; some furniture; and foodstuffs, such as carbonized bread, olives, grapes, onions, figs, and dates. A five-room exhibit features restored objects and magnificent frescoes from the *Temple of Isis,* first discovered at Pompeii in 1765. Two other important displays are the Santangelo collection of ancient coins and the Borgia collection of Egyptian and Etruscan art. Admission charge. Piazza Museo (phone: 440166).

CATACOMBE DI SAN GENNARO (CATACOMBS OF ST. JANUARIUS) The remains of San Gennaro lay in these catacombs from the 5th to the 9th century. On two levels, the catacombs date from the 2nd century and probably began as the tomb of a noble family that was later donated to the Christian community as a burial place. They are important for their early Christian wall paintings. Guided visits (most are in Italian, but some English-speaking tours are available) take place daily in August; Fridays through Sundays in July and September; and Thursdays through Sundays from October through June. Admission charge. 16 Via di Capodimonte, past the *Chiesa della Madre del Buon Consiglio* (phone: 881232).

MUSEO E GALLERIE NAZIONALI DI CAPODIMONTE (CAPODIMONTE MUSEUM AND PICTURE GALLERY) One of Italy's best collections of paintings from the 14th through the 16th century is displayed in the grandiose 18th-century palace of a former royal estate on the hills in the northeastern part of the city. A Simone Martini panel (1317) of Robert of Anjou being crowned King of Naples is one of the museum's treasures; also represented are Bellini, Masaccio, Botticelli, and Correggio. In the Titian room is a well-known portrait of Pope Paul III and other members of the Farnese family. The royal apartments on the first floor include a marvelous parlor, the *Salottino di Maria Amalia,* completely built and decorated in Capodimonte ceramics (some were shattered in the 1980 earthquake). Surrounding the palace is a favorite among Naples's parks. Closed Mondays and after 2 PM October through May; closed Sundays after 2 PM and Mondays the rest of the year. Admission charge. *Parco di Capodimonte* (phone: 744-1307).

CERTOSA DI SAN MARTINO (CARTHUSIAN MONASTERY AND NATIONAL MUSEUM OF ST. MARTIN) Now a museum, this enormous monastery founded by the Angevin dynasty is beautifully situated on Vomero Hill, next to an Angevin fortress, *Castel Sant'Elmo.* The monastery was renovated in the 16th and 17th centuries (in the latter period by Cosimo Fanzago), so it is today a monument to the Baroque. The church immediately to the left as you enter is lavishly done in Baroque inlay of variously colored marbles and stones (see, too, the rooms behind the altar, including the one to the left with an intricate inlay of wood). In the museum the marvelous view from the belvedere of Room 25 is said to have inspired the saying "See Naples and Die." The museum contains a collection of 19th-century Neapolitan painting, a naval section, memorabilia from the Kingdom of Naples, and some striking 18th- and 19th-century *presepi* (nativity scenes). The most famous is the *Presepe Cuciniello,* a room-size installation with countless figures and particularly graceful angels. Another *presepe* fits in an eggshell. The museum remains open until 8 PM Tuesdays, Thursdays, and Saturdays in August and September. Admission charge. Via Tito Angelini (phone: 578-1769).

PORTO DI SANTA LUCIA E IL LUNGOMARE (SANTA LUCIA PORT AND THE WATERFRONT)
One of the best-known Neapolitan songs has immortalized this tiny port abob with picturesque fishing and pleasure boats. It is formed by a jetty that leads out from the mainland to a small island entirely occupied by the Borgo Marinaro, a so-called fishing village now populated largely with restaurants, and *Castel dell'Ovo* (Egg Castle). The fortress dates from the 12th century, but monks lived here even earlier, and in Roman times a patrician villa occupied the site. Santa Lucia is the focal point of seaside Naples: Via Nazario Sauro approaches it from the east; Via Partenope passes in front of it; and Via Caracciolo leads away from it to the west. The three together constitute Naples's *lungomare,* a broad promenade along the water that is *the* place in Naples to take an early evening *passeggiata* (stroll) and watch the sun go down. For at least a half mile of its length, Via Caracciolo is backed by the greenery of the *Villa Comunale* public park, which is filled with Neapolitans enjoying themselves. Ice cream is consumed by all.

ENVIRONS

CAMPI FLEGREI (PHLEGREAN FIELDS) Hot springs and sulfurous gases rise from this dark, violent volcanic area that extends west of Naples from Capo Posillipo to Capo Miseno, along the Gulf of Pozzuoli. Its name comes from the Greek for "burning," and it is as rich in archaeological remains as in geophysical phenomena. The remnants of the Greek colony of Cuma, founded in the 8th century BC (the oldest archaeological site in Italy), are about 11 miles (18 km) west of Naples (closed Mondays; admission charge). To get there by car, take S7 in the direction of Formia, and turn left 3 miles (5 km) past Pozzuoli (8 miles/13 km from Naples) to Cuma. There are remains of Roman baths at Baia (closed Mondays; admission charge), which is 5 miles (8 km) past Pozzuoli on an unmarked road signposted "Baia-Bacoli." Sophia Loren's hometown, Pozzuoli is also home to Italy's third-largest amphitheater, built when the town was a major port in Roman times (closed Mondays; admission charge). Also in Pozzuoli is a Roman temple, partially submerged in water, that reveals the effects of bradyseism, or "slow earthquake," to which the whole area is subject; less or more of the pillars is visible as the earth rises and falls. Lakes—such as Lago d'Averno (said to have been the entrance to the underworld) and Lago Miseno—have formed in the craters of extinct volcanoes in the Campi Flegrei, but the Solfatara crater just north of Pozzuoli is merely dormant (its last eruption was in the 12th century). Full of steaming fumaroles and containing the remains of a Roman spa, it is open daily (admission charge). Pozzuoli is the last stop of the *metropolitana* from Piazza Garibaldi in Naples; Baia and Cuma are stops on the suburban *Ferrovia Cumana* train line leaving from Piazza Montesanto.

VESUVIO (MT. VESUVIUS) About 15 miles (24 km) southeast of Naples is this still-active volcano; it last erupted in 1944 and has averaged one eruption every 35 years over the past 300. For more details, see *Campania and the Amalfi Coast* in DIRECTIONS. Take the Naples-Salerno autostrada to Ercolano; from there it is an 8-mile (13-km) drive with spectacular views. To reach Vesuvius by public transportation, take the *Circumvesuviana* railway (*Napoli–Barra–Torre del Greco–Torre Annunziata* line) from *Stazione Circumvesuviana* on Corso Garibaldi (see *Train*). Get off at Herculaneum (Ercolano) or Pugliano, then take a bus to the *stazione inferiore*, where an English-speaking guide may be hired. Be prepared for a long, steep climb; take comfortable shoes. Don't bother going on an overcast day.

EXTRA SPECIAL

No stay in Naples is complete without a sunny drive up the famed promontory of Posillipo, a few miles southwest of the center, perhaps culminating in an alfresco lunch at Marechiaro (a picturesque fishing village built high above the sea), which overlooks the southern end of the Bay of Naples. The road from the Mergellina port area climbs past fragrant gardens and some of the most lavish villas in Naples—including the summer residence of the President of Italy—becoming Via Nuova di Posillipo, which was begun by order of Murat, King of Naples, and completed in 1830. Don't miss the view of Cape Posillipo (from Via Ferdinando Russo just past Piazza Salvatore di Giacomo) before continuing up Via Nuova di Posillipo, which ends at Marechiaro. It was made famous by a song of the same name written by Salvatore di Giacomo, the first line of which is inscribed in the wall of an old house overlooking the water. On the way back take Via Nuova di Posillipo, turn right onto Via Giovanni Boccaccio, and stop at the *Parco della Rimembranza* for spectacular views of the Bay of Naples on one side and the Bay of Pozzuoli on the other.

Sources and Resources

TOURIST INFORMATION

For general information, brochures, and maps of Naples and its environs, contact the *Ente Provinciale per il Turismo* (*EPT;* 58 Piazza dei Martiri, Staircase B; phone: 405311; fax: 401961). Branches or booths are located at the *Stazione Centrale* (Piazza Garibaldi; phone: 268779); the *Stazione di Mergellina* (phone: 761-2102); and the *Aeroporto di Capodichino* (phone:

780-5761). The *Azienda Autonoma di Soggiorno e Turismo di Napoli (AAST),* or local tourist office, is based in the *Palazzo Reale* (Piazza del Plebiscito; phone: 418744; fax: 418691). Its branches include one at Piazza del Gesù Nuovo (phone: 552-3328 or 551-2701); one at *Castel dell'Ovo* (phone: 764-5688); and another at the hydrofoil terminal in Mergellina (phone: 761-4585). All tourist offices are closed Sundays and for a long (1 to 4:30 PM) midday break June through September; closed weekends and for the same midday break the rest of the year.

LOCAL COVERAGE Among other brochures, the *AAST* puts out the interesting *Naples—The Old City: A Stratified Multiple Itinerary Map*, which traces four itineraries through the historic center (roughly the area between Piazza del Gesù Nuovo and the *Duomo*), each route corresponding to a period in Neapolitan art: medieval, Renaissance, Baroque, and rococo. The office also publishes a useful booklet, *Qui Napoli,* distributed monthly to the better hotels. Listings in both publications are in Italian and English. Another good monthly, bilingual guide is *Napoli Top,* available at bars, hotels, and newsstands. All are free of charge. The Neapolitans' daily newspaper is *Il Mattino.* English-language newspapers can be bought at most news kiosks in the center of town.

TELEPHONE The city code for Naples is 81. When calling from within Italy, dial 081 before the local number.

GETTING AROUND

Many major sights are easily accessible by foot. For others, such as *Parco di Capodimonte* and attractions on the Vomero, alternate means of transportation are desirable. Avoid driving in the city: Neapolitan traffic jams belong in the *Guinness Book of World Records.* If you do drive, *never* leave anything in your car, even for the shortest period of time. Neapolitan car thieves, among the most resourceful in the world, can open and empty a car trunk in a matter of seconds.

AIRPORT *Capodichino Airport* serves mostly domestic (phone: 709-2815) and some international flights (phone: 789-6111). A taxi ride from downtown takes anywhere from 15 to 45 minutes, depending on the traffic, and tends to be expensive; from the airport to downtown, the fare is double the meter. Night and holiday rides cost extra, as does baggage; ask to see the *tabella* (fare table). Bus No. 14 from the main train station, *Stazione Centrale,* stops at the airport. The trip, which takes 30 minutes to an hour, depending on traffic, is very inexpensive; purchase tickets in advance at a tobacco shop or newsstand. It runs every half hour from 6 AM to midnight.

Alitalia passengers flying into Rome's *Leonardo da Vinci Airport* at Fiumicino can take a train directly from the airport to the *Stazione Centrale* in Naples (and return as well). Visitors from the US have the added advantage of being able to buy train tickets when purchasing their plane tickets, and baggage can be checked straight through to Naples from the US departure point. The train leaves twice daily; the trip takes two and a half hours.

BOATS Ferries and hydrofoils for Capri, Ischia, and Procida leave from the *Molo Beverello,* in front of Piazza Municipio and *Castel Nuovo,* or from Mergellina's Porto Sannazaro. In summer, hydrofoils also depart from Mergellina to Sorrento, Positano, Amalfi, the islands of Ponza and Ventotene, Sicily, and the Aeolian Islands. Sailing times are listed in *Il Mattino* and at tourist offices.

BUS AND TRAM Main routes and schedules are listed in the supplement to the telephone directory, *Tutto Città.* Tickets must be bought in advance at a tobacco shop or newsstand. Also available are half-day tickets that allow unlimited bus and tram travel all morning or all afternoon.

CAR RENTAL Major international firms are represented. Note that few gas stations are open at night; check with your hotel or see the listings in *Qui Napoli* or *Napoli Top.*

FUNICULAR Four funicular lines connect lower-lying parts of Naples to neighborhoods on the hills. Of the three that go to the Vomero, the *Funicolare Centrale,* from Via Toledo to Piazza Fuga, is most useful for visiting the *Certosa di San Martino.* (The *Funicolare di Montesanto,* which goes from Piazza Montesanto to Via Morghen, was closed at press time for renovation.) The fourth funicular connects the Mergellina area to the Posillipo area.

SUBWAY The *metropolitana* runs from Napoli Gianturco to Pozzuoli Solfatara, making useful stops at the *Stazione Centrale,* Piazza Cavour (near the *Museo Archeologico Nazionale*), Piazza Montesanto and Piazza Amedeo (near funiculars), Mergellina, Campi Flegrei, and elsewhere en route.

TAXI Hail cabs as they cruise, or pick one up at a stand. For a radio-dispatched taxi, call 556-4444, 570-7070, or 556-0202. Do not use unmetered taxis.

TRAIN Naples's main train station is the *Stazione Centrale* (Piazza Garibaldi; phone: 553-4188), but many intercity trains also use the *Stazione di Mergellina* (phone: 680635), whose seafront location is more convenient for catching ferries to the islands at Porto Sannazaro. Trains to Herculaneum, Pompeii, and Sorrento, operated by the suburban railway, *Ferrovia Circumvesuviana,* leave from the nearby *Stazione Circumvesuviana* (Corso Garibaldi; phone: 779-2444) and can be reached by the down escalator from the *Stazione Centrale.* Trains to Campi Flegrei points, operated by *Ferrovia Cumana* (phone: 551-3328), another suburban railway, leave from Piazza Montesanto.

SPECIAL EVENTS

Twice a year (on the Saturday before the first Sunday in May and on September 19) Neapolitans crowd into the *Duomo* and pray for the *Miracolo,* the liquefying of the dried blood of San Gennaro—their patron saint—that is kept in two vials in a chapel of the church. The miracle is supposed to have occurred first on the hands of a bishop transporting San Gennaro's body after the saint was martyred on the orders of Emperor Diocletian in Pozzuoli on September 19, 305, and it has been happening regularly since the first recorded recurrence in 1389—regularly, but not *always*. The event is something of a mass fortune-telling, because when it fails, disaster is expected to befall the city—in the past it might have been plague, in the future it could be Vesuvius. (The blood failed to liquefy during the last eruption of Vesuvius, in 1944.) Nowhere is the atmosphere more alive with anticipation than in the chapel downstairs, where San Gennaro's bones are kept and the people plead for a sign. (For information on details of the liquefaction, call 449097.) Other important festivals celebrate the feast of *Santa Maria del Carmine* on July 16 and the *Madonna di Piedigrotta,* which lasts several days in early September.

MUSEUMS AND CHURCHES

In addition to those mentioned in *Special Places,* a number of other museums and churches are impressive. All museums charge admission unless otherwise noted.

ACQUARIO (AQUARIUM) One of the oldest in Europe (1872), it houses some 200 species of Mediterranean marine life, all collected from the Bay of Naples. Closed Mondays. *Villa Comunale* (phone: 583-3111).

CAPPELLA SANSEVERO (SANSEVERO CHAPEL) The funerary chapel of the Sangro family contains the *Veiled Christ* by Giuseppe Sammartino and many other 18th-century sculptures. Closed Mondays and Wednesdays through Saturdays for a long (1 to 5 PM) break; closed Tuesdays and Sundays after 1 PM. 19 Via Francesco de Sanctis (phone: 551-8470).

CHIESA DI SAN DOMENICO MAGGIORE (CHURCH OF ST. DOMINIC MAJOR) This frequently restored 13th-century church contains the famous crucifix of St. Thomas Aquinas (who lived and taught in the adjoining monastery) and paintings by Titian, Luca Giordano, Solimena, Simone Martini, and others. Closed Mondays; Tuesdays through Saturdays after 2 PM; and Sundays and holidays after 1 PM. Piazza San Domenico (phone: 551-7006).

CHIESA DI SAN GREGORIO ARMENO (CHURCH OF ST. GREGORY OF ARMENIA) A Baroque church worth a visit for its famous nativity scene (on view only during *Christmastime*). Open daily. Via San Gregorio Armeno.

CHIESA DI SAN PAOLO MAGGIORE (CHURCH OF ST. PAUL MAJOR) This church of the late 16th century, wonderfully Neapolitan Baroque in style, has paintings by Stanzione, Solimena, and Paolo de Matteis. Open daily. Piazza San Gaetano (phone: 454048).

CHIESA DI SANTA MARIA DEL CARMINE (CHURCH OF ST. MARY OF THE CARMELITES) Built in the 12th century and substantially reconstructed between 1283 and 1300, this church is home to a venerated image of the Madonna. An adjacent tower is the scene of a mock burning and other celebrations on the saint's day, July 16 (see *Special Events,* above). Open daily. Piazza del Carmine (phone: 200605).

MUSEO CIVICO FILANGIERI (FILANGIERI CIVIC MUSEUM) Arms, furniture, porcelain, costumes, and paintings are housed in the 15th-century *Palazzo Cuomo.* Closed Mondays; Tuesdays through Saturdays after 2 PM; and Sundays and holidays after 1 PM. 288 Via Duomo (phone: 203175).

MUSEO DUCA DI MARTINA (DUKE OF MARTINA MUSEUM) Ivories, enamels, china, and majolica, European and Oriental, are displayed in the *Villa Floridiana,* a small neoclassical palace in the Vomero section, with splendid gardens and a panoramic view of the bay. Closed Mondays; Tuesdays through Saturdays after 2 PM; and Sundays and holidays after 1 PM. Via Cimarosa (phone: 578-8418).

MUSEO PRINCIPE ARAGONA PIGNATELLI CORTES (PRINCE OF ARAGON PIGNATELLI CORTES MUSEUM) A collection of 19th-century furniture and china, plus a coach museum in the park's pavilion, with French and English carriages. Closed Mondays; Tuesdays through Saturdays after 2 PM; and Sundays and holidays after 1 PM. Riviera di Chiaia (phone: 669675).

SHOPPING

For shopping purposes, Naples is commonly divided into a *zona elegante* (elegant zone) and a *zona commerciale* (commercial zone). The most fashionable shopping area, the *zona elegante,* is centered around Piazza dei Martiri, along Vias Calabritto, Filangieri, dei Mille, and Chiaia. Via Chiaia leads to the more commercial zone between Piazza Trieste e Trento and Piazza Dante along Via Roma (also called Via Toledo, after the viceroy who opened it in 1536; steer clear of this area after dark) and toward the main railroad station along Corso Umberto I. Ceramics and porcelains have been sold here since the 18th century, when Bourbon kings founded the Capodimonte school and factory. Although original Capodimonte pieces are collectors' items, and Capodimonte-style figurines are produced by companies all over Italy, the production of more traditional ceramics, in popular folk styles, continues to thrive in Naples and the vicinity.

Neapolitan street markets are very colorful (always beware of pickpockets and *scippatori,* who speed by on motorbikes, grabbing bags and gold chains from shoulders and necks as they go). Markets are in the neighborhoods of Resina, for new and used clothing and fabrics; Spacca-Napoli, for books and silver objects; Antignano, for fabrics, household goods, and food; and, at *Christmas,* on Via San Gregorio, for traditional Neapolitan nativity figures. Antiques shops are mostly in the area around Piazza dei Martiri and Via Santa Maria di Costantinopoli.

On Via Forcella, between Via Duomo and Piazza Calenda, a daily market of gigantic proportions offers everything from soap to stereos. Bathroom products, lighters, records, electrical appliances, and every sort of cigarette, cigar, and pipe tobacco are all at prices half of those in the shops. Check carefully to be sure the box you take home really contains what you bought, and watch your purse!

Most stores in Naples are open from 9:30 AM to 1:30 PM and 4:30 to 7:30 PM; closed Sundays. Hours often are extended in summer.

Antiquités Hermano Antique clocks, paintings, and unusual objets d'art, plus some furniture. 30 Via Domenico Morelli (phone: 764-3913).

Baracca e Burattini Opposite the entrance to the archaeological museum is this artisans' shop, selling masks, marionettes, and lovely dolls. 2 Piazza del Museo (no phone).

Berisio Antique books. 28 Via Port'Alba (phone: 544-7639).

Bowinkel Lovely old prints of Naples—among other places—framed and unframed. 24 Piazza dei Martiri (phone: 764-4344).

Chiurazzi Bronze reproductions of sculptures in the archaeological museum. 271 Via ai Ponti Rossi (phone: 751-2685).

Lerre For lovers of unusual women's shoes, the designs here are eye-catching, the footwear well made. 21-22 Via Calabritto (phone: 764-3884).

Ospedale delle Bambole Hand-crafted dolls and puppets. 81 Via San Biagio dei Librai (phone: 203067).

Persepolis Fine Persian and other handwoven Oriental rugs, all with certificates guaranteeing their authenticity. 23/D Piazza dei Martiri (phone: 764-3824).

Il Sagittario Curious leather goods, such as masks and sculptures. 10/A Via Santa Chiara (phone: 552-0602).

Simplement Top-quality women's shoes, ranging from classic to more unusual styles. 27 Via Calabritto (no phone).

La Soffitta Hand-painted ceramics. 12 Via Benedetto Croce (phone: 551-6339).

SPORTS AND FITNESS

Most sports facilities belong to private clubs, so check with your hotel's concierge about which are open to the public.

FITNESS CENTERS *Eracles Club* (4 Calata Trinità Maggiore, near Piazza del Gesù Nuovo; phone: 552-9478, men; 551-1228, women).

JOGGING One good place to run is the *lungomare* (seafront promenade) along Via Caracciolo and Via Partenope from the port of Santa Lucia to the Mergellina. The *Villa Comunale,* the park behind Via Caracciolo, is another good spot.

SOCCER From September through April, *Napoli* plays at *Stadio San Paolo* (Piazzale Vincenzo Tecchio, Fuorigrotta; phone: 615623 or 619205). Its capacity is

80,000 often fierce fans, although Neapolitans have the reputation of being the least rowdy among Italians.

SWIMMING There are fine seaside resorts on the nearby islands and along the Amalfi Coast (see *Italy's Best Beaches* in DIVERSIONS). There is a public pool—*Piscina Scandone* on Via Giochi del Mediterraneo (phone: 570-9159)—in the Fuorigrotta area.

TENNIS There are public courts at several tennis clubs, including the *Sporting Club Virgilio* (6 Via Tito Lucrezio Caro; phone: 769-5261); the *Tennis Club Vomero* (8 Via Rossini; phone: 658912); the *Tennis Club Napoli* (*Villa Comunale;* Viale Dohrn; phone: 761-4656); the *Tennis Country Club* (3 Via Guantai Orsolone; phone: 587-3868); and the *Tennis Club Petrarca* (93 Via Petrarca; phone: 575-6714).

THEATER

Even those who speak Italian probably won't understand the Neapolitan dialect, but just for the color and sheer vitality, take in a performance by the renowned *Gruppo Repertorio di Eduardo de Filippo* at the *Teatro San Ferdinando* (Piazza Teatro San Ferdinando; phone: 444500). A fine place to sample Neapolitan music and folklore is the *Circolo della Stampa* (Via Villa Comunale; phone: 764-2588; reserve seats through your concierge). Other theatrical groups perform at the *Politeama* (80 Via Monte di Dio; phone: 764-5016 or 764-5079); *Cilea* (11 Via San Domenico; phone: 646830); *Sannazaro* (157 Via Chiaia; phone: 411723 or 403827); *Bracco* (40 Via Tarsia; phone: 549-5904); and *Bellini* (14 Via Conte di Ruvo; phone: 549-9688).

MUSIC

Naples is well known for its outstanding operatic presentations in one of Italy's—and the world's—most splendid venues.

HIGH NOTES

Teatro San Carlo Built under Bourbon King Charles III in 1737, destroyed by fire in 1816, and thoroughly rebuilt in neoclassical style within six months, the theater features Ionic columns, niches, and bas-reliefs on the outside and a fresco of Apollo and the Muses on the ceiling of the sumptuous auditorium, which has perfect acoustics. Italy's second-most-famous opera house (*La Scala* takes first place, though it is not as old) is worth a visit if only for a view of the flamboyant rococo reception hall. Talented and progressive direction of the theater where Bellini's *La Sonnambula,* Donizetti's *Lucia di Lammermoor,* and many other operatic classics had their premieres makes for one of Italy's most lush musical experiences. Book well in advance. The season generally runs from December through most of June. Then, from mid-September through mid-November, the theater is the scene of a series of symphonic concerts, the *Concerti d'Autunno* (Autumn Concerts). Travelers not attending a performance can tour the theater in the morning by prior arrangement. Closed Mondays. 93/F Via San Carlo (phone: 797-2111; 797-2370, tickets).

RAI (Radio Televisione Italiana) sponsors the *Associazione Alessandro Scarlatti* (58 Piazza dei Martiri; phone: 406011), a symphony orchestra and chorus that produces works from centuries past as well as contemporary times. Still more symphony and chamber concerts, by groups such as the *Accademia Musicale Napoletana* and others, are scheduled frequently at the *Auditorium RAI-TV* (Via Guglielmo Marconi; phone: 725-1111); in the church or cloisters of *Santa Chiara* (Via Benedetto Croce; phone: 522-6209); and in numerous other churches about town. The *Conservatorio di Musica* (35 Via San Pietro a Maiella; phone: 459255) is another music spot. In the summer concerts are held in the gardens at Capodimonte.

NIGHTCLUBS AND NIGHTLIFE

Like most port towns, Naples has a number of seedy bars and rip-off joints to be avoided. *Il Gabbiano,* near the principal hotels (26 Via Partenope; phone: 764-5717), is a piano bar that serves late snacks. One of the most elegant nightclubs in town is *Virgilio* (6 Via Tito Lucrezio Caro; phone: 769-5261), up on the exquisite Posillipo Hill, one of the most posh areas in Naples. Another swanky nightspot is *Rosolino* (see *Eating Out*), which also is a piano bar and restaurant. Also worth looking into is *Chez Moi* (13 Parco Margherita; phone: 407526), a nightclub. The enormous *Kiss Kiss* discotheque (47 Via Sgambati; phone: 546-6566) is a Neapolitan institution. Two other good discos are *Bella di Notte* (83 Via G. de Bonis; phone: 769-5074) and *My Way* (30/C Via Cappella Vecchia; phone: 764-4735). The *Otto Club* (23 Salita Cariati; phone: 666262) has good live jazz and serves drinks and light meals (closed Mondays). Most nightspots close at 4 AM.

Best in Town

CHECKING IN

A very expensive hotel charges $240 or more per night for a double room; expensive ones run from $160 to $240; moderately priced hotels range from $110 to $160; and an inexpensive place costs from $50 to $110. All hotels feature air conditioning and private baths. Those listed below as having "business services" usually offer such conveniences as an English-speaking concierge, meeting rooms, photocopiers, computers, translation services, and express checkout, among others. Call the hotel for additional information. All rates include breakfast. All telephone numbers are in the 81 city code unless otherwise indicated.

VERY EXPENSIVE

Excelsior Part of the CIGA chain, this hotel dominates the port of Santa Lucia, with terraced seaside rooms overlooking 12th-century *Castel dell'Ovo*, the old fishing village of Borgo Marinaro, and the whole bay. The *Casanova Grill* takes some prizes (see *Eating Out*). There are 136 rooms (some are in need of renovation), 24-hour room service, business services, and a garage nearby. 48 Via Partenope (phone: 764-0111; 800-221-2340; fax: 411743).

EXPENSIVE

Britannique Offering Swiss management and efficiency, it's hospitable and very clean. Most of the 86 rooms in this old converted villa are large, and since it's set on a hillside up and back from the waterfront, most have attractive views. The dining room is for hotel guests only, and there's 24-hour room service and business services. 133 Corso Vittorio Emanuele (phone: 761-4145; fax: 669760).

Holiday Inn In a new business district, this 22-story hotel caters largely to a corporate clientele. With its 330 rooms and 12 meeting rooms, the accent is on service, especially for the business traveler. There are a gym and sauna, plus a courtesy shuttle to downtown (about 1 mile/1.6 km away) and to the airport (2 miles/3 km away). Twenty-four-hour room service and business services are available. Centro Direzionale (phone: 225-0111; 800-HOLI-DAY; 1678-77399 toll-free in Italy; fax: 562-8074).

Miramare Conveniently located, with the added attraction of the waterfront, this hotel is reputable, comfortable, and small (31 rooms). In it are a restaurant and a lovely breakfast terrace. 24 Via Nazario Sauro (phone: 764-7589; fax: 764-0775).

Oriente Owned by the same proprietors as the *Santa Lucia* (see below), this renovated 132-room establishment is centrally located. The style is strictly modern; the emphasis, on comfort, service, and efficiency. There's a restaurant and business services. 44 Via Armando Diaz (phone: 552-1133; fax: 551-4915).

Paradiso A breathtaking panoramic view of the entire Bay of Naples, seen from the front guestrooms and the roof terrace, makes this 71-room place with a restaurant and 24-hour room service particularly appealing. Business services. 11 Via Catullo (phone: 761-4161; fax: 761-3449).

Parker A sweeping staircase, chandeliers, and old-fashioned elevators are all part of the charm of this fine, renovated 83-room Belle Epoque–style property. There is a restaurant, 24-hour room service, and business services. 135 Corso Vittorio Emanuele (phone: 761-2474; fax: 663527).

Santa Lucia Once shabby, this seafront property was spruced up with considerable taste to match its smarter neighbors, which include the *Excelsior* and the *Vesuvio*. Old paintings and antiques lend an Old World touch to this 108-room hostelry, but the amenities are strictly 20th century. No restaurant. Business services. 46 Via Partenope (phone: 764-0666; fax: 764-8580).

Vesuvio Facing the picturesque port of Santa Lucia, this luxurious hotel has 174 rooms, good baths, a decor ranging from period style to modern, a restaurant, 24-hour room service, a garage, and business services. 45 Via Partenope (phone and fax: 764-0044).

MODERATE

L'Angioino Part of the reliable French-owned Mercure chain, this new hotel is centrally located, clean, and well run. The 86 rooms are comfortably furnished, and the beds are made up with that fast-disappearing luxury—crisp linen sheets. There is no restaurant, but light meals can be ordered through room service. Business services. 123 Via de Pretis (phone: 552-9500; fax: 552-9509).

INEXPENSIVE

Le Fontane al Mare Nicely located (close to the seafront) and a very good value. Its 21 rooms are tastefully furnished, in keeping with the 19th-century palazzo in which it is housed. No restaurant. Keep a supply of coins on hand to feed the elevator. 14 Via N. Tommaseo (phone: 764-3470 or 764-3811).

EATING OUT

While Italian food is not all pasta and pizza, both originated in Naples and are a staple of southern Italy. Here pasta is almost always a first course at lunch, while it is usually replaced in the evening meal by a light broth or soup. Pizza is generally served only in the evenings. Naples is the home of *spaghetti c'a pummarola* (Neapolitan dialect for *spaghetti al pomodoro* in Italian), born of the mating of pasta with the tomato not too long after the latter arrived in Italy from South America in the 16th century. It is still the most popular pasta dish, easily prepared, vividly colorful, fragrant with additions of basil or parsley and garlic, and topped with tangy parmesan cheese. Other Neapolitan favorites are *vermicelli con vongole* (pasta with clams, with or without tomatoes, in a garlic and olive oil sauce) or *con zucchine* (with zucchini, garlic, and oil) and *pasta e fagioli* (a thick white bean soup with short pasta).

As Naples is seafood country, the best main course here is simple fresh fish grilled and seasoned with olive oil and lemon. But if you're watching your budget, be careful. Most quality fish is sold by weight at restaurants, and you'd do well to avoid those whose prices are listed on the menu *al chilo* (per kilogram), which can turn an otherwise modest bill into a major monetary setback. Exceptions to this rule are lesser fish such as *alici* (anchovies), which, when fresh, can be tastily prepared in oil, garlic, and parsley, and *fritto misto,* a mixture of fried shrimp, squid, and small local fish. *Never* eat raw seafood (it may have come from the polluted Bay of Naples).

Dinner for two (including house wine, tip, tax, and cover charge) will run $90 or more at a restaurant listed as expensive, from $60 to $90 at a moderate one, and from $30 to $60 at an inexpensive place. All restaurants are open for lunch and dinner unless otherwise noted. All telephone numbers are in the 81 city code.

EXPENSIVE

La Cantinella This eatery is a favorite among Neapolitans, visiting dignitaries, and tourists staying nearby along the picturesque port of Santa Lucia. Fresh fish is at a premium, but local clams and mussels mated with a hint of garlic, parsley, and tomato and lavished on a steaming plate of linguine constitute one of the great pleasures of southern Italian life, within reach of everyone's pocket. The service is friendly and efficient. Closed Sundays and August. Reservations advised. Major credit cards accepted. 23 Via Nazario Sauro (phone: 764-8684).

Casanova Grill A delightfully intimate dining room in the *Excelsior* hotel, it offers a wide selection of enticing antipasti, plenty of fresh fish, Neapolitan specialties such as pasta with seafood, a remarkable fish soup, and roast baby lamb with rosemary and garlic. Open daily. Reservations advised. Major credit cards accepted. 48 Via Partenope (phone: 417911).

Il Gallo Nero In this elegant, antiques-filled 19th-century villa, classic favorites and innovations are on the menu, plus fresh fish and imaginative meat dishes. The terrace commands a splendid vista of Mergellina. Closed Mondays, for lunch (except Sundays), and August. Reservations advised. Major credit cards accepted. 466 Via Tasso (phone: 643012).

Giuseppone a Mare Traditionally one of Naples's best fish restaurants, with incomparable views from Cape Posillipo, it sometimes suffers vicissitudes in quality, service, and price. Still, it's worth trying if you're in the Posillipo area. Closed Sundays and *Christmas* through *New Year's.* Reservations advised. Major credit cards accepted. 13 Via Ferdinando Russo, Capo Posillipo (phone: 769-6002).

La Sacrestia Dine alfresco on delicious Neapolitan dishes such as *scazzette di Fra' Leopoldo* (homemade pasta stuffed with ricotta cheese) or fresh fish. On a hillside beyond Mergellina, it affords splendid views from the terrace. Closed Mondays from September through June; Sundays in July and August. Reservations advised. Major credit cards accepted. 116 Via Orazio (phone: 664186).

MODERATE

Amici Miei Traditional Neapolitan fare is served in an elegant ambience in one of the more posh residential zones, near the *Teatro Politeama.* Closed Sundays for dinner, Mondays, and August. Reservations advised. Major credit cards accepted. 78 Via Monte di Dio (phone: 764-6063).

Brandi This favorite claims to have invented the famous *margherita* pizza back in 1889 in honor of one of its most distinguished clients—Bourbon Queen Margherita. Today the pizza is still memorable, and the display of vegetable and fish antipasti is hard to resist. Usually crowded, but the waiters are friendly and helpful. Closed Mondays and the last week of August. Reservations advised. Diners Club accepted. 1-2 Salita Sant'Anna di Palazzo (phone: 416928).

La Cantina di Triunfo The owner-chef of this former wine cellar continues the oenological tradition by offering an exceptional array of wines and grappas. The menu varies seasonally, but the food is always fresh and well cooked, using the best traditional Neapolitan recipes. Closed Sundays and August. Reservations advised. No credit cards accepted. 64 Riviera di Chiaia (phone: 668101).

Ciro a Mergillina For 150 years this has been *the* place to see and be seen in Naples. Its fish always is top quality, and the pizza is among the best in town. Closed Mondays. Reservations advised. Major credit cards accepted. 21 Via Mergellina (phone: 681780).

Ciro a Santa Brigida In the center of town, this has been one of the best and busiest of Naples's trattorie/*pizzerie* since the 1920s. Sample the great variety of fresh fish or pasta such as lasagna *imbottita* (with meatballs) and *maccheroni alla siciliana* (pasta with eggplant). This is also a good place for *pastiera* (a typical Neapolitan dessert made of ricotta cheese and wheat). Closed Sundays. Reservations advised. No credit cards accepted. 71 Via Santa Brigida (phone: 552-4072).

Don Salvatore A longtime Neapolitan favorite where everything is good, from antipasto to pasta, fish, meat, and pizza (served evenings only). Closed Wednesdays. Reservations advised. Major credit cards accepted. 5 Via Mergellina (phone: 681817).

Dora The ambience here is that of a small fishing boat, and the fish served is first class. Try the linguine *all'aragosta* (with crayfish). Closed Sundays and August. Reservations advised. No credit cards accepted. 30 Via Ferdinando Palasciano, Riviera di Chiaia (phone: 680519).

Lombardi a Santa Chiara This family-run restaurant has been known to generations for its unfailingly good pizza and wickedly tempting *frittature* (platters of piping-hot, deep-fried pieces of mozzarella and vegetables such as artichokes and fennel). Closed Sundays and August. Very popular, so reservations are strongly advised. Visa accepted. 59 Via Benedetto Croce (phone: 552-0780).

Osteria al Canterbury Like many Neapolitan eating places, this one keeps its doors locked to ward off holdups. But don't be put off—inside, the atmosphere is warm and welcoming, the walls lined with wine bottles. Try the *maccheroni di casa Canterbury* (homemade pasta topped with mozzarella, eggplant, and a tomato-meat sauce). The set lunchtime menu is particularly inexpensive. Closed Sundays. Reservations advised. Major credit cards accepted. 6 Via Ascensione a Chiaia (phone: 413584).

Pizzeria Bellini One of the city's oldest *pizzerie* serves a vast assortment of pizza (the most famous is with fresh basil and tomato) plus pasta, fish, and meat dishes. Closed Wednesdays. Reservations unnecessary. No credit cards accepted. 80 Via Santa Maria di Costantinopoli (phone: 459774).

Rosolino An elegant supper club, piano bar, and nightclub in the Santa Lucia quarter, it's close to the *Excelsior* and *Vesuvio* hotels. Closed Sundays. Reservations necessary for dinner. Major credit cards accepted. 5-7 Via Nazario Sauro (phone: 764-8600).

INEXPENSIVE

Gorizia One of the Vomero's older *pizzerie* is now a full restaurant with traditional Neapolitan cuisine. The pizza (available at dinner only) still is noteworthy. Closed Wednesdays and August. Reservations unnecessary. No credit cards accepted. 29 Via Bernini (phone: 578-2248).

Osteria Castello Terra cotta tile floors, cheerful red-and-white checkered tablecloths, and the wafting aroma of homemade sauces beckon all who are looking for traditional, no-frills Neapolitan cooking. The menu changes every three days. Closed Sundays. Reservations advised. American Express accepted. 38 Via Santa Teresa a Chiaia (phone: 400486).

Osteria della Mattonella One of Naples's prettiest and most unusual trattorie has walls covered with hand-painted majolica tiles from the 17th century. The food is Neapolitan home cooking at its best, with antipasti of fried mozzarella and eggplant rolls, and pasta courses that include an excellent *fusilli con ricotta e ragù* (short pasta with meat sauce and ricotta cheese). Diners select their favorite wine from groaning shelves and finish off their meals with a dish of brightly wrapped *torroni* (sweets made of nougat, nuts, and sometimes chocolate). Closed Sundays for dinner. Reservations advised. No credit cards accepted. 13 Via G. Nicotera (phone: 416541).

Vini e Cucina The food is delicious—real home cooking, Neapolitan-style—and at rock-bottom prices, so this little Mergellina restaurant is often impossibly crowded. Closed Sundays. Reservations unnecessary. No credit cards accepted. 762 Corso Vittorio Emanuele (no phone).

BARS AND CAFFÈS

Neapolitans pride themselves on serving the best coffee in Italy, and they may well be right. It tends to be darker, denser, and more aromatic than brews found elsewhere, whether you take it straight (espresso), in a cappuccino, or, in summer, iced *(caffè freddo)*. Naples boasts more than its fair share of bars and *caffès*, many of them historic landmarks. Most also serve a dazzling array of tempting pastries for the sweet-toothed Neapolitans. And don't forget that Naples produces some of the best gelati in Italy. The following is a selection of some of the city's best *caffès* and *gelaterie*. None accept credit cards, and all are inexpensive (but remember that the bill easily can triple if you sit down rather than stand at the counter).

Bilancione Brothers Pietro and Vicenzo Bilancione have turned this into Naples's most popular bar for ice cream. On Sundays traffic jams form outside as locals stop by to pick up their favorite flavors for an after-lunch treat. Try the prize-winning hazelnut ice cream. Closed Wednesdays. 238 Via Posillipo (phone: 769-1923).

La Botteghina Bar Up on spectacular Posillipo Hill, this is a gathering place for lovers of traditional Neapolitan *pasticceria*—cakes and pastries of every type imaginable. Closed Wednesdays. 104 Via Orazio (phone: 660516).

La Caffettiera A favorite place for well-dressed Neapolitan women to drop in for a *caffè* after an exhausting morning spent shopping in the chic shops of nearby Via Chiaia, it is elegant and restful inside. Outside, tables are set up in one of Naples's prettiest piazze. Closed Mondays. 25/26 Piazza dei Martiri (phone: 764-4243).

Caflish Opened in 1825, one of Naples's most popular bars is justly famous for it pastries, especially the ricotta-filled *sfogliatella*. Redecorated to a more modern design, it's still a favorite among young and old alike. Closed Thursdays. 253 Via Toledo (phone: 412339).

Chalet Ciro On the seafront at Mergellina, this is a classic place to meet for an *aperitivo*, a rum baba, or an ice cream, served with flair at the outdoor tables. It's also a perfect spot for people watching. Closed Wednesdays. Via Caracciolo (phone: 669928).

Gran Bar Riviera This third-generation *caffè* invented the wickedly delicious *tartuffo*—homemade chocolate ice cream filled with marrons glacés—which has since been copied (but never quite as well) all over Italy. Closed Mondays. 183 Riviera di Chiaia (phone: 665026).

Gran Caffè Gambrinus The walls of this Old World institution are still lined with paintings and sketches, a throwback to the days when it was a gathering place for the city's artistic and intellectual community. Nowadays you're more likely to find the city's well-heeled residents here, for whom the white-

jacketed waiters, hushed tones, and linen tablecloths offer a glimpse of
Naples's glorious past. Closed Tuesdays. 1/2 Via Chiaia (phone: 417582).

Remy Gelo A temple for ice cream lovers, this *gelateria* offers a choice of a hundred flavors, as well as a mouthwatering display of ice cream cakes and
granite—crushed ice flavored with fresh lemons, oranges, or coffee. Closed
Mondays. 29 Via Galiani (phone: 667304).

Palermo

The capital of Sicily, Palermo (from the Greek *panormos,* meaning "broad harbor") is bordered on one side by the blue Tyrrhenian Sea and on the other by dusty-brown mountains. It nestles on the edge of a fertile valley known as the Conca d'Oro (Golden Conch Shell), said to be named for the exquisitely scented orange and lemon groves that once encircled the city.

Throughout history, Palermo has drawn from its European and Mediterranean heritages. Unlike much of Sicily, it was never Greek but was founded in the 6th century BC by seafaring Phoenicians from Carthage. In 254 BC, it was conquered by the Romans. Over succeeding centuries, it was invaded by Saracens, Normans, Swabians, Angevins, and Spaniards, each influencing the city's monuments and customs. Under the Arabs, who conquered the city in AD 831 and ruled it until their defeat in 1072 by the Norman King Roger I, Palermo became a major Mediterranean center (in the 10th century the city reportedly had 300,000 inhabitants). Subsequent wars among the European monarchs led to alternating periods of prosperity and decline (including a 19th-century "wine boom," spurred by British fondness for wines like marsala) until the city was annexed by Italy in 1860. Scholars date the birth of the contemporary Mafia to the mountain banditry of that turbulent era.

Since Garibaldi's day, Palermo—like much of Sicily—has been under the influence of the Mafia, Sicily's criminal organization. Allied bombings racked Palermo during World War II, and during the ensuing military occupation some members of the Mafia were installed as mayors of Sicilian towns. Since World War II—and during the semi-autonomy that Sicily enjoyed for the following three decades—the Mafia has exerted significant economic and political influence, subjecting the city to a succession of bloody gang wars. Although during the last two decades much of the Mafia's activity shifted toward the more financially active city of Catania in the eastern part of the island, Palermo has had several Mafia-related murders in recent years. While in 1992 and 1993 there was overwhelming electoral support for La Rete, an anti-Mafia party, in the national elections last year the National Alliance—a coalition of three rightist parties considered to be the Mafia's party of choice—carried the vote in Palermo, indicating a desire to return to the past.

Today, the historic center of Sicily's major port city, with a population of about 900,000, is a hodgepodge of narrow streets, broad squares, snarled traffic, bustling outdoor markets, luxuriant subtropical gardens, Arab mosques with red domes, Gothic churches and cathedrals, Spanish Baroque chapels, decaying 17th-century palaces, and Liberty-style (as Art Nouveau is known in Italy) buildings—most of the latter designed by Sicilian Ernesto Basile.

Downtown, in the business and exclusive shopping district along Viale della Libertà, people still stroll unhurriedly or linger over a *caffè*. Prince Giuseppe Tomasi di Lampedusa wrote his early-20th-century masterpiece *Il Gattopardo* (The Leopard) while seated in a *caffè* near Piazza Politeama. The tale is considered the best introduction to Sicily as cultivated Sicilians see it.

The Sicilian regional government sits in a 12th-century Arab-Norman palace (*Palazzo dei Normanni*, or *Palazzo Reale*). Long neglected, the downtown area is at last getting a face-lift (expected to go on for several years), and some shopping streets are closed to automobiles. Palermo has many points of international artistic interest. The imposing Norman cathedral, from which Cardinal Salvatore Pappalardo now frequently rails against the city's criminals, dates back to the 12th century. The center of town is the four-cornered Quattro Canti intersection, with its Spanish Baroque design. And the majestic Baroque fountain in Piazza del Municipio casts a spell of the past in the fading evening light. The small *Martorana* church in central Piazza Bellini has beautiful Byzantine-influenced mosaics, as does the incomparable cathedral in the nearby town of Monreale. The 8,000 mummies lining the walls of the Capuchin convent's catacombs are an eerie reminder of those who came before.

But if the waves of invaders left their mark on the city's art and architecture (as well as on the local dialect, many words of which are derived from Arabic, and on the physical traits of its populace—witness the blond, blue-eyed Sicilians who claim descent from Normans), they left an even more obvious imprint on the island's distinctive dishes. Because of its hot, sunny climate and variable topography, which includes some extremely fertile areas, Sicily has always been blessed with a surfeit of high-quality culinary resources. Its vegetables and fruits are among the tastiest in Italy.

Palermo At-a-Glance

SEEING THE CITY

Palermo is bordered on the north by 1,800-foot Monte Pellegrino (Pilgrim's Mountain), which Goethe described as "the most beautiful promontory in the world." The headland, defended by Carthage against Rome for three years during the First Punic War, is 9 miles (14 km) from Palermo by car and can be reached by the winding Via P. Bonanno. There are impressive views of the city below and of the fertile Conca d'Oro Valley beyond at almost every turn. The best view is from the terrace of the *Castello Utveggio*. Formerly a hotel, the castle is now a management school. The road continues to the *Sanctuario di Santa Rosalia* (see *Special Places*) and then down to the beach of the resort of Mondello.

SPECIAL PLACES

The Old City center, near the bay, can be covered fairly easily on foot, but some sites worth seeing require transportation. When visiting churches, carry a handful of 100- or 200-lire pieces to operate the machines that provide extra lighting or recorded explanations. Note that many sites of interest in Palermo close for a midday break, generally from noon or 1 PM to anywhere from 3 to 5 PM; we suggest calling ahead to check exact hours.

QUATTRO CANTI (FOUR CORNERS) Sometimes called Piazza Vigliena, this four-cornered crossroads is the heart of the Old City. From here it is a short walk to many of Palermo's principal monuments. The four façades at Quattro Canti, built in the early 17th century, are fine examples of Spanish Baroque architecture. The fountains are decorated at ground level with statues representing the four seasons; at the next level, with four of Sicily's Spanish kings; and yet higher, with four of the city's women saints. Intersection of Via Maqueda and Corso Vittorio Emanuele.

CHIESA DI SAN GIUSEPPE DEI TEATINI (CHURCH OF ST. JOSEPH OF THE THEATINE FATHERS) Although its Genoese façade on the southwest corner of the Quattro Canti is simple, this church's Spanish Baroque interior is notable for its rich detail. The frescoes on the roof of the vault are copies of the originals that were destroyed when the church was bombed in 1943. Corso Vittorio Emanuele (no phone).

PIAZZA PRETORIA, OR PIAZZA DEL MUNICIPIO (CITY HALL SQUARE) A few steps from the Quattro Canti on Via Maqueda is Piazza Pretoria. In its center is a huge, slightly elevated fountain designed by 16th-century Florentine sculptors. Beautifully illuminated at night, the fountain is known by local residents as the *Fontana di Vergogna* (Fountain of Shame) because of its naked statues. The *Municipio* (City Hall), originally called *Palazzo delle Aquile* (Palace of the Eagles), dates from 1463 and has been restored several times. A small street on the left of the palace leads to Piazza Bellini, the third part of this central monumental complex.

CHIESA DI SANTA CATERINA (CHURCH OF ST. CATHERINE) This church was built between 1580 and 1596. Its late Renaissance façade (the cupola is especially lovely) suggests little of the polychrome marble decoration within, a splendid example of Spanish Baroque. Except for Sundays from 10 AM to noon, the church is rarely used for services (and rarely open). Piazza Bellini (no phone).

LA MARTORANA, OR CHIESA DI SANTA MARIA DELL'AMMIRAGLIO (CHURCH OF ST. MARY OF THE ADMIRAL) Facing *Santa Caterina* is Palermo's most famous church and one of the few Greek Orthodox houses of worship in Italy today. The first visible feature is the strikingly beautiful campanile, which dates from the 12th century. The interior, where the original central Greek cross plan can still be detected, is decorated with intricate Norman mosaics.

Originally named for its founder, George of Antioch, admiral to the fleet of King Roger II, the church was later ceded to the nearby Benedictine convent founded in 1193 by Eloisa Martorana. Closed Sundays after 1 PM; closed Mondays through Saturdays for a short (1 to 3:30 PM) break. Piazza Bellini (phone: 616-1692).

CHIESA DI SAN CATALDO (CHURCH OF ST. CATALDO) Opposite *La Martorana,* this tiny church, which dates from the Norman period, shows its Arab heritage in its three small red domes. Because of the untimely death of its founder, Admiral Maione of Bari, it was never fully decorated. It does have its original mosaic floor and rows of original columns, and the altar still bears the ancient symbols of the lamb and the cross. Visit during daylight, as there is no electricity. Ask the caretaker of *La Martorana* for the key. Piazza Bellini.

CHIESA DEL GESÙ (CHURCH OF JESUS) Across Via Maqueda, the narrow Via Ponticello leads to the first church built by the Jesuits in Sicily (1564), now their local headquarters. The church, which was completely restored after being badly bombed in 1943, has a somber façade and a richly decorated interior. Located in the heart of the Alberghiera quarter, one of Palermo's poorest and liveliest neighborhoods, it is only a few steps from Piazza Ballaro, where a colorful morning market flourishes. Open daily, with a long (10 AM to 5 PM) closing. Piazza Casa Professa (phone: 329878).

DUOMO (CATHEDRAL) A small park with palm and other trees stands before the imposing *Cattedrale di Santa Maria Assunta* (Cathedral of St. Mary of the Assumption). Dedicated in 1185 by an English archbishop, the cathedral blends northern European Gothic (the original towers to the east) with Arab styling, but was much altered in the late 18th century by Baroque architect Ferdinando Fuga, who added a large dome and a transept. The main entrance, from the park, is through the great south porch, with its carved wooden doors; the column on the left is inscribed with a verse from the Koran. The spacious interior houses the tombs of the great King Frederick II and five other former Sicilian monarchs and their relatives. The *Duomo,* once a mosque, is interesting, too, for its exceptionally long nave, its choir, and treasury. Usually open daily, with a long (noon to 4 PM) closing. Piazza della Cattedrale (phone: 334373).

PALAZZO DEI NORMANNI, OR PALAZZO REALE (PALACE OF THE NORMANS, OR ROYAL PALACE) Originally built by the city's Arab occupiers and subsequently modified by both the Normans and the Spaniards, this building has always been the residence of Sicilian rulers. The restored palazzo houses the Sicilian regional government. The royal apartments on the top floor have beautiful mosaics. The *Cappella Palatina* (Palace Chapel), with its Saracen carved ceilings and columns and Byzantine mosaics, is considered one of the finest examples of Arab-Norman art in Sicily. At press time, the royal apartments were closed to the public (except by telephone appointment) for security reasons. The chapel is open Mondays through Saturdays from 9 AM to noon and, weekdays, from 3 to 5 PM; Sundays and holidays from 9 to 10 AM and noon to 1 PM. No admission charge. Piazza del Parlamento (phone: 656-1111).

CHIESA DI SAN GIOVANNI DEGLI EREMITI (CHURCH OF ST. JOHN OF THE HERMITS) Not far from the *Palazzo dei Normanni* is a lovely Arab-Norman church built in 1132 at the request of the Norman King Roger II. It has picturesque pink domes and a cloister with elegantly wrought columns and a luxuriant tropical garden. Open Mondays, Thursdays, and Saturdays from 9 AM to 2 PM; Tuesdays, Wednesdays, and Fridays from 9 AM to 1 PM and 3 to 5 PM; Sundays from 9 AM to 1 PM. 18 Via dei Benedettini (phone: 651-8223).

CHIESA DI SAN DOMENICO (CHURCH OF ST. DOMINIC) Many well-known Sicilians are buried inside this large church, located just beyond the entrance to the *Vucciria* market. The *Oratorio del Rosario di San Domenico* behind it boasts a masterpiece, the *Madonna del Rosario,* painted by Van Dyck after he fled the plague in Palermo in 1628. Closed weekday afternoons; closed weekends for a long (11:30 AM to 5 PM) break. Piazza di San Domenico (phone: 585293).

MUSEO ARCHEOLOGICO REGIONALE (REGIONAL ARCHAEOLOGICAL MUSEUM) One of the most important historical museums in Italy, it boasts an excellent collection of Phoenician, Egyptian, Punic, Greek, and Roman artifacts, including the famed metopes of the Selinunte Greek temples. Open Mondays, Wednesdays, Thursdays, and Saturdays from 9 AM to 1:30 PM; Tuesdays and Fridays from 9 AM to 1:30 PM and 3 to 5:30 PM; Sundays and holidays from 9 AM to 12:30 PM. Admission charge. 4 Via Olivella (phone: 587825).

GALLERIA REGIONALE DELLA SICILIA (REGIONAL GALLERY OF SICILY) The *Palazzo Patella,* or *Abatellis*—a late Gothic-Catalan structure on the edge of the Kalsa neighborhood near the port—houses this tastefully arranged and well-documented gallery. There are interesting paintings and sculptures from many Sicilian periods, including a superb half-length *Annunciation* by Antonello da Messina (1430–79). Open Mondays, Wednesdays, Fridays, and Saturdays from 9 AM to 1:30 PM; Tuesdays, Thursdays, and Fridays from 9 AM to 1:30 PM and 3 to 5 PM; Sundays and holidays from 9 AM to 12:30 PM. Admission charge. 4 Via Alloro (phone: 616-4317).

CONVENTO DEI CAPPUCCINI (CONVENT OF THE CAPUCHIN FRIARS) For even the most unimpressionable, the catacombs of this ancient convent are an amazing sight, as they contain the desiccated bodies (some naturally mummified) of more than 8,000 priests, professionals, workers, women, and children of old Palermo. Open daily, with a long (noon to 3 PM) break. Donations requested. Via Cappuccini (phone: 212117).

ORTO BOTANICO (BOTANICAL GARDEN) On the eastern edge of Palermo, this is one of the finest gardens in Europe. Its design is 18th-century, and the vegetation is lush and subtropical. Closed Sundays; weekday afternoons; and Saturdays after 11 AM. Admission charge. 2/B Via Lincoln (phone: 616-2472).

PALAZZO DELLA ZISA (PALACE OF ZISA) From the Arabic *El Aziz* (The Magnificent), this is one of several pleasure palaces built by the Norman kings outside the city proper. The former residence of King William (1156–66), this restored palazzo is a splendid example of Arab-Fatimid architecture. It is one of the most important surviving Arab-Norman secular monuments in Sicily. Open Mondays, Wednesdays, Thursdays, and Saturdays from 9 AM to 1:30 PM; Tuesdays and Fridays from 9 AM to 1:30 PM and 3 to 5:30 PM; Sundays and holidays from 9 AM to 12:30 PM. No admission charge. Take bus No. 24 from Piazza Castelnuovo, downtown, to Vicolo Zisa (phone: 652-0269).

SANTUARIO DI SANTA ROSALIA (SANCTUARY OF ST. ROSALIE) Built in 1625, this sanctuary has a convent and grotto where Palermo's patron saint lies. Palermans come here to pay homage to St. Rosalie and for the beautiful view of their city. Closed Saturdays after 11 AM and Sundays. Donations requested. Monte Pellegrino (phone: 540326).

PALERMO'S ART NOUVEAU At the turn of the century, Palermo was one of the most economically active capitals in southern Europe. Mercantile families from England, seeking a sweet wine to export home, found the famous sherry in Marsala on the northern coast of Sicily. During the Belle Epoque, the English were the first in Palermo to construct buildings and homes in the Liberty style (named after the renowned London fabric store), known worldwide as Art Nouveau. Ernesto Basile, the son of the architect of the *Teatro Massimo,* was most responsible for adapting the Liberty style to Palermo. He used the city's Arab-Norman tradition as a springboard for this design, which uses writhing lines and flower forms, particularly in ironwork and decoration.

Basile's designs included the *Chiosco Ribaudo* (Piazza Castelnuovo, on the corner of Via Ruggero). This now-abandoned kiosk is a good example of how the architect took elements of Arab architecture—arches, open marquetry, and mosaic insets—and melded them into a new form. Across the piazza, at the start of the wide Viale della Libertà and at the corner of Via Siracusa and Via Villafranca, stands the *Villino Basile.* Constructed in 1904 as the architect's home, it is now a government building. Note the corner balcony with its floral, wrought-iron detail. Other Basile-built palazzi include the *Villa Utveggio,* constructed in 1903 (Via Siracusa and Via XX Settembre), with its flowing stucco reliefs around the windows, and the *Villino Florio* (38 Viale Regina Margherita), which many consider Basile's best work—perhaps because of its storybook, castle-like appearance (though like many of Palermo's monuments it is now neglected). One of the earliest examples of the Liberty style is the *Villino Favaloro* (Via Dante and Via Malaspina), built by Basile and his father in 1889.

Basile wasn't the only Liberty-style architect. Vincenzo Alagna, one of his disciples, designed the *Palazzo Dato* (Via XX Settembre and Via XII Gennaio) in a more fanciful manner than his master—closer to the style of the Spaniard Antonio Gaudí. Note the swirling stone decorating the façade and framing the windows and doorways. Filippo La Porta built the *Villino Caruso* (159 Via Dante) in 1908, with its wonderful wrought-iron marquee at the back of the mansion. Other examples of Art Nouveau architecture can be found at two hotels—the *Grande Albergo e delle Palme* downtown (originally the *Palazzo Ingham)* and the *Grand Hotel Villa Igiea* in Acquasanta (see *Checking In* for both)—and in the suburb of Mondello, where Basile built luxury homes.

ENVIRONS
There are a few interesting day trips from Palermo. Most can be made by train or bus, but for speed and convenience we suggest a taxi or car. Beware of poor signposting, commonplace in Sicily.

PIANA DEGLI ALBANESI One of the island's most interesting settlements, this Albanian community was founded in 1488. Its inhabitants retain their ancient dialect and observe Greek Orthodox traditions. *Easter* and *Epiphany* are especially colorful celebrations. About 14½ miles (23 km) from Palermo; buses leave several times a day from *Stazione Centrale* on Piazza G. Cesare.

CASTELDACCIA On the coastal road (S113) just after Bagheria are the presses of the Duke of Salaparuta's vino corvo, Sicily's most famous wine (for details, see *Italy's Most Visitable Vineyards* in DIVERSIONS). Corvo conducts tours in Italian and wine tastings. Hours and tours vary according to season; call ahead for a current schedule (phone: 91-953988).

MONREALE Five miles (8 km) southwest of Palermo is this hilltop town, site of the famous *Cattedrale di Santa Maria la Nuova,* built by King William II between 1172 and 1176. Indisputably the most important Norman church in Sicily, it contains some extraordinary medieval artwork. The grand façade is nothing to compare with the vast interior, whose walls are almost entirely covered with mosaic scenes from the Old and New Testaments. One of the most stunning depictions, the full-length figure of Christ kneeling in benediction, is in the apse. The wooden choir is beautiful, as are the sarcophagi of several Sicilian kings and queens. (One hundred–lire coins will operate temporary lights for viewing the art.) There is an admission charge to the roof, which affords a view of the cloister next door and the fertile Conca d'Oro Valley below the town. Open daily, with a long (12:30 to 3:30 PM) closing.

On the south side of the cathedral is a 12th-century *chiostro* (cloister), enclosed by double rows of individually designed columns, many of which are decorated with reliefs and mosaics. It's closed Sunday afternoons and Mondays through Saturdays after 1:30 PM. Admission charge.

Monreale is a good place to buy ceramics (there is a local school), which may be less expensive here than in Palermo. Buses to Monreale leave from 8-9 Via Stabile in downtown Palermo.

EXTRA SPECIAL

Palermo has several colorful open-air street markets that hark back to the days of the Arabs. The biggest of these, and the best known—immortalized in a painting by Sicily's most celebrated 20th-century artist, Renato Guttuso—is the *Vucciria*. Depending on who you talk to, the name means "The Place of the Voices," or it comes from the French word *boucherie*, or slaughterhouse. Originally a meat market, it now also sells fish, cheeses, fresh produce, dried herbs, fried balls of stuffed rice, dried fruits and nuts, and even transistor radios and cassettes. Not far from the port, the *Vucciria* stretches from Via Roma to the sea and from the *Chiesa di San Domenico* to Corso Vittorio Emanuele. It is noisy and crowded (be careful with your wallet or purse) but wonderfully vivid and alive. Although it is open all day (closed Sundays), the mornings are cleaner and more colorful.

Added attractions here include a small trattoria, the *Maestro del Brodo* (7 Via Pannieri), where soup can be the basis of an inexpensive meal; the *Shangai* (34 Vicolo dei Mezzani), a terrace restaurant overlooking Piazza Caracciolo that serves pasta *con le sarde* (with sardines), *con broccoli,* or *alla norma* (with eggplant) and delicious baked squid; and the tiny *Taverna Azzurra* (Discesa dei Maccheronai), where locals gather for a glass of *zibibbo* (sweet wine), *sangue siciliano* (Sicilian blood, another sweet wine), or marsala.

Sources and Resources

TOURIST INFORMATION

General information on Palermo and its environs, including lists of hotels, is available at the *Azienda Autonoma Provinciale per l'Incremento Turistico Palermo (AAPIT)* office downtown (35 Piazza Castelnuovo; phone: 583847). It is closed Saturdays after 2 PM and Sundays. Other *AAPIT* branches are at the international terminal of the airport (phone: 591698), which is open daily, and at the *Stazione Centrale* (Piazza Giulio Cesare; phone: 616-5914), which is closed Sundays. The *CIT* travel agency (12 Via Libertà; phone: 586333 or 582294) offers tours of the city and of the island.

LOCAL COVERAGE *Giornale di Sicilia* is Palermo's daily paper. *Ciao Sicilia,* a monthly magazine in Italian, is available at newsstands. *Libreria Flaccovio* (see *Shopping*) and *Feltrinelli* (459 Via Maqueda) have good selections of guidebooks and other books in English.

TELEPHONE The city code for Palermo is 91. When calling from within Italy, dial 091 before the local number.

GETTING AROUND

Downtown thoroughfares are few, so traffic in Palermo is chaotic. Rush hour often lasts for most of the day. Allow plenty of time to get where you're going. Note one peculiarity in street addresses: They often do not correspond from one side of the street to the other; odd numbers may run one way while even numbers go the other.

AIRPORT Flights operate from *Punta Raisi Airport* (phone: 591275, general information; 601-9111, domestic flights; 591295, international flights), 20 miles (32 km) outside the city. The 45-minute taxi ride from downtown is prohibitively expensive. Much more reasonable are airport buses, which leave from the *Stazione Centrale* (phone: 580457) and from the corner of Via Isidoro La Lumia behind the *Teatro Politeama Garibaldi* roughly every hour from 5:25 AM to 9:45 PM; from the airport, from 6:15 AM to 11 PM or later, depending on the arrival of the last flight.

BOAT Boats to Naples (daily), Sardinia (once weekly), Tunisia (once weekly), and some of the Sicilian Islands leave the maritime station at the *Vittorio Veneto* dock. Principal carriers are *Tirrenia* (*Stazione Marittima;* phone: 602-1111) and *Siremar* (120 Via Francesco Crispi; phone: 582403). Boats and hydrofoils also depart daily for Ustica, an unspoiled island off the Palermo coast, and in summer, for the Aeolian Islands. Contact *SNAV* (51 Via Principe di Belmonte; phone: 333333). Also check local newspapers for schedules.

BUS Because of traffic jams, travel by crowded public bus can be hard work and a waste of time. Buy tickets at shops with a sign reading "Biglietti A. M. A. T." Efficient by contrast (especially to Catania), the Sicilian intercity bus company, *SAIS* (16 Via Balsamo; phone: 616-6028), provides daily bus service between Palermo and most Sicilian cities. *AST* (*Azienda Siciliana Transporti*) operates between Palermo and nearby towns. Buses depart from Piazza Lolli (phone: 681-6002) and Piazza Marina (phone: 688-2738). *Giornale di Sicilia* publishes daily schedules.

CAR RENTAL Most international firms are represented. Driving is recommended for excursions outside Palermo, but not in the city itself, given traffic and parking difficulties.

CARROZZE Sometimes called *carrozzelle,* these ever-less-frequent horse-drawn cabs—pleasant when there is little traffic—can be hired only at the *Stazione Centrale.* Work out the price with the driver beforehand; otherwise you may find the hansom's meter conveniently broken when your drive is over.

TAXI Relatively affordable, cabs can be picked up at a downtown stand or called, though this costs slightly more. For a radio taxi, call 513311, 513198, or 625-5911/2/3.

TRAIN Service is less efficient in Sicily than elsewhere in Italy; better to try one of the bus companies listed above. The main train station is the *Stazione Centrale* (Piazza Giulio Cesare; phone: 616-1806 or 616-4808). Train schedules are listed in daily local newspapers.

SPECIAL EVENTS

On March 18, bonfires rage throughout the city in celebration of *Festa di San Giuseppe*. In nearby Piana degli Albanesi, *Epiphany* and *Easter* are celebrated according to Greek Orthodox rites. In Prizzi, also nearby, the *Ballo dei Diavoli* (Dance of the Devils) takes place just before *Easter*. In May, drivers from around the world leave Palermo for Cefalù in the *Targa Florio* car rally. The *Festino di Santa Rosalia* (Feast Days of St. Rosalie) is a three-day event, culminating on July 15 with a street procession in which a statue of Palermo's patron saint is carried joyfully through the city. In early September there is a procession to the sanctuary on nearby Monte Pellegrino. In December, February, March, and April, the *Festival delle Marionette* takes place at the *Museo Internazionale delle Marionette* (see *Museums,* below) and other theaters; performers come from as far as Sweden, Malaysia, France, and India.

MUSEUMS

Besides those mentioned in *Special Places,* Palermo has a number of interesting museums.

GALLERIA D'ARTE MODERNA (MODERN ART GALLERY) Works by painters from Sicily and elsewhere in southern Italy. Open Tuesdays through Saturdays from 2 to 8 PM; Sundays from 9 AM to 1 PM. Admission charge. 1 Via F. Turati (phone: 588951).

MUSEO ARCHEOLOGICO DELLA FONDAZIONE MORMINO (MORMINO FOUNDATION ARCHAEOLOGICAL MUSEUM) Prehistoric and ancient pottery. Open weekdays from 9 AM to 1 PM and 3 to 5 PM; Saturdays from 9 AM to 1 PM. No admission charge. 52 Viale della Libertà (phone: 625-9519).

MUSEO ETNOGRAFICO PITRÈ (PITRÈ ETHNOLOGICAL MUSEUM) The art, crafts, and folklore here illustrate all aspects of Sicilian life. In the *Parco della Favorita* estate, reachable by taxi or bus No. 14, 15, or 45. Closed Fridays; mid-week holidays; and after 1 PM. Admission charge. Via Duca degli Abruzzi (phone: 671-1060).

MUSEO INTERNAZIONALE DELLE MARIONETTE (INTERNATIONAL MUSEUM OF MARIONETTES) Here are puppets from Sicily and other parts of the world, including China, Java, Burma, and points west, all housed in an 18th-century baronial palace. Open Mondays, Wednesdays, and Fridays from 9 AM to 1 PM and 4 to 7 PM; Tuesdays, Thursdays, and Saturdays from 9 AM to 1 PM. Admission charge. 1 Via Butera (phone: 328060).

SHOPPING

Palermo's compact, central shopping district boasts several stores as elegant as those in Rome, Florence, and Milan. Some streets off Via della Libertà are closed to traffic. All the famous Italian designers have shops or outlets here. Hand-crafted items include ceramics, willow baskets, embroidered fabrics, clay crèche figures, and replicas of the famed Sicilian puppets and horse carts. For fun and perhaps a serendipitous find, try your luck at the colorful *Mercato delle Pulci* flea market (in Piazza Peranni, just behind the cathedral) for used and antique furniture, paintings, and decorative objects. It is open every morning except Mondays. The open-air *Vucciria* market, which takes place Mondays through Saturdays, is well worth exploring (see *Extra Special,* above). For objects made from metal, a good place is the street market–like Via dei Calderi, where local craftspeople display their wares outside their workshops. Marsala wine and marzipan candy are two prime gastronomic products available. Some pastry shops prepare *cassatte,* traditional Sicilian sponge cakes, for air shipment.

Most of Palermo's stores are open Mondays from 4 to 7:30 PM; Tuesdays through Saturdays from 9 AM to 1 PM and 4 to 7:30 PM. Food stores are closed Wednesday afternoons.

Battaglia Where Palermo's high society shops for top-label women's and men's clothing. 74/M Via Ruggero Settimo (phone: 580224).

Fecarotta Fine Sicilian, Italian, and other European antiques. Specializes in silver. 103/B Via Principe di Belmonte (phone: 331518).

Fecarotta Gioielli Jewelers with top-label watches and high-quality gifts, including antiques. 68 Via Ruggero Settimo (phone: 586282) and 88/C Via Principe di Belmonte (phone: 581208).

Fratelli Magrì One of the city's oldest and best-known bakeries. 42 Via Isidoro Carini (phone: 584788).

Frette A vast array of fine linen in a city where the dowry still has its cult. Three locations: 12 Via Ruggero Settimo (phone: 585166); 85 Via G. Sciutti (phone: 343288); and 36/B Via della Libertà (phone: 625-0075).

Giovanni Alongi Menswear, from shoes to eveningwear. 46/A Via Ruggero Settimo (phone: 582927).

Libreria Flaccovio The best bookstore in town has a wide selection of art books, guidebooks, and books in English. 37 Via Ruggero Settimo (phone: 589442).

Ma Gi Fine jewelry and silver. 45 Via Ruggero Settimo (phone: 585446).

Mangia Charcuterie Fine regional food products, well packaged and fresh, as well as an international charcuterie. 116 Via Principe di Belmonte (phone: 587651).

Meli Genuine and simulated tortoise shell frames in traditional 18th-century designs. 294 Via Dante (phone: 682-4213).

Miroslava Tasić Fine handmade tablecloths, sheets, bedspreads, curtains, and upholstery fabrics made of silk, linen, and cotton with lace and embroidery. By appointment only. 2 Largo Cav. di Malta (phone: 588126).

Napoleon An elegant shop with a vast range of styles and labels for women, as well as leather jackets and handbags. 1 Via della Libertà (phone: 587173).

I Peccatucci di Mamma Andrea Beautifully packaged handmade cakes, cookies, marzipan, and *rosolio* (a traditional Sicilian liqueur). 67 Via Principe di Scordia (phone: 334835).

De Simone Colorful, even gaudy, decorative ceramics. Two locations: 33 Via M. Stabile (phone: 580427) and 2 Piazza Leoni (phone: 363190).

Verde Italiano Well-designed, handmade ceramics, plus food and herb products (33 Via delle Croci; phone: 326002). You can also visit their small, charming ceramics studio (42 Via Principe di Villafranca; phone: 320282).

Vicenzo Argento The last of the great Sicilian puppet makers sells his exquisite work in this tiny shop in the shadow of the cathedral. 445 Via Vittorio Emanuele (no phone).

SPORTS AND FITNESS

HORSE RACING Trotters and bettors assemble at *La Favorita* racecourse (Viale del Fante; phone: 670-3462) on Wednesdays and Saturdays at 2:30 PM from January through June; races are in the evening in summer.

HORSEBACK RIDING For information, reservations, and directions for day trips, call *Manostalla* (Balestrate; phone: 878-7033).

SCUBA DIVING Obtain information on this and underwater fishing from *FIPS* (93 Via Terrasanta; phone: 302302). Favored areas are Punta Raisi, Sferracavallo, and the lovely island of Ustica, site of international diving competitions.

SKIING For information on lifts and slopes (including one for beginners) in the nearby Madonie Mountains, contact the *Club Alpino Italiano* (*CAI*; 30 Via Agrigento; phone: 625-4352) or the *Club Alpino Siciliano* (43 Via Paternostro; phone: 581323).

SOCCER From September through May, *Palermo* plays at the *Stadio Comunale* (11 Viale del Fante; phone: 513643 or 523869).

SWIMMING Palermo's many pleasant beaches are the city's pride and joy, but watch for pollution warnings, posted on signs. The beaches tend to be over-crowded in August. The city's main beach resort is Mondello, 7 miles (11 km) north. Most of the long, sandy beach is taken up by *stabilimenti balneari* (bathing establishments), which charge an entrance fee. By Italian law, anyone is free to use the beach without paying, as long as he or she stays within 15 feet of the shoreline. Those who pay the admission fee, however, may also rent chairs, take showers, and use the pool if there is one. Another beach, in the small fishing village of Sferracavallo, lies beyond the rocky spur of Monte Gallo, a few miles farther west. It is somewhat less commercial, and the water is delightfully clear. Solunto and Porticello, east of Palermo, also have good beaches. One hour away are the popular beaches of Cefalù.

The *Piscina Olimpica Comunale* (a municipal pool) is at 11 Viale del Fante (phone: 670-3558).

TENNIS A good place is *Circolo del Tennis* (3 Viale del Fante; phone: 544517). The regional *Federazione Italiana di Tennis* (*FIT*; 115 Via Alpi; phone: 501266) can provide additional information.

WATER SPORTS For information on sailing, try the exclusive *Circolo della Vela Sicilia* (1 Viale Regina Elena, Mondello Valdesi; phone: 450182 or 450333). *Club Sci Nautico Mondello* (Via Piano Gallo, Mondello; phone: 455500) will get you onto water skis. For windsurfing, there's *Albaria Windsurfing Club* (9 Viale Regina Elena, Mondello; phone: 453595). At Cefalù there is a popular summer sports resort complex, the *Club Valtur*. Make reservations in advance in Rome (phone: 6-678629).

THEATER AND MUSIC

Palermo has a century-long tradition of *opera dei pupi* (puppet theaters). Our favorite follows:

CENTER STAGE

Museo Internazionale delle Marionette Marionette and puppet theater, which made its way to Sicily through Spain and Naples in the mid-19th century, has been a fundamental part of the island's peasant culture. But only fairly recently has it begun to be acknowledged as a real art form. This entrancing museum houses a theater where marionette and puppet shows regularly take place. Call to find out schedule of performances. 1 Via Butera (phone: 328060). Also see *Museums,* above.

Other theaters sometimes used for puppet shows are *Figli d'Arte Cuticchio* (95 Via Bara all'Olivella; phone: 323400); the *Teatro Ippogrifo* (6 Vicolo Ragusi; phone: 329194); and *Bradamante* (25 Via Lombardia; phone: 625-9223).

Palermo's other theaters are the *Teatro Politeama Garibaldi* (Piazza Ruggero Settimo; phone: 584334), which generally produces opera or ballet; *Teatro Biondo* (Via Roma; phone: 588755); and *Teatro Golden* (60 Via Terrasanta; phone: 300609). In summer, a program of ballet, jazz, and classical music is offered at the *Teatro del Parco di Villa Castelnuovo* (Viale del Fante; phone: 518287), an open-air theater by the sea. Tickets are available through the *Politeama*. Concerts are also held at the *Sala Scarlatti* of the *Conservatorio di Musica* (Music Conservatory; 45 Via Squarcialupo; phone: 240241) and at *SS Salvatore Auditorium* (396 Corso Vittorio Emanuele; phone: 26654).

NIGHTCLUBS AND NIGHTLIFE

There are several small piano bars, where conversation and liquid (and sometimes solid) refreshments can be enjoyed against a musical background. The best are at *Grande Albergo e delle Palme* and the *Grand Hotel Villa Igiea* (see *Checking In* for both); *Mazzara* (15 Via Generale Magliocco; phone: 321366); and the *Bar Notarbartolo* (6 Via Notarbartolo; phone: 308333). *Villa Verde Mondello* (36 Via Piano Gallo; phone: 454237) also has a piano bar. For live music, try *Il Ritrovo degli Artisti Golosi* (37 Via Gerbasi; phone: 325742; it serves food too) and *Metropolis* (Piazza Marina; no phone). Those yearning to dance should try *Speak Easy* (34 Viale Strasburgo; phone: 518486), popular with the younger set, or *Axys* (55 Via dei Nebrodi; phone: 527265), both discos. The *Coca Cola Club* (also called *Waikiki,* Viale Galatea, at Mondello Beach; phone: 454196) is a popular outdoor discotheque, open in summer. But you will find that most Sicilian nightlife takes place at home. There is much socializing among families and friends, either at each other's homes or in the many fine neighborhood restaurants.

Best in Town

CHECKING IN

In Palermo, as throughout Sicily, hotels are less expensive than elsewhere in Italy. A very expensive hotel charges $250 or more per night for a double room; an expensive one, from $140 to $250; a moderate place, from $90 to $140; and an inexpensive one, $90 or less. All hotels feature air conditioning, private baths, TV sets, and telephones unless otherwise indicated. All telephone numbers are in the 91 city code unless otherwise noted.

VERY EXPENSIVE

Grand Hotel Villa Igiea Europe's visiting monarchs once stayed in this sprawling, turn-of-the-century villa in a seaside park 2 miles (3 km) from the city center. Palermo's only luxury hotel, it boasts 117 rooms and six suites, a tennis court, and a pool. It is one of the city's best examples of Art Nouveau architecture, particularly the elegant *Sala Basile,* a banquet and conference room. The service is excellent, and *La Terrazza* restaurant (see *Eating Out*) and the piano bar are good. 43 Salita Belmonte, Acquasanta (phone: 543744; fax: 547654).

EXPENSIVE

Excelsior Palace Built in 1891, this 129-room downtown establishment a short walk from the main shopping center is a jewel of comfort. Some rooms overlook the fashionable Via della Libertà, others the public English garden. The elegant dining room boasts Murano glass chandeliers and good food. An American-style breakfast is included. 3 Via Marchese Ugo (phone: 625-6176; fax: 342139).

Grande Albergo e delle Palme Richard Wagner stayed here, and the word is that Mafia bigwigs once held summit meetings here. Today, this centrally located, 187-room hotel is a home away from home for Italian businesspeople, politicians, and traveling journalists. It has many touches of Liberty-style architecture, added by Basile at the turn of the century. Among its attractions are efficient service, good food in the *Terrazza Fiorita* restaurant (see *Eating Out*), and Old World grandeur, but some guestrooms are small and noisy. 398 Via Roma (phone: 583933; fax: 331545).

MODERATE

Astoria Efficient, modern, and fairly close to downtown (though not within walking distance), this hotel has 325 rooms and a pleasant restaurant. 62 Via Montepellegrino (phone: 637-1820; fax: 637-2178).

Cristal Palace Centrally located, this modern hotel is a good value. There are 90 rooms, a restaurant, and parking. 477/D Via Roma (phone: 611-2580; fax: 611-2589).

Jolly Located near the *Villa Giulia* and the *Orto Botanico*, this modern member of the well-known chain offers 277 rooms, many with sea views. There also is a pool (rare in Palermo) and a pleasant restaurant with alfresco dining. Slightly outside the center, but the hotel has a van that regularly transports guests downtown. 22 Foro Italico (phone: 616-5090; fax: 616-1441).

Mondello Palace Seven miles (11 km) north of town, this is a pleasant, 83-room resort hotel with a restaurant, a piano bar, a pool, a garden, and a private beach. Mondello's best. 2 Viale Principe di Scalea, Mondello (phone: 450001; fax: 450657).

Politeama Palace Across the street from the *Teatro Politeama Garibaldi*, these 102 guestrooms are fine for short stays. 15 Piazza Ruggero Settimo (phone: 322777; fax: 611-1589).

INEXPENSIVE

Europa Just off Via della Libertà and close to the shopping district, this 73-room hotel has a restaurant. 3 Via Agrigento (phone: 625-6323; fax: 625-6323).

Splendid Hotel La Torre On the far end of Mondello Beach, about 7 miles (11 km) from town, this modern 179-room property has an outdoor pool and a park.

The restaurant and bar offer alfresco dining on a terrace overlooking the Tyrrhenian Sea. 11 Via Piano Gallo, Mondello (phone: 450222; fax: 450033).

EATING OUT

Food in Palermo is distinctive for its combination of Arab, Norman, and Spanish influences and for the quality of its super-fresh ingredients. Local fish is abundant and sometimes is prepared in unusual ways—slivers of swordfish stuffed with raisins and pine nuts, sardines *a beccafico* (stuffed and flavored with laurel), and *neonato* (a fish cake made from minnows). The local meat, primarily kid and lamb, is a little less plentiful but excellent. Many Sicilian recipes include almonds, pine nuts, raisins, and sweet-and-sour condiments. Desserts of almond paste, ricotta cheese, and candied fruits may also be of Arab origin. Besides homemade sorbets, the best-known desserts are *cassatta siciliana* (sponge cake filled with ricotta cream and candied fruits), cannoli (pastry cones filled with sweet ricotta cream), and *frutta della Martorana* (marzipan) in the shapes of fruits, vegetables, and even pasta.

Sicily's best dishes are probably its pasta—with a sardine and fennel sauce, with tomatoes and eggplant, or with broccoli and pine nuts. Swordfish, sliced in steaks or formed into meatballs or cold stuffed rolls, is also among the island's favorites, as is the famous *falsomagro* (a veal roll stuffed with eggs, cheese, tomatoes, and fresh herbs).

Expect to pay over $70 for a dinner for two, including wine, at the city's expensive eating places; from $40 to $70 in the moderate category; and less than $40 for an inexpensive meal. All restaurants are open for lunch and dinner unless otherwise noted. All telephone numbers are in the 91 city code unless otherwise indicated.

EXPENSIVE

Friend's Bar Despite its out-of-the-way location, this place is favored by Palermo's smart set for its outdoor dining and light, full-flavored food, such as *risottino al pesto* (rice with pesto). Closed Mondays and August. Reservations necessary. Major credit cards accepted. 138 Via Brunelleschi (phone: 201401).

Il Gambero Rosso The imaginative menu includes such interesting selections as pasta with oysters, risotto with seafood sausage, and delectable shrimp. Closed Mondays in winter, and November. Reservations advised. Major credit cards accepted. 30-32 Via Piano Gallo, Mondello (phone: 454685).

Gourmand's Palermo's businesspeople and politicians favor its modern decor, discreet service, good Sicilian cooking, and small bar. Try the *fettuccine alla Nelson* (homemade pasta in a sauce of zucchini, eggplant, tomato, basil, oregano, anchovies, and mozzarella). Closed Sundays and August 10 to 20. Reservations advised. Major credit cards accepted. 37/E Via della Libertà (phone: 323431).

Regine International dishes made with the local fish and produce is offered at this downtown eatery. Specialties include *pasta alla Lido* (with chunks of swordfish, clams, shrimps, and tomato) and mixed grilled fish. Closed Sundays and two weeks in August. Reservations advised. Major credit cards accepted. 4/A Via Trapani (phone: 586566).

Renato–L'Approdo This attractive restaurant is known for its excellent wine cellar, with over 91,000 bottles, and its varied menu of traditional Sicilian dishes. Closed Wednesdays and two weeks in August. Reservations advised. Major credit cards accepted. 224 Via Messina Marina (phone: 6302881).

Sympathy 2 Great fish dishes are served at this sister eatery to *Sympathy Trattoria* (see below), 30 minutes from town and near the beach. Closed Tuesdays. Reservations necessary in summer. No credit cards accepted. Piazza Sferracavallo (phone: 532389).

Sympathy Trattoria At this tiny, colorful eatery on the Mondello waterfront, the fish is excellent and Brooklynese is spoken as well as Sicilian. Closed Thursdays. Reservations advised. Major credit cards accepted. 18 Via Piano Gallo, Mondello (phone: 454470).

La Terrazza In the *Grand Hotel Villa Igiea,* this Art Nouveau restaurant has a refined Sicilian kitchen. Specialties include swordfish antipasto and *capellini trinacria* (thin pasta with olive oil, eggplant, tomatoes, mozzarella, and parmesan cheese). Save room for the *semifreddo* (Italian ice-cream cake). There is a vast assortment of wines, and alfresco dining on the terrace in spring and summer. Reservations advised. Major credit cards accepted. 43 Salita Belmonte, Acquasanta (phone: 543744).

Il Trittico In the new section of town, this spacious restaurant features classic (some even ancient) Sicilian recipes, reinvented. Sauces are somewhat light, and vegetables or fish are often substituted for meat. Try the *spigola al finocchio* (sea bass baked in a sauce of braised fennel, orange slices, arugula, and parsley on a bed of radicchio). The dessert tray offers such Sicilian treats as espresso jello. Closed Mondays. Reservations advised. Major credit cards accepted. 126/B Principe di Paternò (phone: 345035).

MODERATE

A'Cuccagna In the heart of downtown, this well-known, relaxing trattoria features an impressive self-serve antipasto display and typical Palermo dishes. Closed two weeks in August. Reservations advised. Major credit cards accepted. 21/A Via Principe Granatelli (phone: 587267).

La N'grasciata Habitués of this simple, harborside restaurant call first to ask if the catch is in, and the proprietor has been known to tell customers to come on a better day. You could start with *u'sciabbacheddu* (tiny fried baby fish) or slices of *bottarga* (pressed tuna roe). Pasta with *bottarga* is also a specialty. Closed Sunday dinner. Reservations advised. Major credit cards accepted. 12 Via Tiro a Segno, in the Sant'Erasmo neighborhood (phone: 616-1947).

La Playa On the outskirts of town, this seaside restaurant has a warm tone, and the seafood antipasto, smoked swordfish, and lemon sorbet are special. Open daily. Reservations necessary. Major credit cards accepted. 120 Viale Europa, Ficarazzi (phone: 496538).

Roney Known for its people watching, this bar/restaurant with a spacious verandah serves a wide range of dishes, including outstanding pasta, fresh fish, and roast meat. There also is a topnotch *pasticceria* (see *Bars and Caffès*, below). The kitchen stays open until midnight. Open daily. No reservations. Major credit cards accepted. 13 Viale della Libertà (phone: 328427).

La Scuderia The name means "The Stable," but this is more of a carriage house; it offers elegantly prepared Sicilian rustic specialties. Take a taxi. Closed Sunday dinner. Reservations advised. Major credit cards accepted. 9 Viale del Fante (phone: 520323).

Terrazza Fiorita On a summer evening, try this rooftop garden restaurant whose choice of antipasti and main dishes is enticing. Open only for dinner, and only July through August. Reservations necessary. Major credit cards accepted. In the *Grande Albergo e delle Palme,* 398 Via Roma (phone: 583933).

Da Totuccio Very popular with locals, this vast and boisterous trattoria conceals an entire floor above with a patio overlooking the sea. There's an impressive array of antipasti and desserts. Closed Tuesdays. Reservations advised. Major credit cards accepted. 26 Via Torre, Mondello (phone: 450151).

INEXPENSIVE

Antica Focacceria San Francesco Established in 1834, this simple place has wrought-iron interior grillwork and marble-top tables. Fresh pizza and *focaccia* sold by the slice is the fare here—try the *sfincione* (thick-crusted pizza with onions, breadcrumbs, and artichokes). Open daily. No reservations. No credit cards accepted. 56 Via Alessandro Paternostro (phone: 320264).

Il Mirto e la Rosa This co-op restaurant offers vegetarian dishes with a Sicilian accent, including pumpkin dishes and vegetable couscous. Open daily. Reservations advised on Saturdays. Major credit cards accepted. 30 Via Principe Granatelli (phone: 324353).

BARS AND CAFFÈS

Hectic Palermo nonetheless has its share of spots for relaxing and enjoying a *caffè*, cocktail, ice cream, or fresh pastry. Following are our first choices; no credit cards are accepted unless otherwise noted. Most bars and *caffès* listed below are in the inexpensive price range.

Bar Gelateria Ilardo This large bar specializing in ice cream is located at the harbor, across the street from the city's amusement park. Its sidewalk tables are virtually steps away from Palermo's most trafficked and noisy thoroughfares. But Palermitans swear by its nearly 20 flavors of always fresh gelato. 12 Via Foro Umberto I (phone: 616-4413).

Gran Caffè Nobel Centrally located in the shopping district, this Old World–style *caffè*/tearoom is elegantly appointed with Murano glass chandeliers, plush upholstered armchairs, and antique Sicilian ceramics. Particularly good is the naturally sweet, specially blended Arabic coffee. The cappuccino arrives with a separate pitcher of steamed milk. Seventy-three international cocktails are offered; try the house drink, the *Nobel Star* (dry vermouth, vodka, champagne, and a drop of Campari). Canapés, small sandwiches, and outstanding Sicilian pastries also are served. Weather permitting, tables are set up on the sidewalk. 35 Viale della Libertà (phone: 611-0750).

Roney Half of the enclosed verandah of this slick, well-known establishment (see *Eating Out*) is reserved for bar patrons indulging in the exceptionally black and potent espresso, a cocktail, or tea. Its *pasticceria* offers some of the best and most elegantly presented cannoli and other sweets. There is a stand-up coffee bar as well. Major credit cards accepted. 13 Viale della Libertà (phone: 328427).

Spinnato Antico Caffè On an elegant shopping street next to a big, colorful flower stand, this bar's outdoor tables attract everyone from tired tourists to local merchants to Palermitan bankers. It boasts great coffee and Sicilian pastries, including *cornetti* (croissants) with eight different fillings. 115 Via Principe di Belmonte (phone: 583231).

Rome

To a visitor, Rome's most prominent characteristic is probably its sensuality—a quality evoked by its sun-drenched ruins, its Baroque flourishes, and its powerful religious art. Throughout the ages this ancient city has provided inspiration to a number of writers, including Goethe, Keats, Byron, Shelley, and Henry James. If these men were alive today, they might well be repelled by the traffic and general chaos of modern Rome; nevertheless, it remains the Eternal City, ancient capital of the Western world, center of Christianity for nearly 2,000 years, brimming with joie de vivre—or *gioia di vivere,* as they say here.

The city lies roughly in the center of the Lazio region of Italy, with the Tiber River (called *il Tevere* in Italian) forming an S-curve as it snakes through it. Ancient Rome, including the original seven hills, is on the east bank, Città del Vaticano (Vatican City) and Trastevere (*tras* means across; *tevere,* Tiber) on the west. (For the record, the seven hills of ancient Rome are the Aventine, Caelian, Capitoline, Esquiline, Palatine, Quirinal, and Viminal.) The *Mura Aureliane* (Aurelian Walls), built to protect the city in the 3rd century, still stand, as do the vestiges of later walls and many buildings and monuments from Rome's long and glorious past: There are traces of the Etruscans; ancient Rome, including the famous ruins of the *Colosseo* (Colosseum) and the *Pantheon;* the early Christian period, with such buildings as the *Basilica di Santa Maria Maggiore* (Basilica of St. Mary Major); and a wealth of dazzling Renaissance and Baroque architecture, from the *Basilica di San Pietro* (St. Peter's Basilica) to Piazza del Campidoglio, the square designed by Michelangelo. The city is a collection of scattered piazze, which, with their *caffès,* news kiosks, and shops, form the center of daily life. Even the simplest piazza is accented with the sculpture and architecture for which Rome is so famous—magnificent churches, palaces, fountains, and statuary.

Legend attributes the city's birth to Romulus and Remus, twin sons of the war god Mars and Rhea, a vestal virgin. The babies, left to die on the shore of the Tiber River, were rescued and suckled by a wolf and grew up to lead a band of adventurers and outlaws. Romulus, the stronger leader, is said to have founded Rome in 753 BC; he killed his brother (who refused to obey his laws) and thus became its first king.

Traces of habitation found on Monte Palatino (Palatine Hill), however, indicate that there was a settlement and trading site here a century or more earlier than the legend indicates. The traditional founding date is thought to refer to when settlements of Latin, Sabine, and Etruscan shepherds and farmers on the Palatine took on the shape of a city and became fused under one system of laws; eventually, the settlement extended to the Quirinal and Esquiline Hills. By the 6th century BC the city was the center of an Etruscan monarchy; Roma probably derives from Ruma, an Etruscan noble name.

Following a succession of seven legendary kings (the first three of whom were Etruscan), a republic was declared in 509 BC, and a period of expansion began. By about 270 BC the entire Italian peninsula was under the protection of Rome. Political unification brought cultural unity as well, fostering a new style in art and literature. With Hannibal's defeat in 201 BC, Rome dominated the Mediterranean, and eventually also gained supremacy over Alexander the Great's empire in the east and over Spain and Gaul in the west.

A long period of civil war ended with Julius Caesar's defeat of Pompey in 48 BC, but the brilliant conqueror of Gaul was assassinated four years later. His great-nephew and heir, Octavian, with the honorific name of Augustus, became Rome's first emperor and one of its best administrators. Augustus is said to have found Rome a city of brick and to have left it a city of marble; the *Teatro di Marcello* (Theater of Marcellus) and the *Mausoleo di Augusto Imperatore* (Mausoleum of Emperor Augustus) are among his many fine buildings that survive today.

It was during the reign of Augustus (27 BC–AD 14) that Roman civilization reached its peak, ushering in two centuries of peace known as the Pax Romana. Brilliant feats of engineering and architecture as well as advances in culture, government, and law mark this period. Persecution of the Christians, which began during Nero's reign, ended in the early 4th century, when Constantine the Great issued the Edict of Milan, guaranteeing freedom of worship. But by that time the empire, which stretched from Ireland to what is now Turkey, had grown too large to be governed effectively; it was divided in 395, with the eastern section of Byzantium overseen by Constantinople (now Istanbul). This was the beginning of the end of the Roman Empire.

By the 5th century a series of economic crises, internal decadence and corruption, and repeated barbarian invasions led to the collapse of the empire. The last emperor, Romulus Augustulus, was deposed in 476.

Thus began the Dark Ages, marked by struggles between the crumbled empire and the church, which was centered in the papacy at Rome. With its aqueducts shattered and its great baths and other buildings vandalized, the city declined. Its population—which had reached a million at the time of Augustus—shrank to less than 50,000. Monte Capitolino (Capitoline Hill) and the *Foro Romano* (Roman Forum) became grazing pastures for goats.

In the 11th century, Rome and the Italian peninsula shared in the general revival of trade throughout Europe. Southern Italy and, soon after, Rome benefited from the intellectual advances of the Arab world, along with the scholasticism and organization of monastic life. By 1377 the city was safe enough for the Holy See—which had fled to Avignon, France, 70 years earlier—to return, and Rome again became the capital of the Catholic world. Under papal patronage, it was soon reborn artistically and culturally. During the 15th century, restoration of the *Basilica di San Pietro* began; the *Vatican* complex of buildings was erected; and churches and well-planned streets changed the face of the city. Powerful popes and the papal aristocracy commissioned artists and architects to create sumptuous palaces, splendid villas, and piazze adorned with fountains and obelisks. The late 16th century brought the birth of Baroque Rome, which was later dominated by architect, sculptor, and painter Gian Lorenzo Bernini, whose masterpieces still epitomize the magnificent theatricality of Rome.

The security of the popes remained inviolate until Napoleon Bonaparte invaded in 1798 and deported Pope Pius VI to France. Napoleon was crowned King of Italy in 1805, proclaiming Rome a sort of second capital of the French Empire. A decade later, however, the Napoleonic regime had collapsed, the papal kingdom was reconciled with France, and the pope returned to Rome once again.

By 1849, with renewed nationalistic pride, Rome was again proclaimed a republic under the leadership of patriot Giuseppe Mazzini. The French twice tried to restore the temporal power of the pope in Rome, but they met with strong resistance from republican forces led by Giuseppe Garibaldi. Finally, in 1870, the Italians entered Rome through a break in the *Mura Aureliane* at the *Porta Pia* and incorporated the city into the Kingdom of Italy. That act dissolved the pontifical state and made Italian unity complete. A year later Rome became the capital of the kingdom and the *risorgimento* (rebirth) began. The new prosperity was reflected in the city's architecture, known as Umbertine style after turn-of-the-century King Umberto I.

World War I set Italy back and paved the way for fascism. In 1922 Benito Mussolini began a regime that was to last until his downfall some 20 years later. During World War II Rome was occupied by the Germans until its liberation in 1944 by the Allies. In 1946 a referendum was held and Italy was declared a republic—just as it had been nearly two and a half millennia earlier.

Today Rome is still the capital of Italy and of the Catholic church, as well as the home of some 3.2 million people. The city's standard of living is high, and despite significant problems—insufficient housing, impossible traffic, a soaring cost of living, worrisome pollution, and the need to absorb new arrivals from Pakistan, Ethiopia, and the Philippines—today's Romans still enjoy a relaxed way of life. Perhaps nowhere north of Naples is the *arte di arrangiarsi*—the art of making do, or surviving with style—practiced with such skill. Although the *dolce vita* nightlife has become subdued, an unmistakable air of conviviality still prevails. Escalating prices have not dampened the traditional Roman pastimes of lingering lunches and late-night dinners at the city's 5,000 or so restaurants and trattorie. Returning visitors will even notice a spruced-up look—there are newly renovated palazzi everywhere, painted in the pale pastels popular at the turn of the century.

Those who tire of the urban bustle have only to travel into the neighboring countryside, which offers seascapes, medieval towns, picturesque lakes, and green hills and meadows of umbrella pines, cypresses, and wildflowers. Take an organized excursion to Tivoli; to the Castelli Romani (Roman hill towns), where the pope has his summer home; or to the excavations at Ostia Antica, the ancient port of Rome.

Be sure to take time to enjoy the city itself as well. See the *Foro Romano,* the *Terme di Caracalla* (Baths of Caracalla), and the *Colosseo* by day, and stroll by them again at night when the ruins are bathed in moonlight. Watch the play of water at any of Rome's nearly 1,000 fountains. Visit the ancient *Teatro di Marcello,* a medieval fort, or a Renaissance palace. Sip an *aperitivo* at one of the many *caffès* that appear in unexpected corners across the city. You're sure to find that, despite its modern-day problems, the Eternal City remains eternally entrancing.

Rome At-a-Glance

SEEING THE CITY

The magnificent overview of Rome and the surrounding hill towns from Piazzale Garibaldi at the top of Monte Gianicolo (Janiculum Hill) is best at sunset. There's another splendid panorama from the dome of the *Basilica di San Pietro.* For a view of Rome dominated by the basilica, go to the Colle del Pincio (Pincio Hill), next to the *Villa Borghese,* above Piazza del Popolo. To see the city and the basilica from an unusual angle, look through the keyhole in the gate to the priory of the *Cavalieri di Malta* (Knights of Malta), at Piazza dei Cavalieri di Malta on Monte Aventino (Aventine Hill).

SPECIAL PLACES

Rome cannot be seen in a day, a week, or even a year. If your time is limited to a few days, an organized tour is your best bet (see *Getting Around*). After your organized excursion, grab a pair of comfortable walking shoes and a map and explore on your own. The ancient center of the city is very close to Piazza Venezia, the heart of the modern city, making Rome delightfully walkable.

The "must sees" below are organized under the headings "Ancient Rome," "Papal Rome," and "Modern Rome," with a separate section on "Piazze, Palazzi, and Other Sights." Elements of all categories often are found in one location, however. A bit of trivia: The initials "SPQR," seen on buildings throughout the city, stand for *Senatus Populusque Romanus* (Senate and People of Rome). They've been used since ancient times to indicate public structures.

Most museums, monuments, and archaeological sites run by the state or city are closed on Sunday afternoons, and many close Mondays as well. Also, many attractions close for a two- to four-hour break in the afternoons.

Because of ongoing strikes and personnel shortages, opening and closing hours change often. The numerous restorations under way mean that some museums are closed and others have only limited displays. Check with your hotel, the *Ente Provinciale per il Turismo* (*EPT;* Provincial Tourist Office), or the daily newspapers before starting out. The *EPT* (see *Tourist Information*) publishes an annual pamphlet in four languages with information on Rome's museums and monuments, including addresses, phone numbers, and schedules. Where possible, we have listed operating schedules that seem relatively reliable.

Warning: Pickpockets work all around the city, but are especially busy on such bus lines as the No. 56 to Via Veneto and Nos. 62, 64, and 492 to the *Vatican,* and at the most popular tourist spots, even though plainclothes police scour these areas. Beware of gangs of children who may surround you and make straight for your wallet or purse. They haunt the Tiber bridges, the *Colosseo,* and the quayside walk to the *Porta Portese.* On Via del Corso, carry your shoulder bag on the arm *away* from passing vehicular traffic to avoid bag snatchers on motor scooters. Do not hang purses on *caffè* or restaurant chairs. Avoid carrying your passport and any significant amount of money, and be sure to store valuables in a hotel safe-deposit box.

ANCIENT ROME

COLOSSEO (COLOSSEUM) The grandest and most celebrated of all Rome's monuments, this amphitheater is a logical starting point for a tour of ancient Rome. The enormous arena, one-third of a mile in circumference and 137 feet high, was built by Vespasian and Titus between AD 72 and 81. At the time 50,000 spectators regularly would pack the stadium for an afternoon of gory fun. Hundreds of professional gladiators did battle to the death and numerous unarmed condemned criminals wrestled hungry lions here; on state occasions the *Colosseo* was flooded and naval battles staged. Gladiatorial contests were held here until 404; animal combats were stopped toward the middle of the 6th century. The *Colosseo* was abused by later generations. It was a fort in the Middle Ages, and Renaissance construction workers regularly chopped away at the structure when they needed marble for the *Basilica di San Pietro* and assorted palazzi, destroying a large chunk of the outer wall. Buttresses were erected by Pius VIII (1800–23) to keep the structure from caving in on itself. Later, the luxuriant vegetation (420 exotic species that prompted two books on the *Colosseo*'s flora and countless rhapsodies by Dickens, Byron, and other famous writers) was entirely weeded out. The floor was then excavated to reveal the locker rooms underneath—with separate but equal facilities for lions and men.

The lions have long since been replaced by stray cats, but the allure of the structure is as strong as ever. Visitors instinctively appreciate the genius of the engineers who found a way to erect such a gigantic structure on marshy ground, and who designed it so that immense and often rowdy crowds could enter and exit with ease through its 80 doors. Now in the midst of being restored, it remains the very symbol of Rome's grandeur. It's easy to understand why Romans said that should the *Colosseo* fall, Rome—and the world—would follow. Closed Wednesday and Sunday afternoons. Admission charge to the upper level. Piazzale del Colosseo.

MONTE PALATINO (PALATINE HILL) Adjacent to the *Colosseo* and the *Foro Romano* (Roman Forum), the Palatine Hill is where Rome began. The Emperors of Rome subsequently built their palaces here, turning the hill into an imperial preserve (its Latin name is the source of the word "palace"). Other great men—including Cicero, Crassus, and Mark Antony—also lived here. In ruins by the Middle Ages, the ancient structures were incorporated into the sumptuous *Villa Farnese* in the 16th century, and the *Orti Farnesiani* (Farnese Gardens) were laid out, the first botanical gardens in the world.

The Palatine Hill is a lovely spot for a walk or a picnic, offering fine views of ancient and modern Rome. Fields of flowers are scattered with ruins of the luxurious villas that once covered most of the hill. They stand next to the foundations of the mud huts where Rome's founders settled in the 8th century BC. Be sure to see the *Casa di Livia* (House of Livia)—actually that of her husband, Augustus—with its remarkable frescoes; Domitian's *Domus Flavia* (Palace of the Flavians), designed by his favorite architect, Rabirius; the impressive stadium; the view from the terrace of the *Palazzo di Settimio Severo* (Palace of Septimius Severus); and the remains of the *Orti Farnesiani* at the top, with another superb panorama of the nearby *Foro Romano* and *Fori Imperiali* (Imperial Forums). Closed Tuesday and Sunday afternoons. Admission charge includes the *Foro Romano*. Enter at Via di San Gregorio or by way of the *Foro Romano* on Via dei Fori Imperiali.

FORO ROMANO (ROMAN FORUM) Following in the footsteps of early Romans, climb down from the Palatine Hill to the low area that grew from a meeting ground of hilltop tribes into the commercial, civil, and religious center of ancient Rome. Actually made up of many different forums, it was once an agglomeration of open-air markets, shopping malls, public meeting spots, and large ceremonial structures, including three triumphal arches, two public halls, half a dozen temples, and numerous monuments and statues. Along its Via Sacra, Julius Caesar returned from the wars in triumphal processions, and at its *Rostra* (Platform), Mark Antony harangued the crowd after Caesar was killed. Still embedded in the floor of the *Basilica Emilia* (Aemilian Basilica) are the coins that melted in fires during the sack of Rome in the 5th century. During the Middle Ages the forum was covered with dirt and garbage and called *Campo Vaccino* (Cow Field); when excavations began in the 19th century, a good deal of it was 20 feet underground. Today much of the forum lies beneath the roaring traffic of Via dei Fori Imperiali. What is left is a white, open jungle of fallen columns and headless statues.

Highlights today include the triumphal *Arco di Settimio Severo* (Arch of Septimius Severus), built by that emperor in AD 203; the *Arco di Tito* (Arch of Titus), built in AD 81 and adorned with scenes depicting his victories;

the *Tempio di Antonino e Faustina* (Temple of Antoninus and Faustina), with its 10 magnificent marble columns—and a 16th-century Baroque façade; the eight columns of the *Tempio di Saturno* (Temple of Saturn), which was built in 497 BC and was the site of the *Saturnalia,* the precursor of our *Mardi Gras;* three splendid Corinthian columns of the *Tempio di Castore e Polluce* (Temple of Castor and Pollux), erected in 484 BC; and the *Tempio di Vesta* (Temple of Vesta) and the nearby *Casa delle Vestali* (House of the Vestal Virgins), where highly esteemed women guarded the sacred flame of Vesta and their virginity. The *Basilica di Massenzio* (Basilica of Maxentius)—otherwise known as the *Basilica di Constantino* (Basilica of Constantine) because it was begun by one emperor and finished by the other)—still has imposing proportions: 328 by 249 feet. Only the north aisle and three huge arches remain of this former law court and exchange.

As this is one of the city's most bewildering archaeological sites, a guide is extremely useful, especially for short-term visitors. A detailed plan and portable taped tour (in English) are available at the entrance. Keep in mind that this neighborhood becomes extremely hot at midday in summer. Closed Tuesday and Sunday afternoons. Admission charge includes *Monte Palatino.* Entrance on Via dei Fori Imperiali, opposite Via Cavour.

FORI IMPERIALI (IMPERIAL FORUMS) Next to the *Foro Romano* and now divided in two by Via dei Fori Imperiali is the civic center begun by Caesar to meet the demands of the expanding city when the *Foro Romano* became too congested. It was completed by Augustus, with further additions by later emperors, and abandoned in the Middle Ages. Sections of the *Fori Imperiali* were excavated by Mussolini, who then partially paved them over when he constructed Via dei Fori Imperiali in 1932.

Two of the major sights of this area are a forum and a market built by Emperor Trajan. Although the *Foro di Traiano* (Trajan's Forum) is not open to visitors, it can be seen either from the sidewalk that surrounds it or from the market. It's noteworthy for the formidable 138-foot-high *Colonna Traiana* (Trajan's Column), composed of 19 blocks of marble. The column is decorated with a spiral frieze depicting the Roman army under Trajan during the campaign against the Dacians. Some 2,500 figures appear to be climbing toward the top where, since 1588, a statue of St. Peter has stood instead of the original one of Trajan. The market (entered at 94 Via IV Novembre) is a three-story construction that once housed about 150 shops and commercial exchanges. Now it is mostly empty, with terraces and huge vaulted rooms where the city's supplies of wheat and olive oil were once stored. However, it is still worth a look. Closed Mondays. Admission charge for *Mercati Traiani* (Trajan's Market). Entrance to the forums is on Via XXIV Maggio.

CARCERE MAMERTINO (MAMERTINE PRISON) Just off Via dei Fori Imperiali between the *Foro Romano* and the *Campidoglio* (City Hall) is the prison where the Gallic rebel leader Vercingetorix died and where, according to legend, St.

Peter was imprisoned by Nero and used a miraculous spring to baptize his fellow inmates. From 509 to 27 BC it was a state prison where many were tortured and slaughtered. Much later the prison became a chapel called *San Pietro in Carcere.* The gloomy dungeons below, made of enormous stone blocks, are among the oldest structures in Rome. Open daily, with a short closing (12:30 to 2 PM). Admission charge. Via San Pietro in Carcere off Via dei Fori Imperiali.

CIRCO MASSIMO (CIRCUS MAXIMUS) A few ruins dot the open grassy valley that once was the site of the great 4th-century BC arena. Originally one-third of a mile long and big enough to accommodate 250,000 spectators, the horse-shoe-shaped racetrack was the model for later Roman circuses. The obelisks that once decorated a long central dais here are now in Rome's Piazza del Laterano and Piazza del Popolo. The medieval tower is one of the few remains of the great fortresses built by the Frangipane family. Behind the Palatine Hill.

PANTHEON This best-preserved ancient Roman building, sometimes called *La Rotonda,* was founded in 27 BC by Agrippa, who probably dedicated it to the seven planetary divinities, and was rebuilt by Hadrian in AD 125. It became a Christian church in 606 and contains the tombs of Raphael and the first two Kings of Italy. The building is remarkable for its circular plan combined with a Greek-style rectangular porch of 16 Corinthian columns, for the masterful engineering of its immense dome (which is wider than that of the *Basilica di San Pietro*), and for its balanced proportions (the diameter of the interior and the height of the dome are the same). Closed Mondays. No admission charge. Piazza della Rotonda.

TERME DI CARACALLA (BATHS OF CARACALLA) This grandiose tribute to the human body was built on 27 acres by Emperor Caracalla in the 3rd century AD. Each of the sunken, mosaic-covered floors visible today was the bottom of a single, huge pool. Each of the pools was heated to a different temperature by an elaborate underground central-heating system, and the whole complex was open to the public. For a nominal fee, the citizens of Rome could pass from tub to tub, soaking in the steaming water of the circular *caldarium,* rubbing elbows with friends in the *tepidarium,* and talking brisk business in the *frigidarium.* Changing rooms, dry steamrooms, gymnasiums, a snack bar, and a library flanked the pool rooms. Located in the southern part of the city, near the beginning of Via Appia Antica, what's left are sun-baked walls and some wall paintings, but the vast scale makes a picturesque ruin. Closed Sunday and Monday afternoons. Admission charge. Enter on Viale delle Terme di Caracalla, just short of Piazzale Numa Pompilio.

MURA DI ROMA ANTICA (ANCIENT ROMAN WALLS) Set in the 3rd-century *Mura Aureliane* (Aurelian Walls), which snake around the city for 12 miles, the magnificent gates at the *Porta San Sebastiano* mark the beginning of Via Appia Antica (see below). They were rebuilt in the 5th century and restored again in the 6th century. Every Sunday morning guided walks (in Italian only) are conducted along the walls from the ancient Roman wall to *Porta Latina,* affording good views of the *Terme di Caracalla,* Via Appia Antica, and the Alban Hills in the distance. The *Museo delle Mura* (Museum of the Walls), housed within two medieval towers of the gate, contains local archaeological finds. Closed Mondays as well as Sunday, Wednesday, and Friday afternoons; the museum closes for an afternoon break (1:50 to 4 PM) on Tuesdays, Thursdays, and Saturdays. Admission charge. 18 *Porta San Sebastiano* (phone: 704-75284).

VIA APPIA ANTICA (APPIAN WAY) Portions of this famous 2,300-year-old road are still paved with the well-laid stones of the Romans. By 190 BC the Via Appia Antica extended all the way from Rome to Italy's southeastern coast. Although its most famous sights are the *Catacombe di San Callisto* (see below), many other interesting ruins are scattered along the first 10 miles (16 km) of the route. Via Appia Antica was used as a graveyard by patrician families because Roman law forbade burial within the city walls. Among the sights worth seeing is the *Chiesa di Santa Maria in Palmis,* better known as the *Domine Quo Vadis Chapel,* about a half mile beyond *Mura di Roma Antica.* It was built in the mid-9th century on the site where (according to legend) St. Peter, fleeing from Nero, had a vision of Christ. St. Peter said, *"Domine quo vadis?"* ("Lord, whither goest thou?"). Christ replied that he was going back to Rome to be crucified again because Peter had abandoned the Christians in a moment of danger. Peter then returned to Rome to face his own martyrdom. The marble-lined *Tomba di Cecilia Metella* (Tomb of Cecilia Metella), where the daughter of a Roman general is buried, is a very picturesque ruin not quite 2 miles (3 km) from *Mura di Roma Antica.* The tomb is closed Sunday and Monday afternoons. No admission charge. From here a bus will take you back to the center of Rome.

CATACOMBE DI SAN CALLISTO (CATACOMBS OF ST. CALIXTUS) Of all the catacombs in Rome, these are the most famous. Catacombs are burial places in the form of galleries, or tunnels—miles of them, arranged in as many as five tiers—carved underground. Marble or terra cotta slabs mark the openings where the bodies were laid to rest. Early pagans, Jews, and Christians prayed and were buried in the catacombs from the 1st through the 4th centuries. After Christianity became the official religion of Rome, the catacombs became places of pilgrimage because they contained the remains of so many early martyrs, including St. Cecilia, St. Eusebius, and many popes (though these remains were later moved to churches for safekeeping). Take a guided bus tour or a public bus. At the catacombs guides (who are often priests) conduct regular tours in English. Closed Wednesdays and for an afternoon break (noon to 2:30 PM). Admission charge. 110 Via Appia Antica.

BASILICA DI SAN CLEMENTE (BASILICA OF ST. CLEMENT) This basilica is one of Rome's most complex buildings, a physical testimony to the city's long history. Beneath this 12th-century structure near the *Colosseo* are a frescoed church and vestiges of several other buildings, including a 1st-century Mithraic temple dedicated to Apollo (the Roman sun god) and a house where early Christians worshiped. The church was built in the 4th century after Emperor Constantine put an end to the persecution of Christians. Open daily, with a midday closing (noon to 3:30 PM). Admission charge to the belowground areas. On the corner of Via San Giovanni Laterano and Piazza San Clemente (phone: 704-51018).

ANTIQUITIES MUSEUMS West of the city center, not far from the train station, are three neighboring museums which amomg them display a great number of Rome's splendid antiquities. The first museum is set in the *Terme di Diocleziano* (Baths of Diocletian; 79 Via Enrico de Nicola; phone: 488-0530), which were the largest baths in the empire, built in AD 305 to hold 3,000 people. The site now houses the *Chiesa di Santa Maria degli Angeli* (Church of St. Mary of the Angels), adapted by Michelangelo from the hall of the baths' *tepidarium.* Although part of the museum is presently closed, visitors can view much of its impressive collection, including the *Trono Ludovisi* (Ludovisi Throne), a finely carved marble throne belonging to an aristocratic family prominent during the Renaissance; tour the *Chiostro Grande* (Great Cloister), which also was designed by Michelangelo; and stroll through the 16th-century gardens. The museum is closed Mondays and afternoons. Admission charge.

Next door to the *Terme di Diocleziano,* on Piazza della Repubblica, is *Il Planetario* (The Planetarium), a brick Roman rotunda (built around AD 300) that houses about a dozen ancient marble and bronze statues of gods and goddesses as well as a splendid bronze figure of a gladiator. Formerly linked with the *Terme di Diocleziano,* the building served as a planetarium (hence the name) and then a movie theater until the 1980s. It's open daily. No admission charge (no phone).

The third antiquities museum is the new *Museo Nazionale Romano* (National Museum of Rome), which is scheduled to open early this year. Set in the huge, bright pink *Palazzo Massimo,* across from *Il Planetario,* it contains a large number of historic artifacts and treasures, including a collection of Roman coins and several restored marble statues dating to the days of the Roman Empire. At press time its operating schedule was not yet determined; contact the tourist office (see *Tourist Information*) for an update. There's an admission charge. The museum is on Piazza dei Cinquecento, to the right of the *Stazione Termini* (Central Railway Station).

CASTEL SANT'ANGELO Dramatically facing the 2nd-century Ponte Sant'Angelo (St. Angelo Bridge)—lined with statues of angels (including two reproductions of originals by Bernini)—this imposing monument was built by Hadrian in AD 139 as a burial place for himself and his family (thus, it is also known as the *Tomba di Adriano*—Hadrian's Tomb). It has undergone many alterations, including the addition of the square wall with bastions at each corner named after the four evangelists. Later converted into a fortress and prison, the building has seen a lot of history: Popes took refuge here from antipapal forces (a secret passage connects it to the *Vatican*), some of the victims of the Borgias met their ends here, Benvenuto Cellini was imprisoned here for some time, and the last act of Puccini's opera *Tosca* takes place here. It is now a national museum containing relics, artworks, ancient weapons, a prison cell, and a restored 300-year-old papal bathroom with a tub. Closed Mondays and afternoons. Admission charge. Lungotevere Castello.

TEATRO DI MARCELLO (THEATER OF MARCELLUS) Begun by Julius Caesar, completed by Augustus, and named after the latter's nephew, this was the first stone theater in Rome and is said to have been the model for the *Colosseo*. It seated from 10,000 to 14,000 spectators and was in use for over 300 years. During the Middle Ages it became a fortress, and during the 16th century the Savelli family transformed it into a palace, which later passed to the powerful Orsini family. The sumptuous apartments at the top still are inhabited by the Orsinis, whose emblem, a bear *(orso)*, adorns the gateway on Via di Monte Savello, where the theater's stage once stood. Every summer a concert series is performed here in the evenings; contact the tourist office (see *Tourist Information*) for more details. The theater is closed to the public except during performances. Via del Teatro di Marcello.

LARGO ARGENTINA Just west of Piazza Venezia are the remains of four Roman temples, still unidentified, which are among the oldest ruins in Rome. Julius Caesar was assassinated nearby, in the *Teatro di Pompeo* (Pompey's Theater); the Senate was meeting here temporarily because of fire damage to the *Foro Romano*. The area is slated for much-needed restoration. Visits must be arranged in advance with the *Soprintendenza Comunale ai Monumenti Antichi* (Superintendent of Antiquities, Monuments, and Excavations; 29 Via del Portico d'Ottavia; phone: 671-02070). No admission charge. Corso Vittorio Emanuele II.

PIRAMIDE DI CAIO CESTIO (PYRAMID OF GAIUS CESTIUS) Rome's only pyramid is located in the southern part of the city, near the Protestant cemetery. Covered with white marble and 121 feet high, it contains a burial chamber decorated with frescoes and inscriptions. Piazzale Ostiense. The interior can be visited only with special permission from the *Soprintendenza Comunale ai Monumenti Antichi* (see above). No admission charge. Piazzale Ostiense.

PAPAL ROME

CITTÀ DEL VATICANO (VATICAN CITY) Vatican City, the world's second-smallest country (the smallest is also in Rome, the Sovereign Military Order of Malta, on Via Condotti), occupies less than 1 square mile within the city and is headquarters of the Roman Catholic church. An independent state under the sovereignty of the pope since the Lateran Treaties were concluded in 1929, the *Vatican* has its own newspaper *(Osservatore Romano)*, its own currency, railway, and radio station, as well as its own post office and stamps. (Since Italian post offices function so badly, do all your mailing from here. *Vatican* stamps may be used in Rome but not elsewhere in Italy, while Italian stamps may *not* be used in *Vatican* mailboxes. Souvenir packets of stamps can be purchased at the *Servizio Filatelico*—Philatelic Service—in the office building to the left of the *Basilica di San Pietro,* entered under the *Arco delle Campane*—Arch of the Bells.) The *Vatican*'s extraterritorial rights cover other major basilicas (such as *Basilica di Santa Maria Maggiore* and the *Chiesa di San Giovanni in Laterano*—see below for both), the pope's summer home at *Castel Gandolfo,* and a few other buildings. Vatican City is governed politically by the pope and protected by an army of Swiss Guards (formed in 1506 by Pope Julius II), whose uniforms were designed by Raphael. The *Vatican*'s central telephone number is 6982; most of its operators speak English.

General audiences are held by the pope every Wednesday at 10 or 11 AM, usually in the *Sala Nervi* (Nervi Auditorium), within the *Vatican* walls. Special audiences can be arranged for groups of 25 to 50 persons. Given John Paul II's propensity for travel, however, it is a good idea to check on his whereabouts before trekking off to see him. To arrange for free tickets to papal audiences, write to Bishop Dino Monduzzi (*Prefettura della Casa Pontificia,* Città del Vaticano 00120, Italy). Be sure to include your address in Rome. Reservations will be confirmed by mail before the audience, but tickets will be delivered by messenger the day before. Last-minute bookings (space permitting) can be made in person on Mondays and Tuesdays from 9 AM to noon at the *Prefettura* office, located at the bronze doors of the right wing of the colonnade of Piazza San Pietro. Tickets also are available through the *North American College* (30 Via dell'Umiltà; no phone) and the *Chiesa di Santa Susanna* (Church of St. Susan; 14 Via XX Settembre; phone: 482-7510).

Guided tours in English of Vatican City's underground excavations, the gardens, and the *Cappella Sistina* (Sistine Chapel) are offered daily year-round. Sign up at the *Ufficio Scavi* (Excavations Office; near the *Arco delle Campane;* phone: 698-85318) for a 90-minute tour of the pre-Constantine necropolis in the *Vatican,* where it is believed that St. Peter is buried. You can also see a wall of the original, smaller medieval church (closed Sundays; admission charge). Book a tour of the gardens at the *Ufficio Informazioni* (Vatican Tourist Information Office; see *Tourist Information*). Tours are offered daily (except Wednesdays and Sundays) at around 10 AM. There's an admission charge. Ask at the information office about guided tours of the *Cappella Sistina* (or make prior arrangements for a group visit through a travel agency). The tourist office also can arrange visits to the famous *Laboratorio del Mosaico* (Vatican Mosaic Workshop), where students have been making miniature and full-size mosaic pictures for centuries.

PIAZZA SAN PIETRO (ST. PETER'S SQUARE) This 17th-century architectural masterpiece was created by Gian Lorenzo Bernini, the foremost practitioner of the Baroque style in Rome. The vast, open, elliptical area is framed by two colonnades, each four deep in Doric columns, leading to the façade of the *Basilica di San Pietro* (see below). Atop the colonnades are statues of saints. An 83½-foot obelisk, shipped from Heliopolis, Egypt, to Rome by Caligula, marks the center of the square and is flanked by two fountains that are still fed by the nearly 400-year-old *Acqua Paola* aqueduct. Find the circular paving stone between the obelisk and one of the fountains and turn toward a colonnade: From this vantage point it will appear to be only a single row of columns.

BASILICA DI SAN PIETRO (ST. PETER'S BASILICA) The first church here was built by Constantine on the site where it is believed St. Peter was martyred and subsequently buried. Some 11 centuries later the church was totally reconstructed. Michelangelo deserves a great deal of the credit for the existing church, but not all of it: Bramante began the plans in the early 16th century, with the dome of the *Pantheon* in mind; Michelangelo finished the plans in mid-century, thinking of Brunelleschi's dome on the *Duomo* in Florence. Giacomo della Porta took over the project at Michelangelo's death, actually raising the dome by the end of the century. In the early 17th century Carlo Maderno made some modifications to the structure and completed the façade, and by the middle of the century Bernini was working on his colonnades.

The door farthest to the right of the portico is the Holy Door, opened and closed by the pope at the beginning and end of each *Jubilee Year,* usually only four times a century. (It was last opened in 1983.) The door farthest to the left is by the modern Italian sculptor Giacomo Manzù and dates from the 1960s. Among the treasures and masterpieces inside the basilica are the famous *Pietà* by Michelangelo (now encased in bulletproof glass since its mutilation and restoration in 1972); the *Baldacchino* by Bernini, a colossal, seven-story Baroque amalgam of architecture and decorative sculpture weighing 46 tons; and Arnolfo di Cambio's 13th-century statue of St. Peter, whose toes have been kissed smooth by the faithful. Also inside is the *Museo Storico* (Historical Museum; phone: 698-83410), which houses part of the *Vatican*'s treasures. The interior of the basilica is gigantic and so overloaded with decoration that it takes some time to get a sense of the whole. *Note:* Visitors must obey a strict dress code. Although casual clothing is permitted, shorts, miniskirts, and revealing tops are prohibited.

The vast dome can be seen from nearly everywhere in the city, just as the entire city is visible from the summit of the dome. Visitors may go up into the dome by elevator, then take a staircase to the top for a panoramic view of Rome or a bird's-eye view of the pope's backyard. The basilica, the dome, and the *Museo Storico* are open daily. Separate admission charges to the latter two. Piazza San Pietro.

MUSEI VATICANI (VATICAN MUSEUMS) The *Vatican*'s museum complex houses one of the most impressive collections in the world, embracing works of art of every epoch. It also contains some masterpieces created on the spot, foremost of which is the extraordinary *Cappella Sistina* (Sistine Chapel), with Michelangelo's Old Testament frescoes on the ceiling (painted from 1508 to 1512) and his *Last Judgment* on the altar wall (1534–41). The splendid $13-million restoration of the ceiling, a 10-year project involving the removal of centuries of soot, has revealed unexpected vibrancy in Michelangelo's colors. Air conditioning and lighting systems also have been installed in the chapel, and footnotes have been added to art histories. The second phase of the project—restoration of the *Last Judgment*—was completed last year, and other frescoes are in the process of being restored.

While Michelangelo was painting the ceiling of the chapel for Pope Julius II, the 25-year-old Raphael was working on the *Stanza della Segnatura* (Hall of the Chancery), one of the magnificent *Raphael Rooms* commissioned by the same pope, which would occupy the painter until his death at the age of 37. Half of the rooms in the *Museo Gregorio Etrusco* (Gregorian-Etruscan Museum), which houses the *Vatican*'s Etruscan collection—including the famous *Tomba Regolini-Galassi* (Regolini-Galassi Tomb) from Cerveteri, two Etruscan carts, and an extensive funereal dowry of pots, jewelry, and votive offerings—are now open to the public. The remaining rooms are still closed for renovation, and at press time no date had been set for reopening. Also part of the *Vatican* museum complex are the *Museo Pio-Clementino* (Pius-Clementinus Museum), containing Greco-Roman antiquities, including such marvelous statues as *Laocoön and His Sons* and the *Apollo Belvedere;* the *Pinacoteca* (Picture Gallery); the *Biblioteca* (Library); and the *Gregoriano-Profano* (Gregorian Profane), *Pio-Cristiano* (Christian), and *Missionario-Etnologico* (Missionary-Ethnological) sectors. Closed Sundays (except the last Sunday of the month), all Catholic holidays, and afternoons from October through June (except during *Easter* week). No admission charge on the last Sunday of the month. Entrance on Viale Vaticano (phone: 698-83333).

CHIESA DI SAN GIOVANNI IN LATERANO (CHURCH OF ST. JOHN LATERAN) Founded by Pope Melchiades in the 4th century, this is the cathedral of Rome—the pope's parish church, in effect. Over the centuries it has suffered barbarian vandalism, an earthquake, and several fires. Most recently it was the target of a terrorist bombing in 1993, which caused structural damage inside the courtyard. The interior of the church was largely rebuilt in the 17th century by Borromini, who maintained the 16th-century wooden ceiling. The principal façade belongs to the 18th century. Older sections are the lovely cloisters, dating from the 13th century, and the baptistry, which dates back to the time of Constantine. The adjoining *Palazzo di San Giovanni Laterano* was built in the 15th century on the site of an earlier palace, destroyed by fire, that had been the home of the popes from Constantine's day to the

Avignon Captivity. A small museum houses a collection of papal robes, uniforms, coats of arms, and the original 1929 *Lateran Treaty,* which created the sovereign state of Vatican City and recognized Roman Catholicism as Italy's state religion. The church has reopened, but at press time the museum remained closed due to the damage sustained in the bombing; call for current information (phone: 698-86433). In front of the palace and church is the *Scala Santa* (Holy Staircase), traditionally believed to have come from the palace of Pontius Pilate in Jerusalem and to have been ascended by Christ at the time of the Passion. The 28 marble steps, climbed by worshipers on their knees, lead to the *Cappella di San Lorenzo* (Chapel of St. Lawrence; also known as the *Sancta Sanctorum*), once the popes' private chapel; while it's closed to the public, it is visible through the grating. In the piazza is the oldest obelisk in Rome. Piazza di San Giovanni in Laterano.

BASILICA DI SANTA MARIA MAGGIORE (BASILICA OF ST. MARY MAJOR) This 5th-century church, rebuilt in the 13th century, has an 18th-century façade and the tallest campanile in Rome. It has particularly interesting 5th-century mosaics and a ceiling that was, according to tradition, gilded with the first gold to arrive from the New World. Piazza di Santa Maria Maggiore.

PIAZZE, PALAZZI, AND OTHER SIGHTS

PIAZZA DEL CAMPIDOGLIO The Capitoline, the smallest of the original seven hills, was the political and religious center of ancient Rome. In the 16th century Michelangelo designed the harmonious square seen today, with its delicate, star-patterned pavement. At the center is a copy of the magnificent 2nd-century bronze equestrian statue of Marcus Aurelius (the original is in the museum in the *Palazzo dei Conservatori*). The piazza is flanked on three sides by palaces: the *Palazzo Nuovo* and *Palazzo dei Conservatori* (Palace of the Magistrates)—facing each other and together making up the *Musei Capitolini* (Capitoline Museums)—and between the two, the *Palazzo Senatorio* (Senate Building), which houses officials of the municipal government. The *Musei Capitolini* (phone: 671-02475) are famous for their especially valuable collection of ancient sculptures, including the *Capitoline Venus,* the *Dying Gaul,* a bronze statue (known as the *Spinario*) of a boy removing a thorn from his foot, and the *Capitoline Wolf,* an Etruscan bronze to which Romulus and Remus were added during the Renaissance. Closed Sundays and Mondays. Admission charge.

PIAZZA DI SPAGNA (SPANISH STEPS) One of the most picturesque settings of 18th-century Rome was named after a palace that housed the Spanish Embassy to the Holy See. The famous Piazza di Spagna actually was built by the French to connect their quarter above with the Spanish area below. One of Rome's finest French churches, *Trinità dei Monti* (Holy Trinity on the Hill), hovers at the top of the 138 steps, as does an ancient obelisk placed there by Pius VI in 1789. At the bottom of the steps—which in the spring are covered with hundreds of pots of azaleas—is the *Fontana della Barcaccia* (Barcaccia Fountain), the oldest architectural feature of the square, believed to have been designed by either Pietro Bernini or his son, Gian Lorenzo. Over the years the steps have become a meeting place for young people, crafts sellers, caricature sketchers, and musicians. The house where John Keats spent the last three months of his life and died, in February 1821, is on Piazza di Spagna at No. 26. It is now the *Keats-Shelley Memorial House,* a museum dedicated to the English Romantic poets, containing a library of more than 9,000 volumes of their works. Open weekdays, with a short closing (12:30 to 2:30 PM). Admission charge. 26 Piazza di Spagna (phone: 678-4235).

VIA CONDOTTI The Roman version of New York City's Fifth Avenue, this street is lined with the city's most exclusive shops, including *Gucci, Bulgari,* and *Ferragamo* (see *Shopping*). Only a few blocks long, it begins at the foot of Piazza di Spagna, ends at Via del Corso, and is a favorite street for window shopping and the ritual evening *passeggiata,* or promenade, since it is—like much of the area—pedestrians-only. Via Condotti's name derives from the water conduits built under it by Gregory XIII in the 16th century.

One of Via Condotti's landmarks is the famous *Caffè Greco,* long a hangout for Romans and foreigners (see *Bars and Caffès*). Another noteworthy spot, at No. 68, is the smallest sovereign state in the world, consisting of one historic palazzo. If you peek into its charming courtyard, you'll see cars with license plates bearing the letters "SMOM" (Sovereign Military Order of Malta), denoting an order founded during the Crusades.

PIAZZA DEL POPOLO This semicircular plaza at the foot of Pincio Hill was designed in neoclassical style by Valadier between 1816 and 1820. At its center is the second-oldest obelisk in Rome, dating from the 13th century BC. Two twin-domed churches, *Santa Maria di Montesanto* (St. Mary of Montesanto) and *Santa Maria dei Miracoli* (St. Mary of the Miracles), face a ceremonial gate where Via Flaminia enters Rome. Next to the gate is the remarkable early-Renaissance *Chiesa di Santa Maria del Popolo* (Church of St. Mary of the People), containing two paintings by Caravaggio, sculptures by Bernini, and frescoes by Pinturicchio, among others. The piazza's two open-air *caffès, Rosati* and *Canova,* are favorite meeting places (see *Bars and Caffès*).

PIAZZA NAVONA This historic square, built on the site of Emperor Domitian's stadium, is a fine example of Roman Baroque. In the center is Bernini's fine *Fontana dei Fiumi* (Fountain of the Rivers), the huge figures representing the Nile, Ganges, Danube, and Plata. On the west side of the square is the *Chiesa di Sant'Agnese in Agone* (Church of St. Agnes in Agony), the work of a Bernini assistant, Borromini, which contains statuary and frescoes from the same period. During the *Christmas* season the square is lined with booths selling sweets, toys, and nativity figures.

PIAZZA FARNESE This square is dominated by the *Palazzo Farnese,* the most beautiful 16th-century palace in Rome. Commissioned by Cardinal Alessandro Farnese (later Pope Paul III), it was begun in 1514 by Sangallo the Younger, continued by Michelangelo, and completed by Della Porta in 1589. Opera fans will know it as the location of Scarpia's apartment in the second act of Puccini's *Tosca.* Today it is occupied by the *French Embassy* and can be visited only with special permission. Send your request a few days in advance of the date you want to visit, along with a copy of the first page of your passport, to the *Ufficio Culturale* (Cultural Office; Ambasciata di Francia, Piazza Farnese, Rome; phone: 686011). However, anyone is welcome to sit outside the palazzo on the long stone bench in front. The two fountains on the square incorporate Egyptian granite bathtubs from the *Terme di Caracalla.*

PIAZZA CAMPO DEI FIORI Very near Piazza Farnese, one of Rome's most colorful squares is the scene of a general market every morning (except Sundays). In the center—surrounded by delicious cheeses, salamis, ripe fruit and vegetables, and *fiori* (flowers) of every kind—is a statue of the philosopher Giordano Bruno, who was burned at the stake here for heresy in 1600. Watch your wallet or purse—this is a favorite hangout for pickpockets.

PIAZZA MATTEI This delightful small square on the edge of the ancient Jewish ghetto contains the famous *Fontana delle Tartarughe* (Fountain of the Tortoises), sculpted in 1585 by Giacomo della Porta and Taddeo Landini. Four naked boys lean against the base and life-size bronze tortoises adorn the marble basin. The water moves in several directions, creating a magical effect.

PIAZZA DEL QUIRINALE The *Palazzo del Quirinale,* built by the popes in the late 16th and early 17th centuries as a summer residence, became the royal palace after the unification of Italy, and is now the official residence of the President of Italy. The *Fontana dei Dioscuri* (Fountain of the Dioscuri) has ancient Roman statues depicting Castor and Pollux (who were known as the Dioscuri) dominating wild horses; the granite basin is from the *Foro Romano* and was once used for watering livestock. The square affords a marvelous view of Rome and the *Basilica di San Pietro.* A band plays daily at 4 PM in winter and 4:30 PM in summer.

FONTANA DI TREVI (TREVI FOUNTAIN) Designed by Nicola Salvi and completed in 1762, the fountain took 30 years to build and was the last important monumental Baroque work in Rome. Set in a tiny square reached by narrow, cobblestone streets, it depicts a colossal Oceanus riding a chariot drawn by sea horses surrounded by a fantasy of gods and tritons. According to legend, you will return to Rome if you stand with your back to the fountain and throw a coin over your left shoulder into the water. Piazza di Trevi.

PIAZZA BARBERINI At the foot of Via Veneto, this square has two of Bernini's famous fountains: the *Fontana del Tritone* (Triton Fountain), which depicts a triton kneeling upon a scallop shell supported by four dolphins; and the *Fontana delle Api* (Fountain of the Bees), with three Barberini bees (the family's crest) spurting thin jets of water into a basin below.

CHIESA DI SAN CARLO ALLE QUATTRO FONTANE (CHURCH OF ST. CHARLES AT THE FOUR FOUNTAINS) A masterful achievement of fantastical Roman Baroque architecture, this tiny church and its adjacent convent, begun in 1634, were Borromini's first important commission. The dome of the church features unusual geometric coffers that make it appear to float above the curved walls. The crypt, with curves echoing the church above, and the small convent are true lessons in architectural economy. The church façade, completed in 1668, was Borromini's last work. Open daily, with a long closing (noon to 4 PM). At the corner of Via del Quirinale and Via delle Quattro Fontane.

CHIESA DI SANT'IVO ALLA SAPIENZA (CHURCH OF ST. IVES OF KNOWLEDGE) With its star-shaped church, elaborate white marble corkscrew campanile, and courtyard of noble proportions, this is considered Borromini's masterpiece. The dome has six windows, so the church is filled with light. Commissioned by Pope Urban VIII, the church—the original seat of the *Università La Sapienza di Roma* (Roman University of Knowledge)—was completed in 1650 after eight years of work. Open Sunday mornings only. 40 Corso Rinascimento.

VILLA BORGHESE In the northern section of the city, this former estate of Cardinal Scipione Borghese is Rome's most magnificent park, with hills, lakes, villas, and vistas. It is a wonderful place for a picnic in the shade of an umbrella pine. Two museums are here: the *Galleria Borghese* (phone: 854-8577), housed in the cardinal's small palace and noted for its Caravaggios (including the dramatic *Madonna and Child with St. Anne*), its Bernini sculptures, and Antonio Canova's statue of the reclining Pauline Borghese; and the *Galleria Nazionale d'Arte Moderna* (National Gallery of Modern Art; phone: 322-4152), with a collection of works by modern Italian artists. At press time half of the *Galleria Borghese* was closed for restoration; part of its collection, including masterpieces by Caravaggio, Bernini, and Raphael, is displayed in the *San Michele a Ripa* building complex (22 Via di San Michele in Trastevere; no phone) along the Tiber River. Both galleries are closed Mondays. Admission charge to the *Galleria Borghese*. *San Michele a Ripa* is closed Mondays and for a long afternoon break (1 to 4 PM). Admission charge. Enter the *Villa Borghese* through the *Porta Pinciana,* at the top of Via Veneto, or walk up Pincio Hill from Piazza del Popolo. The main entrance is at Piazzale Flaminio, just outside the *Porta del Popolo.*

CIMITERO PROTESTANTE (PROTESTANT CEMETERY) In the southern part of the city, behind the *Piramide di Caio Cestio,* is the Protestant cemetery where many non-Catholics who lived and died in Rome are buried: Keats (look for his gravestone, with the inscription, "Here lies one whose name is writ in water"), Shelley, Trelawny, Goethe's illegitimate son, and the Italian Communist leader Antonio Gramsci. The cemetery is another favorite haunt of pickpockets, so keep tabs on your wallet or purse. 6 Via Caio Cestio.

GHETTO E SINAGOGA (JEWISH GHETTO AND SYNAGOGUE) On the banks of the Tiber River, near the Ponte Garibaldi (Garibaldi Bridge), is this vibrant, though somewhat shabby section of town, once a walled ghetto, today rich with tiny shops and restaurants offering Roman-Jewish specialties. The synagogue is located by the Tiber; next door is the *Museo di Arte Ebraica* (Museum of Hebraic Art), a permanent exhibit of ritual objects from the 16th to the 19th century plus documents of recent history. Closed Saturdays and Jewish holidays. Admission charge. On the Lungotevere dei Cenci (phone: 687-5051).

ISOLA TIBERINA (TIBER ISLAND) In the oldest part of the city, between Trastevere and the Jewish ghetto, this small, 900-foot-long island in the Tiber grew, according to legend, from a seed of grain tossed into the river after the Etruscan kings were forced out. Noteworthy is the *Chiesa di San Bartolomeo* (Church of St. Bartholomew), built on the site of the earliest-known temple to Asclepius, the Greek god of healing. This is where victims of the city's 3rd-century plague were sent, and today a hospital still operates here. There also is a tiny park on the marble-paved, downriver point of the island, a good spot to read or enjoy a picnic. The *Antico Caffè dell'Isola* (Via di Quattro Capi; no phone) offers snacks; next door is the popular trattoria *Sora Lella* (see *Eating Out*).

MODERN ROME

MONUMENTO A VITTORIO EMANUELE II (MONUMENT TO VICTOR EMMANUEL II) Sometimes called the *Vittoriano,* this most conspicuous landmark of questionable taste was completed in 1911 to celebrate the unification of Italy. Built of white Brescian marble and overwhelming Capitoline Hill, it is often derided by Romans as the "wedding cake" or the "typewriter." It contains Italy's *Tomba del Milite Ignoto* (Tomb of the Unknown Soldier) from World War I. Turn your back to the monument and note the 15th-century *Palazzo Venezia* to your left. Formerly Mussolini's official residence (and home to Pope Paul II before that), it was from the small balcony of this building that the dictator made his speeches. Piazza Venezia.

VIA VITTORIO VENETO Popularly known as Via Veneto, this wide street extends from a handsome gate in the ancient Roman wall, the *Porta Pinciana,* down past the *US Embassy* to Piazza Barberini. Recently spruced up with flowers, trees, and other greenery, the area also boasts several fashionable shops and restaurants; however, the elegant atmosphere is becoming marred by more and more hamburger joints springing up alongside the smart *caffès.* Late at night the street can attract a mixed crowd—from down-and-out actors and decadent Roman nobility to seedy gigolos and male prostitutes. Well-to-do Americans stay in the fine hotels, and young people flock to the discos in the area, which, along with adjacent Via Bissolati with its many foreign airline offices, is well patrolled by police.

PORTA PORTESE Rome's flea market takes place on the edge of Trastevere on Sundays from dawn to about 1 or 2 PM. It's a colorful, crowded, and chaotic happening. Genuine antiques are few and far between—and they're usually scooped up before most people are out of bed. Still, you'll find some interesting junk, new and secondhand clothes, shoes, jeans, items brought by Eastern European immigrants, pop records, used tires and car parts, black-market cigarettes—everything from Sicilian puppets to old postcards and broken bidets. Keep a sharp eye on your wallet or purse here. Via Portuense.

OUT OF TOWN

ESPOSIZIONE UNIVERSALE DI ROMA (EUR) Mussolini's ultramodern quarter southwest of the city center was designed for an international exhibition that was supposed to take place in 1942 but never did. It's now a fashionable garden suburb and the site of international congresses and trade shows as well as of some remarkable sports installations built for the *1960 Olympic Games,* including the *Palazzo dello Sport* (Sports Building). Also noteworthy here is the *Museo della Civiltà Romana* (Museum of Roman Civilization; 10 Piazza Giovanni Agnelli; phone: 592-6135). Although half the museum remained closed for renovations at press time, it's still worth seeing for its thorough reconstruction of ancient Rome during the time of Constantine. The museum is closed Mondays and Sunday, Wednesday, Friday, and Saturday afternoons; on Tuesdays and Thursdays it also closes for a short break (1:30 to 3 PM). Admission charge.

OSTIA ANTICA (ANCIENT OSTIA) This immense excavation site about 15 miles (24 km) southwest of Rome was the great trading port of the ancient city, much closer to the mouth of the Tiber than it is today. The ruins—picturesquely set among pines and cypresses—first were uncovered in 1914, and new treasures are being discovered constantly. They reveal a great deal about the building methods and management of the far-flung Roman Empire.

A visit takes at least half a day. Among the chief sites are Piazzale delle Corporazioni (Corporations' Square), once 70 commercial offices, with mottoes and emblems in black and white mosaics indicating that the merchants were shipwrights, caulkers, rope makers, furriers, and shipowners from all over the ancient world; the *Capitolium* (a temple); the *Foro* (Forum); baths; apartment blocks; several private houses, most notably the *Casa di Amore e Psiche* (House of Cupid and Psyche); and the restored theater. This onetime community boasted remarkable cultural and religious diversity, obvious today from the remains of its synagogue, several Christian chapels, and a number of temples to the Persian sun god, Mithras. The site is open daily. Admission charge. A local museum (phone: 565-0022) traces the development of Ostia Antica and displays some outstanding statues, busts, and frescoes. It is open daily. Admission charge included in the park entry fee. To reach Ostia Antica, take either the *metropolitana*'s *Linea B* towards *EUR,* transferring to the local train at *Stazione della Magliana* (Magliana Station); an *ACOTRAL* bus from Via Giolitti; or the *Tiber II* boat (see *Getting Around*).

CASTELLI ROMANI (ROMAN CASTLES) Rome's "castles" are actually 13 hill towns set in the lovely Alban Hills region southeast of the city, an area where popes and powerful families built fortresses, palaces, and other retreats. The mountains, the volcanic lakes of Nemi and Albano, chestnut groves, olive trees, and vines producing the famous Castelli wine make the area a favorite day trip for Romans. Particularly charming are Frascati, known for its villas and its wines; Grottaferrata, famous for its fortified monastery, which can be visited; beautiful Lago di Nemi (Lake Nemi), with its vivid blue waters and wooded surroundings, where the goddess Diana was worshiped; and Monte Cavo (Mt. Cavo), a mountain whose summit offers a panorama of the *Castelli* from a height of 3,124 feet. The *Castelli Romani* are best seen on an organized tour or by car—but beware of Sunday traffic.

EXTRA SPECIAL

Fountain fans should not miss Tivoli, a charming hilltop town on the Aniene, a tributary of the Tiber, about 20 miles (32 km) east of Rome. It's famous for its villas, gardens, and, above all, cascading waters—all immortalized by Fragonard's 18th-century landscapes. Called Tibur by the ancient Romans, it was even then a resort for wealthy citizens, who bathed in its thermal waters, considered therapeutic to this day.

The *Villa d'Este,* built for a cardinal in the 16th century, is the prime attraction—or, rather, its terraced gardens are. They contain some 500 fountains, large and small, including the jets of water lining the famous Viale delle Cento Fontane (Avenue of the Hundred Fountains) and the two-story *Fontana dell'Organo* (Organ Fountain), so named because it once worked a hydraulic organ. The villa and gardens are open daily. Admission charge. Nearby, the *Villa Gregoriana,* built by Pope Gregory XVI in the 19th century, has sloping gardens and lovely cascades, which are best on Sundays, since most of the water is used for industrial purposes on other days. It's open daily. Admission charge.

Only 4 miles (6 km) southwest of Tivoli is *Villa Adriana* (Hadrian's Villa), the most sumptuous ancient Roman villa, almost a city in itself. It was built from AD 125 to 134 by the Emperor Hadrian, an amateur architect who enjoyed this stately pleasure dome for only four years before his death. Every detail of the villa's dozens of buildings, two swimming pools, two libraries, gymnasium, theater, thermal baths, courtyards, and tree-lined avenues was perfect. Each window was placed for the best possible view, jets of water spouted strategically in every corner, statues from all over the empire surrounded the pools, and romantic nooks were sculpted out of nature to appear as if they'd always been there. Still standing in a huge, rambling, and somewhat abandoned archaeological park are numerous buildings, including a marine theater—a delightful little island construction accessible by bridges. There's a scale model of the entire original layout at the entrance gate. The villa is closed Mondays. Admission charge.

You can see Tivoli with a guided tour or take an *ACOTRAL* bus from Via Gaeta or a train from the *Stazione Termini* (Central Railway Station). The *Villa Adriana* also can be reached by bus from Via Gaeta, but note that while one bus, which leaves every hour, stops first at the *Villa Adriana* and then at Tivoli, the other, which leaves every half hour, goes directly to Tivoli—to reach the *Villa Adriana*, you must get off at a crossroads and walk about a half mile. If you rent a car (a wiser choice), take the Autostrada per l'Aquila to the Tivoli exit, then follow the signs; the town is about an hour's drive from the city.

Sources and Resources

TOURIST INFORMATION

The *Ente Provinciale per il Turismo* (*EPT;* Provincial Tourist Office) for Rome and Lazio has a main information office (5 Via Parigi; phone: 488-99253) that is open weekdays. There are branches at the *Stazione Termini* (phone: 487-1270), in the customs area at *Aeroporto Leonardo da Vinci* (Leonardo da Vinci Airport; phone: 650-10255), and at the Feronia "Punto Blu" and Frascati Est service areas of the A1 and A2 highways, respectively, for those arriving by car (no phone). All branches stock useful (and free) booklets, maps, and hotel listings. Ask for *Carnet,* the English-language monthly listing of events.

The *Ufficio Informazioni* (Vatican Tourist Information Office) is on the left side of Piazza San Pietro, facing the basilica (phone: 698-84866). It's closed on some Catholic holidays.

LOCAL COVERAGE The *International Herald Tribune,* now also printed in Rome, is available at most newsstands in the city center; it often lists major events in Italy in its Saturday "Weekend" section. *A Guest in Rome* is published by the *Golden Key Association of Concierges. La Repubblica, Corriere della Sera,* and *Il Messaggero* are daily newspapers that list local events on weekends; *La Repubblica* has an interesting Thursday supplement called "TrovaRoma" that lists the week's events, shows, theater, new movies, and more. *Wanted in Rome,* a useful biweekly publication sold at downtown newsstands, details the latest happenings.

The Rome telephone directory's *TuttoCittà* supplement is an invaluable resource. It lists every street in the city and contains detailed maps of each zone as well as postal codes, bus routes, locations of taxi stands, and other useful information. There are many useful English-language books about Rome, some of which are available in Italy. (However, you should purchase them in the US whenever possible, as the prices are far more reasonable.) They include *Italian Hours* by Henry James (Ecco Press; $10.50), first published in 1909; and Georgina Masson's *Companion Guide to Rome* (HarperCollins; $19), which provides handy information on the city presented in an amusing, readable style. An excellent source for readers who can understand Italian is the two-volume *A Piedi nella Roma Antica* (Edizoni Iter; 18,000 lire/about $12 per volume), describing several walking tours through various sections of Rome. The best map of the city is *A-Z Roma Autostradario* (Guidaverde Editrice; 35,000 lire/about $22).

FOOD *La Guida d'Italia* (L'Espresso; 35,000 lire/about $22)—updated annually—is a comprehensive guide to restaurants and wine throughout Italy. Written in Italian, it is available at newsstands. *Ristoranti d'Italia del Gambero Rosso* (Gambero Rosso; 35,000 lire/about $22) is another helpful Italian-language restaurant guide. *Eat Like the Romans* (Alphabyte; 10,000 lire/about $6.25), by Maureen Fant, a food writer for *The New York Times,* is available only in Italian bookstores. Another useful guide is *Dove Mangiare a Roma e Dintorni* by Marco Santarelli (Edizioni Iter; 35,000 lire/about $22), which not only reviews restaurants but has a map showing their locations.

TELEPHONE The city code for Rome is 6. When calling from within Italy, dial 06 before the local number.

GETTING AROUND

AIRPORTS *Aeroporto e Leonardo da Vinci e Fiumicino* (phone: 6595; also called *Fiumicino Airport*) in Fiumicino, about 16 miles (26 km) from downtown Rome, handles both international and domestic traffic. Check in at least 40 minutes before your flight or risk losing your reservation. The trip between the airport and downtown Rome takes between a half hour and 45 minutes by taxi, depending on traffic. *Ferrovie Italiane dello Stato (FS)*—also known as *Italian State Railways*—provides the quickest and least expensive service between the airport and the city. The *Servizio Navetta* (also called the *Collegamento Non-Stop*) express train runs between the airport and Rome's *Stazione Termini;* the trip takes about 30 minutes and costs 12,000 lire (about $7.50) each way. Trains leave the airport for Rome from 7:50 AM to 10:25 PM, and leave *Stazione Termini* for the airport from 7 AM to 8:50 PM. The local *Servizio Metropolitana* train runs between the airport and *Stazione Tiburtina* (Tiburtina Station) in Rome, making several stops en route. The fare is 7,000 lire ($4.50); the trip takes about 40 minutes. Trains leave the airport from 6:55 AM to 10:50 PM, and leave *Tiburtina* for the airport between 6 AM and 10 PM. *Aeroporto Ciampino* (Ciampino Airport; phone: 794921), located about 8 miles (13 km) from downtown, handles mostly charter traffic.

BOAT The *Tiber II* carries 300 passengers on half-day cruises along the river to Ostia Antica and back (water levels and weather permitting). From May to September the *Acquabus* also plies the river. For information and reservations for both, contact either *Tourvisa* (phone: 445-0284) or the *EPT* (see *Tourist Information*). To rent a boat, contact *Acquario* (41 Via V. Brunelli; phone: 501-0360); charters are available from *Axa-Riga Yachts* (191 Via Eschillo, Room 51; phone: 509-0222; fax: 509-17530).

BUS *ATAC (Azienda Tramvie e Autobus Comune di Roma)*, the city bus company, is the (weak) backbone of Rome's public transportation system. Most central routes can be extremely crowded, pickpockets are rampant, and some lines discontinue service after 9 PM, midnight, or 1 AM. During August the number of buses in use is greatly reduced while drivers are on vacation. Tickets, which currently cost 1,280 lire (about 80¢), must be purchased before boarding and are available at some newsstands, tobacco shops, and bars. (Be aware that these outlets frequently exhaust their ticket supply, and the fine for riding without a ticket is steep.) You also can buy a single ticket (also costing 1,280 lire) that can be used on all three forms of local transportation—buses, subways, and trains. Remember to get on the bus via the back doors, stamp your ticket in the machine, and exit via the middle doors (the front doors are used only by *abbonati*, season-ticket holders). There are no transfer tickets, but all tickets are valid for 90 minutes.

Consider buying day passes, called "Big," at the *ATAC* information booth in Piazza dei Cinquecento or at principal bus stations, such as those at Piazza San Silvestro and Piazza Risorgimento; they cost 4,000 lire (about $2.60). A weekly pass called the *Carta Settimanale per Turisti* is also economical; costing 10,000 lire (about $6), it may be purchased only at the *ATAC*'s *Ufficio Informazioni* (Information Office; Largo Giovanni Montemartini) and at the information booth in Piazza dei Cinquecento. Tourists will appreciate the tiny, electric-powered No. 119 bus, which loops through downtown Rome between Piazza del Popolo and close to Piazza Navona, passing Piazza di Spagna. Route maps—*Roma in Metrobus*—are sold at the *ATAC* information booth and at the *Ufficio Informazioni*, as well as at some newsstands. For information, call 46951. Bus service to points out of town is run by *ACOTRAL*. For information, call 593-5551.

CAR RENTAL Major car rental firms such as *Avis* (phone: 470-1229 in Rome, 167-863063 toll-free in Italy), *Budget* (phone: 488-1905), *Europcar* (phone: 481-9103 or 482-5701), and *Hertz* (phone: 321-6886), as well as several reliable Italian companies such as *Auto Maggiore* (8/A Via Po; phone: 229351), have offices in the city, at the airport, and at railway stations. *Tropea* (60 Via San Basilio; phone: 488-1189) has rental and chauffeur-driven cars.

HORSE-DRAWN CARRIAGES Rome's *carrozzelle* accommodate up to five passengers and are available at major city squares (Piazze San Pietro, di Spagna, Venezia, and Navona), in front of the *Colosseo,* near the *Fontana di Trevi,* on Via Veneto, and in the *Villa Borghese.* They can be hired by the half hour, hour, half day, or full day. Arrange the price with the driver before boarding.

SCOOTERS AND MOPEDS Pollution and insufferable traffic jams have made scooters and mopeds popular alternatives to cars for some Romans. But a word to the two-wheeled: Some Italian automobile drivers consider these vehicles a nuisance and often are loath to give them their fair share of the roadway. Use extreme caution—and wear a solid helmet. To rent a moped, scooter, or motorbike, try *Scoot-a-long* (302 Via Cavour; phone: 678-0206); *Scooters for Rent* (66 Via della Purificazione, near Piazza Barberini; phone: 488-5485), which also rents bikes; or *St. Peter Scooters* (43 Via Porta Castello, near the *Basilica di San Pietro;* phone: 687-5714).

SUBWAY The *metropolitana,* Rome's subway, consists of two lines. *Linea A* runs roughly east to west, from the *Stazione Ottaviano* (Octavian Station) near the *Vatican,* across the Tiber, through the historic center (Piazza di Spagna, Piazza Barberini, the *Stazione Termini,* and San Giovanni), and over to the eastern edge of the city past Cinecittà, the filmmaking center, to the Alban Hills. *Linea B,* which is partly an underground and partly a surface railroad, runs north to south, connecting the *Tiburtina* train station (where numerous long-distance trains stop) with the *Stazione Termini* and the *Colosseo* and, with a stop at the *Ostiense* station at Piazza Piramide to connect with the train to *Aeroporto Leonardo da Vinci,* down to the southern suburb of *EUR.* Tickets, which cost 1,280 lire (about 80¢), are sold at some newsstands, tobacco shops, bars, and at most stations. Only a few stations are staffed with ticket sellers, however; most have ticket-dispensing machines that accept only coins, so be prepared. Subway entrances are marked by a large red "M."

TAXI Cabs can be hailed in the street or found at numerous stands, which are listed in the yellow pages. The *Radio Taxi* telephone numbers are 3570, 3875, 4994, and 88177. Taxi rates are quite expensive (and increase regularly); drivers are required to show you, if asked, the current list of added charges. After 10 PM a night surcharge is added, there are surcharges for holidays and for suitcases, and an additional surcharge is added for trips to the airport at Fiumicino. Don't hire free-lance taxis; drivers usually are unlicensed and charge up to double the price of the regular taxi fare.

TOURS A quick and interesting tour on Bus No. 110 covers some 45 major sights in three hours. Although there is no guide, a short brochure in English gives the highlights. The bus leaves Piazza dei Cinquecento around 3 PM (2 PM in winter). It runs daily in season and on weekends only the rest of the year. For additional details, either call 46951 or check with the *ATAC* booth in the square. The Roman Catholic, pro-ecumenical Fathers of Atonement (30 Via Santa Maria dell'Anima; phone: 687-9552) lead walking tours of the city and the *Vatican* on Friday mornings. They also offer lectures on Thursday mornings. Both are given in English; there's no charge, but a donation is appreciated.

Secret Walks in Rome (6 Via dei Quattro Cantoni; phone: 397-28728) offers imaginative tours of the city. Excursions include bicycle tours of Rome and half-day walking tours focusing on wines and wine shops. Advance reservations required.

For those especially interested in art history and archaeology, a team of professionals in both fields is available to take individuals or groups on private English-language tours of Rome, or on one- and two-day trips outside the city. For information, contact Peter Zalewski (6 Via Cristoforo Colombo, Marcellina di Roma; phone: 774-425451; fax: 774-425122). An English-speaking German, Ruben Popper (12 Via dei Levii; phone: 761-0901), who has lived in Rome for more than 30 years, also leads city tours (mostly walking).

For a bird's-eye view of the city, take a helicopter tour, which leaves from the *Centro Sperimentale d'Aviazione* at *Aeroporto dell'Urbe* (Urbe Airport; 825 Via Salaria; phone: 8864-0035). A minimum of five passengers is required for the breathtaking—but pricey—20-minute ride; reserve a week in advance.

TRAIN Rome's main train station is the *Stazione Termini* (Piazza dei Cinquecento; phone: 4775, information). There are several suburban stations. The ones most often used by visitors are the *Stazione Ostiense* (Ostiense Station; Piazzale dei Partigiani; phone: 575-0732), one of the stations from which trains depart for *Aeroporto Leonardo da Vinci;* and the *Stazione Tiburtina* (Tiburtina Station; Circonvolazione Nomentana). Because of the increase in crime in many of Italy's train stations, the police have anticrime units patrolling all trains and stations, but remain alert anyway.

SPECIAL EVENTS

The events of the church calendar—too numerous to mention here—are extra special in Rome. Below is our recommended festival choice, followed by other celebrations throughout the year.

A FAVORITE FETE

La Festa di Noantri (The Feast of Ourselves) For a boisterous week in late July, when the richest Romans have fled to the sea or the mountains, the teeming Trastevere quarter becomes one sprawling outdoor trattoria. As night falls and the air cools, streetlights illuminate rows of tables stretching for blocks, restaurant blending with pizzeria melting into *caffè*. Merrymakers pack the streets, musicians stroll, gaudy stands jam the main avenue, piazze host live jazz and become open-air cinemas, and—because there is a religious foundation to all this—the *Chiesa della Madonna del Carme* (Church of the Carmine Madonna) stays open nearly as late as the watermelon stands. The *noantri* of the celebration are the people of Trastevere, who consider themselves the only true Romans and choose to honor their neighborhood when the rest of town has fled the heat.

During *La Settimana Santa* (Holy Week), the city swarms with visitors. Religious ceremonies abound, particularly on *Venerdì Santo* (Good Friday), when the pope conducts the famous *Via Crucis* (Way of the Cross) procession to the ruins of the *Colosseo,* where Christian martyrs met their deaths. On *Easter Sunday* itself Romans go to mass, then indulge in a huge family feast (often featuring roast lamb and concluding with a dove-shaped cake). The celebration continues through the next day, which is known as *Pasquetta* (Little Easter); on this day almost everything in the city closes down, and it seems like the entire population is out picnicking in the sunshine.

The arrival of spring is celebrated in April with a colorful display of potted azaleas covering Piazza di Spagna, and in May a picturesque street nearby, Via Margutta, is the site of an exhibition of paintings by artists of varied talents. The *Fiera di Via Margutta* (Via Margutta Art Fair) is repeated in the fall. Also in May the *Villa Borghese*'s lush Piazza di Siena becomes the site of the *Concorso Ippico Internazionale* (International Horse Show), and soon after that is the *Campionato Internazionale di Tennis* (Italian Open) tennis tournament (see *Tennis*). An antiques show also takes place in spring and fall along charming Via dei Coronari (near Piazza Navona), and there's the *Mostra Internazionale di Rose* (International Rose Show) in late spring at the delightful *Roseto Comunale* on Aventine Hill. In late May or June the vast *Fiera di Roma,* a national industrial exhibition, takes place at the fairgrounds along Via Cristoforo Colombo.

For *Natale* (Christmas), relatively modest decorations go up around the city, almost all churches display their sometimes movable, elaborate *presepi* (nativity scenes), and a colorful toy and candy fair is held in Piazza Navona. The season, including the fair, lasts through the *Festa dell'Epifania* (Feast of the Epiphany; January 6), when children receive gifts from a witch known as the Befana to add to those Babbo Natale (Father Christmas) or the Bambino Gesù (Baby Jesus) brought them at *Christmas.* The intervening *Capodanno* (New Year's Eve) is celebrated with a bang here as in much of the rest of Italy—firecrackers snap, crackle, and pop from early evening on.

There are also innumerable characteristic *feste* or *sagre* (festivals, usually celebrating some local food or beverage at the height of its season) in the many hill towns surrounding Rome, particularly in the Castelli Romani, about 15 miles (24 km) south of the city. The most notable of these are *L'Infiorata* (The Flowering) at Genzano di Roma in June and the *Sagra dell'Uva* (Rite of the Grapes) at Marino in October.

MUSEUMS

In addition to those described in *Special Places,* Rome has many other interesting museums. Included in the following list are churches that should be seen because of their artistic value. Unless otherwise indicated, the churches are open daily and do not charge admission. You will, however, need a supply of 500-lire coins to operate the electric lights that illuminate the frescoes and other paintings in many churches. The museums and galleries listed below are closed Mondays and charge admission unless otherwise specified (though some waive their admission charges on Sundays). Always check the operating schedules before setting out; many places close for several hours in the afternoon.

CHIESA DI SAN LUIGI DEI FRANCESI (CHURCH OF ST. LOUIS OF THE FRENCH) The French national church, built in the 16th century, contains three Caravaggios, including the famous *Calling of St. Matthew.* Via della Dogana Vecchia.

CHIESA DI SAN PIETRO IN VINCOLI (CHURCH OF ST. PETER IN CHAINS) Erected in the 5th century to preserve St. Peter's chains, this church contains Michelangelo's magnificent statue of Moses. Piazza di San Pietro in Vincoli.

CHIESA DI SANT'AGOSTINO (CHURCH OF ST. AUGUSTINE) The *Madonna of the Pilgrims* by Caravaggio and the *Prophet Isaiah* by Raphael are found in this 15th-century church. Piazza di Sant'Agostino.

CHIESA DI SANT'ANDREA AL QUIRINALE (CHURCH OF ST. ANDREW OF THE QUIRINAL) A Baroque church by Bernini, to be compared with the *Chiesa di San Carlo alle Quattro Fontane* (see *Special Places*), Borromini's church on the same street. Via del Quirinale.

CHIESA DI SANT'ANDREA DELLA VALLE (CHURCH OF ST. ANDREW OF THE VALLEY) This fine 17th-century church was designed by Carlo Maderno and Carlo Rainaldi and has an elegant cupola (Rome's second-highest after the *Basilica di San Pietro*) that dominates the skyline. Giorgio Lanfranco's celebrated fresco, *The Glory of Paradise,* is inside. Both the exterior and interior recently were cleaned. Piazza Sant'Andrea.

CHIESA DI SANTA MARIA D'ARACOELI (CHURCH OF ST. MARY OF THE ALTAR OF HEAVEN) In this Romanesque-Gothic church are frescoes by Pinturicchio and a 14th-century staircase built in thanksgiving for the end of a plague. Piazza d'Aracoeli.

CHIESA DI SANTA MARIA IN COSMEDIN (CHURCH OF ST. MARY IN COSMEDIN) This Romanesque church is known for the *Bocca della Verità* (Mouth of Truth) in its portico—a Roman drain or treasury cover in the shape of a god's face whose mouth, according to legend, will bite off the hand of anyone telling a lie. Piazza della Bocca della Verità.

CHIESA DI SANTA MARIA SOPRA MINERVA (CHURCH OF ST. MARY OVER MINERVA) Built over a Roman temple to the goddess Minerva, this church has a Gothic interior (unusual for Rome), frescoes by Filippino Lippi (which have been freshly restored), and two versions of Michelangelo's statue of *St. John the Baptist.* Piazza della Minerva.

CHIESA DI SANTA MARIA IN TRASTEVERE (CHURCH OF ST. MARY IN TRASTEVERE) Another recently restored ancient church, this one was the first in Rome dedicated to the Virgin, with 12th- and 13th-century mosaics. Piazza Santa Maria in Trastevere.

CHIESA DI SANTA MARIA DELLA VITTORIA (CHURCH OF ST. MARY OF THE VICTORY) It is Baroque to the core, especially in Bernini's *Cappella Cornaro* (Cornaro Chapel). Via XX Settembre.

CHIESA DI SANTA SABINA (CHURCH OF ST. SABINA) A simple 5th-century basilica, it offers original cypress doors, a 13th-century cloister and bell tower, and stunning views of the city. Piazza Pietro d'Illiria.

GALLERIA COLONNA The Colonna family collection of mainly 17th-century Italian paintings, including some works by Veronese and Tintoretto, are displayed in the *Palazzo Colonna,* where the family still lives. Open Saturday mornings only; closed in August. *Palazzo Colonna,* 17 Via della Pilotta (phone: 679-4362).

GALLERIA DORIA PAMPHILI Displayed here is the Doria Pamphili family's private collection of Italian and foreign paintings from the 15th to the 17th century, including Caravaggio's *Mary Magdalene.* Closed Mondays, Wednesdays, and Thursdays. *Palazzo Doria Pamphili,* 1/A Piazza del Collegio Romano (phone: 679-4365).

GALLERIA NAZIONALE D'ARTE ANTICA (NATIONAL GALLERY OF ANCIENT ART) This museum exhibits paintings by Italian artists from the 13th through the 18th century plus some Dutch and Flemish works. *Palazzo Barberini,* 13 Via delle Quattro Fontane (phone: 481-4591).

GALLERIA NAZIONALE D'ARTE MODERNA (NATIONAL GALLERY OF MODERN ART) Particularly noteworthy are works by pre–World War I Italian painters and the futurists. 131 Viale Belle Arti (phone: 322-4151).

GALLERIA PALAZZO CORSINI Displayed in a regal palace are paintings, classical sculptures, and other artworks, all created in the 16th and 17th centuries. 10 Via della Lungara (phone: 654-2323).

GALLERIA SPADA Renaissance art and Roman marble work from the 2nd and 3rd centuries; also two huge, rare antique globes that were used on Dutch ships in the 16th century. The building itself is noteworthy for its exterior, designed by Borromini. *Palazzo Spada,* 3 Piazza Capo di Ferro (phone: 686-1158).

MUSEO BARRACCO (BARRACCO MUSEUM) This fine, extensively restored 19th-century mansion, boasting a private collection of fascinating pre–Roman era sculptures, belonged to Baron Giovanni Barracco, who donated it to the city in 1904. Two famous German archaeologists, Wolfgang Helbig and Ludwig Pollak, helped assemble the collection, which includes a sphinx uncovered near the *Chiesa di Santa Maria sopra Minerva* on the site of a temple to the Egyptian goddess Isis, ca. 43 BC. 168 Corso Vittorio Emanuele II (phone: 654-0848).

MUSEO NAPOLEONICO (NAPOLEONIC MUSEUM) Housed here is memorabilia of the emperor's family during their rule in Rome. Closed weekends and for an afternoon break (2 to 5 PM). 1 Via Zanardelli (phone: 654-0286).

MUSEO NAZIONALE DI VILLA GIULIA (VILLA GIULIA NATIONAL MUSEUM) The country's most important Etruscan collection is displayed in a 16th-century villa by Vignola. 9 Piazzale di Villa Giulia (phone: 320-1951).

MUSEO DI PALAZZO VENEZIA (MUSEUM AT PALAZZO VENEZIA) Tapestries, paintings, sculpture, ceramics, and other art objects are featured, as well as important temporary exhibits. A hall of medieval art recently reopened after a 10-year renovation. 118 Via del Plebescito (phone: 679-8865).

GALLERIES

Rome has many art galleries with interesting shows of Italian and foreign artists. They generally close Mondays and for an afternoon break (1 to 4 PM). The following offer an excellent selection of contemporary and modern art:

GABBIANO 51 Via della Frezza (phone: 322-7049).

GALLERIA L'ARCADIA 70/A Via Babuino (phone: 679-1023).

GALLERIA GIULIA 148 Via Giulia (phone: 688-02061).

GALLERIA IL SEGNO 4 Via di Capo Le Case (phone: 679-1387).

L'ISOLA 5 Via Gregoriana (phone: 678-4678).

SHOPPING

In Rome you'll find the great couturiers, but even though their designs will cost less here than back home, don't expect any bargain-basement finds. The best buys are in high-quality, hand-finished leather goods, jewelry, fabrics, shoes, and sweaters. Almost all stores observe the Anglo-Saxon rite of *prezzi fissi* (fixed prices). A particularly good time to shop is in early

January, when most stores in Rome lower their prices significantly (sometimes by as much as 50%) for several weeks.

The chicest shopping area is around the bottom of Piazza di Spagna, beginning with elegant Via Condotti, which runs east to west and is lined with Rome's most exclusive shops. Via del Babuino, which connects Piazza di Spagna to Piazza del Popolo, has traditionally been known for its antiques shops, but is also a high-fashion street, as is nearby Via Bocca di Leone, where there are a number of designers' boutiques. Running parallel to Via Condotti are several more streets—such as Via Borgognona, Via delle Carrozze, and Via Frattina—mostly pedestrian zones with more fashionable boutiques. These streets end at Via del Corso, the main street of Rome, which runs north to south and is lined with shops geared to the younger set. There are some fine shops along Via del Tritone, Via Sistina, and in the Via Veneto area, and small, chic boutiques around the *Pantheon,* Campo dei Fiori, and Via del Governo Vecchio. On the other side of the river toward the *Vatican* are two popular shopping streets that are slightly less expensive—Via Cola di Rienzo and Via Ottaviano. Also explore Via Nazionale, near the *Stazione Termini.*

Antiques hunters should stroll along Via del Babuino, Via dei Coronari, Via del Governo Vecchio, Via Margutta, and Via Giulia. Rome's finest food shops are on Via della Croce and Via Cola di Rienzo.

If shopping is entertainment, Rome's street markets are its best theater. Most of the country's most intriguing goods can be found here. High-quality shoes, new and secondhand clothes, a few genuine antiques, and lots of interesting junk are sold at the city's gigantic Sunday morning labyrinth at the *Porta Portese,* which operates from 5 AM (the bargain hour) until 1 PM. If you wish to join the fray, stuff a little cash in a tight inside pocket, leave camera and purse at home, and prepare to shuffle through the packed streets. The vast clothing market at the weekday shops and stands on Via Sannio, near San Giovanni, is the place for good buys on a wide assortment of casual clothes—army surplus, jeans, down jackets, mode-of-the-moment sweaters; beware of imitations.

One of the most rewarding Roman experiences is to pore over new and used books, modern reproductions of etchings of Rome's monuments, and the occasional authentic antique print in the stalls at Piazza di Fontanella Borghese, which are open weekday mornings. Fine prints also may be found at the following auction houses: *L'Antonina* (23 Piazza Mignanelli; phone: 679-4009); *Christie's* (114 Piazza Navona; phone: 687-2787); *Finarte* (54 Via Margutta; phone: 320-7630); *Semenzato* (93 Piazza di Spagna; phone: 676-6479); and *Sotheby's* (90 Piazza di Spagna; phone: 678-1798). For typical shopping hours, see GETTING READY TO GO.

Below are some of our favorite shops in Rome:

Apolloni Mostly 17th- and 18th-century paintings, sculpture, and furnishings. 133 Via del Babuino (phone: 679-2429).

Armando Rioda Hand-crafted copies of Italy's luxury leather goods at lower prices than the originals. 90 Via Belsiana (phone: 678-4435).

Arturo Ferrante Rare antiquities, also paintings and furnishings. 42-43 Via del Babuino (phone: 678-3613).

Balloon Italian-designed, low-cost women's shirts made of Chinese silk. 35 Piazza di Spagna (phone: 678-0110) and 495 Via Flaminia Vecchia (phone: 333-3352).

Bassetti High-fashion ready-to-wear for both men and women at discounted prices; the best clothes bargain in the Eternal City. 5 Via Monterone (phone: 689-2878).

Battistoni Men's elegant but conservative clothing. 61/A Via Condotti (phone: 678-6241).

Beltrami Sophisticated women's clothing. 19 Via Condotti (phone: 679-1330).

Beppino Rampin Custom-made shoes and boots for men and women. 31 Via Quintino Sella (phone: 474-0469).

Bertè Old and new toys. 107-111 Piazza Navona (phone: 678-5011).

Borsalino World-renowned hats. 157/B Via IV Novembre (phone: 679-4192).

Bottega Veneta Fine leather goods in the firm's trademark soft, basketweave design. 16/B Via San Sebastianello (phone: 678-2535).

Bruno Magli Top-quality shoes and boots, classic elegance. Three locations: 70 Via Veneto (phone: 488-4355); 1 Via del Gambero (phone: 679-3802); and 237 Via Cola di Rienzo (phone: 324-1759).

Buccellati For connoisseurs: A fine jeweler with a unique way of working with gold. 31 Via Condotti (phone: 679-0329).

Bulgari One of the world's most famous high-style jewelers. 10 Via Condotti (phone: 679-3876).

Carlo Pasquali Old prints, engravings, original lithographs, and drawings. Near the *Fontana di Trevi* at 25 Largo di Brazzà (no phone).

Cerruti 1881 This trendy clothier is a favorite among Italian men. 20 Piazza San Lorenzo in Lucina (phone: 687-1505).

Cesari Exquisite upholstery and other decorator fabrics. 195 Via del Babuino (phone: 361-0495).

Davide Cenci Italian diplomats and their spouses buy their pin-striped suits, tweeds, and trench coats here. 1-7 Via Campo Marzio (phone: 699-0681).

Fallani Antiquities, ancient coins, and archeological items. 58/A Via del Babuino (phone: 320-7982).

Fendi Canvas and leather bags, genuine and faux furs, luggage, costume jewelry, and clothing. 36-40 Via Borgognona (phone: 679-7641/2/3).

Ferragamo Classic shoes. Women's: 73 Via Condotti (phone: 679-1565); men's: 66 Via Condotti (phone: 678-1130).

Franco Maria Ricci Sumptuously printed coffee-table books by a discriminating publisher, sold in an elegant setting. 4/D Via Borgognona (phone: 679-3466).

Fratelli Merola Handmade gloves of fine leather, produced in their own atelier. 143 Via del Corso (phone: 679-1961).

Galleria dell'Antiquariato Europeo Porcelain, bronzes, marbles. 76 Via Margutta (phone: 320-7729) and 112 Via dei Pastini (phone: 678-0195).

Galleria delle Stampe Antiche Old prints. 38 Via del Governo Vecchio (no phone).

Galtrucco All kinds of fabrics, especially pure silk. 23 Via del Tritone (phone: 678-9022).

Gherardini Fine leather fashions. 48/B Via Belsiana (phone: 679-5501).

Gianfranco Ferré High fashion for women. 42/B Via Borgognona (phone: 679-0050).

Gianni Versace The Milanese designer's Rome outlets. 41 Via Borgognona and 29 Via Bocca di Leone (phone: 678-0521).

Giorgio Armani Smart, fashionable clothing for men and women. 140 Via del Babuino (phone: 678-8454) and 77 Via Condotti (phone: 699-1460).

Gucci Men's and women's shoes, luggage, handbags, and other leather goods. Be prepared to wait. 8 Via Condotti (phone: 678-9340).

Laura Biagiotti Elegant womenswear. 43 Via Borgognona, corner of Via Belsiana (phone: 679-1205).

Libreria Editrice Vaticana A vast selection of books on art, archaeology, religion, and theology (some in English) at the *Vatican*'s own publisher's outlet. Next to the *Vatican* post office in Piazza San Pietro (phone: 6982).

Lion Bookshop The city's oldest English-language bookstore, chock-full of volumes on Rome's history, travel, and food. 181 Via del Babuino (phone: 322-5837).

Mario Valentino Fine shoes and leather goods. 84/A Via Frattina (phone: 679-1242).

Marisa Pignataro Outstanding knit dresses and tops in pure wool. 20 Via dei Greci (phone: 678-5443).

Massoni Fine handmade jewelry with a distinctive look. 48 Largo Goldoni (phone: 679-0182).

Medison One of the city's best custom shirtmakers for men. 6 Via Gregoriana (phone: 678-9618).

Missoni High-fashion knitwear for men and women in unique weaves of often costly blended yarns. 78 Piazza di Spagna (phone: 679-2555).

Ai Monasteri Products ranging from bath oils to honey to liqueurs from some 20 monasteries. 76 Piazza Cinque Lune (phone: 688-02783).

Myricae Hand-painted ceramics and such, made by Italian artisans from Sardinia to Deruta. 36 Via Frattina (phone: 679-5335).

Nazareno Gabrielli Excellent leather goods. 36-37 Via Condotti (phone: 679-0862).

Perrone Leather and fabric gloves. 92 Piazza di Spagna (phone: 678-3101).

Petochi Imaginative jewelry and grand old clocks. 23 Piazza di Spagna (phone: 679-3947).

Pineider Italy's famed stationer. 68-69 Via Due Macelli (phone: 678-9013).

Polidori Exclusive menswear and tailoring (21 Via Condotti and 4/C Via Borgognona). Finest pure silks and other fabrics (4/A Via Borgognona; phone: 678-4842).

Prada Fine-quality leather goods, including bags, shoes, and luggage, at relatively reasonable prices. 28-31 Via Nazionale (phone: 488-2413).

Le Quattro Stagioni Handmade ceramics by artisans from all over Italy. Shipping to the US can be arranged. 30/B Via dell'Umiltà (no phone).

Richard Ginori This shop has sold fine porcelain dinnerware and vases since 1735. 87-90 Via Condotti (phone: 678-1013) and 177 Via del Tritone (phone: 679-3836).

Ritz The classic look of Tuscany in women's clothing, including dressy loden coats. 188-189 Via del Babuino (phone: 361-2057).

De Sanctis Gift items, including Murano glass objects, Ginori porcelain, Florentine ceramics, and Alessi stainless household items. 80-84 Piazza Navona (phone: 688-06810).

Al Sogno Giocattoli Huge stuffed animals and a wide selection of amusing toys. 53 Piazza Navona (phone: 686-4198).

Tanino Crisci Chic women's shoes. 1 Via Borgognona (phone: 679-5461).

Trimani Founded in 1821, this is Rome's oldest and most famous wine shop. 20 Via Goito (phone: 446-9661).

Valentino Bold, high-fashion clothes for men. 12 Via Condotti (phone: 678-3656). Branches include a womenswear shop (15-18 Via Bocca di Leone; phone: 679-5862); *Oliver,* a shop for men, women, and children (61 Via del Babuino; phone: 679-8314); and an haute couture salon (24 Via Gregoriana; no phone).

SPORTS AND FITNESS

AUTO RACING At the *Autodromo di Roma* (*Valle Lunga* racetrack, Campagnano di Roma, Via Cassia, Km 34; phone: 904-1027). Take a bus from Via Lepanto.

BICYCLING A pleasant excursion through Rome by bicycle is along the Villa Circuit, which travels 18 miles (29 km) from one major public park to another, all former private estates. You can get a perspective of the city that few tourists—and even fewer Romans—ever see. Start on the silent residential Aventine Hill, cross the Tiber, and climb up Monte Gianicolo to the vast *Villa Doria Pamphili.* Dozens of muskrats, descendants of a single pair brought here as part of an experiment, waddle and paddle around the lake in the park's center. Pass by the *Basilica di San Pietro,* cross the river again, and pedal through the gardens of the *Villa Borghese.* From the *Villa Borghese* due north to Via Salaria, it's a short ride to our final suggested stop—the wooded, aristocratic *Villa Ada. Nino Collati* (81 Via del Pellegrino; phone: 654-1084) rents bikes, including tandems. Bicycles are also available at *Bike Rome* (phone: 322-5240), located in the parking lot of the *Villa Borghese;* at Piazza San Silvestro and Piazza del Popolo; and on Via di Porta Castello near Piazza San Pietro. Be sure to take the same precautions when biking as when riding a scooter or moped (see *Getting Around*).

FITNESS CENTERS Rome has relatively few fitness centers and gyms, and those that exist tend to be cramped. An exception is the roomy, well-equipped, and (unusual for Rome) air conditioned *Roman Sport Center* (in the underground passage to the *metropolitana* stop at the top of Via Veneto in the *Villa Borghese,* 33 Via del Galoppatoio; phone: 320-1667). Although it is a private club, its American owner allows visitors to attend aerobics classes and to use the pool, squash court, sauna, Jacuzzi, and two gyms. Another private club, the *Navona Health Center* (39 Via dei Banchi Nuovi; phone: 689-6104), also opens its three-room gym in an ancient historical palazzo to non-members. Another fitness center accessible to the public is the *Barbara Bouchet Bodyshop* (162 Viale Parioli; phone: 808-5686).

GOLF There are several courses in and around Rome. The following are our two favorite fairways.

TOP TEE-OFF SPOTS

Circolo del Golf Roma Located 7 miles (11 km) southeast of Rome, this undulating 6,344-yard layout is well loved by golf devotees. The course is rough, and strong winds sweep across its pines, cypresses, and oaks, but in the background are ruins of ancient Roman aqueducts. Accuracy is a must. Closed Mondays; book well ahead for weekends. 716A Via Appia Nuova (phone: 780-3407).

Olgiata British course architect C. K. Cotton started with plenty of space, so there's never a feeling of congestion. At the same time, he gave every hole a character all its own, balancing the course as a whole to challenge every facet of a player's skill and strategic abilities. The large greens have narrow bunkered entrances, the levels change (though never too drastically), and there's scarcely a straight hole on the course. The *West* course is for international tournaments, the nine-hole *East* course for duffers. Closed Mondays; visitors may not play on weekends. 15 Largo Olgiata (phone: 378-9968).

HORSE RACING Trotting races take place at the *Ippodromo Tor di Valle* (Via del Mare, Km 9.3; phone: 529-0269). Flat races are held at the *Ippodromo delle Capannelle* (1255 Via Appia, Km 12; phone: 718-3143) in the spring and fall.

HORSEBACK RIDING There are several riding schools and clubs inside the capital, and dozens more in the countryside surrounding the city. A regional branch of the *Associazione Nazionale per il Turismo Equestre* (*ANTE;* National Association for Equestrian Tourism; 5 Via A. Borelli; phone: 444-1179 or 494-0969) arranges special events for riders and can provide a complete list of local facilities. For lessons at various levels of proficiency, rentals by the hour (sometimes a subscription for several hours is required), or guided rides in the country, contact the *Centro Ippico Monte del Pavone* (Via Valle di Baccano; phone: 904-1378) or *Società Ippica Romana* (30 Via dei Monti della Farnesina; phone: 324-0591 or 324-0592). For weekend or week-long riding vacations, contact *Turismo Verde* (20 Via Fortuny; phone: 320-3464).

JOGGING There are two tracks in the *Villa Borghese;* enter at the top of Via Veneto or from Piazza del Popolo. The *Villa Glori* (in the Parioli quarter) has a 1,180-meter track, which is illuminated at night; the large *Villa Doria Pamphili,* on the top of Monte Gianicolo (Janiculum Hill), has three tracks, as does the *Villa Ada* (off Via Salaria), which once was Mussolini's private park; and the *Villa Torlonia* (off Via Nomentana) has a pretty track flanked by palm and acacia trees. These villas are generally safe places to run, even at night.

SOCCER Two highly competitive teams, *Roma* and *Lazio,* play on Sundays from September through May at the *Stadio Olimpico* (Olympic Stadium at the *Foro Italico;* 1 Via dei Gladiatori; phone: 36851), site of the final game of the 1990 *World Cup.*

SWIMMING The pools at the *Cavalieri Hilton International* (see *Checking In*) and the *Aldrovandi Palace* (15 Via Ulisse Aldrovandi; phone: 322-3993) hotels are open to non-guests for a fee. Public pools include the *Piscina Olimpica* (*Foro Italico;* phone: 323-6076) and the *Piscina delle Rose* (20 Viale America, *EUR;* phone: 592-1862). Swimming in the sea near Rome is dangerous because of the high levels of pollution. Southeast of Ostia, at Castel Fusano and Castel Porziano, are stretches of free beach which are fine for a stroll, but are not suitable for swimming. Lago di Bracciano (Lake Bracciano), about 20 miles (32 km) north of Rome, is good for swimming, but there are no changing facilities. Note that the lake can get very crowded on weekends.

There are several water parks in the area, complete with swimming and wading pools, Jacuzzi-type basins, long, snaking water slides, and playpens for small children. Among them are: *Acqualand,* 30 miles (48 km) southeast of Rome near Anzio (41 Via dei Faggi, Lavinio; phone: 987-8247); *Acquasplash,* 20 miles (32 km) from the city (Via Palo Laziale, Ladispoli; phone: 991-2942); and *Acquapiper,* 15 miles (24 km) from Rome near Tivoli (Via Maremanna Inferiore; phone: 774-326538).

TENNIS Most courts belong to private clubs. Those at the *Cavalieri Hilton International* (see *Checking In*) and at the *Sheraton Roma* (Viale del Pattinaggio; phone: 5453) hotels are open to non-guests for a fee. Public courts are occasionally available at the *Foro Italico* (phone: 321-9021). Also open to the public are the *Società Ginnastica Roma* (5 Via del Muro Torto; phone: 488-5566), which has five courts; and, in the Via Appia Antica area, the four-court *Oasi di Pace* (2 Via degli Eugenii; phone: 718-4550), which also has a swimming pool.

The *Campionato Internazionale di Tennis* (Italian Open) takes place in Rome in May, and although tickets for the semifinals and finals are difficult to come by without advance purchase (at least four months ahead), daytime tickets for same-day events are relatively easy to obtain at the *Foro Italico* box office (phone: 36851). For information on purchasing advance tickets, contact the *Federazione Italiana Tennis* (70 Viale Tiziano; phone: 323-3807 or 324-0578).

WINDSURFING Sailboards and lessons are available at Castel Porziano (*primo cancello,* or first gate); in Fregene at the *Stabilimento La Baia* (phone: 665-61647) and the *Miraggio Sporting Club* (phone: 665-61802); and at the *Centro Surf Bracciano* at Lago di Bracciano (no phone).

THEATER

Italy has been a land of patrons and performers since the days of the Medicis. Now, in areas where the aristocracy is too impoverished to treat, the government has rushed in, and virtually every fair-size city has its *teatro stabile* (repertory theater). As a result, ticket prices are far more reasonable than in the US, which is why you'll often see *esaurito* ("sold out") pasted across the poster outside the theater. During the theater season, approximately October through May, check *A Guest in Rome* or any daily newspaper for listings (see *Local Coverage*).

We begin with the *teatri stabili* in Rome, followed by other choices that offer a variety of theatrical and cinematic entertainment.

CENTER STAGE

Teatri di Roma (Theaters of Rome) The government-subsidized regional theaters premiere most contemporary Italian plays, as well as their share of foreign works—varying the diet of Goldoni and Pirandello that more traditional Italian companies serve up to the Sunday matinee crowd. The *Teatri di Roma* perform at three principal locations, each a splendid historic theater: the recently restored *Teatro Argentina* (Argentine Theater; Largo Argentina; phone: 688-04601), the *Teatro Valle* (Valley Theater; 23/A Via Teatro Valle; phone: 688-03794), and the *Teatro Quirino* (Quirinale Theater; 73 Piazza dell'Oratorio; phone: 679-4585).

Another major theater is the *Teatro Eliseo* (Eliseo Theater; 183/E Via Nazionale; phone: 488-2114), which presents both classic and avant-garde works. A season of classical drama (in Italian and sometimes Greek) is held each July in the open-air *Teatro Romano di Ostia Antica* (Roman Theater of Ostia Antica; phone: 565-1913). The *Teatro Sistina* (Sistine Theater; 129 Via Sistina; phone: 482-6841) is Rome's best music hall. The charming, turn-of-the-century cabaret theater *Salone Margarita* (Margarita Lounge; 75 Via Due Macelli; phone: 679-8269) offers late-night shows and occasional Sunday afternoon concerts. Check the newspapers for the *Cinema Pasquino* (in Trastevere at Vicolo del Piede; phone: 580-3622) and the *Cinema Alcazar* (14 Via Merry del Val; phone: 588-0099), which often have English-language movies.

MUSIC

Aside from Italian opera, Rome offers visitors a wealth of musical experiences. We begin with the city's most venerable venue, followed by a list of other musical treats. Check *A Guest in Rome* or the daily newspapers for information about performances (see *Local Coverage*).

HIGH NOTES

Accademia Nazionale di Santa Cecilia (National Academy of St. Cecilia) Named for the patron saint of music and established in 1566 by Pierluigi da Palestrina, this organization serves a host of functions, including managing Rome's symphony orchestra in residence, staging concerts in the *Vatican*'s stark *Pio Auditorium* on Sunday afternoons (with reprises on Monday and Tuesday evenings) from October through June, and orchestrating Bach-to-Berg chamber performances in the academy's own delightful hall on Friday evenings. A guest conductor system has attracted Maazel, Abbado, Giulini, Sawallisch, and other notables. Yuppies and university students are swelling the once rather elderly ranks of the city's concertgoers, and large chunks of tickets are sold by subscription, so be prepared to queue up to snare a seat. In summer *Santa Cecilia* presents evening concerts in the hilltop Piazza del Campidoglio. Since seats here are not numbered, it's wise to find your place an hour or more before the music begins, settle down with a picnic supper, and enjoy the summer sunset in the company of majestic architecture. During intermission, stroll behind the square for Rome's best overview of the *Foro Romano* by night. 4 Via della Conciliazione (phone: 679-0389).

The regular season at the *Teatro dell'Opera* (Opera Theater; 1 Piazza Beniamino Gigli, corner of Via Firenze; phone: 481-7003) runs December through May. The best way to get tickets for good seats is through your hotel concierge or major travel agencies. Tickets also are sold at the box office several days before a performance, but they go fast—and be prepared to wait in line. The *Rome Ballet* also performs at the *Teatro dell'Opera*. Between October and May concerts and ballets are offered at the *Teatro Olimpico* (Olympic Theater; 17 Piazza Gentile da Fabriano; phone: 323-4890). The *Istituzione Universitaria dei Concerti* (University Institute of Music) holds concerts at the renovated *Aula Magna IUC* (50 Lungotevere Flaminio; phone: 361-0051/2) and at the university's *Aula Magna* (1 Piazzale Aldo Moro; phone: 361-0051). Other concerts occasionally are held at the *Auditorio del Gonfalone* (Banner Auditorium; 32 Via del Gonfalone; phone: 687-5952) and elsewhere around Rome by the *Coro Polifonico Romano* (Roman Polyphonic Chorus). Still more musical groups use the *Teatro Ghione* (Ghione Theater; 37 Via delle Fornaci; phone: 637-2294). There are concerts in many churches throughout the year, especially around *Christmas,* and during the summer there are occasional musical performances in the parks and piazze.

NIGHTCLUBS AND NIGHTLIFE

Nightspots slip into and out of fashion so easily that visitors would do well to check Thursday's "TrovaRoma" supplement to the daily *La Repubblica* for an up-to-date survey of what's going on. Since the 1950s the few nightclubs here have clustered around Via Veneto and Piazza di Spagna, but they are pricey, with high minimums. For the younger set on the lookout for disco, jazz, and general hanging-out spots, a walk through Trastevere or the Testaccio area around Rome's old general markets and slaughterhouse (the newer bohemian area now that Trastevere has become gentrified) will turn up a host of intriguing places.

Among the nightclubs, the small, swanky, expensive restaurant and piano bar *Tartarughino* (near Piazza Navona at 1 Via della Scrofa; phone: 686-4131) is popular with the political set; there's no dancing. A slightly younger crowd gathers at fashionable *Gilda* (near Piazza di Spagna at 97 Via Mario de' Fiore; phone: 678-4838), known for its live music and pricey restaurant.

Also popular are the *Open Gate* (4 Via San Nicola da Tolentino; phone: 488-4604 or 482-4464) and, off Via Veneto, *Jackie O* (11 Via Boncompagni; phone: 488-5754), which has an expensive restaurant, a piano bar, and a disco.

The disco *Piper* (9 Via Tagliamento; phone: 841-4459) has been packing people in, literally, for generations. The show here changes every night. *Le Stelle* (22 Via Cesare Beccaria; phone: 361-1240) plays pop, rap, soul, and funk until dawn. The *Bulli e Pupi* disco (on Aventine Hill at 11/A Via San Saba; phone: 578-2022) is not for executives, but for their offspring. The posh *Hostaria dell'Orso* (25 Via dei Soldati; phone: 683-07074) has something for everyone—the dimly lit, comfortable *Blu Bar* on the main floor offers laid-back piano or guitar music, and *La Cabala* upstairs is a disco for titled young Romans. It's in one of Rome's loveliest centuries-old buildings, not far from Piazza Navona (closed Sundays). There also is a restaurant (see *Eating Out*). *Veleno* (27 Via Sardegna, off Via Veneto; phone: 493583), which often has "theme" evenings, packs in the motor-scooter crowd. For live music and dancing in downtown historical Rome, there is the very special *Casanova* (36 Piazza Rondanini; phone: 654-7314). The live music at *Club 84* (84 Via Emilia; phone: 482-7538) lures dancers of all ages. *L'Alibi* disco (44 Via di Monte Testaccio; no phone) attracts a gay clientele. *Alien* (17 Via Velletri; phone: 841-2212), is another popular disco, located near the *Porta Pia*. *Yes Brazil* (in Trastevere at 103 Via San Francesco a Ripa; phone: 581-6267) offers live music from 7 to 9 PM and Latin disco until 1 AM. *Caffè Latino* (96 Via di Monte Testaccio; phone: 574-4020) also has live music (including blues). Things get hot at *Regine* (50 Via del Moro; no phone), where there is live Caribbean music and South American food. *Zelig* (74 Via Monterone; phone: 687-9209) is a disco for the younger crowd.

Karaoke, that Japanese import where audience members perform onstage to recorded background music, has hit the Eternal City; good *karaoke* bars include *I Soliti Ignoti* (Via delle Tre Cannelle; phone: 678-9424) and the *Karaoke Club* (2 Via Ludovisi; phone: 489-04044).

Especially good jazz can be heard (despite the noise of diners in its restaurant) at *St. Louis Music City* (13/A Via del Cardello; phone: 474-50706) and the *Sax Club* (51 Vicolo dei Modelli; phone: 699-42260), near the *Fontana di Trevi.* Also try well-regarded *Caffè Caruso* (36 Via Monte Testaccio; phone: 574-5019), which plays both disco and jazz.

If you're just an amiable barfly who might like to strike up a pleasant conversation in English, the place to go is the bar at the *D'Inghilterra* hotel (see *Checking In*); there is no music except for the tinkling of ice cubes, but the bartender is one of the nicest in town. Other American haunts include the *Little Bar* (54/A Via Gregoriana; phone: 699-22243) and a pub called *Jeff Flynn's* (12 Via Zamardelli; phone: 686-1990). The *Fox Pub* (9 Via di Monterone; no phone) is jumping nightly around happy hour (from 9:30 to 10:30 PM), when drinks are very inexpensive. Many hotels have pleasant piano bars, including the *Excelsior, Holiday Inn Crowne Plaza Minerva, Majestic,* and *Plaza* (see *Checking In* for all).

Caffè Picasso (Piazza della Pigna; no phone) is a relaxing, upscale hangout for young intellectuals and hip artists; it also features a rotating art exhibit. *La Vetrina* (20 Via della Vetrina; no phone) is another bohemian enclave, complete with live music, art exhibits, and occasional poetry readings.

Best in Town

CHECKING IN

Of the more than 500 hotels in Rome, the following are recommended either for some special charm, location, or bargain price in their category. Those without restaurants are noted, although all serve breakfast if desired. All have private baths, air conditioning, TV sets, and telephones in the rooms unless otherwise stated. In high season prices can be staggering; expect to pay more than $500 for a double room per night in the hotels listed as very expensive; from $300 to $500 for hotels in the expensive price range; from $150 to $300 in the moderate category; and less than $150 in the inexpensive category. Off-season rates are about 10% lower. Most of the major hotels in Rome have complete facilities for the business traveler. Those listed below as having "business services" usually offer such conveniences as an English-speaking concierge, meeting rooms, photocopiers, computers, translation services, and express checkout, among others. Call the hotel for additional information. All telephone numbers listed below are in the 6 city code unless otherwise indicated.

VERY EXPENSIVE

Cavalieri Hilton International It's far from the historic center of Rome at the top of a lovely hill (Monte Mario) overlooking much of the city, but shuttle buses to Via Veneto and the Piazza di Spagna run hourly during shopping hours. The swimming pool is especially desirable in summer, and the rooftop restaurant, *La Pergola,* wins high praise from food critics. A 387-room resort, it further offers tennis, a sauna, other diversions, and business services. 101 Via Cadlolo (phone: 31511; 800-HILTONS; fax: 315-12241).

Excelsior Big (383 rooms), bustling, but efficient, this member of the CIGA chain dominates Via Veneto, next to the *US Embassy.* It's a favorite with Americans, and the bar is a popular meeting place. There's a restaurant, and business services and 24-hour room service are available. 125 Via Veneto (phone: 4708; 800-221-2340; fax: 482-6205).

Le Grand This old-fashioned, luxurious property, near the railroad station and the *Palazzo del Quirinale* (the residence of Italy's president), and not too far from the *US Embassy,* has a courtly, sober, and somewhat ambassadorial air. Still among the proudest links in the CIGA chain, it has 171 large and well-appointed rooms; 24-hour room service; and *Le Restaurant* (see *Eating Out*), which offers some of the finest food in Rome. There also are two cozy bars, and afternoon tea is served to the strains of soothing harp music. Business services are available. 3 Via Vittorio Emanuele Orlando (phone: 4709; 800-221-2340; fax: 474-7307).

Hassler Villa Medici At the top of the Piazza di Spagna and within easy striking distance of the best shopping in Rome, this hotel is favored by a loyal clientele of Hollywood stars and European royalty. The guestrooms could stand some refurbishing, and the public rooms have seen better days, yet the bar remains a popular and traditional meeting place for local personalities. Each of the 85 rooms is individually decorated, and half overlook the city; a small number of penthouse suites with private terraces afford breathtaking views. The service is friendly and efficient. The rooftop restaurant has splendid views and serves a Sunday brunch popular with Romans and other lovers of Rome. Business services are offered. 6 Piazza Trinità dei Monti (phone: 678-2651; fax: 678-9991).

EXPENSIVE

Ambasciatori Palace Across the street from the *US Embassy,* it has 145 generally spacious rooms, old-fashioned amenities, a restaurant, 24-hour room service, a convenient location, and business services. 70 Via Veneto (phone: 47493; fax: 474-3601).

Atlante Star Near the *Vatican,* this modern 61-room hotel boasts a magnificent rooftop terrace. The *Roof-Garden Les Etoiles* restaurant offers a sweeping view of Rome with the *Basilica di San Pietro* in the foreground. There's also 24-hour room service; parking and business services are available. 34 Via Vitelleschi (phone: 687-9558; fax: 687-2300).

Boston The roof garden is just one of the selling points of this 120-room hostelry, well located between Via Veneto and Piazza di Spagna and across from a parking garage. Although there is no restaurant, the breakfast buffet is a delightful plus. Business services are offered. 47 Via Lombardia (phone: 473951; 800-223-9862; fax: 482-1019).

Forum Few hotels anywhere in the world can boast rooms with such views. The roof garden and adjacent rooftop restaurant, which abut the wall of a medieval church tower, overlook the *Foro Romano* and *Fori Imperiali.* This is not, strictly speaking, a luxury property, but the 81 rooms are comfortably sized, if not huge; the service is pleasant; the elevator works; and all around are lively restaurants in the Subura quarter. It's also within walking distance of Piazza Venezia and near a *metropolitana* (subway) stop. 25 Via Tor de' Conti (phone: 679-2446; fax: 678-6479).

Holiday Inn Crowne Plaza Minerva Any resemblance to US members of this chain begins and ends with its moniker. Located in the historical section of the city, adjacent to the *Pantheon,* it offers 118 rooms, 13 junior suites, and three presidential suites, all with color satellite TV and electronic safes. The suites are elegantly decorated with Napoleonic-period furnishings—even the meeting rooms have fine frescoes and statues. There's a restaurant, a comfortable piano bar, and a rooftop terrace that offers alfresco dining in summer with a unique view of the *Pantheon* and the ancient city. Business services are available. 69 Piazza della Minerva (phone: 684-1888; 800-HOLIDAY; fax: 679-4165).

D'Inghilterra Popular with knowledgeable travelers—Anatole France, Mark Twain, and Ernest Hemingway have stayed here. Some of the 102 rooms are small—inevitable in older, downtown hotels—so be sure to ask for one of the larger ones. Some top-floor suites have flowered terraces. There is a small and *simpatico* restaurant, and the ever-crowded bar is a cozy haven for English-speaking tourists and Roman patricians. Business services are available. Near Piazza di Spagna, in the middle of the central shopping area. 14 Via Bocca di Leone (phone: 672161; fax: 684-0828).

Lord Byron Once a private villa, this small (47 rooms) elite inn in the fashionable Parioli residential district still maintains its club-like atmosphere. There isn't a swimming pool or spa—nothing but discreet personal attention, subdued opulence, and what general opinion holds is the finest restaurant in the capital, *Relais le Jardin* (see *Delightful Dining*). Business services. 5 Via Giuseppe de Notaris (phone: 322-0404; fax: 322-0405).

Majestic The lobbies and some of the halls are richly adorned with frescoes, sumptuous carpeting, and draperies; the 105 rooms and baths are well appointed and spacious. On the premises is the turn-of-the-century *La Veranda* dining room. The service is professional, and the downtown location across from the *US Embassy* and close to airline offices is particularly convenient in this traffic-bound city. 50 Via Veneto (phone: 486841; fax: 488-0984).

Raphael Behind Piazza Navona, it's a favorite of Italian politicians (it's near the *Senate* and the *Chamber of Deputies*). Several of the 83 rooms are small, and some could use a bit of refurbishing, but loyal patrons love the antiques in the lobby, the cozy bar, the restaurant, and the location. The roof terrace has one of Rome's finest views. Business services. 2 Largo Febo (phone: 650881; fax: 687-8993).

Rex This 50-room hotel close to the *Teatro dell'Opera* is named for the fabled pre–World War II Italian luxury liner (the ship in Fellini's *Amarcord*), which gives an idea of the Art Deco aura to which it aspires. There's a bar but no restaurant; breakfast is included in the room rate. Business services are available. 149 Via Torino (phone: 488-1568 or 482-4828; fax: 488-2743).

Sole al Pantheon One of Rome's most venerable hostelries—and one of the more sought after and priciest in town—this 28-room hotel is also among the most convenient because of its entrance on Piazza della Rotonda, facing the *Pantheon*. Be sure to ask for a room with a view—a few on the top floor have whirlpool baths, balconies, and panoramas of the spectacular skyline. Don't be put off by the kitschy downstairs lobby. There is no restaurant. Business services are available. 63 Piazza della Rotonda (phone: 678-0441; fax: 684-0689).

MODERATE

Columbus In a restored 15th-century palace right in front of the *Basilica di San Pietro,* this 107-room hotel (under the same ownership as the *Rex* hotel—see above) offers antique furniture, paintings, a handsome restaurant, a garden, and a lot of atmosphere for the price. 33 Via della Conciliazione (phone: 686-5435; fax: 686-4874).

Fontana A restored 13th-century monastery next to the *Fontana di Trevi,* it offers 30 cell-like rooms (no TV sets)—though 10 have great views of the fabulous fountain—and a lovely rooftop bar and restaurant. It's a bargain in every way. Business services are offered. 96 Piazza di Trevi (phone: 678-6113).

Gregoriana In the heart of Rome's high-fashion district, on the street of the same name, this tiny gem (19 rooms) attracts a stylish crowd. Its Art Deco–like decor features room letters (rather than numbers) created by the late illustrator Erté. There's no restaurant, though a continental breakfast is included. No credit cards accepted. 18 Via Gregoriana (phone: 679-4269; fax: 678-4258).

Locarno Near Piazza del Popolo and Piazza di Spagna, this Belle Epoque hotel often attracts artists, writers, and intellectuals. The 36 rooms have Victorian furniture, and many are large enough to accommodate sofas and desks. A pleasant plus: Bikes are available to guests free of charge. Although the hotel does not have a restaurant, drinks and breakfast are served on the terrace during warm weather. Business services are available. 22 Via della Penna (phone: 361-0841; fax: 321-5249).

Manfredi Located on a charming street chockablock with artists' studios and galleries, this is the perfect romantic hideaway for those who don't fancy big hotels. The 15 elegant rooms—decorated in dusty rose and cream—are soundproofed from the noise of the busy street below. There's a small breakfast room but no restaurant. 61 Via Margutta (phone: 310-7676; fax: 320-7736).

Plaza This property in a 19th-century historic building has aged gracefully. Its lobby, with a stained glass ceiling, period wallpaper, and plush furniture, is one of Rome's prettiest, and the old-fashioned bar at one end is a great place for a nightcap. Former guests include Empress Carlota of Mexico and Sir Edmund Hillary. All but 11 of the 207 spacious guestrooms have private baths. Although some of the rooms could use refurbishing, this hotel is a good choice because of its location near Via Condotti and its ambience. There is no restaurant, but a complimentary breakfast is offered. Business services are available. 126 Via del Corso (phone: 396-672101; fax: 684-1575).

La Residenza On a quiet street just behind Via Veneto, this old-fashioned place feels much more like a private villa than a hotel. The 27 rooms are comfortable and artistically decorated (all but two have private baths). Full American breakfast is included, but there's no restaurant. Book well in advance. Business services are available. No credit cards accepted. 22 Via Emilia (phone: 488-0789; fax: 485721).

Sant'Anselmo In a small palazzo-style building on Aventine Hill, this bargain hotel has 46 rooms (all but three with private baths) and a family atmosphere, but no restaurant or air conditioning. Nearby are two other similar properties under the same management—the *San Pio* with 65 guestrooms (no air conditioning) and the *Aventino* with 23 rooms (no air conditioning, no TV sets). Reservations are necessary well in advance. Business services are available. 2 Piazza di Sant'Anselmo (phone: 578-3214; fax: 578-3604).

Teatro di Pompeo The hotel's foundation was originally laid in 55 BC and is said to have supported the *Teatro di Pompeo* (Pompey's Theater), where Julius Caesar met his untimely end. It's on a quiet street and offers 12 charming rooms, with hand-painted tiles and beamed ceilings. There's no restaurant. Business services are available. 8 Largo del Pallaro (phone: 687-2566; fax: 654-5531).

Trevi In a renovated palazzo only a few steps from the fabled fountain, this four-story hotel has 20 guestrooms but no restaurant. 20 Vicolo del Babuccio (phone: 678-9543; fax: 684-1407).

INEXPENSIVE

Casa Stefazio Here is a great bargain: a bed-and-breakfast place set in a sprawling, tree-shaded house and run by Orazio and Stefania Azzola, a hospitable Italian couple. The five bedrooms are attractive and comfortable, and there is a surprising number of amenities: several lovely gardens, a tennis court, a pool, a sauna, and a billiards table on the premises, and horseback riding nearby. The food, prepared by Cordon Bleu chef Orazio, is sumptuous (dinner is available upon request). The property is a 45-minute bus ride from the city center, but the privacy, greenery, and quiet are powerful compensations. Open April through December. 553 Via della Marcigliana (phone/fax: 871-20042).

Fortis Guest House This small, friendly hotel offers 22 guestrooms, 17 with private baths or showers. The accommodations are basic (no air conditioning or TV sets), but the property is well managed, the ambience is homey, and the location (in the Prati quarter across the Tiber River) is pleasant and convenient. There is no restaurant. 7 Via Fornovo (phone: 321-2256; fax: 321-2222).

Margutta This 21-room hotel near Piazza del Popolo has an English-speaking concierge but no restaurant. The rooms are basically furnished (no TV sets, phones, or air conditioning), but all have private baths. The two rooms on the roof (Nos. 50 and 51) feature fireplaces and are surrounded by terraces. 34 Via Laurina (phone: 679-8440).

EATING OUT

Although influenced by Greece and Asia Minor, the ancient Romans were the originators of the first fully developed cuisine of the Western world, the progenitors of a gastronomic tradition still felt in kitchens the world over.

While the lavish banquets described in detail by Petronius and Pliny no doubt existed, genuine Roman gastronomy more likely began in humble kitchens, based on such staples as lentils and chick-peas, still popular entries on many menus. Unfortunately, the old-fashioned, inexpensive trattorie are becoming rare; in their stead are growing numbers of Chinese restaurants and fast-food emporiums—none of them too terrific. So don't be surprised if your favorite casual dining spot is now all tarted up and pricey. Be aware too that fad menus continue to show up everywhere. In addition, some chefs are cutting corners—for example, using truffle-flavored pastes in dishes described on the menu as *con tartufi* (with truffles); the real thing is customarily grated at your table. The trendy dessert continues to be *tiramisù*, a Tyrolean calorie bombe of mascarpone cheese, liqueur, and coffee; easy to prepare, it is elbowing out better and more interesting desserts. Worst of all, an increasing number of desserts are factory-made frozen confections, rather than freshly prepared dishes.

The bright side is the new generation of well-trained cooks who are reviving forgotten regional dishes and devising new, less fatty, and more refined versions of old standbys; they call their fare *cucina creativa* (creative cuisine).

Traditional Roman cooking is robust and hearty. Cholesterol and calorie counters guiltily succumb to steaming dishes of *spaghetti all'amatriciana* (with tomato, special bacon, and tangy pecorino—sheep's-milk cheese), deep-fried *filetti di baccalà* (salt cod filets), or *coda alla vaccinara* (oxtail stewed in tomato, onion, and celery).

Restaurants usually offer abundant fresh fish, particularly on Tuesdays and Fridays, but prices are steep. Fresh fish or Florentine steaks priced *al chilo*—by weight—may inflate a bill way out of proportion, even at moderate-priced restaurants. (All restaurants are required to identify frozen fish as well as other frozen ingredients—look for the word *congelato*.) Don't hesitate to try the *antipasto marinara* (a mixture of seafoods in a light sauce of olive oil, lemon, parsley, and garlic), the *spaghetti alle vongole* (with clam sauce—the shells included), and as a main course, trout from the nearby lakes or (at a higher price) rockfish from the Mediterranean.

Veal is typically Roman, served as saltimbocca (literally "hop into the mouth," flavored with ham, sage, and marsala wine) or roasted with the fresh rosemary that grows in every garden. *Abbacchio al forno* is milk-fed baby lamb roasted with garlic and rosemary, and *abbacchio brodettato,* ever harder to find, is lamb stew topped by a tangy sauce of egg yolks and lemon juice. *Abbacchio scottadito* ("finger burning") are tiny grilled lamb chops. On festive occasions *maialetto* (suckling pig) may appear on the menu; it is stuffed with herbs, roasted, and thickly sliced. Its street-stand version, *la porchetta,* is eaten between thick slabs of country bread. Another traditional meat dish is *bollito misto* (boiled beef, tongue, chicken, and pig's trotter). Watch too for such Roman specialties as *trippa* (tripe flavored with mint, parmigiano cheese, and tomato sauce), *coniglio* (rabbit), *capretto* (kid), *coratella* (lamb's heart), *animelle* (sweetbreads), and in season, *cinghiale* (wild boar). Dried boar sausages are popular in antipasti, along with salamis; the local Roman salami is prepared with tasty fennel seeds.

Among the traditional pasta dishes is the incredibly simple *spaghetti alla carbonara* (with egg, salt pork, and pecorino cheese). *Penne all'arrabbiata* are short pasta in a tomato-and-garlic sauce with hot peppers. The familiar *fettuccine all'Alfredo* depends upon the quality of the egg pasta in a rich sauce of cream, butter, and parmigiano.

Fresh seasonal vegetables are served in many ways: as a separate first course; as the base for a savory antipasto; accompanying the main dish; or even munched raw—for instance, *finocchio al pinzimonio* (fennel dipped into purest olive oil, seasoned with salt and pepper)—after a particularly heavy meal to "clean the palate." Several local greens are unknown to visitors, such as *agretti, bieta, cicoria,* and *broccolo romano*—the last two often boiled briefly, then sautéed with olive oil, garlic, and hot red peppers. Salad ingredients include red radicchio, wild aromatic herbs, and the juicy tomatoes so cherished during the sultry summer months, when they are served with ultra-aromatic basil—the sun's special gift to Mediterranean terraces and gardens (don't spoil their wonderful taste by adding vinegar). Tomatoes also are stuffed with rice and roasted. Yellow, red, and green sweet peppers, eggplant, mushrooms, green and broad beans, and zucchini are favorite vegetables for antipasto, while asparagus and artichokes are especially prized in season. The latter are stuffed with mint and garlic and stewed in olive oil *alla romana,* or opened out like a flower and deep fried *alla giudia* (Jewish-style).

After such a meal Romans normally have fresh fruit for dessert, although there is no shortage of sweet desserts, such as *montebianco* (a rich chestnut-purée confection), zuppa inglese (a trifle-like dessert consisting of liqueur-soaked strips of cake served with pudding), and of course, gelato (ice cream). For a final *digestivo,* bottles brought to the table may include sambuca (it has an aniseed base), grappa (made from the third and fourth grape pressings and normally over 60 proof), and an herbal liqueur to aid digestion known as *amaro* (which means bitter, but is more often quite sweet).

Most dining is à la carte, although a *menù turistico* is offered at some unpretentious trattorie for reasonable prices, and a few tony establishments have a *menù degustazione* (sampler menu) that is sometimes (but not always) less expensive. An even better value are the quick-service, often cafeteria-style, *rosticcerie* and *tavole calde* (literally "hot tables"). There are also several small wine-tasting establishments that offer inexpensive light snacks at lunch with a glass of fine wine; some also serve pasta or a mixed vegetable platter (see *Bars and Caffès*, below).

Dinner for two (with wine) will cost more than $200 in restaurants listed below as very expensive; $120 to $200 in restaurants described as expensive; $75 to $120 in moderate places; and less than $75 in inexpensive spots. Restaurants serve lunch and dinner unless otherwise noted. Always ask prices when ordering wine. Good Italian wines can cost $30 or more per bottle. All telephone numbers are in the 6 city code unless otherwise indicated.

For an unforgettable dining experience, we begin with our favorites (we admit that they're pricey), followed by our cost and quality choices, listed by price category.

DELIGHTFUL DINING

Checchino dal 1887 Serious diners flock to this bustling place (which has earned a Michelin star) for traditional Roman specialties and samples from the city's best wine cellar. The current generation of Mariani brothers, Francesco and Elio (whose family has run the restaurant since 1887), are consummately professional. The *spaghetti alla carbonara* and *all'amatriciana* alone are worth a visit. Other notable specialties include oxtail stew with celery and the unlikely sounding *rigatoni con pajatta* (pasta in a tomato sauce with lamb's intestines). The ubiquitous pecorino cheese is served with raw acacia honey for dessert. Closed Sunday dinner, Mondays, August, and a week at *Christmas*. Reservations necessary. Major credit cards accepted. 30 Via Monte Testaccio (phone: 574-6318 or 574-3816).

Relais le Jardin The sumptuous dining room of the *Lord Byron* hotel has been hailed as Rome's foremost restaurant by a wide consensus of Italian food critics and restaurant guides. Chef Antonio Sciullo's creations transform the unlikely into the surprising and sometimes sublime. The menu follows the seasons—you might find zucchini blossoms stuffed with bean purée, ravioli with a delicate pigeon ragout, or watercress flan with scallops. The dessert soufflé has a crunchy hazelnut topping. Service is appropriately sophisticated, as are the wines. Closed Sundays and August. Reservations necessary. Major credit cards accepted. *Lord Byron Hotel,* 5 Via Giuseppe de Notaris (phone: 322-0404).

VERY EXPENSIVE

Alberto Ciarla Acclaimed chef Alberto is renowned for what he does with fresh fish, although his herbed pasta sauces also are a delight, and the pâté of wild game in season is divine. Be sure to leave room for one of his picture-perfect desserts. (The restaurant recently began offering a slightly less expensive prix fixe menu.) The ever-large, noisy crowd brightens up the somber all-black decor, and in good weather there are a few outdoor tables on a Trastevere street. Open for dinner only; closed Sundays. Reservations advised. Major credit cards accepted. 40 Piazza San Cosimato (phone: 581-8668).

Antica Enoteca Capranica A 16th-century palace that has served as housing for seminary students and as a wine shop is now one of Rome's smartest dining spots. The food, prepared under the watchful eye of famed chef Angelo Paracucchi, is light and elegantly presented. The menu changes seasonally, but specialties might include ravioli stuffed with ricotta and zucchini, boiled meat, and seafood. The knowledgeable sommelier can help you select just the right wine to go with your meal. Closed Sundays. Reservations advised. Major credit cards accepted. 99 Piazza Capranica (phone: 684-0992).

Le Restaurant This outstanding dining room at the *Grand* hotel serves continental and regional specialties that change with the seasons. The decor, flowers, and waiters in tails all reflect the *Grand* approach to luxury. Open daily. Reservations necessary. Major credit cards accepted. 3 Via Vittorio Emanuele Orlando (phone: 4709).

La Rosetta Famous for its excellent fish dishes, this swanky, one-Michelin-star bistro is small, jam-packed, and chic. The chef grills, fries, boils, or bakes to perfection any—or a mixture of all—of the seafood flown in from his native Sicily. Try the *pappardelle al pescatore* (wide noodles in a piquant tomato sauce with mussels, clams, and parsley) or Sicilian-style *pasta con le sarde* (with sardine chunks and wild fennel). Closed weekends and August. Reservations necessary. Major credit cards accepted. 9 Via della Rosetta (phone: 656-1002 or 683-08841).

El Toulà The well-heeled, well-traveled, and aristocratic literally rub elbows here (the place is small) for Cortina- and Venice-inspired fare. The menu changes continually, but chef Daniele Repetti can be counted on to prepare excellent seafood year-round (such as poppy seed–daubed salmon in oyster sauce) and game (including venison) in winter. Try the *menù degustazione.* There's an impressive list of 500 wines, and the desserts are exceptional.

Prices are lower at midday. Closed Saturday lunch, Sundays, and August. Reservations necessary. Major credit cards accepted. 29/B Via della Lupa (phone: 687-3750 or 687-3498).

EXPENSIVE

Alvaro al Circo Massimo Let Alvaro suggest what's best—be it fresh fish, game such as *fagiano* (pheasant) or *faraona* (guinea hen), or mushrooms (try grilled *porcini*). The ambience is rustic; there are outdoor tables during the summer. Closed Mondays. Reservations advised. Major credit cards accepted. 53 Via dei Cerchi (phone: 678-6112).

Andrea The best dining place in the Via Veneto area. In season there's fettuccine with artichoke sauce; always on the menu is ricotta-stuffed fresh ravioli. Also try the *insalata catalan,* a Spanish-style seafood salad. Pleasant service, a good house wine, and rich desserts are other pluses. Closed Sundays, Monday lunch, and three weeks in August. Reservations necessary. Major credit cards accepted. 26 Via Sardegna (phone: 474-0557).

Dal Bolognese The menu is nearly as long as the list of celebrities who frequent this eatery, run by two brothers from Bologna. Try the homemade *tortelloni* (pasta twists stuffed with ricotta cheese) and the popular *bollito misto.* There are tables outdoors in good weather. Closed Sunday dinner, Mondays, and two weeks in August. Reservations necessary. Major credit cards accepted. 1 Piazza del Popolo (phone: 361-1426).

Camponeschi In summer dinner is served on an outdoor terrace overlooking the *Palazzo Farnese* and a tranquil square with ancient Roman fountains. Some say the view is better than the pricey fare, which tends to be refined, well-prepared versions of traditional Italian dishes. Others swear by such rarified offerings as corn polenta with Alba truffles or partridge *en croûte.* Open for dinner only; closed Sundays. Reservations advised. Major credit cards accepted. 50 Piazza Farnese (phone: 687-4927).

Il Capitello This elegant addition to the ancient Campo dei Fiori area is an understated 50-table dining room crowned by a frescoed ceiling; piano music in the background adds to the ambience. The menu is decidedly Calabrian: Try the spicy pasta dishes and the fresh seafood. Closed Sundays. Reservations necessary. Major credit cards accepted. 4 Campo dei Fiori (phone: 683-00073).

Al Fogher This special restaurant not far from Via Veneto offers a taste of Venice in the heart of Rome. Every ingredient is carefully selected to ensure peak freshness and taste, and the dishes are meticulously prepared. Good choices include *taglioni* flavored with cinnamon, ham, and lemon; *fegato alla veneta* (liver with onions and white wine); and osso buco (veal shanks). Be sure to save room for the wonderful homemade desserts, including apple strudel, *panna cotta* topped with seasonal fruit, and *crème brûlée.* There's also a fine wine list, and the atmosphere is quiet and elegant, almost somber. Closed Saturday lunch, Sundays, and August. Reservations advised. American Express accepted. 13/b Via Tevere (phone: 841-7032).

Hosteria dell'Orso Although this restaurant housed in an elegant 14th-century building is widely known as a tourist place, the traditional Italian fare is quite good. Upstairs is a disco (see *Nightclubs and Nightlife*), and downstairs is a piano bar. Closed Sundays. Reservations necessary. Major credit cards accepted. 25 Via dei Soldati (phone: 683-07074).

La Lampada Specialties here are truffles and wild mushrooms, but don't expect the former to be fresh beyond the autumn/winter season. The risotto is made with white truffles, the carpaccio with a grating of both black and white truffles (from Norcia and Alba, respectively). Closed Sundays. Reservations necessary. Major credit cards accepted. 25 Via Quintino Sella (phone: 481-5673).

Quinzi e Gabrieli Seafood, prepared as simply as possible, is a very serious subject here. In season the oyster bar is popular; the small dining room seats only 22. Open for dinner only; closed Sundays and August. Reservations necessary. Major credit cards accepted. Near the *Pantheon,* at 6 Via delle Coppelle (phone: 687-9389).

Romolo In this famed tavern in the heart of Trastevere, near a particularly picturesque ancient city gate, the painter Raphael supposedly courted (and painted) the baker's daughter—the resulting portrait is called *La Fornarina.* The fare and the good wine list cling to the traditional, with such hearty dishes as *spaghetti alla boscaiolo* (with mushrooms and tomato) and *mozzarella alla Fornarina* (melted cheese wrapped in prosciutto and accompanied by a fried artichoke). Closed Mondays and August. Reservations necessary, especially in summer. Major credit cards accepted. 8 Via di Porta Settimiana (phone: 581-8284).

Taverna Flavia It's been fashionable with the movie crowd, journalists, and politicians for over 30 years. Owner Mimmo likes autographed pictures—one entire room is devoted to Elizabeth Taylor—and the *Sardi's* style survives, despite the demise of "Hollywood on the Tiber" long ago. Good pasta dishes and fine grilled fish are served until quite late. Closed Saturday lunch, Sundays, and August. Reservations necessary. Major credit cards accepted. 9-11 Via Flavia (phone: 474-5214).

Taverna Giulia This reliable old favorite is set in a 600-year-old building. Genoese specialties include pesto over *trofie* noodles, wild mushroom soup, *stoccafisso* (dried cod), and smoked fish. Closed Sundays and August. Reservations advised. Major credit cards accepted. 26 Vicolo dell'Oro (phone: 686-9768).

Vecchia Roma Located in a handsome piazza of Baroque churches and Renaissance buildings, only steps away from some of the finest monuments of ancient Rome, this is where tradition reigns. The menu tends toward Italian classical specialties, with a broad selection of justifiably beloved favorites like prosciutto with melon, veal in a tuna sauce, grilled baby lamb chops, and fresh country salad greens; there's also an impressive wine list. The setting is classic trattoria: whitewashed walls, rustic furniture, and an agreeably old-fashioned air. It is especially pleasant in warm weather, when tables are set up outdoors under giant market umbrellas, but it's comfortable inside as well (thanks to air conditioning—a rarity in Rome restaurants). Closed Wednesdays and two weeks in August. Reservations advised. Major credit cards accepted. 18 Piazza Campitelli (phone: 686-4604).

MODERATE

Il Barroccio *Pane rustico* (crusty country-style bread) is made here daily, and Tuscan-style beans are slow-baked in a wood-burning oven. On a side street near the *Pantheon,* this is the place to try *crostini* (fried bread offered with an assortment of toppings) in all its permutations, *bruschette* (slices of toast covered with tomatoes and herbs), and pizza. Across the street at No. 123 is its twin, *Er Faciolaro,* owned by the same people. One or the other always is open during conventional hours. Reservations necessary on weekends. Major credit cards accepted. 13 Via dei Pastini (phone: 679-3797).

La Campana This 400-year-old, truly Roman restaurant has become a beloved institution. The waiters can help you decipher the handwritten menu, which tempts most with *carciofi alla romana* (fresh artichokes in garlic and oil), *tonnarelli alla chitarra* (homemade pasta in an egg-and-cheese sauce), lamb, truffle-topped poultry dishes, and homemade desserts. Closed Mondays and August. Reservations advised. Major credit cards accepted. 18 Vicolo della Campana (phone: 686-7820).

La Cannaccia Sicilian owner Salvatore Ruggieri has gone overboard decorating his trattoria; fortunately, the fare is more straightforward. The fresh swordfish is a favorite among regular patrons, who have included Federico Fellini and Marcello Mastroianni as well as politicians from the nearby *Chamber of Deputies.* Closed Sundays and part of August. No reservations or credit cards accepted. 63 Via della Guglia (no phone).

La Carbonara On the square where Rome's most colorful morning food market has been held for centuries, this is where *spaghetti alla carbonara* is said to have been invented. The windows of the ancient palazzo look out over the scene; inside are high-ceilinged, wood-beamed rooms—try for a table near the window. The menu is as authentically Roman as the decor. Closed Tuesdays. Reservations advised for dinner in summer. Major credit cards accepted. 23 Campo dei Fiori (phone: 686-4783). Moderate.

Il Cardinale In a restored bicycle shop off stately Via Giulia, decorated in a some-what precious turn-of-the-century style, this popular spot specializes in regional dishes: pasta with green tomato or artichoke sauce, grilled eels, a sweetbread casserole with mushrooms, and *aliciotti con l'indivia* (an anchovy and endive dish). Closed Sundays and August. Reservations advised. Visa accepted. 6 Via delle Carceri (phone: 686-9336).

Cesarina Year in and year out diners return for the *bollito misto,* well prepared from the rich cart of meat and sausage, with green sauce. In summer the fresh fish may appeal more, as will the air conditioning. Year-round the pasta Bolognese-style is a traditional favorite. Closed Sundays. Reservations necessary. Major credit cards accepted. 109 Via Piemonte (phone: 488-0828).

Le Colline Emiliane Eateries like this are becoming a rarity: Service is prompt, the decor is simple, and homemade pasta is the specialty—the *maccheroncini al funghetto* (large macaroni with mushrooms) is delicious. This spot has a well-deserved reputation for consistency over the years. Closed Fridays and August. Reservations advised in winter. No credit cards accepted. Near Via Veneto at 22 Via degli Avignonesi (phone: 481-7538).

Costanza A narrow alleyway leads to this spacious, traditional trattoria, a long-time Roman favorite, now among the smartest eateries in the capital. The stuffed homemade pasta—varieties change with the seasons—is delectable; look for ravioli plump with puréed artichoke, or try the wild *porcini* mush-rooms on pasta. The antipasto offerings are of the highest quality. The rus-tic decor—terra cotta floors and white walls—includes a bit of the *Teatro di Pompeo,* still visible on the back wall. Don't bother with the handful of outdoor tables in summer unless you arrive very early in the evening or don't mind a long wait. Closed Sundays and August. Reservations advised. Major credit cards accepted. 65 Piazza Paradiso (phone: 686-1717 or 688-01002).

Er Cuccurucù A garden overlooking the Tiber provides one of Rome's most pleas-ant summer settings for dining alfresco, while inside all is cozy and rustic. The antipasti are good, as is the meat grilled over an open wood fire. Ask for the *bruschetta con pomodori* (toasted country bread smothered in fresh tomatoes and oregano), homemade pasta with wild mushroom sauce, and a *spiedino misto* (a grilled kebab with big chunks of veal, pork, and sausage interspersed with onions and peppers). Closed Mondays in winter, Sundays in summer, and July 15 to September 15. Reservations advised. Major credit cards accepted. 10 Via Caporati (phone: 325-2571).

Il Dito e la Luna Sicilian fare and *cucina creativa* are featured at this lovely restau-rant with white walls, terra cotta floors, and antique furnishings. Specialties include *lasagnette con scampi, pomodori, e zucchini* (flat pasta with shrimp, tomatoes, and zucchini), *anitra in pasta sfoglia* (duck in puff pastry with an orange sauce), and a good selection of homemade desserts. Open for dinner only; closed Sundays and August 11 to 31. Reservations advised. No credit cards accepted. 51 Via dei Sabelli (phone: 494-0276).

Il Drappo Drapes softly decorate the two small rooms of this *ristorantino* run by the Sardinian brother-sister team of Paolo and Valentina Tolu. They offer delicate versions of the island's fare, fragrant with wild fennel, myrtle, and herbs. The innovative menu, recited by Paolo and prepared by Valentina, always begins with mixed antipasti, including *carta di musica* (hors d'oeuvres on crisp Sardinian wafers). Try the classic Sardinian dessert *seadas* (cheese-stuffed, fried cake in a special dark honey). Open for dinner only; closed Sundays and two weeks in August. Reservations necessary. Major credit cards accepted. 9 Vicolo del Malpasso (phone: 687-7365).

La Fiorentina This favorite Roman pizzeria, with its wood-burning oven and grill, is in residential Prati on the *Vatican* side of the river. It serves pizza even at lunchtime, a rarity in Italy. There are tables on the street in good weather. Closed Wednesdays and Thursday lunch. Reservations advised. Major credit cards accepted. 22 Via Andrea Doria (phone: 312310).

La Gensola Located in Trastevere, this *simpatico* Sicilian trattoria offers delicious antipasti based on eggplant, and the pasta with broccoli is superb. Closed Saturday lunch, Sundays, and a week at *Christmas*. No reservations or credit cards accepted. 63 Via della Guglia (no phone).

Giggetto al Portico d'Ottavia In Rome's Jewish ghetto, this is the place to sample the delicious and well-prepared fried artichokes that most Roman menus identify as *alla giudia,* as well as zucchini flowers stuffed with mozzarella and *crostini.* This place is a continual favorite, even if the waiters do tend to be cheerless. The experience is absolutely authentic. Closed Mondays. Reservations advised. Major credit cards accepted. 21/A Via del Portico d'Ottavia (phone: 686-1105).

Il Gladiatore This old-fashioned, cozy trattoria overlooking the *Colosseo* is known for its fresh fish. Closed Wednesdays. No reservations. Major credit cards accepted. 5 Piazza Colosseo (phone: 700-0531).

Da Mario A favorite, with such Tuscan specialties as Francovich soup, Florentine steaks, and delicious game in season, all prepared with care and dedication by Mario himself. Try the famed *ribollita* (twice-boiled vegetable soup, which depends upon a deep purple cabbage for its special taste). Service is brusquely Tuscan; the decor is dark and old-fashioned; and the location is near Piazza di Spagna. Closed Sundays and August. Reservations advised. Major credit cards accepted. 55 Via della Vite (phone: 678-3818).

Nino A reliable place, frequented by artists, actors, and aristocrats, near Piazza di Spagna. The authentic Tuscan fare is simply but ably prepared, and the service is serious. Specialties: *zuppa di fagioli alla Francovich* (thick Tuscan white-bean soup with garlic), *bistecca alla fiorentina* (thick, succulent T-bone steak), and *castagnaccio* (semisweet chestnut cake). There's an excellent wine list. Closed Sundays. Reservations advised. Major credit cards accepted. 11 Via Borgognona (phone: 679-5676).

Osteria Picchioni Serving the most expensive—some say the best—pizza in town, this family-style, old-fashioned trattoria uses only top-quality ingredients; unfortunately, the decor runs to plastic flowers. Watch out for the prices—a plate of spaghetti with truffles can run around $100! Closed Wednesdays and August. Reservations necessary. No credit cards accepted. 16 Via del Boschetto (phone: 488-5261).

Otello alla Concordia A delightful trattoria in the middle of the Piazza di Spagna shopping area, it has certain tables reserved for habitués and a colorful courtyard for fine-weather dining. The menu is Roman and changes daily, depending a great deal on the season. Closed Sundays and for two weeks beginning at *Christmas.* No reservations. Major credit cards accepted. 81 Via della Croce (phone: 679-1178).

Paris The Cappellanti family adds a creative zing to traditional Roman-Jewish and Roman dishes such as deep-fried artichokes (in season) and *pasta e ceci* (with chick-peas). The delicious desserts are homemade—a rarity in Rome nowadays. Closed Sunday dinner, Mondays, and August. Reservations necessary. Major credit cards accepted. 7/A Piazza San Calisto (phone: 581-5378).

Pierluigi The fish is fresh, the piazza is charming, the prices are reasonable, and in summer the dining is alfresco. As a result, this popular trattoria in the heart of old Rome is usually full. Closed Mondays and Tuesday lunch. Reservations necessary. Major credit cards accepted. 144 Piazza de' Ricci (phone: 686-1301/2).

Piperno A summer dinner outdoors on this quiet Renaissance *piazzetta,* next to the *Palazzo Cenci*—which still reeks "of ancient evil and nameless crimes"—is sheer magic. Indoors it is modern and less magical, and the classic Roman-Jewish cooking can be a bit heavy. The great specialty is *fritto vegetariano* (zucchini flowers, mozzarella cheese, salt cod, rice and potato balls, and artichokes *alla giudia*). Closed Sunday dinner, Mondays, *Easter,* August, and *Christmas.* Reservations necessary. Major credit cards accepted. 9 Monte de' Cenci (phone: 688-02772).

Polese This place offers simple food at reasonable prices, which makes it a good value any time of the year. You can choose to eat outside under the trees of the spacious square or inside the intimate rooms of a Borgia palace. Begin with *bresaola con rughetta* (cured beef with arugula, seasoned with olive oil, lemon, and freshly grated black pepper), and continue with the *pasta al pesto.* Closed Tuesdays. No reservations. Major credit cards accepted. 40 Piazza Sforza Cesarini (phone: 686-1709).

Al Pompiere Visiting firemen and other travelers adore this bright, old-fashioned restaurant (whose name means "The Fireman"), situated in a 16th-century palazzo near the Campo dei Fiori. The menu includes deep-fried artichokes, mozzarella-stuffed zucchini blossoms, and osso buco (veal shanks). Closed Sundays and July 24 to September 1. Reservations advised for dinner. No credit cards accepted. 38 Via Santa Maria Calderari (phone: 686-8377).

Quadrifoglio The spicy and flavorful Neapolitan fare—like *vermicelli con colatura di alici* (with anchovy paste) and *tortino di alici e patate* (anchovy and potato tarts)—served in this award-winning restaurant is in sharp contrast to its spartan decor. Don't pass up the rich pastries. Closed Saturday dinner, Sundays, and August. Reservations advised. Major credit cards accepted. 7 Via Marche (phone: 484575).

Settimio all'Arancio Simple but good food, served right in the heart of downtown Rome, near the old Jewish ghetto. It's always crowded. Particularly noteworthy are the *fusilli con melanzane* (pasta with eggplant) and the fresh fish (served Tuesdays and Fridays). Closed Sundays and August. Reservations advised. Major credit cards accepted. 50 Via dell'Arancio (phone: 687-6119).

Sora Lella On Isola Tiberina (Tiber Island), this trendy, always-crowded trattoria serves authentic, hearty Roman dishes such as *pasta e ceci* (with chick-peas), *penne all'arrabbiata,* tiny sautéed lamb chops, and beans with pork rind. Ring the bell to gain entry. Closed Sundays and July. No reservations or credit cards accepted. 16 Via di Quattro Capi (phone: 686-1601).

La Tana de Noantri There is delightful dining at this Trastevere trattoria, both in the garden in summer and in the rustic indoor room the rest of the year. The pasta and meat dishes respect Roman tradition (as does the pizza), and the fish is always fresh. Closed Tuesdays. Reservations advised. Major credit cards accepted. 1-3 Via della Paglia (phone: 580-6404).

La Tavernetta It looks like a take-out pasta shop, but there are actually four narrow dining rooms set one above the other. At this tiny, tidy spot between Piazza di Spagna and Piazza Barberini, the homemade pasta is nearly perfect and seafood is the specialty. Closed Mondays and August. Reservations advised. Major credit cards accepted. 3-4 Via del Nazareno (phone: 679-3124).

Toto alle Carrozze A trattoria with a banquet spread of strictly Roman antipasti, good pasta, and Roman fish and meat dishes. This is a *giovedì gnocchi, sabato trippa* (Thursday gnocchi, Saturday tripe) kind of traditional place. Closed Sundays. No reservations. Major credit cards accepted. Just off Via del Corso at 10 Via delle Carrozze (phone: 678-5558).

Tullio Up a narrow hill, just a few yards from Via Veneto, this Tuscan trattoria serves superb *ribollita* (Tuscan vegetable soup) and baked beans *al fiasco* (in the bottle). It's a custom to place a straw-covered bottle of chianti on the table—diners pay only for what they drink. Try the grilled steaks Florentine-style. Closed Sundays and August. Reservations advised. Major credit cards accepted. 26 Via di San Nicola da Tolentino (phone: 474-5560).

Le Volte Under the frescoed ceiling of the 16th-century *Palazzo Rondanini,* diners can enjoy linguine in lobster sauce, pizza baked in a wood-burning oven, and wild boar with polenta (in autumn and winter). Closed Tuesdays and two weeks in August. Reservations advised. Major credit cards accepted. 47 Piazza Rondanini (phone: 687-7408).

INEXPENSIVE

Buca di Ripetta This delightfully old-fashioned trattoria is always packed with locals, who flock here for the delicious food, including a variety of pasta dishes, vegetable soup, and osso buco (veal shanks). The atmosphere is lively and friendly. Closed Sunday dinner, Mondays, and August. Reservations advised. No credit cards accepted. 36 Via di Ripetta (phone: 321-9391).

Fiaschetteria Beltramme The fashion crowd—plus painters, potters, plumbers, and frame makers—crams into this tiny place to enjoy the home-cooked broth, spaghetti, boiled beef, and oxtail Roman-style. The strictly traditional menu may take some deciphering, but the staff will be happy to translate. No fancy decor, not even a telephone—just good food and a pleasant house wine from Frascati. Closed Sundays and August. No reservations or credit cards accepted. Between Piazza del Popolo and Via Condotti at 39 Via della Croce (no phone).

Grotte Teatro di Pompeo Julius Caesar met his untimely end nearby—some say right here, amid the massive and still visible stone vaults of the *Teatro di Pompeo.* The *zuppa di verdura* (vegetable soup) is untheatrical but wholesome, and the *fettuccine verdi alla gorgonzola* (green noodles in a rich cheese sauce) is a wonderful pasta choice. Try the typically Roman osso buco *con funghi* (with wild mushrooms) or the saltimbocca. Closed Mondays and August. Reservations unnecessary. Visa accepted. 73 Via del Biscione (phone: 688-03686).

Lucifero Pub A fondue-and-beer tavern tucked into a side street off the Campo dei Fiori, it offers an inexpensive alternative to pizza. Open daily. No reservations or credit cards accepted. 28 Via dei Cappellari (phone: 654-5536).

Pizzeria Panattoni Popular with university students, this always-crowded eatery in Trastevere is nicknamed "The Morgue" because of its long, white marble tables. But there's nothing morbid about the delicious pizza, garlic bread, *supplì al telefono* (rice balls stuffed with cheese), and baked beans served here. Closed Wednesdays. No reservations or credit cards accepted. 53 Viale Trastevere (phone: 580-0919).

La Sagrestia The best pizza in town—or at least a top contender—with pies fresh from the wood-burning oven. There's also good pasta and draft beer at this ever-crowded and cheery place, with a kitschy decor. Closed Wednesdays and a week in mid-August. Reservations advised for large groups. Major credit cards accepted. Near the *Pantheon* at 89 Via del Seminario (phone: 679-7581).

Trearchi da Gioachino Among the declining numbers of true Roman trattorie, this one stands out. The chef, who comes from the Abruzzo region, prepares such tasty specialties as homemade ravioli, *pappardelle* noodles with hare sauce and lamb, and other pasta made in various delectable ways. Closed Sundays and August. Reservations advised. Major credit cards accepted. 233 Via dei Coronari (phone: 686-5890).

BARS AND CAFFÈS

Perhaps no other institution reflects the relaxed Italian lifestyle as much as the ubiquitous *caffè* (or bar, as it is called in Rome). From small emporiums with three tin tables (where locals perpetually argue world politics and the Sunday soccer results) to sprawling drawing rooms to tearooms to wine bars, life slows to sit and sip. Romans order Campari, cappuccino, or a light lunch and put the world on hold. Inside they meet friends and suitors, read the paper, or write the great Italian novel. Some regulars even get their mail at their local *caffè*. Outside, in summer, the *caffè* is for appraising the passing spectacle. Remember that prices are usually far higher outdoors than in, so when you're charged $6 or $7 for an espresso, don't grumble—just think of it as rent for the sidewalk table. You can stay the whole afternoon if you like. Also increasingly popular are small wine bars, which offer samples of regional and continental wines as well as light fare, making for an ideal lunch. Most of these places do not take credit cards or reservations; those listed below are open daily unless otherwise indicated.

Below is the most evocative of the breed, as well as a world-famous *gelateria* (ice-cream parlor), followed by a sampling of the other *caffès*, bars, and *gelaterie* that Rome has to offer.

BEST CAFFÈS

Caffè Greco When this *caffè* was opened in 1760 by Greek-born Nicola della Maddalena, its clients were local working people. Later, at the tranquil little marble tables in the three back rooms, Stendhal and Schopenhauer paused, and Hans Christian Andersen no doubt had this place in mind when he characterized Rome as the only city in the world that made him feel instantly at home. Casanova mentioned the establishment in his memoirs, Mark Twain loved the place, Nicolay Gogol scribbled *Dead Souls* seated on its austere benches, and the painter Giorgio de Chirico said he couldn't paint without stopping here for his daily dose of the Italian drink *Punt e Mes*. After World War II local intellectuals dubbed the narrow room where John Keats, Washington Irving, and Oscar Wilde had taken coffee "The Omnibus." Today the place is full of busts and statues of such famous habitués, and the front bar is jammed with the expensive furs and suede pumps of shoppers catching their collective breath between jaunts to *Fendi* and *Ferragamo*. Couturier Valentino comes here, as do members of the Bulgari clan, whose atelier is nearby. *Caffè Greco* has been declared a part of Italy's national patrimony, and even the waiters, who dress in tails, look as if they're being preserved for posterity. Closed Sundays. 86 Via Condotti (phone: 678-2554).

Tre Scalini Not surprisingly, this place is a perennial favorite with both Romans and foreigners, particularly in summer, when the cone seekers are often three deep at the ice-cream counter inside. The setting—ringside on Rome's beautiful and car-free Piazza Navona, facing Bernini's famous *Fontana dei Fiumi*—is incomparable, the cast of characters, colorful. The renowned specialty is *tartufo*, a grated bitter chocolate–covered chocolate ice-cream ball swathed in whipped cream and named for its resemblance to the knobby truffle. 28 Piazza Navona (phone: 688-01996).

For a pre-lunch or -dinner *aperitivo*, try fashionable *Baretto* (Via Condotti), *Rosati* (5/A Piazza del Popolo; phone: 322-5859; closed Tuesdays), or *Canova* (Piazza del Popolo; no phone), which also offer light lunches and late-night snacks. *Babington's* (23 Piazza di Spagna; phone: 678-6027; closed Tuesdays) is an English tearoom that serves expensive snacks and luscious cakes, as well as light lunches. Currently *alla moda* is the little *Bar della Pace* (Piazza della Pace, behind Piazza Navona; no phone), popular with the young crowd and open until 3 AM. *Eustachio il Caffè* (82 Piazza Sant'Eustachio; phone: 686-1309; closed Mondays), a stand-up espresso bar, serves what is reputed to be the best coffee in town (made from fine coffee beans roasted over a wood-burning fire). For one of the city's best *cornetti* (a sweetish croissant, not on any list of low-cholesterol food), walk across the piazza to the *Bernasconi Caffè*. *Ciampini* (Piazza Trinità dei Monti; phone: 678-5678) boasts a fine hilltop view of the entire city, as well as excellent food.

Wine shops–cum–wine bars serve light lunches of well-prepared vegetables, pasta, cheese, and good wine (November through March, try a glass of the wonderful *vini novelli*) for around $15 to $20 per person. They are scattered all over old Rome but are tiny and dark. Simply look for their sign: *Enoteca*. The shops usually have only a few tables and close before 8 PM. Try the *Bottega del Vino da Bleve* (9/A Via Santa Maria del Pianto;

phone: 683-00475) in downtown Rome; tiny *Cul de Sac 1* (73 Piazza Pasquino; phone: 688-01094), which re-creates the atmosphere of an old *osteria; Il Piccolo* (74 Via del Governo Vecchio; no phone) near Piazza Navona; or *Spiriti* (5 Via di Sant'Eustachio; phone: 689-2499).

On summer evenings the after-dinner crowd often moves toward one of the many *gelaterie* in Rome, some of which are much more than ice-cream parlors, since they serve exotic long drinks and *semifreddi* (semisoft ice cream). Perhaps the best-known *gelateria* in town is the very crowded *Giolitti* (40 Via Uffici del Vicario; phone: 699-1243), not far from Piazza Colonna—try any of the fresh fruit flavors (closed Mondays). Others include the sleek, high-tech *Gelateria della Palma* (at the corner of Via della Maddalena and Via delle Coppelle; no phone), *Fiocco di Neve* (51 Via del Pantheon; no phone), and *Caffè di Rienzo* (5 Piazza della Rotonda; phone: 687-7404)—all near the *Pantheon;* the lively *Gelofestival* (29 Viale Trastevere, in Trastevere; phone: 581-3363); and the more sedate *Biancaneve* (1 Piazza Pasquale Paoli, where Corso Vittorio Emanuele II meets the Lungotevere dei Fiorentini; phone: 688-06227). Favorites in the fashionable Parioli residential district are *Gelateria Duse* (1/E Via Eleonora Duse; no phone) and the *Casina delle Muse* (Piazzale delle Muse; no phone) for a fabulous *granita di caffè con panna* (iced coffee with whipped cream). In the Jewish ghetto try *Dolce Roma* (20/B Via Portico d'Ottavio; phone: 587-972) for chocolate-chip cookies and Austrian pastries. The *Gran Caffè Europeo* (33 Piazza San Lorenzo in Lucina; no phone) is another place for indulging in high-calorie pastries.

Siena

The late Italian writer Curzio Malaparte wrote that if you ask a Florentine saint for news about heaven, you will get an answer, but in a tone of voice that casts doubt on your worthiness to go there. Ask San Bernardino of Siena, however, and you will be told not only what heaven is, where it is, and the shortest road to take, but also how many rooms it has, how many kitchens, and what's cooking in the pot. Something of the same air of affectionate intimacy pervades this city. Sienese speech is peppered with diminutives (it is said the Sienese speak Italy's purest Italian), and Sienese Renaissance painting continued to delight in pretty Madonnas while the Florentines wrestled with problems of perspective.

Florence was a menacing presence through much of Siena's history; it was largely Florence that arrested Siena's development and caused it to remain the medieval gem it is today. One legend has it that Siena was founded by the Senes Gauls; another, that it was founded by Senio, son of Remus, one of the founding brothers of Rome, hence the Roman she-wolf on the Sienese arms. What is certain is that Siena was an Etruscan city and then a military stronghold under the Romans. Overtaken by the northern Lombards, it did not flourish as a center of commerce, finance, and culture until the late Middle Ages, when its wealth and trade became the envy of its Tuscan neighbors, prompting continual warfare, particularly with the Florentine city-state. By 1235 the mightier military strength of Florence forced Siena to accept harsh peace terms.

But that was merely round one. In 1260, the Sienese dealt the Florentines a resounding defeat at Montaperti, a hill east of the city. Under a nine-member government of merchant families (called the Governo dei Nove), peace was made, and Siena embarked on one of its most enlightened and prosperous periods. The university (founded in 1240), some of the city's most noteworthy buildings, such as the *Palazzo Comunale,* the *Palazzo Chigi-Saracini,* and the *Palazzo Sansedoni,* as well as plans to enlarge the cathedral, date from this time. It was a golden age for painting, too—Duccio di Buoninsegna and Simone Martini were making names for themselves beautifying palaces and churches.

The good times lasted until 1355, when, following a severe drought and an outbreak of plague in 1348, civil discontent brought about a rebellion of leading noble families and a series of short-lived governments. The decades of the Black Death also brought a heightened spirituality; the city's two beloved saints, Catherine and Bernardino, emerged during that period. Would-be conquerors came from farther afield until, in 1554, a 24,000-man army of Spanish, German, and Italian troops under the command of the Florentine Medici family laid siege to the city. A year later Siena fell. Cosimo I de' Medici became its ruler, and Siena became part of the Grand Duchy of Tuscany, first under the Medicis and then under the French House of Lorraine, until it passed, with Tuscany, to the Kingdom of Italy in 1860.

Absorption by Florence kept Siena as small and medieval-looking as it is. Loss of independence also led the Sienese to invest their annual *Palio*—the reckless bareback horse race around the treacherous Piazza del Campo held on July 2 and again on August 16—with vibrant civic passion. The August 16 *Palio,* the more important of the two, has been documented as far back as 1310; the July 2 *Palio* was instituted in 1656 (for details, see *Special Events*).

Now as then, the city is divided into *contrade* (districts). The 17 *contrade* (once, 59) have allegorical names such as Bruco (Caterpillar), Tartuca (Tortoise), Chiocciola (Snail), Drago (Dragon), and Leocorno (Unicorn). Keep an eye on the corners of buildings as you walk around town, and you'll see the *contrade* marked off with their symbols, just as streets are with their names. Each *contrada* has its own patron saint, a church where the saint is worshiped, and a feast day in the saint's honor, and each has its own fountain, outside the church, where its babies are baptized a second time.

Palio time is the time to visit Siena only *if* you don't object to what seems (and is) cruel to the horses—the curves are too sharp for safety, and many accidents occur—*if* you don't mind massive crowds, and *if* you make reservations and other arrangements well in advance. If you miss the event itself, you still may catch sight of a clutch of little boys, perhaps standing in a slice of late afternoon shade by the *Duomo,* practicing wielding, waving, and throwing the flag. The image will stay with you.

Siena At-a-Glance

SEEING THE CITY

The best spot for a bird's-eye view of Siena is the top of the *Torre del Mangia,* next to the *Palazzo Comunale* in Piazza del Campo, from which one can see not only the Campo below and across a sweep of red tile roofs to Siena's other major monumental complex, the *Duomo,* but also out to the surrounding hills. Another vantage point is from the top of what the Sienese call the *Facciatone* (Big Façade), actually the front of the never-finished *Duomo Nuovo* (New Cathedral), which now houses the *Museo dell'Opera del Duomo* (see *Special Places*). It affords a good view of Piazza del Campo and the *Torre del Mangia,* among other things. Still another vista is that from the *Fortezza Medicea* (see *Extra Special*), which should be saved for the end of a visit.

SPECIAL PLACES

A glance at the map shows that all of Siena seems to gravitate toward seashell-shaped Piazza del Campo. In fact, since Siena's *centro storico* (historic center) is no bigger than a large provincial town, almost all of its sights are within walking distance of this piazza. Be aware, however, that the town's narrow streets wind uphill and down and sometimes turn into steps. *Note:* Cars are not permitted in much of the downtown area; there are well-marked parking areas just outside the city walls.

Some sites of interest in Siena close for a midday break, usually from 12:30 or 1 PM to anywhere from 2:30 to 3:30 PM; we suggest calling ahead to check exact hours.

PIAZZA DEL CAMPO From the hazy horizon of Tuscan hills beyond the city walls, all Siena seems to slide down into Piazza del Campo, one of Europe's most beautiful old squares. It's on a slant, and its brick paving is divided into nine sectors, a number that harks back to the 13th and 14th centuries, when the city was ruled by the Governo dei Nove. The sectors converge on the piazza's lower side, in front of the *Palazzo Comunale* and the adjacent *Torre del Mangia.* Facing them on the higher side is the *Fonte Gaia,* a monumental fountain decorated with reliefs by Jacopo della Quercia (reproductions take the place of the 15th-century originals, which are now in the *Museo Civico* in the *Palazzo Comunale*). All around the semicircular edge of the piazza are medieval and Renaissance buildings. One of the most noteworthy is the *Palazzo Sansedoni,* with its curved façade. Dating from the 13th and 14th centuries, it became a single residence in the 18th century. At *Palio* time the windows of the palaces are hung with ancient banners, the center of the piazza is stuffed with spectators, and the roadway all around turns into the route of the historical procession—and then the *Palio* racetrack.

PALAZZO COMUNALE The elegant façade of this Gothic building is slightly curved, in keeping with the unusual outline of the Campo. Siena's *City Hall* since it was built between 1297 and 1310, it also houses an art museum. The adjacent bell tower, the *Torre del Mangia,* was added in the mid-13th century. It takes its name from a onetime bell ringer, Giovanni di Duccio, who was evidently a man of prodigal habits and better known to the Sienese as Mangiaguadagni (Spendthrift). The pillared and roofed structure at the base of the tower is the *Cappella di Piazza,* built from 1352 to 1376 to fulfill a vow made during the plague of 1348.

Inside the *Palazzo Comunale* is the *Sala del Mappamondo*—a room named for a world map no longer there—which houses the somewhat deteriorated but splendidly restored *Maestà* (1315) of Simone Martini, the great Sienese painter's first masterpiece. The fresco of Guidoriccio da Fogliano (1328) in the same room has long been attributed to Martini (now considered doubtful). Below that is a Madonna and Child by the earlier Sienese painter Guido da Siena, dated 1221; it may have been repainted a half century or so later by Duccio di Buoninsegna. The adjacent *Sala della Pace* is decorated with a series of allegorical frescoes on the subject of good and bad government. Painted between 1338 and 1340 by Ambrogio Lorenzetti, they show Giotto's influence. One, which offers a fine view of the city, was daring for its day because of the use of landscape as a subject in its own right. Lorenzetti is believed to have died from the plague not long after completing the fresco cycle. The museum also contains the originals of Jacopo della Quercia's reliefs for the *Fonte Gaia.* Closed daily after 12:45 PM from November 16 to March 15; closed Sundays and most holidays after 1:30 PM the rest of the year. Admission charge. Piazza del Campo (phone: 292263).

DUOMO (CATHEDRAL) Dedicated to Santa Maria dell'Assunta (Our Lady of the Assumption), this is one of the most beautiful medieval churches in Italy. It was begun in 1196, during the early stages of Siena's development as a city-state, and much of what is seen today was completed in the 13th century. Construction began again in 1339, when it was decided that the existing church should form the transept of a newer, much larger church. By 1355 money problems and the plague had put an end to the super-church dream, but not before the façade of the new church had been built. (It is this piece of unfinished architecture, to the right of the *Duomo,* that the Sienese call the *Facciatone,* or Big Façade.) Attention returned in the late 14th century to finishing the old *Duomo,* and the result is an imposing, if somewhat irregular, white marble basilica with characteristic black stripes. The lower level of the façade, largely Romanesque, is dominated by the stone carving of Giovanni Pisano, whose work decorates many Tuscan churches. The upper level is full 14th-century Gothic. The mosaics with gold backgrounds at the top are from the 19th century.

The interior of the church is rich in art treasures. The floor, installed from the mid-14th to the mid-16th century, is divided into 56 squares, each recounting a different biblical story in inlaid marblework. The scenes are the work of more than 40 different, mostly Sienese, artists (there are several by Beccafumi). While many are visible year-round, the most precious are kept covered in the interests of conservation and can be seen only from August 15 to September 15. Another treasure is the magnificent marble and porphyry pulpit by Nicola Pisano, Giovanni's father, sculpted with the help of his son and Arnolfo di Cambio. The Renaissance *Cappella di San Giovanni Battista* has frescoes by Pinturicchio (note the two portraits of Alberto Aringhieri). Pinturicchio also painted the lively, vivid frescoes recounting the life of Pope Pius II (Enea Silvio Piccolomini) in the *Librera Piccolomini,* off the left side of the nave. Built in 1495 by the pope's nephew (who later became Pope Pius III) to house his uncle's precious collection of books, the library also contains a famous Roman statue of the Three Graces. The *Duomo* is open daily, with a midday closing. The library is closed Sundays after 1 PM, and Mondays through Saturdays for a midday break. Admission charge to the library. Piazza del Duomo (no phone).

BATTISTERO Siena's baptistry is down a flight of stairs to the right of the cathedral, behind the apse. The 14th-century building is best known for its baptismal font, designed by Jacopo della Quercia and considered a work of transition from the Gothic to the Renaissance. A collaborative effort, it has two bronze angels by Donatello, as well as bas-reliefs around the basin by Donatello, Lorenzo Ghiberti, and others. Piazza San Giovanni.

MUSEO DELL'OPERA DEL DUOMO (CATHEDRAL MUSEUM) Also known as the *Museo dell'Opera Metropolitana,* this museum contains mainly works that have been taken from the cathedral. Almost as interesting as the works themselves is their setting: the *Duomo Nuovo,* the unfinished extension of the cathedral that was planned and then abandoned in the mid-14th century. A visitor can only imagine its potential magnificence from the five huge Gothic arches that still stand and would have been the nave. Three of these were closed off to form the museum. On the ground floor are ten statues of Old Testament figures carved by Giovanni Pisano for the *Duomo* façade (the statues on the façade now are reproductions) and a stone relief panel of the Madonna and Child carved by Jacopo della Quercia for one of the side altars. Upstairs is the masterpiece that made Duccio di Buoninsegna's career, the *Maestà* (1308–11), which was carried from his workshop to the high altar of the cathedral in solemn procession. Originally it showed the Madonna and Child on the front and the 26 scenes of the Passion on the back (it was sawed in two in the 18th century), with smaller scenes of the life of Christ and the Virgin above and below. (Nineteen of these smaller panels remain; others are in museums in the US and Great Britain.) Still another masterpiece is Simone Martini's *Blessed Agostino Novello and Four of His Miracles* (1330). Open daily, March 14 through October; closed after 1:30 PM, November to March 15. Admission charge. Piazza del Duomo (phone: 49153 or 42309).

PINACOTECA NAZIONALE The *National Picture Gallery* is a must for a clear understanding of Sienese art from the 12th to the 17th century. In the beautiful 15th-century *Palazzo Buonsignori* are 40 rooms filled with Sienese masterpieces by Guido da Siena, Duccio, Simone Martini, Pietro and Ambrogio Lorenzetti, Beccafumi, and others. Closed Sundays after 1 PM in summer; closed daily after 1:30 PM in winter. Admission charge. 29 Via San Pietro (phone: 281161).

CHIESA DI SANT'AGOSTINO Built during the 13th and 14th centuries, this church underwent Baroque modifications in the 18th century. It houses Perugino's *Crucifix and Saints* (1506) and, in one of the chapels, the *Massacre of the Innocents* (1482) by Matteo di Giovanni, *Madonna and Child with Saints* by Ambrogio Lorenzetti, and the *Epiphany* by Sodoma over the altar. Prato di Sant'Agostino (no phone).

PALAZZO CHIGI-SARACINI Like many Sienese palaces and churches, this was begun in the 12th century, finished in the Gothic style in the 14th century, and later altered and restored. Originally built for one of the leading families of Siena, it is now the seat of the *Accademia Musicale Chigiana* and a music school whose international summer students congregate around the carved stone well in the delightful courtyard. The interior can be visited on request: Its lofty ornate rooms are decorated with gems of Sienese art from the 13th to the 17th century. Concerts are held in the palace's music room, which is adapted from the noble apartments and is Siena's main concert hall. Closed Mondays. No admission charge. To visit the interior, apply to the *Accademia,* 89 Via di Città, Siena 53100 (phone: 46152).

PALAZZO PICCOLOMINI A mid-15th-century Renaissance palace in the midst of medieval Siena, this was once the home of the family of Pope Pius II. It now houses the state archives, with a wealth of documents and statutes pertaining to Siena's turbulent history. Farther down the street are the *Logge del Papa,* three graceful Renaissance arches that Pius II had built in his family's honor. The archives are closed Sundays. No admission charge. Via Banchi di Sotto (no phone).

MUSEO ARCHEOLOGICO NAZIONALE (NATIONAL ARCHAEOLOGICAL MUSEUM) Exhibits ranging from prehistory to the Roman period include Etruscan funeral urns from the 3rd century BC and Greek and Roman statues and statuettes dating from the 6th century BC. Closed the first and last Mondays of every month and daily after 1 PM (open afternoons in summer). Admission charge. 3 Via della Sapienza (phone: 49153).

BASILICA DI SAN DOMENICO Approach from Via della Sapienza for a breathtaking glimpse of the *Duomo*, its bell tower, and the *Torre del Mangia*. *San Domenico* is a massive, severe-looking, monastic Gothic building begun in 1226 and completed in the 15th century, while the graceful bell tower next to it was built in 1340. Inside, the spacious, simple majesty of this austere church—in the unusual T-shape of an Egyptian cross—is interrupted with shafts of light from modern stained glass windows. See the *Cappella di Santa Caterina,* a chapel adorned with Sodoma's early-16th-century frescoes of the mystic Sienese saint who was a member of the Dominican order and who eventually became one of the two patron saints of Italy (with Saint Francis of Assisi). A reliquary in the same chapel contains the head of St. Catherine, while another chapel, the *Cappella delle Volte,* contains a fresco of her by a contemporary, Andrea Vanni, which is held to be the only authentic portrait of the saint in existence. Piazza San Domenico (no phone).

SANTUARIO CATERINIANO (ST. CATHERINE'S SANCTUARY) St. Catherine lived from 1347 to 1380; by 1464, only a few years after her canonization, her house was turned into a sanctuary. Despite the sacred transformation, the addition of chapels, and the 15th- and 16th-century paintings showing scenes from her life, there is still a homey atmosphere. The adjoining *Chiesa di Santa Caterina,* facing Via Santa Caterina, is part of the sanctuary; once the dyer's shop of her father, it too contains frescoes and statues of the saint. Open daily, with a long (12:30 to 3:30 PM) break. No admission charge. Costa di Sant' Antonio (no phone).

FONTE BRANDA One of Siena's oldest and best-loved fountains is at the end of Via Santa Caterina, not far from the sanctuary. References to it date as far back as 1081, but it was rebuilt in the mid-13th century, when it was given its present triple-arched mini-fortress form with the arms of Siena in the middle.

BASILICA DI SAN FRANCESCO Begun in the 14th century and originally Gothic in style, this church was much changed externally by Baroque additions following a 17th-century fire and by a modern façade. Still, the interior, in the shape of an Egyptian cross, retains the characteristic alternating layers of black and white marble. Detached frescoes by Pietro Lorenzetti (the *Crucifixion*) and Ambrogio Lorenzetti are in the side chapels. The church opens onto the former *Convento di San Francesco* and a wonderful Renaissance cloister. Piazza San Francesco (no phone).

ORATORIO DI SAN BERNARDINO This structure was built in the 15th century on the spot where Siena's beloved second saint, the Franciscan San Bernardino (1380–1444), preached his sermons (quite lively ones, evidently—his gift for persuasion caused him to be made the patron saint of advertising and public relations by Pope John XXIII). Its upper floor is gracefully decorated with stucco and is frescoed with images of the Madonna and saints (including San Bernardino) by some notable 16th-century artists: Sodoma, Girolamo del Pacchia, and Beccafumi. Open daily, with a midday closing, April through October; open at the discretion of the custodian (who may accept a tip to open the oratory) the rest of the year. Admission charge. 6 Piazza San Francesco (phone: 289081).

BASILICA DI SANTA MARIA DEI SERVI Away from the center, on a rise that offers a splendid view of the *Duomo,* it has a simple 13th-century façade and bell tower. Its interior mixes Gothic severity with Renaissance splendor. Among the works of art are a Madonna (1261) by Coppo di Marcovaldo and one by Lippo Memmi. Piazza Alessandro Manzoni (no phone).

EXTRA SPECIAL

Besides the *Torre del Mangia* and the *Facciatone,* one spot in Siena offers a panoramic view of all the palaces and churches, the red-roofed expanse cut through by winding streets. This is the *Fortezza Medicea,* also known as the *Forte di Santa Barbara,* a defensive fortress built in 1560 by Cosimo I of the Florentine Medici family shortly after his arrival in Siena as the city's conqueror. But the vista is not the only reason to visit this well-preserved fort and city park at the end of a long day's sightseeing. Inside, part of the space is given over to the *Enoteca Italica Permanente,* a showroom and outlet for all the best Italian wines, including the excellent chianti bottlings for which the province is famous. The most demanding restaurateurs do their shopping here, but so can the enthusiastic individual, and tasting is encouraged for a small charge. With advance notice, a guided visit to a wine estate can be arranged here; the price varies with the excursion. The cellars are open daily from noon to midnight. No admission charge. *Fortezza Medicea* (phone: 288497).

Sources and Resources

TOURIST INFORMATION

Siena's tourist organization, the *Azienda di Promozione Turistica* (*APT*; 56 Piazza del Campo; phone: 280551), is an information office and travel agency. It is closed Saturday afternoons; Sundays; and weekdays for a long (12:30 to 3:30 PM) break (open all day in summer). The services of Donatella Grilli, a private guide, are recommended (phone: 285188). Others include Vittoria Adami (phone: 47174); Monika Buchstaller (phone: 364408); and Paolo Faldoni (phone: 49050). The *APT* has a list of more English-speaking, licensed guides as well as a list of drivers with cars.

LOCAL COVERAGE The Sienese read Florence's daily newspaper, *La Nazione*. The weekly *La Voce del Campo* lists local events. Many shops in the heart of town carry English-language guidebooks.

TELEPHONE The city code for Siena is 577. When calling from within Italy, dial 0577 before the local number.

GETTING AROUND

Since so many of the narrow streets in the center of this city are closed to traffic, the only way to get around is on foot. Several car parks situated around the walls make walking to the center easy enough for even the most reluctant pedestrian.

BUS Siena has local bus service; one of the main stops for most of the buses is Piazza Matteotti. Buses for destinations in and around Tuscany usually leave from Piazza San Domenico; for information, call *TRA-IN* (phone: 204245). For tickets and information, go to the booth at Piazza Gramsci or at the railway station.

CAR RENTAL Most international chains are represented. Among reputable smaller firms are *Benito Minucci* (11 Viale Sardegna; phone: 282000) and *Balzana* (2 Via P. Fracassi; phone: 285013), which offers chauffeur service.

TAXI There are cabstands at the train station and at Piazza Matteotti, or call *Radio-Taxi* (phone: 49222).

TRAIN The main station is at the foot of the hills, a short taxi ride from the city center, at Piazzale Fratelli Rosselli (phone: 280115). The information office keeps varying hours, depending on the day of the week and the season; in summer it is usually closed Sundays and Mondays.

SPECIAL EVENTS

Siena's annual *Palio* horse races are one of Italy's major traditions.

FAVORITE FETE

Palio The city's celebrated bareback horse race around the outer edge of the Piazza del Campo has been going on since the 14th century. It is run twice, on July 2 in honor of Santa Maria di Provenzano and on August 16 in homage to Santa Maria dell'Assunta. The races involve months of preparation on the part of each *contrada,* but the actual *Palio* activities begin three days or so before each race, with the selection of horses, a lottery to choose which of the 17 *contrade* will run (the track can accommodate only 10 horses), and several rehearsals. The night before the race a banquet is held in each of the participating *contrade* (visitors with tickets may attend). The next day various religious activities fill up the morning; in the afternoon horses are blessed in the local churches. In late afternoon the *Torre del Mangia* bell sounds, and a spectacular parade files into Piazza del Campo—representatives of the city and of all the *contrade* march in historic costume. This is followed by the race itself. There are no rules, so rumors of the drugging of horses and bribing of jockeys go on right up to post time. The Sienese are by now worked up to a fever pitch, and even though the race is over in only a few minutes, celebration in the winning *contrada* goes on all night and the next day. Finally, in September, the two winning *contrade* of the July and August races hold a huge outdoor banquet, with the winning horses at the head of the table.

Tickets for the *Palio* are not easy to come by. Most grandstand seats on the perimeter of the course belong to the Sienese almost by birthright. Remaining seats sell out many months in advance, and are expensive in the rare instances that they are available. Merchants in the town's better shops are the best source; ask around the Piazza del Campo. The demand for tickets is so great that spaces at the windows of homes around the Campo are sold, too, and scalping is rampant. Non–ticket holders can stand in the mass of humanity in the middle of the piazza without charge, but early arrival (before noon) is imperative to ensure a view (pick a high spot near the *Fonte Gaia*). Another alternative is to buy a ticket for one of the rehearsals that take place on the three days preceding each *Palio,* though this is becoming increasingly impossible, as city officials usually buy up all the tickets. The regal pageantry is missing at these trial heats, but you can still feel a bit of the spirit. Occasionally, a third *Palio* may be declared for some special reason.

For those not planning to visit Siena at *Palio* time but still looking for a taste of it, each *contrada* has days when its church and the museum in which it keeps the silk *Palio* banners are open to the public. The tourist information office (see above) can provide a list of these days and phone numbers, but make arrangements a week in advance.

MUSEUMS

Siena's most important museums are listed under *Special Places.* In addition, the following (none charges admission) are also of interest:

BIBLIOTECA COMUNALE DEGLI INTRONATI Ancient religious and civic manuscripts and beautifully illuminated sacred books. Closed Sundays, and Saturdays after 2 PM. 5 Via della Sapienza (phone: 280704).

MUSEI DELL'ACCADEMIA DEI FISIOCRITICI A geomineralogical and zoological museum with prehistoric fossils, shells, and skeletons found in the surrounding area. Closed Thursday afternoons; weekends; holidays; and Mondays, Tuesdays, Wednesdays, and Fridays for a midday break. 4 Piazza Sant'Agostino (phone: 47002).

ORTO BOTANICO A botanical garden. Closed Sundays, Saturday afternoons, and holidays. 4 Via Pier Andrea Mattioli (phone: 298874).

SHOPPING

Sienese shops are a mixture of extreme sophistication and rustic simplicity. While leading names in Italian fashion are in evidence in clothing and shoe stores, local craftsmanship can be found in the numerous shops selling ceramics, pottery, and excellent copies of medieval and Renaissance Sienese items. The shops lining the main streets near Piazza del Campo—Banchi di Sopra, Banchi di Sotto, and Via di Città—are fertile ground for all of Siena's specialties, including the numerous culinary delicacies to be found in this area. Siena is particularly famous for *panforte,* a rich, spiced fruit-and-nut cake; *ricciarelli* (almond cookies); and salami. Buy wine at the *Enoteca Italica Permanente* in the *Fortezza Medicea* (see *Extra Special,* above) or at any local grocer. One favorite souvenir quest is the attempt to collect a set of flags, mugs, or plates that carry the crests of each of Siena's 17 surviving *contrade.*

A colorful outdoor market takes place Wednesdays at Piazza La Lizza (near the *Basilica di San Domenico*), where you can buy everything from flowers to handbags, dresses, kitchenware, and pottery. And every February brings an important antiques fair to the splendid halls of the old salt warehouse, the *Magazzini del Sale* (Piazza del Campo; phone: 292355).

Most shops are open from 9 AM to 1 PM and 4 to 8 PM in summer (from 3:30 to 7:30 PM in winter), and closed Monday mornings and Sundays year-round.

Antica Drogheria Manganelli The best place to buy Tuscan fruitcakes and *vin santo,* a dessert wine. 71 Via di Città (no phone).

Antichità Saena Vetus High-quality antiques and some small pieces for the bargain hunter. 53 Via di Città (phone: 42395).

Art Shop Exquisitely made paper products—notebook covers, picture frames, large folders, tiny boxes—made by 17th-century methods. 17 Via di Città (no phone).

La Balzana Tuscan and other Italian antiques and bric-a-brac. Piazza del Campo (phone: 285380).

Bianco e Nero Handmade ceramics with Sienese motifs. 8 Via dei Fusari (phone: 280026).

Ceccuzzi Beautiful Italian fabrics as well as made-to-measure and ready-to-wear clothes. Two entrances: 1 Banchi di Sopra and 32-36 Via dei Montanini (phone: 289219).

Ceramiche Santa Caterina One-of-a-kind, hand-painted ceramics. 9/A Via Camporegio (phone: 45006).

Enoteca San Domenico Tuscan wines and fine foods, including Siena's famous fruitcakes. 56 Via del Paradiso (phone: 271181).

Mercatissimo della Calzatura e Pelletteria Fine, reasonably priced leatherwork. 1 Viale Curtatone (phone: 281305).

Mori An extensive selection of shoes, bags, and belts. 30-32 and 68-70 Via Banchi di Sopra (no phone).

Il Papiro Hand-decorated paper—including the unusual *papier à cuvé*—and marbleized paper designs applied to fabrics that are then affixed to wallets and handbags. 37 Via di Città (phone: 284241).

Provvedi One of the best stocked of the many ceramics shops in the area. 96 Via di Città (phone: 286078).

Quercioli Jewelry, some of it from the nearby workshops of Arezzo, a leading jewelry-making town. 5 Via Banchi di Sopra (no phone).

Siena Ricama Hand-embroidered table linen and pillow covers in the colors and designs of Renaissance Siena. 61 Via di Città (phone: 28009).

La Stamperia Marbleized paper and bookbinding by fine artisans. 80 Via delle Terme (no phone).

Il Telaio Beautifully designed and handloomed women's jackets. 2 Chiasso del Bargello (phone: 47065).

SPORTS AND FITNESS

HORSEBACK RIDING The *Club Ippico Senese* (Località Pian del Lago; phone: 318677) offers riding lessons and countryside treks.

SOCCER From September through May *Siena* plays at the *Stadio Comunale Artemio Franchi* (3 Viale dei Mille; phone: 281084), near the *Fortezza Medicea.*

SWIMMING The outdoor municipal pool in Piazza Amendola (phone: 47496), on the northwest edge of the city, is open in summer. There also is the *Piscina Quattro Querce* (31 Via di Marciano; phone: 40013).

TENNIS There are courts at *Circolo Tennis La Racchetta* (2 Via Vivaldi; phone: 221110), a private club that welcomes visiting players. Some hotels allow non-guests to rent courts (see *Checking In*).

MUSIC

Siena has no opera company, but the *Accademia Musicale Chigiana* more than makes up for this deficit in July and August, when its summer school for professional and advanced musicians is in session. During the program students make regular concert appearances, as soloists or in ensembles, and at the same time the academy sponsors a series of concerts, the *Estate Musicale Chigiana,* featuring well-known guest artists. An annual week-long festival in late August, the *Settimana Musicale Senese,* features rarely played or forgotten works as well as those of contemporary composers. The events take place in the *Palazzo Chigi-Saracini* music room—Siena's main concert hall for performances at other times of the year as well—or in any of the city's innumerable palaces and churches. For information, contact the *Fondazione Accademia Musicale Chigiana* (89 Via di Città; phone: 46152; fax: 288124).

NIGHTCLUBS AND NIGHTLIFE

As in most Italian cities, at least in the summer, nightlife to the average Sienese simply means wandering through the city and stopping at the occasional *caffè* in the Campo that's open late. Greater stimulation is possible at three discotheques: *Club Enoteca,* adjacent to the wine cellars of the *Fortezza Medicea* (phone: 285466), closed Mondays through Wednesdays; *Barone Rosso* (9 Via dei Termini; no phone); and the more centrally located *Gallery* (13 Via Pantaneto; phone: 288378), closed Wednesdays. *Al Cambio* (48 Via Pantaneto; phone: 43183), open to 2 AM and closed Thursdays, is a popular gathering place for drinking, music, and conversation. *L'Officina* (3 Piazza del Sale; phone: 286301) is a piano bar/watering hole.

Best in Town

CHECKING IN

Do not arrive in Siena without a hotel reservation between May and October. Because of the small size and popularity of the town, its 30 or so hotels, both inside and outside the walls, usually are booked solid for most of the prime tourism season. It is definitely a mistake to arrive in town unexpectedly on *Palio* days and the days immediately preceding them. You can make reservations through the *Siena Hotels Promotion* office (Piazza San

Domenico; phone: 288084; fax: 280290), which is closed Sundays and holidays. Prices vary greatly. The very expensive hotel will charge $450 or more per night for a double room; an expensive hotel, from $300 to $450; a moderate one, from $130 to $275; and an inexpensive one, from $80 to $120. All hotels feature air conditioning, private baths, TV sets, and telephones unless otherwise indicated. All telephone numbers are in the 577 city code unless otherwise noted.

VERY EXPENSIVE

Certosa di Maggiano Among cypress trees and vineyards, this 14-room hotel has a unique atmosphere of seclusion and meditation—not surprising, since it began in the 14th century as a Carthusian monastery. A short taxi or bus ride outside the city walls, this member of the Relais & Châteaux group has several spacious sitting rooms, Renaissance furniture, and a permanent show of ancient manuscripts and documents. A large, well-kept garden contains a heated pool and tennis courts, and the restaurant of the same name is highly recommended (see *Eating Out*). 82 Strada di Certosa (phone: 288180; fax: 288189).

EXPENSIVE

Jolly Excelsior There are 126 well-appointed rooms, a restaurant, and a bar in this comfortable, traditional hotel, with the efficient service that characterizes the chain. Centrally located near the town gate, at Piazza La Lizza (phone: 288448; fax: 41272).

Park The building originally was a castle-cum-villa, built in 1530 for the well-to-do Gori family. They chose the spot for its dominating position (and, therefore, its easy defense) as well as for the healthy air and attractive countryside views of olive trees and rolling hills. A pool and tennis courts are unobtrusively integrated into a romantic, slightly decadent-looking Italian garden surrounded by a small wood of oak and beech trees. There are 69 rooms with color TV on request, and the *Magnolia Terrace* restaurant is good (see *Eating Out*). A short taxi or bus ride from the city center, at 16 Via di Marciano (phone: 44803; fax: 49020).

MODERATE

Palazzo Ravizza An old-fashioned pensione within easy walking distance of the main sights of Siena, this 17th-century villa is surrounded by its own garden and provides a peaceful, yet central, vantage point from which to enjoy the city. Most of the 30 rooms have a private bath, but none has air conditioning or a TV. The pleasant restaurant is for guests only (full board required in high season). 34 Pian dei Mantellini (phone: 280462; fax: 271370).

Villa Catignano On a hilltop 15 minutes from town, 16 meticulously restored suites are available for weekly rental in a 16th-century villa's renovated farm buildings. There is a splendid view, a formal Renaissance garden, and a pool under ancient cypress trees. The rooms are not air conditioned and have no TVs, and there's no restaurant, but each suite has a kitchenette. Pianella, Castelnuovo Berardenga (phone: 356755; fax: 356755).

Villa Scacciapensieri A bit over a mile (1.6 km) from the city center, this handsome 28-room family villa, built a little over a hundred years ago, is another romantic spot in the countryside. With its large garden and view of both the city and the surrounding vine-clad hills, as well as a tennis court, a pool, excellent cuisine, and regular bus service into town, this is an ideal stopping place from which to enjoy sightseeing trips in Siena or forays into the Chianti hills. Open March through December. 10 Strada di Scacciapensieri (phone: 41441; fax: 270854).

INEXPENSIVE

Castagneto Below the city walls on the western side of Siena, this small but comfortable hotel offers splendid panoramas from its own garden. There are 11 rooms with private showers; no air conditioning or restaurant. Open mid-March through November. No credit cards accepted. 39 Via dei Cappuccini (phone: 45103).

Chiusarelli Set just below the imposing walls of the *Basilica di San Domenico* and the *Fonte Branda* on the western outskirts of the city, this hotel still is within easy reach of the center. Three of the 50 rooms have no private bath, and none is air conditioned. There are a restaurant, a glassed-in terrace, and a small garden. 15 Viale Curtatone (phone: 280562).

Duomo This attractive hotel is perfect for a comfortable, reasonably priced stay in town. It's in the heart of medieval Siena, a five-minute walk from the *Duomo,* and within easy reach of Via di Città, one of the main shopping streets. Many of the 23 quiet rooms offer a view of the *Duomo.* There's no restaurant. 34 Via Stalloreggi (phone: 289088; fax: 43043).

Garden Housed under two roofs are 150 rooms (none air conditioned) in the main building and a new, more posh annex. This hostelry has plenty of charm, a pool, a garden, and a restaurant. 2 Via Custosa (phone: 47056; fax: 46050).

Santa Caterina In this 18th-century palazzo are 19 tastefully furnished rooms. There's a large, pleasant verandah for breakfast and a delightful garden for an aperitif. Located just outside the city walls, but only a 10-minute walk from the city center. 7 Via Enea Silvio Piccolomini (phone: 221105; fax: 271087).

La Torre Here are eight small but tastefully refurbished rooms in a renovated medieval tower within walking distance of the Campo. No restaurant. 7 Via Fiera Vecchia (phone/fax: 222255).

Villa Belvedere Just 7 miles (11 km) outside Siena in Colle Val d'Elsa, this lovingly restored villa—built in 1795—was once the residence of the Grand Duke of Tuscany. The 15 rooms are not air conditioned. There is a lovely garden and a good restaurant. Località Belvedere, Colle Val d'Elsa (phone: 920966; fax: 924128).

Villa Liberty More than a century old and in the center of town, this very attractive villa has 12 rooms, all decorated in contemporary style (no air conditioning, though). No restaurant, but there's a bar. 11 Via Veneto (phone: 44966; fax: 50431).

EATING OUT

Siena (as part of Tuscany) is one of the few places in Italy to sample good beef as well as game—venison, wild boar, hare, pheasant, quail, and wild pigeon. Whether in salami, in rustic pâtés to be spread on rounds of toasted bread, or served with lentils or beans, these seasonal delights are a staple of the area's hearty country fare. Sienese cooks are also handy with vegetable dishes and are well versed in the making of soups, such as the rich vegetable broth with bread and poached egg known as *acqua cotta* (literally, "cooked water") and *ribollita* ("reboiled"), the Rolls-Royce of vegetable soups. Wild mushrooms, gathered fresh from the surrounding wooded areas and served in a variety of ways, can be a main course or a side dish. Cheeses are traditionally made from sheep's and cow's milk, the most prevalent being *caciotta* and pecorino, which can be mild and soft or seasoned to become salty and hard. Wines range from the local chianti to the reds made from the brunello grapes of nearby Montalcino. The dry but robust Tuscan whites include vernaccia from San Gimignano and bianco vergine della Valdichiana. And then there is the traditional sweet dessert wine, *vin santo.*

Siena is essentially informal, and while the more expensive hotels offer an elegant ambience befitting their ratings, the average restaurant tends to be more homey—though the food is no less delectable for being served in relaxed surroundings. In the listings below dinner for two in a very expensive restaurant will cost $150 to $250; expensive restaurants charge from $90 to $140; moderate, from $70 to $90; and inexpensive, $65 or less. Prices include wine but not service or tip. All restaurants are open for lunch and dinner unless otherwise noted. All telephone numbers are in the 577 city code.

VERY EXPENSIVE

Certosa di Maggiano The fare in this sophisticated country hotel ranges far beyond the Tuscan border to include such nouvelle-style dishes as tortellini soufflé, shrimp fricassee, and sole with asparagus. Most dishes are made from locally grown ingredients, the choice of dessert changes daily, and there is an excellent selection of wines. Closed Tuesdays, except to hotel guests. Reservations advised. Major credit cards accepted. 82 Via di Certosa (phone: 288180).

EXPENSIVE

Botteganova A creative approach to traditional Tuscan fare results in high-quality dining at this elegant spot. Truffles abound, and the desserts are homemade. Closed Mondays for lunch, Sundays, the first week in January, and July 20 to August 10. Reservations advised. Major credit cards accepted. 29 Strada Chiantigiana (phone: 284230).

Magnolia Terrace For traditional Tuscan cooking, try this restaurant in a 16th-century villa–turned-hotel. Offerings include salads of mushrooms and white beans in the purest olive oil, soups made from freshly gathered mushrooms, and fish fresh from the Tuscan coast, plus homemade cheeses and cakes and a vast selection of wines. It's all reliable, if uninspired. Open daily. Reservations advised. Major credit cards accepted. In the *Park* hotel, 16 Via di Marciano (phone: 44803).

Al Marsili A handsome 15th-century, vaulted restaurant near the *Duomo,* this prime Sienese eating place is rooted in Tuscan tradition, but it serves its own original dishes as well. Fresh vegetables form the basis of some of the regulars' favorites: zucchini casserole, chick-peas with garlic and rosemary, and vegetable *sformati* (mousse). Mushroom pâté is spread on toasted country bread for an hors d'oeuvre, and game—guinea fowl, wild duck, or pigeon, roasted or served with one of the inimitable house sauces—is prominent among the poultry dishes. Closed Mondays. Reservations advised. Major credit cards accepted. 3 Via del Castoro (phone: 47154).

MODERATE

Il Biondo At the edge of the old city center, this large, modern restaurant with an outdoor terrace adds fresh fish dishes, such as homemade spaghetti with shrimp, to an otherwise Tuscan menu, which often features roast lamb with artichokes, grilled pork liver, and pork and sausage on skewers. Closed Wednesdays, two weeks in January, and two weeks in July. Reservations advised. Major credit cards accepted. 10 Vicolo del Rustichetto (phone: 280739).

Le Campane The menu includes house variations on classic Tuscan soups such as *ribollita* and an artichoke quiche. Fresh fish, charcoal-grilled meat, and veal scaloppine with fresh tarragon are other entrées. Closed Mondays. Reservations advised. Major credit cards accepted. Between the *Duomo* and Piazza del Campo, at 4 Via delle Campane (phone: 284035).

Cane e Gatto Owners Paolo and Sonia Senni have their collection of modern lithographs by Picasso, among others, hung on the walls of this chic, tiny eatery. There is no menu, but there is art in the creative cooking and fine wines. Closed Thursdays and after the August 16 *Palio* for about a week. Reservations necessary. Major credit cards accepted. 6 Via Pagliaresi (phone: 287545).

Grotta di Santa Caterina–Da Bagoga Founded by Bagoga, a former *Palio* jockey, this lively restaurant is jammed during *Palio* time and often during the rest of the summer as well. *Palio* mementos decorate the walls, and the menu is classic Tuscan fare—pasta with hare sauce, roast meat, and game. Closed Sundays for dinner, Mondays, and 10 days in mid-July. Reservations advised. Major credit cards accepted. 26 Via della Galluzza (phone: 282208).

Da Guido In the heart of the old city, one of the most characteristic of the wood-beamed restaurants serves equally characteristic Tuscan cuisine. This is one of Siena's favorite haunts, and photos of its famous habitués line the brick walls. Closed Wednesdays. Reservations advised. Major credit cards accepted. 3 Vicolo Pier Pettinaio (phone: 280042).

Le Logge This is where the connoisseurs congregate. Taste the delectable rustic Sienese bean soup, *crostini* (toasted rounds of bread) with game and mushroom pâté, or classic meat and game dishes with a sprinkling of truffles in season. A home-produced *caciotta* dominates the cheese selection. Forget the mediocre house wine. Closed Sundays, June 1 to 15, and November 15 to 30. Reservations necessary. Major credit cards accepted. 33 Via del Porrione (phone: 48013).

Al Mangia Since it's right on Piazza del Campo, this well-known Sienese eatery, with alfresco dining in warm weather, is inundated in summer by *Palio* fans and other visitors. At other times, however, it's a pleasant eating place, with tables outside looking toward the handsome *Palazzo Comunale.* The menu is particularly good for game and mushroom dishes, and the wine list is decent. Closed Mondays. Reservations advised. Major credit cards accepted. 43 Piazza del Campo (phone: 281121).

Da Mugolone Serving excellent Tuscan fare in a rustic setting, it's a favorite, and not only with locals. Try the *pappardelle alla lepre* (wide noodles in hare sauce) or *capretto* (kid) in a tasty sauce. Closed Thursdays and 10 days in mid-July. Reservations advised. Major credit cards accepted. 8 Via dei Pellegrini (phone: 283235).

Nello La Taverna An informal, friendly atmosphere makes this a popular place with locals and visitors alike. It's a good place to try traditional Tuscan game, or pasta served with any of a variety of sauces, or, as in the *tagliatelle* with tarragon, simply with fresh herbs. The *menù gastronomico sienese* likewise is recommended. Closed Mondays and February. Reservations advised. Major credit cards accepted. 28 Via del Porrione (phone: 289043).

INEXPENSIVE

Il Ghibellino Paper cloths on marble tables mark this eatery, whose menu features leek soup, rabbit stewed with artichokes, and homemade desserts. Closed Thursdays. Reservations unnecessary. No credit cards accepted. Near Piazza del Campo, at 26 Via dei Pellegrini (phone: 288079)

Papei The perfect place to try home-style Sienese cooking—homemade pasta, beans, steaks *alla fiorentina*. This friendly trattoria is frequented by locals and offers alfresco dining in the summer. Closed Mondays and late June. Reservations advised. Major credit cards accepted. 6 Piazza del Mercato (phone: 280894).

Turrido In warm weather dine on the terrace or in the garden on Tuscan fare such as *pappardelle alla lepre*, grilled lamb, and wild *porcini* mushrooms in various guises. There is an inexpensive tourist menu. Closed Mondays. Reservations necessary during *Palio* season. No credit cards accepted. 60-62 Via Stalloreggi (phone: 282121).

BARS AND CAFFÈS

Siena is at once smaller, more sophisticated, and more politely provincial than most Italian cities, and its student population is tiny. So unlike Milan, with its swarms of lively after-work watering holes, or Rome, with its chattering crowds, tiny Siena has only a few *caffès*. Here are the best, as well as other informal snacking spots. Most bars and *caffès* listed below are in the inexpensive price range. Unless otherwise indicated, they do not accept credit cards.

Caffè del Corso This is not much larger than a postage stamp, but it does have demure charm and a tiny upstairs tearoom, where Sienese ladies meet to sip tea, eat a piece of cake, and chat. 25 Via Banchi di Sopra (no phone).

Costa Pizza, snacks, and such are the draws here, one of Siena's more attractive places for a light meal. Try the pizza *della casa*—a rich concoction of sausage, mozzarella, and tomatoes. Closed Wednesdays. Major credit cards accepted. 37 Piazza del Campo (phone: 280614).

Enoteca Caffè Not to be confused with the vintners' asssociation store of the same name, this is a reliable, old fashioned *caffè* with a pleasant decor. Inside or out, it's a good place to enjoy a *prosecco* (dry white sparkling wine). Piazza del Campo (no phone).

Il Palio The most popular of the traditional *caffès,* it has an ample selection of appetizers. You can linger for an hour over an espresso, and no one will bother you. Piazza del Campo (no phone).

La Speranza Offering reliable cafeteria fare, this is where the locals pop in for a quick lunch. Closed Tuesdays. Piazza del Campo (phone: 281184).

Victoria Caffè Tea Room This is the largest, newest, and most comfortable tearoom in town, with comfy wicker furnishings and an ample menu of potables (including champagne), ice cream, and other snacks. Closed Mondays. Major credit cards accepted. 130 Via di Città (phone: 46720).

Taormina

Set on the slopes of Monte Tauro (Mountain of the Bull) and looking out at snow-capped Mt. Etna and the blue Ionian Sea, this little town is easily one of the world's loveliest resorts. For 20 centuries, Taormina has offered visitors the amenities of a restful vacation against the backdrop of exquisite natural beauty—ancient and medieval stone buildings framed by palm trees and vivid bougainvillea vines. Recently, Taormina has been known primarily as a refuge for rich and cultured Europeans. Along with swarms of day visitors, in a typical year Taormina hosts nearly three-quarters of a million overnight travelers.

Taormina's roots reach far back in time. Tombs built by the Siculi (Italian tribes that migrated to Sicily 1,300 years before Christ) have been discovered nearby. In 735 BC, Greek sailors founded the nearby city of Naxos. For several centuries, there was bitter rivalry among Greek colonies in Sicily. After Naxos was destroyed by Dionysius of Syracuse in 403 BC, the Siculi survivors founded Tauromenium. This town, too, was wiped out by Dionysius but was soon refounded. In 358 BC, a new state was established by Andromachus, with the support of the Naxian survivors.

The Romans, who arrived in 263 BC, gave Taormina considerable autonomy. Despite the vicissitudes of the empire (and the emperors' internal rivalries), it seems to have enjoyed centuries of peace and prosperity, attracting patrician vacationers. The area was known for its olives, grapes, and other fruits, vegetables, and marble, but its primary importance was military—the natural harbors below and the rocky lookout points above lent the region a strategic advantage.

After the fall of Rome and a brief period of domination by barbarian tribes, Taormina—like the rest of Sicily—fell under the influence of the Byzantine Empire. It became an archbishopric and, for a while, was the most important city in eastern Sicily. It fell to the Arabs in 902, and for the next several centuries it was variously dominated by the Swabians, the Normans, the Angevins, and the Aragonese. When King Martin died without heirs in 1410, King Ferdinand sent his son John to the island, and for the next three centuries all of Sicily was ruled by Spanish viceroys. During the latter part of this period, Taormina suffered a major fire and a severe earthquake, subsequently declining in population and sinking into obscurity. Little changed during the 18th and 19th centuries under the Spanish Bourbons, the Savoys of Piedmont, and the Hapsburgs of Austria.

The town's fortunes began to turn after Italian unification in 1860. With the stabilization of government and development of transportation, Taormina was soon discovered by wealthy German and British travelers. In a short time, its hotel industry burgeoned; by the turn of the century, it was popular with crowned heads of state and the families of European financiers. It was not unusual for the Rothschilds, the Krupps, and the Vanderbilts to vacation here; still later it became a favorite spot for artistic personalities such as D. H. Lawrence and German photographer Wilhelm von Gloeden.

Taormina today is known for its yield of citrus fruits, olives, and the wine commonly known as the "red wine of Etna." But mass tourism is the city's principal source of revenue, which has led to some problems. The traffic jams on the few narrow, steep roads leading from the sea to Taormina's position on a rocky balcony can be overwhelming, especially in August. Steps are being taken, however, to alleviate the congestion—a new road and underground parking facilities are being built below the town, as well as elevators to carry people up to Taormina. And a newly rebuilt *funivia* (cable car) is in operation between the town and Lido di Mazzarò (Mazzaro Beach). Noisy construction along the road leading to town and general chaos getting in and out of Taormina is expected to continue through next year. Fortunately, its price tag and governors have succeeded in protecting Taormina from the defacement that can result from invasions of vacationers. It has taken on a role in Italian cultural life as well—theater, film, and literary festivals are held here annually—so this enchanting city of gardens and medieval monuments continues to offer its visitors, in the words of Guy de Maupassant, "all that seems made on the earth to entice eyes, spirit, and imagination."

Taormina At-a-Glance

SEEING THE CITY
With its stone buildings, flowered balconies, and lush subtropical vegetation, Taormina appears to be a physical outgrowth of the surrounding mountainous landscape. The ruins of the *Castello* (Castle) on the summit of Monte Tauro command a good view of the town; the sea is accessible from here by foot or by car along the road descending from the village of Castelmola or by bus from the center of Taormina, just beyond *Porta Messina*. There's an even better view from Castelmola itself, about 3 miles (5 km) away. Taormina, however, is best known for the stunning view it affords of the town, the sea, and—in the distance—volcanic Mt. Etna, visible from the well-preserved Greek theater. In town, Piazza IX Aprile, off central Corso Umberto I, offers a lovely vista of the sea and coastline below.

SPECIAL PLACES
Taormina itself is tiny, with most shops, restaurants, and other attractions on or just off Corso Umberto I. The smaller crossroads are often merely pedestrian staircases hewn into the rock. Note that some sites of interest in Taormina close for a midday break, generally from 1 or 2 PM to 4 or even 5 PM; we suggest calling ahead to check exact hours.

CORSO UMBERTO I (UMBERTO I AVENUE) Closed to automobiles, Taormina's central street runs horizontally through the town, from *Porta Messina* to *Porta Catania*. The street marks the outskirts of what was the ancient Greek city of Tauromenion and what is still known as the Borgo Medioevale (Medieval Township). The street is unusually beautiful, with bougainvillea-filled balconies, shady piazzas, outdoor *caffès,* and irresistible pastry shops. The *corso* is undoubtedly the best place in Taormina for strolling and people watching.

TEATRO GRECO (GREEK THEATER) One of Sicily's most impressive and well-preserved archaeological ruins, the structure, probably built in the 3rd century BC, is the second-largest ancient amphitheater in Sicily after the one in Syracuse. The *cavea* (graduated rows of seats) was carved out of the hillside and surmounted by a portico of marble columns. Under the Romans, the theater was significantly rebuilt for use as a gladiatorial arena. The view from the theater is fine, and the acoustics are so good that it is still used for summer arts and film festivals. The theater closes two hours before sunset. Admission charge. 40 Via Teatro Greco (phone: 23220).

PALAZZO CORVAJA (CORVAJA PALACE) Built on the site of the ancient Roman forum, this impressive late-14th-century building with a crenelated façade is Taormina's most important medieval building. Originally the seat of the first Sicilian parliament, it also is thought to have been the residence of Queen Bianca of Navarre. In the 16th century it was passed on to the Corvaja family. Windows and other decorations, such as the black and white lava inlay ornamentation, are typically Catalan-Gothic in style. In the picturesque inner courtyard is a 13th-century stone staircase. Open daily, with a short (2 to 4 PM) closing. No admission charge. Piazza Vittorio Emanuele.

CHIESA DI SANTA CATERINA (CHURCH OF ST. CATHERINE) Next to *Palazzo Corvaja,* this small church has a fine statue of St. Catherine, three handsome Baroque altars, and a gloomy downstairs funeral chamber. Behind the church are the remains of a small Roman theater, or *odeon,* where musical performances were held in ancient times. Open daily, with a long (1 to 5 PM) closing. Piazza Santa Caterina.

NAUMACHIAE Via Naumachiae leads to the remains of an ancient cistern and its arcaded retaining wall. The Romans used naumachiae (artificial ponds or lakes, surrounded by seating for spectators) to stage mock sea battles. Some archaeologists believe this one may have been part of a gymnasium. Via Naumachiae.

PIAZZA IX APRILE (NINTH OF APRIL SQUARE) This charming square features jacaranda trees and a lovely 19th-century iron lamppost. Passersby stop here for an *aperitivo* at one of the several outdoor *caffès,* including the popular *Mocambo Bar* (see *Bars and Caffès*). The square is also a good place to enjoy the panoramic view of the Greek theater, Mt. Etna, and the sea below. To the left as you enter the square (which is simply a broadening of the *corso*) is the tiny 15th-century *Chiesa di Sant'Agostino,* now the public library, which often hosts temporary exhibits of contemporary paintings, antique books and sculptures, and photographs. It's open daily (phone: 23310). On the right, up a double staircase, is the *Chiesa di San Giuseppe,* with a charming Baroque façade. Open daily, with a long (1 to 5 PM) closing. At the end of the square stands the *Torre dell'Orologio* (Clock Tower), entranceway to the Borgo Medioevale (Medieval Township). The present tower dates from the 12th century, but its foundations are believed to be much older.

BORGO MEDIOEVALE (MEDIEVAL TOWNSHIP) Many architectural details from the Middle Ages are preserved in this district. Note especially the Gothic windows and doors at Nos. 122, 176, 190, 228, and 241. Up a staircase on the right is the *Palazzo Ciampoli,* which dates back to 1412.

DUOMO (CATHEDRAL) *San Nicola di Bari* (St. Nicholas of Bari), Taormina's *Duomo,* is a severe 14th-century church of rough-hewn stone. Its crenelated walls have a decidedly Norman appearance. Its interior is in the form of a Latin cross—the nave and two aisles are separated by columns of Taormina rose marble. Note the 15th-century triptych, *Visitation of Mary to Elizabeth, St. Joseph, and St. Zachariah* by Antonio Giuffrè, and other medieval religious paintings. Open daily, with a long (1 to 5 PM) closing. Piazza del Municipio.

PIAZZA DEL MUNICIPIO AND PORTA CATANIA (MUNICIPAL SQUARE AND CATANIA GATE) The *Duomo*'s main portal opens out onto Piazza del Municipio, where a Baroque fountain supports a female centaur, symbol of the town. Across the *corso* is what is left of the *Chiesa del Carmine,* including its campanile. The *corso* comes to an end at the arch of *Porta Catania,* which is also called *Porta del Tocco* (Tolling Gate) because in Norman times the people of Taormina gathered here when the bells were rung. It is inscribed with the date 1440, as well as the Taormina and Aragon coats of arms. To the left is the *Palazzo del Duca di Santo Stefano,* a massive Gothic residence.

CONVENTO DI SAN DOMENICO (CONVENT OF ST. DOMINIC) Just downhill from Piazza del Municipio is the *Chiesa di San Domenico,* whose campanile commands a lovely view. The nearby convent has been a hotel—the *San Domenico Palace*—since 1896 (see *Checking In*). With its original monastic furnishings, the hotel is a treasure trove of art objects. The 15th-century cloister, with its fine marble well, has been enclosed in glass. The gardens are lush; the views of the sea and Mt. Etna are spectacular. (The management does not encourage uninvited guests—especially those who are too casually dressed—though both the bar and restaurant are open to non-residents.)

GIARDINO PUBBLICO (PUBLIC GARDEN) Via Roma winds down from the *San Domenico,* providing exceptional panoramas. At the end, turn right into ·Via Bagnoli Croce, which leads to the *Giardino Pubblico.* Once part of the nearby *Villa Cacciola,* the park was taken over by the city in 1923. Not only

are the views from the park splendid, but the colorful Mediterranean subtropical vegetation is enhanced by odd Babylonian-style structures erected
in the last century for the villa's owner, Lady Trevelyn. A springtime stroll
in these well-tended formal gardens is truly a sensual experience. Open
daily. No admission charge.

ENVIRONS

LIDO DI MAZZARÒ (MAZZARO BEACH) A summer vacation in Taormina also means
sun and sea, with the accompanying gastronomic delights. Most people
staying in Taormina swim at the Lido di Mazzarò, a long, well-equipped
beach lined with numerous hotels, *caffès*, and restaurants. There are footpaths to the beach and the *funivia*, which operates daily between Mazzarò
and a point on Via Luigi Pirandello near the *Villa Nettuno* hotel from 7:30
to 3:30 AM July through September; to 1 AM the rest of the year. Other
pleasant beaches in the area are Spisone and Giardini-Naxos, for which
there is regular bus service, and Capo Schisò.

CASTELMOLA Three miles (5 km) away from Taormina and 1,800 feet above sea
level is this tiny village, which overlooks Taormina and the ruins of its
medieval castle. Historians believe Castelmola may have been the ancient
city of Mylai, which was used as a place of hiding by refugees of various
wars in the area. It was destroyed by the Arabs in AD 902. *SAIS* buses (phone:
625301) run to the top from the terminal on Via Luigi Pirandello; the ride
takes 20 minutes.

GIARDINI-NAXOS Naxos was the oldest Greek colony in Sicily. There are few traces
of the ancient city, but excavations begun in 1967 have unearthed some of
the basalt blocks from the town's defense walls. Its location on Capo Schisò,
a peninsula of lava rock, is striking. Giardini, the sea resort, is less than 3
miles (5 km) south of Taormina. It was from this spot that the Italian patriot
Giuseppe Garibaldi sailed with about 5,000 troops to fight for Italian unification in 1860.

FORZA D'AGRÒ AND CAPO SANT'ALESSIO The tiny medieval town of Forza d'Agrò
is only a short drive north of Taormina. Both the *Chiesa della Trinità* (Church
of the Trinity) and the *Chiesa di San Francesco* (Church of St. Francis) contain interesting paintings and artifacts. Capo Sant'Alessio, a twin-peaked
rock cliff separating two beaches and topped by a medieval castle, is nearby.

ALCANTARA GORGE A winding road toward the interior (S195, signposted
"Francavilla") from Giardini leads to the scenic Alcantara Valley, the setting for various Greek myths. After the viaduct in Contrada Larderia, one
comes to the gorge, a narrow split in the lava rock, plunging precipitously
down to the river.

MT. ETNA The biggest volcano in Europe—and still very active—Etna was believed
by the ancients to be the forge of Hephaestus, the Greek god of fire. It was

also associated with the legend of the Cyclops Polyphemus, who waylaid Ulysses on his way through the Straits of Messina. (*Etna* comes from the Greek *aitho,* or "eye burn.") The mountain's earliest known eruption, in 475 BC, was recorded by Pindar and Aeschylus. We know of 136 eruptions since. Several times—notably in 1669, when it destroyed Catania—its lava has reached the sea, and in 1983 eruptions lasted a full three months. It still smokes and rumbles frequently—Etna has been particularly active since 1990—indicating that a major eruption is possible at any time. Occasionally, at night, incandescent magma flows from a huge fracture about a half-mile long below the volcano's southeast crater. The red glow from this and some 200 other minor craters can be seen from as far away as Taormina. The main caldera is fascinating geologically, and the view from the summit, including most of Sicily, the Aeolian Islands, and Calabria, is awesome. Take note of weather conditions and the volcano's current activity before going up the mountain.

There are several approaches to Etna from Taormina. The nearest is by way of Fiumefreddo. Drive south on S114, then take S120 northwest to Linguaglossa; bear left to the village of Mareneve. A minibus carries visitors from there to within a short walk of the caldera, and the fee includes an English-speaking guide. There also is a small train that goes around the base. Farther south there are easy approaches from either Nicolosi or Zafferana. At Nicolosi-Nord a cable car climbs to within about 8,500 feet; four-wheel-drive vehicles are available from there to the top, where visitors can get to within 900 feet of the central crater. Plan to spend at least half a day on the volcano; wear warm clothing and sturdy shoes. It's also fun to make the trip at night, when lava glows eerily red in the caldera, and then stay to see the sunrise—a poetic experience. Locals make a habit of skiing on the volcano in winter. The *CIT* bus company (101 Corso Umberto I; phone: 23301/2/3) offers all-day excursions to Etna with English-speaking guides. Pay a base rate to ascend approximately 3,280 feet, or pay a supplement to leave the guide behind and continue up by four-wheel-drive (with a driver) another 1,640 feet toward the crater. *CIT* also has an afternoon trip (same cost as the all-day excursion) for those who wish to watch the sun set from Etna.

Sources and Resources

TOURIST INFORMATION

Taormina's *Azienda Autonoma di Soggiorno e Turismo* (*AAST;* in the back of *Palazzo Corvaja,* Piazza Santa Caterina; phone: 23243; fax: 24941) is closed Sundays; Saturdays for a long (noon to 4 PM) break; and weekdays for a short (2 to 4 PM) break. The office provides brochures and pamphlets on Taormina, its services, and its surroundings, as well as information about hotels, although it does not make reservations. The *CIT* bus company (see above) or any private agency can help.

LOCAL COVERAGE *Giornale di Sicilia, Gazzetta del Sud,* and *La Sicilia,* Italian-language newspapers published in Palermo, Messina, and Catania respectively, are the best sources of local information.

TELEPHONE The city code for Taormina is 942. When calling from within Italy, dial 0942 before the local number.

GETTING AROUND

Walking is the easiest and most enjoyable way around town, whereas a car is useful for excursions.

AIRPORT A taxi ride to the *Fontana Rossa Airport* (33 miles/53 km from Taormina, in Catania; phone: 95-578392) takes about one hour.

BUSES *SAIS* bus company (phone: 625301) offers regular service from the terminal on Via Luigi Pirandello, in front of the *Miramare* hotel, to most nearby towns, including Mazzarò, Castelmola, Forza d'Agrò, and Giardini-Naxos, and to Agrigento, Alcantara, and Siracusa. Many hotels have minibuses that make round trips to the beach. Bus tours of the island are available through local travel agents.

CAR RENTAL The major companies all have offices in Taormina. *CIT* (see above) offers special rates to foreigners. Some also rent scooters, though your hotel can also make arrangements.

TAXI Cabstands are at Piazza Badia (phone: 23000); Piazza Duomo (phone: 23800); the *Taormina–Giardini-Naxos* train station (phone: 51150); and Mazzarò (phone: 21266). Cabs can also be hired for special excursions. Prices are registered by meter or negotiable beforehand.

TRAINS Trains to and from Messina and Catania and other points arrive regularly at *Taormina–Giardini-Naxos* station (phone: 51026), where taxi and bus service to Taormina are available.

SPECIAL EVENTS

Every summer, beginning in mid-July, Taormina hosts *Taormina Arte,* a two-month arts festival that consists of about eight days of films and a month or more of theatrical and dance productions, many held in the *Teatro Greco* (see *Special Places*). Although less important than in the past, it is still very much a part of the international film festival circuit and draws critics, directors, and stars. The program and tickets for the festival are available in June from *Taormina Arte* (*Palazzo Congressi;* phone: 21142).

SHOPPING

Taormina has perhaps the best selection of antiques, ceramics, jewelry, and lace handiwork in all of Sicily. Conveniently, most of the shops are concentrated on the main street, Corso Umberto I, which stretches from one end of the Borgo Medioevale to the other and is off limits to cars. Don't be afraid to browse farther afield, such as around the area just below the *corso,* which can yield some interesting finds.

Shops are open daily from 9 AM to 1 PM and 4 to 9:30 PM in summer; from 9 AM to 1 PM and 3:30 to 7:30 PM in winter.

Antichità Pandora Quality, often outlandish, antiques. 2 Salita Lucio Denti (no phone).

La Baronessa Tasteful clothes and accessories for men and women. 148 Corso Umberto I (phone: 24960).

Carlo Panarello Decorative Sicilian ceramics and antiques. 122 Corso Umberto I (phone: 23910).

Casa d'Arte M. Forin Fine silver, porcelain, antique furniture and prints, and other art objects. 148 Corso Umberto I (phone: 23060).

Daneu An unusual and imaginative gift shop, it features handmade pottery, fabrics, and prints. 126 Corso Umberto I (no phone).

Estro High-quality gems and gold jewelry. 205 Corso Umberto I (phone: 24991).

Galeano (Concetta) Beautiful hand-embroidered lace tablecloths and bedspreads in linen and cotton. 233 Corso Umberto I (phone: 25144).

Gioielleria Giuseppe Stroscio Finely crafted antique jewelry. 169 Corso Umberto I (phone: 24865).

Giovanni Panarello A collection of antique bits (pieces of marble, candlesticks, etc.) from local churches at reasonable prices. 110 Corso Umberto I (phone: 23823).

Giovanni Vadalà Designer clothes for men and women. 189-191 Corso Umberto I (phone: 625163).

Marù Fendi furs and leathers. 83 Corso Umberto I (phone: 24218).

Mazzullo Elegant clothing and accessories for men and women. 35 Corso Umberto I (phone: 23152).

Pasticceria Roberto Marzipan, Sicilian strudel, and other pastries are made here in full view. Packing for overseas shipment is available. 9 Via Calapitrulli (phone: 626263).

SPORTS AND FITNESS

Activities here are mostly limited to water sports and tennis. Most major hotels have arrangements with bathing establishments at Mazzarò, Spisone, Isolabella, and Mazzeo; a list is available at the tourist information office (see above).

GOLF About a half-hour's drive from Taormina toward Etna is the 18-hole *Il Piccolo Golf Club* (55 Contrada Rovittello, S120, Castiglione di Sicilia; phone: 986252), noted for its dramatic views.

HORSEBACK RIDING Although slightly pricey, this is an excellent way to explore Mt. Etna's strange lava terrain, much as Goethe did. Sturdy beasts depart from *Villa Maria* near Linguaglossa at 9:30 AM sharp. For further information, contact Linguaglossa's tourist office (8 Piazza Annunziata, Linguaglossa; phone: 95-643094).

SCUBA DIVING Instruction and equipment are available through *Circolo Taormina Sub di S. Vinciguerra e A. Magri* (Spiaggia Mazzarò; phone: 626151).

SKIING In winter, when tourism and Etna are dormant, the volcano provides 13 miles of slopes at the Linguaglossa pine forest.

TENNIS Book a court through the *Taormina Sporting Club Circolo Tennis* (Via Bagnoli Croce; phone: 23282).

WATER SKIING Arrangements can be made with the *Water Ski Club* (Villagonia, Via Nazionale; phone: 52283).

WINDSURFING Rent a board from *Wind Surf* (Lido Mazzarò; phone: 625167).

THEATER AND MUSIC

In August a concert and ballet series is offered at the *Teatro Greco* (see *Special Places*). A schedule of performances is usually available from the tourist information office (see above) or *Taormina Arte* (see *Special Events*) at the beginning of the summer.

NIGHTCLUBS AND NIGHTLIFE

Taormina's classiest nightclub is *Tout Va* (70 Via Luigi Pirandello; phone: 23824), a former casino set in a huge park. Offering a restaurant of the same name (see *Eating Out*), piano bar, and discotheque, it is open daily to 4 AM June through September; weekends only the rest of the year. Other nightclubs with live music and dancing are *La Giara* (see *Eating Out*), which serves very good food, and *L'Ombrello* (Piazza Duomo; phone: 23733). In the evenings, people gather until late either at the *Mocambo Bar* or at *Wunderbar* (see *Bars and Caffès* for both). At the *Casanova* pub (Vico Francesco Paladini, an alley off the *corso;* phone: 23965), young people and music spill out of the interior as the sun goes down. A popular late-night discotheque for gays is *Le Perroquet* (Piazza San Domenico; phone: 24462); it's open daily in summer and weekends only the rest of the year.

Best in Town

CHECKING IN

Hotels are Taormina's major commercial resource—there are nearly 70 hotels and *pensioni* in the town itself and another 20 in Mazzarò. Usually modern, comfortable, attractive, and well equipped, they are occasionally elegant as well. Service is generally good to excellent. Expect to pay from

$175 to $300 per night for a double room at an expensive hotel; from $90 to $175 in a place listed as moderate; and $90 or less at those rated as inexpensive. All hotels feature private baths unless otherwise indicated. Many hotels encourage guests to take half board; it's worth considering as it usually is a good value. Note that many of the hotels close for several months during the winter. All telephone numbers are in the 942 city code unless otherwise indicated.

For an unforgettable Taormina experience, we begin with our favorite *albergo,* followed by our cost and quality choices, listed by price category.

A SPECIAL HAVEN

San Domenico Palace In 1896, after 500 years as a Dominican monastery, this regal Renaissance structure, dramatically positioned high above the sea, was reborn as a singularly unaesthetic hotel, and it has been playing host to the famous ever since. Such luminaries as Marlene Dietrich and Sophia Loren have marveled at the spectacle of sunset from the terrace and inhaled the scents of lemon and jasmine in the garden overlooking the azure Ionian and nearby Etna. Elsewhere, shady cloisters, tapestry-hung corridors, immense salons, and 111 luxurious, antiques-furnished guestrooms artfully blend the extravagant and the severe. Life at the arcaded edge of a heated pool is a side of earthly existence the friars never imagined. Private beach facilities, *Les Bougainvilles* restaurant (see *Eating Out*), a huge baronial parlor transformed into an elegant bar, and impeccable service round out the superlative amenities—all worth the exorbitant price tag. Open year-round. 5 Piazza San Domenico (phone: 23701; fax: 625506).

EXPENSIVE

Grand Albergo Capo Taormina Right on the water, this large and modern property offers 207 comfortable rooms, each with a sea view. There is a beautiful saltwater pool with a vista of Mt. Etna, excellent beach facilities, a good restaurant, and a bar. Run by the same management as the *San Domenico.* Open *Easter* through December. 105 Via Nazionale (phone: 24000; fax: 625467).

Villa Sant'Andrea Once the summer home of a British family, this small hotel overlooking the bay has 61 charming rooms (most have balconies and sea views); a beautiful terrace restaurant, *Oliviero* (see *Eating Out*); a lush private garden; and a private beach. Open March through December. 137 Via Nazionale, Mazzarò (phone: 23125; fax: 24838).

Bristol Park Elegant, with 50 rooms, a good restaurant, a pool, splendid views of the Ionian and Mt. Etna, and a private beach. Half board is encouraged. Open mid-March through October. 92 Via Bagnoli Croce (phone: 23006; fax: 24519).

Excelsior Palace At the edge of town by the *Porta Catania,* this property offers beautiful views of Etna and the hotel's exquisite garden. The 89 rooms are tastefully arranged. There is a low-key atmosphere, a restaurant, a private pool, and a beach. Open year-round. 8 Via Toselli (phone: 23975; fax: 23978).

Villa Belvedere True to its name, this simple hotel offers great views of Mt. Etna and the sea. Its 44 rooms are sparely but tastefully decorated; some have terraces. The pool is set in a tranquil garden. Ask for a room with a sea view. No restaurant. Open *Easter* through October and at *Christmastime.* 79 Via Bagnoli Croce (phone: 23791; fax: 625830).

Villa Ducale This former country villa, about 1 mile (1.6 km) from the center of town on the road to Castelmola, was recently transformed into a 10-room relais by a young couple. Warm and elegant, it offers breathtaking views of Taormina, the Ionian Sea, Etna, and Castelmola. The rooms, each individually named, are tastefully and comfortably furnished with antiques and wrought iron beds, wool rugs, and damask bedspreads (our favorites are *Gli Angeli* and *Les Fiancés*), and each has a private balcony or a terrace with a view. Breakfast, included in the rate, is delivered to your room or served on the hotel's terrace. There's no restaurant, but there are several within walking distance. Transportation to the beach (3 miles/5 km away) and beach facilities (changing rooms and so on) are included. Open March to mid-January. 60 Via L. da Vinci (phone: 28153; fax: 28154).

Villa Paradiso Small (35 rooms) and centrally located, it overlooks the sea, has an excellent restaurant, and boasts one of the best views of Mt. Etna. Half board is encouraged. Open mid-December through October. 2 Via Roma (phone: 23922; fax: 625800).

INEXPENSIVE

Pensione Svizzera Most of the 18 rooms in this clean, comfortable property have splendid vistas of the Ionian Sea; some guestrooms have terraces. Breakfast is served in a lovely garden. There's also a restaurant. Open March to mid-November and mid-December to mid-January. 26 Via Luigi Pirandello (phone: 23790; fax: 625906).

Villa Fiorita Restful stays and magnificent views (many of the 24 rooms look onto the sea, and some have balconies) are offered at this hostelry. There also is a garden, a pool, and excellent service, all in a clean, but somewhat worn, environment. No restaurant. Open year-round. 39 Via Luigi Pirandello (phone: 24122; fax: 625967).

Villa Sirina This 15-room villa feels more like a private home than a hotel, a restaurant, a pool, and a location right near the beach. Open through October. Contrada Sirina (phone: 51776; fax: 51671).

Villino Gallodoro A small pensione set at the foot of the cable car stop in Mazzarò, it has 15 simple and clean rooms, most with private baths. Near the beach, it is ideal for sun lovers on a budget. Breakfast is served on a lovely shaded terrace, and there's a dining room. Open February through October. 147 Via Nazionale, Mazzarò (phone: 23860).

EATING OUT

Most hotels have their own dining rooms, but don't hesitate to sample the local restaurants. For the most part, they are pleasant, often have lovely views, and can offer better value than comparable restaurants in northern Italy. Whenever possible, try the local specialties, particularly the fish and succulent fresh vegetables such as eggplant, artichokes, and squash. The pasta is delicious. Expect to pay $70 to $100 or more for a dinner for two at restaurants categorized as expensive; between $45 to $70 at those listed as moderate; and $45 or less at inexpensive restaurants. Prices do not include wine or tip. All restaurants are open for lunch and dinner unless otherwise noted. Generally, restaurants in Taormina are open daily in summer and take their appointed day off only when the season slumps. All telephone numbers are in the 942 city code unless otherwise indicated.

EXPENSIVE

Les Bougainvilles In the *San Domenico,* this elegant dining room serves an assortment of refined Sicilian dishes (although the quality is uneven) and grilled meat and fish. In summer, dine on the terrace and enjoy the breathtaking view of the Ionian Sea. Open daily. Reservations necessary. Major credit cards accepted. 5 Piazza San Domenico (phone: 23701).

La Giara Just a few steps down from the *corso* is this fashionable late-night restaurant and nightclub that is frequented by locals and visitors alike. The menu features both continental and Sicilian fare, all prepared with attention. Excellent Sicilian wines are served. Closed Mondays. Reservations advised. Major credit cards accepted. 1 Vico Floresta (phone: 23360).

Da Lorenzo In the center of town, with a pleasant garden for outdoor dining, this eatery is noted for its fresh fish and traditional Sicilian fare, including an excellent spaghetti *alla norma* (with eggplant). Closed Wednesdays. Reservations advised. Major credit cards accepted. 4 Via M. Amari (phone: 23480).

Oliviero By the sea, this restaurant in the *Villa Sant'Andrea* hotel has a lush outdoor terrace and a piano bar. Specialties include crabmeat risotto, grilled mixed fish, filet of beef, dessert crêpes, and excellent Sicilian wines. Closed

January and February. Reservations advised. Major credit cards accepted. 137 Via Nazionale, Mazzarò (phone: 23125).

Il Pescatore Perched above the bay, this is considered by many to be Taormina's best trattoria. The menu features mainly fish, usually caught in the restaurant's own boat, with very good cannelloni and risotto *alla pescatora* (with seafood). Closed Mondays and November through February, except for 15 days at *Christmastime*. Reservations advised. Major credit cards accepted. 107 Via Nazionale, Isolabella (phone: 23460).

Tout Va A fashionable establishment in a private park, with a piano bar and discotheque, this restaurant serves continental and Italian fare. Closed for lunch and mid-October through May. Reservations advised. Major credit cards accepted. 70 Via Luigi Pirandello (phone: 23824).

MODERATE

La Botte A favorite late-night spot, this eatery serves excellent pizza, a vast assortment of Sicilian appetizers and main courses, and grilled meat and fish, all at reasonable prices. Closed Mondays in winter, and January. Reservations advised. Major credit cards accepted. 4 Piazza Santa Domenica (phone: 24198).

La Bussola An attractive establishment that serves very good food and affords a great view. Closed Wednesdays except in August. Reservations unnecessary. Major credit cards accepted. Via Nazionale, Isolabella (phone: 21276).

Al Castello da Ciccio Recently opened, this local favorite has a terrace with wonderful sea views. Seafood is the specialty: Try the risotto *al Castello* (with seafood) or *pennette alla Ciccio* (cut pasta with a salmon-and-crab cream sauce). Closed Wednesdays. Reservations advised. No credit cards accepted. On the road to Castelmola, at 11 Via Madonna della Rocca (phone: 28158).

Il Fico d'India This beachside eatery features pasta with sardines and an excellent entrée of fish simmered in a sauce of capers, tomatoes, and olives. Closed Mondays, January, and February. Reservations unnecessary. No credit cards accepted. 14 Via Appiano, Mazzeo, Letojanni (phone: 36301).

Da Giovanni Good fish dishes are served at this bright, family-run restaurant, with a spectacular view of the sea. The enormous fish soup, made with the catch of the day, is a meal in itself. Closed Mondays. Reservations advised on weekends and in high season. Major credit cards accepted. Via Nazionale, Isolabella (phone: 23531).

INEXPENSIVE

Da Antonio It's never a bad idea to follow the locals, and in Taormina they all come here. Excellent fresh seafood is the lure: Try the risotto *alla frutta di mare* (with seafood). Pizza is served, too. Closed Mondays. Reservations advised for dinner. Major credit cards accepted. Via Crocifisso, along the descent by road to Giardini-Naxos, soon after leaving the *Duomo* end of the *corso* (phone: 24570).

Il Barcaiolo Great food at great prices is the reason this wonderful local beachfront place has a big following in summer. Closed in winter. Reservations advised in summer. No credit cards accepted. Spiaggia Mazzarò, reached from Via Castellucio (turn off Via Nazionale at the *Atlantis Bay* hotel), then down the steps (phone: 625633).

BARS AND CAFFÈS

One would be hard pressed to find a city better suited to leisurely outdoor *caffès* than Taormina. From several spots along the *corso,* the *Giardino Pubblico,* Ionian Sea, and Mt. Etna are visible. These faraway sights would be exhilarating enough, but the endless parade of people strolling along the *corso* provides still more entertainment. Most bars and *caffès* listed below are in the inexpensive price range.

A. Chemi Known for its mouth-watering Sicilian candies and pastries like *paste di mandorla* (almond pastries with lemon, orange, or pistachio), *pignolata* (soft dough meringued in chocolate and lemon), candied orange peel, and marzipan, it also serves drinks, ice cream, and *granita* (flavored shaved ice served in a glass or cone). There are some outdoor tables across the street. Closed Tuesdays, except in summer. No credit cards accepted. 102 Corso Umberto I (phone: 24260 or 28766).

Al Duomo This bar has outdoor tables facing Taormina's simple, serene cathedral. Specialties are homemade ice cream, cocktails, and such fruit drinks as *frullati* (fresh fruit milk shakes). Closed Mondays, except in July and August. No credit cards accepted. 6 Piazza Duomo (phone: 625444).

Etna Cannoli, *cassatta siciliana,* and beautifully packaged marzipan are the hallmarks of this pastry shop on the *corso.* Closed Mondays. No credit cards accepted. 112 Corso Umberto I (phone: 24735).

Mocambo Choice for people watching from the outdoor tables, inside it reeks of the Old World, with upholstered chairs, grand chandeliers, and a painted mural from the early 20th century. Try the gelati or the long drink Mocambo (fruit juice with Campari and spumante). There's live piano music from 9 PM to midnight from April through September. Open to 1:30 AM. Closed Mondays, except July through September. American Express accepted. Piazza IX Aprile (phone: 23350).

Saint Honoré The proprietor here recently returned to Sicily after spending several years in Brooklyn. Among the specialties are exquisite cactus-shaped marzipan, eight flavors of *granita*, and 10 varieties of ice cream, including the irresistible *cassatta* (with ricotta cheese, nuts, chunks of chocolate, and dried fruit). Closed Tuesdays, except in July and August. No credit cards accepted. 208 Corso Umberto I (phone: 24877).

Shatulle This moody nightspot (open from 6:30 PM to 3 AM) is the most chic in town, the favorite of local and visiting artists, actors, and filmmakers. With photographs on the walls inside by William von Gloeden and others of old Taormina, and lovely rattan armchairs in the small quiet piazza outside, crepes of all kinds, sandwiches, and drinks are served. Closed Mondays. No credit cards accepted. 4 Piazza Paladini (no phone).

Wunderbar Outdoor tables on the piazza and spectacular open views of Mt. Etna and the Ionian Sea are the main attractions here, though the drinks—try the house aperitif, *Wunderbar* (freshly squeezed orange and lemon juices with dry spumante)—are also a draw. There is a piano bar nightly from 9 PM to midnight March through October and on *Christmas*. Closed November and Tuesdays from December through April. No credit cards accepted. 7 Piazza IX Aprile (phone: 625302).

Trieste

At one time the major port of the Hapsburg Empire, this once-glamorous commercial and cultural center on the Adriatic suffered a steady decline after World War I and today is a city far overshadowed by its past. All but forgotten by the rest of Italy, it is tucked away in the northeasternmost corner of the peninsula, 90 miles (144 km) northeast of Venice and right on the border of the independent republic of Slovenia. But if present-day Trieste seems faded compared with the bustling seaport of a century ago, much of its old fascination still lingers.

Visitors find very few of the great monuments, antiquity, and art treasures that are so plentiful in other Italian cities. Trieste's special appeal is its ambience and people, Old World elegance, and interesting mixture of cultures. Traces of Trieste's cosmopolitan past are evident in its religious and ethnic diversity, grand old hotels, strong Slavic flavor, richly varied local cuisine, and Viennese-style cafés. Yet it is essentially a quiet little town, which the Italian Census Bureau has ranked as the most livable in Italy, with an easy pace and tranquillity that can make a visitor's stay here quite pleasant.

Trieste also boasts a wonderful natural setting, from the beautiful harbor and coastline to the surrounding mountains in the Carso, its limestone highlands (which include some of the most spectacular caves in Europe). Its handsome examples of 18th- and 19th-century neoclassical architecture are interesting, its piazze magnificent and lively, and its seafront worth a long and leisurely stroll.

To understand Trieste is to grasp the sense of loss that permeates the air, creating a nostalgic, somewhat romantic mood. The city still laments the transferral of its environs to Yugoslavia after World War II, and there is a growing sense of isolation from the rest of Italy. Much like the local weather, which can be gloriously sunny in summer but suffers from a cold, sometimes fierce, wind from the north called the *bora,* the Triestine character is a curious blend of Mediterranean and more northern elements. In casual contact this comes across as exuberance tempered by melancholy.

Trieste's origins go back to Roman times, when it was a small port known as Tergestum. By the Middle Ages it had become an independent municipality that periodically fell under domination by Venice, then the major power in the Adriatic. In 1382 Trieste placed itself under the protection of the Austro-Hungarian Empire, where it remained for more than 500 years (interrupted briefly in the early 1800s, when Napoleon's armies occupied the town). Only after the Hapsburg Emperor Charles VI declared the city a free port in 1719 did Trieste attain real importance. The decree launched the city's fortunes as the empire's major gateway to the world. But it was Charles's daughter, Empress Maria Theresa, who is generally credited with creating modern Trieste. In the mid-18th century the empress enlarged the seaport and revamped the city, laying out a neat grid of streets in the quarter named after her, the Borgo Teresiano, which is still considered the "new" part of town. She improved public education, encouraged local industry, and lifted the constraints that confined Trieste's Jewish community to a ghetto.

The lure of commerce attracted foreign merchants and entrepreneurs from all over the Mediterranean and Central Europe. By the mid-1800s Trieste's population had grown tenfold from the previous century. The newcomers blended into the city's fabric without losing their distinct identities. This mutual tolerance is evident in the variety of churches in Trieste: Catholic, Protestant, Serbian Orthodox, Waldensian, Anglican, and Methodist. A magnificent synagogue built in 1912 is still active, although the once sizable Jewish community, whose roots in Trieste go back at least seven centuries, has shrunk to only a few hundred.

By the end of the 19th century Trieste had become a center of trade, finance, and banking, the birthplace of the modern insurance company, and Austria-Hungary's great emporium for Central Europe. A prosperous bourgeoisie built stately homes in the Teresiano quarter, several of which are museums today. The city also nurtured some great writers, including James Joyce, who lived here with his family from 1904 to 1915, supporting himself by teaching English. Much of his autobiographical novel *A Portrait of the Artist as a Young Man* was written here, as were parts of his masterpiece, *Ulysses*. The local tourist board distributes a small free booklet in English that provides a Joycean walking tour of the city, pointing out his haunts and homes. One of Joyce's most devoted pupils, the businessman Ettore Schmitz, launched a writing career of his own under the name Italo Svevo and, together with fellow Triestine writer Umberto Saba, helped launch a new trend in Italian literature.

Although Trieste had strong Austrian and Slavic overtones, it remained essentially Italian. In the late 1800s the struggle for union with Italy gained force. The Italian composer Giuseppe Verdi (who created two works for Trieste's opera house) became a symbol of this cause, and disorders usually erupted wherever his music was played.

Sadly, unification with Italy in 1918 signaled the city's demise. The new frontier severed Trieste from its German and Slavic hinterland, leaving it, in the words of historian Denis Mack Smith, "a head without a body." World War I seriously damaged the port and local industry, and Trieste never regained the prosperity of its prewar days. The Nazis occupied it in 1943 and established a concentration camp at an old rice-processing plant outside town. Today the *Risiera di San Sabba* (1 Ratto della Pileria; phone: 826202) is a memorial to the Resistance. It's on the northeast outskirts of town, a 10-minute taxi ride from the center (closed afternoons and Mondays; no admission charge). After the war the territory bordering Trieste—most of the Istrian Peninsula and the Karst (Carso), predominantly Slovenian—

was transferred to Yugoslavia, and in 1947 the city itself, also in dispute, was proclaimed a free territory under United Nations administration. Trieste remained a city without a country for seven years until it was finally returned to Italy in 1954, along with a sliver of Istrian coast. Ten years later it became the capital of the Friuli–Venezia Giulia region.

Today about a quarter of the city's 140,000 residents are retired (it has the highest per capita pensioner population in the country). Most of the others are involved in Trieste's traditional occupations: banking, insurance (it is Italy's insurance capital), trade, and import-export. A large Slovenian minority continues to run its own cultural and educational facilities, while the location here of the prestigious *International Center for Nuclear Physics* has given Trieste a certain stature in the scientific community, too.

A dividing point between East and West, Trieste is vulnerable to policies on both sides of its frontier. Its port has suffered from the crisis in Italy's steel and shipbuilding industries. Civil war in the former Yugoslavia halted the flow of people who once crossed the border to buy blue jeans, coffee, appliances, and machine replacement parts. The conflict also disrupted trade from nearby Slovenia, an important source of raw materials for Trieste's industry.

Visitors, however, have a hard time perceiving these civil and economic hardships. The city is full of elegant shops and fine restaurants, and Triestines enjoy a comparatively high standard of living. Most important, Trieste's appealing ambience and the echoes of its glorious past are still here for all to savor.

Trieste At-a-Glance

SEEING THE CITY

For a spectacular panorama of Trieste, its harbor, its coast, and the mountains of Istria, take the No. 2 tram or the No. 4 bus from Piazza Oberdan to the village of Opicina, a thousand feet above sea level. Get off two stops before the end, at the *Obelisco di Opicina.* Both the tram and the bus run every 20 minutes from 7:40 AM to 10:10 PM. Another good vantage point is the hilltop *Castello di San Giusto* (see *Special Places*), which can be reached by foot, taxi, or the No. 24 bus. The *Molo Audace,* a pier that juts out into the harbor near Piazza dell'Unità d'Italia, is a favorite promenade and offers a beautiful view of the city, sea, and hills.

SPECIAL PLACES

The heart of Trieste, Piazza dell'Unità d'Italia is the natural starting point for a walking tour of the city, as most of the major attractions are nearby. To the north of it is Borgo Teresiano, the business, cultural, and commercial center, encompassing Trieste's opera house in Piazza Verdi, the neoclassical palace of the *Borsa Vecchia* (the former Stock Exchange) in Piazza della Borsa, and avenues and side streets lined with elegant boutiques, old *caffès,* and colorful food shops. The district is bisected by the Canal Grande, which once allowed ships to sail right into Piazza Ponte Rosso. South of Piazza Unità the winding streets of the old medieval city lead past the Roman amphitheater and a Roman gateway, the so-called *Arco di Riccardo,* to the Colle di San Giusto, a hill named after Trieste's patron saint. Perched on top of the hill are the old fortress and the 14th-century church that dominate the town. It's a good walk to the hill (or, better, take bus No. 24 up and walk down), but vehicular transportation is needed to get to *Castello di Miramare,* the most unusual and spectacular of Trieste's sights, as well as to the Grotta Gigante (see *Environs,* below, for both).

Note that some sites of interest in Trieste close for a midday break, generally from noon to 3 PM; we suggest calling ahead to check exact hours.

CENTER

PIAZZA DELL'UNITÀ D'ITALIA This spacious, truly breathtaking square is enclosed on three sides by stately 19th-century palazzi—the *Palazzo Comunale* (Town Hall), the *Palazzo del Governo* (Prefecture), and the building housing the once powerful *Lloyd Triestino* shipping line. The piazza is open to the sea on its west side, which sweeps right up to the Adriatic. By all means, find an outside table at *Caffè degli Specchi* (see *Bars and Caffès,* below) from which to take it all in.

CASTELLO DI SAN GIUSTO The bastions of this 15th-century castle built by the Venetians on the site of a Roman fort command a wonderful view of Trieste. In recent decades the castle has been tastefully restored, and today it houses an extensive collection of old arms and armor. The castle is open daily; the museum is closed afternoons and Mondays. Admission charge. Piazza della Cattedrale, Colle di San Giusto (phone: 313636).

CATTEDRALE DI SAN GIUSTO Dedicated to the city's patron saint, the 14th-century cathedral is a curious amalgam of two earlier churches, from the 5th and 11th centuries, which in turn were built on the site of an ancient Roman temple. The decision to incorporate the previous structures into the new, grander cathedral reflects the characteristic practicality of the Triestines, and the result is a unique but appealing blend of styles. The simple, Romanesque façade is embellished by a Venetian Gothic rose window. The five-nave interior contains some handsome Byzantine mosaics, a 9th-century baptismal font, a 16th-century wooden *pietà,* and a small collection of holy relics and artworks. Open daily. Piazza della Cattedrale, Colle di San Giusto (phone: 313636).

TEATRO ROMANO Greek tragedies were performed at this Roman amphitheater, built in the 1st century BC. Under the Roman Empire it was the setting for gladiator fights. Open daily. No admission charge. Via del Teatro Romano (no phone).

ORTO LAPIDARIO (LAPIDARY GARDEN) Just downhill from San Giusto, this is one of the most romantic spots in Trieste, with a Byronesque feel to it. Formerly the church's graveyard, it was transformed in the middle of the last century into a stone garden of archaeological finds. Strolling among the ruins one comes across Roman tombstones, fragments of altars, memorial tablets, urns, and other statuary. Off to one side a neoclassical temple, built in the last century, houses a sculptured monument to the German archaeologist Johann Winckelmann, who was murdered in Trieste in 1768. The garden also contains the *Museo Civico di Storia e d'Arte* (Civic Museum of History and Art), which has a small, eclectic collection of ancient art and artifacts. Of particular interest are Egyptian burial objects and several mummies; Roman jewelry, busts, and urns; pre-Roman bronzes; and an extensive coin and medal exhibit. Closed afternoons and Mondays. Admission charge. 1 Piazza della Cattedrale (phone: 308686 or 310500).

CIVICO MUSEO REVOLTELLA Baron Pasquale Revoltella, a Venetian financial tycoon of the mid-19th century and one of the main financiers of the Suez Canal, bequeathed his palazzo and private art collection to the city. Revoltella specified, however, that his home should also be used as a showcase for contemporary art, and the renovated gallery now ranks among Italy's best modern art galleries, with works by Picasso, Braque, and Kokoschka. Of particular interest are the museum's upper floors, which have been maintained as they were in the baron's day. Closed Sunday afternoons, Tuesdays, and for a long midday break. Admission charge. 27 Via Diaz (phone: 311361).

MUSEO DEL MARE (MARITIME MUSEUM) Tastefully modernized, this delightful museum contains all kinds of objects that illustrate the history of navigation and fishing. In addition to nautical instruments and maps, there are wonderful scale models of a wide variety of vessels. One room is devoted to Guglielmo Marconi; upstairs, superbly crafted three-dimensional scenes depict various kinds of fishing. Closed afternoons and Mondays. Admission charge. 1 Via Campo Marzio (phone: 304987).

MUSEO MORPURGO The home of a wealthy family has been turned into a museum, complete with original furniture, gilded mirrors, Venetian chandeliers, paintings, and sculpture. While it's officially closed afternoons and Mondays, the museum's hours are extremely erratic, depending on the availability of its small staff. Ring a downstairs doorbell to be admitted. Admission charge. 5 Via Imbriani (phone: 636969).

ENVIRONS

CASTELLO DI MIRAMARE (MIRAMARE CASTLE) At the tip of a wooded promontory overlooking the Bay of Grignano, this white turreted castle is surrounded by a magnificent park. It was built in 1860 for Archduke Maximilian and his wife, Princess Carlotta of Belgium, who spent three happy years here before Maximilian was persuaded to become Emperor of Mexico. The ill-fated Hapsburg prince was soon executed by the Mexican republican army of Benito Juárez, and his wife went insane. The sumptuous rooms of the castle are maintained exactly as they were when the royal couple was in residence. The throne room, chapel, several parlors, royal bedrooms, and Maximilian's fine library—all filled with precious furniture, paintings, antique vases, and art objects—are open to the public. Visitors are also free to stroll through the beautiful 55-acre park, which contains a small *caffè.* The castle is closed afternoons; the park is open daily. The guided tours in English are a must. Admission charge to the castle only. On evenings in July and August the royal couple's sad tale is told in a dramatic hour-long sound-and-light show (English version on Tuesdays at 9 PM). Miramare is about 5 miles (8 km) north of Trieste, a 10-minute taxi ride. An alternative is to take the No. 6 bus from the train station to Barcola, and then change to the No. 36 bus. In summer transportation to the castle from Trieste is available by boat (phone: 224143).

GROTTA GIGANTE (GIANT GROTTO) About 10 miles (16 km) north of Trieste, this enormous cave is the largest natural cavern known today, and it is considered a speleological wonder, with stalactites and stalagmites up to 50 feet long. The cave has been equipped with stairways and lighting, and there are 45-minute guided tours in English every half hour. There is also a small museum of local archaeological finds. Closed Mondays and for a midday break. Admission charge (phone: 327312). The cave can be reached by the bus or tram to Opicina.

MUGGIA Some 7 miles (11 km) southwest of the city (about a 20-minute ride by car or the No. 20 bus), this tiny fishing village is well worth a visit. The jewel of a harbor, once part of the Republic of Venice, is virtually unknown to tourists and, indeed, to most Italians outside Trieste. Its miniature main square features an exquisite 13th-century cathedral, and the whole village is dominated by a castle built in 1375. Several excellent seafood restaurants make this a perfect lunchtime excursion. The town's *Carnevale* celebration is famous throughout Italy (see *Special Events*). Muggia's tourist office is at 20 Via Roma (phone: 273259).

MONRUPINO Nine miles (14 km) east of Trieste is this small village, worth the 15-minute taxi ride from the city's center. It is dominated by the *Rocca di Monrupino,* a castle built by local inhabitants in 1300 to defend themselves against Turkish incursions. The castle offers an extraordinary panorama of the spectacular Carso region. At the end of August in even-numbered years the village's Slovenian population hosts the *Nozze Carsiche* (Weddings of the Carso), four days of dancing, merrymaking, and other costumed festivities.

EXTRA SPECIAL

To fully grasp the special nature of Trieste, every visitor must stroll along the *riva,* its waterfront promenade, and take in the harbor, ships, surrounding hills, fishermen's shops, and restaurants. One of James Joyce's favorite walks, it has been an inspiration to generations of Trieste writers. The stroll should include a stop at the huge enclosed fish market—the *Grande Pescheria*—on the waterfront just south of Piazza dell'Unità d'Italia. Another must is a visit to Piazza Ponte Rosso. The Grand Canal that bisects this unusual square was dug in the 18th century to allow trading ships to sail into the business district. Today it serves as a dock for pleasure craft. But the piazza is still a lively center of commerce, with outdoor food and flower markets and numerous clothing stalls. Rising like an ancient Greek temple at its far end is the *Chiesa di Sant'Antonio,* one of Trieste's most striking neoclassical monuments and one of the city's best-loved places of worship since its completion in 1842.

Sources and Resources

TOURIST INFORMATION

General tourist information is available at the main office of the *Azienda Autonoma di Soggiorno e Turismo* (*AAST;* 20 Via San Nicolò; phone: 369881; fax: 369981) and at a smaller office at the railroad station (8 Piazza Libertà; phone: 420182). Both are closed Saturday afternoons, Sundays, and for a very long (1 to 5 PM) midday break. During open hours there's a toll-free number (phone: 1670-16044) for tourist inquiries.

LOCAL COVERAGE The tourist office publishes various English-language brochures that list museums, special events, theater and concert halls, and day excursions. The tourist office also has a weekend program, *Trieste for You,* that offers discounts on selected hotels, and a card that grants to the holder free excursions and reduced prices at a variety of restaurants, shops, and museums. Hotels have information about evening activities. The local Italian-language daily newspaper is *Il Piccolo.*

TELEPHONE The city code for Trieste is 40. When calling from within Italy, dial 040 before the local number.

GETTING AROUND

The city is small, and most of the main points of interest are easily accessible on foot.

AIRPORTS Trieste's airport, *Ronchi dei Legionari* (phone: 773224), is 20 miles (32 km) northwest of the city and served mainly by domestic flights. An airport bus operates between the airport and the central railroad station on Piazza Libertà. The nearest major international airport is Venice's *Marco Polo.*

BUS Service is good within the city and to nearby points of interest. Tickets, which are sold at newsstands and tobacconists, must be purchased before boarding. For bus information, call 77951.

CAR RENTAL Most international firms are represented.

TAXI Cabs are quite expensive, but given the city's small size, rides to the most likely tourist spots should be less than $20. There are numerous stands and two 24-hour taxi services: *Taxi Radio Trieste* (phone: 307730) and *Co-operativa Alabarda* (phone: 54533).

TRAIN *Stazione Trieste Centrale* is at 8 Piazza Libertà (phone: 418207).

SPECIAL EVENTS

Every February the nearby fishing port of Muggia (about a 20-minute car ride from Trieste) holds a daylong, colorful *Carnevale,* with huge floats (the whole city participates in building them) and costumed parades through the town. For information, call Muggia's tourist office (phone: 273259). From July through mid-August a popular *Festival dell'Operetta* takes place at the *Teatro Stabile–Politeama Rossetti* (phone: 567201). Other summer events include outdoor concerts, ballets, and plays at the *Castello di San Giusto;* classical drama performances amid the ruins of the *Teatro Romano;* and evening sound-and-light shows at *Castello di Miramare.* Every September the *Settembre Musicale* festival features classical concerts by first-rate guest musicians and ensembles in the city's churches.

MUSEUMS

The museums of most interest to visitors are discussed in *Special Places,* but several others are worth a visit. Unless otherwise indicated, they are closed afternoons and Mondays and charge admission.

ACQUARIO MARINO A public aquarium on the waterfront, it is home to a wide variety of Adriatic marine life. Open to 6:30 PM May through September; closed afternoons the rest of the year. 1 Riva Nazario Sauro (phone: 306201).

MUSEO FERROVIARIO *The* place for railway buffs. Housed in the former railroad station that was the departure point for trains to Austria and Bavaria, this museum has 11 steam trains, as well as trams—both electric and horse-drawn—and a lovingly constructed, hand-built model railway depicting trains and trams in use in the Trieste area at the beginning of the century. 1 Via G. Cesare (phone: 379-4185).

MUSEO DEL RISORGIMENTO A small collection of artifacts and paintings illustrates Trieste's struggle to become part of Italy. 4 Via XXIV Maggio (phone: 361675).

MUSEO TEATRALE (THEATER MUSEUM) Housed in the *Teatro Verdi,* this small museum contains several thousand old librettos, manuscripts, books, and photographs related to opera, and a fine collection of musical instruments. Open during intermissions and Tuesday and Thursday mornings. 1 Piazza Verdi (phone: 366636).

SHOPPING

Trieste has a fine selection of the designer clothes, sportswear, shoes, and other leather goods for which Italy is famous, and it is an easy and extremely pleasant place to shop. Most of the best boutiques are concentrated in the area from Piazza della Borsa to Piazza Goldoni, including the main avenue, Corso Italia, the elegant 19th-century *Galleria Tergesteo* shopping arcade (Piazza della Borsa), and numerous side streets. An added attraction are the nautical shops that line the waterfront, selling boating accessories and clothing. Two hidden alleyways (Via del Ponte and Via delle Beccherie) behind Piazza dell'Unità d'Italia are lined with antiques shops and old curio shops—a kind of mini–flea market—that are great for browsing and for some good buys. Stop by Piazza Ponte Rosso any morning to buy fresh fruit and vegetables. Trieste is not particularly known for handicrafts, but a few bottles of the excellent wines produced in the region make a worthwhile purchase. Most shops are open from 8:30 AM to 1 PM and 3:30 to 7:30 PM (7 PM in winter); closed Monday mornings and Sundays.

La Bomboniera More than a century old, this tiny sweets shop has etched glass doors, carved walnut shelves, and an original Bohemian glass chandelier. It sells pastries and beautifully wrapped chocolates. 3 Via XXX Ottobre (phone: 62752).

Christine Pelletterie Fine leather clothes, shoes, and accessories for men and women. 15 Piazza della Borsa (phone: 366212).

Fabbrica Jurcev Fine liqueurs, especially grappa, made on the premises by a firm whose history goes back more than a hundred years. 24 Via Romagna (phone: 68530).

Fendi Chic women's clothing, including furs, faux furs, and leather goods. 1 Capo di Piazza (phone: 366464).

Max Mara Fine womenswear at significantly less than what this fashionable label costs in the US. 23 Via Carducci (phone: 636723).

Le Monde Trendy fashions for men and women. 1 Passo San Giovanni (phone: 62237).

Spangher A large, slickly modern waterfront shop selling the latest in nautical equipment and elegant sailing clothes, shoes (including designer rubber boots), and accessories. 8 Riva Gulli (phone: 305158).

Trussardi Elegant sportswear and accessories for men and women by the well-known Milanese designer. 27 Via San Nicolò (phone: 68087).

V. Zandegiacomo Elegant smoking and grooming articles for men, and quality silver, china, and glassware. 1 Corso Italia (phone: 60974).

Vecchia Europa A tasteful selection of antique objects, art, furniture, and jewelry. 1/C Via Armando Diaz (phone: 366852).

SPORTS AND FITNESS

The tourist office (see *Tourist Information,* above) has information on sports facilities in the city.

GOLF The *Golf Club Trieste* (80 Padriciano; phone: 226159) has an 18-hole course about 4 miles (6 km) from the city center. Closed Tuesdays.

HORSE RACING Trotting races are run Wednesdays and Sundays at the *Ippodromo di Montebello* (4 Piazzale de Gasperi; phone: 393176 or 947100).

SAILING In the summer rent sailboats at the *Società Triestina della Vela* (8 Pontile Istria; phone: 313257) or *Società Triestina Sport del Mare* (1/D Molo Venezia; phone: 303580).

SOCCER From September through April *Triestina* plays at *Stadio Comunale Grezar* (2 Via Macelli; phone: 812210).

SWIMMING There's an indoor municipal pool (3 Riva Gulli; phone: 306024). Trieste's coastline is dotted with rocky beaches (the ones in Muggia and the resort town of Barcola are particularly nice), several of which have water sports facilities in the summer.

TENNIS Book courts by the hour at the *Tennis Club Park Hotel Obelisco* (1 Via Nazionale, Opicina; phone: 211756) or at the *Tennis Club Triestino* (Padriciano; phone: 226179).

THEATER

The *Teatro Stabile–Politeama Rossetti* (45 Viale XX Settembre; phone: 567201) is Trieste's major theater for top national productions. The *Teatro Cristallo* (also known as the *Teatro Popolare la Contrade*; 12 Via Ghirlandaio; phone: 391947) offers a mixture of avant-garde and traditional theater by repertory groups from all over Italy. Plays for the local Slovene community are staged at the *Teatro Sloveno* (4 Via Petronio; phone: 632664/5). Two other theaters that regularly stage plays are the *Teatro Armonia* (Via Arianan; phone: 370667) and the *Teatro Miela* (3 Piazza Duca degli Abruzzi; phone: 365119).

MUSIC

Music-loving Trieste hosts classical concerts year-round, but its major attraction is the beautiful 19th-century opera house *Teatro Comunale Giuseppe Verdi* (1 Piazza Verdi; phone: 366636), similar to Milan's *La Scala* and one of the best run in Italy. The opera season lasts from mid-October through April. Concerts and other musical events are held at the *Conservatorio Tartini* (12 Via Ghega; phone: 363508), the *Teatro Cristallo* (see *Theater,* above), and the auditorium of the *Civico Museo Revoltella* (27 Via Diaz; phone: 366636).

NIGHTCLUBS AND NIGHTLIFE

Despite its cosmopolitan aspects, Trieste closes down rather early in the evening, but it does have its pockets of after-hours vitality. The hot discotheque is *Il Mandracchio* (1 Capo di Piazza; phone: 366292). Other good discos are the *Vertigo Club* (26 Via Canale Piccolo; phone: 368116); *Opera* (2 Strada Costiera; phone: 224544); *Macchiavelli* (285 Viale Miramare, about 5 miles/8 km outside the city in Barcola; phone: 44104); and *Nepenthes* (67 Duino, near the airport; phone: 208607). The *Bottega del Vino* (phone: 309142), an elegant piano bar and restaurant occupying the former stables of the *Castello di San Giusto,* offers romantic dining and dancing until 1 AM, except Tuesdays (see *Eating Out*). Another popular late-night restaurant is the stylish *Elefante Bianco* on the waterfront (near Piazza dell'Unità d'Italia at 3 Riva III Novembre; phone: 365784). Most bars in Trieste are open daily and close in the wee hours of the morning.

Best in Town

CHECKING IN

For a small city, Trieste has a surprisingly varied selection of hotels, some of which recall its glamorous past. As it is still relatively undiscovered by foreign tourists, local prices are quite reasonable. The best hotels in town, listed as expensive, charge $170 or more per night for a double room. Hotels in the moderate category charge $70 to $160; an inexpensive one, expect to pay $70 or less. All hotels feature air conditioning and private baths unless otherwise indicated. All rates include breakfast unless otherwise noted. Some of Trieste's major hotels have complete facilities for the business traveler. Those listed below as having "business services" usually offer such conveniences as an English-speaking concierge, meeting rooms, photocopiers, computers, translation services, and express checkout, among others. Call the hotel for additional information. All telephone numbers are in the 40 city code.

EXPENSIVE

Duchi d'Aosta Small and truly elegant, it boasts an ideal location right on Piazza dell'Unità d'Italia. Built in the late 19th century, the 52 rooms have been tastefully modernized and equipped with television sets and mini-bars. Exquisite decor and friendly service make it a delightful place to stay. Ask for a corner room overlooking the square and the waterfront. The ground-floor *Harry's Bar* offers an intimate setting for cocktails, and the adjoining *Grill Room* (see *Eating Out*) is one of the city's finest restaurants. Business services are available. 2 Piazza dell'Unità d'Italia (phone: 7351; fax: 366092).

Savoia Excelsior Palace Some critics claim the modernization of this grand old hotel overlooking the waterfront destroyed its Old World elegance, but guests will find that all of its 150 rooms are comfortable and feature all the amenities. Nostalgic patrons can still find some of the former ambience in the spacious lobby. Many of the rooms (including several suites and apartments) have wonderful views. There is a restaurant and a piano bar. Business services are available. 4 Riva Mandracchio (phone: 7690; fax: 77733).

Abbazia A favorite of Italian businesspeople, this renovated small hostelry near the train station is nicely decorated. Most of the 21 rooms have private baths but no air conditioning. No restaurant. 20 Via della Geppa (phone: 369464; fax: 369769).

Colombia The pick of properties in this price category, this place near the train station is a real value. There are 40 modern, carpeted rooms (not air conditioned); an attractive lobby and bar; and a particularly nice concierge. No restaurant. 18 Via della Geppa (phone: 369333; fax: 369644).

Continentale It's pleasant and small, opposite a house where James Joyce once lived, on a quiet side street in the center of town. The 53 rooms are spacious and very clean; about 20 of them have private baths, but none has air conditioning. There's a bar and a small breakfast room. 25 Via San Nicolò (phone: 631717; fax: 631718).

Al Teatro Near the opera this old-fashioned hotel is popular with musicians. The 47 rooms (some with parquet floors) are simple but comfortable; most have private baths, but none has air conditioning. No restaurant. 1 Capo di Piazza (phone: 366220; fax: 366560).

EATING OUT

Trieste's cuisine is a hearty blend of northern Italian and middle-European cooking, and it offers a wide variety of characteristic dishes. As might be expected in a port city, the fish is superb, and there are plenty of fine seafood restaurants. Pork, beef, veal, and venison are also local specialties. One pleasant Triestine tradition that's especially convenient for visitors is the informal "buffet," which offers home-cooked meals that are consumed with beer or wine at stand-up counters (some have stools) or at small tables. Buffets serve the best sausages, ham, and salami, in addition to such typical dishes as goulash, *tafelspitz* (boiled beef), and *jota,* a thick bean soup with sauerkraut, served at room temperature. Trieste has the added advantage of being in wine country. Excellent regional wines include pinot grigio, tocai, and merlot. Beer is also extremely popular; in addition to the full range of Italian brands, there are plenty of imports from Germany and Austria. Desserts—rich cakes and strudels, coffee rings, and Sacher tortes—are decidedly Austro-Hungarian in origin.

Expect to pay $60 to $90 or more for a three-course meal for two at restaurants we categorize as expensive; $40 to $60 at moderately priced restaurants; and $40 or less at inexpensive ones. Prices include tip, tax, and cover charge, but not wine. All restaurants are open for lunch and dinner unless otherwise noted. All telephone numbers are in the 40 city code.

EXPENSIVE

Antica Trattoria Suban A well-known restaurant in a country house a few miles from the center of town, it has been in the same family for over a hundred years. It has a lively, elegantly rustic atmosphere and an excellent menu and wine list. Try the *crespelle al radicchio rosso* (crêpes with grilled radicchio) or the crêpes with basil and cream sauce as an appetizer, followed by one of the superb steak or veal dishes. This is regional cooking at its best. Closed Mondays, Tuesdays, and three weeks in August. Reservations advised. Major credit cards accepted. 2 Via Comici (phone: 54368).

Città di Cherso Fish is the specialty here, and the chef has a fine touch with it, whether served in risotto *con scampi* (with shrimp), in spaghetti *ai frutti di mare* (with mixed shellfish), or simply grilled with oil and lemon. It is a welcoming place, with stone walls, soft lights, and friendly service. Closed Tuesdays and mid-July through August. Reservations advised. Major credit cards accepted. 6 Via Cadorna (phone: 366044).

Grill Room Old World charm and a refined cuisine of regional and international inspiration are the draws of this elegant dining room in the *Duchi d'Aosta* hotel. The filet mignon is excellent, and there is a good selection of pasta and fish dishes. Indulgent diners may want to try some beluga caviar at about $130 per portion, but there are other appealing appetizers that cost considerably less. Open daily. Reservations advised. Major credit cards accepted. 2 Via dell'Orologio (phone: 7351).

Hosteria Bellavista One of Trieste's finest eating places serves sophisticated dishes such as *crespelle al caviale* (crêpes filled with caviar); ravioli *all'anatra* (stuffed with duck); and filet of lamb cooked with honey, wild thyme, and truffles. Another reason to dine here is the spectacular view of the Gulf of Trieste. The wine cellar is well stocked, and there also is a wide selection of grappe and over a hundred varieties of whiskies. Closed Sundays, *Easter,* and *Christmas.* Reservations advised. Major credit cards accepted. 52 Via Bonomea (phone: 411150).

Marinella A pleasant, 10-minute walk from the *Castello di Miramare,* this huge restaurant on the sea has a beautiful view of the coast and excellent seafood. The risotto with shrimp is particularly good. Closed Sundays for dinner and Mondays. Reservations advised. Major credit cards accepted. 323 Viale Miramare, Barcola (phone: 410986).

MODERATE

Bottega del Vino There are superb views of the city from this medieval-style restaurant inside *Castello di San Giusto.* The chef specializes in meat cooked over a charcoal fire. One part of the restaurant is given over to wine tasting.

Closed Tuesdays. Reservations unnecessary. Visa accepted. 3 Piazza Cattedrale (phone: 309142).

Al Bragozzo Fish is the specialty at this cheerful, wood-paneled restaurant on the waterfront. Customers help themselves to a wide variety of fish antipasti and choose their main dish from the fresh catch of the day. The homemade ravioli *miramare* (stuffed with shrimp, salmon, and heavy cream) is not to be missed. Closed Mondays. Reservations unnecessary. No credit cards accepted. 22 Riva Nazario Sauro (phone: 303001).

Buffet Benedetto One of the best buffets in town, it also has ample room for sit-down dining, and its homey, wood-paneled decor, much like an Alpine tavern, is nicely complemented by the friendly service. This is a place for hearty meat and potato dishes such as goulash and *stinco di maiale* (roast shank of pork); it also serves excellent gnocchi with a meat or cheese sauce. For quicker, stand-up meals, the buffet offers a tantalizing array of salami, other cold meat, and salads. Try the exquisite marrons glacés (candied chestnuts), made fresh every day, for dessert. Closed Mondays and August. Reservations unnecessary. No credit cards accepted. 19 Via XXX Ottobre (phone: 632964).

Elefante Bianco The menu of this excellent restaurant has a distinctly Central European flavor. Interesting specialties include *gamberoni all'arancia* (shrimps cooked in an orange sauce) and *costate di cervo gratinate* (ribs of venison served au gratin). There's also a tempting selection of homemade desserts. Closed Sundays. Reservations advised. Major credit cards accepted. Riva III Novembre (phone: 362603).

Ai Fiori Traditional food with a touch of fantasy is served in a charming and intimate setting. The menu changes daily, but the focus remains finely prepared pasta and fish dishes. Try the artichoke soup or the risotto with oysters and champagne. Closed Sundays for dinner, Mondays, *Christmas* through *New Year's Day,* and three weeks in August. Reservations advised. Major credit cards accepted. 7 Piazza Hortis (phone: 300633).

Al Granzo This favorite seafood place has a waterfront terrace overlooking the huge, enclosed fish market. Specialties include spaghetti with crabmeat, fish soup, and a delicate seafood risotto, as well as delicious homemade desserts—particularly *rigojanci* (a chocolate cream pastry), a local specialty of Hungarian origin. Closed Wednesdays. Reservations advised. Major credit cards accepted. 7 Piazza Venezia (phone: 306788).

Nastro Azzurro A popular lunch spot for businesspeople, it's considered one of the best seafood restaurants in town. It consists of one large room with brass chandeliers and a sumptuous display of shellfish appetizers, the catches of the day, and rich desserts. Fish, prepared every way possible, also appears in delicious pasta and risotto dishes. Closed Saturdays for dinner and

Sundays. Reservations advised. Major credit cards accepted. 10 Riva Nazario Sauro (phone: 305789).

Sacra Osteria Housed in a former inn where a Hapsburg prince once slept, this landmark restaurant, a block from the sea, has the feel of a modernized old tavern. Open all day for drinks and cold-cut snacks, the restaurant also has a fine menu of fish and meat dishes, a legendary homemade Sacher torte, and an exceptional wine list. Meals are served until midnight, and there is a pleasant outdoor garden for summer dining. Closed Mondays. Reservations advised. Major credit cards accepted. 13 Via Campo Marzio (phone: 304791).

INEXPENSIVE

Cantina Sociale Another good seafood restaurant, with a down-to-earth style and extremely reasonable prices. The house specialty is a very good *zuppa di pesce* (fish soup). Closed Tuesdays. Reservations unnecessary. No credit cards accepted. 18 Riva Nazario Sauro (phone: 300689).

Osteria da Giovanni This typical trattoria is bursting with atmosphere, with hams and salami strung from the ceiling, slices of which are served up as antipasti with carafes of excellent local wine. Hearty portions and remarkably low prices make this one of the best deals in town. Closed Sundays and two weeks in August. Reservations unnecessary. No credit cards accepted. 14 Via San Lazzaro (phone: 639396).

Siora Rosa A small, lively neighborhood buffet, it's characterized by a cozy atmosphere and an irresistible aroma wafting from the kitchen. The food is genuine Triestine fare: *jota* soup, roast pork, *cotechino* (cooked salami), hot boiled ham with horseradish, and liver with onions. For a light lunch there are sandwiches and salads. Closed weekends. Reservations unnecessary. No credit cards accepted. 6 Piazza Hortis (phone: 301460).

Trieste Pick The city's most famous buffet is a favorite with locals, who come here to sample this spot's main fare—pork. It is cooked in every way imaginable, served with *crauti* (sauerkraut), and washed down with jugs of wine or beer. It's good fun, if you don't mind the crowded tables (it's especially jammed at lunch), and a very good value. Closed Sundays and the last two weeks of July. Reservations unnecessary. No credit cards accepted. 3 Via della Cassa di Risparmio (phone: 307997).

BARS AND CAFFÈS

The coffeehouse tradition is an important part of Trieste life, and there are several historic cafés in which to enjoy a leisurely coffee or light snack. When ordering, keep in mind that, here, cappuccino means espresso in a small cup with a bit of steamed milk. For the standard large cup of cappuccino served in the rest of Italy, ask for a *caffè latte*. The following are our two favorites, followed by our quality choices (all are inexpensive, and none accept credit cards):

BEST CAFFÈS

San Marco For true Old World atmosphere nothing beats this restored *caffè*, with its two high-ceilinged, cavernous rooms, black wrought-iron lamps, golden wall friezes, and red marble tables where regulars play cards or read newspapers all day. Writers Italo Svevo and Umberto Saba were regulars. Linger for hours over a cup of coffee or toasted sandwich. Unfortunately, there are no notable pastries other than a large jam-filled cookie. Closed Wednesdays. 18 Via Battisti (phone: 371373).

Tommaseo Lovingly restored, this *caffè* is a landmark on the blowy seafront. The marble tables on cast-iron bases, ornate coat stands, mirrors, and cupids are all as they were when James Joyce lived in the city, hanging out here, teaching at Berlitz, and trying to scrounge a few lire for a glass of *birra*. Closed Mondays. Riva III Novembre (phone: 366765).

Bar Tergesteo Antique wooden tables and glittering Venetian crystal chandeliers make this a good spot for a light snack or pastry or a late drink after the opera. Closed Mondays. In the *Galleria Tergesteo,* 15 Piazza della Borsa (phone: 365812).

Caffè degli Specchi The splendid outdoor setting of this more-than-160-year-old bar—a fashionable meeting place—makes it the best place to see and be seen while sipping an *aperitivo* or savoring a gelato. Closed Mondays. Piazza dell'Unità d'Italia (phone: 365777).

Pirona James Joyce is said to have written the draft outline for *Ulysses* at this fine old *caffè*. Closed Mondays. 12 Largo Barriera Vecchia (phone: 636046).

Turin

Turin (Torino) is one of the richest cities in Italy—and one that has held on to its aristocratic traditions most tightly. Although it is populated by immigrants who arrived from the country's south in search of work after World War II, the city is deeply marked both by class distinctions and a desire for privacy. The aristocratic Turinese have created a city center filled with beautiful piazze, flowering parks, and elegant *caffès*—an ideal place for visitors. A stroll down Turin's main shopping street, Via Roma, proves that the inhabitants are blessed with excellent taste and the means to indulge it.

It is obvious that the almost one million Turinese work hard to enjoy the fruits of their labors, and the favorite image the Turinese present to the rest of the country is one of hardworking sobriety, though this is not quite accurate. In fact, there seems to be a curious dichotomy at work here— a second face carefully concealed from outsiders. For example, Turin's vast wealth derives from the massive heavy industrial projects ringing the city, notably the enormous plants producing Fiat automobiles, yet it is also home to the finest names in automotive haute couture, car designers like Bertone, Pininfarina, and Giugiaro. The Turinese are not known for being heavy drinkers, yet they created some of the best-known drinks in the world: Martini, Cinzano, and Carpano vermouths were invented and still are made in Turin. Turinese cuisine is elaborate and delicious; fanciful pastries and sweet and bitter chocolate concoctions are prized, yet Turin also is the birthplace of the simple *grissino*—the breadstick.

Turin's roots lie deep in history. Conveniently located on the banks of the Po River, the original city was laid out as a garrison town for the Romans, who were working their way north in their ultimate conquest of Gaul. These ancient founders left a notable legacy, including the grid street pattern still visible today.

The city's Roman heritage notwithstanding, it is impossible to divorce the history of Turin from a great noble family, the House of Savoy. Possessed of the longest lineage in Europe, this aristocratic clan made Turin the capital of its vast duchy in the 11th century. Over nine centuries the citizens of Turin saw their fortunes soar under such enlightened rulers as Charles Emmanuel III and at times sink to sickening depths as their city was threatened by many enemies. For every enlightened Savoyard ruler, however, there seemed to be a dozen soldier-dukes. The history of Turin is, therefore, a martial rather than a cultural one.

Twice in its history Turin experienced lengthy and severe sieges at the hands of the French. Both lasted months, yet at neither time was the city taken. From their strong capital, the House of Savoy spent much of their tenure conquering additional territory (they acquired the Kingdom of

Sardinia in the 18th century) or repulsing invaders. Along with the rest of northern Italy, Turin fell to Napoleon's armies in 1798, and Charles Albert of Savoy expelled the Austrians from his lands in the early 19th century.

But Turin and the House of Savoy had a greater role to play in the destiny of nations. It was here that the first murmurs of the new Italian state—a unified Italy—were heard. The able and intelligent Victor Emmanuel II and his prime minister, Count Camillo Cavour, became the chief movers and shakers of unity. Cavour enlisted the aid of the French in a war against Austria (which was the major impediment to Italian unity) and, following two stunning victories at Magenta and Solferino (battles said to have been so bloody that the sites gave their names to dark red pigments on a painter's palette), broke the power of foreign interventionists in Italy. By 1861 the kingdom of Italy had been proclaimed, with Turin as its capital. In 1870 Rome was given that honor, but the king who ruled in Rome was Turinese, Vittorio Emanuele II of the House of Savoy.

In its dynamic struggles for independence, Turin rapidly caught up with its European economic rivals, whose industrial revolutions had a two-decade head start on Italy's. Fiat and, later, Lancia were the leaders of this industrialization. Throughout the Fascist period, anti-Fascist cells were at work in this traditionally independent-minded city; when the Germans assumed control of northern Italy in 1943, open warfare broke out between partisan bands and the Nazis in and around the city. In addition, there were almost daily air attacks by the Allied air forces.

Yet the city survived and ultimately prospered. It was the cornerstone of the Italian economic miracle that followed World War II, and it became the center of modern Italian writing. First published out of Turin were such important authors as Italo Calvino, Primo Levi, and Cesare Pavese. The city and the Turinese continue to flourish today.

Turin At-a-Glance

SEEING THE CITY

In the heart of the city is the dramatic and rather oddly designed tower of the *Mole Antonelliana* (20 Via Montebello; phone: 817-0496). It is some 500 feet high, and the viewing platform at the 275-foot mark commands a view of the city and the Alps beyond. The structure was begun by Alessandro Antonelli in 1863 as part of Turin's synagogue, but the congregation that commissioned it objected to its unorthodox design (it looks like a cross between a very large greenhouse and a very thin pagoda), leaving it to the city to either demolish or finish. Completed in 1897, it is now something of a city symbol. An elevator takes visitors to the base of the spire. It's closed Saturdays and Mondays; admission charge.

Situated on the far bank of the Po, the terrace of the *Convento dei Cappuccini* affords a magical nocturnal view of the city. Cross the river at Ponte Vittorio Emanuele I and follow signs for Via M. Giardino.

SPECIAL PLACES

At the heart of this busy town is Piazza San Carlo, an impressive architectural unity that incorporates the twin churches of *Santa Cristina* and *San Carlo,* which frame Via Roma. The 1831 equestrian statue dominating the square is of Emanuele Filiberto, the first of the House of Savoy to make Turin a capital. Elegant shops front the square, particularly some fine antiques shops and antiquarian bookshops. The *caffès* that ring Piazza San Carlo are ideal spots for sampling one of Turin's famous *aperitivi*. Not far away is the smaller, quieter Piazza Carignano. Packed into this tranquil square are some of Turin's best-known sights: the massive Baroque *Palazzo Carignano,* home of the first Italian parliament, and the *Palazzo dell'Accademica delle Scienze* (Academy of Sciences), which houses the world-famous Egyptian collection. There is also the ancient and venerable *Del Cambio* restaurant (see *Eating Out*), a favorite haunt of Cavour.

Most of the places noted here are in the city center, an area flanked on the south by Corso Vittorio Emanuele, on the east by Corso Inghilterra, on the north by Corso Regina Margherita, and on the west by the Po River. Many are within walking distance of each other. Note that some sites of interest in Turin close for a midday break, usually from noon or 12:30 PM to 2 or 3 PM; we suggest calling ahead to check exact hours.

CAPPELLA DELLA SANTA SINDONE (CHAPEL OF THE HOLY SHROUD) Within the 15th-century *Duomo di San Giovanni* (St. John's Cathedral) is the chapel that contains Turin's most famous possession, the *Santissima Sindone* (Holy Shroud). Behind the apse stands the awesome black marble, 17th-century chapel. On the altar is a black marble urn containing the shroud, in which it is said the body of Christ was wrapped following His crucifixion. The shroud has not always been in Turin. Although specifically mentioned in the Gospel of Matthew, no trace of cloth was known until it turned up in Cyprus centuries after Christ's death. From Cyprus it traveled to France, where it is thought to have been acquired by the Savoys in 1578. The rarely exhibited sheet reveals the features of a man who suffered crucifixion— specifically in the manner described in the Gospels. While millions believe the features to be those of Christ, the Vatican is reluctant to acknowledge them as such. The church, however, treats the shroud as a holy relic, and belief in its validity has been enhanced since the present pope agreed to accept it as a gift from the Archbishop of Turin to the Holy See.

Tests have been performed on the cloth, and some say evidence exists to suggest that the cloth is of the correct age (early 1st century) and that its origins are in the Middle East. But tests of the cloth conducted at *Oxford University* in 1988 place its date of origin at about 1350. As for the imprint of the man on the cloth—how and when it appeared—dozens of theories exist (none is irrefutably supported by scientific data).

Although now technically belonging to the Vatican, the shroud will remain in Turin. It is kept in a silver casket within an iron box, enclosed in the marble urn on display. The only two keys are held by the Archbishop of Turin and the Palatine Cardinals, the group of senior churchmen based permanently at the Vatican. A large reproduction of the shroud, itself shown to the public on very rare occasions, stands in the chapel (which was closed at press time for several years for renovation). Piazza San Giovanni (phone: 436-6101).

PALAZZO DELL'ACCADEMIA DELLE SCIENZE (ACADEMY OF SCIENCES) This 17th-century palace designed by Guarino Guarini houses a number of collections, the two most important of which follow. Both are at 6 Via Accademia delle Scienze.

Museo Egizio (Egyptian Museum) It is said that Turin's collection of Egyptian artifacts is second only to that of the *National Museum* in Cairo. By far the most exciting exhibit in the museum is the entire *Temple of El-Elessiya* (dating from 15 BC). The presentation of this stone temple to the museum was a reward for the museum's work in saving ancient sites lost forever by the building of the *Aswan High Dam*. All told, the museum includes some 30,000 precious and rare objects dating from the earliest civilization in Egypt to the full flowering of its culture during the 17th and 18th Dynasties. It's open Mondays through Saturdays, with a short (2 to 3 PM) closing; Sundays from 9 AM to 2 PM. Admission charge (phone: 561-7776).

Galleria Sabauda (Savoy Gallery) The collection of Flemish and Dutch paintings here, including works by Van Eyck, Memling, and Rembrandt, is probably Italy's richest. Italy is well represented by various Piedmontese, Tuscan, and Venetian masters, among them Mantegna, Guardi, Fra Angelico, and Veronese. Of particular interest is Bronzino's *Eleonora of Toledo*. Most of the treasures were collected by the Savoys throughout the years. It's open daily to 2 PM. Admission charge (phone: 547440).

PALAZZO MADAMA (MADAMA PALACE) It is possible to see every phase of Turin's history in the architecture of this, one of the town's most imposing buildings, which incorporates the remains of a gate dating from the time of the Roman founders. In the Middle Ages the palazzo became a Savoy stronghold, and over the years it was enlarged until, in the 17th century, its military value diminished and it became the household of the Madama Reale (loosely, dowager duchess) Maria Cristina of France, widow of Vittorio Amedeo II of Savoy and mother of Charles Emmanuel II. In 1721 the Baroque façade was added by the brilliant Sicilian architect Filippo Juvarra. The palazzo now houses the *Museo d'Arte Antica* (Museum of Ancient Art), something of a misnomer, as the bulk of the collection—certainly the masterpieces—dates from the late Middle Ages, the Renaissance, and the 17th and 18th centuries. One large gallery contains a Venetian state barge that once belonged to the Kings of Sardinia. At press time the palazzo was closed for restoration; call for reopening information and hours. Admission charge. Piazza Castello (phone: 535265).

PALAZZO REALE (ROYAL PALACE) Until 1865 this rather plain 17th-century building was the home of Savoy rulers. The first floor has excellent examples of furniture and decoration from the 17th and 18th centuries. There is a fanciful Chinese room with some excellent porcelains. In the gallery attached to the library is a Leonardo self-portrait. Closed Mondays. Admission charge. Piazza Castello (phone: 436-1455).

PARCO DEL VALENTINO (VALENTINO PARK) In the southern part of the city, along the banks of the Po River, is a broad swatch of park containing an imitation castle constructed in the mid-1600s by Maria Cristina of France. The castle is an almost perfect reproduction of a French château. Nearby is a newer (1884) reproduction, the *Borgo Medioevale* (Medieval Village). The houses of the village are patterned after those in the Piedmont region, the castle after Valle d'Aosta. Closed Mondays and holidays. No admission charge on Fridays (phone: 669-9372).

PALAZZO CARIGNANO (CARIGNANO PALACE) Originally built for the Carignano princes in the 17th century, this palace has two noteworthy façades: The one toward Piazza Carignano was designed in the Baroque style by Guarini; the other, toward Piazza Carlo Alberto, was added nearly two centuries later by Ferri and Bollati. The palace was the seat of the first Italian parliament and the birthplace of Victor Emmanuel II. It houses the *Museo Nazionale del Risorgimento* (National Museum of the Risorgimento), which displays documents and relics of the Italian unification movement. Closed Sunday afternoons. Admission charge. 5 Via Accademia delle Scienze (phone: 562-1147).

MUSEO DELL'AUTOMOBILE CARLO BISCARETTI DI RUFFIA Started by an aficionado of things automotive in the mid-1950s, this museum is devoted to the history of the automobile and its ancestors from 15th-century wind-powered contraptions to the development of the city's sprawling Fiat industrial complex. It now houses 160 vehicles, including a steam-powered tricycle from 1891 and the car that won the 1907 Paris-to-Peking motor race by covering the distance in 44 days. The first tentative efforts of such distinguished makers as Lancia, Ferrari, and Alfa Romeo are on display, along with some perfectly preserved legends—a 1916 Rolls-Royce Silver Ghost, a 1933 Bentley, and a 1916 Model T Ford. There is a vast research library as well. Closed Mondays. Admission charge. 40 Corso Unità d'Italia, south of the city center (phone: 677666).

ENVIRONS

SACRA DI SAN MICHELE (MONASTERY OF ST. MICHAEL) Perched at 3,155 feet on the edge of the San Michele ravine high above the Dora Riparia Valley, this Benedictine monastery was built by a group of French monks in 998. It takes its name from the appearance of St. Michael, who is said to have appeared miraculously in midair to catch a falling child. The abbey, now overseen by Rosminian priests, commands an astonishingly beautiful position. The "Staircase of the Dead" leads to the marble portal, which has strong Romanesque bas-reliefs—some decidedly more profane than sacred (symbols of the zodiac, women offering their breasts to serpents, and the like), as well as the stories of Cain and Abel and of Samson and Delilah. The esplanade surrounding the Romanesque-Gothic church at the summit offers beautiful views of the Dora Riparia Valley and the Po and Turin plains. Open daily, with a long midday break. On S25, 23 miles (37 km; about a half-hour drive) west of the city (phone: 939130).

PALAZZO STUPINIGI (STUPINIGI PALACE) Built in the 18th century as a hunting lodge for the Savoy family, this beautiful palace (sometimes called the *Villa Reale* or the *Palazzina di Caccia*) boasts a design based on that of *Versailles*, and it has all the clarity and authority of a great work of art. Filippo Juvarra, whose signature is indelibly stamped on Turin, was the architect. Although "merely" a hunting lodge, it was Napoleon's home before he assumed the crown of Italy. It is now the *Museo dell'Ammobiliamento*, a museum of 18th-century furniture—some of it lovely—but it is the building, with its frescoes and noble sculpture of a stag stamped against the alpine sky, that one comes to see. Visitors must take guided tours (only in Italian). Open daily, with a midday closing. Admission charge. On the Pinerolo road (S23), about 7 miles (11 km) south of Turin (phone: 358-1220).

BASILICA DI SUPERGA (SUPERGA BASILICA) In 1706, when King Vittorio Amedeo II feared defeat at the hands of a French army that was besieging Turin, he promised to have a basilica built if the Turinese forces won. They did, and the result is this Baroque jewel designed by Sicilian architect Juvarra, which sits at 2,205 feet on top of Superga—one of Turin's highest hills. It then became the Savoy royal family's mausoleum *(Tombe Reali)*. At press time the basilica was being restored, but it remains open to the public daily, with a long midday closing. The royal tombs are closed Fridays, holidays, and for a midday break. On S590, 15 miles (24 km) east of Turin (phone: 898-0083).

CASTELLO DI RIVOLI (RIVOLI CASTLE) In an industrial suburb west of town is this restored Baroque castle designed in part by the prolific Juvarra. Now home of the *Museo d'Arte Contemporanea* (Contemporary Art Museum), it hosts special shows of both Italian and foreign artists and has a permanent collection emphasizing the Italian school known as "Arte Povera": In the 1950s conceptual and minimalist artists used worthless materials—rags, stones, and paper—to escape commercialism. Closed Mondays. Admission charge. On S25, 13 miles (21 km) west of Turin, on Piazza Castello Rivoli (phone: 958-1547).

Sources and Resources

TOURIST INFORMATION

The main tourist office in Turin (226 Via Roma; phone: 535901 or 535181) offers advice and assistance in English. It is closed Sundays.

LOCAL COVERAGE Turin's daily newspaper is *La Stampa,* considered one of the finest in Italy. Its readership and influence extend well beyond the city. The *International Herald Tribune* can be purchased on its day of publication at larger newsstands and at the train station. A useful English and Italian booklet, *A Guest in Turin,* is available free at hotels, the tourist office, the main train station, and the airport.

TELEPHONE The city code for Turin is 11. When calling from within Italy, dial 011 before the local number.

GETTING AROUND

AIRPORT There are daily flights to all major European cities from newly renovated and expanded *Turin International Airport* (in Caselle; phone: 567-6361). Bus service and taxis to Turin are available.

BUS/TRAM/TROLLEY Turin has extensive bus and tram service, and a country trolley line serves the outskirts of the city. Very few buses, trams, or trolleys run all night. Purchase tickets in advance at tobacco shops or some newsstands; they are validated on board. For information about schedules, call *Trasporti Torinesi* (*T.T.;* phone: 538376) or ask at the information office (19 *bis* Corso Turati).

CAR RENTAL All major international firms are represented.

TAXI Hail cabs as they cruise; find one at a taxi stand on a major street; or call 5730 or 5737.

TRAIN Turin is an important railway center for northern Italy. The *Stazione Porta Nuova* (not to be confused with the secondary *Stazione Porta Susa*) is on Corso Vittorio Emanuele II (phone: 538376).

SPECIAL EVENTS

As might be expected in a city that makes much of its living from automobiles, Turin's biggest event is the *Salone Internazionale Automobile* (International Car Show), held in even-numbered years in late April or early May at the *Lingotto Fiere* (294 Via Nizza; phone: 664-4111). Since the city is overrun with conventioneers who crowd every hotel, restaurant, and shop, it is suggested that only devoted autophiles visit Turin during this period. The center also hosts the two-week *Biennale dell'Antiquariato* (Biennial Antiques Fair) at the end of February and beginning of March in odd-numbered years, and the important yearly *Salone Internazionale del Veicolo Industriale* (International Industrial Vehicle Exposition) in

November. Annual events at the fairgrounds (15 Corso Massimo d'Azeglio) include the *Expocasa* (International Salon of Domestic Arts) in February; the *Expovacanze* (International Show on Vacations, Sport, and Leisure) in March; and the *Tecnomont & Expomontagna* (International Shows of Technology and Mountain Sports) in October. May marks an annual book show at the *Torino Esposizioni* (15 Corso Massimo d'Azeglio; phone: 6569). In September the annual four-week *Settembre Musica* takes place. This major cultural event focuses on classical and contemporary music; concerts are performed in churches and theaters around the city (phone: 576-5564; fax: 644927).

MUSEUMS

Besides those mentioned in *Special Places*, Turin has two other museums of interest:

ARMERIA REALE (ROYAL ARMORY) Nowhere is the martial past of the House of Savoy more clearly documented than in the *Armeria Reale*, which houses a rich collection of arms and armor dating from Roman times to the Napoleonic era. Open Tuesdays and Thursdays from 2:30 to 7:30 PM; Wednesdays, Fridays, and Saturdays from 9 AM to 2 PM; and Sundays from 9:15 AM to 1 PM. Admission charge. 191 Piazza Castello (phone: 543889).

MUSEO NAZIONALE D'ARTIGLIERIA (NATIONAL ARTILLERY MUSEUM) Housed in the *Mastio della Cittadella,* the only remaining tower of the 16th-century citadel, this collection contains firearms from the history of Turin. The museum was closed for renovation at press time; call for hours. Admission charge. Corso Galileo Ferraris (phone: 562-9223).

SHOPPING

The most elegant shopping street is Via Roma, which runs from the *Porta Nuova* railway station to Piazza Castello. Pedestrians-only Via Garibaldi is also a mother lode of fine shops, some less expensive than those on Via Roma. Also worth window shopping are Via Po, Via Lagrange, Via Carlo Alberto, and Via Amendola.

Turin has a colorful, sprawling flea market called *Il Balon* (in the Porta Palazzo area) all day Saturday and *Il Gran Balon* (antiques only) in the Piazza della Repubblica on the second Sunday of each month. The best time to go to both is dawn. At the *Mercato della Crocetta* (Via Marco Polo) on weekday mornings and all day Saturdays, eagle-eyed shoppers can some-times find sample-sizes in cashmere, silk, and leather goods left over from last year's fashion shows—their labels neatly removed.

The Turinese are artists when it comes to producing and consuming chocolate. *Peyrano* (76 Corso Vittorio Emanuele II; phone: 543940; and 47 Corso Moncalieri; phone: 660-2202) has been making chocolate for a number of royal houses for centuries. The firm specializes in bitter and liqueur chocolates; the prices are rather high. Other top-quality makers of

Turin's favorite sweet are *Stratta* (191 Piazza San Carlo; phone: 541567) and *Caffarel* (no retail address; distributor to the city's best *caffès* and *pasticcerie*), the original creator of the *gianduiotto,* a velvety-smooth, hazelnut-flavored Turinese chocolate candy.

Most shops are open from 9 or 9:30 AM to 1 PM and 3:30 or 4 to 7:30 or 8 PM; many are closed Sundays and Monday mornings as well.

Bambi High-quality children's shoes at good prices. 10 Via Amendola (phone: 518204).

De Candia For the well-dressed Turinese male. 175 Piazza San Carlo (phone: 543800).

Durando Turin's sole retailer of fine Fendi furs. 77 Via Roma (phone: 537087).

De Filippis Pasta in every imaginable size, shape, and composition. 39 Via Lagrange (phone: 596953).

Mariangela One of the city's best boutiques for top designer women's clothing and accessories. 149 Piazza San Carlo (phone: 519380).

Olympic This extremely elegant shop is known for its classic women's and men's clothing. 182 Piazza San Carlo (phone: 518090).

Visetti Beautiful lingerie in silks, satins, crêpes de Chine, and cotton. 247 Piazza Comitato Liberazione Nazionale (often abbreviated to C. L. N.), Via Roma (phone: 546120).

SPORTS AND FITNESS

GOLF There are several courses within easy reach of Turin. The following is our favorite fairway:

A TOP TEE-OFF SPOT

Golf Club Torino On a classic championship layout with wide fairways, these 36 holes in *Parco Mandria* unwind along flat terrain scattered with trees and water hazards. Even Sunday players have a fighting chance here; the fairly forgiving course allows for errors and recovery. Site of many Italian championships, the club is very exclusive. The clubhouse is quite charming. Closed January, February, and Mondays. Twelve miles (19 km) out of town, at 137 Via Grange, Fiano Torinese (phone: 923-5440; fax: 923-5886).

There also are courses at *E Roveri* (24 Rotta Cerbiatta, Fiano Torinese; phone: 923-5719); *Stupinigi* (506 Corso Unione Sovietica; phone: 347-2640; fax: 397-8038); *Vinovo* (182 Via Stupinigi, Vinovo; phone: 965-3880; fax: 962-3748); and *Le Fronde* (68 Via Sant'Agostino, Avigliana; phone: 935083; fax: 930928).

HORSE RACING Flat races are run most of the year, except in August and the dead of winter, at *Vinovo* (see *Golf,* above; phone; 965-3285).

SOCCER From September through May, both *Torino* (phone: 562-3941) and *Juventus* (phone: 65631)—"la Juve" in headlines and graffiti—play at *Stadio delle Alpi* (131 Strada Altessano; phone: 738-0081).

SWIMMING The municipal swimming center (*Stadio Comunale*; 294 Corso Galileo Ferraris; phone: 319-9309) has both covered and uncovered pools. There's an admission charge.

THEATER AND MUSIC

Operas, symphonies, ballets, and any number of plays may be running concurrently. There is no "season" as such—productions go on year-round. The best way to find out what Turin is offering on a daily basis is to consult *La Stampa* or your hotel desk. The following are some of our favorite venues:

HIGH NOTES

Auditorium della RAI Symphony concerts and chamber music sponsored by the state's performance network are heard here year-round. The group produces works from the past as well as contemporary pieces. Best of all, ticket prices are affordable. 15 Via Rossini (phone: 880-74961).

Teatro Regio An 1,800-seat hall that opened in 1973 with Maria Callas singing Verdi's *I Vespri Siciliani,* this theater is the national testing ground for budding young vocal talent, and a significant portion of the works staged here are contemporary. The hall publishes extensive calendars of events. 215 Piazza del Castello (phone: 881-5241; fax: 881-5214).

Other theaters of note are the *Teatro Nuovo* (17 Corso Massimo d'Azeglio; phone: 655552 or 669-0668); *Teatro Carignano* (6 Piazza Carignano; phone: 537998; the box office is on 49 Via Roma; phone: 544562); and *Teatro Alfieri* (2 Piazza Solferino; phone: 562-3800). In summer opera and other productions are often offered outside in the *Palazzo Reale* gardens.

NIGHTCLUBS AND NIGHTLIFE

The Turinese generally do not dance the night away, and what nightlife there is seems to be restricted to those lucky few in the know. Such nightclubs as the city possesses are located mostly in the area around the *Porta Nuova* railway station. Some come and go so quickly that they are known by word of mouth only. Hotel porters are the best sources of information on the discotheques, pubs, and piano bars that have brilliant, but brief, life spans. A few worth noting at press time are *Wisky Notte* (5 Via S. Pio V; phone: 687563); the aptly named *Pick Up* (8 Via Barge; phone: 447-2204); and the *Cotton Night Club* (9 Via Bernardino Galliari; phone: 655795).

Best in Town

CHECKING IN

Turin has a parking problem, so visitors who are driving should ask hotel management whether garage space is available. Rates tend to be high because the city thrives on weekday business travelers (check for special weekend rates). Hotels that charge from $200 to $275 a night for a double room are classified here as expensive; those that ask between $100 and $150 are moderate. All hotels feature private baths. All telephone numbers are in the 11 city code unless otherwise indicated.

For an unforgettable Turinese experience, we begin with our favorite villa, followed by our cost and quality choices, listed by price category.

A SPECIAL HAVEN

Villa Sassi In the wooded hills just outside the city—3 miles (5 km) from downtown (follow signs for Pino Torinese and Chieri)—this noble, splendidly restored, and pricey 18th-century mansion set in a beautifully landscaped park is a world unto itself. Enjoy the tranquillity of the 15 elegant, antiques-filled guestrooms, and wine and dine in the villa's eminent restaurant, *El Toulà* (see *Eating Out*). 47 Strada al Traforo del Pino (phone: 898-0556; fax: 898-0095).

EXPENSIVE

City Small (44 rooms) and modern, it has an attractive little garden and a late-night grill that serves hot snacks (no restaurant). 25 Via F. Juvarra (phone: 540546; fax: 548188).

Jolly Ligure Directly opposite the *Porta Nuova* train station, this contemporary 169-room hotel offers every modern amenity and a restaurant. 85 Piazza Carlo Felice (phone: 55641; 800-247-1277 in New York State; 800-221-2626 elsewhere in the US; fax: 535438).

Jolly Principi di Piemonte One of Turin's finest hotels (and the nicest of the three Jolly properties in Turin) is in the heart of town, not far from the *Porta Nuova* train station. Public areas retain some Belle Epoque character, while the 107 rooms are large, with classic decor, and the service is superlative. The restaurant is small and romantic. 15 Via P. Gobetti (phone: 562-9693;

800-247-1277 in New York State; 800-221-2626 elsewhere in the US; fax: 562-0270).

Sitea The lobby of this popular hotel is a blend of Old World elegance and contemporary accents. There are 119 spacious guestrooms; ask for one of the *camere in stile* (rooms with a Jacuzzi), whose handsome, turn-of-the-century character outshines the contemporary rooms. The place has a central location, excellent service, and a restaurant. There are discounts on weekends when there are no trade fairs in town. 35 Via Carlo Alberto (phone: 5570171; fax: 548090).

Turin Palace Most of the 125 rooms in this elegant, stately hostelry have been renovated, and the restaurant has an excellent reputation. This, Turin's only five-star deluxe hotel, is the only one pretending to be "grand" that actually is. Across from the *Porta Nuova* train station, at 8 Via Sacchi (phone: 562-5511; fax: 561-2187).

MODERATE

President Several of the 72 rooms in this cheerful, modern hotel overlook an enclosed garden. Another plus is the helpful staff. Only breakfast is served, but there is a small bar. 67 Via A. Cecchi (phone: 859555; fax: 248-0465).

Victoria Centrally located, this little-known hostelry is a real find. Its first class amenities, charm, and period furniture—such as 19th-century sleigh and canopy beds—make each of the guestrooms unique. At press time 55 rooms were being added to the existing 65 (most guestrooms will have Jacuzzis when the work is completed). No restaurant, but the sunlit breakfast room evokes a country ambience. 4 Via N. Costa (phone: 561-1909; fax: 561-1806).

EATING OUT

The cuisine of Turin, like northern Italian cooking in general, is similar to that of France in method—but very different in ingredients. Piedmont is especially rich in delicacies, some as simple as the *grissino* (breadstick). Others are more exotic: Fabulous white truffles, for instance, are hunted at night—not by pigs, as in France, but by dogs. This range of culinary delights and a plethora of cheeses and hot appetizers make dining in Turin a distinctly different experience.

A dinner for two that costs from $100 to $150 is categorized here as expensive; one between $60 and $100, moderate; and $50 or less, inexpensive. Prices include house wine and tip, but not tax. All restaurants are open for lunch and dinner unless otherwise noted. All telephone numbers are in the 11 city code.

EXPENSIVE

Bontan On the city's outskirts, this more-than-70-year-old villa is decorated with Oriental carpets and Gobelin tapestries. Piedmontese cooking is the order of the day, with such specialties as tortellini stuffed with *robiole* cheese and green squash. Fish and vegetarian menus are available. Closed Sundays and Mondays. Reservations necessary. Major credit cards accepted. 55 Via Canua, San Mauro Torinese (phone: 822-2680).

Del Cambio A faded scarf in the Italian colors still marks the table that Cavour frequented. The braised beef in barolo wine is exceptional, but diners also come here for the history and the 19th-century atmosphere—the waiters wear tails, white gloves, and aprons. Closed Sundays and August. Reservations necessary. Major credit cards accepted. 2 Piazza Carignano (phone: 546690).

I Due Lampioni di Carlo The atmosphere recalls a 19th-century drawing room, with a high, barrel-vaulted ceiling and somber decor. A wide range of Piedmontese hot appetizers is served, as are excellent *agnolotti* (large ravioli) stuffed with pheasant. Closed Sundays and August. Reservations advised. Major credit cards accepted. 45 Via Carlo Alberto (phone: 817-9380).

Al Gatto Nero Turin's best seafood restaurant has no street sign, but behind its large windows are usually some 80 diners enjoying excellent fish, shellfish, and steaks. Closed Sundays and August. Reservations advised. Major credit cards accepted. 14 Corso Filippo Turati (phone: 590414).

Neuv Caval d'Brôns The food at this very stylish and centrally located restaurant—including many sublime vegetarian dishes—is excellent, the menu at times a little daring. Closed Sundays and early July. Reservations necessary. Major credit cards accepted. 157 Piazza San Carlo (phone: 545785).

L'Oca Nera "Slow food," a culinary movement committed to combining traditional cuisine with a creative presentation, is the draw here. The vegetable flans and *branzino* (bass) marinated in basil make this place worth visiting, but there's an added attraction—for a small charge, you can enjoy an after-dinner cabaret or puppet show. Closed for lunch, Sundays, and August. Reservations advised. Visa accepted. 14 Via San Massimo (phone: 882336).

La Prima Smarrita A former country inn, this restaurant is a downtown meeting place for executives. It offers variations on traditional dishes such as *ovoli* mushroom and watercress salad and pasta stuffed with *porcini* mushrooms. The service, by waiters dressed in tunics, is excellent. Closed Mondays and three weeks in August. Reservations necessary. Major credit cards accepted. 244 Corso Unione Sovietica (phone: 317-9657).

San Giorgio Enjoy an evening of dining and dancing at this lakeside restaurant with a lovely view. Closed Wednesdays for lunch and Tuesdays. Reservations advised. Major credit cards accepted. Borgo Medioevale al Valentino (phone: 669-2131).

El Toulà One of the best restaurants in Turin is ensconced in the *Villa Sassi* hotel outside the city center. Specialties include salmon marinated in raspberry vinegar, and breast of duck with local herbs. Any pork dish is sure to be outstanding, and the wine list boasts an excellent selection of exclusive house wines, including champagne. The service is excellent. Closed Sundays and August. Reservations necessary. Major credit cards accepted. 47 Via Strada al Traforo del Pino (phone: 898-0556).

Vecchia Lanterna Quiet and hospitable, this longtime favorite makes the most of local duck and pork. Any meal begun with a terrine of duck pâté is bound to be a success. Duck even finds its way into stuffed pasta such as *agnolotti*. Closed Saturdays for lunch, Sundays, and two weeks in August. Reservations necessary. Major credit cards accepted. 21 Corso Re Umberto (phone: 537047).

MODERATE

Cafasso Owner/chef Mario Albano offers a wonderful selection of local dishes in this restaurant on the outskirts of town. Try the *cotechini* (fresh pork sausages), *bollito misto* (a variety of boiled meat), or the *toma piccante* (aged cow's milk cheese). Closed Wednesdays. Reservations advised. Major credit cards accepted. 178 Strada Val Salice (phone: 660-1495).

Montecarlo Abundant portions of home-cooked food, such as *orzo e fagioli* (small rice-like pasta with beans), are served in surroundings worthy of a film set. Closed Saturdays for lunch and Sundays. Reservations advised. Major credit cards accepted. 37 Via San Francesco da Paola (phone: 888763).

INEXPENSIVE

Buca di San Francesco A popular spot near the main train station, it serves a wide choice of pasta and meat dishes, all prepared in northern Italian and Tuscan styles. Closed Fridays and August. No reservations. Major credit cards accepted. 27 Via San Francesco da Paola (phone: 812-5950).

Porto di Savona Sample herb omelettes, risotto with radicchio, and homemade desserts at this pleasant, family-style trattoria. Closed Mondays, Tuesdays for lunch, and mid-July through mid-August. No reservations or credit cards accepted. 2 Piazza Vittorio Veneto (phone: 817-3500).

BARS AND CAFFÈS

Turin is home to some of Italy's most celebrated coffeehouses—many in 19th-century palaces—where customers can overdose on pastries and chocolates. Most bars and *caffès* mentioned below are in the inexpensive price range. Among the best known, and certainly the oldest *caffè*, is *Baratti e Milano* (29 Piazza Castello). This grand old establishment is dark, intimate, and a great place to people watch; try the famous fruit jellies and chocolates. Dating from the same era yet ages away in decor are *San Carlo* and *Torino* (144 and 204 Piazza San Carlo, respectively), whose interiors are a riot of mirrored gilt and stucco. Not to be forgotten is *Platti* (72 Corso

Vittorio Emanuele II). Opened in 1876, the original structure, decor, and *liquoreria* (liquor store) sign have all been preserved. Another historical place is *Fiorio* (8 Via Po), a *caffè/gelateria* that serves some of the city's best ice cream. In addition to a vast assortment of sandwiches, cocktails, and freshly baked pastries, you can enjoy lunch in its buffet and restaurant rooms. Off Via Garibaldi is the *Confetteria al Bicerin* (5 Piazza della Consolata). Its name comes from the traditional blend of hot coffee, chocolate, and milk—*bicerin*—that once was served in all the best coffeehouses in Turin, but today can be sipped only here and at a handful of other places. With its small white tables and the old wooden counter overflowing with colorful candies, this establishment maintains the atmosphere of a 19th-century *cioccolateria* (a coffeehouse that specialized in chocolate products).

Venice

Venice is luminously beautiful, both in radiant, peak-season June and in bleak, wet November. And it is painfully beautiful when suddenly, on some late-winter morning, the rain trickles to a halt, the cloud curtains part, and trapezoids of sunlight reheat the ancient stones.

A romance with the "Queen of the Adriatic" easily flourishes in a city that has long been conducive to flirtation and fairy tale. For centuries, the constant breath of the salty sea has washed the princely palaces along the Canal Grande (Grand Canal) and its sleepy back canals—these grand buildings framed by walls of muted green, brown, and Venetian-red hues. The tranquil waters of Venice's snaking *rii* (small canals) dissect the city—rippled, distorted reflections through which gondolas glide.

Venice is ingeniously built on and around 117 islands and islets, separated by 177 small canals (and the appropriately named Canal Grande) on Italy's northeastern Adriatic Coast. These small land bodies are joined together by 400 small iron and concrete bridges; the three largest and most historically important—Rialto, Accademia, and degli Scalzi—span the Canal Grande. In addition, a 3-mile bridge reaches across the Laguna Veneta (Venetian Lagoon), connecting it to the mainland near the sprawling town of Mestre. The city is protected from the force of the Adriatic Sea by the natural breakwater of the Lido, a long, narrow sandbar that continues to be one of the more fashionable resorts on the Adriatic.

With some know-how or by sheer serendipity, there is nowhere in Venice that a visitor cannot reach by foot. The rewards of exploring these labyrinthine alleyways are many. Aside from the major sites, every characteristic neighborhood *campiello* (small square), filled with the screams of delighted children, every typical old-fashioned *bacaro* (wine bar), lends insights to one of the world's truly great and unique travel destinations.

The lagoon city began as a place of refuge from the violent barbarian invasions of the 5th century; mainland inhabitants fled to the isolated islands that were then no more than swamplands. As communities grew, the islands became connected to one another. In about 800, Venice gained its independence from Byzantium and started its illustrious millennium as a maritime republic (called La Serenissima). By about 1000, Venice had developed into a powerful, flourishing city-state, and for the next six centuries it was a magnificent imperial power, holding dominion throughout the lands around the Mediterranean, in northern Africa, and in Asia Minor. It was the city of Marco Polo, the most famous of the many Venetian merchants who became extravagantly rich by going to the Levant, where they collected such exquisite products as silks and spices to be sold at a substantial profit throughout Europe and the rest of the Western world. What wasn't brought back under conventional contracts of sale was taken as war booty during such aggressions as the Crusades and used to decorate, embellish, and lend Venice a permanent air of East-meets-West that still distinguishes it from other cities in Europe, perhaps even the world.

In 829, two Venetian sailors found themselves in Alexandria during one of their routine voyages. Every city and nation in the Roman Catholic world had its own patron saint, and the two mariners were determined to secure the protection of one of the church's most important figures—the apostle and evangelist St. Mark. In a daring feat, they smuggled the saint's remains out of Egypt by packing the relics in a crate of lard, which was especially abhorrent to Moslems and thus a guarantee that the remains would escape notice. The sailors returned with their prize to a jubilant Venice, whose citizens proclaimed St. Mark (San Marco) La Serenissima's exalted patron. This coup secured prestige and a modicum of clout for Venice.

Shortly after the arrival of St. Mark's relics, a modest private chapel adjacent to the *Palazzo Ducale* (Doge's Palace) in today's Piazza San Marco was constructed to house them. The shrine was glorified with war booty from the Crusades; the most noticeable bounty were four bronze horses, replicas of which grace the façade of the *Basilica di San Marco.* The regal winged lion of St. Mark, the city's patron beast that symbolized Venice, became the emblem of the republic and its far-flung dominion—it stood guard over a network of strongholds from the Strait of Gibraltar to the Bosporus Strait.

Venice was the focal point for the great trade routes from the Middle East, and the money-lending and commercial market around the city's Ponte di Rialto (Rialto Bridge) was the vibrant pulse of European commerce. The Venetian court was the most luxurious in Europe. The well-heeled of European courts converged on the city to experience its incomparable theater, opera, gambling in private casinos, and the wild days of *Carnevale* that could go on for months at a time.

The doges celebrated their mastery of the Mediterranean with an annual ceremony of marriage to the sea, and the golden ducats that overflowed the city's coffers financed some of the world's most spectacular art and architecture, much of which still adorns the city today. The Venetian school of painting, which produced magnificent colorists, began with Giorgione and achieved its apogee in the 16th century with Titian Vecellio (Tiziano), Paolo Veronese, and Jacopo Tintoretto. The proud, thousand-year Venetian independence ended with the Treaty of Campoformio in 1797, when a young Napoleon traded the territory to Austria. In 1866, after nearly 70 years of Bonaparte and then Hapsburg domination, the city was joined to newly unified Italy.

Today, Venice proper has a meager population of 70,000, which steadily decreases by about 1,500 annually due to the city's extraordinarily high cost of living and increasing pollution. The millions of tourists who swarm through its narrow streets and tiny squares make up Venice's chief industry. A gaudy party atmosphere reigns from *Easter* to October, with a midsummer explosion sometimes as crass as it is colorful. In its way the scene is as vibrant, insistent, exotic, and chaotic as anything from the days of the international market on the Ponte di Rialto.

And yet it's still possible to turn from the main thoroughfare and, after a few random rights and lefts, find yourself in a haven of quiet back alleys, on a tiny bridge across a deserted canal, in the middle of a silent, sunbaked *campo,* with a fruit stall—and not a tourist in sight.

Venice in winter is a totally different experience: placid, gray, and startlingly visual. Suddenly, there is no one between you and the noble palaces, the soaring churches, the dark canals. Only the mysterious masked merriment of *Carnevale* (a 10-day celebration ending on March 1 this year) interrupts the chilly repose of the time when Venice is most emphatically a community of Venetians.

Few cities have attracted so many illustrious admirers. Shakespeare set one of his best-known plays, *The Merchant of Venice,* here (though most historians believe he never set foot in Venice, or even Italy). Galileo Galilei used the bell tower in Piazza San Marco to test his telescope. Richard Wagner composed here. Lord Byron and Henry James wrote here. It's not hard to feel the ghosts of these and others who, as James said, "have seemed to find [here] something that no other place could give."

Venice At-a-Glance

SEEING THE CITY

The traditional vantage point from which to admire Venice is the summit of the 324-foot red campanile (bell tower) in Piazza San Marco. The view on all sides is breathtaking—from the red-shingled rooftops and countless domes of the city to the distant islands dotting the wide lagoon. Take the elevator, or climb the stairs to the top. It's open daily; admission charge.

For a bird's-eye view of Piazza San Marco (and the rest of the city), take a short boat ride to the Isola San Giorgio (one stop on the No. 82 *vaporetto* from Riva degli Schiavoni), and ride the elevator to the top of the church tower. A masterpiece by Andrea Palladio, the church contains two major works by Tintoretto and beautiful carved wooden choir stalls depicting the life of St. Benedict. For a memorable experience, visit the church on Sundays at 11 AM, when the weekly mass is sung in Gregorian chant by resident monks. It's open daily, with a midday closing; admission charge (phone: 528-9900).

SPECIAL PLACES

Piazza San Marco is the center of life in Venice, a glittering testimony to the opulence of the Venetian Empire in the East. From here sightseers can board boats to the Lido, other islands, and various quarters of the city.

Note that some sites of interest in Venice close for a midday break, usually from noon or 12:30 PM to about 3 or 4 PM; we suggest calling ahead to check exact hours.

DOWNTOWN

PIAZZA SAN MARCO (ST. MARK'S SQUARE) It's easy to understand why Napoleon called this huge marble piazza the finest drawing room in Europe, and why this is the only square in the city that Venetians call a piazza (the other public spaces are known as *campi*—fields—because they were once unpaved). Bells chime, flocks of pigeons crisscross the sky, violins play, couples embrace in the sunset—while the visitor takes it all in from any of its congenial *caffès*. A mere turn of the head allows you to admire the *Basilica di San Marco;* the *Palazzo Ducale;* the early 20th-century copy of the original 9th-century bell tower; the clock tower where two giant bronze Moors have struck the hours for five centuries; the old and new administration offices; and the old library, which now houses the archaeological museum. In the *piazzetta,* through which the square opens onto the Canal Grande, are two granite columns—one topped by the winged Lion of St. Mark, the other by a statue of St. Theodore, Venice's patron saint until he was supplanted by St. Mark. *Vaporetto* stop San Marco.

BASILICA DI SAN MARCO (ST. MARK'S BASILICA) A masterpiece of mosaics and sinuous curves, massive domes, and a profusion of supportive pillars, this monument of Venetian-Byzantine architecture was begun in 830 to shelter the tomb of St. Mark, whose bones had been smuggled out of Alexandria. When first built, it was not a cathedral but a small and private chapel for the doges, who resided next door. Most of the present basilica was constructed during the 11th century, but the phenomenal decoration of the interior and exterior continued well into the 16th century. The basilica has a large dome and four smaller ones; its imposing façade of variegated marble and sculpture has five large doorways. The four famous bronze horses have adorned the central doorway since 1207, when they were brought here after the sack of Constantinople. Today, bronze replicas have taken their place atop the entrance, and the originals are now on permanent display in the basilica's museum. Inside, the walls are encrusted with precious art, rare marbles, and magnificent mosaics. Behind the high altar in the chancel is the famous gold altarpiece, the *Pala d'Oro,* and the basilica's treasury includes rare relics and Byzantine goldwork and enamels. Many of the treasury's prize pieces came from the booty brought home by Crusaders, or by Venice's mercantile elite, from expeditions to the Near and Far East. One of the treasures, the bejeweled 10th-century icon known as the *Madonna Nicopeia,* is exhibited in a chapel of its own to the left of the main altar. Sunday vespers at 6 PM (5:30 PM in winter) is a particularly magical time to visit. Closed Sundays before 2 PM. Separate admission charges to the chancel and treasury. *Vaporetto* stop San Marco. Piazza San Marco (phone: 522-5697).

PALAZZO DUCALE (DOGE'S PALACE) Next to the basilica is this pink and white palace with an unusual double loggia that served as the residence of the doges and the seat of government. The finest room in the palace is the *Sala del Maggior Consiglio* (Grand Council Chamber), containing paintings by Tintoretto and Veronese. You may also visit the doge's apartments and the armory. The palace is connected to the old prisons by the famous Ponte dei Sospiri (Bridge of Sighs), whose name comes from the lamentations of prisoners supposedly taken across the bridge to be executed. Open daily. Admission charge. *Vaporetto* stop San Marco. Piazza San Marco (phone: 522-4951).

CANAL GRANDE (GRAND CANAL) Lined with some 200 marble palaces built between the 12th and the 18th century, the Canal Grande has been called the finest street with the finest houses in the world. On the right (east bank) are the *Palazzo Vendramin-Calergi,* where Wagner died, now the winter home of the *Casino;* the *Ca' d'Oro* (Golden House), so called because its ornate façade once was entirely gilded; the *Palazzo Mocenigo,* where Lord Byron lived; and the *Palazzo Grassi,* a world class art exhibition center. On the left (west bank) are the *Palazzo Pesaro,* which houses the modern art gallery, and the *Ca' Rezzonico,* an architectural jewel that contains the civic museum of 18th-century Venice. A good way to see all of these beautiful palazzi is to take a slow boat ride in an open, front-row seat along the entire 2-mile length of the Canal Grande, on the No. 1 line from the train station to San Marco. Nighttime is a particularly wonderful time to do this; the No. 1 line runs all night.

CHIESA DI SANTA MARIA DELLA SALUTE (CHURCH OF ST. MARY OF GOOD HEALTH) Dedicated to the Madonna for delivering Venice from a plague, this magnificent 17th-century Baroque church is almost directly across the Canal Grande from Piazza San Marco. Its octagonal shape and white Istrian limestone façade are easily recognizable in innumerable paintings of Venetian scenes and panoramas. Inside are paintings of the New Testament by Titian and Tintoretto. Open daily, with a long (noon to 3 PM) closing. *Vaporetto* stop Salute. Campo della Salute, Dorsoduro (phone: 522-5558).

CHIESA DEL REDENTORE (CHURCH OF THE REDEEMER) Also built to thank the Madonna for rescuing the Venetians from an earlier plague, and a must for architectural enthusiasts, this 16th-century church is known for its perfect proportions and remarkable harmony, both inside and out. It was constructed by Andrea Palladio on a point of the Isola della Giudecca, a short boat ride (take the No. 82) from San Marco by way of Isola San Giorgio. Open daily, with a long (noon to 4 PM) break. *Vaporetto* stop Redentore. Campo Redentore. Isola della Giudecca, Dorsoduro (phone: 523-1415).

GALLERIA DELL'ACCADEMIA (GALLERY OF FINE ARTS) Brief but frequent visits are the best way to savor the rich contents of this great gallery. Of particular interest are Veronese's *Supper in the House of Levi,* Titian's *Presentation of the Virgin,* Tintoretto's *Transport of the Body of St. Mark,* and Giorgione's *Tempesta.* The paintings of Venice by Antonio Canaletto, Francesco Guardi, and Gentile Bellini are the academy's most Venetian selections, both by subject and artist. Open Wednesdays through Mondays to 2 PM; Tuesdays to 7 PM. Admission charge. For security reasons, the number of visitors permitted in the *Galleria* at any one time is limited to 180, so summertime waits can be over an hour—come early. *Vaporetto* stop Accademia. Campo della Carità, Dorsoduro (phone: 522-2247).

MUSEO DEL SETTECENTO VENEZIANO (MUSEUM OF VENICE IN THE 1700S) Built in the 17th century, *Ca' Rezzonico*—the palace that has housed the museum since 1936—has a magnificent exterior that is best observed from the Canal Grande (in turn, its windows afford superb views of the canal). A splendid backdrop for some of the more important treasures of 18th-century Venetian art, the palace itself is known for its grandiose decor and its frescoes by Giandomenico Tiepolo and his son Giambattista. Closed Fridays. Admission charge. *Vaporetto* stop Rezzonico. *Ca' Rezzonico,* Dorsoduro (phone: 522-4543).

SCUOLA GRANDE DI SAN ROCCO (GREAT SCHOOL OF ST. ROCH) The Venetian *scuola* was not a school but something of a cross between a trade guild and a religious brotherhood that did works of charity and supplied wealthy patronage for the arts. *San Rocco,* the most important and heavily decorated *scuola,* contains a rich collection of Tintorettos—some 56 canvases depicting stories from the Old and New Testaments. Open daily in summer; closed weekdays after 1 PM in winter. Admission charge. *Vaporetto* stop San Tomà. Campo San Rocco, San Polo (phone: 523-4864).

CHIESA DI SANTA MARIA GLORIOSA DEI FRARI (ST. MARY'S CHURCH) Known simply as the *Frari,* this Gothic Franciscan church is considered by many to be the most splendid in Venice, after *San Marco.* It contains three unquestioned masterpieces: the *Assumption* and the *Madonna of Ca' Pesaro,* both by Titian, and Giovanni Bellini's triptych on the sacristy altar. Also not to be missed are the intricately carved wood choir (15th century), the marble, pyramid-shaped mausoleum for the 19th-century sculptor Canova, and Donatello's wooden sculpture of St. John the Baptist in the apse. Closed Mondays through Saturdays for a midday break; open Sundays and holidays from 3 to 5 PM only. Admission charge. Near the *Scuola Grande di San Rocco. Vaporetto* stop San Tomà. Campo dei Frari, San Polo (phone: 522-2637).

CHIESA DI SANTA MARIA DEL CARMELO (CHURCH OF OUR LADY OF MOUNT CARMEL) Also known as the *Chiesa dei Carmini* (Church of the Carmelites), this Gothic 14th-century church with a 17th-century campanile—crowned by a statue of the Virgin—still has original gilded wooden ornamentation in its nave. Also worthy of attention are its walls, which are lined with many 17th- and 18th-century paintings. Open daily, with a long (noon to 4:30 PM) closing. *Vaporetto* stop Rezzonico. Campo Santa Margherita, Dorsoduro (phone: 522-6553).

CHIESA DI SANTI GIOVANNI E PAOLO, OR SAN ZANIPOLO (CHURCH OF STS. JOHN AND PAUL) One of Venice's most significant, this massive, Gothic Dominican church was consecrated in 1430. Its marble interior is dominated by a profusion of ornate tombs where 25 doges are buried. There also are huge carved monuments to the Mocenigo family dynasty; an urn containing the unfortunate Venetian martyr Marcantonio Bragadin's skin; the important Bellini polyptych *SS Vincent Ferrer, Christopher, and Sebastian*; and a shrine containing the foot of St. Catherine of Siena. Most memorable of all is the 16th-century *Cappella del Rosario,* a richly decorated little chapel. Bring 500 lire to illuminate the newly restored, brilliantly colored oil paintings on the ceiling by Veronese. *Vaporetto* stop Rialto, Campo SS Giovanni e Paolo, Castello (phone: 523-7510).

SCUOLA GRANDE DEI CARMINI (GREAT SCHOOL OF THE CARMELITES) Next to the *Chiesa di Santa Maria del Carmelo,* this gracious 17th-century palace contains the most extensive collection of works by Giambattista Tiepolo anywhere in Venice. Closed Sundays and for a long (noon to 3 PM) break. Admission charge. *Vaporetto* stop Rezzonico. Campo Santa Margherita, Dorsoduro (phone: 528-9420).

SCUOLA SAN GIORGIO DEGLI SCHIAVONI (SCHOOL OF ST. GEORGE OF THE SLAVONIANS OR DALMATIANS) Beyond Piazza San Marco in a part of the city most visitors do not tour, this small building contains some of the city's most overlooked treasures: nine 16th-century masterworks by Vittore Carpaccio depicting stories of St. George (patron of the *scuola*), St. Jerome, and St. Tryphon. Poorly lit and in need of restoration, it's worth a visit if you're in the neighborhood. Closed Tuesdays through Sundays for a long (12:30 to 3:30 PM) break and Mondays and holidays after 12:30 PM. Admission charge. *Vaporetto* stop San Zaccaria. Calle dei Furlani, Castello (phone: 522-8828).

JEWISH GHETTO Venice's ghetto—the world's first—gave its name to all other confined Jewish communities. The word comes from *geto,* which in the old Venetian dialect means foundry. Before 1516, when Venice's entire Jewish population was forced to move to an abandoned arsenal on a small, naturally isolated island in the *sestiere* of Cannaregio, they had lived predominantly on the Isola della Giudecca, "Island of the Jews." The 700 Jews who moved to the Ghetto Nuovo (New Ghetto) grew to 5,000 within a century. In 1541, an adjoining area, the Ghetto Vecchio (Old Ghetto), was annexed, followed by the Ghetto Nuovissimo (Newest Ghetto) in 1633. All three areas are characterized by "skyscrapers"—some seven stories high, with ceilings as low as six feet—that utilized every inch of the area's limited space to accommodate the waves of Jewish immigrants who arrived here from all over Europe. It was not until Napoleon arrived in 1797 that Venice's Jews were declared free citizens and allowed to live where they pleased. A small number of Jewish families continue to live here today. Five synagogues in the ghetto (the oldest is the *German Synagogue,* built in 1528 and home of the *Museo Ebraico*—see *Museums*) still stand in the three adjacent ghettos. The synagogues can be visited only as part of a frequent, multilingual tour that begins at the museum. Take *vaporetto* No. 1 or 82 to San Marcuola, or walk northeast from the train station for five minutes (phone: 715359).

ENVIRONS

LIDO For most of the 20th century, this shoestring island—across the lagoon from Venice proper—was one of the world's most extravagant resorts. Indeed, the word *lido* has come to mean any fashionable, luxuriously equipped beach resort. There has always been a touch of decadence to the Venetian Lido, with its elegant, rambling hotels, sumptuous villas, swank casino, and world-weary, wealthy clientele. Thomas Mann used the Lido's posh *Grand Hotel des Bains* (see *Checking In*) as a background for his haunting novella *Death in Venice.*

Tourists still come by the thousands—some drawn by the water activities and sports, others by the tinsel of an international film festival, many by the trendiness of the biennial art celebration, still others by the comfort of being able to keep a car while in Venice (there also are buses on the island). Most, however, are lured by the legendary Lido ambience, though the resort has lost some of its glamour. If you are not staying at a Lido hotel, you'll have to settle for sunning on the public beach, or pay a high rental to use a cabaña for the day. You can keep a car on the Lido relatively easily, especially if you take advantage of your hotel's parking arrangements, but you must first get your car there. Car ferry ("Trasporto Automezzi") No. 17 leaves the island of Tronchetto for Lido and vice versa about once every hour and a half. You can always leave the car at Piazzale Roma or Tronchetto and take advantage of the island's public buses. If you bring your car to the Lido and have no hotel arrangements for parking, there is a public parking facility on Via Sandro Gallo, off Via S. M. Elisabetta.

If you're willing to travel away from the center of the island, you might try the white tranquil beaches of Alberoni, an area best known for its world class golf course and very casual lifestyle. Be forewarned: Most of the island shuts down in winter. The Lido can be reached by frequent boat service from *vaporetto* stops throughout Venice (lines No. 1, 6, 14, 52, and 82); it's less than a 15-minute ride from Riva degli Schiavoni.

MURANO The island home of Venetian glass making since the 13th century affords visitors an opportunity to watch the glass blowing and molding processes at one of its factories, but be prepared for the high-pressure tactics used to sell the glass. Also on the island is the *Museo Vetrario* (Glass Museum), which chronicles the history of glass making (see *Museums*). Murano is 15 minutes by the No. 5 or No. 12 *vaporetto* from the Riva degli Schiavoni or five minutes on the No. 52 from Fondamente Nuove.

BURANO The colorful homes, small boats, and nets and tackle of the fishermen who live here add charm to this little island, best known as a center of lace making, which still is practiced by a few island women. Burano is 40 minutes by the No. 12 *vaporetto* from Fondamente Nuove. It is more convenient, though a longer trip, to take the No. 14 from San Zaccaria, which goes on to Torcello (see below) after Burano.

TORCELLO One of the first and most prosperous colonies on the lagoon in the 5th and 6th centuries, Torcello declined as Venice grew. Today the main square is overgrown with grass. Most of the cathedral dates from the 7th to 13th centuries. It has several fine Byzantine mosaics, an interesting iconostasis, and a couple of noteworthy restaurants (see *Eating Out*). During peak seasons and hours, the island can get crowded with organized day trips. It is an hour-long ride from San Zaccaria on the No. 14 *vaporetto*.

SAN LAZZARO DEGLI ARMENI Once visited almost exclusively by tourists of Armenian descent, this small island has become popular among people who have an interest in Venice's past liaisons with the East. Its Benedictine monastery has been home to a small but thriving order of Armenian Mechitarist monks since the early 17th century. The monastery is open daily to the public from 3 to 5 PM, just enough time for a guided tour by one of the monks; the tour includes a visit to its library, which houses 4,000 manuscripts (many of them Armenian and some dating from the 8th century BC). A Tiepolo fresco adorns the ceiling above the monastery's entrance. It's a 10-minute ride on the No. 20 *vaporetto*, which leaves (infrequently) from the San Zaccaria stop. We suggest taking the 2:55 PM boat, which dovetails with the limited hours that the monastery is open to the public. Donation suggested (phone: 526-0104).

EXTRA SPECIAL

South of Venice is the seaside town of Chioggia, once a major stronghold of the Venetian Republic. Now little more than a fishing port, it retains charming traces of its past glory. The 13th-century *Chiesa di San Domenico* displays works by Carpaccio and Tintoretto; the highly decorated Baroque altar contrasts with its simpler surroundings. There are numerous other small churches in Chioggia, some in a poor state of repair, but all with significant works of Venetian art. The *Duomo,* at the end of Corso del Popolo, is a grandiose 17th-century cathedral reconstructed on the ruins of the original 12th-century church. Inside, paintings recount some of the history and sacred legends of Chioggia. Around the corner is the celebrated Piazza Vescovile. Bordered by plane trees and an ornamented balustrade, it has been a favorite subject for painters through the ages. Chioggia can be reached by boat, passing several other lagoon islands on the way, or by bus from the *Piazzale Roma* bus station. On the waterfront is *El Gato* (653 Campo Sant'Andrea; phone: 401806), an excellent, moderately priced alfresco restaurant (closed Mondays and January; major credit cards accepted) specializing in local fish from the Adriatic, served with salads and local wines.

Sources and Resources

TOURIST INFORMATION

Stop in at the *Azienda di Promozione Turistica (APT)* office near *Harry's Bar (Palazzetto Selva*; phone: 522-6356 or 529-8730) or at *Santa Lucia* train station (phone: 719078) for maps and listings of hotels, museum hours, and special events. The *Palazzetto Selva* office is open daily; the *APT* at the station is closed Sundays. The *Assessorato al Turismo* (in the *Ca' Giustinian;* phone: 270-7735) has information about the city's cultural events; it's closed Sundays and after 2 PM. The *Biennale* organization also is housed there. For information about winter activities, particularly cultural events and off-season hotel discounts, contact *Promove* (2233 Corte del Teatro San Moisè, San Marco; phone: 521-0200; fax: 521-0125).

A *Biglietto Cumulativo* pass (available at the *Palazzo Ducale*) grants the holder access for one year to nine of the city's museums, including the *Palazzo Ducale,* the *Civico Museo Correr,* and the *Galleria Arte Moderna.* For visitors ages 14 to 29 years, the handy *Rolling Venice* card allows free or discounted access to most museums, exhibits, and concerts; it is available from the *Assessorato alla Gioventù* (1529 Corte Contarina, San Marco; phone: 270-7646). Passholders also get reduced rates for transportation, hotels, restaurants, and shops. Proof of age and a passport-size photo are required.

LOCAL COVERAGE The biweekly (monthly in winter) *Un Ospite a Venezia* (A Guest in Venice) is a useful multilingual publication, available at the concierge desks of most major hotels. It lists museum schedules, special events, entertainment programs, gondola and motorboat taxi rates, *vaporetto* routes, and other handy information. *The Companion Guide to Venice* by Hugh Honour (London: Collins; $29.50), a sensitive, well-written guide to the city, is available in many bookstores.

TELEPHONE The city code for Venice is 41. When calling from within Italy, dial 041 before the local number.

GETTING AROUND

Losing yourself in Venice is inevitable—and recommended. However, major confusion can be avoided by knowing a few facts. Since 1711, Venice has been divided into six *sestieri* (literally, "sixths", or wards): San Marco, Castello, Cannaregio, San Polo, Dorsoduro, and Santa Croce. The largest of the six—the area surrounding Piazza San Marco—is San Marco. The *sestieri* are used as points of reference and are part of a location's address. All buildings have two addresses: One is the official mailing address; the other is a specific street address. A store's vague mailing address, for instance, could be 2250 San Marco, while its street address (far more useful to the visitor) is 2250 Calle dei Fuseri, San Marco.

There are no cars in Venice, except on the Lido. After crossing the 3-mile-long Ponte della Libertà, which connects the mainland to Venice, visitors must leave their cars in the lots and garages (*autorimessa*) at either the island of Tronchetto (from there take the No. 82 boat to the Lido, San Marco, and other stops) or, slightly farther, the *Garage Comunale* or *San Marco* parking facilities at Piazzale Roma (passenger boats No. 1, 52, and 82 also go to San Marco and other destinations from the Piazzale Roma). All three sites have both *all'aperto* (indoor) and *al coperto* (outdoor) parking; the daily rate is often based on the size of the vehicle. Most spaces at the Piazzale Roma are rented by Venetians, so finding a spot here may be difficult. Many of the finer hotels offer free or discounted parking at the Piazzale Roma; be sure to check when booking. *Note:* Don't leave anything in your car; even though there are attendants and a "security patrol" at all lots, things have been known to disappear. A less expensive alternative (and a way to avoid high-season congestion) for those arriving by car is to park in mainland Mestre, right across from the station, and catch the frequent train to Venice, a journey of only 10 minutes or so. An added advantage of this strategy is that the sight of Venice has a far greater impact when one steps out of the train terminal into the city's beauty.

AIRPORT *Marco Polo Airport* (in Tessera; phone: 260-9260) serves domestic and international flights. Eight miles (13 km) from the city, it is reachable by the public *motoscafo* (motorboat) service, which connects the airport to Piazza San Marco and the Lido (the schedule is casually coordinated with arriving and departing flights; leave yourself plenty of time). A private *taxi acquei* (motorboat taxi) for up to four people is a more expensive option; it will deliver you as close to your hotel door as possible. *ACTV* bus No. 5 is the least expensive way to travel between the airport and the parking area of Piazzale Roma; buy a bus ticket at the newsstand in the airport lobby. Ask for time schedules at the tourist office in the *Palazzetto Selva*; also consult *Un Ospite a Venezia*.

BUS AND TRAIN The main bus station (phone: 528-7886) is at Piazzale Roma; the train station, *Stazione Santa Lucia* (phone: 715555), is on the Canal Grande, not far from the bus station.

GONDOLA A 50-minute tour of the city in one of these sleek, black boats is rather expensive, and the price rises after 8 PM. But it's a unique experience, particularly at night, when the pale moonlight drapes the city's Gothic palaces in silver, and the island of San Giorgio Maggiore and the Rialto Bridge all become a heart-stopping stage that calls to mind Robert Browning's *In a Gondola* and Thomas Mann's *Death in Venice.* Unless you give the gondolier specific directions, he will determine the route and may or may not play tour guide (at no extra cost). Sing, he won't. If you're looking for those romantic *barcaroli* you saw in Katharine Hepburn's *Summertime,* make arrangements through your hotel for a nighttime "Gondola Serenade." Depending on the request, a number of gondolas (from two to ten) will travel together, sharing the accordion music and Italian songs of an accompanying duo. It won't be intimate, but it will be lots of fun. A less costly alternative is a daytime gondola-ferry, called a *traghetto,* that crosses the Canal Grande at seven points. The ride, which lasts only a minute, can be exciting, as the drivers dodge *vaporetti* and *taxi acquei.* When in Venice, the tradition is to stand.

MOTOSCAFI AND VAPORETTI The small boats that make up the *ACTV* municipal transit system are inexpensive and fun. The *motoscafi* are express boats making only a few important stops, and they cost a bit more than *vaporetti.* The *vaporetti* are much slower; Nos. 1 and 82 ply leisurely along the length of the Canal Grande (ironically, the No. 1 is named *accelerato,* although it is the slowest). In peak season, additional boats are added to accommodate the crush. If you're in a big hurry to get to the station or elsewhere, ask your hotel to call a taxi. It's not quite as expensive as a gondola, and it's faster (phone: 522-2303). There is a movement afoot by environmentalists to replace them all with electric boats.

Two passes allow unlimited travel during a specific time period, such as 24 hours or three days. Check pass regulations, as some lines are excluded.

TOURS The *Associazione Guide Turistiche* (5267 Calle delle Bande, Castello; phone: 520-9038; fax: 521-0762) has a list of multilingual tour guides whose fixed rates are approved by the local tourist board. Or contact New York–born, longtime Venice resident Samantha Durell at the *Venice Travel Advisory* (phone: 523-2379; phone/fax: 212-873-1964 in the US; fax: 526-5615) for a private back-street walking tour. Many agencies offer walking and boat tours and day trips to the outer islands or to the Veneto. Two of the most reliable are *Ital Travel* (72b Ascensione San Marco; phone: 523-6511) and *Kele & Teo* (4930 Ponte dei Bareteri, San Marco; phone: 520-8722; fax: 520-8913).

SPECIAL EVENTS
Venice is famous for its spectacles of fantasy and frolic.

FAVORITE FETES

Carnevale While *Carnevale* officially starts about two weeks before *Ash Wednesday* (March 1 this year), Venetians really don't begin festivities until about a week before. *Carnevale* is a pre-*Lenten* festival that was revived in the early 1980s in Venice. Today, it's celebrated with a profusion of amazing costumes, outdoor and indoor entertainment events, a few private (and expensive) masked balls, and, most important, an air of gaiety and lightheartedness rather unique to this otherwise introverted and insular village. Piazza San Marco and the neighboring streets become extremely crowded, noisy, and often difficult to pass through, while back-street routes, restaurants, and hotels remain, as always, relatively tranquil. Bring masks and costumes from home, or buy them from well-stocked mask and costume stores in Venice; bring a camera and lots of color film; purchase concert tickets as soon as you arrive to ensure a place; and then lose yourself in the joyous moment of a city reliving its glorious history. The grand finale involves fireworks over the lagoon on *Shrove Tuesday.* The crowds often swell to more than 100,000.

Festa del Redentore (Feast of the Redeemer) For centuries, Venice has been commemorating the end of a deadly 16th-century plague with this joyous festival. On the third Saturday of July, a bridge of pontoons is built across the Canale della Giudecca, from the door of the *Chiesa del Redentore* to Zattere. The church, designed by Palladio and built as an offering of thanks for the end of the terrible plague, is open that Saturday and Sunday for visiting and mass. Early Saturday morning, the energy building throughout the Canale Giudecca and Bacino San Marco is palpable, as boats of all shapes, sizes, and degrees of luxury arrive from ports far and near, their passengers jockeying for position, opening bottles of wine, and setting out food, flowers, and lounge chairs within minutes of putting down anchor. The Venetians themselves are somewhat casual in their timing—it's their city, and they know where they'll be parking—so they spend the day canalside on the streets, decorating their boats with paper Chinese lanterns and lights and setting up massive "feast" tables that practically take up the whole boat. As dusk approaches, the water-based social event gets under way: Boats take their places, and celebrants eat, drink, and greet their neighbors. At 11 PM the sky explodes for a half hour of spectacular fireworks, followed by a crescendo of the tooting of hundreds of horns. As the frenzy dies down, the great pontoon "bridge" opens, and for the next 24 hours, boats make the trek across the water. Spectators on land crowd the canalside *fondamente* to watch the festivities and then keep San Marco's restaurants busy into the wee hours of the morning.

April 25 is the *Festa di San Marco,* the feast day of Venice's beloved patron saint, when loved ones exchange red roses and a special high mass is celebrated in the *Basilica di San Marco* at 10 AM. In mid-May (usually on a Sunday), Venetians of all ages and in all kinds of boats participate in *Vogalonga,* a local regatta second only in popularity and color to the *Regata Storica* (see below). The regatta starts at 9 AM at the *Molo* off Piazza San Marco. Every four years in early June, the city hosts the *Regata Storica delle Repubbliche Marinare,* the race and procession of costumes and historic boats that hark back to the 11th century, when Venice was one of the most powerful maritime republics (the others were Amalfi, Genoa, and Pisa). The festival rotates among the four cities; Venice's next turn will be in 1998. The annual *Mostra Internazionale di Cinematografica* (International Film Festival) is held on the Lido in late August and early September, and in odd-numbered years, the important *Esposizione Internazionale d'Arte Moderna* (International Exposition of Modern Art), better known as *Biennale d'Arte,* takes place in a small park beyond the Riva dei Sette Martiri from June through October. On the first Sunday in September, gondola races and a magnificent procession of decorated barges and gondolas filled with Venetians in Renaissance dress highlight the *Regata Storica* (Historic Regatta) on the Canal Grande. Every September or October (October 8 this year), a marathon starts along the Veneto's Brenta Canal and follows the tow paths, passing Palladian villas and ending in the center of Venice at the *Basilica di San Marco.* Runners ,who want information about competing can contact the *Venice Marathon Secretariat* (34 Via Felisati, Mestre; phone: 940644; fax: 940349) or the tourist office in the *Palazzetto Selva* (see *Tourist Information,* above). To celebrate the *Festa della Salute* on November 21, another "bridge" of boats is formed from Santa Maria del Giglio to the *Chiesa di Santa Maria della Salute.*

MUSEUMS

Besides those mentioned in *Special Places,* Venice has a number of museums of special interest. Days and hours vary with the season and with the funds available. Last tickets usually are sold an hour before closing. For current schedules, check with the *APT* in the *Palazzetto Selva* (see *Tourist Information*) or look in *Un Ospite a Venezia.*

CA' D'ORO OR GALLERIA GIORGIO FRANCHETTI (FRANCHETTI GALLERY) Venice's second-most famous palace (the first is the *Palazzo Ducale)* is the setting for Baron Franchetti's private collection of bronze sculpture from the 12th through the 16th century as well as important Renaissance paintings from Venice and Tuscany. Closed after 1:30 PM. Admission charge. *Vaporetto* stop Ca' d'Oro. 3932 Canal Grande, Cannaregio (phone: 523-8790).

CIVICO MUSEO CORRER (CORRER CIVIC MUSEUM) Documentary and curio remains of Venetian history are the subject of this museum in Piazza San Marco's *Ala Napoleonica* (Napoleonic Wing). Among the treasures here is a collection of Venetian coins. The museum also has a picture gallery with works from the 13th to the 18th century, along with prints, sketches, and ceramics. Closed Tuesdays. Admission charge. *Vaporetto* stop San Marco. Piazza San Marco (phone: 522-5625).

COLLEZIONE PEGGY GUGGENHEIM (PEGGY GUGGENHEIM COLLECTION) Peggy Guggenheim's private collection of modern art, now managed by New York City's *Solomon R. Guggenheim Foundation,* includes works from the cubist, surrealist, and abstract expressionist movements. Artists represented include Picasso, Braque, Max Ernst (one of Ms. Guggenheim's husbands), and Jackson Pollock (her discovery). Closed Tuesdays. Admission charge. *Vaporetto* stop Accademia. *Palazzo Venier dei Leoni*, 701 Calle Cristoforo, Dorsoduro (phone: 520-6288).

GALLERIA D'ARTE MODERNA (MODERN ART GALLERY) A small (50 paintings at press time) but impressive collection of 20th-century art, it includes works by Kandinsky, Klimt, Morandi, and De Chirico. It is housed in the *Ca' Pesaro*— a handsome 17th-century palazzo sitting directly on the Canal Grande. Closed Mondays, and Tuesdays through Sundays after 1 PM in summer; closed Mondays in winter. Admission charge. *Vaporetto* stop San Stae. *Palazzo Ca' Pesaro,* San Polo (phone: 721127).

GALLERIA DI PALAZZO CINI (CINI GALLERY) Count Vittorio Cini's magnificent private collection of Tuscan artwork and temporary exhibits of paintings are mounted in his home near the *Accademia* and the *Collezione Peggy Guggenheim.* Open Tuesdays through Sundays from 1 to 7 PM in summer only. Admission charge. *Vaporetto* stop Salute or Accademia. 864 San Vio, Dorsoduro (phone: 521-0755).

MUSEO EBRAICO (JEWISH MUSEUM) A visit to the Jewish Ghetto is incomplete without a stop at this small museum, which houses a collection of memorabilia from the early ghetto days. The staff conducts hourly tours of the museum in English as well as interesting visits to some of the ghetto's synagogues otherwise closed to the public. Tours leave on the half hour from 10:30 AM to 3:30 PM. Closed Saturdays. Admission charge. *Vaporetto* stop Ponte delle Guglie or San Marcuola. 2902 Campo del Ghetto Nuovo, Cannaregio (phone: 715359).

MUSEO FORTUNY (FORTUNY MUSEUM) For 42 years, Mariano Fortuny, the Spanish-born fashion designer and master of fabric, made this 15th-century Gothic palazzo his home. Today visitors can view his sketches, collection of paintings and sculpture, and samples of the pleated silk fabrics for which he was famous, as well as changing exhibits of other artists and artifacts from around the world. Closed Mondays. Admission charge. *Vaporetto* stop Sant'Angelo. 3780 Campo San Beneto, San Marco (phone: 520-0995).

MUSEO D'ICONE DELL'ISTITUTO ELLENICO (ICON MUSEUM OF THE HELLENISTIC INSTITUTE) Housed in the 17th-century, Longhena-designed *Collegio Greco,* it boasts one of the largest collections (80 pieces) of Byzantine icons in Western Europe; the works were painted by Greek artists called *madon-*

neri. Next door is the 16th-century *Chiesa di San Giorgio dei Greci* (with its leaning bell tower), the spiritual home of Venice's Greek population. Museum closed Sundays and for a short (1 to 2 PM) break. Admission charge. *Vaporetto* stop San Zaccaria. Calle dei Greci, Castello (phone: 522-6581).

MUSEO NAVALE (NAVAL MUSEUM) During the heyday of the Republic, Venice's naval exploits were legendary. This museum's displays of model ships and historical artifacts tell the story of how the city built a shipping industry on principles of mass production to become master of the Mediterranean. Closed Sundays, holidays, and after 1 PM. Admission charge. *Vaporetto* stop Arsenale. 2148 Campo San Biagio, Castello (phone: 520-0276).

MUSEO VETRARIO (GLASS MUSEUM) A trip to Murano, the island of glass making, is incomplete without a visit to this impressive showcase of Venice's unique and indigenous craft. Most noteworthy is the two-floor display of 4,000 pieces that chronicles the origins, innovations, and diversities of Murano glass making; also on display are glass pieces—from wedding goblets to elaborate chandeliers and mirrors. Closed Mondays. Admission charge. *Vaporetto* stop Museo, Murano. 8 Fondamenta Giustinian (phone: 739586).

PALAZZO GRASSI Designed by Giorgio Massari in the 18th century as a private residence, this palazzo is the city's most-visited (second only to the *Palazzo Ducale*). Splendidly restored by Italy's famous architect Gae Aulenti, it's the site of important artistic expositions of international themes. Open for special exhibits only. Admission charge. *Vaporetto* stop San Samuele. 3231 Campo San Samuele, San Marco (phone: 523-1680).

SHOPPING

Venetian glass is seductive, but much of it made today is of poor quality and design (visit the museum and factories on Murano—see *Special Places*—to get an idea of what to look for). With a keen eye to cut through the trinkets, you'll find winning souvenirs—from inexpensive necklaces of colorful Venetian glass beads to a simple, handsome decanter or perfume flacon. Other items worth purchasing are traditional handmade papier-mâché *Carnevale* masks, which have been enjoying a renaissance since the fete was reinstated in the early 1980s. Almost all souvenir shops carry a sampling—from the authentic and historical to the modern and bizarre. Handmade lace can be exorbitantly expensive, but small, simple pieces can be charming and affordable. The widest selection can be found on Burano and in the shops around Piazza San Marco. In addition, handmade marbleized paper products make lovely and easily transportable gifts.

Two of the city's most colorful outdoor food markets—the *Erberia* for produce (closed Sundays) and the *Pescheria* for fish (closed Mondays)—are held near the Ponte di Rialto. It is fascinating to wander here, even if you aren't shopping.

A twice-annual *Mercantino dell'Antiquariato* (Antiques Fair) sets up in the small Campo San Maurizio (midway between Piazza San Marco and Campo Santo Stefano) the week before *Easter* and *Christmas.*

Venice's main shopping district is the area directly surrounding and west of Piazza San Marco and in the Mercerie area, which leads from the Piazza San Marco to the Ponte di Rialto in the north. Most shops are open from 9:30 AM to 12:30 PM and 3:30 to 7 or 7:30 PM; closed Sundays and Monday mornings. Food stores are closed Sundays and Wednesday afternoons. Most Venetian merchants accept major American credit cards, and though they don't look kindly on bargaining, it's still worth a try.

Anticlea Antiquariato The eclectic treasures here include antique Venetian glass beads, old glass, lace, porcelain, antique maps of Venice, and other collectibles. Just east of Piazza San Marco, at 4719/A San Provolo, Castello (phone: 528-6946).

Arianna da Venezia Convenient if you're visiting the *Ca' Rezzonico* museum next door, this shop is chockablock with exquisite hand-printed velvet items, from bed covers and throw pillows to jackets, wall hangings, and *Carnevale* masks, all done by the owner in the old *Fortuny* textile factory, still operating on Giudecca. 2793 Fondamenta del Traghetto, Dorsoduro (phone: 522-1535).

Bottega Veneta The flagship of this world class store offers beautifully made leather goods in rich colors. 1337 Calle Vallaresso, San Marco (phone: 522-8489).

La Coupole A temple to Milan's highest fashion for men and women, with prices to match. Two locations: 1674 Frezzeria, San Marco (phone: 520-6063), and 2366 Calle Larga XXII Marzo, San Marco (phone: 522-4243).

Dominici A centrally located and interesting collection of antique silverware and china. 659-664 Calle Larga San Marco, San Marco (phone: 522-3892).

Al Duca d'Aosta Sports clothes and accessories for men (4946 Mercerie del Capitello, San Marco; phone: 522-0733) and women (across the street, at No. 4922; phone: 520-4079).

Ebrû Lovely hand-crafted marbled paper and ready-made and custom gift items. Two locations: 3135 Salizzada San Samuele, San Marco (phone: 520-0921), and 3471 Calle Santo Stefano, San Marco (phone: 523-8830).

Elysée Haute designerwear for women from Italian and international high priests of fashion. 4485 Calle Goldoni, San Marco (phone: 523-6948).

F. G. B. Quality handmade Venetian crafts—especially masks in papier-mâché, glass, wood, and ceramics. 2459 Campo Santa Maria del Giglio, San Marco (phone: 523-6556).

Fantoni Libri Arte Illustrated art, architecture, design, and textile books, as well as a number of handsome works on Venice (most in Italian). 4119 Salizzada San Luca, San Marco (phone: 522-0700).

L'Isola Contemporary museum-quality glassware designed by the Carlo Moretti firm—the pieces are simple. 1468 Campo San Moisè, San Marco (phone: 523-1973).

Jesurum & Co. Exquisite lace and other handmade needlework, all displayed in a lovely, deconsecrated church (4310 Ponte della Canonica, Castello; phone: 520-6177), and a much smaller selection at its convenient branch (60 Piazza San Marco; phone: 522-9864).

Legatoria Piazzesi Notebooks, boxes, albums, and other gift articles crafted from handmade marbleized papers in classic Italian style. 2511 Campiello della Feltrina, San Marco (phone: 522-1202).

Livio de Marchi Everyday objects—from rumpled shopping bags to hats and shoes—seem sculpted from putty by this eccentric artist who is said to be to wood what Michelangelo was to marble. 3157 Salizzada San Samuele, San Marco (phone: 528-5694).

Luigi Bevilacqua These silk brocade, damask, and printed velvet fabrics have draped European courts, the Vatican, and the White House. 1320 Campiello Comare, Santa Croce (phone: 721384).

M. Antichità e Oggetti d'Arte Between Piazza San Marco and *La Fenice,* this jewel of an antiques store has exotic and romantic curiosities redolent of Venice's past. 1690 Frezzeria, San Marco (phone: 523-5666).

Marco Polo Vetri d'Arte On this popular store-lined street west of Piazza San Marco is a great selection of contemporary Murano glass, ranging from serious (and pricey) works by master artisans to small, gift-size items. 1644 Frezzeria, San Marco (phone: 522-9295).

Mondonovo The city's best *mascheraio* (mask maker) offers papier-mâché masks—alligators, camels, and mummies, as well as traditional *commedia dell'arte*—for *Carnevale.* 3063 Campo Santa Margherita, Dorsoduro (phone: 528-7344).

Murano Art Shop The city's most interesting collection of locally made artworks—from traditional to innovative. 1149 Frezzeria, San Marco (phone: 528-7543).

Nardi Beautiful high-quality jewelry in the Venetian tradition—both new and antique. 69 Piazza San Marco, San Marco (phone: 522-5733).

Nicolao Atelier *Carnevale* and theater costume maker to the stars, Stefano Nicolao lives in a fantasy world of brocade, lace, and velvet. Orders flood in from around the world year-round for his four-digit-priced creations. 5565 Calle del Bagatin, Cannaregio (phone: 520-7051).

Paola Carraro Unique oversize sweaters made of silk, mohair, or cotton that are hand-knit renditions of some of the world's great contemporary master-pieces—from Klee to Picasso, Magritte to Warhol. On the street from the

Accademia to the *Guggenheim*. 869 Calle Nuova Sant'Agnesa, Dorsoduro (phone: 520-6070).

Pauly Venetian glass by one of the star producers. Two locations: Ponte dei Consorzi, Castello (phone: 520-9899), and 73 Piazza San Marco (phone: 523-5484).

Il Prato Elaborate, fantasy, and traditional *Carnevale* masks and attire. 1770 Frezzeria, San Marco (phone: 520-3375).

Rigattieri Simple white and colorful ceramics, many from the Veneto region. 3532 Calle dei Frati, San Marco (phone: 523-1081).

Rubelli A Venetian landmark and one of Europe's most celebrated names in exquisite fabrics, some still made by hand on 15th-century looms. 1089 Campo San Gallo, San Marco (phone: 523-6110).

Tragicomica One of Venice's more serious mask workshops, at two locations. The original is near Campo San Polo at 1414 Campiello dei Meloni, San Polo (phone: 523-5831); the newer, more impressive selection is across the alley-way from playwright Carlo Goldoni's home at 2800 Calle dei Nomboli, San Polo (phone: 721102).

V. Trois Luxurious Fortuny fabrics and other exquisite new and antique Venetian fabrics. 2666 Campo San Maurizio, San Marco (phone: 522-2905).

Venetia Studium The ultimate Venetian souvenirs—exquisite replicas of fashion and home decorating accessories taken from colorful Fortuny designs. For serious buyers, the store has a large, museum-like palazzo location near *La Fenice* (ask at this shop if you are interested; a salesperson will accompany you there). 2403 Calle Larga XXII Marzo, San Marco (phone: 522-9281).

Venini The only Venetian retail store for this world-famous design company of contemporary hand-blown glass. 314 Piazzetta dei Leoncini, San Marco (phone: 522-4045).

Vogini Venice's oldest (and perhaps finest) leather goods store occupies four convenient locations—all next to each other and just a minute's walk from the Piazza San Marco. 1291, 1292, 1301, and 1305 Calle II dell'Ascensione, San Marco (phone: 522-2573).

SPORTS AND FITNESS

Visitors to Venice get plenty of exercise climbing up, down, and across its hundreds of bridges. For more organized sports, one must move to the open spaces of the Lido, where the CIGA chain pretty much has the monopoly on sports activities. What they don't own, they manage, and with one phone call or fax, you can book tennis, windsurfing, water skiing, golf, or a beach cabaña. Contact them from April through October at 52 Lungomare Marconi, Lido (phone: 526-7194; fax: 526-0058).

BICYCLING A well-stocked place to rent bikes is the Lido's *Giorgio Barbieri* (5 Via Zara; phone: 526-1490).

FITNESS CENTER *International Club* (4249 Campo Manin; phone: 528-9830) is one of the few fitness centers in Venice open to visitors.

GOLF A surprising plus in this water-based wonderland, Venice boasts a first-rate island course.

A TOP TEE-OFF SPOT

Golf Club Lido di Venezia At 6,356 yards, this spectacular 18-hole seaside layout at the far western end of the Lido is long for a continental course. And with tees and greens surrounded by groves of pines, olives, and poplars, it also can be demanding. However, it is extraordinarily well balanced. Certain par 5 holes call for long hitting, while other holes require all the other golfing skills. Concentration is paramount, especially at the seventh hole, the longest par 4, where two bunkers guard the green; the eighth hole, which has a blind approach; and the 14th, which forces a player to avoid a gaggle of scattered traps. Closed Mondays and three weeks over *Christmas*. Via del Forte, Alberoni (phone: 731333; 800-221-2340).

JOGGING The crowded, narrow streets of Venice are not the best place for running, but one 20-minute jog to try is just east of Piazza San Marco; the broad Riva degli Schiavoni runs southeast along the water toward the Riva dei Sette Martiri, the *Giardini Pubblici* (Public Gardens), and the *S. Elena Marina*. Runners also may jog on the beach at the Lido.

SOCCER From September through May, *Venezia* plays at *Stadio Comunale P. L. Penzo* (S. Elena; phone: 522-5770).

SWIMMING The north end of the Lido has municipal beaches, many of which charge admission or make you pay for chair and umbrella rentals. Other beaches along this strip are the domain of the island's luxury hotels, but they rent cabañas for a fee. There is also a public pool at *Piscina Comunale Sacca Fisola* (Via Sandro, Giudecca; phone: 528-5430).

TENNIS On the Lido, the *Tennis Club Venezia* (41/D Lungomare Marconi; phone: 526-7194 or 526-0335) has seven courts (two covered and two lighted). Visitors also can play at the *Tennis Club Lido* (163 Via Sandro Gallo; phone: 526-0954).

THEATER

Music, rather than drama, is the performing art of Venice. If language is not a problem, a pleasant theater for traditional and contemporary productions is *Teatro Goldoni* (4650/B Calle Goldoni, San Marco; phone: 520-

5422). *Teatro Ridotto* (Calle Vallaresso; phone: 522-2939), a delightful little rococo theater, hosts dance performances as well as drama. It's just a two-minute walk from Piazza San Marco.

MUSIC

Venice has a rich musical tradition and a full calendar of musical events—as you will see from the wall posters that announce forthcoming concerts. The following is our favorite forum:

HIGH NOTES

Teatro La Fenice Unprepossessing from the outside, this *istituzione nazionale* is a titan on the local and national arts scene and an architectural marvel within, from its wonderfully symmetrical grand staircase and mirrored corridors to the magnificent chandeliers, the scallop-topped velvet curtain, and the ceiling resplendent with rosy cherubs. *La Scala*'s greatest rival for national preeminence, *La Fenice* premiered Verdi's *Attila, Ernani, Rigoletto, La Traviata,* and *Simone Boccanegra* as well as Stravinsky's *Rake's Progress* and Britten's *Turn of the Screw*. The opera season raises its curtain annually in November or December and runs through July, with many high-quality ballet, orchestral, and recital events interspersed throughout the year. 1977 Campo San Fantin, San Marco (phone: 521-0161; fax: 522-1768).

All year, concerts take place in various churches, where the acoustics can be quite extraordinary, and the setting is as rich in beauty and history as the musical offerings are. Such gifted chamber music groups as the *Solisti Veneti* and talented musical directors like Riccardo Parravicini guarantee rewarding performances. Concerts also are held inside the ornate salons of famous palaces, venues that make for equally unique experiences. There is an admission charge to almost all performances.

The *Chiesa della Pietà* (Church of the Pietà), more commonly called the *Chiesa di Vivaldi* (Church of Vivaldi)—on the Riva degli Schiavoni in Castello—is where Antonio Vivaldi lived, worked, and served as the church's choirmaster and resident priest. Concerts take place here at least five evenings per month; the *Metropole* hotel next door can supply program information, and tickets can be purchased through your hotel concierge, through one of the many travel agencies (such as *Kele & Teo*, 4930 Ponte dei Bareteri, San Marco; phone: 580-8722), or at the church (closed for a midday break) the day before or the day of the concert. Vivaldi's masterpiece *The Four Seasons* is always one of the most popular performances, especially during *Carnevale,* the film festival, and *Christmas* week, when you should secure tickets well in advance.

Another popular setting for classical music concerts is the *Chiesa San Stae* on the Canal Grande in San Polo. Tickets for these performances go on sale the day of the concert at the church or the *Tempio della Musica* music store (5368 Tramo del Fontego, San Marco; phone: 523-4552) in the shadow of the Ponte di Rialto.

NIGHTLIFE

Martini Scala Piano Bar (1980 Campo San Fantin, San Marco; phone: 522-4121), the most chic of Venice's nightspots, is open until 3:30 AM. It shares a kitchen with *Antico Martini* (see *Eating Out*) and offers delicious—albeit limited—light fare at much lower prices than the more upscale restaurant. *Linea d'Ombra* (Fondamenta Zattere, Dorsoduro; phone: 528-5259) has an outdoor dining deck in warm weather on the Canale della Giudecca, with a jazz pianist most weekends. As long as the weather holds, the city's best nightlife is the nonstop show in Piazza San Marco. Take up residence in one of the *caffès,* listen to the schmaltzy orchestra, and watch the world go by. Popular places for rock and disco are the *Acropolis* (Lungomare Marconi; phone: 536-0466), on the Lido, and the *Club El Souk* (1056/A Accademia, Dorsoduro; phone: 520-0371), both open year-round.

For gambling enthusiasts, the *Casino* (Lungomare Marconi, Lido; phone: 526-0626) is open from June through September. During the summer, a special *vaporetto* line leaves the train station about every half hour and deposits visitors just a few steps from the casino. The *Casino/Lido* line also stops at Piazzale Roma and San Zaccaria. The casino's winter home is the handsome *Palazzo Vendramin-Calergi* (on the Canal Grande; phone: 529-7111), open from October through May. Go for the opulent setting, if not to toss some chips. Both casinos are open from 3 PM to 2:30 AM. Bring your passport; men must wear jackets.

Best in Town

CHECKING IN

Your first decision when choosing accommodations in Venice is whether to stay out at the Lido (a summertime consideration only) or in the center of town. Staying in the city, you can look out onto a small picturesque canal or catch a sweeping view of the grand lagoon from the windows of your room. But being on the Lido gets you away from the crowds. Be forewarned—Venice has some of Italy's most expensive hotels and some of its most misleading and deceiving hotel lobbies. Never judge a Venetian hotel by its lobby, and ask to see a room first (a common request). In high season (*Christmas* to January 6, around *Carnevale,* March 15 through June, and September through October), very expensive hotels here charge $300 or more per night for a double room; expensive hotels, from $200 to $300; moderate places, from $135 to $200; inexpensive places, from $65 to $125; and very inexpensive ones, $60 or less. All hotels feature private baths unless otherwise indicated. Most moderately priced hotels tack on a daily supplemental rate for air conditioning. Many offer significant discounts in winter and sometimes in July and August (although the heat and humidity during the summer can make hotels without air conditioning unbearable). Another cost-saving measure is to ask not to have breakfast (generally a less-than-wonderful affair) at the hotel; it can cut your room rate considerably. Those hotels listed below as having "business services" usually offer such conveniences as an English-speaking concierge, meeting rooms, photocopiers, computers, translation services, and express checkout, among others. Call the hotel for additional information.

During peak season, finding accommodations in Venice may be a problem. When the city is sold out, Mestre is a likely, albeit drab, alternative. Just 10 minutes away by train, it has an abundance of hotels in all categories that cost considerably less than those in Venice. All telephone numbers are in the 41 city code unless otherwise indicated.

For an unforgettable stay in Venice, we begin with our favorite *alberghi*, followed by our cost and quality choices, listed by price category.

SPECIAL HAVENS

Cipriani On the serene Isola della Giudecca, this luxurious and elegant three-acre oasis has a beautiful garden surrounding an Olympic-size pool, and stunning views of the nearby Isola San Giorgio. Immaculate but relaxed service and such details as silk Fortuny wallpaper and heavy matching drapes are redolent of days gone by. In addition to the 98 elegant rooms in the main building, there are 10 private apartments and junior suites in the exquisite 15th-century *Palazzo Vendramin* next door. A top-of-the-line one-bedroom suite will cost about $2,000 per night, but more frugal rates are available, starting at $400 per night. A sleek mahogany motorboat whisks guests to and from Piazza San Marco in five minutes, 24 hours a day. The fine restaurant occupies an idyllic setting, and the poolside restaurant is open for lunch and snacks, as well as 24-hour room service. The *Cipriani Culinary Program* offers five-day courses led by experts in various cuisines. Open mid-January through mid-November; *Palazzo Vendramin* open year-round. Business services. The hotel's private launch leaves from *vaporetto* stop San Marco. 10 Isola della Giudecca, Dorsoduro (phone: 520-7744; 800-237-1236; fax: 520-3930).

Gritti Palace Many people—crowned heads of state, film stars, and day dreamers—would rather stay in this one-of-a-kind, 97-room CIGA gem than anywhere else in Europe. Once the Renaissance residence of the Venetian doge Andrea Gritti, who died here in 1538, it is one of the world's most celebrated hotels—famous for excellent service, a classic dining room (see *Antico Martini* in *Eating Out*), and a beautiful dining terrace overlooking the Canal Grande. It also offers its guests 24-hour room service and use of the CIGA sports facilities—private beach, tennis, golf, and horseback riding—on the Lido. Exquisite interiors capture quintessential historical Venice at its best. No two guestrooms are alike, and all are wonderful; those in the front overlook the Canal Grande. The most expensive of CIGA's Venice properties charges as little as $330 for a double and as much as $1,350 for an executive suite. Business services. *Vaporetto* stop Santa Maria del Giglio. 2467 Campo Santa Maria del Giglio, San Marco (phone: 794611; 800-221-2340; fax: 520-0942).

VERY EXPENSIVE

Danieli Once the residence of the 14th-century doge Enrico Dandolo and now one of Venice's largest hotels (three adjoining buildings comprise 222 rooms), this CIGA crown jewel boasts a historic Gothic courtyard, now the hotel lobby in the *Casa Vecchia* (come just for tea if you're not lucky enough to stay here). On the right is the *Casa Nuova,* where rooms are just as opulent, albeit more modern; on the left is the *Danielino,* whose splendid top-floor terrace restaurant affords a bird's-eye view of Isola San Giorgio. There also is 24-hour room service. Rooms in the back may not be worth the price. Business services. *Vaporetto* stop San Zaccaria. 4196 Riva degli Schiavoni, Castello (phone: 522-6480; 800-221-2340; fax: 520-0208).

Locanda Cipriani Even Venetians dream of honeymooning here on the peaceful, otherworldly island of Torcello, 40 minutes from Piazza San Marco. Most settle for a memorable meal (see *Eating Out*), for even though the inn's six country-style rooms are charmingly simple, obligatory half board makes this a costly, albeit gastronomically memorable, escape. You'll never feel so removed from civilization, yet you'll have the luxury of first class dining just downstairs. Opened in 1936 by the man who gave the world *Harry's Bar*, it's now managed by his daughter and grandson. Open mid-March through October. *Vaporetto* stop Torcello. 29 Piazza San Fosca, Torcello (phone: 730150; fax: 735433).

Luna Baglioni A cool marble palace with frescoed ceilings and imposing chandeliers made from Murano glass, this regal 118-room hotel is near the *Giardinetti Reali* (a lovely park) and neighboring *Harry's Bar;* upper floors afford views of the island of San Giorgio. There is a restaurant, and guests have access to numerous sports facilities on the Lido, including discounted access to the golf club. Free parking at Piazzale Roma. Business services. *Vaporetto* stop San Marco. 1243 Calle Vallaresso, San Marco (phone: 528-9840; 800-346-5358; fax: 528-7160).

Bellini Elegant Venetian decor is the hallmark of this 70-room hotel replete with inlaid marble, silk damask wallpaper and matching drapes, authentic period pieces, and impressive Murano chandeliers. Just a block from the train station, it has a restaurant and sun deck with a view of the Canal Grande. Business services. *Vaporetto* stop Ferrovia. 116 Lista di Spagna, Cannaregio (phone: 524-2488; 800-44-UTELL; fax: 715193).

Excelsior Palace Refurbished in an exotic Hispano-Moorish style, this luxurious, 218-room Old World property established the Lido as a luxury seaside resort for Europe's monied set; today, it remains one of Venice's most lavish hotels. Since 1937 it has played a key role in the prestigious *Mostra Internazionale di Cinematografica*, which is held across the street. It has a fine restaurant and 24-hour room service; is right on the beach (the best rooms overlook it); and boasts tennis courts and free transportation to CIGA's horseback riding facilities and a golf course off the hotel's property. The hotel provides guests with free water taxi service to and from Piazza San Marco every half hour. Open *Easter* through October. Business services. *Vaporetto* stop Lido. 41 Lungomare Marconi, Lido (phone: 526-0201; 800-221-2340; fax: 526-7276).

Grand Hotel des Bains On the Lido, this stately, porticoed, old-fashioned hotel is where Luchino Visconti filmed much of *Death in Venice.* Built in 1900, it has been painstakingly renovated to its Belle Epoque splendor. In it are 193 spacious rooms, and across the road are its private beach and luxurious cabañas. Part of the CIGA chain, it shares tennis, golf, and horseback riding facilities, and transportation back and forth from Piazza San Marco every half hour, with its nearby sister hotel, the *Excelsior Palace* (see above). Open *Easter* through October. Business services. *Vaporetto* stop Lido. 17 Lungomare Marconi, Lido (phone: 526-5921; 800-221-2340; fax: 526-0113).

Metropole One of the last big hotels along the stretch of Riva degli Schiavoni toward the *Arsenale,* this hostelry offers 72 antiques-filled rooms and exceptionally amiable service. Room 349, with its elaborately hand-carved wooden bed and one of Venice's famed *altane* (wooden terraces), is our favorite. There is a restaurant, 24-hour room service, business services, and free parking at Piazzale Roma. *Vaporetto* stop San Zaccaria. 4149 Riva degli Schiavoni, Castello (phone: 520-5044; 800-44-UTELL; fax: 522-3679).

Monaco and Grand Canal The intimate seclusion of this elegant and comfortable 72-room hotel is just a minute's walk from Piazza San Marco. Its acclaimed restaurant, suitably named *Grand Canal,* has a lovely flowered terrace directly across from the beautiful *Chiesa di Santa Maria della Salute.* There also is 24-hour room service and business services. *Vaporetto* stop San Marco. 1325 Calle Vallaresso, San Marco (phone: 520-0211; 800-44-UTELL; fax: 520-0501).

Quattro Fontane Transformed from a 19th-century villa, this quiet 68-room hostelry with excellent service offers the peace of an English country garden. It still has the air of a family dwelling, with antique furniture of various origins and a pleasant alfresco restaurant. Open *Easter* through October. Business services are available. *Vaporetto* stop Lido. 16 Via Quattro Fontane, Lido (phone: 526-0227; fax: 526-0726).

Rialto You can almost touch Venice's world-famous bridge from half of this hotel's 71 rooms; the two with small wrought-iron balconies afford incomparable views. Double-paned windows and air conditioning (for an extra charge) keep out the inevitable cacophony of the busiest spot in town. The decor is a cross between modern and 18th-century Venice, with handsome beam ceilings; there is a restaurant next door. *Vaporetto* stop Rialto. 5149 Ponte di Rialto, San Marco (phone: 520-9166; 800-44-UTELL; fax: 523-8958).

Sofitel Venezia On the outskirts of the *Giardini Papadopoli* (Papadopoli Gardens), this attractive hotel with efficient service and a restaurant is on a small canal. It is a very short walk from Piazzale Roma, the train station, and all the must-sees in the Santa Croce neighborhood. All one-hundred rooms are furnished in 18th-century Venetian style; those on the top floor have private balconies. Restoration work was scheduled to be under way this year, without disrupting any guest services. There also is 24-room service and business services. *Vaporetto* stop Piazzale Roma. 245 Giardini Papadopoli, Santa Croce (phone: 528-5394; 800-221-4542; fax: 523-0043).

MODERATE

Accademia In the 17th-century *Villa Maravegie,* this tranquil, rather stately, family-run establishment has 27 rooms (the five without baths are less expensive; renovated rooms are slightly more expensive). Breakfast is served in the lovely garden, which affords a view down a small canal to the Canal Grande (there's no restaurant). Restoration of the wide vestibules and high ceilings has left the informal *ambiente* intact, with the charm of a private home from another era. *Vaporetto* stop Accademia. Near the *Galleria dell'Accademia*, at 1058 Fondamenta Maravegie, Dorsoduro (phone: 523-7846; fax: 523-9152).

Ala In a charming *campo* directly behind its grand luxe neighbor, the *Gritti Palace*, is this convenient and traditional hotel. Its 85 rooms are simply decorated. No restaurant. It's equidistant from Piazza San Marco and the *Galleria dell'Accademia*. *Vaporetto* stop Santa Maria del Giglio. 2494 Campo Santa Maria del Giglio, San Marco (phone: 520-8333; fax: 520-6390).

Amadeus A few minutes' walk from the train station, this link in the Best Western chain adds an elegant luster to the Lista di Spagna strip of souvenir hawkers. All 63 rooms are furnished in 18th-century Venetian style; a few have terraces. One of the two restaurants is in a glass-enclosed garden. Business services. *Vaporetto* stop Stazione. 227 Lista di Spagna, Cannaregio (phone: 715300; 800-528-1234; fax: 524-0841).

Bisanzio Tucked away behind the *Chiesa di Vivaldi* in one of the oldest and quietest corners of town, this hostelry is close to everything. Of the 40 rooms (some decorated in old-Venetian style, with Murano chandeliers, damask curtains, and so on, and others in a more contemporary style), six have private terraces, some overlooking the nearby *Chiesa San Giorgio dei Greci.* No restaurant, but it has a private mooring for gondolas. *Vaporetto* stop San Zaccaria. 3651 Calle della Pietà, Castello (phone: 520-3100; 800-528-1234; fax: 520-4114).

La Fenice et des Artistes Behind the *Teatro La Fenice* in a lively, popular neighborhood, this 61-room hotel has always appealed to opera buffs, as well as renowned performers and musicians (though unless you are one of the "artistes," be prepared for a chilly reception). There is a pretty garden, and marble, beam ceilings, and antique Venetian decor throughout, but no restaurant. Air conditioning is extra, and most rooms are in need of refurbishment. *Vaporetto* stop San Marco. 1936 Campiello della Fenice, San Marco (phone: 523-2333; fax: 520-3721).

Flora A 44-room jewel, this hotel has a beautiful, flowered patio where you can have breakfast, afternoon tea, or an evening *aperitivo.* The atmosphere is tranquil and gracious. Ask for No. 47, a lovely top-floor room that looks out onto Desdemona's palazzo (of *Otello* fame), with the dome of *Santa Maria della Salute* in the distance. Some of the rooms can be small, a common problem with Venice's hotels. No restaurant. *Vaporetto* stop San Marco. Five minutes west of Piazza San Marco, at 2283 Calle Larga XXII Marzo, San Marco (phone: 520-5844; fax: 522-8217).

Giorgione A top-to-bottom refurbishment a few years ago left this 70-room hotel fresh, attractive, and inviting. On a quiet side street off the popular Campo Santi Apostoli, it's a minute's walk from the *Ca' d'Oro* and the Rialto. No restaurant. Meeting rooms for up to a hundred. *Vaporetto* stop Ca' d'Oro. 4587 Salizzada del Pistor, Campo SS. Apostoli, Cannaregio (phone: 522-5810; fax: 523-9092).

Hungaria The mosaic façade of this hotel (built in 1906) is a riveting focus on one of the Lido's main streets. The hundred guestrooms are large, clean, and simple. The comfortable Old World charm is enlivened by a predominantly European clientele. The dining room is for hotel guests only. A private beach shared by a number of the smaller hotels and the lagoon-side *vaporetto* dock are just a 10-minute walk away. Parking is available. Open February through November. *Vaporetto* stop Lido. 28 Gran Viale, Lido (phone: 526-1212; fax: 526-7619).

Kette Tucked in a quiet spot between *La Fenice* and Piazza San Marco, this charming and efficient hostelry is within strolling distance of everything, and it has its own private dock for gondolas. Forty of the 60 rooms are renovated. No restaurant. *Vaporetto* stop San Marco. 2053 Piscina San Moisè, San Marco (phone: 520-7766; fax: 522-8964).

Mapaba There are 60 rooms in this property with a restaurant. Your stay here will be tranquil and relaxing, whether reading on the hotel's flowering patio or biking to nearby beach facilities. Open year-round, but call ahead to confirm winter schedule. *Vaporetto* stop Lido. 16 Riviera San Nicolò, Lido (phone: 526-0590; 800-528-1234; fax: 526-9441).

Marconi In the shadow of the famed Ponte di Rialto, this restored hotel has 28 rooms. Ask for No. 101 or No. 102—both face the canal (it's worth the supplement). The rest of the guestrooms are almost as lovely (and twice as quiet), though most of the hotel's romantic Venetian *ambiente* is in the lobby. No restaurant. *Vaporetto* stop Rialto. 729 Riva del Vin, San Polo (phone: 522-2068; fax: 522-9700).

Panada Three of the 48 Venetian-decorated rooms at this hotel boast Jacuzzis. No restaurant, but there is a cocktail lounge. *Vaporetto* stop San Marco or Rialto. A minute's walk north of Piazza San Marco, at 646 Calle Specchieri, San Marco (phone: 520-9088; 800-44-UTELL; fax: 520-9619).

Do Pozzi Small (29 rooms), attractive, and just a minute west of Piazza San Marco, it has a pleasant atmosphere and a lively canalside restaurant, *Da Raffaele*. Breakfast is served in a charming courtyard. *Vaporetto* stop Santa Maria del Giglio or San Marco. 2373 Calle Larga XXII Marzo, San Marco (phone: 520-7855; fax: 522-9413).

San Cassiano There are 36 rooms in this restored 14th-century Gothic palazzo on the Canal Grande; six of them (all triples, but they can be booked as doubles for a small supplement) look out on the *canalazzo* (as the Venetians call their beloved canal). A private landing overlooks the glorious façade of the *Ca' d'Oro*, just across the canal. No restaurant. *Vaporetto* stop San Stae. 2232 Calle del Rosa, Santa Croce (phone: 524-1768; fax: 721033).

Santo Stefano One of the city's most elegant squares is the setting for this former 15th-century tower–cum-hotel. There are only 11 small rooms (eight overlook the *campo*), each lovingly decorated by the owner's wife. Very friendly service and an excellent location, but no restaurant. Special rates are available for long-term stays. *Vaporetto* stop San Samuele. 2957 Campo Santo Stefano, San Marco (phone: 520-0166; fax: 522-4460).

Savoia e Jolanda Two buildings make up this 78-room hotel. Half the guestrooms in the main palazzo have a balcony and face a canal, but air conditioning hasn't been added yet. In warm weather, you might want to stay in the *ala nuova* (new wing), where there is a cooling system and the rooms are renovated; it overlooks a quiet piazza and the *Chiesa di San Zaccaria*. The hotel's open-air bar/restaurant is on the lagoon. *Vaporetto* stop San Zaccaria. 4187 Riva degli Schiavoni, Castello (phone: 520-6644; fax: 520-7494).

Seguso Obligatory half board doesn't seem to daunt any of the regular guests, making this otherwise inexpensive 33-room family-run hotel moderate in price. On the sunny Zattere promenade, the hostelry offers sweeping views of the Isola della Giudecca. Children are welcome. Open March through mid-November. *Vaporetto* stop Zattere. 779 Zattere, Dorsoduro (phone: 528-6858; fax: 522-2340).

INEXPENSIVE

Campiello In the shadow of big, well-known hotels sits this small family-run property in a quiet little piazza off the Riva degli Schiavoni. The 15 clean, simple rooms have air conditioning and TV sets. No restaurant. *Vaporetto* stop San Zaccaria. 4647 Calle del Vin, Castello (phone: 520-5764; fax: 520-5798).

Canada There's no elevator here, and the lobby is on the third floor, but if you have good legs, ask for either of the top floor's two rooms with beamed ceilings, a terrace, and roofscape view. There are 25 guestrooms, but no restaurant. *Vaporetto* stop Rialto. A minute's walk from the Rialto on one of the main arteries to Piazza San Marco, at 5659 Campo San Lio, Castello (phone: 522-9912; fax: 523-5852).

Casa Fontana The Stainer family prides itself on the hominess of its three-story, 15-room inn, a five-minute walk from San Marco. There's no elevator, but some of the rooms on the top overlook the spires of the nearby *Chiesa di San Zaccaria*. A few have private terraces. No restaurant. *Vaporetto* stop San Zaccaria. 30122 Campo S. Provolo, Castello (phone: 521-0533; fax: 523-1040).

Cristallo One of the Lido's nicest, least-expensive, and best-located hotels (24 rooms) is run by the same congenial family that has made the *Wildner* (see below) an institution. There is no restaurant, but parking is available, and there's access to a private beach 10 minutes away. Closed in winter. *Vaporetto* stop Lido. 51 Gran Viale Santa Maria Elisabetta, Lido (phone: 526-5293; fax: 526-5615).

Locanda Fiorita Conveniently located just two steps from the popular Campo Santo Stefano, this terraced inn has a flowering vine-covered façade. The 10 rooms—two face the *campiello*—are furnished impersonally, but the family-run *ambiente* makes this feel like home. No restaurant. *Vaporetto* stop Sant'Angelo or Accademia. 3457 Campiello Novo, San Marco (phone: 523-4754).

Paganelli Each of the two buildings in this hostelry has 11 rooms. In the noisier half located on the lagoon, the rooms offer wooden beams and occasionally a canal view; some have air conditioning. No restaurant. A good value.

Vaporetto stop San Zaccaria. 4183 Riva degli Schiavoni (phone: 522-4324; fax: 523-9267).

Riva Tucked away on the narrow Canale dei Sospiri (it takes its name from the famed Bridge of Sighs under which it passes), this hotel affords its guests the opportunity to listen to the ballads of gondoliers without having to pay for the ride. Ten of the 12 rooms have white marble bathrooms; the two without baths cost less. Breakfast, served on Ginori china, is included. Open *Carnevale* through November. *Vaporetto* stop San Marco. 5310 Ponte dell'Angelo, Castello (phone: 522-7034).

San Zulian Equidistant from Piazza San Marco and the Ponte di Rialto, this narrow, 18-room hotel is ideally situated. If you don't mind the four-floor hike, ask for room No. 304, with its rustic, beamed ceiling and a private terrace overlooking a sea of rooftops. There is a supplemental charge for air conditioning. No restaurant. *Vaporetto* stop Rialto. 535 Calle San Zulian, San Marco (phone: 522-5872; fax: 523-2265).

Serenissima Midway between the Rialto and Piazza San Marco, this hotel has 37 rooms, some without a bath. Over 400 works of contemporary art make this place a magnet for those who appreciate the blend of modern painting and old-style decor. No restaurant. Open *Carnevale* through mid-November. *Vaporetto* stop Rialto or San Marco. 4486 Calle Goldoni, San Marco (phone: 520-0011; fax: 522-3292).

Wildner Centrally located just east of Piazza San Marco on the most desirable "street" in town, this 16-room pensione-like hotel boasts an informal alfresco restaurant overlooking the lagoon that is perfect for breakfast, a late-afternoon *aperitivo*, or a light meal with a view. Ask Signora Lidia for a room overlooking the Canal Grande. *Vaporetto* stop Zaccaria. 4161 Riva degli Schiavoni, Castello (phone and fax: 522-7463).

VERY INEXPENSIVE

Le Garzette Here are five simply decorated rooms. The beach is nearby, and an 18-hole golf course is a half-mile away. Guests have access to bikes, kayaks, and canoes. The kitchen is run by well-known chef Salvatore Manzi and his family, and most of the produce and herbs they use comes from their gardens. The rustic trattoria downstairs specializes in fresh fish, seafood, and *prodotti genuini* ("natural" foods). Inexpensive half board is not obligatory but highly recommended. Parking available. Open February through November. *Vaporetto* stop Lido. 32 Lungomare Alberoni, Malamocco, Lido (phone: 731078).

Locanda Montin Overlooking a charming stretch of canal with flowered balconies, this seven-room place (two guestrooms have a view of the canal) is ideal for those who want to spend little and be in a quiet, centrally located neighborhood. Ask for the room where Eleonora Duse and Gabriele D'Annunzio stayed. You'll sacrifice a private bath by staying here, but the payoff is the good food served in the restaurant downstairs, which used to be frequented by artists and intellectuals before it became trendy (and quite expensive). There is a collection of original paintings by Venetian artists of the 1950s and 1960s, many of whom were regulars. *Vaporetto* stop Accademia. 1147 Fondamenta Eremite, Dorsoduro (phone: 522-7151; fax: 520-0255).

Noemi None of the 15 rooms here has a private bath, but the shared facilities are clean, and you'll feel as if you're visiting a dear Venetian aunt with your gracious host, Signora Noemi. Most guestrooms have impressive antique pieces that once graced the signora's home, and the stair's banister is an unusual tribute to Murano glasswork. There's a restaurant downstairs. A half-minute's walk from the Piazza San Marco. *Vaporetto* stop San Marco. 909 Calle dei Fabbri, San Marco (phone: 523-8144).

EATING OUT

One of life's great pleasures is dining out in Venice in good weather—alongside a canal, in one of the small, sunny squares, or in a little garden shaded by vine leaves. As for the fare, everyone's perfect idea of Venice is eating a delicious seafood dinner and drinking a good wine from the Veneto. It might be easier to find the idyllic setting than reliably good, fresh seafood dinners, which have become expensive and hard to find. Frozen fish is too often served when an unknowing tourist doesn't ask whether it is *fresco,* although a city law requires that menus specify which are *surgelato* (frozen) and which are fresh (often they don't). Be forewarned—the fish market is closed on Mondays, so the restaurants' pickings are slim. Many smaller establishments close without notice in January or February for two to three weeks before *Carnevale.* Prices for dinner for two, with wine and tip, but not tax, range from $150 to $200 at a very expensive restaurant; $75 to $125 at an expensive one; $40 to $75 at a moderate place; and $40 or less in the inexpensive category. All restaurants are open for lunch and dinner unless otherwise noted. All telephone numbers are in the 41 city code unless otherwise indicated.

For a memorable dining experience, we begin with our culinary favorite, followed by our cost and quality choices, listed by price category.

DELIGHTFUL DINING

Al Covo The two owners—the Texan Diane and the Venetian Cesare—are reason enough to come here every night of your stay in Venice. She's as friendly and enthusiastic as he is talented and creative, and both are passionately dedicated to offering the freshest fish their suppliers can provide. The *moleche* (soft-shell crabs) in season are a must. And don't miss the mixed seafood antipasto, which includes minute shrimp served with polenta, whipped salt cod, and stuffed mussels. The pasta dishes are sauced with clams or scampi, and the simply grilled or fried fish is first-rate. Diane's homemade cookies and chocolate cake are perfect for dessert. The large selection of excellent international wines (in a city with no cellars) is well priced. The amiable staff and handsome, relaxed setting are just icing on the cake. One of the two dining rooms is reserved for nonsmokers, an amenity rare in Italy. Closed Wednesdays, Thursdays, January, and two weeks in August. Reservations advised. Major credit cards accepted. *Vaporetto* stop Arsenale. 3968 Campiello della Pescaria, Castello (phone: 522-3812).

VERY EXPENSIVE

Antico Martini One of Venice's classiest restaurants since 1720, across the square from the *Teatro La Fenice,* serves both international and Venetian specialties in a Belle Epoque setting. It has a fine wine list, and the kitchen accepts orders until 11:30 PM (later for the après-opera, on evenings when performances are scheduled at *La Fenice*). Closed Tuesdays, and Wednesday lunch. Reservations necessary. Major credit cards accepted. *Vaporetto* stop San Marco. 1983 Campo San Fantin, San Marco (phone: 522-4121).

Club del Doge In the *Gritti Palace* hotel, this is the place for a delicious selection of both traditional Venetian and continental dishes served in deluxe surroundings. In good weather, diners eat on a flower-bedecked canalside terrace across from the *Chiesa di Santa Maria della Salute.* Open daily. Reservations necessary. Major credit cards accepted. *Vaporetto* stop Santa Maria del Giglio. 2467 Campo Santa Maria del Giglio, San Marco (phone: 794611).

Harry's Bar The original establishment to carry this moniker and long a Venetian landmark serves light meals in the popular downstairs bar/restaurant, which is crowded with tourists in summer. During the film and art festivals, it is the place to celebrity watch. Upstairs, the setting is elegant, the food, splendid—though a bit overpriced. The Bellini cocktail was born here, as was the delicate raw beef entrée—carpaccio. Closed Mondays. Reservations necessary for the upstairs restaurant. Major credit cards accepted. Directly in front of the San Marco *vaporetto* stop. 1323 Calle Vallaresso, San Marco (phone: 528-5777).

Locanda Cipriani The almost pastoral tranquillity of the garden makes this a perfect place for a leisurely lunch or serene stay (see *Checking In*). The restaurant sits on an ancient piazza on the sleepy island of Torcello. Direct boat service leaves Piazza San Marco near the *Danieli* hotel at noon and returns from Torcello at 3:30 PM. Closed Tuesdays and early November to mid-

March. Reservations advised. Major credit cards accepted. *Vaporetto* stop Torcello. 29 Piazza San Fosca, Torcello (phone: 730757).

La Colomba Sooner or later, everyone drops in at this favorite restaurant near *La Fenice*, as folks have since the 1700s. Large, elegant, and always crowded, it has a lovely outside terrace, a renowned collection of modern art on the walls, and an equally creative array of meat and seafood specialties. Try *cartoccio Colomba*, Adriatic fish baked in a paper bag. Closed Wednesdays from November through April. Reservations advised. Major credit cards accepted. *Vaporetto* stop Santa Maria del Giglio or San Marco. 1665 Piscina di Frezzeria, San Marco (phone: 522-1175).

Corte Sconta Despite its steadily increasing prices, this old neighborhood *bacaro* (wine bar) has held onto its informal and welcoming atmosphere. Old-timers still congregate at the bar, leaving the bare wooden tables to the savvy clientele who've found this hidden spot for inventive and traditional fish dishes prepared by the young chef. Closed Sundays, Mondays, January 15 to February 15, and July 15 to August 15. Reservations advised. Major credit cards accepted. *Vaporetto* stop Arsenale. 3886 Calle del Pestrin, Castello (phone: 522-7024).

Da Fiore This institution is venerated for its simple treatment of fresh fish and shellfish, as well as fresh vegetable specialties and home-baked breads and desserts. Closed Sundays, Mondays, and from *Christmas* to mid-January. Reservations necessary. Major credit cards accepted. *Vaporetto* stop San Tomà. 2202 Calle del Scaleter, San Polo (phone: 721308).

Al Graspo de Ua Colorful and popular, this more-than-a-century-old restaurant is located in a 19th-century blacksmith's shop. It offers very good Venetian and regional dishes, fresh fish, and a good selection of wines. Closed Mondays, Tuesdays, mid-December to mid-January, and the first two weeks of August. Reservations advised. Major credit cards accepted. *Vaporetto* stop Rialto. 5094 Calle Bombaseri, San Marco (phone: 520-0150).

Da Ivo When Venetians can't look another sea bass in the face, they head here to enjoy chef Ivo's renowned *bistecca alla fiorentina* and other Tuscan specialties. Try the *pappardelle alla marinara* (thick, flat pasta in tomato, caper, and black olive sauce). Open to 11:30 PM. Closed Sundays and three weeks in January. Reservations advised. Major credit cards accepted. *Vaporetto* stop San Marco or Rialto. 1809 Calle dei Fuseri, San Marco (phone: 528-5004).

Ai Mercanti Just beyond the colorful *Pescheria* (Fish Market), this small, casually elegant eatery offers sea- and meat-based specialties. Additions to the ever-delicious risotto dish change with the season, and an exceptionally light *frittura di pesce* (fried fish) seems hardly fried at all. The hard-to-come-by steak tartare is at its best here, as is a delicate fish carpaccio. There is an impressive list of regional wines. Closed Sundays, two weeks in January, and two weeks in August. Reservations advised. Major credit cards accepted. *Vaporetto* stop Rialto. 1588 Campo della Beccarie, San Polo (phone: 524-0282).

Osteria del Ponte del Diavolo With only two restaurants on the charming island of Torcello, it won't be hard to find this popular eatery owned by Corrado Alfonso, the former chef at the *Locanda Cipriani*. The menu selection—from appetizers to desserts—is determined by what's in season. Try the *insalata di mare* for openers. Closed Thursdays, December through January, and for dinner (except June through August). Reservations advised, especially on weekends. Major credit cards accepted. *Vaporetto* stop Torcello. Torcello (phone: 730401).

Ai Poste Vecie Low ceilings and wood beams, a roaring fire in the winter, and alfresco dining in the small outdoor garden in summer have made this cozy place an institution. Homemade ravioli are stuffed with fresh scallops, and risotto dishes are embellished with the day's catch from the *Pescheria,* just across a small wooden bridge from the restaurant. Fresh fish prepared in a variety of ways tops the bill, although there are a few first-rate meat dishes. Closed Tuesdays, two weeks in January, and two weeks in July. Reservations advised. Major credit cards accepted. *Vaporetto* stop Rialto. 1608 at the Rialto Pescheria, San Polo (phone: 721822).

Taverna La Fenice Undaunted enthusiasm and a talented chef from the *Gritti Palace* resuscitated this refined restaurant in the shadow of the *Teatro La Fenice.* For openers, try the *fettuccine alla Pavarotti* (with a cream base, black truffles, and slivers of tongue and chicken breast), then move on to the fresh *sogliola alla Fenice* (filet of sole with zucchini, shrimp, and clams). There also are delicious meat entrées and a fine wine selection. Alfresco dining from May through October. Closed Wednesdays and January. Reservations advised. Major credit cards accepted. *Vaporetto* stop San Marco or Santa Maria del Giglio. 1938 Campo della Fenice, San Marco (phone: 522-3856).

Da Valentino On the Lido, this small dining spot with a garden and terrace serves Venetian fish and meat specialties, including game in season. Homemade desserts and good local wines are an integral part of any meal here. Closed Mondays through Wednesdays and November through February. Seating is limited, so reservations are advised. Major credit cards accepted. *Vaporetto* stop Lido. 81 Via Sandro Gallo, Lido (phone: 526-0128).

MODERATE

Antica Bessetta Venetian home-cooking is hard to beat, and here it is at its best in the fresh vegetable and homemade pasta dishes as well as in the more sophisticated (and expensive) fish specialties. Closed Tuesdays, Wednesdays, and mid-July to mid-August. Reservations advised. No credit cards accepted. *Vaporetto* stop Rio Biasio. 1395 Calle Salvio, Santa Croce (phone: 721687).

Al Bacareto Near Campo Santo Stefano, this rustic trattoria has a few tables outside and a welcoming dining room inside where you can sample traditional local dishes, such as *bigoli in salsa* (whole wheat spaghetti with anchovy and onion sauce) or *fegato alla veneziana* (sautéed liver with onions). Closed Saturday dinner, Sundays, and August. No reservations. Major credit cards accepted. *Vaporetto* stop San Samuele. 3447 Calle Crosera, San Marco (phone: 528-9336).

Caffè Orientale In a particularly delightful spot near the *Chiesa dei Frari* with a romantic terrace on the Rio Marin, this family-run restaurant is as popular for lunch with the locals as with foot-weary tourists. The menu (be prepared for Venetian dialect) includes reliably fresh Adriatic fish. Closed Sunday dinner, Mondays, three weeks in January, and two weeks in August. Reservations advised. Major credit cards accepted. *Vaporetto* stop San Tomà. 2426 Calle dell' Olio, San Polo (phone: 719804).

Ai Gondolieri Unusual for Venice, this dining spot serves a menu of traditional meat dishes to a full house of predominantly Italian patrons in a typical trattoria setting. The fresh pasta ushers in a memorable meal. Closed Tuesdays and August. Reservations advised. Major credit cards accepted. *Vaporetto* stop Accademia or Salute. 366 Ponte del Formager, Dorsoduro (phone: 528-6396).

Alla Madonna Brightly lit and lively, on a little side street on the San Polo (not San Marco) side of the Ponte di Rialto, it is a consistent favorite with Venetians because of its professional service (despite the bustle), reasonable prices, and reliably good food in unpretentious surroundings. Closed Wednesdays, two weeks in August, and December 24 through January. No reservations. Major credit cards accepted. *Vaporetto* stop Rialto. 594 Sotoportego della Madonna, San Polo (phone: 522-3824).

Al Mascaron A great stop after a visit to the nearby churches of *Santa Maria Formosa* or *Santissimi Giovanni e Paolo* (*San Zanipolo*). Join the food-wise habitués at communal tables for a good meal and a dose of colorful local bonhomie. Closed Sundays. No reservations. No credit cards accepted. *Vaporetto* stop Rialto. 5225 Calle Longa Santa Maria Formosa, Castello (phone: 522-5995).

Osteria Ca' d'Oro alla Vedova A former *bacaro* (wine bar), this attractive trattoria boasts a well-stocked wine cellar to accompany its Venetian fish and vegetable dishes, polenta (not always so easy to find in Venice), and Veneto cheeses. Closed Sunday lunch and Thursdays. No reservations. No credit cards accepted. *Vaporetto* stop Ca' d'Oro. 3912 Via Nova, Cannaregio (phone: 528-5324).

Riviera Possibly the best restaurant on the wide Zattere promenade overlooking the Canale della Giudecca. The owner and chef, who had decades of experience at the legendary *Harry's Bar,* serves homemade pasta that gives that institution a run for its money. The delicious homemade *gnocchi alla gorgonzola* have a creamy cheese sauce with a bite. Closed Sunday dinner and Mondays. Reservations advised. Major credit cards accepted. *Vaporetto* stop San Basilio. 1474 Fondamenta le Zattere, Dorsoduro (phone: 522-7621).

Al Theatro Few places stay open so late (till midnight) and offer so much. Its neighbor, *Teatro La Fenice,* supplies much of the late-night crowd, but lots of others stop by for an *aperitivo,* a pizza, or full-course dinner served alfresco. Closed Mondays. No reservations. Major credit cards accepted. *Vaporetto* stop Santa Maria del Giglio. 1917 Campo San Fantin, San Marco (phone: 521-0455).

Al Vecio Cantier If you're on the Lido, it's worth the 10-minute taxi ride south to Alberoni and this lovely trattoria, well known for its fresh fish dishes. Try the enormous array of fish-based antipasti, or any of the daily specials, including *branzino,* sweeter than the American sea bass, expertly prepared *alla griglia* (grilled) and served outdoors when the weather is good. Closed Mondays, Tuesday lunch, and November through January. Reservations advised. Visa accepted. *Vaporetto* stop Lido. 76 Via della Droma, Alberoni, Lido (phone: 731130).

INEXPENSIVE

Altanella Four generations have been producing nothing but the freshest fish in a homey, no-frills ambience on the Isola della Giudecca, one of the least touristy areas of Venice. Try any of the daily specials, mostly grilled fresh fish or the very light *fritto misto.* There are a few tables on a charming *altanella* (wooden terrace) over a small, pretty canal, so book in advance. Closed Mondays, Tuesdays, January, and two weeks in August. No credit cards accepted. *Vaporetto* stop Redentore or Traghetto. 268 Calle dell'Erbe, Giudecca (phone: 522-7780).

Al Milion Memoirs of Marco Polo's million exotic tales gave this *bacaro* (wine bar) its name. The food and *ambiente* are simple and unpretentious yet enjoyable; the selection of wines, impressive. Closed Wednesdays and most of August. Reservations advised. No credit cards accepted. *Vaporetto* stop Rialto. 5841 San Giovanni Crisostomo in the Corte Prima del Milion, Cannaregio (phone: 522-9302).

Pizzeria le Oche With 40 varieties to choose from, this is the Baskin-Robbins of Venice's pizzerias. There's a pleasant garden in the back, but if you're lucky or if you come before 7 PM, there will be a free table out in front, the better to enjoy your *disco volante* (flying saucer)—two pizzas face to face like a giant sandwich—or the *mangiafuoco* (fire eater) with spicy salami and chili peppers. Closed Mondays. No reservations. Major credit cards accepted. *Vaporetto* stop San Stae or Rio Biasio. 1552 Calle del Tintor, Santa Croce (phone: 524-1161).

Pizzeria alla Zattere The favorite of pizza aficionados as much for the lengthy list of delicious combinations as for the idyllic views from its terrace on the wide Canale della Giudecca. Closed Tuesdays, November, and two weeks in December. No reservations. No credit cards accepted. *Vaporetto* stop Zattere. 795 Zattere ai Gesuati, Dorsoduro (phone: 520-4224).

Da Remigio The food at this popular neighborhood trattoria is reliably good and the prices surprisingly low for a place so close to San Marco. Fresh fish, however, will hike your otherwise very conservative bill. Closed Monday dinner, Tuesdays, mid-July through early August, and December 20 through January. No reservations. Major credit cards accepted. *Vaporetto* stop San Zaccaria. 3416 Salizzada dei Greci, Castello (phone: 523-0089).

Rosticceria San Bartolomeo The predominantly Venetian, forever loyal clientele—from students to businessfolk—that frequent this convenient place two steps from the Ponte di Rialto confirms its reputation for giving a good value for the lire. Downstairs is informal and bustling, and patrons sit at counters along the windows. Upstairs, there is a subtle rise in price and ambience, as well as waiter service. Reliable pasta, pizza, roast meat, chicken, and grilled fish have made this place a perennial favorite. One catch—no food is served after 8:30 PM. Closed Mondays. No reservations. No credit cards accepted. *Vaporetto* stop Rialto. 5424 Calle della Bissa, San Marco (phone: 522-3569).

San Tomà You might see homemade pasta hanging out to dry in the sun, but most neighborhood regulars seem to return here for pizza while sitting in the lovely garden in the back. There also are a few tables in front in a charming little piazza. Closed Tuesdays and 10 days in August. Reservations advised. Visa accepted. *Vaporetto* stop San Tomà. 2864 Campo San Tomà, San Polo (phone: 523-8819).

La Zucca Its name, "The Pumpkin," hints at its vegetarian menu and some of its specialties, such as cream of pumpkin soup and pumpkin bread. It is always packed with a young and interesting crowd that is mostly Venetian. Desserts are homemade and delicious. Closed Sundays. Reservations advised. No credit cards accepted. *Vaporetto* stop San Stae or Rialto. 1762 Remo del Maggio, Santa Croce, near San Giacomo dell'Orio (phone: 524-1570).

BARS AND CAFFÈS
Join the Venetians in their ritual of drinking an *ombra* (which means "shade" and refers to the break that workers once took in the cool shadow of San Marco's bell tower, where they downed a much-welcome glass of wine) any time during the day at a *bacaro,* a pub named after a *pugliese* wine once

very popular in Venice, or an *enoteca,* a cheerful neighborhood wine bar usually offering simple *cichetti* (hors d'oeuvres) in the style of Spanish *tapas.* You'll also find hearty sandwiches, the occasional hot pasta dish, and, if you're lucky, a few tables. *Bacari* are generally priced very modestly according to the wine choice—the reliable house wine (usually around 50¢ to 75¢ a glass) is de rigueur—while *enoteche* offer more extensive selections for some interesting wine tasting. Venice will sink before you can get to even a small sampling of these ubiquitous, unofficial social clubs. The following are the best-known and most characteristic. All are inexpensive, and none accept credit cards. Also included is our favorite *caffè* (it is expensive and accepts major credit cards), where you also can get a light meal.

BEST CAFFÈ

Florian The show first opened in 1720 and has been running here ever since—both outdoors, on the dizzyingly ornamental and people-packed Piazza San Marco, and indoors, among the salons full of red velvet, parquet, and intricate paneling and painting. To enjoy it all, order a cappuccino outdoors on an early April morning, when the pigeons and the first trans-Alpine arrivals herald Venice's spring opening. Or sip a cold white soave on a balmy summer night and enjoy the lilting rhythm of Strauss or Rossini or Offenbach, as interpreted by the four-piece *Florian* orchestra from late April through October. Or savor a rum punch indoors on a windy November afternoon, standing shoulder to shoulder with soigné Venetians at the coffee-fragrant bar. Or experience this *caffè* with a Brandy Alexander in hand and a pale winter sun outside. Venice is for all seasons, and this favorite of Casanova and Madame de Staël is as important a stop on a Venice itinerary as the *Palazzo Ducale.* Closed Wednesdays in winter. *Vaporetto* stop San Marco. 57 Piazza San Marco (phone: 528-5338).

Caffè Lavena It is said that Richard Wagner found his inspiration here, at one of Piazza San Marco's historic *caffès.* Light food is the specialty, but don't miss the "Lavena's Cup" ice cream extravaganza. An orchestra plays outdoors until midnight from early March through mid-November. Closed Tuesdays in winter. *Vaporetto* stop San Marco. 133 Piazza San Marco (phone: 522-4070).

Leon Bianco Grab a toothpick and spear any number of delicious potato, rice, or cheese croquettes. This is one of Venice's best-stocked sandwich bars, with a wine list to match, and counter seating. Closed Sundays. Near the busy Campo San Luca. *Vaporetto* stop Rialto. 4153 Salizzada San Luca, San Marco (phone: 522-1180).

Do Mori Open since 1750, this is one of the most characteristic of the traditional *bacari*, offering sandwiches, croquettes, and other fresh *cichetti*. It's standing room only; there are very few chairs. Near the *Pescheria*. Closed Wednesday afternoons and Sundays. *Vaporetto* stop Rialto. 429 Calle do Mori, San Polo (phone: 522-5401).

Do Spade Unspoiled and authentic, this *enoteca* is frequented by vendors from the nearby Rialto market and high-brow connoisseurs alike. A variety of delicious sandwiches are made daily, and there are a few wooden tables, although the local crowd prefers to stand. Closed Sundays and most of August. *Vaporetto* stop Rialto. 860 Sotoportego delle Do Spade, San Polo (phone: 521-0574).

Vino Vino Purposely low-key and neighborhoody, this fashionable wine bar near *La Fenice* is owned by the upscale *Antico Martini*. Enjoy light meals and a large selection of Italian and imported wines by the glass or bottle at marble-top tables. Wine tasting from 10 AM to 1 AM for the after-theater set; eating from noon to 2:30 PM and 7 to 10 PM; closed Tuesdays. *Vaporetto* stop Santa Maria del Giglio. 2007 Ponte delle Veste, San Marco (phone: 522-4121).

Al Volto Considered the best in town since it opened in 1936, this Venice institution offers over 2,000 different wine labels from all over the world and 70 foreign beers. There are rare and costly wines as well as the more current and affordable vintages. Open from 5 to 9 PM; closed Sundays. *Vaporetto* stop Rialto. 4081 Calle Cavalli, San Marco (phone: 522-8945).

GELATO

On summer evenings, locals and visitors alike stroll through Venice, stopping for a gelato at one of the many ice-cream shops in the city. Two worth a visit are *Paolin* (2962 Campo Santo Stefano, San Marco; phone: 522-5576; closed Mondays November through April), the oldest and best *gelateria* in town, and the less centrally located *Gelateria Nico,* behind the *Accademia* and on the Zattere promenade (922 Zattere ai Gesuati, Dorsoduro; phone: 522-5293; closed Thursdays), where gelato is made fresh daily.

If you're strolling along the lagoon on the Riva degli Schiavoni, look for the gondola-shaped cart selling homemade gelati in the shadow of the Victor Emmanuel statue. For three generations, the Maier family has been selling their delectable ice cream every day from March through October.

Verona

If the Venetians are all *gran signori* (fine gentlemen and ladies), and the people of Padua are *gran dottori* (very learned), the Veronese—as the old saying goes—are all *tutti matti* (quite mad), a characteristic that runs the gamut from charming eccentricity to an almost surly obtuseness.

Verona's strategic location on the navigable Adige River made the city important in its early days. It became a Roman territory in AD 49 and was known as *Piccola Roma* ("Little Rome"). The massive *Arena,* the arched stone doors such as the *Porta Borsari* (translated as "Money Changers' " or "Toll Collectors' " Gate), and fragments of pillars and walls throughout town are all signs of the importance of Roman Verona. But nowadays the overwhelming impression is medieval. There are battlements, turrets, slits in the walls from which archers shot their arrows, and cobbled streets on which visitors can easily imagine horses clattering as they pass over the Ponte di Castelvecchio.

A border town, Verona played a key role in Italy's past. After the Romans, the city was ruled by the Goths and King Theodoric, followed by two centuries of Lombards. It was conquered by the Franks and Charlemagne in 774. The medieval period was one of religious building fervor. The grand masters left their imprints on the city, especially under the doges and the Venetian republic. Verona's contributions to the Renaissance include painter Paolo Veronese and architect Michele Sanmicheli. The Venetians were ousted in 1797 by Napoleon, whose government was in turn removed in 1814 by the European coalition, then ruled by the Hapsburgs until the Italian unification in 1860.

The rule of the Della Scala family had the most lingering effect on Verona. Known as the Scaligeri, the family reigned from 1262 to 1387, during which time Romeo is supposed to have courted Juliet and "with love's light wings did o'erperch these walls" into the Capulet garden. It was the Scaligeri who gave Verona so many of the city's monuments, such as the *Arche Scaligere* (Scaligeri Arches), aboveground tombs where the family is buried; the *Castelvecchio,* now the city's main museum; and the Piazza dei Signori (Lords' Square) and many of its surrounding buildings, including the *Palazzo del Governo* (Government Palace), also known as the *Palazzo degli Scaligeri.* Many churches grew in splendor during their reign, and it was a time of great cultural awareness. Dante Alighieri stayed in the *Palazzo degli Scaligeri* during his Florentine exile as a guest of Cangrande I della Scala, whom he immortalized in the 17th canto of his *Paradiso.*

During the 13th century, poor people lived under the arches of the Roman *Arena* and had to pay rent for their humble dwellings until they were turned out to make way for the city's prostitutes, who in those days had to wear a cap with a rattle on the peak to differentiate them from "honest" women. In fact, the city's monuments, however ancient and revered, are still just as much a part of day-to-day life as they always were. The *Arena,* which once featured gladiators and lions and, later, medieval jousters, still dominates the city; during Verona's world-famous opera season, the *Arena* plays an important role in civic life. The Scaligeri palaces have become government offices. A daily market is held in Piazza delle Erbe, on the site of the old Roman forum. Lawyers and judges still ascend the *Scala della Ragione* (Stair of Reason), as they did in the 15th century.

Old Verona is small and compact, only a half-hour walk end to end. But it has much to see. Be sure to look up at the façades of the buildings (some of them, like No. 4 on Via San Cosimo, are almost grotesque). The diligent roamer will soon discover that not only Romeo and Juliet but everyone in Verona had a balcony. It will also quickly become apparent that Romeo and Juliet are only one reason to come to Verona, and the least haunting of the impressions visitors will carry home.

Verona At-a-Glance

SEEING THE CITY

The *Torre dei Lamberti* (Lamberti Tower; Piazza delle Erbe; phone: 803-2726) rises to 272 feet in the heart of Old Verona. Fortunately, there is an elevator as well as stairs to the top, which commands a fine view of the city. It's closed Mondays; admission charge (discounted for those who climb the stairs).

On the other side of the Ponte di Pietra (Stone Bridge) from the *Torre dei Lamberti* are the *Teatro Romano* (Roman Theater), founded by Augustus, and the *Castel San Pietro* (St. Peter's Castle), built by the Austrians in the 19th century. Both afford good views of Verona. The *Scalone di San Pietro* (St. Peter's Stairway) is steeped in legend. The higher one climbs, the more of the city is visible on the horizon. Here King Albion, King of the Lombards, was killed at the instigation of his wife, Rosamund. On the same side of the river is the lovely *Giardino Giusti,* a formal 16th-century garden with terraces overlooking the city (see *Special Places*).

SPECIAL PLACES

While other cities may have their museums and picture galleries, Verona has churches, although many are so dimly lit that one can only guess at the artistic and architectural wonders lurking within. There are so many churches, so large, so awe-inspiring, that it is hard to believe there were ever enough Veronese to fill them (most churches were affiliated with monasteries). Note that most sites of interest in Verona close for a midday break, usually from noon to 4 PM; we suggest calling ahead to check exact hours.

DUOMO (CATHEDRAL) The most important church in Verona is this 12th-century Romanesque basilica with a 15th-century Gothic nave. Located in the old section of the city near the Ponte di Pietra, it was probably built on the site of a paleochristian church dating from the late Roman Empire. The choir screen separating the altar from the rest of the church is attributed to Sanmicheli. At the end of the nave, in the *Cappella Nichesola* (Nichesola Chapel), is Titian's *Assumption of the Virgin Mary.* Behind the cathedral is the little 12th-century *Chiesa di San Giovanni in Fonte,* one of the most important examples of Romanesque architecture in Verona. It is named for the huge octagonal baptismal font in red stone, its eight sides showing scenes from the life of Christ. Open daily, with a long midday closing (noon to 4 PM). Piazza Duomo (phone: 595627).

CHIESA DI SANT'ANASTASIA (CHURCH OF ST. ANASTASIA) Although the foundations of this basilica were laid in 1290 by the Dominicans, it was not finished until 1481. The vaulted ceiling is supported by massive red Veronese marble columns. Two *gobbi* (hunchbacks) support the holy water fonts at the foot of the first column on either side of the nave. There is something uncannily realistic in the resigned expressions of the *gobbi,* as if they were carrying the weight of the church on their shoulders. In the sacristy to the left is *St. George and the Princess,* the famous fresco by Pisanello. Put a hundred-lire coin into the machine to illuminate the picture, which, like a fairy-tale painting, features a knight in armor, a damsel in distress, a castle in the clouds, and, in the foreground, the unexpectedly large rump of a white charger. Open daily, with a long midday closing (noon to 4 PM). Corso Sant'Anastasia (phone: 800-4325).

CHIESA DI SAN ZENO MAGGIORE (CHURCH OF ST. ZENO MAJOR) Zeno is the patron saint of Verona, and his laughing, black-faced statue is seated on its bishop's throne in a small apse to the left of the altar. The 48 panels of the magnificent bronze doors show scenes of the Old and New Testaments, and the triptych above the main altar is a depiction by Andrea Mantegna of the Madonna with angel musicians and saints. The ceiling of the nave looks like an upturned wooden ship's keel. Open daily, with a long midday closing (noon to 4 PM). It's a pleasant 15- to 20-minute walk along the banks of the Adige to this fascinating church. Or take bus No. 33 (daily except Sundays) from Via Diaz (a two-minute walk on Via Oberdan from Piazza Brà) or a taxi. 2 Piazza San Zeno (phone: 800-6120).

Note: Do not confuse this basilica with the tiny church called *San Zeno in Oratorio* on Via A. Provolo, near the *Museo Castelvecchio.* The smaller church contains an enormous boulder that is supposedly the stone on which the laughing St. Zeno used to sit fishing by the Adige River.

CHIESA DI SAN FERMO MAGGIORE (CHURCH OF ST. FIRMANUS MAJOR) Both churches here, constructed in the form of a Latin cross, are considered a turning point in local ecclesiastical architecture. The lower church, which parishioners use in winter, is pure Romanesque; the upper and larger church, altered by the Franciscans in the 13th century, has a more Gothic aspect.

The interior is decorated with frescoes by Veronese painters from Turone (see his *Crucifixion*) to Pisanello (the *Annunciation*). The ceiling here, as at *San Zeno,* looks like a ship's keel. Open daily, with a long midday closing (noon to 4 PM). Just before Ponte Navi on Stradone San Fermo (phone: 800-7287).

CHIESA DI SAN LORENZO (CHURCH OF ST. LAWRENCE) Still remaining here are the *matronei* (women's galleries) that run above the two lateral naves. Two cylindrical towers of striped stone and brick were the entrances to the galleries. Open daily from 8 AM to noon (but often inexplicably closed). 28 Corso Cavour (phone: 800-1879).

CHIESA DI SANTO STEFANO (CHURCH OF ST. STEPHEN) Walk over the Ponte di Pietra and visit this church, believed to have been built in the time of Theodoric the Goth. It was constructed in a mixture of styles, tradition dating its foundations to around AD 415. It is thought to have been Verona's cathedral for more than three centuries. More than 20 Veronese bishops are buried here, and the façade is inscribed with records of important events. Open daily, with a long (noon to 4:30 PM) midday closing. Piazza San Stefano (phone: 834-8529).

CHIESA DI SANTA MARIA IN ORGANO (CHURCH OF ST. MARY IN ORGANO) This structure is known for the remarkable marquetry (inlaid designs in wood) on the backs of its wooden choir stalls and in its sacristy, which were executed around 1499 by Fra Giovanni da Verona. The designs contain 32 types of wood, endowing them with extraordinary nuances of light and color. Open daily from 7:30 to 11 AM. Piazza Isolo (phone: 591440).

CHIESA DI SAN GIORGIO MAGGIORE (CHURCH OF ST. GEORGE MAJOR) Also known as *San Giorgio in Braida,* this building (1536–43) lacks the powerful atmosphere of some earlier Romanesque churches, but it is rich in artwork (Goethe once termed the church "a fine gallery"). Paintings include a large Tintoretto, *The Baptism of Christ,* over the entrance and a Veronese, *The Martyrdom of St. George,* on the end wall of the apse. The design of the cupola and the unfinished campanile are attributed to Sanmicheli. Open daily, with a long midday closing (11 AM to 4 PM). Lungadige San Giorgio (phone: 834-0232).

GIARDINO GIUSTI (GIUSTI GARDEN) Across the Adige from Old Verona is this formal garden, which was designed by its 16th-century owner, Count Agostino Giusti. Laid out behind a palazzo of the same name, the garden is composed of formal walks with box-hedge mazes geometrically arranged around statues and fountains. A series of terraces and stairs leads to an upper garden affording wonderful views of the city. Open daily. Admission charge. Via Giardino Giusti (phone: 803-4029).

PIAZZA DELLE ERBE (SQUARE OF THE HERBS) Every morning except Sundays, octagonal white umbrellas shade the stalls of this market square, where fresh produce, flowers, and clothing are sold. On the fountain is a Roman statue known as the *Madonna Verona,* who holds a scroll declaiming, *"Est iusti latrix urbs haec et laudis amatrix"* ("The city is proud of her justice and fond of praise"). The statue is the only visible vestige of the Roman forum that once occupied the site. At the northwest end of the square is the Baroque façade of *Palazzo Maffei,* with statues of Greek gods along the roof. At the same corner is the beautifully frescoed 14th-century *Casa Mazzanti.* Next to the *Casa Mazzanti,* leading into Piazza Mercato Vecchio, is the *Arco della Costa,* an arch from which hangs a prehistoric whalebone, also discovered under the square during excavations, evidence that millennia ago this entire area was under the sea.

ARCHE SCALIGERE (SCALIGERE ARCHES) The tombs of the Scaligeri family are supposedly one of the greatest medieval monuments in Italy. They've been closed for restoration for years, but you can peek through the 14th-century wrought-iron grate to get a view. In the center of town near the Piazza delle Erbe.

PIAZZA DEI SIGNORI Also known as Piazza Dante, for the square's central monument to the great poet (a frequent Scaligeri guest), this square in the medieval heart of Verona is hemmed in by monumental buildings. The 15th-century Gothic exterior staircase in the courtyard of the 12th-century *Palazzo della Ragione* is known, appropriately, as the *Scala della Ragione.* The *Palazzo dei Tribunale* (Palace of the Tribunal) boasts a classic medieval crenelated tower, and the *Palazzo del Governo* (Palace of the Government) was once home to the Scaligeri family. Both have doorways by Sanmicheli. Across the piazza is the Venetian Renaissance *Loggia del Consiglio* (Portico of the Counsel).

ANTICO CAFFÈ DANTE In the heart of Old Verona, this old-fashioned coffeehouse offers light meals and refreshments, as well as a taste of history. In 1865, to mark the annexing of Verona to a unified Italy, the ceiling was painted with oval portraits of Italy's great patriots—Garibaldi, Mazzini, Cavour, et al. Marble tables and plush armchairs have been restored to their former grandeur. Sip an aperitif at an outdoor table when the weather is nice, and enjoy a view of one of Verona's great piazze. Closed Sundays in winter. 2 Piazza dei Signori (phone: 595249).

CASA E TOMBA DI GIULIETTA E CASA DI ROMEO (JULIET'S HOUSE AND TOMB AND ROMEO'S HOUSE) The only thing certain about these monuments is that their association with Shakespeare's "star-crossed lovers" is pure invention— Juliet's balcony was added to the house in the 1920s. Hordes of tourists and graffiti-covered walls at the otherwise empty house make for a singularly unromantic experience. Juliet's house is at 23 Via Cappello (phone: 803-4303). Her tomb occupies a more attractive and evocative spot, the medieval monastery of *San Francesco al Corso* on Via del Pontiere (phone: 800-0361). Romeo's house, on Via Arche Scaligere near Piazza Indipendenza, can be viewed from the street only. Juliet's house and the tomb are closed Mondays. Admission charge.

ARENA Nowadays, the enormous 1st-century Roman arena in Piazza Brà serves as the opera house, thus remaining an important component of Veronese life. Over the years, this site has been a battleground for gladiators and lions, a fortress, a marketplace, a jousting field, and a repertory theater. It was still intact in the 11th century, when an earthquake caused its outside wall to collapse; now only a piece remains of the original structure. Since then, the Veronese have been assiduous in their conservation efforts, maintaining their arena as one of the better preserved Roman amphitheaters. The audience sits on marble benches 2,000 years old; the inner wall, backdrops, and staircase are intact; and the acoustics are perfect. In fact, the structure qualifies as a ruin only because of the crumbled state of its outer ring, of which only a small section remains. The outdoor opera season presented here each summer has been well known to music lovers since it began in 1913 with a staging of *Aïda* in honor of the one-hundredth anniversary of Verdi's birth. Three operas are grandiosely staged every season to sold-out audiences of over 20,000, who have come from every corner of the world. A ballet and a few select concerts also are featured. Closed Mondays and after 1:30 PM in opera season (July and August); closed Mondays the rest of the year. Piazza Brà (phone: 800-3204).

MUSEO CASTELVECCHIO With its drawbridge on the Adige River, this crenelated Scaligeri fortress looks like a Disney castle from the outside. The building fell into disrepair over the centuries, was bombed in World War II, and then was gloriously restored by modern Venetian architect Carlo Scarpa, who also installed the impressive museum collection. Some later buildings dating back to the Napoleonic era contrast in style to the main part of the castle. Situated in the original Scaligeri apartments, the art gallery has frescoed rooms, rough cement walls, and pink, Veronese marble floors. It houses a collection of Romanesque, Gothic, and Renaissance sculpture and paintings by some of the Veneto's greatest artists, including Tintoretto, Tiepolo, and Veronese. There also is a collection of spurs, lances, helmets, armor, and arms. Closed Mondays. Admission charge. 2 Corso Castelvecchio (phone: 594734).

GALLERIA D'ARTE MODERNA E CONTEMPORANEA PALAZZO FORTI (MODERN AND CONTEMPORARY ART MUSEUM) In the first room of this maze of galleries, marble troughs separate paintings (the room was once a stable). In addition to a permanent collection of Italian modern art, there are interesting shows with a more international scope. The permanent collection is closed Mondays. Admission charge. 1 Via Forte (phone: 800-1903; 596371, special exhibits).

MUSEO MINISCALCHI ERIZZO The exterior of the palace of the Miniscalchi family boasts an ornate frescoed façade. Inside are drawings, paintings, armor, weapons, porcelain, and bronzes from different epochs, all the private collection of the heirless Erizzo family. Closed Mondays, Tuesdays, January through February, and for a long (12:30 to 3:30 PM) break. Admission charge. 2/A Via S. Mamaso (phone: 803-2484).

GATES OF THE CITY Verona's gates were built in different epochs and in different architectural styles. *Porta Borsari,* with a façade of red Veronese marble, was built in the age of Flavius. *Porta Leona* was the eastern approach to the Roman city. The classical lines and arches of *Porta Nuova, Porta Palio,* and *Porta Vescovo* were all designed by Sanmicheli, Verona's architectural answer to Palladio.

ENVIRONS

PARCO GIARDINO SIGURTÀ (VILLA SIGURTÀ PARK) There are over a hundred acres of gardens—woods, lawn, aquatic gardens, and lots of flowers—on the road to this villa garden in the Mincio Valley, about 12 miles (19 km) from the city. Closed December to mid-March, Mondays through Wednesdays, and Fridays. Admission charge. Valeggio sul Mincio (phone: 795-0203).

LAGO DI GARDA (LAKE GARDA) The eastern half of Lake Garda—the largest of the Lombardy lakes—is in the Veneto (for information about the western part of the lake, see *The Lombardy Lakes* in DIRECTIONS), with gently sloping hills of vineyards, olive and lemon trees, castles, and medieval towns, and the majestic Alps looming in the distance. Highly developed for tourism, the area offers such freshwater sports as swimming, sailing, and water skiing (see also *The Veneto* in DIRECTIONS).

Travelers with children may want to visit *Gardaland* (15 miles/24 km west of town on S11, in Castelnuovo/Peschiera del Garda; phone: 644-9777; fax: 640-1267), an amusement park with rides, restaurants, variety shows, and other attractions. It's open daily to 6 PM April through June; daily to midnight July through the second weekend in September; closed weekdays the last two weeks of March and in October; and closed the rest of the year. A free shuttle runs from the *Peschiera di Garda* railway station, about a mile (1.6 km) away.

North of *Gardaland,* the *Parco Natura Viva* (Garda Zoological Park) in Pastrengo also offers family fun, with a drive-through safari park and a *Parco Faunistico* (Zoological Park) that nurtures endangered species and includes a tropical aviary, an aquaterrarium, and a dinosaur park. To get to the *Parco Natura Viva,* take S12 northwest for 12 miles (19 km), cross the river, and head south for 2 miles (3 km). The *Parco Faunistico* (phone: 717-0080) is closed Wednesdays from November to March 14; the safari park (phone: 717-0052; fax: 677-0247) is open daily mid-March through October; closed weekdays November through mid-March. Admission charge to all parks.

SOAVE Fifteen miles (25 km) east of Verona on E13 is this medieval town with a castle, 14th-century walls, and towers, all amidst vineyards that produce grapes for crisp white soave wine.

BOLCA Another worthwhile side trip is to this fossil-rich area. Drive east on S11 about 10 miles (16 km) before turning off north toward Tregnago, passing through the Val d'Illasi, which is overrun with cherry blossoms and patrician villas. Many can be visited. For information, contact the central office of the *Azienda di Promozione Turistica* (*APT;* see below). Continue north to Bolca (about 30 miles/48 km northeast of Verona), one of the most important geological sites in Italy. In Bolca and its surroundings are stunning marine fossils that date back 50 million years, when the area was a vast lagoon languishing in a tropical climate. Bolca's *Museo dei Fossili* (Fossil Museum; 50 Via San Giovanni Battista; phone: 656-5111) draws visitors from all over the world. It's closed Mondays and for a midday break; admission charge.

Sources and Resources

TOURIST INFORMATION

General tourist information is available at the *Azienda di Promozione Turistica* (*APT;* 61 Via Leoncino; phone: 592828; fax: 800-3638), which is closed Sundays September through June. An *APT* branch at the railway station (phone: 717-0052; fax: 677-0247) is open daily in summer; closed after 2:30 PM in winter. Available free of charge is *Passport Verona,* a three-language guide that lists monuments and offers itineraries; a hotel guide; a restaurant listing; and a good city map.

Verona has nearly two dozen officially accredited guides, most of whom speak excellent English. To book one, contact the *Associazione di Guide Turistiche* (7 Via da Mosto; phone: 576852; fax: 575612).

LOCAL COVERAGE The daily papers of Verona and its province are *L'Arena* and *La Nuova da Verona.*

TELEPHONE The city code for Verona is 45. When dialing from within Italy, dial 045 before the local number.

GETTING AROUND

Verona is best seen on foot. Park in one of the city's garages or outside the gates and walk from there. (It is unlikely that a car would be stolen, but it would be unwise to leave anything of value visible in it.)

AIRPORT Verona is served by *Verona-Villafranca Airport,* about 7 miles (11 km) out of town (phone: 809-5666). Bus and taxi service into Verona are available.

BUS Verona has an extensive municipal bus service. Tickets are inexpensive; buy them beforehand at tobacconists or at the bus station at *Porta Nuova,* in front of the main railway station (phone: 521200). A tourist day ticket is available. Buses serving the province and Lake Garda depart from the *Porta Nuova* bus station (phone: 800-4129).

CAR RENTAL Representatives of the major car rental firms are at *Porta Nuova* (see *Train,* below).

TAXI Go.to the cabstand at Piazza Brà, or call *Radio Taxi* (phone: 532666) from 6 AM to midnight.

TRAIN The main station, *Porta Nuova,* is at the south end of the Corso Porta Nuova (phone: 590688).

SPECIAL EVENTS

Verona's large trade-fair organization, *Veronafiere* (8 Viale del Lavoro; phone: 829-8111; fax: 829-8288), attracts visitors from all over the world to a number of fairs throughout the year. We start with our favorite, followed by other noteworthy happenings.

FAVORITE FETE

Fieracavalli A gigantic four-day fair and market in mid-November turns Verona into a thousand-horse town, with colorful sales and auctions, and animals of all breeds competing in jumping, dressage, and races. The newest and best gear for the intelligent care and feeding of the horse is on display, and hundreds of dealers and shoppers from all over Europe are on hand to snap it up. Italy's best riders, the mounted carabinieri, are resplendent in their Napoleonic uniforms.

In April, *VinItaly,* Italy's most important wine fair, offers a complete panorama of Italy's wines, including tastings. Also in spring, *Herbora* specializes in herb-based products. And in fall, *Intermarmomach* shows all the marble, granite, and other stone produced in Italy today, much of which comes from the Verona area. For details on all three events, contact *Veronafiere* (see above).

In April of odd-numbered years, Italian and foreign antiques dealers exhibit and sell their wares at the *Itinerari d'Arte e d'Antiquariato* (Antiques Fair). For details, contact Verona's *APT* administration office (phone: 800-0065 or 800-6997; fax: 801-0682) or the *Associazione Provinciale Antiquari Veronesi* (phone: 591688). The *Rassegna del Presepe* (*Christmas* Crèche Exhibition), held in the *Arena* from early December to early February, displays an international collection of antique and modern crèches.

MUSEUMS

Apart from those mentioned in *Special Places,* Verona has a few smaller museums.

BIBLIOTECA CAPITOLARE (CAPITAL LIBRARY) The oldest functioning library in Europe houses manuscripts, parchments, codices, and so on. Open Monday, Wednesday, and Saturday mornings; Tuesdays and Fridays from 9:30 AM to 12:30 PM and 4 to 6 PM; closed Thursdays, Sundays, and July. No admission charge. 13 Piazza Duomo (phone: 596516).

MUSEO CIVICO DI STORIA NATURALE (NATURAL HISTORY MUSEUM) One of Italy's most important geological and fossil collections, it features outstanding finds from the region. Closed Fridays. No admission charge on Sundays. In Sanmicheli's *Palazzo Pompei*, at 9 Lungadige Porta Vittoria (phone: 807-9404).

MUSEO LAPIDARIO MAFFEIANO (MAFFEIANO LAPIDARY MUSEUM) The oldest in Europe, with stone plaques, statues, urns, and reliefs. Closed Mondays and after 1:30 PM. Admission charge. 28 Piazza Brà (phone: 590087).

TEATRO ROMANO E MUSEO ARCHEOLOGICO (ROMAN THEATER AND ARCHAEOLOGICAL MUSEUM) An ancient theater and antiquity museum. Closed Mondays and after 1:30 PM. Admission charge. Rigaste Redentore (phone: 800-0360).

SHOPPING

An important commercial crossroads and a city of wealth, Verona offers some fantastic shopping. Clothes, shoes, antiques, design, and all objects of elegance are easy to find in the city's one-of-a-kind shops and designer boutiques. The province of Verona produces shoes for all of Italy and abroad, representing one-tenth of the country's entire production. Drive along the main road toward Lake Garda, through Bussolengo, and buy directly from the factories at very low prices.

In the center of town are two streets devoted almost exclusively to antiques, Via Sant'Anastasia and Via Sottoriva. Stores here are tucked away under medieval arches, their façades dating from the 3rd and 4th centuries.

The main shopping street is the pedestrians-only Via Mazzini, hub of all the big names in Italian fashion. Most shops are closed Monday mornings and for a long (12:30 to 4 or 4:30 PM) break.

Bertolosi Children's shoes. 24/A Via Mazzini (phone: 803-4806).

Bon Bon Children's clothes. 12/A Via Cappello (phone: 594172).

Calimala Embroidered linen and lace. 6/B Via E. Noris (phone: 800-2427).

Canestrari The oldest jeweler in Verona, in a shop that looks a bit like Aladdin's cave. 50 Via Mazzini (phone: 594763 or 800-6491).

Folli Follie Prada, Granello, and Pitti shoes, bags, clothes, and accessories. 9/A Via G. Oberdan (phone: 592939).

Fulmine del Guanto Great gloves. 44 Via Mazzini (phone: 595512).

G. M. C. Discount designer shoes, bags, and belts. 15/A Via Cattaneo (phone: 800-1251).

Libreria Ghelfi & Barbato An old-fashioned bookstore, including many books in English. 21 Via Mazzini (phone: 597732 or 800-2306).

Mantellero High class men's hats and women's hosiery in a hallowed atmosphere. 59 Via Mazzini (phone: 803-1607).

New Galles Fashion, including Emporio Armani styles. 4 Via A. Cantore (phone: 803-1555 or 803-4133).

Principe Verona's local shoe store. 80 Via Mazzini (phone: 800-7165).

Profumerie Douglas A large selection of perfumes, aftershaves, and colognes, all at discount prices. 35/A Via Capello (phone: 803-6177).

Proposte di Passeroni New and antique silver. 63 Via Mazzini (phone: 596596).

Spega Freshly prepared delicacies, perfect for a picnic by the banks of the Adige River. 11 Via Stella (phone: 800-4998).

SPORTS AND FITNESS

Sports do not seem to be very high on the agenda for visitors to the city, perhaps because they get enough exercise just walking around.

GOLF There's an 18-hole course, *Golf Club Verona,* on Ca' del Sale, in Sommacampagna (phone: 510060).

HORSEBACK RIDING Contact the *Società Ippica Veronese* (Boschetto, Lungadige Galtarossa; phone: 803-1854).

SOCCER Every other Sunday, from September through May, *Verona* plays at *Stadio Bentegodi* (Piazzale Olimpia; phone: 567427).

SWIMMING Try the *Piscina Comunale* (Via Colonello Galliano; phone: 567622).

TENNIS There are courts at the *Circolo Tennis Scaligero* (6 Via Cristoforo Colombo; phone: 568892).

THEATER AND MUSIC

The *Arena* opera season, spanning July and August, is a major musical phenomenon in Europe. Although the soprano can look very small if you're sitting near the lip of the *Arena,* she's still visible and, more important, more audible than in the higher-priced seats farther down. Prices for the best seats are expensive; higher up and to the sides, they are more reasonable. (For more information, see *Special Places.*) The rest of the year, excellent music, including opera, can be heard at the *Teatro Filarmonico* (4/K Via dei Mutilati; phone: 800-2880), where tickets are less expensive. In summer, ballet performances are given on the other side of the river in the *Teatro Romano*, which also hosts a summer Shakespeare festival. Book through the *Ente Lirico Arena di Verona* (28 Piazza Brà, Verona 37121; phone: 590109, 590966, or 590726; fax: 801-1566).

NIGHTCLUBS AND NIGHTLIFE

Popular nightclubs in the city center include *Excalibur Club* (24 Stradone A. Provolo; phone: 594614), which welcomes non-members and is the best in town (closed Mondays); *Campidoglio* (4 Piazzetta Tirabosco; phone: 594448), a piano bar specializing in 1960s music, with live music after midnight (closed Mondays); and *Café Jazz da José* (8 Via Sant'Egidio; phone: 592958), offering jazz in a 14th-century palazzo (closed Tuesdays).

Best in Town

CHECKING IN

Trade fairs and the *Arena* theater and concert season in the summer can easily fill all the city's hotels and those in the surrounding countryside, so book well in advance. Expect to pay $325 or more per night for a double room in the hotel listed as very expensive; from $170 to $320 at an expensive place; from $85 to $160 at a moderate hotel; and $85 and less at an inexpensive one. Prices are lower without breakfast, so make sure you have not been charged for it if you choose not to take it. The *Cooperativa Albergatori Veronesi* (Veronese Hoteliers Asssociation; phone: 800-9844; fax: 800-9372) will book you a hotel room free of charge. All hotels feature private baths unless otherwise indicated. All telephone numbers are in the 45 city code unless otherwise noted.

VERY EXPENSIVE

Gabbia d'Oro Close to Piazza delle Erbe in the center of town, this lodging establishment is perhaps the best in Verona, with eight rooms, 19 suites, and an extremely helpful staff. Fresco fragments, ancient wooden beams, exposed brick, attractive floral arrangements, and subdued furnishings combined with antiques in the intimate sitting rooms create a homey, unhotel-like ambience. Meals are served in an attractive inner courtyard in summer; the view from the roof bar is spectacular. 4/A Corso Porta Borsari (phone: 800-3060; fax: 590293).

EXPENSIVE

Accademia Just off Via Mazzini, this conveniently located hundred-room place has a helpful staff and a restaurant. 10-12 Via Scala (phone: 596222; fax: 596222).

Colomba d'Oro Excellently maintained and just around the corner from the Roman arena, this comfortable 49-room hotel has a garage but no restaurant. 10 Via Cattaneo (phone: 595300; fax: 594974).

Leon d'Oro Close to the trade fair center, though in unattractive surroundings, this ultramodern hostelry with 208 rooms and seven suites is one of the few in Italy with nonsmoking rooms. There's also a restaurant serving sophisticated Italian food, a gym, a sauna, satellite TV, and most conveniences for the business traveler. 5 Viale Piave (phone: 801-0555; fax: 801-0504).

Villa del Quar Set amid gardens and vineyards, this 16th-century villa is in the valpolicella countryside, just 4½ miles (7 km) outside Verona. An architect and his family converted part of their home into a charming and sophisticated hotel, furnishing the 18 rooms and four suites with antiques. All guestrooms have marble-tiled bathrooms, air conditioning, mini-bars, TV sets, and telephones. The lovely and peaceful surroundings, cool breezes, pool, and expert cooking by a Bolognese chef make this a pleasant experience for those who prefer staying outside town. 12 Via Quar, Pedemonte (phone: 680-0681; fax: 680-0604).

MODERATE

Antica Porta Leona Around the corner from Juliet's house and Via degli Amanti (Lovers' Street), this charmingly redecorated hotel with 36 rooms is on one of the quaintest corners in Verona. No restaurant. 3 Corticella Leoni (phone: 595499; fax: 595499).

Bologna Ideally located just off Piazza Brà, this unpretentious, modern 30-room hostelry has a very good restaurant, *Rubiani,* whose sidewalk terrace looks out toward the *Arena.* 3 Piazzetta Scalette Rubiani (phone: 800-6830; fax: 801-0602).

San Luca Quiet and efficient, it has 41 rooms but no restaurant. Conveniently located near Piazza Brà and the *Arena,* at 8 Vicolo Volto San Luca (phone: 591-333; fax: 800-2143).

Touring This turn-of-the-century, 47-room hotel is in the heart of Old Verona. A few rooms share a bath, and there's no dining room. 5 Via Q. Sella (phone: 590944; fax: 590290).

INEXPENSIVE

Aurora These are economical accommodations for those who appreciate a hotel's view more than its comforts (only double rooms have baths), though major improvements were scheduled to be finished this spring. Of the 22 rooms, ask for one overlooking the white umbrellas of the market square. No restaurant. 2 Via Pellicciai (phone: 594717; fax: 801-0860).

Torcolo The 19 guestrooms in this hostelry, just a few steps from the *Arena,* are decorated in a variety of styles—from 18th century to modern. Breakfast is served on a shady terrace, but there's no dining room. 3 Vicolo Listone (phone: 800-7512; fax: 800-4058).

EATING OUT

Veronese menus differ only slightly from those elsewhere in northern Italy, and the overall standard is high. Local specialties include gnocchi with a variety of sauces, from the classic meat or tomato to butter and sage. An interesting pasta sauce is made with *ortiche* (nettles), which taste a little like broccoli. For the main course, Verona is famous for its boiled meat—not just the usual cuts, but less expected parts, such as *testina* (head), which is always served with *pearà,* a bread sauce spiced with pepper. The non-squeamish may want to try another typical dish, *pastissada,* a horse meat stew served with toasted polenta. The town has become synonymous with *pandoro,* a simple but delicious cake that resembles panettone.

To enjoy the local wines (soaves, bardolinos, and valpolicellas), join the Veronese in a traditional *osteria,* a wine bar that has in some cases grown up into a full-fledged restaurant. Wine is available by the glass, and snacks and sandwiches are served at the bar. Most of the *osterie* listed below have evolved from serving only house wine to featuring the region's fine fermentations.

Try to avoid touristy places with inexpensive menus that list dishes in several languages, and those restaurants with entrées named after Romeo and Juliet—they generally offer mediocre food. The *osterie* are a far better choice for an economical meal. In the restaurants listed as very expensive, expect to spend about $150 for a dinner for two, including wine; those rated as expensive will cost from $100 to $150; a moderate meal will run from $50 to $100; and an inexpensive one, $50 or less. All restaurants are open for lunch and dinner unless otherwise noted. All telephone numbers are in the 45 city code unless otherwise indicated.

VERY EXPENSIVE

Le Arche Innovatively prepared fish dishes are served in elegant surroundings. Closed Monday lunch, Sundays, two weeks in January, and the first three weeks of July. Reservations advised. Major credit cards accepted. 6 Via Arche Scaligere (phone: 800-7415).

Il Desco Save this elegant restaurant for a romantic evening; for a perfect start, try the *budino di formaggio con fonduta* (a cheese fondue specialty). Closed Sundays and the second half of June; open late in August after opera performances. Reservations advised. Major credit cards accepted. 5-7 Via Dietro San Sebastiano (phone: 595358).

12 Apostoli One of Italy's most celebrated dining spots dates back over 200 years. It's still a wonderful experience, characterized by original recipes and soups, excellent wines, and Renaissance-style decor. Closed Mondays, Sunday dinner, one week in January, and mid-June through the first week of July. Reservations advised. Major credit cards accepted. 3 Vicolo Corticella San Marco (phone: 596999).

EXPENSIVE

Bottega del Vino The ambience is Old Verona, with plenty of rose marble, frescoed walls, wooden tables, and a bar the length of the front room. The menu and house wines are chalked on a blackboard in the *osteria* up front, with more formal dining on cloth-covered tables in the back rooms. Try the risotto and *bigoli* (thick pasta—a local specialty). The renowned wine list is extensive and well priced. Closed Wednesdays, except during the summer. Reservations unnecessary. Major credit cards accepted. 3 Via Scudo di Francia (phone: 800-4535).

Il Cenacolo Choose from a wide selection of entrées and grilled meat; the fixed-price menu seems endless (even though the restaurant's name means "The Last Supper"). Closed Tuesdays. Reservations advised for dinner. Major credit cards accepted. 10 Via Teatro Filarmonico (phone: 592288).

Nuovo Marconi Elegant Belle Epoque decor is the backdrop for painstakingly prepared Veronese specialties. Fish is the specialty, though everything is delicious. Closed Sundays and late June through early July. Reservations advised. Major credit cards accepted. 4 Via Fogge (phone: 591910).

MODERATE

Al Calmiere The typical Veronese rose marble floor gives this eatery a warm, wonderful feeling. The cooking is simple, home-style, and well prepared; meat and vegetables are cooked in the massive fireplace in the back room. Dine outdoors in the spring and summer, overlooking *San Zeno,* one of Verona's most beautiful churches. Closed Wednesday dinner, Thursdays, and three weeks in July. Reservations advised. Major credit cards accepted. 10 Piazza San Zeno (phone: 803-0765).

Cicarelli An old posthouse, it offers friendly service, a lively atmosphere, and the best pasta, topped with traditional Veronese sauces; also, superb meat served with *salsa verde* (parsley, capers, and egg) and horseradish. Closed Friday dinner, Saturdays, four weeks in July and August, and *Christmas.* Reservations advised. Visa accepted. About 5 miles (8 km) away on the road to Mantua, at 171 Via Mantovana, Madonna di Dossobuono (phone: 953986).

Ciopeta Centrally located, behind the *Arena* and Piazza Brà, this family restaurant serves simple, healthy fare and offers lots of atmosphere. There is alfresco dining in the summer. It also has eight inexpensive rooms, none with private bath. Closed Saturdays except in July and August, and for two weeks during *Christmas.* Reservations advised. No credit cards accepted. 2 Vicolo Teatro Filarmonico (phone: 800-6843).

La Greppia Imaginatively renovated, this vintage dining place serves excellent fresh pasta and boiled and roast meat dishes. Closed Mondays, one week in January, and three weeks in June. Reservations advised. Major credit cards accepted. 3 Vicolo Samaritana (phone: 800-4577).

Osteria la Fontanina The setting is charming, with a bar and two small dining rooms cluttered attractively with flea market finds and dried flower arrangements.

Fish and meat dishes are offered, and a well-priced, three-course lunch is served daily. Choose a local wine from the ample list. Closed Sundays, Monday lunch, most of August, and *Christmas*. Reservations necessary. Major credit cards accepted. 3 Portichetti Fontanelle, S. Stefano (phone: 913305).

Osteria all'Oste Scuro This wine bar–turned-restaurant features an unusually congenial atmosphere and home-style cooking. Reasonably priced tasting menus, with glasses of different wines accompanying the main courses, are organized once or twice weekly between September and May. Closed Saturday lunch, Sundays, two or three weeks in August, and one week at *Christmas*. Reservations advised. Major credit cards accepted. 10 Vicolo S. Silvestro (phone: 592650).

Alla Pigna Veronese food is combined with some Tuscan specialties in this stylish dining spot, decorated with rose-colored marble columns from the 14th century, leafy wallpaper, and framed caricatures of former clients on the walls. The wine list is uneven. Closed Sundays and four weeks in July and August. Reservations advised. Major credit cards accepted. 4 Via Pigna (phone: 800-4080).

Torcoloti Old-fashioned elegance, perfect for a quiet dinner. The appetizers—especially the combination *tris della casa* (three kinds of stuffed pasta)—are excellent. Closed Sundays, Mondays, and June. Reservations advised. Major credit cards accepted. 24 Via Zambelli (phone: 800-6777).

INEXPENSIVE

Armando This unassuming (yet excellent) fish restaurant is next to an *osteria* of the same name. Closed Mondays. Reservations unnecessary. No credit cards accepted. 8 Via Macello (phone: 800-0892).

Al Carro Armato Close to Piazza dei Signori in a 14th-century building, the "Armored Tank" seems like a natural hangout. During the day locals play cards and drink the house wine; in the evening, a younger crowd takes over. Cheese and cured meat are served with a well-chosen selection of wines. Closed Wednesdays. No reservations. No credit cards accepted. 2/A Vicolo Gatto (phone: 803-0175).

Fontanina In a little square close to *Sant'Anastasia,* this friendly, family-run trattoria (not to be confused with *Osteria la Fontanina,* above) enjoys a faithful clientele of locals, who return for its simple home-style cooking and outdoor tables in summer. Closed Tuesdays from November through April. Reservations advised. No credit cards accepted. 5 Piazzetta Chiavica (phone: 803-1133).

Impero A reliable pizzeria in charming Piazza dei Signori, it has plenty of tables outdoors. Closed Wednesdays. Reservations advised. Major credit cards accepted. 8 Piazza dei Signori (phone: 803-0160).

Liston A favorite with musicians and theaterfolk, this relaxed trattoria/pizzeria just behind Piazza Brà offers tasty dishes, and it stays open into the wee hours. Closed Wednesdays and two weeks from January to February. Reservations advised. Major credit cards accepted. 19 Via Dietro Listone (phone: 803-4003).

BARS AND CAFFÈS

Visitors and locals alike gravitate in the morning to the line of *caffès* in Piazza Erbe, with its quaintly umbrella-lined market stalls and the splashing of its fountain. In the afternoons and evenings, they head to the *caffè* terraces on Piazza Brà, right in front of the *Arena,* where the world passes by, *La Dolce Vita*–style. The following places—bars, *caffès*, and other snacking spots—are somewhat off the beaten path. Most bars and *caffès* listed below are in the inexpensive price range.

Antico Caffè Dante The proprietor of the *Nuovo Marconi* took over and carefully restored this historic venue, transforming it into a brasserie-style *caffè*/restaurant with a short but interesting menu. Also offering delicious cakes and pastries, it's an ideal place to sit and enjoy the lovely view of Piazza dei Signori at any time of day. Also see *Special Places.* Closed Sundays in winter. Major credit cards accepted. 2 Piazza dei Signori (phone: 595249).

Bar al Ponte Enjoy the view at this riverside bar, which has a small terrace in the back with a few tables. Closed Wednesdays in winter and for two to three weeks from September to October. No credit cards accepted. Right by the Roman bridge, at 26 Via Ponte Pietra (phone: 803-2812).

Brigliadoro This somewhat serious coffee bar (also known as *Barretto*) offers good wines by the glass and a selection of cold dishes, salads, and cured meat, such as smoked goose breast. There also are a variety of freshly ground coffee roasts and interesting teas. Closed Sundays. MasterCard and Visa accepted. 4 Via S. Michele alla Porta (phone: 800-4514).

Gelateria Mazzini Verona's best ice-cream store offers a huge assortment of delectable flavors. Closed Sundays in winter. Counter service only. No credit cards accepted. 5 Via Mazzini (phone: 590161).

Osteria le Decete With a temping array of freshly prepared sandwiches and cold snacks, this nonsmoking bar does a booming lunch business. Closed Sundays and after 8 PM. No credit cards accepted. 32 Via Pellicciai (phone: 594681).

Diversions
Exceptional Pleasures and Treasures

For the Experience

Quintessential Italy

Any visitor can savor the quintessence of this nation, which has entranced travelers since Homer met Circe, simply by getting away from it all in one of the vintage destinations and diversions that follow. So remember, before you trot off to the *Great Wall* or sail for Bora Bora, there's no place like Rome. At the same time, however, the pollution and frantic pace of Italy's larger cities—and the increasing accessibility to the great museums and piazzas of the smaller towns—make those lesser-known spots especially appealing to today's visitors.

SOCCER SUNDAY *Calcio* is a national religion in Italy, and the Sunday afternoon *partita* is its rite. During the two hours when these games are played throughout the country, an eerie hush, broken only by periodic roars of raw joy, falls over town and country alike. After a team has won a home game and the stadiums empty, triumphant fans wrap themselves in team colors, blow horns, and wave banners from buses, scooters, and cars. Where teams share a home town and a stadium, rivalries are intense, especially during the twice-yearly *derby,* when parents who root for, say, *Inter* disown children who favor, say, *Milan.* By all means go to a match, but if you like to express your sympathies exuberantly, don't sit in the wrong part of the bleachers.

CROSSING THE ALPS TO CORTINA D'AMPEZZO, Trentino–Alto Adige The drive across the Brenner Pass into the Trentino unveils a skier's-eye view of the peninsula that seems to extend almost to the Sicilian shore and, in winter, the spectacle of Cortina: an urbane populace in chic ski outfits and matching goggles, the smell of pine and cedar, narrow valleys, figure-eight roads flanked by giant evergreens, and precipitous drops into snowy nothingness. Where the road stops, the chair lift carries you up to the thin air of the top of Italy, where it's magical to loll on the sun-warmed deck of a mountain restaurant, the craggy pink Dolomites all around, or wait for your ears to thaw while nursing a *caffè corretto* (a coffee "adjusted" with grappa).

VILLAGE ON A VOLCANO, Etna, Sicily In the metropolis of Catania, vendors hawk postcards of villages being destroyed by burning lava and tell of incautious tourists seeking sights too near the crater. In the piazza, the men play a placid game of after-dinner cards, offer glasses of the smoky wine from which they make their living, show off the ruined Norman church that is their local treasure, and otherwise demonstrate their Sicilian pride in home. Ride the tiny train that runs around the base of Mt. Etna, Europe's largest active volcano, to get a better look at the agricultural heart of the area: dark slopes braided with rich vineyards; moonlike hills of hardened rock and ash; farmers, commuting from the towns to their fields, disembarking now and again. When raging Etna drives them away, they will return to build again.

HARVEST TIME, Orvieto, Umbria The serene hills below Orvieto begin bustling in September, as harvest workers armed with shears fan out into the disciplined rows of vines, clip away the clusters of fat trebbiano and malvasia grapes hiding under their protective leaves, and haul away crates of rich fruit. At noon, the laborers rest on blankets scattered through the fields, gnaw slabs of prosciutto between bread, and down swigs of last year's wine. Later, clothes and hands stained a rich scarlet, they bring the piled fruit to be crushed—in some villages by the oaken *torchio.* Some larger vineyards offer tours of the cool cellars where the grapes are pressed by machine and the product is fermented, aged, bottled, and labeled; for weeks, whole villages reek of new wine. Meanwhile, everyone hopes: Maybe some fluke in the weather or an all too rare smile from the gods will make this vintage *speciale.*

A PROVINCIAL PASSEGGIATA, Perugia, Umbria The Sunday-evening stroll, or *passeggiata,* is an Italian ritual, and it is particularly colorful on the handsome Corso Vannucci, the main street of Umbria's attractive regional capital. Bearded university students argue as they amble. A grinning girl in her first-communion lace leads a retinue of proud relatives. A town marching band trumpets, the violinist squeakily serenading *caffè*-sitters in exchange for small change. A clique of teenagers coolly holds court on motor scooters parked in front of a restaurant sign offering "Fast Food All'Italiana." Flow with the crowd along the city's curved Renaissance façades to the fountain in the cathedral piazza. Or take a front row seat in a *caffè.* The cost of this entertaining procession? The price of a Campari and soda.

ROME AT CHRISTMAS Spirits soar along with prices, and stores stay open on Sundays during Italy's holiday jubilee, which lasts from early December until the arrival of La Befana, the national answer to Santa Claus, on January 6. Most years, a giant *Christmas* tree stands guard at Piazza Venezia. Windows are dressed in glitter and Styrofoam snow (about as close as Rome ever gets to the real thing). Lavish nativity scenes are mounted by churches throughout the city. Some evoke images of those found in ancient Rome or even Capri; some are outdoors. Shoppers wrapped in showy furs inspect the king's ransom in gold and jewels along Via Condotti, and Piazza Navona is jammed with stalls selling trinkets, toys, tree ornaments, and the freshly mined hunks of coal-colored spun-sugar candy known as *carbone.* The city offers an elegant gift to visitors and Romans—free concerts in selected ancient churches and palazzi, their organs tuned and frescoes brilliantly illuminated for the occasion.

FOUNTAINS OF ROME In the thick heat of a Roman August, flocks of bare-legged tourists and the few locals who have not migrated to the teeming beaches converge under the spray of the city's innumerable fountains. Clutching fast-liquefying ice-cream cones, these chill seekers stare enviously at the *Fontana di Trevi*'s Neptune riding his marine chariot through cool waves of marble and water, or they enjoy the water alongside the Four Rivers at Piazza Navona, the giant Roman bathtubs that Michelangelo installed at Piazza Farnese, the sea monsters at the 19th-century Piazza Esedra, the fish at the *Pantheon*, or the climbing turtles at Piazza Mattei. At many street corners, cast-iron fountains spout drinking water from springs borne to town on ancient aqueducts. And in the evening, the fountains provide a soothing background gurgle and a civilized place to rinse off the stickiness of that irresistible gelato nightcap.

TRASTEVERE, Rome The people who live in Trastevere, the medieval maze of curving alleys and *piazzette* on the right bank of the Tiber, believe that their neighborhood is the only true Rome and its inhabitants the only true Romans. Gentrification has set in, but it still teems and throbs with life, particularly in summer. Walk across the bridge to the boat-shaped Tiber island known as the Isola Tiberina. Get there when dusk gilds the medieval mosaics in Piazza Santa Maria, and hunt around for one of the area's basement theaters, small jazz clubs, and tiny art cinemas, their signs camouflaged by laundry hung out to dry. Then have supper outdoors at one of the festive *pizzerie* that appropriate sidewalks and parking spaces all summer long. After midnight, stop at the back door of an unassuming bakery a block from Piazza Trilussa to sate yourself on tomorrow's *cornetti* and hot, cream-filled bombe. And at dawn on Sunday, show up at the immense flea market at Porta Portese, which closes by lunchtime, to comb through piles of early Renaissance Levis, stucco busts of Mussolini, and priceless and prongless silver forks.

MASS IN ST. PETER'S, Vatican City There is an opulent sense of secrecy and devotion in the penitent hum emerging from the confessionals, the permanent smell of incense, the smoky glow of candles on gilt-framed paintings and glinting Baroque statues in *St. Peter's Basilica*. Here's where the faithful of Rome share pews with pilgrims from Lithuania, Poland, and Zaire, and stately processions of white-robed men and boys perpetually reenact a ritual that only the initiated can fully understand. Sometimes the dark whispers of the mass are broken by a bright burst of sound as orchestra and chorus deliver the Bach *Magnificat,* the soloists' voices rebounding off the fluted columns and convoluted walls. At the final cadence, the hush sets in again.

GRAND CANAL, Venice Drift down the lavish 2-mile length of the Grand Canal in a sleek gondola—yes, a touristy, expensive gondola. There's more to see than even the observant have time to notice: hundreds of wrought-stone, pink-tinted, marble-edged Gothic and Renaissance palaces; sleek mahogany motor launches moored in front of equally princely hotels; lumbering boat-buses unloading passengers onto listing docks; and a skein of alleyways and slender, twisting canals winding away from this broad, curving boulevard of water. Anyone beholding it all for the first time without a lump in his or her throat surely has a heart of stone.

Italy's Most Memorable Hostelries

Like one big room with a view, Italy is full of princely villas, magnificent monasteries, and other handsome accommodations lovingly and lavishly ransomed from the past. These historic hostelries supply the perfect excuse to avoid the anonymous glass-and-concrete business domes of postwar Italy. We have highlighted exceptional *alberghi* located in the country's main urban centers in the individual reports in THE CITIES. But splendid hotels are not solely the domain of major metropolises. Here are some of our favorite rural retreats.

DEI TRULLI, Alberobello, Puglia One of the main attractions of little-visited Puglia is Alberobello, whose narrow streets are lined with clusters of more than a thousand *trulli*—tiny whitewashed, beehive-shaped houses found only in this part of southern Italy. Their design, believed to be prehistoric and pagan, conjures up images of gnomes' houses or Tolkien land. This hostelry provides the opportunity to actually lodge in one of them. Each of the 20 cozy mini-apartments is an authentic individual *trullo,* complete with bedroom, miniature living room with fireplace, bathroom, and patio. There also is a good restaurant, a pool, and landscaped grounds. The rather steep rates are justified by the unique setting indigenous to Alberobello alone. Open year-round. Information: *Hotel dei Trulli,* 32 Via Cadore, Alberobello (Bari) 70011 (phone: 80-932-3555; fax: 80-932-3560).

QUISISANA, Capri, Campania When Doctor Clark, a British physician, founded his little sanatorium in the middle of the last century, he chose the sunniest and least windy corner of Capri and named the spot *Qui Si Sana,* meaning "Here one gets well." The hotel grew and prospered; today, it enjoys perfect health in the heart of Capri as one of Italy's best-known and most glamorous holiday spots. Its 142 elegant rooms, restaurant, and courtyard for dining attract a well-heeled clientele. Only the service is still superbly old-fashioned, and its three-star oval pool, tennis courts, celebrated terrace bar, and international parade of guests are great for what ails you. And Capri itself makes the rest of the world and its problems seem sweetly irrelevant; the vital issues here are the flawless sea, the endless bouquet of flowers, and the sunny-Italy sunshine. Open April through October. Information: *Quisisana,* 2 Via Camerelle, Capri (Napoli) 80073 (phone: 81-837-0788; fax: 81-837-6080).

VILLA D'ESTE, Cernobbio, Lombardy Between its construction by luxury-loving Cardinal Tolomeo Gallio in 1568 and its conversion to a hotel in 1873, this sumptuous property on mountain-framed Lake Como passed through the hands of the noble families Torlonia and Orsini, who seem to have owned every worthwhile piece of Renaissance real estate under the Italian sun. Nudged into the 20th century with grace and style, the place must rank with the top half-dozen resort hotels on the planet. Stroll through the 20-acre park on pathways across velvet lawns or through groves of pine and cypress, and promenade under the lindens alongside the lake. The 158 air conditioned rooms and suites are opulently decorated with period furniture and 19th-century antiques. There are two restaurants (the *Grill/Sporting Club* is better), a nightclub, eight tennis courts, three pools (one indoor, two outdoor), and facilities for water sports. The nearby mountains and lake guarantee cool weather even during the hottest Italian summers. Open March through November. Information: *Villa d'Este,* 40 Via Regina, Cernobbio (Como) 22010 (phone: 31-511471; fax: 31-512027).

MIRAMONTI MAJESTIC, Cortina d'Ampezzo, Veneto In the craggy heart of the Dolomites, a few kilometers above the glitter of Italy's most sophisticated and *very* expensive mountain resort, and surrounded by a park full of pines, this venerable 130-room hotel still has one courtly toe in the 19th century. But the sybaritic guests of the fin de siècle did without such modern delights as the pool, tennis courts, fully equipped sports center, nine-hole golf course, dining room (for guests only), pub, and disco. If the gabled roofs and romantic balconies look familiar, it's because you saw them in a James Bond film. Come in winter for Cortina's incomparable skiing, or in summer for inspiring mountain rambling. Open *Christmas* to mid-April and July through August. Information: *Miramonti Majestic,* 103 Via Peziè, Cortina d'Ampezzo (Belluno) 32043 (phone: 436-4201; fax: 436-867019).

SANTAVENERE, Maratea, Basilicata The white-arcaded façade, set in a verdant fabric of olive and pine trees, and its dramatic position between a Saracen tower and the turquoise Tyrrhenian would ensure a nomination for an Oscar among Mediterranean hostelries. So it's surprising that this structure, built when Maratea was an innocent fishing village and no one who counted vacationed in the tumbledown region, remained such a well-kept secret for so many years. Maratea's narrow streets, rising and falling over well-trodden steps and twisting and turning under ancient arches, bustle nowadays, but the hotel is as pretty as ever—elegant but not stuffy, with 44 guestrooms and a restaurant and scattered with reproduction antiques, model sailboats, and other nautical touches, rather like a comfortable country home. If you aren't exhausted by climbing up and down Maratea's steps and ramps, there's also tennis and swimming in the pool or sea. The disco-and-boutique option is there when you want it. Open *Easter* through October. Information: *Santavenere,* Fiumicello di Santa Venere, Maratea (Potenza) 85040 (phone: 973-876910; fax: 973-876985).

SPLENDIDO, Portofino, Liguria Since its transformation from a private aristocratic residence at the turn of the century, this special hotel has pampered both well-to-do and ne'er-do-well, and the view from its terraces and balconies—of Portofino's many-colored cottages and bobbing boats in the aquamarine port—has remained miraculously unchanged. This 63-room member of the Relais & Châteaux group is situated in what can only be described as paradise—the perfectly tended grounds, atwitter with birds and perpetually scented with mimosa and orange blossoms, modestly conceal a tennis court and pool. A romantic path leads down to the small town and the irresistible *aperitivo* hour at dockside. Open April through December. Information: *Splendido,* Portofino (Genova) 16034 (phone: 185-269551; 800-237-1236; fax: 185-269614).

ALBERGO SAN PIETRO, Positano, Campania All 60 guestrooms in this stunning and supremely romantic seaside cliff-top hotel have views over the Amalfi Coast. No signs mark the entrance; the building seems tied to the cliff that plunges into the Bay of Salerno. Its architecture and furnishings provide a colorful Italian and Moorish blend. Rooms are tucked into the rock, layer upon layer of them. Their walls are white and dazzling, their floors tiled and scattered with Oriental rugs, and each is embellished with antiques and sea-view balconies. And there are flowers at every turn, inside and out. The pool is on top, with a stunning view, and an elevator that pierces the rock carries guests to the private rocky beach and tennis courts below in style. A convertible jitney brings you into chic little Positano, just a mile away. Film and opera director Franco Zeffirelli, who has a summer palace here, gives the town a kind of perpetual opening-night air when he and his retinue are in residence. Open one week before *Easter* through October. Information: *Albergo San Pietro,* Positano (Salerno) 84017 (phone: 89-875455; 800-223-9832; fax: 89-811449).

The Best Restaurants of Italy

Dining in Italy is filled with many delights. *Cucina creativa*—Italy's answer to France's nouvelle cuisine—is now firmly established. Centuries-old regional dishes are being rediscovered and presented in modernized versions. Old-fashioned cereal staples like barley and *faro*—the porridge that nourished the ancient Roman soldiers—have become popular; give them a try. As expected, there are more pasta dishes in Italy than there are forks, so don't limit yourself to spaghetti. With 5,000 miles of coastline, fish abounds as well, and meat dishes are imaginative and varied. Wind up the meal with a fine distilled grappa, available in most bars and restaurants.

Almost every evening in Italy, the *cena* (dinner) is the principal entertainment. Fine restaurants can be found in every city (and in many an out-of-the-way corner), and family trattorie know how to make the most of their comestible bounties; they offer a mix of homeyness, sophistication, and market-fresh foods (usually written in purple ink in an almost indecipherable scrawl).

We have featured remarkable *ristoranti* in the country's major urban centers in the individual reports in THE CITIES. The delightful dining places listed below are located off the beaten track. *Buon appetito!*

DEI CACCIATORI DA CESARE, Albaretto Torre, Piedmont One of Italy's premier chefs, Cesare Giaccone, has won a cult following for his inspired and unusual dishes, all based on excellent regional ingredients. Delicious local truffles—used with abandon—are the star of the show in the fall, playing the leading role in his "autumn surprise" (a lightly poached egg smothered under a layer of truffles). Other specialties are mushroom salad, ravioli sauced with fontina, *stradette* (wide strips of cornmeal pasta) dressed with leeks, spit-roasted kid, and goose braised with cabbage. For a dramatic finale, try the hazelnut cookies, baked and served on the branches of hazelnut trees. In a tiny village about 19 miles (30 km) from Alba, this simple but elegant restaurant has no sign outside; call ahead for directions. Closed Tuesdays, Wednesdays, January, and August. Information: *Dei Cacciatori da Cesare,* 9 Via San Bernardo, Albaretto Torre (Cuneo) 12060 (phone: 173-520141).

PARACUCCHI–LOCANDA DELL'ANGELO, Ameglia, Liguria A modern, unprepossessing 37-room hotel near the buzzing beaches of Liguria's Riviera is the modest backdrop for Angelo Paracucchi's nationally acclaimed seafood workshop, one of Italy's culinary landmarks. Traditional marine staples like clams, rock lobster, shrimp, and sea bass appear here in enticing and original guises. The pasta is tossed with asparagus, seafood, or the simplest tomato and olive oil sauces. Game appears on the table in fall and winter, raspberries and wild strawberries in early summer, and honey-and-vinegar-flavored duck year-round. Closed Mondays in off-season and the last three weeks in January. Information: *Paracucchi–Locanda dell'Angelo,* 60 Via XXV Aprile, Ameglia (La Spezia) 19031 (phone: 187-64391; fax: 187-64393).

GENER NEUV, Asti, Piedmont Homemade pasta, *finanziere* (stewed sweetbreads and mushrooms), and roast breast of guinea hen, all prepared just right, are typical of the comforting food served at this countrified yet formal, family-run restaurant in the charming medieval town of Asti. Truffles and mushrooms are specialties in late autumn. A tasting plate of desserts is on hand for those with a sweet tooth (and the foresight to have saved room). The beamed ceiling is inscribed with sayings in the Piedmontese dialect (ask for translations). Closed Mondays, Sunday dinner, August, and the week between *Christmas* and *New Year's.* Information: *Gener Neuv,* 4 Lungo Tanaro, Asti 14100 (phone: 141-57270).

LA FRASCA, Castrocaro Terme, Emilia-Romagna That proprietor Gianfranco Bolognesi began life as a sommelier is evident here. The stone walls of the cozy dining room are upholstered with empty wine bottles, the cellars are pavement-to-beams with the best vintages from around the world, and

Bolognesi himself delights in helping guests match, say, a thickly perfumed cannonau from Sardinia with the lobster ravioli in sweet pepper sauce; an ardent aglianico del vulture from Potenza to accompany the stuffed rabbit; or a pale blond müller thurgau to honor the seafood-and-truffle salad. End the celebration with a grappa *digestivo.* Closed Mondays, Sunday dinner in winter, part of January, and August. Information: *La Frasca,* 34 Via Matteotti, Castrocaro Terme (Forli) 47011 (phone: 543-767471; fax: 543-766625).

ALIA, Castrovillari, Calabria The Alia brothers have put Calabria on the culinary map with the help of their mother—who supervises the kitchen—to produce beautifully prepared, simply presented regional dishes made with local ingredients. Anchovy-orange salad, pasta with tomato, ricotta, and mint, fava bean purée, marinated salt cod, and pork dishes are all featured here, as is the family's homemade sausage. Inland, equidistant from the Gulf of Taranto and the Tyrrhenian Sea, the place has a warm and friendly feel to it. The wine list is studded with gems; the unusual, homemade rose liqueur is a must. Closed Sundays. Information: *Alia,* 69 Via Jetticelle, Castrovillari (Cosenza) 87012 (phone/fax: 981-46370).

LOCANDA DELL'ISOLA COMACINA, Comacina Island, Lombardy For more than 40 years, this restaurant perched on a hilltop on the only island in Lake Como has featured the same memorable menu. The feast begins with a bottle of wine and an entire loaf of warm, freshly baked bread placed on the table. Now comes a thick slice of tomato topped with a sliver of lemon drizzled with olive oil and a touch of oregano. Then on to praga ham and melon and tissue-thin slices of *bresola* (dried beef). Next comes a procession of bowls that would send a vegetarian (and almost anyone else) into ecstasy: roast onions; zucchini; marinated carrots; cauliflower; red, yellow, and green peppers; and sensational celery. On to perfectly grilled salmon trout with just the right touches of olive oil, lemon juice, and rough salt, followed by perfectly grilled chicken served with a green salad. The parmesan cheese that comes next is fresh, hacked off a wheel that weighs more than 70 pounds. Dessert is ice cream atop slices of fresh oranges or peaches, all doused in banana liqueur. The meal is concluded with a coffee ceremony calculated to keep the island's old evil spirits at bay. Closed Tuesdays, except June through August, and November through February. Information: *Locanda dell'Isola Comacina,* Sala Comacina, Lago di Como (Como) 22010 (phone: 344-55083).

AL BERSAGLIERE, Goito, Lombardy On the banks of the pretty Mincio River, this more-than-150-year-old restaurant serves wonderful smoked sturgeon, lobster, fresh pasta, risotto with snails, guinea hen, homemade gelato, and other delicious desserts. The wine list is exemplary. Closed Mondays, Tuesday lunch, 10 days in January, three weeks in August, and *Christmas.* Information: *Al Bersagliere,* 258 Via Statale, Goito (Mantova) 46044 (phone: 376-60007; fax: 376-606363).

LA VECCHIA OSTERIA–ANTONELLO COLONNA, Labico, Lazio The fare at this wonderful dining spot with just seven tables is well worth the hour's drive from the Eternal City. Beautiful flower arrangements adorn the elegant, old-fashioned dining room, topped by a domed ceiling. Chef Antonello concocts mouth-watering dishes, including artichokes *alla romana* (stuffed with garlic and mint), freshly made *millefoglie* (literally, one thousand leaves—flakes of puff pastry blended with pastry cream), and house chocolates filled with herbal infusions. Antonello's ricotta cheese puts the anemic American version to shame. The menu changes weekly. Closed Sunday dinner, Mondays, and August. Information: *La Vecchia Osteria–Antonello Colonna,* Via Casilina, Km 38.8, Labico (Roma) 00030 (phone: 6-951-0032).

CA' PEO, Leivi, Liguria The picturesque view from the dining room—of olive tree–covered hillsides, the coastline of the Tyrrhenian Sea, and the sunset in the distance—perfectly complements the food at one of the Italian Riviera's finest restaurants. Traditional yet hard-to-find regional dishes such as stuffed lettuce in broth, chestnut-flour lasagna, and boned and stuffed capon are featured daily. The fresh fish is lightly sauced, the mushrooms splendid in season, the extra-virgin olive oil (locally produced) delicious, and the wine selection superb. Closed Mondays, Tuesday lunch, and November. Information: *Ca' Peo,* 80 Via dei Caduti, Leivi (Genova) 16040 (phone: 185-319696; fax: 185-319671).

SOLE, Maleo, Lombardy In the same family for a century, this rustic converted farmhouse rises among grapevines, birds' nests, and gentle church bells. The menu's offerings suit the setting of wooden ceilings and whitewashed walls. Minestrone precedes traditional Milanese *maccheroni alla verdura* (giant macaroni with vegetables); entrées include such country fare as *faraona alle mele* (guinea fowl with apples) and *fegato di vitello all'uva* (calf's liver with grapes). Proprietor Colombani collects antique recipes and delights in re-creating long-ignored regional dishes. In summer, drink your coffee and grappa on the shady loggia, watch the flight of the swallows, and breathe the herb-scented country air. Closed Sunday dinner, Mondays, January, and August. Information: *Sole,* 22 Via Trabattoni, Maleo (Milano) 20076 (phone: 377-589248; fax: 377-658058).

VILLA MARCHESE, Milazzo, Sicily The industrial city of Milazzo is a must for two reasons: It's the port for ferries to the Aeolian Islands, and it's the place where dedicated food lovers interested in *cucina creativa* congregate. All the dishes in this small and charming eatery 2 miles (3 km) from Milazzo are made with the freshest ingredients Sicily has to offer. Specialties include pasta with fresh anchovies, local lobster cooked in a variety of ways, the catch of the day, and desserts fragrant with Sicilian almonds. The villa is set in a gorgeous garden, and the pleasant outdoor summer patio, with exuberant, purple-magenta bougainvillea, affords a lovely view of the Aeolian Islands (you almost forget about the industrial surroundings). Closed

Mondays and November. Information: *Villa Marchese,* Strada Panoramica, Contrada Paradiso, Capo Milazzo (Messina) 98057 (phone: 90-928-2514).

DOLADA, Pieve d'Alpago, Belluno High up on a mountainside with spectacular views of the Alpago Valley, Santa Croce Lake, and the surrounding peaks, Enzo and Rossana De Pra's restaurant has become a shrine for gastronomic pilgrims. The service is friendly, expert, and unfussy, and the menu is moderate in length but imaginative and varied. For starters, try the delicious *insalata tiepida di rana pescatrice e gamberi allo zenzero candito* (warm salad of monkfish and ginger-candied prawns) or *terrina di fegatini alle erbe e tartufo nero* (chicken liver pâté with truffles and herbs). First courses include *genziane di pasta al ragout di piccione* (gentian-shaped pasta with pigeon sauce) and *pasta croccante farcita alle verdure e caprino* (crisp pasta with vegetbles and goat's cheese). Among the main dishes are local mountain-raised lamb with polenta, and stuffed breast of guinea fowl. The fruit desserts and chocolate mousse are superb, as is the well-selected list of Italian wines. Closed Mondays and Tuesday lunch (except in July and August), and February. Information: *Dolada,* 21 Via Dolada, Plois, Pieve d'Alpago (Belluno) 32010 (phone: 437-479141; fax: 437-478068).

VIPORE, Pieve Santo Stefano, Tuscany Chef Cesare Casella commutes between New York City's popular *Coco Pazzo* and the family's hilltop trattoria. Here, flanked by his parents, he prepares simple Tuscan food flavored with Lucca's famous extra-virgin olive oil and herbs from the garden adjacent to the restaurant. Excellent *salume* (cured meat such as salami and prosciutto), homemade pasta, including *tacconi* (with wild mushroom sauce), grilled meat, and simple fruit desserts are accompanied by fine Italian wines. Mushrooms, prepared in many different ways, are a specialty in the spring and autumn. There are two *menù degustazioni* (tasting menus); you can also order dishes à la carte. If the weather permits, dine on the terrace overlooking the vegetable garden, a fig tree, and, in the distance, the elegant city of Lucca in the valley. Call for directions—it's hard to find. Closed Mondays, Tuesdays through Fridays for lunch, the last two weeks in January, and two weeks in November. Information: *Vipore,* Pieve Santo Stefano (Lucca) 55010 (phone: 583-395107 or 583-394065).

IL SOLE, Ranco, Lombardy The Brovelli family maintains a charming and elegant dining spot in a romantic setting, with a vine-covered terrace overlooking Lake Maggiore. The exquisite offerings—including fresh pasta, fish, and foie gras—are prepared to perfection, and the inventive desserts are equally tempting. The menu changes monthly. Closed Monday dinner (except in summer) and Tuesdays. Information: *Il Sole,* 5 Piazza Venezia, Ranco 21020 (phone: 331-976507; fax: 331-976620).

GAMBERO ROSSO, San Vincenzo, Tuscany Located beside the Tyrrhenian Sea, this is *the* place for fresh bounty from the sea. Try Fulvio Pierangelini's renditions of chick-pea soup with shrimp, oysters in gelatin, and ravioli with beans and seafood. His wife prepares such elegant desserts as a gratin of berries baked in a zabaglione sauce, and delicate small pastries. The wines are superb. Closed Tuesdays and November. Information: *Gambero Rosso,* 13 Piazza della Vittoria, San Vincenzo (Livorno) 57027 (phone: 565-701021).

LE TRE VASELLE, Torgiano, Umbria In the center of a quiet village rising gently above the soft, reassuring Umbrian countryside is this restaurant run by the Lungarotti family, the area's most highly regarded wine producers. Their home-bottled torre di giano, rubesco, and San Giorgio grace tables laden with rabbit with laurel, arugula-and-mushroom salad, zucchini with basil and parmesan, and more. See also *Most Visitable Vineyards.* Closed mid-January to mid-February. Information: *Le Tre Vaselle,* 48 Via Garibaldi, Torgiano (Perugia) 06089 (phone: 75-988-0447; fax: 75-988-0214).

Shopping in Italy

The descendants of Cellini and Michelangelo still boast a sure instinct for what is simply beautiful, including objects for daily use that delight the senses. The result has come to be known as "Italian style."

No matter where the dollar stands relative to the lira, the temptation to shop in Italy is almost irresistible. Although great bargains are now rare, the quality is high, and the choice—of luxurious leathers, hand-finished off-the-rack suits, designer dresses, 18-karat gold trinkets, ceramic plates, delicious comestibles, and more—remains wide. Italy's street markets are its best theater; intriguing goods of all kinds, from garments to espresso pots, can be found here.

Most shops practice the Anglo-Saxon rite of *prezzi fissi* (fixed prices). Especially at outdoor markets, try for the traditional *sconto* (discount), but don't overdo it—those good old haggling days are more or less gone.

BEST BUYS

The following are things to look for while tooling through Italy's small towns and villages. For recommendations of specific stores in the large metropolitan areas, see the *Shopping* entries in the individual reports in THE CITIES.

CERAMICS AND POTTERY In the days when earthenware was made from local clay to stock kitchens, towns in every corner of Italy created their own distinct pottery designs and have continued the traditions down through the centuries. The search for the perfect pot is one of the great Italian delights.

Albisola, Liguria Dozens of factories and workshops produce hundreds of windows full of the Baroque blue style that has been traditional since the 17th century. Little figures for *Christmas* crèches are a specialty, and there's a museum at the *Villa Faraggiana.*

Deruta, Umbria Lavishly supplied showrooms are scattered all along the main road, but some of the best shopping is in the *botteghe* (studios) uphill in town, where you can see the artists at work. Look at the *Museo della Ceramica Umbra* (Museum of Umbrian Ceramics; *Palazzo del Comune,* Piazza dei Consoli) in town and at the *Chiesa di Madonna dei Bagni* a mile south of the city before making a selection.

Faenza, Emilia-Romagna The French word faïence has come to signify any ceramic tableware. But the trademark of Faenza is a cheerful red, blue, and green carnation pattern. The *Museo Internazionale delle Ceramiche* (International Ceramics Museum; 2 Via Campidoro) displays antique pottery from all regions of Italy.

Fratte Rosa, Marches Pots made of the iron-rich local clay, often painted a rich eggplant color, come in many sizes and shapes. Sturdy pots suitable for cooking are particularly attractive, albeit a challenge to carry home.

Grottaglie, Puglia In this town not far from Taranto, an entire quarter is dedicated to ceramics. You can find everything from doll-size pitchers to gigantic urns with the local pattern of blue flowers on a beige background.

Terlizzi, Puglia Royal blue and rust glazes characterize the ceramics of this town.

Vietri sul Mare, Campania The last town (or the first, depending on direction) on the Amalfi Drive is full of potters. Pass the picturesquely tiled food stores en route to the huddle of shops around the main square. Naively painted animals and fish are some of the many motifs on the plates, vases, and colorful whatnots for sale, ubiquitous along the Amalfi Coast in most resort towns such as Positano and Amalfi.

CLOTHING The prospect of picking up an entire wardrobe in Italy is so tempting that some travelers dream of an airline losing their luggage permanently. Famous the world over for its *alta moda* (haute couture), Italy also offers a chance to purchase high-quality fashion at everyday prices.

EMBROIDERY AND LACE Despite inroads by Chinese exporters, Italian lace making and embroidery can still be found, especially at Burano (Venice) and Orvieto (Umbria).

Isola Maggiore, Lake Trasimeno, Umbria Fine handiwork is still practiced in a workshop on an island in the middle of Lake Trasimeno. A permanent exhibition and sale near the castle on the island is accessible by boat from the town of Passignano.

Offida, The Marches When the warm weather comes, the women of this town near Ascoli Piceno sit in their doorways and make lace, sometimes spending as much as a year on a single tablecloth. Meanwhile, local monasteries exhibit 500-year-old examples.

FABRICS Italy is known around the globe for its velvet, linen, silk, and other fabrics. Venice produces the very finest.

Città di Castello, Umbria Tablecloths, towels, and sheets are worked on Renaissance looms in *Tela Umbra* on Piazza Costa in this small city on the left bank of the Tiber.

Como, Lombardy Como has always been *the* Italian silk center, and the *Emporio della Seta* (190 Via Canturina) stocks yard goods as well as scarves, ties, and classic shirts that demonstrate the range of the Italian imagination. Stop by *Ratti* (19 Via Cernobbio) for great prices on silk designer scarves and shawls and fabric.

Santarcangelo, Forlì (Emilia-Romagna) Linen is still hand-printed here with great wooden blocks that have been used since the 17th century. The antique tools and techniques are still visible at the *Stamperia Artigiana* (15 Via C. Battisti), where live demonstrations are offered.

FOOD Seasons are all: Italians pride themselves on knowing when and where to find each special food at its golden moment. A trip to Italy is a voyage through a gastronomic culture. Be bold: Try what you don't know.

Asparagus A tender white variety, delicately tipped with violet, is grown from March through May. Eat it raw, sliced into salad. The best place to find it is *Cooperativa Asparagi* (14 Vicolo Mattiussi) in Tavagnacco (Udine) in Friuli–Venezia Giulia. In Sicily, wild asparagus is a fleeting treat, often served in a *frittata* (omelette).

Cheese Many shops throughout the country stock gift boxes of *parmigiano reggiano,* the perfect cheese—natural and wholesome—for snacks and grating. Also try *grana,* a cheese for grating and eating that is similar to *parmigiano* but less expensive.

Sardinia offers a wide variety of natural, unprocessed cheeses, many made from ewes' milk. Fresh mozzarella is delicate and soft—not the rubbery square stuff seen in American supermarkets. True mozzarella must have a minimum of 30% buffalo milk, the rich ingredient that gives this cheese its unique taste; the rest is properly (and legally) called *fior di latte,* and is cow's milk. Stands line the streets in Mondragone and Formia on the coast between Rome and Naples; don't hesitate to buy.

Excellent varieties of local cheeses also can be sampled in the covered market at Piazza Cavalieri di Vittorio Veneto in Aosta.

Fruit A sour cherry known as the *amarena* appears in Cantiano, near Pesaro in the Marches, in late spring and can be found briefly in outdoor markets in the Abruzzo and Lazio in June and July. Out of season, buy the homemade jam. The year's first peaches ripen in Monte San Biagio, near Latina in Lazio, in mid-May, and the town celebrates with a peach festival in late June. This is also the place to try white peaches, Italy's most succulent fruit.

Nemi, near Rome, is known for its wild strawberries; Trento, for its apples, untreated with chemicals; and Sicily, for its *tarocchi* (ruddy blood oranges), available in winter. Everywhere are amazingly diverse varieties of figs and grapes—try them all, fresh and dried.

Grappa In any season, the best of this powerful grape-based liquor is found in the north. Visit the *Distilleria Rossi d'Angera,* in Angera (Varese) in Lombardy, for a look at the venerable slow methods of maturing it in oak barrels. Or shop at *Romano Levi* (Via XX Settembre) in Neive (Piedmont). The town of Bassano del Grappa (in the Veneto) is renowned for its quality production.

Olive Oil Cities and regions vie for the honor of producing fine olive oil. Try them all; the northern oils are generally less acidic but somewhat more bland. In any case, always choose extra-virgin (first pressing). Balestrino (Savona) in Liguria grows 17 different types of olives. To compare the oil made from each type, visit in March, when samples are offered for tasting. The main oil-producing region in Tuscany is around Lucca, although some oil comes from the Chianti area. Bitonto, near Bari in Puglia, is another olive capital.

Pastries In Assisi in Umbria, eat *mostaccioli di San Francesco,* a honey-and-almond cake that the saint is said to have requested on his deathbed. In the medieval mountaintop town of Erice at the *Pasticceria Grammatico* (14 Vittorio Emanuele), try *bello e brutto* (amorphous-shaped drops of almond paste flavored with lemon peel). Sicily's ricotta-stuffed *cassata* (not an ice cream) is a feast for eyes and palate.

Truffles Norcia in Umbria and Acqualagna, near Pesaro in the Marches, are fragrant with pungent black truffles, especially at the end of October. White truffles reign in Piedmont. To enjoy them in a meal, visit Acqualagna's *Ristorante Ginestra* on Passo del Furlo. Many Umbrian restaurants now feature locally produced black and white truffles in the autumn. A new trend: Truffle oil and pâté are used for flavoring; on a menu, fresh truffles should be specified as such.

Vinegar Balsamic vinegar is the champagne of its breed, and a tiny bottle of the real thing is a result of years of distillation. The best is found in Modena at *Giuseppe Giusti* (77 Via Farini).

JEWELRY Italians have been working with precious stones and metals since the time of the Etruscans. So if you make only one Italian purchase, it ought to be a small (but fine) piece of gold jewelry. Arezzo is the capital of gold manufacturing in the country.

Campoligure, Liguria The family-run workshops in this tiny mountain town export almost all of their precious handmade filigree, a braid of two threads of gold or silver woven into delicate webs and then connected to make feathery jewelry and decorative objects. A silver-and-gold filigree show is held every weekend in September in the *Palazzo Comunale*. Beware of factory-made imitations.

Torre del Greco, Campania The cameo and coral capital of Italy is just outside Naples. But unless your eye is infallible, trust only reputable shops, such as *Orafa International* (35 Via de Nicola); *Coral Orafa International* (17 Via de Guevera); *Cameos at Cammei* (32 Via de Nicola); or *Apa* (1 Via de Nicola). A coral caveat: Because of the threat of water pollution and the dwindling numbers of artisans, the price of local coral has risen, and much of what you see in Italy comes from Asia.

Valenza Po, Piedmont With more than 1,200 companies and studios, this one-industry town works (and then exports along with Arezzo) almost all the gold that Italy imports. Professional jewelers and passionate amateurs should aim to visit during the annual October exhibition.

KNITWEAR The knitted creations of Italian factories are famous for reasons that can be immediately seen in almost every clothing store all over the country. But some of the finest come from the small workshops where you can choose your own wool.

LEATHER GOODS All different kinds of animal skins are used to make the belts, purses, briefcases, and baggage found throughout Italy. Quality is high (and often with prices to match). The center is Florence, whose shops and outdoor markets offer good, if not cheap, buys.

MUSICAL INSTRUMENTS The antique tradition of hand-crafted musical instruments is alive and well in a few renowned centers all over Italy.

Accordions The first accordion was made in 1863 in Castelfidardo, near Ancona in the Marches, and the streets of the town still echo with the sounds of tuning and testing from a dozen workshops. Watch the 8,300 pieces being assembled at the *Brandoni* shop (38 Via Sauro), and see a hundred vintage instruments from all over the world in a museum in Piazza della Repubblica.

Lutes and Violins Cremona, a sizable town in Lombardy, was the home of Antonio Stradivari, the greatest violin maker of all time, and the art of creating stringed instruments has not been forgotten here. On the Corso Garibaldi, look for the *Scuola Internazionale di Liuteria* and the workshops of a number of master lute makers. At No. 95 is the workshop of world class violin maker Istvan Konja, a Hungarian going under the Italianized name of Stefano Conia.

Whistles Comic, brightly painted terra cotta figures of priests, roosters, and puppets are made into whistles in Rutigliano, 24 miles (38 km) outside of Bari in Puglia.

Wind Instruments The traditional craft goes back to the 18th century in the small town of Quarna, near Novara in Piedmont, where 600 workers turn brass, silver, and ebony into clarinets, flutes, and saxophones in family-run workshops.

SHOES You'll find a shoe shop on virtually every corner in Italy, but it's the rare Anglo-Saxon foot that matches an Italian last. Price is generally a clue to what you're getting—as usual, you get what you pay for. When in doubt about the composition, just sniff; the aroma of real leather is inimitable. Varese (near Milan) is the national center for industrial production; Florence is the place for luxury footwear with hand-stitching.

An Antiques Lover's Guide to Italy

Though Italian cities preserve some of the finest collections of antiquities in the world, buying genuine antiques is not an easy matter. Plenty of dealers are willing to sell small relics of ancient Rome or Etruscan civilization, but even if these items were genuine, the strict control on exporting antiquities would make it impossible for foreign purchasers to take them out of the country. At the same time, the kinds of handsome household items of later periods that predominate in the antiques trade of countries like England and Scotland are uncommon in Italy; poorer than other European nations, it never had a large middle class to demand luxury goods in quantity. The objects of value that do exist were almost always made for large noble families who have passed them down—or sold them at prices far beyond the means of the average buyer.

There is, however, a thriving antiques trade in Italy, and many dealers traffic in non-Italian goods. Many moderately priced antiques found here are English; silver is an especially common stock item.

Our favorite antiques shops in Florence, Milan, and Rome are listed in the individual reports in THE CITIES. For a comprehensive listing of antiques dealers by region and specialization and of major fairs, consult the *Guida OPI dell'Antiquariato Italiano,* published by Tony Metz, and the *Catalogo dell'Antiquariato Italiano,* published by Giorgio Mondadori. Both are in Italian.

WHAT TO BUY

Italian antiques exist in several categories. Gilded wood candlestick holders, ceramic plates and painted tiles, Venetian trading beads, old prints and maps, and lamps made from opaline are good finds, as are figurines from the traditional *Christmas presepe* (nativity scene). Expect to pay for quality. Also look for the following:

CHINA AND GLASS There is a lot of Venetian glass about, but it is hard to tell its age without expert advice (some master glass blowers make fine reproductions). The original Venetian crystal tended to be of a darker, smoky hue.

COPPER AND BRASS You don't have to be an expert to find good pieces of domestic copper and brass. These metals were used for domestic utensils, so no imprints were used. The oldest pieces, shaped with a hammer, are of irregular thickness. Northern Italy and the Abruzzo are the most reliable sources.

FURNITURE Most genuinely old Italian furniture is very heavily restored or extremely expensive. What is available is often not nearly as beautifully finished as pieces made in England or France; design was generally considered more important. Renaissance furniture, particularly sought after, is wildly expensive. Popular versions of *barocchetto* (Baroque) furniture, however, as well as *rustico* (rustic), are still available, usually in the provincial cities of central and northern Italy. European walnut is especially prized.

JEWELRY Though Italy is Europe's foremost center for modern goldsmithing and jewelry design, much antique jewelry sold here is imported. However, the market offers such treasures as the ornamental earrings mostly produced in Gaeta in Lazio. These were traditionally used instead of engagement rings by peasant girls who worked in the fields, where a ring would have been a nuisance. Sardinia has fine gold work in rings, earrings, and necklaces. In Rome, look for antique micro-mosaics, much sought after by collectors.

PAINTINGS Since Italians are the world's experts at restoration, plenty of appealing paintings are on the market. But don't assume they'll be as authentic (or as valuable) as they are handsome. Italian regional loyalties, which in past centuries gave rise to distinctive local schools of painting, are expressed today by the high demand among each region's collectors for the works created there. Works by non-Italian artists painted during Grand Tour days may be underpriced. Ask first about export restrictions.

PICTURE FRAMES Gilded-and-carved wood-and-glass frames can still be found fairly easily—though you need a very large wall on which to hang them and a large bank account to pay for those made during the Renaissance. More practical are the little dressing table frames made in mahogany. Not as outrageously expensive, they are widely sold.

POTTERY Production of majolica—the tin-glazed and richly colored and ornamented earthenware pieces Italians know as maiolica or faïence—reached its zenith in the northern Italian towns of Deruta, Faenza, Gubbio, and in Urbino (the Marches) and Castelli (Abruzzo) during the Renaissance. In the mid-16th century, potters in Faenza introduced a lacy, Baroque style of "white" pottery, called *bianchi di Faenza,* which remained popular well beyond the mid-17th century. Both types of pottery are much sought after. There are many clever copies, and antiques dealers tell of colleagues who commission pieces and then have them joined together with copper wire so that the finished vessel looks authentically old. Another trick is to glaze century-old bricks to give them an aged look before turning them into Castelli pottery.

PRINTS The cartographer of the medieval world, Italy created maps by the score beginning in the 14th century. Prints were also widely issued. Some of those available today have been reproduced on old paper; others are original, pulled out of old books. However, shops all over Italy sell the real thing at favorable prices and are very helpful and knowledgeable.

RULES OF THE ROAD FOR AN ODYSSEY OF THE OLD

Buy for sheer pleasure, not for investment. Forget about the carrot of supposed retail values that dealers habitually dangle in front of amateur clients. If you love something, it will probably ornament your home until the *Colosseum* falls.

Buy the finest example you can afford of any item, in as close to mint condition as possible. Chipped or broken "bargains" will haunt you later with their shabbiness.

Train your eye in museums. These are the best schools for the acquisitive senses, particularly as you begin to develop special passions.

Get advice from specialists when contemplating major acquisitions. Much antique furniture and many paintings have been restored several times, and Italian antiques salespeople are more entertaining than knowledgeable. If you want to be certain that what you're buying is what you've been told it is, stick with the larger dealers. Most auction houses have an evaluation office whose experts make appraisals for a fee. Even museums in some cities can be approached. In Rome, a useful contact is *Art Import* (2 Piazza Borghese; phone: 6-687-3633/4; fax: 6-699-41402), a British firm specializing in British antiques but knowledgeable about the trade in general.

Don't be afraid to haggle. Large dealers will have *prezzi fissi* (fixed prices); the others will decide for themselves. The rule of thumb is to bargain wherever you don't see the *prezzi fissi* sign. Also, while most larger dealers take credit cards, smaller shops may not.

When pricing an object, don't forget to figure the cost of shipping. Around 30% of the cost of the item is about right for large items. The bigger international shipping firms offer a door-to-door service to New York as well as advice about required export licenses. The following firms may be helpful:

Emery Worldwide, 48/A Via Passo Buole, Fiumicino, Rome (phone: 6-658-1621; fax: 6-658-4594).

International Freight Consultants, 190 Via Cavour, Rome (phone: 6-482-4616; fax: 6-488-3234) or 28/5 Via Fantoli, Milan (phone: 2-554-00041; fax: 2-554-00310).

Rinaldi, 34 Via Smerillo, Rome (phone: 6-415211; fax: 6-411-1565).

Also note that the Italian government requires that any object of possible historical interest to the Italian state be declared and has levied a tax on goods exported to the US.

Taking the Waters

Italy's water—and its mud—are the base of one of the country's most lucrative industries: There are *terme* (spas) all over the country. Some, such as the Alpine resort of Bormio, flourish on the sites of thermal springs first exploited by those imperial water worshipers, the ancient Romans, who built baths with great fervor. Others trace their origins to antique legends.

Today, for those who are "taking the waters," there is a whole menu of steamrooms and saunas, sprays and whirlpool baths, mud tubs and honey rubs, paraffin packs and vapor inhalations, underwater gymnastics, and regimens of just plain drinking. Every spa has its specialty, and things are so clinical that most spas have doctors on hand; checkups generally are required before any steam treatments or submersions can be undertaken.

The healing comes from the waters that bubble, but also from the related diversions—golf, tennis, horseback riding, fine food, casinos, discos, boutiques, art exhibits, auctions, and concerts. And an increasing number of spas feature special menus for dieters.

Montecatini Terme, an elegant enclave that once belonged to the Medicis, has hosted princes and pashas and their betters. There are eight springs—five for drinking, two for mineral baths, and one for mud bathing—and a multitude of hotels that provide excellent service and a host of activities. For details about this celebrated Italian spa, see *Tuscany* in DIRECTIONS.

Some of the country's best *terme* are described below. For a complete map of spas in Italy, write to *ACI* (8 Via Marsala, Rome 00185).

ABANO, Veneto *Mud* is the magic word at this favorite of the ancient Roman aristocracy and military, whose name derives from the Greek for "pain remover." And after mud, which is mineral-enriched volcanic material at about 189F, comes massage—all available as part of the facilities of most hotels. Then the rest of the day is free for swimming in thermal waters or for golf, riding, tennis, and touring. Abano is a pretty, bustling town of tree-lined streets, just outside Padua and a half hour from Venice. Verona and Vicenza are within reach as well. Of the dozens of comfortable hotels, the exclusive *Grand Hotel Orologio* and the less expensive *Quisisana Terme* have the best food and the most cosmopolitan clientele. At press time, the spa was temporarily closed; call ahead for opening dates. Information: *Azienda di Promozione Turistica,* 18 Via Pietro d'Abano, Abano Terme (Padova) 35031 (phone: 49-866-9055).

CHIANCIANO TERME, Tuscany The origins of this red-roofed town with lovely shaded parks can be traced to the Etruscans and, like many other Italian spas, its springs were much appreciated in ancient times. Today, the lure of the rich Tuscan and Umbrian countryside distracts some visitors from the venerated water regimen that proposes to return their livers to a pristine state. Chianciano's centuries-old establishments draw an international clientiele. Of the seemingly infinite hotels, a few stay open in the winter, but life can be dismal here off-season, despite the beauty of the surrounding countryside. Most hotels require half board during high season. Nearby is Arezzo, with its serene frescoes of Piero della Francesca and a lively, irresistible antiques market the first weekend of every month. Siena is an hour distant, as are the churches of Assisi and the towers of San Gimignano. Body and soul will thrive in the unhurried atmosphere, the fine air, and the cypress- and pine-trimmed landscapes of this beautifully groomed region, whether or not guests drink the waters with the clockwork regularity that a proper cure demands. The season runs from mid-April to mid-November. For grand comfort, stay at the *Excelsior* hotel. Information: *Azienda Autonoma di Cura,* 7 Via Giuseppe Sabatini, Chianciano Terme (Siena) 53042 (phone: 578-63538; fax: 578-64623).

FIUGGI, Lazio When Michelangelo felt the need to flee Rome and the rigors of painting the ceiling of the *Sistine Chapel*—for a breath of clean air and a sip of purifying water—it was to this town (an hour south of Rome and 2,500 feet above sea level) that he came. Carried by papal couriers to Boniface VIII in Rome during the Middle Ages, this water is now bottled and sold all over Italy, but many Italians still consider a summer holiday at the source essential to year-round health. The two springs, each set in a lush garden, are known nationally as cures for kidney disturbances. Hotels range from the splendid—Italy's kings summered here—to the simple and economical. The Italian royalty used to take the waters at the *Grand Hotel Palazzo della Fonte* (phone: 775-5081). In addition to the usual luxury hotel and spa amenities, there is a fitness center here with a personalized exercise program, tennis, a pool, and a small golf course and riding stable nearby. Open February through November. Information: *Azienda Autonoma di Soggiorno,* 4 Via Gorizia, Fiuggi (Frosinone) 03015 (phone: 775-55446 or 775-55019; 800-225-5843).

GRADO, Friuli–Venezia Giulia Up the coast from Trieste and the Slovenian border, this island town with its marine thermal establishment is linked to the mainland by a 3-mile causeway. Grado is renowned for its *sabbiatura* treatments (immersion in sunbaked sand) for relief from arthritis and rheumatism. The classical warm seawater procedures—pool and tub soaks, inhalations, and the like—are also highlights. This far corner of Italy also is a good jumping-off point for visits to Trieste, the Roman ruins of Aquileia, or the unique Slovenian grottoes of Postojna. Information: *Azienda Autonoma di Soggiorno e Cura,* 58 Viale Dante Alighieri, Grado (Gorizia) 34073 (phone: 431-899111).

ISCHIA, Campania The largest island in the Bay of Naples is volcanic, and it bubbles with hot springs and naturally radioactive water. The steamy mud is good for aching bones, and the vapors do wonders for respiratory disorders. All the sloshing and sniffing can be done right in your hotel—and in some cases in your own room, if that's what you want. Of the four main thermal centers, *Lacco Ameno* is the best supplied with luxury hotels with their own thermal establishments: *San Montano,* whose furnishings re-create the atmosphere of a transatlantic ship, right by the sea, with its own private beach, and the outstanding *Regina Isabella,* which offers the most elaborate medical menu of all. Taking the mud cure at Ischia is most popular during its prime season—from April through October. Information: *Azienda Autonoma di Soggiorno,* Via Iasolino, Porto d'Ischia (Ischia) 80077 (phone: 81-991146 or 81-983005) or 104 Corso Vittoria Colonna, Porto d'Ischia (Ischia) 80077 (phone: 81-983066 or 81-991464; fax: 81-981904).

LEVICO TERME, Trentino Just 13 miles (21 km) from the mountain city of Trento, Levico Terme is set on an idyllic, tree-bordered lake at the foot of Monte Fronte at an altitude of 1,800 feet. Its sister town, Vetriolo Terme, is 7 miles (11 km) away at about 4,900 feet. Both offer a wide variety of sports; sailing and windsurfing in summer at Levico and skiing in winter at Vetriolo are the main draws. The colonnaded thermal complex, set in a botanical park remarkable for its variety of exotic trees, dates from the turn of the century; the high arsenic and iron content of spring waters available here is reputed to benefit blood and nerves, cure skin diseases, and even resolve various ailments of the reproductive system. Information: *Azienda di Promozione Turistica,* 3 Via Vittorio Emanuele, Levico Terme (Trento) 38056 (phone: 461-706101; fax: 461-706004).

MERANO, Alto Adige Not far from Brenner Pass and Austria, the mountain town of Merano glows with Tyrolean charms. The spa is across the river from the tightly packed streets of the Old Town. Mud baths and masks, radioactive waters, vigorous rubdowns, and steamy saunas administered at the spacious, greenery-rimmed thermal center not only pamper those in good health but also bring relief to sufferers of arthritis, allergies, asthma, and digestive and circulatory problems. The *Meranerhof* hotel is next to the thermal center and its lake and pool, and the *Schloss Rundegg* has all the facilities of a health and beauty farm. Information: *Terme di Merano,* 9 Via Piave, Merano (Bolzano) 39012 (phone: 473-237724).

ST.-VINCENT, Valle d'Aosta All the deep relaxation of the day's thermal treatments can be cheerfully undone each evening in the gambling casino of this Alpine town. But if guests can resist the charm of chips and late nights around the wheel, they may discover the myriad benefits that St.-Vincent's waters are said to offer the digestive system. The *Billia* hotel, set in its own pretty park, has a pool and medical staff to advise guests on the optimal diet-dissolution ratio. There are footpaths for quiet post-sip rambles; high-altitude hiking trails are just a short drive away. Information: *Azienda Autonoma di Soggiorno e Turismo,* 48 Via Roma, St.-Vincent (Aosta) 11027 (phone: 166-512239; fax: 166-513149).

SALSOMAGGIORE, Emilia-Romagna When a local doctor named Lorenzo Berzieri successfully used the local warm salt springs to cure an ailing patient in 1839, he little imagined the parade of celebrities that would descend on this garden-greened town in the years to come. Equidistant from Milan and Bologna (in the hills between Lake Garda and the Italian Riviera), Salsomaggiore was where Italy's crowned heads of the 19th and early 20th centuries recovered from overdoses of champagne and rheumatism induced by damp palaces. Said to be efficacious in treating chronic inflammations of every sort, the local regimen of massages, baths, mud packs, and irrigations is administered at major hotels with their own thermal facilities. But most visitors still patronize the huge Baroque spa center. More worldly than most Italian spas, Salsomaggiore brims with boutiques and discos, and *caffès* are shoulder to shoulder in the traffic-free town center. The busy morning market and the frequent evening auctions staged by one or the other of the numerous antiques shops give Salsomaggiore a cheerful animation missing at many other Italian health resorts. Information: *Azienda Autonoma di Soggiorno e Cura,* 4 Viale Romagnosi, Salsomaggiore Terme (Parma) 43039 (phone: 524-572100; fax: 524-79047).

SATURNIA, Tuscany In Tuscany between the Aurelia coast road and the Via Cassia, near Manciano (on Rte. 74), this is simply a warm thermal waterfall where 2,000 years of bathers have smoothed and hollowed out sitting places among the rocks. Swimming and soaking here can be done comfortably even on a crisp day in February by anyone brave enough to race from car to springs. If you prefer to soak in greater style, check into the only hotel—the lovely *Terme di Saturnia*—whose two grandiose sulfur-pungent pools are more elegantly accessible. The hot fumes float above the warm water, and, when the evening chill sets in, they swirl foggily above the grass-edged basins, mysteriously concealing, then revealing, their borders. Information: *Terme di Saturnia,* Saturnia (Grosseto) 58050 (phone: 564-601061; fax: 564-601266).

Most Visitable Vineyards

The ancient Greeks knew Italy as "Enotria"—the land of wines—and wine making is still big business here, from the cool Alpine terraces of South Tyrol to the sun-scorched Sicilian isles off the coast of North Africa. With four million acres of vineyards and an ever-growing number of zones of controlled name and origin (known as Denominazione di Origine Controllata or, simply, DOC), the nation produces more wine than any other country in the world—and more varieties. In addition, many good Italian bottlings are still sold as simple *vini da tavola* (table wines); some are merely awaiting the completion of the DOC warranty paperwork. Between November and March, don't miss *vino novello*, Italy's response to beaujolais nouveau. The best comes from the Veneto and Tuscany, but other varieties are also good and getting better every year.

Touring Italy's countless wineries shows off this oenological spectacle in all its many facets, from vast modern plants turning out tens of millions of bottles annually to cramped cellars presided over by a farmer who puts out just a barrel or two in a good year. Signs reading *vendita diretta* (direct sales) invite visitors to stop, sample, and buy wine to take away.

Many wineries, wine shops, and public displays denoted by the term *enoteca* (wine library) welcome browsers; in many cases tastings are offered by the glass for a nominal fee, and some offer substantial snacks. The more humble establishments are known as *bottiglierie*.

THE NORTHEAST

ALTO ADIGE In the province of Bolzano, known as Bozen by the area's German-speakers and as South Tyrol to the rest of the world, many wineries are located along the Weinstrasse (Wine Road) that runs from Bolzano south past Lago di Caldaro to Roverè della Luna. With the Dolomites towering over valleys of neatly kept apple orchards and vineyards, cozy guesthouses, and hearty Austrian food, the area presents an inviting contrast to Mediterranean Italy. It is also one of the few parts of the country where white wines are treated with as much care as reds. There are many fragrant and well-balanced rieslings, sylvaners, and pinots. The traminer aromatico grape originated near Termino (Tramin to the Germans), and the best Italian gewürztraminers still come from here—pale gold and spicily aromatic but more restrained than their Alsatian cousins. The area also makes, in fairly small quantities, cabernets that are delightfully perfumed, clear-flavored, supremely fresh, and notably well balanced.

Alois Lageder, Bolzano Founded in 1855, this family-run winery produces two different lines of wines—barrel-aged löwengang and the Alois Lageder single-vineyard varietals (wines named for the principal grape from which they are made), including a sauvignon blanc (called Lehenhof) and a pinot grigio (called Benefizium Porer). Visit the löwengang cellars outside town or the bottling plant/*enoteca* in Bolzano. Information: *Alois Lageder,* 235 Viale Druso, Bolzano (Bolzano) 39100 (phone: 471-920164; fax: 471-931577).

Schloss Turmhof, Entiklar, Bolzano Run by Herbert Tiefenbrunner and his family, this winery occupies a shady glen with a castle that looks as if it belongs in the Vienna woods. The wines are first-rate—particularly the white pinots, chardonnays, rieslings, sylvaners, gewürztraminers, and goldenmuskatellers. The müller thurgau, which goes by the name of feldmarschall and comes from 3,300-foot vineyards that are the highest in South Tyrol, is exquisite. Plates of cold cuts, sausages, and sauerkraut are served with the wines in the gardens and the cozy, wood-paneled *Weinstuben*. Information: *Schloss Turmhof*, Entiklar, Kurtatsch (Bolzano) 39040 (phone: 471-880122).

FRIULI–VENEZIA GIULIA With Trentino–Alto Adige, this area of northeastern Italy is the center of the country's white wine production. The hilly Collio Goriziano and Colli Orientali del Friuli, near the Slovenian border, produce fruity and flowery whites that range from delicate to light to substantial and full-bodied and rich (depending on the producer). They are generally known by their varietal grape names—pinot bianco, pinot grigio, and riesling Renano. Charming, nicely rounded reds, simple and rather light because they are not wood-aged as in France and California, are made with merlot and cabernet grapes in these two areas and in the flatter districts known as Grave del Friuli and Isonzo. The *Enoteca La Serenissima* (26 Via Battisti, in Gradisca d'Isonzo; phone: 481-99528), 7½ miles (12 km) southwest of Gorizia, was Italy's first public wine library and remains one of the most impressive.

Livio Felluga, Brazzano, Gorizia Founded by patriarch Livio, the Felluga family winery produces highly esteemed wines from its vineyards in both the Collio Goriziano and Colli Orientali areas. The high-quality whites—tocai, sauvignon, pinot grigio, and pinot bianco—and reds—cabernet, merlot, and the full-bodied refosco—are all well worth sampling. Terre Alte, a blend of tocai, pinot, and sauvignon grapes, is considered one of Italy's finest white wines. Information: *Livio Felluga*, 1 Via Risorgimento, Brazzano di Cormons (Gorizia) 34071 (phone: 481-630246; fax: 481-630126).

VENETO In this pretty area of hills and villas, more DOC wines are produced than any other type, and most are of the Veronese trio of bardolino and valpolicella (reds) and soave (white). Known worldwide as everyday wines par excellence, they are never tastier than when drunk young and fresh at the vineyard. Oenologically minded visitors should make the pilgrimage to Verona in April, when *VinItaly*, the nation's most important wine fair, is in full swing. Above all, sample the costly, majestic valpolicella known as amarone. This deep garnet-red, almost port-like wine derives its intense fruity flavors (and an alcohol content of up to 17%) from grapes crushed only after weeks-long aging off the vine on straw pallets. In Treviso province, a number of Italy's best country restaurants serve good local pinot, cabernet, merlot, and the fizzy white prosecco di Conegliano-Valdobbiadene— dry but fruity and distinctively aromatic.

Nino Franco, Valdobbiadene, Treviso Founder Nino Franco's son Primo manages this winery in the soft, vine-covered hills near Conegliano. Its main product is a fine sparkling prosecco with a fruity bouquet; the dry wine is pleasurably pungent, whereas the sweet version has a floral taste. This winery also has a variety of creditable still wines. Information: *Nino Franco*, 167 Via Garibaldi, Valdobbiadene (Treviso) 31049 (phone: 423-972051; fax: 423-975977).

Masi, Gargagnago di Valpolicella, Verona In a zone dominated by the industrialized giants among wine producers, *Masi* treads a civilized middle ground, drawing on choice vineyards to produce highly individualistic wines—soave classico col baraca, valpolicella classico Serego Alighieri, sweet recioto, and two unusual table wines known as masianco and campo fiorin. The latter, a distinctive, dark red, is elegantly flavored and long-lived as a result of having been partly fermented on the skins of grapes pressed to make amarone. The amarones, made in several styles, rank among Italy's most distinguished red wines. Some of the area's wine *cantine* are open to the public. Information: *Azienda di Promozione Turistica,* 61 Via Leoncino, Verona 37121 (phone: 45-592828; fax: 45-800-3638).

THE NORTHWEST

PIEDMONT Well known for its robust, complex, dry reds—authoritative barolo, barbaresco, gattinara, and others like them that develop greatness with aging—this area also makes two whites of renown, the sweetish and sparkling asti spumante and the bone-dry still wine called gavi, as well as delightful lighter reds that are meant to be drunk young. These most notably include barbera and dolcetto. Far from being sweet (as its name might suggest), dolcetto is a soft, intensely fruity, low-acid wine. Well-marked wine roads lead through major DOC zones, including barolo, barbaresco, and asti spumante, and there are impressive public *enoteche* at Barolo, Grinzane Cavour (near Alba), Costigliole d'Asti, and Vignale Monferrato.

Ceretto, Alba, Cuneo Oenologist Marcello and his brother Bruno specialize in first-rate, fresh, vigorous wines in a region known for impressive reds requiring lengthy aging. Try the spritzer-like white arneis, lusty barbera, dolcetto, nebbiolo, and elegant barolo reds, and the barbaresco from the Cerettos' prestigious vineyards. Experimental, non-traditional French varietals are also worth sampling. Information: *Ceretto,* 34 Località San Cassiano, Alba (Cuneo) 12055 (phone: 173-282582; fax: 173-282383).

Abbazia dell'Annunziata, La Morra, Cuneo In the heart of the barolo zone, this 15th-century abbey south of Alba houses a wine museum and produces noteworthy barolo, nebbiolo, barbera, and dolcetto in the cellars adjoining the museum. Information: *Ratti, Antiche Cantine dell'Annunziata,* La Morra (Cuneo) 12064 (phone: 173-50185; fax: 173-509373).

Martini & Rossi, Pessione, Turin Among Piedmont's large wine and vermouth houses, this is perhaps the most visitable. A wine museum on the premises has pieces dating to the times of the Etruscans and Greeks, and the hospitality is impeccable. Arrange guided tours and tastings at the main cellars in Pessione, about 9 miles (14 km) southeast of Turin, are by appointment. Information: *Martini & Rossi, S.p.A.,* 42 Corso Vittorio Emanuele, Torino 10123 (phone: 11-81081; fax: 11-810-8400).

LOMBARDY Wine of virtually every style is featured in this region around Milan. There are dry spumanti and fruity whites, light rosés, and reds of all styles. Rugged and mountainous Valtellina to the north—a growing area praised by Pliny, Virgil, and Leonardo, among others—starts with the hard-to-cultivate nebbiolo grape, grown on south-facing vineyards. Then the pressings are wood-aged to produce a simple, substantial red with rich color and deep flavor that is less austere and more immediate than the barolo, barbaresco, and other nebbiolo-based wines from Piedmont. Valtellina sfursat is produced by methods similar to those used for Veneto's amarone. Oltrepò Pavese, to the southwest, makes a number of full, grapey reds, plus clean, crisp, fruity whites that range stylistically from müller thurgaus to pinots. Franciacorta to the east is the home of some of Italy's best sparkling wines. Some of these are dry, some sweet; those made by the *metodo champenois* (champagne method) tend to be less yeasty than their French counterparts.

Guido Berlucchi, Borgonato di Cortefranca, Brescia About 12½ miles (20 km) northwest of Brescia, near Lake Iseo at the nation's largest producer of champagne-style wines, visitors are welcome to witness the intricacies of the *metodo champenois* and sample the product—Berlucchi cuvée brut, brut millesimata, pas dosé, grand cremant, and Max Rosé—all made from pinot or chardonnay grapes from Franciacorta, Oltrepò Pavese, and Trentino–Alto Adige. Nearby, the firm also has a small estate known as *Antica Cantina Fratta.* Information: *Guido Berlucchi & Compagnia,* 4 Piazza Duranti, Borgonato di Cortefranca (Brescia) 25040 (phone: 30-984381; fax: 30-984293).

Ca' del Bosco, Erbusco, Brescia Maurizio Zanella's state-of-the-art winery has its own helicopter pad, beautiful reception rooms, and *caves* for aging. One of Italy's finest sparkling wines, the aristocratic Ca' del Bosco spumante, is produced here. Zanella's still wines—especially the barrel-fermented chardonnay, the Maurizio Zanella (Italy's premier cabernet-merlot blend), and the Pinero pinot noir—are also notable. Information: *Ca' del Bosco,* 20 Via Case Sparse, Erbusco (Brescia) 25030 (phone: 30-776-0600; fax: 30-726-8425).

CENTRAL ITALY

TUSCANY Tuscan wine makers have long been building their reputations on the strength of imposing reds such as brunello di Montalcino, vino nobile di Montepulciano, and a variety of *vini da tavola.*

Still, chianti remains the quintessential Italian wine, and Tuscany is its home. You'll find it here in all its many styles—from light and easy-drinking classico to spicy and assertive riserva. Don't miss the vineyards of the classico zone along the Chiantigiana road between Florence and Siena, some of the most picturesque in all of Italy, particularly the Castelnuovo Berardenga, Radda, and Gaiole townships. And be sure to stop at the towered town of San Gimignano, known for its white vernaccia. The *Enoteca*

Italica Permanente in the *Fortezza Medicea* in Siena displays and serves choice wines from all over Italy.

Badia a Coltibuono, Gaiole in Chianti, Siena Amid a forest of pine and fir overlooking the Arno Valley, this ancient abbey may have been the place where the first chianti was made nearly a thousand years ago. Today the Gaiole township is known for the delicacy of its chianti classico, particularly in good years; the estate itself is noted for its stocks of fine chianti riserva, as well as good red and white table wines. The local vin santo toscano, made of trebbiano and malvasia grapes that have been left to dry before pressing and then allowed to ferment in small oak barrels for three or four years, is especially interesting. Dark gold, it has a lively bouquet, a velvety texture, and more or less sweetness depending on the sugar content of the original grapes. The establishment also produces a delicious extra-virgin olive oil. Wines and oils can be tasted at a restaurant on the grounds; visits to the abbey and cellars are by appointment only. Information: *Badia a Coltibuono,* Gaiole in Chianti (Siena) 53013 (phone: 577-749498; fax: 577-749235).

Ruffino, Pontassieve, Florence A large, widely respected producer of chianti and other wines, *Ruffino* has its main cellars at Pontassieve, about 10 miles (18 km) east of Florence. The wine house also has 10 estates situated throughout Tuscany. Most of them are in the classico zone, where *Ruffino* also has a guesthouse in the commune of Greve-in-Chianti. *Ruffino* produces galestro, orvieto, and libaio whites; red wine production includes the chianti classicos—aziano, santedame, riserva ducale riserva, Ruffino chianti, and torgaio—as well as a line of premium table wines called "super Tuscans" with the Capitolare designation. In a region whose wines usually vary radically from year to year, Ruffino chianti has the distinction of maintaining its quality from one vintage to the next. Visits by appointment only. Information: *Jon McInnes, Chianti Ruffino,* 42-44 Via Aretina, Pontassieve (Firenze) 50065 (phone: 55-83605; fax: 55-831-3677).

Villa Banfi, Sant'Angelo, Montalcino, Siena One of the leading US wine importers, which California's Robert Mondavi described as "the world's most modern winery," this vast estate of more than 2,000 acres of vines is open to the public by appointment. Notable products include an austere and full brunello di Montalcino, rosso di Montalcino centine, Santa Costanza, the bubbly-and-sweet moscadello di Montalcino, and the California-style chardonnay fontanelle and cabernet sauvignon tavarnelle. A restored medieval castle houses a wine museum. Information: *Elisabeth Koenig, Villa Banfi, S.p.A., Castello Banfi,* Sant'Angelo Scalo, Montalcino (Siena) 53020 (phone: 577-840111; fax: 577-840205).

Tenuta di Capezzana, Seano, Florence About 45 minutes west of Florence, the estate of Count and Countess Contini-Bonacossi has been producing fine wine and olive oil since AD 806. Fresh whites, an easy-drinking rosé, simple chianti, elegant carmignano with a hint of cabernet, one of Tuscany's finest vin santo toscano dessert wines, and even their delectable estate-produced extra-virgin olive oil are available for tasting and purchase at the *Capezzana* wine shop. Stop in at the olive oil mill during the crush in November. Visits by appointment only. Information: *Tenuta di Capezzana,* 100 Via Capezzana di Carmignano, Seano (Firenze) 50040 (phone: 55-870-6005; fax 55-870-6673).

UMBRIA Known as "the green heart of Italy," this region was noted in the past for the sweet white wine from Orvieto. In the last several years its wine makers have experimented with non-Italian grapes like chardonnay and cabernet sauvignon, with the result that Umbria promises to one day produce some of Italy's finest modern wines. The areas of special interest are Orvieto and the hills along the Tiber between Perugia and Todi.

Azienda Vallesanta di Luigi Barberani, Baschi, Terni Right off the autostrada that links Rome with Orvieto (A1), in the beautiful town of Baschi, Barberani has restored ancient wine making traditions using very modern equipment and methods. His orvieto muffa nobile "calcaia" is a venerable dessert wine, whose production depends on the most careful balance of damp growing conditions, a regal variety of mold, and rigid temperature controls. The results are intriguing. Visit his shop in Orvieto, across from the *Duomo,* if you're short of exploring time. Information: *Azienda Agricola Vallesanta,* Loc. Cerreto, Baschi (Terni) 05023 (phone: 763-41820; fax: 763-40773).

Cantine Lungarotti, Torgiano, Perugia About 6 miles (10 km) south of Perugia, this estate winery has become something of a contemporary legend under the supervision of Giorgio Lungarotti, who made his name with the Torgiano DOC white and red wines (most notably the single-vineyard reserve Rubesco red). He also produces prestigious chardonnay, cabernet sauvignon, and San Giorgio wines—this last a blend of cabernet and sangiovese, the grape on which chianti is based. The family also owns *Le Tre Vaselle* (see *The Best Restaurants of Italy*). A major national wine competition known as the *Banco d'Assaggio* is held here each fall. Nearby are an attractive wine museum and a display of local ceramics. Information: *Cantine Lungarotti,* Torgiano (Perugia) 06089 (phone: 75-988-0348; fax: 75-988-0294).

THE MARCHES The area of wooded slopes and medieval towns along the Adriatic coastline is known for its crisp, pale white verdicchio, which goes perfectly with the fish- and seafood-based dishes that are prevalent here. Rich, rustic reds—such as the Montepulciano-based rosso del conero—complement many lamb and veal dishes. In the town of Jesi—nestled in the vast hilly area 20 miles (32 km) west of Ancona—is *La Serva Padrona* (1 Piazza Pergolesi; phone: 731-212550), where most of the region's gems can be sampled.

Villa Bucci, Ostra Vetere, Ancona Milanese marketing expert Ampelio Bucci produces one of Italy's finest, food-friendly verdicchio wines—fruity and fresh—

and a reserve white (Villa Bucci) rich in perfume and structure. Legendary oenologist Giorgio Grai is a consultant to this winery, tucked in the gentle rolling landscape of the Marches. Information: *Fratelli Bucci,* 30 Via Cona, Ostra Vetere (Ancona) 60010 (phone: 71-964179).

SOUTHERN ITALY

CAMPANIA The wines of Campania have been legendary since even before the Roman era. The Greeks recognized prime opportunities in the area, introducing vines that yielded the aglianico and the fruity greco grape. The most prized wine of the Roman Empire, the strong red falernum (based on the aglianico), was grown along the coast north of Naples. Though the wines of this region eventually fell into decline, attempts at upgrading their quality and restoring ancient varieties to their former prestige have brought Campania back as a serious wine-producing region. While most of the area's wines still are modest and intended for mostly local consumption, a few ambitious producers dedicated to a more complex product are worth seeking out.

The region's best-known wine—white lacryma cristi (tears of Christ)—comes from the rich, volcanic soil of Mt. Vesuvius. The vineyards at Pozzuoli and Cumae yield the ancient falerno. Other wines worth looking for include the fruity white greco di tufo, perfect with the ubiquitous *mozzarella in carrozza* (breaded and fried mozzarella sandwich with anchovies), and taurasi, probably the best Campanian red, which complements aged cheeses such as the salty *caciocavallo*. The notorious, potent Strega (Witch) liqueur is made in Benevento.

Mastroberardino, Atripalda, Avellino About 30 miles (48 km) east of Naples in the hilly Avellino region, this state-of-the-art vineyard is Campania's leading wine producer. Working with local varietals, the Mastroberardino family produces a fiano di avellino Vignedora (regarded by many cognoscenti as Campania's best white wine), a greco di tufo Vignadangelo, and a good version of the famous lacryma cristi del Vesuvio. Their elegant red taurasi, made from the historically significant aglianico grape, is best when aged at least four years. Information: *Mastroberardino,* 75/81 Via Manfredi, Atripalda (Avellino) 80342 (phone: 825-626123; fax: 825-624151).

SICILY One of the largest wine-producing regions in Italy, Sicily also has the most vineyards. Most of the island's wine was once exported to the north to be used as a blending wine (for vermouth, for example) or distilled into industrial alcohol. But the quality of Sicilian wine making has improved tremendously in recent years. Many of the grapes are clean and fresh—the whites, light and dry; the reds, full-bodied. Corvo is perennially popular both in Italy and overseas, and the grapes from the vines planted in the volcanic soil of Mt. Etna show distinction.

Most of Sicily's wine making zones are dedicated to the production of marsala and (somewhat less) to muscat dessert wines. British traders discovered marsala in the town of the same name on Sicily's western coast 200 years ago, and it remains Sicily's best-known wine. The sherry-like, fortified wine makes a perfect aperitif or after-dinner drink, and is an essential ingredient in zabaglione. Malvasia delle Lipari, from the islands north of Sicily, is another dessert wine.

Corvo Duca di Salaparuta, Casteldaccia, Palermo Following the tradition established by the Duke of Salaparuta in 1824, wine maker Franco Giacosa continues to produce quality red and white corvo in the hills near Palermo. Aromatic and earthy, corvo is perhaps the best-known Sicilian wine in the US. The winery also produces colomba platino, Duca Enrico, bianca di Valguarnera, and terre d'agala—more refined versions of the corvo grape. Information: *Vini Corvo,* Via Nazionale, S113, Casteldaccia (Palermo) 90014 (phone: 91-953988; fax: 91-953227).

Vecchio Samperi, Marsala, Trapani Marco de Bartoli divides his time between his passion for restoring old cars and his love for producing dry marsala and bukkuram, a dessert wine made from semi-dry muscat grapes. Although his courtyard is usually strewn with sports cars in various stages of completion, his outstanding wines are well worth a stop. Information: *Vecchio Samperi,* 292 Contrada Samperi, Marsala (Trapani) 91025 (phone: 923-962093; fax: 923-962910).

Carlo Hauner, Salina, Isole Eolie Artist Carlo Hauner moved to secluded Salina—one of the Aeolian Islands (sometimes called the Lipari Islands)—to paint. Once there, however, he was so captivated by a vineyard he saw that he took it over. He is known throughout Italy for his lushly dramatic dessert wine—malvasia delle Lipari—and for his bottled capers and sun-dried tomatoes. Information: *Carlo Hauner,* Fraz. Lingua di Salina, Salina (Messina) 98050 (phone/fax: 90-984-3141).

Regaleali, Vallelunga, Palermo Count Tasca d'Almerita and his family produce Sicily's finest table wines at their estate south of Palermo. Fresh, drinkable whites, plus rosés and reds, are all excellent. The well-balanced white Nozze d'Oro is capable of aging, and the rich Rosso del Conte is a winner. Look for the vineyard's experimental, yet highly successful, sparkling wines, chardonnays, and cabernet sauvignons. Information: *Regaleali,* Contrada Regaleali, Vallelunga (Palermo) 90020 (phone: 921-542522; fax: 921-542783).

Cooking Schools

Along with the rest of the world, Italians have rediscovered the pleasures of the nation's regional cooking: Neapolitans now eat Tuscan food at home, and Venetians down Sicily's cannoli and cannelloni—foods that, as often as not, *Mamma's mamma* told her nothing at all about. Enter the cooking school.

Some are taught by superstars of Italian cooking like Marcella and Victor Hazan and Giuliano Bugialli. Many are in English; most are staged in spring and summer; and early booking is a must.

The following programs not only teach food preparation but explore many facets of the Italian culinary experience. Some schools are oriented toward professional chefs who want to hone their skills, while others provide a vacation in someone else's well-equipped kitchen. Some of the best are listed here.

VILLA TABLE, Coltibuono Lorenza de' Medici, author of many cookbooks published in Italy, teaches cooking using simple ingredients, including wine and olive oil produced on the estate (see *Most Visitable Vineyards*). This week-long cooking experience held in May, June, September, and October permits total immersion into the way of life on a Tuscany country estate. Students sleep in the villa's 15th-century guestrooms. In English. Information: *The Villa Table,* Badia a Coltibuono, Gaiole in Chianti (Siena) 53013 (phone: 577-749498), or *The Villa Table,* Judy Ebrey, 7707 Willow Vine Ct., Ste. 219, Dallas, TX 75230 (phone: 214-373-1161; fax: 214-373-1162).

COOKING IN FLORENCE, Florence Giuliano Bugialli is well known as the author of four definitive books on Italian cooking. However, every year in Florence during May, June, September, and at *Christmas,* he also offers several hands-on courses that cover the culinary delights of all Italy. Each of the five classes in the week-long course involves supervised preparation of a complete meal planned by Bugialli—a different menu for each class. In English. Information: *Giuliano Bugialli's Cooking in Florence,* PO Box 1650, Canal Street Station, New York, NY 10013 (phone: 212-966-5325; fax: 212-226-0601).

MANGIA, Florence Judy Witts teaches Tuscan cooking to American college students, but three-hour private lessons, food-related walking tours, and three- to seven-day sessions can also be arranged year-round, with a few days' notice. Her straightforward recipes, easygoing manner, and enthusiasm make the classes enjoyable—the food is memorable, too. Information: *Mangia,* 31 Via Taddea, Firenze 50173 (phone/fax: 55-292578).

RUFFINO TUSCAN EXPERIENCE, near Florence Chef Giovanna Folonari, the wife of winery owner Ambrogio Folonari, teaches her own version of elegant home entertaining on the grounds of the *Ruffino* wine company's vineyards in Chianti. Courses from a day to a week can be scheduled. In English. Accommodations are arranged at a hotel in Florence. Information: *Jon McInnes, Ruffino,* 42-44 Via Aretina, Pontassieve (Firenze) 50065 (phone: 55-83605; fax: 55-831-3677).

ITALIAN COUNTRY COOKING, Positano, Campania In the classes of this eight-day full-participation course in fabled seaside Positano, on the Amalfi Coast, the emphasis is on country cooking with locally available ingredients. Each of the various spring and fall sessions emphasizes a specific area—pasta and other first courses, meat, fish, desserts. All instruction is in English in director Diana Folonari's cliffside home; lodging is in nearby hotels. Information: *Folonari Country Cooking Classes,* c/o *E&M Associates,* 211 E. 43rd St., New York, NY 10017 (phone: 212-599-8280 in New York; 800-223-9832 elsewhere in the US).

SCHOOL OF TRADITIONAL NEAPOLITAN CUISINE, Positano, Campania The Amalfi Coast's premier *Le Sirenuse* hotel started cooking classes in response to its guests' ever-growing interest in the local *cucina napolitana.* At each of five classes (participants sign up for one or more), chef Alfonso Mazzancano, a native of Positano, discusses the use of local ingredients, and students prepare a traditional Neapolitan meal; southern Italian wines are served with the repast. The hotel also offers a "Culinary Package" that includes all five classes, excursions, and accommodations. In English. Information: *Le Sirenuse,* 30 Via Cristofo Colombo, Positano (Salerno) 84017 (phone: 89-875066; fax: 89-811798), or *Judy Ebrey, Cuisine International,* 7707 Willow Vine Ct., Ste. 219, Dallas, TX 75230 (phone: 214-373-1161; fax: 214-373-1162).

WORLD OF REGALEALI, Vallelunga, Sicily Marchesa Anna Tasca Lanza hosts five-day total-immersion sessions on Sicily's unique gastronomic heritage. Participants stay at the immense Tasca estate, where there are vineyards, olive groves, lovely wildflowers, and flocks of sheep, and indulge in cooking, cheese making, bread baking, and tasting the estate's fine wines (deemed some of Sicily's best). Few outsiders have ever enjoyed this quintessentially Sicilian experience. Courses are offered in the spring and fall. In English. Information: *Marchesa Anna Tasca Lanza,* 9 Viale Principessa Giovanna, Mondello (Palermo) 90149 (phone: 921-450727; fax: 921-542783).

CLASSIC ITALIAN COOKING, Venice Marcella and Victor Hazan's master classes at their home in Venice, and Marcella's classes hosted by the legendary Venetian *Cipriani* hotel in spring and fall, are so popular that reservations are made as many as two years in advance. The focus is on food and wine, and the Hazans offer the same kind of practical culinary advice that made their books best sellers (Victor's forte is oenology). Students shop at the *Rialto* market and dine in Venice's finest restaurants with the Hazans. In their 16th-century palazzo/home, a six-day course leading to a diploma teaches the essentials of making pasta, antipasti, and country breads, as well as traditional main courses. Enrollment in the master class is limited to six participants. In English. Information: *Hazan Classics Enterprises, Inc.,* PO Box 285, Circleville, NY 10919 (phone: 914-692-7104; fax: 914-692-2659).

GRITTI PALACE COOKING COURSES, Venice Every year in July and the beginning of August, this splendid old hotel, once the palace of a Venetian doge, is home to a series of five-day cooking courses, covering all of Italy's prime gastronomic areas. Each is taught by a well-known master chef invited for his or her knowledge of some regional cuisine. The venue is the hotel's own ultra-professional kitchen. Lessons are demonstration-style, followed by a lunch accompanied by wines chosen by the hotel's knowledgeable wine steward. Students may sign up for just one or stay for all of the sessions. It's not necessary to stay in the hotel to participate (you get a discount if you do). In Italian with simultaneous English translations on request. Information: *Gritti Palace Cooking Courses, Gritti Palace Hotel,* 2467 Campo San Marco del Giglio, Venezia 30124 (phone: 41-794611), or *CIGA Hotels,* 745 Fifth Ave., Ste. 1201, New York, NY 10151 (phone: 212-935-9540 in New York; 800-221-2340 elsewhere in the US).

VENETIAN COOKING IN A VENETIAN PALACE, Venice Renowned Venetian chef Fulvia Sesani offers a variety of choices for foreign guests who would like to include her well-known classes as part of a vacation in Venice. Options range from one-on-one lessons to morning or afternoon group classes in her palace to a whirlwind seven-day tour that includes day trips to the Veneto wine country and escorted dinners in Venice's most interesting restaurants. Classes are limited to 12 students. Information: *Fulvia Sesani,* 6140 Santa Maria Formosa, Castello, Venezia 30122 (phone/fax: 41-522-8923).

For the Mind

Theater, Music, and Opera

Italy has been a land of patrons and performers since the flushest days of the Medicis and the Gonzagas. Noble courts throughout the peninsula maintained private orchestras. Comedians *dell'arte* found the palace gates flung wide open with welcome. Recent cuts in government subsidies have impacted adversely on orchestras, choruses, and the legitimate theater, but most cities of size vaunt a concert hall and *teatro stabile* (repertory theater), and musical events still crowd the Italian calendar. Ticket prices are more reasonable than in the US.

Even outside the big cities, concerts and ballets attract huge audiences. Ownership of compact disc players and portable cassette players has increased concert attendance by attracting a younger audience. Today's venues are not only local auditoriums but also Renaissance palazzi and medieval churches, piazze, and flower-edged cloisters and courtyards. And you've never really heard Bach until you've heard his music reverberating through a Baroque basilica or against a background of classical columns.

Opera continues to boom. And in recent years, some of the country's dowager opera houses have been refitted with modish new finery, making them even more fashionable. Productions are good in Venice, Naples, Parma, and Rome as well as Milan.

In the theater, Goldoni and Pirandello are perennial favorites—with Guglielmo Shakespeare running a close third. Theatrical activity is more national than metropolitan. Companies usually do a limited run in major cities and then go out on tour—so travelers may well catch something in the provinces that they just missed in the capital.

We have highlighted exceptional performance venues in the country's major urban centers, such as *La Scala* in Milan, *San Carlo* in Naples, and *La Fenice* in Venice, in the individual reports in THE CITIES. Our other favorite Italian theaters, concert halls, and opera houses are listed below.

SOCIETÀ AQUILANA DEI CONCERTI BARATTELLI, L'Aquila, Abruzzo The nation's most impressive example of low-budget, high-quality music can be found in this Apennine city, the jumping-off point for visits to the *Parco Nazionale d'Abruzzo*. That it has a musical reputation of a city many times its size is all the more impressive, given that this is the capital of one of Italy's poorer regions. Behind its reputation is the late local lawyer Nino Carloni, who not only founded the distinguished *Orchestra Sinfonica degli Abruzzi* (Abruzzo Symphony Orchestra) but also was able to recruit some of Europe's most prestigious artists for his *Barattelli Society*'s chamber concert series, held in a tiny auditorium with state-of-the-art acoustics that is nestled picturesquely inside the city's 15th-century castle. A Sunday afternoon here is a perfect finale to a day's ramble in the neighboring wilderness. Information: *Ente Musicale Società Aquilana dei Concerti Barattelli, Castello Cinquecentesco,* L'Aquila 67100 (phone: 862-414161).

AMICI DELLA MUSICA, Perugia, Umbria Held at the 13th-century *Palazzo dei Priori,* the chamber concert series of the *Amici della Musica* (Friends of Music) is both a rare musical experience and the highlight of the social season in this storybook 15th-century town. Despite its small size, Perugia is the capital of the flourishing Umbria region and, as such, attracts artists of the caliber of a Backhaus, Pollini, or Accardo; Claudio Abbado has conducted the *European Youth Orchestra* here. During August, the harmonies switch from Bach to bop for the *Umbria Jazz Festival,* and the cobbled streets swing to the likes of Ornette Coleman as well as a number of younger jazz musicians and blues singers from all over Europe. The *amici della musica* are by this time on the Riviera listening to Stravinsky in stereo. Information: *Associazione Amici della Musica,* 63 Corso Vannucci, Perugia 06100 (phone: 75-572-2271).

TEATRO OLIMPICO, Vicenza, Veneto The last work of the late-Renaissance architect Palladio, this superb classical edifice, with its wood-and-stucco stage, elliptical seating area, playful perspectives, and orgy of ornament, was conceived to amuse the leisure class of 16th-century Vicenza. Modeled on an ancient Roman theater, it was begun in 1580, and it remains among the most stylish theaters in Europe. The stage is surrounded by Corinthian columns and niches between painted street scenes, evoking a masterly trompe l'oeil effect. Local repertory theater alternates with productions by touring companies during the June-through-September season; if you can't make it, visit the building anyway. Information: *Teatro Olimpico,* Piazza Matteotti, Vicenza 36100 (phone: 444-323781).

TEATRI STABILI Italy has no single great national theater. It has instead a dozen or so *teatri stabili*—regionally or municipally sponsored repertory companies that perform in their own theaters in most of the country's major cities as well as tour up and down the peninsula. Giorgio Strehler's *Il Piccolo* in Milan is tops; Genoa's *Stabile* is excellent. Naples has Roberto De Simone as well as traditional melodrama in dialect. Two of the most highly acclaimed companies outside the large metropolitan areas are the *Centro Teatrale Bresciano* and the *Piemontese Gruppo della Rocca* (which tours around Piedmont). Contact local or regional tourist offices for details.

Italy's Most Colorful Festas

Hardly a day passes in Italy without some community of even a few hundred souls celebrating some village-shaking historical event, traditional food, or local saint. There are harvest festivals, banquets of music, and masked carnival balls in candlelit palaces. Pungent Alba celebrates a *Festival of the Truffle;* Cavesana a feast consecrated to San Giorgio, the patron of oxen. Whether at the *Tournament of Noses* in Soragna, the live chess game at Marostica, the goose race of Lacchiarella, the *Mongrel Fair* in Mango, or the *Feast of Celibates* at Casto (which means "Chaste"), banners are draped from every windowsill, lights are strung up, processions shuffle to the rejoicing of the town band, celebrants dance in the piazza—and everyone commemorates whatever it was with a *porchetta* sandwich.

The festivals celebrated in Italy's major urban areas, such as Siena's *Palio,* are described in the individual reports in THE CITIES. Here are some of the most festive of Italian *feste* off the beaten path.

EASTER WEEK Nearly every village and town throughout the nation stages a special procession or ceremony honoring *Easter.* Some are derived from ancient pagan practices, and some from medieval customs. The pageantry in Sicily is particularly colorful. All night long on *Good Friday* in Trapani, the air throbs with haunting Sicilian funeral laments, and groups of men labor down the narrow streets carrying the weight of 20 huge platforms representing scenes of the Passion in an extraordinary display. In Nocera Tirinese, near Catanzaro, Sicily, penitents cut their legs with shards of glass, then walk behind rough-hewn statues of the Madonna and Christ in procession.

Following a 700-year-old tradition, hooded figures in Cascia (near Perugia) carry heavy crosses and wear chains on their legs while trudging through the Stations of the Cross.

And in Chieti, in Abruzzo, in one of the most ancient of rites, the whole town center is illuminated by torch and candlelight, and 150 musicians chant the *Miserere,* as a solemn procession of men in black tunics and gray mantles slowly winds through the streets.

SAGRA DEL TARTUFO, Alba, Piedmont A knobby cratered nugget, worth 10 times its weight in silver, the truffle is the main pleasure of any food lover's autumn and the chief honoree at a series of October goings-on in Alba, Italy's truffle capital. The festivities culminate with an orgy of truffle madness: contests, auctions, truffle hound competitions, cooking demonstrations, and innumerable tastings and sniffings of the gloriously ugly fungus. Information: *Azienda di Promozione Turistica,* Piazza Medford, Alba (Cuneo) 12051 (phone: 173-35833; fax: 173-363878).

FESTA DI SANT'ORSO, Aosta, Valle d'Aosta At the end of every January (30 to 31), following a tradition that goes back a thousand years, artisans from 12 mountain valleys around Aosta gather to show off the goods they've made by hand during the long winter months. Hundreds of stands exhibit items in wood, wrought iron, lace, wool, and straw—all for sale. Visitors can fight the cold with the region's famous cheese *fonduta* and its wicked *coppa dell'amicizia* (literally, cup of friendship, since it is passed around a group), a spiked-and-spiced coffee served in strange, many-spouted wooden receptacles. The bright parkas and brown faces adorning fellow shoppers confirm that you're not far from Italy's finest skiing. Information: *Azienda Autonoma di Soggiorno*, 3 Piazza Narbonne, Aosta 11100 (phone: 165-303725; fax: 165-40134).

VENDEMMIA DEL NONNO, Castagnole Monferrato, Piedmont The second Sunday of October, while the tangy odor of pressed grapes suffuses the streets of small towns all over Italy, this village enacts an authentic old-fashioned grape harvest the way grandfather used to. Families work together in the vineyards, heap carts high with the richly colored fruit, trample it with bare feet, and feast raucously at day's end at a community supper that features the traditional *bagna cauda,* a savory anchovy and garlic vegetable dip. Don't miss the local wines—barbera, grignolino, dolcetto, and the precious ruché, a robust red produced only in small quantities and only in this area. Information: *Pro Loco,* Castagnole Monferrato (Asti) 14030 (phone: 141-292173).

RASSEGNA MEDITERRANEA DEGLI STRUMENTI POPOLARI, Erice, Sicily Folk musicians from all over the Mediterranean—and as far abroad as Scotland and Scandinavia—descend on this pretty Sicilian hill town every year in late December to play and display bagpipes, flutes, lutes, tambourines, Jew's-harps, and other folk instruments. More than two decades old, the festival is a fine time to visit ancient and mysterious Erice, where ivy-covered buildings of Arab, Gothic, and Baroque design line the cobbled streets. The haunting music makes a perfect soundtrack for wide-screen views from the town's Norman castle overlooking Trapani and the Sicilian coast. Information: *Azienda Autonoma di Soggiorno e Turismo,* 11 Viale Conte Pepoli, Erice (Trapani) 91016 (phone: 923-869388).

L'INFIORATA, Genzano, Lazio On the Sunday after *Corpus Domini* in June, the long street sloping up to the *Chiesa di Santa Maria della Cima* in this hill town just outside Rome is completely, fragrantly carpeted with flowers worked into elaborate abstract designs, copies of famous artworks, or biblical scenes. (The next morning, at 10 AM, the children of the town descend on the street like a swarm of locusts, wiping out all the artwork in a matter of minutes.) Everyone in town, and visiting Romans by the score, turns out to see the pretty show and then heads for nearby country restaurants to eat fettuccine and drink amber-hued liters of the local castelli wine. Follow their example. Information: *Azienda Autonoma di Soggiorno,* 2 Via Olivela, Albano Laziale (Roma) 00041 (phone: 6-942-0331 or 6-932-4081).

CORSA DEI CERI, Gubbio, Umbria Ubaldo, the patron saint of this most beautiful and perfectly preserved of Italian towns, is honored on May 15 with an unusual and spectacular event that brings native Gubbini back home from all over the world. Three *ceri*—gigantic wooden structures resembling Brobdingnagian candles that are topped with tiny, but resplendently attired, statues of St. George, St. Anthony, and St. Ubaldo (patron saints of Gubbio's medieval guilds)—are fixed to mammoth litters. Then troupes of bearers tote them at top speed up and down the town's steep, narrow medieval alleys to the summit of Monte Ingino, where St. Ubaldo's glass coffin occupies a crumbling basilica; St. Ubaldo's candle always arrives first. Townspeople and tourists pack the streets to watch the colorful event, and flags, food, and religious fetes are the order of the day. If you're in town on the last Sunday in May, stop by the Piazza della Signoria to see the showy annual crossbow contest, which carries on the tradition of rivalry between the men of Gubbio and those of nearby Sansepolcro. Information: *Azienda Autonoma di Soggiorno e Turismo,* 6 Piazza Oderisi, Gubbio (Perugia) 06024 (phone: 75-922-0693; fax: 75-927-3409).

SAGRA DELL'UVA, Marino, Lazio When this town on the slopes southeast of Rome celebrates its grape harvest on the first Sunday of October, wine actually flows from the fountain in the town's center. After the sacred thanksgiving rites of the morning (a procession, a grape offering to the Madonna, and ritual restaurant feasts), the day turns pleasantly pagan, with allegorical floats, roast suckling pigs, garish street stands, and gushing wine (gratis)—the straw-golden dry white of the Alban hills. Meanwhile, the mood builds from merry to mildly wild, and celebrants routinely stagger on until late at night. Information: *Associazione Pro Loco,* 3 Largo Palazzo Colonna, Marino (Roma) 00047 (phone: 6-938-5555).

SAN RANIERI E GIOCO DEL PONTE, Pisa, Tuscany Every town in Italy has its own saint with his or her own special day and mode of celebration. In Pisa, the saint is Ranieri, and the festivities begin on the night of June 16, as candles flicker enchantingly around the buildings along the Arno. The next day, rowing teams in 16th-century costume compete in a hotly contested race on the river and then scale a high post to claim the victory flag. And the last Sunday in June, the strongest men from each side of the river don medieval finery for the *Gioco del Ponte,* a gigantic tug of war on the Ponte di Mezzo, according to a tradition rooted in far more lethal local skirmishes. Information: *Azienda di Promozione Turistica,* 24 Borgo Croce, Pisa 56100 (phone: 50-40096; fax: 50-40903).

FESTIVAL DEI DUE MONDI, Spoleto, Umbria Founded in 1957 by Gian Carlo Menotti, this celebrated mid-June event brings together performers from both sides of the Atlantic and beyond for three weeks of dance, poetry readings, concerts, drama, opera, and art exhibits notable for their diversity, quality, and sizable number of new works. Equally remarkable is the setting. The capital of the Dukes of Lombardy from the 6th to the 8th century, picturesque Spoleto is full of narrow vaulted passages and interesting nooks and crannies, quaint old shops, and colorful markets. The final concert is traditionally held in front of the 12th-century cathedral, with the audience sitting on the majestic stairway overlooking it in the shadow of handsome palaces and hanging gardens. Menotti himself is still actively involved, though his son has officially taken over directorship. Information: *Festival dei Due Mondi,* 18 Via Beccaria, Roma (phone: 6-321-0288), or 9 Via del Duomo, Spoleto (phone: 743-40396 or 743-220320).

FESTIVAL INTERNAZIONALE DI MUSICA ANTICA, Urbino, the Marches For 10 days every year in late July, instrumentalists, dancers, singers, and theoreticians—both amateur and professional—from the four corners of Europe and the United States converge on this ancient hill town in the Marches, Raphael's birthplace, for Italy's most important Renaissance and Baroque music festival. Courses are offered at all levels and for all ages in the principal ancient instruments, voice, music history, and dance (both folk and courtly), and ambitious artisans learn to construct harpsichords and lutes. There are ample opportunities to perform with other musicians, and the chorus, open to all, serenades in the main piazza on the last day. An evening concert series focusing on music composed before 1750 runs through the summer. Information: *Società Italiana per la Musica Antica,* 33 Via Monte Zebio, Roma 00195 (phone: 6-372-9667).

CARNEVALE, Viareggio, Tuscany During the three weekends before *Lent* and on *Shrove Tuesday,* this summer seaside resort becomes a whirl of *Carnevale* costumes, confetti, and floats poking fun at Italian politicians. It all climaxes in a parade of leering dummies, pert majorettes, and immense, elaborately decorated floats (some as high as a hundred feet), where a festive do-or-dare atmosphere reigns as the procession leaves from the *Royal* hotel and lumbers down the *lungomare,* crowded with confetti-strewn, costumed children and food vendors. There's music, fireworks, and endless pranks, because *"A Carnevale, ogni scherzo vale"* ("At *Carnevale,* any joke goes"). The parade area is closed off; there's an admission charge, and you'll have to pay extra if you want to reserve a seat in the bleachers. Besides Viareggio, the celebration is best exemplified in Venice; Bassano del Grappa (the Veneto), Putignano (Puglia), and Verres (Valle d'Aosta) are other venues for *Carnevale* bacchanalia. Information: *Carnevale di Viareggio, Palazzo delle Muse,* Second Floor, 22 Piazza Mazzini Viareggio 55049 (phone: 584-47503 or 584-962568; fax: 584-47077).

LA SAGRA DEI CUOCHI DEL SANGRO, Villa Santa Maria, Abruzzo For three days every year in mid-October, gifted master chefs who hail from this small town in the Sangro River Valley, where some of the world's finest cooks learned their trade, return to their hometown to demonstrate their art in an appetizing street festival that honors culinary talents stretching back to the Renaissance. Information: *Istituto Professionale Alberghiero di Stato,* Villa Santa Maria (Chieti) 66047 (phone: 872-944422).

Churches and Piazzas

Whether it's a Mussolini-modern space ringed with chic *caffès* or a medieval square sprouting vegetable stalls, Italy's piazze are the acknowledged centers of local activity. In them, revolutions were preached, crowds harangued, heretics burned, and confetti sprinkled. Every day marks a new period in the perennial urchin-league soccer match. Every evening, tables and chairs are hauled onto the sidewalk, and a new hand is dealt in *scopa,* a card game. And every Sunday, at the end of mass in the late morning, the faithful pour out onto the square for a round of political gossip before lunch. The church, which draws its patrons from the teeming society just outside its portals and represents a supremely Italian mix of diversion and devotion, is the raison dêtre of almost every piazza in Italy. Styles range from plain to grandiose, from the peasant church tacked onto the dusty piazza as afterthought to the marble-striped façade of a Renaissance *duomo.*

Do as the Italians do—sit and sip and stretch and stroll on a glorious piazza in front of a splendid church like those listed below. Here, indeed, the *far niente* (doing nothing) for which Italy is well known is truly *dolce* (sweet).

We have highlighted exceptional churches and piazze in the major urban areas, such as Piazza della Signoria in Florence, the *Duomo* in Milan, and Piazza Navona in Rome, in the individual reports in THE CITIES, and the renowned Campo dei Miracoli in Pisa in *Tuscany* in DIRECTIONS. Our other favorites, listed below, are along the coastline or in the countryside.

BASILICA DI SAN FRANCESCO, Assisi, Umbria When this handsome, elaborate double church was erected for the greater glory of St. Francis in 1228—two years after his death—there were strong protests from Franciscans who thought such a structure inconsistent with their sect's consecration to a life of poverty. The colossal complex, which includes the *Sacro Convento,* a Franciscan monastery, and two churches (one on top of the other), looms over the roofs and alleys clustered on the Umbrian hillside town. The façade is a curious mixture of stolid squareness and Gothic fancy embroidered in light pink stone, and the windowless tower dissolves into a row of slender arches at the top. The realm below, the *Chiesa Inferiore,* is spacious, but dark—which is unfortunate, because the walls are covered with frescoes. Those in the nave, by the 13th-century Maestro di San Francesco, are the oldest; others are by Giotto (the right, or south, transept and the third chapel on the right), Pietro Lorenzetti (left, or north, transept), Simone Martini (first chapel on the left), and Cimabue (his striking *Virgin and Child with Four Angels and St. Francis* is in the right transept, right wall). In the bright *Chiesa Superiore* (Upper Church) are frescoes by Cimabue, including a Crucifixion, and Giotto's famed frescoes of the life of St. Francis, 28 scenes running counterclockwise around the nave (the attribution of the last few scenes is in doubt). Painted almost 800 years ago, they are captivating for the views they offer of ordinary life—fabrics, weapons, faces, furniture, landscapes, homes, walls, and towers—as well as for their narrative and inspirational content. As some critics have put it, art with a human dimension was born here, a far cry from the stylized rigidity that went before.

CERTOSA DI PAVIA (CHARTERHOUSE OF PAVIA), near Pavia, Lombardy Wonderfully out of place in the quiet Lombard countryside on the banks of the Ticino, this monumental monastery of glowing brick is just an hour from Milan. When the dozens of architects, painters, sculptors, and builders who pieced it together during most of the 15th century were finished, it was an exuberantly decorated mini-city with its own unique urban sprawl. It has its own train station (stop Certosa) and even a skyscraper of sorts (the octagonal cupola of its church towers five stories above everything else in the area). The arcades of its two cloisters are decorated with terra cotta reliefs, and the roofs are spiky with the chimneys of the Cistercian priests' cottages—tiny villas, each with two floors and a garden, which the religious occupants leave seven times daily to visit the church for prayers. The monastery is open to the public, and several of the cells can be visited.

BASILICA DI SAN VITALE, Ravenna, Emilia-Romagna The naked brick exterior of this knobby, octagonal church, built between 526 and 547—probably based on a much older church in Constantinople—conceals an Oriental treasure of an interior, brilliant with mosaics populated by royalty and gaudy birds and heavily embellished with columns whose capitals are encrusted with gingerbread curlicues. On the outer walls of the chancel are Old Testament scenes: on the left, Abraham and the three angels and the sacrifice of Isaac, and on the right, the death of Abel and the offering of Melchizedek. The imperial decoration climaxes in the apse. Depicted in a majestic fablescape of tiny colored stones at either side of the altar, Emperor Justinian and Empress Theodora, dressed in ornate Eastern robes and with Theodora bearing the chalice containing the wine of the sacrifice of Christ in her hands, lead a stately procession toward Jesus. By the emperor's side stands Archbishop Maximian, who consecrated *San Vitale,* holding the Eucharist. The infinitesimal stones are angled this way and that, and the effect as their blues, greens, golds, and whites catch the light is dazzling.

Remarkable Ruins

The only museums in the world where picnics and dogs are allowed, and where sightseeing is ideally combined with a sunbath, a game of touch football, or a bottle of wine, historic ruins have long been part of Italian life.

There are simply more ruins in the country than anyone can catalogue. Each ruin is in its own distinctive state of decay, and each complex has its own particular mood and its own prime viewing time during the year. Be sure to check schedules in advance; many important sites are closed Mondays or Tuesdays and on holidays, and many shut down Sunday afternoons as well.

We have spotlighted noteworthy ruins in the country's large metropolitan areas, such as the *Baths of Caracalla* in Rome, the *Teatro Greco* in Siracusa, and the *Arena* in Verona, in the individual city reports in THE CITIES. Our other favorites, listed below, are off the beaten track. And always keep an eye peeled for the unobtrusive yellow signs that point down dusty roads. Together with the handful of superbly interesting destinations sketched below, the moss-covered stumps of column in the middle of the woods that are found in this fashion may turn out to be the best part of the journey.

NORA, Gonnesa, Sardinia Jutting out into the sensuously limpid water for which Sardinia is famous, this area on the island's southern tip bears traces of 4,000 years of population. Primitive stone towers called *nuraghi* dating from 1500 to 2000 BC dot the countryside and make up the Bronze Age village of Seruci (not far from the modern town of Gonnesa, on Cape Pula, 19 miles/30 km west of Cagliari). Remains of the ancient city of Nora, founded by the Phoenicians in the 9th century BC on a much earlier site, are here as well, and above them are later, Roman ruins. At the center of the city is the temple to the Phoenician goddess Thanit, made of large, irregular blocks of stone. In addition, much of the Roman city remains, including a well-preserved amphitheater, baths, temples, and stunning mosaic floors. A special bonus of a visit here: Nora lies amid some of Italy's loveliest unspoiled scenery, well off the path taken by most tourists. Information: *Azienda Autonoma di Soggiorno e Turismo,* 97 Via Mameli, Cagliari (Sardegna) 09100 (phone: 70-664195 or 70-664196).

PAESTUM, Campania The massive temples of Paestum, gleaming bone-white against the dark greens and browns of the brush-covered mountains south of Salerno, provide an almost unique opportunity to see a Greek town that has not been surrounded by modern structures. Founded by the Greeks in the late 7th century BC as Poseidonia, it was inhabited successively by the early Italic tribes, the Romans, and the early Christians. Consequently, the ruins are a catalogue of the changing styles of 700 years of art. The most prominent of the ruins are the weathered but ruggedly eternal remains of three amazingly well preserved temples, their parades of columns remarkably intact among the cypress trees, oleander, and fragrant herbs. The *Basilica,* the oldest temple in Paestum, was constructed in the mid-6th century BC and dedicated to the goddess Hera (it was mislabeled by Christians in the 18th century). Facing east, it has 50 fairly bulbous Doric columns that taper dramatically at the top, creating the illusion that the temple pitches outward. Next to it, the *Temple of Neptune* (known as the *Temple of Poseidon*—its Greek cognomen, but also misnamed because it, too, was dedicated to Hera) was built in the middle of the 5th century BC. Perfectly proportioned, it is considered to be one of the most beautiful Doric temples in Italy or Greece, as well as one of the best preserved—it is also the largest (200 feet by 80 feet). Both temples to Hera are at the southern end of the Via Sacra. At its northern end is the so-called *Temple of Ceres,* built in approximately 500 BC to honor the goddess Athena. The smallest of the temples of Paestum, it once had, in addition to its Doric exterior columns, Ionic interior columns (whose scant remains are in the museum). It still contains three medieval tombs dating from a time when the temple was used as a Christian church.

Paestum is also home to the only known examples of classical Greek painting. A museum across the street from the archaeological zone includes funerary wall paintings dating from the late 5th century BC. Among the most interesting is a fresco from the *Tomba del Tuffatore* (Tomb of the Diver), discovered about a half mile (1 km) away, showing an athlete plunging into the water, a look of Olympic concentration on his face. They are the only paintings of figures to have been found in Magna Graecia. Also noteworthy are the 34 metopes (Doric-style low reliefs from the 6th century BC) from the *Temple of Hera Argiva* at the mouth of the Sele River, 8 miles (13 km) north of Paestum. In addition, reproductions of various cornices in the museum show how richly colored the temples across the street once were. Information: *Azienda Autonoma di Soggiorno,* 151/156 Via Magna Grecia, in the archaeological zone, Paestum (Salerno) 84063 (phone: 828-811016).

POMPEII AND HERCULANEUM, Campania Shortly after noon on August 24, AD 79, Mt. Vesuvius erupted. The busy seaport of Pompeii was suffocated by live cinders and ash, and the small, quiet town of Herculaneum was covered by an enormous burning "mud" slide, in some places over 80 feet deep. On that fateful day, Pompeii, which was then, and is now, a thrumming business center of about 30,000, was effectively embalmed. Pliny the Younger described the catastrophe as he watched from Cape Miseno, witnessing the rain of ashes and cinders and the inhabitants' desperate attempt to escape the suffocating heat and fumes. Two thousand people perished, and the city was buried.

Pompeii was "rediscovered" in the 16th century by Domenico Fontana, an architect rebuilding roads. The Bourbon King Charles of Naples, an avid collector, encouraged excavations in 1748, yet systematic digging didn't begin until 1860. It continues today (almost two-thirds of the site has been unearthed), with the current emphasis on restoring artifacts on the spot and exploring the ancient way of life. In 1991 archaeologists found eight mummified bodies of people who had managed to get almost to the sea, over 200 yards away. They were the first victims to be found at the site in 20 years. Some had covered their mouths with their tunics to keep from breathing the poisonous gases that Vesuvius poured out. The discovery provoked a further search for other mummified bodies in the area.

Much of the spectacular artwork found at the site is kept in Naples's *Museo Archeologico Nazionale,* but there's enough here to leave a visitor thoroughly exhausted—and still feeling that there are a few blocks of marble unturned. Be sure to see the *Basilica,* the largest and most important of Pompeii's public buildings, located just off the *Forum,* the religious, civic, and business center of the city. Along the side and at the far end of the *Forum* are the *Temple of Apollo* (which has a copy of the bronze statue of the god that was found here but moved to the *Museo Archeologico Nazionale*) and the *Temple of Giove,* or Jove, with its triumphal arches and a view of Vesuvius in the background.

Walk out of the *Forum* along Via dell'Abbondanza to the well-preserved *Terme Stabiane* (Stabian Baths), which contain a *palestra* (sports arena or gym), a pool, and separate hot and cold rooms for men and women. Both the 5,000-seat *Teatro Grande* and the thousand-seat *Teatro Piccolo* (which was covered) are not far from the baths. The *Anfiteatro,* the oldest Roman amphitheater in existence (ca. 80 BC), with a capacity of 12,000, is some distance away, next to the *Grande Palestra,* where athletes trained.

Of Pompeii's magnificent patrician villas, three stand out. The huge *Casa del Menandro,* named after a portrait of the Greek poet found there, is lavishly decorated with paintings and mosaics. The *Casa dei Vettii,* which belonged to two rich merchants of the Vettio family, is a meticulously restored, sumptuously decorated villa with fine frescoes in the Fourth, or late, Pompeiian style, characterized by mythological and architectural scenes drawn in dizzying perspective. The *Villa dei Misteri* (Villa of the Mysteries) might be called an ancient suburban house, since it's actually outside the ruins (but visitable with the same admission ticket). Thought to have belonged to a female initiate of the Dionysian cult, it contains frescoes depicting the initiation of young brides, painted on a background of Pompeiian red. The frescoes cover the walls of an entire room, the largest paintings to have survived from antiquity.

Scholars initially believed that most of Herculaneum's inhabitants had escaped the wrath of Vesuvius's eruption, but discoveries showed that the people only got as far as the town's gate to the sea. The "mud" hardened to the consistency of concrete, making excavation extremely difficult. (The earliest diggers, in 1709, more interested in plunder than history, simply burrowed tunnels and hauled out the loot. The first serious excavations began in 1738.) The volcanic blanket probably preserved the town's houses, many of which were partly constructed of wood. Unlike Pompeii, where wood went up in flames, the beams, staircases, doors, window frames, and even some furnishings are intact in Herculaneum, giving a far better idea of daily life than Pompeii's more fragmentary ruins. Herculaneum also reveals a wider range of structures and building styles, from the elaborate villas of the patrician classes to shops, multilevel apartment buildings, municipal baths, and a *palestra.* Herculaneum was sacked in 1990 by thieves who carted off more than 300 jewels, statues, coins, and other precious artifacts (valued at $250 million). The cache was recovered by the police, however, and scheduled to be back on view at press time.

Herculaneum's high points are the *Terme* (Baths), built during the reign of Augustus; the *Casa dell'Atrio a Mosaico* (House with the Mosaic Atrium), with its black-and-white mosaic floor; the *Casa a Graticcio* (Wooden Trellis House); the *Casa del Tramezzo di Legno* (House with the Wooden Partition); the *Casa Sannitica* (House of the Samnites), with an atrium surrounded by Ionic columns; the blue mosaic–filled *Casa del Mosaico di Nettuno e Anfitrite* (House of the Neptune and Amphitrite Mosaic); and the *Casa del Bicentenario* (House of the Bicentenary), where a small cross and altar are on display, evidence that the cross was already a symbol of Christianity in the 1st century. Another interesting house is the *Casa dei Cervi* (House of the Stags), with its red and black frescoes and its sculpture of stags attacked by dogs.

The *Villa dei Papiri* (thousands of papyrus scrolls were found here), a grandiose private house that was excavated in the mid-18th century, is now closed. The famous bronze statues of water carriers (or dancers) housed in the *Museo Archeologico Nazionale* in Naples are part of the hundreds of extraordinary works of art discovered here, and the *J. Paul Getty Museum* in Malibu, California, is a reconstruction of the villa.

Both the Pompeii and Herculaneum sites are closed Mondays and holidays; admission charge. Information: *Azienda Autonoma di Soggiorno,* 1 Via Sacra, Pompeii (Napoli) 80045 (phone: 81-863-1041).

SEGESTA, Sicily On the side of a barren, savage hill appropriately called the Monte Barbaro, the massive Doric temple of Segesta sits eerie and solitary and silent, except for the clanging of goats' bells. Destroyed by the Saracens in about AD 1000, it has no roof today and probably had none when it was built in the 5th century BC as a place of open-air sacrifices within a ring of 36 giant columns. The stark Greek amphitheater spread out in the sun-scorched wilderness above the temple is worth the hike up the steep mountain path. For those who prefer to ride, a shuttle bus leaves hourly from the parking area. A classical theater festival takes place at the site from June through mid-August in odd-numbered years. Information: *Azienda Provinciale per il Turismo,* 1/A Piazzetta Saturno, Trapani (Sicilia) 91100 (phone: 923-27077).

TARQUINIA AND CERVETERI, Lazio Virtually all that is known of the remote Etruscan civilization comes not from excavation of its cities but from excavation of its necropoli (burial grounds), virtual cities of underground chambers and dome-shaped tombs. Though their inscriptions are written in a language that still baffles experts, more than 60 excavated tombs at Tarquinia are decorated with bright wall paintings documenting Etruscan life—banquets, sports, dances, religious rites, furnishings, and travel. Many of the burial chambers in Cerveteri (ancient Caere) have lost their paint, but the fascination lies in their furnishings and architectural details—ceiling beams, doorways, divans—all carved in soft tufa stone. The *Tomba dei Capitelli* (Tomb of the Capitals), in particular, built at the height of Caere's wealth and power, shows what the inside of an Etruscan home was like. The walls of the 4th- or 3rd-century BC *Tomba dei Rilievi* (Tomb of the Reliefs), which were the burial vaults of the rich Matuna family, are covered with charming painted stucco reliefs of household scenes. They show everyday life in Caere, right down to the Matunas' stew pots and the family mutt. The *Tomba di Regolini Galassi,* in another location closer to town and dating from the late 7th century BC, is also famous. Its dowry of presents to accompany the dead on their voyage to the afterlife is now in the Etruscan collection at the *Vatican.*

The *Musei Vaticani* and the *Villa Giulia* in Rome both have extensive collections of the angular, modern-looking household objects the Etruscans buried with their dead. Equally worthwhile are the more intimate displays in the medieval towns of Tarquinia and Cerveteri, both of whose museums are closed Mondays. Information: *Ente Provinciale per il Turismo,* 11 Via Parigi, Roma 00185 (phone: 6-488-1851); the *Museo Nazionale Cerite,* Principe Ruspoli Castello, Cerveteri (Roma) 00052 (phone: 6-995-0003); and the *Museo Nazionale Tarquiniense, Palazzo Vitelleschi,* Corso Emanuele, Tarquinia (Viterbo) 01016 (phone: 766-856036).

VILLA ROMANA DEL CASALE, Piazza Armerina, Sicily Built in the 3rd or 4th century at the foot of Mt. Mangone, this sprawling villa probably was the country or summer residence of the Emperor Maximian Herculius. Archaeologists and historians believe that the villa was inhabited throughout the Byzantine-Islamic period, destroyed during the barbarian invasions, restored to glory by the Normans after 1000, and razed by William the Bad in the 12th century. It was gradually buried by repeated flooding and soil erosion; its modern excavation began in 1928. The building is organized in four large groups of rooms linked by corridors, peristyles, and galleries. It had cold- and hot-water baths, gymnasiums, gardens, and halls, whose dimensions testify to their grandeur. But it is most remarkable for the delightful quality, color, design, and state of preservation of the mosaic floors that run through most of the villa. They depict mythical acts of heroism, hunting scenes, races, and cupids harvesting grapes. The busy hunters, struggling heroes, and frightened running bulls and deer are powerfully realistic; tiny colored mosaic stones outline each tensed muscle. One scene of women bathing, remarkable for its subtle shadings of flesh color, shows that bikinis were already in style during the Roman Empire. No textbook of ancient history could ever tell the story of Roman life as vividly as this. Information: *Azienda Autonoma di Soggiorno,* 15 Via Cavour, Piazza Armerina (Enna) 94015 (phone: 935-680201).

For the Body

Italy's Unparalleled Skiing

Italy's large international resorts like Cervinia, Cortina, and Sestriere have it all—a vast array of runs and lifts, troops of multilingual instructors, a selection of winter sporting opportunities such as ice skating and tobogganing, cornucopias of shops, shimmering hotels, high-speed nightlife, and the glossy aura of Europe's leisured classes. But there are also lots of cozier, *famiglia*-oriented villages, many of them linked to a constellation of neighbors by chair lifts and cable cars.

Increasingly available is the all-region *tessera,* a pass that permits a skier to schuss hundreds of miles of trails with a single document. One of the best, the *Superski Dolomiti Pass,* offers access to more than 450 lifts serving more than 675 miles of Alpine ski trails. District passes that permit use of some portion of these 450 lifts—as much territory as most intermediates would be able to cover in a couple of weeks of skiing—are somewhat less expensive.

The best skiing is in the Alpine tier. Resorts in the French-flavored Valle d'Aosta are situated on natural balconies with stunning views of Mont-Blanc (Monte Bianco here), the Matterhorn (which Italians know as Monte Cervino), Italy's own Monte Rosa, and other celebrated Alpine peaks; all are easily accessible by tunnels and *autostrade.*

There also is good skiing (though sometimes less snow) in the German-speaking Alto Adige, with the Dolomites' craggy pink peaks rising fantastically out of valleys. With their spires and towers, deeply grooved boulders and huge terraces, and sheer vertical faces on all sides, the Dolomites do not look particularly skiable. But wide-open ledges and snowfields above, and tree-covered lower slopes below, provide sport enough to last a lifetime. That this area also is known as South Tyrol gives a clue to the culture here—equal parts Teutonic and Mediterranean.

Serviceable but crowded skiing lies within striking distance of more southerly cities: Abetone near Florence; Terminillo, Campo Imperatore, and Ovindoli near Rome; and Roccaraso, equidistant from Rome and Naples. It's even possible to ski on Mt. Etna—volcanic activity permitting—and cool off afterward in the Sicilian sea. (Avoid Sundays, when the crowds are overwhelming.)

Sci di fondo—cross-country skiing—is booming here. A wide choice of trails and excursions (and a good supply of the relatively inexpensive necessary equipment) is readily available. And no matter where you go, there's a very high standard of cooking in the dining rooms adjacent to the slopes.

Words of caution: If you need an English-speaking instructor from the area's ski school, say so when signing up, or risk having to learn to recognize "Bend your knees" when spoken in all too faultless Italian. Know the local trail markings—green for novice, blue for intermediate, red for competent, and black for the very best skiers. Be prepared for sometimes hair-raising traffic, both on the mountain roads and on the slopes; traditions of slope safety and etiquette are uneven. Try to avoid crowded *Christmastime* (when snow conditions can be chancy), and remember that the Italian school vacation extends through *Epiphany* (January 6). And consider summer skiing on glaciers, such as at Bormio in Lombardy. June and September are its prime times for snow, sunny skies, and smaller and fewer crowds.

For each ski center, we have included a few favorite hotels, generally in each price range: Expensive (E), Moderate (M), and Inexpensive (I)—or at least, more moderate.

BORMIO, Lombardy In ancient times, Romans came here to cure gout in the natural hot water bubbling from Bormio's nine springs. Now, year-round, Italians from every corner take to the heights in a two-stage cable lift that carries them above the lower mountain, with its soft snow and forest-edged runs, to 6,500 feet, and on to the wide-open snowfields at about 9,800 feet. Then, at the end of each bracing day's skiing, they return to this small, elegant city and a warm reception, Bormio-style. Many do as the ancient Romans did—relax in the thermal center in town or, a 15-minute taxi ride into the mountains, at the original Roman baths. At nearby Passo dello Stelvio, no fewer than 16 schools help keep the high-altitude glaciers populated even at high noon in July, a fine time to learn to ski. Information: *Azienda di Promozione Turistica,* 10 Via allo Stelvio, Bormio (Sondrio) 23032 (phone: 342-903300; fax: 342-904696). Hotels: *Palace* (E), *Everest* (I).

CANAZEI, Trentino Busy, friendly, and not overly chic, it's surrounded by the most decorative mountains in Italy—the Sella, Marmolada, and Sassolungo sections of the distinctively dramatic Dolomite range. The more than 60 miles of trails here are linked with the extensive networks of neighboring Val Gardena and Val Badia, so there's no shortage of skiable terrain, and the valley ski schools are known for their professionalism and highly developed teaching methods. The covered pool and up-to-date skating rink will burn off any unused energy. Information: *Azienda Autonoma di Soggiorno e Turismo,* 16 Via Roma, Canazei (Trento) 38032 (phone: 462-61113; fax: 462-62502). Hotels: *Diana* (M), *Tyrol* (M to I).

CERVINIA, Valle d'Aosta In the Italian shadow of the Matterhorn, this is one of the most popular Italian mountain resorts—partly because of its open, sun-bathed position; partly because of its majestic mountain-rimmed setting on the Monte Rosa plateau; partly because of its altitude, which begins at over 6,500 feet and guarantees an abundant harvest of snow in an average year; and partly because the spring skiing is superb. The trails are mostly smooth and forgiving—it's possible to stay on the slopes all day without ever bending your knees. The lift system is also one of Italy's most sophisticated, and the town is linked to neighboring Valtournenche; on a clear day it's possible to ski to Zermatt, Switzerland. There is every type of winter sport, from cross-country skiing to ice hockey and bobsledding. The atmosphere is equally frenetic, with chic shops, discos, skiers dressed at least to maim (both on and off the slopes), and Maseratis with roof racks full of Rossignols. Quaint it ain't. Information: *Azienda Autonoma di Soggiorno e Turismo di Breuil-Cervinia,* 29 Via J. A. Carrel, Cervinia (Aosta) 11021 (phone: 166-949136; fax: 166-949731). Hotels: *Cristallo* (E), *President* (M), *Europa* (I).

CHAMPOLUC, Valle d'Aosta Tucked into the end of the sunny Val d'Ayas under Monte Rosa and mercifully ignored by the great mass of European skiers, Champoluc has kept its countrified air. But the facilities are as complete as the town life is simple. Including the neighboring Frachey, Staval, Orsia, and Gressoney, 30 lifts serve over 120 miles of trails, offering skiing for every level. There's even an 18-mile cross-country trail. Glamorous hotels are not part of Champoluc life, and quiet is the order of the evening. Information: *Azienda Autonoma di Soggiorno,* 16 Via Varasc, Champoluc (Aosta) 11020 (phone: 125-307113; fax: 125-307785). Hotels: *Anna Maria, Castor* (M), *Monte Cervino* (I).

CORTINA D'AMPEZZO, Veneto The country's number-one ski resort attracted its first tourists—English, German, and Austrian mountain climbers—in the mid-19th century; skiing began here early in the 20th century. But the ski trade didn't really boom until the town hosted the *1956 Winter Olympics.* Now among the Alps' best-equipped and most cosmopolitan ski resorts, it counts a huge open *Stadio Olimpico del Ghiaccio* (Olympic Ice Stadium) among its special offerings, along with a location amid the toothy spikes of the Dolomites at the heart of the Superski Dolomiti region. Add the resort's own network of four ski areas, and the resulting package draws a stylish international set that nourishes the department stores, big hotels, and scores of smart boutiques and eateries crowding Corso d'Italia, the long, narrow main street. Information: *Azienda di Promozione Turistica,* 8 Piazzetta San Francesco, Cortina d'Ampezzo (Belluno) 32043 (phone: 436-3231; fax: 436-3235). Hotels: *Cristallino, Menardi, De la Poste* (E).

CORVARA IN BADIA, Alto Adige Corvara is the principal departure point for the Sella Ronda, the Dolomite circuit that connects five downhill areas and countless skiing experiences and that, together with a mega ski pass, provides access to about 250 miles of linked trails. Located in one of the few valleys where residents still speak Ladin (a language said to have come down from the Latin of Romans who came here in the 4th century), Corvara itself has a bucolic flavor, despite the modish tone of its shops, *caffès,* and discotheques. For those who prefer the great indoors, there's heated swimming, covered tennis, and high-Alpine bowling. Information: *Azienda*

Autonoma di Soggiorno e Turismo, Palazzo Comunale, Corvara in Badia (Bolzano) 39033 (phone: 471-836176; fax: 471-836540). Hotels: *La Perla* (E), *Posta Zirm* (M), *Tablè* (M to I).

COURMAYEUR, Valle d'Aosta Among the most glamorous of Italian ski resorts and perhaps the friendliest in the Alps, Courmayeur is stunningly situated in the middle of 12 peaks above 13,000 feet. The dramatic south-facing side of the Mont-Blanc massif looms above, and over two dozen lifts make more than 60 miles of ski runs accessible to both beginners and experts. The area is heaven for intermediates, with enough autostrada-on-snow trails to boost any ego and enough moguls to show that there's always more to learn. Meanwhile, snow pioneers accompanied by guides can ski across Monte Bianco and over the French border to Chamonix. Such facilities and terrain attract important skiing competitions all winter and, with them, the sleek international set and modern Milan-Turin managerial money. The even more upwardly mobile use helicopters as transport to powdery plateaus. The beauties of the old-fashioned town itself will satisfy valley types; there are four cross-country circuits ranging in length from 3½ to 12 miles. Summer skiing keeps the Gigante glacier from getting lonely during the off-season. Information: *Azienda Autonoma di Soggiorno e Turismo,* Piazzale Monte Bianco, Courmayeur (Aosta) 11013 (phone: 165-842060; fax: 165-842072). Hotels: *Palace Bron* (E), *Chetif* (M), *Centrale* (I).

LIVIGNO, Lombardy Not so long ago, this curious, little-known village of distinctive wooden houses strung out along a valley on the Swiss-Italian border was the exclusive domain of cross-country ski wanderers; its only road was regularly blocked by heavy snowfalls. Now, thanks to enthusiastic, but not excessive, development and the construction of a tunnel into Switzerland as an alternative means of egress, it offers attractive skiing and accommodations, plus ice skating, tobogganing, a pretty lake, and a gentle landscape. It still caters to a reasonably limited clientele, particularly compared with some of the great ski mills across the border. Thanks to Livigno's border-town dispensation, duty-free items can be purchased in the chalets-turned-shops along the main street. Information: *Azienda di Promozione Turistica,* 55 Via Dala Gesa, Livigno (Sondrio) 23030 (phone: 342-996379; fax: 342-996881). Hotels: *Alpina* and *Europa* (I).

MADONNA DI CAMPIGLIO, Trentino The least cosmopolitan of Italy's Big Five—a group that includes Cervinia, Cortina, Courmayeur, and Sestriere—this resort is not widely known outside the country. Its facilities are world class: Helicopters ascend to the highest peaks for guided all-day descents, and three dozen lifts fan out from the town to serve four separate areas with 60 miles of slopes and trails. The possibilities run the gamut from ballroom slopes for novice snowplowers to the steep, bumpy terrain favored by high-tech slalomers. The town itself is Tyrolean in style, though there are modern structures in the Campo Carlo Magno section, and it is surrounded by beautiful pine forests and lakes—all dominated by the awesome sawtooth skyline of the Brenta Dolomites. Snowcats can haul hardy skiers up to one of the slopeside refuges for dinner and then back down in time for action in one of the town's discos. Information: *Azienda Autonoma di Soggiorno,* 4 Via Pradalago, Madonna di Campiglio (Trento) 38084 (phone: 465-42000; fax: 465-40404). Hotels: *Golf* (E), *Grifone* (E to M), *Il Caminetto* (M).

MOENA, Trentino The Italian capital of cross-country skiing, set in a sunny valley at the bull's-eye of the Dolomites, Moena is the starting point for the annual competition known as the *Marcialonga,* a 43-mile circuit that attracts cross-country fans from all over Europe. During the rest of the season, trails are exceptionally well maintained, and the town is cheerful, bustling, and unpretentious. A favorite of vacationing families, it offers an order of luxury lower than that of some of its glossy neighbors, and prices are the opposite of exorbitant. Information: *Azienda Autonoma di Soggiorno,* 33 Piazza Cesare Battisti, Moena (Trento) 38035 (phone: 462-573122; fax: 462-574342). Hotels: *Catinaccio, Leonardo* (M), *Alpi* (I).

ORTISEI/VAL GARDENA, Alto Adige Tucked below the broad open plateau of the Alpe di Siusi in the lushly wooded Val Gardena, sunny Ortisei is lively and pretty, with ornately decorated houses and shops overflowing with wood-carvings. From the main square, buses fan out to all adjacent valleys, and a five-minute cable car ride hoists skiers 2,625 feet to a bounty of ski trails linked to the 675 miles of the Superski Dolomiti facilities. One of the most attractive sections is the Sella Ronda, over 16 miles of lift-connected runs around the Sella mountain massif. Easy enough even for beginners, it's best done on Tuesdays or Wednesdays, when less-trafficked lifts make it possible to cover the maximum territory. Those who care more about serious skiing than village life should stay at Alpe di Siusi itself at 5,900 feet, where there are nine hours of sunlight in January and guaranteed snow. Information: *Azienda Autonoma di Soggiorno e Turismo,* 1 Via Rezia, Ortisei (Bolzano) 39046 (phone: 471-796328; fax: 471-796749). Hotels: *Adler* (E), *Villa Emilia* (M), *Ronce* (I).

SAN MARTINO DI CASTROZZA, Trentino Under the rose-colored peaks of the Dolomites' theatrical Pale di San Martino, this long-established center in the Valle del Cismon enjoys the twin Italian advantages of a southern exposure and protection from icy northern winds. Yet at 4,760 feet, there is reliable snow on the piney trails that skirt the village, and the local master ski pass admits skiers to the multiple joys of the Superski Dolomiti system. The *Drei Tannen* (Via Passo Rolle, near the *Savoia* hotel) has the best food in town. It is also almost obligatory to swig a little of the incendiary local grappa, especially on gelid early-morning runs from the high Rosetta. Information: *Azienda Autonoma di Soggiorno e Turismo,* 165 Via Passo Rolle, San Martino di Castrozza (Trento) 38058 (phone: 439-768867; fax: 439-768814). Hotels: *Savoia* (E), *Rosetta* (M), *Bel Sito* (I).

SAN SICARIO, Piedmont Designed and built from scratch in the late 1960s with the hard-core skier in mind, this high-powered, very Italian ski center offers a complex of contemporary hotels and mini-apartment residences, all accessible by silent monorail from the covered parking lot. The no-traffic regime guarantees stressless days and sleepful nights, and the location in the middle of an extensive trail network known as the Via Lattea (Milky Way)—a consortium of nine ski towns and their collective lift systems—takes care of the skiing. The comfort, convenience, and quality of the facilities more than make up for the lack of local color—especially for 9-to-5 trailaholics. Information: *Azienda Autonoma di Soggiorno,* 3 Piazza Vittorio Amedeo, Cesana (Torino) 10054 (phone: 122-89202). Hotels: *Rio Envers* (E), *San Sicario* (M).

SAPPADA, Veneto The language is German and the food Austrian. But the currency is still Italian in this town off the beaten trails just south of the border. Ideal for seekers of the small but *bello,* Sappada has 30 miles of varied and well-groomed skiing as well as opportunities for cross-country trekking. The friendly hotels are mostly pocket-sized and family-run, and there is a broad selection of short-term apartment rentals in balconied chalets. Evening entertainment centers on *vin brulé* (hot mulled wine) or cold beer, not brassy disco dancing. The costumed *Carnevale* merriment of February is an added dividend. Information: *Azienda di Promozione Turistica,* 20 Borgata Bach, Sappada (Belluno) 32047 (phone: 435-469131; fax: 435-66233). Hotels: *Bladen* (M), *Oberthaler Park* (M), *Sorgenti del Piave* (I).

SAUZE D'OULX, Piedmont Lift-linked to the bigger, brassier centers of Sestriere and San Sicario and thereby to the 240 trail miles of the Via Lattea, Sauze d'Oulx itself is a smaller, more easygoing, and less sophisticated snow haven. Close to the border, Sauze d'Oulx has been a favorite with the French since the early part of the century. It is also popular with the British, and English—of a sort—is widely spoken. The mountain terrace of the Val di Susa, at 4,900 feet, is a wind-free suntrap, and rows of people in deck chairs usually can be seen with aluminum reflectors under their chins. Wide north-facing slopes and open larch woods mean a long season of powder and fine trails of the calendar art variety. The town itself is a charmer—buildings lean this way and that over the twisting streets, a 15th-century fountain in the piazza. Dedicate evenings to *fonduta* (Italian-style fondue) chased with a local arneis or erbaluce di Caluso wine. Information: *Azienda Autonoma di Soggiorno e Turismo,* Piazza Garambois, Sauze d'Oulx (Torino) 10050 (phone: 122-831596 or 122-831786; fax: 122-831880). Hotels: *Gran Baita* (E), *Sauze* (M), *Miosotys* (I).

SESTRIERE, Piedmont Like Courchevel in France, Sestriere was carved out of snowy emptiness expressly to create a fabulous location where an ordinary skier can become an expert winter mountaineer. The main square is named for Fiat founding father Giovanni Agnelli, whose vision spawned the whole thing. In season, excellent high-altitude runs rise from a base of about 9,200 feet for all levels of skier, and it's possible to ski here for a week without ever repeating a run—especially when you take advantage of the facilities of other Via Lattea resorts. The instruction is excellent, the mood chic and modern, and the condos comfortable. The sun shines abundantly, and there are large terraces with plenty of deck chairs and umbrella tables from which to enjoy it. And although there's no sense of village life, Sestriere is eminently lively in season. It's an especially marvelous place to ski on the quiet weekdays. Information: *Azienda Autonoma di Soggiorno e Turismo,* 11 Piazza Giovanni Agnelli, Sestriere (Torino) 10058 (phone: 122-755444 or 122-755169; fax: 122-755171). Hotels: *Çristallo* (E), *Belvedere* (M), *Olimpic* (I).

VALGRISENCHE, Valle d'Aosta This tiny two-tow valley is a bit off the highway that speeds the world to chic Courmayeur, with no nightlife and no grand hotels. It simply offers the opportunity to travel back in time, to see the Italian mountains as they were 45 years ago, before Italy high-styled skiing for the new leisure class. Go before it's too late, and be prepared for off-trail exploring, strapping on sealskins for steep ascents, and quaffing thermosfuls of *vin brulé* (but bring your own). If all this is too serene and relaxing, rest assured that high society is only a sleigh ride away. Information: *Pro Loco Valgrisenche,* Aosta 11010 (phone: 165-97105). Hotel: *Perret* (I).

Top Tennis

It wasn't too long ago that tennis was the game of the elite; nowadays, it's often hard to find a free court. Most of the activity takes place at private tennis clubs, but admission usually can be arranged by the better hotels for their guests. Hotels in prime resort areas have at least a court or two. Clay is the preferred surface at clubs and some hotels, and regulation tennis shoes, as well as accepted tennis attire, are usually required.

At tennis camps, adults and children can work on their strokes in gorgeous surroundings. Fitness centers, pools, saunas, and solaria are the usual companions to serious instruction (usually in Italian) by *Federazione Italiana Tennis* (Italian Tennis Federation) coaches. And the atmosphere is always friendly and relaxed.

For a complete listing of Italian tennis clubs and for general information about the game in Italy, contact the *Federazione* (70 Viale Tiziano, Roma 00100; phone: 6-323-3807). Here are some of the best net bets.

WHERE TO PLAY

BAIA DI CONTE, Alghero, Sardinia Alghero's Spanish-style resort, overlooking a bay of turquoise water and set amid olive and eucalyptus trees, and the attractive seaside *Baia di Conte* hotel at Porto Conte, 4½ miles (7 km) from town, are ideal for spicing stroke drills with Sardinian scenery. At hotel tennis camps, open to adults and children from April through October, certified instructors and coaches work with groups of eight. A fitness room, a sauna and whirlpool bath, windsurfing, and horseback riding are available; guests can unwind at night in the hotel's disco. Information: *Baia di Conte,* Alghero (Sardegna) 07040 (phone: 79-952003; fax: 79-950293).

IL CIOCCO, Lucca, Tuscany The summer tennis camps of this international vacation center in a vast natural reserve in the Garfagnana hills are organized primarily for eight to 15 year olds. However, adults can use the courts and arrange coaching sessions with the instructor and, off the courts, enjoy the solarium, sauna, health club, and pool, and horseback ride or go on hikes. Lodging is in the hotel or in cozy little chalets in the surrounding woods. Information: *Il Ciocco, Centro Turistico Internazionale,* Castelvecchio Pascoli (Lucca) 55020 (phone: 583-7191; fax: 583-723197).

METAPONTO, Marina di Pisticci, Basilicata An outstanding spot to play is at one of more than a hundred vacation villages of *Club Med. Le Club,* as it's known in its native France, is founded on the formula of Leisure-Sport, so the villages' facilities are extensive, their instruction first-rate, and their settings consistently attractive. Located near pine woods and the gentle waters of the Gulf of Taranto, this *Club Med* collection of village-style houses has 18 tennis courts. An 18-hole golf course is 20 minutes away, with free transportation provided. There's plenty of opportunity for sailing and swimming, and, as at many *Club Med* establishments, children's groups for every age level ensure amusement for every member of the family. Information: *Club Med Metaponto,* San Basilio Mare, Marina di Pisticci (Taranto; phone: 835-470151)—or contact the *Club's* New York office at 3 E. 54th St., New York, NY 10022 (phone: 800-CLUBMED).

KAMARINA, Scoglitti, Sicily The *Club Med Kamarina,* on the Ionian Sea in Sicily, is a fine place to mix tennis and beach life. There are 28 courts, of which 21 are clay and six are floodlit. Accommodations are in a hotel or in separate bungalows. You're assured one hour of instruction daily. Two pools, a sandy shore, sailing and windsurfing, and archery will compete with the cultural pull of the Greek and Roman ruins within easy excursion distance. Closed November to early May. Information: *Club Med Kamarina,* BP25, Scoglitti (Ragusa) 97100 (phone: 932-911333; fax: 932-911719)—or contact the *Club* in New York (see *Club Med Metaponto,* above).

VALTUR VILLAGES Following the French *Club Med* model of sports-oriented vacation villages, the eight *Italian Valtur* summer seaside complexes have cornered the market in the peninsula's glamorous locations. They guarantee luxurious accommodations and provide the same round-the-clock roster of activities as their Gallic counterparts. Near Cefalù, on the northern coast of Sicily, is *Pollina,* with eight tennis courts. (Four are lighted, so it's possible to water-ski all day and save tennis for a nightcap.) *Capo Rizzuto,* on the Ionian coast of Calabria, has eight courts (three lighted), and *Brucoli,* not far from the Sicilian city of Syracuse, has six courts (three lighted). Special tennis weeks with top-ranking coaches are featured in June and July. *Valtur* centers are closed October through April. Information: *Valtur,* 42 Via Milano, Roma 00184 (phone: 6-482-1000; fax: 6-470-6334).

INTERNATIONAL TOURNAMENTS

For those accustomed to the respectful hush of *Wimbledon,* noisy Italian crowds can strike a jarring note. But if you just think of the noise as heart-felt enthusiasm, attending a tournament in Italy can be a cultural as well as a sporting experience. The top tournaments at which this very Mediterranean show of excitement is most evident are held in the following places:

Milan, February.
Rome and **Bologna,** May.
Florence, June.
San Remo, July.
San Marino, July or August.
Palermo, September.

For exact dates and information on purchasing tickets, contact the *Federazione Italiana di Tennis* (70 Viale Tiziano, Roma 00100; phone: 6-323-3807). For news about the sport in Italy, consult the country's major tennis publications—*Matchball, Il Tennista,* and *Tennis Italiano*—all available on newsstands.

Great Italian Golf

The British brought golf to Italy around the turn of the century, but 50 years passed before the game acquired any degree of popularity. Today, Italy's more than one hundred courses, including 30-plus new ones, offer a beautiful natural setting, an ideal climate nearly year-round, professional-quality layouts, and some rather challenging sport.

Some courses do not allow visitors to play on weekends, and most are closed Mondays. Some, but not all, accept credit cards. The courses are very crowded on weekends, so reserve a tee time well ahead, either through your hotel or by contacting the club directly. All Italian golf clubs extend reciprocal privileges to foreigners with a membership card or other evidence of club membership at home. Our recommended courses in the major urban areas are detailed in the individual reports in THE CITIES. Some of our favorite off-the-beaten-track fairways are listed below.

For complete information about golf in Italy, contact the *Federazione Italiana di Golf* (388 Via Flaminia, Roma 00196; phone: 6-323-1825; fax: 6-322-0250).

GARLENDA, Garlenda, Liguria Winters are mild, springs gentle, and summers temperate on the Italian Riviera, so there's no season to the pleasures and challenges of this 18-hole course. Just as the first holes have lulled you into relaxation, the 12th hole comes along, a long and treacherous par 4. It's followed by a long par 3 that crosses a stream, and, three holes later, a par 4 with a left-hand dogleg. Even then, the average duffer has a good chance of making a few pars here. The course—30 miles (48 km) from Savona and 58 miles (93 km) from Genoa—is closed Wednesdays September through June. The most convenient lodging is next door at the lovely *Golf Hotel La Meridiana* (11 Via ai Castelli, Garlenda; phone: 182-580271; fax: 182-580150), which is open March through November. Information: *Garlenda Golf Club,* 7 Via del Golf, Garlenda (Savona) 17030 (phone: 182-580012; fax: 182-580561).

PEVERO, Porto Cervo, Sardinia When Robert Trent Jones, Sr. created this 18-hole course, one of the world's great seaside layouts, he gave free rein to his sense of the dramatic. The result is a direct reflection of his raw materials—a narrow, rising and plunging, sea-edged neck of land patched with granite outcrops, pine, broom, gorse, lavender, poppy, lupin, and juniper that blazes with color in the spring. Major traps are found at the third, 11th, and 15th holes. The course is open to non-members year-round (bring a handicap card from your home club); clubs and carts can be rented. Closed Tuesdays in winter. The club also has an excellent restaurant (closed in winter and early spring). Information: *Pevero Golf Club,* Porto Cervo (Sassari) 07020 (phone: 789-96072).

PUNTA ALA, Punta Ala, Tuscany Set in southern Tuscany's Maremma, near the meeting place of the Tyrrhenian and the Ligurian Seas opposite the isle of Elba, this 18-hole, 6,720-yard course has been a standout among Italian layouts since 1964, when it was carved out of a pine woods on rolling terrain stretching down to the sea. Long and tough from start to finish, it has been seeded with a Korean grass known for its even growth, so players are almost able to hit a driver off the fairways. Caution is required on the fifth and 12th holes; the eighth confronts players with a long par 4 on a steep uphill slope. High summer temperatures (albeit tempered by sea breezes) add to the challenge. Punta Ala is a prime destination for sports of all types, particularly swimming, sailing, and riding. Open daily. Information: *Punta Ala Golf Club,* 1 Via del Golf, Punta Ala (Grosseto) 58040 (phone: 564-922121; fax: 564-920182).

SAN REMO, San Remo, Liguria Known for the olive groves through which the 18-hole course unfolds, this 6,020-yard layout offers panoramic sea views, narrow fairways, undulating greens, and a valley location that protects players from the sea winds. Tee shots must be precise, but otherwise this is a course for relaxation. Three miles (5 km) north of San Remo. Closed Tuesdays.

Information: *Golf Club San Remo,* 59 Strada Campo Golf, San Remo (Imperia) 18038 (phone: 184-577092; fax: 184-557388).

IN THE HILLS

VILLA D'ESTE, Como, Lombardy On the banks of Lake Montorfano, this interesting hillside course presents an arduous test of skill that some consider the toughest par 69 in Europe. It has hosted several major international tournaments since it was constructed in 1926. Unwinding through chestnut, birch, and pine groves, its 6,066 yards offer not a single opportunity for relaxation. While not cramped, the tree-bordered fairways roll and dip inexorably toward the lake, so that both accuracy and power are essential every step of the way. The 18-hole layout was built by the lush *Villa d'Este* hotel, which no longer is involved in the club's operation. Closed December through February. Information: *Circolo Golf Villa d'Este,* 13 Via per Cantù, Montorfano (Como) 22030 (phone: 31-200200; fax: 31-200786).

SESTRIERE, Sestriere, Piedmont Known as the highest 18-hole course in Europe, this layout in the western Alps is open only in July and August. After then, it's snow, snow, snow. Major challenges are the strong winds that often start up when players least expect them; be prepared. Watch out for the ninth hole, a long, uphill par 4 that plays to a very small green, and the 18th hole, where it's all uphill—and steep. Information: *Golf Club Sestriere,* 4 Piazza Agnelli, Sestriere (Torino) 10058 (phone: 122-76276 or 122-76243).

CANSIGLIO, Vittorio Veneto, Veneto Robert Trent Jones, Jr. designed this 18-hole course on a limestone plateau with a good deal of wide-open space peppered with natural obstacles and double tees. Careful shots are in order. Closed November through April. The course is 41 miles (65 km) from Treviso and 15½ miles (25 km) from Vittorio Veneto. Information: *Golf Club Cansiglio,* CP152, Vittorio Veneto (Treviso) 31029 (phone: 438-585398).

Italy's Best Beaches

Italy's 5,000 miles of coastline are continually washed by the historic dark waves of the Ligurian, Tyrrhenian, Ionian, Adriatic, and Mediterranean seas. Sun worshipers can sprawl on wide swaths of downy sand at Viareggio, hike down a cliff-hanging path to a craggy Sardinian cove, or dally in a pedal boat off the sandy Adriatic coast. To get away from everybody else who's getting away from it all, head for the northern coast of the Gargano, near the obscure fishing village of Vieste, where a 40-mile-long strand is punctuated at either end by two huge dunes. Or travel to the garland of islands that rings Italy's coast—Elba, Giglio, Ponza, Ischia & Co.—for the country's freshest fish and crystal-clearest waters. Even these spots are jammed to capacity in August; both in July and August, book well ahead. Windswept and flower-scented Sardinia is a beach paradise in May, June, and even after August 16. Waters are warmest in the Cagliari bays and capes at the southern end of the rocky isle. New resorts are drawing visitors to the eastern and western coasts of the island as well.

Urban sands are described in the individual reports in THE CITIES. Other *bellissime* beachfronts are listed below.

AEOLIAN ISLANDS, Sicily Movie buffs know this chain of ancient volcanoes north of Milazzo, off the Sicilian coast, as the setting for Roberto Rossellini's *Stromboli,* starring Ingrid Bergman; classics majors may remember it as the home of Aeolus, the god of the winds, and a notable stop on Odysseus's grand tour. Each of the landfalls has its own magic. Lipari, the largest, busiest, and easiest to reach, is a subtle mosaic of pastel houses, buff-colored beaches, and turquoise waters. At Vulcano, the adventurous can climb to the summit of the broad crater for fine views over the archipelago and splash in the thermal springs near the shore of Porto di Levante. On Stromboli, hike up the cone-shaped crater on a moonlit night to see the fiery bubbles of lava and showers of stone explode against the sky and then fall tamely back into the crater. Scuba divers choose the clear waters of Panarea or Salina, while those seeking solitude visit wild and secluded Alicudi or Filicudi. In high season, the archipelago can be reached by ferry and/or hydrofoil from three mainland cities, including Naples. Go early in the season; the water is warm enough for swimming by late May. Information: *Azienda Autonoma di Soggiorno e Turismo dell'Isole Eolie,* 231 Corso Vittorio Emanuele, Lipari (Messina) 98055 (phone: 90-988-0095).

AMALFI COAST, Salerno, Campania The Sorrento Peninsula—the finger of land curling around the Bay of Naples and pointing to the island of Capri—is mountainous and brilliant with flowers. Its southern side is edged by a narrow road that has been famous for breathtaking views and heart-stopping curves since it was carved out of the rock in the mid-19th century. Break up the dizzying drive through its tunnels, over its bridges, and atop its cliffs with a stay in Positano, where cubist chunks of houses cling to the hillside that dives down to the pebbled seafront and tiny beach, and minuscule boutiques display trendy summer styles. For the best swimming, rent a boat with enough motor to take you a few miles away from the gladding crowd. Yachts anchor off the coast at the privately owned islands of I Galli. One of the most romantic hotels in Italy, the *Albergo San Pietro* (see *Italy's Most Memorable Hostelries,* above), perched south of town, has its own private beach. In Amalfi, the best beaching is to be enjoyed in early morning, before the carnival comes to town. Information: *Azienda Autonoma di Soggiorno e Turismo,* 4 Via del Saracino, Positano (Salerno) 84017 (phone: 89-875067; fax: 89-875760), or *Azienda Autonoma di Soggiorno e Turismo,* 19 Corsa Repubbliche Marinare, Amalfi (Salerno) 84011 (phone: 89-871107).

CAPRI, near Naples, Campania The most famous, most expensive, and most crowded of all Italian islands, Capri also is one of the most beautiful places in the world. You should keep your distance in July and August, when the little main square and the Marina Piccola beach become twin cans of Mediterranean sardines. But off-season, on a sunny November Wednesday, say, it's incomparable, with sapphire sky and sea and heady aromas from hillside lemon groves perfuming the air. Information: *Azienda Autonoma di Soggiorno,* 1 Piazza Umberto, Capri (Napoli) 80071 (phone: 81-837-0686; fax: 81-837-0918).

COSTA SMERALDA, Sardinia Centuries of invasions by various intruders drove Sardinians inland, leaving the island's coastline largely uninhabited. Then, in 1960, the Aga Khan turned the 35-mile stretch between the eastern port of Olbia and the island's tip at La Maddalena from a natural paradise to a manicured emerald Eden by building the country's most glamorous beach complex. The boulders are still here, and the water is still an incredibly cloudless cobalt, but scattered from cove to cove are myriad elegant hotels. Most have their own pools and a cove or stretch of private beach, separated from the main hotel grounds so that guests can enjoy total seclusion. When the yacht fleet is in at Porto Cervo, you may see movie stars, sheiks, and bluebloods. But everyone on the Costa Smeralda comes here for the laid-back sun-and-sea life, so it all stays superbly simple (and savagely expensive). There are facilities for boating, scuba diving, windsurfing, and water skiing. Information: *Azienda Autonoma di Soggiorno e Turismo,* 36 Viale Caprera, Sassari 07100 (phone: 79-233534; fax: 79-237585).

ELBA, near Piombino, Tuscany Known mainly for Napoleon's brief stay on the island, Elba has beaches, some sandy, for swimmers and toe-dippers; others rocky and suitable for scuba divers. Sandy beaches in the north include Spartaia, Procchio, Campo all'Aia, Biodola, and Scaglieri; in the south, Stella Bay, Lacona, Marina di Campo, Cavoli, Fetovaia, and Seccheto (sand and rock); and on the east coast, Barbarossa Reale, Cavo (sand and rock), Calamita Peninsula, Naregno, Pareti, Morcone, and Straccoligno. The *Hermitage* hotel in Biodola is one of the island's most elegant resorts. Information: *Azienda di Promozione Turistica dell'Arcipelago Toscano,* 26 Calata Italia, Portoferraio 57037 (phone: 565-914671; fax: 565-916350).

FORTE DEI MARMI, Lucca, Tuscany The Italian coastline is really like a gigantic seaside café, and the chief amusement is watching the sprawling parade of candy cane–striped umbrellas, deck chairs, and beach cabins, fleets of pedal boats, sippers of Campari, builders of sand castles, narcissistic waders, and ostentatious volleyball players. The whole expanse of coast between the Lido di Camaiore and the bustling resort town of Viareggio is really one long marina, with the ultra-stylish Forte dei Marmi its high point. Patrician families from Rome, Florence, Milan, and Turin have been coming here every summer since the last century, though many of their pined and palmed seafront villas have been transformed into small hotels. Though the air is perfumed with mimosa and eucalyptus, never expect romantic solitude (though by comparison with other parts of the coast, Forte dei Marmi is almost sedate). Much of the *centro* is a pedestrians-only zone, and everyone gets about by bicycle. Information: *Azienda Autonoma di Soggiorno,* 8 Viale Franceschi, Forte dei Marmi (Lucca) 55042 (phone: 584-80091; fax: 584-83214).

MARATEA, Potenza, Basilicata Fishermen have plied the transparent waters of this enchanted coastline since Greek times, but the pleasantly unpretentious town of Maratea, at the ankle of Italy's boot, was virtually unknown 30 years ago; even today few foreigners make their way this far down the coast. Those who do find beaches ranging from blanket-size to roomy and a shoreline jagged with cliffs, crags, coves, and caves. The Apennines reach almost to the sea here, leaving just enough space for a huddle of russet roofs and a riot of low-growing rosemary, myrtle, and broom between the pines and olive trees. Maratea harbors the sumptuous *Santavenere* hotel, as well as more modest accommodations. Information: *Azienda Autonoma di Soggiorno e Turismo,* 32 Piazza del Gesù, Maratea (Potenza) 85040 (phone: 973-876908).

MONTE ARGENTARIO, Grosseto, Tuscany Halfway between Rome and Pisa on the Tyrrhenian coast, Monte Argentario has all the advantages of an island, including sandy beaches, but none of the drawbacks. The air is clear and tangy, the vegetation is lush and fragrant, the sea spreads out on all sides, and, with a narrow causeway linking the promontory to Orbetello and the mainland coast road, there's no fuss over ferries. The Porto Ercole side of the mountain is frequented by nouveau-*ricco* Roman and landed aristocracy. Summer at the secluded, exclusive *Pellicano* hotel and you won't have to worry your uncrowned head about villa upkeep. Rent a boat at nearby *Cala Galera,* one of the largest marinas on the coast, with space for 750 boats. Try to lunch at tony Porto Santo Stefano when the swordfish catch comes in. And should the water seem bluer on the other side of the strait, catch a ferry to the tiny, unblemished isles of Giglio, with its half-moon beach, and Giannutri. Information: *Azienda Autonoma di Soggiorno e Turismo della Costa d'Argento,* 55/A Corso Umberto, Porto Santo Stefano (Grosseto) 58019 (phone: 564-814208), or *Azienda Autonoma di Soggiorno e Turismo,* 44 Via Umberto, Giglio Porto, Isola del Giglio (Grosseto) 58013 (phone: 564-809265).

SENIGALLIA, Ancona, the Marches With miles of pale, velvety sand sloping gently into a warm and shallow sea, the Adriatic Coast is beloved by Italian and German families. Less frantic in high season than more northerly parts, Senigallia is a prime destination for the sand-castle set. Hundreds of family-run *pensioni* and hotels, in all price ranges, are scattered along a tidily modern beachfront; the historic old center represents the Renaissance and the Baroque in pleasing harmony, with a fortress to visit after a swim and lunch. An aged synagogue recalls the once-flourishing Jewish community. Information: *Azienda Autonoma di Soggiorno,* 2 Piazzale Morandi, Senigallia (Ancona) 60019 (phone: 71-792-2726).

SPERLONGA, Latina, Lazio Attracting an intensely casual crowd of young Romans in June and July and families with station wagons during the national holiday month of August, this tiny village is a Moorish labyrinth of white buildings, staircases, and alleyways stacked compactly on a seaside ledge, with long sand beaches on either side of a rock spur leading into the sea. Sperlonga has only a handful of modest hotels; the *Corallo,* right in town, has a staircase that plummets to the beach. Also in the center is the *Florenza Residence; La Playa* at Fiorelle is on the beach. Information: *Associazione Pro Loco,* 22 Corso San Leone, Sperlonga (Latina) 04029 (phone: 771-54796).

Sailing the Seas of Italy

Think of it: Christopher Columbus, Amerigo Vespucci, Giovanni da Verrazano, and Giovanni Caboto, whom the world knew better as John Cabot, were all Italian sailors. As three-fourths of their country is surrounded by water, it should come as no surprise that Italians still take to the sea with great gusto. The country's four seas—the Tyrrhenian, the Ligurian, the Adriatic, and the Ionian—abound in charming ports, picturesque villages, crumbling ruins, historical monuments, elegant resorts, secluded coves, and incomparable beaches. Dock at any harbor and sample some of the country's finest cuisine, or relax in a waterfront *caffè.* But beware of crowds the first two weeks of August.

In many cases, a license is required for sailing the Italian seas. One crew member must understand sufficient Italian to comprehend and to take notes from the radio *bollettino del mare* and to deal with the local tourist port authorities. Dock space for overnighters becomes iffy in August. Many tourist ports are small, so arrive by 5 PM in peak season, when it's first-come, first-served.

Local yacht clubs can be very helpful. In addition, there are several other reliable sources of information:

For charters in the Tyrrhenian: *Organizzazione Mare,* 172 Via Oderisi da Gubbio, Roma 00146 (phone: 6-556-2169 or 6-558-4707).

For sailing along the Tuscan coast and Sardinia: *Top Service,* 40 Viale Duse, Firenze 50100 (phone: 55-608334).

For sailing in the Tuscan Archipelago and around Sardinia: *Renato Lessi,* Località Porto, Punta Ala, Grosseto 58040 (phone: 564-921098).

For sailing in the Adriatic and Ionian Seas: *Skimar,* 5 Piazza Velasca, Milano 20122 (phone: 2-583-08794).

For sailing around Sicily: *Salpancore,* Via Banchina Lupa la Cala, Palermo, Sicilia 90100 (phone/fax: 91-332128).

WHERE TO SAIL

Once you've made your arrangements, here are some of the best waters for sailing around Italy, as well as our selection of the prime ports of call.

TYRRHENIAN SEA The challenging Tyrrhenian can endanger small craft because of strong breezes, forceful waves, and the treacherous scirocco and libeccio winds. But the coastline—and its sandy beaches, high peaks and promontories, quaint fishing villages, fine resorts, and the world's most beautiful islands, of which Capri, Ischia, and Sardinia are the best known—makes it worth conquering those fears. (Avoid July or August, when human hordes turn this watery paradise into a garbage dump.)

To approach Ischia, volcanic Stromboli, or the fabled Monte Cristo from the sapphire sea is a breathtaking sailing experience. You can explore hidden coves, visit Capri's famed Blue Grotto, call at the less known (but equally dramatic) Green Grotto, and stop at the Tiberian Baths.

The coast near Naples is all cliffs, fantastically sea-carved promontories, Saracen towers, and peaceful seaside towns—legendary Sorrento, villa-studded Posillipo, Moorish-looking Amalfi, and Positano. In May and June, the flowers are at their most glorious, and in September the light from the usually calm sea is hauntingly lovely.

In Tuscany, farther north, visit Monte Argentario and ultra-chic Porto Ercole, walk along centuries-old cobblestone streets, or climb to high lookout points for bird's-eye views of the littoral.

And don't forget the Tuscan Archipelago. Sail around the island of Monte Cristo—"Treasure Island" to Alexandre Dumas—now a nature reserve. On the island of Giannutri are Roman remains to prowl; on Giglio Island, you can tour an ancient castle and its fortifications.

Elba is a gigantic, half-submerged mountain that is the largest landfall in this island group, a splendid combination of rocky shores, sandy beaches, and mountains that descend straight to the sea. The clean waters hide ancient wrecks, rusted anchors, and broken amphoras. The area around Sant'Andrea is particularly favored among boaters equipped with scuba gear.

The ultimate Tyrrhenian sailor's destination may be sun-washed Sardinia. The island's Costa Smeralda (Emerald Coast) is only one of many splendid coastlines; it's hard to go wrong. Don't miss Porto Cervo, Porto Rotondo, Porto Conte, Stintino, the minuscule, barren Isola dei Cavalli, and the Golfo degli Aranci.

LIGURIAN SEA The going is a bit smoother in this body of water that laps at the strands of the Italian Riviera in central and northern Italy. Along the Tuscan and Ligurian coasts, beautiful old villas stand proudly on seaside cliffs. Portovenere, an important harbor in Roman times and now a reference point for all sailors, is dreamy, picturesque, and worth a special trip. In Genoa, the Gothic *Chiesa di San Pietro* rises dramatically out of sheer rock.

Portofino is the celebrated port and resort near Genoa. The rich and famous come here for the luxurious *Splendido* hotel, the superb restaurants, and the stylish boutiques, all in a setting of brightly colored houses, fisherfolk's boats, crystal-clear blue sea, olive trees, sea pines, and a lighthouse.

ADRIATIC AND IONIAN SEAS The coastline here is linear and sandy rather than rocky and craggy, except in the south, so avid sailors usually prefer the Ligurian and Tyrrhenian. Given the smaller crowds, several ports can make a cruise here eminently enjoyable.

Muggia, an ancient Venetian village near Trieste, is justly famous for its summer music festivals and folklore exhibits. The ancient seaside fishing town of Chioggia, in the Veneto region, has one of the largest and most picturesque fish markets in Italy and two canals photogenically packed with fishing boats.

In Puglia, to the south, fishing villages, historical sites, and archaeological remains abound. The mountain promontory of Gargano, the spur of Italy's boot, is edged with long, luxurious strands, exotic rock formations, fantastic caves, and tiny coves perfect for picnicking. Vieste, an ancient fishing village with a medieval castle, is coming into its own as a resort. Manfredonia, Rodi Garganico, and whitewashed, cliff-top Peschici are other worthy ports of call. Just off shore are the jewel-like Tremiti Islands, virtually beachless fragments of rock that attract snorkelers and divers.

As the Adriatic flows into the Ionian, it becomes the Mediterranean's deepest sea, extending from Puglia to Basilicata and Calabria over to Sicily.

LAKE CRUISING

With the exception of the Po River, Italy's largest, Italian rivers are so shallow and rocky that river cruising is virtually nonexistent. But an organized boat excursion on Lake Maggiore may well prove a highlight in an Italian adventure.

The shores of this 40-mile-long, island-studded expanse of blue, nestled beneath high Alps, are sometimes rugged, sometimes lush with subtropical vegetation—magnolias, azaleas, palms, and orange and lemon trees. Lake cruises here provide a view of the 14th-century *Castello di Rocca di Angera,* the lovely town of Ispra, and the *Santuario di Santa Caterina del Sasso.* In the center of the lake are the sweetly scented Borromean Islands. Isola Bella (Beautiful Island), the busiest and most famous, has gracious gardens inhabited by lacy albino peacocks; ignore the tacky souvenir stands. Isola Madre (Mother Island) has splendid gardens, luxuriant with nearly 150-year-old cypress, massive palms, and 80-yard-long wisterias. Isola dei Pescatori (Fishermen's Island) is small and quaint. On the mainland is Stresa, a touristy resort that livens up in September, when the annual festival of lyrical music comes to town. Information: *Skimar,* 5 Piazza Velasca, Milano 20122 (phone: 2-583-08794).

Horsing Around, Italian Style

Italy's equestrian tradition goes back to the *condottieri*—the great mounted warrior-princes of the Renaissance. The Italians still gallop off with countless *Olympic* medals in the four-footed competition. And there are many opportunities for the horse-loving tourist to pursue his or her avocation, from the Alpine top of the boot to the Sicilian stirrup.

There are manicured manors where counts cantered, informal farmhouses converted to equitation to supplement faltering agricultural income, and all manner of establishments in between. For information, contact the *National Association for Equestrian Tourism* (*ANTE;* 5 Via Alfonso Borelli, Roma 00161; phone: 6-444-1179; fax: 6-444-1604). In Sardinia, contact *Agriturismo a Cavallo* (CP107, Oristano 09170; phone: 783-418066). For more information about riding in and around the capital, see *Rome* in THE CITIES.

A representative selection of Italy's equitation establishments follows.

ALA BIRDI, Arborea, Sardinia Surrounded by pine woods near the beach on Sardinia's west coast, this complex of hotels, bungalows, and mini-apartments—one of Italy's best-equipped equitation centers—offers dedicated riders a choice of 45 horses and three first-rate instructors. The high-powered training emphasizes acquiring close-to-professional expertise. But there also are rambling excursions along the shore and into the neighboring countryside. The nearby beach is especially welcome at the end of a day in the saddle. In spring and fall, vast flocks of birds migrate to the area, and exotic flamingos and herons are regular winter visitors. Information: *Ala Birdi*, 24 Strada a Mare, Arborea (Oristano) 09092 (phone: 783-801084; fax: 783-801086).

TENUTA LA MANDRIA, Candelo, Piedmont In a day's ride from La Mandria you'll still see hopefuls panning for gold in the shallow riverbeds that cross the wild Baraggia plateau, where this equestrian holiday center is situated. The skilled and exacting management offers holidays in all-sized portions, from the equivalent of an afternoon's snack to a fortnight-long banquet that has riders traveling past ancient Roman gold mines or recently reclaimed trails between abandoned medieval castles. The plateau is on thousands of acres of state property, all forest-covered and uninhabited. Riding out from this once-fortified medieval village seems almost like time travel, though Candelo is only about an hour's drive from either Turin or Milan. Some 20 horses and a half dozen ponies are available to the 15 guests who can be accommodated in the restored farmhouse and the 10 who lodge in the annex; overnight trips include accommodations in modest inns en route. Expert riders can go wherever they wish and leave their youngsters in experienced hands. The food here features local country dishes, complemented by some very urbane wines. Information: *Tenuta La Mandria,* Candelo (Vercelli) 13062 (phone: 15-253-6078).

LA SUBIDA, Cormons, Friuli–Venezia Giulia The countryside in this rural northeast corner of Italy bordering Slovenia is a patchwork of meadows and pastures, orchards and vineyards, chestnut forests and rustic churches. A handful of small houses set on a verdant hillside provides lodging, and the handsome family-run trattoria serves grilled specialties typical of the nearby Julian Alps. Ride to the ruins of the castle at Monte Quarin, or enjoy the pool, a children's playground, a stable of bicycles, and a lighted tennis court. Long hours of riding will help work off the rich cuisine. The wine of the local Collio area, which is superb and in short supply elsewhere, makes for a festive end to a day on the trail. Closed February and July. Information: *La Subida,* 22 Località Monte Subida, Cormons (Gorizia) 34071 (phone/fax: 481-60531).

RENDOLA RIDING, Montevarchi, Tuscany The proprietor of this pastoral riding center goes by the very Anglo-Saxon name of Jenny Bawtree. But the setting, the excellent food, and the gracious simplicity of the farmhouse accommodations are pure Tuscan, and the bridle paths rise and fall over the vineyard-clad hills of Chianti itself. This is art and wine country, and Arezzo, Florence, and Siena are comfortable day trips away—by motorized horsepower for the saddle-weary. Animal lovers will enjoy the farm's barnyard, populated by goats, ducks, cats, and dogs. Beginners start with a few lessons in the *maneggio* (training ring) before going out for brief outings; experts join two- to five-day trips around the area. *Rendola Riding* has 20 horses and can house 15 people in eight bedrooms (four with private bath) year-round. Information: *Rendola Riding,* Montevarchi (Arezzo) 52020 (phone/fax: 55-970-7045).

RIFUGIO PRATEGIANO, Montieri, Tuscany At this stone-faced, wooden-shuttered hotel with 24 rooms high in the hills between Siena and the Tyrrhenian coast, beginners can alternate riding lessons with lounging sessions around the pool and garden, while more experienced equestrians can range over the establishment's woods and meadows, along Etruscan roads, across burbling streams, and to hidden ruins. Tiny lakes, miniature churches, stark castles, and winding pathways to the sea, discovered during the day's ride, make for animated dinnertime conversation. Choose from a dozen guided itineraries, with the mountaintop village of Gerfalco, the glorious abandoned abbey of *San Galgano,* and the Merse River, where riders can swim in late spring and summer, as prime points of interest. There also are longer organized trips to various places such as Volterra. The area is perfect for hiking and biking as well, though the hills are awesome in the heat of July and August. Montieri itself is attractive and unspoiled, and Siena, Volterra, and San Gimignano are all within easy reach by car. Closed January 7 through March. Information: *Rifugio Prategiano,* Montieri (Grosseto) 58026 (phone: 566-997703; fax: 566-997891).

FATTORIA CERRETO, Mosciano Sant'Angelo, Abruzzo For sea and saddle, this is the best bet. Guests can headquarter in one of the four rooms at the farm itself, ride all morning, and then stretch out in the sun in the afternoon. The atmosphere is cheerful and countrified, and the nearby town of Giulianova has several good restaurants. The farm's 17 horses are well trained, with good mounts for riders of any level of skill. Mounted exploration of the area, and week-long trips that cover a hundred miles or more in the Abruzzo foothills, can be arranged. Information: *Fattoria Cerreto,* Colle Cerreto, Mosciano Sant'Angelo (Teramo) 64025 (phone: 85-806-1632).

LE CANNELLE, Parco dell'Uccellina, Tuscany The atmosphere at this parkland establishment is rough and ready, the devotion to riding single-minded. Paths wander through wild Mediterranean brush or along vast deserted expanses of parkland beach. Wild boar, fox, and horned white cattle are the only intruders. Housing is in eight unadorned bungalows, and guests bring and prepare their own provisions. Since only one Land Rover is permitted on the single bumpy road connecting *Le Cannelle* to civilization, visitors must call ahead to request pickup at the entrance to the protected area. Open year-round. Information: *Le Cannelle, Parco dell'Uccellina,* Talamone (Grosseto) 58010 (phone: 564-863618).

VALLEBONA, Pontassieve, Tuscany Visitors to Vallebona can spend mornings on horseback and afternoons on foot exploring Florence, only a 20-minute drive away. A maximum of 15 guests stay in the simple rooms in this restored Tuscan farmhouse, help care for one of the 25 horses, putter in the garden, and participate in the busy, informal life on the farm. The center also organizes three- to 10-day excursions to Etruscan sites, mountain trail rides, and sightseeing along the river valleys between Siena and Grosseto. Accommodations along these routes are in tents or on farms. Information: *Centro Ippico Vallebona,* Fattoria Lavaccho, 32 Via di Grignano, Pontassieve (Firenze) 50064 (phone: 55-839-7246; fax: 55-831-7395).

Freewheeling Through Italy

With the Alps across the top and the Apennines down the middle, there's not a great deal of flat terrain left for leisurely pedaling, nor many trails. But this is a nation of great bicycling traditions, and every Sunday on country roads all over the boot, legions of capped and uniformed bicyclists hunch over their handlebars, pretending to be Saronni or Fausto Coppi.

The bicycle is dangerous in traffic-strangled cities, especially in hilly Rome (for a cycling circuit of the capital, see *Rome* in THE CITIES). And wherever you are in the country, ride with extreme caution—and a solid helmet.

In addition to those listed below, many suggested itineraries for trips all over the country can be found in *Cicloturismo,* one of several monthly biking magazines in Italian available at newsstands.

ITALIAN LAKES Italy's lake region provides some of best cycling in the country. The roadways are fairly flat, the summer temperatures moderate, the towns attractive and well spaced, and the landscape a lyrical mix of lemon groves, palm trees, and other subtropical vegetation against an Alpine backdrop. Visitors can stop at each of the five lakes, one by one; cyclists with two weeks' vacation and the stamina to go 500 miles (800 km) can take a once-in-a-lifetime two-wheel ride around them all.

Begin at Lake Como in Menaggio, an inviting resort town of considerable charm, then travel north to Gravedona, following the lake shore around its northern tip, and head southward, skirting Lago di Lecco's eastern shore.

To visit Lake d'Iseo and Lake Garda, the next destinations, the route passes through the busy center of Bergamo, with its charming medieval quarter, set high above the Lombardy Plain, before continuing on to Lake d'Iseo. The dominant scenic elements are wild mountainsides and gray-green olive trees. Circle this less-developed lake, passing through Sarnico, Lovere, and Iseo, and then head for Garda.

The largest and the most spectacular of the Italian lakes, Garda is wild and Alpine in the north, softer and greener to the south. The stretch between Salò, Mussolini's last headquarters, and Riva del Garda is lush, verdant, and entirely spectacular, particularly when the late afternoon sunlight gilds the eastern shore. In 27 miles (43 km), this road follows the corniche over 56 bridges and burrows through 70 tunnels; watch out for trucks.

Having pedaled through vineyards on the eastern shore, head back to Como and its shores, crowded with fig and mulberry trees. Pedal alongside wilder and more exotic Lake Lugano and finally to Lake Maggiore, where Hemingway set *A Farewell to Arms,* and the little town of Luino. From there, circle broad Lake Maggiore, weaving in and out of Switzerland, or bike to Laveno and take the ferry to the western shore. Hostels, campgrounds, and hotels dot the way. Avoid August, Italy's vacation rush hour. Como's *APT* sponsors an annual one-day Giro del Lago di Como, offering three routes around the lake: 119 km, 162 km, and 200 km. Information: *APT del Comasco,* 17 Piazza Cavour, Como 22100 (phone: 31-27.4064).

PARCO NAZIONALE D'ABRUZZO Two hours east of Rome, this national park is crisscrossed by 50 miles (80 km) of an almost carless asphalt road, as well as by a network of neglected country roads that are good for those with mountain bikes. The park has a healthy population of bears, foxes, mountain goats, and even wolves—all of which you're most likely to get a glimpse of if you plan an early morning ride in the spring or fall. It's wonderful for walking, too. Good maps are available from the park authorities. From *Easter* through early autumn (depending on snow), mountain bikes are available for rent from *Cooperativa Ecotur,* 13 Via Santa Lucia, Pescasseroli (Aquila) 67032 (phone: 863-912760).

TUSCANY An interesting circuit of about 50 miles (80 km) starts in the busy medieval city of Prato, not far from Florence. Take the road to Figline, Schignano,

Migliana, Vernio, and Montepiano, all charming country towns way off the
tourist track. From Montepiano the road passes through green and golden
farmland to Barberino, Calenzano, and back to Prato, whose *centro storico*
is worth a look.

IL GIRO D'ITALIA If you have a spare semester to train, a 10-speed Bianchi bike,
and the stamina of Stallone, you might attempt to follow in the tire treads
of the speed demons who participate in this three-week-long May (or early
June) bike race—one of Italy's great annual sports events. The competition, which has been going on for over 70 years, covers 2,400 miles and
climbs a grueling assortment of Alpine passes. Followed passionately both
on television and by cheering crowds along the nation's roads, this galva-
nizing marathon is the *Wimbledon* and *Kentucky Derby* of biking championships. The route, which changes each year, is announced in February by
its newspaper sponsor, *La Gazzetta dello Sport.* Information: *Federazione
Italiana Ciclistica*, 2 Via L. Franchetti, Roma 00196 (phone: 6-368-57255).

Take a Hike: Walking Through Italy

A striking 21% of all Italy is still wooded, and wild mountains loom over
a good deal more. The Valle d'Aosta alone offers a dozen peaks over
13,000 feet (4,000 meters) and a hundred-odd glaciers. The available wilderness ranges from northern tundras to subtropical woods and is home to
wolf, brown bear, mouflon, ibex, and other fauna largely extinct in the rest
of Europe. Despite the web of *autostrade* that now laces this passionately
automotive country, hikeable dirt roads still veer off the most beaten tourist
tracks. In the Alps, many are dotted with *rifugi* (mountain huts) that provide bed, blankets, and board tasty enough that you don't forget where
you are.

Tromp from Tuscan hill town to Tuscan hill town, trek from *rifugio* to
rifugio along the spiky, soaring ridges of the Dolomites, or wander from
cliffs down to the sea along the old Roman mule paths of Capri. For those
who read Italian, Stefano Ardito's guide *Sui Sentieri della Storia* (On the
Paths of History), available in bookstores in Italy, describes 25 hiking itineraries and paths. Included are maps, photographs, and historical notes.
Our favorite hiking areas follow:

WHERE TO HIKE

PARCO NAZIONALE DEL GRAN PARADISO, Aosta, Valle d'Aosta Some of Europe's
highest mountains—Monte Bianco (a.k.a. Mont-Blanc), Monte Cervino
(known outside Italy as the Matterhorn), and Monte Rosa—stand on the
border between Italy, France, and Switzerland and protect this green rib-
bon of valley from the colder, wetter weather of the north. But the relatively mild climate is only one reason that this spacious park, tucked in a

large corner of the Valle d'Aosta, lives up to its name for dedicated walkers. When Italy was a kingdom, royal hunting parties rode in these hills along 43 miles of high-altitude bridle paths—and all of these can be hiked today. There are also a number of well-appointed *rifugi*—open all summer—and wildlife galore, which is most often visible at day's end by those who lodge in one of the *rifugi;* when the day-trippers have gone, the ibex and chamois that populate the park arrive. Otherwise, the best base for walking is either small, quiet Degioz in the neighboring Valsavaranche or busy, cheerful Cogne, which organizes guided mountain excursions for visitors. There are plenty of marked trails, but for advice about routes, distances, and difficulty, and a copy of a free hikers' guide in Italian and English, *Alte Vie* (High Roads), with excellent directions and maps, contact the *Cogne Tourist Office,* Piazza E. Chanoux (phone: 165-74040; fax: 165-749125).

PARCO NAZIONALE DELLO STELVIO, Bormio, Lombardy The largest protected area in Italy, this park just south of Switzerland offers some of the most attractive hiking in the Alps. Deer, chamois, ibex, marmots, and wild goats populate the park, and hikers may encounter many of them on most local rambles. One particularly interesting tour is the five-day trip to the massif of the Gran Zebrù, which represents about 25 hours of solid trekking from Sant'Antonio near Bormio, up the Gran Zebrù, and back to Santa Caterina Valfurva. En route are several refuges and marvelously varied scenery—glaciers, Alpine tundra, and evergreen forests. Since the paths can be steep, this is definitely for experienced walkers only. For treks suited to hikers with less expertise and for information about expert guides, contact the park management: *Direzione Parco Nazionale dello Stelvio,* 56 Via Monte Braulio, Bormio (Sondrio) 23032 (phone: 342-905151).

LAGO DEL MIAGE, Courmayeur, Valle d'Aosta A three-hour ramble from the mountain town of Courmayeur leads to this sky-blue glacier lake surrounded by beautiful woods. The vista of the neighboring Monte Bianco group is stupendous. The area offers many other mountain hikes, including a demanding 10-day circuit of Monte Bianco itself. Information: *Azienda Autonoma di Soggiorno e Turismo,* Piazzale Monte Bianco, Courmayeur (Aosta) 11013 (phone: 165-842060; fax: 165-842072).

ISOLA DI CAPRAIA, Livorno, Tuscany Two and a half hours by ferry from Livorno (daily departures in summer) and the teeming Italian Riviera is this island with a tiny port village, a castle, no boutiques, no nightlife, very few tourists, and some wonderful walking through untouched Mediterranean landscape. One path leads to the Punta della Bella Vista, which commands a perfect panorama of the coast and the shimmering Ligurian Sea. Other walking routes wind along hillsides perfumed with wild lilies and jasmine, brilliant with heather, rosemary, and cyclamen. Bird watchers will find kindred souls and expert guides. The rare Corsican gull nests on these shores; it can live only where the sea is pure and limpid. The prettiest among the handful of hotels and *pensioni* is *Il Saracino*, with 34 rooms, most overlooking the sea. Rooms are more likely to be available after August 20 or in the early summer. Information: *Il Saracino,* Isola di Capraia (Livorno) 57032 (phone: 586-905018; fax: 586-905062), or, for general information and hotel and apartment bookings, *Agenzia Parco,* Isola di Capraia (Livorno) 57032 (phone/fax: 586-905071).

BRENTA DOLOMITES, Madonna di Campiglio, Trentino Only the most fearless walkers will want to tackle the hiking trails of this region. Along these *vie ferrate* (iron trails), bracelets and necklaces of iron cable have been anchored to the mountain at just the point that most sensible mortals would elect to turn back. Elsewhere, ladders are embedded in scrambles too steep for hands and knees. For the less ambitious, there are countless excursions and hikes to some of the most scenic spots, and tramways and chair lifts are available for many of these. The best by far are trips to the Grosté, to Monte Spinale, and to Pradalago. Information: *Azienda Autonoma di Soggiorno,* 4 Via Pradalago, Madonna di Campiglio (Trento) 38084 (phone: 465-42000; fax: 465-40404).

MONTE BALDO, Malcesine, Veneto The little chain of mountains that separates Lake Garda from the Adige River is a haven for walkers interested in plants and flowers. The unusual varieties found here attract professional and amateur botanists. Dramatic views over the lake are an added delight at this spot, approximately 25 miles (40 km) north of Verona. Information: *Azienda Promozionale di Turismo,* 1 Via Capitanato, Malcesine (Verona) 37018 (phone: 45-740-0044).

CATINACCIO DOLOMITES, Nova Levante, Alto Adige About 12 miles (19 km) north of Bolzano, this sturdy, simple mountain town, known as Welschnofen by its German-speaking population, makes a fine base for walkers of every degree of expertise. Gentle, shady forest paths strike out in all directions. To the west is hill country and a descent to the Adige Valley and civilization. To the south is the rugged Latemar massif. East are the long, rose-colored ridges of the Dolomites' Catinaccio range, whose dramatic footpaths have been made more accessible since the construction of cable cars and chair lifts. But the ambitious and experienced will find challenging *vie ferrate,* with cables and ladders at crucial points; experts can try the towering spirits of the Vaiolet. Refuges at frequent intervals provide lunches and overnight lodging. Information: *Azienda Autonoma di Soggiorno e Turismo,* 5 Via Carezza, Nova Levante (Bolzano) 39056 (phone: 471-613126; fax: 471-613360).

SAN FRUTTUOSO, Portofino, Liguria Instead of taking the pleasant half-hour boat ride from the resort town of Camogli (about an hour from Portofino) to this fascinating medieval abbey, walk an extraordinary hour and a half from Portofino, with the sea and shoreline at your feet around every bend. The final reward is a picture-book inn/trattoria, *Da Giovanni,* on the beach and accessible only by water or walking trail. Information: *Azienda Autonoma di Soggiorno*, 35 Via Roma, Portofino (Genova) 16034 (phone: 185-269078).

PARCO NATURALE ALTA VAL SESIA, Rima, Piedmont The austere trails of this protected mountain area lead out from several neighboring towns. The perfectly preserved village of Rima is the most beautiful starting point, with its carefully restored rustic houses of stone and wood, built to resist the heaviest snowfalls. Information: *Comunità Montana Val Sesia*, 5 Corso Roma, Varallo Sesia (Vercelli) 13019 (phone: 163-51555).

PARCO NAZIONALE DEL CIRCEO, Sabaudia, Lazio A dangerous land of sorcery and spells when Odysseus passed through 3,000 years ago, the scene of Circe's mythical magic is now an enchanting national park on the edge of the Tyrrhenian Sea, home to wild boar, fox, and hare. An experienced hiker can scramble over the promontory of Monte Circeo. From there, trekkers see the Pontine Islands; one, Zannone, is under park jurisdiction and can be visited by hiring a private boat from the popular resort island of Ponza. In the park itself are easy walks through oak forests and low Mediterranean brush, often on trails used long ago by woodcutters and the *carbonai*, who once made charcoal here. The four coastal lakes, part of the park complex, teem with birdlife in spring and fall. Open daily. Information: *Parco Nazionale del Circeo*, 107 Via C. Alberto, Sabaudia (Latina) 04016 (phone: 773-511386).

CINQUE TERRE, La Spezia, Liguria Perched on the rocky coast north of La Spezia, these five villages, world-famous for their white wine, once were accessible only by dirt road or by sea; now they're reachable by paved road or train. An experienced hiker could cover all five villages in one long day's march (about 12 miles/19 km), but it is more enjoyable to take one's time, strolling over the steeply terraced, vine-covered slopes (be careful—some paths are narrow and without railings). There's a chance to ogle the magnificent, craggy coast views all along the way. From Riomaggiore, a favorite walk is along the Via dell'Amore, the most picturesque and most beautiful. The northernmost town, Monterosso al Mare, has a few hotels, but simple accommodations can be found in the other four. Information: *Ente Provinciale per il Turismo*, 47 Viale Mazzini, La Spezia 19100 (phone: 187-770900; fax: 187-770908).

FORESTA UMBRA, near Vieste, Puglia The Gargano promontory in the southern region of little-visited Puglia, on the spur of the boot, is best known for its beaches and animated resorts. But high above the coastal commotion is a shady, miraculously surviving 30,000-acre Eden of firs, oaks, maples, beeches, and giant ferns, such as Aeneas must have seen in his wanderings; even wild boar still roam free. Stay in the simple refuge-hotel, and spend a piney and pensive day walking along the silent forest paths. Information: *Azienda Autonoma di Soggiorno e Turismo*, 1 Piazza Kennedy, Vieste (Foggia) 71019 (phone: 884-708806; fax: 884-707130).

LONG-DISTANCE HIKES

E-5 LONG-DISTANCE EUROPEAN FOOTPATH The international long-distance footpaths that have been marked by modern pilgrims since 1969 are maintained by walking clubs and associations in 15 countries. Two of the six footpaths that crisscross Europe pass through Italy. The E-1 *Sentiero Europeo* (European Path) is unmarked for most of its length in Italy, and only about 24 miles (38 km) near Genoa are kept up with care. The E-5, a better choice, is 370 miles (592 km) and 26 days long. It reaches Italy at the Timmelsjoch, north of Merano, then winds down the Passerier Valley, rich in fruit trees and vineyards; climbs into the Sarntal Alps; rolls and dips along a series of ridges and high valleys to Bolzano; heads south above the Adige River Valley to Lake Santo, just north of Trento; and then swings through the southern Dolomites and heads southeast to Venice. Two compact German publications describe the complete route in detail, with maps, addresses, photos, and other information needed to walk each section: *EuropÄischer Fernwanderweg E-5,* published by Fink-Kümmerly & Frey (41 Gebelsbergstrasse, Stuttgart 7000, Germany), and *Deutscher Wanderverlag,* c/o Dr. Mair & Schnabel & Co. (44/1 Zeppelinstrasse, Ostfildern 7302, Germany). Information: *Azienda Provinciale per il Turismo,* 132 Corso III Novembre, Trento 38100 (phone: 461-914444; fax: 461-896511).

GRANDE ESCURSIONE APPENNINICA Inaugurated in 1983 by the celebrated Italian climber Reinhold Messner, this "green autostrada" through the central Apennines is evidence of Italians' interest in hiking and the environment. Its approximately 250 miles (400 km) extend from the tricornered border of Umbria, the Marches, and Tuscany to the point where Tuscany joins Liguria and Emilia-Romagna, near the Tyrrhenian coast. Presenting no particular technical difficulties, it offers superb walking through the heartland of Italy's most poetic areas. Information: *Gruppo Trekking Firenze,* 12 Piazza San Gervasio, Firenze 50100 (phone: 55-585320; fax: 55-574457).

GRANDE TRAVERSATA DELLE ALPI A challenging itinerary, the "Great Crossing of the Alps" stretches east and north of Turin, from the Maritime Alps near the French border almost to Switzerland, above Lake Maggiore. Its more than 400 marked miles (640 km) cross the region's most beautiful valley and take in 84 refuges (open July through September). One of the most interesting sections begins in Susa, a town easily reached from Turin, and leads north to Il Truc, Usseglio, Balme, and Ceresole. It's also possible to continue into the Valsavaranche in the *Parco Nazionale del Gran Paradiso.* All hiking is at fairly high altitudes, from 4,900 to 8,200 feet, and often follows old mule paths between abandoned mountain villages. The Grande Traversata does require a good level of physical fitness but is not a particularly difficult route. There are, however, a few strenuous ascents and descents that may inspire wistful memories of the mules. Information:

Comitato Promotore GTA, 1 Via Barbaroux, Torino 10100 (phone: 11-562-4477).

SENTIERO ITALIA For serious trekkers, the *Sentiero Italia* stretches all the way from Trieste, crossing the Alpine arch to Liguria on the Tyrrhenian coast, running down through the Apennine rib of Italy to the Calabrian Aspromonte, and extending into Sicily, Sardinia, and Corsica, for an itinerary of 3,125 miles (5,000 km). Information: *Associazione Sentiero Italia,* 12 Piazza San Gervaso, Firenze 50131 (no phone).

Directions

Introduction

With its land a living history text—and despite its often delinquent drivers—Italy lends itself to an infinite variety of driving tours. While visits to the major metropolitan areas reveal something of this diverse country and its people, other aspects of Italian life can be experienced only outside city limits—in small fishing villages or mountain campsites in the Abruzzo, on rocky beaches along the Amalfi Coast or hairpin turns in the Dolomites, through the lush hills of Tuscany or the rugged terrain of Sardinia, or in the wildlife preserve of *Gran Paradiso National Park* in the Valle d'Aosta.

On the following pages are 28 driving tours through Italy's varied regions, on the mainland and on irresistible islands. From Piedmont to Puglia they traverse the country's most spectacular routes and roads and most arresting natural wonders, offering unforgettable views of azure lakes, winding rivers, dramatic mountain peaks, and virgin forests. They are journeys, too, into Italy's fascinating past. Along the routes are monuments left by ancient civilizations—*sassi* (prehistoric caves), *trulli* (cylindrical limestone huts), and ruins of Greek, Etruscan, and Roman temples and houses—as well as structures built in later times, such as the churches, bell towers, and monasteries of the Middle Ages; the basilicas, chapels, and palazzi of the Renaissance; and modern-day *gallerie* and sports centers, to name only a few. Along the way, too, are communities where traditional ways of life are still followed—fishing and farming support families as they have for centuries, dress and celebrations date back to the dimmest past, saints and sacred icons are religiously revered, and people still speak dialects that reflect the numerous foreign invasions the country has endured.

Each route begins with an introduction to the region, followed by suggested driving tours designed to take five to seven days. It is possible to string together several routes to form longer itineraries, but if you are pressed for time, you will find that by following any single itinerary you will see most of the sites and sights in the area. Each route also suggests the most outstanding hotels and dining spots along the way, from simple *pensioni* to deluxe villas, from cozy trattorie to elegant restaurants.

These tours are not exhaustive—there is no effort to cover absolutely everything in each region—but the places recommended and activities described were chosen to make your trip a memorable one.

The Italian Riviera

What is pine green and bay blue, has more than 18 million wisteria petals, and collects 3,000 annual hours of sunlight—most of which seem to be crammed into any average summer afternoon? Answer: The Italian Riviera. And as anyone who has spent a part of summer hereabouts will gladly agree, there is no satisfactory answer to the riddle of why this glorious arc of Mediterranean coast has remained so long in the shadow of its showy French cousin to the northwest.

Given a snorkel and a little wanderlust, it's easy to polish off the itinerary offered below in a week—provided there's no dallying over lunch. But then, why *not* dally? With a little preplanning, the most strenuous afternoon activity could be ordering another bottle of chilled vermentino or a slushy *granita di caffè*. (With no preplanning in the summer, however, you may spend most of your time seeking accommodations.) Who needs Nice?

The backdrop for this *dolce vita* is a 220-mile-long crescent along the Ligurian Sea that's divided in the middle by the sprawling port city of Genoa. Everything to the west is known as the Riviera di Ponente; everything to the east and south, the Riviera di Levante—referring to whether the sun will be setting or rising as you gaze from your seafront window. In midsummer the resident population of Liguria is outnumbered four to one by beach umbrellas. Hundreds of wild, craggy coves are carved into the wall of the coastline, however, and a 15-minute dinghy ride will take you far from the madding crowd. Some of Italy's classiest vacationers indulge in cove hopping, from Ventimiglia to Lerici, via sleek sloops, eliminating the risk of being cast ashore at a less-than-hallowed hotel.

The Italian Riviera has a lot more to offer than superb climate and beaches. The Ligurians themselves are proud and reserved, but they are welcoming toward visitors. The narrow coastline is protected by a semicircle of mountain ranges, the Alps to the north and the Apennines to the east, making Liguria one of Italy's most scenically varied regions. The terraced hills that look like giant staircases are devoted to growing grapes for the region's delicate wines and olives for its well-respected olive oil industry. The seafood here is some of the best in Europe.

Liguria has always been a seafaring region. Even today, 70% of the population of 1.7 million lives on the coast. Many of these people work at the ports, especially Genoa, or in the production of slate, olive oil, or pasta, but most are involved in tourism or related industries. Liguria is famous for hand-crafted filigree, macramé, ceramics, and especially floriculture. As early as the 16th century, the Italian nobility of other regions sent to Liguria for fresh flowers—roses, carnations, strelitzias, gladioli, and daisies, to name only a few of the varieties grown here.

The most famous date in Ligurian history is the discovery of America in 1492 by the Genoese Christopher Columbus. But the oldest evidence of Ligurian citizenry comes from the Balzi Rossi caves of Ventimiglia, near the French and Italian border. Over 200,000 years ago, humans took shelter in these caves. Other parts of the western coast are also rich with traces of prehistory: Neanderthal people (who existed from about 100,000 to 30,000 BC) lived in caves in the San Remo and Finale districts. Farther inland, Paleolithic people (about 30,000 to 10,000 BC) left burial mounds and funeral artifacts.

The Romans made their appearance after the first Punic War (3rd century BC). The fierce Ligurian tribes fought savagely for independence, but by 14 BC Augustus Caesar had conquered the whole Alpine arc region, and Liguria became completely Romanized. Towns sprang up at Albingaunum (Albenga) and Albintimilium (Ventimiglia) in the west and at Luna (Luni) in the east. Archaeological remains of these Roman towns are still in existence, most notably in Luni, near the Tuscan border.

Liguria was considerably larger in the past than it is today; its western borders stretched well into what is now France. Alaric, King of the Visigoths, destroyed Albenga in AD 409. Other barbarian tribes wreaked havoc in the area until the Lombards invaded in AD 568 and dominated for 200 years. Liguria's Middle Ages properly began only toward the end of the 8th century, when the Franks established a Tuscan-Ligurian feudal mark.

The ports along the coast had been important as trading centers. After the fall of the Roman Empire and throughout the Middle Ages, the Arab Saracens, highly organized plunderers from North Africa and what is now the Middle East, repeatedly stormed the entire Ligurian coast. In AD 935 they sacked Genoa, and for the next two centuries, largely in response to the continuing Saracen threat, Genoa slowly built itself up as a powerful maritime center.

In the 12th century, Genoa began its conquest of the rest of the Riviera, although other independent Ligurian cities, particularly Savona and Ventimiglia, fought to retain their individual liberty. The conquest was complete by the end of the 14th century, but trouble was brewing from within. Factions that supported the pope, including the Guelphs, fought bitterly with those who supported the Holy Roman Empire, the Ghibellines. This, and the devastation caused by wars with Venice and Pisa, so weakened the region that, between 1499 and 1522, Louis XII of France was able to impose his authority over the area. A few years later, the French were ousted by the great Ligurian leader Andrea Doria, with the help of the Spanish. Doria, a brilliant admiral as well as a politician, known as Father of the Country, also framed a constitution and helped to create a unified Republic of Genoa that remained intact for nearly 200 years.

In 1746 the region was occupied by the Austrians, who remained in control until the French Revolution. In 1797 the Ligurian republic became a battleground for the Napoleonic Wars. For the first decade of the 19th century, it was annexed to France, but, with Napoleon's defeat in 1815, the newly titled Duchy of Genoa became united to the Kingdom of Sardinia.

The following decades witnessed the struggle for Italian unification. In 1831, Giuseppe Mazzini founded the Young Italy movement, which led to the growth of a national spirit otherwise known as the Risorgimento, "Revival" or "Rebirth." Another hero was Nice-born Giuseppe Garibaldi, a charismatic military leader who was responsible for bringing Sicily and Naples into the growing union. Garibaldi achieved the liberation of the south with his famous "Thousand" Red Shirts, all fierce Ligurian sharp-shooters.

Today's visitors to the Italian Riviera will see not the fierce and inde-pendent side of the Ligurians, only their hospitality. All the towns and many of the villages have extremely efficient and friendly information offices that go under the name *Azienda di Promozione Turistica (APT)*, but just ask for *"informazione turistica"* and you can't go wrong. The offices give advice on sights to see, hotels, tours, and festivals—also on where to find the best water skiing instructor or the best local wine.

This route, starting in Ventimiglia (near the French border not far from Nice), winds along the arc-shaped coast, passing through such renowned resorts as San Remo and ancient fishing villages like Noli. It is bisected by the port city of Genoa, then continues south toward such internationally famous playgrounds as Portofino. Halfway along the Riviera di Levante, the route turns slightly inland, skirting the insular Cinque Terre (Five Lands) to finish at Portovenere, on the small peninsula just south of the port town of La Spezia.

Distances between towns are short—few are more than a 10-minute drive from one another, although Sunday traffic can be brutal. A number of trains stop at the villages along the coast, and an energetic hiker could even cover some of the area on foot. Two roads traverse the Riviera, almost parallel to each other; each averages 164 miles (262 km; the coastline itself is closer to 200 miles/320 km long). The autostrada (A10 west of Genoa and A12 east; follow the green signs), which commands some stunning views, generally runs inland and at a higher altitude. The older Via Aurelia (S1; follow the blue signs) clings to the coast, running through all the towns and villages. The coast road can be congested with traffic, so, unless you are very patient, use the autostrada, exiting to visit particular places.

Accommodations range from very expensive, where a double room for one night will cost $225 or more; to expensive, which costs from $125 to $225; to moderate, which runs from $75 to $125; to inexpensive, which will cost $75 or less. (A warning for visitors arriving in July or August: Sometimes as much as four to six months' advance booking is required during this period by the more popular hotels or those with limited accommodations, and that does not necessarily mean the most expensive.) Most hotels are not open year-round, but those that are may offer unofficial discounts in the winter. All hotels feature private baths unless otherwise indicated.

Despite the accessibility to fresh fish, a seafood dinner will nonetheless be a costly, albeit memorable, affair. With this in mind, here are estimated meal prices: A very expensive dinner for two costs $150 or more; an expensive dinner, from $100 to $150; a moderate repast, from $50 to $100; and an inexpensive one, $50 or less. All restaurants are open for lunch and dinner unless otherwise noted. Prices include wine but not liquor. For each location, hotels and restaurants are listed alphabetically by price category.

Note that most sites of interest on the Italian Riviera close for a midday break, usually anywhere from noon or 12:30 PM to 2:30 or 3:30 PM; we suggest calling ahead to check exact hours.

En Route from the French Border Whether on A10 or S1, stop at Mortola Inferiore, 3 miles (5 km) before Ventimiglia, to visit the *Giardini Hanbury* (Hanbury Gardens). Now with more than 6,000 species of flora, the gardens were founded by the Englishman Sir Thomas Hanbury in 1867. They are regarded as one of the most important sites in Europe for the cultivation of exotic plants. They are closed Wednesdays; admission charge (phone: 184-229507).

VENTIMIGLIA The medieval section of town stands on a hill to the west of the River Roja. This ancient port was independent until 180 BC, when it became subject to Rome. Invasions by Goths and other barbarians forced the citizens to move uphill from the coast, where some fine Roman archaeological sites, such as a well-preserved amphitheater, remain. The fortified hill city is very much as it was during the 13th century, when it was conquered by Genoa. The *Chiesa di San Michele,* near the Corso Francia, is a large, somber Romanesque building (11th to 13th century), with the original crypt incorporating Roman columns and milestones. The modern section of Ventimiglia—to the east of the river—is important principally as a center for the production and sale of flowers. A yearly *Festival di Musica Antica* (Festival of Ancient Music) is held sometime between July and August, and a colorful historical folk festival takes place around the middle of August. The nearby *Balzi Rossi* prehistoric caves (near the French border; phone: 184-38113) are open daily in summer, with a short midday closing; closed Mondays and for a short midday break in winter; admission charge. Tourist information is available at 61 Via Cavour (phone: 184-351183) and at the main train station (*AVAST;* phone: 184-358197). Both are closed Sundays and for a midday break.

BEST EN ROUTE

Balzi Rossi If ever there was an outstanding restaurant at this end of the Riviera, this must be it. The fresh fish–based menu is topnotch, and the terrace is a delight; considering the quality, so are the prices. Closed Mondays, Tuesday lunch, the first two weeks in March, and the last two weeks in November.

Reservations necessary. Major credit cards accepted. Five miles (8 km) from Ventimiglia toward the French border, at Piazzale de Gaspari, Ponte San Ludovico (phone: 184-38132). Very expensive.

La Riserva On the outskirts of the medieval city, 1,300 feet above sea level, this secluded 30-room hotel offers a homey atmosphere, a superb restaurant next to a heated pool, and a wonderful view of the coast. Open April through September and three weeks at *Christmas.* Castel d'Appio, Ventimiglia (phone: 184-229533; fax: 184-229712). Moderate.

En Route from Ventimiglia Only a mile or so (2 km) out of Ventimiglia on A10, the exit to Pigna leads to Dolceacqua, which means "Sweet Water" (4 miles/6 km from the exit). In keeping with its name, the village produces some of the best wine in the region, a delicate, light red called rossese. Perched on a hill are the impressive 12th-century ruins of the Doria family castle. Many of the interior narrow passageways that run up to the castle are completely cut off from daylight. It's closed Tuesdays and for a long (noon to 3 PM) break; admission charge (phone: 184-206561). Among the many traditional craft shops here, the most notable may be that of Jean Perrino (43 Via Barberis; phone: 184-206090), who sculpts fantastic shapes from 300-year-old local wood.

Back on the autostrada, it is 3 more miles (5 km) to Bordighera, where there are a number of good hotels, and another 7 miles (11 km) to Ospedaletti. Both small towns are popular winter resorts. The British have been coming to Bordighera for over a century; Queen Margherita of Savoy chose this palm-shaded resort—known for its Baroque architecture—as her principal residence. The tourist office (1 Via Roberto; phone: 184-262322; fax: 184-264455) is open daily, with a midday closing. The Vatican gets its supplies of palms for *Holy Week* exclusively from this district.

BEST EN ROUTE

Cap Ampelio Set in a park with views of the sea, this well-established, elegant establishment has more than a hundred modern rooms and a good restaurant. In addition to a pool, there is the *Centro Maurice Mességué* (part of the well-known chain of spas throughout Europe). Guests can enjoy individual services or sign up for an all-inclusive week of pampering from Sunday through Saturday. Open mid-December through October. 5 Via Virgilio, Bordighera (phone: 184-264333; 184-266767, spa; fax: 184-264244; 184-264324, spa). Expensive.

Carletto Friendly owners, delicious pasta, a mouth-watering selection of antipasti, and fresh fish make this attractively decorated spot a sure winner. Closed Wednesdays, June 20 to July 5, and mid-November to mid-December. Reservations advised. Major credit cards accepted. 339 Via Vittorio Emanuele, Bordighera (phone: 184-261725). Expensive.

Del Mare A modern hundred-room complex with gardens, a pool, a restaurant, and a private beach, this is one of the area's best. Open mid-December to September. About 1 mile (1.6 km) outside the town center on Via Aurelia, at 34 Via Portico della Punta, Bordighera (phone: 184-262201; fax: 184-262394). Expensive.

La Réserve Tastevin Sublime seafood is served in this elegant setting, appropriate for the *zuppa di pesce* (fish soup). Alfresco dining with lovely port views and an excellent wine selection overseen by two world class sommeliers/owners make this a place for a perfect evening. Closed Sunday dinner, Mondays in off-season, and mid-October to mid-December. Reservations advised. Major credit cards accepted. 20 Via Arziglia, Campo Sant'Ampelio, Bordighera (phone: 184-261322). Moderate.

SAN REMO The capital of the Riviera di Fiori (Riviera of Flowers), San Remo is an elegant Edwardian resort reminiscent of Cannes. Made fashionable at the turn of the century by Russian and German aristocrats, it is still a favorite watering spot of Italy's rich and powerful, as evidenced by the number of luxurious yachts moored in the harbor.

The origins of the town are Roman, but its most potent era was the Middle Ages, when the Genoese bishops resided here. San Remo was, in fact, named after the first of the bishops, San Romolo. Over the centuries, it was heavily fortified, having to endure persistent invasion by the Genoese, the pirate Barbarossa (who sacked the town in 1543), and the English. The town's medieval nucleus, known as La Pigna ("The Pine Cone") for its shape, is perched on a hill. Its tall houses are joined by small arches for reinforcement against earthquakes. At its top is the Baroque *Chiesa di Nostra Madonna della Costa* (Church of Our Lady of the Coast), whose origins go back to the 6th century, when there was a sanctuary on the site. Another noteworthy building is the Russian Orthodox *Chiesa di Santa Maria degli Angeli;* the building, on Via Nuvoloni, is not often open to visitors, but the colorful exterior is delightful in itself.

A visit to the *Mercato dei Fiori* (Flower Market) in Valle Arnica just outside of town, open weekdays from about midnight to 8 AM (it's busiest from October through June), will reveal an abundance of roses, jasmine, carnations, narcissi, tulips, and countless other varieties: 20,000 tons of blossoms are shipped from the Riviera each year. The *Municipal Casinò* (18 Corso degli Inglesi; phone: 184-534001) is one of only four casinos in Italy; players must have some form of identification, such as a passport, to get in. It's open daily from 2:30 PM to 2:30 AM. Winnings can be spent immediately at the fashionable boutiques on nearby Corso Matteotti, one of the most exclusive shopping areas in this part of the Riviera. The *Festival di San Remo* song celebration takes place here each year, usually in February. The 18-hole *Golf Club San Remo* is 3 miles (5 km) outside of town (for details, see *Great Italian Golf* in DIVERSIONS). For a spectacular view of the coast, as well as Cannes on a clear day, which is nearly always, take the funicular (when it's working) from Via Isonzo up to Monte Bignone. The tourist office (*Palazzo Riviera,* 1 Via Nuvoloni; phone: 184-571571; fax: 184-507649) is closed Sundays and holidays after 2 PM.

BEST EN ROUTE

Royal One of the most grand and luxurious properties on the Riviera di Ponente, it has 148 rooms, manicured gardens, a noted restaurant, a garden pool, tennis courts, a nightly dance orchestra (in high season), and impeccable service. At least one member of European royalty or international celebrity usually is in residence. Although the hotel is located in the center of town, the surrounding parkland lends a secluded atmosphere. Open mid-December to mid-October. Rates vary for sea or hill views. 80 Corso Imperatrice, San Remo (phone: 184-5391; 800-223-6800 in the US; fax: 184-61445). Very expensive.

Astoria West-End This 120-room hotel is considerably more modern than the *Grand Hotel Londra* next door (see below); it has a high standard of service, a restaurant, a lovely park, and a pool. Open year-round. 8 Corso Matuzia, San Remo (phone: 184-667701; fax: 184-65616). Expensive.

Da Giannino A small, simple place, it's well known for its *tagliolini integrali al nero di seppia* (whole-wheat pasta in squid-ink sauce). The *branzino in salsa di ribes* (sea bass with currant sauce) is another specialty. Closed Sunday dinner and May 15 to June 1. Reservations necessary. Major credit cards accepted. 23 Lungomare Trento e Trieste, San Remo (phone: 184-504014). Expensive.

Grand Hotel Londra Dating from 1860 and still a favorite, this large, elegant establishment—San Remo's first hotel—has a restaurant, a verdant park, and a pool. Open mid-December to mid-October. 2 Corso Matuzia, San Remo (phone: 184-668000; fax: 184-880359). Expensive.

Liberty del Casinò Compared with some Italian restaurants, the atmosphere here at the *Municipal Casinò* is formal, but this does not deter the devoted. Both the kitchen and the service are excellent. Open daily. Reservations advised. Major credit cards accepted. 13 Corso Inglesi, San Remo (phone: 184-534001). Expensive.

Mediterranée A little out of town, this modern but tastefully decorated hostelry boasts delightful gardens surrounding the pool, as well as an alfresco restaurant. Many of its 67 rooms have balconies overlooking the sea. Open year-round. 76 Corso Cavallotti, San Remo (phone: 184-571000; fax: 184-541106). Expensive.

Pesce d'Oro Stop for the homemade pasta dishes with pesto and excellent fresh fish; together with either the local pigato or rossese wine, dining here is a particularly memorable experience. Closed Mondays. Reservations advised. American Express accepted. 300 Corso Cavallotti, San Remo (phone: 184-576332). Expensive.

En Route from San Remo Take a short but worthwhile detour to Bussana Vecchia. Exit from A10 about 2 miles (3 km) out of San Remo, or take the Via Aurelia. This medieval village was leveled by an earthquake in 1887, and all its inhabitants, who were nicknamed, ironically, Bissana (Twice Healthy), were killed when the church where they had taken refuge collapsed. For years the town was left abandoned, but today a community of artists (specializing in ceramics and wrought iron) have built charming homes and studios within the old buildings without changing their exteriors. Beyond Bussana Vecchia, for the next 30 miles (48 km) or so, the route is lined with industrial developments, but there is a fine strip of beach at Alassio. Alassio's tourist office is located at 26 Viale Gibb (phone: 182-640346). There are also two very good restaurants along this stretch, in Imperia (see below).

BEST EN ROUTE

Lanterna Blu-da Tonino With a friendly, relaxed atmosphere, this restaurant is one of the best on the Riviera. Its specialties are scampi, *bianchetti* (tiny anchovies and sardines), a variety of fish soups, and delicious pasta. The building, one of the most attractive in an otherwise busy, modern harbor, dates from the 1600s. In summer, dine at the open windows and watch the fishing boats go by. Closed Tuesday and Wednesday lunch in summer; Wednesdays the rest of the year; the first two weeks of July; and December 12 to 25. Reservations advised. Major credit cards accepted. 32 Via Scarincio, Borgo Marina, Porto Maurizio, Imperia (phone/fax: 183-63859). Expensive.

Beau Rivage This family-run, 19th-century villa is conveniently situated near the beach and the town's *centro storico*. The 20 airy rooms have wrought-iron beds and carefully selected antiques. In the two reading rooms are original frescoed ceilings. Open December 27 to mid-November. 82 Via Roma, Alassio (phone/fax: 182-640584). Moderate.

Salvo ai Cacciatori Fish is the thing to eat here, especially *bottarga* (caviar) served as a first course with *tagliatelle*. Closed Mondays, mid-June to mid-July, and the first half of November. Reservations advised. Major credit cards accepted. 14 Via Vieusseux, Oneglia, just east of Imperia (phone: 183-23763). Moderate.

ALBENGA This small, flourishing market town, a little bit inland on a fertile plain, is the most important historic site on the western Riviera. From the 6th century BC, Albenga was the seat of the Ingaunian tribes, until it was conquered by Rome in 181 BC. It then became a prosperous commercial center whose territorial supremacy stretched from Finale in the east to San Remo in the west. The fortified walls of the historic center in the Piazza Duomo still are largely intact; the layout of the medieval buildings within reveals the early Roman influence. The most distinctive and evocative features of the town are the 50 brick tower houses, many still in excellent condition. Except for an early invasion by the Goths, the city enjoyed a long period of peace. This accounts for the preservation of the most important Christian monument extant in Liguria, the 5th-century cathedral baptistry, with its decagonal exterior, octagonal interior, and fine blue and white mosaic, *Christ Amidst Doves*. Except for the baptistry, the cathedral was reconstructed in the 13th century; architectural features have not changed for centuries, most notably the Piazzetta dei Leoni, which lies behind the apse. Although subject to Genoese authority since 1251, Albenga retained considerable independence; building continued here until the 15th century. Obtain tickets to the baptistry at the *Museo Civico* (12 Piazza San Michele; phone: 182-51215). The museum itself has a collection of prehistoric artifacts and Roman exhibits relating to the town. Also in the piazza and of interest are the *Museo Navale Romano* and the *Museo Preistorico*. All three museums are closed Mondays and for a long midday break; separate admission charge to each. The tourist office (1 Viale Martiri della Libertà; phone: 182-50475) has information on Albenga and nearby towns; it's closed Sundays and for a long midday break.

BEST EN ROUTE

Italia Modest, with only eight rooms, it also boasts a restaurant that turns out some of the best food in town. Restaurant closed Mondays and most of November. Reservations necessary Saturday evenings. Major credit cards accepted. 8 Viale Martiri della Libertà, Albenga (phone/fax: 182-50405). Hotel, inexpensive; restaurant, moderate.

En Route from Albenga About 7 miles (11 km) out of town, take the exit for Borghetto. Just north of A10 is the village of Toirano, where at the *Palazzo Comunale* (corner of Via Bernardo Ricci and Piazza San Michele), visitors can get tickets for a guided tour of the nearby grottoes, filled with stalagmites and stalactites in pastel shades of rose and green. At the grotto's entrance is the *Museo Preistorico della Val Varatella "Nino Lamboglia."* The grotto and museum (phone: 182-98062) are open daily, with a midday closing. There's an admission charge to the grotto but not to the museum. Tourist information is available in Albenga (address above). Ten miles (16 km) farther along the coast is the pleasant resort of Finale, which has a very good beach.

FINALE-LIGURE On the west side of town is a charming historic section known as Finalborgo. The harshness of the surrounding countryside makes the ornate, colorful buildings, many with trompe l'oeil effects, all the more attractive. The *Convento di Santa Caterina*, with its serene inner courtyards, is in vivid architectural contrast to the ruins of the 12th-century *Castel Govone*, which stands above the town in massive isolation. The tourist office, at 14 Via San Pietro (phone: 19-692581; fax: 19-680052), is open daily, with a midday closing, in high season.

BEST EN ROUTE

La Residenza Punta Est One of the region's most delightful small hostelries is on the outskirts of Finale, in a shady hilltop garden. The elegant 18th-century complex of buildings with 37 rooms has an ambience that's more like that of a private villa than a hotel. There are a pool and a restaurant. Open May through September. 1 Via Aurelia, Finale (phone: 19-600612; fax: 19-600611). Expensive.

SAVONA There are some attractive fishing villages, such as Noli and Spotorno, on the way to Savona, 15½ miles (25 km) from Finale, and nearby Garlenda has an excellent golf course (for details, see *Great Italian Golf* in DIVERSIONS). For the most part, however, the coastline from here to Genoa is dominated by industry and shipping. Savona, the largest town on the Riviera di Ponente, is itself a large industrial complex. Well worth a visit is the *Pinacoteca Civica* in its small historic center (Civic Picture Gallery; 7 Via Quarda Superiore; phone: 19-828601); it contains a rich collection of 14th- to 18th-century paintings, both Lombard and Ligurian, including works by Foppa and Magnasco. It's closed Mondays; Tuesdays through Saturdays for a long (noon to 3 PM) break; and Sunday afternoons; admission charge. Tourist information is available at 23 Via Paleocapa (phone: 19-820522; fax: 19-827805), which is open weekdays, with a midday closing, and Saturdays from 8 AM to 1 PM.

BEST EN ROUTE

La Farinata In this very lively, crowded spot, fish is delicious, fresh, and best with *farinata,* roasted flat cakes made from chick-peas. From the street this restaurant looks like a bakery, but don't be put off: Behind the shopfront are two large rooms. Closed weekends and the last two weeks of August. Reservations advised. No credit cards accepted. 15 Via Montesisto, Savona (phone: 19-826458). Inexpensive.

GENOA About 28½ miles (46 km) from Savona, this dynamic city sprawls up the Ligurian hillsides and along the coastline for nearly 25 miles (40 km). Italy's principal port, it's also one of the most important maritime centers on the

Mediterranean. For details on its sights, hotels, and restaurants, see *Genoa* in THE CITIES.

En Route from Genoa About 17 miles (27 km) from the center of Genoa is Rapallo, one of Italy's renowned resorts.

RAPALLO Hannibal is said to have passed through here after he crossed the Alps; the Roman single-span bridge on the east side of the bay is named after him. The town was under the jurisdiction of the Bishops of Milan until 644, after which Genoese influence prevailed. Its most notable monuments, all dating from the 14th and 15th centuries, include the *Casa di San Lazzaro* (Leper House of St. Lazarus; Via Bana), which still bears the original frescoes on its exterior, and the *Cattedrale di Santi Gervasio e Protasio* (Cathedral of Saints Gervasio and Protasio; 1 Via Filippo Neri), which was founded in the 6th century but reached its present proportions only in 1606. Behind the modern, palm and orange tree–lined promenade lie the remains of the medieval quarter, where over 500 years ago the wives of sailors and fishermen developed a lace making technique still in use today. In the quaint shop of *Emilio Gandolfi* (1 Piazza Cavour; phone: 185-50234), dedicated shoppers can still find exquisite lace; although it is extremely expensive, it's suitable to pass on as a family heirloom. Golfers can take advantage year-round of the superb 18-hole course about a mile (2 km) out of town at the *Rapallo Golf and Tennis Club* (377 Via Mamelli; phone: 185-261777; fax: 185-261779), which is closed Tuesdays. The tourist office (9 Via Diaz; phone: 185-51282; fax: 185-63051) is closed Sundays and for a midday break.

BEST EN ROUTE

Bristol Rapallo With 193 rooms, the town's most renowned hotel is housed in a stately 19th-century palazzo whose 1970s glass façade gives it the appearance of a convention center. Besides seclusion, it offers the usual comforts, including a heated pool, a park, and a superb rooftop restaurant, as well as exquisite views of the bay. Open March to January 6. 369 Via Aurelia Orientale, Rapallo (phone: 185-273313; fax: 185-55800). Very expensive.

Eurotel Well established but smaller (68 rooms) than the *Bristol Rapallo* (see above) and close to the harbor, it has a garden-surrounded pool and a good restaurant. Open February 16 to January 6. 22 Via Aurelia Ponente, Rapallo (phone: 185-60981; fax: 185-50635). Expensive.

Da Ardito *Pansotti* (stuffed tortellini in a creamy walnut sauce) and *coniglio alla ligure* (rabbit with olives) are two of many appetizing dishes served in this popular trattoria. There is terrace dining in summer. Closed Mondays. Reservations advised. Major credit cards accepted. 9 Via Canale, San Pietro di Novella, Rapallo (phone: 185-263174). Moderate.

En Route from Rapallo The Penisola di Portofino (Portofino Peninsula) is a little off the beaten track, but it's far too good to miss. The two main towns here are bustling Santa Margherita Ligure and exclusive Portofino. From Rapallo, detour onto southbound S227; 2 miles (3 km) down the road is Santa Margherita Ligure.

SANTA MARGHERITA LIGURE This more charming, less commercial version of Rapallo has a small, stony beach (unlike Portofino), a wide variety of hotels (also unlike Portofino), and good fish restaurants. The tourist office (2/B Via XXV Aprile; phone: 185-287485) is closed Sundays and for a long midday break.

BEST EN ROUTE

Imperial Palace Set in a spacious park, this luxury property combines all the modern comforts (including a heated pool) with Old World elegance—the 102 bedrooms and public spaces are furnished with museum-quality antiques. It boasts a very good restaurant and has access to a private beach and tennis courts. Open April through November. 19 Via Pagana, Santa Margherita Ligure (phone: 185-288991; fax: 185-284223). Very expensive.

Miramare A stately, turn-of-the-century façade decorated with a charming, typical trompe l'oeil creates the appropriate tone for this 84-room hotel. Many of the rooms overlook the ocean and have white wrought-iron balconies. There's a lovely garden, a beautifully landscaped pool, and a restaurant. Open year-round. 30 Via Milite Ignoto, Santa Margherita Ligure (phone: 185-287013; 800-223-6800; fax: 284651). Very expensive.

La Trattoria Cesarina This place has a good wine cellar—pigato is a favorite—and the specialties are fresh regional fish and meat dishes. Closed Wednesdays, two weeks in March, and two weeks in December. Reservations advised. Major credit cards accepted. 2/C Via Mameli, Santa Margherita Ligure (phone: 185-286059). Expensive.

Trattoria dei Pescatori Characteristic and charmingly rustic, this family-run restaurant sits directly in front of the small port from whence come its delicious daily specialties. Closed Thursdays. Reservations advised. Visa accepted. 43 Via Bottaro (phone: 185-286747). Expensive.

Da Alfredo Tucked away under arches in front of the port, this colorful trattoria has alfresco dining. Here locals mix with visitors, including opera tenor Luciano Pavarotti, who often stops by when in town. The wonderful seafood risotto bears his name. Closed Thursdays and November. Reservations advised. Major credit cards accepted. 37 Piazza Martiri della Libertà, Santa Margherita Ligure (phone: 185-288140). Moderate.

Minerva There are 28 rooms with balconies overlooking the sea and surrounding green hills in one of this town's nicest middle-range hostelries. The tranquillity of the hotel contrasts with the lively waterfront, just a minute away. There is a restaurant, sun deck, and parking. Open year-round. 34 Via Maragliano, Santa Margherita Ligure (phone: 185-286073; fax: 185-281697). Moderate.

Fasce In addition to 16 clean, modest rooms, there also is a pretty garden, rooftop sun deck, and parking. A good value, amiably run by young hosts. Open year-round. 3 Via Bozzo, Santa Margherita Ligure (phone: 185-286435; fax: 185-283580). Inexpensive.

Ulivi The perfect find for the traveler who revels in a family ambience. Each of the eight rooms has a TV set, and it's only a two-minute walk to the beach and port. Half board required during high season. Open mid-December to mid-October, except for the two weeks before *Easter*. 28 Via Maragliano, Santa Margherita Ligure (phone: 185-287890; fax: 185-282525). Inexpensive.

En Route from Santa Margherita Ligure Continue for 3 miles (5 km) to Portofino. Rather than driving, however, it's better to leave your car at Santa Margherita (at times it's obligatory), and take a boat (departures are every half hour) to Portofino (contact *Servizi Marittimi del Tigullio,* 24 Via Marsala, Rapallo; phone: 185-55814) or a regular bus, which leaves every 15 minutes in high season (contact *Tigullio Pubblici Trasporti,* 36 Corso Italia, Rapallo; phone: 185-51306).

PORTOFINO This exquisite, tiny fishing village is known as the Pearl of the Riviera for its unspoiled charm and romantic land- and seascapes. It has two castles: *Castello Brown* was renovated by an Englishman in the 19th century (follow the footpath signs for *Faro,* or Lighthouse; you'll recognize it as the setting of *Enchanted April*); *Castello San Giorgio,* on the tiny peninsula across from the harbor, was completely rebuilt at the beginning of this century by an American millionaire. *Castello Brown*'s hours are erratic; call the tourist office (see below) for a current schedule. *Castello San Giorgio* is closed Tuesdays. Admission charge to both. Each April 23, to commemorate St. George's feast day, Portofino's residents burn a huge pine tree in the center of the village. It is believed that good luck will follow those living on the side of town where the burning tree falls. During the bonfire, there's a feast of wonderful food and delicious local wines. Normally, however, the town is quiet and fiercely concerned with repelling "barbarian" tourists, hence the high prices and restrictions. Nighttime entertainment centers around outdoor *caffès* and bars, and would-be disco dancers are relegated to the exclusive *Carillon* restaurant (phone: 185-286721) in Paraggi, just outside town on the road to Santa Margherita Ligure. As you arrive at Portofino's small port, on the right is the entrance to the *Museo del Parco,* an open-air sculpture museum where more than 50 works by predominantly Italian artists grace the terraced hillside. Lucio Fontana, Arnaldo Pomodoro, and Man Ray (one of his rare pieces of sculpture is here) are just a few of those represented. At press time, the museum was closed due to lack of funds; call for hours. There's an admission charge (phone: 185-269498). The tourist information office (35 Via Roma; phone: 185-269024) is closed Sunday afternoons in summer; closed Sundays the rest of the year.

From Portofino, you might take one of the frequent 30-minute boat excursions to San Fruttuoso, on the peninsula but accessible most easily by sea. You also can get there on foot—it's a beautiful one-and-a-half-hour walk (about 2 miles/3 km) on a well-marked, though occasionally steep, trail. The tiny village has a small beach and an abbey in its center. The original monastery, built in 711, was destroyed in a Saracen raid and then rebuilt after the 10th century (it's closed in February). The church beside it is a young relation, founded only in the 13th century. This hidden medieval enclave was revitalized and restored by the *Italian Trust* in the 1980s. Boats are available from Portofino to and from Rapallo, Santa Margherita Ligure, and Camogli; for information, contact the tourist information office (see above).

The Penisola di Portofino also has some delightful hiking routes. You might even attempt the four-hour walk to Camogli (see below) and take the boat back. Detailed maps are available at various tourist.information offices. But be aware that during the summer, even a short walk (of an hour or so) can be fatiguing because of the heat; good shoes and sensible planning are essential. (See also *Take a Hike: Walking Through Italy* in DIVERSIONS.)

BEST EN ROUTE

Nazionale The only hotel directly on the marina, it has 12 comfortable suites, five of which overlook the colorful, world-famous port and its *piazzetta*. No restaurant, but breakfast is served outdoors in good weather. Open mid-March through November. 8 Via Roma, Portofino (phone: 185-269575; fax: 185-269578). Very expensive.

Splendido Supreme among the many wonderful hotels along the Riviera or elsewhere, this paradise of a hostelry has 63 guestrooms and a notable restaurant. For more information, see *Italy's Most Memorable Hostelries* in DIVERSIONS. Open April through December. 10 Salita Baratta, Portofino (phone: 185-269551; fax: 185-269614). Very expensive.

Eden Once a private home, this old villa has retained its charming *ambiente*. A two-star hotel with three-star rates, it has nine rooms, plus an enclosed garden for alfresco dining. Open from *Christmas* through November. On a quiet side street behind the picturesque port, at 18 Vico Dritto, Portofino (phone: 185-269091; fax: 185-269047). Expensive.

Piccolo Pleasant and recently refurbished, it's a good alternative for those who can't splurge on the *Splendido*. Half of the 23 suites (some with terraces) overlook the sea. No restaurant, but there are plenty of dining places in the village. Open mid-March through October. 31 Via Duca degli Abruzzi, Portofino (phone: 185-269015; fax: 185-269621). Expensive.

Il Pitosforo A popular waterfront fish restaurant–cum–verandah, it was made famous by film stars who flocked here and even lent their names to some of the dishes, most of which are excellent. Closed Mondays, Tuesday lunch, and December 20 to February 20. Reservations advised. Major credit cards accepted. 19 Molo Umberto, Portofino (phone: 185-269020; fax: 185-269290). Expensive.

Puny There is no better combination than the portside setting and acclaimed menu (and clientele) of this attractive restaurant. When weather permits, it's nice to sit outside. Try the *pappardelle a Portofino* (flat noodles with a pesto and tomato sauce) or the fresh oven-baked fish sprinkled with fragrant laurel. Closed Thursdays and January through most of February. Reservations advised. No credit cards accepted. 5 Piazza Martiri dell'Olivetta, Portofino (phone: 185-269037). Expensive.

Da Giovanni It's an idyllic half-hour boat ride (or a one-and-a-half-hour walk) to the hidden medieval enclave of San Fruttuoso, where this charming restaurant on a small gulf specializes in fresh fish. There are a handful of simply furnished rooms upstairs. Restaurant closed Wednesdays and January; hotel open May through September. No reservations. No credit cards accepted. San Fruttuoso (phone: 185-770047). Restaurant, moderate; hotel, inexpensive.

Trattoria Concordia There are just eight tables at this family-run place, but everyone prefers to dine outdoors under a covered verandah, where the simple *cucina casalinga* (home cooking) seems to taste better. Closed Tuesdays and January through February. No reservations. Visa accepted. 5 Via del Fondaco, Portofino (phone: 185-269207). Moderate.

CAMOGLI Southwest of Rapallo on the peninsula, this charming fishing port can be reached by car, train, or boat from Genoa, Rapallo, Santa Margherita Ligure, and Portofino. Built in layers, the small port looks like a palette of colors tumbling into the aquamarine sea. The *Sagra del Pesce* (Festival of the Fish), held the second Sunday in May, and *Stella Maris* (Star of the Sea), held the first Sunday in August, are the two most important and colorful holidays. Camogli is also a good starting point by foot or boat (it's inaccessible by car) for a visit to lovely San Fruttuoso (see above). The tourist office (33r Via XX Settembre; phone: 185-771066) is closed Sundays and for a long midday break.

BEST EN ROUTE

Cenobio dei Dogi This is one of Italy's very special places, though the rooms and baths are in need of a face-lift. Once a nobleman's home, this 88-room hotel is surrounded by verdant parkland that is a government reserve. There are an excellent terraced restaurant, two private pebbly beaches, a pool, and tennis courts. Open March to early January. 34 Via Cuneo, Camogli (phone: 185-770041; fax: 185-772796). Very expensive.

Da Rosa Seafood is served alfresco and portside amid marvelous views. Closed Tuesdays, most of January, February, and November. Reservations advised. Major credit cards accepted. 11 Largo Casa Bona, Camogli (phone: 185-773411). Expensive.

Primula Pull up a chair at this popular open-air *caffè,* perfect for people watching, and take in the sun and the view of the Golfo Paradiso and the Penisola di Portofino. The homemade ice cream is the draw, but you can also enjoy an informal and leisurely lunch or dinner. There's a selection of *panini caldi* (hot sandwiches), salads, and *primi piatti* (first courses)—the *pasta con pesto* is a reliable choice. Closed Thursdays. No reservations. No credit cards accepted. 149 Via Garibaldi, Camogli (phone: 185-770351). Inexpensive.

Stella Maris The tiny fishing village of Punta Chiappa cannot be reached by car—all the more reason for "escapists" to search out this rustic pensione. A 15-minute boat trip from Camogli—or a somewhat longer though equally enjoyable trip from Portofino—delivers you to this 14-room (only two have private baths), family-run seaside hotel. Half board is obligatory in summer. Nature lovers and trekkers will be delighted with the hiking paths leading to Portofino and Camogli. Usually open April through October. 68 Via San Nicolò, Punta Chiappa (phone: 185-772818). Inexpensive.

LEVANTO Back on A10 or S1, another 12 miles (19 km) along the coast from Rapallo, the route turns inland, away from Sestri Levante (a tiny peninsula famous for its ceramics and ship models). Turn right at Passo del Bracco onto S332, and drive south for 8 miles (13 km) to Levanto. A small resort with the last good stretch of beach for the next 20 miles (32 km), Levanto has a delightful historic section with a number of interesting buildings. One is the 13th-century *Comune* (Town Hall) in Piazza Cavour, with five arcades gracefully adorning its exterior. Another is the 15th-century *Chiesa di San Francesco* (Piazza Nostra Signora Annunziata), which contains an impressive painting of the miracle of San Diego by Bernardo Strozzi. There are also some very pleasant trompe l'oeil paintings on the exteriors of the townhouses. Levanto is the most convenient point—as an alternative to the larger town of La Spezia—for a base for touring the neighboring Cinque Terre. The tourist office (12 Piazza Colombo; phone: 187-808125) is closed Sunday afternoons and for a long (12:30 to 4 PM) break.

Hostaria Da Franco A wonderful selection of fresh seafood and local pasta is served on a flower-filled verandah. Try the *trenette* with pesto. Closed Mondays (except in July and August) and November. Reservations advised. No credit cards accepted. 8 Via Privata Olivi, Levanto (phone: 187-808647). Moderate.

Stella d'Italia In this well-run hostelry are 40 rooms; the building itself is an elegant villa with a garden and a restaurant. Half board is encouraged. Open mid-March to November 4 and two weeks at *Christmas*. 26 Corso Italia, Levanto (phone: 187-808109; fax: 187-809044). Inexpensive.

Stella Maris All seven rooms in this pensione have frescoes on the walls and 18th-century furniture. The owners prepare the delicious food themselves, including homemade ice cream, so half board is a temptation. Closed November. Reserve well in advance. 4 Via Marconi, Levanto (phone: 187-808258; fax: 187-807351). Inexpensive.

CINQUE TERRE A string of five small fishing hamlets—nearly hidden between the mountains and the sea—much of the Cinque Terre has changed very little over the centuries. Until fairly recently, they were accessible only by donkey or boat. Now all the villages along this enchanting 15-mile (25-km) stretch of coast can be reached relatively easily by train; Monterosso al Mare and Manarola are accessible by car. Exit the Via Aurelia at the fork at Pian di Barca. This leads to Monterosso al Mare, where the area's tourist office is located (Piazza Colombo; phone: 187-817506); it's closed November to *Easter*, except around *Christmas*. Monterosso al Mare also is the only town with any kind of beach. Park your car here and walk the length of all five towns (12 miles/19 km), or take one of the frequent trains to the other villages. For more information, see *Take a Hike: Walking Through Italy* in DIVERSIONS. Vernazza is the most colorful of the five villages. Like Manarola and Riomaggiore, the two towns linked by the lovely, rock-hewn "Via dell'Amore" footpath, Vernazza sits on a tiny strip of coastline backed by a wall of sheer cliffs. Corniglia, in the center of the strip, is perched high on a hill, offering a fine view of the whole area. There are many little places in the Cinque Terre to take a break for a snack. Try a piece of the delicious *focaccia col formaggio* (a flat cheese-flavored bread) and a glass of sciacchetrà, the region's celebrated white wine. All the hotels are small, simple, and functional, albeit sometimes not as charming as one would imagine, but the hamlets more than make up for it, and the hiking trails are spectacular. The hostelries usually offer good dining, but don't order anything other than pasta with pesto or seafood, the local specialties.

Aristide Diners will have to walk from the communal parking lot to get to this attractive, old trattoria in the lower reaches of town, since cars are not permitted in the area. Naturally, all the fish and seafood comes from the sea below. Try the sampling of 12 antipasto dishes. Closed Mondays in off-season. Reservations advised. No credit cards accepted. 138 Via Discovolo, Manarola (phone: 187-920000). Expensive.

Il Gambero Rosso High on the rocks of Vernazza, this establishment is worth a visit for its seafood and bustling atmosphere. Ask for a table outside and try the *ravioli di pesce* (seafood ravioli). Closed Mondays off-season; February through March; and most of November. Reserve in advance, and arrive early. Major credit cards accepted. 7 Piazza Marconi, Vernazza (phone: 187-812265). Expensive.

Porto Roca This modern hotel with 43 rooms (most with dramatic views), perched on a cliff above Monterosso and surrounded by quiet, shady gardens, is one of the nicest options in the Cinque Terre. It offers first class service and a restaurant serving fresh fish caught virtually outside your door. Open April through October. 1 Via Corone, Monterosso al Mare (phone: 187-817502; fax: 187-817692). Expensive.

I Due Gemelli Fresh seafood—try the house specialty, spaghetti *all'aragosta* (with lobster)—and a dramatic view of the Ligurian Sea are the hallmarks of this family-run place; there also are 14 rooms with sea views. Open year-round; restaurant closed Tuesdays off-season. Reservations advised. No credit cards accepted. Six miles (9 km) from La Spezia or Riomaggiore on Via Littoranea, Località Campi, Riomaggiore (phone: 187-920111 or 187-29043). Restaurant, moderate; hotel, inexpensive.

Gianni Franzi This spot is a favorite with locals, day-tripping Genoese, and travelers, almost all of whom come here for the *penne con scampi* (quill-shaped pasta with shrimp) or *acciughe al forno* (local baked sardines). A seaview and the distinctive white wine from these terraced hills makes this place heaven indeed. Closed Wednesdays off-season, and January through February. Reservations advised. Major credit cards accepted. 2 Via Visconti, Vernazza (phone: 187-812228). Moderate.

Il Gigante A guaranteed winner here is the first-course *minestrone alla genovese* (bean and vegetable soup with pesto). Closed Tuesdays and November through February. Reservations advised. Major credit cards accepted. 9 Via IV Novembre, Monterosso (phone: 187-817401). Moderate.

Marina Piccola This port-side perch is a front-row seat for the mesmerizing seascape at the foot of the vertical town of Manarola. Try the traditional *trenette con pesto* (thick pasta with pesto sauce) or *taglierini alla Marina Piccola* (pasta with seafood). There also are nine simple, clean rooms with balconies.

Closed Thursdays and January. Reservations advised. Major credit cards accepted. 38 Via Discovolo, Manarola (phone: 187-920103; fax: 187-920966). Restaurant, moderate; hotel, inexpensive.

Pasquale This hostelry has 15 simple rooms, all overlooking the water. Half board in high season (required) is a pleasure. Reserve ahead in season. Open *Easter* through October. 4 Via Fegina, Monterosso al Mare (phone: 187-817477; fax: 187-817550). Moderate.

Ca' d'Andrean A simple 10-room hotel, it's located midway between the parking lot at the edge of Manarola (you'll see why cars aren't allowed) and the small port at the bottom of the town's winding main road. It is modern and clean, with a small but inviting garden to relax in after an afternoon's hike. Closed most of November. 25 Via Discovolo, Manarola (phone: 187-920040). Inexpensive.

En Route from Cinque Terre Return to S1 or A12 and drive about 8 miles (13 km) to La Spezia, Italy's largest dockyard.

LA SPEZIA The indented Golfo della Spezia is a natural safe harbor for the huge naval arsenal here, which can be visited only once a year—on March 19, the feast of the city's patron saint. La Spezia is a modern, highly industrialized city. Consequently, it often can offer accommodations on short notice when the smaller, nearby resorts are booked. An interesting naval museum (Piazza Chiodo; phone: 187-717600) exhibits relics of the Battle of Lepanto and objects relating to sailing and steamships. It's closed Sundays; Tuesdays, Wednesdays, Thursdays, and Saturdays for a short (noon to 2 PM) break; and Mondays and Fridays until 2 PM; admission charge. The *Museo di Baldo Formentini,* also known as the *Museo Civico* (9 Via Curtatone; phone: 187-27228), contains remarkable statues from the Bronze and Iron Ages and a collection of traditional costumes and household implements from the Cinque Terre. It's closed Mondays; Tuesdays through Saturdays for a midday break; and Sundays after 1 PM; admission charge. Tourist information, boat tours, and information on ferries for Corsica, Cinque Terre, Portofino, San Fruttuoso, and other destinations can be obtained at 47 Viale Mazzini (phone: 187-770900; fax: 187-770908). The office is closed Sundays; Mondays, Tuesdays, Thursdays, and Fridays for a midday break; and Wednesdays and Saturdays after 1 PM.

BEST EN ROUTE

Jolly Not beautiful, but the service is dependable and good, and the 110 rooms and facilities are modern. It's a reliable alternative when seaside spots are full or when you want to catch an early-morning ferry from the nearby port. There is a restaurant. Open year-round. 2 Via XX Settembre, La Spezia (phone: 187-27200; 800-221-2626; fax: 187-22129). Expensive.

Da Dino A popular local restaurant, it offers outdoor dining with mostly seafood served. Closed Sunday dinner, Mondays, and the last two weeks of July. Reservations advised, particularly for lunch. Major credit cards accepted. 19 Via da Passano, La Spezia (phone: 187-21360). Moderate.

Ghironi Conveniently located on the edge of town, near the motorway, this place has 50 comfortable, pleasant rooms. It's not particularly quaint, but it's convenient for ferry departures. There is a bar but no restaurant. Open year-round. 62 Via Tino, La Spezia (phone: 187-504141; fax: 187-524724). Moderate.

La Posta This eatery has been in the same family for four generations, and its house specialty, chateaubriand with mushrooms, prosciutto, and cognac, is a welcome change from the fish restaurants along the coast. Closed weekends. Reservations advised. Major credit cards accepted. 24 Via Don Minzoni, La Spezia (phone: 187-34419). Moderate.

En Route from La Spezia Head 5 miles (8 km) southwest on the S530 to Portovenere.

PORTOVENERE Prehistoric humans first settled this area; then came the Romans. The 12th century saw the ascendancy of Genoa, which began to give the little town the heavily fortified appearance it maintains today. Despite its isolation, many poets and writers have made their way to this once idyllic place. Among the famous who have sought inspiration here were D. H. Lawrence, Percy Bysshe Shelley (who drowned nearby), and Lord Byron. The town's two ancient churches, noteworthy for their beautiful architecture, are worth a visit. The older, dating back to 1130, is *San Lorenzo* (above the port), with a Romanesque façade. At the extreme edge of the village, standing high on a mass of rocks, is the *Chiesa di San Pietro*, a 13th-century Gothic-Genovese construction with 6th-century interior elements still visible. Evidence suggests that the building was originally pagan and perhaps dedicated to the goddess of the sea. The town is dominated by the Genoese *Castello*, which offers a panoramic view of the surrounding area. It's open daily in summer, with a midday closing; open from 2 to 5 PM only in winter. The tourist office (1 Piazza Bastreri; phone: 187-900691) is closed Wednesdays and for a long (noon to 3 PM) break.

Portovenere also can be reached by boat, and from here the trip can be extended to Isola Palmaria, with its famous blue grotto; Isola del Tino, site of the ruins of the 11th-century abbey of *San Venerio*; and Isola Tinetto and its 6th-century monastery. Gold-veined black marble is quarried on these islands; purchase marble items in Portovenere. This is an excellent place from which to tour other places on the Riviera. In high season, boats leave often for Portofino, Cinque Terre, and Lerici; ask at the harbor or the tourist office.

Royal Sporting A stay at this modern, 62-room hostelry, with its lovely gardens and views, is a perfect alternative to the rush of nearby La Spezia. On the outskirts of town in an isolated spot, it has a private sand beach, a pool, and a restaurant. Open *Easter* through September. Località Seno dell'Olivo, Portovenere (phone: 187-900326; fax: 187-529060). Expensive.

Taverna del Corsaro Protected by the *Chiesa di San Pietro* perched above, with open-air dining on a wide terrace with views of the nearby island of Palmaria, this well-known seafood restaurant combines an idyllic setting with fine dining. The owner's reputation as one of the country's best sommeliers is confirmed after a memorable evening here. Closed Tuesdays off-season and the first two weeks in June. Reservations necessary. Major credit cards accepted. 102 Calata Doria, Portovenere (phone/fax: 187-900622). Expensive.

Della Baia This modern hotel is popular with those who want a quieter stay than can be found in Portovenere, 2 miles (3 km) away. All 40 guestrooms have TV sets; their nondescript decor is made up for by the small terraces looking out on the harbor and pool. Open year-round. 111 Via Lungomare, Località Le Grazie (phone: 187-900797; fax: 187-900034). Moderate.

Iseo Right on the harbor, this eatery serves local fresh fish and seafood. Try the house specialties, spaghetti *al curry* (with olive oil, curry, herbs, and calamari) and *alla Giuseppe* (with mussels, clams, and squid in a tomato base). Closed Wednesdays and November through January. Reservations necessary. Major credit cards accepted. 9 Calata Doria, Portovenere (phone: 187-900610). Moderate.

La Medusa Slightly more formal than the waterfront restaurants, this eatery has an equally delicious fish-based menu. An alfresco terrace opens onto the tiny Piazzetta del Centario, a timeless, quiet spot. Closed Mondays and November. Reservations advised. Major credit cards accepted. 74 Via Cappellini, Portovenere (phone: 187-900603). Moderate.

En Route from Portovenere Take S530 back to La Spezia, then head 7 miles (11 km) southeast to Lerici.

LERICI This seaside town is best known for its 16th-century hilltop *Castello* and sandy beach. The imposing silhouette inspired Mary Wollstonecraft to write *Frankenstein*, and it was in the Gulf of La Spezia (still known as the Gulf of the Poets) that her husband, Percy Bysshe Shelley, drowned after his sailboat capsized. Other literati drawn to the area include D. H. Lawrence, Lord Byron, and Baroness Orczy, who wrote *The Scarlet Pimpernel* while in residence here.

In season, the port and its shops, restaurants, and bars stay open late. A drive to the nearby town of Ameglia offers memorably dramatic coastal scenery. Boats leave daily from Lerici to Cinque Terre and Portovenere, and the Tuscan border is a minute's drive away. The tourist office (47 Via Roma; phone: 187-967346) can provide information on the area; it's closed Sunday afternoons and for a long (12:30 to 4 PM) break.

BEST EN ROUTE

Paracucchi–Locanda dell'Angelo Twenty minutes from Lerici is the backdrop for one of Italy's culinary landmarks. For more information, see *The Best Restaurants of Italy* in DIVERSIONS. There also are 37 modern rooms. Closed Mondays off-season, and the last three weeks of January. Reservations necessary. Major credit cards accepted. 60 Via XXV Aprile, Ameglia (phone: 187-64391; fax: 187-64393). Restaurant, very expensive; hotel, moderate.

La Barcaccia The morning's local catch will gladly be shown to you at your outdoor table before it is perfectly prepared. Closed Thursdays off-season and February. Reservations advised for the few tables outside. Major credit cards accepted. 8 Piazza Garibaldi, Lerici (phone: 187-967721). Moderate.

La Conchiglia This small restaurant with alfresco dining offers pasta with any one of a number of fish-based sauces, and baked or grilled fish entrées. Closed Wednesdays and February. Reservations advised. Major credit cards accepted. 3 Piazza del Molo, Lerici (phone: 187-967334). Moderate.

Due Corone The pretty, outdoor dining area here is a good place to try homemade *gnocchetti in salsa di mare* (small gnocchi in a seafood sauce) or any of the fresh, simply grilled fish. Closed Thursdays and December 22 to January 22. Reservations advised. Major credit cards accepted. 1 Via Vespucci, Lerici (phone: 187-967417). Moderate.

Europa Shelley and Byron were not guests at this modern 37-room hotel, but the spectacular view from high atop this hill no doubt was the same one that won their hearts. Climb down hundreds of stone stairs to a sandy beach or just stay on the wide sun deck. This tranquil spot is removed from the center of town. Open year-round. 1 Via Carpanini, Località Maralunga, Lerici (phone: 187-967800; fax: 187-965957). Moderate.

Florida Just outside Lerici on the coast, this modern hostelry offers access to the sandy beach directly in front of it. All 32 rooms have balconies with views of the gulf. Open February to mid-December. 35 Via Biaggini, Località La Vallata, Lerici (phone: 187-967332: fax: 187-967344). Moderate.

En Route from Lerici A lovely 4-mile (7-km) drive leads to Sarzana.

SARZANA This ancient Roman site was founded in 177 BC. In addition to two interesting medieval fortresses, the town has a handsome Renaissance cathedral, original 15th-century ramparts, and narrow streets. Try to visit in the spring, when one of the town's three antiques fairs takes place. Starting on

Good Friday, hundreds of stalls offer everything from everyday collectibles to unusual and rare items. The *Soffitta nella Strada* (Breath of Air in the Street), another fair, has drawn dealers and antiques buffs from all over Italy for over 25 years. Beginning August 1, it lasts for two weeks, sprawling through narrow streets east of Piazza Matteotti in the center. The *Mostra Nazionale dell'Antiquariato* (National Antiques Fair) takes place at the same time in the *Palazzo degli Studi* (phone: 187-624095) but has more valuable, museum-quality pieces. The tourist office is at 1 Piazza Matteotti (phone: 187-623025).

BEST EN ROUTE

La Scaletta Less than a mile out of town in the countryside is this family-run eatery, which offers alfresco dining in a shaded garden in summer. A refreshing change from the predictable fish-based menus at other restaurants in the area, this place offers *coniglio alle olive* (rabbit with olives) and delicious grilled steaks. Also worth trying are the homemade pasta and salami. It is rustic but tastefully decorated with lots of artwork. Closed Tuesdays, September, and December 23 to January 2. Reservations advised. Major credit cards accepted. 5 Via Bradia, Sarzana (phone: 187-620585). Inexpensive.

Piedmont and Valle d'Aosta

Tucked into northwestern Italy and dominated by the Alps, these two regions impress visitors not only with their unique topography but also with the hearty spirit of their people. Piedmont (meaning "at the foot of the mountain") borders France in the west and abuts Valle d'Aosta, a tiny, semi-autonomous region of green valleys and glaciers wedged between Piedmont, Switzerland, and France.

The history of the two regions is not as closely linked as geography would suggest. The Valdostans—*valdostani* to the Italians—always have been removed from the rest of Italy, both culturally and politically. They speak a patois closer to French than Italian, and their sense of their separate identity has generated a modest "independence movement" whose intent is to loosen ties to the central Italian government. This separation movement has an ancient historical precedent. Although both Piedmont and Valle d'Aosta were fiefs of the powerful House of Savoy, Piedmont was the personal possession of the Savoyard dukes, whereas Valle d'Aosta managed to gain a constitution granting it a degree of freedom as early as the 12th century. But the House of Savoy made its presence felt—Valle d'Aosta was a favorite Savoy playground, so the area is dotted with hunting lodges, castles, and sanctuaries all built to serve the ruling family.

Valle d'Aosta's strategic position has made it a crossroads of history. Evidence remains of the original inhabitants, the Salassi, a pre-Roman tribe that may have drifted in from France. In the 3rd century BC, Hannibal, with his troops and elephants, passed through the region. The Romans, heading in the other direction, entered Gaul through one of the numerous passes in the Valdostan Alps. Part of the Roman road to Gaul can still be seen at various points, and the regional capital at Aosta (once known as the "Rome of the Alps") contains extensive Roman remains. In 1800 Napoleon led his army through Valle d'Aosta on his way to conquer northern Italy.

For centuries pilgrims walked through Valle d'Aosta en route to Rome. It was here that the famous St. Bernard dogs were first bred and trained to rescue travelers lost in the snow. St. Bernard himself, a canon of Aosta's cathedral and patron saint of alpinists and mountain climbers, was charged with clearing the Alpine passes of robbers and keeping track of the pilgrims intent on making their way south. It's disappointing to learn that the dogs—known for carrying little flagons of brandy tied under their necks—were not trained by their namesake. They were bred many years after his death (and still are today) and only named in his honor.

Formed millennia ago by a vast glacier, Valle d'Aosta is shaped like an oak leaf, with a main valley as its spine. Running laterally like veins from this central valley are side valleys, usually not more than 25 miles of twisting road, most of which end in soaring mountains 12,000 and 14,000 feet high: Monte Bianco (Mont-Blanc), Il Cervino (the Matterhorn), Monte Rosa (Mt. Rosa), and *Parco Nazionale del Gran Paradiso* (Grand Paradise National Park). Lying south of the central valley, the park runs over the mountains into Piedmont. The width of the central valley, the Vallata della Dora Baltea, varies in places, but wherever topography permits, local inhabitants make the best of a beautiful, if inhospitable, landscape. Where the valley is widest, there are vineyards and apple orchards.

The valley's hundred-plus castles served as defense as well as residences, as Valle d'Aosta was the beginning of the main "highway" into central Italy. Castle watchmen kept a sharp lookout for invaders, but they also watched for ordinary travelers, who were a source of taxes levied by the Savoyard and local rulers.

This tour runs from Turin, Piedmont's capital, through the major provincial town of Ivrea and on into Valle d'Aosta. The distance from Turin to Aosta, the capital city of the Valle d'Aosta region, is just under 80 miles (128 km). The ancient and charming town makes a good base for trips throughout the region. This itinerary explores the "lateral" valleys of Gressoney and Valtournenche, visiting the most interesting castles along the way. From Aosta our route travels south to Cogne in *Parco Nazionale del Gran Paradiso*. From there you will double back to the chic ski resort of Courmayeur, near the French border, for an Italian-side view of Mont-Blanc.

From June through October all but the highest roads can be negotiated without snow tires or chains, which are essential on some stretches from November through May. In winter many passes are closed (though the Great St. Bernard tunnel is open year-round). The autostrada (A5) runs directly from Turin to Aosta, but after Ivrea we recommend taking the state highway (S26), which passes through many picturesque Valdostan towns and villages.

Those heading for Valle d'Aosta during prime ski season (advance booking is essential from *Christmas* through *Easter*) might stop at the ski resorts of Ayas, Breuil-Cervinia, Chamois, Champorcher, Cogne, Courmayeur, Gressoney, Pila (Aosta), La Thuile, Torgnon, and Valtournenche.

Expect to dine well and heartily in Valle d'Aosta. The climate encourages stick-to-the-ribs sustenance of beef, game, and mountain trout. Also look forward to delicious dairy products, such as fondue of fontina cheese, polenta, and thick meat and vegetable soups. *Valdostani* drink a heady mixture of hot black coffee, grappa, genepy liqueur, and lemon peel from a giant beaker called a *grolla* or *coppa d'amicizia* (cup of friendship), multi-spouted for passing round the table. The region's altitude and climate, one of the driest in Italy, are ideal for wine production. Noteworthy examples of the local vinoculture are the pinot noir, the rich ruby-red arnad-montjovet, the fresh white wines from Morgex (near Courmayeur), the coppery donnas (often spelled donnaz), and the sang des salasses produced by the monks of the *Abbazia di Gran San Bernardo* (Great St. Bernard Abbey).

Valle d'Aosta has both a winter and a summer season, the former lasting from *Christmas* through *Easter* and the latter from June through August. During both, hotel reservations are necessary. A double room in a very expensive hotel will cost about $230 a night; those rated as expensive charge $110 or more; moderate, from $70 to $110; and inexpensive, $70 or less. All hotels feature private baths unless otherwise indicated, and rates include breakfast. An expensive meal for two costs $90 or more; moderate, from $60 to $90; and inexpensive, $60 or less. Prices include a bottle of wine, tip, tax, and cover charge. All restaurants are open for lunch and dinner unless otherwise noted. For each location hotels and restaurants are listed alphabetically by price category. Note that many sites of interest in Piedmont and Valle d'Aosta close for a midday break, usually from 12:30 to 2 PM; we suggest calling ahead to check exact hours.

TURIN For a detailed report on the city, its sights, its hotels, and its restaurants, see *Turin* in THE CITIES.

En Route from Turin Stop at Chivasso, Caluso, or Strambino to visit minor ruins. Otherwise, it is a quick drive north about 35 miles (56 km) on A5 or S26 through the Po Valley.

IVREA Considered the gateway to Valle d'Aosta, Ivrea is really in the region of Piedmont. It has some industry (the main Olivetti plant is on the outskirts), a well-preserved old town, and a fine castle, built by the Savoys in the 14th century, that is still largely intact. One of Ivrea's great attractions is its unique two-week-long *Carnevale,* usually held at the end of February. It seems that in the 12th century the local lord insisted on *droit du seigneur* with a young miller's daughter. She pretended to agree to the marquis's demands, but when the opportunity presented itself, she decapitated her would-be lover and set fire to his castle. Far from decrying her actions, the local *ivreasi*—presumably sick of this sort of thing—supported her and celebrated her freedom. Greatly embellished over the years, this story is reenacted yearly in a parade in which, oddly enough, Napoleonic officers appear, along with medieval pipers and squires. A feature of the *Carnevale* is the battle of oranges, in which two teams—one on foot, the other mounted—pelt each other with fruit. If you are a spectator, be prepared to duck an unexpected dose of vitamin C. Ivrea's tourist office (*Informazione e Assistenza Turistica;* 1 Corso Vercelli; phone: 125-618131; fax: 125-618140) is closed Saturday afternoons, Sundays, and for a long midday break.

L'Aranciere For tasty local cuisine and attentive service, try this cozy, wood-paneled restaurant set under the arcades of a fine neoclassical square. Closed Sundays. Reservations advised. Major credit cards accepted. Piazza Ottinetti, Ivrea (phone: 125-641332). Moderate.

Caffè del Teatro Bask in period decor reminiscent of a 19th-century coffeehouse, and in the back room, indulge on excellent food amid furnishings that could belong to an English gentlemen's club. Try the sandwiches. Closed Sundays. Reservations unnecessary. No credit cards accepted. 29 Via Palestro, Ivrea (phone: 125-641186). Moderate.

Sirio A little over a mile (1.6 km) north of Ivrea, overlooking Lago Sirio, this modern 53-room hotel offers rowing, swimming, fishing, and sailing. In addition, it houses the town's finest restaurant. Open year-round. 85 Via Lago Sirio, Ivrea (phone: 125-424247; fax: 125-48980). Moderate.

Monferrato An attractive mountain ambience combined with delicious food and friendly owners make this trattoria (with a pensione across the street) a more than worthwhile stop. Especially good pasta, such as *fettuccine al limone* (noodles with lemon and cream), and mouth-watering local desserts vie with the regional *brasato* (beef sautéed with red barolo wine). On occasion a guest will sit down to play the piano. Closed Mondays. Reservations unnecessary. Visa accepted. 1 Via Gariglietti, Ivrea (phone: 125-641012; fax: 125-40566). Inexpensive.

Moro A homey downtown establishment, it serves a good prix fixe dinner and also offers 33 rooms, most with private bath. Closed weekends from October through March, and *Christmas Eve* through January 7. Reservations unnecessary. Major credit cards accepted. 43 Corso Massimo d'Azeglio, Ivrea (phone: 125-40170 or 125-423136). Inexpensive.

Trattoria del Ponte This pretty dining place, which takes its name from a nearby 15th-century stone bridge, is a real bargain. Locals come here for such excellent home-cooked dishes as polenta with different cheeses and *coniglio in umido* (braised rabbit). Closed Fridays and the second week of September. Reservations unnecessary. No credit cards accepted. Fondo di Val Chiusella, Ivrea (phone: 125-749124). Inexpensive.

En Route from Ivrea Continue north on S26 for 15 miles (24 km) to Pont-St.-Martin.

PONT-ST.-MARTIN The climb into the Valle d'Aosta proper begins at this tiny hamlet, a pretty little town that seems more French than Italian. Here a restored Roman bridge from the 1st century BC still spans the Lys River.

Dora Stazione Besides serving tasty hot hors d'oeuvres and good game dishes, this hotel-restaurant offers customers a painted ceramic plate as a souvenir of the meal. Some of the seven rooms have private baths. Closed Mondays and the second half of September. Reservations unnecessary. Visa accepted. Near the railway station, at 10 Via della Resistenza, Pont-St.-Martin (phone: 125-82035). Inexpensive.

Ponte Romano A well-maintained 13-room hostelry and restaurant, it overlooks the Roman bridge. Restaurant closed Wednesdays. Reservations unnecessary. Visa accepted. 10 Piazza IV Novembre, Pont-St.-Martin (phone: 125-804320 or 125-804329; fax: 125-807108). Inexpensive.

En Route from Pont-St.-Martin Drive north into the beautiful Gressoney Valley on a winding 25-mile (40-km) road that leads ever higher into the mountains and closer to the towering majesty of Monte Rosa. The mountain is said to have acquired its name from its deep, rose-red color at sunset (although it probably derives from the local word for "glacier"), a sight worth seeing despite the drive down afterward in total darkness. More Swiss than Italian, valley inhabitants are descended from the Walser people, who crossed over from Switzerland during the Middle Ages and have clung tenaciously to their old customs, colorful costumes at *festa* time, and language.

GRESSONEY-ST.-JEAN Here, in the largest town in the valley, the former villa of Queen Margherita (of the Italian royal family) houses the local tourist authority (phone: 125-355185; fax: 125-355895).

BEST EN ROUTE

Il Gressoney A very modern hotel, built with considerable charm, it has a pretty covered garden in the center and spectacular views of Monte Rosa from all 27 rooms and the piano bar. There's also a dining room. Gressoney-St.-Jean (phone: 125-355986; fax: 125-356427). Expensive to moderate.

Lo Stambecco Named for the local mountain goat (ibex in English), this is an excellent place to rest and "refuel" after a long drive in the mountains. The game dishes, open fire–roasted meat, and cornmeal polenta will revive the weariest traveler. Closed Wednesdays. Reservations unnecessary. No credit cards accepted. Via Deffeyes, Gressoney-St.-Jean (phone: 125-355201). Moderate to inexpensive.

Lyskamm This 24-room hostelry is quiet and clean, with magnificent views of the surrounding countryside and a restaurant. Open mid-December through October. Gressoney-St.-Jean (phone: 125-355436; fax: 125-355917). Inexpensive.

En Route from Gressoney-St.-Jean To visit the next valley, which runs parallel to the Gressoney Valley, retrace the route to Pont-St.-Martin and then follow signs for Aosta. Near Donnas, famous for its rich, almost copper-colored wines, a yellow sign indicates the location of part of the Roman road to Gaul. (Because of the danger of falling rocks, the section of ancient road is fenced off.) Just beyond Donnas is the great fortress of *Bard*. Built in the 10th century by Ottone of Bard, it commands the narrow gorge below. Napoleon had the road covered with straw and his troop's cart wheels wrapped in sacking and then led an entire army up the gorge at night without raising the alarm of the garrison. Four miles (6 km) along the road from *Bard* a signpost marks the turnoff to *Castello di Issogne*.

CASTELLO DI ISSOGNE From the outside this unprepossessing castle seems to be nothing more than the largest building in the village. Inside it is fascinating, both historically and artistically. It was the residence of the Challont family, one of the most powerful in Valle d'Aosta, who in the 15th century created a cultured oasis here. The atrium and portico are decorated with frescoes that, because of the rarefied climate, remain almost intact. The pictures offer a charming record of local life, with scenes of butcher shops, tailors, fruit and vegetable markets, and the local pharmacy. As the exterior walls of the castle tell much about the life of the common folk of the age, so the interior tells the tale of their "betters." The noble bedrooms have attached chapels, and a room is set aside to store carpets and thick wall coverings that helped retain precious heat in the winter. Even here, in the remoteness of the Alps, protocol had to be observed—elaborate assembly halls and opulent rooms were kept just in case the noblemen had to entertain a passing Savoy duke or French king. It is open daily, March through September; open daily with a midday break, October through February; admission charge (phone: 125-929373).

En Route from Castello di Issogne Immediately beyond *Issogne* on the main highway is the village of Verrès.

VERRÈS The castle here was built by the Challonts, the same family that constructed *Castello di Issogne*. A much earlier structure, however, it was built for defense rather than gracious living. The huge cube, which measures some 90 feet along each wall, has a square courtyard and a number of large, high-ceilinged rooms. Completed in 1391, it was designed to display the power of Ibleto di Challont, the Duke of Savoy's regent in the district. It still makes a strong impression. The castle is closed Wednesdays; admission charge (phone: 125-920338).

BEST EN ROUTE

Chez Pierre The chef makes the most of good local ingredients, with outstanding selections that include mushroom and game dishes in season, homemade pâtés, delicious *agnolotti* (crescent-shaped ravioli) stuffed with a variety of fillings, and trout with almonds. The desserts are excellent, especially the *gelato di crema con zabaglione caldo* (vanilla ice cream with warm zabaglione). There also are 12 rooms. Restaurant closed Tuesdays. Reservations advised. Visa accepted. 43 Via Martorey, Verrès (phone: 125-929376; fax: 125-920404). Restaurant, expensive to moderate; hotel, moderate.

Evançon It's pleasant and quiet, with a charming garden and a small restaurant. The 20 rooms are spacious and bright, if a touch spartan. 9 Via Circonvallazione, Verrès (phone: 125-929152; fax: 125-929259). Inexpensive.

ST.-VINCENT Before entering the Valtournenche Valley, spend some time in St.-Vincent, often called the "Riviera of the Alps." Protected by the imposing bulk of Mt. Zerbion, the village has a mild climate and lush vegetation. Its curative hot springs have drawn visitors since the 18th century (for more details, see *Taking the Waters* in DIVERSIONS). It is still one of the most fashionable places in Valle d'Aosta, home to Europe's largest casino (*Casino de la Vallée;* open year-round) as well as fine hotels and a wide range of shops and restaurants.

BEST EN ROUTE

Batezar–Da Renato Small and elegant, it boasts a limited but exquisite menu and fine service. Specialties include *pazzarella* (pizza garnished with mushrooms and truffles), cannelloni, and filet of lamb with mint. Closed weekdays for lunch and Wednesdays. There are only 10 tables, so reservations are necessary. Major credit cards accepted. 1 Via Marconi, St.-Vincent (phone: 166-513164). Expensive.

Billia Set in a lovely parkland, this handsome, turn-of-the-century, 250-room hotel offers a heated pool, three tennis courts, a fitness center with a sauna, a private fishing reserve, and direct access to the hot springs. There is a fine restaurant and a passageway that leads from the hotel to a nightclub and the *Casino de la Vallée.* The whole effect is not unlike a miniature Palm Springs or Monte Carlo in the middle of the Alps. 18 Viale Piemonte, St.-Vincent (phone: 166-5231; fax: 166-523799). Expensive.

Le Grenier After having cocktails on the upper level, diners descend to the warm, rustic dining room for excellent fondues and trout. Closed Mondays for lunch and Tuesdays for dinner. Reservations advised. Major credit cards accepted. 1 Piazza Zerbion, St.-Vincent (phone: 166-512224). Expensive.

Elena Modest in size (48 rooms), extremely well run, and centrally located, this hostelry is less magnificent than the *Billia* but luxurious in its own way. No restaurant. Piazza Zerbion, St.-Vincent (phone: 166-512140; fax: 166-537459). Moderate.

La Stella Alpina A welcome change to some of the more elegant restaurants in smart St.-Vincent, this lively eatery offers homemade pasta dishes and desserts. In the late evening coproprietor Maura Sasanna often gets out her guitar and sings. Closed Tuesdays for dinner and Wednesdays. Reservations advised. Major credit cards accepted. Località Pallu-Col de Joux, St.-Vincent (phone: 166-513527). Moderate.

Posta Here are 39 rooms and an inexpensive, first rate restaurant, all efficiently managed and well staffed. Piazza XXV Aprile, St.-Vincent (phone: 166-512250; fax: 166-537093). Inexpensive.

En Route from St.-Vincent The entrance to the long, deep Valtournenche Valley is approached from Chatillon on S406, a few miles north of St.-Vincent. The Matterhorn, rising to 14,700 feet, stands at the head of this valley, with the town of Breuil-Cervinia just beneath it.

BREUIL-CERVINIA Most attempts on the mountain have been made from this base. The town had little importance as a resort until 1937, when it was linked to the outside world by the first proper roadway and a cable car. Since then intrepid climbers have had to share the neighborhood with skiers, who come in droves to enjoy the Matterhorn's long ski runs (also see *Italy's Unparalleled Skiing* in DIVERSIONS), and with non-skiers, who come merely to see the magnificent mountain and the surrounding scenery. Development of the little town, unfortunately, has been too rapid to be entirely tasteful.

BEST EN ROUTE

Cristallo Amid quiet luxury and unobstructed views of the Matterhorn and its surrounding mountains, guests are pampered by an extremely attentive staff. There are 96 rooms, an indoor pool, tennis courts, a restaurant, and a lovely garden where guests can admire the view and take the mountain air. Open December through May; July; and August. Breuil-Cervinia (phone: 166-943411; fax: 166-948377). Expensive.

Hermitage The roaring fireplace in the lobby is indicative of the cozy and friendly mountain atmosphere throughout this 36-room hotel. The restaurant's giant windows look out at the Matterhorn; it's not unusual to find the owner seated at one of the tables following with his binoculars the progress of a climb on the mountain. Amenities include a pool. Open mid-November to mid-May and early July to mid-September. Restaurant reservations advised. Major credit cards accepted. Breuil-Cervinia (phone: 166-948998; fax: 166-949032). Hotel, expensive; restaurant, moderate.

Copa Pan Casual atmosphere and local Valdostan specialties (particularly good fondues) are the draws here. Closed Mondays. Reservations unnecessary. Visa accepted. Via Jumeaux, Breuil-Cervinia (phone: 166-949140). Moderate.

Hostelerie des Guides Opened to coincide with the hundredth anniversary of the conquest of the Matterhorn, this 14-room establishment has the atmosphere of an English gentlemen's club. The lobby is a mini-museum dedicated to the feats of mountaineering; although emphasis is on the exploits of the Matterhorn guides (who have their office in the hotel), the museum also features arcana from points as diverse as Canada and Nepal. There is a fine bar (no restaurant) and a billiards room. Via J. A. Carrel, Breuil-Cervinia (phone: 166-949473; fax: 166-948824). Moderate.

En Route from Breuil-Cervinia Returning via S406 to the state highway (E21–A5, in the direction of Aosta), you pass the village of St.-Denis before reaching the 14th-century castle of *Fénis,* one of the best preserved and most picturesque in Europe. Its powerful double walls and jumble of square and cylindrical towers make the castle look virtually impregnable. Within, surrounded by loggias and galleries, is a courtyard giving access to richly decorated rooms. The frescoes adorning the various apartments have been restored to some degree; in the *State Room,* a magnificent *St. George and the Dragon* is a first class example of Gothic painting. The castle is open daily, March through September; open daily with a midday break, October through February; admission charge (phone: 165-764263).

AOSTA The capital of the region is an ancient settlement; the old town (founded by the Emperor Augustus as Augusta Praetoria) is still contained within the walls built by the Romans a hundred or so years before Christ. Among the many Roman remains are the *Arco di Augusto* (Arch of Augustus), a well-preserved theater, the *Porta Praetoria* city gate, and the restored single-arched bridge spanning the Buthier River. There are a number of imposing medieval sights as well. The town's cathedral (Piazza Giovanni XXIII) contains important Limoges enamels and reliquaries, as does the *Chiesa di Sant'Orso* (Church of St. Ursus; 14 Via Sant'Orso). The church has a magnificent cloister, on whose 40 elaborate columns are carved scenes from the life of Sant'Orso, as well as biblical and bestiary figures, although the interior of this 11th-century structure has suffered two overzealous restorations. The towers set in the city walls look as strong today as they must have been when they were built between the 12th and 13th centuries. One such tower is called the *Torre del Lebbroso,* commemorating the internment there of a lone leper for the greater part of his life. The part of the city enclosed by Roman walls has been closed to cars. Various shops stock both Italian and French products, as well as typical Valdostan handicrafts—lace, wood-carvings and stone carvings, and such local delicacies as *tegole* (almond cookies) and, for those who fancy it, *mocetta* (dried goat meat)—which are featured at the thousand-year-old *Festa di Sant'Orso* held on January 30 and 31. (For details on the festival, see *Italy's Most Colorful Festas* in DIVERSIONS.) *Note:* As Aosta is not a ski resort, restaurants close early in winter; arrive by 8 PM or reserve ahead if planning to eat later.

Hostellerie du Cheval Blanc The Vai brothers, well-known Aosta restaurateurs, are behind this new venture, a well-designed hotel with 55 rooms, a fitness center, and a heated indoor pool. The excellent (two-Michelin-star) *Petit Restaurant* is one of the finest of the region. Its several fixed menus offer sophisticated French, Italian, and local dishes, all served with flair and accompanied by fine wines. There's also a less formal brasserie. *Petit Restaurant* closed Wednesdays; brasserie open daily. Reservations advised for both. Major credit cards accepted. A 10-minute walk from the old town center, at 20 Via Clavalite, Aosta (phone: 165-239140; fax: 165-239150). Hotel and *Petit Restaurant,* expensive; brasserie, moderate.

Europe Clean and modest, it offers 71 rooms, a restaurant, excellent service, and a central location at 8 Piazza Narbonne, Aosta (phone: 165-236363; fax: 165-40566). Expensive to moderate.

Valle d'Aosta The best place to stay if you are traveling by car is less than a mile out of town (it even has a heated garage). The 104 rooms are clean, quiet, and comfortable. Its restaurant, *Le Foyer,* and bar are popular with *aostani* (closed Tuesdays; reservations advised). 146 Corso Ivrea, Aosta (phone: 165-41845; fax: 165-236660). Expensive to moderate.

Borgo Antico A bustling restaurant on two floors, it's usually filled with locals who come to sample the large variety of seafood, frogs' legs, or escargots. The pizza with fondue, wild mushrooms, and local fontina cheese is worth the wait if you've forgotten to make reservations. Closed Mondays. Reservations advised, especially on weekends. Major credit cards accepted. 143 Via Sant'Anselmo, Aosta (phone: 165-42255). Moderate.

Casale Although it is a short distance from Aosta in the hamlet of St.-Christophe, many locals willingly make a pilgrimage to this justifiably famed restaurant. Arrive hungry, as the waiters will bring you a huge array of local antipasti before you even get to the wide selection of pasta and meat courses. Closed Mondays and December. Reservations advised. Major credit cards accepted. Take the E21–A5 highway toward St.-Vincent for 3 miles (5 km), and turn left at the St.-Christophe sign. 1 Regione Condemine, St.-Christophe (phone: 165-541203). Moderate.

Valdôtaine In this typical mountain *birreria* (brasserie) with wood-paneled walls and a warm and inviting atmosphere, good local specialties such as grilled meat and sausages and Valdostan fondue are featured. Closed Thursdays. Reservations unnecessary. Visa accepted. 8 Via Xavier de Maistre, Aosta (phone: 165-235708). Moderate.

Vecchia Aosta This family-run venture has a reputation as one of the best eateries in town. The setting is a tastefully restored palazzo in the shadow of the ancient *Porta Pretoria* city gate. Try the house specialty, *trenette con sugo di* *trota* (flat pasta with trout sauce). Closed Wednesdays and two weeks in June and October. Reservations advised. Major credit cards accepted. 4 Piazza Pretoria, Aosta (phone: 165-361186). Moderate.

Il Vecchio Ristoro Housed in an old mill, one of Aosta's prettiest restaurants produces some very good fish dishes, especially trout and salmon. Closed Sundays and mid-July through August. Reservations advised. Visa accepted. 4 Via Tourneuve, Aosta (phone: 165-33238). Moderate.

Piemonte The owner/chef turns out dishes that include various home-cured hams and fresh *tagliatelle* and peppers in a *bagna caôda* (literally "hot bath") of anchovies, oil, and garlic. Closed Fridays. Reservations advised. No credit cards accepted. 13 Via Porta Pretoria, Aosta (phone: 165-40111). Moderate to inexpensive.

Turin Spotlessly clean and cheerfully run, this 51-room establishment and restaurant is in the middle of town. 14 Via Torino, Aosta (phone: 165-44593; fax: 165-361377). Inexpensive.

En Route from Aosta About 4 miles (6 km) west toward Mont-Blanc on the S26 is the sign for Cogne. Watch for the two magnificent castles visible from the turnoff. One, standing on an isolated rock, is *St.-Pierre,* the most fairy tale–like of all the Valdostan castles. The locals claim that this is the one that Walt Disney must have had in mind when he built *Disneyland.* A good time to visit is the summer, when there are archaeological exhibitions. The castle is open daily, March through September; daily with a midday break, October through February; admission charge (phone: 165-903485). Above *St.-Pierre* is the 13th-century fortress/castle of *Sarre.* This imposing building was once used as a hunting lodge by the Savoy family, a fact attested to by the enormous number of hunting trophies on display. *Sarre* is open only in the summer and has no fixed hours (no phone). Nearby, also on the road to Cogne, is the four-towered castle of *Aymaville,* dating from the mid-15th century. It, too, is only open in the summer, with no fixed hours (no phone).

COGNE A mountain village known for lace making and woodcarving, Cogne is the gateway to *Parco Nazionale del Gran Paradiso.* Founded in 1922, it is the best-preserved alpine nature reserve in the world. Its flora and fauna are representative of the Alps in general: Edelweiss, gentian, artemisia, and juniper grow in profusion or can be seen at the *Giardino Alpino* in the park itself. The chamois and the ibex—once threatened by extinction—are now quite plentiful here, as are the fox, hare, marmot, and stoat. The rarest alpine birds, notably the eagle, owl, and imperial raven, are occasionally visible. While hunting and scavenging are strictly forbidden in the park (fines are as high as $80,000!), hiking is encouraged. For more details, see *Take a Hike: Walking Through Italy* in DIVERSIONS. In winter there are some

40 miles (64 km) of cross-country skiing trails around Cogne. The park is open year-round. Cogne's tourist office is at Piazza E. Chanoux (phone: 165-74040; fax: 165-749125).

BEST EN ROUTE

Lou Ressignon Just beyond Cogne on the main road is a family-run restaurant that dispenses good local food. Chamois, served either as an hors d'oeuvre or as a main course, delicious polenta, an extremely filling *soupe à la cogneintze* (rice and bread soup), and veal *carbonada* (marinated in red wine) are specialties. Closed Mondays for dinner, Tuesdays, and the last two weeks of June and September. Reservations unnecessary. Major credit cards accepted. 81 Via Bourgeois, Cogne (phone: 165-74034). Moderate.

Brasserie du Bon Bec At Cogne's most popular restaurant the staff, attired in traditional costume, loads tables with homemade regional specialties, including a fine version of the traditional *fonduta* (cheese fondue) and some mouth-watering desserts. Closed Mondays. Reservations necessary. No credit cards accepted. 68 Via Bourgeois, Cogne (phone: 165-749288). Moderate to inexpensive.

Mont Blanc Centrally located, this modern, clean, and comfortable 22-room hostelry has a good restaurant that turns out well-cooked local specialties. In high season (*Christmas, Easter,* July, and August) guests are required to take full or half board. 18 Via Gran Paradiso, Cogne (phone: 165-74211; fax: 165-749293). Moderate to inexpensive.

Notre Maison The restaurant attached to this 12-room hotel is a local favorite. Try the juniper-smoked trout caught nearby. Restaurant closed Mondays. Reservations advised. Major credit cards accepted. Frazione Cretaz, Cogne (phone: 165-74104; fax: 165-749186). Moderate to inexpensive.

Sant'Orso Popular with skiers in winter and hikers in summer, this modern 30-room hotel is conveniently located close to the town's main piazza, but most guestrooms have views of the national park. There is a sauna and solarium. Half board required. 2 Via Bourgeois, Cogne (phone/fax: 165-74821). Moderate to inexpensive.

En Route from Cogne Return along S507 to St.-Pierre and rejoin the S26 to Courmayeur.

COURMAYEUR Courmayeur was not popular as a resort until the British discovered it in the late 18th century. These prototypical alpinists came for the fine air, the beautiful views, and the excellent climbing and skiing on the slopes of Mont-Blanc (conquered in 1786) and environs (for more information, see *Italy's Unparalleled Skiing* in DIVERSIONS). The town gained importance—and many more visitors—with the 1965 opening of the Mont-

Blanc Tunnel. Today it is an elegant resort, the equivalent of Gstaad or Klosters in Switzerland. But unlike other winter vacation spots, here the sheltering effect of Mont-Blanc makes the summer climate far more agreeable than that of Chamonix on the other side of the border, so there is also an active season for walkers, hikers, and those who come just to take the air, as well as for summer skiers. One of the most exciting cable car journeys in the Alps is that from La Palud, just 2 miles (3 km) away, over the Mont-Blanc massif, with views of the "sea of glaciers" that wend their way down the sides of the mountain. The highest point on the ride to Punta Helbronner is about 11,000 feet, easily worth the price of the round-trip ticket for the breathtaking panoramic view of the entire Chamonix Valley.

Courmayeur attracts the sorts of vacationers that make it worthwhile for the best Roman, Milanese, and international retailers to keep permanent branches here, so the shopping is excellent. Especially on Via Roma, such names as *Cartier, Trussardi, Valentino, Fendi,* and *Armani* are found. In the center of town is the *Museo Duca degli Abruzzi,* one of the best mountaineering museums in Europe. It is closed Mondays and for a long midday break; admission charge (phone: 165-842064). There are many high-decibel discotheques and a simpatico watering hole called the *American Bar* (Via Roma).

BEST EN ROUTE

Most hotels close for extended periods twice a year, from after *Easter* through June and from late September to early December. Call ahead for dates.

Royal e Golf A sleek, modern 89-room place with a good restaurant, it's set in a lovely garden with beautiful views of the mountains and glaciers. Guests can swim in the heated pool and purchase ski lift passes here. 81-83 Via Roma, Courmayeur (phone: 165-846787; fax: 165-842093). Very expensive.

Des Alpes Popular with skiers in winter and hikers in summer, this modern 62-room hotel is geared to the sports-minded. It is about 200 yards from the slopes, close to the main Val Veny ski lift and the ski school. There is a restaurant. Strada Statale, Courmayeur (phone: 165-89981; fax: 165-89983). Expensive.

Les Jumeaux One of Courmayeur's chicest hotels is the perfect place for the dedicated skier—the cable car is nearby. In addition to 86 rooms and a restaurant, there is a sauna and fitness center. 35 Strada Regionale, Courmayeur (phone: 165-846796; fax: 165-844122). Expensive.

Palace Bron Situated in a pine forest, overlooking Courmayeur proper with a spectacular view of the mountains beyond, this is a delightful place for people who prefer not to be in the town itself. Its small size (27 rooms), fine service, and restaurant make it a prized find. 41 Via Plan Gorret, Courmayeur (phone: 165-846742; fax: 165-844015). Expensive.

Pavillon A member of the prestigious Relais & Châteaux group, this fine establishment has 50 rooms and suites, all boasting balconies with stupendous views. Beautifully situated, it is only two minutes from a ski lift, with a covered, heated pool, a lovely solarium, and a sauna. The superb restaurant, *Le Bistroquet*, is known for its delicious local delicacies, such as *bagna caôda* (a hot dipping sauce for vegetables that sometimes contains the local thistle); a wide range of fondues; excellent pasta and risotto; and fine cuts of meat, grilled to perfection. There also is a relaxing bar for après-ski. Restaurant closed Mondays and for lunch. Reservations advised. Major credit cards accepted. 60-62 Via Regionale, Courmayeur (phone: 165-846120; fax: 165-846122). Expensive.

Le Relais du Mont Blanc The menu changes daily in this large, busy restaurant according to the season and the whims of the very capable chef. Always available is a variety of classic Valle d'Aosta dishes, as well as some good fresh fish (surprising, since Courmayeur is far from the sea). Save room for the excellent cheese board, with its selection of local mountain cheeses and Italian favorites. Closed Tuesdays, June, and November. Reservations advised. Visa accepted. 26 Strada Statale, Courmayeur (phone: 165-846777). Expensive.

Cadran Solaire A serious rival to *Le Bistroquet* for the title of best area restaurant, this place—exquisitely decorated with stone arches and wooden floors— is smack in the middle of town. Try the locally raised roast duck and the numerous delicate starters. Excellent service and value. Closed Mondays. Reservations advised. Major credit cards accepted. 122 Via Roma, Courmayeur (phone: 165-844609). Expensive to moderate.

Brenva Built in 1897 as a place for mountaineers to rest their weary limbs after attempts on Monte Bianco, this 14-room, Old World–style hotel is in the picturesque village of Entrèves. The restaurant attracts many a diner from Courmayeur proper, 2 miles (3 km) up the road. Entrèves (phone: 165-869780; fax: 165-869726). Moderate.

La Maison de Filippo In what is known as the "most famous restaurant in the Alps," the prix fixe meal includes an incredible number of courses—dozens of appetizers make up the bulk of the menu. The restaurant is rustic and intimate, with outdoor dining in the summer. Closed Tuesdays, May, and November. Reservations necessary. Major credit cards accepted. There is also a very popular pensione with six inexpensive rooms. North of Courmayeur in Entrèves (phone: 165-89968). Moderate.

Pierre Alexis This bustling place has a downstairs room with an attractive balcony. The good prix fixe menu may include such dishes as risotto with *porcini* mushrooms, *vitello alla carbonada* (veal cooked in a tangy wine sauce), or braised chamois. Closed Mondays, October, and November. Reservations advised. Major credit cards accepted. 54 Via Marconi, Courmayeur (phone: 165-843517). Moderate.

Vacherie A few miles south of Courmayeur on the state highway between Morgex and Pré-St.-Didier, this restaurant specializes in seafood, a nice change of pace for the region. The ground floor holds an expansive bar with an open fireplace, a charming place to sit before or after dinner. Closed Wednesdays. Reservations advised. Major credit cards accepted. Mont Bardon (phone: 165-809209). Moderate.

Moulin Small and friendly, this restaurant is in Entrèves. Try the homemade *agnolotti* (pasta triangles) stuffed with *porcini* mushrooms. The chef also produces a good *carbonada* (ragout of veal in a piquant wine sauce). At the end of the meal grappa lovers can sample from the patron's vast selection. Closed Wednesdays. Reservations advised. No credit cards accepted. 6 Via Colle del Gigante, Entrèves (phone: 165-89636). Moderate to inexpensive.

Dolonne Housed in a tastefully remodeled 17th-century house are 26 spacious and comfortably furnished rooms. A nearby cableway gives immediate access to the ski slopes of Val Veny. Breakfast only. 62 Via delle Vittorie, Courmayeur-Dolonne (phone: 165-846671). Inexpensive.

En Route from Courmayeur A few miles along S26 toward the Little St. Bernard Pass is La Thuile.

LA THUILE From this small resort town ski lifts link directly with the La Rosière–Montvalenza resort area in France.

BEST EN ROUTE

Planibel This vast hotel complex, which accommodates the bulk of the skiers who come to La Thuile, has a skating rink, squash courts, restaurants, pubs, pizzerias, and a complete range of shops, including a supermarket. (Some of the 338 rooms have cooking facilities.) Very much a "fun for the whole family" kind of place, it's open year-round. La Thuile (phone: 165-884541; fax: 165-884535). Expensive.

La Bricole Lively atmosphere and very good food make this a favorite with residents of La Thuile. Closed Mondays, May, June, and September through November. Reservations advised. Visa accepted. Frazione Entrèves, La Thuile (phone: 165-884149). Moderate.

En Route from La Thuile If it's summer, drive through the Little St. Bernard Pass (it's closed in winter) to Bourg St.-Maurice in France, and then descend the beautiful Val d'Isère. Reenter Italy at the Colle di Liseran, in the Piedmont section of *Parco Nazionale del Gran Paradiso*. At San Giorgio, just outside Ivrea, rejoin the Turin-Aosta autostrada (A5), which connects with highways leading to Milan and Genoa.

The Lombardy Lakes (including Lugano, Switzerland)

The Italian lakes have been a playground since the Romans conquered Gaul and Cicero set up a summer house on Lake Como. So magical is the scenery of the Italian lake district that Leonardo chose it for the background of the *Mona Lisa,* Hemingway made it a setting in *A Farewell to Arms,* and Liszt composed music in response to its natural beauty. Poets have called the lakes Italy's sapphire necklace. They are in the far north of Italy, in the region of Lombardy, although they also touch the region of Piedmont to the west and the Veneto and Trentino–Alto Adige regions to the east. South of them is the rest of Lombardy, and to the north is Switzerland, into whose territory the topmost segment of Lake Maggiore projects. The lakes are long crevices that glaciers carved into the Alpine arc that crosses Italy's far north, where lemon and olive groves and vineyards are cut into the rock on steep terraces. Dolomitic cliffs seem to hang over the lake villages that hug the water's edge, and for half the year, a mantle of snow covers the peaks that soar up to 8,000 feet high. Moving south, the foothills allow space for more vineyards and for the elegant, centuries-old gardens of the villas.

The mood and character of each lake differs significantly, as seen in the marked contrasts among the fine aristocratic bearing of Stresa (Lake Maggiore's chief city, whose attractions have been seriously eroded by relentless heavy traffic along the lake shore) and its famed trio of islets (the Isole Borromee), the charm and intimacy of Lake Orta, the dreaminess of Lake Como, the more rugged scenery around Lake Iseo, and the magnificent mountain countryside surrounding the highly sophisticated and developed Lake Garda, with its network of delightful towns.

Lombardy's 3,000-year history has been scarred by war and domination, but the turbulent past left a splendid heritage of crenelated castles, fortresses, and towers in ancient cities and hill towns throughout the region. There are Stone Age sites in the Val Camonica, where early peoples etched on stone slabs religious symbols and pictures of animals and of men brandishing weapons. Among the vestiges of imperial Rome is the villa at the little town of Desenzano, at the foot of Lake Garda, whose famed mosaics show cupids making wine. In the medieval and Renaissance cities nearby— Cremona, Mantua, and Brescia—where nobles entertained lavishly at their courts, richly decorated cathedrals and palazzi and delightful piazze tempt the visitor to linger.

The mountain passes made the area tempting to invaders. The Gauls descended from the north through the Alps in the first half of the first millennium before Christ. In the 4th century BC, the Etruscans came from Tuscany, in the south to settle in the fertile Lombard plain, just south of the lake district. They were later defeated and subjugated by the Romans. In the 6th century, the Lombards (a Germanic tribe that left the region its name) ousted the Romans and successfully occupied the broad plain of the Po Valley, just south of the lakes. After their departure, Charlemagne, the Bishops of Milan, the Holy Roman Emperor Otto I, sundry feudal lords, and some independent city-states, or communes, all laid claim to some part of Lombardy at some time. In the 12th century, the Holy Roman Emperor Frederick I was defeated by the Lombard League, a group formed by various communes that had joined forces. But Lombardy's newfound freedom was brief: Foreign domination was replaced by civil strife, and the territory was carved up among the powerful families whose names—Visconti, Sforza, Pallavicino, and Gonzaga, among others—are remembered today in the wealth of beautiful villas, castles, and works of art they built or acquired during this early Renaissance period.

At the beginning of the 15th century, the powerful Republic of Venice moved into the eastern part of the region, annexing Bergamo and Brescia, among other areas. The Venetians were followed by a wave of foreign invaders who penetrated farther afield: first the French, in the 16th century, then the Spanish, who stayed for 200 years, and finally the Austrian Hapsburgs. Apart from a brief hiatus under Napoleon in the early 19th century, Lombardy remained under Austrian control until 1859, when an allied French and Piedmontese victory finally ousted them. Lombardy thus became part of the independent kingdom of Italy just a year before Garibaldi and his "Thousand" achieved unification for most of the rest of the peninsula.

Visitors to Italy and to Lombardy sometimes neglect the lakes in favor of towns with more established traditions as cultural and artistic capitals. But within the lake region itself are numerous fine cities whose architecture, museums, and monuments are wonderfully rich. The region has the bonus of a breathtaking natural landscape with clear air, piercingly blue water that usually is safe for swimming, and miles of glorious rolling hills, woods, and mountains to be explored or simply admired. This is an area endowed with all the natural beauty of Switzerland, combined with the unmistakable warmth of the Italian people.

Lombardy also is a fertile and prosperous region. Its cooking reflects the richness of the soil and the relative wealth of its people, including wild game such as boar, berries and mushrooms from the dense forests, and prized fish from the lakes—trout, perch, and *coregone* (a small delicate fish with shrimp-colored flesh), all prepared with skill and sophistication. Rice and cornmeal polenta are staples. Mantua is known for its *tortelli di zucca* (pasta stuffed with pumpkin and almonds), Varese for its risotto, and Brescia for its *casonsei* (ravioli stuffed with vegetables). In Cremona, renowned for its delicate veal dishes, try the *marubini,* the local ravioli served in broth or with a sauce. The area appeals to wine buffs: Lake Como has damaso, and the town of Bardolino, which lends its name to the prized wine, is on the eastern shores of Garda. The wines of the Franciacorta zone include some first class sparkling whites.

Many of the fine villas around the lakes, especially those at Maggiore and Como, have magnificent gardens, so visitors in late April, May, or June will be rewarded with the spectacle of a riot of colors and scents. July and August attract huge crowds, and though October brings some days of rain, there is often sunshine with an autumnal glow. On Lake Garda, the peculiarly Mediterranean climate makes both spring and fall attractive times. But to take advantage of all that the lakes have to offer, the summer is best. Most lakeside hotels and many restaurants close from November to *Easter*.

The route outlined here heads northwest from Milan, Lombardy's capital, to Varese. It then proceeds west to Lake Maggiore and, taking a short detour west to Lake Orta, cuts east to explore Lake Lugano and a bit of its Swiss surroundings before arriving at Lake Como, of the distinctive upside-down "Y" shape. From here, the route continues eastward to the ancient hill town of Bergamo, to the smaller, lesser-known Lake Iseo, and to the historic city of Brescia. It ends still farther east, with a circle around Lake Garda, the largest and best-known of the Lombardy lakes, and then stops at lovely Mantua and Cremona. Both are small, diverse cities whose wealth permitted great patronage of the arts over many centuries, as testified to by their splendor today.

Some of the world's finest hotels are found here, and a tour of the area would be incomplete without the magical experience of spending at least a night in an aristocratic villa on the lakeshore, although travelers who savor the very grand will pay for it. Prices for a double room at the palatial *Villa d'Este* on Lake Como *begin* at $500 a night; expect to pay $350 or more at other hotels listed as very expensive. An expensive hotel will cost from $250 to $350; moderate, from $150 to $250; and inexpensive, $150 or less. All hotels feature private baths unless otherwise indicated. At an expensive restaurant, dinner for two will cost $120 or more; at a moderate place, from $70 to $120; and in an inexpensive one, $70 or less. Prices include house wine. All restaurants are open for lunch and dinner unless otherwise noted. For each location, hotels and restaurants are listed alphabetically by price category.

Note that many sites of interest in the Lombardy Lakes region close for a midday break, usually from noon or 12:30 PM to 2 or 3 PM; we suggest calling ahead to check exact hours.

MILAN For a detailed report on the city, its sights, its hotels, and its restaurants, see *Milan* in THE CITIES.

En Route from Milan Take S233 northwest for 32 miles (51 km) to Varese.

VARESE This prosperous commercial center is known for its production of shoes and for its macaroons and liqueur. During the Middle Ages, Varese was a feudal town that belonged to the Bishops of Milan, then to the Visconti and Este families. The town's most striking monument is the 254-foot-high bell tower of the *Basilica di San Vittore* (Piazza del Podestà), designed by Varese architect Giuseppe Bernascone in the early 17th century. At the foot of the tower stands Varese's most ancient building, the Romanesque 12th-century *Battistero di San Giovanni,* which contains some interesting 14th- and 15th-century frescoes. Worth a visit is the *Palazzo Estense* (Via Sacco), built in the 18th century as the summer home of Francesco III d'Este, Duke of Modena and Lord of Varese. Today the palace is used as the *Town Hall,* but its splendid classical Italian Renaissance garden is open daily to the public.

About 5 miles (8 km) outside town is the Sacro Monte (Sacred Mountain), for centuries a focal point for pilgrims. Follow the signs for Sant'Ambrogio on the road leading northwest out of Varese. From the *Prima Cappella* (First Chapel), a footpath leads past 14 shrines to the rococo *Santa Maria del Monte* sanctuary. The shrines, designed by Bernascone in the early 17th century, contain frescoes and life-size terra cotta statues depicting the mysteries of the rosary. (Those in the tenth chapel—representing the Crucifixion—are by Dionigi Bussola.)

BEST EN ROUTE

Lago Maggiore Excellent Lombard food is served at this small, popular restaurant in the historic center. There is a good selection of wines. Closed Sundays, Monday lunch, the first two weeks in July, and *Christmas.* Reservations advised. Major credit cards accepted. 19 Via Carrobbio, Varese (phone: 332-231183). Expensive.

Palace Built at the beginning of this century in Art Nouveau style, this 108-room hotel is magnificently set in its own parkland in the hills overlooking Varese. Spectacular views of the lake and Monte Rosa, Old World comfort, occasional classical concerts on the grounds, a good restaurant, tennis courts, and a pool make this an excellent choice. Open year-round. 11 Via Manara, Varese (phone: 332-312600; fax: 332-312870). Expensive.

Teatro At Angelo Mario Mogavero's sophisticated establishment, diners enjoy delicious, imaginative dishes and superb service. The restaurant was once the refreshment area of the *Teatro di Varese.* Although still housed in the same building, it is now an entity unto itself, and the theater's history is inscribed on the walls. Closed Tuesdays and July 23 to August 25. Reservations advised. Major credit cards accepted. 3 Via C. Croce, Varese (phone: 332-241124). Inexpensive.

En Route from Varese Follow signs for Vergiate and Sesto Calende on the road leading southwest out of town to the old Roman market town of Sesto Calende (about 16 miles/26 km from Varese), passing over the bridge that spans the Ticino River. Ahead lies Lake Maggiore, with magnificent mountains in the background. Follow the road (S33) up the western side (the Piedmont side) of the lake to Arona. The road proceeds northward through some of the loveliest scenery on Lake Maggiore, with villa after villa perched on the left, some with spectacular gardens. At La Sacca, just before Stresa (15½ miles/25 km from Sesto Calende), the remarkable *Santa Caterina del Sasso,* a 13th-century Carmelite convent built into the sheer cliff face, can be glimpsed across the water.

A worthwhile side trip is to head west about 7½ miles (12 km) on S394 from Varese to Gavirate, where *brutti e buoni* (macaroons) are the local delicacy. Then visit the *Museo delle Pipe* (Pipe Museum; 1 Via del Chiostra; phone: 332-743334), a private collection of over 20,000 pipes gathered from all over the world. Closed Sundays; no admission charge. At nearby Voltorre is the *Chiesa di San Michele*'s Romanesque cloister, a jewel dating from the 11th to 12th century.

STRESA Surrounded by mountains and facing the three Isole Borromee (Borromean Islands), one of the area's main attractions, this town enjoys a superb position on Lake Maggiore, despite the endless stream of traffic and a slightly tawdry tourist atmosphere. This is the town where Ernest Hemingway's protagonist stayed in *A Farewell to Arms* before escaping by rowboat on the lake into Switzerland. The *Grand Hotel des Iles Borromées,* described in the novel, still dominates the waterfront (see *Best en Route*). Two giant cedars of Lebanon, illuminated at night, stand guard just outside the town. At the entrance to Stresa (coming up from Arona) is the privately owned *Villa Pallavicino,* whose splendid gardens are closed November through *Easter*; admission charge (phone: 323-31533).

Boats for the Isole Borromee—Isola Madre (Mother Island), Isola Bella (Beautiful Island, but also a variation of the name Isabella), and Isola dei Pescatori (Fishermen's Island)—leave frequently from the landing stage. Take the public *traghetto* (ferry); the small, private boats can be expensive. Information about the *traghetto* can be obtained at the landing on the waterfront.

The islands are named after the Borromeo family, one of the greatest among the Italian aristocracy, and, except for the Isola dei Pescatori, they still belong to the family, as do the fishing rights to the lake. Isola Bella, the closest island to Stresa, is all but taken up by the 17th-century *Palazzo Borromeo*, built by Count Charles III Borromeo for his wife, Isabella (thus the name of the island). The terraced gardens of the palace are closed from late October through late March, and for a short (noon to 1:30 PM) break; admission charge (phone: 323-30556). Try not to let the tacky souvenir stands discourage you; once you're inside the palace grounds, the view improves perceptibly. Have lunch at *Delfino* (on the waterfront; phone: 323-30473), one of the oldest trattorie on the lake.

A real fishing village, the Isola dei Pescatori is full of narrow cobbled alleys and contented cats. The popular *Ristorante Italia* (on the waterfront, near the landing; phone: 323-30456) is a good place to stop for a meal on the island. Isola Madre, the largest of the group, has the most spectacular gardens, especially in May, when the azaleas are in bloom. The gardens and the 18th-century palace, where a puppet theater is on display, are closed from late October through late March, and for a short (noon to 1:30 PM) break; admission charge (phone: 323-31261). There also is an excellent trattoria, *La Piratera* (see *Best en Route*).

Each year, from mid-August to mid-September, Stresa holds an international music festival, the *Settimane Musicali di Stresa* (Stresa Musical Weeks), which offers three to four weeks of symphony and chamber concerts with world-famous soloists, as well as performances by young winners of international competitions. The concerts regularly take place at the *Palazzo Borromeo* on Isola Bella and other locations.

BEST EN ROUTE

Grand Hotel des Iles Borromées Built in 1862, this lakefront deluxe hotel opened up the whole area to tourism. Its charm today, however, is much reduced by the very noisy road that divides it from the lake. There are 130 rooms and suites, as well as an annex with 20 studio rooms and mini-apartments that are rented by the week or month in the summer. There are a private beach on the lake, two heated outdoor pools, tennis courts, a bar, and a restaurant. Open year-round. 67 Corso Umberto I, Stresa (phone: 323-30431; fax: 323-32405). Very expensive.

Emiliano This eatery's imaginative culinary repertoire has earned it a reputation as the best in town. Meals start with small samples of appetizers. The fresh local produce and the desserts are particularly good. Closed Tuesdays and mid-November to mid-December. Reservations necessary. Major credit cards accepted. 52 Lungolago Italia, Stresa (phone: 323-31396). Expensive.

Regina Palace Built in the 1890s, this grand, 150-room lakeside hotel (also affected by the traffic noise) has gardens, a fitness center, tennis, squash, and the *Charleston* restaurant. Open April through December. Corso Umberto I, Stresa (phone: 323-31160; fax: 323-30176). Expensive.

Elvezia Traditional lake dishes, including risotto *con pesce* (with fish) and grilled fish, are served at this charming inn. There also are a few guestrooms. Closed November through March. Reservations necessary on weekends. Major credit cards accepted. 18 Lungolago Vittorio Emanuele, Isola Bella (phone: 323-30043). Moderate.

La Piratera Dine alfresco at the edge of Lake Maggiore or indoors at this rustic island hideaway on such robust fare as spaghetti *alla Piratera* (with hot red peppers and tomato sauce) and lake fish; traditional meat dishes are also available. Closed November through February. Reservations advised. No credit cards accepted. Isola Madre (phone: 323-31171). Moderate to inexpensive.

ORTA SAN GIULIO Before continuing to explore Lake Maggiore, take a short detour west for 9½ miles (15 km) to Lake Orta. S56 leads up close to the peak of *Mt. Mottarone,* a small popular ski resort with superb views, then down to the lake itself. Much smaller than Lake Maggiore, Orta is encircled by hills and mountains that give it an intimate and protected air. Charming towns circle the lake, all easily reached by road. Narrow cobbled streets lead to the town square of Orta San Giulio, which is on the lake. Once there, sip an *aperitivo* at a *caffè* while enjoying the frescoed buildings; the *Palazzo Comunale* (built in 1582), a fairy tale–like town hall; and the splendid lake view. In April and May, Orta's gardens are illuminated as part of its annual flower festival. Sacro Monte (a hill dedicated to St. Francis of Assisi) overlooks the town. Twenty chapels were built here from 1591 to 1770; they contain almost life-size terra cotta statues set in tableaux. The island of San Giulio has a 12th-century Romanesque basilica in its center, surrounded by small villas. Regular ferries leave Orta San Giulio for the island; the more adventurous can hire rowboats. Every June, the town hosts a 10-day festival of ancient music, and in September there is a series of classical concerts. For information, contact the tourist office (9-11 Via Olina; phone: 322-911937; fax: 322-905678).

BEST EN ROUTE

Villa Crespi This exotic Moorish folly with a minaret tower, built by a 19th-century cotton magnate, has been recently restored and is now a luxury hotel. There are only eight suites and six bedrooms, plus a restaurant, a sauna, and a fitness center. Open year-round. 8/10 Via C. Fava, Orta San Giulio (phone: 322-911902; fax: 322-911919). Very expensive.

San Rocco A luxurious 75-room hotel, it's the perfect place to idle summer days away. Ask for the more charming older rooms or one of the deluxe guestrooms. The pool and terrace restaurant seem to float on the lake. There is a tennis court, a fitness center, a bar, and private parking. Open year-round. 11 Via Gippini, Orta San Giulio (phone: 322-905632; fax: 322-905635). Expensive.

Orta The somewhat elaborate 19th-century façade of this 36-room property conceals what is actually a simple, family-run hostelry. There is a good traditional restaurant and a bar on the lake. Open mid-March through October. 1 Piazza Motta, Orta San Giulio (phone: 322-90253; fax: 322-905646). Moderate to inexpensive.

San Giulio A large informal restaurant on the lake, it offers indoor and alfresco dining. Fresh lake fish is the specialty, but the pizza and gelato are also worth trying. Closed Mondays and November through December. Reservations advised. Major credit cards accepted. 4 Via Basilica, Orta San Giulio (phone: 322-90234). Inexpensive.

En Route from Stresa The lakeside road (S33) runs north for 12½ miles (20 km) to Verbania (the Roman name for Lake Maggiore was "Lacus Verbanus," from the plant that grows abundantly on its shores, and even today the lake is sometimes called Lake Verbano), which includes the two villages of Pallanza and Intra. Pallanza is renowned for its botanical gardens at *Villa Taranto*. The gardens are closed November through March; admission charge (phone: 323-440555). Fed by Alpine snows, the Ticino River flows into the lake at this northern point. The river lies in a narrow valley, now a natural park. Horses can be rented for guided tours; for information, contact *Centro Ippico Galliatese La Soliva* (3 Via Porto Vecchio Galliate; phone: 321-862047) or *Centro Ippico La Picchetta* (Via Picchetta, Cameri; phone: 321-518998). From here, it is possible to follow the lakeside road (now S34) all the way up to the Swiss town of Locarno (about 24 miles/38 km from Verbania) and return via the lakeside road (S394) along the eastern shore to Laveno (33 miles/53 km beyond Locarno). It is also possible to explore the upper part of the lake by boat. A steamer from Arona to Locarno can be boarded at various interim points, including Stresa and Intra. Or cross directly to the eastern shore of the lake, using the car ferry that leaves Intra every few minutes for the 20-minute ride to Laveno. Obtain information, tickets, and boat timetables from the *Navigazione sul Lago Maggiore* offices at the various landing stages, or contact the head office in Avona (phone: 322-46651; fax: 322-249530).

LAVENO On the Lombardy side (eastern shore) of Lake Maggiore is this picturesque port with a harborfront of warm ocher buildings. A resort town, it is also known for its ceramics factories. Take the cable car that runs from Laveno almost to the summit of the Sasso del Ferro; it stops at Poggio Sant'Elsa and is worth the ride for the superb panorama over the lake and the mountains. Just short of 2 miles (3 km) south of town, in the fishing village of Cerro, a ceramics museum is housed in the 15th-century *Palazzo Guilizzoni-Perabò* (5 Lungolago; phone: 332-666530), whose courtyard is used for concerts in summer. The museum is closed Mondays; Tuesdays through Thursdays until 2:30 PM; and Friday, Saturday, and Sunday afternoons; admission charge.

BEST EN ROUTE

Bellevue As its name suggests, this hotel/restaurant affords its guests splendid views of the lake and the port of Laveno. The chef is a specialist in cooking lake fish; try the *salmerino al pepe rosa* (salmon trout in pink pepper sauce). Also heavenly are the *ravioli ripieni di pesce del lago* (homemade ravioli stuffed with fish). There also are a few guestrooms. The hotel is closed for two weeks in late January; the restaurant is closed Wednesday lunch in summer and all day Wednesday the rest of the year. 40 Via Fortino, Laveno (phone: 332-667257; fax: 332-666753). Expensive to moderate.

En Route from Laveno Luino is 10 miles (16 km) north of Laveno on S394 along Lake Maggiore's eastern shore. For those with time to spare, however, it's a very pleasant drive south from Laveno along the lakeside, passing through Cerro and continuing to Ispra (about 9½ miles/15 km south of Laveno), where you'll spot the *Santa Caterina del Sasso,* the 13th-century Carmelite convent built into a cliff. After Ispra, take a right turn to the enchanting village of Ranco, an idyllic spot with the bonus of the excellent *Il Sole* restaurant (see *Best en Route*). The road continues south 4½ miles (7 km) to the *Rocca in Angera,* a fortress owned by the noble Borromeo family, which now houses an important doll collection. The fortress is closed November to late March, and for a midday break; admission charge (phone: 331-931300).

Return to Laveno and turn right (east) onto S394 toward Cittiglio. Beyond Cittiglio, turn left into the hills at Casalzuigno, and head toward Arcumeggia, an ancient village nestled in the woods and remarkable for the frescoes painted on the outside of its houses, all by contemporary artists. Continue through the hills to Sant'Antonio, which affords a marvelous view of Lake Maggiore and the Alps, and then down to Nasca. Once back on the lake, turn right onto S394 toward Castelveccana and continue north 5 miles (8 km) to Luino. (The detour from Laveno to Castelveccana is about 14 miles/24 km.)

BEST EN ROUTE

Il Sole This restaurant is regarded by many as among the top ten dining spots in Italy. For more information, see *The Best Restaurants of Italy* in DIVERSIONS. Closed Monday dinner and Tuesdays. Reservations necessary. Major credit cards accepted. There also are nine miniature apartments next door, each beautifully decorated in modern style. Hotel closed January through early February. 5 Piazza Venezia, Ranco (phone: 331-976507; fax: 331-976620). Expensive.

LUINO Originally a fishing village, this attractive town sits at the mouth of the Tresa River, which connects Lakes Maggiore and Luino. Luino flourished during the 19th century as a textile manufacturing center that was run mostly by Swiss proprietors (it's only a few miles from the border). Today most of the textile mills have closed, and many townspeople make the daily trip over the border to work in Swiss chocolate and watchmaking factories and to fill up on Swiss gasoline—it's 25% less expensive than in Italy. The town's long promenade along the lake is especially lovely in spring. The more-than-200-year-old Wednesday market on the streets around the lake has some 900 stalls offering a variety of goods and draws bargain hunters from miles around.

BEST EN ROUTE

Camin Staying in one of the 13 rooms at this attractive hotel in a former lakeside villa is like being a guest at a 19th-century nobleman's country residence; beautiful gardens add to the illusion. It's known for exceptional service, and the restaurant—the finest in the area—offers such specialties as *gnocchi Camin* (red, white, and green gnocchi with tomato and ham in a cream sauce) and a mouth-watering *carré d'agnello alle erbe aromatiche* (lamb roasted with herbs). Closed Tuesdays, except in the summer. 35 Viale Dante, Luino (phone: 332-530118; fax: 332-537226). Hotel, expensive to moderate; restaurant, moderate.

Le Due Scale On the lakefront, this eatery has a cloistered courtyard for outdoor dining in summer. The prix fixe menus are a good value. Closed Fridays, except in the summer, and December. No reservations. Major credit cards accepted. 30 Piazza della Libertà, Luino (phone: 332-530396). Moderate.

I Tre Re Patrons are invited to select their own trout at this dining spot housed in an attractive old building. There also are local delicacies such as *prosciutto di cervo* (cured venison) and *salame di cinghiale* (salami made from wild boar). Closed Mondays, two weeks in January, and two weeks in September. No reservations. No credit cards accepted. 29 Via Manzoni, Luino (phone: 332-531147). Moderate to inexpensive.

En Route from Luino Take the road marked Fornasette, which climbs out of Luino through some lovely mountain pasture, crosses over the Swiss border, and leads into the town of Ponte Tresa (about 7½ miles/12 km from Luino), remarkable in that half of it is in Switzerland and half in Italy. Then turn northward and head almost 7 miles (11 km) along Strada Cantonale 23 to Lugano.

LUGANO The main city of Ticino, Switzerland's Italian-speaking canton, Lugano lies on the border of Italy's lake district, and it seems as Italian as it is Swiss. It has some of both countries—Swiss efficiency and tidy building façades, and the energy and vitality typical of the Italian north. Lugano is an elegant resort with a beautiful lakefront on the body of water from which it takes its name. Across the water lies the tiny enclave of Campione d'Italia, a bit of Italian soil entirely surrounded by Swiss territory—it even uses Swiss currency and the Swiss postal and telephone systems. Campione, best known for its casino (one of only four legal ones in Italy), can be reached by boat from Lugano or by road by the bridge at Melide, south of Lugano. While in Lugano, try the splendid *Da Bianchi* restaurant (3 Via Pessina; phone: 91-228479 in Switzerland), which is closed Sundays.

A visit to *Villa Favorita* (on the outskirts of Lugano at Castagnola) is well worth the trip. Owned by Baron Thyssen-Bornemisza, the 17th-century villa contains his private art gallery. The villa's Old Masters now are in the *Palacio de Villahermosa,* an annex of Madrid's *Prado Museum,* but the collection of 19th- and 20th-century paintings and watercolors on display is worthwhile in itself. The villa is closed Mondays through Thursdays April through June; closed Mondays July through October; closed November through March. Hours vary, so call ahead; admission charge (phone: 91-516152 in Switzerland). The villa can be reached by cab, bus, or boat from the main landing stage.

En Route from Lugano The lakeside road leading northeast out of Lugano (S340) is spellbinding, with calm blue water to the right and mountains and tiny perched villages to the left. It crosses the border back into Italy just before the town of Oria and hugs the shore as far as Porlezza, at the eastern end of the lake (9½ miles/15 km from Lugano). Then it leaves Lake Lugano behind and crosses the Porlezza Plain to Lake Como, entirely in the Lombardy region. The first glimpse of the lake comes as the road curves around above Menaggio, about 7½ miles (12 km) from Porlezza.

BEST EN ROUTE

Regina A splendid view overlooking the lake in Porlezza is one reason to eat here. The *antipasto Regina* (a selection of warm hors d'oeuvres) is another. There also are 22 guestrooms. Closed Mondays and mid-January through March. Reservations advised. Major credit cards accepted. 11 Piazza Matteotti, Porlezza (phone/fax: 344-61228). Moderate.

Stella d'Italia Between Oria and Porlezza, the village of San Mamete is worth an overnight stop for the sheer pleasure of staying in this most romantic of settings. Here are 35 rooms, a terraced garden for outdoor eating, a private beach, and a hotel rowboat. Open March through October. San Mamete (phone: 344-68139; 344-69001 out of season; fax: 344-68729). Moderate to inexpensive.

Europa The service is warm and personal at this comfortable hotel overlooking Lake Lugano. All 35 rooms have balconies, and there's a good restaurant and parking. Closed January through early February. 17 Lungolago G. Matteotti, Porlezza (phone: 344-61142; fax: 344-72256). Inexpensive.

MENAGGIO This resort town is set on what many consider the most beautiful stretch of Lake Como. Just south of it, the lake splits into two, one branch pointing southwest, with Como itself at its southernmost tip, and the other point-ing southeast, with the town of Lecco at its tip. On a promontory across the water, in an angle between the two branches, is the picturesque town of Bellagio. Directly opposite, on the far shore, is the enchanting fishing village of Varenna. Menaggio, Varenna, and Bellagio are connected by car ferry.

BEST EN ROUTE

Grand Hotel Victoria A superbly situated lakeside property, it has a pool; most of the 53 rooms have spectacular views. The highly regarded restaurant, *Le Tout Paris,* features classic French and Italian dishes. Open year-round, with off-season discounts for bed and breakfast arrangements. 7 Lungolago B. Castelli, Menaggio (phone: 344-32003; fax: 344-32992). Expensive to moderate.

En Route from Menaggio The lakeside road south (S340) to Como (21 miles/34 km from Menaggio) passes through the resorts of Cadenabbia and Tremezzo, about 3 miles (5 km) south of Menaggio. Between the two towns is the exquisite *Villa Carlotta,* which was built in the mid-18th century and further embellished in the 19th century. The villa's garden is a spectacle, especially in April and May, when its world-famous azaleas and rhodo-dendrons are in bloom. The villa is open daily April through September; open daily, with a midday closing, March and October; closed the rest of the year; admission charge (phone: 344-40405). The little hill town of Mezzegra, up on the right, is where Mussolini and his mistress Claretta Petacci were shot by partisans after they were captured farther north at Dongo as they were fleeing toward Switzerland.

Continue 3 miles (5 km) south on S340 to the town of Sala Comacina. Just offshore here is Lake Como's only island, Isola Comacina—with a sen-sational restaurant, *Locanda dell'Isola Comacina* (see *Best en Route*); it can be reached by a traditional lake boat called a *lucia* (they have oval hoops over the hull), the local equivalent of a Venetian gondola. About 13 miles (21 km) farther, the road passes through another lake resort, Cernobbio. Continue along S340 to Como.

BEST EN ROUTE

Villa d'Este The most elegant retreat in the lake district, this hostelry has 158 rooms and suites and two restaurants. For more information, see *Italy's Most Memorable Hostelries* in DIVERSIONS. Open March through November. 40 Via Regina, Cernobbio (phone: 31-511471; fax: 31-512027). Very expen-sive.

Locanda dell'Isola Comacina The prix fixe menu at this rustic restaurant, a five-minute boat ride from Sala Comacina (the landing stage is difficult to find;

ask a local), hasn't changed much in half a century. For more information, see *The Best Restaurants of Italy* in DIVERSIONS. Closed Tuesdays (except June through July) and November through February. Reservations advised. No credit cards accepted. Isola Comacina (phone: 344-55083). Expensive.

Villa Flori Not nearly as grand as the *Villa d'Este,* this pleasant 43-room (many with balconies) hotel midway between Cernobbio and Como offers 19th-century elegance with modern comforts, lake views, and a good restaurant. 12 Via Cernobbio, Como (phone: 31-573105; fax: 31-570379). Expensive.

Terzo Crotto This is one of the best restaurants on Lake Como for northern fare—a wide variety of soups, excellent meat, and pasta. The spaghetti and seafood cooked *al cartoccio* (in a paper bag) is a treat. There are several inexpensive guestrooms upstairs. Closed Mondays and November. Reservations advised. Major credit cards accepted. 21 Via Volta, Cernobbio (phone: 31-512304). Moderate.

Trattoria del Vapore Small and friendly, this is a fine spot for pasta and fresh fish. Closed Tuesdays and December. Reservations advised. American Express accepted. 17 Via G. Garibaldi, Cernobbio (phone: 31-510308). Moderate.

Albergo Giardino Though a variety of entrées are available, the many kinds of tasty pizza make this a pleasant place for dinner—try more than one in the garden. It also has 11 small rooms. Restaurant closed Wednesdays and December through February; hotel closed for three weeks at *Christmas.* Reservations advised. Major credit cards accepted. 73 Via Regina, Cernobbio (phone: 31-511154; fax: 31-341870). Inexpensive.

COMO Twice a year, in late March and at the beginning of October, fashion buyers from all over the world flock to this bustling lakeside town to see what's new in silk fabrics. Como is not only the largest resort on this lake but also a famous silk-producing town since the 14th century. Silk fabric as well as designer scarves and shawls are for sale at huge discounts at the *Ratti* factory outlet store (19 Via Cernobbio; phone: 31-233111). A good discount place for silk clothing and accessories, about 3 miles (5 km) out of town, is *Seta* (15 Via Manzoni, Montana Lucino; phone: 31-474393). Both stores are closed Sundays.

Como enjoys a spectacular position at the southern end of the lake, with mountains all around and lovely villas scattered among the hills outside the city. The town is laid out in a grid fashion that dates back to its origins as a Roman fortress. It began as a Gallic colony, and the Romans took it over in the 1st century BC. Two famous Romans, Pliny the Elder and Pliny the Younger, were born here. In the medieval period, it was an independent commune. The Old Town is well preserved, with the three towers of the city walls still standing, as well as traces of the walls themselves, several old churches, and a wealth of old cobbled streets and colonnades that house an array of shops. Vestiges of the Roman past can be seen in the small *Museo Archeologico* (*Palazzo Giovio,* Piazza Medaglie d'Oro; phone: 31-27-1343). The museum is closed Mondays; Tuesdays through Saturdays for a short (12:30 to 2 PM) break; and Sundays after 1 PM; admission charge. Piazza del Duomo is the heart of town. Here, side by side, are the black-and-white-marble *Broletto* (the ancient Town Hall), built in 1215, with the *Torre del Comune* on one side and the *Duomo* on the other. Begun in 1396, the *Duomo* combines Gothic and Renaissance elements in its façade (the rose window is renowned) and interior, and it was finished in the 18th century with a Baroque cupola. Among Como's other notable churches are the 11th-century *Sant'Abbondio* (outside the town walls), in the Lombard Romanesque style, and the 12th-century *San Fedele* (Via Vittorio Emanuele II).

Como is an excellent starting point for boat trips—by far the best way to explore the lake. A fleet of 50 or so paddle steamers and motor boats plies the water from here to the northern point of the lake at Colico, criss-crossing from bank to bank and stopping at lakeside villages on the way. A pass granting unlimited travel for one or more days can be purchased. Tickets and timetables are available at the office by the landing stage in Piazza Cavour, where there also is an office of the *Azienda di Promozione Turistica* (*APT;* 17 Piazza Cavour; phone: 31-274064), or at the railway station (Piazzale San Gottardo; phone: 31-267214). Have lunch on board one of the boats that leave the landing stage twice daily, usually at 10:30 AM and at midday. The food is good, the scenery unparalleled, and the prices reasonable. The boats go to the north of the lake, with stops en route, and return in the early evening. From July through September, Saturday-evening cruises on the lake are offered, with restaurant, bar, and orchestra on board. Timetables are posted at the landing stage, or contact *Navigazione Lago di Como* (phone: 31-273324; fax: 31-260234) for details.

BEST EN ROUTE

Barchetta Excelsior Conveniently situated on the lakefront main square, this modern property offers 82 rooms, three suites, and a restaurant. Open year-round. 1 Piazza Cavour, Como (phone: 31-3221; fax: 31-302622). Expensive.

Palace The best in town, this late 19th-century hotel set in a garden on the waterfront has magnificent lake views. Completely refurbished, it has a restaurant, an outside bar in summer, and efficient service. Open year-round. Centrally located at 16 Lungo Lago Trieste (phone: 31-303303; fax: 31-303170). Expensive.

Santandrea Golf Ten minutes from Como on Lake Montorfano, this elegant 12-room hotel offers tranquillity, a patch of private beach, and golf close by. The excellent restaurant serves nouvelle cuisine alfresco in summer. Closed January. 19 Via Como, Montorfano (phone/fax: 31-200220). Expensive.

Sant'Anna Several charming wood paneled rooms offer an intimate atmosphere for delicious dining. The bill of fare lists unpretentious *nuova cucina*—try the fresh lake fish or *taglialini* with salmon and peppers and the *costoletta di vitello alla pizzaiola* (veal cutlet with diced tomato). Closed Fridays, Saturday lunch, July 25 to August 25, and *Christmas*. Reservations advised for dinner. Major credit cards accepted. 1-3 Via Filippo Turati, Como (phone: 31-505266). Expensive.

Imbarcadero Good food is served in elegant surroundings, overlooking Lake Como. Closed the first week in January. Reservations advised. Major credit cards accepted. 20 Piazza Cavour, Como (phone: 31-277341). Expensive to moderate.

Da Angela Owner/chef Mario Clovis carries on the tradition begun by his family 50 years ago. Elegant table settings, attractive decor, and an innovative menu make this one of Como's best. Closed Sundays and August. Reservations advised. Major credit cards accepted. 16 Via Foscolo, Como (phone: 31-304656). Moderate.

En Route from Como The slow, winding road (S583) leading up the eastern shore (of the western branch) of the lake passes through small lakeside towns and villages, such as Blevio, Torno (just beyond which is *Villa Pliniana/Pliny's Villa*—a 16th-century villa with an unusual intermittent waterfall on its grounds that was described by Pliny the Elder and Leonardo), Riva, Nesso (which has a dramatic waterfall), and Lezzeno. Beyond Lezzeno is Bellagio, about 19 miles (30 km) from Como.

BELLAGIO This enchanting little town occupies a promontory at the inner angle of Lake Como's upside-down "Y," right where the eastern branch of the lake, commonly called the Lago di Lecco, or Lake Lecco, takes leave of the main branch, which retains the Como name. Its waterfront, which boasts some exceptionally pleasant hotels, has preserved an Old World, 19th-century ambience unparalleled anywhere else on the lakes. Bellagio has the enormous advantage of having no through traffic, and its steep streets rise from the lake shore almost like stairs. The gorgeous gardens of the *Villa Serbelloni* occupy much of the promontory itself. Built in the 16th century and renovated in the 17th, the villa passed into the hands of the Serbelloni family in the 18th century and was donated to the Rockefeller Foundation in this century; today, it's used as a study and conference center. It is closed to the public, but the gardens open at 10:30 AM and 4 PM for two-hour guided tours from *Easter* through mid-October; closed Mondays; admission charge. These tours, restricted to a maximum of 30 people, are organized by the municipality of Bellagio. Because of the popularity of group visits, especially in May, you may want to ask your hotel to book you on a tour in advance, or contact the *Assessore al Turismo di Bellagio* (phone/fax: 31-951551) before you arrive.

Nearby is the early-19th-century *Villa Melzi*, which was built by Duke Francesco Melzi, vice president of the short-lived Italian Republic set up by Napoleon. The villa's gardens are worth a visit, especially for the marvelous view across the lake toward Tremezzo, the same view Liszt enjoyed the year he spent here with his mistress, Countess Marie d'Agoult (one of their daughters, Cosima, who was to marry Wagner, was born here). The villa and gardens are closed November to late March; admission charge (phone: 31-950318).

Stroll through the town to look over the racks of silk ties—some with famous labels—outside the boutiques on Salita Serbelloni. The tourist information center (*APT*) is at 14 Piazza della Chiesa (phone: 31-950204).

BEST EN ROUTE

Grand Hotel Villa Serbelloni Built over a century ago, this wonderful grand hotel combines modern comforts with the gracious service and elegant surroundings of a bygone age. Its public rooms, including the restaurant, have frescoed, vaulted ceilings. The 95 rooms and suites have garden or lake views, and the hotel also offers 13 new, reasonably priced apartments in a separate annex above a well-equipped fitness center. Also on the premises are tennis courts, a heated pool, and a private beach. Hotel open mid-April to mid-October; apartments open February through December. 1 Via Roma, Bellagio (phone: 31-950216; fax: 31-951529). Very expensive.

Florence Spacious, immaculate, and replete with antique, stuccoed charm, this property has been run by the same family for over a century. Among other pluses, there is a dining room, which in good weather, alfresco dining on the lakeside terrace in good weather, and an attractive bar. A few of the 40 rooms share baths. Open *Easter* to mid-October. 36 Piazza Mazzini, Bellagio (phone: 31-950342; fax: 31-951722). Inexpensive.

Du Lac This comfortable, welcoming hostelry, run by an Anglo-Italian family, has 48 rooms, an airy restaurant, and a sun terrace with panoramic vistas. Open late March through October. 32 Piazza Mazzini, Bellagio (phone: 31-950320; fax: 31-951624). Inexpensive.

La Pergola A few minutes' walk from the eastern side of the promontory, this traditional trattoria serves excellent meat and fish dishes, incuding *riso e filetto di persico al curry* (rice and perch in a curry sauce). There also are 12 inexpensive rooms upstairs. Closed Tuesdays and two weeks from January to February. Reservations advised. Major credit cards accepted. In the picturesque fishing village of Pescallo di Bellagio (phone: 31-950263). Inexpensive.

En Route from Bellagio Take the car ferry across the lake to Varenna, a colorful little marble-quarrying port with pink and red houses in the harbor and steep, narrow alleyways leading up to the main piazza. Its lovely lakeside promenade is shaded with fragrant bougainvillea. Also in town and worth a visit is the *Villa Monastero* (1 Piazza Venini; phone: 341-831261), founded as a monastery in 1208 and today serving as the *International Center of Physics.* The house and its gardens are open daily April through October with a short (noon to 2 PM) closing; admission charge.

The steep backdrop of the Grigna Mountains, home to one of the most famous climbing schools in Europe, accompanies the S36 south from Varenna along Lake Lecco. The landscape here differs sharply from that of the western arm of Lake Como; it so fascinated Leonardo da Vinci that it is believed to be the background for his famous *Mona Lisa.* At the end of the lake and 14 miles (22 km) south of Varenna is Lecco, an unattractive iron manufacturing center but notable as the setting for *I Promessi Sposi* (The Betrothed), the classic novel by the 19th-century author Alessandro Manzoni. The *Villa Manzoni,* where the author lived as a boy, houses the *Museo Manzoni* (1 Via Gualella; phone: 341-481249). It is closed Mondays and for a short (1 to 3 PM) break; admission charge. Continue south of Lecco on S639 and then turn east onto S342 to Bergamo, 20 miles (32 km) from Lecco.

BERGAMO The roads leading in and out of Bergamo are busy, but this historic city is well worth a visit. Founded by Celtic Gauls and then conquered by Rome, it was subsequently a free commune within the Lombard League, came under the control of the squabbling noble families of Lombardy, and later still belonged to Venice and then to Austria. It is divided into a modern, busy Città Bassa, or Lower City, built largely during the Fascist period (with the exception of several fine Renaissance churches), and a quiet, medieval Città Alta, or Upper City, which stands majestically on a hill at the foot of the Bergamesque Alps. The *Accademia Carrara* (82/A Via San Tomaso, in the Città Bassa; phone: 35-399425) is one of the best art museums in the country, with works by Botticelli, Raphael, Tintoretto, Canaletto, Bellini, Tiepolo, and Carpaccio. Closed Tuesdays and for a short (12:30 to 2:30 PM) break; admission charge.

The Città Alta, with its well-preserved fortifications, cobbled streets, and tiny shops, is by far the most interesting part of the city. It is reached by foot or by a funicular that drops its passengers in Piazza Mercato delle Scarpe, inside the walls of the Città Alta and not far from Piazza Vecchia, its heart (cars are not permitted inside the Città Alta). In and around this square is a collection of medieval buildings, including the severe *Palazzo della Ragione* and its massive tower. Built in the 12th century, the palace was damaged by fire and restored in the 16th century (note the lion of St. Mark on the façade, a relic of the city's centuries in Venetian possession). Through the archways of the palace is the Piazza del Duomo, where a number of interesting structures are found. The most impressive is the 15th-century *Cappella Colleoni,* a funerary chapel housing the tomb of

Bartolomeo Colleoni, the daring *condottiere* (military leader) and a native *bergamasco*. The chapel's façade, in Lombard-Renaissance style, is a striking composition of colored marble and delicate carvings. The chapel is attached to the 12th-century Romanesque *Basilica di Santa Maria Maggiore*, which houses four beautiful inlaid wood panels partly designed by Lorenzo Lotto in the 16th century (they are in front of the choir and may be covered up—ask to see them). There also is a small 14th-century baptistry, which was once inside the basilica but is now freestanding. And, if you're an opera lover, go inside *Santa Maria Maggiore* to pay your respects at the tomb of Gaetano Donizetti, another native. The small *Museo Civico Archeologico* (9 Piazza Cittadella; phone: 35-242839) contains finds from local excavations. It is closed Mondays and afternoons; no admission charge.

Make your way back to Piazza Mercato delle Scarpe, from which Via Rocca leads off to the medieval lookout post, *La Rocca,* in the middle of a spacious park. It commands a glorious view of upper and lower Bergamo and over the surrounding mountains and plain. There are branches of the local tourist office, *APT,* in the Città Bassa (106 Viale Papa Giovanni XXIII; phone: 35-242226) and in the Città Alta (2 Vicolo Aquila Nera; phone: 35-232730).

BEST EN ROUTE

Da Vittorio *Foiada con porcini* (foie gras with *porcini* mushrooms), *fettuccine con ovoli in fricassea* (fricasseed pasta with mushrooms), and snails, among other delicacies, are the claims to fame at this culinary temple. Closed Wednesdays and most of August. Reservations advised. Major credit cards accepted. 21 Viale Papa Giovanni XXIII, Bergamo, Città Bassa (phone: 35-218060). Expensive.

Trattoria da Ornella A family-run restaurant in the heart of the Città Alta, this is a good stop in the midst of sightseeing. Try the *casonsei bergamaschi* (homemade ravioli filled with meat and served with butter, cheese, and sage). Closed Thursdays, Friday lunch, and July. No reservations. No credit cards accepted. 15 Via Gombito, Bergamo, Città Alta (phone: 35-232736). Moderate to inexpensive.

En Route from Bergamo Take S42 east out of Bergamo through the suburb of Seriate and the hilly Val Cavallina, past the tiny Lago di Endine for 22½ miles (36 km) to Lovere, on the shores of Lago d'Iseo.

LAGO D'ISEO This is one of the smallest and most rugged of the main Lombardy lakes, and though it doesn't have the range of sophisticated amenities found on the larger lakes, the beauty and peace of the surroundings make it a worthwhile stop. The main attraction of the lake is its beautiful island. At 2 square miles, Monte Isola is the largest lake island in Europe, a peaceful oasis where only a handful of local people are allowed cars, and even bicycles are restricted. The island rises to a point, with four fishing villages clustered around its base and the *Santuario della Madonna della Ceriola* at the top. Boats to the island leave daily from Iseo and other locations around the lake, with a very frequent *traghetto* (ferry) from Sulzano.

The Oglio River, at the head of the lake, is at the bottom of the beautiful Val Camonica, an Alpine valley filled with prehistoric rock drawings. To get to the valley, take S42 north from Lovere, leaving the lake behind and following the Oglio River about 24½ miles (39 km) to the town of Capo di Ponte, headquarters for the *Centro Camuno di Studi Preistorici*, a small museum of prehistory. The national park of *Capo di Ponte* covers about 75 acres; the oldest etchings in the area date back some 6,000 years, and it is an intensely studied site. The park and museum are closed Mondays and holidays; admission charge (phone: 364-42091).

Return to the lake and head 18 miles (29 km) down its east side via S510 to the pleasant little port town of Iseo itself, with a 14th-century castle, *Castello Oldofredi.*

South of Iseo lies the small wine producing area of Franciacorta, whose red, white, and sparkling wines are developing a well-deserved reputation. Don't miss a visit to one of the wine cellars. The best known is that of *Guido Berlucchi* (4 Piazza Duranti, in the tiny village of Borgonato di Cortefranca; phone: 30-984381; fax: 30-984293). For more information, see *Most Visitable Vineyards* in DIVERSIONS. To get there, take the coast road westward from Iseo for Sarnico and turn left down through the village of Timoline to Borgonato.

BEST EN ROUTE

L'Albereta Gualtiero Marchesi, the renowned Milanese chef, has combined talents with Vittorio Moretti, one of the area's leading wine producers, to create a sophisticated hotel and restaurant in a luxurious country villa. A few minutes south of Iseo, this hostelry is set on a wooded rise with views of vineyards, Lake d'Iseo, and the Lombardy plain; there are 39 suites, an indoor pool, and a tennis court. The restaurant offers lunch for a good value. 11 Via Vittorio Emanuele, Erbusco (phone: 30-776-0550; fax: 30-776-0573). Expensive.

Le Maschere In an attractive setting of an old vaulted chamber furnished in elegant modern style, imaginative chef Vittorio Fusari offers excellently prepared dishes with a touch of nouvelle cuisine but firmly based on the best local products. Try the *terrina di tinca con salsa all'aceto balsamico* (tench terrine with balsamic vinegar sauce) or the *tagliolini alle vongole con salsa di peperoni dolci* (thin pasta with clams and sweet-pepper sauce). Closed Sunday dinner, Mondays, 10 days in January, the last week in August, and the first two weeks of September. Reservations advised. Major credit cards accepted. 7 Vicolo della Pergola, Iseo (phone: 30-982-1542). Expensive.

I Due Roccoli A tranquil country villa on wooded grounds, with a large terrace and a panoramic view of the lake, this stylish hotel is a few minutes' drive from Iseo. It has 11 rooms and two suites, as well as a pool, a restaurant, and a wood-burning fireplace for cozy evenings. Closed January and February. Via Silvio Bonomelli, Iseo (phone: 30-982-1853; fax: 30-982-1877). Expensive to moderate.

Osteria Gallo Rosso Warm and friendly, this restaurant is loved by locals for the atmosphere and excellent cooking. Try the inviting array of *antipasti misti* and the remarkable *petto d'oca affumicato* (smoked goose breast). Meat is grilled over the open fire in the dining room, the salads are a work of art, and the wines are mostly from the family vineyard in the hills. Closed Tuesdays and two weeks in August. Reservations advised. No credit cards accepted. 19 Vicolo Nulli, Iseo (phone: 30-980505). Moderate.

Trattoria del Pesce The Archetti family, who run this simple but first class seafood restaurant, buy only the very best of the local catch. Among the expertly cooked dishes are *fritto di Alborella con filetti di persico* (fried white bait and perch filets), *tinca e anguilla al forna* (oven-baked tench and eel), and *salmerino alla griglia* (grilled lake salmon trout). Closed Tuesdays and the first two weeks of November. Reservations necessary. No credit cards accepted. Peschiera, Monte Isola (phone: 30-988-6137). Moderate to inexpensive.

La Foresta If you don't mind leaving your car behind and taking your luggage over on the boat to the island, this charming, if very simple, hotel has only 10 rooms, good food, friendly service, and ample doses of serenity. Book well ahead in the summer. Open March through November. Peschiera, Monte Isola (phone: 30-988-6210). Inexpensive.

En Route from Iseo Drive southeast on S510 to Brescia, about 15 miles (24 km) away.

BRESCIA Set in the Valtrompia plain at the edge of the Alpine foothills, Brescia (pop. 200,000) is Lombardy's second-largest city after Milan. Its industrial plants have made it wealthy, and it was already an important Gallic center of power when the Romans conquered it and named it Brixia. In the center of town is Piazza della Vittoria, a modern square dating from the Fascist era; Mussolini gave public addresses from the red marble *Arengario,* or *Rostrum,* here. Just north is another square, Piazza della Loggia, the heart of the city since the Renaissance, surrounded by Renaissance buildings largely in the Venetian style. (Brescia, like Bergamo, was a Venetian possession for nearly 400 years.) One of these buildings, the *Palazzo del Comune,* also known as the *Loggia,* was begun during the late 15th century and finished in the late 16th century by numerous architects, sculptors, and painters, including Sansovino, Palladio, and Titian. In front of it is the exquisite *Torre* *dell'Orologio,* a clock tower designed after the one in Venice's Piazza San Marco, with two statues striking the hours. Pass beyond the tower to Piazza del Duomo, which was the civic and religious center of town until it was superseded in the former capacity by Piazza della Loggia. Of interest here is the *Duomo Nuovo* (New Cathedral), whose huge cupola is the third largest in Italy. It was begun in the 17th century to replace the 11th-century *Duomo Vecchio,* the old cathedral next door, which is better known as the *Rotonda* because of its circular plan. Also in the square is the *Broletto,* a medieval town hall with an 11th-century tower, the *Torre del Popolo* (Tower of the People).

The heart of Roman Brescia is Piazza del Foro, which covers part of the ancient forum and has in the background the spectacular remains of the *Tempio Capitolino* (Capitoline Temple), built in 73 AD and partially restored at the beginning of the 19th century. The *Museo Civico Età Romana*, an archaeological museum, occupies part of the temple. The museum is closed Mondays and for a short (noon to 2 PM) break; admission charge (phone: 30-46031). Next to it is the vast *Teatro Romano,* an amphitheater that held an audience of 15,000. Brescia has other monuments of interest; it was known as the "city of a hundred convents" before the anticlerical Napoleon closed most of them. From May through November, concerts, plays, and operas are staged at various sites throughout the city. The provincial tourist office (*APT;* 34 Corso Zanardelli; phone: 30-43418) can provide information about these events. It is open weekdays, with a midday closing.

BEST EN ROUTE

Pergolina A comfortably furnished trattoria near the *Tempio Capitolino*, it serves good home cooking, such as *tortellini di zucca*. An open fireplace in the middle of the restaurant is used to roast meat. Closed Sunday dinner, Mondays, and August. Reservations advised. No credit cards accepted. 65 Via Musei, Brescia (phone: 30-46350). Moderate.

Raffa Elegant and refined, this restaurant is especially popular at lunch for its good Brescian cooking. Closed Sundays and August. Reservations advised. Major credit cards accepted. In the heart of the city, at 15 Corso Magenta, Brescia (phone: 30-49037). Moderate.

En Route from Brescia The S11 and the A4 lead to the southwestern corner of Lake Garda, the largest of all the Italian lakes. Its shores, which border the Lombardy, Veneto, and Trentino–Alto Adige regions, are dotted with cypresses, olive groves, vineyards, and flowering shrubs. Head first for 17 miles (27 km) on S11 for Desenzano del Garda, which has an attractive harbor and Old Town center.

Desenzano is a northern Portofino with plenty of its own charm. A popular outdoor flea market is held the first Sunday of every month at Piazza

Malvezzi (except in January and August), and there is a surplus of sumptuous shops for the well-to-do Milanese who spend summers and weekends year-round in the villas here. The town's *Villa Romana* (Via Scavi Romani; phone: 30-9143547) was one such pleasure palace, probably belonging to a Milanese even back in Roman times; it has splendid mosaic floors. The villa is closed Mondays; admission charge. In the *Duomo di Santa Maria Maddalena,* built in the late 16th century, is a *Last Supper* by Tiepolo. Before leaving Desenzano, drop in at the *Enoteca la Vite* (50 Via Castello; phone: 30-914-1292) to taste some of the fine local wines and grappas. It stays open until 2 AM and is closed Sundays.

Pick up S572 north, the first leg of the Gardesana Occidentale (the road along the western shore). After passing through the Moniga area, known for its production of red chiaretto wine, take the turnoff for Salò (about 12½ miles/20 km north of Desenzano), where it is believed that the ancient Romans maintained an important salt warehouse—hence the name. This beautiful spot was the seat of Mussolini's puppet government, the Italian Social Republic, set up in September 1943 and backed by Hitler. It is also the birthplace of Gasparo Bertolotti, held by some to have been the inventor of the violin. Much of the town was destroyed by an earthquake in 1901, but the two ancient town gates remain, as does the 15th-century late-Gothic cathedral with three paintings by Paolo Veronese and, in the baptistry, Romanino's *Madonna and Saints.* On Saturday mornings, a large market stretches along the lakefront. The resort town of Gardone Riviera is just 3 miles (5 km) north of Salò, but if you have time, leave the lake road at Barbarano, turning left into the Via Panoramica, which leads up into the hills, for a marvelous view over the lake and the tiny island of Isola di Garda before winding down into Gardone.

BEST EN ROUTE

Laurin This Art Nouveau villa was Mussolini's *Ministry of Foreign Affairs* during World War II. Its owners have restored it beautifully, leaving many original features but furnishing the 36 large and airy guestrooms in a comfortable, modern style. Golf and tennis courts are just five minutes away. The elegant, frescoed restaurant serves exquisite *trota in picedo* (fresh lake trout in a piquant wine sauce). Closed mid-December through most of January. 9 Viale Landi, Salò (phone: 365-22022; fax: 365-22382). Expensive to moderate.

GARDONE RIVIERA A point of interest in this lakeside resort is the villa that belonged to the flamboyant poet, patriot, and novelist Gabriele D'Annunzio, who died here in 1938. D'Annunzio was also a hero of World War I. After the Treaty of Versailles ignored Italy's claim to the port city of Fiume, on the Dalmatian coast, D'Annunzio rounded up a band of volunteers, captured the city himself, and ruled it for 15 months, much to the embarrassment of the Italian government. The estate in the upper part of town—Gardone di Sopra—reflects the author's eccentricities, not to mention his delusions of grandeur, which he transmitted to his admirers, including Mussolini. Called *Il Vittoriale degli Italiani,* it is a complex of gardens, monuments, and memorials to his wartime and postwar achievements, containing the mausoleum where he and his comrades in the march on Fiume are buried, a car and airplane used in various exploits, and even a ship stuck into the flank of a hill. Visitors can walk around the grounds and are led through the villa, where the poet's study and his bathroom, chock-full of *objets,* including a marvelous, deep-blue glazed tub, are most interesting. Concerts are given in the amphitheater. The house is closed Mondays and for a midday break; admission charge. Go early in the day in the summer—only a limited number of visitors are permitted in the house.

BEST EN ROUTE

La Stalla Near *Il Vittoriale,* this place serves traditional meat and fish dishes, with alfresco dining in summer. Closed Tuesdays and January. Reservations advised. Major credit cards accepted. 14 Via dei Colli, Gardone (phone: 365-21038). Moderate to inexpensive.

En Route from Gardone Traveling north 7½ miles (12 km) through the former Roman colony of Maderno along the Gardesana Occidentale (S45 *bis*), one comes to Gargnano, where Mussolini had his villa (*Villa Feltrinelli*—not open to the public). Continue 12 miles (19 km) to Limone sul Garda (see below) and then to Riva del Garda, or, if time is no object, take a left turn toward Tignale, about 2 miles (3 km) beyond Gargnano. This small, winding mountain road (with a few towns along its route) is spectacular, with views of the lake stretching for 30 miles. (The *Santuario della Madonna di Monte* Castello is a superb panoramic point.) Following signs for Limone and Riva, the road eventually winds down through the pretty hill village of Tremosine into Limone sul Garda, an enchanting, old-fashioned town that was loved by Goethe and D. H. Lawrence and until a half century ago was accessible only by boat. Its steep mountain backdrop prevents it from expanding too much and also acts as a remarkable sun trap—which accounts for the lemons growing at this northerly point. These groves are Europe's oldest, and the steep terraces and tall posts are all that remain of the area's hundreds of "lemon houses."

Continue 6 miles (10 km) north on S45 *bis* from Limone to Riva del Garda. A spectacular feat of engineering, the road passes through tunnel after tunnel hewn from the rock, with splendid vistas out over the lake. Riva itself has been Italian only since the defeat of the Austrians in World War I (this is the Trentino–Alto Adige region). At Riva, round the northern segment of the lake and turn southward along its eastern shore, most of which touches the Veneto region. The road (the Gardesana Orientale—

S249 the whole way) leads into Malcesine (11 miles/18 km from Riva), which was a favorite holiday spot of Greta Garbo and has an impressive 13th-century castle housing a small museum. Another well-preserved castle is at Torri del Benaco, where the car ferry crosses over to Maderno. The road follows the outline of a lovely promontory—Punta di San Vigilio (15½ miles/25 km beyond Malcesine), where Winston Churchill painted just after the war—and continues through the town of Garda and on to Bardolino, home of the light, fruity wine of the same name. There are several wine cellars in Bardolino where visitors are welcome. From here drive south 14 miles (22 km) to Peschiera del Garda. Here, pick up S11 and drive 6 miles (10 km) to Colombare and turn right toward the pretty walled town of Sirmione.

BEST EN ROUTE

Park Hotel Imperial A beauty to look at, this posh hostelry on the lake has 48 rooms, tennis courts, two pools, gardens, and an upscale restaurant for dieters and non-dieters alike. Open year-round. 10/B Via Tamas, Limone sul Garda (phone: 365-954591; fax: 365-954382). Expensive.

Villa Fiordaliso Mussolini installed his mistress Claretta Petacci in this lovely lakefront villa, where her red bedroom and marble bathroom are still on view. It has six guestrooms and an impeccable restaurant. Closed Mondays and early January through mid-March. 132 Via Zanardelli, Gardone Riviera (phone: 365-20158; fax: 365-290011). Expensive.

Hotel du Lac Each of the 88 rooms in this modern hostelry has a balcony with a view of the lake and mountains. There is also an outdoor grill at lunchtime, a pool, and two tennis courts. A family favorite, with half board required and full board available April, May, and October. Open April through October. 1 Via Fasse, Limone (phone: 365-954481; fax: 365-954258). Moderate to inexpensive.

Al Torcol Housed in a converted stable, this lively, attractive restaurant specializes in meat and fish grilled on an outdoor barbecue. Closed Mondays and Tuesdays in winter, Mondays in spring, and late October to mid-December. No reservations. No credit cards accepted. 44 Via IV Novembre, Limone sul Garda (phone: 365-954169). Inexpensive.

Villa Giulia Small and cozy, this century-old, family-run hostelry has 16 rooms, a pool, a terrace, a sauna, and a fine lake view. The living and dining rooms are decorated with antiques. Half board is required, but the food is excellent. Open mid-March through mid-October. 20 Via Rimembranza, Gargnano (phone: 365-71022; fax: 365-72774). Inexpensive.

SIRMIONE This resort town runs the length of a narrow, 2-mile-long peninsula projecting into Lake Garda from the middle of its southern shore, dividing the water into the two bays of Desenzano and Peschiera. It has been a favorite holiday spot since Roman times, largely because of its hot sulfur springs, which have given rise to numerous spa clinics treating a wide variety of ailments. The Roman poet Catullus loved the place and wrote about it, although the Roman villa that has been excavated here—and is named for him—was not necessarily his. In the 13th century, the town, formerly independent, fell to the powerful Della Scala (or Scaligeri) family of Verona, who immediately put a wall around it and built a fortress to guard the gate. This well-preserved castle, the *Rocca Scaligera*, its towers and crenelations intact, still guards the entrance to the town. The castle is closed Mondays and Sundays after 1 PM in summer; closed daily after 1 PM the rest of the year; admission charge (phone: 30-916468). Beyond it are the narrow streets of the Old Town, a pedestrian island, and, at the very tip of the peninsula, the archaeological zone, where the so-called *Grotte di Catullo* (Grottoes of Catullus; phone: 30-916157), actually the remains of a large, imperial-era Roman villa, can be visited. The villa is closed Mondays; admission charge. Sirmione offers plenty of swimming, boating, and other activities.

BEST EN ROUTE

Locanda San Vigilio Since the 16th century, visitors have found this lakeside inn a peaceful oasis. Winston Churchill used to come here with his painting gear. The inn is on the site of a 12th-century chapel, and there are four rooms and three suites. The restaurant specializes in fish prepared to perfection. Open mid-March through mid-November. Northeast around the lake from Sirmione, about 20½ miles (33 km), just beyond Garda, to the town of San Vigilio (phone: 45-725-6688, hotel; 45-725-5190, restaurant; fax: 45-725-6551). Expensive.

Vecchia Lugana Refined versions of local specialties reign at this old tavern, with tables outside under a pergola in summer. Most entrées feature fish fresh from the lake, but there also are venison and rabbit dishes. Try the eggplant and ricotta stuffed with pasta to start. The desserts are delicious, and there is a vast wine selection. There is a piano bar upstairs. Closed Monday dinner, Tuesdays, and January. Reservations advised. Major credit cards accepted. 1 Piazzale Vecchia, Lugana, Sirmione (phone: 30-919012). Expensive.

Villa Cortine Palace Set in a cypress-studded park beyond town on the way to the *Grotte di Catullo*, this hotel has 50 rooms and two suites, a garden restaurant, a pool, and a private pier. Open *Easter* through October. 12 Via Grotte, Sirmione (phone: 30-990-5890; fax: 30-916390). Expensive.

Aurora The setting in a historic building is lovely, and there is a terrace for dining. Proprietor/chef Ezio Giorgio Erbifori is a well-known gastronome, and his inventive specialties include truffled *taglioni* (thin egg noodles), salmon trout with fresh grapes or with pink pepper, rabbit stew with olives, and veal scaloppine with calvados. Closed Sundays. Reservations advised. Major credit cards accepted. Northeast around the lake, about 16 miles (26 km) from Sirmione, at Piazzetta San Severo, Bardolino (phone: 45-721-0038). Expensive to moderate.

Piccolo Castello Just inside the ramparts of town, this restaurant near the *Rocca Scaligera* offers good regional fare. Closed Tuesdays and December through January. No reservations. No credit cards accepted. 7 Via Dante, Sirmione (phone: 30-916138). Moderate to inexpensive.

Mon Repos Among the olive groves at the end of the promontory, this small hotel boasts a restaurant and pool. Most of the 24 rooms have balconies. Open *Easter* through October. 2 Via Arici, Sirmione (phone: 30-990-5290; fax: 30-916546). Inexpensive.

En Route from Sirmione Two historic towns beyond the Lombardy lake district beckon: Mantua (Mantova in Italian) and Cremona. Leave Sirmione and head back to Peschiera del Garda; from there, turn south, following signs for Ponti sul Mincio, Monzambano, Volta Mantovana, and Goito. From Goito, take S236 into Mantua, 30 miles (48 km) from Sirmione.

MANTUA Although it is built of brick, Mantua is warm, its red and ocher buildings in contrast with the marsh lakes that surround it on three sides. It is also a delight for visitors, with its traffic-free piazze, soaring towers, a castle in the center of town, and smart shops and *caffès*. What the Medici, Visconti, Sforza, Este, and Farnese families were to Florence and other Italian cities, the Gonzagas were to Mantua—a ruling dynasty that held sway for centuries and left behind a priceless heritage in works of art. Something of the grandeur of their court can be seen in the city's major attraction, the *Palazzo Ducale,* which is not one but several buildings, comprising, it is said, some 500 rooms, including 15 courtyards, gardens, and internal squares (enough are open to make a visit unforgettable). The palace was begun in the 13th century by the powerful Bonacolsi family, who had imposed their rule on the formerly free commune of Mantua, and was later taken over by the Gonzagas in 1328. Thereafter, the building was continuously expanded and transformed until the early 18th century, although it was undoubtedly at its most resplendent at the height of the Renaissance, when the Gonzagas patronized such luminaries as the painter Andrea Mantegna, the architect Leon Battista Alberti, and the humanist Politian. The beautiful and learned Isabella d'Este, wife of Giovanni Francesco Gonzaga II, also became one of the era's leading lights. The family's glory endured through Vincenzo I, who was a friend to Tasso and who commissioned the world's first operatic masterpiece, Monteverdi's *Orfeo,* and produced it at court. The glory declined after the senior branch of the family died out in 1627, and the last family member died in 1708.

Enter the palace from Piazza Sordello. Given its size, visits are by guided tour only. Since tours are conducted in Italian, those wishing more than a cursory commentary may want to book a private guide through the *Azienda di Promozione Turistica* (*APT;* 6 Piazza Mantegna; phone: 376-350681; fax: 376-363292) or the *Ufficio Guida* (23 Piazza Sordello, *Casa di Rigoletto;* phone: 376-368917). The highlight of the tour is the *Camera degli Sposi,* where Mantegna's famous frescoes (1472–74) of the family of Ludovico II (including a portrait of the painter himself) line the walls, and his charming view of children and blue sky decorates the ceiling. Also of interest are the remains of frescoes by an earlier painter, Antonio Pisanello; Rubens's portrait of Guglielmo and Vincenzo Gonzaga and their wives, Eleonora of Austria and Eleonora de' Medici; and the apartments of Isabella d'Este. The palace is open Sundays and Mondays from 9 AM to 1 PM, and Tuesdays through Saturdays from 2:30 to 5 PM as well, April through September; open Sundays and Mondays from 9 AM to 1 PM, and Tuesdays through Saturdays from 2:30 to 4 PM as well, March and October; closed November through February. There's an admission charge.

Before leaving Piazza Sordello, note the 18th-century façade of the *Duomo* and the 13th-century buildings opposite the *Palazzo Ducale,* especially the *Palazzo Bonacolsi.* Then walk under the archway to the adjacent Piazza Broletto and continue through the handsome porticoed Piazza delle Erbe, passing, to the left, the 13th-century *Palazzo della Ragione,* the 15th-century clock tower, and a tiny Romanesque church, the *Rotonda di San Lorenzo,* built by one of Mantua's 11th-century rulers, Countess Matilde di Canossa. Around the corner, in Piazza Mantegna, is the *Basilica di Sant'Andrea,* a Renaissance landmark designed by Leon Battista Alberti in the late 15th century. Mantegna's tomb is inside, in the first chapel on the left.

One last sight in Mantua, not to be missed, is the *Palazzo del Te* (15 Viale Te; phone: 376-365886), designed and decorated by Giulio Romano as a summer palace for Federico II. It is a fair walk across town (at least 15 minutes), since it was built (1525–35) as a Gonzaga "country" retreat and horse-breeding farm. Its Mannerist style parodies the classicism of the previous generation. The *Sala dei Cavalli,* with frescoes depicting Federico's favorite horses; the *Sala di Psiche,* with its voluptuous scenes on the theme of the marriage of Love and Psyche; and the *Sala dei Giganti,* floor-to-ceiling with colossal giants, are among the most striking rooms painted by Romano and his collaborators. There is a snack bar and a good bookshop. The palazzo is closed Mondays; admission charge. En route to the palace or on the way back, stop to see Mantegna's house (47 Via Acerbi; phone: 376-360506). A square building with a cylindrical courtyard, it's now used for art exhibits. When there's a show, it's open daily, with a long (noon to 3 PM) closing; otherwise, call ahead for an appointment. There's no admission charge.

Try to be in town on Thursday for the province's biggest market: It is like an outdoor traveling department store, with stalls selling all kinds of goods.

A word of caution: Always drink mineral water in Mantua, as the tap water has an excessively high sulfur content.

BEST EN ROUTE

Albergo San Lorenzo Furnished with antiques and artworks, this comfortable, old-fashioned hotel feels like a private home. There are 41 rooms (some overlooking the splendid Piazza delle Erbe) and a restaurant. Open year-round. 14 Piazza Concordia (phone: 376-220500; fax: 376-327194). Expensive.

Il Cigno Gaetano Martini and his wife, chef Alessandra, are renowned for their creative and outstanding Mantuan cooking. A *menù degustazione* lets you sample specialties from a centuries-old cookbook of the Dukes of Mantua. Closed Mondays and Tuesdays, the first 10 days of January, and the first half of August. Reservations advised. Major credit cards accepted. 1 Piazza Carlo d'Arco, Mantua (phone: 376-327101; fax: 376-328528). Expensive.

Grifone Bianco In summer, candlelit tables in a gently lit piazza make this a soothing place to dine. The building dates from about 1400, making it one of the oldest in the city. The fare is typical Mantuan—try the *tortelli di zucca*, then move on to the *filetto al pepe verde* (filet of beef with green peppercorns) or the carpaccio (thinly sliced raw beef). Closed Tuesdays and two weeks in June. Reservations necessary. Major credit cards accepted. 6 Piazza delle Erbe, Mantua (phone: 376-365423). Moderate.

Rechigi Modest but comfortable, this hotel is conveniently located in the historic center of town. There are 50 rooms and a restaurant. Open year-round. 30 Via Calvi, Mantua (phone: 376-320781; fax: 376-220291). Moderate.

L'Ochina Bianca An excellent dining spot for high-quality fare and low prices, it offers elegant versions of traditional Po Valley fare, including horsemeat. Vegetarians will like the homemade ravioli stuffed with vegetables. The desserts are homemade; the wines, selected with great care. Try the dessert wine of chilled red fragolino made with concord grapes. Closed Mondays, Tuesday lunch, and the first week of January. Reservations advised. Major credit cards accepted. 2 Via Finzi (phone: 376-323700). Inexpensive.

En Route from Mantua Head west to Cremona, 38 miles (61 km) away via S10. Set at the southernmost edge of Lombardy, Cremona is only a short distance from the banks of the Po River, on the other side of which is Emilia-Romagna.

CREMONA Founded by the Gauls and later a Roman colony, this city is where the world's first modern violin was made. Andrea Amati, who passed the art on to his sons and particularly to his grandson, Niccolò, made this instrument in the 16th century. The latter taught his technique to Andrea Guarneri, whose grandnephew, Giuseppe Guarneri del Gesù, fashioned instruments that were surpassed only by those of Niccolò's other pupil, Antonio Stradivari, or, as he signed his work in Latin, Antonius Stradivarius. Even today, while Cremona is better known for its fine foods industry (pasta, cheese, and more), the world's finest violins continue to be those made in the 17th and 18th centuries by these two most celebrated masters of Cremona's three great violin making families. While examples of their superb Cremonese craftsmanship can be heard in concert around the world, five violins—by Andrea and Niccolò Amati, Giuseppe Guarneri (the father of "del Gesù"), Giuseppe Guarneri del Gesù ("of Jesus," so called because he signed his work with a cross and the letters IHS), and Stradivarius— have come home to Cremona and are on permanent display in the 13th-century *Palazzo Comunale* (Piazza del Comune; phone: 372-4071). The palazzo is closed Mondays, and Sundays for a midday break; admission charge.

An open-air, municipal living room, Piazza del Comune is considered one of the most harmonious medieval squares in Italy. Next to the *Palazzo Comunale* is the *Loggia dei Militi* (Soldiers' Loggia), also dating from the 13th century. Across from them in a magnificent piazza is the city's *Duomo*, founded in Lombard Romanesque style in the 12th century, enlarged with Gothic transepts in the 13th and 14th centuries, and later completed with Renaissance touches to the façade. The octagonal baptistry, dating from the 12th century, is on one side of the church, while the 13th-century bell tower, better known as the *Torrazzo* (and Italy's highest), is on the other side. The latter is closed November through March; Mondays through Saturdays for a long (noon to 3 PM) break; and Sundays for a long (12:30 to 3 PM) break; admission charge. The intrepid who manage all 502 steps to the top are rewarded with a view that extends, on a clear day, to the Alps and Apennines; a third of the way up is an inside view of the works of the 16th-century clock.

Among Cremona's other churches are *Sant'Agostino* (Via Guido Grandi) and *San Sigismondo* (about 1½ miles/2 km from the center), both worth a look. The 16th-century *Palazzo Affaitati* (4 Via Ugolani Dati; phone: 372-461885) houses the *Museo Civico*, which contains Cremonese paintings from the 13th through the 19th century; ceramics and coins; and sections devoted to local archaeology, treasures from the cathedral, and the Risorgimento. The museum is closed Sundays for a midaay break, and Mondays; admission charge.

The *Museo Stradivariano,* where the master's tools, paper patterns, and construction notes are displayed, is in the same building but reached through an entrance around the corner at 17 Via Palestro (phone: 372-461886; same hours as the *Museo Civico;* admission charge). For those looking to purchase a stringed instrument, Cremona's streets, especially Corso Garibaldi, are dotted with workshops. The tourist office, *Azienda di Promozione Turistica* (*APT*), is at 5 Piazza del Comune (phone: 372-23233).

BEST EN ROUTE

Ceresole A very popular, pretty restaurant, it features an imaginative and varied menu that emphasizes Cremonese and other Italian fare. Closed Sunday dinner, Mondays, the first three weeks in August, and *Christmas*. Reservations advised. Major credit cards accepted. 4 Via Ceresole, Cremona (phone: 372-23322). Expensive.

Trattoria del Fulmine It's well worth the trip for the outstanding traditional Po Valley fare. Specialties include *fegato d'oca con polenta* (goose liver with polenta). There is also a selection of fine wines. Closed Mondays, Sunday dinner, January, and August. Reservations advised. Major credit cards accepted. Head 23 miles (37 km) northeast on S415 to Crema, then follow the signs to Trescore Cremasco, another 4 miles (6 km). 12 Via Carioni, Trescore Cremasco (phone: 373-273103). Expensive.

Centrale Locals come to this classic, old-style restaurant to savor *marubini* and succulent meat dishes such as *cotechino di Cremona* (a rich boiled sausage) served with *mostarda* (mustard-hot crystallized fruit). Closed Thursdays and July. Reservations advised. No credit cards accepted. 4 Vicolo Petrusio, Cremona (phone: 372-28701). Moderate to inexpensive.

Impero A block from Piazza del Comune, this hostelry has 36 rooms with baths or showers, plus a restaurant. Hotel open year-round; restaurant closed November through March. 21 Piazza della Pace, Cremona (phone: 372-460337; fax: 372-458785). Moderate to inexpensive.

Continental This convenient hotel is a few minutes' walk from the town center, with ample parking. The 57 rooms have all the modern amenities; there also is a good restaurant. Open year-round. 27 Piazzale Libertà, Cremona (phone/fax: 372-434141). Inexpensive.

The Dolomites

The Italian Dolomites are one of Europe's most beautiful and striking mountain ranges. Part of the eastern Alps, they extend from the region of Trentino–Alto Adige and the Adige River Valley east to the Veneto region and the Piave River Valley, both only a short distance from the Austrian border. To the south, they continue as far as the Brenta River Valley. Named after Déodat Guy Silvani Tancrède Gratet de Dolomieu, an 18th-century French geologist who spent his life studying them, they are home to some of Italy's most popular ski resorts. Eighteen of the many Dolomite peaks rise above 10,000 feet. The highest, the Marmolada, "Queen of the Dolomites," a great glacier at its side, rises to 10,964 feet. The Marmolada range is one of the principal mountain groups of the western Dolomites, which also include the Pale di San Martino, Cima d'Asta, Latemar, Catinaccio, Sassolungo, and Sella groups. The principal mountain groups of the eastern Dolomites—the area around Cortina—are the Sorapis, Civetta, Pelmo, Antelao, Tofane, and Tre Cime di Lavaredo.

At certain times of day, the mixture of dolomitic limestone and porphyry transforms the Dolomites from a hundred shades of pink at dawn to an intense, almost inflamed red at sunset. It is also the angle and intensity of the sun that breathes life into these massive and bizarre rocks. But the word "rock" doesn't really say it all. Pinnacles, towers and turrets, pyramids and columns, all pointing straight to the sky, have been sculpted by the forces of erosion.

Historically, the Dolomite regions have undergone countless vicissitudes. Stone weapons and utensils reveal that part of the area was inhabited as far back as the 5th millennium BC. Barbarian Celts then arrived, and in the year 15 BC they fell under domination of the Romans, who opened roads in the Dolomites that were forerunners of what is today one of the best networks of mountain highways in the world. Next came invasions by the Franks, Ostrogoths, Lombards, and Bavarians. The invasions, lootings, and battles culminated when Charlemagne gained control, and the ensuing events of several centuries eventually led to Austrian dominance. It wasn't until 1919 that the last of the area, now the autonomous region of Trentino–Alto Adige, returned to Italy.

The Dolomites remain a crossroads where different cultures, languages, and customs meet. En route, travelers come across Roman ruins, medieval castles, Baroque churches, and Tyrolean chalets. The Trentino—the province of Trento—is predominantly Italian-speaking. But north of it, South Tyrol or Alto Adige—the province of Bolzano, which was Austrian until 1919 (the Italian name derives from the Adige River)—is predominantly German-speaking. Newspapers, radio, and television are bilingual, as are most road signs. If you know some German, you will be better received than if you were to speak Italian (inhabitants of the Südtirol still resent Mussolini's attempts to Italianize the area).

Another population in the Alto Adige speaks Ladin, a mixture of Celtic dialect and the vernacular Latin brought to the area by the Roman soldiers and colonizers in the 1st century BC. The Rhaeto-Roman descendants of this historical encounter still live in the Ladin valleys of Badia, Gardena, Fassa, and Ampezzo. Numbering not quite 80,000, these proud people are determined to keep their heritage and national identity alive.

On holidays or even on Sundays, the mountain people don ancient costumes and dance elaborately to the tune of yodeled music. Their mountain folklore is a central part of their lives. In fact, the Dolomites themselves are a way of life; agriculture, especially fruit and wine growing, is as important to the economy as tourism. So begin by exploring the villages, the museums of arts and crafts, and the local shops of the woodcarvers and sculptors. Walk through the tiny farm settlements that dot the valleys and look for signs of the past in the decorations encircling the windows, the carved symbols over the doors, and the painted façades. The balconies of these rustic houses are usually framed by geraniums, and even the *baite,* typical Alpine wood structures used to stack hay and stable animals, have a special charm.

As to natural beauty, keep in mind that the almost unreal peaks and bizarre massifs that are fascinating when seen from the valley become an unparalleled reality up close. If time allows, take some hikes up the mountains or ride the chair lifts and tramways. And if possible, stop in at one of the many *rifugi,* or rustic lodges (at times little more than wood huts), scattered all over the mountains and at the base of the peaks. Some of them are repositories of another kind of mountain lore—that concerning the daring pioneer climbers who came from all over the world, especially England, in the mid-19th century. Their pictures hang on the walls along with their old-fashioned climbing equipment. A hike up to a *rifugio* (in many places, a chair lift or tramway will also get you there) will allow you to watch as the modern-day climbers start out on their ascents or to enjoy a hearty mountaineer meal.

The main attraction of the Dolomites in winter is its ski slopes. Adding luster to the region are the international *World Cup* races, held annually in Val Gardena, Val Badia, and Madonna di Campiglio. The exceptional network of lifts provides access to hundreds and hundreds of miles of great skiing. Most impressive of all is the Dolomiti Superski pass, available at all the resorts. This one pass grants access to some 650 miles of groomed runs and 464 lifts leading into and out of nearly 40 separate facilities.

Cultural activities—art exhibits, theater, dance, and ballet performances, and jazz and classical music festivals—have become as much a part of the mountain scene as skiing and hiking. The local tourist information offices can provide a complete list of events. Local traditions and folklore, however, have not been forsaken. In the summer, the villages and the valleys come to life with folk and wine festivals and parades in ancient costumes, while the mountains and the mountain lakes become a vast playground for young and old: Recreation includes swimming, sailing, windsurfing, fishing, taking jeep excursions, biking (mountain bikes—the current fad—can be rented at most resorts), playing tennis, golf and miniature golf, and going on nature walks.

The largest group of visitors to the Dolomites is the hikers, who can be seen on just about every peak in any season. The climate is generally mild: Winters are cold but not frigid; summers are pleasantly warm and sunny. Storms, especially in August, do sneak up, so hikers should be prepared with lightweight and waterproof gear. A word of warning: These splendid mountains can be treacherous. It's easy to get lost, and darkness descends quite rapidly. All excursions are marked by painted symbols on stones or tree trunks. Before starting out, stop in at the local tourist board for detailed trail maps that also give the approximate time and distance of each excursion, as well as information on lodges and huts. Only an expert mountaineer, or someone familiar with the area, should stray from the marked trails. The Dolomites also offer an excellent opportunity to experience the thrill of mountain climbing; it's safest to go with a guide from one of the area's many rock climbing schools. Contact the local tourist boards or *Associazione Guide Alpine* in each of the resorts for more information.

In addition, trekking on horseback is becoming increasingly popular, especially in the Alto Adige region, where locals boast of having their very own, homebred horse—the Avelignese, named after the village of Avelengo. For information, contact the tourist office in Bolzano (11-12 Piazza Parrocchia; phone: 471-993808; fax: 471-975448). The Trento (or Trentino) region is also promoting tours on horseback as the ideal way to experience the mountains. Some 265 miles (424 km) of specially designated riding trails now run through valleys, along ridges, and over passes, and old huts and shelters are being reclaimed and refurbished for overnight accommodations. For more information, contact Trento's tourist office (4 Via Alfieri; phone: 461-983880; fax: 461-984508) or the *Federazione Italiana Sport Equestri* (13 Piazza Fiera, Trento; phone: 461-985080). Though seemingly abundant, the many multicolored flowers decorating the grassy plains and valleys are actually rare; some, such as the edelweiss, even face extinction. It's illegal to pick certain flowers, especially the edelweiss, so note the signs posted on all hiking trails to avoid stiff fines.

The most scenic and popular driving route through the Dolomites is the Grande Strada delle Dolomiti (Great Dolomite Highway), from Bolzano to Cortina d'Ampezzo, which leads across grassy meadows and valleys, over famous mountain passes, close to majestic peaks, and into lovely Alpine villages. For the most part, the route outlined here follows that highway, with some detours to the most important and beautiful valleys and resorts. After Cortina, the route circles north and west to take in Brunico and Bressanone on its way back to Bolzano. A side trip to Merano is suggested before proceeding from Bolzano to Trento, after which a side trip to Madonna di Campiglio is possible. The Great Dolomite Highway is fairly wide, but, as with all mountain driving, bends and hairpin turns are unavoidable, so take it slow. In winter, higher passes may be closed due to snow, but there are alternative routes. And an excellent network of buses serves the entire region, making it easy to travel from one town to another. The Trentino area is covered by the *Atenisa Bus Company* (3 Via Marco, Trento; phone: 461-82100), and Alto Adige is covered by the *SAD Bus Company* (phone: 1678-46047 toll-free in Italy). Local tourist offices can provide a list of destinations and schedules.

There are literally hundreds of hotels all over the Dolomites, ranging from luxurious chalets to family-run *pensioni* and bed and breakfast accommodations (tourist offices have listings). Yet another way to fully savor local mountain life and discover authentic customs and traditions is to stay in a *maso,* or a family-run farm. The accommodations are charmingly rustic and the fare simple and hearty, much of it homegrown. For information, contact *Unione Agriturismo* (7/A Via Brennero, Bolzano; phone: 471-972145) or Bolzano's tourist office (see above). For similar accommodations in the Trentino region, contact the *Associazione Agriturismo* (23 Via Brennero, Trento; phone: 461-824211). Almost all hotels have dining facilities, and the food is generally quite good everywhere. The fare, mostly Austrian, includes specialties such as *knödel,* as they are called in Alto Adige, *canederli* in Trentino, and polenta (cornmeal mush), a good hearty dish served with assorted meat or mushrooms. *Speck* is an excellent smoked prosciutto, delicious in a sandwich. Strudel is excellent all over. Pizzerias have experienced a boom in recent years, offering simple but excellent meals in addition to pizza. And with some 2,500 years of experience in viniculture, the region produces many fine wines. Grape seeds and fragments of wine cups dating back to the 5th century BC have been found in the area. The most renowned wines are teroldego rotaliano, pinot nero dell'Alto Adige, termeno aromatico, merlot dell'Alto Adige, and St. Magdalener.

Expect to pay $170 or more per night for a double room in hotels listed as very expensive; $110 to $170 in the expensive category; $60 to $110 in a moderate place; and $60 or less in an inexpensive one. These rates almost always include breakfast. All hotels feature private baths unless otherwise indicated. Weekly rates include breakfast, lunch, and dinner or just breakfast and dinner. A meal for two without wine in a restaurant listed as very expensive will cost over $120; expensive will cost $80 to $120; moderate, $50 to $80; and inexpensive, $50 or less. All restaurants are open for lunch and dinner unless otherwise noted. March to *Easter,* August, and *Christmas* are peak times, when prices may be higher and accommodations difficult to find, so reserve ahead. Many hotels close from May to early June and from October to mid-December. For each location, hotels and restaurants are listed alphabetically by price category.

Note that many sites of interest in the Dolomites close for a midday break, usually from noon to 2 or 3 PM; we suggest calling ahead to check exact hours.

BOLZANO (BOZEN) Capital of the Alto Adige, Bolzano (Bozen in German) is an important industrial and commercial city, as well as a tourist center. Its position on the way to the Brenner Pass has made it a gateway to northern Europe since its earliest days; now it is also the holiday maker's gateway to the western Dolomites. Don't be surprised to hear the Italians speak German here or to eat food more common in Austria. Until the end of World War I, Bolzano was the capital of Austria's South Tyrol, and it is still bilingual and bicultural. In fact, the sensation of being in two countries at once is one of its most distinctive and attractive features.

Life in Bolzano is pleasant and unhurried, as is immediately apparent while strolling through the Old Town. This district is set in an angle formed by the confluence of the Isarco and Talvera Rivers (which flow into the Adige south of town) and is entirely Tyrolean. Piazza Walther (Waltherplatz) is dominated by a splendid 14th- and 15th-century Gothic cathedral with a characteristic colored roof. Not far away is the 13th- and 14th-century *Chiesa di Dominicans,* also Gothic, containing a chapel with an important cycle of frescoes of the Giotto school. North of it is one of the main streets of the Old Town, Via dei Portici (Laubengasse), narrow and flanked by medieval arcades along which more modern buildings—16th and 17th century—house shops offering the best Italian and German products. Shops are closed Saturday afternoons. The buildings, carved wood doors, and elaborate windows are uniquely Tyrolean. Via dei Portici leads into Piazza delle Erbe, where a colorful outdoor fruit market is held daily. Nearby is the 14th-century *Chiesa di Francescani,* noted for its altarpiece. It's closed for a midday break. After Piazza delle Erbe, Via dei Portici becomes Via del Museo, named after the *Museo Civico* (Civic Museum; 14 Cassa di Risparmio; phone: 471-974625), which houses a vast archaeological and ethnographic collection, paintings, precious wood sculptures, and a colorful array of typical Alto Adige costumes. The museum is closed Mondays, Sunday afternoons, and for a midday break; admission charge.

Take the Guincina (Guntschna), a 1½-mile (2-km) botanical walk, for a fine view of the town and the mountain backdrop. Bolzano's tourist information office (*APT;* 11-12 Piazza Parrocchia; phone: 471-993808; fax: 471-975448) offers free, guided, multilingual tours Tuesdays from *Easter* through October. The meeting point is in front of the Benedictine abbey at Piazza Gries at 9:30 AM. Lastly, take a walk across the Talvera River past the newer sections of the city into picturesque, suburban Gries. Once a resort town of its own and now part of Bolzano, Gries has an old parish church with a 15th-century carved wood altarpiece by Michael Pacher, one of the most famous Tyrolean painters and sculptors of his time, as well as the 18th-century Baroque church of the *Monastero dei Benedettini di Muri* (Benedictine Monastery), noted for frescoes by Martin Knoller.

For the finest Tyrolean artisan products, visit the *Artigiana Atesini* (Alto Adige Artisans; 39 Via Portici; phone: 471-978590). Here, you can inspect woodcarvings, delicately embroidered and lace fabrics, ceramics, wrought-iron objects, and etchings on glass—a traditional art form for which Bolzano is renowned. It's open daily, with a long midday closing. Bolzano's ceramic artists are as adept at creating knickknacks, such as the much sought-after Angels of Bolzano, as at making wood-burning majolica stoves. They are as magnificent as those that once adorned and heated medieval castles. Locals dress up in traditional south Tyrolean attire for the outdoor *Christmas* market; held daily in Piazza Walther from November 29 to December 24, it attracts shoppers from all over. Thursday through Sunday afternoons, the shopping experience is heightened by bands, choirs, parades, street theater, and art shows. Hotels and restaurants offer special rates during this period. Other outdoor markets include Bolzano's picturesque daily fruit market (in Piazza delle Erbe) and a delightful open-air flea market on Saturdays. An annual flower market is held April 30 and May 1 from 10 AM to 10 PM.

The tourist information office (see above) has a listing of Bolzano's cultural events; most noteworthy is the *Estate in Bolzano* (Summer in Bolzano). Held in July, it includes the *Festival Internazionale di Jazz* (International Jazz Festival) and the *Festival di Danze* (Dance Festival).

Several ancient castles on the edge of town are worth a visit. Begin with the 12th-century *Castel Mareccio* (Via Claudia de' Medici; phone: 471-976615), an easy walk along the Lungotalvera, on the left side of the Talvera River. Now a well-equipped conference and cultural center, the castle can be visited by appointment. Its restaurant is closed Sundays. Approximately 1½ miles (2 km) north of Bolzano on Via Sarentina is the medieval *Castel Roncolo* (Schloss Runkelstein; Via Sarentina; phone: 471-974625 or 471-980200). One of the most famous in the area, it rises high on a steep cliff and dominates the valley below. The interior is notable for its 14th- and 15th-century frescoes depicting feudal and court life. It's open for guided visits (except Sundays and Mondays) March through November; admission charge. For information on other castles in the vicinity, some of which have been turned into fine hotels and restaurants, contact the tourist office (see above).

Wine plays an important role here. In and around Bolzano's wine-producing districts, all sorts of festivals are organized in the fall to celebrate the grape harvest. The most important one is called *Torggelen*. The name actually comes from *Torggl*, meaning winepress, which refers to the tasting of the new wine. For aficionados of wine and wine making, a side trip along the Strada del Vino (Wine Route) is in order. To get there, take S38, which goes from Bolzano to Merano. Just outside of Bolzano, at the first intersection, is a sign marked *Weinstrasse* (Wine Route). Follow the route south about 6 miles (10 km) into the heart of wine making country, surrounded by hillside vineyards and picturesque castles, to the town of Caldaro (Kaltern). On its outskirts is the 12th-century *Castello Ringberg* (follow the signs), which houses the *Museo del Vino* (Wine Museum; 1 Via dell'Oro; phone: 471-963168 or 471-21287), entirely devoted to the evolution of wine making through the centuries. The museum is closed Mondays, Sunday afternoons, and for a midday break April through November; closed December through March; admission charge. The castle's restaurant serves local fare and, of course, the best regional wines. It's closed Tuesdays and mid-November to mid-March (phone: 471-960010).

Another excursion outside town is to Collalbo (follow the signs on the old *statale*, or state road, to Brenner) to visit the Renon Plateau and the majestic Earth Pyramids, sculpted by the erosive forces of nature. Few geological formations are as bizarre as these pinnacles made from reddish, clay-like earth. Some stand as high as 130 feet; many are topped by huge boulders. To get to the plateau, take the cable car from Via Renon to Soprabolzano. From there, a small electric train takes visitors to the town of Collalbo and the pyramids. It's also a good starting point for many easy walks on the plateau, where rustic chalets, farmhouses, lodges, and restaurants abound. While there, stop in at the *Museo del Miele e Api* (Honey and Bee Museum) at Plattnerhof di Castalovara, one of the region's oldest *masi* (typical Tyrolean farmhouses). Indoor and outdoor exhibits illustrate apiculture and the process of honey making. Locals refer to the area as the bee pasture. It's open daily April through November; closed December through March; no admission charge. For more information, contact Mr. Glaser (phone: 471-345350; fax: 471-979468); contact Renon's tourist office (phone: 471-345245; fax: 471-356799) for more information about the museum and the area's other attractions.

BEST EN ROUTE

Grifone-Greif Guests enjoy modern comforts in an atmosphere elegantly reminiscent of the past. There are 130 rooms (with TVs and radios), plus an outdoor pool in a park. The very good *Grifone* restaurant is characterized by old-fashioned Tyrolean elegance. The cuisine, both regional and Italian, and the local wines—sylvaner, Santa Maddalena, and lago di caldaro—are very good, and there's outdoor dining in summer. Hotel open year-round; restaurant closed Sundays. Reservations necessary for restaurant. Major credit cards accepted. On the main square, near the cathedral, at 7 Piazza Walther, Bolzano (phone: 471-977056; fax: 471-980613). Hotel, expensive; restaurant, expensive to moderate.

Park Hotel Laurin Bolzano's most luxurious hotel, built in 1900, offers excellent service and a very elegant ambience. Set in a park in the old center of town, it has 95 rooms, a fine restaurant (appropriately called *La Belle Epoque*), and a heated pool. Hotel open year-round; restaurant closed Sundays. 4 Via Laurin, Bolzano (phone: 471-980500; fax: 471-970953). Expensive.

Da Abramo In a building that was once the *Town Hall* of Gries, it's enlivened by flowers and plants. Traditional Italian dishes—risotto is a specialty—and seafood are served, and there's alfresco dining in summer. Closed Sundays and most of August. No reservations. Major credit cards accepted. 16 Piazza Gries, Bolzano (phone: 471-280141). Expensive to moderate.

Chez Frederic The ambience and style are French, the cuisine and wines, a combination of the best French and the best Italian, both of which can be savored outdoors in summer. Closed Monday dinner, Tuesdays, and July 5 to 27. Reservations necessary. Major credit cards accepted. 12 Via Armando Diaz, Bolzano (phone: 471-271011). Moderate.

Luna-Mondschein Somewhat less refined than the other hotels in its category, it is nonetheless very pleasant and rustic. There are 85 rooms, a garden, and a restaurant. Open year-round. 15 Via Piave, Bolzano (phone: 471-975642; fax: 471-975577). Moderate.

Scala-Stiegl This Tyrolean 60-room hotel on the edge of town has extremely good service and an outdoor pool (all rooms have TVs and mini-bars). In summer, meals are served outside in a lovely garden. Open year-round. 11 Via Brennero, Bolzano (phone: 471-976222; fax: 471-976222). Moderate to inexpensive.

En Route from Bolzano Head northeast for 1³/₄ miles (3 km) to pick up S241 at Cardano (Kardaun). For 5 miles (8 km), S241 leads east through a narrow, and somewhat frightening, gorge called Val d'Ega (Eggental), whose entrance is guarded by the *Castello di Cornedo*. Continue through Nova Levante, a pretty summer resort surrounded by pine forests. As the road climbs, look up through the treetops for a glimpse of two impressive Dolomite peaks—the highest peak (9,236 feet) of the Latemar group and the 9,756-foot Catinaccio, in whose German name, Rosengarten (Rose Garden), the legend of Laurino lives on. Farther up the road is a grand view of Lago di Carezza (Karersee), a typical Alpine lake whose emerald green waters mirror the Latemar peaks. S241 continues up and over the 5,671-foot Passo di Costalunga, also known as the Passo di Carezza (Karerpass), which marks the boundary between the provinces of Bolzano and Trento. On the approach to the top of the pass, the view suddenly opens up: To the west, in the far distance, are the Ortles and Venosta Alps; to the east, beyond the Fiemme and Fassa Dolomites, the renowned Pale di San Martino.

After the pass, the road descends into the Val di Fassa, and the Marmolada, or Queen of the Dolomites, the most majestic of all the mountains, comes into view. At Vigo di Fassa, time permitting, take the tramway to Ciampedie, where there is a natural panoramic terrace at the foot of the Rosengarten. From Vigo, take S48 south 3 miles (5 km) to Moena, the gateway to the Fassa Valley, the Italian capital of cross-country skiing and home to one of the world's most famous competitions—the *Marcialonga* (for details, see *Italy's Unparalleled Skiing* in DIVERSIONS). Then turn north on S48 for 10 miles (16 km) to Canazei.

CANAZEI A summer and winter resort in the Alta Val di Fassa (High Fassa Valley), Canazei is surrounded by the peaks of three Dolomite groups—Sassolungo, Sella, and Marmolada—and is also central to three Dolomite passes—Passo del Pordoi, Passo di Sella, and Passo di Fedaia. In the center of town is the delightful late-Gothic *Chiesa di San Floriano,* decorated with Baroque wood altars. The façades of many buildings are painted with narrative and symbolic frescoes. A hike or the chair lift takes visitors to scenic high spots such as Pecol and Col dei Rossi. Another way to see the area is on horseback. While in town, take time to visit the highly recommended wine cellar of *Enoteca Valentini* (2 Via Antermont; phone: 462-61135), which boasts a great selection of the best Trentino and Alto Adige wines, as well as other Italian and German vintages. Typical Trentino products—such as *speck,* honey, and marmalade—can be purchased on the ground floor. For more information on Canazei, contact the Valle di Fassa's tourist office (Via Costa, Canazei; phone: 462-62466; fax: 462-62278) or Canazei's tourist board (16 Via Roma; phone: 462-61113 or 462-61145; fax: 462-62502).

Don't leave town without taking a side trip to Marmolada. Follow S641, a somewhat narrow but panoramic road, east to the Fedaia Pass, the boundary between the provinces of Trento and Belluno (the latter in the Veneto region), and continue on to Malga Ciapela. From here, catch the tramway to Marmolada for an unequaled view of the entire Dolomite range. The Marmolada glacier is famous for some great summer skiing.

BEST EN ROUTE

Diana Near a small pine forest, this characteristic mountain lodge has 30 rooms and a restaurant. Open December 20 to April 20 and July to September 20. 84 Via Roma, Canazei (phone: 462-61477; fax: 462-62694). Moderate.

Tyrol This rather refined, 36-room chalet-like hotel is near the center of town, on the edge of a pine forest. The restaurant is very good. Open mid-December through mid-April and mid-June through mid-September. 3 Viale alla Cascata, Canazei (phone: 462-61156; fax: 462-62354). Moderate.

En Route from Canazei Pick up S48 northeast. Approximately 9 miles (14 km) from town, to the left, detour onto S242, which travels over the Sella Pass, with the mountains of the Sella group to the east and Sassolungo to the west. The road then descends into tiny Plan de Gralba and right into the heart of the Val Gardena—one of the most beautiful resort areas in the Dolomites, a skiers' paradise in winter and a playground for mountain climbers and hikers in summer. The valley is part of the Ladin-speaking region of Alto Adige, and its inhabitants still conserve their enthusiasm for mountain culture and folklore. Its craftspeople are renowned—the expert woodcarvers are especially famous for hand-carved furniture, statues, and toys. The route traverses the entire valley, passing through its three most important villages—Selva di Val Gardena, Santa Cristina, and Ortisei—all within a few miles of each other.

SELVA DI VAL GARDENA AND SANTA CRISTINA Known in German as Wolkenstein in Gröden and St. Christina, these two villages are equally charming. A number of excursions begin in each town. The Passo di Gardena can be reached by tramway from Selva di Val Gardena. After the 20-minute ride, passengers are rewarded with an incomparable view of the Sella, Sassolungo, and Sciliar mountains and of the Alpi di Siusi, a high Alpine plain. From Santa Cristina, a chair lift ride of less than 10 minutes leads to Monte Pana, where weary visitors can relax at the ski lodge *Sporthotel Monte Pana* and enjoy the magnificent view. For more altitude, another 10-minute chair ride carries visitors up to the *Rifugio Mont de Soura* at 6,565 feet, and a three-hour hike reaches the top of the famed Sella Pass.

In Selva during the summer, there is a variety of musical events to enjoy, such as the *Settimane Musicali Gardenesi* (Gardenese Musical Weeks) in July and August, and the *Festival del Folklore Gardenese* (Gardena Folklore Festival) in August. For a list of events, check with the *Azienda Autonoma di Soggiorno e Turismo Selva/Gardena* (*AAST; Palazzo Cassa Rurale*; phone: 471-795122; fax: 471-794245). In September, Santa Cristina attracts many visitors to the *Settimane Autunnali* (Autumn Weeks), a pleasant event that combines guided hikes and excursions with cultural and musical events, local folklore, and superb food. For information about this and other events in Santa Cristina, contact the tourist office in the *Palazzo Comunale* (phone: 471-793046; fax: 471-73198).

For a delightful shopping experience, explore the colorful and picturesque outdoor markets, Wednesdays in Santa Cristina and Thursdays in Selva di Val Gardena.

ORTISEI (ST. ULRICH) The chief town of Val Gardena, this summer and winter resort village lies at the foot of the Alpe di Siusi, the most extensive plateau in the Alps. Grassy and wildflower-strewn in summer and snow-covered in winter (for details, see *Italy's Unparalleled Skiing* in DIVERSIONS), it can be reached by tramway from Ortisei and offers wonderful views. Ortisei is another village with a Ladin heritage, and the *Museo Ladin* (Ladin Museum; 83 Via Rezia, just behind the *Sparkasse Bank;* phone: 471-797554) has a display of 300 years of the art of woodcarving. Look for old wooden toys, as well as paintings by famous Gardena artists. In addition, the fascinating mineral and fossil collection provides insight into the geological vicissitudes of the Dolomites. The museum is closed Sunday afternoons and for a long midday break in July and August; open Tuesdays and Fridays only from 4 to 6:30 PM the rest of the year; admission charge. Ortisei also is a village of woodcarvers, and there are shops selling carvings everywhere. For a more cultural glimpse of the artistry of local woodcarvers, visit the permanent exhibition of Gröden handicraft at the *Palazzo dei Congressi* (Congress Hall) on Piazza Stetteneck; the *Associazione Turistica* (Tourist Board) is also located here (phone: 471-796328; fax: 471-796749). The palazzo is closed Sundays and for a long midday break. And don't forget the outdoor market on Fridays in the main square of Piazza Stetteneck.

The tourist office organizes walks in the mountains once a week in July, August, and part of September. They are led by a qualified guide who also provides a wealth of information about the mountains, geology, flora, and fauna. For details, stop by or call the *Associazione Turistica* (see above). For equine excursions, contact *Maneggio S. Durich* (phone: 471-796904).

BEST EN ROUTE

Aquila-Adler Undoubtedly the best hotel in Ortisei, it boasts a golden book of famous guests and offers 85 rooms, a covered pool, a garden, tennis, a sauna, a solarium, and a restaurant. Open mid-December through mid-April and mid-May through mid-October. 7 Via Rezia, Ortisei (phone: 471-796203; fax: 471-796210). Very expensive to expensive.

Angelo-Engel A typical Alpine lodge, cozy and pleasant, it has 37 rooms, good service, a sauna, a garden, and a restaurant (open to hotel guests only). Open mid-December through October. 35 Via Petlin, Ortisei (phone: 471-796336; fax: 471-796323). Moderate.

Ronce It boasts a cozy family atmosphere, all wood decor, and proximity to the ski slopes. There are 24 rooms, a garden, a sauna, and a restaurant (for guests only). Open *Christmas* through *Easter* and mid-June through mid-October. 1 Via Ronce, Ortisei (phone: 471-796383; fax: 471-797890). Inexpensive.

En Route from Ortisei There are two ways to approach Corvara in the Val Badia. One way is to backtrack through Santa Cristina and Selva di Val Gardena to Plan de Gralba, and pick up S243 at the intersection. From there, travel north-northeast 2 miles (3 km) to the Passo di Gardena (taking in yet another view of the Sella group as you climb) and into the village of Colfosco. To the right, after 1¼ miles (2 km), is Corvara in Badia.

Unfortunately, this approach cuts out what some consider the most splendid Dolomite pass of all—the 7,692-foot Passo di Pordoi, which affords an exhilarating view of the Marmolada, Catinaccio, Sassolungo, and Sella mountains. One way to see the Passo di Pordoi is to head for Corvara straight from Canazei. Take S48 14 miles (22 km) over the pass and on to S244 at Arabba, which leads into the Val Badia and to Corvara in Badia.

Since the Val Gardena is only a stone's throw from Val Badia, side trips from Corvara are easy (via the Passo di Gardena), or stop there after having visited the Val Badia.

CORVARA IN BADIA In the heart of the Alta Val Badia, another Ladin valley, is this dreamy mountain village. On the approach to town, the sight of a massive rock that seems to rise out of the earth is dazzling. This is the Sassongher (8,668 feet), Corvara's pride and joy. The small town sits at the foot of this lone giant. Not as fashionable as the other resort areas (for information on winter sports, see *Italy's Unparalleled Skiing* in DIVERSIONS), it is friendly and probably as authentic today as it was in 1880, when visitors began to discover it.

The first tourists were English climbers, who came not only because of the challenging mountain but also because of the reputation of a local Alpine guide, Franz Kostner, who had spent much of his life as a guide in the Himalayas and was the first to lead the English to the top of the Matterhorn. The village rapidly became the place to go, especially to avoid frivolity and to live close to nature. Corvara is still basically the same today; its townsfolk take pride in an old-fashioned hospitality. In return, they—Ladins, as they consider themselves—ask only that visitors respect and learn to love their mountains.

The valley can be explored using Corvara as a base. The tiny town of Colfosco is literally around the bend and within walking distance (1¼ miles/2 km). Other villages—Pedraces, La Villa, and San Cassiano—are only a few miles away, easily reachable by daily, regularly scheduled bus service; accommodations are in fine hotels or cozy, family-style, chalet-like *pensioni*. Short hikes into the mountains will turn up a variety of rustic farmhouses and barns or entire tiny settlements of mountain farmers. Some farmhouse and barn façades are frescoed, while their windows are framed by classic Ladin decorations. Look carefully for sundials or carved or painted flowers with six petals set inside a circle—the wheel of life, a Celtic symbol.

Hikes, excursions, and nature walks are organized one day each week by the Corvara/Colfosco *AAST* (on the main thoroughfare in the *Palazzo Comunale*; phone: 471-836176 or 471-401555; fax: 471-836540). Contact the *Arlara* hotel (phone: 471-836146) or *Trapper's Home* (phone: 471-836643) about tours on horseback. Bus excursions are also available; inquire at the *AAST* (see above) or at the *Tourdolomit* travel office (also on the main thoroughfare; phone: 471-836232). In summer, as part of its promotion of Ladin culture, the tourist board organizes weekly visits to *viles,* ancient Ladin settlements, and to *masi,* typical farmhouses, as well as Ladin cooking classes. August brings many costumed processions and other Ladin festivities.

BEST EN ROUTE

La Perla There's a touch of sophistication in a typically Tyrolean atmosphere in this 50-room hotel. Besides a restaurant, it has an indoor pool, a gym, a sauna and solarium, a boutique, and an art gallery. Open mid-December through mid-April and mid-June through September. 44 Centro, Corvara in Badia (phone: 471-836132; fax: 471-836568). Very expensive to expensive.

Posta-Zirm Corvara's oldest and most prestigious hotel is an international gathering spot where friends meet in a characteristically Ladin ambience. There are 45 rooms, a restaurant, a disco, an indoor pool, a sauna, and a solarium. Open December to mid-April and May through October. 16 Centro, Corvara in Badia (phone: 471-836175; fax: 471-836580). Expensive.

Sassongher A 50-room hotel, it combines rustic Tyrolean elegance and a cozy atmosphere, enhanced by locally produced antique furniture. There is a restaurant, gym, indoor pool, sauna, solarium, hot tub, and boutique. Open December through mid-April and mid-June through mid-September. 29 Via Pescosta, Corvara in Badia (phone: 471-836085; fax: 471-836542). Expensive to moderate.

L'Fana For beautiful mountain ambience and local fare presented with a touch of refinement, this is the place. It is popular among villagers and visitors alike for its vast selection of dishes and excellent service. There's terrace dining in summer. Closed May through June and November through mid-December. Reservations necessary. Major credit cards accepted. In the nearby town of La Villa (phone: 471-847022). Moderate.

Speckstube Peter Typical Tyrolean decor is an appropriate backdrop for the excellent Ladin cuisine and the fine selection of vintage wines served here. A wonderful place to get tasty snacks or to indulge in some wine tasting, it is especially popular among the locals, who come here for midnight snacks. Closed Wednesdays; April through May; and October through November. No reservations. No credit cards accepted. In Colfosco, about 2 miles (3 km) from Corvara (phone: 471-836071). Moderate.

La Tambra A traditional Alpine chalet, small but lively, this is where locals go for a good mountain meal. The regional fare includes barley soup, goulash, and game in season. Closed Wednesdays; May through mid-June; and October through mid-December. No reservations. No credit cards accepted. 159 Via Pescosta, Corvara in Badia (phone: 471-836281). Moderate.

Tablè Tastefully furnished according to the mountain tradition, this 27-room hotel organizes special gastronomic evenings and candlelight dinners and is renowned in the valley for its pastries and homemade ice cream. Open mid-December through March and mid-June through mid-October. 127 Via Pescosta, Corvara in Badia (phone: 471-836144; fax: 471-836313). Moderate to inexpensive.

En Route from Corvara Head north on S244 for 2½ miles (4 km) to La Villa, and then turn right into the Valle di San Cassiano. Travel through

Armentarola to the Passo di Valparola (7,046 feet), and past the foot of another mountain, Lagazuoi. The road then hooks into S48 and the Passo di Falzarego, a pass that is open only in summer. The next stop is Cortina d'Ampezzo, in the eastern Dolomites, about 21 miles (34 km) from Corvara.

CORTINA D'AMPEZZO Of all the ski resorts in the Dolomites, Cortina is the only one that requires little introduction. The splendid town sits in a large basin called the Valle del Boite, framed by the Tofane, Pomagagnon, Cristallo, Sorapis, and many more gold-pink peaks. Cortina has been known as a mountaineers' paradise since the mid-19th century, although it wasn't until near the turn of this century that the first hotels were built. It then developed quickly, and even before World War I it was on the map as one of the best resorts in the Dolomites. For more information, see *Italy's Unparalleled Skiing* in DIVERSIONS.

Cortina is a small but cosmopolitan city with exclusive shops, luxury hotels, refined restaurants, nightclubs, and discos. Such glamorous and sophisticated accoutrements have made it *the* place to be and ski in Italy, and at least once a year the jet set meets here to renew acquaintance. But Cortina is not glitter alone. Its more rustic side is sought by mountain climbers who test their courage on the high peaks and hikers who pitch camp at the quaint *rifugi,* or small, lone lodges.

Corso Italia, the main avenue, is largely a pedestrian island, where you'll find the *Ciasa de ra Regoles* (67 Corso Italia; phone: 436-86622), which houses an important museum of geology and mineralogy and the Rimoldi collection of modern art. It's open from 4 to 8 PM; closed Sundays; admission charge. Stop in at the *Artigianato Artistico Ampezzano* (Corso Italia; phone: 436-868440), a permanent exhibit of the crafts of local artisans, to see woodcarvings with precious inlays of ivory and mother-of-pearl; wrought-iron, brass, and copper objects; and splendid filigree necklaces, clasps, and brooches. It's open daily; no admission charge. And don't miss the *Cooperativa di Consumo* (40 Corso Italia; phone: 436-861245), a store featuring locally made handicrafts. For many, boutiques take precedence over mogul or downhill skiing on the magical mountains. Several of the world's greatest fashion designers have set up shop in Cortina through the years, making it the couture capital of the Dolomites.

After a day on the slopes, visit Cortina's most exclusive pastry shop, *Embassy* (44 Corso Italia; phone: 436-86377). Sharing the limelight of sweet success is the *Lovat Pastry Shop* (65 Corso Italia; phone: 436-3307), where tired skiers gather in late afternoon to replenish calories lost on the slopes. And you can while away the evening hours with a glass of fine wine and a smoked pork sandwich at the tiny but well-supplied *Enoteca Cortina* (5 Via del Mercato; phone: 436-862040), which is closed Sundays. Three miles (5 km) from the center of town is one of Cortina's most colorful shops, *El Touladel* (follow the signs to the village of Col; no phone), selling exquisite tablecloths, napkins, fabrics, loden-covered sofas, and marvelous terra cotta lamps.

But since Cortina's real wealth is the mountains, it would be a mistake not to take a few excursions to some of nature's best belvederes: The same mountains that are breathtaking when seen from the town will leave you speechless close up. There are tramways and chair lifts (not all of them depart from town) to some of the most scenic spots, such as the 10,673-foot summit of the Tofana di Mezzo or the foot of the Tofane group, west of Cortina, and the foot of the Cristallo group, east of town. The *Rifugio Cinque Torri*, the *Rifugio Col Drusciè*, and the *Belvedere di Pocol* shouldn't be missed. For more details about these and other excursions, contact the *Azienda di Promozione Turistica* (*APT;* 8 Piazzetta San Francesco; phone: 436-3231; fax: 436-3235; or 1 Piazza Roma; phone: 436-2711).

BEST EN ROUTE

Miramonti Majestic Without question, this luxurious 106-room hotel is the grande dame of Cortina's hostelries. Open *Christmas* to mid-April and July through August. For more information, see *Italy's Most Memorable Hostelries* in DIVERSIONS. 103 Via Peziè, Cortina d'Ampezzo (phone: 436-4201; fax: 436-867019). Very expensive.

De la Poste Dating back to 1805, this hotel has 80 homey rooms and a restaurant. Elegant, sophisticated, and fashionable, it is in the center of town. Open *Christmas* to mid-April and June through mid-October. 14 Piazza Roma, Cortina d'Ampezzo (phone: 436-4271; fax: 436-868435). Very expensive.

El Toulà Housed in a former hayloft, which is what its name means in the local dialect, this sister to *El Toulà* in Rome serves exceptional international cuisine. Closed *Easter* to mid-July and mid-September to *Christmas*. Reservations necessary. Major credit cards accepted. 123 Via Ronco, Cortina d'Ampezzo (phone: 436-3339). Very expensive.

Cortina This establishment is rustic yet refined, with Persian rugs adorning the floors. The 48 rooms are furnished with beautiful objects made by Cortina's artisans—including headboards hand-sculpted in Val Gardena. There is a restaurant. Open *Christmas* to mid-April and mid-June to mid-September. 94 Corso Italia, Cortina d'Ampezzo (phone: 436-4221; fax: 436-860760). Expensive.

Europa The very rustic Alpine atmosphere of this 52-room establishment is complemented by beautiful pieces of antique furniture. The restaurant's international fare is highly recommended. Open mid-December through October. 207 Corso Italia, Cortina d'Ampezzo (phone: 436-3221; fax: 436-868204). Expensive.

Il Meloncino Tiny and rustic, the best eatery in town is known for its remarkable grilled meat platters. There's alfresco dining in summer. The panorama from the terrace may distract you from the fine food. Closed Tuesdays, June, and mid-October through November. Reservations necessary. No credit cards accepted. Località Gillardon, Cortina d'Ampezzo (phone: 436-861043). Expensive.

Tana della Volpe The dark wood decor and pink accessories accentuate this eatery's quaintness. Reserve a table in the *Stube,* a typical Tyrolean dining area. In summer, dine alfresco on international fare. Closed Wednesdays in low season, mid-June to mid-July, and November. Reservations necessary. No credit cards accepted. 27A/B Via della Stadio, Cortina d'Ampezzo (phone: 436-867494). Expensive.

Da Beppe Sello Traditional but exquisite food is served in a rustic, cozy atmosphere. Closed Tuesdays, *Easter* to mid-May, and mid-September through October. Reservations advised. Major credit cards accepted. 68 Via Ronco, Cortina d'Ampezzo (phone: 436-3236). Expensive to moderate.

Capannina The Venetian and Tyrolean dishes are excellent, as is the selection of fine wines (both regional and international). The small, cozy dining room is decorated with style and elegance. Closed Wednesdays, *Easter* to late June, and October to *Christmas.* Reservations advised. Major credit cards accepted. 11 Via Stadio, Cortina d'Ampezzo (phone: 436-2950). Expensive to moderate.

Menardi On the outskirts of town, this 40-room hotel with a restaurant was once a large, old farmhouse. Chalet-like furnishings give it a warm and cozy atmosphere. Open *Christmas* through mid-April and mid-June through mid-September. 110 Via Majon, Cortina d'Ampezzo (phone: 436-2400; fax: 436-862183). Expensive to moderate.

Sport Tofana An older 88-room, chalet-like hotel—3 miles (5 km) west of Cortina on S48—is in a peaceful spot away from the crowds. There is a restaurant. Open *Christmas* to mid-April and July through mid-September. Via Pocol, Pocol (phone: 436-3281; fax: 436-868074). Moderate.

En Route from Cortina Take S48 east out of town through the Passo Tre Croci and enjoy an impressive view of Monte Cristallo. Seven and one-half miles (12 km) from Cortina, turn left onto S48 *bis* for Lago di Misurina, north about 2 miles (3 km). Although this lake is not as pretty as other, lesser-known Alpine lakes, it is famous for the way it mirrors the majestic 9,746-foot Tre Cime di Lavaredo (Drei Zinnen), a truly breathtaking visual effect. Route S48 *bis,* which becomes S51, leads to the outskirts of Dobbiaco (Toblach), 22 miles (35 km) from Cortina by this route. Dobbiaco is another lovely village in a very green valley, the Alta Val Pusteria, and its parish church offers one of the best examples of Baroque art in the whole Alto Adige. For one week in July every year, the mountains and valleys surrounding Dobbiaco reverberate with the sounds of Mahler as the village honors its adopted musical son, who spent many years here in search of refuge and inspiration. For information about the festival, contact the *Associazione Turistica* (Tourist Information Office; 21 Via Roma, Dobbiaco 39034; phone: 474-72132; fax: 474-72730).

If the glitz and glitter of Cortina have failed to meet your expectations of a rural and rustic ambience, take a detour to Sesto in Val Pusteria. From Dobbiaco, head east on S49 to San Candido. Take S52 southeast about 9½ miles (15 km) to Sesto, a favorite in both winter and summer for those looking for quiet relaxation. The resort is surrounded by grassy plains and gentle peaks. Less than a mile away is the tiny village of Moso, which competes with Sesto for being the most picturesque and quaint. At the edge of town, follow the signs for Val Fiscalina, considered by many to be one of the most beautiful and magical places in the Dolomites. The tourist board in Sesto (9 Via Dolomiti, Sesto 30930; phone: 474-70310; fax: 474-70318) can provide information about hotels. Return to Dobbiaco and pick up S49 westbound for Brunico, about 17 miles (27 km).

BRUNICO (BRUNECK) The capital of the Val Pusteria is famous for the spacious and gentle slopes that surround it. Although it's dominated by a 13th-century castle, the area's greatest attraction is the panoramic view from the Plan de Corones, reached by cable car. On a plateau 7,460 feet high, the Plan de Corones has an extensive network of lifts and great winter skiing.

The *Museo Etnografico* (Ethnographic Museum; Via Duca Teodone; phone: 474-32087) offers an informative glimpse of life on a mountain farm. This re-creation of a typical farm village centers around a 300-year-old manor, *Main am Hof.* The museum is closed Sundays and Mondays November through March; closed Sundays before 2 PM and Mondays April through October; admission charge. From June through August, Brunico hosts a variety of concerts and musical events, held in the *Casa Rogen,* the *Chiesa Parrochiale,* and the *Parco de Tschurtschenthaler.* Check with the Brunico *AAST* (at the bus station on Via Europa; phone: 474-555722; fax: 474-555544) for information. They also organize guided tours (in English) of the town every Friday at 5 PM from mid-June through August, as well as botanical excursions.

BEST EN ROUTE

Andreas Hofer Pine-paneled walls and typical Tyrolean furniture are the most distinctive decorative features of this modern hotel with 54 rooms. There is a solarium and sauna, as well as a pleasant garden. The restaurant is cozy and friendly, and the Tyrolean cuisine is reputed to be the finest around (an entire dynasty of chefs comes from here). The specialty is game with polenta. Open January through March and June through October; restaurant closed Saturdays. Reservations advised for restaurant. Major credit cards accepted. 1 Via Campo Tures, Brunico (phone: 474-31469; fax: 474-31283). Moderate to inexpensive.

En Route from Brunico Continue for about 22½ miles (36 km) to Bressanone on S49.

BRESSANONE (BRIXEN) On the road to the Passo dell Brenneo (Brenner Pass), this charming Alto Adige town claims an eclectic combination of architecture and monuments, from the medieval to the Baroque. From the 11th century to the first decade of the 19th century, it was dominated by prince-bishops, who also ruled much of the surrounding area. Its 13th-century cathedral, redone in the Baroque style in the 18th century, is imposing, and its adjoining cloister is covered with 14th- and 15th-century frescoes, as well as an even older (begun in the 11th century) frescoed baptistry. The *Palazzo dei Principi Vescovi* (Palace of the Prince-Bishops; phone: 472-30505) is also worth a visit. Daily from 2 to 5 PM from mid-December to mid-February, visitors can see the palace's unique collection of 97 18th- and 19th-century nativity scenes, all beautifully arranged and comprising delicately carved wood figurines. As each story unfolds through the eyes of the people of Alto Adige, it is not surprising to find shepherds in Tyrolean attire and hats. Most impressive is a colossal scene (1758–1807) by Augustin Alois Probst, who filled his crèche with 5,000 pieces. Even the more modest crèches have 500 figurines. The palace is closed Sundays, holidays, and from November to mid-March (except as stated above). There's an admission charge.

Like Bolzano, Bressanone has a lively outdoor *Christmas* market, which is open daily from late November to December 22. The local artisans are renowned for their wax creations; most appealing are the elaborately decorated candles with bas-reliefs. Even if you see nothing else in Bressanone, stop at the *Elefante* hotel (see below), a beautifully preserved 16th-century building with one of the best restaurants in the Dolomites. On Wednesdays from July through September, the tourist board (*APT*; 9 Viale Stazione; phone: 472-22401 or 472-36401; fax: 472-36067) organizes free guided tours of Bressanone's historic district. On Thursdays in July and August, it offers guided hikes and other excursions.

BEST EN ROUTE

Elefante In the mid-16th century, this inn stabled an elephant the King of Portugal was sending over the Passo di Brenner as a gift to the Hapsburg emperors in Vienna. A fresco remains on the hotel's façade to commemorate the event, and the inn looks much as it did then. The public rooms and some of the 30-plus guestrooms have antique furnishings; across the street is an annex with 14 rooms and a heated pool. The restaurant serves Tyrolean fare (the produce and dairy products come from the hotel's farm) and homemade pastry, but no dish is as famous as its *Elefantenplatte* (*piatto elefante* in Italian), or elephant platter—a mountainous heap of meat and vegetables served to no fewer than four diners. Open March through mid-November and at *Christmastime*; restaurant closed Mondays. Reservations advised. Visa accepted. 4 Via Rio Bianco, Bressanone (phone: 472-32750; fax: 472-36579). Expensive to moderate.

Fink The fine local reputation of this restaurant comes as much from its excellent selection of regional dishes as from the *Menhir Stube,* a precious, stone-carved stela used in ancient times for burials, on display here. The owner exhibits other archaeological artifacts and documents that he has collected. Closed Wednesdays, part of July and August, and Tuesday dinner from November through June. Reservations unnecessary. Major credit cards accepted. 4 Portici Minori, Bressanone (phone: 472-34883). Moderate.

En Route from Bressanone Pick up A22 for a quick return to Bolzano, about 25 miles (40 km). Before leaving the Alto Adige, however, a side trip to charming Merano, approximately 18 miles (29 km) from Bolzano northwest on S38, is recommended for those who have the time.

MERANO (MERAN) An old-fashioned spa town, Merano has few major monuments but definite character—steep-roofed houses with painted façades, oak-beamed wine cellars with wrought-iron signs, flower-bordered streets and balconies, *caffè*-lined promenades, and 6,560-foot-high trails that can be reached by skiers or hikers by cable car in a few minutes. It is picturesque and quaint—see Via dei Portici in the Old City center—as well as cosmopolitan. The town is also very lively, thanks to events such as international horse races, summer evenings of folk dancing, and the two concerts held daily from April through October along the Passeggiata Lungo Passirio (only one of Merano's promenades offering tranquillity or scenic views—others are the Passeggiata Tappeiner and the summer and winter promenades, the Passeggiata dell'Estate and the Passeggiata d'Inverno). Colors explode and fragrances permeate the pure mountain air during the first week of June, when thousands of flowers and plants line the promenades (admission charge). In August, some of the world's most prestigious orchestras come to Merano for the *Festival Internazionale di Musica Classica* (International Festival of Classical Music). For information about this and other events, contact the tourist board (*APT*; 45 Corso Libertà; phone: 473-235223; fax: 473-235524).

Europeans also visit Merano in the spring and fall for their health, since its mineral waters are supposed to be very beneficial. Others come for such beauty treatments as mud baths, massages, and diets. For details, see *Taking the Waters* in DIVERSIONS. In summer, the town draws walkers; in winter, skiers. The *Gran Premio di Merano,* the most prestigious Italian horse race, is held here on the last Sunday of September. The Tyrolean equivalent of the *Kentucky Derby*, it is just as exciting. In fall, the town, which is situated in the center of a grape growing district, has been the traditional place to take the grape cure, although the distinction between grape cure and wine therapy is sometimes fuzzy.

Local grape festivals are organized in October, with the *Festival Autunnale* (Autumn Festival) taking place on the second Sunday of the month. Events include parades with allegorical floats, folk dances, a display of local costumes, and much more. For a delightful shopping experience, visit the city's outdoor market (Via IV Novembre) on Fridays.

The *Museo Civico* (43 Via Galilei; phone: 473-37834) has several interesting collections, ranging from art and archaeology to local crafts, fossils, and minerals from the Alto Adige region. Noteworthy is the first wooden typewriter, conceived and built by Parcines Peter Mitterhofer, a local carpenter, in 1863. Closed Sunday afternoons and for a long midday break; admission charge. The *Castello Principesco* (Via Galileo; phone: 473-37834), where Tyrolean princes once lived, houses a noteworthy collection of period furniture and antique musical instruments. It's closed November through March; Sundays; holidays; Saturday afternoons; and for a midday break. There's an admission charge. Women's attire from 1870 to the present is the central theme of the *Museo della Donna* (Woman's Museum; 68 Via Portici; phone: 473-31216); one room has only hats and headdresses. It's closed weekdays before 3 PM, Saturday afternoons, and Sundays; admission charge. Merano 2000, a nearby plateau, affords a wonderful panoramic view. To get there, take city bus No. 3 (from the train station) to Val di Nova, where the Ifinger Seilbahn (Ifinger Tramway) goes up to the plateau. The area offers a variety of lodges for snacks and drinks, as well as some fine excursions.

Also worth visiting is the *Tyrol Castle*. Built in 1140 on a steep rock near the town of Tyrol, it was the official residence of the Counts of Tyrol. Noteworthy are the reliefs surrounding the main portal, the chapel, and the capitals in the *Cavalier Room*. An interesting archaeological museum also is housed in the castle. The castle is closed November to mid-March, Mondays, and for a midday break; admission charge (phone: 473-220221). Buses for Tyrol leave regularly from Merano's train station.

BEST EN ROUTE

Castel Freiberg Built in the 14th century, this former castle stands on a hill in total isolation. Although it's reminiscent of ancient times, the quality of service, facilities, and level of comfort in the 36 rooms are all up-to-date. There is a restaurant, a sauna, a solarium, a garden, indoor and outdoor pools, and tennis. Open mid-April through October. Four miles (6 km) southeast of Merano off S38 in Località Fragsburg (phone: 473-244196; fax: 473-244488). Very expensive to expensive.

Palace Kurhotel This majestic, 124-room structure is set in a park and surrounded by exotic plants. Furnished in the elegant Empire style, it is both traditional and comfortable. There is a restaurant, a spa, indoor and outdoor pools, a sauna, and beauty treatments. Open April through December. 2 Via Cavour, Merano (phone: 473-211300; fax: 473-234181). Very expensive to expensive.

Kurhotel Schloss Rundegg Another castle that has been transformed into a hotel, and since this one was built in the year 1100, a stay in one of the 30 rooms is like taking a leap into the past. Its restaurant is for hotel guests only; other amenities include an indoor pool, tennis, a garden, and spa facilities (sauna, solarium, diet consultation, and beauty treatments). Open January 1 to 5 and February through December. 2 Via Scena, Merano (phone: 473-234100; fax: 473-237200). Expensive.

Andrea The tone of this highly recommended restaurant is traditional; the cuisine, regional with a modern twist. Spinach *Krapfen* and crêpes with parmesan and beer are among the specialties, and the selection of local and national wines is very good. Closed Mondays. Reservations necessary. Major credit cards accepted. 44 Via Galilei, Merano (phone: 473-237400). Expensive to moderate.

Museumstube Onkel Taa The name refers to a display of ancient artifacts, and the walls of the *Hapsburg Room* are covered with imperial portraits. Owner-chef Carlo Platino (Uncle Taa) grows organic vegetables and breeds trout. His specialties include grilled vegetables, meat, or trout; the butter, cheese, and bread are homemade. Closed Mondays, mid-January to mid-March, and mid-November through mid-December. Reservations advised. Major credit cards accepted. Five miles (8 km) from Merano on Via Stazione, Toll (phone: 473-236604). Expensive to moderate.

Naif This classic Austrian beer hall serves regional food. Closed Mondays and November 7 to 20. No reservations. No credit cards accepted. 35 Via Val di Nova, Merano (phone: 473-32216). Moderate.

Augusta In this beautiful villa are 26 rooms and a restaurant. Open March 15 to November 15. Centrally located, at 2 Via Otto Huber, Merano (phone: 473-222324; fax: 473-220029). Moderate to inexpensive.

Schloss Labers This former medieval castle has a highly evocative interior and 32 rooms. An outdoor restaurant is used in warm weather; there is a typical Tyrolean bar, tennis courts, and a heated pool. Open April through October. 25 Via Labers, Merano (phone: 473-234484; fax: 473-34146). Moderate to inexpensive.

Terlaner Weinstube Located under the arches of a picturesque street, its furnishings are antique, and the food is regional and international. Closed Wednesdays and parts of February and March. Reservations necessary. No credit cards accepted. 231 Via dei Portici, Merano (phone: 473-235571). Moderate.

En Route from Merano Return to Bolzano on S38, and pick up the A22 southbound to Trento, 18 miles (29 km) away.

TRENTO A noble, albeit somewhat austere, city on the Adige River, Trento is surrounded by the Dolomites to the east and the Brenta group, a prolongation of the Dolomites, to the west. Roman in origin, Trento became an important town on the way to the Passo di Brenner for the same strategic reasons its northern neighbor, Bolzano, did. From the 11th century until 1803, it, along with the rest of the Trentino province, was ruled by Prince-Bishops of Trent, whose rule extended into Alto Adige for part of that time. The city gained lasting fame in the mid-16th century as the seat of the Council of Trent, which sat from 1545 to 1563 in an attempt to reform the church and curtail the spread of the Protestant Reformation. After a brief stint of Napoleonic rule, Trento became Austrian until the end of World War I although, unlike Bolzano, it has always been largely Italian-speaking and Italian in character. Today it is the capital of the Trentino–Alto Adige region.

Much remains in Trento from the medieval period and much also from the early 16th century, due to the influence of a particularly humanistic prince-bishop, Bernardo Clesio. Among the city's highlights (in the Piazza del Duomo) is the *Cattedrale di San Vigilio,* 12th- and 13th-century Lombard Romanesque to Gothic in style. Inside is the *Cappella del Crocefisso* (Crucifix Chapel), containing the crucifix before which the Council of Trent's decrees were proclaimed. From the *Duomo,* walk north along Via Belenzani, the city's most beautiful avenue, lined with Venetian-style Renaissance palaces, some with frescoed façades. Turn right onto Via Manci, another notable street, and follow it to Trento's most celebrated monument, the *Castello del Buonconsiglio* (Castle of Good Counsel; Via B. Clesio; phone: 461-233770), the residence of the prince-bishops. It consists of several parts, including the 13th-century *Castelvecchio,* the oldest, and the 16th-century *Palazzo Magno,* a Renaissance addition by Bernardo Clesio. Inside the castle walls are sections devoted to archaeology and medieval and modern art. It is closed Mondays and for a short (noon to 2 PM) break; no admission charge the first and third Sunday of each month.

Trento has gained worldwide recognition for the *Festival Internazionale Film della Montagna e della Eplorazione Avventura "Città di Trento"* (International Mountain and Exploration Film Festival) held here each year in May and June. In April and May is Trento's annual *Festival Musica Sacra* (Sacred Music Festival), held at many of the city's churches. For information about both, contact the *APT* (Tourist Board; 4 Via Alfieri; phone: 461-983880; fax: 461-984508). On Fridays and Saturdays, Piazza d'Arogno is the site of a crafts market where local artisans sell their wares—look for the colorful, hand-painted trays, a typical Trentino craft. And don't miss the wild mushroom market; featuring about 260 species, it is held daily from June through October in the Piazza Lodron.

Trento's palaces, with their frescoed façades, are not to be missed. The oldest frescoed house is the *Casa Balduini* (29 Piazza Duomo), whose decorations date back to the 15th century. Others include the *Casa Cazuffi Rella* (northeast side of Piazza Duomo), whose allegorical frescoes depict mythological figures and symbolic scenes. One of the most prestigious Renaissance buildings is the *Palazzo Geremia* (22 Via Belenzani), whose frescoed façade illustrates many historical episodes, including the arrival in Trento of Maximilian I of Austria. The local tourist office can supply a list of Trento's frescoed structures. And the *Consorzio Trento Iniziative* (78 Via Solteri; phone: 421-88011) offers free guided tours of the city on Wednesdays from July through September.

Trento's pride and joy is Monte Bondone, the broad, roundish mountain that dominates the city. Only 30 minutes from downtown, it boasts great skiing in winter, while in summer its flowery meadows are ideal for nature walks, climbing, or simply viewing the higher peaks—such as the Brenta Dolomites—in the distance. Take S45 *bis* 12 miles (20 km) toward Lake Garda. At the Montevideo signpost, turn left for Sardagna and continue to Monte Bondone. Along the way are the villages of Candriai, Veneze, Norge, and Vason. About 1½ miles (2 km) from Vason is the beautiful basin of Viote, now the site of the *Giardino Botanico Alpino* (Alpine Botanical Gardens; phone: 461-47540), which afford a rare glimpse of Alpine flora. The gardens are open daily, with a short (noon to 2:30 PM) closing, from June through September; closed the rest of the year; admission charge.

Excursions to several places in the area can be made easily from Trento. Take the cable car (near the train station) to the lush green valley sitting directly above Trento. Nestled here is the picturesque village of Sardagna. From the edge of town there is a spectacular view of Trento, with high Dolomite peaks in the background. And 2 miles (3 km) east of Trento along SS47 is the Ponte Alto Gorge, with an impressive waterfall inside a grotto. The gorge was built in 1537 to stop the destructive Fersini River, which threatened to flood Trento. There's an admission charge. Many of Trentino's most impressive castles have now opened their gates to visitors. An easy and pleasant way to see them is to ride on one of the *Trenini dei Castelli* (Castle Trains) into the Valley of Valsugana, Vallagarina, or the Non Valley. These trips include a multilingual guide, admission charges, transportation, and lunch or dinner at one of the castles. The trains run from June through September on either Fridays, Saturdays, or Sundays.

Trento also is close to many resorts. Take S47 south to Levico Terme, just 13 miles (21 km) away. At the foot of Monte Fronte, it is one of the most popular thermal and holiday spots in the area. For more information, see *Taking the Waters* in DIVERSIONS.

Accademia A private residence in medieval times, this tranquil 44-room hotel near Piazza del Duomo boasts its original vaulted ceilings and exposed beams. Some rooms have private balconies, and there is a garden courtyard and a terrace with views over the rooftops of Trento. No restaurant. 4-6 Vicolo Colico (phone: 421-233600; fax: 421-230174). Expensive.

Chiesa In this 16th-century palace, the accent is on sophistication. The refined fare is regional Trentino, and a selection of local wines is offered. Closed Sundays, Wednesday dinner, and the last two weeks of August. No reservations. Major credit cards accepted. *Parco San Marco,* Trento (phone: 461-238766). Expensive.

Grand Hotel Trento A cozy place, it has 94 rooms and a private garden. Its restaurant, *Il Caminetto,* is good. 1 Via Alfieri, Trento (phone: 461-981010). Expensive.

Osteria Due Spade The fare at this friendly and cozy eatery descends directly from old Trentino recipes. There also is an excellent selection of wines. Closed Monday lunch and Sundays. Reservations necessary. Major credit cards accepted. 11 Don Rizzi, Trento (phone: 461-234343). Expensive to moderate.

America A very cordial family atmosphere is a plus at this renovated 43-room hotel. There also is a restaurant. 52 Via Torre Verde, Trento (phone: 461-983010; fax: 461-230603). Moderate.

Villa Madruzzo Located 2 miles (3 km) east of Trento in Cognola, this is a converted 18th-century villa with 51 comfortable rooms, a restaurant, and a pleasant garden. 26 Via Ponte Alto, Cognola (phone: 461-986220; fax: 461-986361). Moderate to inexpensive.

Birreria Forst Don't miss a chance to eat in this very popular beer hall. The cooking is regional, as are the wines. Pizza is served as well. Closed Mondays and late June to mid-July. No reservations. No credit cards accepted. 38 Via Oss Mazzurana, Trento (phone: 461-235590). Inexpensive.

En Route from Trento One last side trip leads to the Dolomiti di Brenta and to the popular resort of Madonna di Campiglio. Take A22 north 9 miles (14 km) to Mezzolombardo. Exit and follow S43 north 14½ miles (23 km) to Cles. If its name rings a bell, it's because this pretty medieval village was once the home of the Clesio family, one of whose members figured prominently in Trento's past and whose ancestral castle is outside of town. After Cles, at the intersection, take S42 west for 7½ miles (12 km) through Male; at Dimaro, pick up S239 south into Madonna di Campiglio.

MADONNA DI CAMPIGLIO If ever a resort came close to competing with Cortina, it's Madonna di Campiglio. It has all the ingredients: first class hotels, excellent facilities, fashionable shops, and a marvelous setting at the bottom of a large valley, dominated to the east by the beautiful Brenta Dolomites and to the west by the magnificent Presanella and Adamello groups. Dense fir woods surround the village.

In 1110, Madonna di Campiglio was merely a shelter, built by a monk named Raimondo for the few wayfarers brave enough to cross the Alpine passes with their cattle. It remained farmland until 1862, when the entire Campiglio Valley was purchased by Giambattista Righi to create a summer resort. And although the first hotel was built in Madonna di Campiglio in 1872, the resort really came into its own between the two world wars. It owes its popularity above all to skiers (for details, see *Italy's Unparalleled Skiing* in DIVERSIONS), but the area is also a paradise for mountain climbers— it has one of the best mountain climbing schools in the Alps. For more information, check with the *APT* (Tourist Board; 4 Via Pradalago; phone: 465-42000; fax: 465-40404) or *Trentino Holidays* (78 Via Soltieri; phone: 451-82200). Also see *Take a Hike: Walking Through Italy* in DIVERSIONS. In addition, Madonna di Campiglio boasts one of the highest golf courses in Europe. Situated in the Campo Carlo Magno area, the nine-hole layout is surrounded by the majestic Dolomite scenery and has hosted many prestigious summer tournaments. Contact *Golf Club Carlo Magno* (at the *Golf* hotel; see *Best en Route*).

The accent in Madonna is on ecology. In keeping with this trend, local mountain guides organize nature excursions along some of the most beautiful trails in the area and week-long mountain treks with stays in rustic alpine lodges. Contact the *Ufficio Guide Alpine* (Piazza Brenta Alta, Madonna di Campiglio; phone: 465-42634) and ask for Fabio Stedile, an expert guide who speaks English. Reserve at least a day ahead for one of these trips.

BEST EN ROUTE

Golf Located 1¼ miles (2 km) north of Madonna di Campiglio, this very fashionable 124-room hotel in Campo Carlo Magno is the former summer residence of the Hapsburg family. It is both elegant and cozy, with an excellent restaurant and a nine-hole golf course. Open December through mid-April and mid-July through mid-September. Campo Carlo Magno (phone: 465-41003; fax: 465-40294). Very expensive.

Grifone Modern yet cozy, the atmosphere of a mountain lodge prevails in this 40-room hotel, which also has a nursery and a fine restaurant. Open December to mid-April and July through August. 7 Via Vallesinella, Madonna di Campiglio (phone: 465-42002; fax: 465-40540). Very expensive to expensive.

Carlo Magno Zeledria Set in a lovely pine forest, this cozy Alpine lodge (a tavern in the 18th century) has 94 rooms, a restaurant, and an indoor pool. Open December to mid-April and mid-June through mid-September. Passo di Campo Carlo Magno (phone: 465-41010; fax: 465-40550). Expensive to moderate.

St. Hubertus Each of the 32 rooms at this hotel has a balcony and a great view. The decor is both charmingly rustic and elegant, interspersed with Tyrolean touches. The owner is a profound believer in authentic Austrian hospitality and tradition. There is a heated pool, a garden, and a restaurant. Open December through April and July through August. 7 Viale Dolomiti Brenta, Madonna di Campiglio (phone: 465-41144; fax: 465-40056). Expensive to moderate.

Cozzio This cozy, family-run establishment is close to the town's main square, yet it sits right behind the famous *Tre-Tre World Cup* ski course. It has a disco, a games room, and a TV room. The restaurant offers fine traditional fare. Once a week in summer, the family takes guests on an easy hike to the nearby woods, where meat is grilled and polenta is cooked over an open fire, mountain-style. Open December through April and July through September. 31 Via Cima Tosa, Madonna di Campiglio (phone: 465-41083; fax: 465-40003). Moderate.

Crozzom Centrally located, this rustic, wood-paneled eatery serves excellent regional dishes and wines. Carrot cake and strudel are two of the specialties. Fresh flowers on each table add elegance to the warm and friendly *ambiente*. In summer, dinner is served on a flowery terrace or in the garden. Open daily. No reservations. Major credit cards accepted. Via Dolomiti di Brenta, Madonna di Campiglio (phone: 465-42217; fax: 465-42636). Moderate.

Il Caminetto A cozy and warm air pervades this 33-room establishment, especially in the *caminetto* (fireplace) room. There is a restaurant. 17 Via Adamello, Madonna di Campiglio (phone: 465-41242). Moderate to inexpensive.

The Veneto

Stretching from the soaring pink-hued peaks of the Dolomite Mountains to the flat, green plains of the Po River, the Veneto is one of the most diverse regions in Italy. Aside from the Dolomites and their rambling foothills, which define the Veneto's northern frontier with Austria, other highlands include the Asolan and Euganean hills, whose tranquil, vine-covered slopes have long been relished by those escaping the often oppressive heat of the lowland summer. Even more typical of the region are its vast plains and its mighty rivers—the Po, Adige, Brenta, Piave, Sile, and Livenza.

The area also is abundantly rich in agriculture. Unlike the rural scenery found throughout much of Europe, the farms of the Veneto still are maintained on a small scale, and many of the ingredients waiting to be savored on the local trattoria tables, including the wines, have been grown no more than a few minutes' drive from the kitchen.

After touring the hinterlands of the Veneto, vacationers will appreciate its beaches—or rather its beach, for almost all the coastline constitutes one continuous, fine strand, interrupted only by the mouths of rivers and lagoons. But the flavor of its many parts varies, from the busy resorts of Jesolo and the Lido of Venice to miles of deserted horizons that remain the exclusive territory of birds and other wildlife. Inland, the Veneto offers its visitors another shoreline—more than 30 miles of beach on the eastern coast of Lake Garda, Italy's largest lake. Like the region's hillier retreats, the Riviera-like resorts of Garda have been popular since ancient times.

But the Veneto region is more than a place of natural beauty. Historically and artistically, it reflects the Byzantine influences imported through Italy's eastern trading routes. Roman influence also left its mark, for the conquering legions of the emperor Augustus based themselves here to repulse the invading barbarian tribes of northeastern Europe. During the Middle Ages, under the influence of rich local families who ruled the Veneto cities (the Scaligeri of Verona, the Carraresi of Padua, and the Camino of Treviso), the Veneto became, together with Tuscany, economically and artistically one of the richest areas of the peninsula.

The Veneto was also subject to the central government of Venice at the zenith of its career as a republic (during the 14th and 15th centuries). Venice's ascendancy resulted in the creation of some of the world's greatest works of art and supreme examples of architectural grandeur—most notably the magnificent Palladian villas, many of which still grace the Veneto landscape.

The rich, lively paintings and frescoes that adorn so many Veneto interiors are the work of such Renaissance greats as Giotto, Pisanello, and Andrea Mantegna in the 14th and 15th centuries, Veronese in the 16th century, and the Tiepolo father and son Venetian painters of the 17th and 18th centuries.

Venetian cooking is as diverse as its geography. Its hearty mountain fare, featuring dumplings, soups, rich desserts, and cakes, shows a strong Austrian influence. The fertile hills and plains around Verona, Vicenza, and Treviso offer wonderful meat and vegetable dishes. In the hilly forests around Belluno, there is a wealth of wild mushrooms and game, while *cucina casalinga* (home cooking) on the coast boasts the culinary delights of Adriatic fish and shellfish, such as bream, sardines, cuttlefish, and clams. Venetian wines are world famous, from the dry white pinot bianco and grigio to the red cabernet and merlot, not to mention the fiery, highly alcoholic grappa made from the final grape pressings.

From Venice, our route follows the Brenta and the magnificent country villas that overlook it to Padua (with an optional detour to the Euganean Hills); then, bypassing Vicenza, it heads for Verona. The route then returns via Vicenza—the city of Palladio—branches out to the Dolomite foothills and Bassano del Grappa on the Brenta, and then continues on to the mountain town of Belluno via the delightful panoramic setting of Asolo. The road then takes a detour through the mountains to the town of Vittorio Veneto and then on to Treviso. Allow nine or 10 days for a leisurely drive, since the countryside is as spectacular as the towns in this northeastern border region of Italy.

The Veneto has a network of efficient tourist information offices. Most towns and cities have either an *Azienda di Promozione Turistica* (*APT;* Local Tourist Board) or an *Ente Provinciale per il Turismo* (*EPT;* Provincial Tourist Board). The latter will have information not only on the town but also on the surrounding province.

Prices in the Veneto vary greatly depending on whether an establishment is in a historic center, such as Padua, Verona, or Treviso, or slightly off the beaten track, as in Belluno, Bassano del Grappa, or the Euganean Hills. Expect to pay $200 or more per night for a very expensive double room with breakfast; from $125 to $200 for an expensive room; from $75 to $125 for a moderate one; and $75 or less for an inexpensive room. All hotels feature private baths unless otherwise indicated. An expensive dinner for two with wine will cost $100 or more; a moderate one, from $60 to $100; and an inexpensive one, $60 or less. All restaurants are open for lunch and dinner unless otherwise noted. For each location, hotels and restaurants are listed alphabetically by price category.

Note that many sites of interest in the Veneto close for a midday break, usually from noon or 12:30 PM to anywhere from 2 to 3:30 (and occasionally 4) PM; we suggest calling ahead to check exact hours.

VENICE For a detailed report on the city, its sights, its hotels, and its restaurants, see *Venice* in THE CITIES.

En Route from Venice Take the road for Marghera and then follow signs for Malcontenta on the Brenta River, where, escaping the steamy heat of Venice, noble Venetian families took their ease in magnificent villas, some designed in the 16th century by the seminal local architect Andrea Palladio or his followers. About 15½ miles (25 km) from Venice via S11 is Dolo.

BRENTA RIVIERA The Brenta villas are strung out along the river between Malcontenta and Stra (the S11 runs along the north bank). *Villa La Malcontenta,* the first of the grand villas, constructed by Andrea Palladio for the Foscari family in 1560, is a gracious masterpiece half hidden behind weeping willows. Sitting placidly on the shores of the Brenta River, this superbly simple villa, to which a Foscari family member banished his wife, has a Greek-temple façade like many aristocratic homes in this area, designed by Palladio. His classicism influenced notable 18th- and 19th-century English and American buildings, from *Knole* to the *White House.* The villa is open May through October on Tuesdays and Saturdays only, from 9 AM to noon. There's an admission charge (phone: 41-547-0012).

The next villa worth stopping for is *Widmann-Foscari,* an impressive house with French Baroque overtones to its original early-18th-century Venetian façade. Here the family portrait is a frescoed ceiling in the hall, and there are mythical frescoes by Giuseppe Angeli. The garden is a typical example of Venetian mannerism of the 18th and 19th centuries. The villa is closed Mondays; November through March; and for a short (noon to 2 PM) break; admission charge (phone: 41-560-0272).

DOLO This town is dotted with 17th- and 18th-century family villas, many of them still inhabited, as well as the domed and pillared 18th-century *Chiesa di San Rocco.*

BEST EN ROUTE

Villa Ducale This recently refurbished 18th-century country home is the perfect base for touring the neighboring aristocratic villas. There are 10 generous-size rooms, most with terraces overlooking formal gardens and some with the original painted wall panels and frescoed ceilings. There's also a restaurant. Closed January. 75 Riviera Martiri della Libertà, Dolo (phone/fax: 41-420094). Very expensive to expensive.

En Route from Dolo Just beyond Dolo lies one of the Brenta's pièces de résistance, *Villa Lazara Pisani.* Unfortunately, the villa is closed to visitors, though it can be glimpsed from the road through the trees. Six miles (10 km) from Dolo is Stra.

STRA The climax of this waterside tour is the place where the *Villa Pisani* (also called *Villa Nazionale*), now a national monument, dwarfs all other Brenta villas both in size and magnificence. In the villa, which was built in the mid-

18th century for the Pisani family (who owned 50 villas in all), are 164 rooms (eight are open to the public) bearing original frescoes, including the spectacular ballroom ceiling, a work by Giambattista Tiepolo that depicts the power and success of the Pisani family. As befits such a palatial residence, it was visited by monarchs, grand dukes, and czars traveling around Europe. In 1807, Napoleon bought it and gave it to his brother, the Viceroy of Italy. Then, in 1934, it served as the first rendezvous for Hitler and Mussolini. On the grounds is a box-hedge maze, designed by Girolamo Fregimelica, the architect of the villa. The villa and grounds are closed Mondays May through October; closed Mondays and after 3 PM the rest of the year (the labyrinth is open in summer only); admission charge (phone: 49-502074).

En Route from Stra Just beyond Stra is Padua.

PADUA Padua (or Patavium, as it was known in 10 BC—Padova in modern Italian) is one of the most important industrial, commercial, and agricultural centers in northern Italy. An artistic, scientific, and scholastic gem, Padua is also a historic jewel: The buildings in the city center are reminiscent of a stage set for a Shakespearean play. The first wall around Padua was built in 1200; its university, founded 22 years later, was one of the first in Europe, second in age only to Bologna's. Dante and Petrarch attended the university and Galileo taught here. Padua's artistic landmarks are relics of its dramatic history, and some of the world's major treasures of art and architecture are housed here, including those of Giotto and Donatello, both Florentines.

The *Cappella di Scrovegni* (Piazza Eremitani; phone: 49-875-1153 or 49-875-2321), erected by the noble Paduan family of the same name, is most renowned for Giotto's 1305 frescoes that set the style for three-dimensional space in Renaissance painting. The frescoes depict scenes from the lives of the Virgin Mary and Christ, the Last Judgment, seven virtues, and seven vices, all based on the idea of redemption. The chapel was built by Enrico Scrovegni as penance for the material sins of his wealthy father, depicted among "The Blessed" in *The Last Judgment.* It is open daily March through December; closed Mondays January through February and public holidays; admission charge. Nearby is the *Chiesa degli Eremitani* (Church of the Hermits; phone: 49-31410), known for its extensive Mantegna frescoes. Built in the late 13th century, the church and frescoes were destroyed during World War II, but the church was later rebuilt in its original Romanesque style. The church is open daily, with a long (noon to 3:30 PM) closing.

When Padua's patron, St. Anthony, was canonized in 1231, a Gothic basilica was built around his tomb in Piazza del Santo. Known simply as *del Santo,* the church is one of Italy's most famous sanctuaries, a wonderful mixture of Romanesque, Gothic, Venetian, and Byzantine architecture, with arched doorways, eight-tiered domes, and bell towers that look like minarets. The main altar, notable for its ornate gold bas-reliefs, is the work of Donatello, as are the nine sculpted reliefs along the top of the saint's enormous tomb (phone: 49-663944). Ask the sacristan for access to the cloisters, which were built between the 13th and the 16th centuries and which afford a fine view of the basilica. On August 13, the *Festa di San Antonio* is enthusiastically celebrated with processions through the town.

In the square outside *del Santo* is Donatello's famed masterpiece, an equestrian statue of a Venetian *condottiere* (military commander), Erasmo da Narni, better known as Gattamelata. Across the square (to the right as you face the church) is the *Oratorio di San Giorgio,* a burial chapel of the Soragna family frescoed by Jacopo Avanzi and Altichiero. Next door, the *Scuola del Santo* (School of St. Anthony; phone: 49-663944) is lined with 16th-century frescoes, three by Titian. Both are open daily, with a midday closing, from February through November; closed afternoons December through January; admission charge to both.

The neoclassical, "doorless" *Caffè Pedrocchi* (Piazzetta Pedrocchi; phone: 49-875-2020) is Padua's most famous 19th-century monument, designed by Giuseppe Jappelli in 1831. Standing in the precincts of the university just off Piazza Cavour, the *caffè*'s columned loggias with tables and chairs quickly became the "living room" of patrician Paduans. The ground floor was open to the public; the upstairs rooms with swirling frescoed ceilings were the domain of nobles. The ground floor is still a *caffè*, its outside seating a popular vantage point over the bustling heart of town. Art shows and cultural events are held in the restored upstairs salons, which are closed Mondays; Tuesday through Friday mornings; and weekends for a midday break; admission charge. (For information on events taking place in the *caffè*, contact Padua's department of culture; phone: 49-661377.) Not far away are two interesting squares, Piazza delle Erbe and Piazza della Frutta, which contain outdoor fruit and vegetable markets. The huge building between them, girded with loggias and topped by a sloping roof, is the *Palazzo della Ragione*. Built as a meeting hall, courthouse, and administrative center during the 13th century to celebrate Padua's newly won independence as a republican city, it was remodeled in the 14th century to include exterior arcades and a vaulted roof. The interior frescoes, on religious and astrological themes, are 15th-century replacements of originals by Giotto and members of his school. Also inside is a large wooden statue of a horse, built for a tournament in the 15th century and for some time erroneously attributed to Donatello. The palazzo is closed Mondays and public holidays in summer; closed Mondays, public holidays, and after 1 PM the rest of the year; admission charge (phone: 49-820-5006).

Another historic square not to be missed is Piazza dei Signori. It is surrounded by the onetime local government seat, the 14th-century *Palazzo del Capitanio,* the early-15th-century clock tower, and the Renaissance *Loggia del Consiglio*. In another of the city's beautiful squares, the 18th-century Prato della Valle, there is an open-air market every Saturday, selling, among other items, footwear manufactured along the Brenta River, including top-quality designer shoes for which Brenta is renowned. The largest piazza in Italy, it is surrounded by canals and has a garden in the center. More flora can be seen at the nearby *Orto Botanico* (Botanical Gardens; 15 Via Orto Botanico; phone: 49-656614). Founded in 1545, these gardens are the oldest in Europe and among the most extensive. The gardens are open daily, with a midday break, in summer; closed Sundays, and Mondays through Saturdays after 1 PM, the rest of the year; admission charge. A single, combined entry ticket to some of Padua's most important sites is available from the local tourist offices. There's one in Piazza Eremitani (phone: 49-875-1153), which is open daily, and another at the railway station (phone: 49-875-2077), which is closed Sunday afternoons. A one-day tourist bus ticket that allows unlimited travel on city routes for a small fixed charge can be obtained from *ACAP* offices at the railway station (phone: 49-662055) and from other authorized agents.

BEST EN ROUTE

Antico Brolo Close to the Prato della Valle, this fairly formal eatery serves creative regional cooking made with seasonal vegetables. Try the *gamberi al zafferano* (shrimp saffron) or the *sella di coniglio ai asparagi e funghi* (rack of rabbit with asparagus and mushroom sauce). There's alfresco dining in the garden in the summer. Closed Sundays and August. Reservations necessary. Major credit cards accepted. 14 Vicolo Cigolo, Padua (phone: 49-664-5555). Expensive.

Belle Parti Formerly *El Toulà* (and still affiliated with the prestigious chain), this comfortable restaurant, with high, wood-beamed ceilings, is run independently by Angelo Rasi. The menu offers delicious regional fish and meat dishes with imaginative variations. Try the *prosciutto Belle Parti* (wafer-thin slices of marinated beef), polenta *pastissada* (oven-baked polenta-and-meat cake), prawn risotto, and stuffed pigeon, or one of the fish dishes. Local wines from the Euganean Hills make an ideal accompaniment. Closed Sundays, Monday lunch, and August. Reservations necessary. Major credit cards accepted. 11 Via Belle Parti, Padua (phone: 49-875-1822). Expensive.

Padovanelle Just outside the city in a park surrounding Padua's racecourse, this modern 40-room hotel complex has indoor and outdoor pools, a tennis court, private parking, and lovely gardens. Its *Ippodromo* restaurant looks out onto the track, and bets can be placed when the course is open. 4 Via Ippodromo, Ponte di Brenta, Padua (phone: 49-625622; fax: 49-625320). Expensive.

San Clemente Outside the city center, this beautiful restaurant is in a restored 15th-century hunting lodge attributed to Palladio. The food is as elegant as the setting—creative cooking that frequently features fish and seafood. The kitchen smokes its own fish and meat and makes excellent pasta. In summer, dine outdoors surrounded by herbs in the botanical garden. Closed

Sundays, Monday lunch, August, and December 26 through January 6. Reservations necessary. Major credit cards accepted. 142 Corso Vittorio Emanuele II, Padua (phone: 49-880-3180). Expensive.

Le Calandre Four miles (6 km) outside town is this culinary find, where both traditional and innovative food are prepared by the Alajmo family. Risotto, beet dumplings, homemade pasta, boned squab, and mushrooms in season are cooked to perfection. The pastries are always fresh, and the other desserts are first-rate as well. The popular *caffè* next door serves croissants at breakfast and sandwiches from mid-morning on. Closed Sunday dinner, Mondays, and two weeks in August. Reservations advised. Major credit cards accepted. 1 Via Liguria, on the route from Padua to Vicenza, Sarmeola di Rubano (phone: 49-630303). Expensive to moderate.

Donatello In the heart of town, this hostelry affords a splendid view of Donatello's equestrian statue. It has 49 rooms (a few without private bath) and a restaurant. 102 Via del Santo, Padua (phone: 49-875-0634; fax: 43-875-0829). Moderate.

Europa A large, centrally located, efficient establishment, it offers 59 rooms and a good restaurant serving local specialties. A short walk from the *Cappella di Scrovegni*, at 9 Largo Europa, Padua (phone: 49-661200; fax: 49-661508). Moderate.

Da Giovanni A must for meat lovers, this restaurant specializes in huge whole roasts or boiled meat, all carved at the table, and homemade pasta as a hearty first course. Wines, whether of the house or from local vineyards, are excellent. Closed Saturday lunch, Sundays, August, and from *Christmas* through *New Year's Day.* Reservations advised. American Express accepted. 22 Via Maroncelli, Padua (phone: 49-772620). Moderate.

Grande Italia One of Padua's more popular hotels has 62 rooms (a few without private bath) and a restaurant (closed Sundays). Directly opposite the main station, at 81 Corso del Popolo, Padua (phone: 49-650877; fax: 49-875-0850). Moderate.

En Route from Padua South of Padua, in the middle of the plains, is an unexpected collection of small, cone-shaped, densely vegetated volcanic hills called the Colli Euganei (Euganean Hills). This is one of Italy's most romantic corners. From Padua's main station, follow the city's ancient walls to the turnoff for the airport (Via Sorio). Take the small, signposted road to the left about 8 miles (13 km) outside Padua on the road to Teolo to the magnificent *Abbazia di Praglia*, a Benedictine monastery founded in the 11th century. It's set against a backdrop of sharply rising hills with a magnificent view over the surrounding plains, and the church, the *Chiesa dell'Assunta,* dedicated to the Madonna, was reconstructed in the 15th century in Venetian Renaissance style. Guided visits are available Tuesdays through Sundays (except on religious holidays) on the half-hour from 3:30 to 5:30 PM in summer; from 2:30 to 4:30 PM in winter (phone: 42-990-0010).

From the abbey, return to the main road, turn right, and follow the signs to Torreglia, Galzignano, and Valsanzibio—the site of *Golf Club Padova,* an excellent 18-hole course (47 Via Noiera; phone: 49-913-0078), and the beautiful gardens of the *Villa Barbarigo.* The villa is closed Sunday and Monday mornings; for a long (noon to 3 PM) break; and November through mid-March; admission charge (phone: 49-913-0042). Then head to Arquà Petrarca, one of the most picturesque medieval villages in the region. There, the retirement home of 14th-century poet Petrarch (15 Via Valleselle; phone: 429-718186 or 429-718294) is worth a visit. His house is closed Mondays, public holidays, and for a midday break; admission charge. At this point you may return to Padua by way of Montegrotto Terme and Abano Terme, both important spa towns where hotels continue the tradition of mud baths and similar therapies that have been enjoyed since Roman days (for more information on the latter, see *Taking the Waters* in DIVERSIONS). Today the area boasts over 200 indoor/outdoor swimming pools. It is also well endowed with simple trattorie—many offering quail and meat grilled on an open fire—and inexpensive *alberghi.*

Instead of returning to Padua, continue south from Arquà Petrarca on S16, following signs for Monselice. A stroll down Via al Santuario is a good way to see Monselice's highlight—the *Ca' Marcello,* once an awesome fortress. Its castle, which houses one of Italy's finest collections of armor and weapons, also is filled with beautiful 15th- to 18th-century furniture. The castle is open Tuesdays, Thursdays, Saturdays, Sunday mornings, and the second and third Sunday of each month from April to mid-November; closed mid-November through March. Guided tours in Italian are offered at 9 and 10:30 AM and 3:30 and 5 PM on Tuesdays, Thursdays, and Saturdays, and at 3:30 and 5 PM on the second and third Sunday of each month; admission charge (phone: 429-72931). Continue past the Romanesque-Gothic *Duomo* (Passeggiata delle Sette Cappelle) to the *Santuario delle Sette Chiese* (Sanctuary of the Seven Churches), tiny shrines situated among the cypress trees that line the road. At the end of the lane is the 17th-century *Villa Duodo,* whose lovely gardens are open to the public daily.

From Monselice, head west 6 miles (10 km) on S10 to Este. The town is dominated by its castle (ca. 1339) with pretty grounds. The *Museo Nazionale Atestino* (National Atestino Museum; 9 Via G. Negri; phone: 429-2085) houses Iron Age and Roman relics, for which Este is renowned. The museum is closed Mondays and public holidays; Tuesdays through Saturdays for a short (1 to 3 PM) break; and Sundays after 2 PM; admission charge. The local ceramics industry prospers at *Este Ceramica Porcellane* (31 Via Sabina; phone: 429-2270); seconds and surplus items are sold at a small shop outside the factory. Continue west on S10 to romantic and medieval Montagnana, where Franco Zeffirelli filmed parts of *Romeo and Juliet.* The town's 14th-century walls are still intact; Palladio's unfinished

Villa Pisani stands outside the eastern gate. Sansovino designed the beautiful portal on the Renaissance cathedral, which also contains Veronese's *Transfiguration of Christ.*

Return to Padua. The 55 miles (88 km) separating Padua from Verona can be covered on either the state highway (S11) or the autostrada (A4), which runs more or less parallel and gives splendid views of the luscious green vine-clad hills of one of the most fertile areas of the country.

VERONA Of *Romeo and Juliet* and *Two Gentlemen* fame, Verona is one of Italy's oldest and most beautiful cities, already in existence when it was occupied by the pre-Roman Etruscans. For a more detailed report on the city, its sights, its hotels, and its restaurants, see *Verona* in THE CITIES.

En Route from Verona From the northern outskirts of town, follow the green signs for A4 to Vicenza (about 32 miles/51 km toward Padua) and exit at Vicenza Ovest (West).

VICENZA Beautiful enough to be dubbed "the Venice of Terra Firma," Vicenza is best known as the city of Andrea Palladio. Born in Padua in 1508, Palladio fled from his apprenticeship as a stone carver in 1524 to Vicenza, where he spent most of the rest of his life, influencing not only Vicenza's architecture—hence its common name Città del Palladio—but also the development of buildings throughout Europe and America.

The hub of activity is Piazza dei Signori, no less busy now than in the heyday of Vicenza's civic life. Like other Venetian cities, Vicenza was first and foremost a Roman colony, which eventually flourished under the Venetian Republic. By the end of the 16th century the city was resplendent with new buildings, many of them built by Palladio, that survive to this day. Piazza dei Signori is flanked on one side by the *Basilica,* formerly the Gothic *Palazzo della Ragione* (Town Hall), which Palladio converted to High Renaissance style. Many consider this to be his masterpiece. Palladio simply enveloped the preexisting façade with his classic columns on two levels, transforming it into one of the finest Renaissance buildings in the world. One corner of the *Basilica* is flanked by a tall, elegant clock tower, the *Torre di Piazza* (also known as the *Torre Bissara*), dating from the 12th century. The basilica is closed Mondays and public holidays; Tuesdays through Saturdays for a midday break; and Sunday afternoons; admission charge to special exhibitions (phone: 444-323681).

Across the square from the *Basilica* is the *Loggia del Capitaniato,* a building with enormous red brick columns. Formerly the residence of the Venetian local governor, it is one of Palladio's most imposing works. The town's main shopping street, Corso Andrea Palladio, is a visual delight and worth a stroll. At the end of the street, stop at the Dominican Gothic *Tempio di Santa Corona,* containing Bellini's *Baptism of Christ* and Veronese's *Adoration of the Magi.* It's open daily, with a midday closing (phone: 444-323644).

Contrà Porti is a street studded with private palaces of the rich and famous (and not-so-famous). Don't miss No. 6-10, the Venetian-Gothic 14th-century *Palazzo Cavalloni-Thiene;* No. 11, Palladio's *Palazzo Porto Barbaran;* and No. 12, the Renaissance *Palazzo Thiene,* with a terra cotta portal and a rear façade by Palladio. At No. 14 is the Gothic *Palazzo Sperotti-Trissino;* No. 16 is the Renaissance Palazzo *Porto-Fontana;* No. 17, the Venetian-Gothic *Palazzo Porto-Breganze;* No. 19, the Gothic-Venetian *Palazzo Colleoni-Porto;* and No. 21, Palladio's unfinished *Palazzo Iseppo da Porto.*

Another of the architect's outstanding works of genius is the *Teatro Olimpico* (Piazza Matteotti; phone: 444-323781). Still in use, the theater is closed Sunday afternoons, and Mondays through Saturdays for a midday break; admission charge. Purchase tickets for performances from the *Agenzia di Viaggi Palladio* (16 Contra Cavour; phone: 444-546111). For more details on the theater, see *Theater, Music, and Opera* in DIVERSIONS.

Palazzo Chiericati (Piazza Matteotti) is yet another of Palladio's imaginative projects, with its entire façade, except for the doorway, composed of two tiers of columns. This is now the home of the *Museo Civico* (Municipal Museum, Piazza Matteotti; phone: 444-321348) and a fine collection of Venetian paintings by such artists as Paolo Veneziano, Battista da Vicenza, Carpaccio, Paolo Veronese, and Giovanni Buonconsiglio. The museum is closed Sunday afternoons, Mondays, public holidays, and for a midday break; admission charge.

Vicenza sits in the middle of a countryside peppered with villas, many of which are included in a booklet called *The Villas,* produced by Vicenza's tourist board (*APT;* 5 Piazza Duomo; phone: 444-544122; fax: 444-325001; available from the tourist information office at 12 Piazza Matteotti; phone: 444-320854). A series of concerts of Baroque music played by Italian and foreign orchestras that are held on the grounds of some of these villas is now a well-established summer event. For information and booking, contact *Vicenza E—Convention & Visitors Bureau* (37 Corso, Fogazzaro, Vicenza 36100; phone: 444-327141; fax: 444-544430). One of the closest and most important villas is *Villa Valmarana* "ai Nani" ("of the dwarfs" because of the tiny statues on the garden wall; phone: 444-543976). Built in the 17th century by Mattoni, a follower of Palladio, it is decorated with frescoes by Giambattista Tiepolo and his son Giandomenico. From mid-March through April, the villa is open Wednesdays, Thursdays, weekends, and public holidays from 10 AM to noon and 2:30 to 5:30 PM, and Tuesdays and Fridays in the afternoons only; from May through September, the villa is open Wednesdays, Thursdays, weekends, and public holidays from 10 AM to noon and 3 to 6 PM, and Tuesdays and Fridays in the afternoons only; from October through November, the villa is open Wednesdays, Thursdays, weekends, and public holidays from 10 AM to noon and 2 to 5 PM, and Tuesdays and Fridays in the afternoons only; the villa is closed Mondays, and December through mid-March. There's an admission charge. Another villa is *La Rotonda,* just beyond *Villa Valmarana* and usually visible only from the grounds. This view, however, is enough for you to be able to admire the mastery of this perfectly proportioned villa begun by Palladio in the 16th century. Its four pillar-fronted façades have been copied by numerous English and French architects. The grounds are open Tuesdays through Thursdays (and often on weekends), and the villa itself is open Wednesdays, from 10 AM to noon and 3 to 6 PM from mid-March through October; admission charge (phone: 444-321793). For a wonderful view of the city, stop by the 17th-century *Basilica Monte Berico* (south of town on Viale X Giugno). Don't miss Veronique's *Banquet of St. Gregory the Great* in the church's refectory. It's closed Mondays through Saturdays for a short (12:30 to 2:30 PM) break; no admission charge (phone: 444-320999).

BEST EN ROUTE

Campo Marzio The best in town, this modern, 35-room hotel and restaurant stand at the edge of the *Campo Marzio* park, a short walk from the *Duomo* and Corso Andrea Palladio. Open year-round. 21 Viale Roma, Vicenza (phone: 444-545700; fax: 444-320495). Expensive.

Cinzia & Valerio The house specialty here is Adriatic fish, prepared in inimitable Venetian pâté, risotto, or a casserole and accompanied by excellent local white wines. Closed Mondays and August. Reservations necessary. Major credit cards accepted. 65-67 Contrà Porta Padova, Vicenza (phone: 444-505213). Expensive.

Villa Michelangelo A luxury villa with a palatial feeling, this hotel has beautiful grounds and a pool. There are 34 rooms and a restaurant that serves local food. Open year-round. 19 Via Sacco, Arcugnano (phone: 444-550300; fax: 444-550490). Expensive.

Scudo di Francia Housed in one of the city's many delightful old palazzi and dispensing cuisine as authentically local as its antique furniture, this is a good place to try the traditional dish of the area, *baccalà* (codfish) with polenta, or pasta with white beans. Game or *faraona al forno in salsa al melograno* (pheasant with pomegranates) also are noteworthy. The wine list has an excellent selection of local vintages. Closed Sunday dinner, Mondays, one week in February, and 10 days in August. Reservations advised. Major credit cards accepted. 4 Contrà Piancoli, Vicenza (phone: 444-323322; fax: 444-326465). Expensive to moderate.

Bere Alto Simple dishes accompanied by fine wines are served in a stylish modern setting, a perfect spot for a light meal or do-it-yourself wine tasting. Closed Mondays and Tuesday lunch. Reservations advised. Visa accepted. 57 Via Pedemuro San Biagio, Vicenza (phone: 444-322144). Moderate.

Continental A small, elegant hotel and restaurant situated in front of the stadium, not far from the center of town. A few of the 57 rooms have shared baths.

Open year-round. 89 Viale G. G. Trissino, Vicenza (phone: 444-505476; fax: 444-513319). Moderate.

Antica Osteria da Penacio The fireplace in the winter at this rustic country dining room seems to heighten the taste of the delicious mushrooms and truffles sliced over homemade pasta and poultry. Bright yellow polenta garnishes most main dishes. The wine list is well chosen and well priced. Watch out for weekend banquets, when service may suffer. Closed Wednesdays and January. Reservations advised on weekends. Major credit cards accepted. A few miles south of town, at 13 Via Sorghe, Sorghe di Arcugnano (phone: 444-273081). Inexpensive.

Vicenza Hills Janice and Paolo dal Pra's guesthouse in the hills outside Vicenza sleeps up to eight; minimum stay is two days. The extensive library and the owners' knowledge of the area make this a special place. No restaurant. Open year-round. 133 Viale X Giugno, Vicenza (phone/fax: 444-543087). Inexpensive.

En Route from Vicenza Take S248 to Bassano del Grappa, some 25 miles (40 km) northeast, via the splendid medieval town of Marostica, a remarkable setting for a chess game played with living figures in Renaissance costume the second weekend of September in even-numbered years. There are a number of villas along this route, some that can be glimpsed from the road and some that can be visited, mostly by special arrangement. Obtain details from Vicenza's *APT* office (see above).

BASSANO DEL GRAPPA On the banks of the Brenta River, this delightful little town is filled with medieval and Renaissance streets, arcades, and houses with painted façades. From here, the Venetian plains to the south and the mountains to the north, including Monte del Grappa, are visible. The town is famous for its covered wooden bridge over the Brenta. Designed by Palladio, it was immortalized in an immensely popular song of World War I, when Bassano was at the center of fierce fighting between the Austrian and Italian armies (a war cemetery on Monte del Grappa holds the bodies of more than 20,000 victims, and the bridge is now known as the *Ponte dei Alpini,* in tribute to Italy's Alpine troops). Among the many monuments to fallen soldiers in Bassano is Viale dei Martiri (Avenue of the Martyrs), which leads to the town's finest viewpoint. Bassano is also famous for its grappa, the fiery alcoholic drink made from the last grape pressings (the distillery on *Ponte dei Alpini,* founded in 1779 by Bortolo Nardini, has been run by the same family ever since), and for its lovely white pottery. It is the home of Remondini, the 18th-century printworks, famous for its decorative work.

Housed in an old convent behind the medieval *Chiesa di San Francesco* (Piazza Garibaldi), the *Museo Civico* (4 Via Museo; phone: 424-522235) includes works by Jacopo da Ponte, a local 16th-century realist painter generally known as Bassano, who excelled in pastoral scenes, as well as many examples of Remondini's distinctive prints. The museum is closed Mondays; Tuesdays through Saturdays for a long (12:30 to 3:30 PM) break; and Sundays before 3:30 PM; admission charge. The ceramics section of the museum, with important locally produced pieces from the 17th century to the present day, is housed in the *Palazzo Sturm* on Via Schiavonetti. It's closed Mondays through Thursdays; Friday afternoons; and weekends before 3 PM; admission charge.

For an interesting side trip, we suggest a detour to Castelfranco. Take S47 south about 9 miles (14 km) to Citadella, then go west on S53 for 7½ miles (12 km) to Castelfranco. This charming village is the home of a turreted castle that dates from 1199. The *Duomo* (Piazza del Duomo) houses the *Castelfranco Madonna* by its native son, the painter Giorgione, and frescoes by Veronese. Nearby, Giorgione's house (with his first-floor frieze of frescoes) is a small museum (next to the Piazza del Duomo; phone: 423-491240). The house is closed Mondays and for a long (noon to 3 PM) break; admission charge. There are more villas and gardens to see outside town. To reach Palladio's *Villa Emo-Capodilista* in Fanzolo di Vedelago, follow S53 east about 5 miles (8 km), and turn north following signs for the village of Fanzolo and *Villa Emo*. Still owned by the Emo family, the villa is open Tuesdays, weekends, and national holidays from 3 to 7 PM April through September; weekends and national holidays from 2 to 6 PM October to December 23 and February through March; closed the rest of the year. There's an admission charge (phone: 423-476334). Guest accommodations on the grounds of the villa were due to become available as we went to press; call ahead for details. Also worth visiting is *Villa Corner-Chiminelli* in Sant'Andrea, about 2 miles (3 km) southwest of Castelfranco (2 Via Lama; phone: 424-525103), with frescoes attributed to the school of Veronese. It's open April through October by advance arrangement only; admission charge.

BEST EN ROUTE

Ca'7 Housed in an 18th-century Venetian villa, it has an excellent fish-based menu that can be enjoyed either in the garden or in the gracious dining room. Closed Sunday dinner, Mondays, the first two weeks of January, and the first two weeks of August. Reservations advised. Major credit cards accepted. 4 Via Cunizza da Romano, Bassano del Grappa (phone: 424-52005). Expensive to moderate.

Belvedere A popular dining spot in the hotel of the same name that attracts locals and travelers alike, it offers traditional *cucina veneta* with a light touch. Try the *bigola all'anatra* (tube-like spaghetti with duck sauce); the unusual *insalata di granchio ed asparagi* (crab and asparagus salad); or the *brodetto di scampi* (shrimp consommé). A daily prix fixe menu is offered. Closed Sundays and August. Reservations advised. Major credit cards accepted. 1 Viale delle Fosse, Bassano del Grappa (phone: 424-524988). Moderate.

Ai Due Mori In this charming rustic eatery, beautifully prepared regional and creative dishes are served. The pasta is fresh, the fish lightly sauced, and desserts first-rate. There is also a good wine list. Dine outside in the summer under a large canopy surrounded by Castelfranco's medieval walls. Closed Wednesdays and Thursday lunch. Reservations advised. Major credit cards accepted. 24 Vicolo Montebelluna, Castelfranco (phone: 423-497174). Moderate.

Al Moretto In this hostelry are 35 cozy rooms but no restaurant. Open year-round. 10 Via San Pio X, Castelfranco (phone: 423-721313; fax: 423-721066). Moderate.

En Route from Bassano del Grappa It is a 9¹/₂-mile (15-km) drive east on S248 to Asolo, through countryside dotted with villas and green hills but mostly lined with unsightly ceramics factories (their showrooms, open to the public, are most interesting, however).

ASOLO Known as the "Town of a Hundred Horizons" because of its immense panoramas, Asolo is a small farming market village. Perched on a hill and built around a small square filled with leafy horse-chestnut trees and 15th- to 17th-century buildings, it was much loved by British writers and painters in the last century. The *Museo Civico* (Via Regina Cornaro; phone: 423-952313) houses documents and manuscripts belonging the English poet Robert Browning, who spent many years in Asolo (his son is buried here in the *Cimitero di Sant'Anna,* as is the Italian actress Eleonora Duse). It also has a couple of sculptures by the immensely successful 18th-century artist Antonio Canova. The museum was closed at press time for restoration; contact the tourist office (258 Via Caterina; phone: 423-524192 or 423-529046; fax: 423-524137) for opening hours.

BEST EN ROUTE

Villa Cipriani Among the green hills overlooking Asolo stands this 16th-century villa, the epitome of rural romanticism and seclusion. A member of the luxury CIGA hotel chain, it has 31 rooms and an excellent restaurant. Open year-round. 298 Via Canova, Asolo (phone: 423-952166; 800-221-2340; fax: 423-952095). Very expensive.

Charly's One Like the clientele, the menu here is both local and foreign, with *salmone affumicato* (smoked salmon), various *zuppe* (soups), *oca affumicata* (smoked goose), and chateaubriand with tarragon and béarnaise sauce. Fresh fish is served Tuesdays through Thursdays. Closed Thursday dinner, Fridays, and November. Reservations advised. Major credit cards accepted. 55 Via Roma, Asolo (phone: 423-952201). Moderate.

Ca' Derton Enjoy excellent local fare in this 16th-century house with a 19th-century wood interior. The menu offers such traditional dishes as *pasta e fagi-*

oli (pasta with beans), risotto with fresh mushrooms, asparagus or radicchio from Treviso, and, according to season, game and other meat dishes accompanied by fresh artichokes or peppers. Desserts are homemade. Closed Monday dinner, Tuesdays, several days in February, and the last two weeks of August. Reservations advised. Major credit cards accepted. 11 Piazza d'Annunzio, Asolo (phone: 423-952730). Moderate to inexpensive.

Duse A tiny hostelry in the center of town, it offers a low-frills alternative to the *Villa Cipriani*. There are 13 charming rooms and a small restaurant. Open year-round. 190 Via Browning, Asolo (phone: 423-55241; fax: 423-950404). Moderate to inexpensive.

En Route from Asolo Along the minor road between Asolo and Cornuda La Valle in Maser is the *Villa Barbaro,* the most perfectly preserved of Palladio's farm villas. The architecture is complemented by the stupendous frescoes by Veronese and the trompe l'oeil allegories of classical subjects mixed in with likenesses of the Barbaro family. Once inside, it's not easy to follow the multilingual directions to locate all the different frescoes, but the big slippers that all visitors are required to wear over their shoes to protect the floor are fun. The villa is open Tuesdays, weekends, and national holidays from 3 to 6 PM March through October; weekends and holidays from 2:30 to 5 PM the rest of the year; closed from December 24 through January 6 and on *Easter;* admission charge (phone: 423-923004). Across the street is the only church that Palladio designed outside Venice.

Continue to Cornuda La Valle, turn left onto S348 north, and head for the mountains. The road follows the Piave River (of World War I fame) and rises to fresher, purer mountain air. For some 30 miles (48 km), pastures, woods, and mountain peaks are occasionally interrupted by small villages of wooden chalets and smoking chimney pots. At the intersection of S348 and S50, turn right and drive 22 miles (34 km) to Belluno.

BELLUNO The approach to Belluno, as with a number of Italian towns, is a disappointing confusion of small industries and roadside billboards, with only glimpses of field and mountain between. Press on to the heart of the town, however, where its pretty piazze and cobbled streets, embodying the characteristic layout of a Roman city, lead to the market square and the 15th-century fountain with four water spouts. Some streets are still lined with shady, Renaissance porticoes.

Belluno's inhabitants are blessed with magnificent views of the northeastern Dolomites. Nearer home, the skyline is dominated by the huge Baroque cathedral (Piazza del Duomo) with its green, onion-shape dome and bell tower, which still has its 14th-century crypt. Also on the square, the 15th-century *Palazzo dei Rettori* (Rectors' Palace), with its carved stone balconies and huge clock, retains its Venetian splendor but is now an administration center and, unfortunately, is no longer open to the public. The same applies to the *Palazzo dei Vescovi* (Bishops' Palace), across the piazza, which, although largely rebuilt in the 17th century, is the only town building with medieval characteristics.

The town's museum, in the ancient *Palazzo dei Giuristi* (Jurists' Palace; 16 Via Duomo; phone: 437-24836), contains works by famous artists (such as Bartolomeo Montagna) and lesser-known local ones, plus archaeological remains dating from prehistoric, Roman, and medieval times that were found in the area. The museum is closed Mondays through Saturdays for a long (noon to 3 PM) break, and Sunday afternoons, in summer; closed Monday and Saturday afternoons, and Tuesdays through Fridays for a long (noon to 3 PM) break, the rest of the year; admission charge. Stop in at the *Caffè Pasticceria Manin* (39 Piazza Martiri; phone: 437-940375), dating from 1793, for an *aperitivo* or a pastry.

BEST EN ROUTE

Dolada Captivating mountain and lake views, combined with mouth-watering dishes, make a visit here truly memorable. For details, see *The Best Restaurants in Italy* in DIVERSIONS. There also are seven rooms. Closed Mondays and Tuesday lunch (except in July and August), and February. Reservations advised. Major credit cards accepted. Go to Pieve d'Alpago, then follow signs to Plois and the restaurant. 21 Via Dolada, Plois, Pieve d'Alpago (phone: 437-479141; fax: 437-478068). Expensive to moderate, restaurant; moderate, hotel.

Delle Alpi This comfortable, well-run, 40-room hotel, very close to Belluno's ancient center, is the best in town. The third-floor attic rooms are smaller than the others, but they offer better views of the surrounding mountains. There is a reliable restaurant (under different management) and parking in the rear courtyard. Open year-round. 13 Via Jacopo Tasso, Belluno (phone: 437-940545; fax: 437-940565). Moderate.

Al Borgo Regional Veneto cooking is expertly prepared in this simple 18th-century villa, amid gardens on a hill with vistas of Belluno and the mountains. Highlights include *zuppe* (soups), gnocchi mixed with meat or ricotta cheese or with local radicchio, and *crespelle* (pancakes) made with field herbs or mushrooms. The homemade desserts are often based on *frutta del bosco* (wild strawberries and other berries). Closed Monday dinner, Tuesdays, and two weeks in September. Reservations advised. Major credit cards accepted. Take the road to Mel, turning left at the sign for Anconetta. 8 Via Anconetta, Belluno (phone: 437-926755). Moderate to inexpensive.

En Route from Belluno For a taste of the Dolomites, head north along the Piave River on S50 5 miles (8 km) to Ponte nelle Alpi, then turn right onto the main Venice road (S51), and almost immediately take the left turn marked Cansiglio onto S422. Here the villages, meadows, and pine- and chestnut-covered mountains, their summits often hidden by cloud, are a refreshing change from the sultry summer heat of the towns and lagoons. The road winds around the mountains past the red, overhanging eaves of tiny holdings, sudden trattorie, and the occasional *albergo*. Continue across the flatter, lush meadows of the Alto Piano before descending steadily to Vittorio Veneto.

VITTORIO VENETO In the foothills of the Dolomites, the former twin cities of Céneda and Serravalle are linked by a wide modern boulevard. Joined in 1866, they were renamed for Italy's King Vittorio Emanuele II (although locals still refer to them individually by their old names). The area was the site of the most important of Italy's battles during World War I, as the *Museo della Battaglia* (Battle Museum, in front of Céneda's cathedral; phone: 438-57695) attests with its collection of relics from the Austrian occupation (1917–18) and the October–November 1918 victory. The museum is closed Mondays and for a very long (noon to 4 PM) break May through September; closed Mondays and for a short (noon to 2 PM) break the rest of the year; admission charge. Stroll down Via Martiri della Libertà to view Serraville's well-preserved Gothic and Renaissance palaces. The *Duomo* contains a Titian *Madonna and Saints.* The *Chiesa di San Lorenzo* (Via Martiri della Libertà) inside the 14th-century *Ospedale Municipale* (Municipal Hospital) is decorated with Venetian Gothic frescoes. To arrange a visit, see the custodian at the *Museo del Cedense* in Piazza Flaminio (phone: 438-57103).

Vittorio Veneto also is the site of a good 18-hole golf course—*Golf Club Cansiglio* (phone: 438-585398). For more information, see *Great Italian Golf* in DIVERSIONS.

BEST EN ROUTE

Gigetto Studied rusticity adorned with strange bronze statues, this place is for those who appreciate fine food and superb wines. Traditional country dishes compete with Gigetto's fantasies. Desserts are elegant. Closed Monday dinner, Tuesdays, and most of August. Reservations necessary. Major credit cards accepted. 4 Via de Gaspari, Miane (phone: 438-893126). Expensive.

Abbazia Here are 15 rooms, including a few suites; each is individually decorated to feel more like a home than a hotel. Breakfast only is served, although there is a bar and a banquet room. Piazzale IV Novembre, Follina (phone: 438-971277; fax: 438-970001). Moderate.

Al Castelletto Once part of the noble Brandolini d'Adda property, this wonderful eatery serves local dishes. *Bollito misto* (boiled chicken, beef, and sausage) served with *salsa verde* (green parsley sauce) and horseradish, and grilled meat are specialties. Closed Tuesdays except in July, and two weeks in August. Reservations advised. American Express accepted. 15 Via Castelletto, Pedeguarda (phone: 438-842484). Moderate.

En Route from Vittorio Veneto Follow S51 south for about 8 miles (13 km) and take a right onto S13. Continue along S13 for another 21 miles (35 km) to Treviso.

TREVISO Founded during the Roman Empire, this charming walled city houses many medieval and Renaissance palaces—some with frescoed façades—even though the city was bombed during World War II. Two rivers and a series of canals (with water-powered mill wheels) give Treviso a Venice-like atmosphere—perfect for strolling on cobblestone streets and under arcades that stay cool in the summer. The central Piazza dei Signori is flanked on one side by the Romanesque *Palazzo dei Trecento,* named after the city's 13th-century governing council of 300 citizens; it now houses the town's administrative offices. Nearby is the Romanesque *Loggia dei Cavalieri,* an open-air, arcaded structure where nobles gathered in the 12th and 13th centuries.

A short walk down the Calmaggiore, the main street, with its elegant shops behind 15th-century porticoes, leads to the *Duomo,* with its seven hemispherical domes in lead and copper and its neoclassical façade, a 17th-century addition to the original Romanesque design. Inside is an altar painting of the Annunciation by Titian.

Stop by the Gothic *Chiesa di San Nicolò* (Via San Nicolò) to see its impressive soaring brick façade and tile roofs. The interior is solemn, with massive frescoed columns and chapels. The seminary next door houses frescoes by Tomaso da Modena. The *Museo Civico* (22 Borgo Cavour; phone: 422-658442) contains frescoes and paintings by Venetian artists, including works by Cima da Conegliano, Titian, and Gino Rossi. There also is a collection of over 24,000 Italian and foreign posters dating from 1800 to 1962. The museum is closed Mondays and public holidays; Tuesdays through Saturdays for a short (noon to 2 PM) break; and Sunday afternoons; admission charge. The *Casa da Noal* (38 Via Canova; phone: 422-544895), a Gothic building from the 15th century, has such a large, eclectic collection of local artifacts, including medieval and Renaissance marbles, frescoes, wooden sculptures, weapons, and wrought iron, that it now displays only one aspect of its collection at any given time. These exhibits are held annually, from spring through summer. Call ahead to check opening times; admission charge.

In the center of town—on an island reachable by a footbridge—is Isola della Pescheria, a commercial hub with a lively morning fish-and-vegetable market. There are some typical Treviso *osterie* here; they are usually closed Sundays, as is the market.

BEST EN ROUTE

Relais El Toulà There are only 10 deluxe rooms at this inn, which seems like a country club for area VIPs. It has beautifully manicured grounds, a pool, and fine food served in the restaurant. 63 Via Postumia, Paderno, Ponzano (phone: 422-969191; fax: 422-969994). Very expensive.

Villa Condulmer Surrounded by a pool, 27 holes of golf, riding stables, and tennis courts, this 53-room hotel offers the ultimate in Venetian hospitality, in an 18th-century villa standing in its own parkland. There's also an excellent restaurant. Open April to mid-November. Ten miles (16 km) south of Treviso just east of the S513, Zerman (phone: 41-457100; fax: 41-457134). Very expensive.

Villa Corner della Regina Magnificent golf courses and parks surround this 18th-century Palladian villa, with its seven exquisite suites, five handsome rooms, and 35 annex rooms. Amenities include a restaurant (in season), lawn tennis, a pool, a sauna, and air conditioning in a period setting, enhanced by a doting Venetian staff. The 50% fall/winter discounts make this a more affordable off-season choice. Just south of S53, 11 miles (18 km) west of Treviso, at 10 Via Corriva, Cavasagra di Vedelago (phone: 423-481481; fax: 423-451100). Very expensive to expensive.

Park Hotel Villa Braida A totally restored eight-room villa, this hotel is convenient for touring Veneto's countryside. The restaurant is decent. Open year-round. 16/B Via Bonisiolo, Zerman (see *Villa Condulmer*, above; phone: 41-457222; fax: 41-457033). Expensive.

El Toulà da Alfredo The original establishment from which the other members of this haute cuisine chain sprang respects and develops the highest traditions of *mittel*-European cuisine with local *trevigiano* flavor. *Blinis* with caviar, sirloin steaks with herbs, and feather-light sorbets are just some of the culinary delights. Closed Sunday dinner, Mondays, and two weeks in August. Reservations necessary. Major credit cards accepted. 26 Via Collalto, Treviso (phone: 422-540275). Expensive.

Le Beccherie Tucked away behind Piazza dei Signori, this immensely popular restaurant is family-run. The menu changes with the seasons, so all ingredients, whether vegetable or game, are garden- or field-fresh and exquisitely cooked. Closed Sunday dinner, Mondays, and July 15 to 30. Reservations advised. Major credit cards accepted. 10 Piazza Ancilotto, Treviso (phone: 422-540871). Moderate.

A l'Oca Bianca Near the central square, this is a must for lovers of *cucina casalinga* (home cooking). Closed Tuesday dinner, Wednesdays, and three weeks in August. No reservations. No credit cards accepted. 7 Vicolo della Torre, Treviso (phone: 422-541850). Moderate to inexpensive.

Toni del Spin Located behind the magnificent *Palazzo dei Signori,* this trattoria is a family affair; its equally popular country restaurant and farm provides much of the fresh ingredients and meat served here. A blackboard menu features such dishes as *baccalà* (codfish), *pasta e fagioli* (pasta and bean soup), risotto, and game in season (look for *colombaccio,* or wild pigeon). Closed Sundays, Monday lunch, and three weeks in August. Reservations advised. Visa accepted. 7 Via Inferiore, Treviso (phone: 422-543829). Moderate to inexpensive.

En Route from Treviso Follow A27 due south for 19 miles (30 km) to Venice.

Emilia-Romagna

The Emilia-Romagna region lies north of Tuscany and south of Lombardy and the Veneto, nearly stretching from sea to sea from east to west. Its eastern edge is on the Adriatic, and its western tip reaches almost to the Ligurian coast, stopped short only by the Apennine range. Although part of the region is hill or mountain—a southerly strip that runs northwest to southeast along the Apennines—most of it is flat and low-lying, the fertile plain of the Po River, which forms the region's northern boundary. That geographical fact has made the region home to some of Italy's most abundant agriculture, which in turn has supported the rich and varied local cuisines. Bologna, the regional capital, wallows in this abundance and revels in its nickname, *Bologna la Grassa* (Bologna the Fat).

The geographical reality of a low-lying wedge driven into an essentially mountainous country has also contributed to making Emilia-Romagna one of Italy's most prosperous commercial centers. The region takes its name in part from the Via Emilia, the ancient Roman road that runs, almost in a straight line, from Milan to the sea at Rimini. Laid out by Marcus Aemilius Lepidus in 187 BC to connect the Roman Empire with its newly acquired lands in northern Europe, the road became the region's lifeblood, a communications link and a trade conduit that played a role in virtually every social, political, and military development in the area, from the Roman Empire to World War II.

Despite modern Italy's having made Emilia-Romagna one region, the area is easily divided into two quite different sections. Emilia is the territory to the west, embracing the cities of Piacenza, Parma, Modena, Ferrara, and Bologna. Romagna is the smaller zone to the east, including Rimini and Ravenna. Until the unification of Italy in the 19th century, Emilia's cities and towns—first free communes, then medieval and Renaissance duchies or principalities—spent the greater part of their history fighting against outsiders and among themselves. The region that today is noted for its beautiful, flourishing cities and small-town hospitality was not always so trusting of strangers.

The history of Romagna, on the other hand, tended toward internal cohesiveness and a wider identification with the world beyond its borders. The existence of the seaport at Rimini, once a major Western entrepôt for trade with the East, fostered a more cosmopolitan view of outsiders. That attitude lives on today: Rimini and the numerous seaside resorts nearby draw tens of thousands of holiday makers, all anxious to play on the wide beaches and swim in the warm Adriatic. At high season in Rimini it is rare to hear Italian spoken in the streets.

A more detailed account of the separate past of the two areas might begin in 5th century, when Emilia was first invaded by Goths, then Lombards, then Franks. By the 8th century, foreign domination had left the region's cities in ruins and completely disunited, so that no sooner had they driven the invaders out than they began warring with their neighbors. With the outbreak of the struggle between the Guelphs and the Ghibellines, the bloody, internecine warfare gradually became codified along political lines. By the 13th century, there was hardly a city on the entire Italian peninsula that hadn't been drawn into this seemingly interminable dispute between the forces of the pope and the Holy Roman Empire, and Emilia was no exception. Cities formed allegiances, betrayed them, were subjugated, and rebelled throughout the medieval period. It was only with the establishment of some of the great ruling families that a semblance of order was restored. Parma and Piacenza initially fell under the sway of the Visconti of Milan. Ferrara became the seat of the Este clan, which gradually extended its power to Modena and Reggio. The Pepoli and the Bentivoglio families dominated Bologna.

Although the brilliant, erratic, and ruthless Malatesta family seized Rimini and held it from the 13th to the 16th century, most of Romagna managed to stay aloof from the torment experienced by the Emilian cities. In 402, after the division of the Roman Empire into an Empire of the East and an Empire of the West, Honorius made Ravenna the capital of the latter. After the fall of Rome in the West (476), a short-lived kingdom of the Goths, under Odoacer and Theodoric, maintained Ravenna as a capital city. In the 6th century, however, the great emperor of the East, Justinian, defeated the Goths, and Ravenna became part of the Byzantine, or Eastern Roman, Empire, ruled by exarchs (civil governors), with an eye to what was going on back home in Constantinople.

The world-famous, Byzantine-inspired mosaics of Ravenna are a legacy of that time when the city, in effect, turned its back on Italy and looked to Byzantium for culture and guidance. By the 8th century, however, the Lombards had established themselves in much of northern Italy. They even took Ravenna, but only briefly, and Romagna owes its name to the fact that it remained Roman while the Lombards prevailed in the region that bears their name. Then, in a rapid turn of events, the pope asked the help of the Frankish Kings Pepin and Charlemagne in stemming the Lombard tide. Each proved willing and able, and Romagna came under papal domination, which lasted until the nation of Italy was born in the 19th century.

Papal forces had, in the meantime, made some headway in Emilia, gaining a foothold in Bologna and its environs, but by and large this region remained fragmented. Then, in 1545, Pope Paul III, a member of the noble Farnese family, took control of Parma and Piacenza, creating a duchy for his illegitimate son. By the 17th century, most of Emilia was in the hands of either the Farnese or the Este family, and the question of political power seemed more or less settled—until Napoleon invaded in the late 18th century, reversing the balance of power again. When the dust had settled, the Empress Marie Louise of France had become Duchess of Parma, and

Austria had taken the rest of the province (along with Venice and a huge chunk of northern Italy). Romagna stayed safely in papal hands.

But it was not to last. By 1848, popular feeling for a united Italy, free of foreign occupiers, had become too great to suppress. Piacenza was the first city to throw in its lot with Piedmont (the birthplace of a unified Italy), and the rest of the region rapidly followed. In 1860, the area, now known as Emilia-Romagna, joined with Piedmont to form the nucleus of the modern Italian state.

Despite all the blood spilled in settling the fate of the region, Emilia-Romagna is today a peaceful, prosperous part of Italy. After World War II, the region had the foresight to invest heavily in both industry and agriculture. Some of the country's most famous exports originate here. Parma is the home of parmesan cheese and Parma ham. From Modena come such great Italian automobile marques as Ferrari and Maserati. Bologna has given the world *spaghetti alla bolognese* and mortadella, the granddaddy of American "baloney"; Faenza is the home of faïence pottery. Perhaps the most enduring gift of all is the genius of composer Giuseppe Verdi, who was born in the tiny hamlet of Le Roncole, just outside Piacenza.

Piacenza, in the west and 40 miles (64 km) southeast of Milan, is the logical starting point for a tour of Emilia-Romagna. From here, following the ancient route—in some cases over the actual cobblestones—of the Via Emilia (S9 on modern maps), our itinerary passes through Parma, Modena, Bologna, and Faenza to Rimini. From Rimini, it takes the coast road north to Ravenna and then turns inland to end in the majestic medieval town of Ferrara. In a hotel listed as very expensive, expect to spend $200 or more for two per night. In an expensive hotel, a room will cost $110 to $200; in a moderate one, from $70 to $110; and in an inexpensive place, $70 or less. All prices are for high season. All hotels feature private baths unless otherwise indicated. Although some hotels have parking on the premises or at nearby garages, there may be an additional charge; it is best to inquire beforehand. Expect to pay $90 to $130 at an expensive restaurant; $55 to $90 at a moderate one; and $55 or less at an inexpensive place. All restaurants are open for lunch and dinner unless otherwise noted. For each location, hotels and restaurants are listed alphabetically by price category.

Note that many sites of interest in Emilia-Romagna close for a midday break, usually from noon or 1 PM to 3 or 4 PM; we suggest calling ahead to check exact hours.

PIACENZA Founded by the Romans, Piacenza is now a modern industrial city, but the medieval underpinnings of the old town remain largely intact. The city has always had considerable strategic value—it lies at the point where the Via Emilia touches the Po River—and, in keeping with the history of settlements in this region, a great deal of blood was shed over the centuries to keep it in one camp or another. In 1545, Alessandro Farnese, otherwise known as Pope Paul III, created the Duchy of Parma and Piacenza, which the Farnese family ruled until the early 18th century. Piacenza, however, has a history of independent thinking, a trait that showed itself on two notable occasions. In 1547, a group of Piacenza nobles tired of the tyranny and debauchery of their overlord, Pier Luigi Farnese, and murdered him. Since the Farnese family was extraordinarily powerful, and Pier Luigi was the (illegitimate) son of the pope, the tyrannicide required great courage. In 1848, Piacenza took another step into the unknown as the first Italian city to vote for annexation to Piedmont, the nucleus of the new unified Italian nation, and for this it became known as the *primogenita,* or first-born.

The medieval heart of the town is Piazza dei Cavalli, so called because of the two massive 17th-century equestrian statues (by Francesco Mochi, considered one of the great Baroque masters) dominating the square. Sixteen years in the making, the statues are of two Farnese dukes, Alessandro and Ranuccio I, both descendants of the murdered Pier Luigi but obviously held in higher esteem. Facing them, looming over the piazza, is the graceful *Palazzo del Comune,* built in 1281 in Lombard-Gothic style and also known as the *Gotico.* The *Palazzo del Governatore,* opposite, is a building of the late 18th century, and to one side of the square is the 13th-century *Chiesa di San Francesco,* at the beginning of Via XX Settembre. Piacenza's *Duomo,* just down Via XX Settembre from Piazza dei Cavalli, is a towering Lombard-Romanesque building constructed between the 12th and 14th centuries. It rises on the ruins of the city's first cathedral, which was dedicated to St. Justine and destroyed in 1117. The *Duomo* appears to have been built more for fortification than for worship, and its most curious feature is a thick-barred iron cage set in the masonry at a dizzying height on the side of the soaring bell tower. Miscreants of the town were tossed naked into this *gabbia* and forced to endure the jeers of the townspeople in the marketplace below. Inside, the cathedral shows evidence of the evolution from Romanesque to Gothic style, and there are frescoes by Guercino.

The *Museo Civico* (Civic Museum; Piazza Cittadella; phone: 523-28270 or 523-26981) is housed in the renovated *Palazzo Farnese,* built in the latter part of the 16th century for that illustrious family. It contains paintings (note the *Adoration* by Botticelli and other works of the 17th and 18th centuries) and a variety of archaeological specimens, one of which—the *fegato di Piacenza*—is an odd relic of the days when Emilia was the land of the ancient Etruscans. This bronze cast of a liver inscribed with the names of various Etruscan deities is thought by archaeologists to have been a sort of religious road map, a guide to be consulted when Etruscan priests were called upon to read the entrails of a sacrificial beast. The museum also has an interesting collection of 18th- and 19th-century carriages and coaches and an exhibit of antique weapons. Closed Mondays; Tuesday, Wednesday, and Friday afternoons; and Thursdays and weekends for a midday break; admission charge.

If time permits, other sights to see in Piacenza include two Renaissance churches, *San Sisto* (Via San Sisto) and the *Chiesa di Santa Maria di Campagna* (Via di Campagne), the latter with frescoes by Pordenone; and *Sant'Antonino,* an 11th-century Romanesque church with 14th-century Gothic additions. The town also has a modern art gallery, the *Galleria d'Arte Moderna "Ricci Oddi"* (13 Via San Siro; phone: 523-20742), whose collection of works, ranging from Romanticism to the 1930s, ranks among the best in Italy. Closed Mondays and for a long (noon to 3 PM) break; no admission charge. The tourist office, *Azienda di Promozione Turistica* (*APT;* 17 Via San Siro; phone: 523-34347), or the tourist information office (*IAT;* 10 Piazzetta dei Mercanti; phone: 523-29324; fax: 523-34348), can provide further information. Both are closed Thursday afternoons, Sundays, holidays, and for a long (12:30 to 4:30 PM) break.

Piacenza hosts a number of annual trade shows and fairs, most reflecting the city's commitment to industry and agriculture. In April, the focus shifts to the *Vacanze Tempo Libero* (Vacation and Leisure Time Trade Show), which attracts vast crowds in search of ways to have fun. And in May, the *Casa 1995* showcases the latest Italian trends in home furnishings and interior decoration. Contact the tourist office or the *Quartiere Fieristico* (Trade Show Center; 17 Via Emilia Parmense; phone: 523-593920; fax: 523-62383) for dates and locations of these expositions. You also might want to pay a visit to the city's colorful outdoor market, held Wednesdays and Saturdays in Piazza del Duomo and Piazza dei Cavalli.

Also worth exploring are the beautiful valleys surrounding Piacenza, including Valdarda, Valditone, Valnure, and Valtrebbia. Here, you will find picturesque medieval villages and 400 castles, whose turrets and towers stand high above the tree line. Piacenza's tourist office (see above) has a detailed list of the castles open to the public.

BEST EN ROUTE

Antica Osteria del Teatro One of the best in the entire region, this quaintly elegant and atmospheric restaurant is set in a narrow, picturesque street in the oldest part of town. It's famous for ravioli stuffed with duck and, in season, *flan di ortiche ai dadini di pomodoro* (a mousse of local greens and tomatoes). There also is a wide array of other local delicacies, meat, and produce. Service is excellent. Closed Sunday dinner, Mondays, the first two weeks of January, and most of August. Reservations necessary. Major credit cards accepted. 16 Via Verdi, Piacenza (phone: 523-323777). Expensive.

Grande Albergo Roma Only a block from Piazza dei Cavalli, it has an excellent restaurant with a good view of the city. Amenities include mini-bars, TVs, and radios in all 90 rooms. This is a perfect location for exploring the city on foot, and there is ample parking for guests, plus services for the business traveler. Restaurant closed Saturdays and one week in August. 14 Via

Cittadella, Piacenza (phone: 523-23201; fax: 523-330548). Expensive to moderate.

En Route from Piacenza For a glimpse back in time, take S654 southeast for 8 miles (13 km) to Grazzano Visconti, a reconstructed medieval village. It was named after Graccus Garrianum, a wealthy lord who owned much of the land surrounding the town; the original settlement dates back to the year 300. Set against the backdrop of a 12th-century castle, Grazzano Visconti today is a living museum and artisans' workshop. Craftspeople use traditional techniques and tools to create fine wrought-iron, ceramic, and silver objects, as well as elegant pieces of furniture. The last Sunday in May, the townspeople don medieval costumes to take part in a historical parade and jousting tournament. Throughout the day, along narrow cobblestone streets and in the picturesque squares, the past and present come face to face as visitors mingle with costumed jesters, jugglers, minstrels, and dancers. There is an admission charge, but it is well worth it to be a part of medieval pageantry at its finest. On the second Saturday in July, 14th-century recipes are resurrected as lords and ladies, squires and pages, and troubadours and other music makers gather in the town for a sumptuous outdoor banquet. For information, contact the tourist office (Piazza del Biscione; phone: 523-870997, April through September; 523-870205, the rest of the year). Grazzano Visconti boasts a collection of some 25 vintage cars from the 1930s, as well as 30 basic motorcycles and scooters, in its *Museo delle Auto e Moto d'Epoca* (Antique Car Museum; at the edge of town; phone: 523-870170). Two folding bicycles are also on display—one from 1915, and its 1880 predecessor. It's closed December through February and for a short (noon to 2 PM) break; admission charge.

For another medieval experience, head southeast of Piacenza 18 miles (29 km) on Route 9 to Castell'Arquato (exit at Alseno). High on a hilltop, the thousand-year-old town's towers and monuments stand out above the terraced vineyards that surround the town. Most noteworthy are the *Palazzo Pretorio* with an outside staircase, loggia, and bell tower; the *Collegiata* (a Romanesque church; phone: 523-805151; open daily, with a midday break; admission charge); and the remains of a 14th-century castle. The tourist office (1 Viale Remondini; phone: 523-803091) can provide information.

Halfway to Parma (38 miles/61 km away by the direct route), a road running parallel to the Via Emilia travels through flat, bucolic countryside to the village of Busseto. The great opera composer Giuseppe Verdi was born in the tiny hamlet of Le Roncole (now known as Roncole-Verdi), 3 miles (5 km) southeast of Busseto; lived for a time in Busseto itself; and later built an estate at Sant'Agata, 2 miles (3 km) northwest of town. Verdi lived there from 1853 until 1901, during which time he composed *Il Trovatore* and *Falstaff*. In the villa, visitors can see the composer's bedroom studio and a library; the bedroom of his second wife, singer Giuseppina Strepponi; a death chamber replicating the Milan hotel room where he died; and the surrounding gardens. Still a private home, the villa is open daily (by appointment only), with a long (11:40 AM to 3 PM) break, April through October; admission charge (phone: 523-830210). Call ahead to arrange for a guided tour in English.

Head over to Busseto's *Rocca* (Castle) to purchase a ticket allowing entry to three other Verdi landmarks: the *Teatro Verdi* (Piazza Verdi), a small opera house built by the town in honor of its famous son; a museum in the *Villa Pallavicino* (Roncole-Verdi) containing Verdi memorabilia, including a piano he played as a child; and the rough stone farmhouse in the center of Roncole-Verdi in which he was born (in 1813) and raised. The opera house is open daily, with a midday break. The museum is closed December through March, Mondays, and for a midday break. For more information, contact the tourist information office (24 Piazza Giuseppe Verdi; phone: 524-92487), which is closed October through May.

Every June, Busseto hosts a prestigious international singing competition in search of singers for Verdi's operas. In July, performances take place in Busseto's piazze and streets. For information, contact the *Gruppo Attività Verdiane* (Roncole-Verdi; phone: 524-91753). Busseto's otherwise tranquil pace is accelerated the second Sunday of every month in winter, when the outdoor *Mercato dell'Antiquario* (Antiques Market) takes over the streets of the *centro* (center).

Return to Via Emilia and continue east (toward Parma) for 4 miles (6 km) to Fidenza, and follow the signs to Salsomaggiore. At the foot of the Apennine Mountains, it is one of Italy's most renowned spas. For more information, see *Taking the Waters* in DIVERSIONS. The tourist office (*APT*; 7 Viale Romagnosi; phone: 524-572100; fax: 524-579047) can provide information on the town's events and hotels, some of which are striking examples of Art Nouveau design. Most noteworthy are the *Grand Hotel des Thermes* and the *Terme Berzieri*. In and around town, some monuments, balconies, and storefronts also echo the Art Nouveau theme. Salsomaggiore is a good stepping stone to other towns in the area. *CIT* (10 Viale Romagnosi; phone: 524-577058) offers excursions to Grazzano Visconti, Piacenza, Busseto, and Castell'Arquato.

Return to Via Emilia and head east 13 miles (21 km) to Parma.

BEST EN ROUTE

Biscione If you missed the pageants in Grazzano Visconti, you can still enjoy a taste of the past at this reconstructed medieval restaurant, where costumed pages and ladies-in-waiting serve authentic medieval and regional dishes. Try the mushroom or truffle risotto and the veal cutlet topped with mushroom mousse. The ambience is convivial; the fare, top quality. Closed Monday dinner, Tuesdays, January, and November. Reservations advised.

Major credit cards accepted. Piazza del Biscione, Grazzano Visconti (phone: 523-870149). Expensive to moderate.

I Due Foscari Originally owned by tenor Carlo Bergonzi and now run by his son, this hotel in Gothic-Moorish style offers 18 pleasant rooms. The restaurant has a terrace for outdoor dining in summer. Restaurant closed Mondays, January, and most of August. Near the center of town, at 15 Piazza Carlo Rossi, Busseto (phone: 524-92337; fax: 524-91625). Moderate.

Ugo At this tastefully modern, small restaurant, Ugo and family prepare delicious pasta, grilled meat, and excellent desserts. Closed Mondays, Tuesdays, and July. Reservations advised. Major credit cards accepted. 3 Via Mozart, Busseto (phone: 524-92307). Moderate to inexpensive.

PARMA Despite heavy bombing during World War II, Parma retains the splendor it knew as the capital of the Farnese dukes from the mid-16th to the early 18th century. The French Bourbons succeeded the Farnese family, and then Napoleon annexed the duchy to France for a time. After his downfall, the Congress of Vienna awarded it to Marie Louise of Austria, Napoleon's second wife, who settled in for a long stay as duchess (1816–47) and added her own touches to the city.

Parma's elevated reputation among Italians is based largely on two factors. First, it is said to be one of Italy's most graceful and gracious towns, known not only for its architectural and artistic treasures but also for the courtly good manners of its people. Second, it has given Italy and the world *parmigiano* (parmesan cheese) and *prosciutto di Parma* (Parma ham). Free guided tours in English of parmesan and prosciutto factories can be arranged by request through *Consorzio del Prosciutto di Parma* (8 Via Marco dell'Arpa; phone: 521-243987) and *Consorzio del Parmigiano Reggiano* (26/C Via Gramsci; phone: 521-292700). *Cibus,* a gastronomic fair held in May, is said to rival those in Paris and Cologne. *Salumeria Garibaldi* (42 Strada Garibaldi; phone: 521-235606; and 5 Via Gramsci; phone: 521-292366) is a good place to buy Parma food products. Parma's antiques market is set up every Thursday afternoon on Via d'Azeglio. The regular outdoor flea market takes place Wednesdays and Saturday mornings in Piazza Ghiaia.

Two painters of the early 16th century are associated particularly closely with Parma: Antonio Allegri (known as Correggio because he was born in that nearby town), who worked extensively in Parma, and Il Parmigianino, who was born and worked here. In addition, Parma was the setting for Stendhal's classic novel *The Charterhouse of Parma,* and it has quite a few musical associations besides its nearby links to Verdi. Arturo Toscanini was born in Parma, and music aficionados can visit the maestro's birthplace (13 Via Tanzi; phone: 521-285499). It is closed Mondays and after 1 PM; no admission charge. A small museum next door also has some of Toscanini's music and other memorabilia on display. In a special room, visitors can listen to recordings and view videos of the maestro. It's closed Mondays; Wednesdays and Fridays through Sundays after 1 PM; and Tuesdays and Thursdays for a short (1 to 3 PM) break; no admission charge (no phone). Niccolò Paganini, the virtuoso violinist, was born elsewhere but is buried here. The opera house built by Marie Louise, the *Teatro Regio* (Via Garibaldi; phone: 521-218910), is considered one of the most beautiful in Italy, and its audience is believed to be perhaps the toughest in the world: Even the world's virtuoso and most unperturbable artists are fearful here. The theater can be visited by appointment only.

The architectural beauty spots of the town are many, although the *Duomo,* the *Battistero* (Baptistry), and the *Chiesa di San Giovanni Evangelista* (Church of St. John the Evangelist)—all part of the *centro episcopale,* on an ancient cobbled square in the historic heart of town—must have first claim to a visitor's attention. The Lombard-Romanesque *Duomo* was built in the 11th century, its campanile in the 13th century. Inside, the chief works of art are the *Deposition* bas-relief (on the west wall of the south transept) carved by sculptor Benedetto Antelami in 1176; the bishop's throne, which also has reliefs by Antelami; and Correggio's famous restored *Assumption of the Virgin* fresco on the dome's ceiling, painted from 1524 to 1530. This swirling ascent of concentric circles of figures is a stunning sight, anticipating the Baroque in feeling, even though it was once unkindly described as a "hash of frogs' legs." The *Duomo* is open daily, with a long (noon to 3 PM) break (phone: 521-235886).

Construction of the extraordinary, multi-tiered, octagonal *Battistero* began in 1196; when it was completed in the next century, Parma was graced by one of the finest ecclesiastical structures of the age. The work of Antelami adorns the doors, and the series of reliefs of the months and the seasons inside is also his, but some of the 13th-century ceiling frescoes are by an unknown hand. The baptistry is open daily, with a midday break; admission charge (phone: 521-235886). *San Giovanni Evangelista,* behind the *Duomo,* is noted for another ceiling fresco by Correggio, this time of St. John (the scene of St. John writing the Apocalypse over a doorway in the left transept is another Correggio), and for numerous frescoes by Parmigianino. It is also possible to visit the beautiful cloisters. Open daily, with a long (noon to 3:30 PM) break (phone: 521-235592).

Not far from the *centro episcopale,* on the banks of the Parma River, is the giant and rather gloomy-looking *Palazzo della Pilotta* (Piazza Pilotta; phne: 521-233309), begun as a complex of barns, an armory, and barracks by the Farnesi in the late 16th century but never finished. Its name derives from *pelota,* a Basque version of handball that was played in its vast, echoing chambers. Today the palace houses the *Galleria Nazionale* (National Gallery), the *Biblioteca Palatina* (Palatine Library), and the *Teatro Farnese,* as well as the *Museo Nazionale Archeologico* (National Archaeological Museum). The *Galleria Nazionale,* considered one of Italy's best art museums, has some fine paintings by non-Emilian masters, such as Fra Angelico and Leonardo, and a variety of works by Correggio and Parmigianino. In the *Biblioteca Palatina* is a museum dedicated to Giambattista Bodoni, the 18th-century printer who worked in Parma. The most extraordinary sight in the *Palazzo della Pilotta,* however, is the *Teatro Farnese.* Built in 1618, it was the first Italian theater to have movable scenery. Although the original was lost when the palace was bombed in World War II, a precise reconstruction gives 20th-century visitors a sense of the lavish life lived at a ducal court. Made entirely of wood, this giant Palladian-style folly was in use from 1628 to 1732, but it's too much of a fire hazard to be used today. The palazzo is closed after 1:45 PM; the *Museo Nazionale Archeologico* closes on Mondays as well; admission charge.

For more of Correggio's work, go to the *Camera di San Paolo* (off Via Melloni, not far from Piazza Marconi). It's actually a room in the former *Convento di San Paolo* decorated with the artist's earliest frescoes, whose spirit and subject matter (mythological scenes, greenery, and *putti*) hardly seem monastic. Closed Mondays and after 1:45 PM; no admission charge. Also worth a look is the majestic 16th-century *Chiesa della S. Maria della Steccata* (Via Dante), damaged by bombs in World War II but admirably restored. In it are Parmigianino frescoes, tombs of the Farnese family, and the tomb of Field Marshal Count Neipperg, Marie Louise's second husband. It's open daily, with a long (noon to 3 PM) closing.

Parma also has some fine Art Nouveau buildings, including the *Palazzo delle Poste* (Post Office Building; Vias Pisacane and Belloni) and the interior of the *Cassa di Risparmio,* a bank (Piazza Garibaldi). Parma's tourist office (*APT*; 5 Piazza del Duomo; phone: 521-233959; fax: 521-238605) has information on still other sights.

Before leaving Parma, step into the mysterious world of potions, herbs, and mortars and pestles in the historical *Antica Spezieria di San Giovanni* (1 Borgo Pipa; phone: 521-233309). Next to the *Convento di San Giovanni,* the pharmacy was established in 1201 and operated until 1881, when it was closed to the great consternation of the people of Parma who swore by the ancient remedies. Frescoes from the 16th century still adorn the three rooms open to the public, and the wood paneling, furniture, and shelves are from the 16th to 18th centuries. Most noteworthy is a collection of 192 ceramic vases from the 15th to 17th centuries; also impressive are the giant mortars. Closed Mondays and after 1:45 PM; admission charge. The history of Italian perfumes (including Marie Louise's favorite, Parma violet) and associated paraphernalia from 1870 to 1950 have been assembled at the *Borsari Collection 1870* (30/A Via Trento; phone: 521-771011). It's closed weekends after 1 PM and weekdays for a midday break; no admission charge.

Nine miles (14 km) south of Parma via the provincial road signposted Traversètolo is the *Fondazione Magnani-Rocca*, in the *Villa di Corte di Mammiano* (18 Via Vecchia di Sala; phone: 521-848327 or 521-848148; fax: 521-848337). Housed here is a rich collection of classic and contemporary paintings from Gentile da Fabriano, Filippo Lippi, Tiziano, Dürer, Rubens, Van Dyck, Goya, Monet, Renoir, Cézanne, De Pisis, Morandi, and others. Equally interesting are the original decor and the antique furniture left in the museum to maintain a lived-in feeling. The museum was the brainchild of musicologist Luigi Magnani, who embarked on the transformation of his home into a museum in 1930. A centuries-old park surrounds the villa; inside, visitors can savor authentic food and wine from the nearby farms owned by the foundation. The museum is closed Mondays and December through February; admission charge.

Once back in town, relax at the *Pasticceria Torino* (61 Via Garibaldi; phone: 521-35689), a family-run pastry shop that has been catering to Parma's sweet tooth since 1910. Specialties, which are served in a 19th-century decor on antique silver trays, include Hungarian cake and sweet spinach tortellini. It's closed Mondays and Sunday afternoons.

BEST EN ROUTE

Grand Hotel Baglioni Just minutes from the center of town, it faces the splendid *Parco Ducale.* While the outside is modern, the interior offers the elegance of turn-of-the-century furnishings. Most of the 170 spacious, quiet rooms have Jacuzzis. The restaurant serves typical Parma fare. Business facilities and parking are available. 14 Viale Piacenza, Parma (phone: 521-292929; fax: 521-292828). Very expensive to expensive.

Palace Hotel Maria Luigia Not far from the train station and within easy walking distance of the major sights, this modern, elegant hotel has 105 rooms and a well-regarded restaurant, *Maxim's* (no relation to the one in Paris). Closed Sundays and August. 140 Viale Mentana, Parma (phone: 52l-281032; fax: 521-231126). Expensive.

Park Hotel Stendhal Modern, comfortable, and well-run, it's in the center of town. All 60 rooms are air conditioned. The restaurant, *La Pilotta,* is excellent; the bar next to the foyer is exceptionally friendly and well stocked. Restaurant closed Mondays. 3 Via Bodoni, Parma (phone: 521-208057; fax: 521-285655). Expensive.

Angiol d'Or The specialties that made Parma famous are served here, and any pasta dish *alla parmigiana* is sure to be a winner. Follow with one of the excellent beef, veal, or pork dishes. There's outdoor dining in a garden in summer. Closed Sunday dinner, Monday lunch, early January, and late August. Reservations necessary. Major credit cards accepted. 1 Vicolo Scutellari, Parma (phone: 521-282632). Expensive to moderate.

La Filoma A longtime favorite, this stylish restaurant offers unusual dishes such as *tortelli d'erbetta,* large ravioli-type pasta stuffed with beetroot greens, ricotta, and parmesan cheese. Traditionally made for the town's *Festa di San Giovanni* (June 24), the tortellini are now produced year-round. Closed

Sundays and August. Reservations necessary. Major credit cards accepted. 15 Via XX Marzo, Parma (phone: 521-234269). Expensive to moderate.

Parizzi One of Parma's best-known—and busiest—restaurants offers excellent renditions of local specialties, particularly seafood and crêpes stuffed with parmesan cheese. A good *secondo* is *stinco del santo,* a complicated pun (*stinco* is a cut of beef; in slang, a *stinco del santo* is someone who is too good to be true), but it adds up to a delicious beef casserole. Closed weekdays for lunch, Sunday dinner, and Mondays. Reservations necessary. Major credit cards accepted. 71 Strada della Repubblica, Parma (phone: 521-285952). Expensive to moderate.

Savoy These 21 rooms are a good choice for budget travelers, and the service is first rate. No restaurant. Closed August and December 23 to *New Year's Day.* On a quiet side street in the center of town, at 3 Via XX Settembre, Parma (phone: 521-281101; fax: 521-281103). Moderate.

Vecchio Molinetto A fine, old-fashioned, family-run dining place, it features rustic decor and a menu that falls squarely in the hearty country category. Excellent homemade pasta and veal dishes are served, and a delicious stuffed, boned chicken is the specialty of the house. All can be enjoyed in a nice little garden in summer. There's a good choice of wines, especially the local colli di Parma selections, which include a refreshing malvasia white. Closed Fridays, Saturday lunch, and August. Reservations necessary. No credit cards accepted. 39 Viale Milazzo, Parma (phone: 521-52672). Moderate to inexpensive.

En Route from Parma Bypass Reggio Emilia and continue on to Modena, the next stop along the Via Emilia (S9), 35 miles (56 km) from Parma.

MODENA The Este family brought it out of the bloody Middle Ages and conferred a long period of prosperity and prominence on it, through the Renaissance and beyond. The relative calm of the ducal period came to an abrupt end with the Napoleonic wars and subsequent Austrian domination, but the city rebelled twice and, by the middle of the 19th century, had dispatched the foreigners for good. Like Piacenza and Parma, it was an early member of the "new" Italy. Today, Modena is, above all, a large, industrial city, and three of the greatest names in Italian automobile design—Ferrari, Maserati, and De Tomaso—have their factories here. Modena also is famous for its sparkling red lambrusco wine, for the walnut liqueur nocino, for *aceto balsamico* (balsamic vinegar), and for a local delicacy, *zampone* (stuffed pig's trotter), eaten all over Italy at *New Year's Eve* dinner. The great Italian opera singer Luciano Pavarotti is a local made good.

Today, most of Modena is newly built, a large part of it dating from the postwar period. However, a kernel of the Old Town remains around the *Duomo.* Begun in 1099 and consecrated in 1184, it was designed by

Lanfranco, an architect from Lombardy, and decorated by Wiligelmo, a master sculptor who did the four friezes on the façade. Dedicated to Modena's patron saint, St. Geminiano, it is one of Italy's best-preserved Romanesque cathedrals. The *Torre Ghirlandina,* the tall, graceful Lombardian bell tower next to the cathedral, is one of the city's most conspicuous landmarks, completed in the early 14th century. Climb the tower and admire the bas-reliefs, sculpture, and other decorations along the way. Also noteworthy are the 15th-century frescoes adorning the room at the end of the second flight of stairs. Behind the cathedral is Modena's Piazza Grande, the traditional marketplace of the city for centuries. Even today, on the last Sunday of every month (except July and December), it is the focal point of a giant antiques market, where all kinds of goods are available for prices far lower than those at comparable flea markets in Rome or Florence. In the northeast corner of the piazza, opposite the *Comune* (Town Hall) stairs, look for the *pietra ringadora* (speaker's stone), where, in bygone times, anyone brave or eccentric enough could address the crowd. This burst of civic freedom was short-lived; it assumed a much less noble function when it became the site of public beatings of debtors.

This town of motor racing and legendary factories is worth discovering from the factory floor. *Maserati Automobile* (322 Via Ciro Menotti; phone: 59-219577; fax: 59-219669) offers tours (English-speaking guides are available) Saturday mornings, except in August, by appointment only; contact Mr. Manfredini (admission charge). Although only owners of the car can gain access to Ferrari's legendary plant (proof of ownership required), anyone can visit the *Galleria Ferrari* (43 Via Dino Ferrari; phone: 5366-943204) in Maranello, 7 miles (11 km) south of Modena via S12. This museum's three floors are a visual narration of the many stages the car has gone through over the years. On display are vintage vehicles and the latest racing models. Closed Mondays and for a midday break; admission charge.

Another worthwhile sight is the *Palazzo dei Musei,* on Via Emilia (Largo Porta Sant'Agostino; phone: 59-222145). It contains various museums and picture galleries, but the most noteworthy installation is that of the *Biblioteca Estense* (Este Library; phone: 59-222248), which houses thousands of books and illuminated manuscripts. Among the treasures on display is the 1,200-page *Bible of Borso d'Este*—a tour de force of 15th-century illumination. The *Museo Civico d'Arte Medioevale-Moderna* (Civic Museum of Medieval and Modern Art; phone: 59-243263) is home to several unique displays of musical instruments, ancient weights and measures, scientific tools, weapons, and ceramics. The Gandini collection, an enticing array of over 2,000 samples of fabric, lace, and embroidery, also is here. The library is closed Fridays and Saturdays after 1:30 PM, and Sundays. The *Museo Civico* is closed Mondays; Sundays for a long (1 to 4 PM) break; and Tuesdays through Saturdays for a very long (noon to 4 PM) break. Other museums in the palazzo are closed Mondays and after 2 PM; all charge admission.

Permanent exhibits of contemporary painting, sculpture, figurative arts, architecture, and photography can be seen at the *Galleria Civica* (Civic Gallery; 5 Via Veneto; phone: 59-222100 or 59-237475). It's closed Thursdays through Saturdays for a long (12:30 to 3:30 PM) break, and Sundays through Wednesdays; no admission charge. Don't pass up the opportunity to visit the Panini picture-card collection of more than 750,000 cards from France, Germany, Switzerland, and Great Britain, including old labels, ex libris stickers, letter seals, chocolate and candy wrappers, matchbox covers, and more. These unusual treasures are on view at *Panini Publishers* (9 Via Scaglia; phone: 59-344133, or contact the *Palazzo dei Musei*—see above—for information), the world's largest printer of picture cards.

Modena's tourist office (*APT*) is at 3 Corso Canalgrande (phone: 59-220136; fax: 59-220686) and at 30 Via Scuderi (phone: 59-222482; fax: 59-214591). Among other things, it will provide a list of local bike rentals for those who want to take advantage of Modena's flat terrain.

If time permits, you should visit a balsamic-vinegar factory, where centuries-old techniques are still used to produce Modena's renowned condiment. For information, contact the *Consorzio Produttori di Aceto Balsamico Tradizionale di Modena* (Consortium of Producers of Modena's Balsamic Vinegar; c/o *Camera di Commercio,* 134 Via Granaceto, Modena 41100; phone: 59-208298).

BEST EN ROUTE

Fini Modena's best hotel has 92 attractively decorated rooms and all the modern amenities, including hair dryers in the bathrooms. It's on the outskirts of town toward Bologna, and thus not near the restaurant of the same name and under the same management (see below). But there is a complimentary limousine for guests to the dining spot. Business services are available. Closed August. 441 Via Emilia E., Modena (phone: 59-238091; fax: 59-364804). Very expensive to expensive.

Fini The best restaurant in town is very elegant—the clientele tends to be Modena's first citizens or out-of-town sports dropping by to pick up their new Ferraris. The Fini company is one of the region's major producers of sausages, salami, and other foods; this is a good place to try *zampone* (stuffed pig's trotter); *fritto misto,* a combination of meat, vegetables, and fruits, fried in light butter; or the rich selection of boiled meat known as *bollito misto.* Closed Mondays, Tuesdays, August, and *Christmastime.* Reservations necessary. Major credit cards accepted. 54 Rua Frati Minori, Modena (phone: 59-223314). Expensive.

Aurora An intimate restaurant with good service and excellent food, it is very close to Piazza Grande. The roast veal, pasta *alla zucca* (in squash sauce), and seafood dishes (served Thursdays through Saturdays) are particularly good. Closed Mondays and mid-August to mid-September. Reservations necessary. Major credit cards accepted. 9 Via Taglio, Modena (phone: 59-225191). Moderate to inexpensive.

Roma The ideal place to stay, given its central, yet quiet, location. Its 55 rooms are spacious and comfortable. No restaurant. 44 Via Farini, Modena (phone: 59-222218; fax: 59-223747). Moderate to inexpensive.

En Route from Modena Follow the Via Emilia for 24 miles (38 km) to Bologna.

BOLOGNA This city of red slate roofs, long arcades, and distinctive domes is a hub of commerce and learning, renowned for its university—one of the oldest in Europe—and a gastronomic center of no small repute. For a detailed report of the city, its sights, its hotels, and its restaurants, see *Bologna* in THE CITIES.

En Route from Bologna Continue southeast in the direction of Imola and Faenza, respectively 20 miles (32 km) and 30 miles (48 km) from Bologna via the Via Emilia (S9). About halfway between Castel San Pietro Terme and Imola is the turnoff for Dozza, a charming hill town crowned by the *Rocca,* a majestic castle built between 1200 and 1600. In September of odd-numbered years, the outside walls of many of Dozza's houses are painted with murals, the work of artists taking part in a painting festival of sorts. The best frescoes—among them some of the works of internationally known artists—are eventually removed and put on display in a gallery in the *Rocca.* With its bulwark and battlement walls and Renaissance loggia, the castle still impresses, and its dungeons serve as the headquarters of the wine growers' guild of Emilia-Romagna, an *enoteca* where wine can be sampled and bought. The *Rocca* is closed Mondays and for a midday break; no admission charge (no phone).

BEST EN ROUTE

Canè This tiny restaurant is just down the street from Dozza's castle. Its shaded terrace offers spectacular views of the fertile countryside. For the pasta course, try the handmade *garganelli.* Closed Mondays and most of January. Reservations advised. Major credit cards accepted. 27 Via XX Settembre, Dozza (phone: 542-678120). Moderate.

FAENZA Faenza is small, most of it encircled by its medieval walls. It is best known for the majolica ceramics it has produced since the Middle Ages. Indeed, by the early Renaissance, Faentine potters enjoyed such wide renown that a variation of maiolica (the word refers to the Spanish island of Majorca, where the technique was brought from the Middle East) became known in France as *faïence.* Today, some of the buildings in town are faced with ceramic tiles, and the street signs are ceramic plaques. Any number of artisans are at work in and around Faenza, and any number of shops offer vast assortments of their wares. Although modern examples are generally but a shadow of the glory achieved in earlier work, among the best places to purchase them are the *Bottega d'Arte Ceramica Gatti* (4 Via Pompignoli; phone: 546-30556; showroom, 21 Piazza Libertà; same phone); *Morigi Mirta* (19/4 Via Barbavara; phone: 546-29940), which offers summer ceramic courses in English; and *Geminiani Silvana* (21 Vicolo Pasolini; phone: 546-26566). The tourist office (1 Piazza del Popolo; phone: 546-25231) has a complete list of Faenza's reputable ceramic artists. The *Consorzio Ceramisti di Faenza* (2 Voltone della Molinella; phone: 546-22308), a permanent showroom with their current production, is open daily. The industry that put Faenza on the map has also spawned a museum, the *Museo Internazionale delle Ceramiche* (International Museum of Ceramics; 2 Via Campidoro; phone: 546-21240). Large and well designed, it covers the history, manufacture, and decoration of ceramics from every corner of the globe, from the dawn of time to the present, but especially interesting are the pre-Columbian ceramics and the extensive collection of old Italian pieces. The modern section contains ceramics by Matisse, Chagall, and Picasso. The museum is closed Mondays April through October; closed Mondays and after 1:30 PM the rest of the year; admission charge.

Among the events highlighting ceramics is the *Estate Ceramica* (Summer of Ceramics), held annually from the fourth Sunday in June through September in the Piazza del Popolo, which offers an opportunity to examine the latest creations and to indulge in a shopping spree. And from July through September in even-numbered years, the *Mostra della Maiolica Antica* (Exhibit of Antique Ceramics) is held at the *Palazzo delle Esposizione* (92 Corso Mazzini; phone: 546-28664 or 546-62111). The *Manifestazione Internazionale della Ceramica d'Arte Contemporanea* (International Show of Contemporary Artistic Ceramics) takes place in odd-numbered years at the Piazza del Popolo. In July and August, Faenza's Piazza della Molinella becomes an open-air stage where musical, theatrical, and dance performances are held every evening. But the highlight of the year for the locals is in June, when the *Niballo Palio,* a reenactment of a medieval tournament of the city's five *rioni* (districts), takes place. The object of the event is an intricately embroidered silk cloth, which bears esteem and glory. For information, contact the tourist office.

En Route from Faenza Keep to the Via Emilia; the Adriatic coast at Rimini is 40 miles (64 km) away. A few small towns make interesting deviations from the straight and narrow. One is the spa town of Brisighella, just south of Faenza on S302. This beautiful little hill hamlet is dominated on one peak by a 14th-century castle and on another by a 13th-century clock tower. The whole town is extremely picturesque, particularly its central piazza, overlooked by a curious, arcaded main street, Via del Borgo. In the castle (Via Monticino; phone: 546-81225) is a small museum depicting the simple, rustic lifestyle of old Romagna. It is closed Mondays and for a long (noon to 3:30 PM) break; no admission charge. A variety of medieval feasts and pageants are held in Brisighella the last 10 days of July. For details, contact the *Associazione Feste Medioevali* (Association of Medieval Festivals; 54 Via Maglioni; phone: 546-83126 or 546-83177). An antiques market takes place in the town's historic center on Via degli Asini Friday evenings from June through September. The local tourist office, *Pro Loco,* is in Piazza Stazione (phone: 546-81166).

Just before Rimini comes the epic crossing of the Rubicon. Travelers pass over the legendary river just as Julius Caesar did in 49 BC, except that Caesar was moving south from Gaul to Rome when he forded it. Regrettably, the event is hardly notable these days, for the river is now an uninspiring ditch at Savignano, between Cesena and Rimini.

BEST EN ROUTE

La Grotta An intimate, first class eatery, it's housed in a hollow scraped out of the giant rocks of Brisighella's mountainside. The food is excellent, the service flawless, and the prices astonishingly reasonable. The three set menus range from a small sampling of one or two courses to a full four-course meal. Closed Tuesdays, January, and the first two weeks in June. Reservations advised. Major credit cards accepted. 1 Via Metelli, Brisighella (phone: 546-81829). Inexpensive.

RIMINI The Via Emilia comes to an end here, at what was once an ancient town and the most popular holiday resort on the Adriatic. The Lido di Rimini is a long, wide stretch of beach lined with hotels, bars, restaurants, souvenir stands, and discos that can be, by turns, sleazy, ultra-chic, or fun for the whole family. Foreigners descend on it by the tens of thousands each summer; in fact, always have a reservation in hand unless you enjoy cruising crowded streets in desperate quest of accommodation. Bear in mind, too, that although there is much beach in Rimini, there is not much *public* beach (and there is a fee for the use of changing rooms, chairs, and umbrellas). A sunny note: Most smaller hotels have joined forces to share beaches and make them available to their guests.

Difficulties notwithstanding, Rimini is just the place for those who like a fun-in-the-sun, dance-until-dawn summer vacation. At last count, there were 200 restaurants, 240 pizzerias, 435 *caffès,* and 140 discos. Add to these countless daytime activities and you have a gigantic fun machine geared to both young and old. While totally nude sunbathing is a no-no, topless women are the norm rather than the exception. At night, the beachfront main drags—Lungomare Tintori, Lungomare Murri, and parallel Viale Vespucci—draw hordes of people on the make, some "professional" talent, and carousers of every nationality. A novel way to spend the night in Rimini is to hop aboard a *Blue Line* bus for a ride straight into the town's frenzied nightlife. During July and August the buses shuttle all night between Rimini and neighboring resorts, stopping en route at the liveliest, loudest, and most "in" discos, restaurants, and pizzerias. There is live entertainment on board, and a guide offers insight into the hottest spots. The bus leaves from many central points, including the train station; purchase tickets on board. And the local night train, *Azzurro,* makes continuous runs between Rimini and neighboring resorts; contact the *APT* tourist office (3 Piazzale Indipendenza; phone: 541-51101; fax: 541-26566) for details.

For a respite from Rimini's incessant partying, walk to the left side of the port, the last remnant of the real Rimini. Here you'll find bustling docks, the fresh morning catch, boats under repair, and many unpretentious but good trattorie and wine cellars.

Cycling around town is as much a part of the Rimini experience as sunbathing and discoing until dawn. There are over 20 places to rent bikes throughout the town; check with the tourist office (see above) for a complete list. They also have a booklet describing 19 different bicycle excursions. Also available are mopeds and scooters—and, for the less daring, rickshaws.

Rimini's historic center, about half a mile (1 km) from the beachfront and separated from it by railroad tracks, contains one sight of exceptional historic interest. This is the *Tempio Malatestiano,* a Gothic church converted in the 15th century into one of the most influential buildings of the Renaissance. Designed by the Florentine architect Leon Battista Alberti, who based the façade on Rimini's ancient Roman *Arco di Augusto* (Arch of Augustus), it was one of the earliest Renaissance buildings to be based on an actual classical model. (The *Arco di Augusto* is the breach in the city wall at the end of Corso di Augusto.) Alberti was in the employ of Sigismondo Malatesta, the tyrant of Rimini at the time but also a patron of the arts. Contemporaries have recorded that Malatesta was a brilliant man, with the ability to be very amiable when he chose, but it seems his wives saw little of that charm. He denounced one, poisoned the second, and strangled the third. Yet he was so full of love for his mistress Isotta that he raised the *Tempio Malatestiano* as a monument to her memory. The spacious interior is finely decorated with works of art and dotted here and there with the fanciful symbols of the Malatestas, the elephant and the rose. (The "S" superimposed by an "I" seen everywhere stands not for the dollar but for Sigismondo and Isotta.)

Rimini's colorful and eclectic outdoor market, where everything from produce and cheese to beach toys and "I Love Rimini" T-shirts are for sale, is held Thursdays and Saturdays from 8 AM to 1 PM in Piazza Malatesta. For antiques of all sorts, visit the outdoor market in Piazza Cavour on Friday evenings.

Rimini is a main jumping-off point for trips to the independent republic of San Marino, which is about 15 miles (24 km) away on S72 and which maintains its own information office in Rimini (Piazzale Cesare Battisti;

phone: 541-56333). Many of the town's travel agencies organize excursions to this tiny country and to nearby villages, such as Santarcangelo, which nestles picturesquely on a hillside and is a source of hand-printed linen.

Italia in Miniatura, an open-air park displaying over 250 miniature models of Italian monuments, sights, and daily life, was designed by the creator of the movie creature E.T.; there is a 1½-mile (2½-km) walking tour or an overhead monorail (239 Via Popiglia, Viserba di Rimini; phone: 541-732004; fax: 541-732203). It's open daily; admission charge.

BEST EN ROUTE

Grand The grande dame of the Adriatic coast was built in 1908, and this giant Edwardian building still recalls the opulent, pre–World War II days of seaside resorts. The entire hotel—renovated from top to bottom a few years ago—is decorated in lavish fin de siècle style, and the service does not disappoint. The 119 rooms have air conditioning, TVs, radios, and mini-bars. The finest bit of Rimini seafront is reserved for its guests, but there is also a giant, heated pool. Other amenities are tennis courts, a garden, and a sauna. There's a fine bar; the restaurant, facing the water, serves very good food and keeps a kosher kitchen. Open year-round. 2 Piazzale Indipendenza, Rimini (phone: 541-56000; fax: 541-56866). Very expensive to expensive.

Lo Squero Wonderful seafood and desserts are the draw at this attractive seaside dining spot. Closed Tuesdays in low season, and November through December. Reservations advised in high season. Major credit cards accepted. 7 Lungomare Tintori, Rimini (phone: 541-27676). Expensive.

Caffè delle Rose The "Liberty" theme (as Art Nouveau is known in Italy) predominates in this very stylish place. Wicker tables and chairs, complemented by pink accessories, and meals on a large covered verandah amid plants all create a pleasant *ambiente.* The food is well prepared and refined, offering traditional fare with a sophisticated twist. You can sip after-dinner coffee or a *digestivo* in the piano bar, if you wish. Closed Mondays. Reservations advised. Major credit cards accepted. 2 Viale Vespucci, Rimini (phone: 541-25416). Expensive to moderate.

Club House Squarely on the beach, each of its 28 rooms has a terrace, and the entire hotel is the last word in modern, high-tech convenience. From bed, guests can raise or lower the blinds, close the curtains, lock the door, and turn on a variety of gadgets, all at the touch of a button. No restaurant. Open year-round. 52 Viale Vespucci, Rimini (phone: 541-391460; fax: 541-391442). Expensive to moderate.

Chicchibio A small dining spot with wood paneling, reminiscent of an old English library, it serves typical local fare. Its specialties include homemade pasta and grilled and roast meat. Closed Sundays in low season. Reservations necessary Saturdays. Major credit cards accepted. 11 Via Soardi, Rimini (phone: 541-26778). Moderate.

En Route from Rimini Head northwest for 5½ miles (9 km) on S9 to the small city of Cesena, worth a stop to visit the *Biblioteca Malatestiana* (Malatesta Library; 1 Piazza Bufalini; phone: 547-21297). More than five centuries old, it is Europe's only perfectly preserved medieval library. Built by the Umbrian architect Matteo Nuti in 1452 for Prince Malatesta Novello, Cesena's enlightened ruler (1429–65), it steers away from rectangular halls and instead celebrates the arched vault, naves, and pillars. Multilingual guides take visitors past the *plutei* (reading desks made from cypress wood, carved with family crests), where you can stop and look at leaden tomes of superb illuminated manuscripts. The oldest is the *Etymologiae* of St. Isidore of Seville, dating from the 7th century. Closed Mondays and for a long (12:30 to 5 PM) break mid-June to mid-September; closed Mondays, Sunday afternoons, and Tuesdays through Saturdays for a midday break the rest of the year; admission charge.

The Adriatic coast is lined with seaside resorts, each one more tawdry than the last. A notable exception is Cesenatico, 14 miles (22 km) north of Rimini via S16. Today the town is a very pretty fishing village, but it was born in the early 14th century as a military port for the town of Cesena and was laid out in part by Leonardo on behalf of Cesare Borgia. The central canal, dividing the town in two, is home to a permanently moored fleet of old fishing vessels and sailing barges. Five miles (8 km) farther on S16 is Milano Marittima, an elegant resort.

Just south of Ravenna, 9 miles (15 km) from Milano Marittima, S16 turns inland toward Ferrara, while the main coast road proceeds to Ravenna, passing the *Chiesa di Sant'Apollinare in* Classe, about 3 miles (5 km) south of the city. Stop here for a first look at Ravenna's magnificent mosaics. This beautiful building, standing where the ancient Roman port of Classis once stood, is notable for the simplicity of its 6th- and 7th-century designs. Ravenna's first bishop and martyr, St. Apollinaris, is shown with the faithful depicted as lambs; Christ is surrounded by Apostles depicted as lambs; there is a great Latin cross surrounded by stars; and trees, birds, and flowers are in abundance.

BEST EN ROUTE

Gambero Rosso At this terraced restaurant, fresh fish is the specialty. Closed Mondays and mid-November to mid-December. Reservations advised on weekends. Major credit cards accepted. 21 Molo Levante, Cesenatico (phone: 547-81260). Expensive.

Gianni Delightful and unusual, this spot is not only the best restaurant in Cesena, it's also the best value. The *zuppa di pesce* (fish soup)—locally known as *padella*—is unlike any other, and the pasta dishes are superb. Closed Thursdays. Reservations advised. Major credit cards accepted. 9 Via Natale dell'Amore, Cesena (phone: 547-21328). Expensive.

Trattoria al Gallo Try the mixed grill of fish in this friendly establishment, which serves fresh seafood and mouth-watering homemade desserts. Closed Wednesdays. Reservations advised. Major credit cards accepted. 21 Via Baldini, Cesenatico (phone: 547-81067). Expensive.

La Buca On the canal with tables outside in summer, this eatery is run by a sea-faring family. The food is good, especially the fish and seafood, and the desserts are out of this world—but the prices are not. Closed Mondays, except in high season, and part of January. Reservations advised. Major credit cards accepted. 41 Corso Garibaldi, Cesenatico (phone: 547-82474). Moderate to inexpensive.

RAVENNA Ravenna's position in the history of Western Europe is unique. It existed as a Roman city even before Emperor Augustus founded the port of Classis just to the south. In the 5th century, after the Roman Empire split into an eastern and a western section, it became the capital of the Empire of the West. It then went through a short period as a kingdom of the Goths. But at the height of its splendor, from the 6th century to the 8th century, while the western portion of the empire fell into the hands of many chiefs, it was part of the Eastern Roman Empire—the Byzantine Empire—and its dominant influence came not from the Italian peninsula, or even the rest of Europe, but from Constantinople. This eastern-facing stance marked the art and architecture of the city with the indelible imprint of Byzantium, first and foremost in the mosaic masterpieces that are the chief glory of Ravenna's early Christian churches. The most famous are in the *Basilica di San Vitale* (17 Via San Vitale) and the adjacent *Tomba di* (Tomb of) *Galla Placidia,* in the *Battistero degli Ortodossi* (Orthodox Baptistry) and the *Battistero degli Ariani* (Arian Baptistry), and in the *Basilica di Sant'Apollinare Nuovo* (Via di Roma).

San Vitale is an octagonal church built between 526 and 547 and probably based on a much older church in Constantinople. For more information, see *Churches and Piazzas* in DIVERSIONS. Concerts are held on Mondays in July and August, when the church hosts the city's *Festival per la Musica d'Organo* (Festival of Organ Music).

In the same complex as *San Vitale* is the exquisite *Tomba di Galla Placida*, the sister of the Emperor Honorius. It dates from the mid-5th century, and its mosaics are the oldest in Ravenna, still Roman rather than Byzantine in style. In some ways, the mosaics in this tiny, dark room are more affecting than the ones in the main church, since they are closer to the eye and their symbolism is more personal, their execution more natural. The tomb is dominated by a tympanum mosaic of Christ the Good Shepherd and, facing that, one of St. Lawrence with the instrument of his martyrdom (a gridiron—he was roasted alive). In the transepts are some charming stags—representing souls—drinking from the Fountain of Life. The ceiling of the dome is deep blue, studded with countless stars. (*Note:* The coin box to light the tomb is outside, set in the wall facing the front door of the building.) The complex is open daily; admission charge.

The *Battistero degli Ortodossi,* also known as the *Battistero Neoniano,* adjoins the *Duomo* of Ravenna, which is largely an 18th-century Baroque building. Originally a Roman-era bathhouse, the baptistry was dedicated to Christianity in the mid-5th century and is thus contemporary with the *Tomba di Galla Placida.* The centerpiece of the mosaics in the dome here—betraying telltale signs of 19th-century restoration—is the baptism of Christ, the figures surrounded by Apostles as by the spokes of a wheel. The *Battistero degli Ariani* is on a quiet side street (Via degli Ariani) not far from Ravenna's main square, the Piazza del Popolo. Thought to have been built by Theodoric in the early 6th century, this structure houses another set of brilliant mosaics with the sacrament of Baptism as a major theme.

The *Basilica di Sant'Apollinare Nuovo* is the last great treasurehouse of mosaics in the city. It was erected by Theodoric in the early 6th century and adapted for Christian use toward the mid-6th century by Justinian. Most, but not all, of the mosaics are from Theodoric's time—in fact, the transition from a classical Roman style to pure Byzantine is evident here. The mosaics of the two upper registers on either side (scenes from the life of Christ and prophets or saints) are from the era of Theodoric, as are the two city scenes on the lower friezes: the port of Classis, with its two lighthouse towers on the left frieze, and the palace of Theodoric, with the city of Ravenna behind it on the right frieze. The two glorious processions on the lower friezes, however, are from the time of Justinian, fully Byzantine. On the left is a procession of 22 virgins, preceded by the Magi marching toward the enthroned Virgin and Child. On the right, a procession of 26 martyrs moves toward Christ enthroned. The largest mosaics in Ravenna, they are absolutely stunning. The basilica is open daily; admission charge.

A monument of an entirely different era is near the restored *Chiesa di San Francesco,* not far from *Sant'Apollinare Nuovo* and the Piazza del Popolo. This is the *Tomba di Dante,* Italy's greatest poet. Exiled from his native Florence for political reasons, Dante spent his last years in Ravenna at the court of Guido da Polenta, where he finished the *Divine Comedy.* He died on September 13, 1321, and his ashes are still in Ravenna (some of the ashes were kept in a Florence library until 1986, when they were proclaimed missing)—his tomb in *Santa Croce* in Florence is empty. Each year amid much pomp a Florentine delegation is dispatched to Ravenna to pay homage. The tomb seen here today dates from 1780, covering another one of the late 15th century, beneath which is the actual resting place. Open daily, with a short (noon to 2 PM) closing; no admission charge.

Ancient and modern mosaic tiles and figures remain a Ravenna art form. Two notable studios are *Studio il Mosaico* (22 Via Fiandrini; phone: 544-36090) and *Artemosaico di Puglisi Liborio* (137 Via Cavour; phone: 544-23904). Check with the local *APT* (see below) for information on other studios. A permanent exhibit of contemporary mosaic art can be seen at the *Pinacoteca Comunale—Loggetta Lombardesca* (13 Via di Roma; phone: 544-35625). It is closed Mondays and for a short (1 to 2:30 PM) break; admission charge. On the third weekend of each month, an antiques market is set up in Piazza Garibaldi and along city streets.

Ravenna's tourist office (*APT*) is close to the town center (8 Via Salara; phone: 544-35404), north of Piazza del Popolo. A personal guide to the treasures of Ravenna is recommended: *Verdiana Conti Baioni* (9 Via Carrale; phone: 544-63154), with a guide who grew up in one of Ravenna's museums and speaks flawless English.

About 5 miles (8 km) from Ravenna on S16 Adriatica in Savio is the *Museo degli Strumenti Musicale Meccanici Marino Marini* (Marino Marini Museum of Mechanical Musical Instruments; phone: 544-560547), which houses a prestigious collection of mechanical organs, pianolas, music boxes, and other instruments. It is closed Mondays and for a short (1 to 2:30 PM) break; admission charge. Also about 5 miles (8 km) out of town, on S253 San Vitale to Godo, is the *Museo dell'Arredo Contemporaneo* (Museum of Contemporary Furniture; phone: 544-419299), which displays masterpieces from 1880 to the present, including the works of Frank Lloyd Wright, Le Corbusier, and Charles Rennie Mackintosh. It's closed Mondays, Tuesdays, and before 3:30 PM; admission charge.

BEST EN ROUTE

Tre Spade Originally located in the heart of town, this restaurant has moved to a nearby villa, surrounded by a park. The menu is unchanged, the food, excellent. Try the turkey smothered in walnut sauce; the risotto with shrimp, *porcini* mushrooms, and saffron will appease even the most demanding palate. Closed Sunday dinner. Reservations advised. Major credit cards accepted. 136 Via Faentina, Ravenna (phone: 544-500522). Expensive.

Bisanzio Thirty-six comfortable rooms (most have radio, TV, and mini-bar) and a prime location for sightseeing and shopping make this modern hotel an excellent choice. No restaurant. 30 Via Salara, Ravenna (phone: 544-217111; fax: 544-32539). Expensive to moderate.

Diana A 33-room hotel that has recently undergone extensive renovation, it is a no-frills but very comfortable place to stay, with a garden. Most rooms have a TV, a radio, a telephone, a mini-bar, and air conditioning. No dining room. Centrally located, at 47 Via Rossi, Ravenna (phone: 544-39164; fax: 544-30001). Expensive to moderate.

Ca' de Ven An institution, this huge old *enoteca* (wine cellar) is famous for a local creation called *piadina:* a bready pancake fried on a griddle and brought to the table warm, along with a huge platter of ham, salami, mortadella, and cheese. The wines served here, as might be expected, are exquisite, particularly the local pagadebit. Closed Mondays. Reservations unnecessary. No credit cards accepted. 5 Via Ricci, Ravenna (phone: 544-30163). Moderate.

Centrale Byron For location rather than spacious quarters, try this very well run, simple hostelry with 57 rooms (most with a TV, a radio, a mini-bar, and air conditioning), just steps from the central piazza and in the middle of Ravenna's very good shopping district. No restaurant. 14 Via IV Novembre, Ravenna (phone: 544-21225; fax: 544-32539). Moderate to inexpensive.

En Route from Ravenna Take S16 north to Ferrara, 45 miles (72 km) away.

FERRARA Like Bologna, Ferrara has—unjustly—been left off the itineraries of most foreign visitors to Italy, although it is familiar to some as the setting of Giorgio Bassani's novel *The Garden of the Finzi-Continis*. While not very large, it has a colorful history and is rich in art and architecture, most of it in the beautiful, quaint medieval heart of town dominated by the giant *Castello Estense* (Castle of the Este Dukes). The castle's size and prominence reflect the importance of the family in the history not only of the city but also well beyond its walls. Ferrara was the seat of the Este family from the 13th century through the 16th century, and during that time it was a cultural stronghold of the Renaissance in northern Italy. Few royal families lived with quite the splendor of the Dukes and Duchesses of Ferrara, who were famous for the luxury of the palaces they built, for the lavishness of their hospitality, and for the richness of their garb. They were also noted patrons of the arts, their court a meeting place for the most famous poets, painters, and philosophers of their age. Ludovico Ariosto and Torquato Tasso, writers of two of the great classics of Italian literature, were in the dukes' service.

The city flourished under Este patronage; in fact, at the end of the 15th century, Duke Ercole I embarked on a plan to double Ferrara's size by building a new urban quarter—the area known as the Herculean Addition—north of the castle. Later dukes consolidated the family's power and prestige. Ercole's son Alfonso I married Lucrezia Borgia; their son Ercole II married Renée, daughter of Louis XII of France (another son, an Este cardinal, built the *Villa d'Este* at Tivoli, near Rome). The marriage didn't work out, and Ercole exiled his royal wife for political reasons. That the move was accomplished without any repercussion is a sign of just how powerful the Estes had become. The end came swiftly, however. In 1598, the duchy was annexed to the Papal States, because the Estes failed to produce a legitimate male heir. A branch of the family lived on in Modena and Reggio Emilia, but with the loss of Ferrara its glory days were gone.

Begin by visiting the castle, right in the center of town (and opposite the tourist office, which is at 22 Largo Castello; phone: 532-299279). Protected by a moat and three drawbridges, this giant building was begun in 1385 as a response to the townspeople's revolt over a tax increase, which led to the beheading of the ducal tax collector. The castle was finished some two centuries later. It now houses provincial offices, but some of the rooms in which the Estes lived are open to the public. Among these are the large and small *Games Rooms,* so called because of the theme of the frescoes decorating the ceiling—athletic games—and the *Aurora Room,* decorated with four frescoes showing different hours of the day. Beyond is the tiny chapel of the unhappy princess Renée (Renata, in Italian), one of the few old Protestant places of worship in Italy. (Princess Renée, an ardent Protestant, sheltered John Calvin in the city during the 1550s.) The last act of a particularly sordid chapter in Este family history was played out in the dungeons beneath the northeast tower. A 15th-century duke, Niccolò d'Este, discovered that his wife, Parisina Malatesta, was having an affair with Ugo, his illegitimate son. Niccolò imprisoned the two lovers in the dungeons and had them decapitated in 1425. The dungeons were in use as late as World War II, when first the Fascists and later the Nazis held political prisoners and resistance fighters here. Closed Mondays; admission charge.

Behind the castle lies the old ghetto, which once housed one of the largest and most important Jewish populations in Italy. A block from the castle is Ferrara's beautiful cathedral. Begun in 1135, it is remarkable for a wide marble triple façade, the upper portion of which is Gothic, the lower Romanesque. There is a stern Last Judgment over the main portal by a sculptor whose name has been lost to time. The museum within contains two early-15th-century statues by the Sienese sculptor Jacopo della Quercia, late-15th-century works by Cosimo Tura, a master of the Ferrarese school of painting, and an unknown 12th-century master's sculptured reliefs of the months of the year that were part of a door on the south side of the cathedral. The interior of the cathedral has been much altered, but outside, the cathedral itself, the beautiful and large adjacent piazza, and the towering campanile (a 15th-century addition) are so perfectly preserved they look as if they were copied from a medieval painting illustrating the benefits of a just prince or good communal government. The cathedral is open daily, with a midday closing. Stroll down nearby Via San Romano and Via delle Volte for a touch of medieval Ferrara.

On the edge of the historic center is the *Palazzo Schifanoia* (23 Via Scandiana; phone: 532-64178), a home away from home for the ruling family. This noble building, begun in 1385 for Alberto V and greatly modified by Borso d'Este (whose famous Bible is in the museum in Modena) and by Ercole I in the late 15th century, was used primarily for the Estes' extravagant entertainments. It was their pleasure palace—hence the name, taken from the Italian words meaning "disgust" and "boredom." The frescoes in the *Salone dei Mesi,* by Francesco del Cossa, Ercole de' Roberti, and others of the Ferrarese school, make up one of the most important fresco cycles of the Renaissance bearing a profane theme. Zodiacal motifs and triumphs of the gods occupy the upper levels, but the lower levels, showing scenes of courtly life with Borso d'Este figuring prominently in each one, are invaluable documents of the everyday existence of a great ducal family of the Renaissance. The palazzo now houses the numerous collections—illuminated manuscripts, ceramics, coins, medals, and so on—that make up the *Museo Civico.* It is closed Mondays; admission charge.

Still another Este palace, the *Palazzo dei Diamanti,* is at the corner of Corso Ercole I d'Este and Corso Rossetti. Built in the late 15th century by Duke Ercole I as the centerpiece of his Herculean Addition, the Renaissance quarter he built (but never finished) to the north of the medieval part of town, it takes its name from the 8,500 diamond-shaped blocks of stone on its façade (the diamond was an Este family symbol). Inside the palace is the *Pinacoteca Nazionale,* the city's most important picture gallery. The street is important in itself: Ercole I had it built and lined it with palaces, one after another, descending in height toward the end, where he had trees planted. From the castle, it looked like a long boulevard leading to the country, which was far from the truth. Closed Mondays; Tuesdays through Fridays after 2 PM; and weekends and holidays after 1 PM; admission charge (phone: 532-205844).

Other notable palaces built by members of the ruling family are not far from the *Palazzo Schifanoia.* The *Palazzo di Ludovico il Moro* was built at the end of the 15th century by the Sforza husband of Beatrice d'Este. It is now the home of the *Museo Archeologico Nazionale* (National Archaeological Museum; 124 Via XX Settembre; phone: 532-66299), which houses, among other curiosities, two Roman boats found in the region, each carved out of a single gigantic tree trunk, and Etruscan antiquities from the seaport of Spina. Also visit the *Palazzina di Marfisa d'Este* (far end of Corso della Giovecca; phone: 532-207450), a small but beautiful 16th-century residence with elaborately painted ceilings, an outdoor theater, and a delightful garden. It's closed Mondays and for a short midday break. At press time, the archaeological museum was closed for renovation; both sites charge admission.

Today Ferrara is a uniquely friendly city that, with its perfect brick houses, swarms of bicycles (there isn't a hill in sight), and wintertime pea-soup fogs, resembles Bruges or Amsterdam rather than any place Italian. Because of its flat terrain and green-bordered city walls, half the population jogs, so it's no surprise that Ferrara has produced winners in marathons the world over, including New York's. Bicycles can be rented at *Bicincittà* (Via Kennedy; phone: 532-337-628072).

An event not to be missed is the *Palio di San Giorgio,* a reenactment of four medieval races with horses, donkeys, and children, which takes place the last Sunday in May. The festivities begin with a parade of 800 costumed people who look as if they had just stepped out of one of *Palazzo Schifanoia*'s frescoes. For information, contact the tourist office (see above). In the last week of August, the town hosts the *International Buskers Festival,* a curiosity that draws street-corner musicians from all over the world. And don't miss the delightful open-air market with collector's items, held the first weekend of each month except August. Stop by the *Ceramiche Artistiche Ferraresi* (125 Via Baluardi; phone: 532-66093) to look at its collection of engraved pottery. Of ancient Asian origin, the fine art of engraving pottery came to Ferrara in the 15th and 16th centuries, where, at the hands of masterful local artisans and thanks to the Estense patronage, it flourished and achieved new heights of color and expression. The decline of the Este family led to this art's demise, until a group of Ferrara potters recently revived it. For more information about the city, contact the tourist office *(APT)* at 19 Piazza Municipio (phone: 532-209370 or 532-239269; fax: 532-210844).

About 38 miles (61 km) from Ferrara is the *Parco del Delta del Po* (Po River Delta Park), an intricate network of waterways, canals, and islets—punctuated with small towns like Comacchio, Porto Garibaldi, Gorino, and Goro—where Italy's largest river meets the Adriatic. Biking, hiking, and horseback riding are great ways to get around the park, but boat tours are the most popular modes of transportation. For boat excursions departing from Ferrara, contact *Itinerando* (85 Via Ripagrande; phone: 532-765123); from Gorino, contact *Albergo Ristorante USPA* (9 Piazza Libertà, Gorino; phone: 533-99817 or 533-999815), which also offers guided bicycle tours and rentals.

BEST EN ROUTE

Ripagrande In this restored 14th-century palazzo are 40 modern rooms, many with sitting areas, kitchens, and second bathrooms, as well as TVs, radios, and mini-bars. The top-floor rooms (under the eaves) have beautifully beamed ceilings and terraces with magnificent views. The attentive staff bends over backward to please. There is a good restaurant and bar, and a pleasant courtyard for alfresco breakfasts. The hotel will arrange guided city tours, excursions to nearby towns, treks on horseback, and bicycle rentals. Services are available for the business traveler. In the heart of the medieval section, at 21 Via Ripagrande, Ferrara (phone: 532-765250; fax: 532-764377). Expensive.

Buca San Domenico The pizza here is the best in town; there are many other good dishes as well. Closed Mondays and August. Reservations advised. Major credit cards accepted. 22 Piazza Sacrati, Ferrara (phone: 532-200018). Moderate.

La Provvidenza The rustic atmosphere and a lovely garden provide a perfect setting in which to enjoy prodigious quantities of fine fresh pasta, grilled meat, and great desserts. Closed Mondays and part of August. Reservations advised. Major credit cards accepted. 92 Corso Ercole I d'Este, Ferrara (phone: 532-205187). Moderate.

Grotta Azzurra This popular place specializes in northern Italian cuisine. Closed Wednesdays, Sunday dinner, part of January, and August. Reservations advised. Major credit cards accepted. 43 Piazza Sacrati, Ferrara (phone: 532-209152). Moderate to inexpensive.

La Romantica Across the street from the *Ripagrande* (see above), this small spot lives up to its name, offering intimacy and discreet but attentive service. Start with *cappellacci di zucca alle noci,* a pasta stuffed with pumpkin and served with a walnut sauce. The filling harks back to the Middle Ages, when kosher cooking was prevalent around Ferrara—it has no dairy or meat in it and thus could be served with a meat second course. Closed Tuesday dinner, Wednesdays, part of January, and August. Reservations advised. Major credit cards accepted. 36 Via Ripagrande, Ferrara (phone: 532-765975). Moderate to inexpensive.

San Marino

Every year more than three million tourists visit San Marino, the world's oldest and second-smallest republic (the smallest is Nauru, in the South Pacific). You might think that this number of visitors would overwhelm a country whose population numbers a mere 24,000 and whose area measures only 23 square miles—and to a certain extent it does. At high noon on a midsummer day it is sometimes hard to see San Marino's quaint charm beyond the droves of day-trippers and the gaudy displays of countless souvenir shops vying for their attention. But if that day is a clear one, look again. From any number of points in San Marino the panorama embraces the Apennines to the south, expansive plains and hills to the north, the brilliant blue Adriatic to the east, and the Croatian coast, 156 miles (250 km) away. There's no doubt that San Marino's mountaintop setting is spectacular, and it is this, along with interesting historic sites and colorful remnants of the republic's long past, that makes a visit worthwhile.

San Marino lies 11 miles (18 km) from the Adriatic coast of north-central Italy, bordering the regions of Emilia-Romagna to the north and the Marche (Marches) to the south. Most visitors arrive from the coastal town of Rimini, and as you approach, the republic's distinctive "skyline" comes into view: Monte Titano (Mt. Titanus), at a height of 2,470 feet, with its three fortified peaks. The territory of San Marino comprises this mountain, at whose top is the capital, San Marino City, and the surrounding hills, scattered with eight small villages, or "castles" (*castelli*). The climate is temperate, thanks to its altitude and the ever-present *garbino* wind, with summer temperatures rarely exceeding 80F.

According to tradition San Marino dates back almost 1,700 years, to AD 301 and the arrival of a Christian stonecutter from Dalmatia named Marinus. Fleeing the religious persecution of the Roman Emperor Diocletian, Marinus sought out the secluded safety of Monte Titano, where he built a chapel and began to live a saintly life. Other Christians soon followed, giving rise to a free community that very early developed the democratic institutions still governing it today.

San Marino's inaccessibility protected it throughout the fall of the Roman Empire and the subsequent barbarian invasions. Later, when covetous neighbors cast eyes in its direction, it struggled to remain independent. Only twice was it unsuccessful: once in the 16th century, when it was occupied by Cesare Borgia, and again in the 18th century, when Cardinal Giulio Alberoni, legate in Romagna, annexed it to the Papal States. In each case the loss of liberty lasted only a few months.

Along with its freedom, the country prides itself on a long tradition as a place of asylum. The Italian patriot Giuseppe Garibaldi was one of the most famous figures to have found refuge here, in 1849. During World War

Il 100,000 refugees found a haven within its borders. Sadly, the republic was bombed in 1944, despite its proclaimed neutrality. In 1992 San Marino was granted membership in the *United Nations*, a matter of considerable local pride.

San Marino has a small volunteer army. The blue uniforms, blue-and-white plumed headgear, and old-fashioned muskets and sabers of the militia and the *Guardia del Consiglio Grande e Generale* (Guard of the Great and General Council, an honor guard to the country's rulers) can be seen on special occasions. Guardsmen of the *Guardia di Rocca,* however, are on regular duty at the entrance to the government palace, and their green jackets, red trousers, red-and-white feathered caps, and vintage pistols are no less decorative.

The economy of the country is based on tourism, light industry, some farming, and the sale of postage stamps, which have considerable philatelic value. While the Italian lira is the local currency in common use, the minting of coins, mainly for collectors, is another source of revenue.

The border is marked by a banner proclaiming, in Italian, "Welcome to the Ancient Land of Liberty." A passport is not needed to enter from Italy, and there is no customs control, despite the customs station.

Within minutes you are in Serravalle, the most populous of the *castelli.* Here is evidence of industrial growth alongside one of the country's oldest and best-kept castles. Since the bestowal of Serravalle to San Marino in 1463, the republic's territory has not grown by a single inch. Not even Napoleon's offer to extend its borders in 1797 was accepted.

Continuing along the winding road is Domagnano, another of the *castelli,* to the left before arriving at Borgo Maggiore.

BORGO MAGGIORE Established in the 12th century, this market town was originally known as Mercatale. Its open-air market, held on Thursday mornings, has been taking place since 1244. The porticoed Piazza di Sopra remains practically unchanged. Just off Piazza Grande, the main square, is one of San Marino's most important museums, the *Museo Postale, Filatelico e Numismatico* (Stamp and Coin Museum). As we went to press, it was closed for repairs (see *Museums*). Stop also for a look at the ultramodern *Santuario della Beata Vergine della Consolazione* (Sanctuary of the Blessed Virgin of Consolation), an extraordinary church designed by the famous Florentine architect Giovanni Michelucci in the 1960s.

En Route from Borgo Maggiore San Marino City can be reached by foot along the shortcut called the Costa, by car, or via cable car.

SAN MARINO CITY Enter the Old City through the *Porta di San Francesco* (St. Francis's Gate), begun in the 14th century as the doorway to a convent. Once inside the city walls, to the right, you will see the convent and the small *Chiesa di San Francesco,* both founded in 1361. Though this is the oldest church in the republic, only its façade gives away its age; much of the original character of the interior was lost in 17th- and 18th-century restorations. The cloister next door houses a gallery of changing exhibitions and a museum with some noteworthy old paintings, including one of St. Francis by Guercino, and a magnificent fresco, *The Adoration of the Magi*, by Antonio Alberti da Ferrara. There also is a collection of modern paintings. Open daily, mid-June through the first week in September; closed for a midday break the rest of the year; admission charge (phone: 991160).

From the *Porta di San Francesco*, San Marino's narrow streets must be explored on foot, and the ascent can be quite steep at times. Via Basilicius leads upward to tiny Piazzetta del Titano, one of the social centers of the town. Not far off the square, on Contrada Omerelli, is the *Palazzo Valloni*, a structure partly of the 15th and partly of the 18th century. It houses the state archives, with documents dating from 885, as well as the government library. The street ends at the *Porta della Rupe*, the gate through which you enter the city if you take the shortcut from Borgo Maggiore.

To continue the ascent, return to Piazzetta del Titano and take the short walk up the hill to Piazza Garibaldi and the government stamp and coin office *(Azienda Autonoma di Stato Filatelica e Numismatica)*, where you can buy stamps and coins and sign up for a free subscription service that will send you details of new issues and first-day covers. It's closed Sundays and for a long midday break. Then turn and follow Contrada del Collegio up to Piazza della Libertà, the largest and most elegant of San Marino's squares. It takes its name from the 19th-century statue of liberty in the middle, but it's also known as the Pianello, since it's one of the few flat spaces within the walls. To the left is the mountain shelf and a spectacular view; directly in front, dominating the square, is the *Palazzo Pubblico* (Government Building). Although there has been a public building here since the early 14th century, today's *Palazzo Pubblico* dates only to the end of the 19th century, but it was built in an old-fashioned neo-Gothic style. For a small fee the office here will stamp your passport with an unnecessary, but official, San Marino visa. At press time the *Palazzo* was closed for renovations and was due to reopen sometime this year. Until then government offices are operating in temporary headquarters across the street.

San Marino is governed by two captains regent chosen twice a year for six-month terms by the *Guardia del Consiglio Grande e Generale*, whose 60 members, in turn, are elected by popular vote and hold office for five years. Incidentally, Abraham Lincoln was made an honorary citizen of San Marino in 1861. The *sammarinesi* (as the locals are known) are proud of the thank-you letter, preserved in the state archives, in which he said, "Although your dominion is small, nevertheless your State is one of the most honoured throughout history."

Beyond the *Palazzo Pubblico*, Contrada del Pianello leads to the cable car station. En route it passes the Cava dei Balestrieri, the field on which the country's famous *Palio delle Balestre Grandi*, or crossbow competition, is held each year in September. From here you can continue the climb by following Contrada Omagnano or by returning to Piazza delle Libertà. Either way, follow signs to the *Basilica di San Marino*. The remains of the republic's founding saint are buried under the altar of this neoclassical church, which was built in the 19th century to replace an older one that stood on the spot.

From the basilica, signs point through the oldest quarter of the city to the first of the three fortified towers that figure on the country's coat of arms. Known as the *Rocca* or *Guaita,* the tower dates from the 11th century, although its overall appearance is of the 15th century. San Marino is 2,465 feet above sea level at this point. You can climb to the top of the tower and enjoy the cool breezes blowing off the Adriatic as well as a splendid view. It's open daily in July and August; closed for a midday break the rest of the year; no admission charge (phone: 991369). The *Rocca* is joined by a watch path to the second tower, the *Fratta* or *Cesta,* on the highest point of Monte Titano (2,470 feet). Dating from the early 14th century, this tower contains the *Museo delle Armi Antiche* (see *Museums,* below). If your legs have held out thus far, you may want to go along the less beaten path to the third tower, the *Montale,* which is closed to the public. This narrow, graceful structure was in use from the 13th to the 16th century.

From the *Montale* a path leads down the slope to the modern *Palazzo di Congresso* (Congress Palace). Turn back toward the center along Viale J. F. Kennedy, Via Giacomo Matteotti, and Viale Antonio Onofri to see other modern buildings and, just up the hill, tennis facilities, all evidence of the present in this most ancient state.

TOURIST INFORMATION

The main tourist office is in the historic center on Contrada Omagnano (phone: 882998 or 882400; fax: 990388). It is closed weekends; for a short (2:15 to 3 PM) break; and Friday afternoons. The office offers information about various events, including classical musical concerts. You can get your passport stamped with a San Marino visa at the smaller outlet at Piazza Mario Tini (phone: 905414), which is closed October through April, weekends, and for a midday break. There also are branches of the tourist office at Contrada del Collegio (phone: 882914 or 990452), which is closed October through April and weekends, and on Via XXVIII Luglio (phone: 902701), which is closed weekends and for a midday break. Hire English-speaking guides (sanctioned by the tourist office) from *Ufficio Guide* (Piazzale della Repubblica di San Marino; phone: 991529 or 882400).

LOCAL COVERAGE The tourist office publishes *Practical Guide to San Marino,* an excellent free booklet in English that covers everything from cable car timetables to advice on how to cope with an overheated engine in traffic jams on the town's steep, narrow streets.

TELEPHONE San Marino's phone code is scheduled to change from 549 to 378 sometime this year, but at press time it was uncertain whether this would indeed happen. If the prefix does change, note that when calling San Marino from Italy, telephone numbers should be preceded by 0378 (0549); from the US they should be preceded by 39-378 (39-549).

GETTING AROUND

The nearest airports are at Miramare di Rimini (9 miles/14 km away) and Forlì (38 miles/61 km away). The closest train station is in Rimini. Travel by car is on the scenic four-lane highway from Rimini, though you also can reach the border along other well-paved but winding routes. San Marino also is accessible by bus.

BUS Buses depart from Rimini several times a day year-round, arriving about 45 minutes later in San Marino at either Piazzale della Stazione or Piazzale Marino Calcigni. Both stops are within easy walking distance of the historic center. Service within the country itself is good, with frequent buses available to most points of interest. Purchase tickets in advance from tobacconists or at newsstands. Measure your children before getting on; if they are under three feet tall, they ride free.

CABLE CAR Running nonstop in summer from Borgo Maggiore to Contrada Omagnano from 7:45 AM to 9 PM (on a reduced basis in winter), the service is headquartered right next door to San Marino's main tourist office. Buy tickets at any cable car stop.

CAR Leave your vehicle in one of the 12 parking lots dotting the city. Small, with steep, winding streets, San Marino is best explored on foot.

TAXI The main taxi stand is in Piazzale della Repubblica (phone: 991441), but you also can order a cab by calling 903360, 900591, 902049, 997444, 901266, or 991219.

SPECIAL EVENTS

San Marino is at its traditional best during holidays. In addition to the festivities at *Christmas* and *Easter,* two other choice days are April 1 and October 1, when members of San Marino's *Guardia del Consiglio Grande e Generale* meet to elect two new captains regent. The investiture ceremony, which takes place at these times, dates back to 1244 and attracts thousands of spectators. September 3 is set aside each year for a centuries-old crossbow competition, in which the people of San Marino gather at the Cava dei Balestieri, in the piazza near the main tourist office. Complete with buglers and Renaissance costumes, the contest celebrates the founding of the republic. Don't assume that this spectacle is staged for tourists alone. Actually, it was mandated by law in the early 17th century, even as crossbows were beginning to be superseded by more modern weaponry. Exhibitions are held at other times throughout the year as well. Other public holidays recognized in San Marino occur on February

5, the *Festa di Sant'Agata* (Feast of St. Agatha), San Marino's patron saint; March 25, when the republic's small army marches through the streets wearing colorful 18th-century uniforms; and July 28, which marks the fall of fascism in Italy. Banks may close, but most shops are open on these days.

MUSEUMS

Unless otherwise noted, the museums listed below are open daily to 8 PM, mid-June through early September; daily, with a midday closing, the rest of the year. All charge admission, though there is a discount should you visit three or more.

MUSEO DELLE ARMI ANTICHE Housed in the *Fratta* (or *Cesta*), the tower occupying the highest point of Monte Titano, it features arms and armor from medieval times to the 20th century—as well as some magnificent views from its lookout points (phone: 882679).

MUSEO DELLE ARMI MODERNE (MUSEUM OF MODERN ARMS) Weapons from around the world, dating from 1850 to today. Contrada della Pieve (phone: 991999).

MUSEO AUTO FERRARI This small, well-designed museum contains 26 gleaming Ferraris, from the earliest models to the famous Testarossa. Open daily from 10 AM to 1 PM and 2 to 6 PM. Via Tonnini (phone: 990390).

MUSEO DELLE CERE (WAX MUSEUM) Wax models of famous characters from San Marino's history, as well as figures from farther afield: the current pope; Garibaldi and his wife, Anita; and Abraham Lincoln. For those with a strong stomach a special section re-creates the gory torture techniques of medieval times. 17 Via Lapicidi Marini (phone: 992940).

MUSEO DELLE CURIOSITÀ (CURIOSITY MUSEUM) These strange-but-true exhibits include a life-size model of the world's heaviest man and the skull of a dinosaur born with two brains. Open daily from 9 AM to midnight in summer; from 9:30 AM to 5:30 PM in winter. 26 Via Salita alla Rocca (phone: 992437 or 991075).

MUSEO POSTALE, FILATELICO E NUMISMATICO (STAMP AND COIN MUSEUM) One of San Marino's most important museums contains examples of all the stamps and coins issued by the republic, along with stamps from other countries. As we went to press, the museum was closed for repairs; call ahead for reopening dates. Borgo Maggiore, just off Piazza Grande (phone: 882996).

SHOPPING

Souvenirs of a pedestrian nature are the most conspicuous items for sale in San Marino. More legitimate buys include stamps and coins, local wines (sangiovese, a rich, robust red, and grilet, a naturally fermented sparkling dry white), and good liqueurs. You can sample and purchase these at the local wine cooperative, *Consorzio Vini Tipici* (Strada Serrabolino, 87

Valdragone, Borgo Maggiore; phone: 903124; fax: 902866). For an idea of the local craft products available, go to the *Mostra dell'Artigianato* (Handicraft Exhibition), above the Piazzale Mario Giangi parking area, just off Viale Federico d'Urbino. Most stores in San Marino are open from 9:30 AM to 1 PM and from 4:30 to 7:30 PM; closed Sundays.

Other stops to include on your shopping list include the following:

Costa Valerio e Susanna Ceramics—both modern and antique—plus pottery, mostly hand-painted, by local artisans. 15 Salita della Rocca (phone: 991182).

Gioielleria Arzilli This large, serious jewelry store is on a par with the best in Italy. The *Arzilli* links with goldsmithing go back several generations, and their wares—though certainly not inexpensive—are becoming known worldwide. 1 Via Donna Felicissima (phone: 902128 or 992038).

Marino Cesarini One of San Marino's oldest dealers in stamps and coins, many of which are rare. Small antiques and objets d'art also are for sale. 2 Piazzale lo Stradone (phone: 991149).

Pasticceria Liberty A bakery that features local cakes and pastries. You also can drop in for a spot of tea or an aperitif before dinner. 1 Contrada San Francesco (phone: 991986).

Rafaella Antiquariato Antique furniture and paintings—strictly Italian, French, and English. 104 Via III Settembre (phone: 905254).

Sir Paul Men's and women's clothing, including some of Italy's best-known designer labels. 28 Contrada Santa Croce (phone: 992635).

SPORTS AND FITNESS

FITNESS CENTERS Arrange workouts in Serravalle, one of the eight small towns just outside San Marino City, at the *Palestra di Atletica Pesante* (Strada la Ciarulla; phone: 901067) or the *Palestra Centro Sportivo* (Via Rancaglia; phone: 901054).

SWIMMING Two pools (one's for kids) are at the *Tavolucci* center, on the road from Borgo Maggiore to Serravalle (Via XXVIII Luglio; phone: 903354).

TENNIS There are courts at the *Tennis Club San Marino* (Via del Paron; phone: 991298), the *Tavolucci* center (see above), and in Serravalle at *Tensport Serravalle* (Via Rancaglia; phone: 900111). Municipal courts are located in Borgo Maggiore (Strada Sottomontana; phone: 903176).

NIGHTCLUBS AND NIGHTLIFE

San Marino's clubs tend to cater to the over-21 crowd. The *Club Française* (Via Rivo Fontanelle, Gualdicciolo; phone: 999009); *Devotion* (Via Rivo Fontanelle, Gualdicciolo; phone: 999393); and the *Symbol Club* (Via Ornera, Domanagnano; phone: 906136) stay open at least until 2 AM.

Expect to pay $70 or more per night for a double room in hotels rated as expensive; about $50 to $70 in those listed as moderate; and $50 or less in inexpensive hotels. All prices include breakfast and all rooms feature private baths unless otherwise indicated. Most San Marino hotels close for a month or two in winter. If all hotels are full (very possible during high season), the tourist offices have names and phone numbers of people who rent rooms in their homes. A meal for two will cost from $50 to $75 in expensive restaurants and from $40 to $50 in moderate ones. Prices include tax, cover, and tip. All restaurants serve an economical fixed-price tourist menu, and most close for a month or two in winter. All are open for lunch and dinner unless otherwise noted. Hotels and restaurants are listed alphabetically by price category.

Grand Hotel San Marino Just outside the Old City walls, this modern, 57-room place is probably the most comfortable in town. Every front room features a balcony with a beautiful view of the Apennines. There is a restaurant, the *Arengo*; a health center; and a garage. Open mid-February through November. Viale Antonio Onofri (phone: 992400; fax: 992951). Expensive.

Righi–La Taverna In summer the tables right on the piazza are filled with tourists feasting on one-dish platters, pizza, and the grand view of the *Palazzo Pubblico*. The local specialties also served at this two-story restaurant make it popular with the *sammarinesi* as well. Closed Wednesdays in winter and mid-December through January. Reservations advised. Major credit cards accepted. Piazza della Libertà (phone: 991196). Expensive.

Titano San Marino's first hotel opened in the 1890s just a few steps from Piazza della Libertà. Each of the 50 rooms has a bath or shower; some afford a view. The panoramic terrace restaurant is one of the loveliest spots in town. Open mid-March to mid-November. 21 Contrada del Collegio (phone: 991006; fax: 991375). Expensive to moderate.

Il Beccafico Centrally located and close to the *Rocca,* this eatery is decorated with crossbows and other ancient weapons with which the country has come to be identified. Specialties include ravioli stuffed with ricotta cheese and herbs, and *caciatello,* a dessert similar to *crème caramel.* Open year-round. Reservations unnecessary. Major credit cards accepted. 35 Via Salita alla Rocca (phone: 992430). Moderate.

Bolognese There are only five rooms in this small, family-run hotel, but each is furnished with character, including solid wood antique bedsteads in some. The restaurant has a terrace for outdoor dining on warm summer evenings. Open year-round. 28 Via Basilicius (phone/fax: 991056). Moderate.

Buca San Francesco Straightforward cooking of San Marino and the neighboring Romagna region is featured here. Pasta dishes include *tagliatelle,* tortellini, and green lasagna; main courses range from *scaloppine al formaggio e funghi* (veal with cheese and mushrooms) to grilled and mixed roast meat. Closed November through February. Reservations unnecessary. Major credit cards accepted. 3 Piazetta del Placito Feretrano (phone: 991462). Moderate.

Excelsior Not as grand as its name suggests, it's nevertheless a clean, comfortable 25-room hotel with parking facilities. Even if you are not staying in the hotel, it is worth stopping at the excellent restaurant for the house specialty, *filetto del Monte Titano* (steak filet with mushroom sauce). Hotel and restaurant open year-round. Reservations advised for the restaurant. Major credit cards accepted. 50 Via J. Istriani (phone: 991163 or 991940; fax: 990399). Moderate.

La Fratta This busy, cheerful restaurant specializes in spit-roasted meat. It also turns out a very fine dish of homemade *tagliatelle con funghi porcini* (flat pasta with *porcini* mushrooms). A panoramic terrace offers alfresco dining. Open year-round. Reservations advised. Major credit cards accepted. Via Salita alla Rocca (phone: 991594). Moderate.

La Grotta This charming hostelry has 14 rooms, each with private bath or shower, and a pleasant restaurant. Open year-round. 17 Contrada Santa Croce (phone: 991214). Moderate.

Grotta dei Nani The restaurant's name comes from *Snow White and the Seven Dwarfs* (*nani* means dwarfs), but there is nothing small about the portions, so come hungry. Hearty local cooking is served in a cellar converted to look like the dwarfs' den. Open year-round. Reservations advised. Visa accepted. Contrada dei Magazzeni (phone: 992636). Moderate.

Joli Just outside the city walls, this 20-room hotel is comfortable and friendly, with the added bonus of a garage and restaurant. Open March through December. 38 Viale Federico d'Urbino (phone: 991008; fax: 991009). Moderate.

La Rocca Most of the 10 rooms in this pleasant hotel on the way up to the *Rocca* have private balconies. It also boasts a pool (albeit small), a rarity in San Marino, and a restaurant. Open year-round. Via Salita della Rocca (phone: 991166). Moderate.

Vecchia Stazione Owned and operated by the Andreani brothers, who also operate the *Joli* hotel next door (see above), this eatery enjoys a reputation for good traditional San Marino cooking. Try *nidi di rondine* (pasta rolls stuffed with ham, cheese, and tomato and baked in a bechamel sauce) and *coniglio porchetta disossato* (oven-roasted rabbit stuffed with fennel). Open year-round. Reservations unnecessary. Major credit cards accepted. Viale Federico d'Urbino (phone: 991008). Moderate.

Da Lino Centrally located in the main piazza of Borgo Maggiore, this well-run hotel has 25 comfortable rooms, 18 with private baths. The *Hosteria da Lino* restaurant is one of San Marino's prettiest, with beamed ceilings, terra cotta floors, and checkered tablecloths. The food and wine live up to the decor—rustic rather than sophisticated. Hotel and restaurant open year-round. Reservations advised. Major credit cards accepted. 48 Piazza Grande (phone: 903975 or 902300; fax: 906630). Hotel, moderate to inexpensive; restaurant, moderate.

Diamond Here are seven rooms and one of the best restaurants in town. The unusual building was dug out of rock. Open mid-March to mid-October. Contrada del Collegio (phone: 991003). Hotel, inexpensive; restaurant, moderate.

Tuscany

Nature has bestowed great gifts on almost every area of Italy, but it is widely agreed that Tuscany must be the most richly endowed region of all. There is nothing predictable about Tuscany's character—the open, cattle-raising plains of the southern Maremma area are the perfect antithesis to the haughty grandeur of the Apennine Mountains—but there is one constant: a remarkable wealth of beauty, mellowed by history and tempered ever so gently by the hand of man.

If the landscape evokes a peculiar sense of familiarity, it is because you likely have seen it all before. These gently undulating hills, punctuated by lone, dark cypresses and pines and crowned by hilltop bastions, are the bucolic backdrop of every Raphael Madonna and every Botticelli nymph. The Renaissance masters superimposed the image of the Holy Land itself onto the Tuscan landscape.

The ancient race that D. H. Lawrence described as "the long nosed, sensitive footed, subtly smiling Etruscans," first "appeared" in Tuscany. They were one of the most sophisticated Mediterranean civilizations of all times, yet only recently have advanced studies lifted a corner of the veil of mystery surrounding their lives and times. For centuries, Tuscan peasants left their land untilled, lest they disturb the Etruscans' reposing souls. What's more, nothing is left of their civilization aboveground, since they built their homes with wood. Still, numerous brightly painted necropoli have been excavated beneath forest-covered hills—the Etruscans were avid believers in a happy afterlife and left elaborate provisions for it. They were wise in the ways of agriculture, mining, and goldsmithing (industries still alive in Tuscany today), and they were surprisingly advanced in the manufacture of arms, for which they were known throughout Europe. Only now is it understood that they did not merely fade into oblivion but were gradually and perfectly integrated into a new Roman society by the 1st century BC.

The Roman Empire grew from the seed of Etruria, the land of the Etruscans, actually a loose federation of 12 city-states that extended down into present-day Umbria and northern Lazio. The Roman Emperor Augustus declared Etruria a region, and Diocletian reorganized it as Tuscia. During the Middle Ages, Tuscany (Toscana in Italian), as it came to be known, was a theater of constant warfare among the free communes of Lucca, Pisa, Florence, and Siena, with the continuing strife between the two medieval political factions—the pro-papal Guelphs and the pro-imperial Ghibellines—an added complication. Caught in the crossfire, small, lofty hill towns fortified their naturally strategic positions with massive walls that became one with the hillside. Many of these towns never grew beyond their medieval walls or mentalities. They tend to be tucked far back from the main arteries, but travelers who take the time to wend their way up are likely to find a one-tower, one-church settlement with a handful of families who seem indifferent to the staggering view of mountains, valleys, and occasional plains that extend from their hushed *piazzetta*. Yet although their power and prestige are long gone, the Tuscans remain particularly proud of their resplendent patrimony. They are not entirely joking when they tell you that, while the Creator may be responsible for the beauty that is Tuscany, the designs were drawn up by Michelangelo.

Michelangelo and his contemporary Leonardo da Vinci were archetypal Tuscan and Renaissance men who headed an extensive roll call that was the greatest company of genius ever assembled in one place at one time. It is difficult to circumscribe the Renaissance with actual dates, but the 15th and 16th centuries were the indisputable apogee of this great period. The 14th century, however, had already seen the arrival of the artist Giotto and three outstanding Tuscan men of letters—Dante, Petrarch, and Boccaccio. They put the seal of approval on the Tuscan dialect by writing in the vernacular rather than in Latin, developed Italian literary style, and put Tuscan culture and manners on the map; in fact, they literally made Florence, and indeed all Tuscany, in D. H. Lawrence's words, "the perfect center of man's universe."

Florentine and other Italian artists, such as Donatello, Botticelli, and Raphael, later flourished under the tutelage of the Medici family, rulers of Florence and eventually Grand Dukes of Tuscany as well as insatiable patrons of the arts. The frescoes of Masaccio, Piero della Francesca, Fra Filippo Lippi, and Luca Signorelli can be found today in small country chapels or in the magnificent urban cathedrals that were the unprecedented engineering feats of architects such as Brunelleschi, the Pisano family, or Michelangelo.

By the early 15th century, Florence had become an active and wealthy banking and commercial city whose political domain extended over most of the region. The Medici, clever bankers themselves, even supplied the Vatican with a number of popes, and other family members soon assumed political positions. There is little doubt that the glorious period of the Renaissance was born as a result of the state of relative stability and unbounded prosperity the Medicis inspired and nurtured. The unusual enlightenment and enthusiastic support of the arts and humanities of Lorenzo de' Medici, called Lorenzo il Magnifico, assured that Florence would become a hotbed of cultural innovation.

The sumptuous Medici courts, which were alive with theater, spectacle, banquets, salons, and important festivities, rivaled those of Paris and Vienna. To escape epidemics, summer heat, or urban ennui, the Medicis built regal country villas and hunting lodges in the cool, game-populated hills outside Florence. They elevated the garden to an art form that was soon imitated all over Europe as the "Renaissance garden"—embellished with geometric parterres and terraces, labyrinths, topiary hedges, Roman statues, pergolas, outdoor theaters, and manmade grottoes. Tuscany's aristocracy followed the new Medici mode, and for the first time the elite of Florence, Lucca, Siena, and other powerful Renaissance cities left their handsome palazzi within the protection of the fortified walls to carry rural villa life to the height of aristocratic refinement.

The Medici family ceased to exist with the death of Gian Gastone in 1737, and many of the aristocracy's country villas became empty. However, a convergence of outstanding individuals in the arts brought a second and new kind of Renaissance to Tuscany. Goethe, Shelley, Stendhal, the Brownings, Dostoyevsky, Twain, Gorky, and Dylan Thomas all made Tuscany their home and escape—the goal of a spiritual pilgrimage that became a source of inspiration for some of their finest works. They spoke and wrote about art, history, love, God, and, always, the landscape. Today, it is this same landscape that draws millions of lesser-known tourists who come to study the frescoes of Giotto or that treasure trove that is Florence's *Uffizi* and then return home remembering nothing but the gentle hills that the Tuscans call *dolci* (sweet).

More than 70% of Tuscany consists of these characteristic hills—only one-tenth of the region is flat plain, mostly in the Maremma, Pisa, and Lucca area—and entire tracts of land are works of art. Slopes have been terraced to stop erosion, improve drainage, and increase the amount of arable land. Some forests have been cleared to provide more room for crops, while others have been planted in compensation. Mountains were (and still are) being carved away, their quarries supplying the needs of the world with the same white Carrara marble that supplied the geniuses of the Renaissance.

According to an ancient legend, the Etruscans introduced the one element that has come to be recognized as the most Tuscan of all: the cypress. Originally, the stately rows of these slender trees, so often seen in dark profile along the curve of a hill, had a specific function: They marked property boundaries and blocked the wind. Since ancient times, their longevity (many trees thrive for well over a thousand years) and evergreen nature have lent them a sacred aura, and they have always been used to flank churches and adorn cemeteries.

Besides the cypresses, olive trees, characteristic hills, and hilltop villages still peaked with fortified castles and church steeples—the two ever-contending symbols of power in medieval Italy—there are other characteristics of this very peaceful landscape, particularly the vineyards. The heart of the region is braided with vines. Then there is the purest example of Romanesque art, the *pieve,* the country parish church, along with the cluster of buildings that served it. Often built on Etruscan or Roman foundations, they are scattered across Tuscany like jewels, many still being used as religious seats.

The most indigenous architecture of all, however, is the *casa colonica,* or Tuscan farmhouse. Frequently set atop a hill and built of whatever stone was immediately available, the farmhouse grew stylistically from a response to the simple needs of the *contadino* (peasant) into a natural, unpretentious elegance, its color and texture in rustic harmony with the tones and shapes of its surroundings. The extended family lived over the animal quarters for warmth, an outside staircase usually joining the two floors. For centuries, the farmers of the region had worked the land under a system known as *mezzadria,* where the laborers shared profits with the wealthy landowners. The practice died out in the early part of this century due to poor returns and a gradual exodus to the city. For modern-day visitors to Tuscany interested in a long stay, renting one of these villas or an apartment in a home may prove to be an attractive (and sometimes more economical) alternative to a hotel. Several companies handle rentals of properties, ranging from Renaissance castles to converted stables. Two reputable firms that have extensive accommodations all over Tuscany are *Tuscan Enterprises* (22-24 Via delle Mura, Casella Postale 34, Castellina in Chianti 53011; phone: 577-740623; fax: 577-740950) and *Casaclub Toscana* (83 Via dei Termini, Siena 53100; phone: 577-46484; fax: 577-286211); each requires a one-week minimum stay. If you prefer to be near the water, *Salogi Agenzia* (11 Via Fatinelli, Lucca 55100; phone: 583-48717; fax: 583-48727) has more than 60 villas and restored farmhouses (almost all with pools) that are mostly in the lovely Lucchesia area in western Tuscany, minutes from the sea (two-week minimum stay or one-week with a supplement). For information on US-based operators offering rentals in Italy, see GETTING READY TO GO.

It was from the economical hearth and frugal spirit of the Tuscan *contadino* that the regional cuisine evolved: High-quality Tuscan meat is grilled over a hearty fire using only herbs (the frequent use of tarragon, sage, rosemary, and thyme came from the Etruscans) and a brushing of extra-virgin olive oil (unfiltered and from the first pressing). Long bouts of famine gave rise to *cucina povera* (poor cuisine), consisting of simple, unsophisticated dishes. Stale bread thickens such winter soups as *pappa al pomodoro* (roughly, "tomato pap") and *ribollita* (literally, "reboiled"); another regional specialty is *farro* (a hearty vegetarian country soup made with emmer, a grain similar to barley). Game has always been important—the Tuscans are Italy's keenest hunters, and the region's thick woods are rich in *cinghiale* (wild boar), pheasant, wild pigeon, and hare. Here also are the most beloved mushrooms of all: the *porcini* that grow wild, the size of T-bone steaks. With the discovery of America came white beans, an important and favorite source of protein in the peasant diet (Tuscans are insultingly called "bean eaters"). The favorite cheese, the pungent pecorino, originated in Roman times. Made from sheep's milk, it comes in over a hundred varieties.

In addition, the olive oil from the Lucchese hills vies with that of the Chianti area as the world's best. Chianti wines, both red and white, cost a fraction of their price abroad; many of the finest reserve bottlings never leave the country. Most restaurants also offer vin santo, a dessert wine something like old sherry that is difficult to find elsewhere.

As in much of Europe, Tuscany's prime touring months are May, June, September, and October. But with the exception of erratic rains and not-so-central heating systems, there are very few months of the year that do not have a certain beauty, thus guaranteeing an enjoyable stay. August is particularly hot, but Tuscany has 200 miles of long, sandy beaches lined with pine groves that alternate with a dramatic, rocky coast, and the Tuscan archipelago's eight islands offer delightful respite. During high season, ferries leave frequently for the islands from Livorno and Piombino. Summer is also the time for Tuscany's medieval *feste*, involving jousts, crossbow contests, Siena's wild bareback horse race, and other events that date back to the volatile Middle Ages. They are re-created with an attention to authenticity and detail that is amazing.

The following circular itinerary begins 12 miles (19 km) northwest of Florence in Prato and continues west to Pistoia, Montecatini, Lucca, and the coastal resorts of Viareggio and stylish Forte dei Marmi, before turning inland to Pisa. It then proceeds south and inland, to Volterra, and east to San Gimignano, in Chianti, and the glorious medieval city of Siena. From there it loops in a southeasterly direction, taking in several charming hill towns on its way up to Arezzo. At Arezzo, it's possible to return to Florence, to turn south into the neighboring region of Umbria (and pick up the *Umbria* route at Perugia), or to see the rarely visited northeastern corner of Tuscany, which offers cool mountains, monasteries, and solitude. The route can be followed in full or sampled in bits and pieces (many destinations can even be visited as day trips from Florence), with optional detours. A detailed road map is necessary, but don't be inhibited for fear of getting lost—just follow your instincts and peek in the back door of Tuscany by following those turnoffs that appeal to your imagination.

Whenever possible, reserve both hotels and restaurants in advance. For one night, hotels listed below as very expensive will cost $200 or more for a double room; those listed as expensive, from $150 to $200; moderate, from $90 to $150; and inexpensive, $90 or less. All hotels feature private baths unless otherwise indicated. A meal for two (with house wine) will cost $125 or more in restaurants listed as very expensive; $75 to $125 in an expensive place; $50 to $75 in a moderate restaurant; and $50 or less in an inexpensive one. All restaurants are open for lunch and dinner unless otherwise noted. For each location, hotels and restaurants are listed alphabetically by price category.

Note that many sites of interest in Tuscany close for a midday break, usually from 12:30 or 1 PM to 3 or 4 PM; we suggest calling ahead to check exact hours.

PRATO Much medieval and Renaissance wealth went into the embellishment of this prosperous town, which has been known for its high-quality textiles, especially its wool, since before the 8th century. Like all modern cities with ancient origins, however, there is an old and a new Prato. Bypass the lifeless apartment buildings, textile factories, and peripheral reminders of the 20th century and head right to the heart of the well-preserved *centro storico* (historic center). The imposing 13th-century *Castello dell'Imperatore* (Emperor's Castle; Piazza delle Carceri) is the principal landmark. Medieval Prato was a staunch supporter of the Ghibellines (those favoring the emperor and opposing the temporal power of the pope), and in thanks for its loyalty the flattered Emperor Frederick II had this massive fortification with crenelated walls built, one of the very few examples of this type of architecture outside Sicily. A lofty view from any of its eight lookout towers is enchanting. Independent Prato eventually fell to the Florentine Guelphs (archenemies of the Ghibellines) in the 14th century, and the same Renaissance masters who lavished their arts on Florence were sent here to do the same. Witness the 15th-century *Santa Maria delle Carceri* (St. Mary of the Prisons), a fine Renaissance church by the noted Florentine architect Giuliano da Sangallo, just across the square from the castle. The magnificent interior is a study of harmonious proportions, highlighted with beautiful white-on-blue glazed terra cottas by Andrea della Robbia.

Undoubtedly the most renowned of all the Renaissance artists to work in Prato was native son Fra Filippo Lippi. An orphan, he was put in a monastery at the age of 15, but, more suited to an unorthodox (and slightly licentious) life, he fled. He was captured by pirates, sold as a slave in Africa, and freed by the Saracens, who marveled at his artistic talents. Upon his return to Prato, he succumbed to the beauty of Lucrezia Buti, a young nun whose angelic face soon appeared as that of the Madonna in most of his paintings. She gave birth to a son who would also become a prominent figure in Renaissance art (Filippino Lippi), and Cosimo de' Medici had Fra Filippo released from his vows, freeing him to cover Prato's fine *Duomo* (Cathedral), and much of the rest of Tuscany, with his delicate frescoes.

The *Duomo* stands in Piazza del Duomo, on a site originally occupied by the 10th-century *pieve* (parish church) of *Santo Stefano.* One of the best examples of Romanesque-Gothic architecture in Tuscany, it has the typical white and green marble stripes adorning its façade, with a della Robbia lunette over the entrance. To the right is an exterior pulpit, the work of Donatello and Michelozzo (1428–38); the *Dancing Putti* reliefs decorating it are copies of Donatello's originals, which are now in the *Museo dell'Opera del Duomo* (Cathedral Museum; 49 Piazza del Duomo; phone: 574-29339). The museum is closed Tuesdays and for a midday break; admission charge. Several times a year, on special occasions (including May 1, August 15, and September 8), the Holy Girdle of the Virgin Mary is put on display in the pulpit. This precious relic was brought to Prato in the Middle Ages by a Tuscan merchant who had a Palestinian wife. Ordinarily, it's kept in a chapel of the *Duomo,* where frescoes by Agnolo Gaddi tell the story. The frescoes in the chancel of the church—stories of the lives of St. John the Baptist and of St. Stephen—are of greater significance, however. These early Renaissance masterpieces took Fra Filippo Lippi 14 years to finish and are considered his finest work. Frescoes by another master, Paolo Uccello, are in the *Cappella Boccherini* (Boccherini Chapel), to the right.

The old civil law court building, the 13th- and 14th-century *Palazzo Pretorio,* is in picturesque Piazza del Comune. It houses the *Galleria Comunale,* one of the region's major collections of Renaissance, mainly Florentine, masters. It is closed Tuesdays and for a midday break; admission charge (phone: 574-452302). The region's most ambitious modern art center, *Luigi Pecci,* is at 277 Viale della Repubblica. It is closed Tuesdays; admission charge (phone: 574-570620). Prato's tourist information office is at 48 Via Cairoli (phone: 574-24112; fax: 574-607925); it is closed late afternoons.

BEST EN ROUTE

Il Piraña A modern yet elegant restaurant, it is best known for its specialties of fresh fish from nearby Tyrrhenian waters. Closed Saturday lunch, Sundays, August, and *Christmas* through *Epiphany.* Reservations necessary. Major credit cards accepted. 110 Via Valentini, Prato (phone: 574-25746). Very expensive.

Il Tonio A rustic place in the *centro storico* with outdoor tables facing a picturesque piazza, it includes fish specialties on its extensive menu of Tuscan dishes. Closed Sundays, Mondays, and three weeks in August. Reservations advised. Major credit cards accepted. 161 Piazza il Mercatale, Prato (phone: 574-21266). Expensive.

Palace Here are 85 well-managed rooms with TV sets and air conditioning, plus a pool. The restaurant (closed August) is highly regarded. 230 Viale Repubblica, Prato (phone: 574-5671; fax: 574-595411). Moderate.

Villa Santa Cristina This 18th-century villa is a perfect introduction to Tuscan hospitality. Its 23 rooms are decorated with period furniture; there's also a pool, gardens, and modern features. Game, especially wild boar in season, is a specialty at the restaurant, which is closed Sunday dinner, Mondays, and August. The hotel is closed in August. Follow signs for Calanzano. 58 Via Poggio Secco, Prato (phone: 574-595951; fax: 574-572623). Moderate.

En Route from Prato Pistoia is due west, but about 10 miles (16 km) directly south of Prato is the village of Poggio a Caiano and the delightful wine-producing zone of Carmignano. The village is the setting of one of the most splendid Medici summer villas, the *Villa Medicea a Poggio a Caiano,* which was originally a fortress but was transformed (from 1480 to 1485) into a showplace for Lorenzo il Magnifico by the very busy Giuliano da Sangallo. Lorenzo's son, the future Pope Leo X, was mostly responsible for the villa's impressive art collection. The villa's gardens are closed Sundays, Mondays, and afternoons; admission charge. For information on visiting hours for the villa, call 55-877012. From the villa, follow signs for the village of Artimino. It's a 6-mile (10-km) drive along a twisting, hairpin road through lovely, rolling countryside to another Medici outpost, the *Villa di Artimino.* This magnificent 16th-century structure, sometimes called the *Villa of the Hundred Chimneys* (for obvious reasons) or *La Ferdinanda,* was designed in the 16th century by Buontalenti as a hunting lodge for Ferdinando I de' Medici. It sits atop a prominent hill overlooking elaborate gardens and olive groves, thick pine and ilex woods, and the vineyards that produce the famous red carmignano wines. The grounds of Artimino are open daily, and it is possible to actually eat and spend the night in the villa's former staff quarters, now the *Paggeria Medicea* (see *Best en Route,* below).

From the Poggio a Caiano area, it's a 20-minute, approximately 15-mile (24-km) ride (pick up S66) to the important agricultural and commercial center of Pistoia.

BEST EN ROUTE

Biagio Pignatta This eatery's specialties are wild game from the hills of Tuscany and recipes that purportedly pleased many a Medici palate. Closed Wednesdays, and Thursday lunch in low season. Reservations advised. Major credit cards accepted. 1 Via Papa Giovanni XXIII, Artimino (phone: 55-871-8086). Expensive to moderate.

Da Delfina A rustic place within the medieval walls of the village of Artimino, it offers the finest in local cooking. The specialty of the house is *coniglio con olive e pignoli* (rabbit with olives and pine nuts). There is also a wide selection of excellent carmignano wines and alfresco dining on the terrace in the summer. Closed Monday dinner, Tuesdays, December 28 through January 10, and August. Reservations advised. No credit cards accepted. 1 Via della Chiesa, Artimino (phone: 55-871-8074; fax: 55-871-8175). Moderate.

Paggeria Medicea A stay in the renovated 16th-century pages' quarters of the Medicis' *Villa di Artimino* comes close to fulfilling any fantasy of being a guest of that illustrious family. Bucolic surroundings and modern decor steeped in historical ambience provide a magic combination in this 37-room hotel. There also is a pool, tennis courts, and the restaurant, *Biagio Pignatta* (see above). 5 Via Papa Giovanni XXIII, Artimino (phone: 55-871-8081; fax: 55-871-8080). Moderate.

PISTOIA The hidden treasures of this town easily merit a day's visit. Once you penetrate the ring of small industry that surrounds it, you'll find that it is full of character, still girdled by a handsome set of 14th-century walls that were fortified by the Medicis and once accommodated over 60 lookout towers. Like its neighbor, Prato, Pistoia was a firm supporter of the Ghibellines, and it, too, eventually fell to that most puissant of rivals, Florence.

From a map of the city, it is possible to pick out a square plan (harking back to Pistoia's Roman origins) inside a trapezoid (the walls), right in the center of which is Piazza del Duomo. The *Duomo* itself was built on 5th-century foundations during the 12th and 13th centuries, Pistoia's wealthier days. The Pisan-style façade has three tiers of arcades and terra cotta decorations by Andrea della Robbia around the central door. The simple interior sets off an ecclesiastical masterpiece, the famous silver altar of St. James, housed in the *Cappella di San Jacopo* (St. James's Chapel). Begun in the late 13th century, the altar contains more than 600 silver figures created by numerous artists through the mid-15th century—a compendium of Tuscan sculpture from the Gothic to the Renaissance. It's open daily, with a midday closing. The *Duomo*'s *Museo Capitolare* (in the *Palazzo Rospigliosi*) is worth a visit just for the dazzling array of antique gold plates, chalices, trays, and other treasures. It is closed Sundays, Mondays, and for a long midday break; admission charge. The 14th-century, white-and-green marble *Battistero* (Baptistry), across from the *Duomo,* was built according to the design of renowned architect Andrea Pisano. Two other buildings in the same square are the austere 14th-century *Palazzo del Podestà*, adjoining the *Battistero*, and the 13th- and 14th-century *Palazzo del Comune.*

Not far away from Piazza del Duomo is the 13th-century *Ospedale del Ceppo* (Piazza Ospedale), which takes its name from the *ceppo,* or box, in which offerings were once left. The hospital's most striking feature is the beautiful multicolored terra cotta frieze decorating the early-16th-century portico, a splendid work by Giovanni della Robbia and the Della Robbia workshop. Elsewhere among this labyrinth of medieval streets are the city's two oldest churches—the 12th-century *Sant'Andrea* (Via Sant'Andrea) and *San Giovanni Fuorcivitas* (Via San Giovanni), which dates from the 8th century but was reconstructed from the 12th to the 14th centuries. Each is the proud possessor of an elaborate pulpit, the former a masterpiece carved (from 1298 to 1301) by Giovanni Pisano, and the latter finished in 1270 by Fra Guglielmo da Pisa, a student of the Pisanos.

It's hard to believe today, but thousands of Pistoia's buildings were damaged during World War II; the city's pride and a timeless expertise have re-created history. The tourist information office (*IAT; Palazzo dei Vescovi;* Piazza del Duomo; phone: 573-21622; fax: 573-34327) can tell you all about it. It is closed Sundays and for a midday break.

Il Convento One of the nicest places to stay in the area, this 24-room hostelry is 2½ miles (4 km) outside town. Housed in a former 19th-century convent, it is a peaceful spot, with a pool and gardens to cool off in after a day's sightseeing. There also is a good restaurant. Open year-round. 33 Via San Quirico, Pistoia (phone: 573-452651; fax: 573-453578). Expensive.

En Route from Pistoia Meticulously groomed *vivai*, extensive nurseries of fledgling trees, from exotic palms to the ubiquitous cypress and everything in between, make up the outskirts of Pistoia. Just beyond them, following S435, lies the elegant spa town of Montecatini Terme, less than 10 miles (16 km) from Pistoia.

MONTECATINI TERME What Vichy is to France and Baden-Baden is to Germany, Montecatini is to Italy. The resort's heralded mineral waters have had a salutary effect on many people—including Giuseppe Verdi (who wrote the last act of *Otello* here), Arturo Toscanini, and La Loren. To "take the waters" in Montecatini means to settle into a hotel, undergo an obligatory clinical consultation with a hydro expert, and make tracks each day, almost always in the morning and on an empty stomach, to one or the other of the town's *stabilimenti termali* (thermal establishments) to down the prescribed measure from any of the five springs—*Tamerici, Torretta, Regina, Tettuccio, Rinfresco*—that are used for drinking. The waters of two other springs—*Leopoldina* and *Giulia*—are for mineral baths, and an eighth spring, *Grocco,* is expressly for mud baths. The *termi* were once the private property of the Medicis, but it was not until the late 1800s that the waters' curative powers became well known. Early in this century, all the various springs were taken over by the state, a massive building program was undertaken, and fashionable hotels were constructed. Now numbering well over 400, the hotels usually operate from *Easter* through November, with a select few operating year-round.

A serious treatment should last 12 days, so if you're here just a day or two, don't expect miracles. But even for those who don't take the cure, a peek at one of the *stabilimenti,* all laid out in a vast green park, is enlightening. The most beautiful is the *Stabilimento Tettuccio,* built in 1927 in a classical style. Here, from early morning until noon, an orchestra plays under a frescoed dome, attendants fill cups at fountains spouting from counters of inlaid marble set before scenes of youth and beauty painted on walls of ceramic tile, and patrons stroll through the colonnades, peruse newspapers, or chat. The entrance fee is stiff because it includes water for those who are taking the cure as well as the otherworldly atmosphere, and there is a lovely, conventional coffee bar inside. Off-season, only the less theatrical *Stabilimento Excelsior,* built in 1915 and with an ultramodern wing, is open.

Montecatini also has expensive boutiques, sports facilities (including horse racing from April through October), and seemingly endless, beautifully groomed flower gardens and forests of centuries-old oaks, pines, palms, cedars, magnolias, and oleanders. The tourist information office (66-68 Viale Verdi; phone: 572-772244; fax: 572-70109) has booklets on different walks through this luxurious vegetation as well as walks up into the nearby hills. It is open daily, with a long midday closing. Spa information also can be found at *Direzione delle Terme* (41 Viale Verdi; phone: 572-7781). The *Montecatini Golf Club,* 6 miles (10 km) away (Via dei Bragi, Monsummano Terme; phone: 572-62218; fax: 572-617435) has 18 challenging holes.

BEST EN ROUTE

Grand Hotel e La Pace Open since 1870, this elegant Old World (though sometimes stuffy) property still has a grandiose period decor and a pampering staff that keeps the clientele feeling like VIPs. There are 150 air conditioned rooms, a heated pool set in an extensive park, tennis courts, and a natural health center. Of the three restaurants, the most formal is graced with a frescoed ceiling, ornate chandeliers, and crisp napery and serves a continental menu. Half board is heavily encouraged in July and August. Open April through October. 1 Via della Torretta, Montecatini Terme (phone: 572-75801; fax: 572-78451). Very expensive.

Tamerici & Principe Everything at this 157-room hotel has been chosen with care. The service is excellent, and there is a well-equipped fitness center with a gym, sauna, solarium, and indoor pool. The restaurant uses ingredients fresh from the owners' farm in the heart of chianti country. Half board is heavily encouraged in July and August. Open April through November. 2 Viale IV Novembre, Montecatini Terme (phone: 572-71041; fax: 572-72992). Expensive.

Gourmet An exquisite meal here—the city's best restaurant—is worth every calorie (there's fresh fish, however, for truly determined dieters). Closed Tuesdays, two weeks in mid-January, and three weeks in August. Reservations advised. Major credit cards accepted. 6 Viale Amendola, Montecatini Terme (phone: 572-771012). Expensive to moderate.

Grand Hotel Croce di Malta Although most of the 120 guestrooms could use some sprucing up, this is one of the rare hotels in town that's open year-round. Within walking distance of everything, it has a surprisingly good restaurant (half board required in July and August). The public areas and pool are lovely. 18 Viale IV Novembre, Montecatini Terme (phone: 572-75871; fax: 572-757516). Expensive to moderate.

Cappelli–Croce di Savoia Intimate and affordable, this pleasant 72-room hotel has been run by the amiable Cappelli family since the 1930s. The spacious lobby, with marble floors, Persian carpets, and pots and vases of flowers, is a bit grander than the more modest rooms, but there is a beautiful flowering, back patio with a pool and a good restaurant, all only a hundred yards or so from the spa facilities. Half board is heavily encouraged in July and August. Open April through mid-November. 139 Viale Bicchierai, Montecatini Terme (phone: 572-71151; fax: 572-770545). Moderate to inexpensive.

Lido Palace This popular, family-run hotel with a restaurant is well located in a quiet area next to the *Tamerici & Principe* (see above) and near the thermal establishments. A few of the 50 rooms have small terraces. It is one of the few hotels in town that doesn't require board during high season. Open March through November. 14 Viale IV Novembre, Montecatini Terme (phone: 572-70731; fax: 572-72494, attn. Alb Lido). Inexpensive.

En Route from Montecatini Terme Continue west toward Lucca on S435, until a detour beckons at Pescia. If time permits, take the detour and turn south to Montecarlo (watch for signs), well-known for its white wine. The drive to this hill town should be made when there is still enough light to watch the Tuscan plains gradually spread out before you. The town's delightful isolation lends it a storybook quality, and it has some surprisingly fine restaurants. After the visit, return to S435 and drive the remaining 10 miles (16 km) to Lucca.

BEST EN ROUTE

Forassiepi This old restored farmhouse lies just outside the 15th-century walls of Montecarlo. Indoors everything is pink linen and orchids, but outdoors the unforgettable view vies with the menu for attention. For the first course, ask for the *assaggio di primi* (a variety of homemade pasta specials). Then sample from the extensive menu of pheasant, thrush, quail, rabbit, and wild boar, as well as less gamey choices. Closed Mondays and Tuesdays. Reservations advised. Major credit cards accepted. 800 Porta Belvedere, Montecarlo (phone/fax: 583-22005). Expensive to moderate.

La Nina There's outdoor dining in a lovely garden at the first hint of warm weather at this pleasant restaurant. Find it by following the signs just before entering town. Closed Monday dinner, Tuesdays, two weeks following *Epiphany*, and two weeks in mid-August. Reservations advised. Major credit cards accepted. 54 Via San Martino, Montecarlo (phone/fax: 583-22178). Expensive to moderate.

LUCCA A fair-size city with the air of an elegant town, Lucca is too often overlooked by travelers speeding on to nearby Pisa or the coast. In the 9th century, the city already had 40 churches listed in its archives; today, there are more than 60 of them. During the 12th and 13th centuries, Lucca's power equaled that of Florence or Pisa, and its silk was considered the finest in all of Europe. During the 16th and early 17th centuries, Lucca gained its third and final set of city walls, a girdle of ramparts that are intact today and constitute a unique feature—they are broad and low enough to be topped with a tree-lined promenade, a public thoroughfare that is an intrinsic part of city life. Within the walls, Lucca's architecture is an interesting mélange of Roman to medieval to 16th century, with Baroque, neoclassical, and Art Deco (called "Liberty" in Italy) interventions. Giacomo Puccini was born here—the old-fashioned *Fanciulla del West* bar on Via Mordini is one of the gayer memorials to him, but Puccini himself preferred the *Caffè di Simo* (Via Fillungo), a bar where excellent ice cream is still served amid marble, brass, and antique mirrors.

The center of town is Piazza Napoleone. Take Via del Duomo out of the square and pass the *Chiesa* and *Battistero di San Giovanni* to find Lucca's *Duomo,* dedicated to San Martino, in the piazza of the same name. Although a church has occupied the spot since the 6th century, this one dates only from the 13th century. It has an asymmetrical Romanesque façade of columned loggias and an interior of largely Gothic design, as a result of a 14th- and early-15th-century renovation. One of the treasures of the church is the very beautiful tomb of Ilaria del Carretto, wife of Paolo Giunigi, a powerful ruler of independent Lucca. The tomb, created in 1408, a few years after her death, is a marble masterpiece of Jacopo della Quercia, who breathed life into the silk-like folds of her gown and headrest. In the middle of the nave is another treasure: a small marble temple by Matteo Civitali that houses the *Volto Santo* (Holy Visage), a wooden crucifix with the image of Christ, probably of 12th-century Eastern origin. According to legend, however, it was carved by Nicodemus immediately following the Crucifixion and procured by a Lucchese bishop during a pilgrimage to the Holy Land; it was famous enough throughout Europe to have been mentioned by Dante in the *Inferno.* After dark each September 13, it is paraded through town in a candlelight procession.

After returning to Piazza Napoleone, head toward Piazza San Michele. The piazza that hums today (in September, a colorful, daily open-air market sells everything from souvenirs to housewares to clothing) was once the old Roman Forum; in fact, the unusual church on the piazza is called *San Michele in Foro* (St. Michael in the Forum). Built in the 12th and 13th centuries, it has a Romanesque façade in the Pisan-Lucchese fashion, with four decorative arcades of sculpted columns (no two are alike), topped by a colossal statue of St. Michael. Inside the church are a *Madonna and Child* by Andrea della Robbia and a panel painting of four saints by Filippino Lippi. Follow Via Fillungo, one of Lucca's busiest streets, lined with medieval houses and towers, to reach another interesting church, *San Frediano,* in Piazza San Frediano. Have a look at the bell tower of this 12th-century church and, inside, in the *Cappella Trenta,* at the reliefs by Jacopo della Quercia. Then cross over Via Fillungo to the 2nd-century *Anfiteatro Romano,* another of Lucca's Roman sites (and the site of a three-day flower market at the end of April in even-numbered years). All that remains of the amphitheater is the oval outline, traced by soft yellow medieval-style houses. Exit from the opposite side and proceed to Via Giunigi, a medieval street containing several palazzi built by the Giunigi family in the 14th century. One of them is easily recognized, since it sports a tower with holm oak trees on top. A small but interesting antiques fair takes place the third weekend of every month at Piazza San Giusto.

The *lucchesia* area, the wooded and olive-crowded hills outside Lucca, produces the coveted *olio d'oliva lucchese* and is home of a number of stately private villas that cropped up in the 16th and 17th centuries. The *Villa Torrigiani, Villa Reale* (once home of Napoleon's sister Elisa Baciocchi), and *Villa Mansi* are just a few that are open to the public. The main office of the local tourist bureau, *Azienda di Promozione Turistica (APT;* 2 Piazza Guidiccioni; phone: 583-491205; fax: 583-490766), is closed Sundays and afternoons; calls, however, can be received from 8 AM to 2 PM except Sundays. The other *APT* office (Vecchia Porta S. Donato, Piazzale Verdi; phone: 583-419689) is open daily.

BEST EN ROUTE

Il Bottaccio Guests lucky enough to stay in one of the eight suites in this former 17th-century olive oil mill in the village of Montignoso, just northwest of Lucca, are cosseted from the moment they arrive to the minute they leave. Rooms are decorated with antique furnishings, the tile floors are heated, and the bed linen is made of Como silk. In season, baskets of freshly picked apricots, peaches, strawberries, and raspberries are left in the guestrooms. The one-Michelin-star restaurant lives up to the hotel's high standards. Meals are served at tables around a lotus-flower-strewn goldfish pond. 1 Via Bottaccio, Montignoso (phone: 585-340031; fax: 585-340103). Very expensive.

Principessa Elisa Tuscany's newest deluxe country inn is ensconced in an early 18th-century villa once owned by a French army official in the employ of Elisa Baciocchi, Napoleon's sister. The common areas and 10 suites were re-created to befit a princess's every caprice, with furniture, fabrics, and carpets designed from period prints. Luxuriant gardens and landscaping include a brook, walking paths, and a large pool. The restaurant, situated in the villa's Victorian-style conservatory, overlooks the lovely grounds. Two miles (3 km) outside Lucca, on Via Nuova per Pisa, Massa Pisana (phone: 583-379737; fax: 583-379019). Very expensive.

Villa La Principessa A 13th-century villa, reconstructed in the early 19th century, is now an elegant 44-room hotel and restaurant just 2 miles (3 km) outside Lucca on the road to Pisa (follow the blue signs for Pisa). The spacious gardens, large pool, staff, and total serenity make this member of the Relais

& Châteaux group an exquisite choice. Open February 15 to January 6; restaurant closed Sundays. Via Nuova, Massa Pisana (phone: 583-370037). Very expensive to expensive.

Solferino Another confirmation of Lucca's importance as a gastronomic center, this excellent, family-run establishment is 3 miles (5 km) outside town, on the road to Viareggio. The fare is basically local, but innovative touches are evident in dishes such as baby water buffalo and duck in cream sauce. Closed Wednesdays, Thursday lunch, January 7 to 14, and two weeks in mid-August. Reservations advised. Major credit cards accepted. San Macario in Piano (phone: 583-59118; fax: 583-329161). Expensive to moderate.

Buca di Sant'Antonio Set in the medieval quarter near *San Michele,* this rustically elegant restaurant serves the best local fare, including *porcini* mushrooms cooked *al cartoccio* (in paper wrapping) and game in season. Closed Sunday dinner, Mondays, and the last two weeks of July. Reservations advised. Major credit cards accepted. 1-3 Via della Cervia, Lucca (phone: 583-55881; fax: 583-312199). Moderate.

Universo The best to be found within the old walls. Its 60 rooms are clean and comfortable, if rather old-fashioned; there also is a restaurant. The unbeatable advantage, however, is its central location, at 1 Piazza Puccini, Lucca (phone: 583-493678; fax: 583-954854). Moderate.

Vipore Cesare Casella's welcoming eatery 5 miles (8 km) from Lucca is well worth the trip, as many locals will attest. For more information, see *The Best Restaurants of Italy* in DIVERSIONS. Closed Mondays, Tuesdays through Fridays for lunch, the last two weeks in January, and two weeks in November. Reservations necessary. Major credit cards accepted. Leave Lucca from Ponte Monte San Quirico and go 3 miles (5 km) on the road to Via Sant'Alessio; then take the picturesque road signposted Via Pieve Santo Stefano. Pieve Santo Stefano (phone: 583-395107 or 583-394065). Moderate.

Hambros Parc This 19th-century villa in the town of Lunata, 3 miles (5 km) from Lucca, has been converted into a country hotel. The 57 rooms are simply furnished and wonderfully quiet, and the villa is set in its own parkland dominated by two lush magnolia trees. The *Chez Pascal* restaurant is on the grounds but operates under different management. 197 Via Pesciatina, Lunata (phone/fax: 583-935355). Moderate to inexpensive.

Da Giulio in Pelleria At this large, simple, and informal first-rate trattoria, try the *spezzatino di vitello con olive nere* (veal and black olive stew) or *farro.* Closed Sundays, Mondays, the first two weeks of August, and two weeks at *Christmas.* Reservations necessary. Major credit cards accepted. 45 Via delle Conce, near Lucca (phone: 583-55948). Inexpensive.

En Route from Lucca Before heading to Pisa, you might want to consider stopping at the seaside resorts of Viareggio and the posher Forte dei Marmi—especially if the weather is fine and the idea of relaxing under a striped umbrella on a white sandy beach is appealing. For a picturesque ride through western Tuscany's lush green hills at the foot of the Apuan Alps, take S429 west for 15 miles (24 km), following the signs for Viareggio. If time is a factor, head west on the faster (but equally lovely) A11 autostrada for 15 miles (24 km).

VIAREGGIO Visitors have been coming to this resort town on Tuscany's coast for years. Its easy proximity to Florence, refreshing forest of umbrella pines, miles of fashionable stores and crowded bars along the Viale Carducci, building façades in the Liberty style (as Art Nouveau was known in Italy), and the seemingly endless stretch of sandy beach in a country where rocky coastline is the norm, all keep Viareggio a perennial favorite. There are no hotels directly on the beach (most are on the other side of the *lungomare*), and most of the beach belongs to *bagni* (private clubs) that rent cabañas, umbrellas, and chairs for the day, week, or season. Some *bagni* have special deals with the hotels; be sure to ask at yours.

While this is a summer town, a number of the fashion boutiques and many of the fine fish restaurants for which Viareggio is known stay open year-round. And in late winter, the town becomes abruptly alive for *Carnevale;* Viareggio is home to Italy's oldest (122 years) pre-*Lenten* celebration and one of the two most popular in the country (Venice has its own equally splendid festivities). For more details, see *Italy's Most Colorful Festas* in DIVERSIONS. Viareggio's tourist office, *Azienda di Promozione Turistica Versilia (APT)*, is at 10 Viale Carducci (phone: 584-48881; fax: 584-47406). It is closed Sunday afternoons and for a midday break June through September; closed Sundays and for a midday break the rest of the year.

The cultural highlight of the summer takes place annually from the end of July to mid-August 3 miles (5 km) from Viareggio in Torre del Lago, home of the *Festival Pucciniano* (Puccini Festival). The outdoor theater alongside the lake that inspired Puccini to compose such masterworks as *Tosca* and *Madame Butterfly* draws opera buffs from all over the world. The tourist office in Viareggio has information on the program and ticket sales, as does the provincial tourism office, *Pro Loco* (225 Viale Marconi, Torre del Lago; phone: 584-359893 or 584-350567). It's closed from 12:30 to 5 PM and on Sundays.

BEST EN ROUTE

Tito del Molo A bountiful selection of fish and seafood in a large aquarium near the entrance to this pretty, well-known restaurant promises a memorable meal. There's outdoor dining in the summer. Closed Wednesdays and January. Reservations advised. Major credit cards accepted. At the very end of the avenue parallel to the sea, alongside a narrow canal, at 3

Longomolo Corrado del Greco, Viareggio (phone: 584-962016). Very expensive.

Palace Housed in an elegant 1920s palazzo on the main street parallel to the sea, this hotel stays open year-round. Some of the 68 air conditioned rooms have terraces, and 12 face the sea, though the dozen overlooking the courtyard are recommended for their tranquillity. The decor and service are unusually formal and serious for a seaside resort, the restaurant surprisingly sophisticated. 2 Via Flavio Gioia, Viareggio (phone: 584-46134; fax: 584-47351). Expensive.

Scintilla This simple and elegant restaurant is an impressive endeavor by an owner who takes his fish seriously; no meat dishes are offered. The menu changes daily, but be sure to have the *branzino con patate al forno* (fresh sea bass baked with potatoes) if it's offered. Closed Sunday dinner, Mondays, two weeks in January, and August 10 to 20. Reservations advised. Major credit cards accepted. 33 Via Pisano, Viareggio (phone: 584-387069). Expensive to moderate.

San Francisco This pleasant 31-room hotel is modern and cool, with shades of blue and green, marble floors, and leafy green plants. Guestrooms on the upper floors have ocean views, but the four on the courtyard are much quieter. An overall restoration is scheduled to be completed this summer. There's no restaurant, but breakfast, a large buffet of fresh fruit and croissants, is served in a charming room with white wrought-iron chairs. Open January through October. 68 Viale Carducci, Viareggio (phone: 584-52666; fax: 584-55222). Moderate.

La Pace Peace is not exactly what you'll find in this small family-run hostelry on the main drag in the very heart of town. But of the 21 simply furnished rooms, a few face a quiet courtyard. A pretty restaurant on the ground floor offers half or full board, but the real pull here is the convenient location and value for the money. No credit cards accepted. 35 Lungomare Manin, Viareggio (phone: 584-47341). Inexpensive.

En Route from Viareggio If the crowd interests you more than the sea, and an inevitable hike in price is of no concern, drive the additional 8 miles (14 km) farther north on S328 along the hotel-developed coastline of this area—known as Versilia—to the upscale resort of Forte dei Marmi.

FORTE DEI MARMI Named for the fort built by the Grand Duke Leopold I in 1788 to store marble quarried in the nearby Apuan Mountains, Forte dei Marmi has an innate chic and prestige not found in Viareggio. The summertime regulars—Milan's idle rich and Turin's big-time industrialists—promote an air of understatedness. The town is set back from the beach amid an expansive pine forest that provides an exceptionally green, shady area to escape from the summer's heat. And on the beach are over a hundred private *bagni* with individual cabañas and other de rigueur luxuries for a day in the sun. There's no dearth of high-fashion boutiques, and command-post *caffès,* such as the well-known *Principe* (2 Via Carducci) or *Roma* (2 Via Mazzini), are must-stops for homemade gelato. You might even see Giorgio Armani if he's opened his villa for the season. The 18-hole *Versilia Golf Club* (40 Via della Sipe; phone: 584-881574; fax: 584-752272) is closed Tuesdays in winter.

Forte dei Marmi's tourist office (*APT;* 8 Viale Franceschi; phone: 584-80091; fax: 584-83214) is closed afternoons.

An enjoyable day trip from both Forte dei Marmi and Viareggio is the nearby town of Pietrasanta. Small and unassuming, this 13th-century village is a home of marble (located south of the world-famous quarries of Massa and Carrara) and continues to draw artists and sculptors from all over the world. Pull up a chair at the *Bar Michelangelo* in Piazza Duomo, perhaps sharing a table with Fernando Botero, the famous South American artist who frequents this *caffè.* A plaque on the outside lets all know that here Michelangelo negotiated contracts for the façade of Florence's *Chiesa di San Lorenzo*—a project he never completed. And if you're in town the first Sunday of each month, a small antiques fair fills this piazza.

BEST EN ROUTE

Augustus A favorite with well-heeled Europeans and northern Italians, this luxurious 67-room hostelry has lush flower gardens and a beautifully landscaped pool (one of the few in town). Though half or full board is not obligatory, the management prides itself on the fresh seafood that guarantees memorable meals in its restaurant. Open mid-May to mid-October. 169 Viale Morin, Forte dei Marmi (phone: 584-80202; fax: 584-89875). Very expensive to expensive.

Augustus Lido In the 1920s this intimate, 19-room hotel was the private holiday villa of the Agnelli family of Fiat fame, who—among other things—built an underground passageway directly to the sea. No restaurant. Open mid-May through September. 72 Viale Morin, Forte dei Marmi (phone: 584-81442; fax: 584-89875). Expensive.

Villa Roma Imperiale Built in the 1930s as the private home of aristocrats, this villa now offers 19 rooms decorated in pastels and chintz. It is surrounded by pines and open green lawns dotted with canvas-covered lounge chairs, and is only a short walk to the beach or to a downtown *caffè.* One of the few hostelries to stay open year-round, it's as charming in winter as it is cool and welcoming in summer. There is a restaurant. 9 Via Corsica, Forte dei Marmi (phone: 584-80841; fax: 584-82839). Expensive.

Franceschi This lovely, romantic, turn-of-the-century villa with a restaurant is set in a cool pine forest. A separate building houses 22 rooms added to the 33 in the original awninged, ochre-colored villa. The hotel offers a legion of red bikes for guests' use. Open year-round. 19 Via XX Settembre, Forte dei Marmi (phone: 584-787114; fax: 584-89016). Moderate.

San Martino With its exposed brick archways and wooden beams, the back room of this family-run trattoria dates back to the 1200s. The cooking is rustic and appealing, with homemade pasta made daily and delicious, fresh fish dishes. Save room for the wonderful desserts. Unlike most places in town, this restaurant stays open in August, for fear that its artist habitués won't have anywhere to go for a good meal. Closed Tuesdays and 10 days in January. Reservations advised for dinner. American Express accepted. 17 Via Garibaldi, Pietrasanta (phone: 584-790190). Moderate to inexpensive.

Lo Sprocco Casual, yet elegant, this restaurant in a restored 17th-century building with arched ceilings and salmon-painted walls is an all-time favorite. Standard Tuscan fare is well prepared, with an emphasis on pasta and fresh fish. Closed Wednesdays, and lunch in July and August. Reservations advised. Major credit cards accepted. 22 Via P. Barsanti, Pietrasanta (phone: 584-70793). Moderate to inexpensive.

En Route from Forte dei Marmi Take S1 to Pisa, 21 miles (35 km) to the southwest.

PISA Visitors invariably rush to Piazza del Duomo, otherwise known as the Piazza dei Miracoli (Field of Miracles), to see the *Torre* (Leaning Tower). Then what to their wondering eyes should appear on this spacious green lawn but three stunning white buildings—the *Torre,* the *Duomo,* and the *Battistero* (Bapistry)—flanked by a fourth structure, the white wall of the *Camposanto.* The *Duomo,* which set the style known as Pisan Romanesque, or simply Pisan, was one of the most influential buildings of its time; regardless of whether a visitor appreciates the fine points of architecture, it's hard not to be impressed by the Pisan triad.

This city on the Arno was a naval base for the Romans, and during the darkest days of the Middle Ages it kept the Tyrrhenian coast free from marauding Saracens. A fleet of Pisan ships sailed off to the First Crusade. By the 11th century, Pisa had developed into a maritime republic to rival Genoa and Venice. By the 12th century, it had reached the height of its supremacy—it defeated the maritime republic of Amalfi in 1135—and also of artistic splendor. But the seeds of decline were already planted, in the form of internal rivalries and external strife with nearby Lucca, Genoa, and Florence (which was moving farther along the Arno toward the sea). Pisa never fully recovered from a defeat by the Genoese in 1284, which decimated its fleet and aggravated its internal problems, and in 1406 it was defeated by the Florentines. Although there was a period of well-being under the Medicis and even a brief period of independence from 1494 to 1509, from the early 1500s its history merges with that of Florence.

The *Duomo* was begun in 1064 and finished by the end of the 13th century. Consisting of four graceful galleries of columns, its façade was much imitated (as visits to Lucca and Prato will attest). The bronze doors facing the *Battistero* are from the 16th century, replacing originals lost in a fire, but the highly stylized bronze doors facing the *Torre* are by Bonanno Pisano and date from 1180. The interior is cavernous, close to 400 feet long and interrupted by 68 columns, but find the way to Giovanni Pisano's ivory *Madonna with Child*, leaning backward along the curve of the elephant's tusk out of which it is carved, and his intricately sculpted pulpit (1302–11), perhaps the cathedral's greatest treasure. The 16th-century bronze *Galileo Lamp* that hangs opposite the pulpit is of special interest, too. According to legend, Pisa-born Galileo came up with his theory of pendulum movement by studying the swinging of the lamp set in motion by a sympathetic sacristan. (Historians, however, say Galileo arrived at this theory six years before the lamp was made.)

The *Battistero,* begun in 1152 but not finished until the end of the 14th century, is most famous for its pulpit, carved by Nicola Pisano in 1260. Not long after construction had begun on the *Battistero,* ground was broken for the elegant cylindrical campanile, the bell tower standing (now leaning) behind the *Duomo.* The tower rose quickly, but at the third floor, the complication that's very evident today appeared, suspending work for a century. Construction was resumed in 1275, and the finishing touches were made between 1350 and 1372. A few romantic historians contend that the leaning was purposely brought on by the architect, who sought to prove his inordinate skill. Most, however, attribute it to a shifting of soil. The 187-foot tower leans five meters off the perpendicular; its tilt continues to increase by an average of about one millimeter a year, although recent experiments have arrested its leaning for the first time. The walk up the tower's 294 steps has been barred to visitors for several years, pending the completion of extensive repairs to the structure (check with the tourist office for a possible reopening). From the top terrace, Galileo dabbled in his experiments to establish the laws of gravity.

The long, low rectangular building running along the side of the Pisan Triumvirate, its absolute simplicity relieved only by a tiny Gothic tabernacle, is actually a cemetery, the *Camposanto,* begun in 1277. It is said that some of the earth enclosed inside was brought from the Holy Land aboard Pisan ships. Many of the frescoes that once decorated the interior of the *Camposanto* walls were destroyed or heavily damaged in World War II, but some by Benozzo Gozzoli escaped unscathed, and enough remains of the enormous and famous *Triumph of Death, Last Judgment,* and *Inferno,* by the Florentine artist Bonamico Buffalmarco, to suggest the uneasy turn of the 14th-century mind. Sinopias (preparatory designs drawn directly on the walls) of the frescoes, uncovered during postwar restoration, are now in the *Museo delle Sinopie* (Sinopia Museum; Piazza Duomo), across the street from the *Duomo.* It is open daily, with a midday closing. The frescoes themselves can be seen in the nearby *Museo Camposanto Monumentale* (Cemetery Museum; Piazza Duomo), which is open daily. On the other side of the cathedral is the fascinating and little-known *Museo dell'Opera del Duomo* (Museum of the Work of the Duomo; 6 Piazza Arcivescovado), in a former Capuchin monastery. Fine examples of Islamic art—remnants of Pisa's tradition as a trading power—sculptures by father and son Nicola and Giovanni Pisano, and a magnificent frescoed dining room are on display in the museum's 19 rooms. It is open daily. There's an admission charge to all museums (phone for all three museums: 50-560547).

Unless time is short, make your way to the Arno for a look at *Santa Maria della Spina* (St. Mary of the Thorn; Lungarno Gambacorti), a little jewel of a church in Pisan Gothic style. It was built in the early 14th century to house a relic from Christ's crown of thorns (no longer kept here), and it once stood much closer to the river—in the late 19th century it was moved piece by piece to its present spot. Another stop should be the *Museo Nazionale di San Matteo* (National Museum of St. Matthew; Piazza San Matteo in Soarta; phone: 50-541865), which contains many works of 12th- and 13th-century sculpture (the Pisano family is well represented) as well as a *Madonna and Child with Saints* by Simone Martini. The museum is closed Mondays and Sunday afternoons; no admission charge. The feast day of the city's patron saint, San Ranieri, is celebrated on June 17, and the *Gioco del Ponte* (Battle of the Bridge) takes place the last Sunday in June. For more details on these two events, see *Italy's Most Colorful Festas* in DIVERSIONS. The *Regata Storica delle Repubbliche Marinare* (Regatta of the Ancient Maritime Republics) rotates among Pisa, Venice, Amalfi, and Genoa; this year is Pisa's turn. Boat excursions are available up the Arno River to Cinque Terre, the unusual quintet of towns on the Italian Riviera. Contact the city's tourist information office in Piazza del Duomo (phone/fax: 50-560464) for more information. It is open daily, with a midday closing. There's another office at the train station (phone: 50-42291), which is open daily, with a midday closing.

BEST EN ROUTE

Sergio This small, hospitable restaurant on the banks of the Arno has long been considered Pisa's best. Try the *ravioli al tartufo,* and then choose from an extensive selection of à la carte meat and fresh fish dishes. Closed Sundays, the last three weeks of January, and two weeks in mid-August. Reservations advised. Major credit cards accepted. 1 Lungarno Pacinotti, Pisa (phone/fax: 50-580580). Very expensive.

Cavalieri Named after the order of the Knights of St. Stephen, who had their seat in Pisa during the time of the Saracen invasions, this hundred-room hostelry is a member of the Jolly hotel chain. Its international air, modern comforts, bar, and restaurant make it Pisa's best. 2 Piazza della Stazione, Pisa (phone: 50-43290; fax: 50-502242). Expensive.

Emilio Pisans are avid fish eaters, and this establishment keeps them happy with a fine selection of the day's freshest. The homemade pasta is also superb. Only a few blocks from the Piazza dei Miracoli. Closed Mondays. Reservations advised. Major credit cards accepted. 44 Via C. Cammeo, Pisa (phone: 50-562141; fax: 50-562096). Expensive to moderate.

Il Campano A short stroll from the main Piazza dei Cavalieri will lead you to this picturesque trattoria, housed inside a 12th-century tower. In summer, some tables are moved outside. Traditional dishes are served, with the emphasis on fish from the nearby coast. Closed Wednesdays and two weeks in August. Reservations advised. Major credit cards accepted. 44 Via Cavalca, Pisa (phone: 50-580585). Moderate.

Duomo A modern, busy establishment with 94 rooms and a restaurant, it's only a minute's walk from the Piazza dei Miracoli. 94 Via Santa Maria, Pisa (phone: 50-561894; fax: 50-560418). Moderate.

Villa Kinzica Hard to beat in terms of location, this 30-room hotel is just a few steps from the major monuments—the tower can be seen from some of the rooms. There's a small restaurant. 2 Piazza Arcivescovado, Pisa (phone: 50-560419 or 50-561736; fax: 50-551204). Inexpensive.

En Route from Pisa Take S67 for 14 miles (22 km) southeast to Pontedera, then turn south onto S439, following signs to Volterra. The blue-green Cecina Hills on the right stretch for miles, and as Volterra (about 25 miles/40 km from Pontedera) comes closer, the countryside of green velvet hills turns lonely and scarred, with only an occasional flock of sheep to soften its appearance. The gashes marring the landscape are the alabaster quarries that have been Volterra's chief source of income since Etruscan days. More remarkable are the yawning rifts, or *balze,* a peculiar earth flaw caused by intense erosion. The edges of the city have been eaten away by this unrestrainable and continuous movement, which has already consumed a portion of onetime Volterra—Etruscan and Roman temples and dwellings and the 7th-century *Chiesa di San Giusto.*

VOLTERRA Seen from a distance, Volterra rises up isolated, gaunt, and aloof from abandoned countryside. It has been the site of 3,000 years of continuous civilization, and the walled medieval city stands within the perimeter of another, larger set of walls. Ancient Velathri was the northernmost and strongest of the 12 city-states of the Etrurian federation, three times larger than Volterra is today. The medieval city dates mostly from the 12th and 13th centuries. Built largely of a local gray stone, *panchina,* it has taken on something of a golden hue, but Volterra is neither flirtatious nor charming, as are some other Italian hill towns.

The beautiful, central Piazza dei Priori is bounded by sober medieval palaces, of which the *Palazzo dei Priori* (Town Hall), built from 1208 to

1254, is the most prominent. It is the oldest working town hall in Tuscany, and its top commands an unrivaled panorama that can reach as far as the Tuscan coast on a clear day. The church behind the *Palazzo dei Priori* is the *Duomo,* a Romanesque edifice consecrated in 1120, with Pisan touches added in the 13th century. The *Battistero* (Baptistry), too, dates from the 13th century. Close by is the *Porta all'Arco,* an original Etruscan gate to the city, which affords more extensive and breathtaking views. A handsome, 15th-century palazzo of Antonio da Sangallo houses the *Pinacoteca* (Picture Gallery; 1 Via dei Sarti; phone: 588-87580), with a small but impressive collection of predominantly 14th- through 17th-century Tuscan artists, highlighted by Luca Signorelli's *Annunciation* and Rosso Fiorentino's *Descent from the Cross.* It is open daily mid-June to mid-September; closed afternoons the rest of the year; admission charge. The *Museo Etrusco Guarnacci* (Guarnacci Etruscan Museum; 11 Via Don Minzoni; phone: 588-86347) has one of the best and largest collections of Etruscan objects in all Italy, including the famous elongated bronze figure known as the *Ombra della Sera* (Evening Shadow) and some 600 funerary urns of tufa, terra cotta, and alabaster that demonstrate the Etruscans' skill in working the local alabaster. The museum is open daily, with a midday closing, in summer; open from 10 AM to 2 PM in winter; admission charge. The climb to Volterra's 14th- and 15th-century *Fortezza* begins not far away from the museum. Lorenzo de' Medici was largely responsible for this massive installation, which serves as a reminder that independent Volterra, like many other Tuscan towns, eventually fell to the superior force of Florence. Lorenzo modified an existing 14th-century fortress (the *Rocca Vecchia,* or Old Fortress, which has a tower referred to as the *Torre Femmina,* or Female Tower) and added a *Rocca Nuova* (New Fortress) of five towers, one of which is known as the *Torre Maschio,* or Male Tower. Only the park of the *Fortezza* is open to the public (the rest is used as a prison), but the whole is an impressive feature of Volterra's silhouette.

The Volterra *Tourist Information Office* is just off Piazza dei Priori (2 Via Giusto Turazza; phone/fax: 588-86150). It is closed Sundays and for a long midday break.

BEST EN ROUTE

L'Etruria Typical Tuscan fare is served in this medieval palazzo with vaulted ceilings and turn-of-this-century frescoes. Specialties such as *farro, agnello al forno* (roast lamb), and game are delightful. There's alfresco dining on the piazza in warm weather. Closed Thursdays, January, and the last two weeks of June. Reservations advised. Major credit cards accepted. 6/8 Piazza dei Priori, Volterra (phone: 588-86064). Moderate.

A Biscondola A renovated farmhouse just a few minutes' drive southwest of the city walls, it boasts friendly service and straightforward, delicious food—*pappardelle alla lepre* (broad, flat noodles with hare sauce) and grilled or roasted meat. Closed Mondays and the last three weeks of January. Reservations unnecessary. Major credit cards accepted. On the road to Saline, Direzione Cecina (watch for the signs), S68 (phone: 588-85197). Moderate to inexpensive.

Ombra della Sera This small, pleasant restaurant is just 300 feet from the *Museo Etrusco Guarnacci*. Game is the specialty in season, but the whole Tuscan menu is delicious. Closed Mondays and the last two weeks of November. Reservations advised. Major credit cards accepted. 70 Via Gramsci, Volterra (phone: 588-86663). Inexpensive.

Il Porcellino Tista, the gregarious owner, keeps the traditions of Tuscan home cooking vibrantly alive. Tables are moved outdoors in spring, but the quaint pocket-size dining room inside is far more charming. Try the *piccata al funghetto* (roast lamb with mushroom sauce) or the *coniglio alla cacciatore* (rabbit with tomato sauce). Closed Tuesdays and September through *Easter*. Reservations advised. No credit cards accepted. 16 Canto delle Prigioni, Volterra (phone: 588-86392). Inexpensive.

San Lino Named after a Volterrano, the first pope to succeed St. Peter, and formerly a cloistered convent built in the 12th century, this is a modern 44-room establishment with air conditioning, a delightful enclosed garden terrace, and a small pool. The restaurant (closed November through March) is highly recommended. 26 Via San Lino, Volterra (phone/fax: 588-85250). Hotel and restaurant, inexpensive.

Villa Nencini In this family-run, 17th-century villa are 14 rooms, plus 26 in a new wing. Some guestrooms overlook the green Val di Cecina; on a clear day, you can see the island of Corsica. There also is a pool. Excellent Tuscan wines and local produce are served in the restaurant. Open year-round. 55 Borgo Santo Stefano, Volterra (phone: 588-86386; fax: 588-86686). Inexpensive.

En Route from Volterra Proceed east 17 miles (27 km) on S68 in the direction of Colle di Val d'Elsa. At Castel San Gimignano turn north onto a less-frequented road signposted San Gimignano, and travel 8 miles (13 km) through incomparable Tuscan countryside, above which rises the characteristic skyline of this small hill town.

SAN GIMIGNANO Ringed by three sets of historic walls, San Gimignano bristles with 14 (or 13 or 15, depending on exactly what you count) of its original 72 medieval towers and thus is known as San Gimignano delle Belle Torri—San Gimignano of the Beautiful Towers. Each tower, attached to the private palazzo of a patrician family, was used partly for defense against attack from without and partly for defense against attack by feuding families within the walls. As with today's skyscrapers, height was an indication of prestige. (Note: No cars are allowed inside the city walls.)

The town takes its name from a Bishop of Modena who died here in the 4th century. It became a free commune in the 12th century, and life would have been tranquil had it not been for the destructive conflict between two families in particular, the Guelph Ardinghelli and the Ghibelline Salvucci (the city was predominantly Ghibelline). In 1300, Guelph Florence sent Dante as ambassador to make peace between the warring factions, but he was unsuccessful; internal strife grew so volatile that 53 years later, an exasperated San Gimignano willingly surrendered to the Florentines it had resisted for so many centuries.

The two main streets of this perfectly preserved town, Via San Giovanni and Via San Matteo, feed into two splendid squares, Piazza della Cisterna and Piazza del Duomo. At the center of Piazza della Cisterna is the 13th-century well from which it takes its name. The piazza is paved with bricks inlaid in a herringbone pattern and surrounded by an assortment of medieval palazzi and towers. In the adjoining Piazza del Duomo, the 12th-century cathedral, known as the *Collegiata,* is flanked by more stately palazzi and seven towers. The *Palazzo del Popolo,* to one side of the cathedral, is the home of San Gimignano's small *Museo Civico,* which contains, besides paintings from the 14th and 15th centuries, the room from which Dante delivered his harangue in favor of the Guelphs. It also provides access to one of San Gimignano's towers (*Torre Grossa*), which affords a view of the town and hills in all directions. It is closed Mondays in summer; closed Mondays and for a midday break in winter. Admission charge to the museum (phone: 577-940340) permits entry to the *Cappella di Santa Fina* in the *Duomo,* a Renaissance addition that is decorated with Domenico Ghirlandaio's frescoes of the life of the saint, who was born here and died at the age of 15.

Stop in the 13th-century *Chiesa di Sant'Agostino* (Piazza Sant'Agostino) at the far end of town to see the frescoes by Benozzo Gozzol. For another view out over the surrounding countryside—or back toward the town and towers—climb to *La Rocca,* a onetime fortress and now a public park. While away an hour at one of the sidewalk cafés with a glass of local *vino bianco*— San Gimignano's famous vernaccia is considered the finest white wine in the region and one of the finest whites in Italy. Movie buffs will be interested to know that *Where Angels Fear to Tread,* an adaptation of E. M. Forster's novel, was filmed here. In July and August, the town hosts a series of concerts, ballets, and operas. For information, contact the tourist office (1 Piazza Duomo; phone: 577-940008; fax: 577-940903), which is open daily, with a midday closing.

BEST EN ROUTE

La Mangiatoia Cozy and candlelit, this trattoria is an alternative to any of the well-known hotel restaurants below, and specializes in homemade pasta dishes. Closed Tuesdays and January. Reservations advised. Major credit cards accepted. 5 Via Mainardi, San Gimignano (phone: 577-941528). Moderate.

Relais Santa Chiara The loveliest hotel in the area is just a minute's drive from the town walls. All 41 rooms in this sprawling villa have terraces—half overlook San Gimignano, and the other half face the rolling Tuscan hills and the pool. The public areas are an attractive blend of Tuscan rustic and contemporary styles, while the guestrooms are simple and modern. Open mid-February to mid-January. No restaurant. 15 Via Matteotti, Località Santa Chiara, San Gimignano (phone: 577-940701; fax: 577-942096). Moderate.

Bel Soggiorno The former 13th-century *Convento di San Francesco,* its façade barely distinguishable from the other medieval buildings on this central street, is comfortable in a simple Tuscan fashion. The back rooms afford a view of the morning mist swirling over the fields, and the vista from the restaurant vies for attention with a delicious representation of Tuscan specialties. There is a shower or bath in each of its 18 simply furnished rooms. Open year-round; restaurant closed Mondays. 91 Via San Giovanni, San Gimignano (phone/fax: 577-940375). Hotel, inexpensive; restaurant, moderate.

La Cisterna This rustic 50-room hotel is housed in a 13th-century palazzo on the central piazza. The windows and large wooden balconies of some rooms overlook the surrounding valley. The hotel's *Le Terrazze* restaurant is the domain of some very fine Tuscan dining. Scenes from the film *Where Angels Fear to Tread* were shot here. Hotel and restaurant open April through October; restaurant closed Tuesdays and Wednesday lunch. 23 Piazza della Cisterna, San Gimignano (phone: 577-940328; fax: 577-942080). Hotel, inexpensive; restaurant, moderate.

Leon Bianco A comfortable, 24-room, centrally located hotel, it's housed in a beautifully restored medieval palazzo. No restaurant. Open March through January 15. 8 Piazza della Cisterna, San Gimignano (phone: 577-941294; fax: 577-942123). Inexpensive.

Pescille On a hilltop overlooking the towers of San Gimignano, this former farmhouse, now an idyllic 49-room country inn, is 3 miles (5 km) outside town on the road to Volterra. The owners have kept the rustic feeling, decorating rooms with terra cotta tiles, straw chairs, and country furniture. Outdoors, the tennis courts and a pool are set among olive trees. Its acclaimed *Cinque Gigli* restaurant turns out well-cooked dishes, making good use of the area's wealth of fresh, natural ingredients. Restaurant closed Wednesdays; inn and restaurant closed December through February. Reservations advised. Major credit cards accepted. Località Pescille (phone/fax: 577-940186). Hotel, inexpensive; restaurant, moderate.

Le Renaie If San Gimignano's hotels are full—and they fill up very quickly—this attractive country property is a pleasant alternative, just 3 miles (5 km) out of town. It has 26 rooms; a very good restaurant, *Il Leonetto;* a pool; and fine views over the Tuscan countryside. Hotel and restaurant open December 6 to November 4; restaurant closed Tuesdays. Follow the signs for Certaldo and then for Pancole. Località Pancole, San Gimignano (phone: 577-955044; fax: 577-955126). Hotel, inexpensive; restaurant, moderate.

En Route from San Gimignano About 30 miles (48 km) southeast of San Gimignano, Siena can be reached directly by taking the picturesque road east to Poggibonsi and then turning south and taking the old Roman consular road, the Via Cassia (S2). Avoid the Florence-Siena superstrada. Nine miles (14 km) north of Siena is the tiny hill town of Monteriggioni, created by Siena as an elevated lookout fortress against the archenemy, Florence, in 1213. Ownership of Monteriggioni passed from one combatant to the other, and the town never grew beyond its original perimeters. Its walls have been left perfectly intact, although its 14 towers must have been considerably higher to have elicited Dante's likening them to looming giants.

A pleasant alternative to the direct route to Siena is to explore the chianti classico zone, driving east from Poggibonsi to Castellina in Chianti, there picking up S222, romantically referred to as La Chiantigiana because it cuts through the heart of Chianti country. The chianti classico zone measures only 30 miles in length between Florence and Siena and 20 miles at its widest point, but its landscape is considered one of the most Italian in all Italy. From Castellina, one option is to follow S222 up to Greve, the unofficial capital of the wine producing region. Another is to simply zigzag through the network of country roads, visiting Radda in Chianti and Gaiole in Chianti, both east of Castellina. The best way to explore this stretch is to drift from castle to roadside shrine, following the signs for *degustazione, vendita diretta,* or *cantina.* Producers at private, centuries-old *fattorie* (literally, "farmsteads") usually are happy to invite potential wine buyers for a taste (see *Most Visitable Vineyards* in DIVERSIONS). Afterward, take either the Chiantigiana or the Via Cassia south into Siena.

BEST EN ROUTE

Relais La Suvera The estate of a marquis is the setting for this lovely inn in the heart of Tuscany. There are 25 handsome rooms and 10 princely suites in the main palazzo and stables, while the converted olive press is used as a restaurant serving Tuscan cuisine and estate-bottled wines. If the sweeping panorama doesn't soothe you, a few laps in the pool or a visit to the sauna will. The estate's own wine and olive oil are used in the hotel's restaurant, and horseback riding, a mile (1.6 km) down the road, can be arranged. Open *Easter* through October. Head 6 miles (10 km) south on S541 from Colle di Val d'Elsa to Pievescola di Casole d'Elsa (phone: 577-960300; 800-367-4668; fax: 577-960220; 212-689-0851 in the US). Expensive.

Residence San Luigi Once a working *podere* (farm), this is 4 miles (6 km) west of Monteriggioni, at Strove. The old farm buildings have been tastefully restored and turned into 42 small apartments, and they are surrounded by acres of peaceful grounds, including a pool and tennis, basketball, and volleyball courts. Rustic elegance best describes the whole, which includes a restaurant that excels in local cuisine. Although the apartments are rented weekly in high season (May through September), single-night stays can be arranged when there is a vacancy. Open mid-March through mid-January. 38 Strada della Cerreta, Strove (phone: 577-301055; fax: 577-301167). Expensive.

Il Pozzo This highly regarded restaurant occupies an idyllic setting within the walls of Monteriggioni. Typical of most rustic Tuscan establishments, the menu turns to game specialties such as *cinghiale in dolce e forte* (wild boar in a sweet-and-sour sauce, a Sienese specialty). Closed Sunday dinner, Mondays, January 7 to February 14, and the first two weeks of August. Reservations necessary. Major credit cards accepted. 2 Piazza Roma, Monteriggioni (phone: 577-304127; fax: 577-304701). Moderate.

Trattoria dei Montagliari Such Tuscan dishes as grilled *chianina* beef and other meat are the specialty at this rustic eatery. In warm weather, dine outside with a view of Chianti's hills; in the winter, enjoy a meal inside with the welcoming fire. Closed Mondays and one week in August. Reservations advised. No credit cards accepted. 28 Via dei Montagliari, Panzano in Chianti (phone: 55-852184). Moderate.

Villa Vignamaggio For those who loved the 1993 release of *Much Ado about Nothing,* which was filmed here, this six-suite inn on a 400-acre wine estate in the heart of chianti country gets top billing. Each suite has a wrought-iron bed, oak furniture, and terra cotta tiles, plus a refrigerator, sink, and stove tucked inside a pine *armadio* (wardrobe). The pool and tennis court are surrounded by olive trees and grapevines. Open year-round. No restaurant. Three miles (5 km) from Greve, at 5 Via Petriolo, Ninchianti (phone: 55-853007; fax: 55-854-4468). Moderate.

Bottega del Moro Simple, tasty fare is served at this cozy trattoria. Homemade pasta, roast rabbit with herbs, and *trippa alla fiorentina* (tripe in a tomato sauce) are just a sampling of the offerings. Closed Wednesdays and November. Reservations advised. Major credit cards accepted. 14 Piazza Trieste, Greve (phone: 55-853753). Inexpensive.

SIENA A wonderfully well-preserved medieval city, Siena has an artistic heritage, and it is the site, twice each summer, of the running of the *Palio,* a famous bareback horse race that traces its origins to the Middle Ages. Siena is also a wine center, hardly remarkable considering its setting in the midst of chianti country. For a detailed report of the city and its sights, see *Siena* in THE CITIES.

En Route from Siena To get to Montalcino, about 25 miles (40 km) south, follow the Via Cassia (S2) past Buonconvento and turn off (either at Torrenieri or before) to Montalcino. If there is time for a detour along the way, however, turn east at Buonconvento to visit the *Abbazia di Monte Oliveto Maggiore,* a famous abbey that was a major cultural center in the 15th and 16th centuries. The few miles to the cypress-sheltered mother-house of the Olivetan monks, a congregation of the Benedictine Order founded in 1319, is a marvelous drive, and readers who found Umberto Eco's *The Name of the Rose* intriguing will be fascinated by this extensive compound still known for its skilled restoration of ancient illuminated manuscripts. Of greatest interest is the *Chiostro Grande* (Great Cloister), decorated with splendid frescoes of the life of St. Benedict by Luca Signorelli (nine frescoes, done from 1497 to 1498) and Sodom (the remainder, painted from 1505 on) that alone are worth the trip. The abbey is open daily, with a midday closing.

BEST EN ROUTE

La Torre The restored 16th-century tower that houses this restaurant run by the monks goes back to the abbey's earliest days. Dine outdoors from a menu that is simple and good. Closed Tuesdays. Reservations advised. Major credit cards accepted. *Abbazia di Monte Oliveto Maggiore* (phone: 577-707022). Inexpensive.

MONTALCINO This hill town is extraordinarily perched in the midst of a pretty area known for its noble wines and subtle light. In its early days, the site belonged to an abbey, the *Abbazia di Sant'Antimo,* 7 miles (11 km) to the south. Then Montalcino became a free commune—fought over by the Sienese and the Florentines, however, until the former defeated the latter in 1260 and the town became Sienese. When Siena fell to Medici Florence in 1555, Sienese patriots fled to Montalcino to form a short-lived Sienese republic-in-exile, until Montalcino itself was forced into submission by Cosimo I. In recognition of this hospitality, a delegation from Montalcino occupies a place of honor in the historical procession that precedes Siena's twice-yearly *Palio* race. Most of Montalcino's stately architecture shows medieval Sienese influence. Be sure to visit the 14th-century *Fortezza,* or *Rocca,* the fortress from whose aerial lookouts the city kept its enemies at bay and whose main attraction these days is its informal *enoteca* (wine bar), serving thick *panini* sandwiches, cheese, and glasses of the local brunello di Montalcino, one of the most celebrated (and costly) wines in all Italy. It's open daily; no admission charge (no phone). The town's other command post is the handsome 19th-century *Caffè Fiaschetteria Italiana* (in the central Piazza del Popolo), where the townsfolk converge to talk for hours. The *Sagra del Tordo*—part archery contest, part thrush festival (eating them, not listening to them sing)—is held here on the last Sunday in October. If visiting at this time, make reservations well in advance. The tourist office (66 Via Mazzini; phone: 577-849471) organizes visits to wineries and farms in the area. It is closed Sundays and for a long midday break.

To visit the *Abbazia di Sant'Antimo,* follow signs for Castelnuovo dell'Abate along the 7-mile (11-km) drive south from Montalcino. One of the most noted examples of medieval monastic architecture, the abbey is visible from afar, isolated in an open expanse of olive groves. According to legend, Charlemagne founded it in the 9th century, but most of what is seen today dates from the 12th century. Best preserved of the buildings is the church, built of travertine now turned golden, with alabaster used for much of the trim, column capitals, and windows—at sunset there is nothing quite as beautiful. To visit the church, contact the custodian at 12 Via del Centro, in Castelnuovo dell'Abate, at the top of the hill. And if at all possible, be on hand for the service sung with Gregorian chant, when the Augustine monks walk down from their quarters in Castelnuovo for an hour of singing that fills this sanctum sanctorum to its aged beams. Vespers currently are held on Sunday afternoons, but services with chant are expected to be changed to mornings; call to confirm (phone: 577-835669).

BEST EN ROUTE

Poggio Antico This working farm/restaurant 2½ miles (4 km) out of town has garnered much acclaim. Most of the produce used in the rustic kitchen is grown on the enormous property that surrounds this refurbished *casa colonica;* the menu offers both reliable Tuscan standbys as well as more innovative twists, such as melt-in-your-mouth goose liver cooked in *vin santo.* Closed Mondays. Reservations advised. No credit cards accepted. Località Poggio Antico, Montalcino (phone: 577-849200). Expensive.

La Cucina di Edgardo The best dining choice in town serves very good local cuisine. Closed Wednesdays and the last three weeks in January. Reservations advised. Major credit cards accepted. 33 Via Soccorso Saloni, Montalcino (phone: 577-848232). Moderate.

Bar Sassetti Bassomondo A stone's throw from the *Abbazia di Sant'Antimo,* 7 miles (11 km) outside of Montalcino, is a country trattoria in the best Tuscan tradition, serving classics such as *zuppa di funghi* (soup of wild mushrooms) and casserole of wild boar. Closed Mondays. Reservations unnecessary. No credit cards accepted. 7 Via Bassomondo, Castelnuovo dell'Abate (phone: 577-835619). Inexpensive.

Giardino Here are a dozen clean, modest rooms, as well as a good restaurant stocked with the best chianti and brunello vintages. Restaurant closed Wednesdays. 2 Piazza Cavour, Montalcino (phone: 577-848257). Inexpensive.

Il Giglio Convenient, clean, and unpretentious, it has about a dozen renovated rooms, an interesting restaurant, and a well-stocked wine cellar. Open March through

January; restaurant closed Mondays. No credit cards accepted. 49 Via Soccorso Saloni, Montalcino (phone: 577-848167). Inexpensive.

Il Grappolo Blu Here is the perfect spot to get a late-night plate of pasta or linger over a jug of wine when every other place is closed. There also is a simple, but good, cold buffet. Open from lunch to well after midnight; closed Tuesdays. Reservations unnecessary. Major credit cards accepted. Scale di Moglio, Montalcino (phone: 577-849078). Inexpensive.

Da Idolina A small (four rooms with two shared baths), charmingly furnished pensione, with canopied beds in some rooms. There is also a delightful attic apartment, complete with a kitchen and a sun terrace. No restaurant. No credit cards accepted. 70 Via Mazzini, Montalcino (phone: 577-848634). Inexpensive.

En Route from Montalcino Return to Torrenieri and the Via Cassia and follow it south to S146, the turnoff for Pienza.

PIENZA This little town was once called Corsignano and belonged to the powerful Piccolomini family, one of whose number, Aeneas Sylvius Piccolomini, was born here and grew to be an exceptionally clever Renaissance man and, in 1458, Pope Pius II. An acclaimed humanist, he dreamed of creating the perfect Renaissance city, executed to a precise urban plan, and so he commissioned a famous architect, Bernardo Rossellino, to create this small jewel. It became a papal annex and summer home for Pius, who officially changed its name to Pienza in 1462. Today this unusual miniature city is so pristinely preserved that director Franco Zeffirelli chose to film his *Romeo and Juliet* here. A simple Renaissance cathedral stands in Piazza Pio II, the center of town, and to the right of it is the *Palazzo Piccolomini,* where the Piccolomini family lived until just after World War II, when the last family member died. Also in the square are the *Palazzo Vescovile,* the *Palazzo Comunale,* and a small cathedral museum. Be sure to walk behind the church for a sweeping view of the whole Val d'Orcia and Monte Amiata, a dormant volcano. Every September in San Quirco d'Orcia, 5½ miles (9 km) from town, an outdoor sculpture exhibit is held. The information office is on Piazza Pio II (phone: 578-748502).

BEST EN ROUTE

La Saracina Nearly 5 miles (7½ km) northeast of Pienza is this lovely 19th-century Tuscan farmhouse owned and run by the McCobbs, an amiable American couple. Each of the four elegantly cozy guestrooms and the one apartment has a fireplace. The beautifully landscaped pool and tennis court both offer magnificent views of the surrounding medieval hill towns. No restaurant. Special weekly rates. Open March through December. Km 29.7, S146, Pienza (phone/fax: 578-748022). Expensive.

Dal Falco A rustic place, it features tables in the shady square just outside the town gate. Try the *pici,* tasty homemade pasta of flour and water. Wednesday is the day for fish, not commonly served in this landlocked, game-loving part of Tuscany. Closed Fridays and the last two weeks of November. Reservations advised. Major credit cards accepted. 7 Piazza Dante Alighieri, Pienza (phone/fax: 578-748551). Inexpensive.

En Route from Pienza Continue 8 miles (13 km) east on S146 to Montepulciano.

MONTEPULCIANO Famous for its wine—vino nobile di Montepulciano—and several times larger than Pienza, it is still something of a perfect miniature Renaissance city, except that it owes its harmonious aspect more to the continuing patronage of the Medicis than to the utopian dream of one man. A major determinant of the Medicis' favor, no doubt, was Agnolo Ambrogini, one of the great Renaissance poets and a friend and protégé of Giuliano de' Medici and Lorenzo il Magnifico. Born in Montepulciano, he was better known as Il Poliziano, from the ancient name given to the town's residents. Since Etruscan times, Montepulciano has perched 2,000 feet above sea level, with the spacious and grandiose Piazza Grande at its highest point. Its major claim to fame is the number of handsome palazzi lining that square as well as its two main arteries—Via Roma, which begins at Porta al Prato but leads to the other end of town under several different names, and Via Ricci. Montepulciano is most noted for its monuments of the 16th century. There are few "must-see" attractions (discounting the view from the tower of the *Palazzo Comunale,* a 14th-century building with a 15th-century façade, possibly designed by Michelozzo, in Piazza Grande), but the town itself is a joy to discover, with its winding *vicoli* (alleys), majestic door knockers, window ironwork, and the aged clock tower with the masked Pulcinella striking the hours in front of the *Chiesa di Sant'Agostino* (on the outskirts of town). Also outside of town (a mile-long walk down the Strada di San Biagio) is the *Tempio di San Biagio,* a 16th-century church in pale gold travertine. A High Renaissance masterpiece by Antonio Sangallo the Elder, it sits in an open field, overlooking the whole valley. The information office (Via Ricci, near the Piazza Grande; phone: 578-758687) is closed Mondays and for a long midday break.

BEST EN ROUTE

La Chiusa This farmhouse restaurant can be reached by backtracking a few miles west of Montepulciano on S146 and then turning north to the town of Montefollonico (which is roughly equidistant from Pienza and Montepulciano, so a meal here can be combined with a visit to either one). If the drive through hilly vineyards seems too far to go, consider that some discriminating diners make the trip from Paris, so the inconvenience is worth the culinary reward (there also are 12 delightfully decorated guest-rooms if you're too full to leave). Imaginative cuisine is blended with rarely found Tuscan dishes, such as *farro* and *piccione al vin santo* (wild pigeon in a sherry-based sauce). Closed mid-January through March, November 15 to December 15, and Tuesdays from October through July. Reservations necessary. Major credit cards accepted. Via della Madonnina, Montefollonico (phone: 577-669668; fax: 577-669593). Restaurant, very expensive; hotel, expensive.

Panoramic A simple hostelry 1 mile (1.6 km) southeast of town, in the direction of Chianciano Terme, it offers 25 rooms, tennis courts, pleasant gardens, a fishing lake, and expansive views. No restaurant. Open *Easter* through October. S146, 8 Via Villa Bianca, Montepulciano (phone/fax: 578-798398). Moderate to inexpensive.

Diva A noisy, friendly, and unpretentious trattoria right in town. The decor may be a little nondescript, but the local dishes that grace the table make it a memorable dining experience. Specialties include the homemade *strozzapreti* pasta and delicious roast meat dishes. Closed Tuesdays and the first two weeks in July. Reservations unnecessary. No credit cards accepted. 92 Via di Gracciano nel Corso, Montepulciano (phone: 578-716951). Inexpensive.

Fattoria Pulcino Out of town in the direction of Chianciano Terme, this is a medieval monastery–turned-farm-turned-restaurant. Walk past the open wooden ovens and through a tempting maze of farm products (olive oil, wines, pecorino cheese, and beans) before entering the large dining room, where meals are served at communal tables. There are excellent steaks, sausages, and some very delicious first courses. Closed weekends for lunch. Reservations unnecessary. Major credit cards accepted. On S146 (phone: 578-716905). Inexpensive.

Il Marzocco This small, family-run hotel with a restaurant has two things going for it—its central location and the views of the countryside from many of the 18 rather threadbare rooms, some with terraces. No credit cards accepted. 18 Piazza Savanarola, Montepulciano (phone: 578-757262). Inexpensive.

La Terrazza A renovated 16th-century residence–turned-hotel, it's only a minute's walk from Piazza Grande. Each of the 14 rooms is furnished differently, most rather handsomely, and there are three mini-apartments with kitchenettes. No dining room. No credit cards accepted. 16 Via Piè al Sasso, Montepulciano (phone: 578-757440). Inexpensive.

En Route from Montepulciano If you care to "take the waters," head south 8 miles (13 km) on S146 to the spa town of Chianciano Terme.

CHIANCIANO TERME Tuscany's second-most-popular spa town has springs that date back to the Etruscans. For more information, see *Taking the Waters* in DIVERSIONS. The *Azienda di Promozione Turistica* (*APT;* 7 Via Sabatini; phone: 578-63538; fax: 578-64623), which is closed Sundays and for a late midday break, and the local tourist office (67 Piazza Italia; phone: 578-63167), which is closed Sunday afternoons and for a long midday break April through October (closed Sundays and for a long midday break the rest of the year), can provide spa information.

BEST EN ROUTE

Spadeus A US-style spa in a tastefully furnished 71-room villa, it is an anomaly for the Italian approach to "taking the cure." Guests participate in a balanced beauty and weight-loss program that includes both pampering treatments and early-morning walks and optional aerobics classes to burn up the delicious 1,200-calorie-a-day menu. There also are organized trips to fill cultural needs. The two-night package rates include full board, classes, and spa treatments. Open mid-February to mid-December. 35 Via delle Piane, Chianciano Terme (phone: 578-63232; fax: 578-64329). Very expensive.

Grand Hotel Excelsior The grande dame of hotels in Chianciano is a stately 78-room property. It has a heated pool and a well-respected restaurant where guests gladly take half board, which is encouraged but not required, in high season. The staff is efficient and friendly. Open *Easter* through October. 6 Via Sant'Agnese, Chianciano Terme (phone: 578-64351; fax: 578-63214). Expensive.

Grand Hotel Ambasciatori Most of the 116 rooms in this centrally located, modern hotel have balconies. The atmosphere is friendly, and there's a large pool and a restaurant. Half or full board is offered but not required. 512 Viale della Libertà, Chianciano Terme (phone/fax: 578-64371). Moderate.

Il Morellone Just outside Chianciano in a restored 19th-century Tuscan farmhouse atop a hill is the city's best (and most picturesquely set) restaurant for rustic Tuscan fare. House specialties include *pici* (a spaghetti-like pasta) and roast meat and game. In warm weather, there's alfresco dining on an outdoor terrace overlooking the town and its surrounding hills. Closed Mondays and the last two weeks of November. Reservations advised. Major credit cards accepted. 8 Strada del Morellone, Chianciano Terme (phone: 578-60401). Moderate.

En Route from Chianciano Terme Return to Montepulciano. To reach Arezzo, take the winding, bucolic road to Nottola, and then head north toward Torrita di Siena and onward to Sinalunga. At Sinalunga, either head east and pick up the autostrada north (A1) to the exit for Arezzo, or continue northward along minor roads to Monte San Savino and then to Arezzo. The latter route passes by (or near) three tiny walled hamlets left over from the Middle Ages. Both have a farm family or two still living within the walls, and both are primarily visited now for the restaurants featuring country cooking and small, charming hotels operating in some of the estate buildings. The first hamlet, the *Fattoria dell'Amorosa,* is seen from a distance, gently elevated above its own rolling farmlands south of Sinalunga. The second—*Gargonza*—and third—*Le Gorghe*—are both just outside of Monte San Savino.

BEST EN ROUTE

Locanda dell'Amorosa (Lover's Inn) A regal sweep of cypress trees leads up to this unique establishment, a tiny 14th-century walled village-cum–farming enclave turned into a restaurant with rooms to rent. Those only passing through can sit in the small, airy *piazzetta* in the warm Tuscan sun, nursing a long lemonade. Those staying in any of the 12 light and spacious rooms (once farmworkers' quarters) are more able to partake of the pool, grounds, and gastronomic genius of the kitchen, which is built into the old oxen's stalls and has garnered high praise for its local cuisine with an imaginative nouvelle twist. As its name implies, this is a paradisiacal spot to call home while jaunting off to nearby Siena and other Tuscan towns. Restaurant closed Mondays, Tuesday lunch, and mid-January through February. Località l'Amorosa (phone: 577-679497; fax: 577-678216). Very expensive.

Castello di Gargonza Dante once used this 13th-century walled hamlet in miniature as a refuge. For over 300 years it has belonged to the noble Guicciardini family, who today runs it as a storybook hotel. There are seven spacious rooms in the simple, renovated *castello* (castle) and 18 skillfully renovated stone cottages, with kitchenettes and working fireplaces. A short walk beyond the town walls is the establishment's attractive, rustic restaurant, where tables are moved outside during the summer amid the fireflies and the scent of pine. Restaurant closed Tuesdays. Castello di Gargonza, Monte San Savino (phone: 575-847021, hotel; 575-847065, restaurant; fax: 575-847054, hotel). Moderate.

Le Gorghe Americans Dee and Warren Sweet have restored this more than 200-year-old inn to offer their guests a variety of accommodations—from guestrooms with shared or private baths to two- and three-room suites to the whole farmhouse (by special arrangement). Picnic baskets are prepared on request for alfresco lunches on the 10-acre grounds that have a lake or for forays into the Tuscan-Umbrian hills—but there's no restaurant. Weekly rates available. Le Gorghe, Monte San Savino (phone: 575-844332; 510-930-2864 in the US). Inexpensive.

AREZZO A hill town set at the confluence of green valleys—the Valdarno, the Casentino (the upper valley of the Arno), and the Valdichiana—ancient Arretium has been of strategic importance since its earliest Etruscan and Roman days. A free commune with Ghibelline leanings during the Middle Ages, it fell to Guelph Florence in 1289. Early in the next century, however, the short but decisive reign of Guido Tarlati, a bishop who ruled Arezzo from 1312 to 1327, lifted the city to prominence, and it is its early-14th-century character that remains most in evidence today. After Tarlati's death, Arezzo's fortunes waned, and in 1384 it fell once again, definitively this time, to Florence. Some very prominent Italians were born here: Guido d'Arezzo, the 11th-century Benedictine monk who invented the musical scale; the great pre-Renaissance poet Petrarch; and Giorgio Vasari, the Renaissance painter, architect, and historian. Piero della Francesca may have been born in nearby Sansepolcro, but Arezzo holds him as one of its dearest sons. The town's *Basilica di San Francesco* (see below) is filled with his works.

At the top of the series of terraces on which the town is built stretches a spacious public park—the *Passeggio del Prato*—that overlooks the surrounding farmland. Arezzo's Gothic *Duomo* stands to one side of the *Prato*. Begun in the late 13th century and not finished until the beginning of the 16th century, it is home to a host of artworks, from the stained glass windows of Guillaume de Marcillat (a 15th-century French artist) to a famous fresco of Mary Magdalene by Piero della Francesca and, to the left of that, a memorial to Guido Tarlati (he is not buried here), completed in 1330 by Agostino di Giovanni and Agnolo di Ventura. A few blocks north of the *Duomo* is the 13th-century *Chiesa di San Domenico* (Piazza San Domenico), which has a beautiful wooden crucifix, one of the earlier works of Cimabue. Not far away is the house of Giorgio Vasari (55 Via XX Settembre; no phone), who supervised its construction, took care of its furnishing, and decorated it himself with frescoes between 1540 and 1548. Call the tourist office (see below) for hours, which are erratic; admission charge.

Pace yourself, because Arezzo's main attractions are still to come. Piero della Francesca's remarkable fresco cycle illustrating *La Storia della Croce* (The Legend of the True Cross) is behind the high altar of the *Basilica di San Francesco* (Piazza San Francesco), a large, barren 14th-century church that is the spiritual nucleus and geographical center of the Old Town. A painstaking, multiple-year restoration still has many of the frescoes behind scaffolding, though enough remains visible to make this a must for art lovers. And not far from that is the Piazza Grande, center of urban life for centuries. This sloping, trapezoid-shaped plaza is surrounded by palazzi reflecting the architectural styles of several centuries: Giorgio Vasari's 16th-century *Palazzo delle Logge* (Loggia Palace), with its open portico of shops, is on the north side, flanked by several handsome Renaissance palazzi and medieval homes; the *Palazzo della Fraternità dei Laici* (Palace of the Lay Fraternity) has a Gothic-Renaissance façade; and the magnificent *Pieve di*

Santa Maria, a 12th-to-14th-century church with a Pisan-Lucchese Romanesque façade of the 13th century, backs into the square, with its tall campanile of "a hundred holes" (it actually has 40 mullioned windows) standing alongside it. The first Sunday of every month, and the Saturday preceding it, Piazza Grande and the surrounding streets become the site of an antiques fair, with hundreds of vendors. On the last Sunday in August and the first Sunday in September, the market moves elsewhere to make room for the annual *Giostra del Saracino,* a colorful re-creation of a medieval jousting tournament in which eight knights representing the town's four quarters attack an effigy of the Saracen. Accompanying the joust is a historical procession of lance-bearing knights in full armor on brilliantly caparisoned horses, a fitting spectacle for this evocative and picturesque old square. Tickets are sold at the tourist office (26 Piazza della Repubblica; phone: 575-20839; 575-377678, *Giostra* tickets; fax: 575-28042). To order in advance, call the *Giostra* number to reserve tickets and then send an international money order to the tourist office. The tourist office is closed Sundays.

Other places of interest in Arezzo include the remains of a Roman amphitheater and the nearby *Museo Archeologico Mecenate* (Mecenate Archaeological Museum; Via Margaritone; phone: 575-20882), which contains a collection of the *corallini* vases made by Aretine artists from the 1st century BC to the 1st century. It is closed Mondays, after 2 PM, and Sundays after 1 PM. Admission charge.

BEST EN ROUTE

Buca di San Francesco The dining room is the beautifully frescoed former *cantina* (wine cellar) of a 14th-century palazzo, and if that's not enough, the food here is some of the best in the region. There's a timbale of spinach and chicken livers, vegetable *sformati* (soufflés), and a hearty white bean soup. Closed Monday dinner, Tuesdays, and two weeks in July. Reservations advised. Major credit cards accepted. 1 Piazza San Francesco, Arezzo (phone: 575-23271). Moderate.

Al Principe Aretines love this warm and busy trattoria, one of the oldest still operating in the area. It's in the rural periphery, almost 5 miles (8 km) north on S71, a five-minute drive from the center, but the ride is more than compensated for by the pleasant culinary experience in store: lamb cooked in a crust or the local specialty, *cee* (baby eels) in terra cotta casseroles. Closed Mondays, January 7 to 14, and mid-July to mid-August. Reservations advised. Major credit cards accepted. 25 Località Giovi (phone: 575-362046). Moderate.

Continentale Popular with businesspeople, this modern 74-room hotel is only a few minutes' walk from the medieval quarter. It has a restaurant. 7 Piazza Guido Monaco, Arezzo (phone: 575-20251; fax: 575-350485). Inexpensive.

Minerva Modern, clean, and comfortable, it has 118 rooms and a restaurant. 4 Via Fiorentina, Arezzo (phone/fax: 575-370390). Inexpensive.

En Route from Arezzo To return to Florence, 45 minutes away, hop on the A1. Those who intend to explore the neighboring region of Umbria should take S71 south to Lake Trasimeno, then skirt the lake to Perugia, visiting a final Tuscan hill town, Cortona (18 miles/29 km from Arezzo), before reaching the lake.

CORTONA The birthplace of Luca Signorelli, Cortona has an Etruscan background and a medieval appearance, with steep, narrow streets, only one of which, Via Nazionale, the main street, is level. It leads into Piazza della Repubblica, with the *Palazzo Comunale* (Town Hall), and then on into the adjoining Piazza Signorelli, where the *Palazzo Pretorio* (or *Palazzo Casali*) houses the *Museo Accademia Etrusca* (Etruscan Academy Museum; phone: 575-62767 or 575-630415), most famous for its 5th-century BC bronze Etruscan chandelier, the largest and most richly decorated of its kind. It's closed Mondays and for a long midday break; admission charge. The *Museo Diocesano* (Diocesan Museum; phone: 575-62830), in a former church in front of the *Duomo,* contains—besides several Signorellis—an especially beautiful *Annunciation* by Fra Angelico. It's closed Mondays and for a midday break; admission charge. The tourist office is on 72 Via Nazionale (phone: 575-630352).

BEST EN ROUTE

Il Falconiere Traditional Tuscan fare is offered at this rustic yet elegant restaurant located in a tiny, 17th-century hamlet just 3 miles (5 km) north of Cortona. In the summer, there is alfresco dining on a flagstone terrace overlooking Cortona; in cooler weather, meals are served in the former *limonaia* (lemon house), with stucco walls and vaulted brick ceilings. The old villa has been converted into nine delightful guestrooms, all air conditioned and tastefully furnished with antiques and embroidered white linen curtains. Restaurant closed Wednesdays; hotel open year-round. Reservations advised. Major credit cards accepted. Località San Martino (phone: 575-612679; fax: 575-612927). Moderate.

San Michele The only good hotel in the *centro storico* is in the restored 16th-century Renaissance *Palazza Baldelli.* Some original detail has been preserved in the 32 rooms and three suites. There is no restaurant, but you'll want to drive out into the countryside to *Il Falconiere* (see above) for the finest dinner in this part of Tuscany. Open *Easter* through January 9. 15 Via Guelfa (phone: 575-604348; fax: 575-630147). Inexpensive.

En Route from Cortona Take S71 north out of Arezzo to explore the northeastern corner of Tuscany. The road follows the Arno into a sparsely populated, forest-dense area known as the Casentino, site of powerful monastic developments in the late Middle Ages that were instrumental in paving the way for the Renaissance. The monasteries were usually set in inaccessible mountain sites along the backbone of the Apennines, and the overwhelming beauty of their natural surroundings predisposed residents to extraordinary meditative heights. Contact with the secular world was not totally severed, however, and artistic works and rich architecture are evident, if not abundant. At Bibbiena, 20 miles (32 km) north of Arezzo, turn onto S208 and climb 17 miles (27 km) through pine and beech forests to the most famous of the Casentino monasteries, *La Verna,* at 3,500 feet. The noble Cattani family of Chiusi in Casentino donated this mountain to St. Francis in 1213, and it was here, in 1224, that the saint from Assisi received the stigmata. A cluster of churches sprang up in the century after his death (1226), many, as in the *Chiesa Maggiore,* filled with very beautiful terra cottas by Andrea della Robbia. A community of about 30 Franciscans still lives in seclusion at *La Verna,* carrying on the 800-year-old tradition of the 3 PM procession, 4 PM mass, and 6 PM singing of vespers. The monks also maintain a modern but modest *foresteria* (quarters with accommodations for visitors); inexpensive, modest, clean rooms are available, and the price includes three obligatory meals (good and honest fare, and there really is no other place to eat). It's open year-round. To reserve a room, contact the *Santuario della Verna* (Chiusi della Verna 52010; phone: 575-599356, general information; 575-599357, price information; fax: 575-599320).

Camaldoli, the oldest monastic center in all Tuscany, can be reached from La Verna by a pine-shaded road (about a 20-mile/32-km drive) or by returning to Bibbiena and there taking S71 north (from Serravalle, follow signs to Camaldoli). What functions as the monastery today was founded in the 11th century as the *foresteria* for pilgrims visiting the renowned *Eremo* (Hermitage) of the Camaldolese division of Benedictine monks, another mile (1.6 km) up the road. Gradually, it turned into a monastery itself and was a famed center of learning during the Renaissance—Giuliano and Lorenzo de' Medici used to meet here to discuss classical texts and philosophy with Marsilio Ficino, Leon Battista Alberti, and other 15th-century intellectuals. The monastery has an interesting 16th-century pharmacy with the original cabinets and ceramic containers, and it still sells the herbal panaceas for which the monks have always been known. It also has its original 11th-century *Hospitium Camalduli* for receiving guests—90 simple, clean, inexpensive renovated rooms, some with baths. (Unlike *La Verna,* which participates in retreats, the tiny town features two good, modest restaurants.) For reservations, contact the *Monastero di Camaldoli* (*Foresteria,* Camaldoli 52010; phone: 575-556013). The *Eremo,* where the monks still live in seclusion under the Benedictine rule, is also open to the public. Founded in 1012 by St. Romualdo, it consists of 20 isolated, single cells, each with a sleeping area, study, and small outdoor garden.

Return to Bibbiena and take S70 north to Poppi, where a quick slip through the Old Town will be of interest. Medieval home of the powerful Guidi counts, who ruled the Casentino from the 11th to the 14th century, Poppi has a superb castle (now the *Palazzo Pretorio*) with a small but elaborate courtyard and a tower offering sweeping views of all that was once the Guidi domain. From Poppi, bear west on S70, up and over the Passo di Consuma, and then, after about 7 miles (11 km), turn left at the signs for Pelago and Vallombrosa. The latter, an ancient fir forest between the Casentino Valley to the east and the Valdarno to the west, is a traditional summer escape for Florentines and the site of another ancient monastery, the seat of the Vallombrosian division of the Benedictines. The monastery dates from 1230, although the nucleus of monks founded by St. Giovanni Gualberto goes back to the year 1000. The body of buildings has undergone changes over time, but the 13th-century campanile and a 15th-century dungeon still exist. Nearby Saltino has a number of good restaurants and hotels, some with open vistas over the valley below.

To return to Florence, head south toward Reggello and then west to Leccio.

Elba

Whether a visitor chooses to relax on the more than 50 wonderful beaches along 90 miles of coastline, to climb and picnic in forests on rugged mountains, to hike inland roads with breathtaking views of the sea and wooded slopes, or to drive along spectacular coastal roads, it's hard to miss Elba's natural charm, Tuscan hospitality, and timeless beauty.

Five and a half miles from the mainland, Elba is just difficult enough to reach, and sufficiently out of the way, to deter hordes of package tour travelers—except in July and August. (Many posh pleasure boats from the nearby Argentario Peninsula yacht basin make port at Elba during this time as well.) Travelers who come by ferry from Piombino—or by plane from Pisa—find the journey well worth the effort. They tend to come back again and again, preferring Elba's quiet dignity to the more fashionable vacation spots along the frenetic Mediterranean-Ligurian coastline.

Called Ilva by the Ligurians and Aethalia ("Smoky Place") by the Greeks, Elba passed from the Etruscans to become part of the Roman Empire. It was ruled by the Pisans during the Middle Ages and served as a haven for the Barbary pirates in the 16th century. The Medicis also left their mark—their influence can be seen in the fortifications of Portoferraio, built after Cosimo I de' Medici bought Elba in the 16th century.

The island also was influenced by Napoleon Bonaparte, who reigned over Elba during his first exile from France in 1814. Although he lived here less than a year, the emperor did much to improve the island, altering street plans and building new roads, modernizing agriculture, and developing the iron mines once used by the Etruscans. His summer home, the *Villa di San Martino,* can be visited, and the hardy can climb the hillside beyond to the island's oldest fortress, *Volterraio;* situated atop the ruins of an Etruscan temple, it is also the place where residents once gathered to protect themselves from the notorious pirates Barbarossa and Dragut.

A limited amount of iron ore is still mined in the hills above Rio Marina and then shipped from Portoferraio ("Port of Iron") exactly as it was in the age of the Etruscans, part of whose fortunes in central Italy derived from these very mines. With 11,500 inhabitants, Portoferraio is the largest of the island's eight towns, and it's considered the "capital." More than 150 minerals and semi-precious stones can be found in Elban soil, the result of the seismic turmoil that created the island, and there are more varieties of granite here than anywhere in Europe. The astonishing range of colors of the island's hydrangeas is due to the soil's rich mineral composition.

Elba bathes in sunshine most of the year. It is small but dramatic, with 3,000-foot-high mountains that create an east-west wind break from the prevailing scirocco, which brings hot air and sometimes dust from Africa, and the *maestrale,* which blows cool air south from the Alps. As a result of its peculiar formation, the eastern and northern parts of the island tend to be green and wooded, while the west is rocky, barren, and striking, and the south is buff-colored and sandy.

The island is shaped like a fish, and Portoferraio's pretty port, marked by the stout ancient ramparts of the *Fortezze Medicee,* is tucked within the underside of the top fin. In ancient times Elba had just two important towns, both set on high hills well inland because of the frequent incursions by pirates—Marciana (where the eye of the fish would be) and Rio nell'Elba (at the center of the tail). Both tiny, gracious towns, whose somber medieval cast is enlivened by today's lush gardens, the many restored homes and general air of prosperity are only a half-hour drive from the splendid coastline.

The high season begins around *Easter,* when the sea begins to warm and the island bursts into bloom—daisies, broom, and other wildflowers cover the hills crowned with pine, beech, chestnut, and ilex trees, and potted geraniums, bougainvilleas, roses, and hydrangeas brighten every doorstep and windowsill. It ends in mid-October, when the smell of autumn is in the air and many hotels close for the winter. Swimming is possible from mid-May through September. In summer rain seldom lasts more than a day or two.

For all the bustle of summer tourism, farm life, which is regulated by the seasons, has its own rural charm. Every town and village has its own well-cared-for *bocce* court, where the traditional game is played almost every evening. The grass on the airport runway is kept trimmed by flocks of sheep and goats from a nearby farm that produces some extraordinary fresh ricotta cheese. At night the lights of the island's fishing boats can be seen bobbing up and down at sea; in the morning their catch—swordfish, cuttlefish, clams, mussels, prawns, and small spiny lobsters—is displayed in ice-filled boxes on marble slabs at the market.

Whatever a visitor fancies, from beaches to scenic drives to mountain hikes, this relatively undeveloped vacation paradise delivers.

Note that some sites of interest on Elba close for a midday break, usually from 1 or 2 PM to anywhere from 3 to 5 PM; we suggest calling ahead to check exact hours.

TOURIST INFORMATION

Numerous free guides, including lists of hotels and restaurants, are available from the *Azienda Autonoma di Soggiorno Cura e Turismo dell'Isola d'Elba* (26 Calata Italia, Portoferraio; phone: 914671; fax: 916350), which serves the entire island. Information also is available from the following sources: In Portoferraio: *Aethaltour* (30 Calata Italia; phone: 917148); *Centro Guide Isole d'Elba* (171 Viale Elba; phone: 933017 or 914818); *Agenzia Viaggi TESI* (Calata Italia; phone: 930222); and *Ilva Viaggi e Turismo* (20 Calata Italia; phone: 915555; fax: 917865); in Marino di Campo: *Ufficio Turistico CIPAT* (Via Mascagni; phone: 977766); in Procchio: *Agenzia Viaggi*

Bruno (Via Provinciale; phone: 907380); in Marciana Marina: *Brauntour* (2 Via Mentana; phone: 996874); in Rio Marina: *Forti* (25 Via Palestro; phone: 924087); in Cavo: *Estelba* (phone: 949934). The offices generally are open weekdays from 9 AM to 1 PM.

TELEPHONE The area code for the entire island is 565. When calling from within Italy, dial 0565 before the local number.

GETTING AROUND

Traveling to and around Elba often sounds more difficult than it really is. Transportation and route depend only on personal preference and available time.

AIR The closest international airport is in Pisa. There is a small airport at Marina di Campo on the southern part of the island near the coast (phone: 976008), but you'll have to fly on a regularly scheduled flight from Pisa or on a charter. *Alitalia* operates daily flights to Pisa from Rome, Milan, Turin, Sicily, and Sardinia, and there are daily flights to Pisa from other European cities such as London, Frankfurt, and Paris. From Pisa, Bologna, Bergamo, and Florence, *International Flying Services* (phone: 565-977938 or 35-311255) has connections to Elba from June through early September; reserve through *Alitalia* or the small airline itself.

BOAT EXCURSIONS Regular excursions around the island operate from Portoferraio throughout the summer; inquire at the main tourist agencies (see *Tourist Information,* above), hotels, or the principal bar on the waterfront. A few excursions operate from Porto Azzurro as well; contact *Agenzia Mantica* (at the port; phone: 95351) for information.

BUS All Elba's towns are connected by bus. The main station in Portoferraio is next to the *Grattacielo,* Elba's 10-story "skyscraper." Pick up a schedule at *ATL*'s office (20 Viale Elba, Portoferraio; phone: 914392).

CAR RENTAL Rent cars at Pisa's airport from any of the major international firms represented there. The drive from Pisa to Piombino takes about two hours. There also are several major car rental agencies at the ferry terminal in Piombino. On all but weekdays in May, June, September, and October, you *must* have reservations to put your car on any of the ferries (see *Ferry,* below); make them through most travel agents.

Cars also can be rented on Elba. The main agencies in Portoferraio are *Maggiore Autonoleggio* (8 Calata Italia; phone: 930222); *Happy Rent* (Viale Elba; phone: 914665); and *Segnini* (Calata Italia; phone: 916374). Arrange to have a car meet you at the ferry in Portoferraio or at the airport. Renting on the island is more expensive than on the mainland.

FERRY Ferries travel from Piombino to Portoferraio and vice versa about every 50 minutes from 5:30 AM to 9:30 PM in July and August (reserve in advance). Departures during other months are less frequent and more variable; inquire directly from the ferry companies (see below). All ferries accept cars and caravans; the journey takes an hour. Some ferries go to Cavo, Rio Marino, and Porto Azzurro as well. The hydrofoil, for foot passengers only, takes half an hour; it operates between Piombino and Portoferraio.

Toremar has six offices: 4 Via Calafati, Livorno (phone: 586-896113); 22 Calata Italia, Portoferraio (phone: 918080); 13-14 Piazzale Premuda, Piombino (phone: 565-31100); 9 Banchina dei Voltoni, Rio Marina (phone: 962073); Banchina IV Novembre, Porto Azzurro (phone: 95004); and 114 Via Appalto, Cavo (phone: 949871). *Navarma* can be found at two locations: 13 Piazzale Premuda, Piombino (phone: 565-221212), and 4 Viale Elba, Portoferraio (phone: 914133 or 918101). *Moby Lines* (4 Via Elba, Portoferraio; phone: 9361; fax: 916758) runs efficient, frequent, clean, and regular service between Piombino and Portoferraio. *Elba Ferries* (phone: 565-220956, Piombino; 930676, Portoferraio) operates between the same two towns.

GUIDED TOURS The main travel agencies offer a number of half- and whole-day guided tours. Obtain details in Portoferraio from *Aethaltour* (30 Calata Italia; phone: 917148) or *Intourelba* (1 Via Tesei; phone: 917236; fax: 500467). There also is a guides' association (171 Viale Elba; phone: 933017 or 914818). For an individual guided tour in English, contact the *Gruppo Guide Turistiche* (188 Casella Postale, Portoferraio; phone: 914224).

MOPED AND BIKE RENTAL Either is a good alternative to a car for day trips. *Brandi* (11 Via Manganaro, Portoferraio; phone: 914359) and *TWN* (phone: 914666) rent mountain bikes, mopeds, and motorcycles. *TWN*'s Portoferraio office is on Viale Elba, by the bus terminal; it also has branches in Marina di Campo, Lacona, Porto Azzurro, and Marciana Marina.

TAXI Call *Molo Massimo* (phone: 915212).

TRAIN There are no trains on Elba, but to reach Piombino (and the ferries) by train, take the main rail line that runs along the west coast of Italy and get off at Campiglia Marittima. From Campiglia Marittima a branch line runs 9 miles (14 km) to Piombino Marittima, its quayside terminus. Leave plenty of time, and get off at the third stop in the town of Piombino. In summer several trains run daily.

SPECIAL EVENTS

Easter is a special time on Elba, although tourist services are quite limited during that period. On *Good Friday* evening young men carry the cross and an effigy of Christ through village streets, while others in the procession sing Gregorian chants. Early on *Easter* morning villagers from Sant'Ilario and San Piero, hill towns above Marina di Campo, meet in procession on the way to worship in each other's churches. On *Easter Monday* worshipers make a pilgrimage to the *Santuario della Madonna del Monte* (Shrine of the Madonna del Monte) above Marciana and, on

Ascension Thursday, to the *Santuario di Santa Lucia* (Shrine of Saint Lucia) outside Portoferraio. A mass for Napoleon is celebrated annually on May 5 in Portoferraio.

On August 12 the island celebrates the *Festa di Santa Chiara,* the patron saint of Marciana Marina, with a religious procession, dancing in the piazza, and fireworks. Celebrations, which start in the evening, go on until the early hours. Similar rites are held on August 7 for San Gaetano in Marina di Campo. On August 16 San Rocco is feted with a rowboat competition with rowers in folkloric costumes, followed by a free meal of grilled sardines and wine served in the main piazza at Rio Marina.

SPORTS AND FITNESS

Summer brings myriad competitions, including boat races, tennis matches, and water skiing and windsurfing championships, all with vacationers in mind. In general water sports are the most popular; equipment can be rented at most large beaches.

BEACHES Elba has a variety of wonderful beaches, some sandy and safe for swimmers and waders, others rocky and suitable for deep diving. The best sandy beaches on the north coast are Spartaia, Procchio, Campo all'Aia, La Biodola, and Scaglieri; on the south coast, try Golfe Stella, Lacona, Marina di Campo, Cavoli, Fetovaia, or Seccheto (sand and rock); on the east coast go to Barbarossa Reale, Cavo (sand and rock), the Calamita Peninsula, Naregno, Pareti, Morcone, or Straccoligno. Usually, hotels and bars near the beaches own concessions for deck chairs, umbrellas, changing cabins, and toilets; charges are by the day or week. During the high season deck chairs at popular beaches are reserved months in advance by regular residents.

BOATING For rentals, contact *Corsi* (Località Magazzini; phone: 933396) or the *Agenzia Viaggi TESI* (see *Tourist Information*) in Portoferraio, or *Circolo della Vela* (phone: 99027) in Marciana Marina.

FISHING Both underwater and by boat, fishing is free except in the protected area between Le Ghiaie pebble beach at Portoferraio and the submarine nature reserve at Capo Bianco. Inquire at your hotel or at the waterfront. The village of Chiessi is a favorite base for spear fishers.

GOLF The *Acquabona Golf* hotel has a beautifully situated, well-maintained, nine-hole course inland on the main road between Portoferraio and Acquabona (phone: 960064).

HORSEBACK RIDING To make arrangements, contact *Paolo Rossi Fattoria* (Località Buraccio, between Portoferraio and Porto Azzurro; phone: 940245) or *Azienda Agricola Sapere* (Località Mola, Porto Azzurro; phone: 95033).

SAILING For lessons in Portoferraio, contact the *Segal Club Elba* (Località Magazzini; phone: 933176); *Casa di Vela* (50 Schiopparello Spiaggia; phone:

933265); or *Le Grotte del Paradiso* (Località Le Grotte; phone: 933329); in Marciana Marina, contact the *Circolo della Vela* (phone: 99027).

SKIN DIVING Elban waters are wonderful for skin diving, especially along the rocky northwest and west coasts and also along the east coast of the Calamita Peninsula, which is accessible only by boat. The fishing village of Chiessi is a favorite base. Fill oxygen tanks at the *Enfola* campsite (phone: 915390) and at *Armeria Elbana* (phone: 914770). In Marciana Marina the *Centro Sub* (15 Via Aldo Moro; phone: 904256) offers courses in diving and underwater photography. It also rents boats to groups.

TENNIS It is hard to find courts near the beaches because of the steep terrain. Many hotels, however, have floodlit courts. In and around Portoferraio non-guests may sometimes be able to play at the *Park Hotel Napoleone* (Località San Martino; phone: 916973); the *Hermitage* (Località Biodola; phone: 969932); *Le Grotte del Paradiso* (Località Acquabona; phone: 933057); *Picchiaie Residence* (Località Picchiaie; phone: 933072); *Galletti Fabrizio* (Località Schiopparello; phone: 933017); or *Fabricia* (Località Magazzini; phone: 933181).

WINDSURFING The *Elba Windsurfing School* is headquartered at *La Perla* hotel in Procchio (phone: 907371). In Marina di Campo *La Foce* campground has a school (phone: 976456), and there is another at Tropical beach (phone: 97006). The *Yachting Segel Club* is at Località Magazzini, Portoferraio (phone: 933176).

NIGHTCLUBS AND NIGHTLIFE

Discos and nightclubs dot the island, and almost every Friday, Saturday, and Sunday evening one village or another has dancing in the open air. Indoor entertainment in Portoferraio is best at *Norman's Club* (Località Capannone; phone: 969943); *Club 64* (Località Capannone; phone: 969988); *Moulin Rouge* (Via delle Conserve; phone: 918400); and the *Music Bar* (Via Provinciale; phone: 915432). However, the favorite Elban evening pursuit is definitely *bocce,* the Italian version of French *boules.* The game is played with great fun and seriousness, and each town has lighted courts.

FOOD AND WINE

Elba offers an unusual combination of food—the fresh seafood dishes typical of a Mediterranean island plus the hearty peasant fare of the bountiful Tuscan farmland. Seafood dishes include *cacciucco* (a bouillabaisse-like soup), and *gamberi* (prawns) and *polpi* (octopus) served in many ways. Fish offerings include *dentice* (sea bream), *nasello* (whiting), and *triglia* (red mullet). A tradition of *cucina casalinga* (home cooking) combines pasta, often handmade, with wonderful fish and shellfish—*alla margherita* (with spider crab), *all'aragosta* (with lobster), or *alle seppie* (with cuttlefish). More familiar is spaghetti with fish sauce, *alle vongole* (with tiny clams), or *al pesto. Gurguglione* is a tasty vegetable soup. *Cinghiale* (wild boar) may also appear on the menu. *Focaccia di pignoli* (a flat cake studded with pine nuts) is typical of Portoferraio. Don't be bashful about having the waiter explain the many dialectical names for foods.

Colorful outdoor markets—food, household goods, and clothing—are held in Rio Marina on Mondays, Marciana Marina on Tuesdays, Marina di Campo on Wednesdays, Procchio and Copliveri on Thursdays, Portoferraio (Piazza della Repubblica) on Fridays, and Porto Azzurro on Saturdays.

The island produces a variety of pleasant table wines—white, red, rosé, and sparkling—and several dessert wines. Of the former, the white is outstanding; try the procanico and Elba bianco. A favorite red is sangiaveto. Moscato and aleatico dessert wines are delicious served with fresh fruit or with cookies called *crostate*. If you have a special interest in wines, drive to Marciana Marina to visit the bar-tasting platform at the end of the Lungo Mare. While on that side of the island, drive a little farther toward Poggio and taste the local brandy. Near Portoferraio is a century-old wine estate, *La Chiusa,* run by Giuliana Foresi, a top producer of the prized aleatico, which visitors can sample and purchase there. Another Elba specialty is its bracing white grappa, an after-dinner drink.

TOURING ELBA

Roads on tiny Elba are quite good, so it's easy to drive around it in just a day. With this in mind, choose accommodations from the variety of resorts, and explore from one base. For the sea lover there is every kind of beach and aquatic facility. Inland the mountains offer a completely different experience, even though they are only a mile or two from the beaches.

In general costs on the island are about 10% lower than on the mainland, but as everywhere, seafood can be expensive. Elba has relatively few restaurants, because most hotels require guests to take at least half board. Even in the more expensive hotels, full board costs little more, making it perhaps the wisest choice. The price ranges listed below are for high season (officially mid-June to mid-September); some hotels offer savings of up to 40% for bookings in late May or early October. Hotels rated as expensive charge $240 or more per night for a double room; moderate, from $120 to $230; and inexpensive, $110 or less. Most hotels open after *Easter* and shut down in late October. Their prices rise month by month, peaking in July and August. All hotels feature air conditioning, private baths, TV sets, and telephones unless otherwise indicated. A dinner for two, including wine and tip, in a restaurant rated as expensive costs from $120 to $150; moderate, from $60 to $110; and inexpensive, $50 or less. All restaurants are open for lunch and dinner unless otherwise noted. For each location hotels and restaurants are listed alphabetically by price category.

PORTOFERRAIO Well worth exploring, Elba's "capital" is recommended as a base during the off-season, when many resort hotels elsewhere on the island close. It lies on the northwest promontory at the entrance to Portoferraio

Bay. Walk from the harbor through the walled arches (stopping for a treat at the *gelateria*), and continue onward and upward along beautiful, steep streets flanked by yellow houses. On Via Garibaldi, the main street, is the *Palazzo Comunale* (Town Hall), the boyhood home of Victor Hugo. To the northeast, on Via Napoleone, is the *Chiesa della Misericordia;* mass is said here every May 5 for Napoleon. Continue to the highest point in town, Piazza Napoleone, for spectacular views: To the west is *Forte del Falcone;* to the east, above the lighthouse, *Forte della Stella.* Both were originally Medici fortresses, built in 1548 and later completed by Napoleon. On the ridge between the two lies the *Villa dei Mulini* (made from two older windmills that were joined together; phone: 915846), which was Napoleon's principal residence; it has a pretty garden and contains his library and other memorabilia. It's closed Mondays and Sunday afternoons; admission charge includes entry to his country residence, the *Villa di San Martino* (see *En Route from Portoferraio*).

If markets intrigue you, stop by *Galleaze,* the covered one in Piazza Cavour; it is open weekday mornings. There also is a bustling open-air market in Piazza della Repubblica on Friday mornings. Local craftspeople are centered in Portoferraio, and several shops sell their wares. The headquarters for the *National Confederation of Craftsmen (CNA)* is at 64 Via Manganaro (phone: 917485). *Terra e Mano* (2 Via G. Marconi) is the workshop and showroom for Oreste May's elegant modern ceramic plates and pots with tasteful designs. For a wide selection of rock crystals and Tuscan stones, some for collectors, others worked into jewelry and gift items, stop by *Cosebelle* (Piazza del Popolo and Calata Mazzini) or its factory and showroom (Località Antiche Saline). Works also are made on commission. *Enoteca la Botte* (Via Guerrazzi) in the downtown area sells Elban wines by the case (and will deliver to yachts). Visitors are welcome to a free tasting at one of the shop's handful of tables. Snacks, sandwiches, and wine by the glass are available, as are other traditional products such as the island's beloved *schiaccio di Rio Marino* (dry tea cake). Most shops are open from 10 AM to 1 PM and 5 to 7:30 PM; food and wine stores are open from 8:30 AM to 1 PM and 5 to 7:30 PM; closed Sundays.

To view an interesting collection of ancient prehistoric, Etruscan, and Roman artifacts, visit the *Museo Civico Archeologico* (*Fortezza della Linguella;* phone: 917338). It's closed Sundays, and Mondays through Saturdays for a long (12:30 to 4 PM) break, September through June; closed Sundays, and Mondays through Saturdays for a longer (1 to 6 PM) break, July and August; admission charge.

BEST EN ROUTE

Park Hotel Napoleone Turn-of-the-century elegance is found in this 64-room hotel on a wooded hillside, five minutes from the port. There also is a restaurant, a meeting room, two tennis courts, miniature golf, mountain bikes for rent, and a minibus to the beach. A riding stable is nearby. Open *Easter* through October. San Martino di Portoferraio, Portoferraio (phone: 918502; fax: 917836). Expensive to moderate.

La Barca The locals say this is the best eatery in town. The wood-burning oven turns out delicious fish baked in paper. Located downtown, this friendly trattoria is cozy inside and offers a few tables outdoors. Closed Wednesdays in winter. Reservations necessary. Major credit cards accepted. Via Guerrazzi, Portoferraio (phone: 918036). Moderate.

Crystal Close to the beach, with 15 rooms, it is located on a thoroughfare, but all the guestrooms are soundproof. The front rooms have terraces with good sea views. No restaurant. Closed November. Località Le Ghiaie (phone: 917971; fax: 918772). Moderate.

Al Solito Posto The seafood dishes in this charming eatery include *antipasto di mare* and baked fish; desserts are white or dark chocolate mousse. Veal saddle à la Orloff is a house specialty. Closed Thursdays, January, and February. Reservations necessary. Major credit cards accepted. Via Carducci, Portoferraio (phone: 916238). Moderate.

Acqua Marina Some of the 36 rooms in this agreeable bed and breakfast establishment have balconies overlooking a splendid bay; none has a TV or air conditioning. No restaurant. Open March through October. Località Padulella, Portoferraio (phone: 914057). Inexpensive.

Ape Elbana An older building in downtown Portoferraio, it has a wide verandah, 24 comfortable rooms (all but one has a private bath, none has a TV), a homey restaurant, and an Old World charm, although with a bit of the shabby about it. Hotel open year-round; restaurant closed November through March. No credit cards accepted. 2 Salita Cosimo de' Medici, Portoferraio (phone: 914245). Inexpensive.

La Ferrigna The best-known restaurant in Portoferraio specializes in Elban cookery. Try the prawns, risotto with squid, or stuffed zucchini. Closed Tuesdays in low season, two weeks in November, and January through February. Reservations advised. Major credit cards accepted. 22-23 Piazza della Repubblica, Portoferraio (phone: 914129). Inexpensive.

Villa Ombrosa Close to both Portoferraio and a lovely beach, this charming hostelry has its own restaurant. All but three of the 47 rooms have private baths. Ask for a front room with a balcony. Open year-round. 3 Viale de Gasperi, Portoferraio (phone: 914363). Inexpensive.

En Route from Portoferraio The *Villa di San Martino* (Località San Martino; phone: 914688), Napoleon's summer residence, lies 1 mile (1.6 km) south of Portoferraio on a hill overlooking the sea. Although Napoleon lived here only a few months before his departure for the Hundred Days, the villa houses his personal library and a statue of Pauline, his sister. Above all, it's imbued with his mystique. The central room is decorated with trompe l'oeil paintings depicting the Egyptian campaign. On one wall the emperor's graffito, "Napoleon is happy everywhere," is still legible. The villa is closed Mondays and Sunday and holiday afternoons; the *palazzina* is closed Tuesdays. A combined visit on a single ticket is possible Wednesdays through Sundays. Museum hours and days are subject to change, so check first.

BIODOLA West of Portoferraio toward Procchio, Biodola is one of the most beautiful resort areas on Elba's north coast. Boasting a broad, sandy beach, it is set well off the road.

BEST EN ROUTE

La Biodola Favored by a loyal clientele, this place has 76 tastefully decorated rooms overlooking the magnificent bay, a restaurant, a seawater pool in a lovely, landscaped garden, eight tennis courts, volleyball, windsurfing, boat rentals, and a beginner's golf course. Open April through September. Golfo della Biodola, Biodola (phone: 936811). Expensive.

Hermitage The pride of the island, this elegant, modernized luxury hotel is tucked into a corner of Biodola Bay. Accommodations include 123 guestrooms, as well as cottages on the steep, wooded slopes overlooking the bay. There are two pools, a private beach, a garden, eight tennis courts, a six-hole golf course, a fine restaurant with attentive waiters and a sophisticated menu, and a dining spot on the beach. Open April through October. Golfo della Biodola, Biodola (phone: 936911). Expensive.

Casa Rosa Neat and unpretentious, this hotel overlooks Biodola Bay. It has a good dining room, a pool, and a pleasant garden. None of the 35 rooms has a TV or air conditioning. Open *Easter* through October. No credit cards accepted. Località Biodola (phone: 969919). Inexpensive.

En Route from the Portoferraio Bay Area Bordering the bay, 3 miles (5 km) southeast of Portoferraio at Località Antiche Saline, are the pleasant, modern *Terme San Giovanni* (phone: 914680), specializing in medicinal mud baths for the treatment of arthritis, cellulitis, rheumatism, and sinusitis.

The wooded foothills in this area lead to the low mountain range of the central section of Elba. The road then climbs in sharp curves to the promontory of Punta delle Grotte. An open gateway to the left leads to the remains of the tremendous *Villa Romana,* thought to have been built during the reign of Emperor Augustus. The view across the bay to Portoferraio is lovely, and what has been excavated of the villa is easily explored.

From Portoferraio follow the coastal road east around the bay; after Magazzini turn right and take the road signposted Rio nell'Elba for 9 miles

(14 km) to Volterraio. Volterraio's fortress, probably constructed in the 13th century by the Pisans, is perched high on the hillside, dominating the skyline. Park halfway up the hill and take the footpath. The rugged climb takes about 45 minutes, but the breathtaking views and the grandeur of the fortress, with its ruined walls and fig trees growing wild in the courtyards, make it well worth the effort.

BEST EN ROUTE

Villa Ottone Less than 2 miles (3 km) southeast of Portoferraio on Portoferraio Bay, this old-fashioned, 64-room hostelry is known for its sailing school. It also has a large garden, a restaurant, a private beach, a windsurfing school, and lighted tennis courts. Open April through September. Ottone (phone: 933042; fax: 933257). Expensive.

Garden Overlooking the bay from pretty, pine-shaded grounds, it has 51 rooms (none has a TV), a sailing school, and its own sand and gravel beach, but no restaurant. Open *Easter* through October. No credit cards accepted. Schiopparello (phone: 933043). Moderate.

RIO MARINA There are many different minerals to be found on Elba, and it is easy to collect samples while exploring the island. Most indigenous minerals are also for sale at the stalls in the open market in Rio Marina. (*Note:* The ropes of rock necklaces sold to tourists usually are made from gemstones imported from Africa. Most Elban rocks are too soft for polishing.) Rio Marina also has a small mineral museum in the *Palazzo Comunale* (Via Principe Amedeo, Third Floor; phone: 962747). It is closed October through March, Sunday afternoons, and for a midday break; admission charge. North of Rio Marina is Cavo, an old mining town where evidence of Etruscan iron smelting has turned up at the shoreline (and quickly disappears into private collections) and in the mining district.

BEST EN ROUTE

Rio This attractive hotel has a restaurant overlooking the harbor. The 37 rooms have no TV sets. Open April through September. 31 Via Palestro, Rio Marina (phone: 962722). Moderate.

Dal Moro The seafood here is served by a cozy fireplace on chilly evenings or at outdoor tables on warm days. Closed Wednesdays and *Christmas* week. Reservations necessary in summer. Major credit cards accepted. 3 Via Traversa, Rio Marina (phone: 962448). Moderate to inexpensive.

Mini Hotel Easy Time On a steep hill overlooking a magnificent bay, this hotel is just a few minutes' walk from town. Four of the eight rooms have small terraces with views; none has a TV set. Its restaurant is open to hotel guests only. Open year-round. Via Porticciolo, Rio Marino (phone: 962531). Inexpensive.

PORTO AZZURRO Originally called Porto Longone, this small town is the southern terminus of the ferry lines. The main life revolves around the harbor, which usually is full of yachts and fishing boats. During high season, day-long excursions to the island of Montecristo are possible (see *Boat Excursions,* above). Shops selling Tuscan minerals include *Age* (Località Pianetto) and *Giannini* (2 Via Italia).

BEST EN ROUTE

Cala di Mola Overlooking the estuary just outside Porto Azzurro harbor, this attractive hotel has a well-appointed restaurant and public rooms, beautiful gardens, and a double pool. There are no TV sets or air conditioning in the 41 rooms. Open May through September. No credit cards accepted. Mola (phone: 95225). Moderate.

La Lanterna Risotto pirate-style (with fish), *cacciucco* (fish soup), and other fish specialties are served at this trattoria with a terrace overlooking the sea. There also are a few guestrooms. Open daily in season. Reservations necessary. Major credit cards accepted. Porto Azzurro (phone: 95026). Moderate.

CAPOLIVERI An ancient town dating from the Roman occupation, Capoliveri enjoys a position 500 feet above sea level, which affords spectacular views.

BEST EN ROUTE

Il Chiasso Considered one of the island's top restaurants, this eccentric eatery is known for its shellfish soup, spaghetti with anchovies and pine nuts, roast kid in yogurt, and whole fresh fish baked in parchment. There's alfresco dining in summer. Closed Tuesdays in winter and January to *Easter* week. Reservations advised. Major credit cards accepted. 20 Via Nazario Sauro, Capoliveri (phone: 968709). Expensive to moderate.

En Route from Capoliveri Follow the coastline 7½ miles (12 km) along the low wooded cliffs down to the plain of Lacona, an area popular with campers. This leads to the principal bays of the south coast: Golfe Stella, which has two main sandy beaches, Lido and Margidore; and Golfo della Lacona, a tremendous, wide, sandy beach with very good, well-run campsites nestled among the trees.

BEST EN ROUTE

Lacona Large (128 rooms), modern, and only 300 feet from the sea, it has its own stretch of beach, a pool, two tennis courts, and a restaurant. Open May through early October. Lacona (phone: 964054). Expensive to moderate.

Antares This hostelry overlooking Golfe Stella features a restaurant and access to the beach. None of the 43 rooms has a TV set. Open mid-March through September. Lido di Capoliveri (phone: 940131; fax: 940084). Moderate.

Da Gianni One of the best seafood restaurants on the island is near the airport, only 1½ miles (2 km) from Marina di Campo. Owner Gianni is from the Puglia, and his great specialty is risotto with clams, mussels, and other shellfish in a rich wine-based stock, but some think the delectable baked mussels are his real pièce de résistance. Closed October to mid-March. Reservations advised. Major credit cards accepted. La Pila (phone: 976965). Moderate to inexpensive.

MARINA DI CAMPO Lively and pretty, Marina di Campo is a good base for expeditions. Stroll around or sit at a little bar and watch the fishing boats in the harbor. Some Elban enthusiasts feel it is the best place to stay on the island; accordingly, there are many good hotels along or near the excellent sandy beach. Market day is Wednesday.

BEST EN ROUTE

Montecristo Named for the island due south, this is the best place in town, with 43 rooms. Situated on the beach, it has a restaurant, a pool, and excellent service. Open April through October. 11 Via Nomellini, Marina di Campo (phone: 976861 or 976782). Expensive.

La Triglia Authentic Elban cuisine, including very good fish. Closed Thursdays and November to mid-February. Reservations advised. Major credit cards accepted. Via Roma, Marina di Campo (phone: 976059). Expensive.

Bahia A cluster of whitewashed, tile-roofed cottages, each with a view, is nestled on a hillside of olive groves. There are 40 guestrooms (none with a TV) and a restaurant. It's a three-minute walk from a splendid beach. Open *Easter* through October. Località Cavoli, Marina di Campo (phone: 987055). Moderate.

Barcarola Seconda Very comfortable and close to the beach, here are 28 rooms (none with a TV), a restaurant, and a pretty garden. Open mid-April through October. Località San Mamiliano, Marina di Campo (phone: 976255). Moderate.

Bologna In the center of town, it offers a wide variety of consistently good food. Closed November to mid-April. Reservations advised. Major credit cards accepted. Via Case Nuove, Marina di Campo (phone: 976105). Moderate.

Dei Coralli A comfortable hotel on the edge of town, it has a pool, a tennis court, and a restaurant with good food and service. None of the 62 rooms has a TV set. Open June through September. 81 Via degli Etruschi, Marina di Campo (phone: 976336). Moderate to inexpensive.

Meridiana A pleasant 27-room hotel that's close to the beach and the pine belt on the edge of town. No TVs or restaurant. Open *Easter* through October. 69 Via degli Etruschi, Marina di Campo (phone: 976308). Moderate to inexpensive.

Villa Nettuno Adjoining the beach on the edge of town, this 32-room hostelry is set in the pine belt. There's no air conditioning or TVs in the rooms, but it does offer good service and a pleasant restaurant. Open mid-April through October. 30 Via degli Etruschi, Marina di Campo (phone: 976028). Inexpensive.

En Route from Marina di Campo Follow the main road north a little more than 1 mile (1.6 km) to a signposted intersection; turn right, and head 4 miles (6 km) to Sant'Ilario. This beautiful little town was an ancient village fortified in the 12th century, probably by the Pisans. A lovely walk around the outer walls affords spectacular views in every direction.

From Sant'Ilario take the main road out of the piazza west, then south, for 2½ miles (4 km). Bear right to visit the village of San Piero and the ruins of the large Romanesque *Chiesa di San Giovanni*. Nearby is the impressive watchtower, *Torre di San Giovanni*. From the top a sentry could see the whole of Campo Bay and often as far as the island of Pianosa. Take the road up to the main ridge behind Monte Perone; the stopping place here has excellent picnic areas and fabulous views in all directions.

Return to the main road and bear right for the village. San Piero is bigger than Sant'Ilario and even older, built on the site of a Roman colony. The *Chiesa di SS Pietro e Paolo* contains the remains of some 14th-century frescoes.

BEST EN ROUTE

La Cantina The best food in the area can be found on the typically Elban menu here (try the *menù degustazione*). Closed Tuesdays and November through March. Reservations advised. Major credit cards accepted. 21 Via Giovanni XXIII, La Pila (phone: 977200). Expensive to moderate.

MARCIANA Also called Marciana Alta, this is one of the oldest and prettiest villages on the island—it dates from Roman times. Like some other Elban towns, it was fortified in the 12th century by the Pisans. It is set high in the hills overlooking a steep valley full of vineyards and olive, chestnut, and fig trees. The minuscule *Museo Archeologico* (Via del Pretoria; phone: 901215) displays the island's early relics, from prehistoric times through the Roman era. The museum is closed (except by appointment) mid-October through mid-April; Wednesdays; Sundays after 1 PM; and the rest of the week for a short (2 to 3 PM) break; admission charge.

Just south of Marciana, cable cars ascend Monte Capanne, the highest point on Elba. Park and follow a path through the trees to the terminal. The cars run from mid-May to mid-September; they are closed in cloudy and windy weather. Quite primitive-looking, they rather resemble bird cages, but bravery is rewarded by the view from the top, which includes all of Elba and the coasts of mainland Italy and the island of Corsica.

The Fonte di Napoleone (Napoleon's Spring) lies just off the signposted road between Marciana and Poggio. Toward Poggio is the small factory where Elba's own very good mineral water, Acqua di Napoleone, is bottled.

BEST EN ROUTE

Da Luigi Beautifully set on the hillside outside Poggio, it's approached by an improbable track, but the food and the outdoor dining in summer are definitely worth the drama of getting here. The food and ambience are excellent—try the fresh gnocchi, the heavenly zucchini fritters, and the grilled lamb, chicken, or steaks. Closed Mondays. Reservations advised. Major credit cards accepted. Località Feno, Poggio (phone: 99413). Moderate.

Publius With a magical night view from its terrace overlooking the valley and bay, this country inn offers the island's best food and service. Try any of the *crostini* (toast covered with chicken liver pâté or olive or mushroom paste) and home-pickled wild mushrooms. Closed mid-November through mid-March. Reservations advised. Major credit cards accepted. 6 Piazza XX Settembre, Poggio (phone: 99208). Moderate.

MARCIANA MARINA A very pleasant seaside resort, Marciana Marina has an excellent harbor for yachts and small boats. Its wide waterfront promenade ends near the medieval watchtower, *Torre Saracena*.

BEST EN ROUTE

Gabbiano Azzurro Due An inland establishment with 21 rooms, an indoor pool, and a fitness center, it's nestled among the vineyards on the lower slopes of a hill near Poggio. No restaurant, but terrific service. Open year-round. 48 Viale Amedeo, Marciana Marina (phone: 997035; fax: 99497). Expensive. Its inexpensive annex, *Gabbiano Azzurro Uno,* has 39 rooms (phone: 99226).

Rendez-Vous da Marcello Dine very well on mussels, clams, crab, and lobster on the terrace at the water's edge. Other specialties are spaghetti *alla margherita* (with crab) and *crème caramel.* Closed Wednesdays in winter, January 10 to February 10, and November 10 to December 10. Reservations advised. Major credit cards accepted. Piazza della Vittoria, Marciana Marina (phone: 99251). Moderate.

La Primula Ideally located in the center, a short distance from the waterfront, this place is the best in town. There are 71 rooms and a restaurant. Open *Easter* through October. Viale Cerboni, Marciana Marina (phone: 99010; fax: 996819). Inexpensive.

En Route from Marciana Marina To return to the Portoferraio Bay area, take the signposted main road east along the coast to Procchio (another seaside village where accommodations are quite good) and Bivio Boni.

BEST EN ROUTE

Desirée On Spartaia cove, just west of Procchio, this place has its own sandy beach and sheltered harbor. The 75 secluded, comfortable bedrooms have private terraces. There is a restaurant. Open *Easter* through September. Località Spartaia, Procchio (phone: 907311). Expensive.

Del Golfo At the western end of a long, sandy beach, it has 102 rooms, a restaurant, gardens, a pool, and tennis courts. Open year-round. Procchio (phone: 907565). Expensive.

La Perla Close to the beach, this comfortable 51-room hotel offers a seaside buffet, tennis courts, windsurfing, and a pool. Open *Easter* through October. Via Provinciale, Procchio (phone: 907371). Expensive to moderate.

Lo Schioppo A pleasant restaurant off the main road on a quiet hillside, it serves good fish and shellfish. Closed for lunch, Tuesdays, and October through *Easter*. Reservations advised. Major credit cards accepted. Località lo Schioppo, between Procchio and Marciana Marina (phone: 99038). Expensive to moderate.

Umbria

It is often said that Umbria, the small, landlocked region that lies at the heart of the Italian peninsula, takes its name from *umbra*, the Latin word for shade. In fact, these hills, pitted with caves and mountain watersheds through which the mighty Tiber River passes, are lush and verdant, particularly in contrast to the arid and stony Abruzzo next door. More academic-minded travelers may point out that three of the ruling families in Umbria's Etruscan past had names—Umria, Umruna, and Umrana—that may have been taken to identify the region.

There is something soothing about this pleasant, humble region, and it may be characteristic that several of Christendom's most beloved saints were born here: St. Valentine, a 3rd-century Bishop of Terni, which is today an Umbrian industrial town; and St. Clare, founder of the Order of Poor Clares, are just two. Foremost among all the region's saints was Clare's friend, St. Francis of Assisi, founder of the Franciscans. Umbria's saints and their followers prayed in the mountain grottoes and preached in the cobbled streets and among the daisies and wild red poppies of the field. Their spirit pervades the Umbrian atmosphere today, just as the graceful abbeys of the orders they founded crown the green hilltops. Umbria's monastic orders left an indelible mark not only on the region but on the entire Western world.

Monasticism came to Western Europe from the deserts of the Middle East. The two worlds met in Umbria when a large number of Syrians migrated to live as hermits in the hills, spreading the concept of monastic life. St. Benedict, born in the Umbrian town of Norcia around 480, gave a Western imprint to the tradition of hermit prayer by adding the concept of work. Hence the Umbrian monks prayed, but they also farmed, studied, and copied manuscripts, maintaining a wondrous intellectual and social order that can be seen even in the tidy ledgers of abbey farm and vineyard holdings and the monks' treatises on agriculture displayed in the fascinating *Museo del Vino* at Torgiano, near Perugia. This Umbrian monasticism, with the work ethic it incorporated, spread throughout Italy and then throughout the West, carrying culture and stimulating commerce as it went.

This is not to portray Umbria as solely a clerical state. In fact, disobedience to the papacy became so serious at one point in 16th-century Perugia that Pope Paul III had to use troops to put down an uprising over a church-imposed salt tax (even today, the *perugini* use salt sparingly in cooking, and most bread in Umbria is baked without it). Many of the region's festivals hark back to pagan rites. Most famous is the *Festa di Calendimaggio* (Calendimaggio Festival) at Assisi, a romantic rite of spring. During the Middle Ages, young minstrels sang ballads and love songs in the streets; today, each April 29 to May 1, Assisi is illuminated by torches, decked with medieval flags, and populated by damsels and knights in sumptuous costume.

Nor is Umbria locked into its past. Every June and July, Spoleto plays host to the *Festival dei Due Mondi* (Festival of the Two Worlds), a panoply of international arts. Also renowned is the annual *Umbria Jazz,* a 10-day celebration in July that attracts some of the biggest names in jazz. It takes place in Perugia, Terni, and other locations.

In the beginning, the Umbri were a Villanovan tribe, believed by scholars to have reached Umbria from across the mountains around Bologna. Shepherds and farmers, the Umbri were soon pushed aside by the more sophisticated and aggressive Etruscans, who invaded from the Tyrrhenian coast. Perugia, for instance, a Villanovan settlement perched on a rocky stronghold that dominated the upper Tiber Valley, had already fallen to the Etruscans by the 5th century BC. The Etruscans considerably improved the region, teaching the illiterate Umbri an 18-letter alphabet, and their ambitious public works can be seen in the city walls and mighty arched gate at Perugia. They also left beautiful painted tombs at Orvieto.

The Romans, in turn, overwhelmed the Etruscans and the Umbri in 310 BC. Quintessential builders, they bequeathed an amphitheater at Assisi; a temple, a theater, and a high, many-arched bridge at Spoleto; and a theater and another bridge at Gubbio. Hostile Lombards from the Po Valley were next. With the fall of the Roman Empire, they won control of the region and set up the powerful duchy of Spoleto, which ruled much of Umbria from the 6th to the 11th century and became an important center for the arts.

The age of communes began in the 11th and 12th centuries, when Italy's city-states experimented with self-government. Umbria's chief communes—Perugia, Assisi, Foligno, Spoleto, Orvieto, Gubbio, and Città di Castello—are all fascinating for what they reveal about that era. True, they fought each other with dismaying regularity, allying themselves, as convenient, with one or another of the great powers, which in those days meant either Rome or Florence, pope or emperor. Geographically close to Rome, Umbria was perennially a tempting morsel for the papal powers.

During the late 14th and the 15th century, Umbria's cities were run by powerful noble families. In Perugia these *signori,* or lords, included two bitter rivals, the Oddi and Baglioni. The Trinci ruled in Foligno, the Gabrielli and later the Montefeltro in Gubbio, the Vitelli in Città di Castello, and the Orsini in Terni. Flanking them in the latter part of the period were war leaders called *condottieri,* whose presence possibly reflected the warrior tradition of the old Lombard dukes. When their power bids in Umbria failed, they did not hesitate to put themselves at the service of foreign rulers. Nevertheless, local autonomy came to an end in the 16th century. Perugia's bitter revolt against the pope's salt tax in 1540 was the last gasp, and when its leading city finally fell to the troops, the region passed definitively into the papal empire. Umbria then remained part of the Papal States until the 1860s.

Umbria's painters came into their own during the Renaissance. Giotto's frescoes of the life of St. Francis in the cathedral at Assisi marked a point of departure for painting in the West. Pietro Vannucci, who grew to fame as "Il Perugino," was born at Città della Pieve but worked in Perugia, where his lyrical works can be seen in the *Galleria Nazionale dell'Umbria*. He taught Raphael—Raffaello—to paint. Other great masters who worked in Umbria included Pinturicchio from Perugia, Piero della Francesca, and the architect Bramante. If, as in Tuscany, the landscape in Umbria has an awe-inspiring familiarity, it is because we have seen it before in the paintings in our museums.

Next to its artists, Umbria's artisans stand out. Besides weaving hand-loomed fabrics, embroidering, potting, and turning furniture, they are today celebrated for their fine wrought-iron work. For the value, prices of hand-spun linen and tablecloths or of finely decorated ceramic ware are reasonable, but visitors should not expect bargain-basement prices.

Umbrian food is more subtle than that of Rome and lighter than that of Tuscany. Satisfy a taste for *nuova cucina* elsewhere; specialties here include antipasto hams and salami from Norcia, served with pickled wild mushrooms; thin egg noodles tossed with grated black truffle and olive oil; fresh fish from a mountain stream or eel from Lake Trasimeno; wild game dishes; ewe's and goat's milk cheeses, delightfully unpasteurized; and fresh fruit or dried figs from the orchards that carpet the valleys. Dessert may include an almond *torta* in the form of a serpent, gaily decorated with sugar candies.

The olive is king in Umbrian cuisine. Some consider Umbrian olive oil, especially that produced around Spoleto, to be Italy's best. Soil conditions give it an especially low acid content, and Umbrians swear it is also lighter, or less fatty, than other oils. It is never better than when eaten on slices of *bruschetta* (crusty country bread toasted over an open fire, salted, and drenched with garlic). Another special Umbrian treat is the truffle. Five varieties, from white to gray to black and resembling small potatoes, grow wild in the woodlands, and local dogs are trained to retrieve them with rewards of chocolate. Three towns have truffle festivals: Terni, in June; Gubbio, in November; and most important, Norcia, in February. Olive oil is celebrated each February in a *festa* in Spello, with villagers dressed in local costume. Orvieto stages a wine show each May and June. A mushroom festival takes place at San Leo, near Città di Castello, in September, and a chestnut frolic, at which *marrons glacés* hold the place of honor, goes on at Preggio di Umbertide in October. There is even an onion festival at Cannara, near Assisi, in late September, when the village's best cooks show off their recipes.

Especially in wintertime, menus may include the tiny, tasty lentils grown in the high, wildflower-filled valley of Castelluccio, in the mountains above Norcia. A prized local salami, *mazzafegato,* is made of pork liver, pine nuts, raisins, sugar, and orange peel. *Castagnaccio* is a flat bread made of chestnut flour, seasoned with pine nuts, raisins, and fresh rosemary and served with a glass of dessert wine. Around the *Christmas* holidays comes *pan pepato*—"peppered bread"—a fruitcake of walnuts, almonds, raisins, chocolate, candied fruit, pine nuts, honey, "must" from the grapes, and ground black pepper.

Pliny the Elder was among those who have rhapsodized over the wines of Umbria, and well he might. Umbrian wines were so prized in the 15th century that Torgiano vintners pushed through laws severely punishing anyone doctoring Torgiano's wine or improperly using the label. Today, the region's wines include half a dozen fine DOC labels. Best known is the light, straw-colored orvieto; orvieto classico comes from grapes grown on the oldest wine estates, closest to the town of Orvieto. Torgiano comes red and white, as does the wine grown on the hills around Lake Trasimeno (Colli del Trasimeno). Montefalco is an especially prized red. The name Colli Altotiberini DOC specifies that these fine red, rosé, and white wines come from grapes grown on the hillsides facing the upper Tiber River Valley. Perugia's red, rosé, and white DOC wines are named Colli Perugini.

Our circuit of Umbria begins at Perugia, its capital, and passes through hilly, chestnut-wooded countryside interspersed with broad rolling valleys of olive groves and vineyards to Assisi, a hill town with a soft, saintly aura. The route loops southward to Spoleto, a jewel of a town, and then, rather than continue south to Terni (an industrial center with some historical monuments), cuts west and north to Todi, another small hill town with fine art and architecture. After Todi, a detour to Orvieto is strongly recommended; its cathedral should not be missed. The route goes to Deruta (for pottery browsing) and Torgiano (for the *Museo del Vino*) on its way back to Perugia; at the end, a side trip to Gubbio is suggested for those who have the time.

Hotels listed here as very expensive charge $185 or more per night for a double room; an expensive hotel will cost $115 to $185; moderate, $70 to $115; and inexpensive, $70 or less. All hotels feature private baths unless otherwise indicated. For longer stays, a pleasant alternative to hotels is renting a villa, often in a converted castle, olive mill, or farmhouse. (For information on US-based operators offering rentals in Italy, see GETTING READY TO GO.) In a restaurant listed as very expensive, expect to pay $170 or more for a meal for two; restaurants listed as expensive charge from $85 to $135; moderate places run from $55 to $85; and those listed as inexpensive charge from $35 to $55. Prices include wine. All restaurants are open for lunch and dinner unless otherwise noted. Note that in an especially popular place such as Spoleto, where fashionability strikes quickly, prices in any establishment rise fast from season to season. For each location, hotels and restaurants are listed alphabetically by price category.

Note that many sites of interest in Umbria close for a midday break, usually from 12:30 or 1 to 3 or 3:30 PM; we suggest calling ahead to check exact hours.

PERUGIA Umbria's regional capital is set on a hill, and the best way to see it is to leave the car at the public parking lot halfway up the road that winds to the top. From there, five escalators whisk visitors up a thousand feet into the heart of town. Interestingly, the escalators tunnel straight through the *Rocca Paolina,* the fortress that Pope Paul III raised in the 16th century to show the Perugini who was boss. The fort incorporated the mansion belonging to one of the leading rebel families, the Baglioni, and the surrounding neighborhood, including three churches and several streets from earlier centuries. The *Rocca* was largely destroyed in the 19th century, debris was dumped into it, and its upper walls were used as the foundations of nearby palazzi. Excavations began in the 1950s, and it is through this time-warped ghost city that the escalators climb to the top, even passing a tiny Renaissance-era basketball court.

It becomes immediately obvious to a visitor that Perugia is a university town. International students taking courses at the *Università Italiana per Stranieri* (Italian University for Foreigners) and Italian students from the nearly 700-year-old *Università di Perugia* (University of Perugia) throng the main street, Corso Vannucci, a wide pedestrian island lined with outdoor *caffès,* hotels, fine shops, and the tourist information office, or *APT* (No. 30; phone: 75-572-3327; fax: 75-573-6828), which is closed Sunday afternoons and for a midday break in summer; closed Sundays and for a midday break in summer. There is another, smaller *APT* office at 21 Via Mazzini (phone: 75-572-5431). While at the tourist office, pick up a copy of *Perugia: What Where When* (also available in major hotels), which lists museums and other worthwhile sights. At the end of Corso Vannucci is the main square, Piazza IV Novembre, with one of Perugia's most celebrated monuments, the 13th-century *Fontana Maggiore,* in the center. This notable achievement was built to celebrate the completion of an aqueduct bringing water to Perugia from Monte Paciano, 3 miles (5 km) away. Designed and executed by Nicola and Giovanni Pisano, it consists of two marble basins and a bronze cup decorated with 24 relief sculptures and 24 statues. On the north side of the square is Perugia's *Duomo,* or, rather, its side, since it faces onto Piazza Danti. Begun in 1345 to replace an earlier building, it was finished in 1490—finished, that is, except for the pink and white marble stripes that were to have covered it; only a patch was completed.

On the south side of the square (corner of Piazza IV Novembre and Corso Vannucci) is the *Palazzo dei Priori,* built from 1293 to 1443 and which for hundreds of years was Perugia's *Town Hall.* The part facing the square, with the grand staircase and the doorway topped by the Perugian griffin and the Guelph lion in bronze, was completed by 1297 and is the oldest part of this fine example of medieval civic architecture. Inside the palace (enter from Corso Vannucci) is the frescoed *Sala dei Notari* (Notaries' Room), which is closed Mondays and for a midday break; no admission charge (no phone). Also within is the *Collegio della Mercanzia,* a sort of Renaissance chamber of commerce covered with 15th-century woodcarvings and marquetry. It's closed Mondays and for a midday break; admission charge (phone: 75-573-0366). The highlight of the palace, however, is the recently restored and extended *Galleria Nazionale dell'Umbria* (National Gallery of Umbria; phone: 75-572-0316), which covers the entire development of Umbrian painting—from the stiff religious art of the 13th century to the breathtaking explosion of color and grace in Pinturicchio and Perugino—in addition to works by Beato Angelico, Piero della Francesca, and others. Closed Sunday afternoons and for a midday break; admission charge. Those interested mainly in Perugino, however, should stop in at the *Collegio del Cambio* next door. It was built for the use of money changers in the 15th century, and its most important chamber is filled with vibrant frescoes by Perugino and his pupils. On the middle pilaster is Perugino's self-portrait, and in the painting of the Prophets and the Sibyls, presumed to be by Perugino's pupil Raphael, is that young painter's self-portrait as the prophet Daniel. The fine inlaid woodwork in the lobby is from the 17th century. Closed Mondays, Sunday afternoons, and for a midday break; admission charge (phone: 75-572-8599).

Going out the west end of Piazza IV Novembre, it's possible to approach Perugia's *Etruscan Arch* by way of a medieval street, Via delle Volte. This winding street is also called Via Maestà delle Volte, for a 14th-century fresco in a small church at its end. Adjacent streets such as Via Fratti and Via Ritorta are worth a detour. Via Maestà delle Volte leads to Piazza Morlacchi, from where Via Cesare Battisti leads along a wall built by the Etruscans and then, via a stairway, to Piazza Fortebraccio. Here, the 18th-century Baroque *Palazzo Gallenga-Stuart,* seat of the *Università Italiana per Stranieri*, stands next to the *Etruscan Arch,* or the *Arch of Augustus,* as the Romans called it. Where Roman builders raised the wall higher is readily seen, but the arch itself is pure Etruscan. A delicate porch on top dates from the Renaissance.

At the other end of town, take Via Marzia out of the *Giardini Carducci* (Carducci Gardens) to the *Porta Marzia,* a 2nd- or 1st-century BC gate in the walls. It was moved 10 feet away and reconstructed by the architect (Antonio da Sangallo the Younger) working on the *Rocca Paolina,* and it provides access to the underground Via Bagliona, the subterranean world that once was sealed off by the fortress. The *Museo Archeologico Nazionale dell'Umbria* (National Archaeological Musuem of Umbria) is also at this end of the city, next to the Gothic *Chiesa di San Domenico* (Church of St. Domenic; Piazza G. Bruno; phone: 75-572-7141). It houses a collection of prehistoric, Etruscan, and Roman sarcophagi, vases, coins, and jewelry. Its greatest treasure, however, is the *Cippus,* a marble slab inscribed with 151 words in the Etruscan language. Some urns in the collection are engraved in Etruscan with the translation into Umbria's Latin dialect. Closed Sunday afternoons and for a midday break; admission charge.

The tradition of the *passeggiata*—the evening promenade—is very much alive in Perugia: On Corso Vannucci it seems that everyone who is ambulatory is out for a stroll. For an *aperitivo* any time of the day, visit the *Enoteca Provinciale* (16 Via Ulisse Rocchi; no phone), which offers samplings of the 150 wines from the 60 vineyards in Umbria.

BEST EN ROUTE

Brufani An old favorite of travelers, this pleasantly old-fashioned grand hotel is the best in town. There are 24 rooms and a restaurant. 12 Piazza Italia, Perugia (phone: 75-573-2541; fax: 75-572-0210). Very expensive.

Locanda della Posta Onetime guests Goethe, Hans Christian Andersen, and King Frederick III of Prussia would have been pleased with the renovation done on this, Perugia's oldest hotel, housed in a patrician palazzo on the town's main street. The 40 good-sized rooms are decorated with flair, and there's a lovely frescoed dining room. 97 Corso Vannucci, Perugia (phone: 75-572-2413; fax: 75-572-8925). Expensive.

Osteria del Bartolo This attractive restaurant offers sophisticated cooking. Many of the dishes are based on old recipes, some dating back to medieval times. Closed Sundays and January. Reservations advised. Major credit cards accepted. 30 Via Bartolo, Perugia (phone: 75-573-1561). Expensive to moderate.

Aladino Marco Sciamanna is a friendly and energetic host, always ready to make suggestions about specialties created by his wife, Loredana. The food is a cut above the usual Umbrian fare. Closed for lunch, Tuesdays, and August. Reservations advised. Major credit cards accepted. 11 Via delle Prome, Perugia (phone: 75-572-0938). Moderate.

Falchetto With its 14th-century walls, it looks like a medieval tavern, and visitors interested in sampling authentic Umbrian cuisine should make this their first choice. Among the dishes to try are grilled trout from the Nera River, truffled veal, and delectable roast pheasant. The wines are from Torgiano and other local vineyards. Closed Mondays. Reservations advised. Major credit cards accepted. 20 Via Bartolo, Perugia (phone: 75-573-1775). Moderate.

Giò, Arte e Vini Run by the Guarducci family, well known in Perugia for their fine wine and food emporium next door, this hundred-room hotel has a restaurant that serves Umbrian fare at reasonable prices. The wine list comprises more than 700 labels. Restaurant closed Sunday dinner. Reservations advised. Major credit cards accepted. 19 Via Ruggiero d'Andreotto, Perugia (phone/fax: 75-573-1100). Moderate.

La Taverna Refreshingly different from run-of-the-mill Perugian restaurants, this eatery offers unusual additions to traditional Umbrian fare, including some excellent fish dishes. Try the *maccheroncini con seppioline* (short pasta with baby squid). Host Claudio Brugalissi provides sophisticated service and reasonable prices. Closed Mondays and the last half of July. Reservations advised. Major credit cards accepted. 8 Via della Streghe, Perugia (phone: 75-572-4128). Moderate.

Lo Spedalicchio About 6 miles (10 km) out of town in the direction of Assisi, inside a gate, an ancient castle that once guarded the approach to Perugia has been converted into a 25-room hotel. The furnishings are handsome, modern interpretations of traditional regional styles. There is an elegant dining room; drinks are served in the garden. 3 Piazza Bruno Buozzi, Ospedalicchio (phone/fax: 75-801-0323). Moderate to inexpensive.

Dal Mi'Cocco A good place for hearty local fare at very reasonable prices. The soups are especially noteworthy—try the delicious minestrone or the *pappa al pomodoro* (thick tomato soup). The meat dishes are grilled over an open fire. Closed Mondays and August. Reservations unnecessary. No credit cards accepted. 12 Corso Garibaldi, Perugia (phone: 75-573-2511). Inexpensive.

En Route from Perugia Take the S75 *bis* southeast toward Foligno and Assisi. On the left, after about 3 miles (5 km), is the rocky *Ipogeo dei Volumni,* an Etruscan necropolis (Ponte San Giovanni, Via Volumnia; phone: 75-393329). The Volumni were an important Etruscan family in the 2nd century BC, and these are serious excavations. Closed Sunday afternoons and for a long midday break in summer; closed Sundays and for a long midday break in winter; admission charge. The road crosses the Tiber River at Ponte San Giovanni; at Ospedalicchio, S147 branches off to Assisi, 16 miles (26 km) from Perugia.

ASSISI Set on the slopes of Monte Subasio, commanding panoramic views all around, and full of medieval houses of pink stone, this town seems as gentle and charming as the saint who was born here (1182) and who lies buried in the crypt beneath its prime monument. Begun in 1228, two years after his death, the *Basilica di San Francesco* is a commanding structure whose unmistakable outline appears, from a distance, to be almost as large as the town itself. For details, see *Churches and Piazzas* in DIVERSIONS.

Several other sites associated with St. Francis are situated in and around Assisi. About 2½ miles (4 km) east of town is the mountainside *Eremo delle Carceri* (Hermitage of the Prisons), to which St. Francis and his followers retreated to "imprison" themselves spiritually in prayer. A small Franciscan monastery soon developed, carved out of bedrock; adjacent is a tiny grotto in which St. Francis lived—his rude stone bed can still be seen. The setting is extraordinarily beautiful and imbued with an aura of holiness, much more in keeping with the spirit of St. Francis than the huge basilica in town. The *Convento di San Damiano,* another of Italy's most revered shrines, is a bit more than a mile (1.6 km) south of Assisi. St. Francis restored the little church here, and his friend St. Clare lived in the humble convent with her nuns, the Poor Clares, until her death in 1253. This is also the spot where St. Francis composed the "Cantico delle Creature" in praise of all creation. Almost 3 miles (5 km) west of Assisi is the 16th-century *Basilica di Santa Maria degli Angeli* (on the piazza of the same name), really no more than a huge covering for an area where St. Francis spent much of his life, was joined by his first followers, and died. It contains several tiny shrines, including the *Porziuncola,* an almost toy-like chapel he restored and to which crowds of pilgrims come each August 1 and 2 for the *Festa del Perdono* (Pardon of Assisi), instituted by the saint in 1216.

If you have more time to spend in Assisi, visit the Gothic 13th-century *Chiesa di Santa Chiara* (Church of St. Clare; Piazza di Santa Chiara), which contains the blackened and shriveled remains of the saint herself, and the *Duomo,* begun in the 12th century and dedicated to San Rufino. Assisi also has Roman remains, including the *Tempio di Minerva* (Temple of Minerva), transformed into a Baroque church in Piazza del Comune, the medieval main square. Also medieval is the *Rocca Maggiore,* or Fortress, set on a hill north of the center and reached by a stepped street leading out of the square in front of the *Duomo* (signposted); the view from the top is well worth the climb.

BEST EN ROUTE

Fontebella Here are 43 quiet rooms, most overlooking the broad Umbrian Valley, plus a renowned restaurant, *Il Frantoio.* Among its specialties are *stringotti* (egg noodles) with artichoke sauce and *tortelloni* (big ravioli) stuffed with cream cheese. In season, truffles garnish nearly everything, and there is a choice selection of local wines. Restaurant closed Fridays. Reservations advised. Major credit cards accepted. 25 Via Fontebella, Assisi (phone: 75-812883, hotel; 75-812977, restaurant; fax: 75-812941, hotel). Hotel, expensive; restaurant, expensive to moderate.

Giotto Assisi's largest hotel has 69 clean, pleasantly decorated rooms and a restaurant, where you can dine on a lovely outdoor terrace in summer. Some rooms have dramatic views of the valley. Book early, as this place is popular with groups. 41 Via Fontebella, Assisi (phone: 75-812209; fax: 75-816479). Expensive.

Subasio It's in the heart of town adjacent to Piazza San Francesco, but some of the 65 rooms overlook the valley and are therefore quiet. This charming place has a restaurant known for good food. 2 Via Frate Elia, Assisi (phone: 75-812206; fax: 75-816691). Expensive.

Buca di San Francesco One of Assisi's most popular restaurants is housed in a medieval *cantina* (cellar). Dishes include *prosciutto di cinghiale* (wild boar ham) and spaghetti *al sugo d'oca* (with a rich goose sauce). Closed Mondays and the first three weeks of July. Reservations advised. Major credit cards accepted. 1 Via Brizi, Assisi (phone: 75-812204). Moderate.

Il Medio Evo This highly recommended dining spot features an evocative decor. The mixed fry is a tempting abundance of stuffed olives and meat. Closed Wednesdays and July. Reservations advised. Major credit cards accepted. 4 Via Arco dei Priori, Assisi (phone: 75-813068). Moderate.

Umbra A romantic place, it's downtown on a narrow street away from the more noisy thoroughfares. A few of the 27 rooms afford a splendid vista over the rooftops, and some are furnished with antiques. There's a garden restaurant. 6 Via degli Archi, Assisi (phone: 75-812240; fax: 75-813653). Moderate.

Country House One mile (1.6 km) out of town, in a peaceful country setting, this nine-room hotel is furnished with Umbrian antiques. No restaurant. 178 San Pietro Campagna, San Pietro Campagna (phone: 75-816155; fax: 75-816363). Inexpensive.

La Stalla Halfway up the hill leading to the lovely *Eremo delle Carceri,* this lively trattoria is in a converted stable. The rustic fare—homemade pasta and pizza topped with green vegetables—is complemented by good red and white house wines. Closed Mondays. Reservations advised. Visa accepted. Via Eremo delle Carceri (phone: 75-812317 or 75-813636). Inexpensive.

En Route from Assisi Drive south on S75 and S3 to Spoleto (30 miles/48 km away), passing through picturesque hill country filled with olive groves. Eight miles (13 km) from Assisi is the old town of Spello, whose stone houses cling to the terraced mountain slopes within ancient Roman walls. If you stop, visit the *Chiesa di Santa Maria Maggiore,* particularly its *Cappella Baglioni,* which has a 16th-century majolica floor from Deruta and frescoes by Pinturicchio, including an Annunciation with a self-portrait of the painter. It's open daily, with a midday closing; no admission charge. On the first Sunday after *Corpus Christi,* in the second half of June, Spello's streets are carpeted with giant religious images made from millions of fresh flower petals.

BEST EN ROUTE

Palazzo Bocci This delightfully restored 13th-century building in the heart of town has 23 rooms, each individually decorated. The fresco in the lounge is by 19th-century artist Benevento Crispoldi. The service and amenities are all modern, and there is a pleasant garden. Right in front of the hotel is *Il Molino* (see below). 17 Via Cavour, Spello (phone: 742-301021; fax: 742-301464). Expensive.

Altavilla Each of the 24 rooms in this hotel has a small terrace from which to admire the Umbrian countryside. The walls of the inn and its dining room are hung with paintings by owner Luigi Proietti's father, Norberto, a well-known Umbrian artist. Via M. Mancinelli, Spello (phone: 742-301515; fax: 742-651258). Moderate.

Il Molino In a 700-year-old flour mill that was itself built in Roman ruins, it has a big fireplace turning out the grilled meat that is among its traditional dishes. The house specialty, named after the painter Pinturicchio, is filet in puff pastry with a wild mushroom sauce. Closed Tuesdays. Reservations advised. Major credit cards accepted. 6 Piazza Matteotti, Spello (phone: 742-651305). Moderate.

SPOLETO Success has not spoiled this ancient Roman town and former head-quarters of the Lombard duchy of Spoleto, which ruled most of Umbria in the early Middle Ages. However, should you want to stay in Spoleto during its all-embracing festival of the performing arts, the *Festival dei Due Mondi* (Festival of the Two Worlds), book hotels and tickets to events far in advance. For details on the festival, see *Italy's Most Colorful Festas* in DIVERSIONS. Lovely frescoes by Fra Filippo Lippi and his school are inside the 12th-century cathedral, as is the tomb of the master painter and defrocked monk. Portraits of him, his two assistants, and his son Filippino figure in the fresco of the *Death of the Virgin.*

No other sight in this hill town ranks with the *Duomo,* but it is filled with other impressive monuments, and the effect of the medieval whole is fascinating. Stop at the tourist information office (*AAST;* 7 Piazza della Libertà; phone: 743-220435 or 743-220311; fax: 743-46241) for information and brochures before setting out on a walking tour. It's closed Saturday afternoons, Sundays, and for a midday break in summer; closed weekends and for a midday break in winter. During the festival, held at the end of June and the beginning of July, every alley and staircase is turned into a showroom for contemporary artists. The late Alexander Calder designed the huge sculpture installed in front of the train station in the lower, modern part of town.

Among the sights out of town is the 13th-century *Chiesa di San Pietro* (Church of St. Peter), 5 miles (8 km) east, right off SS Flaminia. The road that winds upward past the church leads to the top of Monteluco, where St. Francis lived for a time at the monastery, now the *Eremo delle Grazie* hotel (see *Best en Route,* below).

BEST EN ROUTE

Eremo delle Grazie In the quiet hills of Monteluco, this lovely 11-room hostelry—formerly a Franciscan monastery—has a restaurant, a pool, and a well-tended garden. Strada per Monteluco, Monteluco (phone: 743-49624; fax: 743-49650). Very expensive.

Il Barbarossa This former country house right outside Spoleto has been tastefully converted into a small but exquisite hotel. The 10 guestrooms have beamed ceilings, antique Umbrian furniture, modern, well-equipped bathrooms, satellite television, and VCRs. Its restaurant serves a refined version of local specialties. Closed Mondays. Reservations advised. Major credit cards accepted. 12 Via Licina, Spoleto (phone: 743-43644; fax: 743-222060). Hotel, expensive; restaurant, moderate.

Duchi Some of the 50 rooms in this modern, efficient, and pleasant place look out at the *Teatro Romano*; others face the valley. There is a restaurant and a nice little bar. 4 Viale Matteotti, Spoleto (phone: 743-44541; fax: 743-44543). Expensive to moderate.

Il Madrigale For a truly memorable—and very Umbrian—eating experience, stop at this wonderfully restored old manor house 7½ miles (12 km) from Spoleto. There is no menu, but local fare may include *pizza al formaggio* (a delicious cheese bread), roughly cut pasta (*strangozzi*) with truffles, and succulent lamb roasted over an enormous fire. Go with a healthy appetite—the food keeps on coming. Closed Tuesdays. Reservations advised. Major credit cards accepted. Take S3 toward Terni until you see the restaurant on your left. Via Flaminia, Km 112, Strettura (phone: 743-54144). Expensive to moderate.

Il Tartufo A temple to the noble fungus, this is *the* place to dine on fresh truffles. Here diners enjoy traditional dishes with gussied-up names such as prisoner's rigatoni, Spoleto-style rags (*stracci*, a type of pasta), and "courtesan-style" steaks. Closed Wednesdays and mid-July to mid-August. Reservations advised. Major credit cards accepted. 24 Piazza Garibaldi, Spoleto (phone: 743-40236). Expensive to moderate.

Apollinaire Here, diners enjoy creative variations on the usual Umbrian theme. The menu changes weekly, depending on the season and the ingredients available. There is a good range of homemade desserts and a well-stocked wine cellar. Closed Tuesdays. Reservations advised. Major credit cards accepted. 14 Via Sant'Agata, Spoleto (phone: 743-223256). Moderate.

Il Gattapone This miniature hotel has just eight elegant rooms, a garden, and a restaurant. Reserve in advance if you hope to be among the lucky guests. 6 Via del Ponte, Spoleto (phone: 743-223447; fax: 743-223448). Moderate.

Il Panciolle During the festival, this is a favorite among performers. It serves traditional Umbrian fare, such as meat grilled over an open fire. The premises have an attractive garden for summer dining and the bonus of seven charming guestrooms. Book early for a room, especially during the festival. Restaurant closed Wednesdays. Reservations advised. Major credit cards accepted. Largo M. Clemente, Spoleto (phone: 743-45598). Moderate.

Villaggio Albergo Parco Ipost A pleasant alternative to staying in Spoleto, which in summer can be hot and crowded, this 41-room hotel is up in the cool hills of Monteluco, 5 miles (8 km) out of town. It has a pool and a tennis court. Monteluco (phone: 743-223441; fax: 743-223443). Inexpensive.

En Route from Spoleto Todi is about 28 miles (45 km) northwest. Take S418 west to Acquasparta; from there, pick up S3 *bis* north.

TODI A growing colony of Americans—as well as wealthy Italian artists, diplomats, and moviemakers—has bought castles and turned them into private villas, transforming Todi from the quiet, undiscovered hill town it once was. Yet it has retained an overall medieval aspect. The town has an especially beautiful setting, centered around its main square, Piazza del Popolo, which is lined with 13th- and 14th-century structures. The most important is the *Palazzo dei Priori,* standing alone at one end with its crenelations and tower. Facing it, at the other end, is the *Duomo,* fronted by a grand staircase, with a Renaissance rose window in its façade and a bell tower. On another side of the square, the *Palazzo del Popolo,* wearing a crenelated crown, and the *Palazzo del Capitano* stand as one, joined by a staircase that affords entry to both. Inside is a delightful museum whose small, eclectic collection ranges from Etruscan artifacts to Umbrian religious art. It's closed Mondays and for a long midday break; admission charge (phone: 75-894-3541). At press time, the museum was closed for extensive restoration work; call ahead to check for reopening dates. The nearby Piazza Garibaldi is a rewarding stop—the view embraces the whole valley below—and two other churches are worth a visit. The *Chiesa di San Fortunato* (Piazza della Repubblica) is a lovely 13th-century structure with an unfinished 15th-century façade set off by the green of the lawn and hedges in front. The town's most famous citizen, the Franciscan monk and medieval poet Jacopone, is buried there. Its setting is not nearly as striking, however, as that of *Santa Maria della Consolazione,* a brief walk (about a half-mile/1 km) south of town. An exquisite white marble church set on a field of green, this Renaissance gem is thought to have been designed by Bramante.

For an extraordinary experience, visit the *Cantina Sociale Tudernum,* 2 miles (3 km) outside Todi on the Rome road (146 Frazione Pian di Porto; phone: 75-898-9403). Here, wine is dispensed by machines that bear an uncanny resemblance to gas pumps. The wine is excellent, and locals flock here on Saturday mornings to fill up for the weekend. Bottled wine also is available, including the justly renowned grechetto di Todi. Open daily, with a midday closing.

BEST EN ROUTE

Vissani Instead of taking S79 to Orvieto, follow S448, which skirts Lake Corbara and ends up in Orvieto, passing through the town of Baschi. The reason for this detour—one of the region's most scenic routes—is a pilgrimage to what is widely considered one of Italy's finest restaurants. Owner/chef Gianfranco Vissani turns out a dazzling array of delicate, perfectly presented courses. The menu changes according to season. Closed Sunday dinner and Wednesdays. Reservations necessary. Major credit cards accepted. S448, Località Civitella del Lago (phone: 75-950396). Very expensive.

Jacopone–da Peppino A relatively modest *osteria* (inn) whose kitchen is part of the rustic decor. Try the *pasticcio Jacopone,* the braised beef in a rich mushroom sauce, and the local wine. Closed Mondays and two weeks in July. Reservations advised. Major credit cards accepted. 5 Piazza Jacopone, Todi (phone: 75-8942366). Moderate.

Lucaroni The Lucaroni family serves quality food at an excellent value, a rarity in increasingly fashionable Todi. The imaginative and well prepared dishes include a good selection of pasta courses and some interesting *secondi* (main dishes), such as *suprema di faraona al tartufo* (breast of woodcock served with black truffles). Closed Tuesdays and the last two weeks of July. Reservations advised. Major credit cards accepted. 57 Viale A. Cortesi (phone: 75-894-2694). Moderate.

Il Padrino Next door to *Vissani* is this less refined eatery. The cooking still is sublime, the fare simpler. Closed Wednesdays and July. Reservations advised. Major credit cards accepted. S448, Località Civitella del Lago (phone: 75-950206). Moderate.

Umbria Good for local cuisine, it has a rustic decor and a terrace for summer dining. Closed Tuesdays and around *Christmas.* Reservations advised. Major credit cards accepted. 13 Via San Bonaventura, Todi (phone: 75-894-2737). Moderate.

Villa Bellago On a promontory overlooking Lago di Corbara, this American-run hotel is ideally situated for exploring Todi and Orvieto. New York restaurateur George Harpootlian and his wife, Davida Shear, converted a cluster of 19th-century farm buildings into a small inn with 12 bedrooms. Amenities include a well-equipped gym, a pool, a tennis court, and a restaurant serving Umbrian classics using fresh seafood and—a rarity in Italy—exceptional beef. S448, Località Baschi (phone: 744-950521; fax: 744-950524). Moderate.

En Route from Todi The route continues north to return to Perugia along S3 *bis,* stopping at Deruta, a town known the world over for its ceramics, and at the wine town of Torgiano. For travelers heading to Lazio or Rome, the recommended route is west to Orvieto, 25 miles (40 km) away, and south from there. The cathedral at Orvieto is so spectacular that even those ultimately headed north should make a detour.

ORVIETO This city clings, somewhat precariously (it has serious landslide problems), to a high, flat table of tufa stone rising up over the gentle, wide valley carved by the Paglia River. During the Middle Ages its name was Urbs Vetus, suggesting to historians that this was probably Volsinii, a large Etruscan city of many temples destroyed by Roman troops in 265 BC and then rebuilt. Two Etruscan necropolises, including several painted tombs, have been found nearby; from one of them came the archaic statue of Venus now in Orvieto's *Museo Claudio Faina,* facing the *Duomo* (see below).

For most people, Orvieto's *Duomo* is what impresses most, no matter how many cathedrals they have seen before. From the gilded mosaics and dainty rose window of the façade to the fresco masterpieces inside, this is one of Italy's greatest treasures. It was begun in 1290 in Romanesque style, possibly according to a design by Arnolfo di Cambio, but in the first decade of the 14th century, Lorenzo Maitani—a master builder, architect, and sculptor from Siena—was called to its rescue. The present church, including the design of the strikingly beautiful Gothic façade, is largely his, even though numerous other architects and artisans succeeded him, and the project was not completed until the early 17th century. Stand back to study the overall effect of the façade and note how it looks something like a giant triptych altarpiece. At the lowest level, on the pilasters between the doors, are bas-reliefs carved in marble. They illustrate scenes from the Old and New Testaments and are thought to have been done (1320–30) by Maitani himself (the central bronze doors are modern).

On the next level, brilliantly colored mosaics depicting the life of Mary point upward to still further mosaic scenes and to a large rose window (the work of Andrea Orcagna in the mid-14th century) surrounded by busts and statues of prophets and apostles. At the apex of the triptych is a Coronation of the Virgin in blue, red, and gold mosaic.

Walk up close to the façade and notice that even the parts that appear plain are actually exquisitely decorated—every graceful, slim column, twist, groove, and strip of surface is studded with color. Inside, the contrast is startling, because most of the interior—its walls of alternating stripes of black and white stone, its alabaster windows—is quite simple. Make a bee-line to the *Cappella Nuova* (New Chapel, also known as the *Cappella di San Brizio*) to see the fresco cycle that influenced Michelangelo and made a name for Luca Signorelli. Fra Angelico began the decoration of the chapel in 1447 but completed only two sections of the ceiling; in 1499 Signorelli was commissioned to finish the work, which took him five years. Among the scenes of the *End of the World,* the *Coming and Fall of the Antichrist,* and the *Last Judgment* are two men dressed in black. The blond is his self-portrait, the other a portrait of Fra Angelico. Dante is pictured in one of the decorative squares of the wainscot. At press time, these frescoes and some of the statues were undergoing an extensive restoration.

In the left transept is the *Cappella del Corporale,* housing a cloth on which the blood of Christ is supposed to have appeared miraculously in nearby Bolsena in 1263. The relic—its possession was the original impetus for building the *Duomo*—is carried through the streets of Orvieto on the *Festa di Corpus Christi* (Feast of Corpus Christi) each June, a holy day that originated in Orvieto in 1264.

The severe Gothic building to the right of the *Duomo* is the *Palazzo Soliano,* formerly the *Palazzo dei Papi* (Papal Palace; phone: 763-41039).

Commissioned by Pope Boniface VIII in 1297, it today houses the cathedral's collection of religious treasures, artworks, and historical bibelots. Closed Sundays and for a midday break; no admission charge. In front of the *Duomo* is the *Museo Claudio Faina,* whose collection includes, among other things, Greek vases. It is closed Mondays and for a midday break; admission charge (phone: 763-41511). As we went to press, the museum was closed for restoration; call ahead for reopening dates.

Orvieto's oldest building is the *Palazzo del Popolo,* begun in 1157. It's open to the public only when there are conferences. Not far from that is the *Chiesa di San Domenico* (Piazza XXIX Marzo), begun in 1233; inside is the tomb of Cardinal Guglielmo de Braye, a masterpiece by Arnolfo di Cambio, who carved it in 1285. The *Pozzo di San Patrizio* (St. Patrick's Well; Piazzale Canen) is at the far end of town, at an overlook called the *Belvedere.* Designed by Sangallo the Younger and built in 1528, the 200-foot-deep well was supposed to provide water for the city in case of a siege. Visitors walk to the bottom and back up via two separate spiral staircases of 248 steps each, one superimposed on the other so they never meet. Open daily; admission charge.

The Orvieto *APT* (Tourist Information Office) is right across from the *Duomo* (phone: 763-41772 or 763-42562; fax: 763-44433). Open daily with a midday closing, it offers an excellent brochure that includes a map and hotel, restaurant, and tourist site listings.

Orvieto is synonymous with fine white wine, either dry or *abboccáto* (mellow). The wine is a blend of several grapes—Tuscan trebbiano, verdello, grechetto, and Tuscan malvasia—grown on local hillsides. Each May and June, the town sponsors a wine show. The countryside is dotted with *cantine* (wine cellars) open to visitors. For serious wine tasting, take a detour to the Decugnano dei Barbi vineyard at Corbara, just outside of Orvieto. Proprietor Claudio Barbi produces a fine orvieto classico, a rich, red decugnano, a rare pourriture noble dessert wine, and an excellent sparkling white wine, or spumante. Call first for an appointment and directions (phone: 763-308118).

BEST EN ROUTE

La Badia A beautifully restored and gracious ancient cloister, it has 26 rooms, tennis courts, a pool, and an elegant dining room. About 3 miles (5 km) south of Orvieto in Località La Badia (phone: 763-90359; fax: 763-92796). Expensive.

Maitani Right in the heart of town, this charming hotel has 41 rooms and a terrace with a superb view of the *Duomo,* but no restaurant. 5 Via Maitani, Orvieto (phone/fax: 763-42011). Expensive to moderate.

Etrusca The house specialty here is *coniglio all'etrusca* (rabbit served with a piquant green sauce). The welcoming trattoria has warm terra cotta tile floors and whitewashed walls, and there's an excellent selection of Umbrian and Tuscan wines. If you're lucky, there may be an impromptu wine tasting. Closed Mondays and the last three weeks of January. Reservations advised. Major credit cards accepted. 10 Via L. Maitani, Orvieto (phone: 763-44016). Moderate.

Virgilio This beautifully restored old palazzo across from the *Duomo* has 13 modern rooms. It also is next door to one of the best wine *cantine* in Orvieto, where you can sample a glass before choosing a bottle. Piazza Duomo, Orvieto (phone: 763-41882). Moderate.

I Sette Consoli Husband-and-wife team Mauro and Anna Rita Stopponi have turned this into one of Orvieto's most welcoming trattorias, with friendly service, a pretty garden for alfresco dining, and a range of fixed menus that offer good food at hard-to-beat prices. Closed Wednesdays and February. Reservations advised. Major credit cards accepted. 1/A Piazza Sant'Angelo (phone: 763-43911). Moderate to inexpensive.

Trattoria dell'Orso Right off Piazza della Repubblica, this eatery serves *ombrichelli,* the region's traditional pasta. Try it *alla campagnola* (with zucchini, eggplant, and onions). All the pasta is homemade. Closed Tuesdays. Reservations unnecessary. No credit cards accepted. 18-20 Via della Misericordia, Orvieto (phone: 763-41642). Inexpensive.

En Route from Orvieto Return to Todi and proceed north on S3 *bis.* About 13 miles (21 km) farther on, Deruta deserves a stop for its multitude of workshops selling painted ceramic ware. Typical Deruta ware has arabesques, dragons, and grotesques harking back to the 14th century; reference to a shipment of vases and jugs for the *Basilica di San Francesco* in Assisi appears in a document of 1358. The industry was at the height of its fame in the early 16th century; in fact, the *Victoria and Albert Museum* in London has a plate made at Deruta by Raphael. The *Museo della Ceramica Umbra* (Museum of Umbrian Ceramics; *Palazzo del Comune,* Piazza dei Consoli; phone: 75-971-1143 or 75-971-1246) has a good collection of pottery and majolica from the 14th century to the present. Closed Mondays and for a midday break; admission charge. Real Deruta ceramic ware is hand-painted, though some stores sell cheaper, mass-produced imitations. To be sure you're getting the real thing, head to Via Tiberina, Deruta's main street and site of *Ubaldo Grazia* (phone: 75-971-1572) and *Antonio Margaritelli* (phone: 75-971-0201). Both stores are open daily, and they will arrange shipping. Other notable sites in Deruta include its 13th-century *Palazzetto Municipale* (Town Hall; Corso Vannucci; no phone). In the atrium is a headless Roman statue of a seated man holding a small boat, which is believed to represent the god of the Tiber River, Tiberino. Upstairs is a collection of 500 paintings by Umbrian masters. Closed Mondays and for a long midday break; admission charge.

Continue on S3 *bis* for another 4 miles (6 km; watch for the turnoff) to Torgiano. A visit to the tastefully arranged *Museo del Vino* (Wine Museum; 11 Corso Emanuele; phone: 75-988-0069) begins, as does local history, with the ancient Etruscans. On view are wine vases and jugs from an Etruscan funeral dowry and dozens of Roman amphoras. A monumental winepress from the 17th century occupies most of one room, and a series of gorgeously decorated antique plates shows versions of Dionysius and Bacchus. A head of Bacchus is by Giovanni della Robbia. Open daily, with a long midday closing; admission charge.

From Torgiano, follow the signs back to Perugia, about 8 miles (13 km) away. It's possible to prolong the exploration of the region with a side trip to Gubbio, 24 miles (38 km) northeast of Perugia via S298.

BEST EN ROUTE

Le Tre Vaselle The same vintner—Giorgio Lungarotti—who founded the *Museo del Vino* established this 48-room hotel in a handsomely restored old country house. For more information on its renowned restaurant, see *The Best Restaurants of Italy* in DIVERSIONS. Closed mid-January to mid-February. Reservations advised. Major credit cards accepted. 48 Via Garibaldi, Torgiano (phone: 75-988-0447; fax: 75-988-0214). Hotel, very expensive; restaurant, expensive.

GUBBIO On the slopes of Monte Ingino, reached by a winding road that twists and turns through chestnut woods, this town is just far enough off the beaten track to have a wondrous flavor of authenticity. Leave the car in the parking area next to Piazza Quaranta Martiri and look up to the Città Alta (Upper City) for an introduction to all its main buildings—especially the Gothic *Palazzo dei Consoli*—seen from here with the green mountain as backdrop. Then take the plunge, following Via della Repubblica inward and upward. The narrow streets, stone houses, and tiny churches give Gubbio a medieval charm, so even an aimless amble through town is rewarding (but try to include Via Galeotti, Via dei Consoli, Via Baldassini, and the banks of the Camignano in your route). The tourist office (*APT*; 32 Via Ansidei; phone: 75-922-0693 or 75-922-0790; fax: 75-927-3409) has information about walking around the town, including a bilingual booklet called *Gubbio Card* that details a number of itineraries. It's closed weekends and for a midday break in winter; closed Saturday afternoons, Sundays, and for a midday break in summer.

Note the tiny door next to the main door in many buildings; this is the so-called *porta del morto,* the doorway for the dead. While such doors are seen elsewhere in Italian churches, only in Gubbio are they a typical feature of domestic architecture (supposedly, only coffins passed through them, but another explanation is that these were the doors to the medieval living quarters above, while the larger doorways led to ground-floor shops and workshops).

Via della Repubblica crosses Via Baldassini, above which a staircase leads to Via XX Settembre. Suddenly, the vast Piazza della Signoria opens up, with a breathtaking vista out over the valley to one side. The facing *Palazzo dei Consoli* (or *Palazzo del Popolo*), constructed between 1332 and 1337, and the *Palazzo Pretorio* facing it, constructed in 1349, were conceived as one civic whole, along with the other buildings of the piazza, in Gubbio's most florid period. Today the *Palazzo dei Consoli* houses a small painting gallery and archaeological museum whose greatest treasures are the seven 3rd- to 1st-century BC bronze plaques known as the *Tavole Eugubine*. Discovered nearby in the 15th century, they are written in the ancient Umbrian language, some using an Etruscan-derived alphabet and others the Roman alphabet. They prescribe the omens for which priests should watch to divine the future and other rituals that shed light on the Etruscans' daily life. Open daily, with a midday break, in summer; open daily from 3 to 5 PM in winter; admission charge (phone: 75-927-4298). Before leaving the museum, go up to the loggia for a panoramic view of the whole red-roofed town.

Gubbio is almost as well known for ceramics as Deruta. Here, too, the industry dates back at least as far as the 14th century and was at its height in the early 16th century, after a certain Mastro Giorgio developed a particularly intense, iridescent ruby red that allowed the Gubbians to subdue much of the nearby competition. Even today, workshops are everywhere, and lovely flowered plates line walls to the left and right of shop doorways.

Each year on May 15, the eve of the *Festa di Sant'Ubaldo*, Gubbio's patron saint, the town stages the *Corsa dei Ceri* (Race of the Candles), an event that's been going on since the Middle Ages (and probably since pagan days). On the last Sunday in May, Piazza della Signoria is the scene of another medieval event, the colorful *Palio della Balestra*, a crossbow match pitting Gubbio against a team from nearby Sansepolcro (a return match is played in Sansepolcro in September). For details on both events, see *Italy's Most Colorful Festas* in DIVERSIONS.

BEST EN ROUTE

Park Hotel ai Cappuccini The owners of this extraordinary hotel, 2 miles (3 km) from Gubbio, have gone to great lengths to preserve what was a 17th-century Franciscan monastery. Inside, however, is every modern convenience, including a mini-computer in each of the 95 rooms—guests can use them to send and receive messages within the hotel and book the property's many facilities, including a fitness center, sauna, and pool. The conference rooms are adorned with well-restored frescoes by Capogrossi. There's a restaurant. Via Tifernate, Gubbio (phone: 75-9234; fax: 75-922-0323). Expensive.

Il Bosone There really are no first class hotels in Gubbio itself, but there are a variety of good family-run establishments. Among these is this attractive old building, tastefully restored, with 33 rooms, a restaurant, and a central location. 22 Via XX Settembre, Gubbio (phone: 75-922-0688; fax: 75-922-0552). Moderate.

Alla Fornace di Mastro Giorgio One section of this fine 14th-century building was once the workshop of the famous ceramics designer Mastro Giorgio, from whom it takes its name, and another was formerly an ice house, where snow was made into ice for use in ice-cream making. Try the *ravioli di polpa di granchio* (pasta cushions stuffed with fresh crabmeat). Closed Mondays, Sunday dinner, and February. Reservations advised. Major credit cards accepted. Via Mastro Giorgio, Gubbio (phone: 75-927-5740). Moderate.

Taverna del Lupo An Umbrian restaurant in an authentic 14th-century setting. Its menu reflects Gubbio's proximity to mountain and forest: risotto with mushrooms or truffles, rabbit, broiled meat with polenta, and duckling. Try the local *eugubini* (Gubbian) wines. Closed Mondays and January. Reservations advised. Major credit cards accepted. 60 Via Ubaldo Baldassini, Gubbio (phone: 75-927-4368 or 75-927-1269). Moderate.

The Abruzzo

The Abruzzo, the rugged, rustic area east of Rome, is one of Italy's most intriguing and least known regions. Much of the mystery derives from the austere Apennine Mountains crushed one upon the other to form a sort of single huge fortress whose walls must be carefully studied before they are scaled. With the exception of scattered ski resorts, the same mountains have hindered tourist development and stalled the arrival of good highways. Poverty, too, has contributed to the area's slow economic development. But for those who appreciate authenticity, the Abruzzo provides a rare glimpse of the old, unspoiled Italy.

The region lies on the Adriatic Sea facing Albania, just about where the back of the "calf" would be on the Italian boot. There are nearly 70 miles of beaches, wide and sandy to the north, toward the Marches region, and the beginnings of rocky outcroppings to the south, after Vasto. At midpoint is the bustling seaport of Pescara. There—at the mouth of the Pescara River—a broad flat valley begins, and fields of grain, carrots, sugar beets, spinach, peppers, and tomatoes abound.

Moving inland, that bucolic flatland rises astride the river and its tributaries, first into foothills terraced for grapes, fig and olive trees, and then into mighty knotted fists of gray limestone mountains whose harshness is legendary. At Pescara, fisherfolk are left behind mending their nets in torpid sunshine, and with only an hour or two of driving inland, you enter nearly alpine scenery whose mountains may still wear caps of snow in May. Above the tree line the deep gouges and distant whorls in the limestone are the legacies of ancient glaciers (a piece of glacier can still be seen in the western border of the region).

Farther inland, penetrating into the more than 200 square miles of valley and highland forest in the *Parco Nazionale d'Abruzzo,* brown Marsican bears hunt blueberries, and chamois goats leap from crag to crag. There and at regional parks on Mount Sirente and Mount Maiella, wolves still prowl, and eagles soar overhead. Lovers of untamed flora may come upon rare bronze and yellow wild orchids, deep blue gentian, orange tiger lilies, white perfumed narcissi, and even the furry edelweiss.

On the flat valleys 4,000 feet and higher, Sardinian shepherds bring their flocks of sheep by ferry in summer to graze here. Time has stopped: in the fields farmers bring in the hay using wooden rakes, as did their forefathers. In the high valleys where farming the stony soil is a perennial challenge, lentils and potatoes grow in handkerchief plots that were laid out in the Middle Ages.

The highest and most dramatic of all the mountains in the Abruzzo and, indeed, in all of Italy (except for the Alps) is the elongated, severe chain of the Gran Sasso. At 9,555 feet, its Corno Grande peak rises to about the average height of the Alps in the north. The Gran Sasso is a watershed; its melting snows and spring waters flow into the Adriatic to the east and into the Tyrrhenian to the west.

Next in size and importance comes the range of the Maiella, whose huge dome-shaped mass is home to several small wolf packs studied and monitored by zoologists. Early man dwelled here, in the Alento and Foro Valleys, where flintstone knives and a large axehead (now in the *Museo Etnografico e Preistorico* in Rome) were found, a few dating from the early Stone Age and more from the glacial era. To the ancient Romans, the Maiella was known as the *Pater montium,* the father of mountains, and here they built, on its slopes, a temple to Jove, the father of the gods.

Other stretches of mountains are the Monti del Morrone, 6,000 feet high, which link the Maiella to the Gran Sasso; toward the Lazio border, the Monti Simbruini; and, overlooking the now prosperous flat farm valley of the Fucino, once a lake that was drained in a spectacular engineering project of the mid-19th century, the Monte Velino chain of four high peaks, including the gracious Monte Magnola, a favorite of skiers. Interspersed are several small lakes—the loveliest of which is the elongated, picturesque Scanno—which cut through the valleys. In addition to the 70-mile-long Pescara River, with its tributary, the Aterno, are the Vomano and the Sangro Rivers.

There is a rapid shift from seaside to mountain clime. The coastal region averages from 53 to 61F year-round, but in the rugged hills and mountains daytime temperatures hover in the low 50s, with nighttime plunging to subzero numbers. Rainfall is concentrated and heaviest in late autumn, especially in November. In the high mountains it may rain every afternoon even in August, although the past decade or so has produced drier-than-usual years. Even so, at high altitudes, furious blizzards and a snowfall of three feet or more are an almost annual occurrence in some spots, and skiing is usually possible at the numerous winter resorts from December through March.

The Abruzzo's population of 1.2 million, scattered over a rugged, often uninhabitable area of more than 6,000 square miles, is barely a third that of Rome. Its 305 townships are often small and scattered throughout the mountain areas. Its four sizable cities are Chieti, the largest, on a plane overlooking the Pescara River Valley; L'Aquila, in the shadow of the Grand Sasso; Pescara; and Teramo.

The area has been inhabited since ancient times; skeletal remains estimated at 40,000 years old (*Homo marsicanus*) were found near Avezzano. After the linguistic unification (only one Abruzzese dialect exists today in the Marsican region; most everyone else speaks Italian with a distinct accent) of the numerous Abruzzo tribes in the millennium before Christ (including the Marsi, Picenti, Paeligni, Pretuzzi, Marrucini, Aequi, Vestini, and Praetutii), they joined with powerful Samnites from the south to form a single culture. Gradually, Romans overran the territory. In 90 BC, the Roman conquest was complete, and soldiers marched on the Via Tibertina from Rome through the valleys, establishing Alba Fucens on the borders of the now dried-up Lake Fucino; located on the site of an earlier prehistoric city, Alba Fucens's ruins make for a fascinating visit.

In 493, with the collapse of the Roman Empire, conquering Goths descended from the north under Theodoric. For two decades after 535, they fought the Byzantines for possession of Italy; the Byzantines won, claiming the Abruzzo as booty. In 571 the Germanic Longobard domination began, and the region was split between the Longobard Dukes of Spoleto and Benvenuto until 774, when Charlemagne unified the region. In 1140 the Norman domination was complete, and the region became a part of the Kingdom of Sicily. The city of L'Aquila, founded in 1254, flourished, as its many fine churches and castle testify. The French Angevin dynasty owned the region after 1266; the Aragons of Spain after 1442.

This was the time of the greatest flowering of the Abruzzo, a passageway for Florentine merchants who bought wool here, or passed en route to Naples. Their influence is still seen everywhere: almost every village features a medieval church, abbey, castle, tower, or fortress with elegant rose-colored windows or finely carved doorways. Monumental fortified castles and romantic Romanesque churches are found in myriad humble villages and in the countryside as well.

The 15th-century Longobard influence can be seen in cities like Sulmona, where late Gothic doorways and other architectural details were designed by Pietro da Como from Lake Como, among others. And in the 16th century, the Umbrian influence is apparent in frescoes in Atri by Abruzzo painter Andrea De Lito and in L'Aquila by Francesco da Montereale.

In 1503, with the rest of southern Italy, the Abruzzo passed into Spanish hands as the kingdom of Naples, taken over by the Austrians from 1707 to 1734. In 1799 Napoleon's troops arrived, bringing the Bourbon Restoration. From 1806 to 1815, the kingdom of Naples was run by Murat during the Napoleonic Restoration. And in 1860 the Abruzzo joined newly unified Italy.

Many of the Abruzzo's native sons were men of letters, beginning with Roman historian Caius Sallustius Crispus, born in the Sabine city of Amiternum in the year 86 BC. The poet Ovid, author of the *Metamorphoses,* was born at Sulmona in 43 BC. Pietro da Morrone, born in 1215 at Isernia, in the adjacent Molise region, was a Benedictine monk who turned hermit in the Sulmona mountains, where he founded the Hermits of San Damiano, a monastic order. In 1294, Pietro wrote a stinging letter of criticism to the quarrelling College of Cardinals, who ironically responded by electing him pope. As the idealistic Celestino V, he was soon frustrated and resigned, turning his back on decadent Rome. He is buried in the *Basilica di Collemaggio* at L'Aquila, where he had proclaimed the *Perdonanza,* a plenary indulgence where everyone's sins are pardoned. The event is solemnly celebrated there each August 28.

In the 18th century, the poet Gabriele Rossetti was born at Vasto. Gabriele D'Annunzio, ardent political leader, journalist, poet, and dramatist, was born at Pescara in 1863, where he lived until the age of 11. The brilliant Benedetto Croce, one of the great 20th-century philosophers, was born in the mountain village of Pescasseroli in 1866; in another mountain village—Pescina—the author of *Bread and Wine* and *Fontamara*, partisan fighter and novelist Ignazio Silone, was born.

Far more than elsewhere in Italy, the past still lives on the Abruzzo. In tiny towns like Scanno, older women still wear traditional black-pleated skirts with turquoise petticoats and black tops. The numerous celebrations of the passage of the liturgical year, of the seasons, and of social occasions have special importance here, and some date back to the dimmest past. (Their dates, too, can be mysterious, varying with the church year, so check first with tourist agencies and hotels.) The *Processione dei Serpari* (Procession of the Serpent-Bearers) is celebrated in Cocullo on the first Thursday in May, in honor of San Domenico. In this pre-Christian ritual, people enter the town's main church with live snakes writhing around their necks and arms, and drape the saint with the serpents. The town of Loreto Aprutino celebrates another ancient rite, the *Processione del Bue di San Zopito* (Procession of the Ox of St. Zopito), in mid-May. Adorned with ribbons and decorations, an ox leads a religious procession into the church; then it is made to kneel down before the altar. Also in late May at Buccianico is the *Bandieresi*, when women weave wildflowers into exquisite miniature floats set in baskets that they carry on their heads.

The Abruzzo's craftspeople are world famous for their production of ceramics. These painted earthenware plates, cups, bowls, and coffee and tea services—still made in the tiny mountain town of Castelli on a steep slope of the Gran Sasso—hark back to the 16th century. The art was developed by the Grue family and other master ceramists who, rather than ape the designs of Faenza and Florence, painted their own majestic landscape. Also famous among Abruzzo crafts is the increasingly rare gold filigree work, like the rosetta brooch the young men of Scanno still give their brides-to-be. More humble handicrafts sold in shops and the outdoor markets are copper pots, thick woolen fringed bedspreads woven in an ornate pattern of two colors, cotton (and sometimes linen) yard goods, and precious *tombola* (bobbin) lace. Sulmona's streets are lined with shops selling single flowers, as well as whole bouquets made from gaily colored sugared almonds.

Food is also an Abruzzo art form. Many of Italy's top chefs, such as Antonio Sciullo of Rome's renowned *Relais e Jardin,* are from the region. In general, tradition reigns in the Abruzzo kitchen, where nouvelle cuisine and elegance are a rarity. Cooking is rustic, for the most part, or what the Italians call *genuina*—uncontaminated by large-scale industrial production. Two separate and distinct cuisines faithfully reflect the two spirits of the region—sea and mountain. The Adriatic area abounds in splendid fresh fish, and hot and cold mixed seafood salads, pasta and risotto with shellfish, and grilled fish of astounding variety are available in the colorful water-front restaurants. Mountain fare includes roast kid and baby lamb (especially at *Easter*), hearty soups and meat in winter, and pasta with mushrooms in the autumn. Inland, freshwater trout is delicious. Local cheeses include mozzarella made from cow's milk, the delicate globe of the *scamorza*, and pecorino (ewe's milk cheese), delicate or aged and tangy. ·

The high plain of the Navelli in the province of L'Aquila is today the sole Italian producer of saffron, the rare delicacy that colors many Abruzzo dishes a deep yellow. Harvested in October, saffron is derived from the flower of the *Crocus sativus*, and it has been grown in the Abruzzo since the late 15th century. It is costly—to make a single pound requires the filaments of 75,000 flowers, and the annual harvest is a mere 135 pounds. In the Abruzzo, it is used in *scapece alla vastese*, a seafood stew of wine-marinated fried squid and fish fillets. The industrial production of pasta (and other food, such as dried figs, tomatoes, and artichokes) is increasingly important in the Abruzzo, but in most restaurants and humble trattorie, visitors are likely to find at least one of the pasta offerings homemade. Most probably it will be the region's *maccheroni alla chitarra*, named for the small rectangular wooden frame upon which it is made. The pasta sheet is placed on top of the frame over taut thin wires and rolled. The traditional sauce for the resulting square, thickish strands is spicy with *peperoncino rosso* (red pepper), *pancetta* (bacon), tomatoes, and pecorino cheese. A delectable baked lasagna, rich with thin egg pasta, is layered with chunks of *scamorza*, *ragù*, and dried *porcini* mushrooms.

One famous Abruzzo dish is "the Virtues"; it is made from seven kinds of dried beans, fresh legumes, springtime vegetables, pasta, condiments, and meat—all simmered for seven hours. What makes it virtuous is its husbandry: It empties the cupboard at winter's end, down to the last dried bean.

The Abruzzo produces its own agreeable wines, including those with the DOC certification. The most noteworthy are the reds and whites of the montepulciano d'Abruzzo and the trebbiano d'Abruzzo. Look for the labels of Bruno Nicodemi of Notaresco and of Giandomenico of Villamagna's farm, *Ai Piedi della Quercia*, for a fine trebbiano. Other top labels are zaccagnini from Bolognano, monti and montori of Controguerra, and pepe of Torano Nuovo. Meals are topped off with a powerful peppery brew called *centerbe* ("one hundred herbs"), whose vivid green color evokes images of alpine fields.

The Abruzzo offers both summer and winter sports. The 84-mile (140-km) coastline boasts a broad sweep of beaches that tend to be wall-to-wall umbrellas, noisy and dirty in midsummer. The least crowded are in the north, such as Alba Adriatica in Teramo province. The 10-mile (16-km) sand beach north of Pescara attracts 500,000 tourists annually, and the city itself has a thousand-boat marina. South of Pescara is Francavilla, a quiet town of gracious villas overlooking the sea. Farther south, the coastline is more varied, especially at Ortona and the Bay of Vasto. Good beaches are at Fossacesia, Ortona, San Vito, and San Giovanni in Venere. Mountain resort areas offer horseback tours of the alpine scenery. Hikers—whether novice or experienced—should make a beeline for the *Parco Nazionale d'Abruzzo,* where there are well-marked paths and mountain bikes for rent. Other scenic mountain areas include the Gran Sasso (between Teramo and L'Aquila) and the Gole di Celano near Ovindoli.

The best ski resorts are Campo Felice and nearby Ovindoli in the Monte Magnola-Velino chain, Campo Imperatore on the Gran Sasso, Pescasseroli in the *Parco Nazionale d'Abruzzo*, Prati di Tivo, and Roccaraso and the lovely town of Pescostanza, both near Sulmona. All have small hotels and inns that are jam-packed at *Christmas* and most winter weekends, so plan well ahead. For details, contact the *Ente Provinciale per il Turismo* (*EPT;* 8 Via XX Settembre, L'Aquila 67100; phone: 862-25140). Information about snow conditions is available from a 24-hour snow bulletin source (phone: 862-420510); it's also listed in Rome's newspapers on Fridays in season. Downhill and cross-country ski equipment can be rented at all localities. The best conditions are from February to mid-March. Downhill runs are short and costly, and lines are long; cross-country skiing may be more pleasant.

The Abruzzo is best explored by car. Below are two driving routes, each of which can be rushed through in two or three days or savored in five or more. Both start in Avezzano, a two-hour drive east from Rome. The first is a tour of the main towns and a few selected villages, mostly by autostrada toll roads whose high viaducts offer breathtaking views, with detours on country roads to visit picturesque towns and villages. The second is a visit to the largest of several huge forested parks—the *Parco Nazionale d'Abruzzo.*

Accommodations in the Abruzzo generally are not in the luxury category, but there are many high-quality and/or comfortable, family-owned places. For a double room for one night, expensive hotels range from $100 to $150; a moderate place will cost between $80 and $100; and an inexpensive hotel, from $60 to $80. All hotels feature air conditioning, private baths, TV sets, and telephones unless otherwise indicated. Book mountain resort hotels months ahead during ski season, and, at all places, try to make reservations beforehand by telephone or in writing (the fax machine has yet to come to many places), as some hotels close during their off-seasons. A meal for two, including wine, at a very expensive restaurant costs $160 or more; at an expensive place, from $80 to $150; at a moderate one, from $65 to $80; and at an inexpensive spot, $60 or less. All restaurants are open for lunch and dinner unless otherwise noted. The prices rise as the altitude drops; seaside restaurants cost more than those in the highlands. For each location, hotels and restaurants are listed alphabetically by price category.

Note that some sites of interest in the Abruzzo close for a midday break, usually from noon or 1 PM to 3 or 4 PM; we suggest calling ahead to check exact hours.

AVEZZANO TO L'AQUILA
From Rome, take the Autostrada per l'Aquila A24 for 65 miles (104 km). After about 40 minutes of driving and seven tunnels, the A24 forks; take the right branch, A25, in the direction of Pescara. The road slices through the same long, flat valley pass where ancient Romans marched toward the Adriatic Sea.

AVEZZANO Exit A25 at Avezzano and take the well-marked country road north 6 miles (9 km) for a short detour to the important ruins of Alba Fucens, a Roman settlement from the 1st century BC that has been under excavation since 1949. In a dramatic setting beneath the massive double mountain of Monte Velino are the remains of baths, a villa, a theater, a basilica, and a huge amphitheater. Note the ancient Roman milestone post that marks the Via Tiburtina from Rome. Before the Romans, the Equi had their acropolis here; remains of their ancient walls still can be seen.

Return to the autostrada and, following the Avezzano signs, take the country road 2 miles (4 km) south to S578, then turn left to Avezzano, which was largely destroyed by an earthquake early this century. Its 15th-century *Castello d'Orsini*, still intact, has an interesting exterior. The *Raccolto Lapidario Marsicano* at the *Comune* (Town Hall; Via Vezia; phone: 863-5011) has minor artifacts and epigraphs from Alba Fucens. Make arrangements to visit it at the *Comune;* no admission charge.

BEST EN ROUTE

Aquila Clean and comfortable, this trattoria offers well-prepared regional dishes such as lasagna, *pasta e fagioli* (pasta and bean soup), and fresh grilled trout. Closed Mondays and late July. Reservations unnecessary. Major credit cards accepted. 26 Corso della Libertà, Avezzano (phone: 863-413152). Moderate.

Umberto One of the oldest restaurants in the whole Marsica area (as this part of the Abruzzo is called), this is the place for regional specialties, including *pasta alla chitarra,* charcoal-broiled lamb chops, and roast pork, and local wines. Closed Thursdays. Reservations unnecessary. Some credit cards accepted. 56 Monte Grappa, Avezzano (phone: 863-413888). Moderate.

En Route from Avezzano Return to A25 and head 8 miles (13 km) east to the exit for Celano, a mountainside farm town (pop. 10,000). Celano's seven medieval churches and stone dwellings cluster around the massive walls of an immense and well-preserved 14th-century castle. In late August every year, the town hosts a week of festivities for its patron saints, with concerts in the piazza and fireworks. Eight miles (13 km) north on S5 *bis* is the lovely village of Ovindoli; horseback riding (the town has three stables that rent horses in the summer) and hiking are excellent in the surrounding area. A challenging hike in dry summer weather is through the canyon-like Gole di Celano, walking from Ovindoli through the magnificent Val d'Arano and then down a steep descent to the town of Celano. The path is marked every summer by the local *Club Alpino Italiano* (*CAI*).

Returning once again to A25, head east toward Pescara and continue 12 miles (20 km) to Cocullo. Try to visit this tiny hilltop town the first Thursday in May, when the *Processione dei Serpari* (Procession of the Serpent-Bearers) takes place in the *Chiesa di San Domenico.* There are ruins of a medieval tower and, from the same era, the *Chiesa della Madonna delle Grazie,* with its fine paintings and altar. Continue 11 miles (18 km) on A25 to Pratola, then take S17 south for 4 miles (6 km) to Sulmona.

SULMONA The main piazza of this especially gracious medieval town (pop. 25,000) resembles a stage setting, crossed by part of a Roman aqueduct. Visit its 11th-century cathedral, *San Panfilo* (Via Ovidio), and the 13th-century aqueduct and the *Chiesa di San Francesco della Scarpa* (both on Piazza del Mercato). Best of all, however, is the fascinating *Annunziata* abbey complex, dating from the 14th century (Piazza all'Annunziata; no phone). It's open daily from 10 AM to 1 PM; no admission charge. Modern Sulmona's main source of income is sugar-coated almonds; gold filigree work is a local craft tradition. For sugared almond flower (*confetti*) arrangements, the most famous shop is *Fratelli Pelino* (55 Via Introdacqua), but local manufacturers all make the same high-quality product, including wreaths that adorn doorways. For typical Abruzzo bedspreads, used more often in the US as area rugs, stop at the factory of *Santarelli* (15 Via Stazione Introdacqua, on the road toward Scanna right outside town; phone: 864-51777). It is closed Sundays.

A pleasant detour is to continue 19 miles (32 km) southeast on the uphill, winding S17 and then take a left onto S84 to Pescocostanzo (near Roccaraso, a popular ski resort). One of the Abruzzo's most picturesque towns, Pescocostanzo has a beautiful square, the Piazza Santa Maria del Colle, site of an 11th-century church, *Santa Maria del Colle.* Its wooden ceiling is carved and gilded, and the 13th-century altar and seated Madonna del Colle were carved in wood by local craftsmen. The magnificent doorway of the nearby *Collegiata* (Abbey School) should not be missed. This is still a village of craftspeople—on Corso Roma, blacksmiths display their wrought-iron wares for all to see. *Vito Sciullo* (Piazza del Municipio) sells traditional Abruzzo gold and silver filigree jewelry, although other shops throughout the town also have high-quality goods. And in some of the tiny *mercerie,* which sell a hodgepodge of everything, a few prized bits of handmade Abruzzo *tombolo* lace can be found.

Europa Park Just outside of town, this 105-room hostelry has a pleasant restaurant, an outdoor tennis court, and a garage, but is not long on charm. Km 93, S17N, Sulmona (phone: 864-251260; fax: 864-251317). Moderate.

Italia The mood is rustic, but with a few surprising touches, such as lemon-flavored cannelloni. In summer, dine alfresco at tables overlooking the main piazza. Closed Mondays and early July. Reservations necessary on the weekends. Major credit cards accepted. 26 Piazza XX Settembre, Sulmona (phone: 864-33070). Moderate.

Rigoletto In an elegant, welcoming atmosphere, diners find rustic regional specialties "updated" with some antique recipes. The vermicelli with local saffron and stuffed roast leg of lamb are memorable. Closed Sunday dinner, the last two weeks of July, and two weeks at *Christmas*. Reservations necessary. Major credit cards accepted. 46 Via Stazione Introdacqua (phone: 864-55529). Moderate.

Italia Centrally located and charming, it has 27 rooms (16 with private baths; none with phones or TVs). No restaurant. No credit cards accepted. 3 Piazza Salvatore Tommasi, Sulmona (phone: 864-52308). Moderate to inexpensive.

En Route from Sulmona Head northwest on S17, which turns into S5, for 65 miles (109 km) to Chieti.

CHIETI Poised on a bluff overlooking the vast Pescara River plain, Chieti was once the home of the Marrucini tribe, which first fought hard against the Romans and later joined them in defending their common territory from the Phoenicians during the Punic wars. A Roman center of power, for a time it ruled over Pescara—then called Aternum—but later was brought to its knees by the barbarians. Sites of interest include the medieval *Duomo* (Piazza della Villa Comunale) and the Baroque 17th-century *Chiesa di San Domenico* (Corso Marrucino). Paintings from the 14th century on can be found in the *Pinacoteca Barbella* in the *Palazzo Martinetti,* a former 17th-century convent (13 Via de Lollis; phone: 871-330873). It is closed Mondays and holidays; Wednesdays, Fridays, and Saturdays after 1 PM; Tuesdays and Thursdays for a long (1 to 4 PM) break; and Sundays, except the first Sunday of every month. There's an admission charge. The town's pièce de résistance is the *Museo Nazionale Archeologico* (National Archaeological Museum; *Villa Comunale,* Viale R. Paolucci; phone: 871-65704), the most important museum in the Abruzzo, whose prize possession is the *Warrior of Capestrano,* dating from about 500 BC. When it was found buried in a vineyard in 1934, the statue became a worldwide sensation, not only for its perfect condition and elegant style but also because it showed that an unknown and sophisticated civilization, a contemporary of the Etruscans, existed in the Abruzzo. The collection also includes a celebrated statue of Hercules found at Alba Fucens, a splendid bed from Amiternum, and elegant polychrome mosaic marble pavements from other ancient Abruzzo cities. The museum is open daily; call ahead for hours. There's an admission charge. Also worth visiting are the ruins of the 2nd-century Roman theater (Via Zecca) and the small Roman temple (one block west of Corso Marrucino, behind the central post office) built by the Teati, the original Roman inhabitants of the city. The mountainous region between Chieti and the *Parco Nazionale d'Abruzzo* has recently been named a national park, the *Parco Nazionale della Maiella*. For English-language information about tours, contact *Linea Verde* (2 Largo Cicciotto, Guardiagrele; phone: 85-800023; fax: 85-85290). Possibilities include hikes and rentals of mountain bikes and cross country skis. The local tourist office, the *Azienda per il Soggiorno,* is at 29 Via B. Spaventa (phone: 871-65231).

BEST EN ROUTE

Dangio' A charming, 38-room inn overlooking the river valley, it has an outstanding restaurant, *La Regine,* that offers a modern and creative interpretation of traditional dishes. Closed Mondays and most of December. Reservations advised. Major credit cards accepted. 20 Via Solferino, Chieti (phone: 871-347356; fax: 871-346984). Moderate.

Venturini The Abruzzo specialty, *pasta alla chitarra,* is angel-hair-fine at this eatery in the historic center. Try *timballino di crespelle* (baked crêpes filled with mushrooms, mozzarella, and prosciutto) and the turkey breast stuffed with chestnuts. Closed Tuesdays. Reservations advised. Major credit cards accepted. 10 Via de Lollis, Chieti (phone: 871-330663). Moderate.

En Route from Chieti On A25, head 6 miles (9 km) east to Pescara, a pre-Roman city on the Adriatic Sea at the mouth of the Pescara River.

PESCARA Pescara was destroyed twice by the Longobards, once by Ottone IV, and now again by today's urban architects, who are constructing unsightly, modern buildings here. Ladislao of Naples, and later Charles V, fortified the city so well that it withstood a siege in 1566 by the Turks and another by the Austrians in 1707. Gabriele D'Annunzio went to school here, and his boyhood home (on Corso Manthonè) now houses three museums—the *Museo della Fondazione Gabriele D'Annunzio* (phone: 85-60391); the *Museo Archeologico* (phone: 85-690656), which has a collection of local Roman artifacts; and the *Museo delle Arti Populari Abruzzesi* (phone: 85-690656), with a permanent exhibit of Abruzzese folk arts and crafts. All three are closed Mondays through Saturdays after 1 PM; closed Sundays after 12:30 PM; admission charge. Pescara is a large fishing port—berth to colorful boats, and home to countless seafood restaurants. Local specialties include the *parrozzo* torte made with hazelnuts and *aurum,* a local liqueur said to derive from the ancients. Nearby are wide, sandy beaches popular with swimmers and sunbathers. The local tourist office, the *Azienda per il Soggiorno,* is at 171 Via Nicola Fabrizi (phone: 85-421-1707).

BEST EN ROUTE

Guerino Among the traditional dishes offered at this reliable old favorite are seafood-stuffed ravioli, and sole with mayonnaise. The fish is always fresh in what has been a leader in the Abruzzo restaurant world (and a steady magnet for tour groups) for over half a century. Closed Thursdays (except July through August) and one week at *Christmas.* Reservations advised. Major credit cards accepted. 4 Viale Riviera, Pescara (phone: 85-421-2065). Expensive.

Duilio Fish takes center stage at this well-managed modern restaurant. Prepare to dine abundantly on such fare as *antipasto alla Duilio* (a splendid array of fish, crayfish, squid, and other shellfish), *fusilli alla pescatrice* (pasta with fish sauce), delicate *rombo* (turbot) with zucchini, or *palombo* (a shark-like fish) with artichokes. Service is attentive, and the wine list is carefully selected. Closed Sunday dinner and Mondays. Reservations necessary. Major credit cards accepted. 9 Via Regina Margherita, Pescara (phone: 85-378278). Expensive to moderate.

Carlton Well appointed and comfortable, this seaside hotel with 70 rooms has a decent restaurant. Parking is available. Open year-round. 35 Viale Riviera, Pescara (phone: 85-373125; fax: 85-421-3922). Moderate.

Franco Crowded with admirers, big and cheery, this riverside trattoria offers a prix fixe menu with at least five types of *antipasto del mare,* as well as risotto with fish and baby shrimp, and a generous mixed fish plate—grilled or fried, with wine and dessert. Closed Mondays. Reservations advised. No credit cards accepted. 58 Via Doria, Pescara (phone: 85-66390). Moderate to inexpensive.

En Route from Pescara Take coastal road S16 north about 13 miles (21 km) to Pineto, the turnoff for Atri, and head west 6 miles (10 km). Of notable interest in Atri is the *Museo Capitolare* (Via Roma; phone: 85-87241). Its collection includes Abruzzo ceramics, sacred vestments, and other articles. The museum is open daily, with a long break (noon to 4 PM) in summer; hours are less fixed in winter (it's best to call ahead). Admission charge. In the Piazza del Duomo, the town's more than 1,100-year-old cathedral (on the ruins of a Roman bath) houses fine frescoes by Andrea De Lito—the most important Renaissance works in the Abruzzo.

Follow A14 north for 10 miles (17 km) and exit at Giulianova. Equestrians might want to stop at *Fattoria Cerreto* in nearby Mosciano Sant'Angelo (Colle Cerreto; phone: 85-806-1579). For more information, see *Horsing*

Around, Italian Style in DIVERSIONS. From Giulianova, take S80 15 miles (24 km) west to Teramo.

TERAMO A pre-Roman city, Teramo lies between the Tordino and the smaller Vezzola Rivers. The Romans later built another city on top of it. Today's modern city has few traces of its proud ancient heritage, but the 12th-century *Cattedrale di San Berardo* (Via Tirso) is of interest, as are the 1st-century Roman theater and amphitheater (Via del'Anfiteatro). The small *Museo e Pinacoteca Civica,* at the *Villa Comunale* (Piazza Garibaldi; phone: 861-247772), houses artifacts from the Roman era, Renaissance paintings, and Castelli ceramics. The museum is closed Sundays and after 1:30 PM; call ahead for afternoon hours in summer. There's an admission charge. The local tourist board is on Via del Castello (phone: 861-244222).

BEST EN ROUTE

Il Duomo In a pleasant setting, brothers Carlo and Marcello Rossi offer such regional seasonal specialties as *porcini* mushroom salad, *tagliatelle* with *porcini,* and lamb prepared in various delectable ways. Other dishes include an 18th-century pasta recipe called *lu rentrocele* (a sauce made with three kinds of meat—beef, lamb, and pork) and, in spring, *le virtù,* the famed peasant soup. There is a good selection of national and regional wines. Closed Mondays and most of August. Reservations advised. Major credit cards accepted. 9 Via Stazio, Teramo (phone: 861-241774). Moderate.

Sporting Very modern for the Abruzzo, this hotel offers an indoor pool, a gym, and a good restaurant, *Il Carpaccio.* The 55 rooms are spacious and comfortable if somewhat uninspired, and they are noisier than they should be. 41 Via de Gasperi, Teramo (phone: 861-414723; fax: 861-210285). Moderate.

Antico Cantinone *Zuppe di ceci e castagne* (chick-pea soup with chestnuts), *crespelle* (light crêpes) stuffed with cheese, and roast lamb are the specialties of this authentic regional trattoria, which has been pleasing diners for half a century. Among the wines are those from the Val Vibrata. Closed Sundays. No reservations. No credit cards accepted. 5 Via Ciotti, Teramo (phone: 861-248863). Inexpensive.

En Route from Teramo Take S80 3 miles (5 km) east to A24, then head southwest for 15 miles (24 km) to the Isola di Gran Sasso exit. For information about climbing the Gran Sasso, contact the *Azienda Soggiorno e Turismo* (8 Via XX Settembre; phone: 862-22306) or the *Club Alpino Italiano* (*CAI;* 15 Via XX Settembre; phone: 862-24342), both in L'Aquila. Against a majestic sweep of high mountains, take Route 491, an easy but winding country road, northeast for 5 miles (8 km). Turn right on to the Castelli provincial road and follow it for 6 miles (10 km) to Castelli, a center for master ceramists for the past four centuries. Across from the village, a deep gouge in the cliff shows where the craftspeople get their fine clay. Dozens of old kilns lie under the village's stone buildings. Scores of small stores sell the ceramics, but before stopping at the first roadside shops to buy, visit the small *Museo della Ceramica*, just outside the village. Among its beautifully displayed ceramics are centuries-old works by the Grue master potters, including painted plates, vases, and panels. The museum is closed Mondays and after 1 PM; admission charge (phone: 861-979398). Although modernizing influences are starting to appear in Castelli pottery, the old ways continue, and a leisurely tour of the shops in the village—after seeing the originals in the museum—is a good way to decide what to buy. Of the many skillful craftspeople, the Antonio D'Egidio family stands out—son Giovanni now paints pottery and runs the shop (18 Scesa del Borgo).

The adventurous should drive up the steep, narrow dirt road to the small country *Chiesa di San Donato.* It is kept locked, so if you want to see the church's precious 200-year-old painted tile ceiling up close, make arrangements in advance at the *Comune* (Piazza Roma; phone: 861-979142). Otherwise, it can be glimpsed only through a window at the front.

Head back to A24 and take it for 29 miles (46 km) to L'Aquila, the loveliest city of the Abruzzo. The autostrada passes through a half-mile-long tunnel directly under the Gran Sasso.

L'AQUILA Built in the 13th century, L'Aquila flourished in the mid-14th century; most of its most important monuments were constructed during those two centuries. They include the outstanding *Basilica di Santa Maria di Collemaggio* (Viale di Collemaggio), which was started in 1287 by the monk Pietro da Morrone, who would later become Pope Celestino V; his mausoleum is inside. The church façade has horizontal stripes, and a finely carved doorframe and rose windows; inside are 14th-century frescoes. The *Chiesa di Santa Maria Paganica* (Piazza Santa Maria Paganica) dates from 1308, and *Santa Maria di Róio* (Via di Róio) was built in 1332. The *Fontana delle 99 Cannelle* (Piazza di Porta Rivera), a restored fountain with 99 spouts, was built in 1272. The renowned *Madonna and Angels* fresco by Francesco da Montereale is in the *Chiesa di San Silvestro* (Via Garibaldi). The churches are open daily, with a long (noon to 4 PM) break. The immense, square, fortified castle, the 16th-century *Castello Cinquecentesco* (bordered by Via Castello and Viale Gran Sasso), houses paleontological and archaeological collections, paintings (especially medieval), 17th-century ceramics from Castelli, and speleological displays of minerals and objects found in the area's numerous caves. The castle is closed Mondays; Tuesdays through Saturdays after 1:30 PM; and Sundays after 1 PM in winter. It's closed Mondays, and Tuesdays through Sundays for a midday break, in summer. There's an admission charge (phone: 862-6331). The tourist office is at 5 Piazza Santa Maria di Paganica (phone: 862-410340).

Tre Marie A national monument, this restaurant is exceptional for its unique decor (including heavy wooden furnishings from the Abruzzo and an 18th-century fireplace) and for its elegantly prepared Abruzzo specialties. Paolo is the latest member of the Scipioni family to oversee the painstaking preparations of the delicate *zuppa della salute* (crêpes in broth), *ravioli ripieni* (homemade stuffed pasta), *maccheroni alla chitarra,* sizzling grilled trout, and *torta di ricotta* (ricotta tart). Look for recipes with *zafferano* (saffron). Closed Sunday dinner, Mondays, and from *Christmas* to *New Year's Day.* Reservations advised. No credit cards accepted. 3 Via Tre Marie, L'Aquila (phone: 862-410109). Very expensive.

Grand Hotel del Parco Close to the Piazza Duomo, this establishment is a real find, offering 36 relatively spacious rooms with parquet floors and well-appointed bathrooms. There is a restaurant and a health center with sauna and hydromassage. Rooms at the rear are less noisy. 74 Corso Federico, L'Aquila (phone: 862-413248; fax: 862-65938). Expensive to moderate.

Il Caminetto The *frittelle* (crêpes) and potato gnocchi here are made with saffron. Another specialty comes from the ancient Romans—*abbacchio in brodetto* (lamb with egg and lemon sauce). Closed Mondays and November. Reservations advised. Some credit cards accepted. S80, Località Cansatessa, L'Aquila (phone: 862-311410). Moderate.

Duca degli Abruzzi Centrally located, this modern, comfortable hostelry has 120 rooms, a garage, and an excellent penthouse restaurant, *Il Tetto,* overlooking the red-tile rooftops. Open year-round. 10 Viale Giovanni XXIII, L'Aquila (phone: 862-28341; fax: 862-61588). Moderate.

En Route from L'Aquila To visit the *Parco Nazionale d'Abruzzo,* take A24 west to Avezzano. Otherwise, follow A24 back to Rome.

PARCO NAZIONALE D'ABRUZZO

Italy has few national parks of such dimensions: 200 square miles of mountains, sunlit valleys, and dense forests of pine, beech, and chestnut trees. The park is bounded by two mountain chains, the Mainarde to the southeast and the Marsicani to the east; by two rivers, the Sangro and the Liri, to the south and southwest; and by the broad, flat farm valley of the Fucinoto in the northwest.

The area was set apart as park land in 1872, but it didn't become a national park until 1950, and after lively debate—the villagers opposed it, fearing it would destroy their livelihood gained from cutting down trees. Today nature lovers wage an ongoing battle to protect the surrounding semi-protected park border areas from development. The park proper, which has remained largely intact, is home to 40 species of mammals and

30 varieties of bird—cuckoos and nightingales can sometimes be heard on a summer evening in the woods. Wild chamois roam the mountains, and among the dozens of snakes is the deadly Abruzzo viper. (Carry a walking stick and wear appropriate footwear when on the woodland paths.) There also are Marsican bears and a few surviving wolves.

Meadows and fields glow with yellow gorse and red poppies, and hilltop towns are poised against a backdrop of gray mountain peaks, long narrow fjord-like lakes, and dramatic canyons. In June and July, wildflowers carpet the high meadows, wild strawberries can be found, and wild mushrooms are in season. In August, when the lowlands turn dry, the park is ideal for hiking, biking, and horseback riding. In winter, the best time for a lingering visit is February, when downhill and cross-country skiers find many sunny days.

Because of its proximity to Rome, Pescasseroli, a major ski center, can become quite crowded over *Christmas*. An alternative is to go later in January, when "white week" discounts are available. For information, contact the *Aziende Autonome di Turismo* (Via Piave, Pescasseroli; phone: 863-910461). Trails are short, but there are plenty of slopes for skiers of all levels. In midwinter, chains may be obligatory for cars.

En Route from Avezzano Take the A25 autostrada 10 miles (16 km) to Pescina. Although it is prosperous today, Pescina was the poverty-stricken farm village so movingly described by writer Ignazio Silone in *Fontamara*. Silone was born here, and his ashes are buried near the stark tower of the town's more-than-600-year-old castle at the edge of the village, as was his wish. Another native son is Cardinal Giulio Mazzarino (1601–61), astute counselor to Louis XIV of France; a small museum (Piazzale Rancilio; phone: 863-842156) commemorates him. It's closed Wednesdays; Sunday afternoons; and Mondays, Tuesdays, and Thursdays through Saturdays for a long (noon to 4 PM) break; admission charge.

Leaving behind the fields of sugar beets and potatoes, take S83 south into the mountains, entering the park area at the village of Gioia Vecchio. At the lofty Passo del Diavolo (Devil's Pass), you descend slightly to enter a high valley through which the small Sangro River snakes. In the center of this broad valley, ringed with higher mountains marked by ski runs, is the immensely popular summer and winter resort of Pescasseroli, 29 miles (46 km) from Pescina and 3,829 feet above sea level. This is the gateway to the park proper and the birthplace of the 20th-century philosopher Benedetto Croce.

PESCASSEROLI Unusual for a ski resort center, Pescasseroli (pop. 2,220) has an ancient heritage. Its small Lungobard *Castello Mancino,* perched at the end of a path on a hilltop overlooking the town, dates from the Middle Ages. The Romanesque *Chiesa di San Pietro e di San Paolo* (in the piazza of the same name) was built in the 14th century. During the 1800s the area became the property of the powerful *Monastery of Farfa* in Lazio.

In Pescasseroli, the *transumanza* (the ancient custom of walking flocks great distances) was observed for many centuries. Shortly before the deep snows arrived, the men from Pescasseroli and other nearby high mountain towns would set out with their herds of sheep and goats to walk down through Molise to Candela, near Foggia in Puglia, where they had winter grazing rights. They walked what is called the *trattura reale*—the royal route.

Visits to the *Parco Nazionale d'Abruzzo* can be arranged (though travelers are free to roam on their own) at the *Azienda Autonoma di Turismo* (67 Via Piave; phone: 863-910461); at the *Ente Parco* headquarters at the *Museo Naturalistico e Parco Faunistico,* a small museum of folklore and natural history with an adjacent zoo on the outskirts of town (Viale Santa Lucia; no phone; open daily, with a long midday break; admission charge); or at *Cooperativa Ecotur* (13 Via Santa Lucia; phone/fax: 863-912760). The latter two sell maps showing 25 suggested itineraries for hikers of all levels and capabilities. Keep to the marked paths, and do not pick wildflowers or mushrooms. Rock climbing is strictly forbidden.

For information on hiking excursions for all skill levels, mountain refuges, and campsites—and there are many—contact the *Cooperativa Servizi Turistici* (Via Umberto I; phone: 863-88152). *Cooperativa Ecotur* (see above) offers five-hour guided walking tours daily in summer, when half-day bus excursions also are available. Reserve ahead in July and August, as the number of people permitted into the chamois-viewing areas—the Valle di Rosa and Monte Amaro—is limited. The *Agenzia Wolf* (Civitella Alfedena; phone: 863-839336) also organizes walking trips.

Ecotur rents mountain bikes from *Easter* through early fall (for more information on cycling in the park, see *Freewheeling Through Italy* in DIVERSIONS) and arranges tailor-made guided trekking, cycling, or horseback excursions of several days, with an English-speaking guide, along the old *transumanza* route. For horseback or pony rides and lessons, also contact *Centro Ippico Vallecupa* (Via della Difesa; phone: 863-910444).

BEST EN ROUTE

Grand Hotel del Parco With 120 rooms, this hostelry is considered the best in town. There is a restaurant and an outdoor pool. 3 Via Santa Lucia, Pescasseroli (phone: 863-912745; fax: 863-912749). Expensive.

Relais Il Salotto Dine alfresco in summer, or in winter by a huge fireplace in a room handsomely paneled in wood. Leave your hiking gear behind—this place is elegant, and the food is a refined adaptation of traditional Abruzzo fare. Specialties include *risotto al limone* (rice with a tangy lemon sauce) and regional homemade pasta dishes. Closed June. Reservations necessary for dinner. No credit cards accepted. 4 Via Collacchi, Pescasseroli (phone: 863-91911). Moderate.

Cerbiatto Try the homemade *codetti ai peperoni* (green pasta with green pepper sauce) at this small, rustic trattoria. Also recommended is *gnocchetti* (small pasta) with beans. Closed Wednesdays. Reservations unnecessary. No credit cards accepted. 19 Via Principe di Napoli, Pescasseroli (phone: 863-910465). Moderate to inexpensive.

Edelweiss A comfortable 25-room hotel, it offers a restaurant, a disco, and a garage. Via Colli dell'Oro, Pescasseroli (phone: 863-912577; fax: 863-912798). Moderate to inexpensive.

En Route from Pescasseroli Four miles (6 km) south on S83 is Opi. It dates from prehistoric times, and even today its houses huddle into a defensive wall protecting the village. Opi is a jumping-off point for a drive on a narrow road through handsome maple and beech woods toward the Forca d'Acero *rifugio,* one of ten in the park.

Ten miles (16 km) east of Opi on S83 is Barrea, a picture-postcard village. Founded nearly a thousand years ago, Barrea suffered from frequent attacks by Saracen pirates and invaders from the north. Despite a catastrophic earthquake in 1915, this medieval center is in fair condition, and vestiges of the ancient walls can be seen. The 13th-century castle has cylindrical towers, as does the *Chiesa di San Tommaso.* The town is a lovely collection of small, ancient stone buildings, towers, and 14th-century churches, against a dramatic background of mountain peaks. The elongated Lake Barrea stretches beyond.

Take S83 for 4 miles (7 km) to Villetta Barrea and turn north onto S479, which winds its way 16 miles (27 km) to Scanno slowly downhill over high alpine meadows reminiscent of Switzerland.

BEST EN ROUTE

Tre Camini Near the crossroad for Opi on S83, this rustic country inn offers the traveler a shaded verandah and tasty dishes such as *fazzoletti verdi* (large pasta filled with ricotta and spinach), grilled salmon trout, and homemade desserts, including apple tart. Closed Thursdays. Reservations necessary on Sundays. No credit cards accepted. Km 48.7, S83, Opi (phone: 863-91936). Moderate.

SCANNO Historians believe that the Scannesi, with their unique customs and costumes, were descended from a nomadic Red Sea tribe—Macau Scammos, who named their town Scamnum. Paliano, as the Old Town is called, is believed to have been named for the Greek god Pan.

Like the rest of the Abruzzo, Scanno flourished in the Middle Ages, but plagues, politics, famine, and earthquakes so decimated it that in 1447 a census showed only 302 surviving inhabitants. By the Renaissance, however, Scanno had returned to life, with a population of 2,420 people and 130,000 sheep. Today there are still the same number of human inhabitants, but the sheep population has shrunk to about one sheep per person. Herding was always important, and until the 1800s a rare variety of black Egyptian sheep was raised here.

The graceful, 13th-century *Chiesa di Santa Maria della Valle* (Piazza Santa Maria della Valle), whose foundations stand on the ruins of a small pagan temple, gazes serenely out over a peaceful valley far below; the church portal and the window above are exquisite. Inside, the polychrome high altar of marble dates from 1731. Behind the church unfolds the tiny Old Town, once within walls pierced by four gates; you can still see remains of a venerable wall and one arched gate. Look in at the *Chiesa di Santa Maria di Costantinopoli* (Piazza San Rocco), built before 1400; an elegant fresco inside shows the Madonna and Child on a throne and the name "De Ciollis" and the date "AD 1478." Whether De Ciollis was painter or patron of what is the town's greatest art treasure, no one knows.

Scanno is popular in both summer and winter. Summer visitors can hike or take the chair lift (when it operates) up Monte Rotondo for magnificent views of the area. In winter, three lifts operate, and skis can be rented at *Bruno Sport* (6 Via del Lago) in town or, close to the slopes at the *Paradiso* hotel, *Rifugio Passo Godi* or *Rifugio Lo Scoiattolo,* all at Passo Godi. Tourist information is available at the *Azienda per il Turismo* (12 Piazza Santa Maria della Valle; phone: 864-74317). Small boats are for hire at Lake Scanno; bicycles, at *Prati del Lago* (a park by Lake Scanno), where there are also three tennis courts. Fishing is popular by the dam at San Domenico a Villalago. *Il Ranch* (Variante La Foce; phone: 864-747714) rents horses and also will arrange horseback tours around the lake and through the hills. Also try *Le Prata* stables (phone: 864-747263) and *Miralago Maneggio* (phone: 864-747390).

Goldsmithing is a time-honored art in this town, and many small workshops offer fine examples to purchase. Brothers Fronterotta (their eponymous shop is in Piazza Santa Maria della Valle) reinterpret traditional motifs, like the *presentosa* (engagement pin), in attractive ways, using solid gold or inexpensive versions of silver. *Di Rienzo* (1 Via Roma) and *Giancarlo Montesi* (Piazza Santa Maria della Valle) offer traditional gold and silver filigree work in earrings, pins, and bracelets. Locally made bobbin lace for inserts in sheets, collars, or centerpieces, as well as Abruzzo bedspreads and a few patchwork quilts, are available at *Violetta* (30 Via Roma), where you can also rent a Scanno costume in which to have your picture taken. *Chiusolo Artigianato* (13 Via Vincenzo Tanturri) sells hand-embroidered bobbin lace collars and other accessories, plus sheepskin wear.

Garden In this modern hotel are 35 rooms, a restaurant, a disco, a bar, a garden, and a garage. 79 Viale del Lago, Scanno (phone: 864-74382; fax: 864-747488). Expensive to moderate.

Gli Archetti Homemade vegetable antipasti and flavorful salami and prosciutto are offered at this longtime Old Town favorite. There is the ubiquitous *pasta alla chitarra,* but also try polenta in a spicy sauce, lamb from the nearby hills, trout, and vegetables prepared the traditional Abruzzo farm way (sautéed in oil and seasoned with dried red peppers). Closed Tuesdays in winter. Major credit cards accepted. 8 Via Silla, Scanno (phone: 864-74645). Moderate.

Vittoria There is a tennis court at this 27-room inn, but no restaurant. 46 Via di Rienzo, Scanno (phone: 864-74398). Moderate to inexpensive.

En Route from Scanno Continue north on S479 12 miles (19 km) past the elongated Lake Scanno, where the road plunges into a narrow rock canyon and the scenery is breathtaking, to Cocullo and the A24 autostrada, which leads back to Rome.

Lazio

If all roads lead to Rome, they lead away from it as well. There are few better ways to discover Rome than to explore the ancient roads radiating from the city the ancients knew as *Caput Mundi,* the center of the world. From Mediolanum in the north—today's Milan—to Brindisi and Taranto at the heel of the Italian boot, all the great cities of the Roman Empire were linked to the capital by roads so enduring that their engineering remains a benchmark for road builders into our own century. Financed by tribute, the 400 major Roman roads were built to last, with up to five feet of layered sand, lime, crushed rock, and, often, flat paving stones of basalt. Down them went settlers in covered wagons, sandal-clad soldiers trudging off to war, and tradesmen in horse carts hustling everything from Greek pottery to wool.

Beginning northwest of Rome and moving clockwise, the main roads were the Via Aurelia, which ran up the peninsula along the sea; the Via Cassia; the Via Flaminia; the Via Salaria, so named because it brought inlanders to the salt flats at the mouth of the Tiber River; the Via Praeneste, which led to one of antiquity's greatest shrines; and the great Appian Way, heading south.

Leaving the city today by any of these ancient roadways is initially painful because of traffic jams and urban blight; occasional serendipitous glimpses of a section of Roman aqueduct, a stretch of ancient wall, or a brickwork tomb, do, however, offer some relief. And surprisingly quickly, the city comes to an abrupt end. Lazio (from the ancient name Latium), the region around Rome, has only a limited industrial belt, mostly around the Via Pontina south of Rome and the Via Tiberina, which meanders along with the Tiber.

On a map, Lazio resembles an ivy leaf. One of its trinity of lobes points north, into Tuscan Italy, where gently rolling countryside and olive orchards and vineyards alternate with lofty cliffs of ruddy brown tufa stone. Here, where the plain of Lazio begins to turn into the foothills of the Apennines, villages perch on a hilltop and cluster around castles. Many were founded by the Etruscans, who liked the safety of an acropolis. Of uncertain origin, the Etruscans were an aristocratic class of merchant sailors who came to dominate Italy from the Arno River to the Tiber—their ancient land, Etruria, extended into present-day Tuscany and Umbria, as well as northern Lazio. While Rome was still a shepherds' trading post, the Etruscans reigned in a federation of 12 city-states. One of these, Tarquinia, was important enough to give Rome three early kings, the Tarquins. The ruins of three other city-states lie close to modern Rome: Cerveteri (ancient Caere), close to the sea off the Via Aurelia; Vulci, off the Via Aurelia; and Veii, off the Via Cassia. Considered the greatest of the Etruscan city-states, landlocked Veii fell to the Romans in the 4th century BC, when it lost control of the Tiber River passage and the overland route south on the Via Praeneste.

The central lobe, surrounding Rome and pointing east into the rugged limestone fastnesses of the Apennines, borders Umbria and Abruzzo. It has a harsher look, and its steep mountains and their springs provide the water for the cascades feeding, among others, the fountains at Tivoli. The area was roughly the hilltop territory of the Sabine and Latin tribes that merged to conquer Rome, Etruria, and finally the Mediterranean, North Africa, northern Europe, and western Asia. Although they were farmers, less cultivated (and less economically advanced) than the Etruscans, the Latin tribes were quick studies and dedicated pragmatists.

The third and largest lobe sprawls southward. Its sand beaches, hopelessly crowded in July and August, form one border. Then flat, rich farmland stretches toward rocky hilltops ablaze with yellow broom in summer; here the hills are crowned with monasteries, some built on the foundations of pagan temples. Several, including the abbey at Monte Cassino, were founded by St. Benedict. The Greeks and a powerful local tribe, the Samnites, ruled here. The area was inhabited far earlier, however. On Monte Circeo, which juts into the Tyrrhenian Sea (from *Tyrrhenoi,* the Greek name for the Etruscans), Ulysses was seduced by a bewitching shepherdess named Circe. Long before that, a Neanderthal tribesman killed a rival, broke a hole into his skull for magical purposes, and left the skull inside a ring of ritual stones in a cave on Monte Circeo. The skull was found there in the 1930s, 40,000 years later.

To travel in Lazio today is to travel through time, seeing traces of three distinct cultures—Etruscan, Latin, and Magna Graecian—that profoundly influenced Western civilization. Then there is Lazio's modern aspect. Among its larger towns are, in the north, the port of Civitavecchia (Rome's own port was silted over during ancient times) and, inland, Viterbo. Heading into the Latin towns, there is the fairly large walled city of Rieti, of Sabine origin—nearby is the magnificent, once powerful Benedictine abbey at Farfa—and, continuing to circle Rome clockwise, the volcanic horseshoe that includes the Alban Hills and two lakes, Albano and Nemi. The Alban Hills are home to 13 small towns, known collectively as the Castelli Romani. They are cool and airy when Rome is not.

The Ciociaria is a mountainous district between Rome and the relatively modern town of Frosinone. Nearby Fiuggi is an old-fashioned spa with waters that are reputed to help kidney sufferers and a bracing hill climate in the summer. Another modern town, Latina, lies in the midst of the Pontine Plain. Once a malaria-plagued swamp, the plain was drained by Mussolini in 1932. It's now a rather dull industrial and agricultural center, and its farmlands support water buffalo imported centuries ago from India. The milk is used to make Lazio's fresh mozzarella, one of the world's finest cheeses. Various beach resorts bask in the sun of the coast west and south of Latina, including Anzio, with its vast American military cemetery nearby;

Terracina; and the loveliest, Sperlonga. Inland on a mountaintop is the splendid *Monastero di Monte Cassino,* bombed by the Allies during World War II and meticulously rebuilt.

The food of the Roman countryside is, like the old Latins themselves, rustic rather than elegant. It employs ingredients unavailable elsewhere and, in certain cases, more flavorful because of the soil and climate. The Lazio diet is made up of mozzarella or piquant pecorino (ewe's milk) cheese, baby lamb or roast kid for a feast day, and pork in all its forms, including a fennel seed–laced salami. With an abundance of imagination rather than a surfeit of raw ingredients, the cooks of Lazio learned to turn poorer cuts of meat into dishes fit for a king (or pope). These included a shepherd's pie of lamb heart, potatoes, and onions; oxtail chunks stewed in wine, celery, and tomatoes; and tripe dressed in a sauce of tomatoes, grated cheese, and fresh mint (still a favorite Lazio dish today).

Spaghetti *alla carbonara* (with a sauce of egg, bacon bits, cheese, and a dash of nutmeg) was supposedly brought to Lazio by Umbrian coal peddlers. But the most authentic Lazio pasta style is *all'amatriciana,* from the town of Amatrice, in the province of Rieti. Purists hold that the diced salt pork must come from Amatrice itself, that only the faintest dab of tomato sauce suffices, and that tasty *pecorino romano,* made from ewe's milk— never parmesan cheese—must be used. Dotted with lakes, Lazio also offers an abundance of seafood, including trout and lake *coregone,* often flavored with fennel or *martana* sauce (capers, tomato, red pepper, garlic, parsley, and olives). Rabbit is popular, as is *pollo alla diavolo* (flattened, peppery chicken).

The Roman countryside produces an abundance of vegetables. On May 1, Italy's *Labor Day,* fava beans are served raw with chunks of pecorino and a robust red wine. Throughout spring, many restaurants offer *primavera* (a fresh vegetable compote). A medley of fried foods may include batter-fried mozzarella chunks, codfish, zucchini, zucchini flowers with a cheese stuffing, and flattened artichokes. *Puntarelle* (a special salad green) is invariably dressed in an anchovy and garlic vinaigrette. In late summer and autumn, when sun and rain come in just the right doses, the hills around Rome abound in wild mushrooms, which appear on menus in raw salads; as a sauce with noodles, polenta, or risotto; or, when the giant *Boletus edulis,* or *porcini,* are available, as a main course. Cheeses to try, besides *pecorino romano,* include *caciotta* (a mild cheese made from a mixture of ewe's and cow's milk), provolone (with a ripe, tangy or mild flavor), and mozzarella *affumicata* (smoked).

Lazio's desserts are generally uninspired, and these days, industrial frozen desserts are frequent, so fresh fruit is usually a wise choice, especially the tiny, woodland-scented strawberries that grow near Lake Nemi. Lazio cooks rinse them in aromatic frascati wine rather than water. Cultivated strawberries, which grow in fields throughout Lazio, are served with fresh orange or lemon juice.

The region's best wine probably is the *aleatico* of Gradoli and its neighbor from Montefiascone, a wine called est! est!! est!!! Cerveteri reds and whites are popular, as are the Castelli wines from Marino—colli albani, frascati, and velletri.

Lazio's sights can be visited in day trips from Rome. The seven routes that follow presuppose a hotel base in Rome, so a car is a must. A tip: The Raccordo Anulare, the ring road around Rome, connects all the roads that lead to Rome. Another tip: A traveler's most vital motto should be "Never on Monday," when most museums and many restaurants are closed. Each Thursday, Rome's daily paper, *La Repubblica,* carries news of local events in Lazio; on Friday, a column in *Il Messaggero* (another Rome daily) reports which Lazio town has a festival, religious procession, parade, or even a demonstration by the *butteri,* Lazio's authentic cowboys. Lazio towns fete just about anything, in its season: the wine vintage, wildflowers blooming, the artichoke crop, or the chestnut harvest.

In the restaurant listings, expensive means that a dinner for two with a bottle of wine will cost from $100 to $200; moderate, from $70 to $90; and inexpensive, $60 or less. All restaurants are open for lunch and dinner unless otherwise noted. Generally, prices are higher near the seashore, lower inland. For each location, restaurants are listed alphabetically by price category.

Note that many sites of interest in Lazio close for a midday break, usually from noon or 12:30 PM to anywhere from 3 to 4:30 PM; we suggest calling ahead to check exact hours.

DAY TRIP 1: TARQUINIA, TUSCANIA, VULCI

The seacoast town of Tarquinia, one of the 12 city-states of the Etruscan federation and one of the must-sees among Italian archaeological sites, is the first stop on this route. It is noted for the wall paintings found in its extensive necropolis, one of the main sources of our knowledge of Etruscan life. In the past, Tarquinia's pretty beach was polluted. The water quality is currently being monitored; be sure to check the signs before swimming. The walled medieval town of Tuscania is also on the route, as are the ruins of a second prominent Etruscan city, Vulci.

En Route from Rome Leave town by the Rome–Fiumicino Airport Highway (from most places in Rome the Via Aurelia followed by the Raccordo Anulare is the best starting point), then turn north onto the toll highway (A12) toward Civitavecchia. Tarquinia is about 1¼ hours (63 miles/101 km) away.

TARQUINIA Dating back to the early Iron Age, Tarquinia was one of the most powerful Etruscan cities from the 8th to the 4th centuries BC, and well into the 6th century BC it was far more important than Rome, thanks to its powerful fleet and nearby iron mines. For more information, see *Remarkable*

Ruins in DIVERSIONS. The *Museo Nazionale Tarquiniense,* in the elegant 15th-century *Palazzo Vitelleschi* just inside the gate to Tarquinia's Old Town, makes a good first stop. Its collection of Etruscan artifacts is one of Italy's most important, and there's fine Greek and Greek-influenced pottery, gold jewelry, magical mirrors, and sarcophagi. But its prized possessions are two winged horses that adorned a late-4th–century BC temple at Tarquinia's acropolis and several reconstructed tombs decorated with wall paintings detached from the actual site for safekeeping. Admission to the museum includes admission to the necropolis, about a mile (1.6 km) away (the museum attendant can provide driving instructions). To conserve the frescoes, only four tombs are open to visitors on any given day, and exactly which four varies from day to day. The museum and necropolis are closed Mondays; Sundays after 1 PM; and Tuesdays through Saturdays after 2 PM in winter; the necropolis's hours are extended in summer to 7 PM. For current information, call 766-856384.

True enthusiasts may want to visit the Pian di Civita, a hillside site. Take the road toward Viterbo; at Km 3.5 turn left onto a dirt road and follow it for 1¼ miles (2 km). It leads to the 4th-century BC *Ara della Regina* (Queen's Altar), the hilltop temple where the above-mentioned winged horses were found and where archaeological excavations are under way.

BEST EN ROUTE

Il Bersagliere Fresh fish takes center stage here, in the form of spaghetti *alla ghiotta* (with a scampi-and-shellfish sauce), simply grilled, or in a flavorful white wine sauce. Some desserts (*crème caramel* and *panna cotta*) are homemade; the ice cream is not. Closed Sunday dinner, Mondays, and *Christmas* week. Reservations advised for Sunday lunch. Major credit cards accepted. 2 Via Benedetto Croce, Tarquinia (phone: 766-856047). Expensive to moderate.

Velcamare Fish cooked in dozens of ways, including baby squid in its ink and pasta with shrimp and arugula, is served in this roomy place by the sea. There are 24 rooms at the adjacent inn. Closed Tuesdays and November through January. Reservations necessary Sundays and in midsummer. Major credit cards accepted. 1 Via degli Argonauti, Lido di Tarquinia (phone: 766-88024). Moderate.

En Route from Tarquinia Take the main road—the ancient Via Cassia, which parallels S1 along the coast for a few miles—north and follow the signs for Tuscania. After 2 miles (3 km) turn right onto the pleasant country road to Tuscania (15 miles/24 km away), running northeast and passing the hamlet of Quarticciolo.

TUSCANIA A beautiful example of a southern Etrurian walled town, Tuscania was built on a hill of tufa rock. It is surrounded by 5th-century BC Etruscan burial mounds, including one belonging to a family named Vipinana, whose tombs were found with no fewer than 27 sarcophagi. Some 50 members of another Etruscan family, the Statlane, have been counted. Ask at the *Museo Nazionale Etrusco* (Piazza Madonna del Riposo; phone: 761-436209) about visiting them. The museum, located in the former *Convento di Santa Maria del Riposo,* houses a collection of artifacts. It is closed Mondays before 2 PM; no admission charge. After the city was conquered by Rome, it continued to prosper, becoming a bishop's seat in the Middle Ages. Just how wealthy it was then can be seen in its scores of medieval towers that survived the 1971 earthquake that damaged much of Tuscania. The fine 11th-century *Chiesa di San Pietro,* built on the site of an Etruscan acropolis, is just outside the present town. With its myriad columns, the church's crypt is a study in architectural styles dating from the Roman era.

BEST EN ROUTE

Al Gallo The best restaurant in town is in this delightful rustic 18-room inn near the *Duomo.* Signs from the main gate in the city wall lead directly to it. Specialties, which change with the season, may include pasta with truffle stuffing, imported Angus beef, or a delicious *semifreddo* (ice-cream cake) with hazelnuts. Closed Tuesdays and the last week in January. Reservations advised. Major credit cards accepted. 24 Via del Gallo, Tuscania (phone: 761-435028). Expensive to moderate.

La Palombella Traditional cornmeal polenta, prepared with a spicy sauce of mushrooms, sausage, and tomatoes, is served at this family-run restaurant in an unprepossessing modern building. Chops and sausages are lovingly grilled over a wood fire, but the house specialty is game—noodles with hare sauce, roast pigeon, or guinea hen. Closed Saturday lunch and late August. Reservations advised on weekends. Major credit cards accepted. 23 Via Canino, Tuscania (phone: 761-435419). Moderate.

En Route from Tuscania Follow the excellently marked, easy-to-drive country roads about 12 miles (19 km) north to Canino; after another 3 miles (5 km), turn right to Vulci (watch for the yellow signs indicating tourist sights).

VULCI The bare ruins of another of the 12 Etruscan city-states lie in an area of Maremma countryside—the Pian di Voce—where flat fields, poplar lanes, and Roman aqueducts stand out against the brilliant Mediterranean light. Here a Bronze Age town was located on the banks of the Fiora River. By the 9th and 8th centuries BC, its craftsmen's skill in making bronze daggers, helmets, and shields was already known. Relics from the excavation of the town and the four necropolises in the vicinity are found in the world's greatest museums—artifacts from the *Isis Tomb* in the Polledrara necropolis, for instance, are in the *British Museum* in London. The monumental *Cuccumella Tomb* is well worth seeing, as is the *François Tomb* at Ponte Rotto (although its famed interior paintings have been removed to the *Villa*

Albani in Rome). Then see the *Museo Nazionale* (*Castel di Badia;* phone: 761-437787), a short drive from the excavations. This beautifully arranged museum is set up inside a restored 12th-century castle replete with a tiny moat. It is open daily, with a short (2 to 2:30 PM) break; no admission charge. Next to the castle, a humpbacked bridge—its foundations Etruscan, the rest of the structure Roman—arches over the rushing Fiora River. As a fortified monastery at the edge of the Papal States, the castle once controlled a major north-south highway link between Etruria and Rome. Carts en route to market were stopped by customs collectors at the castle's dooryard. Together, castle and bridge are among Italy's most romantic sights.

En Route from Vulci Turn back toward the sea and the town of Montalto di Castro (8 miles/13 km), where the Via Aurelia (S1) provides the best route for the return to Rome.

DAY TRIP 2: CERVETERI, BRACCIANO, VEII

Ideal for families with children, this second tour through Etruscan Lazio visits Cerveteri, another Etruscan city-state, with an important museum and tombs carved into the soft tufa stone. After Cerveteri, the tour proceeds to the town of Bracciano for lunch, perhaps a swim in the lake, and a visit to a magnificent castle. It finishes up with a visit to the excavations of Veii, the Etruscan city closest to Rome.

En Route from Rome From the Via Aurelia, take the Raccordo Anulare to the Rome–Fiumicino Airport Highway and then the toll highway (A12) toward Civitavecchia. Exit at Cerveteri, 32 miles (51 km) away.

CERVETERI Settled 900 years before Christ, Cerveteri lies on a small tufa plateau between two gorges. Its development lagged behind that of Tarquinia, Vulci, and Veii, but it made up for its slow start when the mines in the nearby Tolfa Mountains turned it into an Iron Age boomtown. Cerveteri grew rich as its ships set out from the nearby port of Santa Severa (ancient Pyrgi). In the 6th and 5th centuries BC, its fleet was important enough to make common cause with the Carthaginians in fighting the Greek-dominated colonies of Magna Graecia, which ruled from Naples down through western Sicily. That trio—Carthage, Etruria, and Magna Graecia—continued to jockey for power until Rome conquered all three.

Of the hundreds of tombs from the 8th to the 1st centuries BC in the necropolis at Cerveteri, the most important concentration is at Colle della Banditaccia, about a mile (1.6 km) outside the modern town. For more information, see *Remarkable Ruins* in DIVERSIONS. In Cerveteri itself is the *Museo Nazionale Cerite* (Piazza Santa Maria; phone: 6-994-1354), housed in the 16th-century *Palazzo Ruspoli.* The museum has particularly attractive and coherent displays of Etruscan and other ancient artifacts. It is closed Sundays and after 2 PM (hours may be longer in summer; call ahead);

admission charge. The necropolis is closed Mondays and after 4 PM in winter; closed Mondays in summer; admission charge.

BEST EN ROUTE

L'Oasi da Pino Seafood risotto, homemade fettuccine, and fresh fish are served at this cozy, family-style restaurant. Closed Mondays. Reservations advised on weekends. No credit cards accepted. 2 Via Renato Morelli, Cerveteri (phone: 6-995-3482). Moderate.

En Route from Cerveteri Follow the well-marked road inland 20 minutes or so to the town of Bracciano, on the volcanic lake of the same name. Those with the time should continue up the coast to Civitavecchia, which became the port of Rome after the port at Ostia silted up. Civitavecchia's *Forte Michelangelo,* a 16th-century structure for which Michelangelo designed the keep; its *Museo Nazionale Archeologico* (phone: 6-23604; closed Mondays, and Tuesdays through Sundays after 1 PM in summer; closed Mondays, Wednesdays, Fridays, and Sundays, and after 1 PM in winter; admission charge); and vestiges of an antique Roman port make the detour worthwhile. Then cut inland over country roads through the Tolfa Mountains toward Tolfa and then Manziana. At Manziana, a right turn leads to Bracciano, 35 miles (56 km) from Civitavecchia.

BRACCIANO The outstanding feature of this small resort town on the southwest side of Lake Bracciano is the *Castello degli Orsini.* It was the first sight Sir Walter Scott wanted to see in Rome, and children of all ages will understand why. This dream castle is in fine condition. In fact, it is still inhabited by the Odescalchi, a princely Roman family whose glittering parties and balls are Rome's grandest. Built between 1470 and 1485, the castle has five sides, with a crenelated tower at each juncture. It is closed Mondays and for a midday break; admission charge (phone: 6-902-4003). Escorted tours (in Italian) are given hourly during the week and every half hour on Sundays and holidays.

BEST EN ROUTE

Alfredo For an appetizing risotto *alle ortiche* (with wild nettles) and fresh lake fish, try this colorful lakeside restaurant. Closed Tuesdays. Reservations advised. Major credit cards accepted. Via Sposetta Vecchia, Bracciano (phone: 6-902-4130). Moderate.

Sora Tuta Delectable fare such as a spinach and ricotta–stuffed, veil-thin crêpe, pasta with artichokes, broiled lamb chops, and *crème brûlée* are the drawing cards at this century-old family establishment. The wines are less distinguished, but the house red is agreeable. Closed Mondays and August.

Reservations advised on weekends. Major credit cards accepted. 33 Via Agnostino Fausti, Bracciano (phone: 6-902-4409). Moderate.

En Route from Bracciano Circle the lake to Trevignano (18 miles/29 km away), the prettiest of the lakeside towns. Its *Chiesa dell'Assunta*, with a fresco by a student of Raphael, warrants a visit, as do the waterfront trattorie. The food is good, the service is slow, and lingering over a glass of homemade wine is obligatory. From Trevignano, pick up the Via Cassia (S2) to the ruins of Veii (Veio in Italian), near the town of Isola Farnese (watch for the yellow signs).

BEST EN ROUTE

Acquarella Before dining at this rustic country inn (among the most popular of the many lakeside restaurants), go for a swim at its private beach, then dine on homemade cannelloni and grilled *corrigone,* a local white fish. The white wine is locally produced. Closed Tuesdays and mid-November to mid-December. Reservations necessary on weekends. American Express accepted. Via Trevignanese, Km 6, between Trevignano and Anguillara (phone: 6-998-5131). Moderate.

Antico Belvedere Romeo Grappasonni has taken a traditional village trattoria and given its menu and wine list a thoughtful review. He serves imaginative pasta dishes (we liked the baked lasagna of shredded red radicchio and mushrooms), delicious *coregone* (lake flatfish) grilled in fine olive oil, and home-smoked eel. There usually is a vegetarian menu and mostly home-made desserts. Alfresco dining on a terrace is possible in season. Closed Tuesdays and three weeks in January. Reservations advised on weekends. Major credit cards accepted. 7 Piazza Vittorio Emanuele III, Trevignano (phone: 6-999-9580). Moderate.

Boricella Traditional local recipes are offered at this *simpatico* tavern in a fishing village. Try the spaghetti with fish sauce and the stuffed lake trout. Closed Tuesdays and November. Reservations necessary. Major credit cards accepted. 20 Via Trevignanese, Anguillara (phone: 6-996-8037). Moderate.

VEII Built on the right bank of the Tiber, ancient Veii was the largest of the dozen Etruscan city-states, with 7 miles of walls. It controlled the road to the salt flats and depots at the mouth of the Tiber and thrived on the commercial and military importance of the river itself. Veii was the first Etruscan city to fall to Roman domination. This occurred in 396 BC, after a decade-long siege that was broken only when the slaves of Furius Camillus tunneled through tufa rock into the city. The most famous find uncovered during the past century of excavations was the statue of Apollo, now in the *Villa Giulia* museum in Rome. Today's visitors can see a waterfall; the foundations of a 6th-century BC temple, its altar featuring drains for the blood of the sacrificed; and an adjacent pool for ritual dunkings. Follow the signs to visit the famous *Tomba di Campana*. The excavations are closed Saturdays through Mondays in summer; closed Saturdays through Mondays and after 2 PM the rest of the year. The admission charge permits entry to the site of a nearby Roman-era villa (phone: 6-379-0116).

BEST EN ROUTE

Postiglione A 400-year-old post house has been turned into a delightful rustic restaurant that offers homemade pasta and home-raised meat, including lamb. Closed Mondays. No reservations. Major credit cards accepted. Via Cassia, Km 30, Veii (phone: 6-904-1214). Moderate to inexpensive.

En Route from Veii Follow the Via Cassia (S2) back to Rome.

DAY TRIP 3: BOMARZO, BAGNAIA, VITERBO

Continuing north around Lazio, this tour explores the area around the largest of the region's three volcanic lakes, Lago di Bolsena. The first destination is Bomarzo, where stone monsters disport in a garden. From Bomarzo it goes to Viterbo, stopping to see the terraced gardens of the *Villa Lante*. It then heads north to the town of Montefiascone, from which various lakeside points can be visited. If you travel on the weekend, you may see the regular morning antiques fair held outdoors in the village's medieval quarter, where everything from curios to antique stone fireplaces is offered.

En Route from Rome Take the Via Salaria to the Raccordo Anulare and then the Autostrada del Sole (A1) north to the Attigliano exit (about 45 miles/72 km from Rome). Follow signs to Bomarzo, about 4 miles (6 km) from the exit.

BOMARZO A Renaissance equivalent of *Disneyland* inspired by Dante's *Inferno* is the best description of Bomarzo's *Parco dei Mostri* (Monster Park). It actually is a terraced, wooded slope strewn with carved stone animals and fantastical figures, from larger than life to colossal. The park was conceived and built by Vicino Orsini, a 16th-century nobleman and intrepid traveler whose family palace is nearby. Scholars believe that the house was built to reflect one of the religious beliefs of the time—that monsters from the underworld would materialize. Among its huge carvings, all in *peperino,* a granulated form of tufa, are elephants, lions, dragons, giants, and nymphs, faces with mouths as big as doorways, and a leaning house, just like the fun house in a modern amusement park. It is open daily; admission charge (phone: 761-924029).

En Route from Bomarzo Drop down to S204, following it west toward Viterbo, 15 miles (24 km) away. Stop just short of Viterbo at Bagnaia for the *Villa Lante,* then continue on to Viterbo.

VILLA LANTE The small but elegant twin 16th-century villas, designed by Vignola, are closed to visitors, but the spectacular surrounding garden is open daily; admission charge (phone: 761-288008). This wonderful example of a formal Renaissance garden is laid out on five terraces descending to a pond and decorated with fountains. Only escorted visits through the garden (every half hour) are possible.

BEST EN ROUTE

Beccorosso The elegant dining room of the inn in this 16th-century palazzo steps away from *Villa Lante* was recently refurbished in excellent taste. Taste distinguishes the menu as well, as it refines hearty local dishes like ravioli with *porcini* mushrooms or *tonarelli* (a thick spaghetti) with mushroom sauce. The antipasto involves intriguing pâtés—of anchovies, liver, and olives—fine prosciutto, and local salami. Closed Mondays, two weeks in January, and two weeks in August. Reservations advised Sundays. Major credit cards accepted. 26 Piazza XX Settembre, Bagnaia (phone: 761-289730). Expensive to moderate.

Biscetti Nearly a century old, this country restaurant near *Villa Lante* serves seasonal traditional woodland dishes, such as risotto with rare wild *ovoli* mushrooms, mushroom soup, pasta with hare sauce, and wild boar roasted with juniper berries. Closed Thursdays and three weeks in July. Reservations advised on Sundays. American Express accepted. 11/A Via Generale Gandin, Bagnaia (phone: 761-288252). Moderate to inexpensive.

VITERBO The capital of La Tuscia (as northern Lazio is called), Viterbo is an Etruscan city that became important under the Romans and would remain so through the Middle Ages. The name derives from *Tusci,* the Etruscan people who settled on the central Tyrrhenian coastline in the 10th century BC. In the 13th century—troubled times for the papacy, given the continual struggle between the church and the Holy Roman Empire—several popes found it safer to live here than in Rome, so that in 1261, Pope Alessandro IV built the *Palazzo Papale* (Papal Palace). Several conclaves were held here, including the one that elected Gregory X—the longest conclave in the history of the Roman Catholic church. It ended after 33 months, when the cardinals' food supply was cut off.

The *Palazzo Papale* remains one of Viterbo's major monuments, so head first to Piazza San Lorenzo, where the delicate Gothic palace stands right next to the *Duomo,* a 12th-century building with a Renaissance façade; both were built over the old Etruscan acropolis. Then turn back along Via San Lorenzo, strolling toward Porta San Pietro. The walk leads through the San Pellegrino quarter, one of Europe's most completely medieval cityscapes. Every weekend, this neighborhood is the venue for a lively antiques and bric-a-brac market (follow the signs). Be sure to visit the tiny Piazzetta San

Pellegrino, the haunting, medieval heart of the quarter, and Piazza Cappella, another characteristic spot. The exterior stone stairways leading to second-story balconies and front doors, called *profferli,* are typically Viterbese. The quarter seems like a living museum; visitors can glimpse artisans hard at work in their *botteghe* (workshops) off the narrow streets. Many shops sell pretty copies of black Etruscan-style terra cotta pots and vases. Two fountains, the 13th-century *Fontana Grande* (Piazza Fontana Grande) and the 14th-century *Fontana di Piano Scarano* (Piazza Fontana di Piano), are of interest. The latter was at the center of a popular uprising in the 14th century, when a member of the papal court of Urban V attempted to wash a puppy in the fountain, which the townspeople used for drinking water. The *Museo Municipale* (2 Piazza Crispi; phone: 761-340810) houses paintings from the Middle Ages. The museum was closed for restoration at press time but due to reopen shortly; call for updated schedule information. The city's tourist office (*EPT*; 4/A Piazza Verdi; phone: 761-226666) can provide information on other sights and special events, such as the *Festa di Santa Rosa* (September 2–3), when a parade in historic costume takes place, followed by a procession featuring a hundred men carrying a four-ton, 90-foot tower through the streets.

BEST EN ROUTE

Aquilanti Two miles (3 km) out of town toward Bagnaia, this outstanding country-style dining room serves hearty pasta and tasty steak, lamb, and pork chops grilled on an open fire. Closed Sunday dinner and Tuesdays. No reservations. Major credit cards accepted. 4 Via del Santuario, Madonna della Quercia (phone: 761-341701). Expensive to moderate.

Richiastro Refined culinary concepts are put to the test in a millennium-old setting. Offerings include mushroom soup and local specialties such as chickpea soup with chestnuts. Closed Sunday dinner, Mondays through Wednesdays, August, and part of December. Reservations advised. No credit cards accepted. 18 Via della Marrocca, Viterbo (phone: 761-223609). Expensive to moderate.

En Route from Viterbo Head north on Via Cassia to Montefiascone (about 12 miles/19 km), which stands on the edge of the crater of an extinct volcano, now Lago di Bolsena. The drive, which threads its way along a stretch of the ancient Roman consular road, offers rolling scenery and pleasant vistas of vineyards and olive orchards.

MONTEFIASCONE On a hill overlooking Lago di Bolsena is the home of the wine called est! est!! est!!! The reason for its name? Once upon a time, a cardinal's servant quenched his thirst so well at Montefiascone that he left his master, Giovanni Fugger, a sign outside the wine shop exclaiming, three times, "This is it!" The name stuck, and the wine is considered among

Lazio's finest. Fugger's tombstone at the Romanesque *Chiesa di San Flaviano* has the words Est! Est!! Est!!! carved on it. Castle ruins in the town's upper reaches offer a fine view of the lake and of the mountains beyond.

LAGO DI BOLSENA The largest of Italy's many volcanic lakes, Bolsena takes its name from an early Italian tribe, the Volsinienses. The lake is nearly a perfect circle averaging 8 miles in diameter, and it contains two small islands, Isola Bisentina and Isola Martina. On the former is a chapel housing the bones of St. Christine; the latter has a horrific Gothic history. In 532, Queen Martana of the Ostrogoths was strangled on Isola Martina by her cousin Theodahad, to whom she was betrothed but who coveted her throne. The lake so abounds in eels that a particularly gluttonous pope, if Dante is to be believed, gorged himself to death on them. On the western shore are ruins of what was first a Villanovan, then an Etruscan, and finally a Roman town, Visentium. For the Etruscans, the lake held special meaning, and scores of Etruscan tombs have been found nearby. From mid-March through October, boats to Isola Bisentina, dotted with rustic eateries and small swimming beaches, leave from Bolsena (two trips daily, at 10 AM and 4 PM) and Capodimonte (see below); the trip includes a guided tour of the island. For more information, contact *Navigazione Alto Lazio* (60 Corso Repubblica, Bolsena; phone: 761-798033).

Drive to Capodimonte, a tiny summer resort with a sleepy old-fashioned air on the southwest shore of the lake. For a pleasant side trip, circle the lake to the town of Bolsena, on the northeast shore, to visit the *Chiesa di Santa Cristina*. On its portal is a terra cotta panel from the Della Robbia school, and a chapel inside contains a Della Robbia terra cotta portrait of the saint. Ancient Etruscan walls still encircle part of the town.

BEST EN ROUTE

Da Picchietto This rustic garden restaurant specializes in fresh fish and eel from the lake. Closed Mondays in winter, and October. Reservations unnecessary. Major credit cards accepted. 15 Via Porta Fiorentina, Bolsena (phone: 761-799158). Moderate to inexpensive.

En Route from Lago di Bolsena To return to Rome, two routes are possible. Either cut seaward from Capodimonte to pick up the Via Aurelia (S1) at Montalto di Castro, and follow the coastal road south to Rome. Or return to Viterbo from either Capodimonte or Bolsena, and take a leisurely ride on the Via Cimino through the densely wooded (chestnut and oak) hills and past a tiny volcanic lake, Lago di Vico. En route are towns with pleasant historic quarters, such as Ronciglione, just south of the lake, and Sutri, where Pontius Pilate was born. At Sutri, site of an ancient Roman amphitheater (visible from the Via Cassia), pick up the Via Cassia (S2) south. The best route, however, is to continue on to Orvieto, visiting the fine cathedral there, following the clearly marked directions, and returning to Rome via the autostrada (A1) south.

DAY TRIP 4: PALESTRINA, ANAGNI, SUBIACO, TIVOLI

This route turns away from Etruscan Lazio toward areas where Latin tribes such as the Sabines, who conquered the Etruscans, lived before settling Rome. The region has suffered far more than Etruscan Lazio from the construction of tasteless modern buildings, but some extremely interesting sights, such as the ruins of the Roman temple at Palestrina, the medieval town of Anagni, and the monasteries of Subiaco, remain. On the way back, stop at Tivoli.

En Route from Rome Take Via Prenestina east to Palestrina, 24 miles (38 km) away.

PALESTRINA Known to the ancient world as Praeneste, Palestrina, birthplace of the musician of that name in the 16th century, dates at least as far back as the 7th century BC. The ancients believed it was founded by the son Circe bore to Ulysses. It passed to the Romans in 499 BC, and various Roman emperors, including Augustus, Tiberius, and Hadrian, later built pleasure palaces here. But the wonder of Palestrina was its shrine to the goddess of fortune, Fortuna Primigenia, so important to the Romans that they built the Via Praeneste (Via Prenestina now) so that they could make the journey to consult the oracle more regularly. In 82 BC, the Roman statesman Sulla tore down the old buildings—which had been there for at least a century—and replaced them with a many-terraced majestic temple, the largest religious complex in the entire Roman world. It remained in use until the 4th century and then gradually became the foundation of a medieval city.

In 1640, the Barberini family of Rome built a palace in the sacred area, where the small *Museo Archeologico Prenestino* (Piazza della Cortina; phone: 6-953-8100) is located today. Visit the museum before the excavations. One of its treasures is a very large and beautiful 1st-century BC mosaic—showing scenes of the Nile during a flood—that once decorated a floor of the temple. A scale model of the temple as it was in ancient times shows the shrine to the goddess, Jupiter's first daughter, laid out in a triangle on a hillside extending from the level of the present Piazza Regina Margherita, where the *Duomo* now stands, up to the museum's entrance. Vast ramps and staircases adorned with elegant columns, colonnades, vaults, and arches lead toward a vast open terrace. At the top was a semicircular portico in whose center stood a gold statue of Primigenia, long since lost. The Romans were so proud of the monument that they lighted bonfires on the terraces so sailors at sea could see the sanctuary at night. Even today, the ruins are highly evocative, and the windows of the museum offer a wonderful view. The museum is closed Mondays; Sunday afternoons; and after 3:30 PM in winter; one admission charge to museum and excavations.

La Vecchia Osteria–Antonello Colonna Worth a trip in its own right for the chef's version of *alta cucina,* this temple of gastronomy requires a detour from this excursion. For more information, see *The Best Restaurants of Italy* in DIVERSIONS. Closed Sunday dinner, Mondays, and August. Reservations necessary. Major credit cards accepted. From Palestrina, take the country road southeast for 5 miles (8 km); at the Via Casilina turnoff, go left (south) and continue for about 2 miles (3 km) to the Km 38 marker and Labico (phone: 6-951-0032). Expensive.

Taverna delle Tre Fontane Near the *Duomo,* this century-old dining spot is often recommended by the locals. Homemade pasta—including fettuccine with *porcini* mushrooms, and cannelloni with either meat or ricotta and spinach filling—and roast or grilled lamb and veal are served. Closed Wednesdays. No reservations. Major credit cards accepted. 16 Piazza Garibaldi, Palestrina (phone: 6-953-8916). Moderate.

En Route from Palestrina Proceed south to Valmontone and follow the Autostrada del Sole (A2) for about 10 miles (16 km) southeast to the Anagni exit.

ANAGNI Cicero had an estate in this hilltop town, and four popes—Innocent III, Gregory IX, Alexander IV, and Boniface VIII—were born here in the Middle Ages. Its medieval quarter is particularly harmonious, as almost all of its buildings date to the 13th century, and it has one of medieval Europe's more noteworthy cathedrals. This basically Romanesque structure, built in the 11th and 12th centuries atop a former Roman temple and then modified in the 13th century, stands on the highest point of the town. Inside, the loveliest sight is the crypt (open daily from 3 to 5 PM), whose walls are solidly covered with 13th-century frescoes (a painting of Hippocrates adorns one lunette). In 1160, an archbishop announced the excommunication of Frederick Barbarossa from Anagni's cathedral. And in 1303, at the *Palazzo di Bonifacio VIII,* another old building, an emissary of French King Philip the Fair slapped the aged, frail Pope Boniface full in the face with his iron gauntlet, an episode that lives on in Dante. The *Museo Civico* (238 Via Vittorio Emanuele; phone: 775-727053) houses archaeological artifacts. It's open daily, with a long midday closing; no admission charge. Medieval religious art can be seen at the *Museo del Tesoro del Duomo* (by the cathedral; phone: 775-727228). The museum is open daily, with a long (noon to 4 PM) closing, in summer; open daily, with a noon to 3:30 PM closing, in winter. There's an admission charge.

En Route from Anagni Follow the signs to Fiuggi, about 10½ miles (17 km) away.

FIUGGI Fiuggi is a two-part town. There is Fiuggi Città, the actual town, but the real draw is Fiuggi Fonte, a spa whose *fonte* (spring) attracts health seekers, especially elderly ones. For more information, see *Taking the Waters* in DIVERSIONS. The spa bustles in summer and languishes in winter. Its quaint Victorian-era hotels have great charm, its shops sell a fair sampling of local products, from salami to cheese and honey, and its tea shops offer good pastries.

The famed pre–World War I *Grand Hotel Palazzo della Fonte* (7 Via dei Villini; phone: 775-5081; 800-225-5843; fax: 775-506752) has been restored to its early-century splendor. Today's travelers may want to spend an elegant (and expensive) night or two and enjoy swimming, golf at the nearby nine-hole layout, tennis, and overall pampering. The hotel is open March through October.

BEST EN ROUTE

Villa Hernicus Creative cooking has reached Fiuggi, and here it takes the form of fresh lobster risotto with zucchini flowers, potato-filled lasagna with pesto, and roast duckling with a béarnaise sauce. A fine wine list, perfect appointments, and impeccable service mark this elegant restaurant. Leave room for the mouth-watering desserts. There also are four spectacular guestrooms. Open year-round. Reservations advised. Major credit cards accepted. 30 Corso Nuova Italia, Fiuggi (phone: 775-55254). Expensive.

En Route from Fiuggi Drive north to pick up S411 in the direction of Subiaco, a distance of about 19 miles (30 km). Just before the town, turn right onto the Vallepietra road, where Subiaco's most famous sights are found.

SUBIACO According to legend, workmen building a villa for Nero by a long-gone lake needed a place to stay. Their work camp of huts became the town of Sublaqueum, meaning "Under the Waters." The ruins of Nero's villa, about 2 miles (3 km) out of town, can still be visited, but Subiaco—considered the birthplace of Benedictine monasticism—is best known for its monasteries. In the 6th century, St. Benedict came here from his native Norcia, in Umbria. Living as a hermit, he prayed in a cave for three years, and before leaving for Monte Cassino (see *Day Trip 6,* below), he founded several monasteries. One of these original establishments is the *Monastero di Santa Scolastica* (she was Benedict's sister), especially influential from the 11th through the 13th century. The Sacro Speco, the cave in which the saint prayed, is now part of the *Monastero di San Benedetto,* founded in the 12th century. Both monasteries are southeast of town on the road to Vallepietra, one just beyond the other, and both are open daily. There's an admission charge.

En Route from Subiaco Circle north on S411 and west on S5 back to Rome, passing through villages such as Anticoli Corrado, which has a little medieval square, Vicovaro, and Tivoli, the last stop, a total of about 25 miles (40 km).

TIVOLI Already a resort in Roman times, this hilltop town has become a household word because of the *Villa d'Este,* a 16th-century cardinal's palace with terraced gardens that contain 500 of the most famous fountains of Rome. Nearby is the *Villa Gregoriana,* another park with waterworks (actually a waterfall), in addition to the Corinthian-style *Temple of Vesta,* or *Temple of Sibyl,* in the heart of today's small township. But the *Villa Adriana* (Hadrian's Villa), 4 miles (6 km) out of Tivoli in the direction of Rome, is by far Tivoli's greatest archaeological attraction. For details on all three, see *Rome* in THE CITIES. If this is your only chance to see the *Villa d'Este* and the *Villa Adriana,* stop now, leaving the *Villa Gregoriana* for last. The *Villa d'Este* (phone: 774-22070), *Villa Gregoriana* (phone: 774-21644), and *Villa Adriana* (phone: 774-530203) are open daily; admission charge to all three.

BEST EN ROUTE

Sibilla Beloved by travelers since 1730, this trattoria has a terrace that faces one of the loveliest Roman temples extant. Enjoy traditional Roman dishes such as *bruschetta* (garlic bread) and grilled meat or trout under a wisteria-wrapped trellis, and sample the local liqueur, amaretto di Tivoli. Closed Mondays. Reservations advised. Major credit cards accepted. 50 Via della Sibilla, Tivoli (phone: 774-20281). Expensive to moderate.

Adriano Traditional country dishes are served in a family-run establishment near the *Villa Adriana.* The pasta is homemade; the grilled lamb and veal chops are tasty. Closed Sunday dinner. Reservations advised. Major credit cards accepted. 222 Via Villa Adriana, Tivoli (phone: 774-529174). Moderate.

En Route from Tivoli Take Via Tiburtina (S5) back to Rome, 19 miles (30 km) away.

DAY TRIP 5: CASTELLI ROMANI

Southeast of Rome, in the lovely Colli Albani (Alban Hills) region, are 13 hill towns known collectively as the Castelli Romani (Roman Castles). The curious name derives from the castles, or fortresses, palaces, and villas built here over the centuries by various popes and patrician Roman families. This is also wine country, and our route goes directly to Rome's prime wine town, Frascati. It then explores other Castelli towns surrounding the two volcanic lakes of the region, Lago di Albano and Lago di Nemi.

En Route from Rome Take the Via Tuscolana (S215) southeast for 13 miles (21 km) to Frascati.

FRASCATI An ancient Roman town, Frascati is famous both for its wine and for its patrician villas of the 16th and 17th centuries. Although heavily damaged during World War II and then much rebuilt, it still is a favorite Castelli destination among Romans. Its main square, Piazza Marconi, affords a panoramic view over the Roman countryside and the gardens of the *Villa Torlonia.* The gardens are open daily; no admission charge. The 16th-century villa itself was bombed to smithereens during World War II, but the remains of a water theater (a fancy arrangement of fountains) designed by Carlo Maderno, one of the architects of *San Pietro* in Rome, are fascinating. Sitting atop a hill and dominating another side of Piazza Marconi is the *Villa Aldobrandini,* built for a cardinal at the end of the 16th century by Giacomo della Porta. The villa's lovely garden closes after 1 PM (get permission from the *Azienda Autonoma di Turismo;* 1 Piazza Marconi; phone: 6-942-5498); admission charge. Next to it is the privately owned *Villa Lancellotti,* not visitable—but note its gate, by the architect Borromini, Bernini's great rival. Also famous is *Villa Mondragone,* about a mile (1.6 km) east of town. In what is now a Jesuit seminary, Pope Gregory XIII once issued a bull establishing the calendar we use today.

Frascati's well-known wine is mostly from white grapes and, at its best, should be amber in color. Wine consortiums sell the local product everywhere, and some wineries encourage visits. Another Frascati specialty are *pupazze,* honey cakes baked in animal or human forms. One favorite is a three-breasted fertility goddess who harks back to the area's pagan days.

BEST EN ROUTE

Cacciani The menu at this family-owned place stresses traditional Lazio fare (with a woodland accent in the many mushroom dishes in season), plus a twist of nouvelle. Ask to see the wine cellar: It was carved into a tufa hill a century ago, and today it's well stocked with wines from the family vineyards. Dine on the terrace in summer—the view takes in the hillsides and the famed villas. For those who have eaten themselves into a stupor, there also are 20 guestrooms. Closed Mondays, Sunday dinner (in winter), and two weeks in late August. Reservations necessary. Major credit cards accepted. 15 Via Armando Diaz, Frascati (phone: 6-941-9415). Expensive to moderate.

En Route from Frascati Turning south, drive just short of 2 miles (3 km) to Grottaferrata.

GROTTAFERRATA This town's fortified abbey—a castle-like monastery founded in 1004—still is inhabited by monks of the Greek Catholic rite. The abbey was built on top of the ruins of an ancient Roman summer villa, part of which became a chapel incorporated into the abbey's *Chiesa di Santa Maria* (phone: 6-945-9309). In front of the church is a handsome fountain, and monks sell olive oil and wine from an adjacent shop. The small museum, which has a collection of ancient Roman statuary and artifacts, plus some fine medieval pieces, is open from 8:30 AM to noon and 4:30 to 6 PM; Sundays from 4:30 to 6 PM; closed Mondays; admission charge.

BEST EN ROUTE

Al Fico Even after more than three decades, this large, renovated country-style eatery is a favorite Sunday dining place for Romans. If you can, try the homemade fettuccine with wild mushrooms, chicory in tomato sauce, and succulent lamb chops on a less crowded day. The deviled chicken is diabolically good. Closed Wednesdays. Reservations advised. Major credit cards accepted. 134 Via Anagnina, Grottaferrata (phone: 6-941-2070). Expensive.

La Bazzica Locally made white wine, fresh fish, and baby lamb prepared in the Lazio fashion keep the Romans flocking to this traditional restaurant. Closed Mondays. Reservations necessary on weekends. Major credit cards accepted. 58 Viale J. F. Kennedy, Grottaferrata (phone: 6-943-15766). Moderate.

Nando "Sommeliers at your service" is printed on this trattoria's business cards, and rightly so, since it boasts an extraordinary selection of fine wines in a colorful grotto wine cellar dating from the 1500s. Typical of the countrified fare is polenta with a tasty tomato-sausage sauce; game; fresh wild mushrooms in season, on pasta or alone; fresh fish; traditional Roman dishes such as *coratella* (lamb innards) and *pajatta* (pork innards); and homemade desserts. Closed Mondays. Reservations advised. Major credit cards accepted. 4 Via Roma, Grottaferrata (phone: 6-945-9989). Moderate.

En Route from Grottaferrata Continue to Marino, about 4 miles (6 km) away by S216.

MARINO In summer, this favorite Castelli town is crowded with day-trippers from Rome. Like Frascati, Marino is famous for its wine, and on the first Sunday in October it holds an annual wine festival, the *Sagra dell'Uva* (for more information, see *Italy's Most Colorful Festas* in DIVERSIONS).

BEST EN ROUTE

Al Vigneto Fish, polenta, and homemade *crostate* (tarts) are served here. The restaurant is about 3 miles (5 km) out of Marino in a woodland setting; visitors can sample Marino's fine wines under a grape arbor. Closed Tuesdays. Reservations necessary on weekends. Major credit cards accepted. Km 4.5, Via dei Laghi, Marino (phone: 6-938-7034). Moderate.

En Route from Marino Farther along on S216 in the cool, green hills is Castel Gandolfo, where the pope summers.

CASTEL GANDOLFO A particularly lovely setting overlooking Lago di Albano prompted the popes to select Castel Gandolfo for their summer residence. It is supposed to have been the site of Alba Longa, the most ancient city of Lazio, founded, according to legend, by the son of Aeneas and destroyed by the Romans in about 600 BC. Roman legend also speaks of a duel fought between the Horatii, male triplets of Rome, and the Curiatii, triplets of Alba Longa. Through a ruse, a Horatio won after his two brothers had been slain. When his sister, mourning one of the dead Curiatii, turned on him, he killed her as well. The tomb in which the Horatii and Curiatii were supposedly buried lies farther along the road on the way to Ariccia.

A Bernini fountain and the graceful *Chiesa di San Tommaso da Villanova,* also by Bernini, decorate Castel Gandolfo's main square. Also on the square is the entrance to the *Palazzo Papale* (Papal Residence), designed by Carlo Maderno and built from 1624 to 1629 on the site of a sprawling pleasure palace that belonged to Emperor Domitian in the 1st century. The palace and its grounds, enlarged by the later addition of the grounds of the *Villa Barberini,* are all part of the Vatican city-state; the huge complex extends all the way to Albano (see below). The grounds house the famous *Osservatorio del Vaticano* (Vatican Observatory) and a modern hall that accommodates general audiences on Wednesday mornings when the pope is in residence (attendance during the audience is the only way tourists can visit the property, which is closed to the public). When in residence, the pope also appears at a window in the inner of two courtyards at noon on Sundays and can then be seen from close range.

En Route from Castel Gandolfo Follow the lakeside road south for about 1 mile (1.6 km) to Albano.

ALBANO In the 3rd century, Emperor Septimius Severus established a permanent garrison—the *Castra Albana*—for the Roman army here. The camp evidently took up the entire territory of the present town. Although it was covered by later construction, it was only bombed into view during World War II. Now the main gateway to the camp, the *Porta Pretoria,* can be seen, and a giant Roman cistern, carved out of the rock and still in use, as well as the ancient amphitheater can be visited. The so-called tomb of the Horatii and Curiatii, but more probably the tomb of an unknown Roman from the time of the republic, sits by the side of the road on the way out of town.

En Route from Albano Take the Via Appia (S7) to Genzano and then turn off toward Nemi. Both are short drives away.

GENZANO DI ROMA Each year, on a Sunday in mid-June, the entire Via Italo Belardi (the former Via Livia) leading up to the *Chiesa di Santa Maria della Cima* here is covered with "paintings" made entirely of flowers, in celebration of

Corpus Domini. For more information, see *Italy's Most Colorful Festas* in DIVERSIONS.

BEST EN ROUTE

La Briciola Dine by candlelight at this renovated stable offering culinary wonders. The daily menu isn't posted until 11:30 AM, a half hour after the catch of the day has reached the village market. Homemade desserts include strawberry mousse and a delectable *panna cotta* with blueberries. Closed Sunday dinner, Wednesdays, and August. Reservations advised. Major credit cards accepted. 21 Via E. Imbastari, Genzano di Roma (phone: 6-936-3765). Expensive to moderate.

NEMI Set high above the lake from which it takes its name, Nemi is best known for its strawberries, which are the focus of a festival in June, when they're in season. The ancient Romans referred to the lake as the Mirror of Diana, because it reflected a nearby temple dedicated to the goddess of the hunt in an area called the Sacred Grove of Diana, today known as *Il Giardino.* Festivals in her honor took place here in ancient times, and in the 1930s part of the lake was drained to recover two Roman boats built by Caligula as part of the celebrations. The museum in which the boats were placed was bombed during World War II, and they were destroyed. A scaled-down reconstruction of the boats can be seen in the modest museum Tuesdays through Saturdays from 9 AM to 2 PM; Sundays from 9 AM to 1 PM; admission charge (phone: 6-936-8140).

En Route from Nemi Pick up the Via dei Laghi (Lake Road; S217) northwest, and turn right at the turnoff for Rocca di Papa.

ROCCA DI PAPA The highest of the Castelli clings to the side of Monte Cavo at an altitude of 2,250 feet. Named after a castle built here by the popes in the Middle Ages (and destroyed during the Renaissance), it comprises an elevated medieval quarter and a lower modern town. In Roman times, a temple of Jupiter stood at the 3,124-foot top of Monte Cavo, approachable by a Via Sacra over which the earliest Romans marched in solemn procession to offer sacrifices to the one god they all worshiped. In the 18th century, a monastery was built where the temple presumably stood. On a clear day, the view from the top of the mountain is panoramic, taking in the Castelli, the two lakes, and the surrounding countryside as far as the coast. Getting there, however, requires turning off before Rocca di Papa and following a winding road that eventually turns into a private road (the custodians charge a nominal fee).

En Route from Rocca di Papa Return to Grottaferrata and Frascati; from there, take the Via Tuscolana back to Rome.

DAY TRIP 6: MONTE CASSINO, SPERLONGA, ANZIO

Southern Lazio has a flavor all its own, a mixture of pious abbeys and pagan temples, roadside stands selling delectable mozzarella, beachheads whose names ring with the horrors of war, and chic beaches with frequently top-less bathers. This tour leads south of Rome through a part of Lazio known as the Ciociaria, to visit the *Abbazia di Monte Cassino* (Abbey of Monte Cassino), a fascinating experience for people of all faiths. Then it cuts sea-ward to Gaeta and returns north along the coast via a number of seaside towns—Sperlonga for a swim and lunch, Terracina, Anzio (where the Allied landing took place during World War II), and Nettuno.

En Route from Rome Take the Autostrada del Sole (A2) south 70 miles (113 km) to the Cassino exit. The *Abbazia di Monte Cassino* is 5½ miles (9 km) west of the modern industrial town of Cassino, at the end of a wind-ing mountain road.

ABBAZIA DI MONTE CASSINO Set on a mountaintop, this imposing medieval-style complex of buildings is the headquarters for the Benedictine Order, founded by St. Benedict in 529 after, according to legend, three ravens led him from Subiaco to Cassino. He died in the new monastery 14 years later and was buried here, as was his sister, St. Scholastica. During the Dark Ages, after the fall of the Roman Empire, the abbey became one of the greatest repositories of ancient learning. The zealous efforts of the monks of *Monte Cassino* preserved much ancient Latin literature and thought. Destroyed several times in the distant past, the abbey was always rebuilt. In 1944, it was ravaged by the Allies, who suspected it was occu-pied by German troops (justification for the bombing remains a matter of controversy). The library of medieval books and manuscripts that sur-vived the bombing is still one of the greatest collections in the world. Today, visitors can see the reconstructed basilica, several cloisters, and a moving photo exhibition on the extent of the damage. The abbey and its small museum are open daily, with a midday closing; admission charge to museum (phone: 776-311529). The military cemetery visible on the way up contains the graves of 1,100 Polish soldiers who lost their lives in the final assault.

En Route from the Abbazia di Monte Cassino Cut seaward across the penin-sula on S630 to Gaeta, 29½ miles (47 km) away.

GAETA A handsome fortress of ancient origin, much transformed from the 13th through the 16th century, sits on a promontory jutting into the sea in this port and resort town. The 12th-century cathedral is interesting, but best of all is a stroll through the bazaar-like, narrow alleys parallel to the Lungomare Caboto. The pleasure yachts anchored in the basin are quite posh.

La Scarpetta Seafood takes center stage here, with inventive regional specialties and garden dining in pleasant weather. Closed for lunch in summer, and Tuesdays in winter. Reservations necessary. Major credit cards accepted. 1 Piazza Conca, Gaeta (phone: 771-462142). Moderate.

En Route from Gaeta Head north along the coast for 6 miles (10 km) to Sperlonga.

SPERLONGA Perhaps Lazio's loveliest summer resort, this whitewashed town has a Moorish look. For more information, see *Beaches* in DIVERSIONS. About a half-mile (1 km) south of town is the small, fascinating *Museo Nazionale Archeologico di Sperlonga* (Via Flacca; phone: 771-54028), displaying finds from the area. The museum is open daily; admission charge. A few miles away is the Grotto di Tiberio, a great cave on the beach where the emperor maintained a huge marine theater. Various ancient statues were found in the cave, and some can still be seen there. Others, reconstructed from fragments, are in the museum.

Laocoonte–Da Rocco The best of many pleasant restaurants in town serving fish, it has a covered terrace overlooking the sea. The tourist menu will appeal to the economy-minded. Closed Mondays from September 15 to June 14, and *Christmas* week. Reservations necessary on weekends. No credit cards accepted. 4 Via Colombo, Sperlonga (phone: 771-54122). Expensive.

Grotta di Tiberio Near the cave and the beach, the attraction here is a charming garden in an old orchard. Specialties include classic fish dishes such as risotto *al pescatore* (with fish) and spaghetti with clams. Try the delicate *pesce al cartoccio* (fish sealed in parchment). Closed Tuesdays, November, and part of December. Reservations advised. Major credit cards accepted. 8 Via Flacca, Sperlonga (phone: 771-54027). Moderate.

En Route from Sperlonga The next coastal town north (10 miles/16 km) of Sperlonga is Terracina, where fishing boats jam into a canal leading to the sea. Terracina is a colorful, traffic-plagued town that becomes tourist-clogged in midsummer. Serene on a high cliff above it, however, are the ruins of a famous temple of Jupiter dating from the 1st century BC. Beyond Terracina, the Via Pontina (S148) turns north to Rome, while the coast road heads to San Felice Circeo, a bathing resort on the slopes of the 1,795-foot promontory of Monte Circeo, home to the Neanderthals, to Circe, and now to the very rich. Now a nature reserve called the *Parco Nazionale del Circeo,* the area also is home to a good deal of rare wildlife and four coastal lakes, swamps, dunes, forests of oak and maple, and a variety of archaeological remains.

Among these are the ruins of a lavish lakeside summer residence and spa Emperor Domitian built here in the 1st century. Although the park is regularly open to the public (in fact, both San Felice Circeo and the next seaside resort north, Sabaudia, are in it, and visitors will be driving through it along a good stretch of the coast road), permission is necessary for the obligatory guided visit to the ruins of Domitian's villa, which is on one of the coastal lakes between the promontory and Sabaudia. Address requests to *Parco Nazionale del Circeo* (6 Via Carlo Alberto, Sabaudia; phone: 773-511386).

From Sabaudia, follow the coast road northwest via Lido di Latina and Torre Astura for about 25 miles (40 km) to Nettuno and Anzio.

BEST EN ROUTE

Maga Circe Set in one of the most evocative areas of Lazio, this restaurant has a terrace overlooking a promontory. It offers an abundant selection of seafood (including lobster) and a good wine list, plus 65 rooms, several apartments, and a pool. Open daily. Reservations advised. Major credit cards accepted. 1 Via Ammiraglio Bergamini, San Felice Circeo (phone: 773-547821). Expensive.

Miramare A seaside pizzeria with a garden, it also offers *tagliolini* (fine noodles) with shrimp, and risotto with *frutti di mare* (a mixture of seafood). Closed Tuesdays. Reservations advised. Major credit cards accepted. 32 Lungomare Circe, Terracina (phone: 773-727332). Moderate.

NETTUNO AND ANZIO Modern history remembers the stretch of beach between these two resorts as the blood-drenched strand where American and British troops landed in the "soft underbelly of Europe" on January 22, 1944. The British came ashore at Anzio, the Americans, closer to Nettuno, and together they found that the underbelly was not at all soft: The Germans resisted the Allied onslaught for more than four months. Some one thousand British soldiers are buried in the *British Military Cemetery* at Anzio (on S207, about 2 miles/3 km north). Nearly 8,000 American soldiers lie in the *American Military Cemetery,* off the Via Santa Maria, about a half-mile (1 km) north of Nettuno. In the center of the cemetery, which is always open, is a chapel, and next to it a small museum illustrates Allied military operations from the invasion of Sicily to the end of the war.

Together, Anzio and Nettuno form almost one continuous town. Anzio was already a resort in Roman times: Cicero had a summer palace here, and the emperors Caligula and Nero were born here—ruins of the latter's villa can be seen near the lighthouse. Not far away from the villa are the *Grotte di Nerone* (Nero's Caves), actually ruins of ancient Roman port warehouses. Some famous statues have been found on Nero's property, including the *Apollo Belvedere* in the Vatican collection in Rome. Nettuno is known for its picturesque medieval quarter.

Flora Seafood dishes with a regional accent are served at this small dining spot. Closed Mondays and two weeks in October. Reservations necessary. Major credit cards accepted. 9 Via Flora, Anzio (phone: 6-984-6001). Expensive to moderate.

En Route from Anzio and Nettuno S207 leads back to the Via Pontina (S148) for the return to Rome.

DAY TRIP 7: FARFA, RIETI, GRECCIO

Following the Tiber River Valley, the seventh tour goes to a celebrated medieval abbey in Farfa, to the walled city of Rieti, and finally to Greccio, a mountain hamlet.

En Route from Rome Take the A1 autostrada to the Fiano Romano exit, or the Via Salaria (S4), which goes from Rome to the Adriatic Sea, to Passo Corese—about 49 miles (78 km). Then take the turnoff for Farfa, making sure to carefully follow the signs leading to it.

FARFA Admirers of Umberto Eco's elegant mystery, *The Name of the Rose,* set in a medieval monastery, may wish to visit one of the most magnificent, the *Abbazia Imperiale* (Imperial Abbey). Begun in the 6th century, it became one of the most powerful Benedictine monasteries in Europe; nowadays, it is considered one of the most splendid abbey complexes on the continent. Protected by Charlemagne, it came to rival the *Vatican* itself. Vestiges of its ancient fortifications still can be seen. Scholastically, it was the *Harvard* of its day, and in the Middle Ages, parents lined up outside the monastery, making appeals to have their sons educated here. Little of this power and grandeur is still visible, but a visit is pleasant nonetheless. Note the Germanic look of the half doors leading to the street (unusual in Italy). Guided tours (in Italian) of the abbey take place on weekends from 9:30 AM to noon and 3:30 to 5:30 PM in winter; to 7 PM in summer. The complex is open daily; admission charge (phone: 765-27065). Stop at the ancient pharmacy to purchase liqueurs, honey, jam, and soap made by the monks. The *Casa di Santa Brigida* (near the parking lot) is run by nuns who welcome guests for a delicious, abundant, and wholesome lunch.

En Route from Farfa Return to S4 via Tóffia, and proceed 8 miles (13 km) to Rieti.

RIETI The early spring, when the mountains around the Terminillo ski resort are snow-capped and the almond trees in the valley blossom with clouds of white petals, is when this medieval-flavored city is at its loveliest. Within its 13th-century walls are a cathedral, other early churches, a small municipal museum (open mornings only), and the late Renaissance *Palazzo Vecchiarelli,* which was designed by the famed architect Carlo Maderno.

Da Checco al Calice d'Oro One of Italy's finest traditional restaurants has been in the same family for four generations. Its menu of country dishes includes *bollito misto* (boiled meat), lamb, roast kid, and trout. There also are a few moderately priced, comfortable rooms. Closed Mondays and July 15 to August 10. Reservations necessary on Sundays. Major credit cards accepted. 10 Via Marchetti, Rieti (phone: 746-204271). Moderate.

Il Nido del Corvo Woodlands and mountains are reflected in the game, polenta, and mushroom entrées served in this large, attractive restaurant with pleasant furnishings. This is your chance to try risotto with strawberries, a surprisingly pleasant combination. Closed Tuesdays. Reservations necessary on Sundays. Major credit cards accepted. 15 Via del Forno, Greccio, Provincia di Rieti (phone: 746-753181). Moderate to inexpensive.

En Route from Rieti Make a short detour (follow the signs) to Greccio, a mountain village where nearly 800 years ago St. Francis of Assisi arranged a living *Christmas* crèche in a grotto, which is reenacted every *Christmas*. Its Franciscan convent and the small *Chiesa di San Bonaventura* date from the 13th century. In the distance is the Terminillo ski resort. Take S4 to return to Rome.

Sardinia

Sardinia's Grazia Deledda, an unschooled woman from the mountain town of Nuoro, won the Nobel Prize for Literature in 1926. Deledda was a prolific, lyric writer whose works reflect Sardinian peasant life in the early 20th century. Then, as now, Sards were fiercely independent, proud, and wary of outsiders.

One of Deledda's novels, *Canne al vento* (Reeds in the Wind), immortalizes the heady Sardinian winds. They can turn ferocious in the north, where the 7-mile-wide Strait of Boniface separates Sardinia from French-owned Corsica. Settlers fleeing Crete and later Carthage in frail craft learned to steer clear of Sardinia's churning waters, driven by the Balearic current, and by treacherous winds like the mistral.

These same waves and winds brought the island's first settlers during the Neolithic era. They found a warm climate, hospitable terrain, and, in volcanic mountains like Mt. Arci in the Oristano province, obsidian—black glass made from volcanic ash—that was useful for stone tools. These early people fused with the Nuraghesi, believed to have sailed to Sardinia from the eastern Mediterranean by way of North Africa around 3000 BC. They left behind them about 7,000 tower complexes called *nuraghi,* built of huge stones joined without mortar. Some are like medieval castles: They typically have one cone-shaped central tower of several stories and two or three rings of defensive walls, sometimes enclosing other towers.

Sardinia's location 116 miles west of the Italian mainland—about the same distance as from North Africa—puts it at the center of Mediterranean trade routes. Like other islands, it was in constant danger of invasion, and in rapid succession it was occupied by Greeks, Romans, and Phoenicians. One delight of beach life on Sardinia is the occasional serendipitous discovery of reminders of those days. The traces of brickwork half buried in the sand at water's edge may have come from a fisherman's cottage built in Caesar's day. Remains of Carthaginian colonies can be seen near the sea at the site of ancient Nora, south of Cagliari, at Bithia, Paniloriga, and Sant'Antioco. On the western coast near Oristano are the ruins of Tharros, which include a Phoenician temple.

Later, the coastal villages were looted and destroyed by Vandals, Byzantines, and Arabs. Retreating into the mountainous interior, the refugees built the towns that survive to this day. During the Middle Ages, the maritime republics of Pisa and Genoa battled for supremacy in Sardinia, followed by the Spanish and Austrians. Each new occupier left a stamp— the Genoese and Spanish their towers and ramparts, the Pisans elegant Romanesque churches, with their characteristic horizontal stripes.

Successive invasions pushed islanders farther inland. The resulting insularity helps to explain their tongue, Sardo, a romance language close to spoken Latin. Utterly incomprehensible to most other Italians, its four dialectal variations borrow words from Arabic, Spanish, and Portuguese. The Spanish House of Aragon dominated Sardinia for four centuries, leaving its imprint especially on the western coastline, where the local dialect, one of the four variations, is called Catalàn. The Spanish were ousted by the Piedmontese, blamed for deforesting the island to fuel the fledgling industrial revolution in northern Italy.

Despite unification with the new Italy in 1870, Sardinia remained undeveloped and malaria-ridden, even though Mussolini created new farm colonies like Fertilia, settled by northern Italians. The island achieved limited political autonomy as an independent region after World War II. Progress came to the island only after the 1960s, so that today the old and new sometimes seem incongruously juxtaposed.

Summer winds send shivers through the eucalyptus trees and flowering shrubs lining the roads that wind through broad valleys; they waft the unforgettable fragrance of *macchia,* the low growth of aromatic shrubs that cover most of Sardinia's 9,724 square miles of otherwise largely barren mountain peaks and endless rolling hills.

The coast is ringed by islets whose soft rock has been carved into bizarre shapes by the elements. One of the world's most spectacular coastlines, this is the easiest part of Sardinia for outsiders to get to know. Some sections were defaced by construction during the 1970s, but, thanks to environmentalists, much remains undisturbed. Ideal for snorkeling, Sardinia's rocky inlets alternate with secluded coves or, as at Stintino and Alghero, with mile-long stretches of sandy beaches, the nicest of which are often the private strands at hotels. Breathtaking vistas appear as yet another hairpin turn reveals a beach of white sand, a secluded cove, or a cliff dotted with grottoes and, atop, a centuries-old Saracen tower in ruins. The network of watchtowers was built on the coast, each within sight of the other, to warn of the approach of pirates and other invaders.

The rugged mountain interior is capped by 6,017-foot Punta La Marmora in the Gennargentu range, at Sardinia's heart. Above terraced vineyards, solitary shepherds tending their flocks guard rock-strewn plateaus. Sardinian folk culture is undiluted and genuine, especially in the Barbagia area. From foods to handicrafts, clothing, and home furnishings, the grazing economy has shaped traditional Sardinian life. In addition, schools and folk dance clubs help retain the culture, and in summer many hotels schedule an evening of local culinary specialties, followed by folk dances to the music of a triple-piped flute called a *launeddas.*

Unlike Malta or Sicily, Sardinia was never a military or commercial crossroads. This helped to limit its population, today estimated at 170 people per square mile (by contrast, Sicily has 490). In peak season (late July and August), visitors may endure poor service and unfair prices. But from May through June and in September, swimming, sunning, and touring are delightful, and hotel rates fall by one-half or more. Although some resort hotels are open year-round, those on the coast, including those on the Costa Smeralda (Emerald Coast), usually open a week before *Easter* and close at the end of September. So check ahead, as dates vary.

Golf, tennis, hiking, biking, and trekking on foot or horseback are popular in spring and fall. Temperatures are comparatively warm and rainfall scanty, so that even in January visitors enjoy pleasant touring. Indeed, *cagliaritani* boast that they can swim in January, when the almond trees are already in spectacular bloom.

Note that many sites of interest in Sardinia close for a midday break, usually from noon or 1 PM to about 3 or 4 PM; we suggest calling ahead to check exact hours.

TOURIST INFORMATION

There are tourist offices (*Azienda Autonoma di Soggiorno e Turismo; AAST*) in the following cities: *Alghero* (9 Piazza Portaterra; phone: 79-979054; fax: 79-974881); *Arzachena* (Via Risorgimento; phone: 789-82624; fax: 789-81090); *Cagliari* (97 Via Mameli; phone: 70-664195 or 70-664196); *Nuoro* (19 Piazza Italia; phone: 784-30083); *Olbia* (1 Via Catello Piro; phone: 789-21453; fax: 789-21572); *Oristano* (276 Via Cagliari; phone: 783-74191; fax: 783-302518); *Santa Teresa di Gallura* (24 Piazza Vittorio Emanuele; phone: 789-754127; fax: 789-754185); and *Sassari* (19 Via Brigata Sassari; phone: 79-233534; fax: 79-237585). Most offices close from 1 to 4 PM in summer. Brochures usually include a current *Annuario Alberghi* (Hotel Guide) and *Calendario Manifestazioni Turistiche* (Festival Calendar); they are not always translated into English. Good maps are available as well.

Agriturist, the system whereby farmers accommodate visitors in their homes, is catching on in Sardinia. In exchange for room and board, tourists may be asked to perform small jobs around the farm—anything from milking cows or working handlooms to simply expressing a healthy interest in what's going on. Avoid July and August, when the inland heat can be intense. For information, contact *Cooperativa Allevatrici Sarde* (CP 107, Oristano 09170; phone: 783-73954 or 783-481066); *Agriturist* (6 Viale Trieste, Cagliari 09123; phone: 70-668330); or *Terranostra* (3 Via Sassari, Cagliari 09123; phone: 70-668367).

GETTING AROUND

AIR Sardinia has three airports: at Cagliari (*Elmas;* phone: 70-240047); at Alghero (*Fertilia,* which also serves Sassari; phone: 79-935033), and at *Olbia* (for the Costa Smeralda; phone: 789-69228 or 789-21453), close to the Maddalena Archipelago, with its 14 islands. Flights come to the island from Rome, Milan, Pisa, and Bologna. In summer, additional flights depart from other Italian, and some European, cities as well.

The *Alitalia* office in Cagliari is at 12 Via Caprera (phone: 70-60108), and the *ATI* office is at the *Elmas Airport* (phone: 70-240079). In Sassari,

Alitalia has an office at 30 Via Cagliari (phone: 79-234498). At the *Olbia Airport*, call *Meridiana* airlines (formerly *Alisarda*; phone: 789-52626). In Cagliari, an air-taxi service is available from *Air Sardinia* (22 Piazza Carmine; phone: 70-650767); at Sassari, try *Aerotaxi TAS* (8 Via Porcellana; phone: 79-234733).

On the Costa Smeralda at Porto Cervo, a reservations center handles air and steamship arrangements (phone: 789-9400); also try *Sardinia International Travel* (Piazza Centrale; phone: 789-92225), which offers interesting fly/drive packages. In Cagliari, a free bus run by *ARST* (*Azienda Regionale Sarda Turisti;* phone: 70-657236) runs hourly between the bus station at Piazza Matteotti and *Elmas Airport*. The trip takes 20 minutes.

BUS *PANI* (4 Piazza Darsena in Cagliari; phone: 70-652326), the main bus company, connects major cities. Local buses are too crowded and slow to be recommended.

CAR RENTAL Most major international firms have offices at Sardinia's three airports and other locations.

FERRY Frequent ferry service, especially in summer, links Olbia, Santa Teresa di Gallura, and Porto Torres in the north of Sardinia with the mainland cities of Civitavecchia (near Rome), Livorno, and Genoa, as well as with the south of France and Corsica; except for Corsica, these crossings take from 7 to 12 hours. In addition, *Tirrenia*'s (see below) high-speed hydrofoil—the *Acquastrada*—crosses between Civitavecchia and Olbia in three and a half hours. From Cagliari in the south, ferries connect with Civitavecchia, Genoa, Naples, Palermo, Trapani, and Tunisia; these crossings, which take from 14 to 23 hours, at times can be rough, so bring seasickness pills. You'll sleep better in a *cuccetta* (sleeping berth) than a *poltrona* (armchair). Reserve weeks ahead in the summer, particularly if you are taking a car.

The chief companies running ferries are *Tirrenia, Trans Tirreno Express,* and *Traghetti Ferrovie dello Stato* (Italian State Railways), with offices at all railway stations in Italy. Any travel agency in Italy can make ferry bookings. *Tirrenia* has agencies in Cagliari (1 Via Campidano; phone: 70-666065); Olbia (17 Corso Umberto; phone: 789-24691); Porto Torres (*Stazione Marittima;* phone: 91-514600); La Maddalena (2 Via Principe di Napoli; phone: 789-737508); and Rome (41 Via Bissolati; phone: 6-474-2041 or 6-474-2242). Ferries can be subject to annoying and inexplicable delays. Try to eat before embarking, or bring a picnic; the food at the *tavola calda* restaurant on board can be poor.

TOURS For a bus tour, contact *Karalis Viaggi* (199 Via della Pineta, Cagliari; phone: 70-306991/2). For other tour information, contact the *Touring Club Italiano* (c/o *Centromed Travel Agency,* 43 Via XXIV Novembre; phone: 70-670332) or the *Italian Automobile Club* (*ACI;* 2 Via Carboni Boi; phone: 70-492881), both in Cagliari.

TRAIN Connections between the major cities of Olbia, Sassari, Oristano, and Cagliari are excruciatingly slow, and buses may be preferable. It takes about three and a half hours to travel from Cagliari to either Porto Torres in the northwest or Olbia in the northeast. Local trains creep at a snail's pace, though the old-fashioned daily train running between Cagliari and Arbatax passes through fascinating scenery. For information, contact the *Ufficio Ferrovie Sarde* (Piazza Repubblica, Cagliari; phone: 70-491304). In Cagliari, the *Italian State Railways (FS)* station is at Piazza Matteotti (phone: 70-656293).

SPECIAL EVENTS

The Sards celebrate every possible feast day, and they host more than a hundred traditional religious or folkloric festivals, all involving feasting, pageantry, and general merriment. The most important holidays are *Carnevale,* celebrated everywhere just before *Lent; Sa Sartiglia,* in Oristano the Sunday and Tuesday before *Ash Wednesday;* the evocative *Sos Mamuttones* (Shrove Tuesday) at Mamoiada near Nuoro; the *Sagra di Sant'Efisio,* a historic procession from Cagliari to Nora from May 1 to 4; the *Cavalcata,* at Sassari the next to last Sunday in May (commemorating the routing of the Moors in the year 1000); *Li Candelieri* (Feast of the Candlesticks), in Sassari on August 14; and *Sagra del Redentore,* in Nuoro the last Sunday in August.

SHOPPING

Sassari and Cagliari have excellent craft museums and showrooms that display fine Sardinian artworks. By American standards, the handloomed, pure wool bedspreads and carpets, worked in traditional Sardinian motifs, appear relatively expensive, but they are well worth the price given their rarity and high quality. Other good buys are jewelry incorporating the local rare oxblood-colored coral; the traditional Sardinian engagement ring, the *fede sarda,* hand-crafted in 18-karat gold or silver filigree; shawls in black wool or silk, hand-embroidered in pastel hues and real gold; and handmade, brightly colored or pure white Sardinian pottery, worked into lacy patterns. *ISOLA* (184 Via Baccaredda, Cagliari; phone: 70-492756) is a good place to purchase ceramics, handloomed woolen carpets, and bedspreads. They have numerous other locations, including 10 Via Monsignor Bua, Nuoro; Via Catalogna, Alghero; 23 Corso Umberto I, Olbia; Vias Tirso and Lombardia, Oristano; and Porto Cervo, Costa Smeralda.

SPORTS AND FITNESS

BOATING Rent boats—with or without diving equipment or crews for fishing or cruising—through almost any beach hotel or at the *Marinasarda* (Porto Cervo on the Costa Smeralda; phone: 789-92475) or the *Centro Velico di Caprera*, a sailing club (7/23 Via Vittorio Emanuele, La Maddalena; phone: 789-738529). Excursions are offered by most travel agencies, including

Karalis Viaggi (see *Tours,* above), and through the *Centro Velico di Caprera.* *Karalis* also is a yacht broker; you also may want to contact the *Costa Smeralda Yacht Club* (phone: 789-91332).

FISHING Freshwater fishing requires a permit, which can be obtained from the *Assessorato Regionale alla Difesa dell'Ambiente* (69 Viale Trento, Cagliari 09100; phone: 70-55041). Spearfishing—with or without air tanks—is popular but strictly controlled by the authorities. For further information, contact the local branch of the *Federazione Italiana Pesca Subacqua* (Italian Sport Fishing Association; Viale Elmas, Cagliari 09100; phone: 70-6061).

GOLF Sardinia has two 18-hole golf courses—at the Costa Smeralda in the northeast and at Is Molas near Cagliari in the south. The former, the challenging *Pevero Golf Club* (Cala di Volpe, Porto Cervo 07020; phone: 789-96072), was designed by Robert Trent Jones, Sr. (for details, see *Great Italian Golf* in DIVERSIONS). Near Cagliari is the 6,980-yard *Is Molas Golf Club* (Santa Margherita di Pula, Cagliari 09010; phone: 70-924-1013/4).

HORSEBACK RIDING Roaming the rugged Sardinian mountains on horseback, or enjoying a lazy canter along the beach, is a treat for equestrians. Many hotels can make arrangements, and an increasing number keep their own horses. The best known is the 50-horse *Centro Ippico* at the *Ala Birdi* hotel (25 Strada a Mare, Arborea 09021; phone: 783-801083), which offers riding lessons and horseback excursions year-round (for details, see *Horsing Around, Italian Style* in DIVERSIONS). Also consider the *Cooperativa Allevatrici Sarde* (CP 107, Oristano 09170; phone: 783-418066 or 783-73954), which arranges mountain excursions of one or more days (book well in advance). Near Cagliari, the *Gran Hotel Chia Laguna* (see *Best en Route*) also has horses. *Sardegna a Cavallo,* which offers a year-round program of equestrian touring, has offices in Arbatax (phone: 782-667081); Arborea (phone: 783-800268); and Capoterra (phone: 70-721277). The last-named office arranges excursions from S'Ebba to Mt. Arcosu, a *World Wildlife Federation* reservation, among other places. The local tourist offices have up-to-date listings of equestrian tourism possibilities.

HUNTING The Barbagia highlands are popular with hunters. For information, apply to the *Board of Sardinian Regional Directors* (69 Viale Trento, Cagliari 09100; phone: 70-55041) or the *Federazione Italiana della Caccia* (16 Via Bruseu Onnis, Cagliari 09100; phone: 70-668933).

SWIMMING Swimming is possible May through September, especially in the south, where the water is warm. It is cooler but still pleasant in the north. Away from the big cities, the water is sparklingly clear and unpolluted. Many first class hotels on the coast offer a full panoply of beach facilities, which may include sailing and windsurfing rentals and lessons, a pool (for when the sea is rough), water skiing, and scuba diving, plus lighted tennis and *bocce* courts and horseback riding. Serious scuba and deep-sea divers should check with hotel officials about local restrictions, and all scuba divers, however experienced, should use balloon markers, as boaters like to creep (and even speed) into sea-level grottoes. Water skiing within 550 yards of the coast is illegal.

TENNIS Many resort hotels have courts. On the Costa Smeralda, the *Tennis Club* hotel (Porto Cervo; phone: 789-92244) is open year-round and offers lessons on lighted tennis courts. The *Baia di Conte* outside Alghero (see *Best en Route*) runs courses for adults and children. For more details, see *Tennis* in DIVERSIONS. The *Italian Tennis Federation* has an office in Cagliari (16 Via Lamarmora; phone: 70-669054).

NIGHTCLUBS AND NIGHTLIFE

Among the seemingly infinite number of discos and other nightspots, two especially popular venues are the *Sotto Vento Club,* with a restaurant and a piano bar (Golfo Pevero, Porto Cervo, on the road to the *Cala di Volpe* hotel; phone: 789-96072), and the *Ritual Club,* which offers the same (Monti di Lu Colbu, near the town of Baia Sardinia; phone: 789-99032).

FOOD AND WINE

Along the coast, Sardinia's specialties begin with the freshest fish and shellfish, including prawns, crabs, oysters, octopus, lobsters, sea bass, red snapper, and flounder. Any hors d'oeuvres platter is likely to include mixed shellfish salad or *moscardini* (fried baby octopus). A popular first course is *su ziminu,* Sardinia's version of bouillabaisse, which always includes little *scorfano* fish, small crabs, and often lobster claws in a broth rich with chopped, sun-dried tomatoes and white wine. Pasta with lobster and tomato sauce or with sea-urchin caviar, abundant in winter, is also popular. Year-round, Sardinians grate salted, dried caviar of tuna—or *bottarga* (the far more costly mullet)—onto spaghetti tossed with olive oil.

Horsemeat, much prized locally, often masquerades on the menu as just another fancy steak (*bistecca gran premio*) or as *is coiettas* (rolled and stuffed).

Inland dinners may begin with *salumes de Berchidda,* variations on salami made from pigs that have foraged on the fragrant local heath. This leads to the pièce de résistance of all Sardinian cuisine, *porceddu* (suckling pig roasted on a bed of aromatic myrtle). Lamb is also sometimes roasted this way. Both pork and lamb are served *sa birdura croa* (with chunks of celery and radishes).

Pasta dishes include *malloreddus* (tiny shells served with tomato or meat sauce) and *culonzones* (big ravioli stuffed with herbs and ricotta cheese made from ewe's milk and sometimes flavored with fresh mint). Available everywhere in Sardinia are flat rounds of *carta da musica* (music paper) bread, which is named for the rustling sound it makes when eaten dry; moistened, it becomes as soft as fresh bread.

Aged pecorino cheeses made from ewe's milk range in flavor from gentle to tangy. The most celebrated of all Sardinian cheeses, *casu beccio,* has a creamy center. A rarity, it is cured by worms. (Don't worry—it is too prized to appear on a restaurant menu.) More customary methods are employed for aging the cheeses that go into *seadas* or *sebadas* (delectable, bittersweet honey-dipped fried pastries). *Aranciata* (candied orange peel with almonds and honey) comes from Nuoro.

Sardinian wines are increasingly popular, even abroad: From the south comes the dry white nuragus of Cagliari; from the north, the still white aragosta (good with fish) and the sparkling white vermentino di Gallura. Red wines include cannonau, the most popular, and rosso di Mamoiada. Meals may end with the mellow, sherry-like golden vernaccia often used in sauces, with sweet anghelu ruju (red angel) or with a chilled thimbleful of the strong filu di ferru ("wire string") liqueur.

TOURING SARDINIA

Vacationers can view Sardinia from a rented car or by train, horseback, bicycle, or beach chair. During torrid late July and early August, it may be wisest to stake out a beach; save day trips for cooler days. Beware of the annual summer brush fires, particularly in August; ask your hotel concierge or the tourist authorities about possible danger.

Circling the entire island, this driving tour begins at Sardinia's prettiest town, Alghero, which has its own airport at nearby Fertilia and is less than an hour's drive from Porto Torres, served by ferry boats from Genoa and Livorno. From Alghero, the route goes to Sassari, then to tiny medieval Castelsardo. It dips inland through cork oak groves to Tempio Pausania to rejoin the coast beginning at Palau, which faces the isle of La Maddalena, with its necklace of islets. Proceeding to the Costa Smeralda and neighboring Golfo Aranci, it heads south down the coast past Olbia, another air- and seaport, then turns inland to Nuoro in the mountainous Sardinian heartland. Here begins the Barbagia, a wooded highland of dramatic scenery, prehistoric monuments on a heath, cork oaks, and shepherds' villages where folk costumes are still worn. The slow, winding roads twist through the interesting Gennargentu mountain hamlets before straightening out onto a plain where hundreds of native ponies run free. Next comes Barumini, the island's largest ancient Nuraghesi castle-fortress. The Barumini road leads to the capital, Cagliari, founded on the Costa del Sud by Phoenicians and surrounded by breathtaking beaches and dramatic capes and bays. The northern drive back, studded with Phoenician ruins, stops at Oristano and then heads back to Alghero, taking in ancient Tharros and Bosa.

In resort areas in high season—mid-July to mid-August—make reservations by *Easter*. During this time, expect to pay $450 or more per night for a double room in hotels listed as very expensive (those on the Costa Smeralda can go up to over $1,000 a day!); between $250 and $400 in hotels listed as expensive; between $150 and $225 in those listed as moderate; and $125 or less in those listed as inexpensive. Prices are lowest in May and September—sometimes less than half the August rates—and they vary month by month, rising with the temperature. Rates usually include continental breakfast, service charge, and taxes. All hotels feature air conditioning, private baths, and telephones unless otherwise indicated. In midsummer, a dinner for two, including service and taxes and sometimes wine, will cost $150 or more in an expensive restaurant; from $80 to $140 in a moderate one; and $75 or less in an inexpensive place. All restaurants are open for lunch and dinner unless otherwise noted. For each location, hotels and restaurants are listed alphabetically by price category.

ALGHERO This town on the "Coral Riviera" (pop. 37,000) is coastal Sardinia at its loveliest. The great ramparts by the sea were begun by the Genoese and completed by the Spanish. Distrusting the hostile locals, the Spanish grandees shipped them inland and replaced them with Cataláns. The Spanish flavor of the town is still so pronounced that it is sometimes called *Barcelonetta* ("Little Barcelona"). Streets are *calles,* signs designate monuments in Spanish and Italian, and many of the natives, especially the older ones, still speak Catalàn.

What coral beds remain here lie extremely deep in the ocean, so much of the coral seen in Alghero's goldsmith shops today is imported. Alghero has its own long sandy beach, but you'll find excellent, less crowded stretches at Porto Conte and around Capo Caccia, with its dramatic cliffs and eerie grotto at the water's edge with deep caverns and two lakes within, about 11 miles (18 km) away. The grotto can be visited by tour boat (three hours round-trip) from the port at Alghero or by car. If driving, take the coast road from Alghero 11 miles (18 km) west to Capo Caccia. Be forewarned: There is a 670-step climb down to the grotto and then back up. It is open daily, with a long (noon to 3 PM) closing; admission charge.

BEST EN ROUTE

Baia di Conte Located on a sandy bay 8 miles (13 km) northwest of Alghero, this family-oriented 315-room hotel has three restaurants, disco dancing, shops, and a variety of sports facilities, including two pools, horseback riding, tennis, sailing and canoeing. Open mid-April to October. Località Sant'Impenia, Porto Conte (phone: 79-949000; fax: 79-949001). Expensive.

La Lepanto A terrace on the ramparts helps make this Alghero's favorite dining spot, while the kitchens make it the best. The full seafood menu ranges from humble anchovies to prized local lobster. The menu is in Catalàn. Closed Mondays. Reservations advised. Major credit cards accepted. 135 Via Carlo Alberto, Alghero (phone: 79-979116). Expensive.

Il Pavone The panoramic view from the terrace is spectacular at this eatery, which is renowned for its seafood, spaghetti with rock lobster, and fine local torbato wine. Closed Wednesdays (except in summer). Reservations advised. Major credit cards accepted. 3 Piazza Sulis, Alghero (phone: 79-979584). Expensive.

A Dieci Metri Fish is a must—fish ravioli, seafood risotto, or grilled fresh catch from local waters—in this popular (though noisy) former inn. Closed Wednesdays (except in summer), January, and February. Reservations advised. Major credit cards accepted. 37 Vicolo Adami, Alghero (phone: 79-979023). Moderate.

Villa Las Tronas On a promontory overlooking the sea, with its own fine restaurant, this was once a summer residence of the Italian royal family. There are only 30 rooms; number 31 is tops. Hotel open year-round; restaurant closed Wednesdays and mid-September to mid-May. 1 Lungomare Valencia, Alghero (phone: 79-981818; fax: 79-981044). Moderate.

Dei Pini Nestled among pine trees and just 15 minutes from Alghero, this hostelry has a splendid stretch of beach. Each of the 90 rooms has a balcony; there also is a pleasant restaurant and a tennis court. Half board required. Open *Easter* through September. Località Le Bombarde, near the coastal town of Fertilia (phone: 79-930157; fax: 79-930249). Inexpensive.

SASSARI Take S291 from Alghero 24 miles (38 km) to Sardinia's second-largest city (pop. 120,000), founded during medieval times, when invaders drove the populace inland from Porto Torres. The *Museo Archeologico ed Etnografico G. A. Sanna* (Sanna Museum of Archaeology and Ethnography; 64 Via Roma; phone: 79-272202) contains rare Sardinian artifacts, including some from the Bronze Age *Anghelu Ruju Tombs* near Alghero; costumes richly adorned with gold filigree; and Renaissance paintings. The museum is closed after 2 PM; closed Sundays after 1 PM; admission charge. Craftwork is on sale in a hall in the *Giardino Pubblico* (Public Garden), with a good selection of cork, inlaid wood objects, baskets, and ceramics. The garden is open daily; no admission charge.

Thirty miles (48 km) northwest of Sassari, on the tip of Capo del Falcone, a long promontory, is the summer resort town of Stintino. Facing the prison isle of Asinara, the town has windswept fishermen's cottages and a mile-long sand beach, the Spiaggia di Pelosa.

BEST EN ROUTE

Al Senato A wonderful hideaway in the central labyrinth of town, this restaurant serves fresh fish and such island specialties as snails and horsemeat fillet. Closed Sundays and the last two weeks of August. Reservations advised. Major credit cards accepted. 2 Via Mundula, Sassari (phone: 79-231423). Expensive to moderate.

Da Silvestrino In the Old Town, this is a good place to sample seafood pasta and lobster soup. Closed Thursdays in winter. Reservations advised. Major credit cards accepted. 12 Via Sassari, Stintino (phone: 79-523007). Moderate.

Tre Stelle This modern, roomy restaurant serves fish soup, *pesce fresco marinato in vernaccia* (oven-baked fish marinated in vernaccia wine), and Alghero and Gallura wines. Closed Sundays and two weeks in August. Reservations unnecessary. Major credit cards accepted. Downtown, at 6 Via Porcellana, Sassari (phone: 79-232431). Inexpensive.

En Route from Sassari Take S200 for 17½ miles (28 km) to the charming old seaside fort town of Castelsardo. Its 16th-century cathedral has traces of the original Gothic church. Turn inland on S134 and then onto S127, passing cork oak groves and ancient *nuraghi*. At Tempio Pausania, an old Roman town famed for its wine, swing north on S133 to Palau, the ferry-boat landing for the island of La Maddalena. From Castelsardo, the distance is just under 85 miles (136 km).

BEST EN ROUTE

Da Franco This outstanding restaurant with alfresco dining serves the shepherd foods of Sardinia, including its breads (all homemade here) and myrtle-flavored *capretto al forna* (kid roasted over a wood fire). Seafood dishes include spaghetti *all'aragosta* (with lobster sauce) and fish-stuffed ravioli in shrimp sauce. The array of cheeses is extraordinary; save room for bitter honey on ricotta cheese for dessert. There's also an abundant selection of Sardinian wines. Closed Mondays and for three weeks at *Christmas*. Reservations advised. Major credit cards accepted. 3 Via Capo d'Orso, Palau (phone: 789-709558). Expensive.

La Guardiola A bounteous spread of antipasti, fresh seafood and risotto, and huge portions of pasta are worth the trek (try the *farfalle impazzite*—pasta bowties smothered in a tomato-based pepper-and-cream sauce). Avoid the Sunday lunchtime rush. 4 Piazza del Bastione (phone: 79-470428). In summer, the restaurant turns into *La Guardiola Due* and moves around the corner to a terrace with views. Both closed Mondays, except in summer. Reservations advised. Major credit cards accepted. 2 Via Lamarmora, Castelsardo (phone: 79-470755). Moderate.

Bissoni Try the local specialties at this modest refurbished trattoria (the only one in Tempio Pausania): lemon-flavored, cheese-stuffed ravioli, or *malloreddus* (short, chewy pasta) served in tomato sauce and spicy local sausage. The *seadas* just may be the best in Sardinia. Closed Sundays. No reservations. No credit cards accepted. Follow signs on the main road (no phone). Inexpensive.

LA MADDALENA The isles of Maddalena and, beyond, Caprera, part of an archipelago that shelters a US nuclear submarine base, are reached by ferry from Palau, a 20-minute trip with a sometimes long wait in peak season.

A young Napoleon suffered the first defeat of his military career here after islanders withstood a three-day siege launched from Corsica. The *Museo dell'Archeologia Marina Nino Lamboglia* (Museum of Marine Archaeology; Via Principe Amedeo; phone: 789-737395) has a small collection of Roman-era objects, such as amphorae and anchors, discovered by underwater archaeologists. The museum is closed Sundays and after 1:30 PM; admission charge. The island of Caprera, where Giuseppe Garibaldi is buried, is connected to La Maddalena by causeway. The museum in Garibaldi's home is closed Mondays; Tuesdays through Fridays after 1:30 PM; and weekends after 12:30 PM; admission charge (phone: 789-727162).

BEST EN ROUTE

Cala Lunga Not on the beach but with its own pool, this hostelry at Porto Massimo has 72 rooms (none air conditioned, but most with private baths) and a restaurant. Km 5, La Maddalena (phone: 789-737569; fax: 789-735542). Moderate.

La Grotta The simple but delicious island fare offered here includes grilled fresh fish, lobster, and spaghetti, with an occasional Neapolitan touch (its owner hails from Naples). Closed November through April. Reservations necessary. Major credit cards accepted. 3 Via Principe di Napoli, La Maddalena (phone: 789-737228). Moderate.

Mangana Typical Sardinian seafood dishes, a vast selection of island wines, and, for dessert, an interesting version of *sebadas* with myrtle-flavored jelly are the draws here. Closed Wednesdays and one month at *Christmas*. Reservations advised. Major credit cards accepted. 2 Via Mazzini, La Maddalena (phone: 789-738477). Moderate.

COSTA SMERALDA Drive south from Palau on S125 to the Costa Smeralda, a stretch of yacht basins, shopping plazas and *caffès,* and secluded private homes and beach hotels. This grandiose, somewhat precious 33-mile resort development was built in the 1960s and, though it shows its age, it remains popular with the golf and boating set. Porto Cervo, a bayside town 45 minutes by car from both La Maddalena and Olbia, is at the heart of the Costa Smeralda. The *caffè* at its *piazzetta* is a good people watching place, though during the off-season the town is dead. The surrounding mall's boutiques sell the world's priciest labels. The best show in town is at Porto Cervo's marina, crammed in season buoy-to-buoy with million-dollar yachts. Heavenly bays are overlooked by olive tree–covered hills, and the brilliant light plays tricks with the water, making it appear dappled green and turquoise. Unique in Sardinia, here the salt wind has carved giant boulders into eerie shapes.

The hotels listed below, all members of the *Costa Smeralda Consortium*, are opulent and ultra-expensive (up to $1,000 for a double room!), and many require guests to pay full board during high season. Rates drop by about 35% in the off-season. (Also see *Italy's Best Beaches* in DIVERSIONS.)

Pitrizza A member of the Relais & Châteaux group, this property has a handful of four- to six-room villas (a total of 51 rooms), each with a terrace or garden overlooking the rock-hewn pool. There also is a private beach, a terrace, and a fine restaurant set on the beautiful Liscia di Vacca Bay. The clubhouse has a piano bar. Open May 15 through September (phone: 789-91500; 800-221-1800; fax: 789-91629). Very expensive.

Romazzino Overlooking an islet-dotted bay, this bougainvillea-festooned, Mediterranean-style hotel with 93 spacious rooms is perfect for the sporty crowd and families. Pluses include a restaurant and an outdoor pizza oven, boats for hire, tennis, windsurfing, and dancing. Special events are arranged for children. Open May 15 through September (phone: 789-96020; fax: 789-96258). Very expensive.

Cervo Near the *piazzetta*, it boasts a garden, a pool, 94 rooms, and a shuttle boat to a private beach. The restaurant overlooks the old harbor, and the cozy piano bar is a favorite meeting place. The relatively spartan *Cervo Tennis Club* and *Pevero Golf Club* are nearby. Open April through October (phone: 789-92003; 800-221-1800; fax: 789-92593). Expensive.

Le Ginestre All 79 rooms and four suites are clustered around a pool, with a view of the splendid Gulf of Pevero. There are two restaurants, horseback riding, and a tennis court. Open May through October 10 (phone: 789-92030; fax: 789-94087). Expensive.

Il Pescatore Try such seafood delicacies as spaghetti *alla bottarga* (with mullet roe), *spigola al finocchietto* (fish grilled with fennel), or grilled prawns. For a fine view of the port, reserve a waterside table. The choice of local wines is first rate. Closed for lunch from May through October, and November through April. Reservations necessary. Major credit cards accepted. Piazza Vecchio, Porto Cervo (phone: 789-92296). Expensive.

Il Pomodoro A chic pizzeria-*ristorante*, it serves delectable antipasti and pizza in an attractive rustic setting indoors or under a grape arbor outside. Open year-round. Reservations advised on weekends and in high season. Major credit cards accepted. Porto Cervo (phone: 789-92207). Moderate to inexpensive.

BAIA SARDINIA The advantages of continuing to the westernmost point of this peninsula (only a few miles west of Porto Cervo) are the expanse of beach and a host of tourist spots that wear a lower price tag than is usually associated with the area.

BEST EN ROUTE

Club Hotel Practically a bargain compared with accommodations in Porto Cervo, this 84-room hotel boasts a fantastic restaurant (*Casablanca*) that specializes in fish, usually very imaginatively served. Closed mid-October through April. Baia Sardinia, Arzachena (phone: 789-99006; fax: 789-99286). Hotel, moderate; restaurant, expensive.

PORTO ROTONDO Take the coastal road 12 miles (19 km) south of Porto Cervo toward Olbia, and follow the signs to Porto Rotondo. This yacht basin surrounded by sumptuous private summer houses is Sardinia's answer to fashionable American summer beach towns—and more exclusive than its neighbors.

BEST EN ROUTE

Relais Sporting An Aga Khan property and a member of the Relais & Châteaux group, this deceptively simple retreat, which sprawls on a spit of land overlooking a magnificent bay 7 miles (11 km) from Olbia, caters to the international yachting set. All 28 rooms have sea views. The restaurant, noted for grilled fresh fish, fine wines, and a special evening buffet, is the best around and is *the* place to be seen. Open April through September. Porto Rotondo (phone: 789-34005; 800-677-3524; fax: 789-34383). Hotel, very expensive; restaurant, expensive.

Palumbalza Sporting On a point overlooking the rocky coast with its own tiny port, this sprawling white property has 73 rooms, all with a view of the sea. A variety of meal plans are offered in the restaurant. There are two lighted tennis courts, a sailing school, windsurfing, motorboat and sailboat rentals, horseback riding, and a tiny *piazzetta* surrounded by a few shops and a piano bar. Open April 11 to October 5. Località Marinella, Porto Rotondo (phone: 789-32005; fax: 789-32009). Expensive to moderate.

En Route from Porto Rotondo The drive south toward Cagliari on S125 (214 miles/342 km) via Olbia takes five hours without detours for sightseeing. But those desiring to visit the wild, mountainous Barbagia district around Nuoro should detour from the coast road at Siniscola (36 miles/58 km from Olbia), picking up the inland route (S129) for Nuoro (25 miles/40 km away).

BEST EN ROUTE

Le Rose Situated in a large garden, this elegant *albergo* is a half mile from a white sandy beach; there also is a pool. Each of the 38 guestrooms has a private balcony. The restaurant offers alfresco dining; in the summer, there's a nightly piano bar. Open April through October 15. Twelve and a half miles (20 km) south of Olbia, in village of San Teodoro (phone: 784-865072). Expensive to moderate.

Gallura Worth a stopover en route to Posada, the food and service at this downtown inn are first class, from the incredible choice of antipasti to the risotto *con carciofi* (with artichokes) or spaghetti *al sugo di granchi* (with crab sauce), game, and homemade desserts—fresh fruit tarts, chocolate meringues, and so on. Upstairs is a charming pensione of 16 rooms. Restaurant closed Mondays and two weeks at *Christmas.* 145 Corso Umberto I, Olbia (phone: 789-24648; fax: 789-24629). Hotel, inexpensive; restaurant, expensive.

NUORO Residents of this homey little town where Grazia Deledda was born, at the foot of rugged Monte Ortobene, consider themselves the standard bearers of the real Sardinia. What there is here can be seen in the *Museo della Vita e delle Tradizioni* (Museum of Costumes and Popular Traditions; 56 Via Mereu; phone: 784-31426). It is closed Mondays; Sundays after 1 PM; and Tuesdays through Saturdays for a midday break. There's an admission charge. Grazia Deledda's house (42 Via Deledda; phone: 784-34571) is closed Mondays and for a midday break; admission charge. The *Museo Civico Speleo-Archeologico* (5 Via Leonardo da Vinci; phone: 784-33793) has a small collection of archaeological artifacts. It is closed Sundays and Mondays; Tuesdays and Thursdays for a long (1 to 4 PM) break; and Wednesdays, Fridays, and Saturdays after 1 PM; admission charge. Every year on the last Sunday of August, thousands of islanders wearing traditional costumes walk in the famous historical procession to Monte Ortobene to celebrate the *Festa del Redentore* (Feast of the Redeemer).

BEST EN ROUTE

Grazia Deledda Located downtown, Nuoro's best hostelry has 74 rooms, a spacious restaurant, and parking and conference facilities. Open year-round. 175 Via Lamarmora, Nuoro (phone: 784-31257; fax: 784-34017). Moderate.

Fratelli Sacchi Spotless lodgings and a garden are offered at this country inn 5 miles (8 km) east of Nuoro. Fifteen of the 22 guestrooms have private baths; none is air conditioned. The restaurant serves genuine Sardinian hill-country fare, such as *porceddu* and trout *alla vernaccia.* Open June through September; restaurant closed Mondays. Monte Ortobene, Nuoro (phone: 784-31200; fax: 784-34030). Inexpensive.

En Route from Nuoro A good map and good weather are musts for this crossing of the Barbagia. Take S389 south through the hamlet of Mamoiada

(10½ miles/17 km from Nuoro) to Sardinia's highest village, Fonni (3,250 feet), on Monte Spada (10 miles/16 km beyond Mamoiada). Mamoiada is famous for its bizarre, demonic *Mardi Gras* masks, known as *mamuthones,* that were worn during pre-Christian rites. They still are used today at *Mardi Gras* celebrations. From the road, you'll glimpse a large artificial lake, Lago Gusano, to the north. At this point, either continue on the main road, S389 *dir,* or take the mountain road shortcut to visit Désulo (15 miles/25 km south of Fonni), a shepherd's village noted for its weavers, where men wear a distinctive wool jacket, the *orbace.* Pay careful attention to signs: Travelers skipping Désulo will turn right onto S128 about 5 miles (8 km) after Tiana. Those visiting Désulo will continue past the village and turn right on the main road to Tonara; after 1⅓ miles (2 km), turn left onto S128. The next stop for either route is Sorgono, another typical crafts village. Just after Sorgono, veer left onto S128—a road dating to prehistoric times (count the roadside *nuraghi*)—and go through Laconi to tiny Nuralla (about 31 miles/50 km). Turn right onto S197 to cross the Campidano Plain through the Giara di Gesturi, the plateau where native ponies still range. They are not wild but are branded and belong to villagers.

Continue south on S197 to Barumini, 9½ miles (15 km) from Nuralla.

BEST EN ROUTE

Su Gologone In the heart of the mountainous Barbagia region amid century-old oaks and olive orchards, this rustic, antiques-filled hotel has 65 rooms (none air conditioned); a pool; tennis courts; and eight horses. A favorite with the locals, the excellent dining room serves mountain fare; pasta dishes are doused in wild game sauces. Open April through November. Località Su Gologone, Oliena, 8 miles (13 km) southeast of Nuoro (phone: 784-287512; fax: 784-287668). Restaurant, moderate to inexpensive; hotel, inexpensive.

BARUMINI A haven for history buffs, *Nuraghe Su Nuraxi* is the most complete and best preserved of the *nuraghi* excavated to date. Its huge central tower, three stories high, dates from 1500 BC. Excavations of a Bronze Age village are nearby. The *Complesso Nuragico* (Nuragic Complex) is closed Mondays through Saturdays after 2 PM, and Sundays; no admission charge (phone: 70-668501).

En Route from Barumini The remaining 37 miles (59 km) to Cagliari are an easy drive first on S197 and then, bearing left, on S131. Those fascinated by the ancient Sardinian culture will want to make a stop in Senorbi to visit the small *Museo Sa Domu Nosta* (Piazza Municipio; phone: 70-980-9071), which exhibits archaeological finds from the Nuragic era discovered at nearby excavation sites. To get to the museum, 12 miles (19 km) from Barumini, turn left (northeast) at Monastir onto S128. The museum is closed Mondays and for a long (1 to 4 PM) break; admission charge. From there, return to S131 and continue on to Cagliari.

CAGLIARI Founded by the Phoenicians, Sardinia's capital (pop. 225,000) is its main port of entry by both sea and air. The hilltop Old Quarter, Il Castello, around the medieval castle, offers a spectacular view of the Golfo degli Angeli (Gulf of the Angels) and the outlying salt marshes. The neigborhood itself is a patchwork of ruins, including a Roman amphitheater (where operas are performed in August), Pisan watchtowers, and Spanish townhouses with wrought-iron balconies. An old Spanish fort, the *Belvedere,* is now a park. The *Duomo,* built in the late 12th to early 13th century, reveals a mélange of styles, including a neo-Pisan façade, a fine Romanesque pulpit (carved in 1159 for the cathedral in Pisa and donated to Cagliari), a Gothic transept and apse, and a Baroque crypt. It is open daily, with a long (12:30 to 3:30 PM) closing.

For good shopping, wander up Via Giuseppe Manno, a continuation of Corso Vittorio Emanuele, as it winds toward the *St. Remy Bastion* and Piazza Costituzione. Here, among buildings reminiscent of Genoa or Palermo, pause for a rest at the turn-of-the-century *Caffè Genovese,* which has excellent homemade cakes and ice cream.

Housed in the *Museo Archeologico Nazionale* (National Archaeological Museum; 4 Piazza Indipendenza; phone: 70-654237) is a celebrated collection of hundreds of rare bronze miniatures showing Nuraghesi life 2,500 years ago and Phoenician, Greek, and Roman objects. The museum is open daily; admission charge. At the nearby Piazza Arsenale, modern museum rooms showing Renaissance paintings are tucked into the ancient fortress walls, whose windows overlook Poetto Beach and salt marshes. It's open daily, with a short (1:30 to 2:30 PM) closing; no admission charge (phone: 70-200-2410).

Cagliari's beaches have calmer and warmer water than those in the north, making them a good choice for swimming and wind surfing in late spring and early fall. On the road hugging the coast toward Villasimius are resort hotels.

An interesting excursion from Cagliari is to Pula, site of Nora, Sardinia's oldest city. To get there, head south on S195 for 17½ miles (28 km); bear left onto the side road. For details about the site, see *Remarkable Ruins* in DIVERSIONS. The ruins are open daily (phone: 70-920-9138). A few minutes' drive from Nora is the *Museo Municipale di Archeologia* (Municipal Museum of Archaeology; 67 Corso Vittorio Emanuele; phone: 70-920-9610), which has a collection of ceramics and objects from Phoenician and Roman times, all from the Nora site. It's closed Sundays after 1 PM and for a midday break; one admission charge to the ruins and the museum.

BEST EN ROUTE

Capo Boi Set on a heavenly bay, this luxurious 219-room property has a restaurant, a pool, tennis courts, and a fine beach. Open May through October.

On Cape Carbonaro, about 45 minutes southeast of Cagliari, via the coastal road, at Capo Boi, Villasimius (phone: 70-798015; fax: 70-798188). Expensive.

Dal Corsaro Among the best eating spots on the island (and air conditioned), it features *ravioli di pesce, cozze, e gamberetti* (ravioli stuffed with seafood), *taglioni con gamberi e fiori di zucca* (freshly made thin noodles with a sauce of zucchini blossoms and baby shrimp), and other fine seafood dishes. There is a nice selection of regional wines. Closed Sundays and August. Reservations advised. Major credit cards accepted. 28 Viale Regina Margherita, Cagliari (phone: 70-664318). Expensive.

Dal Corsaro al Poetto The management of *Dal Corsaro* also runs this open-air seaside restaurant. Closed October through May. Reservations advised. Major credit cards accepted. Poetto Beach, about 3½ miles (6 km) from downtown, on Viale Poetto, Marina Piccola (phone: 70-370295). Expensive.

Ottagono Renowned for its excellent seafood, pasta (in January, try the spaghetti with *ricci,* or sea urchins), and local fixed-menu specialties. Closed Tuesdays. Reservations unnecessary. Major credit cards accepted. Viale Poetto, Poetto Beach (phone: 70-372879). Expensive.

Sa Cardiga e su Schirone Stop here on the way to Nora for the unbeatable *aragosta* (lobster), *gamberoni* (prawns), or *zuppa di pesce* (fish soup). There is an ample selection of Sardinian wines, a piano bar, and a terrace overlooking the beach. Closed Mondays and late October through late November. Reservations advised. Major credit cards accepted. On the Pula road (S195) at the Capoterra intersection, in Località Maddalena Spiaggia, Capoterra (phone: 70-71652). Expensive to moderate.

Regina Margherita Some of the hundred rooms in this grand old hotel afford views of the port. No restaurant. Open year-round. 44 Viale Regina Margherita, Cagliari (phone: 70-670342; fax: 70-668325). Expensive to moderate.

Antica Hostaria One of the island's best, this trattoria dates from 1872. Try the *malloreddus alla campidanese* (traditional pasta mixed with a tasty vegetable-and-cheese sauce) and, in season, the delicious *fagiano* (pheasant). Round out the meal with one of the house's excellent desserts and the nectar-like *mirto* liqueur. Closed Sundays, August, and *Christmas* week. Reservations advised. Major credit cards accepted. 60 Via Cavour, near the port (phone: 70-665870). Moderate.

Cormoran The best beach in the vicinity is at this 86-room hotel on a dramatic sandy bay. Good food, windsurfing, a pool, tennis courts, and a view of the romantic islet, Isola dei Cavoli, are all pluses. Open May through October. A 45-minute drive southeast of Cagliari, just past Capo Boi, at Foxi, Villasimius (phone: 70-798101; fax: 70-798131). Moderate.

Mediterraneo Its garden setting and view of the bay make this comfortable 136-room hotel near the air terminal and train station a good choice. Its *Al*

Golfo restaurant (closed Sunday dinner and Mondays) is popular with locals. Open year-round. 46 Lungomare Cristoforo Colombo, Cagliari (phone: 70-301271; fax: 70-301274). Moderate.

Panorama In this modern establishment are 97 rooms, a pool, conference facilities, and a penthouse restaurant (closed Sunday dinner and Mondays). Open year-round. Near the city's sports complex, at 231 Viale Armando Diaz, Cagliari (phone: 70-307691; fax: 70-305413). Moderate.

Italia Centrally located (five minutes from the station and port), this hotel has 113 rooms and a coffee shop that stays open late. Closed the first three weeks of August. 31 Via Sardegna, Cagliari (phone: 70-660410; fax: 70-650240). Inexpensive.

En Route from Cagliari Coastal road S195 south circles the Sulcis Mountains and then goes to the southernmost point of Sardinia—Capo Spartivento—where it swings northwest toward the island of Sant'Antioco (about 69½ miles/111 km from Cagliari), connected by a causeway (S126) to the mainland. The Sant'Antioco ruins at Sulcis, a Carthaginian and then Roman city, include a house, a burial site, and a sacred area called a *tophet*. Sulcis is the name of the original Punic town whose ruins lie partly under Antioca. Under Sant'Antioco's medieval church are ancient Christian catacombs. Also worthwhile on Sant'Antioco is the small *Museo Municipale di Archeologia* (Via Castello; phone: 78-83590), with ceramics, jewelry, objects from the Carthaginian and Roman eras, and some interesting Hebrew inscriptions. The museum is open daily (except for major holidays), with a midday closing; admission charge. Just north of Sant'Antioco is the island of San Pietro (accessible only by boat from the harbor).

Back on the mainland, the route (now S126) winds past the splendid Costa del Sud, a series of small bays and pleasant resort hotels, then through two mining towns—Carbonia and Iglesias (17½ miles/28 km from the Sant'Antioco causeway). Noteworthy in Iglesias is the small *Museo Mineralogico* (4 Via Roma; phone: 781-22502); its 13th-century cathedral, the *Chiesa di Nostro Signore di Valverde*; and the 14th-century *Castello Salvaterra* (closed to the public). The museum, which documents mining in the area, is open weekday mornings by appointment only; admission charge. The church is open daily, with a long (noon to 4 PM) closing. After Iglesias, the road (now S130) heads inland through a flat plain 25 miles (40 km) to Decimomannu. From here take S130 *dir* 7 miles (11 km) to S131, the Oristano–Cagliari highway. While heading toward S131 on S130 *dir*, you may want to take a short detour to visit the "painted" village of Serramanna, reached by taking S196 9 miles (14 km) north of Decimomannu. In this village, the art of mural painting is practiced on many outside walls. Techniques, themes, and degree of talent may vary considerably from wall to wall and town to town, but the murals are quite interesting, especially when they express passionate religious feelings and political protests.

Alternatively, head directly to Oristano from Cagliari on S131, a 55-mile (88-km) trip. The rest of the drive runs through the Campidano Plain. Serious equestrians may detour to Arborea (on the outskirts of Oristano), site of a hotel-equitation complex, *Ala Birdi* (see *Horsing Around, Italian Style* in DIVERSIONS).

BEST EN ROUTE

Gran Hotel Chia Laguna Set on a gorgeous white sand beach at the tip of Capo Spartivento in the shadow of an ancient tower, this 324-room complex of low stone buildings is southern Sardinia's answer to the overpriced Costa Smeralda. Activities include horseback riding on the beach, sailing on the hotel's 120-foot sloop, windsurfing, going on archaeological outings and hikes, playing squash, golfing at the nearby 18-hole *Is Molas* course, and working out in the property's gym. There are four restaurants, five *caffès,* and a disco. Child care is available. Open late March through October. Chia, Domus de Maria (phone: 70-92391; fax: 70-923-0141). Expensive.

Is Molas Golf With an interesting 18-hole golf course, a fine beach, a pool, and a tennis court, this comfortable 84-room property southwest of the Gulf of Cagliari is a perfect vacation spot. Its good restaurant offers such island specialties as *malloreddus,* spaghetti with *bottarga* (dried mullet roe), and *sebadas.* There's alfresco dining on a splendid terrace in summer. Open year-round. Km 37.4 on S195, Santa Margherita, Pula (phone: 70-924-1006; fax: 70-924-1002). Expensive to moderate.

Is Morus Located between the sea and a dramatic fringe of mountains, this 75-room establishment calls to mind a private summer villa. Tucked in a large park of cypresses, pines, and eucalyptus trees, it offers a secluded beach, a fine restaurant, a tennis court, a pool, and a shuttle to the nearby *Is Molas* golf course (greens fees are included in the rate). Open early April through October. Santa Margherita di Pula (phone: 70-921171; fax: 70-921596). Expensive to moderate.

Flamingo Get away from it all at this 194-room, 30-suite hotel on a small peninsula. One section is a traditional complex around a pool; the other is a series of square buildings flanked by pine trees (ask for a room facing the beautiful beach). The hotel is near the *Is Molas* golf course. Open April through October. Km 33.8 on S195, Santa Margherita di Pula (phone: 70-920-8361; fax: 70-920-8359). Moderate.

ORISTANO Oristano's peaceful and serene aura belies its status as the island's largest farming center, as well as a thriving commercial and industrial center and port. Today the smallest of Sardinia's provincial capitals (pop.

30,000), it was founded during the Middle Ages by the refugees of ancient Tharros, who fled when the Saracens destroyed their city. Oristano gave birth to Sardinia's 14th-century Joan of Arc, Princess Eleonora d'Arborea. Defying Spain, she ruled over this cathedral town and drafted a code that became the basis for the island's laws. The town's fine cathedral dates from the 13th century, with an onion-dome tower that was added later. There's a Carmelite church nearby and a statue dedicated to Eleonora in the square bearing her name. A small collection of archaeological artifacts is on display in the *Antiquarium Arborense* (Via Parpaglia; phone: 783-7911). The museum is closed Mondays and for a long (1 to 4:30 PM) break; admission charge. Nearby is the Pisan Gothic *Chiesa di Santa Giusta,* which is closed Sundays and for a long (noon to 4 PM) break.

BEST EN ROUTE

Il Faro There's an excellent seafood menu in this elegant restaurant near Oristano's central market. Closed Sunday dinner, Mondays, and January 6 to 20. Reservations advised. Major credit cards accepted. 25 Via Bellini, Oristano (phone: 783-70002). Expensive.

Da Giovanni Near the lighthouse in the seaside resort of Marina di Torregrande, midway between Tharros and Oristano, this simple dining spot serves wonderful fish soup and excellent ravioli *di aragosta* (stuffed with lobster). Closed Mondays and October or November. Reservations unnecessary. No credit cards accepted. 8 Via Colombo, Marina di Torregrande (phone: 783-22051). Moderate.

Mistral This well-maintained modern hotel has 48 rooms and a reasonably attractive lounge and bar. Its restaurant turns out some of the best food in town. Via Martiri di Belfore, Oristano (phone: 783-212505; fax: 783-210058). Inexpensive.

Mistral 2 In this large, efficient beachfront hostelry are two restaurants; although the 132 guestrooms are on the small side, they are tastefully furnished. Open year-round. Via XX Settembre, Oristano (phone: 783-302445; fax: 783-302512). Inexpensive.

THARROS A Phoenician port founded in 800 BC, Tharros today is one of Sardinia's most fascinating archaeological sites. Its remains—plus later Roman temples—can be seen at water's edge partly submerged on the southern tip of the Sinis Peninsula, about 12½ miles (20 km) from Oristano. After repeated barbarian invasions, Tharros was abandoned in 1070, and Maristanis (today's Oristano) was founded. Also on the peninsula are a 15th-century Spanish tower and the remains of a Jewish temple. The nearby beaches are excellent.

En Route from Tharros or Oristano Take the coastal road, S292, 36 miles (58 km) to Bosa, with its medieval church and castle. Here turn off onto the unmarked road heading for Capo Maràrgiù, and continue on to Alghero, a distance of about 70 winding miles (112 km). Pleasant green valleys, picturesque towns, and smashing sea views enliven the route. The area is known for its woolens, lace, cheeses, figs, artichokes, and malvasia wine.

Campania and the Amalfi Coast

There can be just one reason why a precipitous, gnarled, inhospitable limestone peninsula, segregating the Gulf of Salerno from the Gulf of Naples, has become one of the most important holiday destinations in Europe. As André Gide proclaimed in *The Immoralist*, the road from Sorrento to Ravello "is so beautiful that I had no desire . . . to see anything more beautiful on earth."

Long before travelers discovered the spectacular charms of the Neapolitan Riviera, Italians nicknamed it the "Divine Coast"—clear testimony to the grandeur of its scenery and the delight of its architecture.

Campania has two picturesque gulfs, or bays (the Bay of Naples and the Gulf of Salerno), enclosed by picturesque promontories, including the Sorrento Peninsula. It has a massive volcano (Vesuvius), as well as the more benign, forest-covered Lattari Mountains, which slope into the Tyrrhenian Sea. There are 220 miles of dramatic coastline and several romantic islands (Capri, Ischia, and Procida). Its natural endowments alone are sufficient reason to tour the region, but add to this one of the greatest concentrations of archaeological excavations in the world, including Pompeii, Herculaneum, and Paestum; unforgettable towns of mythological and historical importance, such as Sorrento, Positano, Amalfi, Ravello, and Naples; and, finally, the people themselves, who have cheered the world with their music, hospitality, and cuisine, and the region invites a journey of compelling interest.

The Greeks came to Campania as early as the 11th century BC, setting up colonies in Cumae and Pithecusae (present-day Ischia). The arts flourished, towns such as Paestum, with its impressive temples, were built, and olive trees and vineyards were introduced to local agriculture. The Romans gained the upper hand by 326 BC, forcing the Greeks into an alliance that eventually turned entirely to Rome's advantage. Under the emperors, Campania became a playground for the wealthy, who built splendid villas along the coast.

A period of Byzantine influence followed the disintegration of the Roman Empire, but the Byzantines always had to contend with rebellious tribes, outside invaders (most prominently the northern Lombards, who established themselves in the interior but also managed to take Salerno), and city-states with independent ambitions (Naples achieved autonomy by 763; Amalfi did the same in 786). By the 9th century, Saracen mercenaries were making incursions. Often invited in by warring duchies, these Muslims—who had established themselves in Sicily—brought an Arabic influence that is still seen in Campanian architecture. The 11th century brought the Normans. Thereafter, the south of Italy, including Campania, was dominated by a succession of French, Austrian, and Spanish kings and cross-fertilized with influences from the north of Europe to the Mediterranean, from Vienna to Madrid, until it was annexed to the kingdom of Italy in 1860.

Today Campania is dominated by the city of Naples and—to a lesser degree—Salerno. The area consists primarily of three natural elements, each with a splendor of its own. First, there's the Bay of Naples in the north, a volcanic area with steaming natural hot springs. Vesuvius, still active, stands poised midway along the bay between Naples and Sorrento. The eruptions that buried Pompeii and Herculaneum in AD 79 have not occurred with force since 1944, but its twin peaks still periodically emit trails of smoke.

Second, the three romantic islands off the coast of Naples, natural extensions of the tormented geophysical constitution of the mainland, attract the most visitors. Capri is the international resort, and Ischia and Procida share the same genes as the Phlegrean Fields—the crater-filled, sulfurous area west of Naples that the ancients believed was the gateway to the underworld.

The third section of Campania that draws visitors is the Sorrento Peninsula, a narrow finger of mountainous limestone forming the southern rim of the Bay of Naples. Sorrento is poised on the edge of steep cliffs 165 feet above the sea on the peninsula's northern edge, connected by the Amalfi Drive to the southern resorts of Positano, Amalfi, Ravello, and Salerno.

The scenery of the Costiera Amalfitana (Amalfi Coast) is natural in the wildest sense of the word. The rocky Sorrento Peninsula has been eroded into all sorts of shapes; it is still eroding, in fact, but discreet netting has been installed to catch occasional falling stones. Here, all but the sheerest surfaces are blanketed with vineyards, pinewoods, citrus and olive groves, almond trees, camellias, oleanders, and magenta bougainvillea. For more information, see *Italy's Best Beaches* in DIVERSIONS.

Pompeii, Herculaneum, and Paestum are internationally renowned, but there are also important archaeological sites at Velia, Santa Maria Capua Vetere, and Benevento. Campania has over 6,000 thermal springs, and there are spas at Agnano, Montesano, Telese, and Castellammare di Stabia.

Although Campania is not commonly one of Italy's famed gastronomic regions, the combination of rich soil and the sea makes for a wide range of first-rate produce. The best meals are found in smaller trattorie, where the owner tends to be the chef. Look for *casalinga* or *casareccia* signs—guarantees of home cooking and local ingredients. This is where you'll find *torta caprese,* for example—a crumbly dessert made of almonds and chocolate, best topped with a lava-like flow of Neapolitan ice cream.

The gulf waters produce excellent crustaceans, including *vongole* (clams), which are served in pasta and risotto dishes and in seafood soups and salads. Mozzarella cheese, produced from the buffalo that graze in the region, is a staple. It is served *in carrozza* (batter-fried), on pizza, and with eggplant, *parmigiana*-style. But first and foremost, it is served in *insalata caprese,* a salad of fresh sliced mozzarella and tomatoes garnished with basil and olive oil. The local meat and fish are best grilled over charcoal and lightly seasoned with lemon and salt. Pizza, which was born here, is widely available, usually baked in wood-burning ovens. For dessert, try such typical pastries, nougats, and traditional *Christmas* and *Easter* sweets as *zeppole, taralli,* and *struffoli.*

The best-known wines come from the slopes of Mt. Vesuvius: white or red lacryma Christi (Tears of Christ). The vineyards at Pozzuoli and Cumae yield falerno. Other good wines are greco di tufo, taurasi, ravello, and barbera di Castel San Lorenzo. The well-known and potent Strega (witch) liqueur is made in Benevento. At several shops you can invest in bottles of amaretto and fiery grappa. Positano and its surroundings are known for its liqueurs made from *limone* (lemon) and *mirtillo* (bilberry).

In addition, regional crafts, centuries old, make perfect mementos. Neo-primitive in design, the colorful ceramics from Vietri will look twice as wonderful back home (many shops will even arrange shipping for you). *Intarsia* (hand-inlaid marquetry) from Sorrento and Amalfi's handmade paper products are sought the world over.

The Amalfi Drive—the road between Sorrento and Vietri sul Mare—is both spectacular and perilous. Hacked out of solid rock, it offers superb views, although not for the driver, who must negotiate the narrow, twisting, heavily trafficked route. Parking at the resorts is also difficult, especially from July through August, when most Italians take their holidays, and doubly so on weekends, when the numbers swell with day-trippers from Naples. Travel time from Sorrento to Amalfi is one and a half to two hours, depending on traffic. One solution is to move from town to town between 2 and 4 PM, when most Italians are either eating or taking a siesta. Buses don't travel any faster, but they do allow you to sit back and enjoy the ride, as well as eliminate parking problems once you arrive.

The tourist season at Campania's major resorts runs from *Easter* through October. The coast enjoys hot, dry Mediterranean summers and mild winters. June and September are ideal; July and August, despite occasional short but heavy storms, are by far the most popular months. Make reservations well in advance for high season, and be prepared for long waits and heavy traffic.

Off-season visits offer splendid solitude, rare silence, and unobstructed views but not a Caribbean or Florida climate. The Amalfi Coast can be cold in winter, even on sunny days; it occasionally snows on Vesuvius. The average temperature in January and February is 50F, and at night and on rainy days—lamentably frequent in winter—it is much colder. Be aware, too, that due to legal restrictions, many hotels and restaurants (most close for at least part of the winter) are inadequately heated.

In high season, classical plays are performed in the ruins at Pompeii (these were temporarily suspended last year, due to possible damage; check with the local tourist office for this year's schedule). There are Wagner and classical concerts in the gardens of the *Villa Rufolo* in Ravello, film festivals in Sorrento and Salerno, and carnivals in Minori, Maiori, and Amalfi. In fact, every feast day and holiday in the region, particularly *Easter,* is likely to take on the trappings of a carnival.

Our tour heads first to the island of Procida and then south from Naples, swinging under the shadow of Vesuvius along the curve of the bay through Herculaneum and Pompeii. At Castellammare it turns almost directly west to Sorrento, then crosses the tip of the Sorrento Peninsula to the Amalfi Coast and follows the hairpin coast road eastward through Positano, Amalfi, Ravello, Maiori, and Vietri sul Mare. At Salerno it heads south again to Paestum. Although not much more than 90 miles (145 km) in length, the route passes through ancient towns, historic sites, and exciting resorts. The region is rich in attractions that cannot be sampled in a short time, so set aside at least three days.

It's also possible to travel this route without a car. A *CIAT* bus leaves Rome's Piazza della Repubblica every morning, arriving in Positano three hours later. Naples and Sorrento are well linked by the *Circumvesuviana,* a local train line that makes the journey in a little over an hour. Stops include Herculaneum and Pompeii. From Sorrento, all towns on the Amalfi Coast are reached easily by bus or boat (rough waters limit boat service in winter).

The area features every category of accommodation, from grand hotels that were turn-of-the-century favorites to small, family-run *pensioni.* The area has a long tradition of friendly service and client allegiance. Another alternative is to rent a villa, palazzo, or apartment. For information on US-based operators offering rentals in Italy, see GETTING READY TO GO.

In our accommodations listings for high season, double rooms in hotels listed as very expensive run $275 or more a night; expensive hotels go for $150 to $250; moderate means $80 to $150; and inexpensive, $80 or less. All hotels feature private baths unless otherwise indicated. A full dinner for two will come to $80 or more in the very expensive category (how much more depends on how much fresh fish or seafood is ordered); an expensive meal will run $50 to $80; moderate, $25 to $50; and inexpensive, $25 or less. Prices include service and house wine but not expensive bottled vintages, aperitifs, or after-dinner drinks. All restaurants are open for lunch and dinner unless otherwise noted. At the height of the season, it is not uncommon for hotels at seaside resorts to require half board. For each location, hotels and restaurants are listed alphabetically by price category.

Note that some sites of interest in Campania close for a midday break, anywhere from 12:30 or 2 PM to 3 or 4:30 PM; we suggest calling ahead to check exact hours.

NAPLES For a detailed report on the city and its sights, hotels, and restaurants, see *Naples* in THE CITIES.

En Route from Naples A one-hour ferry ride or an even shorter (half an hour) *aliscafo* (hydrofoil) ride from Naples is Procida, one of the loveliest islands in the Bay of Naples. Ferries and hydrofoils leave Naples from *Molo Beverello* in front of Piazza Municipio; hydrofoils also depart from Mergellina's Porto Sannazaro.

PROCIDA Originally part of Ischia, Procida broke away many millennia ago. The island was formed by volcanic craters flattened by erosion. Though it is the closest of the three islands (the others are Capri and Ischia) in the bay to the mainland, Procida is the farthest from modern, sophisticated life. Islanders are determined to keep Procida free of the international glitz that is a part of their neighbors' lifestyles. It's easy to see why: The scent of jasmine, roses, and lemon hangs like a private cloud over fig and pomegranate trees. Domed churches pop up among the pastel houses along the harbor, and bright flowers burst through the lace of wrought-iron balconies. Rounded arches peer out at the sea between stone staircases that seem to crisscross the outside of buildings at random.

There's plenty of history on this gentle island, which was first inhabited in Neolithic times. Procida was a hunting preserve for both the Romans and the Bourbon kings, and Giovanni da Procida, a Ghibelline noble who loved the island and took it as his name, built a lovely castle here (still standing, although much crumbled). Ferdinand IV, a Grand Duke of Tuscany, made the island into a royal domain in the 19th century and converted its fortress into a prison.

Small (2½ square miles), Procida can easily be seen on foot. North of the ferry landing at Marina Grande is Corricella, Procida's oldest village, built in its own protected little harbor. The Piazza dei Martiri was the site of the execution of 12 islanders who planned an uprising against the Bourbons. Nearby is the domed *Chiesa della Madonna delle Grazie,* dating from the beginning of the 18th century, with its revered and graceful statue of the Virgin, and another church, the simple *Chiesa di San Rocco.*

At the highest point on the island, about a half-mile (1 km) above Corricella, stands the Terra Murata fortification, completed in 1521. Inside the Terra Murata are winding alleys full of tall narrow houses and the *Chiesa di San Michele Arcangelo* (Church of St. Michael the Archangel), Procida's patron saint. Three Arabian Nights domes dominate the sky, but below them the church's walls are plain—frequent pirate raids discouraged elaborate decorations. Inside, however, the church's art reflects the original grandeur of the monastery: San Michele is shown saving Procida from the Turks in Nicola Rosso's impressive painting in the apse, and the ceiling has some remarkable Baroque frescoes. San Michele's feast day is celebrated twice a year, on May 8 with a parade of fishing boats and on September 29 with a smaller religious procession. Also within the walls is the 16th-century *Castello d'Aragon* (Piazza delle Arme); it is now a prison, despite talk of turning it into an international hotel.

On the east side of the island, on the escarpment above Spiaggia Chiaia and below Corricella, are palaces of the noble families from days past. Here, too, is the *Casa di Graziella,* named after the heroine of the island's romantic tragedy. Every summer a beauty contest is held in memory of the young woman who, for love of the French writer Alphonse Lamartine, gave up her prospects for an excellent marriage. When he jilted her she died of grief.

There also are two beaches on the west side of the island. Excellent for sunbathing and swimming is Spiaggia Ciraccello (also called Spiaggia Ciraccio), the site of two Roman tombs; there's also Marina di Chiaiolella, from which you can see Vivara, a tiny island connected to Procida by a pedestrian bridge. Vivara is home to a wildlife refuge where myriad birds have made their nests. Once on Vivara, take in the sweeping views of Procida from its summit or visit its two beaches: Pozzo Vecchio to the northwest and Zi' Lorenzo on the north coast.

Procida's tourist office (*AAST*) is located at the *Stazione Marittima* (Via Marittima; phone: 81-810-1968). A helpful travel agency (*ETP*) is on the waterfront (1 Via Principe Umberto; phone: 81-896-9067). It is closed for a long (1 to 4 PM) break; Sundays after 1 PM; and October through March. Besides providing information and maps, the office will book apartments and villas on the island.

An assortment of ferries (most of which carry cars) and hydrofoils from Naples and Pozzuoli on the mainland and the neighboring island of Ischia serve Procida. Contact *Caremar* (phone: 89-313282 in Naples; 81-896-7280 on Procida); *SNAV* (phone: 89-761-2348 in Naples; 81-896-9975 on Procida); or *Linee Lauro* (phone: 89-867-3736 in Pozzuoli for hydrofoils; 89-551-3236 in Pozzuoli for ferries).

Return to Naples.

BEST EN ROUTE

Crescenzo In Chiaiolella, this portside restaurant with a view serves excellent seafood dishes. There also are 10 very pleasant rooms. Open daily. Reservations necessary in season. Major credit cards accepted. 33 Via Marina, Procida (phone: 81-896-7255). Restaurant, expensive; hotel, moderate.

Il Cantinone Outstanding fried fish—fresh and generously portioned—is served at this modest restaurant, a favorite with the discerning locals. Closed Mondays. Reservations unnecessary. No credit cards accepted. 6 Via Roma, Marina Grande, Procida (no phone). Moderate.

Riviera Located by Spiaggia Chiaiolella, this hostelry has 23 rooms (many with beautiful views) but no restaurant. Open April through September. 36 Via

Giovanni da Procida, Procida (phone: 81-896-7197; fax: 81-896-7611). Inexpensive.

La Rosa dei Venti Typical of the rustic character of the island, this former pensione comprises 15 simple bungalows (each sleeping two to six people) with kitchens and baths in a cool and shady *limoneta* (lemon grove). There is access to a small, rocky private beach and, if you call ahead, complimentary transportation from the port. If you're lucky, Signor Pasquale, the loquacious English-speaking owner/writer, will regale you with a synopsis of his novel. Open year-round. In high season, one-week minimum stay required. 32 Via Rinaldi, Procida (phone/fax: 81-896-8385). Inexpensive.

En Route from Naples Take the autostrada (A3) south toward Salerno (avoid the cluttered and confusing coast road). With only four lanes, A3 narrows to almost country-road proportions from time to time; travel can be tediously slow during rush hours. Get off at the Ercolano (Herculaneum) exit, about 4½ miles (7 km) from Naples.

HERCULANEUM Although only about a quarter the size of Pompeii, Herculaneum is an eminently important archaeological site; in fact, many visitors find it more interesting than Pompeii, and considerably less congested. Both cities were destroyed by the same volcanic eruption of Mt. Vesuvius on August 24, AD 79, but whereas Pompeii was smothered by live cinders and ash, Herculaneum was inundated by something akin to a massive boiling mud slide, in some places over 80 feet deep. For more details, see *Remarkable Ruins* in DIVERSIONS. Note that only the most important buildings are open all the time; others are locked, but a guard stationed in the vicinity will gladly open them if tipped. The Herculaneum site is closed Mondays and holidays; admission charge. For information, contact the *Azienda Autonoma di Soggiorno* in Pompeii (1 Via Sacra; phone: 81-863-1041).

En Route from Herculaneum The easiest way to inspect Vesuvius, the cause of all the destruction in Pompeii, Sorrento, and Herculaneum, is to park outside Ercolano station and hop on the bus that makes the short trip 3,280 feet up the volcano three or four times a day. From there, you can walk the last stretch along a shingle path to the edge of the crater (at 4,189 feet) and look down into the enormous cavity or out toward the sea and the surrounding towns. Comfortable walking shoes are advised, and note that there are no railings. An English-speaking guide is usually present. Make sure to note the time of the last bus down the mountain, as times vary.

A brooding, 10,000-year-old hulk, Vesuvius can be seen looming through the haze from almost anywhere in the vicinity of Naples. Its name derives from two words meaning "the unextinguished," and Vesuvius is indeed alive, one of only three active volcanos in continental Europe. (The other two also are on Italian soil—Mt. Etna, on the island of Sicily, and Stromboli, in the Aeolian Islands.) Vesuvius last erupted in 1944 and has given a few smoky belches and rumbles since then. Yet, though all this adds a slight shiver of excitement, today all that is visible of Vesuvius's cataclysmic power are the vapors rising from its fumaroles. Vesuvius has been cultivated since 1500, and forests extend almost to the rim. In fact, the wealth of ancient Pompeii was largely attributable to the rich volcanic soil, full of chalk, phosphate, and potash.

Return to A3 and continue south a short distance to the Pompeii exit. Along the route, huge black volcanic rock formations, umbrella pines, and orange and lemon groves blanket the terraced hillsides. And despite the presence of today's unattractive modern buildings, it is easy to see what drew the ancient Romans, and before them the Greeks. The land is fertile, the light golden, the sea a deep blue, and the terrain spectacular as it buckles and breaks up into mountains just beyond the coast.

POMPEII Like Herculaneum, Pompeii is an archaeological treasure trove. Entire lives have been spent studying it or uncovering it, yet one-third of the ancient town still remains unexcavated. It is possible to hit the high spots in a single visit, though a few words of advice can be valuable. Pick up a map as you enter; even though the streets are signposted, it's easy to lose sight of your companions. Avoid visiting on Sundays and holidays, and in high season, try to arrive early on any day, between 9 and 10 AM, before the ubiquitous busloads of sightseers. It's not unusual for the immediate environs of the ruins—and sometimes even the site itself—to be swarming with con men of all sorts. Hold on to your camera and purse, and don't park in a lonely spot. If you want a guide, hire one at the gate at a rate agreed upon in advance. For more details on the site, see *Remarkable Ruins* in DIVERSIONS.

The Pompeii site is closed Mondays; admission charge. The 1980 earthquake that devastated vast parts of the interior of Campania did some damage here, and some excavations still are closed. For a bite to eat while visiting the ruins, try *Internazionale* (Via del Foro, Pompeii Scavi; phone: 81-861-0777), near the *Forum*. The local travel agency, *Viaggi Turistici Vilni* (4-6 Via Roma; phone: 81-863-1525), has information on the area; it's closed Sundays. There also are two tourist offices—one in the center of town (1 Via Sacra; phone: 81-850-7255) and another near the excavation site (Piazza Esedra; phone: 81-861-0913).

BEST EN ROUTE

Principe The cooking is sophisticated—try the *insalata di frutti di mare* (seafood salad)—and the staff is pleasant at this excellent eatery. Closed Mondays and the first two weeks in August. Reservations unnecessary. Major credit cards accepted. 8 Piazza Longo, Pompeii (phone: 81-850-5566). Very expensive.

Zi Caterina In the center of town, this place is noted for its lavish antipasto, excellent fresh seafood, and delicious ice cream. Closed Tuesdays and the first week of July. Reservations advised. Major credit cards accepted. 20 Via Roma, Pompeii (phone: 81-850-7447). Expensive.

Del Sole A 65-room hotel, it has its own garden, a restaurant, a bar, and parking on the premises. 15 Via Plinio, Pompeii (phone: 81-863-1700). Moderate to inexpensive.

Del Santuario Ideally located right in the central piazza of Pompeii, with the basilica across the street, this 51-room hotel has a restaurant, a *caffè*, and parking. 2-6 Piazza Bartolo Longo, Pompeii (phone: 81-850-2822). Inexpensive.

Trattoria Pizzeria dei Platani Despite its name, pizza is served only in the evening. However, a wide variety of homemade pasta is available at lunch or dinner. Closed Wednesdays. Reservations unnecessary. No credit cards accepted. 4 Via Colle San Bartolomeo, Pompeii (phone: 81-863-3973). Inexpensive.

Villa Laura On a quiet street two blocks from the main piazza, most of the 27 rooms here have balconies, and each is equipped with air conditioning and a TV set. Other amenities include a lovely garden, a breakfast room (no restaurant), a garage, and an elevator. Open year-round. 13 Via delle Stalle, Pompeii (phone: 81-863-1024; fax: 81-850-4893). Inexpensive.

Villa dei Misteri This convenient 41-room motel right near the train station is endowed with ample parking. Much favored by academics and archaeologists, it has a nice garden and a pool, but no restaurant. 8 Via Villa dei Misteri, Pompeii Scavi (phone: 81-861-3593). Inexpensive.

La Vinicola A relaxing outdoor courtyard, generous servings of country cuisine (try the potato gnocchi with mozzarella), and a good selection of wine make this a pleasant dining experience. Closed Fridays from November to mid-July. Reservations unnecessary. No credit cards accepted. 15 Via San Michele, Pompeii (phone: 81-863-1244). Inexpensive.

En Route from Pompeii Return to A3 and drive a short distance to the Castellammare di Stabia exit, then proceed slowly—there's little choice, given the chaotic traffic and potholed street—through the cluttered and rather ugly though colorful center of town. Park and *lock* the car—leaving no valuables inside—then take a cable car up to Monte San Faito, where the air is fresh and cool and the views spectacular.

To reach Sorrento faster and more easily, shortly after exiting at Castellammare, turn left at the "T" junction, following blue signs for Gragnano, Agerola, and Amalfi to an expressway. At its end, make a U-turn and follow signs for Sorrento, 16 miles (26 km) from Pompeii, bearing left. Afterward, take a more scenic road, S145, that swerves along the northern coast of the Sorrento Peninsula. The road winds lazily through villages and lively towns such as Vico Equense (where pizza is sold by the meter) and finally enters Sorrento. All along the way, signs point down to beaches, and every turn in the road reveals marvelous views of Naples and Vesuvius.

SORRENTO This small city of pastel houses, brilliant flowers, and sea-scented air has been the subject of song, story, and legend throughout the centuries. According to Greek mythology, as filtered through the Romans, Surrentum (now Sorrento) was home to the Sirens, who sang out to seamen to lure them into wrecking their ships against the stony shores. Ulysses was said to have outsmarted the Sirens by plugging his crew's ears with wax and having himself tied to the mast to resist their seductions. The Sirens were so humbled by their failure that they turned into stones—the famous Galli rocks poking their heads out of the sea just off the coast at Positano.

The town's cliff-top location, overlooking the Bay of Naples, is idyllic, and the buildings of the Old Town are typically Italian—peeling pinks and peach, streets lined with palms and orange trees. The main square is the pretty, bustling Piazza Tasso, named after Sorrento's most famous son, Torquato Tasso, the 16th-century author of *Gerusalemme Liberata*, an epic poem that is one of the classics of Italian literature; his statue lurks among the palms. The square is built over a 150-foot ravine, at the bottom of which are the ruins of the old water mill. Aware of the importance of tourism, Sorrento is not only free of most petty theft but is also impeccably clean.

The cool, marbled interior of the *Chiesa di San Francesco* (Piazza San Francesco) is particularly inviting on a hot day; its 13th-century cloisters, with their distinctive Moorish arches, are the site of classical concerts (part of the summer festival called *Estate Musicale Sorrentino*). The *Museo di Correale* (48 Via Correale; phone: 81-878-1846) contains some rare editions of Tasso's work, as well as a small archaeological collection and fine examples of 17th- and 18th-century furniture, mostly Neapolitan. The museum is closed Tuesdays and Saturdays; Mondays and Wednesdays through Fridays for a long (12:30 to 5 PM) break; and Sunday afternoons; admission charge.

The beaches are barely there—narrow, dark-gray volcanic strips reached either by hotel elevator or by steep, zigzag staircases. Sea bathing is mostly from a number of privately owned wooden jetties (which charge admission, plus extra fees for a cabin, deck chair or lounge, and beach umbrella). Marina Grande, the town's main public beach, is hopelessly crowded, but it's ideal for observing local color. The largest public beach is at Meta, one of the town's four boroughs, a mile or so east along the Corso Italia. At the ruins of the *Villa di Pollio* in a park *(Punta del Capo)* on the southwest edge of town are a wonderful swimming hole and idyllic places to picnic.

Sorrento's shopping is the best on the coast. The most interesting stores are in the Old Town's narrow flagstone streets, leading off from the pedestrians-only Via San Cesareo. Kitsch abounds; for quality goods, the best buys include gloves, cameos, embroidered blouses, *intarsia* (marquetry), and Capodimonte ceramics. Most shops stay open until at least 10 PM in high season. After that, stop in at *Fauno Notte* (1 Piazza Tasso; phone: 81-878-1021), a nightclub/disco featuring folkloric "Tarantella" evenings with music, costumes, and dancing; it's open April through October. *Davide* (39 Via P. R. Giuliani; phone: 81-878-1337) may serve the best ice cream in the world. Sample some of the 60 flavors—Indian fig, amaretto, and taurasi wine—to judge for yourself; open April through October. Sorrento hosts a prestigious annual international *Festivale di Film* the first week in December, and the *Estate Musicale Sorrentino* is held yearly in July and August, with concerts taking place almost daily throughout the city. Check with the tourist office (see below) for locations of screenings and receptions.

The tourist office (*AAS*; 35 Via Luigi de Maio; phone: 81-807-4033; fax: 81-877-3397) can provide further information about the town and its environs. It publishes an excellent monthly magazine, *Surrentum* (in English and Italian), that is distributed in most hotels and at the tourist office. The *AAS* is closed Sundays and for a short (2:30 to 4:30 PM) break. Take a sightseeing trip around town in a *carrozza*; the horse-drawn carts are lined up under the Tasso statue in Piazza Tasso. Or rent a scooter or moped. *Sorrento Rent-A-Car* (210/A Corso Italia; phone: 81-878-1386) offers reliable mopeds and scooters with helmets at the best rates. Sorrento also is a popular starting point for ferry and hydrofoil excursions to the islands of Capri and Ischia and tours of the Amalfi Coast, with service to Naples as well. Information is available from kiosks around Marina Piccola. The small *Circovesuviano* railroad, destination Naples, leaves frequently and reaches both Pompeii and Herculaneum in half an hour, making for an easy and enjoyable outing.

BEST EN ROUTE

Don Alfonso 1890 Alfonso Iaccarino and his wife, Livia Adario, own this two-Michelin-star restaurant in the hills 4 miles (6 km) above Sorrento. It's the best in the area, possibly in the whole of southern Italy. In addition to the traditional menu, which highlights fresh fish and *frutti di mare,* innovative à la carte selections also are available. The wines (including a spumante from Ischia) are excellent; fresh vegetables are grown organically in the garden; and turkey, chicken, and pheasant are raised here. Closed Mondays in high season; Tuesdays in off-season; and early January through February. Reservations necessary. Major credit cards accepted. 11 Piazza Sant'Agata sui Due Golfi, Sorrento (phone: 81-878-0026; fax: 81-533-0226). Very expensive.

Excelsior Vittoria In 19th-century Belle Epoque fashion, this 125-room hotel is full of potted palms and ferns, gilded ceilings, marble staircases, mosaic floors, and opulent chandeliers. It's surrounded by manicured gardens and terraces with splendid views of Vesuvius, and it has a pool, as well as elevator access to the sea. The best suite is the one in which Caruso stayed just before he died. There's also a lovely restaurant on a terrace overlooking the sea, good service, and parking. Open year-round. 34 Piazza Torquato Tasso, Sorrento (phone: 81-807-1044; 800-448-8355; fax: 81-877-1206). Very expensive.

Ambasciatori Just off the central square, this modern, 103-room hotel has a garden and a terrace overlooking Vesuvius, a restaurant, a private swimming area accessible by elevator, and parking. Often closed November through February; call in advance. 18 Via Califano, Sorrento (phone: 81-878-2025; fax: 81-807-1021). Expensive.

Antico Francischiello About 3 miles (5 km) outside Sorrento in Massa Lubrense, this more-than-century-old restaurant offers first-rate regional fare—the antipasti are rich, the entrées delicious, and the breads home-baked—and a lovely view, particularly from the large terrace; wines come from the family vineyards. If you are unable to move by the end of the meal, the family rents out 20 air conditioned rooms. Closed Wednesdays in off-season. Reservations advised. Major credit cards accepted. 27 Via Partenope, Massa Lubrense (phone: 81-533-9780; fax: 81-807-1813). Restaurant, expensive; hotel, inexpensive.

Bellevue Syrene Wonderfully positioned over the gulf at the top of Sorrento's most beautiful road, this 18th-century villa—now a 59-room hotel—offers an antiques-filled interior in a setting of gardens and towering cypresses. An elevator takes swimmers down to the water. Next door, the *Villa Pompeana* is a prime nightlife center, with a restaurant, bar, and gameroom. The hotel is open year-round; the villa is open April through October. 5 Piazza della Vittoria, Sorrento (phone: 81-878-1024; 800-366-1510; fax: 81-878-3963). Expensive.

Il Mulino Atmosphere plus local fare—seafood and pizza—combine to earn a top reputation for this spot in the heart of town. Alfresco dining is a summer option. Closed Tuesdays in off-season. Reservations advised. Major credit cards accepted. 7 Via Fuorimura, a block up from Piazza Tasso, Sorrento (phone: 81-878-1216). Expensive.

Parco dei Principi Built around an 18th-century villa that belonged to Prince Leopold of Sicily, this large establishment (95 rooms with balconies on the sea) in a verdant park-like setting has a pool and an elevator to a private beach. Motorboating and water skiing can be arranged, and many special events, concerts, and receptions take place here. The restaurant is one of the best in town. The hotel and restaurant are open *Easter* through October. 1 Via Rota, Sorrento (phone: 81-878-4644; fax: 81-878-3786). Expensive.

President High on a bluff about 2 miles (3 km) outside Sorrento (and therefore less expensive than most), this hotel is set amid a pine grove overlooking the bay. It has 82 rooms (most with views), a pool, gardens, and a restaurant. Open *Easter* through October. 26 Via Nastro Verde, Colle Parise, Sorrento (phone: 81-878-2262; fax: 81-878-5411). Expensive.

Imperial Tramontano Surrounded by one of the most luxurious gardens in the heart of town, this hotel is a converted villa. Many of its 105 air conditioned rooms overlook the bay and a beach (access is by private elevator); some have garden terraces and balconies; and all have TV sets. The public rooms are warm and welcoming, with Italian and English antiques. There is a pool and a restaurant. Open March through December. 1 Via Vittorio Veneto, Sorrento (phone: 81-878-2588; fax: 81-807-2344). Expensive to moderate.

La Favorita O'Parrucchiano On the busiest street in town is a good restaurant offering authentic Campanian cooking, much of it made with fresh local cheeses, wine, oil, and vegetables produced by the owners, the Maniello family. The gnocchi are recommended, as are the *gamberoni alla griglia* (grilled prawns). The terrace garden is delightful in warm weather. Closed Wednesdays offseason. Reservations advised. Visa accepted. 71-73 Corso Italia, Sorrento (phone: 81-878-1321). Moderate.

Giardinello This is the place to sample Sorrento's famous potato gnocchi with spicy tomato sauce and cheese. It's also the best in town for pizza—try the version smothered with mushrooms and prosciutto. Wash it all down with an excellent local wine. Closed Thursdays from October through May. Reservations unnecessary. Visa accepted. 7 Via Accademia, Sorrento (phone: 81-878-4616). Moderate.

La Minerva Somewhat out of the way, but worth considering because of its lovely location on the sea. With 50 rooms, this family-style pensione has charm and a good restaurant. Open *Easter* through October. 30 Via Capo, Sorrento (phone: 81-878-1011; fax: 81-878-1949). Moderate.

Sant'Anna In the picturesque fishing village of Marina Grande, this friendly neighborhood eatery is where fishermen rub elbows with the local well-to-do as they eat *casareccia pasta e fagioli* (pasta and beans with mussels) and fish straight from the sea. Tables are set outside overlooking the ocean in summer. Closed Tuesdays. Reservations unnecessary. No credit cards accepted. 62 Via Marina Grande, Sorrento (phone: 81-878-1489). Moderate.

Loreley et Londres Clean and unpretentious, with an extraordinary view, it has 24 rooms and an excellent restaurant. Ask for a room overlooking the sea. Half board is mandatory in season. Open *Easter* through October. 2 Via Califano, Sorrento (phone: 81-807-3187). Inexpensive.

Taverna dell'800 More than a pub, less than a restaurant, it's run by Tony "the Walking Smile," who receives postcards from fans all over the world. Just the place for a *salsiccia con broccoli* (sausage with broccoli), *insalata caprese*, pasta with parmesan cheese, and a beer. The evening menu is classier, with homemade cannelloni and lasagna. It's one of the few air conditioned eateries in town. Closed Mondays. Reservations unnecessary. No credit cards accepted. 29 Via dell'Accademia, Sorrento (phone: 81-878-5970). Inexpensive.

La Tonnarella On the outskirts of town near the train station, this 16-room hotel sits on a cliff jutting out among fragrant gardens. There are gorgeous views of the sea and an elevator to a private beach. Its restaurant is noteworthy, which makes half board here (heavily encouraged in high season) a real pleasure (and a bargain!). There also is a parking lot. Open mid-March to mid-December. 31 Via del Capo, Sorrento (phone: 81-878-1153; fax: 81-878-2169). Inexpensive.

En Route from Sorrento A narrow, twisting road winds for 11 miles (18 km) around the entire peninsula to Positano. It's worth driving if you have time, since it passes through delightful, cool hilltop villages such as Francescello and Sant'Agata, and you'll pass tiny trattorie where locals eat on shady, dappled terraces looking down the peninsula. But it is far less nerve-racking to turn back on S145 toward Naples, drive a few miles to Meta, Sorrento's easternmost borough, and then take S163, which cuts south for 15 minutes or so across mountainous terrain to the Costa Amalfitana (Amalfi Coast) on the other side of the peninsula. From there, S163 continues on its sinuous course all the way to Salerno. This route, known as the Amalfi Drive, is hardly a superhighway; in fact, it can be treacherous, especially when Italian trucks, buses, and cars jockey for position, even on the sharpest turns. Sundays in high season can be a nightmare. But though the drive may tax the nerves, it is a memorable, not-to-be-missed experience.

The crumbling Lattari Mountains come plunging down to the Mediterranean, and whitewashed houses cling to the cliffs like barnacles. Most buildings show the full extent of the Saracen influence on the architecture. Church domes are covered with gleaming majolica tiles; ceilings are barrel-vaulted to keep houses cool during the sun-dazzled summers. There also is a string of lookout towers left along the coast, some of them now renovated and transformed into hotels, bars, and private homes. In many places the mountains have been terraced and planted with olive trees and citrus groves, carefully protected against hail by tent-like canopies of loose-woven mesh. At the foot of the mountains, the sea has worked at the limestone for centuries, creating caves and grottoes and an occasional miniature beach.

POSITANO John Steinbeck, like many other artistic people, was transported by Positano and wrote that it "bites deep. It is a dream place that isn't quite real when you are there and becomes beckoningly real after you have gone." As the steep hills drop almost vertically to the sea, Positano's houses appear to hang like a canvas of cubistic shapes in a broad spectrum of earth tones and pastels, with the green-and-gold-tiled cupola of *Santa Maria Assunta*—the *Chiesa Madre*—presiding over the point where the hills flatten out to the main beach, Spiaggia Grande. Tiny despite its name, it has military rows of beach lounges and, behind it, a handful of restaurants. The small, less expensive public beach past the *Covo dei Saraceni* hotel is a cross between pebbles and sand. Only two roads pass through town, one for eastbound traffic and the other for westbound. The rest of town is connected by a labyrinth of mostly vertical footpaths and stepped alleyways. Parking is almost impossible in town; if you're lucky, you'll find a private yard converted into a parking lot, and the better hotels offer a handful of spots. After that, the going is by foot, so the streets are blessedly free of traffic.

Unlike Sorrento and Amalfi, Positano is almost exclusively a holiday town. It was one of the country's most important mercantile cities during the Middle Ages, but its prestige dwindled with the coming of steamships. For decades, however, the peaceful picturesqueness here has drawn artists, especially painters, many of whom came for a visit and stayed indefinitely. It now also attracts movie stars and other celebrities, rivaling Capri. For six months of the year, life focuses on the beach and the half-dozen restaurants behind it. Boutiques abound—the colorful cottons and silks for which the town is famous flap in the wind outside little boutiques. For the athlete, a town tennis court is cleverly tucked away atop a large garage, framed by cacti, cliffs, and clouds. If you need information, Positano's tourist office (*AAST*; 4 Via del Saracino; phone: 89-875067; fax: 89-875760) is closed Sundays and after 2 PM.

You also can explore some of the Amalfi Coast and its islands by water. In high season, ferries go from Positano to Capri, Ischia, Amalfi, Salerno, Sorrento, and Naples. Check with the tourist office or with *Positour* (69 Via C. Colombo; phone: 89-875012; fax: 89-811045) for schedules and tours.

BEST EN ROUTE

Albergo San Pietro About one mile (1.6 km) east of town, on the road toward Amalfi, there is nothing so crass as a sign to identify this 60-room member of the Relais & Châteaux group, only a 15th-century chapel. The excellent dining room (alfresco in summer) offers regional specialties and international fare. For more information, see *Italy's Most Memorable Hostelries* in DIVERSIONS. Open one week before *Easter* through October. 2 Via Laurito, Località San Pietro, Positano (phone: 89-875455; 800-223-9832; fax: 89-811449). Very expensive.

Le Sirenuse With its Pompeiian red exterior, John Steinbeck's onetime retreat stands out even amid the splendors of Positano. Once a private villa, it was turned into a classic hotel by the Sersale family, which still runs it. There are more than 60 modern rooms (most with Jacuzzis and balconies), a heated pool, and three dining terraces overlooking the beach and the yellow-and-green-tiled dome of the *Chiesa Madre*. Handsome antiques, colorful tiles, and tasteful paintings fill the guestrooms and public areas. Among the few hotels open year-round. 30 Via Colombo, Positano (phone: 89-875066; 800-223-6800; fax: 89-811798). Very expensive.

La Cambusa On the beach, it serves excellent fish soup, *spaghetti alle vongole*, and risotto with squid. Wash down a meal with a local white wine, greco di tufo, and top it off with a rich chocolate dessert. The verandah affords a lovely view. Open year-round. Reservations unnecessary. Major credit cards accepted. Piazza Amerigo Vespucci, Positano (phone: 89-875432). Expensive.

Chez Black One of Positano's "in" spots, this beautiful wood-and-brass restaurant on the water's edge draws a seemingly endless stream of trendy, bronzed habitués. The seafood is especially good, or try the pizza, for which it's known. Usually closed January and February. Reservations unnecessary. Major credit cards accepted. Via Marina, Positano (phone: 89-875036). Expensive.

Covo dei Saraceni The only accommodations right on the beach, this popular hotel has 58 rooms (all with sea views), an excellent restaurant, and a saltwater pool. Open *Easter* through October. Via Marina, Positano (phone: 89-875400; 800-755-9313; fax: 89-875878). Expensive.

Palazzo Murat The 18th-century palace of Gioacchino Murat (a king of Naples and Napoleon's brother-in-law) has been tastefully restored with some period furniture and wood-beamed ceilings. The best (and slightly more expensive) of the 30 or so rooms are in the original L-shaped palazzo, looking out onto the courtyard where guests can have breakfast (no restaurant) surrounded by lush bougainvillea and lemon trees. Rooms in the new wing are slightly less expensive. Open April through October. Halfway down the main shopping street toward the beach, at 23 Via dei Mulini, Positano (phone: 89-875177; 800-223-9832; fax: 89-811419). Expensive.

Buca di Bacco On the beach, this is a favorite of the young and handsome harbor crowd. It rightly claims that it has the largest and most comfortable terrace. Tempting antipasti, a fine seafood salad, and eggplant pasta are among its other claims to fame. There's also an adjacent 54-room hotel in an old restored palazzo. Open April through mid-October. Reservations unnecessary. Major credit cards accepted. Via Marina, Positano (phone: 89-875699; 800-755-9313; fax: 89-875731). Restaurant, moderate; hotel, moderate.

O Caporale A favorite of locals and visitors alike, this rustic trattoria turns out excellent pasta and seafood dishes, including *La Caporalesa* (pasta with eggplant and capers), served under a canopy of vines overlooking the beach. Closed November through February. Reservations unnecessary. Major credit cards accepted. 12 Via Regina Giovanna, near the tourist office, Positano (phone: 89-875374). Moderate.

Casa Albertina A family-run hotel with personal service, this is a minor jewel, with gilt mirrors and bronze lamps, dramatic sea views, 20 rooms all done in mauve and blue, and a restaurant. Usually open year-round. 4 Via Tarolozza, Positano (phone: 89-875143; fax: 89-811540). Moderate.

La Chitarrina To escape the crowds, take a trip into the mountains behind the town to sample some first class food at this delightful trattoria. The menu includes an extensive antipasti table and some mouth-watering pasta dishes, including spaghetti *alla Chitarrina* (pasta with a tomato-based sauce of red peppers and mushrooms). A surprisingly wide selection of beer is available. Coming from Naples, take the left-hand turn 1 mile (1.6 km) before Positano, signposted Montepertuso, and continue along a climbing road for 3 miles (5 km) until you reach the village. Closed Wednesdays, except in August and November to mid-December. Reservations advised weekends and in August. Major credit cards accepted. 75 Piazza Cappella, Montepertuso di Positano (phone: 89-811806). Moderate.

Poseidon This attractive, family-run establishment makes you feel at home immediately. Of the 50 tastefully decorated rooms, those with a view cost more and usually include a terrace. There's also a restaurant with an excellent kitchen and a lovely pool with a view. Open *Easter* through November. 148 Via Pasitea, Positano (phone: 89-811111; 800-223-9832; fax: 89-875833). Moderate.

Da Adolfo A complimentary seven-minute boat ride with boatman "Sergio il Bello" (Handsome Sergio) past cliffs plunging headlong into the turquoise sea may seem reason enough to take lunch beneath this thatch-roofed place at Spiaggia Laurito. Even die-hard carnivores will be thrilled by the aroma of fresh mozzarella being grilled on lemon leaves or the *polpette di zucchini* (vegetarian meatballs). Most regulars make a day of the jaunt, bringing along a bathing suit and renting umbrellas and chairs to loll in the sun after an abundant portion of pasta followed by this morning's catch. The shuttle boat leaves daily every half hour from 10 AM to 1 PM from *Easter* through October from the main jetty near the *Covo* hotel. No reservations. No credit cards accepted. Spiaggia Laurito, Località San Pietro (no phone). Inexpensive.

Casa Guadagno Renegade fashion designer Moschino and his Milanese crowd have let the word out, so summer vacancies in this family-run pensione are rare. There are 10 terraced rooms facing the sea (there's a public beach below—be prepared for a hike) and another 10 overlooking the town. Half board required in summer. It's a leisurely 20-minute walk to the town center. Open year-round. Via Fornillo, Positano (phone: 89-875042). Inexpensive.

Da Vincenzo Up and away from the congestion of the beach and the crush of tourists, this is a genial place where locals may outnumber vacationers.

There are many homemade pasta dishes, along with fresh vegetables and tasty zucchini with parmesan. Closed November through March. Reservations unnecessary. No credit cards accepted. 172-178 Viale Pasitea, at the Casa Soriana curve (phone: 89-875128). Inexpensive.

En Route from Positano The magnificent cliff road (S163) narrows, winding and twisting, toward Amalfi. The 10-mile (16-km) drive can easily take half an hour or longer (without traffic!)—not simply because of the road, but because of the constant distraction of the view. Other diversions include the village of Vettica Maggiore and the fishing community of Praiano, both worth more than a quick look (oddly, Praiano has the best nightclub on the coast, *L'Africana,* housed in a seaside cave on Via Torre a Mare; phone: 89-874042). Then, between two tunnels, the cliffside corniche passes over the gorges of the Vallone di Furore (Valley of the Furies). A finger of the sea no wider than a river presses deep into the gorge, and a tiny fishing village is nestled into the rock. Farther on are signs for the Grotta di Smeraldo (Green Grotto), with emerald-colored waters, only a shade less famous than the Blue Grotto on Capri. It can be reached by a steep staircase, by elevator, or by boat from Positano or Amalfi.

AMALFI Although not as preciously picturesque as Positano or Ravello, Amalfi has a lovely and friendly charm all its own. It was once much larger (almost 70,000 inhabitants during the Middle Ages, compared with fewer than 7,000 today) and much more important. During the 6th century, Amalfi developed considerable trade with the Byzantine Empire, transporting spices and wood to the West. By the 9th century it was already a maritime republic, Italy's oldest, even minting its own coins. By the 11th century, it had become a mercantile and maritime power that rivaled the Big Three—Pisa, Genoa, and Venice. Amalfi's domain on land extended widely; its naval influence was felt all along the southern Italian coasts, where it fought the Saracens, and as far as Jerusalem, where it built churches and hospitals for pilgrims of the First Crusade. In fact, the rules by which the republic governed all its maritime activity, the Tavole Amalfitane (Amalfi Tables), became the maritime code for all the Mediterranean and remained in force until 1570. Amalfi lost its primacy, however, in the 12th century, after it was captured by the Normans, sacked by the Pisans, and suffered its share of natural disasters. Still, something of the old splendor returns when Amalfi hosts the *Regata Storica delle Republicche Marinare* (Regatta of the Four Ancient Maritime Republics), a race and a colorful parade of boats that rotates annually among Amalfi and the three other former rulers of the sea (it's due in Amalfi again in 1997). Other important local holidays are the two feast days of Sant'Andrea (Andrew), the town's patron saint and patron of fishermen, which take place on June 27 and November 30.

Apart from Amalfi's lovely seaside setting, the town's greatest pride is its *Duomo* (Piazza Duomo), dedicated to St. Andrew (whose remains lie in the crypt—minus his skull, which was removed by Pope Pius II). Dating from the 10th century and restored and expanded on subsequent occasions as recently as 1894, it sits at the top of a broad, tall staircase, its lively façade displaying stylistic influences that range from Moorish to Norman to early Gothic. A Romanesque bell tower next to it, begun in the 12th century, is crowned with green and yellow glazed tiles. The cathedral's bronze entrance doors were cast in Constantinople in 1066. There is also a beautiful cloister, the *Chiostro del Paradiso,* built in the 13th century and distinguished by lacy Arabic arches. A bronze statue of Flavio Gioia, son of Amalfi and inventor of the compass, stands in front of the *Pic Nic caffè* by Corso Roma. The town's arsenal, which dates from the 11th century, can be reached from an entrance just before the Lungomare meets Piazza Flavio Gioia. Amalfi's tourist office is at 19/21 Corso Repubbliche Marinare (phone: 89-871107).

Behind the coastal Corso Roma, a jumble of medieval streets and buildings leads from Via Capuano, which climbs, changing its name at regular intervals, for 20 minutes from Piazza Duomo at the bottom to the Valle dei Mulini (Valley of the Mills), where ancient, river-powered paper mills once produced top-quality parchment. Only one mill remains in operation (*Armatruda*); its products can be found in the town's souvenir shops. The Amalfitani stroll nonchalantly from one end to the other, while tourists puff and pant their way to the top.

Boats to Capri and Ischia depart April through October 15 from the docks near Piazza Flavio Gioia; boats for Sorrento ply the waters in summer only.

BEST EN ROUTE

Santa Caterina This place is right at the water's edge, with an elevator that drops down to the pool and the beach. There are terraces and gardens for alfresco dining and lounging, and most of the 54 rooms and cottages have balconies. Half board is required in high season, but it's no hardship, as the meals here are as impressive as the views. Less expensive rooms are available in an annex. Open year-round. 9 Via Nazionale, Amalfi (phone: 89-871351; 800-223-9832; fax: 89-871351). Very expensive.

Saraceno Grand One of the Amalfi Coast's legendary hotels, it has 50 antiques-filled rooms; those on the top floors have ocean views. Two elevators carry guests down to the hotel's private rocky beach, where patrons enjoy the breezy bar and a lovely summer restaurant. It's about 2 miles (3 km) from town, but there's frequent jitney service. Open year-round. 25 Via G. Augustariccio, Amalfi (phone: 89-831148; fax: 89-831598). Very expensive.

Belvedere Cut into a cliff, its 36 rooms and terraces are well shielded from the sound of passing traffic. It has wonderful views, a pool, and a restaurant. Full board encouraged. Open April through October. About 3 miles (5 km) west of Amalfi in the tiny hamlet of Conca dei Marini, on S163 (phone: 89-831282; fax: 89-831439). *Expensive.*

La Taverna degli Apostoli Originally a 13th-century town prison, this attractive, vaulted restaurant at the foot of the splendid cathedral is known for its good fish dishes and unusual starters. Try the homemade *ditaloni clausura* (short pasta with a sauce of peppers, zucchini, eggplant, white wine, and fresh basil). Closed Wednesdays in off-season. Reservations unnecessary. No credit cards accepted. 6 Supportico Sant'Andrea, Amalfi (phone: 89-872991). *Expensive.*

Amalfi This pleasant place is surrounded by fragrant citrus trees set in sunny terraced gardens. There are 36 rooms, and breakfast is included in the rate, though there's no dining room. Open year-round. 3 Via dei Pastai, Amalfi (phone: 89-872440; fax: 89-872250). *Moderate.*

Cappuccini Convento One of Amalfi's landmarks, this 13th-century monastery was transformed into a 41-room hotel situated in a remarkable location. Although the monks still own the hotel, the town manages it. High on a cliff, it's reached by an elevator that burrows through rock to daylight; various terraces offer views of the coast, and the air is fragrant with the scent of citrus groves. Rooms are enlarged monks' cells (two cells for each room). There's a private beach and a restaurant. Open year-round. 46 Via Annunziatella, Amalfi (phone: 89-871877; fax: 89-871886). *Moderate.*

Dei Cavalieri The main building is on one side of the main street leading into Amalfi; on the other side of the road are three villas for guests and a beach within walking distance. All 60 guestrooms are bright and air conditioned. A substantial buffet breakfast is included. Half board required in high season, but you can also eat in a "dine around" program at selected restaurants in Amalfi or at the hotel. The hotel minibus takes guests to and from town, about 2 miles (3 km) away. Open year-round. 52 Via Maura Comite, Amalfi (phone: 89-831333; fax: 89-831354). *Moderate.*

Centrale Less flashy than others in town, this small, clean 20-room hotel is nonetheless one of the best deals around. No restaurant. Often closed January or February. 1 Largo Piccolomini, Amalfi (phone: 89-871243). *Moderate.*

Da Gemma A short walk from the *Duomo,* this homey and tastefully decorated trattoria has a roof terrace for outdoor dining and offers authentic local cuisine—macaroni with chopped eggplant, linguine with shrimp, fresh fish with lemon, and good local wines. Closed Wednesdays from mid-January to mid-February. Reservations necessary. Major credit cards accepted. 9 Via Fra' Gerardo Sasso, Amalfi (phone: 89-871345). *Moderate.*

Luna Convento Here's where Ibsen wrote *A Doll's House,* Mussolini slept, and Ingrid Bergman and Roberto Rossellini hid away from the world. This 50-room landmark hotel was built around the 13th-century cloisters of a convent founded by St. Francis of Assisi (it still has its own church within its walls). The property is set on a panoramic rocky point where the Amalfi Drive turns in a great arc toward Atrani, and it has a glorious dining room and a pleasant bar in a tower originally built to guard against the Saracens. There is a pool and, across the road, a private "beach" of rock flattened out by concrete. Also on the beach side is Amalfi's only discotheque, the *Torre Saracena;* housed in an old tower, it is also run by the *Luna Convento.* Open year-round. 19 Via Amendola, Amalfi (phone: 89-871002; fax: 89-871333). Moderate.

Lo Smeraldino Everything you'd expect from a seaside restaurant popular with families (especially on Sundays). Late arrivals should be prepared to wait for a table. Closed Wednesdays off-season and most of January. Reservations advised. Major credit cards accepted. Lungomare dei Cavalieri, by the main jetty of the port, Amalfi (phone: 89-871070). Moderate.

Da Zaccaria Tucked into the edge of a cliff with an open terrace overlooking the sea, this restaurant serves some of the best fish and seafood in the entire area; it also offers delicious pasta, served on oversize painted plates. Closed Mondays. Reservations necessary in high season. No credit cards accepted. An easy walk from the center, at 9 Corso Colombo, on the stretch of the main road out of town toward Salerno and just before the tunnel that leads into Atrani, Amalfi (phone: 89-871807). Moderate.

La Bussola Named for Flavio's compass, this smart but plain 64-room hotel stands at the western entrance. It has a good restaurant and a private jetty for swimming. Choose a room at the front for vistas of colorful bobbing row-boats in the marina. Usually open year-round. Lungomare dei Cavalieri, Amalfi (phone: 89-871533; fax: 89-871369). Moderate to inexpensive.

Marina Riviera Traditional regional furnishings and beautiful views of the sea are distinguishing features in this hotel, which is cut into the side of a hill going down to the water. All 20 rooms have mini-bars, television sets, and telephones. Open *Easter* through September. 19 Via Comite, Amalfi (phone: 89-871104). Moderate to inexpensive.

Il Tari This small restaurant serves reliably good food at budget prices in a central location. Ask about their regional wines. Closed Tuesdays from October through May. Reservations advised for dinner in season. Major credit cards accepted. 9 Via P. Capuano, Amalfi (phone: 89-871832). Inexpensive.

Trattoria la Perla Wonderful cannelloni and seafood are served at this charming and relaxed restaurant. Try the wines from Ravello. Closed Tuesdays from October through February. Reservations unnecessary. Major credit cards accepted. 3 Salita Truglio, Amalfi (phone: 89-871440). Inexpensive.

En Route from Amalfi Head east a little over a mile (2 km) toward Atrani, virtually an extension of Amalfi (and only a 10- to 15-minute walk).

ATRANI One of the smallest towns in Italy (pop. about 1,200), Atrani retains a predominantly Arabic layout (the coast enjoyed friendly relations with the Saracens). It is delightful in every respect, with a small, sandy beach; tiny, whitewashed alleys leading up from the square; and everywhere the fragrances of tomato, basil, and lemon. There are endless flights of steps, one going all the way up to Scala on the hills beyond (more than an hour's hard climbing) and another to Ravello. While in Scala—the oldest town on the Amalfi Coast—pay a visit to the *Duomo* and the ruins of the *Basilica di San Eustachio* in the village of Dontone, below. The town that looks across a valley at Ravello was the birthplace of Fra' Gerardo Sasso, founder of the Knights of Malta, and is fascinating by night. The main street is ancient—as in Amalfi, it was once the river—and leads down to Piazza Umbetto I. The main coast road runs above the houses that line the southern flank of the piazza. The fireworks and parades at *Christmas* are a real treat.

BEST EN ROUTE

Le Arcate Near the entrance to town coming from Amalfi, this charming, popular trattoria/pizzeria serves fresh and delicious fare of the sea in a beach setting. Closed Mondays off-season, and mid-January to mid-February. Reservations unnecessary. No credit cards accepted. 4 Via di Benedetto Atrani, Atrani (phone: 89-871367). Inexpensive.

La Margherita Worth the climb up to the town of Scala (also reachable by car, or by bus—probably a better idea—and then take the many steps back down to the Valley of the Mills), this neighborhood trattoria with sea views is Amalfi's favorite local hangout. Specialties include *crêpes al formaggio* (cheese-filled crêpes) and fresh grilled fish. There are simple rooms above the restaurant, along with the 20 next door at the *Villa Giuseppina*, where there's a pool. Closed Tuesdays in winter. Reservations unnecessary. No credit cards accepted. 31 Via Torricelli, Scala (phone: 89-857106). Inexpensive.

En Route from Atrani To reach Ravello—4 miles (6 km) away—turn inland just after Atrani and uphill onto a well-marked road that swerves through the Valle del Dragone (Dragon Valley). After dozens of hairpin curves, the road rises to over a thousand feet above the coast and reaches the main square of this most gloriously positioned town on the Gulf of Salerno. Scala, just over a mile away (2 km), is reached by the same road, before it forks at the final bend. Scandinavians and Germans have claimed Scala as their own, so its accommodations fill up early in the season.

RAVELLO The spectacular panorama visible from so many spots in this tiny town, its narrow stepped streets, and the profusion of flowers and greenery gracing every nook and cranny make it a place of incomparable beauty. The town has become an almost tangible being to its devotees. Boccaccio dedicated part of the *Decameron* to Ravello, and it was John Huston's location for *Beat the Devil*, in which it stole the spotlight. Frequented by the talented and the famous, among them Richard Wagner, André Gide, D. H. Lawrence (who wrote *Lady Chatterley's Lover* here), Greta Garbo, Jacqueline Kennedy Onassis, Princess Margaret, and William Styron—who set his novel *Set This House on Fire* here—Ravello is now the adopted home of Gore Vidal. It has been said that this is where "poets go to die."

Ravello, which reached its peak population in the Middle Ages, retains the more enchanting aspects of its medieval form today. Leave the car in any of the public lots on the right as you approach the town, before reaching the Piazza Vescovado, Ravello's main square. Closed to cars, this is the site of the *Duomo,* dedicated to the patron saint of Ravello, San Pantaleone, whose blood miraculously remains in a cracked container in the chapel. Begun in 1086 but finished in the 12th century, the cathedral has magnificent paneled bronze doors by Barisano da Trani (1179). Inside are two impressive pulpits. The older (1130), less intricate one features two large mosaics of Jonah being eaten and regurgitated by a dragon-like green whale. The other (1272), by Nicolò di Bartolomeo da Foggia, rests on six columns supported on the backs of lions and is covered with mosaic medallions of fantastic animals and birds.

Nearby, the *Villa Rufolo* (Piazza Duomo), built by the same family, also in the 13th century, looks unprepossessing from the outside, but on closer inspection it is easy to understand why Wagner used it as a model for the magic garden of Klingsor in *Parsifal.* Except for the *Cortile Moresco* (Moorish Courtyard), little remains to be visited of the actual villa. The gardens, however, merit superlatives. Terraced on several levels and planted with beds of bright marigolds, red salvia, pink and white phlox, and many other flowers, they are surrounded by umbrella pines and cypresses and open onto a stunning view of the mountains and sea and the town of Maiori below. The villa is open daily, with a midday closing; admission charge (no phone).

It's a 10-minute hike to Ravello's second most famous site, *Villa Cimbrone,* whose gardens are considerably larger. Built in 1904 by Lord Grimthorpe, an Englishman searching for peace of mind, it has a lovely cloister where, at the entrance, marble faces on the far wall represent the seven deadly sins. A cypress-shaded path leads through the magnificent gardens to the *Belvedere,* a ledge that seems to lean out over the Gulf of Salerno. On a clear day you can see as far as Paestum, 30 miles (48 km) south. The villa is open daily; admission charge (no phone).

A *passeggiata* around town leads down vaulted passageways, up broad flights of steps, through cool cloisters, along sunny terraces, past colorful ceramics shops, and into *caffès* and restaurants that are hidden until the last minute. But all streets eventually lead back to the main Piazza Vescovado and the chance to spend some lire. On the main square, *Camo* (phone: 89-857486), a small gem of a jewelry shop, sells exquisite as well as less pricey cameos and precious and semi-precious stone-set jewelry made by the store's owner; *Bric a Brac* (phone: 89-857153) is a small antiques and collectibles shop. Stop at *Pasquale Sorrentino's* on the pedestrian road to *Villa Cimbrone* (16 Via Rufolo; phone: 89-857303) to view his impressive, well-priced ceramics collection; he will arrange shipping. Prices for the colorful hand-painted ceramics from nearby Vietri are often less expensive here than in Vietri itself.

During the first half of July, the *Festivale Musicale di Ravello* brings together some of the top names in classical music. Concerts are held in the *Villa Rufolo* gardens and at the cathedral. A number of other music festivals take place throughout the summer. For information, contact Ravello's tourist office (Piazza Arcivescovado; phone: 89-857096; fax: 89-857977), which also offers visitors excellent advice, accommodations information, and maps. It is closed Sundays.

BEST EN ROUTE

Palumbo An exquisite small hotel in the higher reaches of town, this is *the* place to stay. Once a private villa, built on the ruins of the 12th-century *Palazzo Confalone,* it is stylish and charming, with beautiful majolica floors, antique furnishings, a lovely interior courtyard, a grassy garden terrace, and a rooftop dining terrace with gorgeous views. Most of the 14 rooms look out to the sea. The excellent restaurant features specialties such as *fusilli al gorgonzola, crespelli Palumbo* (a rolled crêpe stuffed with spinach and ricotta), tasty apple pie, and delectable dessert soufflés, all washed down by the hotel's own red and white episcopio wines. A dependency has opened across the road, offering seven rooms at considerably lower prices. Open year-round. 28 Via San Giovanni del Toro, Ravello (phone: 89-857244; 800-223-9832; fax: 89-858133). Very expensive.

Caruso Belvedere Just up the street from the *Palumbo* is another old building—the 11th-century *Palazzo d'Afflitto*—that's been converted into a delightful hotel with charm, character (more in need of a face-lift than the elegant *Palumbo*), and beautiful views. Some of the 26 rooms face the garden; some face out to mountains and sea. The good restaurant (half board is strongly suggested) is famed for its cannelloni, *crespini* (a kind of cheese and ham crêpe), and delicious, light lemon chocolate soufflé, all of which go well with the house wine, Gran Caruso. Open year-round; restaurant closed Tuesdays in winter and mid-November through mid-March. 52 Via San Giovanni del Toro, Ravello (phone: 89-857111; 800-755-9313; fax: 89-857372). Expensive.

Marmorata If all the rooms in Ravello are full, return to the coast road, S163, and drive east a short distance to this delightful hotel. Decorated like a luxury cruise ship and overlooking the sea, it has a terrace restaurant, a pool, and access to a rocky beach. Small (40 rooms), it's run by the family that once operated a pepper mill on the site. It's a half-mile (1-km) walk straight up to Ravello. Open *Easter* through October. Reserve well in advance. Località Marmorata, Ravello (phone: 89-877777; fax: 89-851189). Expensive.

Giordano Among the peaceful trees between the *Villa Rufolo* and the *Villa Cimbrone*, this 16-room hotel shares facilities with *Villa Maria* (see below). The pool is heated in winter; there's also a solarium, a music room, and a path leading down to the beach. Open year-round. 14 Via Trinità, Ravello (phone: 89-857255; fax: 89-857071). Moderate.

Parsifal A tasteful, 20-room hostelry, it incorporates parts of a 13th-century Augustinian monastery. Some rooms have private baths. There's a cloister, a charming garden with a reflecting pool, and a seductive view of the coast. In warm weather, meals are served on the trellised, flower-scented terrace. Open April through September. Half board is a good value for the money. 5 Via d'Anna, Ravello (phone: 89-857144). Moderate.

Rufolo This hotel, in which D. H. Lawrence made his home in 1926, is on the way to *Villa Cimbrone*. The 30 simply decorated rooms (all with a wide terrace) afford a marvelous view of *Villa Rufolo* and the mountains in the direction of Maiori. There is a pool and a restaurant. Open year-round. 1 Via San Francesco, Ravello (phone: 89-857133; fax: 89-857935). Moderate.

Villa Maria En route to *Villa Cimbrone,* this delightful find offers excellent food and exceptional views. Try the *soffiatini* (crêpes filled with vegetables and cheese) and any of the innovative pasta dishes. There also are 17 rooms, almost all facing the sea. Restaurant closed Tuesdays in off-season. Reservations advised. Major credit cards accepted. 2 Via Santa Chiara, Ravello (phone: 89-857255; fax: 89-857071). Moderate.

La Colonna The best bet in town for fresh fish and an alluring array of vegetables direct from the Sorrentino family's garden. The flower-filled courtyard makes a lovely setting. Start with the local specialty—*sciosciolle* (homemade pasta with fresh tomato and eggplant sauce). Closed Wednesdays and part of the winter. No reservations. No credit cards accepted. 22 Via Roma, Ravello (phone: 89-857876). Moderate to inexpensive.

Cumpà Cosimo Specialties here include home cooking, Ravello-style—fresh fish and vegetables, pizza, and minestrone and bean soups, all served with good wine from the family vineyard. Try the *misti di pasta* (a sampling of pasta). Closed Mondays and part of the winter. Reservations advised for dinner. Major credit cards accepted. 46 Via Roma, Ravello (phone: 89-857156). Moderate to inexpensive.

Villa Amore A very pretty garden with a view of the sea, 16 pleasant, no-frills rooms with views, a restaurant, and a bar make this an ideal place to stay. Open year-round; half board required in July and August. 10 Via del Fusco, Ravello (phone: 89-857135). Inexpensive.

En Route from Ravello The road toward Salerno swings down to sea level, running through two resorts, Minori and Maiori, only a few minutes apart. Small, Minori has retained a modicum of personality and charm, at least in the quiet streets around the basilica. Maiori is the bolder, brasher, noisier sister, with a palm-lined boulevard running behind the largest beach on the coast, a half-mile of coarse gray sand practically obscured by beach umbrellas. The main escape from the tourism paraphernalia is up Via Chiunzi, which runs above what was once a river. Lined with delicatessens, bakeries, and produce shops, it offers a taste of authentic Italian street life. Maiori's tourist office is on Corso Regina (phone: 89-877452).

BEST EN ROUTE

Giardiniello Dine in a garden filled with lemon trees and ivy, candlelit at night, and enjoy fish and steak dishes. Closed Wednesdays from October through May. Reservations advised on weekends. Major credit cards accepted. 17 Corso Vittorio Emanuele, Minori (phone: 89-877050). Expensive.

Bristol The façade of this hostelry is a mass of flower-filled balconies. Each of its 60 rooms has a telephone and a terrace. An ornate decor prevails, particularly in the restaurant, piano bar, and disco downstairs. Open *Easter* through September. 70 Corso Vittorio Emanuele, Minori (phone: 89-877013). Moderate.

Club due Torri All 103 rooms in this hostelry offer an excellent panorama of the sea. There's no restaurant. Open *Easter* through September. 8 Via Diego Taiani, Maiori (phone: 89-877699; fax: 89-877726). Moderate.

Reginna Palace A boring structure, but the best hotel in town and a good value, with 64 rooms and its own stretch of beach across the road, in addition to a pool and restaurant. Open *Easter* through September. 1 Via Cristoforo Colombo, Maiori (phone: 89-877183; fax: 89-851200). Moderate.

En Route from Maiori The road begins to climb, growing narrow and winding again. The landscape still shows some of the damage caused by floods and landslides decades ago, as well as the damage of repeated brush fires. Around Capo d'Orso, the countryside becomes wilder and less heavily populated, and the small, colorful fishing village of Cetara is the only real town until Vietri sul Mare, where the Amalfi Drive comes to an end. Vietri is famed for its ceramics, and around the main square of the upper city, shop after shop spill over with colorful plates, pots, jugs, and other pottery. Even shops selling other types of wares, such as the fish store and the greengrocer, have storefronts decorated with images of their products in ceramic tiles. A brief stretch of S18 leads around a bend in the coastline from Vietri straight into Salerno, about 15½ miles (25 km) from Amalfi.

SALERNO Sorrento, Positano, Amalfi, and Ravello are tough acts to follow, and Salerno (pop. 200,000) cannot really compare with the elegance and unearthly beauty of the Amalfi Coast. A slightly seedy and raffish seaport—imagine a miniature Naples or Genoa—it has a long and dramatic history. In the 12th and 13th centuries, its most prosperous period, much of Salerno's fame was due to its *School of Medicine,* the oldest in the Western world, possibly begun in the 9th century (and closed in the 19th century). Just as Paris was preeminent in science and Bologna in law, Salerno became so renowned in the field of medicine that it was called the Hippocratic city. On September 9, 1943, it became famous when the Allies launched their invasion of mainland Europe from here, landing south of the city after an aerial bombardment. They encountered heavy resistance from a German Panzer division, and, when the Americans entered the town the next day, much of the waterfront was destroyed. The area has been rebuilt, and broad walkways curve along the waterfront, shaded by palms and scattered here and there with playgrounds, small amusement parks, and sidewalk *caffès.* In the evening, it seems the entire town takes a *passeggiata* by the sea.

Uphill from the port and the modern part of town, the Old Quarter is well worth a visit, especially for the *Duomo di San Matteo* (Cathedral of St. Matthew; Via Duomo). Built in 845 and rebuilt from 1076 to 1085 by Robert Guiscard, it was heavily redone during the 18th century, but some restorations uncovered its earlier forms. The Romanesque doorway, guarded by statues of lions, leads to a beautiful atrium surrounded by 28 columns that came from the Greek ruins down the coast at Paestum. A freestanding campanile (bell tower) looms above the atrium. Inside the church are two highly decorated pulpits and a candlestick in a mixture of Saracen and Byzantine styles, full of mosaic ornamentation. A stroll through the Old Town along Via dei Mercanti passes elegant shops as well as the poorest street vendors. It's lively, colorful, crowded, and loud. The tourist information office (*EPT*; 1 Piazza Ferrovia; phone: 89-231432), by the train station, can provide information on Salerno and its province, which includes most of the towns on the Amalfi Drive. It's closed Sundays; weekdays for a short (2 to 3 PM) break; and Saturdays for a break (1 to 3 PM).

BEST EN ROUTE

Nave Ristorante al Concord For a change of pace, dine aboard a ship moored on the waterfront in the center of Salerno. It features a variety of pasta as well as seafood, pizza, and a reasonably priced fixed menu. Closed Mondays. Reservations unnecessary. No credit cards accepted. Piazza della Concordia, Salerno (phone: 89-226856). Expensive to moderate.

Alla Brace Just across from the *Jolly delle Palme* (see below), this restaurant/pizzeria specializes in meat and fresh fish cooked over a charcoal grill. The linguine dishes are also quite good, and be sure tŏ try the gragnano wines. Closed Fridays and two weeks in late December. Reservations unnecessary. Major credit cards accepted. 11 Lungomare Trieste, Salerno (phone: 89-225159). Moderate.

Jolly delle Palme At the northern end of the waterfront, looking out over a playground and a public beach, is this comfortable member of the Jolly chain. There are 105 rooms and a restaurant. Open year-round. A short walk from the Old Town, at 1 Lungomare Trieste, Salerno (phone: 89-225222; 800-221-2626; fax: 89-237571). Moderate.

Lloyd's Baia Outside town on the drive in from the Amalfi Coast and Vietri, this hostelry on a bluff overlooking the sea is surrounded by gardens and adequately screened off from traffic. In it are 120 rooms, a restaurant, two pools, and a private beach reachable by elevators. Open year-round. 2 Via Marinis, Vietri Sul Mare, heading toward Salerno on S18 (phone: 89-210145; fax: 89-210186). Moderate.

Nicola dei Principati One of Salerno's best dining spots, perhaps because the seafood is very fresh and the antipasti outstanding. Try the fresh seafood risotto. Closed Sundays. Reservations unnecessary. Major credit cards accepted. 201 Corso Garibaldi, Salerno (phone: 89-225435). Moderate.

Pizzeria del Vicolo della Neve In the oldest part of town, this 500-year-old restaurant serves traditional dishes, seafood, pizza, and local wines. Closed Wednesdays for dinner. No reservations. No credit cards accepted. 24 Vicolo della Neve, Salerno (phone: 89-225705). Inexpensive.

En Route from Salerno It is possible to reach Paestum via the coast, but the first half of the drive is made terribly unattractive by construction sites and industrial zones. It's far better to take A3 out of Salerno, get off at the Battipaglia exit, and follow S18 to Paestum, about 26 miles (42 km) from Salerno.

PAESTUM Called Poseidonia (City of Poseidon) by the Greeks, who colonized it at the end of the 7th century BC, the city was taken over by a local tribe, the Lucanians, about 400 BC. It fell to the Romans 150 years later. But its low-lying position near the sea made it vulnerable to malaria; gradually dwindling in population, it was sacked by the Saracens in AD 877. Crumbling and overgrown with vegetation, Paestum wasn't rediscovered until the 18th century. Arriving from the north, drive past the first two entrances, park, and enter through the Porta della Giustizia, near the *Nettuno* (see *Best en Route*). For more details on the site, see *Remarkable Ruins* in DIVERSIONS. A museum housing exhibits from the site and the surrounding area is across the street from the archaeological zone. It is closed Mondays and afternoons (phone: 828-811023). The archaeological zone is closed on some holidays; the last tickets are sold two hours before sunset. A single admission ticket grants access to the museum and archaeological zone.

Besides its antiquities, Paestum is the closest Italy comes to buffalo country. There are so many grazing in the fields that the area has its own special mozzarella—*mozzarella di bufalo*. In July and August, an international music, dance, and theater festival takes place. For information and tickets, contact the tourist information office (*AAST*; 151/156 Via Magna Grecia; phone: 828-811016).

BEST EN ROUTE

Nettuno Just beyond the Porta della Giustizia, it serves fine food in a rustic beamed dining room and on a trellis-shaded terrace, right among the ruins. Offerings include roast meat when in season, as well as fish and seafood, a good selection of local wines, and more celebrated vintages from other parts of the country. Closed Mondays from September through June, and for dinner, except in high season. Reservations unnecessary. Major credit cards accepted. Zona Archeologica, Paestum (phone: 828-811028). Moderate.

Strand Hotel Schumann One of many hotels on the sea outside Paestum, it is set among pine trees overlooking the Gulf of Salerno. It has 36 rooms (each with a balcony or terrace) and a restaurant. Open year-round. Via Laura Mare, Paestum (phone: 828-851151; fax: 828-851183). Moderate.

Martini This modern, clean, and pleasant place is across from the Porta della Giustizia in the archaeological zone. The 29 rooms are in whitewashed cottages set in a beautiful garden; there's an indoor/outdoor pizzeria/restaurant, bar, and dance floor in the main building. Via Principe di Amadeo, Paestum (phone: 828-811020; fax: 828-811600). Inexpensive.

Ericusa The only hotel on Alicudi has just 12 rooms and a restaurant. Open June through September. Località Pirciato, Alicudi (phone: 90-988-9902 or 90-988-9910). Moderate to inexpensive.

La Canna With only eight rooms, each offering access to the common terrace, this pensione with a restaurant is beautifully situated above the port. Open year-round. 43 Via Rosa, Filicudi (phone: 90-988-9956; fax: 90-988-9966). Inexpensive.

Capri

Capri (pronounced *Kah*-pree, not Kah-*pree*) is a tiny jewel sparkling in the Bay of Naples. Although only 4 miles long and 2 miles wide, the island has almost as many identities as it does visitors. An estimated two million tourists make the short trip over from the mainland every year, and what they find usually depends on what they are looking for.

Wealthy jet setters discover kindred spirits, not to mention a multitude of elegant shops, chic *caffès* and restaurants, plush hotels, and private villas. On summer evenings Piazza Umberto I (nicknamed "the drawing room of the world") looks less like a public square than an exclusive cocktail party. Noël Coward rightly called this island "the most beautiful operetta stage in the world." Yet for those who want privacy and tranquillity, there are a surprising number of out-of-the-way corners, quiet wooded paths, and isolated gorges. One of Capri's enduring charms is its craggy, mountainous landscape, which leaves much of it inaccessible to cars and buses.

The island is nothing more than a geographical continuation of the Sorrento Peninsula, a large chunk of limestone that rises from the deep—precipitously in most places—and comes to two points. The west side culminates in Monte Solaro (1,923 feet), the highest spot on the island. The east side peaks in the somewhat lower (1,100 feet) Monte Tiberio—but here, nevertheless, is the island's highest cliff, from which, according to Suetonius, Emperor Tiberius threw his enemies into oblivion. In a saddle between the two mountains is Capri's main town, also named Capri. Its other town, Anacapri, is twice as high, on a plateau at the base of Monte Solaro. Visitors to the island disembark at *Marina Grande,* the port, and make the ascent to either town by road (or to Capri, directly by funicular). The ancients reached Anacapri by a staircase of 881 steps, built by the first Greek colonizers, restored by the Romans, and in use as late as the 19th century. Relations between the townspeople of Anacapri and those of the more chic Capri have always been touchy, perhaps because of what occurred during the plague in 1493. When the epidemic broke out in Capri, the people of Anacapri built a gate to block off the path leading from the infected lower part of the island. Enraged, a group of citizens from Capri smashed it down and hurled it over the precipice below.

Over the centuries writers, artists, and eccentrics have found a welcome home here. Hedonists as different as arms dealer Baron Von Krupp and the acerbic Oscar Wilde were drawn as much by the island's live-and-let-live attitude as by the cerulean sea and subtropical vegetation. Strange as it is to imagine, Maxim Gorky settled on Capri from 1907 to 1913 and ran a school for revolutionaries attended by Lenin and Stalin. Graham Greene kept returning to write at his house in the Caprile district until his death.

The common denominator among all visitors to Capri seems to be the desire for an intensification of life. Whether it's Tiberius spending the last decade of his licentious rule building sumptuous villas or budget-conscious travelers just over from Naples or Sorrento for the afternoon (although Capri is one of the most expensive places in Italy), people come looking for the ultimate resort, a place where the sun, the sea, the fine wine and food, the seductiveness and sensuality of the entire Italian peninsula are compressed into one tiny spot. That the island's permanent population of 12,000 works so hard to welcome foreigners and expatriates is no doubt part of its popularity. But be forewarned: Capri is a resort with a dress code, written into the island's bylaws. People can be fined for removing their shirts in public, except on the beaches, and for wearing wooden-soled sandals that make too much noise on the cobblestones.

Despite the crowds, it's remarkably easy to escape. Pick up a map at the tourist office booth under the clock in Piazza Umberto I and follow the well-surfaced footpath that starts at the terrace of the chic *Punta Tragara* hotel, past the classic view of the Faraglioni rocks and along the steep cliffs. The path concludes with a tiny flight of heart-thumping steps to lunch on the terrace of the simple but excellent *Grotelle* restaurant. Afterward wander along the spur path to see the island's famous natural arch.

TOURIST INFORMATION

The high-season in Capri is the period around *Easter* and June through September. Given the island's popularity, it's best to visit in May and September, when the weather is warm and the island less crowded. Winter, especially around *Christmas,* also can be an enticing time if—and it's a large *if*—the sun is shining. Visitors in winter will find more than half the hotels and restaurants closed, and despite the drastic differences in climate and attractions between summer and winter, the hotels that remain open year-round do not reduce their rates commensurately. A meager 10% off-season discount is the general rule. The *Ente Provinciale per il Turismo* in Naples (58 Piazza dei Martiri, Scala B; phone: 81-405311; fax: 81-401961) can provide information about Capri. On the island local tourist offices *(AAST)* are at the dock at *Marina Grande* (phone/fax: 837-0634); in the town of Capri (Piazza Umberto I; phone: 837-0686; fax: 837-0918); and in Anacapri (19/A Via G. Orlandi; phone/fax: 837-1524). Off-season, the tourist office on Piazza Umberto I posts the names, addresses, and phone numbers of hotels and restaurants that are open year-round.

Many free guides are available from travel agencies and hotels, which also can arrange short tours of the island. Superior free Italian- and English-language guides are *Isola di Capri,* an illustrated index of hotels and *pensioni,* and *Capri È,* which contains a long list of addresses and telephone numbers of hotels, restaurants, bars, and sports facilities, as well as schedules for buses, taxis, and boats to and from the mainland. The tourist office offers *Capri,* an excellent free brochure (in English) that details nine walks on the island, describing the main sights along each route.

TELEPHONE The area code for the entire island of Capri is 81. When calling from within Italy, dial 081 before the local number.

GETTING AROUND

Visitors are *not* allowed to bring cars to the island from March through October unless they have foreign license plates, but it doesn't make sense to drive at any time of the year, because the roads are narrow, crooked, and already crowded with local traffic. Places of interest are all within easy walking distance or well connected by bus, taxi, or funicular. Taxis and buses meet boats and hydrofoils arriving at *Marina Grande* and transport passengers to Piazza Martiri d'Ungheria in the town of Capri, a few steps from the main square, Piazza Umberto I, or to Piazza della Vittoria in Anacapri. For a small charge, you also can hire a motorized luggage cart to transport bags from ferry or hydrofoil to your hotel (phone: 837-0179 or 837-0896).

BUS In general buses leave *Marina Grande* every 15 minutes for Capri and Anacapri. Buses also leave *Marina Piccola,* the little port on the other side of the island, every 15 minutes (every 30 minutes in winter) for both towns. The trip from Capri to Anacapri is worth the ride just for the stunning views it affords as the bus winds up around hairpin bends. For additional bus information, call 837-0420.

FERRY There is frequent ferryboat and *aliscafo* (hydrofoil) service between Capri and the mainland. From Naples (a 75-minute trip) *Caremar* (phone: 837-0700) provides reasonable and dependable ferry service, which also operates out of Sorrento (45 minutes). More expensive hydrofoil service (approximately 40 minutes from Naples) is provided by both *Caremar* and *Aliscafi SNAV* (phone: 837-7577). *Note:* For hydrofoil service, a colored tag must be purchased for each item of luggage or it will not be allowed on board. Other companies with service between Capri and the mainland are *Aliscafi Alilauro* (phone: 837-7577); *Aliscafi Medmar* (phone: 837-7577); *Giuffre & Lauro* (phone: 837-6171); and *Navigazione Libera del Golfo* (phone: 837-0819). In summer ferries and hydrofoils for Capri leave regularly from additional points such as Salerno, Amalfi, Positano, Pozzuoli, and Ischia. For times and prices, check at local tourist information offices. For travelers arriving at Rome's *Leonardo da Vinci Airport,* there is a summer-only hydrofoil service direct to Capri from the town of Fiumicino (5 miles/8 km from the airport). The two-hour trip is infinitely preferable to the car or train trek via chaotic Naples. For information and reservations, contact *Medmar* in Rome (phone: 6-482-8579). In winter there generally is regularly scheduled service to Capri only from Naples and Sorrento, but it is possible to make private arrangements on small boats.

FUNICULAR The funicular connects *Marina Grande* and the town of Capri daily every 15 minutes from 6:30 AM to 8:40 PM, October through March; from 6:30 AM to 9:20 PM, April through May; and from 6:30 AM to 12:30 AM, June through September. Buses run the same route daily from 6:30 AM to midnight, leaving every 40 minutes. A *seggiovia* (chair lift) makes the 12-minute ride from Anacapri to the top of Monte Solaro daily from 9:30 AM to sunset, April through October; 10:30 AM to 3 PM (except Tuesdays), November through March.

HELICOPTER Arrange service to and from *Capodichino Airport* in Naples or the island of Ischia through *Eliambassador* (phone: 789-6273 or 789-6274; fax: 780-3006) or *Elicampania* (phone: 738-7346).

TAXI For a taxi in Capri, call 837-0543; in Anacapri, call 837-1175.

TOURS One way to see Capri and gain a different and dramatic perspective on its sheer limestone cliffs is to circle it in a boat; indeed, some parts of the island are accessible only by sea. Arrange trips around the island through *Gruppo Motoscafisti* (phone: 837-5646). A tour, which takes about two and a half hours, can be combined with tours to the famous Grotta Azzurra (Blue Grotto) and the lesser-known Spumante, Corale, and Bianca Grottoes, as well as to the Bagni di Tiberio. Trips specifically to the Grotta Azzurra leave *Marina Grande* at regular intervals. If no one answers the phone, go down to *Marina Grande* and ask for information at the stand marked "Gite dell'Isola." Gennaro Alberino (phone: 837-7118 or 837-9191); *Nunzio Esposito* (phone: 837-7849); and the *Consorzio Noleggiatori Capresi,* in Anacapri (phone: 837-2422 or 837-2749), also arrange boating excursions. On many off-season days local boatmen decide there aren't enough customers or the sea is too rough, and they close up shop.

SPECIAL EVENTS

Religious festivals and celebrations take on a pagan guise on Capri, and fireworks are set off on any pretext—a saint's day, *Christmas,* or a baptism. On May 14 the island celebrates the *Festa di San Costanzo,* the feast day of its patron saint, and on June 13 Anacapri celebrates the *Festa di Sant'Antonio.* On September 7 and 8, on Monte Tiberio and Monte Solaro, the *Festa della Madonna* is held. At the end of September a more secular celebration, the annual grape harvest, generates hundreds of impromptu parties.

SPORTS AND FITNESS

BOATING Boats can be rented by the hour or the day, with or without guides, through the *Capri Mare Club* (Bagni Le Sirene, *Marina Piccola;* phone: 837-0221). The same establishment runs a windsurfing and sailing school and can arrange water skiing; there also is a fitness center and sauna. Rent sailboats, windsurfers, and rubber dinghies with outboard engines from *Banana Sport* (*Marina Grande;* phone: 837-5188).

SKIN DIVING AND SNORKELING Although there is no reef around Capri, and the fish are sometimes few and far between, the clear water and the abundance of caves and grottoes make the area interesting for divers. Gennaro Alberino and his American wife, Cindy, run the *Gennaro and Cindy Sub* shop right next to the funicular (17 *Marina Grande;* phone: 837-9191, shop; 837-7118, home). They rent snorkeling equipment and can arrange for scuba diving and instruction. The *Capri Diving Club* (Bagni Le Sirene, *Marina Piccola;* phone/fax: 837-3487) also offers scuba-diving courses.

SWIMMING Capri is not a swimmer's paradise, since there are only a few small, stony beaches on the island's craggy coast. The best swimming is probably at *Marina Piccola,* where there are concrete platforms over the water's edge, or directly from a hired boat. Many hotels have pools.

TENNIS The *Tennis Yacht Club* (41 Via Camerelle; phone: 837-0261 or 837-7980), across from the swank *Quisisana* hotel, has three clay courts, a clubhouse, bar, and shower rooms. The club pro, Giuseppe de Stefano, well known on the *Grand Prix* circuit as an umpire, speaks English and gives lessons at reasonable prices, with court fees included. Make reservations at least a week in advance in high season. There are courts in Anacapri at the *Tennis Capri Sporting Club* (10 Via G. Orlandi; phone: 837-2612).

FOOD AND WINE

While some restaurants here offer standard Italian fare and international cuisine, the food on Capri generally shows the influence of nearby Naples and the sea. There are pasta dishes with tomato or eggplant, or with olive or clam sauces. Pizza has a thicker crust than elsewhere in Italy and is topped with a purée of tomatoes and slabs of *mozzarella di bufalo.* The seafood is marvelous, especially the shrimp, crayfish, and squid, which may be batter-fried or served in a salad or pasta sauce. An *insalata caprese* (sliced tomato and mozzarella, seasoned with fresh basil) makes an excellent start for any meal, and the *torta caprese* (traditional chocolate almond cake) is a tasty dessert.

Local wines are simple and of limited production and make no extravagant claims to merit. The white from Falanghina and Greco (greco del tufo) does go well with seafood.

TOURING CAPRI

Since there are essentially two towns on the island—Capri and Anacapri—it is wise to use one as a base, heading downhill on foot and returning uphill by taxi or bus. No trip will take more than a few hours.

Prices can be higher on Capri than on the mainland, particularly around Piazza Umberto I, where cappuccino and a roll can cost more than $10. Expect to pay $200 or more per night for a double room in hotels listed as expensive; $125 to $200 in those listed as moderate; and less than $100 at the inexpensive ones. All rates include breakfast unless otherwise noted, but these prices do not take into account any minimum half-board requirements that some hotels impose in high season. All hotels feature private baths unless otherwise indicated. The price of meals here, as in so many spots in Italy, depends in large measure on which fish or meat dish is ordered (pasta is reasonably priced almost everywhere) and which wine is drunk. Generally, a full meal for two will cost $75 or more in an expensive restaurant; $50 to $75 in a moderate establishment; and less than $50 in an inexpensive one. Prices include service, tax, and cover charge, but not local wine. The seafood on Capri is delicious but by no means inexpensive. All restaurants are open for lunch and dinner unless otherwise noted. For each location hotels and restaurants are listed alphabetically by price category.

CAPRI TOWN This whitewashed town has the look and feel of a North African *medina*. Many of the streets radiating from tiny Piazza Umberto I, the main square, are as narrow as hallways, as steep as staircases, as dim and cool as tunnels. Occasionally, the cramped passageways open onto small room-like *piazzette* where people sit eating, drinking, and chatting, creating the impression that the town is one immense, rambling house.

The lively, enfolding labyrinth of streets is only one of Capri's charms. There is color and excitement, and at every turn, through every open window, are breath-catching views of the sea, of Monte Tiberio to the east and Monte Solaro to the west, and of villas strewn across terraced hillsides shaded by cypress trees, palms, and citrus groves. Capri's greatest attractions are almost all present-day and physical—the play of sunlight and shadow, the smell of jasmine, the sound of the sea against the rocks—rather than monuments of historic or artistic importance. This is not to say that the island has not preserved its past. *Santo Stefano,* the 17th-century church on Piazza Umberto I, has two exquisite marble floors, both from Roman villas on the island, and the adjacent *Palazzo Cerio* (no phone) contains a small private museum of antiquities and fossils found on the island. It's open weekdays to noon; admission charge. Leave the piazza by its south corner and descend Via Vittorio Emanuele III to Via Federico Serena, which curves down to the *Certosa di San Giacomo* (Carthusian Monastery of St. James; no phone). Built in the late 14th century, it has barrel-vaulted ceilings and domes, making it appear slightly Byzantine. It now houses a school and the town library, as well as some Roman statues from the Grotta Azzurra and a collection of paintings from the 17th to the 19th century. Closed Mondays and after 2 PM; no admission charge.

Roman ruins supply the major part of Capri's historical heritage. In 29 BC Emperor Augustus visited the island, which then belonged to Naples, and was struck enough by its beauty to trade an island already in his possession (Ischia) for it. He built roads, aqueducts, and villas. His successor, Tiberius, arrived in AD 27 and for the last 10 years of his life ruled the Roman Empire from here. He erected more villas on prominent points throughout the island, dedicating them to various Roman deities. Altogether, there are supposed to have been a dozen imperial villas on Capri, but among the various Roman ruins on the island, the *Villa Jovis,* built by Tiberius and dedicated to Jupiter, is the best preserved and has the most spectacular position. It is set at the top of what is now called Monte Tiberio.

To reach the *Villa Jovis* (also called the *Villa Tiberius*), leave Piazza Umberto I by Via Le Botteghe, which becomes Via Fuorlovado and then Via Croce. From Via Croce take Via Tiberio uphill, following the signs. (The hike takes about an hour.) Just beyond the entrance to the villa is the *Salto di Tiberio,* the dizzyingly high precipice from which, as the story goes, Tiberius tossed his unfortunate victims to the stony shore of the sea. The villa itself, up a flight of steps, has been stripped of most of its mosaic pavements and decorative devices. Even in its reduced state, however, the ruins reveal extensive evidence of size and structural complexity. Incongruously, the very highest point of the pagan emperor's estate is crowned by a chapel and an immense, modern bronze statue of the Madonna that was blessed by Pope John Paul II and flown to this site by a US Navy helicopter. *Villa Jovis* is closed Mondays; admission charge (phone: 837-0381).

Other spots well worth a visit include *Punta di Tragara,* which offers a good view of the Faraglioni, twin rock islands that stand needlelike offshore and have become one of the symbols of Capri, and the *Giardini di Augusto* (Gardens of Augustus), a public park with about 850 varieties of plants and trees that offers another good view of the Faraglioni, *Punta di Tragara,* and *Marina Piccola.* From the gardens walk down to *Marina Piccola* on Via Krupp, officially closed because of falling rocks but still passable. The Arco Naturale (Natural Arch), a rock eroded to the shape of an archway, and the Grotta di Matromania, a cave in which the ancient Romans possibly worshiped Cybele, the Mater Magna, are not far from the *Villa Jovis.*

The Grotta Azzurra has been incessantly described, rendered in paintings, and pictured on postcards, but it should be seen firsthand. The discovery of this cave on the north side of the island in 1826 put Capri on the modern tourist map. Visitors are taken by motorboat to the cave entrance—a mere six-foot-wide hole in the rock, three feet high when the sea is normal—and then transfer to a small rowboat to be taken inside, where sunlight refracting through water makes the walls of the cave appear blue and gives submerged objects a silvery phosphorescence.

BEST EN ROUTE

La Canzone del Mare A social institution as well as an excellent restaurant and a bathing establishment, this place attracts a large clientele that comes to soak in the sun, to see and be seen, and to eat lunch (the restaurant closes at dusk). The house specialty is fresh fish, and desserts are excellent, particularly the orange *pastiera.* Closed October to *Easter.* Reservations advised. Major credit cards accepted. *Marina Piccola,* Capri (phone: 837-0104). Expensive.

La Capannina Unprepossessing in appearance, this restaurant serves food as straightforward, unpretentious, and fresh as its decor. As a result, it is patronized by everybody from movie stars to day-trippers to royalty, and is considered one of Capri's temples of gastronomy. *Penne alla siciliana* (pasta with an eggplant and mozzarella sauce) makes a fine first course. The fish is simply seasoned and always fresh. Closed Wednesdays, except in August, and November through March. Reservations advised. Major credit cards accepted. 14 Via Le Botteghe, Capri (phone: 837-0732). Expensive.

Al Geranio Some islanders claim this is even better than *La Capannina*. The service is highly professional; the views of the sea, memorable. Closed Tuesdays, except in July and August, and November through March. Reservations advised. Major credit cards accepted. 8 Viale Matteotti, Capri (phone: 837-0616). Expensive.

La Palma One of Capri's oldest hotels (from 1820), it is also one of its most imposing—the tiered building, which looks like a wedding cake, is set among palm trees, from which it takes its name. The decor is romantic, and the service is excellent. Most of the 80 rooms have balconies or terraces, and there is a restaurant and a gym with massage and sauna facilities. Open year-round. 39 Via Vittorio Emanuele, Capri (phone: 837-0133; fax: 837-6966). Expensive.

Da Paolino Lemon is the theme here, not only in the food and the homemade liqueurs but on the dishes and in the surroundings as well—there is alfresco dining on a terrace dripping with clusters of lemons hanging from the trees. The cooking is excellent—the pasta is homemade and the fish freshly caught. Closed Wednesdays and October to *Easter*. Reservations advised. Major credit cards accepted. 11 Via Palazzo a Mare, *Marina Grande*, Capri (phone: 837-6102). Expensive.

Punta Tragara A 10-minute walk from the main square, this 33-room villa-turned-hotel is beautifully situated with a splendid view of the Faraglioni. Its spa, hydromassage, and other luxurious facilities appeal to those looking for relaxation and privacy, but it also has a saltwater pool and a beach for more active guests, plus an elegant terrace restaurant, *Le Grottelle*. Open mid-April to mid-October. 57 Via Tragara, Capri (phone: 837-0844; fax: 837-7790). Expensive.

Quisisana Elegantly sumptuous, this peach-colored hotel has 142 guestrooms and a restaurant. For more information, see *Italy's Most Memorable Hostelries* in DIVERSIONS. Open April through October. 2 Via Camerelle, Capri (phone: 837-0788; fax: 837-6080). Expensive.

Scalinatella Midway between the *Quisisana* and *Punta Tragara,* this 30-room hotel has an understated elegance and a soothing view of the sea. No restaurant, though light lunches are served from the small poolside kitchen. Open mid-

March through October. 8 Via Tragara, Capri (phone: 837-0633; fax: 837-8291). Expensive.

Flora This charming 19-room hotel is meticulously run by longtime Capri resident Virginia Vuotto. It is housed in a fine villa with views over the courtyard of the *Certosa di San Giacomo,* a Carthusian monastery from which the hotel's excellent restaurant takes its name. Chef Giorgio Baldari's creative repertoire includes *saute di calamari al burro d'acciughe* (baby squid sautéed in anchovy butter), *tagliolini con spada e zafferano* (thin pasta with swordfish and saffron), and *lasagne bianco di ostriche e chiodini* (lasagne with oysters and cloves). Hotel and restaurant open March through December. Reservations advised. Major credit cards accepted. 26 Via F. Serena, Capri (phone: 837-0211; fax: 837-8949). Hotel, expensive to moderate; restaurant, moderate.

La Piazzella A short distance from Piazza Umberto I but hidden among a garden of lemon trees, this small hotel with a restaurant is an oasis of peace. All 20 individually and tastefully furnished (with ceramics and antiques) rooms and two suites have terraces with panoramic views. Both suites have a small private garden. Open year-round. 4 Via Giuliani, Capri (phone: 837-0044; fax: 837-0085). Expensive to moderate.

La Fontelina This popular restaurant is dramatically poised on the rocks close to the towering Faraglioni. It is best to come here at lunchtime as it doubles as a *stabilimento balneare*—a place where diners can sunbathe and dive into the crystal-clear water before repairing to the table. It is easily reached by foot along the shady and panoramic Via Tragara, but at the end of the day, after you've had your fill of spinach gnocchi with salmon and ravioli filled with cheese and arugula, the restaurant has a convenient boat service to ferry tired diners back to *Marina Piccola*. Closed November through March. Reservations advised. American Express accepted. Località Faraglioni, Capri (phone: 837-0845). Moderate.

Gatto Bianco Conveniently situated, this 40-room hotel compensates for its lack of a view with the warmth of its welcome. It has a restaurant. Open April through October. 32 Via Vittorio Emanuele, Capri (phone: 837-0203; fax: 837-8060). Moderate.

Da Gemma A favorite with visitors from the entertainment world, it offers a rare mixture of reasonably priced, good home cooking and a warm atmosphere. The management claims to serve the best pizza in the world, cooked in a 15th-century oven in front of the customers. The other specialty is local fish. Closed Mondays and November to December 5. Reservations advised. Major credit cards accepted. 6 Via Madre Serafina, Capri (phone: 837-0461 or 837-7113). Moderate.

Al Grottino A father-and-son establishment and an old favorite with the islanders, who know they will be served very fresh fish. The chef has a fine touch with fried dishes, including a delicate version of the usual *frittura mista* (mixed fried fish). Meals are served in a light and airy dining room. Closed Tuesdays and November to mid-March. Reservations advised. Major credit cards accepted. 27 Via Longano, Capri (phone: 837-0584). Moderate.

La Pigna One of the island's most popular dining spots includes on its menu *pesce spada affumicato* (smoked swordfish) and *gamberetti al parmigiano* (shrimp with parmesan cheese). For an unusual dessert try the *melanzane alla cioccolata,* an unlikely but successful combination of eggplant and chocolate, taken from an old Caprese recipe. Closed November through April. Reservations advised. Major credit cards accepted. Via Roma, Capri (phone: 837-0280). Moderate.

Villa Brunella A charming, family-run hotel on the panoramic walk to the *Punta di Tragara.* Each of the 19 rooms has a private balcony with magnificent views over *Marina Piccola,* and the hotel has a pool. The small restaurant prepares a good array of antipasti and an excellent spaghetti *Brunella* (with seafood); in summer patrons enjoy alfresco dining on one of Capri's loveliest terraces. Open year-round. 24 Via Tragara, Capri (phone: 837-0122; fax: 837-0430). Moderate.

La Cisterna This restaurant serves tasty pizza with a thick crust, sliced tomatoes, and mounds of mozzarella. Its menu also features the largest, most succulent crayfish you're likely to see and a light red local wine bottled by the owner. Closed Thursdays. Reservations advised in summer. Visa accepted. Via Madre Serafina, Capri (phone: 837-5620). Moderate to inexpensive.

Bocciodromo Tina, the welcoming signora who runs this pretty garden restaurant, is Capri-born and -raised and takes pride in turning out fine homemade dishes such as *ravioli capresi* (stuffed with cheese and fresh marjoram). She also makes an excellent lemon liqueur, *limoncino.* Open daily. Reservations unnecessary. No credit cards accepted. 2 Traversa Il Palazzo, Capri (phone: 837-7414). Inexpensive.

La Savardina (da Eduardo) In the countryside, halfway to the *Villa Jovis,* this simple trattoria offers excellent ravioli in butter and sage, fresh fish, and grilled sausage seasoned with fennel. Closed Tuesdays. Reservations advised in summer. No credit cards accepted. 8 Via Lo Capo, Capri (phone: 837-6300). Inexpensive.

Villa Krupp A favorite of academics and budget-conscious travelers, this 15-room place is set apart from the clamor and conspicuous consumption that dominate much of Capri. It offers a beautiful view but no restaurant. Open year-round. 12 Via Matteotti, Capri (phone: 837-0362). Inexpensive.

ANACAPRI Actually the upper town of *Marina Grande,* often fog-shrouded Anacapri can be reached by a hair-raising bus or taxi trip. Horns blare, tires squeal, and the traffic careens around hairpin turns with little hesitation. The only other alternative used to be the *Scala Fenicia* (Phoenician Staircase), the 881 steps used by the Greeks (who carved them out of the rock), the Romans, and everyone else until 1887, when it was closed to the public because of fallen rocks and the road to Anacapri was built.

Less claustrophobic and more secluded than the town of Capri (and far less chic), Anacapri offers more in the unending series of spectacular views of the Bay of Naples and the mainland. One magnificent view is from the garden of the *Villa San Michele,* built in the 1880s by the Swedish doctor and writer Axel Munthe, who lived here until 1910 and often wrote about the island, most notably in *The Story of San Michele.* Constructed on the site of one of the villas of Tiberius and incorporating some of its remains, the house contains some Roman antiquities but is furnished mostly in 17th- and 18th-century style. Its gardens are exquisitely landscaped. The villa is open daily to 3:30 PM, January and February; to 5 PM, March, April, and October; and to 6 PM, May through September; admission charge (phone: 837-0686). For an even more awe-inspiring view, take the chair lift from Anacapri to the top of Monte Solaro. Airborne riders float over citrus groves and tropical gardens to a summit from which the entire island and, in the distance, the Apennine Mountains running down Italy's spine are visible. The chair lift operates daily from 9:30 AM to sunset, April through October; 10:30 AM to 3 PM the rest of the year, except Tuesdays.

In Anacapri are the ruins of another Tiberius construction, the *Imperial Villa of Damecuta,* discovered in excavations that took place from 1937 to 1948. Be sure to visit the *Torre di Damecuta,* a cylindrical tower that was added to the east wing in the 12th century as a lookout point for pirates. The villa and tower are closed Mondays and after 2 PM; one admission charge to both (no phone).

Also in town is one of the island's lovliest churches, the *Chiesa di San Michele* (Church of St. Michael), famous for its exquisite majolica floor, which depicts Adam and Eve in Paradise. The work of Leonardo Chiaiese, an artist from the Abruzzi region, it dates back to the 18th century. It's open daily, with a short midday closing; no admission charge (no phone).

BEST EN ROUTE

Europa Palace A spacious, contemporary hotel built on three levels, it has 103 rooms, large terraces, broad expanses of glass, a pool, a good restaurant, and other modern amenities. Open April through October. 104 Via Axel Munthe, Anacapri (phone: 837-0955; fax: 837-3191). Expensive.

Add'o Riccio The perfect vantage point from which to watch the flotillas of boats going into the nearby Grotta Azzurra while feasting on some of the best-cooked fish dishes on the island. This memorable restaurant can be reached by car, boat, or a pleasant walk of about an hour from Anacapri, past the ruins of the Roman *Villa of Damecuta.* Closed for part of winter. Reservations advised. Major credit cards accepted. Alla Grotta Azzurra, Anacapri (phone: 837-1380). Moderate.

Il Cucciolo Just outside town, this restaurant has several terraces for alfresco dining, with superb views over the entire Bay of Naples. Closed Wednesdays, except in summer, and November to mid-March. Reservations advised in summer. No credit cards accepted. 52 Via La Fabbrica, Anacapri (phone: 837-1917). Moderate.

San Michele di Anacapri Close to Axel Munthe's villa, this 30-room hostelry has the look and feel of a private house, with traditional furnishings and modern conveniences. Large gardens provide shady nooks for daydreaming and other spots for unobstructed views. There is a restaurant. Open year-round. 14 Via G. Orlandi, Anacapri (phone: 837-1427; fax: 837-1420). Moderate.

Da Gelsomina It is well worth the 20-minute walk to reach this quiet, well-run restaurant with a terrace that overlooks the Faraglioni. Diners enjoy spectacular views and good home cooking, with dishes based on fish and meat. Closed Tuesdays in off-season and January to mid-February. Reservations advised. No credit cards accepted. From the main piazza (Piazza Vittoria), follow the picturesque path known as the Migliara, which is too narrow for even the smallest car. Anacapri (phone: 837-1499). Moderate to inexpensive.

Loreley Economical, clean, cozy, and convivial, this hotel looks out on lemon groves and is flower- and fruit-scented. The 16 rooms are large and well furnished; some have private baths and balconies. No restaurant. Open year-round. 16 Via G. Orlandi, Anacapri (phone: 837-1440). Inexpensive.

Ischia

It is difficult to say when, much less why, Ischia began getting second billing to nearby Capri. Perhaps it goes back to Emperor Augustus, who gave the island to the Neapolitans in a trade for Capri, an island half its size (Ischia measures about 6 miles east to west and 4 miles north to south). Today Ischia is too often overlooked by American travelers, but many Italians prefer it to Capri, which they consider too crowded, and many Germans also have discovered it. They love its clear sparkling waters, its sandy beaches (a marked contrast to Capri), and its extensive pine forests, vineyards, and citrus groves—all the green scenery that has caused it to be known as the "Emerald Isle." A good many visitors also come for the hot mineral waters, to "detox," and perhaps lose a kilo or two.

Just as Capri is a continuation of the Sorrento Peninsula, the southern shore of the Bay of Naples, Ischia is a continuation of the Campi Flegrei (Phlegrean Fields) of the northern shore. This, in fact, was where the "fiery fields" finally got down to business. Ischia is a volcanic island of craters and lava beds, with cone-shaped, 2,590-foot Monte Epomeo, the crux of it all, standing nearly dead center. Monte Epomeo hasn't erupted since the early 14th century, and its slopes are now covered with vines that produce the well-known epomeo wine. The mineral springs, whose beneficial effects were known to the ancients, do endure, however, continuing to issue forth at varying temperatures. Here, with the exception of the Nitrodi spring, the waters are used not for drinking (as they are in Montecatini and many other Italian spas) but for hydromassage, inhalation, thermal mineral baths, and, above all, for mud baths.

The island has had a turbulent history. Beginning with the ancient Greeks, it has been colonized, occupied, ruled, or sacked by a succession of invaders, among them the Neapolitans, Romans, Goths, Saracens, Normans, Pisans, Angevins, Aragonese, the pirate Barbarossa, the Duke of Guise, and Admiral Nelson. And from time to time islanders and invaders alike found it necessary to surrender to the superior force of the island's volcanic nature and evacuate completely. Today the island shows few signs of this tumult except in the variety of its architectural styles and in the accretion of history surrounding, for instance, the *isolotto,* the little island that sits just offshore of the town of Ischia, connected by a pedestrian bridge. The Greeks built a fortress here in the 5th century BC. The *Castello d'Ischia*—a collection of walls, fortifications, and other buildings—seen today, however, was built by the Aragonese in the 15th century. In the meantime the *ischitani* sought refuge here over the centuries, from invaders as well as forces of nature. In fact, when the last volcanic eruption occurred (1301 or 1302) and the original town of Ischia was buried in lava (it was farther northwest than the town is today), the inhabitants took cover here and didn't begin to build the new town until the 16th century.

The town they built, on the island's northeast corner, is now the island capital and has grown enough to consist of two settlements: Ischia Porto, where most visitors arrive, and Ischia Ponte, the older nucleus, connected by bridge to the *isolotto*. Circling the island counterclockwise are the other main centers of resort activity, which coincide with the location of the most important springs: Casamicciola Terme, on the north shore, reborn after destruction by an earthquake in 1883; Lacco Ameno, at the northwest corner, a fishing village grown fashionable; and Forio, on the west coast, a picturesque wine-producing village. Sant'Angelo, on the southern shore, is a tiny fishing village, linked, as is Ischia Ponte, to a tiny islet offshore; it has a beach with fumaroles, the Lido dei Maronti, stretching east of it. Sant'Angelo is somewhat off the beaten track, but well worth the trip; even more so are the mountain villages of the interior whose position has kept them relatively untouched by the tourist activity along the coastline.

TOURIST INFORMATION

The official high season on Ischia runs from July through September, although unofficially it begins around *Easter*. In winter many tourist facilities are closed, but with a permanent population of almost 50,000 people, the island never has the bleak shuttered look of some resorts off-season. The *Ente Provinciale per il Turismo* in Naples (58 Piazza dei Martiri, Staircase B; phone: 81-405311; fax: 81-401961) is a source of information about Ischia. In addition, there are local tourist offices on the island itself (104 Corso Vittoria Colonna; phone: 991464 or 983066; fax: 981904; and Via Iasolino; phone: 991146 or 983005), both in Ischia Porto. Many free guides and maps are available at hotels and travel agencies.

TELEPHONE The area code for Ischia is 81. When calling from within Italy, dial 081 before the local number.

GETTING AROUND

Unlike Capri, Ischia does not prohibit tourists from bringing cars to the island in summer; although there are limitations to keep traffic manageable, they affect only residents of the region of Campania. In July and August, however, cars are banned from the center of Ischia Porto and Ponte.

BUS There is regular and inexpensive bus service to most villages; in fact, it's possible to do a complete circuit of the island by public transportation in about two and a half hours. The bus marked *CS* makes the tour clockwise; *CD* does the same route counterclockwise. Both leave from Piazza Trieste e Trento, near the port. Check at the tourist office for details and times of departure, or call 991808 or 991828.

CAR Since Ischia is much larger than Capri, a car is useful, as many of the prettiest villages and best beaches are some distance away. Rental prices are relatively low. Good local companies are *Rentcar Ischia* (59 Via Alfredo de Luca, Ischia Porto; phone: 992444 or 993259); *Davidauto* (84 Via G. Mazzella, Forio; phone: 998043); and *Autocenter* (Via Mazzella, Ischia Porto; phone: 992451). In Lacco Ameno try *Autonoleggio Aragona* (Via Fundera; phone: 994305; fax: 995855). For mopeds and scooters contact *Autonoleggio-Moto* (16 Via dello Stadio; phone: 981055).

FERRY Ferries and *aliscafi* (hydrofoils) run frequently between Ischia and the mainland. From Naples *Caremar* (phone: 992321 on Ischia) provides dependable service from *Molo Beverello,* near *Castel Nuovo;* it also has service from Mergellina *(Molo Ovest)* and, slightly north of Naples, from Pozzuoli. Service from Mergellina also is run by another hydrofoil company, *Snav* (phone: 996403). In summer one ferry and two hydrofoils run daily to Ischia from Sorrento and Capri. *Alilauro* (phone: 991888 on Ischia) also has hydrofoil service from Naples to Ischia. The ferry trip between Naples and Ischia takes approximately one to one and a half hours; by hydrofoil, the same trip takes about 45 minutes.

TAXI Taxis are plentiful, and some hang around the port offering tours of the island. Before taking such a tour, be absolutely certain of what it will cost; if in doubt, don't do it. You also can call a taxi (phone: 984998, 992550, or 993720).

TOURS *Calypso Boat Tours* (phone: 997547 or 990663) offers excursions around the island to see the volcanic cliffs, the Grotta del Mago (Magician's Cave), and the picturesque beach and village of Sant'Angelo. Boats leave daily from various points, including Ischia Porto, Lacco Ameno, and Forio. Purchase tickets on board or at the tourist office.

SPORTS AND FITNESS

Swimming, skin diving, snorkeling, windsurfing, tennis, and hiking easily can be arranged in season through the tourist office. Be sure to visit the beach at Sant'Angelo. A good way to discover some of Ischia's hidden coves is by boat. You can rent small motorboats from local fishermen by the day or half day (phone: 992383 or 905114). Additionally, the *Centro Nautico Isola d'Ischia* (26 Via Lungomare Aragonese, Ischia Ponte; phone: 982915) rents small motorboats and sailboats.

FOOD AND WINE

Like Capri, Ischia is influenced by Naples and the sea. The cuisine features fresh fish, lobster, mussels and clams, pizza, and pasta with sauces of mozzarella and eggplant, or tomatoes, olives, and capers. Inland trattorie frequently serve rabbit. Local wines include the well-respected biancolella and red and white monte epomeo.

TOURING ISCHIA

Accommodations on Ischia can be luxurious or humble. Mineral baths, mud baths, and other such ministrations are given in many hotels as well as in communal bathing establishments. Dining on the island can be in simple trattorie or in first class restaurants. In season expect to pay $250 or more per night for a double room in a hotel listed as very expensive; $120 or more in hotels listed as expensive; $60 to $120 in those listed as moderate; and $60 or less in the inexpensive ones. (As on Capri and the Amalfi Coast, compulsory meal plans may be in effect in some hotels in some seasons, making for higher prices.) All hotels feature private baths and rates include breakfast unless otherwise noted. A full meal for two will run $70 or more in an expensive restaurant; from $40 to $70 in a moderate establishment; and $40 or less in one listed as inexpensive. Prices include tax, tip, and cover charge. All restaurants are open for lunch and dinner unless otherwise noted. For each location hotels and restaurants are listed alphabetically by price category.

ISCHIA The town of Ischia consists of two settlements, Porto d'Ischia and Ponte d'Ischia (or Ischia Porto and Ischia Ponte). They are separated by a *pineta* (pine woods) and connected by a main street that is called Via Roma at its north end and then becomes Corso Vittoria Colonna; running parallel to a sandy beach, it is lined with *caffès,* restaurants, and shops. Most boats from the mainland dock at Ischia Porto, a harbor formed by an extinct volcano. Once an interior lake, it was opened to the sea in 1854 with the construction of a canal through the rim of the crater. Not far from the port, on Piazza del Redentore, are the *Terme Comunali* (Communal Baths; phone: 981025), open year-round. Ischia Ponte is the older part of town, named for the 15th-century pedestrian bridge—Ponte Aragonese—that links it with the *isolotto,* the cluster of buildings, churches, and 15th-century castle that is the oldest of all. In the early 16th century Vittoria Colonna, whose name lives on in Ischia's main street, spent part of her life in the castle. A member of a prestigious Italian family, with her own reputation as one of the great poets of her time (and as the object of love sonnets written by her friend Michelangelo), she is credited with polishing Ischia's cultural image so that it outshone even Naples.

BEST EN ROUTE

Grand Hotel Punta Molino Once a private villa and now one of Ischia's most charming hostelries, it's on a private beach and has 82 lovely rooms. There's a good restaurant, and the hotel's own thermal baths are located on a flowered terrace. Open mid-April through October. 14 Lungomare Vincenzo Telese, Ischia Porto (phone: 991544; fax: 991562). Very expensive.

Excelsior This extravagantly decorated and furnished building is famed for its fine service and comfortable accommodations. The 72 rooms are less ornate than the lounge, which has a raised fireplace and an intricately carved bar. The hotel is set amid pine trees and gardens; it has a restaurant, a pool, and thermal facilities. A beach is nearby. Open mid-April to mid-October. 19 Via Emanuele Gianturco, Ischia Porto (phone: 991522; fax: 984100). Expensive.

Jolly Grande Albergo delle Terme A member of the Jolly chain, it has 208 comfortable rooms, two pools in a tree-shaded garden (plus a pool for children), an excellent restaurant, and its own thermal facilities. Open March through November. 42 Via Alfredo de Luca, Ischia Porto (phone: 991744; fax: 993156). Expensive.

Moresco An old Moorish structure smothered in bougainvillea, it has 75 rooms, each with beamed or vaulted ceilings, tile floors, ornately carved dressers and beds—the brilliant color scheme contrasts dramatically with the whitewashed walls—plus a terrace and air conditioning. Other features are a restaurant, tennis courts, a solarium, gamerooms, gardens, two pools, and a health and beauty center offering spa services. Open April through October. 16 Via Emanuele Gianturco, Ischia Porto (phone: 981355; fax: 992338). Expensive.

Da Ugo Giardini Eden In a paradise-like setting on the sea, among black lava formations created centuries ago, this eatery boasts excellent salads, lobster, charcoal-grilled fish, house white wine, and efficient service. Closed November through April. Reservations advised. Major credit cards accepted. 50 Via Nuova Cartaromana, Ischia Ponte (phone: 993909). Expensive.

Damiano Fresh fish is the specialty of this modern-looking restaurant with a glass-enclosed terrace. Closed for lunch and October through March. Reservations advised. Major credit cards accepted. Via Nuova Circonvallazione, Ischia Porto (phone: 983032). Expensive to moderate.

Parcoverde Terme This white, Moorish-looking hotel, set in its own gardens with palm trees and umbrella pines, is one of only a handful in Ischia that stay open year-round. It has 60 air conditioned rooms, a good restaurant, lovely gardens, and a beach within walking distance, as well as thermal facilities. 29 Via Michele Mazzella, Ischia Porto (phone: 992282; fax: 992773). Moderate.

O Porticciull Right on the waterfront, this popular restaurant with sidewalk tables is run by a mother-and-daughter team who prepare fish and seafood in every conceivable way. Closed for lunch and mid-November through *Easter*. Reservations necessary. Major credit cards accepted. 10 Via Porto, Ischia Porto (phone: 993222). Moderate.

Zi Nannina a Mare A delightful spot to have lunch after sunbathing on the small but pretty beach directly below. Dine alfresco on a terrace dotted with palms and flowers or indoors on such specialties as *penne alla Sorrento* (quill-shape pasta served with melted mozzarella, tomato, and basil) and fried fish dishes. Open year-round. Reservations unnecessary. Visa accepted. Lungomare Cristoforo Colombo, Ischia Porto (phone: 991350). Moderate to inexpensive.

LACCO AMENO On the northern coast, a short ride from the port, Lacco Ameno has some of the best hotels on Ischia, which in turn contain some of the island's best restaurants. Just offshore is the town's landmark, an outcropping of rock called *il fungo* (mushroom) that juts out of the sea. The center of this onetime fishing village is Piazza Santa Restituta, with a sanctuary dedicated to the island's patron saint (the oldest part of the church dates from the 11th century, but most of it is modern). The mineral springs at Lacco Ameno are said to be radioactive, and remains of ancient baths dating from the 8th century BC have been found here. Victorian baths were built over the Greco-Roman remains in the 19th century, but they were torn down in the 1950s to make way for Lacco Ameno's modern thermal baths—*Terme Regina Isabella e Santa Restituta*—and a connecting luxury hotel. Other hotels followed, many equipped to offer thermal treatments in house, and Lacco Ameno soon became a resort town with an international clientele. The mineral baths, mud baths, inhalations, and beauty treatments claim to cure all ailments known to humankind, but the town's setting has restorative powers of its own.

BEST EN ROUTE

Regina Isabella A deluxe hotel in the grand continental tradition, it is the island's best. At the water's edge in the center of Lacco Ameno, it has 135 comfortable rooms, most with sea-view balconies (others have a village view), two seaside restaurants, two pools (one saltwater, one hot thermal water), a private beach, a tennis court, and a beautiful garden. Water sports and diet, exercise, yoga, dance, and aerobics programs are offered; a full roster of spa treatments is available at the connecting *Terme Regina Isabella e Santa Restituta*. The atmosphere of a private club prevails. Open April through October. Piazza Santa Restituta, Lacco Ameno (phone: 994322; fax: 986043). Very expensive.

San Montano Outside Lacco Ameno on a hill above the tiny bay and beach of San Montano, this place affords lovely views of the coast and town. It has 65 rooms, indoor and outdoor dining, thermal and seawater pools, tennis and *bocce* courts, a large garden, a reserved beach, and baths and beauty treatments in its own thermal establishment. Open April through October. Via Monte Vico, Lacco Ameno (phone: 994033; fax: 980242). Expensive.

La Reginella Across from the *Regina Isabella* and under the same ownership, it is a less expensive alternative. Its 50 rooms are in a large villa with graceful terraces and French doors leading onto balconies. Guests may use some of the facilities of the more celebrated establishment, including the pools. Full board required. Open April through October. Piazza Santa Restituta, Lacco Ameno (phone: 994300; fax: 980481). Expensive to moderate.

Terme di Augusto Centrally located and one of the most modern hotels in Lacco Ameno, it has 119 rooms and suites, all with balconies. There are two restaurants, an indoor pool with thermal water, an outdoor pool, a private beach, tennis courts, and a fully equipped spa. Open April through October. 128 Viale Campo, Lacco Ameno (phone: 994944; fax: 980244). Expensive to moderate.

Al Delfino This friendly, family-run trattoria overlooking the harbor serves well-cooked *frittura della paranza* (small, fresh fried fish), homemade deserts, and good local wines. Open year-round. Reservations advised in summer. No credit cards accepted. Corso Angelo Rizzoli, Lacco Ameno (phone: 986189). Moderate.

O Padrone d'O Mare Diners feast alfresco on dishes that are mainly based on fish. The house specialty is *zuppa di pesce* (a big plate brimming with fish and shellfish). Open year-round. Reservations unnecessary. Visa accepted. Lacco Ameno (phone: 986159). Moderate.

FORIO D'ISCHIA This small village on the west coast is the center of the island's wine production and was once a thriving colony of artists and writers. Its dominant feature is the *Torrione,* a 15th-century tower built to defend the islanders against invaders and pirates.

BEST EN ROUTE

Grande Albergo Mezzatorre A former estate that once belonged to a Roman nobleman and, later, to the famous movie director Visconti, today it is one of the island's best hotels. The current owners have preserved the original features of what is really a small castle, with 60 guestrooms. The grounds are large and well tended, and there is a restaurant, a small private beach, and a pool. Open *Easter* through November. Via Mezza Torre, Forio d'Ischia (phone: 986111; fax: 987992). Expensive.

La Cava dell'Isola Just outside Forio, this dining spot is so close to the sea that you could almost go for a swim between courses. It boasts good home-cooked traditional dishes and friendly service. Closed November through April. Reservations unnecessary. No credit cards accepted. Via G. Mazzella, Forio d'Ischia (phone: 997452). Moderate.

Trattoria da Peppina di Renato The cooking here reflects the restaurant's inland location. Specialties include the classic Neapolitan dish *pasta e fagioli* (macaroni with beans in a rich sauce), meat grilled over a charcoal fire, and *coniglio alla cacciatore* (rabbit cooked with olive oil, garlic, and tomatoes).

The atmosphere is down-to-earth and homey. Closed November through March. Reservations unnecessary. Visa accepted. Overlooking town, at 42 Via Bocca, Forio d'Ischia (phone: 998312). Moderate.

Il Soccorso This restaurant takes its name from the nearby *Santuario del Soccorso,* a picturesque whitewashed church perched on the edge of the cliff at the far end of the village. Diners can be sure of the freshest fish on the island and friendly, efficient service. Closed Mondays and November. Reservations unnecessary. Major credit cards accepted. 1 Via Soccorso, Forio d'Ischia (phone: 997846). Moderate to inexpensive.

SANT'ANGELO Down on the southern tip of the island, this is one of the prettiest spots on Ischia—a peaceful place that still has the air of a fishing village rather than a resort. Although somewhat isolated, it is only a 15-minute drive from Ischia Porto and has some fine restaurants, as well as the best beach on the island.

BEST EN ROUTE

Miramare Located in a superb spot, this 50-room hostelry overlooks the beach, the small fishing harbor, and the picturesque promontory of Sant'Angelo. Guests may eat breakfast on the flower-decked terrace; there's also a restaurant. Open March through October. 29 Via Comandante Maddalena, Sant'Angelo (phone: 999253; fax: 999325). Expensive to moderate.

Ristorante Conchiglia Inside is airy and pleasant, but the real treat is the balcony, where diners can eat plates of *frittura mista* (mixed fresh fried fish) and drink jugs of local white wine while looking out over Sant'Angelo. The restaurant also rents out 10 clean, comfortable rooms, but they fill up quickly, so book early. Closed November through April. Reservations advised, especially for a terrace table. No credit cards accepted. Via Sant'Angelo, Sant'Angelo (phone: 999270). Restaurant, moderate; hotel, inexpensive.

Puglia

Italy's southeasternmost region, Puglia—or Apulia, as it is sometimes known in English—is the "heel" of the "boot," nearly a 250-mile/400-km–long spike heel with a spur. Most of the region is flat, covered with fruit and olive trees, tomatoes, grain, and grapes, and cost-efficient crops such as potatoes and melons. Yet it has one of the longest coastlines of any Italian region, the Adriatic bathing it along the eastern shore and the Ionian Sea sweeping around the heel. Although many Italians come to Puglia for its beaches as well as the Alberobello area, dotted with *trulli* (conical stone dwellings), the region is hardly overrun with tourists, except in summer, when it is favored by northern Italians. It is a little-known, developing region rich in history and with a culture that has been influenced over the centuries by Greeks, Romans, Goths, Lombards, Byzantines, Normans, Swabians, Angevins, Aragonese, Spanish, Bourbons, and French.

Puglia can be divided into four geographic areas. In the north is the Tavoliere, a vast, flat, fertile, wheat-producing zone that has been growing grain since ancient times. The area is commonly known as Capitanata, and the Gargano Massif—the dramatic, jagged limestone promontory jutting 40 miles out from its eastern edge into the Adriatic—is its drawing card. Both peninsula and mountain, the Gargano is the spur of the boot, known for its beautiful beaches, limpid sea, romantic grottoes, rich forests, tall rock formations, and the five tiny Tremiti Islands off the coast. At the center of the region is Bari and its surrounding province, Puglia's richest agricultural area, with the greatest concentration of historic and cultural sights. The area corresponds topographically with a region of low hills covered with vineyards and olive groves and stretches of stony ground known as the Murge. Southward is the Salento Peninsula, which forms the high heel of the boot and offers visitors the chance to easily explore both the Adriatic and the Ionian shores.

Puglia's succession of rulers and invasions is reflected in its cities, ancient villages, and impressive monuments, which incorporate a variety of architectural styles. The influence of the Greeks—especially apparent in Taranto, Gallipoli, Otranto, and Bari—dates from when Puglia was part of Magna Graecia, the early Greek colonization of southern Italy that began in the 8th century BC. Remnants of Magna Graecia and evidence of its tremendous impact on the *pugliese* can be found in the art and artifacts in the region's archaeological museums as well as in many of its customs, dialects, and even cuisine.

Under the Normans, during the 11th and 12th centuries, many churches were built, and the Apulian-Romanesque style of architecture originated, incorporating Norman, northern Italian, and even Asian motifs. The 13th century was Puglia's happiest moment, especially the few decades under the rule of Holy Roman Emperor Frederick II of Swabia (1220–50), who encouraged the building of some 30 splendid castles and extraordinary Romanesque cathedrals; during his reign the region flourished economically, culturally, and artistically.

By the 14th century, Puglia had already begun to decline: Venetians took its trade; the Turks raided its coasts; and famine, plague, malaria, and the insidious effects of the feudal system all played a part in its demise. Not much of the Renaissance is visible in Puglia, but the Baroque did have a grand flowering in 17th-century Lecce, still visible today.

Puglia's unique architectural form is the *trullo*. At its most authentic, this is a cylindrical limestone hut made without mortar, whitewashed and topped with a conical stone roof and often painted with a white cross or other symbols whose meanings have been lost through time. In the *trulli* district, centered in the town of Alberobello (the "capital") and the Valle d'Itria south of the town, from Locorotondo to Martina Franca, the huts are huddled together in villages or scattered about the landscape, gleaming against the red clay earth amid olive groves and almond trees that flower in February and endless miles of stone walls, these also constructed with no mortar. Some believe the houses are of ancient origin, while others say they first came about in the 16th century; the examples seen today are at most a few hundred years old, and some are even brand-new. Many are still inhabited, some are used as shops and storehouses, and some are rented out in summer.

Puglia's countryside has seen the refurbishment of old *masserie* (farmhouses), set in idyllic landscapes, into very attractive country inns. The local tourist boards can provide lists. You might also want to consider bicycling through *trulli* country or studying the local cuisine. For US-based tour operators offering biking trips and other packages, see GETTING READY TO GO.

Puglia has busy commercial ports, beautiful stretches of uncrowded beach, and clear azure waters. Its wonderful regional cooking is based largely on an abundance of seafood and fish (red mullet, spiny lobster, dentex, fresh sardines, and eels) found in its two seas. Specialties include *ciambotto* (a tomato-based fish sauce for spaghetti, native to Bari and Foggia, where it is also called *ciabotta*); the Spanish-inspired *tiella* (baked layers of potatoes, rice, mussels, clams, or other seafood); spaghetti *alle cozze* (with a tomato-based sauce with mussels) or *alle vongole* (with clams); *zuppa di pesce* (fish soup); and *frutti di mare* (a salad of squid, octopus, and cuttlefish).

Regional dishes also use products from the countryside's wheat fields, olive groves, fig trees, and fragrant almond trees—as well as endless vineyards. Local pasta includes the ear-shaped *orecchiette,* served with a variety of sauces (the best-known is *con cime di rapa,* or with bitter, green turnip tops), and *maccheroni al forno* (a casserole of pasta, sausage, meatballs, and cheese); other specialties are *cicoria con fave* (purée of bitter greens and fava beans) and *bruschetta* (toasted crusty country bread brushed with olive oil and topped with chopped tomatoes or arugula). *Pugliese* breads, olive oil, and cheese (particularly the fresh mozzarella-like *buratta*) are superb. Bread is always served, as are *taralli,* small, hard yeast-dough rings made with flour, olive oil, and white wine and sometimes flavored with fennel or pepper (sweeter versions of *taralli,* frosted with sugar icing, are served for dessert). The fruit course is sometimes served with fennel or cucumbers.

Puglia's dessert grapes are the best in Italy, but the region is also one of the country's largest producers of wine. Among the excellent local wines are Castel del Monte, copertino, locorotondo, and salice salentino. The sweet muscato dessert wine comes from the Trani area.

The best times for a visit are spring and fall, when the mild Mediterranean climate is ideal. From the rest of Italy, the region is easy to reach by plane (flights to Bari or Brindisi from Milan and Rome), train (roughly 13 hours from Milan; seven from Rome), or car. Once there, however, seeing Puglia by car is a must—and a pleasure, as most roads and highways are in excellent condition.

The route outlined here begins in Bari and forms two loops, one leading north and the other south. The northern loop follows the Adriatic coast for a stretch, detours inland to a 13th-century castle, *Castel del Monte,* and returns to the coast to Trani and Barletta, before continuing north to the promontory of Gargano and its resorts. Then it turns inland to the Capitanata area and returns to Bari after a visit to Foggia. The southern loop also follows the coast for a stretch, then heads inland to visit Alberobello and the *trulli* district. It returns to the Adriatic via Ostuni and passes through Brindisi on the way to the lovely Baroque city of Lecce. Otranto, on the Adriatic side of the peninsula, and Gallipoli, on the Ionian side, are visited before the route winds up at Taranto and returns to Bari. Two warnings: First, museum hours and other schedules can change without warning or explanation; second, never leave anything in your car, not even in a locked trunk.

Except for the deluxe *Il Melograno* in Monopoli and the *Dei Trulli* in Alberobello—both of which run about $300 for a room for two—a double room per night in all other hotels listed as very expensive will cost $175 to $225; in a hotel listed as expensive, from $125 to $175; in one listed as moderate, from $75 to $125; and in an inexpensive hotel, $75 or less. All hotels feature private baths unless otherwise indicated. Dining in Puglia—three courses plus wine and service—will run $80 or more for two in an expensive restaurant; from $50 to $80 in a moderate place; and less than $50 in an inexpensive one. Fish- and seafood-based dining can increase your bill considerably. All restaurants are open for lunch and dinner unless otherwise noted. For each location, hotels and restaurants are listed alphabetically by price category.

Note that some sites of interest in Puglia close for a midday break, usually from noon or 12:30 PM to 4 or even 5 PM; we suggest calling ahead to check exact hours.

BARI The region's capital (pop. 500,000) is an important trade center and, with Brindisi, one of the two most important commercial ports on the lower Adriatic. Because of its enviable coastal position, it was subjected to countless invasions and foreign domination throughout history and was one of the chief embarkation ports for the Crusades. Possibly of Illyrian origin, it was colonized by the Greeks, then by the Romans (who called it Barium), and later ruled by Goths, Lombards, Byzantines, and Normans. Today it consists of two distinct parts. In its bustling modern section, built from the early 19th century on, streets follow a grid pattern. There are broad, palm-lined boulevards, fashionable shops (in the vicinity of Via Sparano), good hotels, and excellent restaurants. The contrast with its old section, Bari Vecchia, on a promontory between the old and new ports, is striking. In Bari Vecchia, narrow stone streets and tiny arched alleyways wind around pastel buildings, ancient churches, bountiful produce stands, and scenes of colorful local life. Newly washed laundry hangs above the streets, and elderly women dressed in black still scrub the steps in front of their homes. Most of the tales about the potential of danger while strolling in this historic quarter are, unfortunately, true. Tourists, usually identifiable at a glance, are always easy prey. Don't venture here at night; during the day, never visit alone, and leave your valuables at the hotel.

In the heart of Bari Vecchia, on Largo Elia, is the *Basilica di San Nicola* (Basilica of St. Nicholas; 6 Piazza Odegitria), Puglia's first Norman church and an outstanding example of Apulian-Romanesque architecture. It was built between 1087 and 1197 to house the bones of San Nicola, the city's patron saint, stolen from Asia Minor in 1807 by a group of Barese sailors. Bari's San Nicola is the very same St. Nicholas, a 4th-century Bishop of Myra (now in Turkey) who was known for his good deeds on behalf of poor children and who eventually evolved into Santa Claus. (The bones are underneath the altar in the crypt.) The church also is known for its 12th-century bishop's throne. It's open daily, with a long (12:30 to 4 PM) closing. Not far away is the 12th-century *Cattedrale* (Cathedral), also Apulian-Romanesque, and the *Castello Svevo* (Swabian Castle; Piazza Federico II di Svevia; no phone), begun by the Byzantines and Normans but significantly redesigned by Frederick II in the 13th century and later inhabited by Duchess Isabella of Aragon. The castle is open Mondays through Thursdays, with a short (1:30 to 2:30 PM) closing; no afternoon closing Fridays through Sundays; admission charge.

Bari has an art museum, the *Pinacoteca Provinciale* (*Palazzo della Provincia,* on Lungomare Nazario Sauro, the seaside promenade east of the center; phone: 80-334600). It is closed Mondays, and Tuesdays through Sundays after 1 PM; no admission charge. Each September the city hosts the *Fiera del Levante* (Levant Fair), southern Italy's most significant trade fair (and one of Europe's most important commercial events), to encourage trade between East and West. More traditional events include the *Sagra di San Nicola* (Feast of St. Nicholas) on May 7 and 8, when a statue of the saint is put on a boat and sent out to bless the sea (San Nicola is also the patron saint of sailors).

Note: Since Bari is a big city (after Naples, the largest in the south) with a thriving, sometimes unsavory, port, theft can be a real problem here. Leave nothing in your car, even when it's locked, and don't carry valuables.

For more information about sights in Bari, stop at the tourist information office (32/A Piazza Aldo Moro; phone: 80-524-2244 or 80-524-2361), near the train station. Puglia's main airport (phone: 80-538-2370) is about 6 miles (10 km) northwest of the city.

BEST EN ROUTE

Palace One of the city's finest hotels has 210 rooms (all with air conditioning), including seven deluxe suites. Also available are a restaurant, turndown service, and an English-speaking concierge. Conventions are its staple. Within easy walking distance of Bari Vecchia and the shops in the modern part of town, at 13 Via Lombardi, Bari (phone: 80-521-6551; fax: 80-521-1499). Very expensive.

Ai 2 Ghiottoni Very good seafood and Apulian specialties are served in modern surroundings. Try risotto *ai 2 ghiottoni* (with spinach, cream, ham, and parmesan cheese). Closed Sundays and the first two weeks of August. Reservations advised. Major credit cards accepted. 11/B Via Putignani, Bari (phone: 80-5232240). Expensive.

Grand Hotel e d'Oriente Reminiscent of 1950s-era hotels, this sprawling maze of 125 rooms has a few modern touches, including air conditioning and a restaurant. Renovations completed last year converted 35 of the rooms into mini-apartments. 32 Corso Cavour, Bari (phone: 80-524-4011; fax: 80-524-3914). Expensive.

Nuova Vecchia Bari Located in a charming area, this dining spot has a vaulted brick ceiling and elaborate antipasto tables; the *menù degustazione* includes local specialties, homemade desserts, and regional wines. Closed Fridays and Sunday dinner. Reservations advised. Major credit cards accepted. 47 Via Dante Alighieri, Bari (phone: 80-521-6496). Expensive.

La Pignata The two things you can count on here are an elegant atmosphere and superb food. Seafood risotto, spaghetti *alle vongole,* and regional favorites such as *orecchiette con cime di rapa* and *tiella* are among the choices. Closed Sunday dinner and August. Reservations advised. Major credit cards accepted. 173 Corso Vittorio Emanuele, Bari (phone: 80-523-2481). Expensive.

Residence di Villa Romanazzi-Carducci An attractive 18th-century villa, this place offers 89 elegant suites. More intimate than the *Palace,* although without a restaurant, it has a private park and pool and draws a chic clientele. A 15-minute walk to Bari Vecchia, at 326 Via Capruzzi, Bari (phone: 80-522-7400; fax: 80-536-0297). Expensive.

Al Sorso Preferito This eatery is known for its seafood specialties, wide variety of antipasti, and rustic charm. Closed Sundays. Reservations advised. Major credit cards accepted. 46 Via Nicola de Nicolò, Bari (phone: 80-523-5747). Expensive to moderate.

Da Cesare Owing to its relaxed atmosphere and wide range of excellent antipasti, this is a favorite spot. All food is cooked to order. After dinner, try an *amaro,* poured from an ancient amphora. Closed Tuesdays and late August. Reservations unnecessary. Major credit cards accepted. Near the station at 154 Corso Cavour, Bari (phone: 80-524-2486). Moderate.

En Route from Bari Drive northwest for 14 miles (22 km) along S16 (the Adriatica Hwy.) past silvery green olive groves and a succession of vineyards. At Molfetta, a charming town with an old port and a Romanesque cathedral that has three domes and two bell towers, turn inland, continuing 7½ miles (12 km) through Terlizzi and Ruvo di Puglia. Here the landscape is made up mostly of low hills, typical of the Murge area of central Puglia, and vast fields of golden wheat. At Ruvo di Puglia (which has a fine 13th-century cathedral), pick up S170. In about 11 miles (18 km) the road leads to Masseria Castello, where there is a turnoff (marked S179 "Dir A") for *Castel del Monte,* one of the region's primary landmarks.

CASTEL DEL MONTE In an isolated position on the top of a hill stands one of Puglia's architectural masterpieces and one of the finest (and most unique) castles in Italy, if not Europe. It was built by Frederick II of Swabia between 1240 and 1250, some say as a prison, and was later used as a hunting lodge, but no one knows the real reason for its construction. Astronomical, astrological, and mathematical theories abound—it is sort of an Italian *Stonehenge.* A perfect octagon, with eight corner towers and eight trapezoidal rooms on each floor, it is built of locally quarried granite called *pietra di Trani.* The pale, champagne-colored structure—one of the earliest and purest Gothic buildings in southern Italy—was once full of sculptures, its walls faced with marble, but most of its decoration was lost by the 18th century, when the building was more or less abandoned. The windows of the castle, which is fully restored, afford a good view of the Tavoliere and surrounding Murge hills. It's open daily April through September; closed after 1 PM October through March; admission charge (no phone).

BEST EN ROUTE

Ostello di Federico Despite its unrivaled and seemingly touristy position at the foot of the castle, this is the perfect spot for a wonderful meal of *pugliese* specialties. There is a pizzeria with a brick wood-burning oven and a more formal dining room that overlooks the castle, both serving homemade fare. Or enjoy a light snack or fresh lemonade on the pine-shaded terrace. Closed Mondays, January, and November. Reservations advised on weekends. No credit cards accepted. *Castel del Monte* (phone/fax: 883-569877). Moderate.

Vecchia Masseria If the *Ostello di Federico* is full, this restaurant is the only alternative in the immediate area. Housed in a *masseria* (farmhouse) a mile (1.6 km) south of the castle (back at the turnoff for Minervino), it provides a delightful ambience, even though it is inevitably filled with tourists. Order a sampling of several kinds of pasta, followed by *spiedini misto carne* (a shish kebab of lamb, veal, sausage, and pork). Castel del Monte (white, red, or rosé) is the appropriate wine. There also are 20 basic guestrooms, a pool, and tennis courts. Closed Wednesdays, except in high season, and most of January. Reservations unnecessary. No credit cards accepted. Km 22, S170, *Castel del Monte* (phone: 883-569860; fax: 883-24008). Restaurant, moderate; hotel, inexpensive.

En Route from Castel del Monte Return to the coast on S170 north for 10½ miles (17 km) to Andria, then detour northeast to Trani, a 45-minute drive from *Castel del Monte.*

TRANI Trani gained considerable importance in the 12th century, when Frederick II established his tribunal here. The approach to this coastal town runs through vineyard after vineyard of the moscato (muscat) grape used to make the sweet dessert wine for which Trani is famous. Also famous is Trani's exquisite 11th- to 13th-century Apulian-Romanesque cathedral, built of the pale stone called Trani marble. Best seen at sunset, the enormous cathedral, a splendidly off-white building against a backdrop of glistening deep blue sea, is dedicated to San Nicola Pellegrino, a Greek who settled in Trani because he found its inhabitants to be the friendliest in the area—a reputation still enjoyed today. Its bell tower is set on an arch, with the number of windows increasing as it rises. The cathedral's extraordinary bronze doors (ca. 1180), reflecting Byzantine influence, are by Barisano da Trani (who also cast the doors of the *Duomo* at Ravello and the one at Monreale, outside Palermo). Inside, this remarkable church is actually three churches on separate levels: The very old (perhaps 7th-century) *Chiesa di Santa Maria,* on which the main church was built, is reached through the crypt, and under it is the still older *Ipogeo di San Leucio.* The surrounding medieval quarter also is of interest, and the town's charming port has become something of a Riviera-style hideaway for the yachting set. Its lovely public gardens offer a good view of the marina. The tourist office is at Piazza della Repubblica (phone: 883-43295).

La Darsena Almost toppling into the port, this tiny spot is a must for lovers of romantic places, as well as for those who appreciate good food. The menu features fish and seafood, all imaginatively prepared. Closed Mondays. Reservations advised. Major credit cards accepted. 98 Via Statuti Marittimi, Trani (phone: 883-47333). Expensive.

L'Antica Cattedrale Across from the cathedral, this terrace restaurant serves a variety of pizza, grilled meat, and fish against a brilliant backdrop of sea. The piano bar makes it a popular spot with locals. Closed Mondays. Reservations advised on weekends. Major credit cards accepted. 2 Piazza Archivio, Trani (phone: 883-586568). Moderate.

Royal This comfortable, air conditioned, 46-room hotel is in the center of town, near the train station. Its decent restaurant opens onto a delightful, almost tropical courtyard in summer. 29 Via de' Robertis, Trani (phone: 883-588777; fax: 883-582224). Moderate.

Lucy With eight no-frills rooms, this simple hostelry near the public gardens enjoys a unique position by the port. No restaurant. 11 Piazza Plebiscito, Trani (phone: 883-41022). Inexpensive.

En Route from Trani Continue to Barletta, 8 miles (13 km) west along the coast road (SS16).

BARLETTA This port city is best known for the famous Disfida di Barletta (Challenge of Barletta), a bloody battle between 13 Frenchmen and 13 Italians that took place on February 13, 1503. The context of the challenge was the struggle between the French and the Spanish for hegemony of the region (the Spanish won), and its immediate provocation was a disparaging remark made by a Frenchman regarding Italian courage. The Italians won the challenge. The *Cantina della Disfida* (1 Via Cialdini; no phone), the former wine tavern where the challenge actually took place, is closed after 1 PM; no admission charge. Barletta's main attraction, however, the *Colosso* (Colossus), predates this incident. It is a 16-foot-tall bronze statue of a Byzantine emperor (exactly which one is not certain); cast in the 4th century, it is thought to be the finest piece of its type from ancient times. It once stood in Constantinople and was, along with the four famous bronze horses now in *St. Mark's Basilica* in Venice, part of the booty the Venetians took when they sacked the city in the early 13th century. After a shipwreck, the *Colosso* was abandoned on the shores of Barletta. It now stands at the corner of Corso Vittorio Emanuele and Corso Garibaldi, next to the 13th-century *Chiesa di San Sepolcro*. The city also has a lovely Romanesque cathedral by the port and an impressive restored 13th-century castle on the southern edge of town. Each year, on the last Sunday in July, a historical reenactment of the Disfida takes place with participants dressed in 16th-century costumes.

Il Bacco Slightly away from the Old Town, this restaurant with exquisite food and decor is one of the finest in Puglia. Local specialties are treated masterfully, particularly fresh pasta dishes and bounty from the sea. Closed Sundays, Mondays, and August. Reservations necessary. Major credit cards accepted. 10 Via Sipontina, Barletta (phone/fax: 883-57100). Expensive.

Il Brigantino This spacious, family-run, seaside resort restaurant is patronized by local businesspeople as well as tourists. It offers typical Apulian antipasti, such as *insalata di mare* (a salad of squid, octopus, and cuttlefish); *calzone pugliese* (a soft pizza bread stuffed with onions, olives, and anchovies); *cavatelli con fagioli* (pasta with beans); *fichi e prosciutto* (large, moist figs with prosciutto); and *scamorza alla griglia* (grilled scamorza cheese). Closed Wednesdays and January. Reservations advised on weekends. Major credit cards accepted. Litoranea di Levante, Barletta (phone: 883-533345). Moderate.

La Cave In a former bakery, located in the same large 12th-century palazzo where the notorious *disfida* took place, is this informal *enoteca* (wine bar). Diners can taste local wines and enjoy a light meal (the limited menu changes frequently). There are a few hearty pasta dishes, but the real draw is wine-induced bonhomie in the medieval atmosphere. Closed Thursday dinner. No reservations. No credit cards accepted. 17 Via Cialdini, Barletta (phone: 883-302614). Inexpensive.

En Route from Barletta Continue northwest for 48 miles (77 km), first on S16 and then on S159, through Margherita di Savoia and beyond, past mounds of sparkling salt beds and geometric patches of farmland. Stay on the coast road. As it approaches Manfredonia, the strikingly beautiful and rugged promontory of Gargano appears. Farther along, the charming town of Mattinata is a worthy stop for its winding streets and excellent restaurants with spectacular views. The tourist office (5 Piazza Roma; no phone) can arrange trips to grottoes and donkey rides in the surrounding craggy hills of olive trees. The town's most unusual feature, perhaps, is its pharmacy: Dr. Matteo Sansone, an antiquities expert, dispenses Band-Aids and aspirin in a drugstore museum, *Farmacia Sansone* (9 Via d'Azeglio; phone: 881-4170), filled with locally collected Greek stelae, holy water fonts, busts, paintings, and a lifetime supply of curios. Contact the tourist office for hours, which vary; admission chrage. From Mattinata, the winding S89, also known as the Garganica, climbs for 36 miles (58 km) high into the coastal mountains, which eventually soar to over 3,000 feet—affording dazzling panoramas of the dramatic blue-green Adriatic and its craggy, white-rock outline. The road descends to the sea at the ancient town of Vieste. Alternatively, keep on the somewhat quicker coast road (26 miles/42 km), which leads to Vieste via Pugnochiuso.

Apeneste Attractive, modern, and simple, this 26-room hotel has air conditioning, tennis courts, a pool, a private beach 1 mile (1.6 km) away, and a discotheque. Its excellent restaurant, *La Rucola,* has won many awards. Half board required in high season. Open year-round. 3 Piazza Turati, Mattinata (phone: 884-4743; fax: 884-4341). Moderate.

Papone Housed in a sparkling fresh 18th-century olive press factory, this exceptional restaurant features homemade pasta, fresh fish, and roast meat dishes. There is alfresco dining in warm weather. Closed Mondays from October through June 15, and November. Reservations unnecessary. No credit cards accepted. 89N Strada Statale, Km 144, Mattinata (phone: 884-4749). Moderate.

VIESTE Set on a rocky outcropping at the far end of the Gargano, this onetime fishing village has become the area's chief resort town. Its old quarter, a spill of whitewashed houses and narrow step streets, reaches out along a small peninsula, with an old cathedral and a Swabian castle (built by Frederick II) perched on a cliff overlooking the sea.

Although Vieste is surrounded by beaches, its southern (or eastern) side is especially favored. Just at the edge of town, marked by the giant rock called the Pizzomunno, the long, wide Castello Beach begins, and some 14 miles (22 km) along the coast on this same side is the huge resort complex of Pugnochiuso, set on a small, picturesque bay.

Use Vieste or Pugnochiuso as a base for exploring the Gargano area. Not to be missed is the spectacular coastal drive north and west around the promontory to the villages of Peschici and Rodi Garganico, considered one of the most naturally scenic drives in all of Italy. From Rodi Garganico, as well as from Vieste and Pugnochiuso, day ferries travel to the Isole Tremiti, a trio of rocky islands (San Domino, San Nicola, and Capraia) with beaches, historic ruins, and gorgeous views, off the northern coast of Gargano (a three- to four-hour trip from Vieste or Pugnochiuso, considerably shorter from Rodi or Peschici). Departures are infrequent in winter, and accommodations here are very limited. In the Gargano interior, the shady, tranquil *Foresta Umbra* is a good place to hike. For more information, see *Take a Hike: Walking Through Italy* in DIVERSIONS. The tourist office is located in the central Piazza Kennedy (phone: 884-708806; fax: 884-707138).

Pizzomunno Vieste Palace One of Italy's most prestigious beach hotels, this full-service 183-room resort is on its own parkland. It has luxurious accommodations, a stretch of private sandy beach, facilities for a full range of water sports, three tennis courts, and two pools. Its dining room serves excellent regional specialties—try the *agnello al forno* (roast lamb) or fresh seafood.

There also is a fitness and beauty center, a disco/piano bar, and a theater. Open *Easter* through September. Half board mandatory in high season. Spiaggia di Pizzomunno, Vieste del Gargano (phone: 884-708741; fax: 884-707325). Very expensive.

Pugnochiuso Surrounded by pine woods, this lovely resort complex on the coast south of Vieste is a village unto itself, containing two beachfront hotels— *Albergo del Faro* and *Albergo degli Ulivi*—with more than 400 rooms, as well as bungalows and cottages. Amenities include two pools (one Olympic-size), tennis courts, a gym, sailing and water skiing facilities, a theater, a nightclub, a bank, boutiques, a travel agency, and five restaurants. Minimum one-week stay required during high season; full board obligatory. Open from *Easter* to mid-October. Centro Vacanze di Pugnochiuso (phone: 884-709011; fax: 884-709017). Very expensive.

San Michele One of the few good restaurants in town serves both local dishes and seafood, including charbroiled fish. There is alfresco dining in warm weather. Closed Thursdays and January 7 to mid-March. Reservations advised, especially on weekends. Major credit cards accepted. 72 Viale XXIV Maggio, Vieste (phone: 884-708143). Expensive.

Portonuovo Adorned with the works of local artists, it features well-prepared, exceptionally fresh food made from homegrown ingredients. Closed Mondays. Reservations unnecessary. Visa accepted. Lama le Canne, Villagio Olivia, Vieste (phone: 884-700905). Moderate.

En Route from Vieste Take S89 west for several miles, and pick up S528 inland (alternatively, pick up S528 by turning off the coastal drive at Valazzo, between Peschici—where the views are unparalleled—and Rodi Garganico, and driving inland past Vico del Gargano). The road leads through the *Foresta Umbra* to S272, where a turn to the east along a number of hairpin curves leads to Monte Sant'Angelo; a turn to the west, to San Giovanni Rotondo.

MONTE SANT'ANGELO This is the highest town of the Gargano—on a clear day you can see as far as Bari—and an important place for religious pilgrimages. According to tradition, the Archangel Michael (for whom the town is named) appeared here more than once in the late 5th century (to a bishop, according to one story, to shepherds, according to another), leaving behind either a footprint or a red cloak (again, depending on the legend) but certainly enough of an impression for a shrine to be built. The resulting *Santuario di San Michele* (Sanctuary of St. Michael) was especially well known during the Crusades, when the Gargano (particularly the nearby town of Manfredonia, the embarkation point for Crusaders) was a way station en route to the Holy Land. At the edge of town, the sanctuary is entered through impressive bronze doors with 24 illustrated panels cast in

Constantinople in 1076. Across from it is the so-called *Tomba di Rotari* (Tomb of Rotharis), which was built in the 12th century, most likely as a baptistry. Perhaps more interesting is the multilevel medieval town itself, which remains unchanged despite masses of tourists and pilgrims. Surrounded by hollow caves, prickly-pear cactus, and pines, it offers splendid panoramas of chalk-white, lonely countryside. The town also has a castle, originally Norman, that was enlarged by the Swabians and the Aragonese.

SAN GIOVANNI ROTONDO Inland from Monte Sant'Angelo, this is another popular place of pilgrimage, although considerably less picturesque than Monte Sant'Angelo. It gained its status only in the 20th century as the result of its association with Padre Pio, the Capuchin monk who received the stigmata, performed miracles for the sick, lived in the local monastery, and is now buried next door in the crypt of *Chiesa di Santa Maria delle Grazie*. Visitors can see his room and the place where in 1918 he received the stigmata that he bore until his death in 1968. The yearly number of visitors (now about three million) may increase greatly if the beatified Padre Pio is canonized, as rumors from Rome imply.

There are ambitious plans to construct an enormous church here that would seat 10,000. The eminent architect Renzo Piano, most recently associated with Genoa's *Columbus 1992* celebration, intends to build it in the form of a seashell with ultra-sophisticated acoustics. If the plans get beyond the drawing-board stage, the church is projected to be completed by the year 2000.

En Route from San Giovanni Rotondo Leave Gargano via S273 south and turn onto S89, heading inland to Foggia, 25 miles (40 km) from San Giovanni Rotondo.

FOGGIA Capitanata's capital city, in the center of the Tavoliere, was chosen by Frederick II as his residence and was also a favorite of the Angevins and the Aragonese. The city suffered an earthquake in 1731 and was heavily bombed during World War II, but its beautiful 12th-century *Cattedrale della Madonna delle Sette Vele* (Cathedral of the Madonna of the Seven Veils; Piazza Duomo), largely rebuilt in the 18th century and the largest in the province, is worth a visit. It's open daily, with a long (noon to 5 PM) closing. The *Museo Civico* (2 Piazza Negri; phone: 881-26245) is housed in a building sporting an arch that is the only remnant of Frederick II's 13th-century palace; it contains fascinating artifacts and archaeological background on the area. It's closed Saturdays; Mondays, Wednesdays through Fridays, and Sundays after 1 PM; and Tuesdays for a long (1 to 4 PM) break; no admission charge. The tourist office is at 17 Via E. Perrone (phone: 881-723650).

Lucera, 12 miles (19 km) west of Foggia on S19, makes an interesting excursion. On one side of this pre-Roman village is one of the oldest known Roman amphitheaters, dating from the 1st century BC. On the other side, on a hill at the edge of the Tavoliere, is a superb castle, comprising a fortress built by Frederick II in 1233 and a surrounding pentagonal wall built by Charles I of Anjou in the late 13th century. The Swabian structure is virtually dwarfed by the Angevin wall, nearly a kilometer in circumference and articulated with 24 defense towers. The town's strikingly simple Gothic *Duomo* is an Angevin monument from the early 14th century.

BEST EN ROUTE

Cicolella The town's best accommodations and food can be had at this 93-room hotel in the center of Foggia. The well-known restaurant serves exceptionally prepared regional specialties—try the homemade *troccoli* (a local pasta) or *agnello arrosto* (roast lamb)—as well as local wines, such as torre quarto rosso, a fine red. The hotel has another, equally good restaurant in town (on Via Bari), bearing the same name. Restaurant closed Sundays, two weeks in August, and two weeks at *Christmas*. Reservations advised. Major credit cards accepted. 60 Viale XXIV Maggio, Foggia (phone: 881-688890; fax: 881-678984). Hotel, expensive; restaurant, moderate.

En Route from Foggia Return to Bari by A14 (80 miles/129 km), and proceed beyond the city to the *trulli* district and the Salento. Mola di Bari, a lovely fishing village with both an ancient town and a modern quarter, a Romanesque cathedral, and an Angevin castle, is 13 miles (21 km) south of Bari along the coastal S16. The highlight of its three-day *Sagra del Polpo* (Octopus Festival), held each July, is octopus prepared a hundred different ways. The town is also famous for a local variation of lasagna, prepared with anchovies, almonds, and basil and named after its patron saint, San Giuseppe. Continue on the coastal road for 14½ miles (23 km) to Monopoli.

MONOPOLI Here, centuries-old fortified farmhouses, known as *vecchie masserie,* are being converted into restaurants with lodgings and facilities for small conferences. This delightful town of green-shuttered windows and churches includes a fine Romanesque cathedral that houses a statue of the Madonna della Madia, who, legend tells, arrived in Monopoli on a raft in the 12th century. There is also a castle that looks out to sea and a picturesque port that once bustled with trade to the East. A short distance up the coast is Polignano, sun-bleached and perched atop promontories riddled with caves.

BEST EN ROUTE

Il Melograno Named after the pomegranate trees that complement the flowering bougainvillea, cacti, and citrus trees adorning the open courtyards and whitewashed walls of this 16th-century farmhouse, this is Puglia's most elegant lodging establishment—and one of its most expensive. Antiques and rugs grace the building, which houses 36 rooms (eight with Jacuzzis) and a restaurant. Amenities include a spa, tennis courts, a pool, and shuttle service to a nearby private beach. Its location is perfect for interesting day trips, which the staff will gladly help to plan. Open March through January. Contrada Torricella, Monopoli (phone: 80-690-9030; fax: 80-747908). Very expensive.

Castellinaria This tasteful, hacienda-style resort stretches along the sea. It offers 32 air conditioned rooms, water sports, a private beach, and a lovely terrace restaurant. Closed November 5 through December 6. S16, Cala San Giovanni, Polignano a Mare (phone/fax: 80-740233). Moderate.

Grotta Palazzese The 20 air conditioned rooms here sit atop a rocky cliff, but the real treat is the summer dining below, in an enormous natural grotto with the sea on one side and a rushing torrent on the other. The menu includes very good fresh seafood and excellent pasta. Open daily. Reservations advised in high season. Major credit cards accepted. On the coast between Mola di Bari and Monopoli, at 59 Via Narciso, Polignano a Mare (phone: 80-740677; fax: 80-740767). Hotel, moderate; restaurant, expensive.

Villa Meo-Evoli A Venetian-style villa has been reincarnated as a delightful restaurant that serves Apulian and continental fare. Garden paths and dramatic statues make for pleasant strolling. Closed Tuesdays. Reservations advised. No credit cards accepted. Strada Provinciale per Conversano, Km 6.5, Contrada Cozzana, Monopoli (phone: 80-803052). Moderate.

En Route from Monopoli Turn inland on S377 to Castellana Grotte, famous for its stalactite caves, some of the most spectacular in Europe. These are a little over a mile (1.6 km) southwest of town, and their fantastic stalactite, stalagmite, and alabaster flower formations can be visited in one- or two-hour guided tours. The pièce de résistance, the Caverna (or Grotta) Bianca, figures only on the two-hour tour. Tours in English are offered daily, mornings and afternoons in summer, mornings only off-season; admission charge. From Castellana, continue 4 miles (6 km) to Putignano, a small town well known for its late winter *Carnevale* celebration, the largest in southern Italy; parades take place the three Sundays before *Ash Wednesday* and on *Shrove Tuesday.* From Putignano, turn east on S172, following this scenic road 8 miles (13 km) to Alberobello.

ALBEROBELLO This unique village has more than a thousand of the whitewashed conical stone dwellings—*trulli*—characteristic of this part of Puglia. The all-white Zona Monumentale (Monumental Zone) is full of old "urban" *trulli*, attached and semidetached in clusters or lining the narrow streets. Many still are inhabited, whereas others serve as shops selling local crafts, handwoven items, regional wines, and foods. The most famous *trullo* is the 50-foot-high, two-story *trullo sovrano,* but the town also has a modern *trullo* church, *Sant'Antonio,* and a *trullo* hotel. And if you'd like to take a miniature *trullo* home with you, stop in the shop of Giuseppe Maffei (741 Via

Duca d'Aosta; phone: 80-9325). The tourist office (Piazza del Popolo; phone: 80-721916) has information on the town and on rentals of authentic, renovated *trulli* in town or in the country that sleep from two to eight people. Some have kitchens, most are inexpensive, and daily, weekly, and yearly rates are available.

BEST EN ROUTE

Dei Trulli In this hostelry are 20 air conditioned *trulli* of modern construction, each with a sitting room. For more information, see *Italy's Most Memorable Hostelries* in DIVERSIONS. Open year-round. 32 Via Cadore, Alberobello (phone: 80-932-3555; fax: 80-932-3560). Very expensive.

Il Poeta Contadino Considered the best in town, this dining spot has a distinctly medieval atmosphere, with vaulted stone ceilings and shadowy alcoves. Fine local specialties, fresh pasta, and mouth-watering fish and meat dishes are cooked according to Apulian traditions. It's a busy place, so arrive early. Closed Sunday dinner, Mondays (October through June), two weeks in mid-January, and June 28 to July 9. Reservations advised. Major credit cards accepted. 21 Via Indipendenza, Alberobello (phone: 80-721917). Expensive.

Trullo d'Oro The next best thing to staying in a *trullo* is having a meal in one. Despite a touristy location, the standards here are high in this authentic, tastefully restored, 400-year-old *trullo*. The Apulian dishes served may include *calzone di cipolla* (yeast bread stuffed with a sauce of onions, tomatoes, and capers), *orecchiette con ciceri* (ear-shaped pasta with chick-peas in broth), eggplant entrées, *cicoria con fave*, and fresh mozzarella. Closed Sunday dinner, Mondays (except in high season), and the last three weeks of January. Reservations advised. Major credit cards accepted. 27 Via Cavallotti, Alberobello (phone/fax: 80-721820). Expensive.

Il Guercio di Puglia Named for a local overlord who, legend has it, exercised his *droit du seigneur* with his subjects' brides on their wedding night, this restaurant has a pleasant outdoor terrace and specializes in regional cooking. Begin with one of the delicious and unusual starters, such as a strong ricotta cheese that resembles cheddar, and follow with one of the substantial entrées, such as *agnello con patate e lampazioni* (lamb with potatoes and wild baby onions). Closed Wednesdays, except in summer, and January. Reservations advised. Major credit cards accepted. 19 Largo Martellotta, Alberobello (phone: 80-721816). Moderate.

Colle del Solo This pleasant hotel has 20 rooms and five suites. It's on the edge of town, a few minutes' walk from the *trulli* zone, with a friendly staff and a decent alfresco restaurant. Open year-round. 63 Via Indipendenza, Albcrobello (phone/fax: 80-721370). Inexpensive.

En Route from Alberobello Head 5 miles (8 km) southeast on S172 to Locorotondo, a delightful village built on a circular plan. Stroll through the town's *centro storico,* well known for its impeccably cared for narrow streets, balconies, and 18th-century whitewashed homes. Just before the entrance to this historical corner is an open park-like esplanade overlooking the Valle d'Itria.

From Locorotondo, continue 4 miles (6 km) south to Martina Franca. The route passes through the Valle d'Itria, one of Italy's most unusual areas, where isolated *trulli* dot the landscape.

BEST EN ROUTE

Centro Storico Appropriately named, this small, authentic trattoria is a favorite among discerning locals. The changing menu follows the seasons, so take the waiters' knowledgeable suggestions—no one has been disappointed so far. Closed Wednesdays and two weeks in mid-March. No reservations. Major credit cards accepted. 6 Via Eroi di Dogali, Locorotondo (phone: 80-931-5473). Inexpensive.

MARTINA FRANCA Halfway between the Adriatic and Ionian coasts and on the highest point of the Murge, this enchanting town is built in an almost perfect circle. Its historic center has an overall 17th- and 18th-century look, and a walk along its narrow streets reveals Baroque and rococo mansions and balconies, sculpted festoons of flowers, little squares, and whitewashed cottages. The walls and ceilings of the massive 17th-century *Palazzo Ducale,* now the Town Hall and the only example of a building designed by Bernini in the entire south of Italy, were frescoed by a local painter, Domenico Carella, and its terrace commands views of the Valle d'Itria. The tourist office is at 37 Piazza Roma (phone: 80-705702).

BEST EN ROUTE

Dell'Erba This air conditioned hostelry has 50 rooms. Its pool and garden are a welcome respite during the summer, and its restaurant serves local specialties and draws a regular clientele. Open year-round. 1 Viale dei Cedri, Martina Franca (phone: 80-901055; fax: 80-901658). Moderate.

Allo Spiedo da Antonietta Weary, hungry travelers will find this a pleasant place to stop. The homemade pasta and mouth-watering starters alone make a detour here well worth the effort. Closed Wednesdays, except in high season. Reservations unnecessary. Visa accepted. 30 Via Virgilio, Martina Franca (phone: 80-706511). Inexpensive.

En Route from Martina Franca It's 6 miles (10 km) east past vineyards and well-kept *trulli* on S172 to Cisternino, a charming, chalk-white medieval hill town that is worth a stop. From there it is another 9 miles (14 km) east to Ostuni, probably the most remarkable town in Puglia (see below).

About 8 miles (13 km) south of either Cisternino or Ostuni is Ceglie Messapico, a small, whitewashed town that seems to have little to do with Italy. In fact, it was once a center and acropolis of the ancient Messapi, who populated much of the area and the Salento but left little trace except for defense walls, laid without mortar, and a still undeciphered alphabet. Like the Etruscans, the Messapi remain a mystery. Other centers were Miano, Manduria, Oria, and Mesagne—one of the most important—founded in 1600 as Messapia.

BEST EN ROUTE

Villa Cenci In the Valle d'Itria just outside Cisternino is this 30-room country inn housed in an old whitewashed *masseria* and adjoining *trulli*-turned–mini-apartments. The "country club" boasts a pool, gardens, and shaded patios; there's also a restaurant. It's a lovely spot to use as a base to explore the area if you can pull yourself away from the relaxed, family-oriented atmosphere. Open *Easter* through September. Via per Ceglie, Cisternino (phone/fax: 80-718208). Moderate.

OSTUNI From a distance across the plain, this town appears as a mirage of bleached-white buildings covering three hills, with a 15th-century Gothic cathedral at the highest point. Close up, the intricately detailed rose window over the church's central door comes into view, followed by the town's narrow streets spanned by graceful archways, its black wrought-iron balconies and lanterns, and its sparkling white buildings with green or turquoise shutters, all reminiscent of a Greek village. The main square, Piazza della Libertà, has the Baroque obelisk of *Sant'Oronzo* (who rescued Ostuni from a plague in the 17th century), a church, a bookstore, a small *caffè*, and a *gelateria* turning out fresh *granita di limone* (lemon ice). Hand-carved, painted whistles in bird and animal forms are Ostuni's specialty. They make wonderful mementos, and some are folk museum–quality. From Ostuni, it is 4 miles (6 km) to the coast and an unusually sandy beachfront, Marina di Ostuni, that extends for a few miles. The area produces a good dry white wine. The tourist office is in the *Palazzo Comunale* (Piazza Libertà; phone: 831-301268).

BEST EN ROUTE

RosaMarina An outstanding, attractive, modern resort, it's on the coast northwest of Ostuni proper. Its architecture is in the pure-white Moorish vein, and many of the 204 rooms open onto gardens. It has tennis courts, a pool, access to a private beach, and a restaurant serving fine regional specialties and local wines. Minimum stay one week (unless room availability permits a shorter stay). Half board is heavily encouraged, though not obligatory. Open June through September. Centro Vacanze Rosa Marina, Marina di Ostuni (phone: 831-970411; fax: 831-970411). Expensive.

3 Torri This sophisticated, comfortable restaurant serves regional food with panache. Closed Wednesdays. Reservations advised on weekends and in high season. Major credit cards accepted. Take S16 toward Brindisi to 294 Corso Vittorio Emanuele, Ostuni (phone: 831-338885). Moderate.

Vecchia Ostuni Almost every town in Puglia has a restaurant that calls itself *vecchio* (or *vecchia*), but few sport old traditions. The cook here gets up early to get the best that the market and fishing boats have to offer. Closed Tuesdays. Reservations advised. Major credit cards accepted. 9 Largo Lanza, Ostuni (phone: 831-973308). Moderate.

En Route from Ostuni Take S379 to Brindisi (20 miles/32 km from Marina di Ostuni); from there, follow S16, the Superstrada Brindisi-Lecce, another 25 miles (40 km) to Lecce. Brindisi is a major port and departure point for ferries to Greece, but the largely modern city offers little of interest to visitors. One of the two ancient Roman columns that marked the end of the Via Appia Antica (Appian Way) overlooks the port, near the house where Virgil died. The other column, which fell down in the 16th century, is reputed to be in Lecce.

LECCE In the center of the Salento Peninsula and known as the "Florence of the South" (something of a misnomer, as Lecce's heyday was during the Baroque—not the Renaissance—period), Lecce was first a Greek and then a Roman town. It reached its height of cultural and architectural development between the 16th and 18th centuries and is virtually brimming with fine examples of *barocco leccese,* an exuberant version of Baroque architecture that flourished here when Lecce was, after Naples, the most important city in the south—made possible not only by the local temperament but also by the soft local stone unique to Lecce, which can be easily worked but hardens when exposed to air, taking on a warm golden tone (it's used today only on building interiors). The building renaissance was due in large part to important religious institutions such as the Jesuits who threw their money and weight around as Lecce, rich in agriculture and banking, thrived. The city's most striking church, the *Basilica di Santa Croce*, built from the mid-16th to the mid-17th century, has a glorious renovated façade exploding with such Baroque detail as flora, fauna, monsters, and angels. The interior, with its 16 chapels, is in the more restrained style of the Renaissance. The basilica is open daily, with a long (noon to 5:30 PM) closing. The artist responsible for the most ornate parts of the *Santa Croce* façade was Lecce-born Giuseppe Zimbalo, one of the most spirited exponents of the local Baroque style. He was also responsible for the lower levels of the *Palazzo del Governo* next door, while his pupil, Giuseppe Cino, did the upper levels. Several blocks away, in Piazza del Duomo, is a wonderful Baroque ensemble consisting of the cathedral, redesigned by Zimbalo in the mid-17th century; its 210-foot bell tower; the *Palazzo del Vescovo* (Bishop's Palace), where Lecce's archbishop continues to live today; a seminary (more of Cino's work); and, in the seminary courtyard, a fantastic Baroque well embellished with rich clusters of fruit, garlands, flowers, and little *putti.* Leaving the Piazza del Duomo, walk along Via Palmieri (Lecce's "Aristocracy Row") to see and feel the festive spirit of the Baroque façade—a swarm of caryatids, wrought-iron balconies, and decorative figures lend a theatrical touch. Very few buildings in the historical district are higher than four stories, since the light-colored stone could not support any more.

At Piazza Sant'Oronzo, roughly equidistant from *Santa Croce* and Piazza del Duomo, are the most noteworthy of Lecce's Roman remains: a 25,000-seat ampitheater from the 1st century BC and one of two (alleged) remaining columns that marked the end of the Appian Way in Brindisi. Here it's called the *Colonna di Sant'Oronzo,* and it's topped with a statue of one of Lecce's three patron saints. In the same square, the 17th-century *Palazzo del Sedile* houses Lecce's tourist office (phone: 832-304443; fax: 832-314814).

Pâpier-maché, or *cartapesta,* is a centuries-old craft still practiced in Lecce, not only for tourist products but also for the fashioning and repair of religious reliquaries. To see it being made by professionals, go to Mario di Donfrancesco's workshop at 1 Via d'Amelio (phone: 832-642593). Every December, Bari hosts a world-renowned papier-mâché fair. The widest selection of local crafts (terra cotta, ceramics, textiles, and pâpier-maché) can be found at the government-sponsored *Mostra dell'Artigianato* (21 Via Rubichi; phone: 83-46758). Wine lovers might be interested in the town's best wine store, *Enoteca,* located next door (25 Via Rubichi; phone: 83-683205), where a wide selection of reds, whites, and rosés from the Salento area are for sale.

BEST EN ROUTE

President Catering primarily to businesspeople, this 150-room hotel is in the newer section of town, about a 10-minute walk from the old center. The decor is modern and functional, albeit somewhat bland, and the walls are a bit thin, but there's a good restaurant. 6 Via Salandra, Lecce (phone: 832-311881; fax: 832-594321). Expensive.

Cristal Newer and more contemporary than the *President,* this hotel isn't centrally located, though a jitney shuttles to and from the *centro storico.* Some of the 63 rooms have small kitchenettes; there's a tennis court, but no restaurant. 16 Via Marinosci, Lecce (phone: 832-372314; fax: 832-315109). Moderate.

Risorgimento Local politicians frequent this atmospheric hotel in a 19th-century palazzo near Piazza Sant'Oronzo. One of the very few lodgings in the historic quarter, it is old-fashioned and in need of a face-lift. The 57 rooms have been decorated on the dark side, but all are air conditioned. There is a restaurant. 19 Via Augusto Imperatore, Lecce (phone: 832-42125; fax: 832-51775). Moderate.

Il Satirello Out of town, this lovely 18th-century *masseria*-turned–stylish restaurant features heavy vaulted ceilings, a large flagstone patio, and hearty regional fare. Closed Tuesdays and the first week of July. Reservations advised on weekends. Major credit cards accepted. Km 9, Strada Provinciale Lecce–Torre Chianca (turn off at the *Tiziano* hotel; phone: 832-376121). Moderate.

I Tre Moschettieri Warm weather comes early to these parts, heralded by tables on the alfresco patio of this ever-popular restaurant. A menu that changes with the seasons guarantees simple *cucina rustica,* but the real draw is the dozens of varieties of pizza. Closed Mondays and the last two weeks of August. Reservations unnecessary. No credit cards accepted. 9 Via Paisiello, Lecce (phone: 832-308484). Moderate.

Gambero Rosso Ronzino de Santis's eatery has a local feel, with a TV set reigning in the corner. Self-service antipasti are the specialty, as are the pizza and homemade pasta. The grilled meat is reminiscent of Greece; also try the hot, Middle Eastern–style bread. Closed Thursdays. Reservations unnecessary. No credit cards accepted. 16 Via Brancaccio, Lecce (phone: 832-241569). Inexpensive.

En Route from Lecce Otranto and Gallipoli are south of Lecce on opposite coasts. To visit both, take S543 to the Adriatic and then the coast road, S611, southeast to Otranto; afterward, cut directly across the Salento Peninsula via S16 and S459 to Gallipoli, on the Ionian coast. Or explore either city from Lecce as a day trip: Otranto is 27 miles (43 km) away, and Gallipoli is 23 miles (37 km) away; take S101 south out of Lecce.

The area between Lecce and Otranto closely resembles parts of Greece, with olive trees, rocky outcrops, and stone huts. In fact, as in much of the Salento, Greek culture was present not only in relics from the past; it lives on in the very population. Some of the residents of nine towns—Calimera, Martignano, Sternatìa, Zollino, Soleto, Martano, Corigliano d'Otranto, Melpignano, and Castrignano de'Greci, many lying close to S16 southeast from Lecce to Máglie—still speak a dialect resembling ancient Greek, dating back to 7th-century (BC) settlers. Many locals keep alive some Greek culinary bents and folkloric traditions. To reach Otranto afterward, proceed to Máglie and follow S16, which turns east toward the coast. Or cut across to Otranto from the town of Martano.

OTRANTO A ferry departure point for Corfu, Italy's easternmost town is attractive, with its *centro storico* enclosed in the old walls. Much of the old section is undergoing a much-needed face-lift. An important town during

Puglia's Byzantine era, it was later ruled by the Normans and was sacked by the Turks in 1480. An amazing mosaic masterpiece covering the entire floor of Otranto's 11th-century *Cattedrale* (Cathedral), Puglia's largest, is especially worth the trip (enter through the crypt on the side). The work of a monk, Pantaleone, from 1163 to 1166, the mosaic features a tree of life with vivid depictions of biblical, mythological, and secular scenes, months of the year, animals, and more. Also fascinating are the 42 columns (no two alike) in the crypt of the cathedral and the *Cappella dei Martiri* (Chapel of the Martyrs), which houses the artistically stacked bones of 560 martyrs slaughtered by Turks (the custodian will gladly show you) because they refused to embrace Islam. The cathedral is open daily, with a long (noon to 4 PM) closing. Otranto also has a famous castle, begun by the Aragonese in 1485, after they ousted the Turks. The writer Horace Walpole set his novel *The Castle of Otranto* here, although he never actually saw the castle. In summer, ferries leave from here daily for the five-hour trip to the Greek island of Corfu. The local tourist office (*AAST*) is on 1 Via Rondachi (phone: 836-801436).

BEST EN ROUTE

Vecchia Otranto An attractive, rustic hideaway, it has a few outdoor tables where the food is both local and imaginative. Specialties include pasta served with dates and prawns and fresh fish cooked over the fire. Closed Mondays in off-season, and November. Reservations advised in summer and on weekends. Major credit cards accepted. 96 Corso Garibaldi, Otranto (phone: 836-801575). Expensive.

Albania This modern, air conditioned hotel has 10 rooms. Its restaurant serves seafood specialties, and there is alfresco dining in summer. Half board required in high season. Restaurant closed October through June. In the center of town, at 10 Via San Francesco di Paola, Otranto (phone: 836-801183). Inexpensive.

Taverna del Leone Reminiscent of Greece, this delightful taverna has checkered tablecloths and a loyal clientele. Good, simple local food is served in pleasant surroundings, and tables move outside in the summer. Open year-round. No reservations. No credit cards accepted. Corso Garibaldi, Otranto (no phone). Inexpensive.

En Route from Otranto From Otranto, you can cut inland directly west toward Gallipoli (see below), or head south to see the lovely eastern coastline for which Puglia is so well known. Leaving Otranto, follow the signs for Capo d'Otranto and Grotta dei Cervi. As you continue south, this curving road along the coastline becomes S173. Well-paved but only two lanes, it can be heavily trafficked during summer weekends and high season, but the pretty scenery makes it worthwhile. The winding road slices through rocky fields with stone walls and flocks of sheep on the right and the rugged shoreline and crystalline sea to the left. Between one resort town and the next, the only buildings visible are the occasional *masserie*—fortified farm-houses so typical of this area and often like walled-in villages within themselves. Lingering on the outskirts of the small beach towns are private villas of elaborate Moorish-inspired architecture that draw from the area's historic past.

The beaches and coves are alternately rocky and sandy, and many caves and grottoes indent this tract of coastline, once inhabited by prehistoric peoples whose extraordinary murals continue to fascinate anthropologists. The small town of Castro, 13 miles (21 km) farther south, and its satellite, Castro Marina, are busy resting places en route to Italy's easternmost point, Santa Maria di Leuca, famous for its sunsets.

BEST EN ROUTE

Panoramico Almost North African in style, this pretty 30-room, air conditioned hostelry with patios and balconies overlooking the sea is well known for its restaurant, with a mostly fish-based menu. After the homemade pasta, the catch of the day is rolled to your table. Have it *alla griglia* (grilled) or *al forno con patate* (oven-roasted with potatoes and sprinkled with herbs and olive oil). Half board is encouraged in August; given the price of fresh fish, however, it's a reasonable and delicious arrangement for hotel guests. Open year-round. Reservations advised on weekends. Major credit cards accepted. Via Panoramico, Castro Marina (phone: 836-97007; fax: 836-97865). Moderate.

GALLIPOLI This busy fishing port on the Ionian Sea was justly named Kallipolis ("Beautiful City") by the Greeks. It consists of a modern city on a spit of land pointing toward a rocky little island, on which lies the medieval quarter, with an ancient bridge connecting the two. The medieval quarter has narrow winding streets and white houses with iron balconies, giving it a Greek look even today, and it's circled by a panoramic road on the site of the old walls. There is a castle on the island at the bridge where a daily produce and fish market takes place. Begun by the Angevins (but altered in the 16th century), its ramparts seem to emerge directly from the sea. At the opposite end of the bridge is another of the town's attractions, the *Fontana Ellenistica,* a fountain dating from the town's Greek days, although it was rebuilt in the 16th century. The detailed façade of the town's 17th-century Baroque cathedral, dedicated to St. Agatha, shows the influence of Lecce. Gallipoli's old harbor is crowded with fishing boats. Crabs are prolific here, as are sponges; the latter can be picked up for a modest price at shops around the port. The shop-lined Corso Roma is closed to automobiles during high season and is a popular mile-long pedestrian thoroughfare—busiest before and after dinner.

Costa Brada Three miles (5 km) south of town along the coast, this property is well worth the drive. It has 78 pleasant, modern rooms (those on the fourth floor have Jacuzzis), two restaurants, two pools (outdoor and indoor), a fitness center, tennis courts, a nightclub, and a sandy beach. At least half board is obligatory in August. Open year-round. Litoranea per Santa Maria di Leuca, Gallipoli (phone: 833-22551; fax: 833-22555). Expensive.

Al Pescatore In a convenient location just past the bridge connecting the modern section of town with the *centro storico,* this popular place is known for its excellent fish-based menu. Diners choose the size and type of fish, which is then grilled to order. There also are a few inexpensive rooms upstairs. Closed Mondays in winter. Reservations advised. No credit cards accepted. 39 Riv. C. Colombo, Gallipoli (phone: 833-2673656). Expensive.

Joli Park In the center of town and a 10-minute walk from the old city, this comfortable, well-maintained, modern hotel has 90 rooms and a decent restaurant. Open year-round. 2 Via Lecce, Gallipoli (phone/fax: 833-263321). Moderate.

Marechiaro Wonderful seafood is served in a rustic seaside setting reached by a tiny, private bridge. Dine alfresco on the terrace overlooking the castle on dishes such as *zuppa di pesce alla gallipolina* (fish soup, Gallipoli-style). Closed Tuesdays from October through May. Reservations advised. Major credit cards accepted. Scoglio delle Uccolette, Lungomare Marconi, Gallipoli (phone: 833-266143). Moderate.

En Route from Gallipoli Follow the coast road north along the Gulf of Taranto, touching on tiny coastal spots such as Santa Maria al Bagno and Santa Caterina (5 and 6 miles/8 and 10 km, respectively, from Gallipoli), which are more reminiscent of North Africa than of anything Italian. At Santa Caterina the road detours slightly inland to make way for a nature preserve (accessible to pedestrians) before returning to Torre San Isodoro, 7 miles (11 km) on. It is around here and in nearby Porto Cesareo that one finds some of Puglia's most beautiful coves, where the clear water of the Ionian Sea ranges in hue from jade green to lapis blue. Not all of the beaches are open to the public, but those that are make wonderful summer rest or relaxation stops en route to Taranto.

BEST EN ROUTE

Riviera This modern establishment overlooking the sea is the newest and best along this stretch of coastal road. Guests can escape the summer heat in acres of cool, private pine forest, with a dip in the hotel's pool, or under an umbrella at the private, rocky beach across the road. All hundred rooms have terraces, half with ocean views, half overlooking the woods (some offer air conditioning at additional cost). The hotel prides itself on its restaurant, particularly the fresh fish, and half board is obligatory in August. Open June through September. Santa Maria al Bagno (phone: 833-573221; fax: 833-573024). Moderate.

La Pergola An excellent trattoria specializing in seafood, a stone's throw from the town's tiny gem of a beach. Egyptian owner Mario Ezzat blends North African dishes with local fare. The risotto *verde* (with a vegetable purée sauce) is especially good. Closed Tuesdays and November. Reservations advised in season and on weekends. No credit cards accepted. 5 Piazza Nardò, Santa Maria al Bagno (phone: 833-573008). Inexpensive.

TARANTO A city of ancient origins, Taranto was founded by the Spartans in 708 BC. Called Taras by the Greeks, it was a major center of Magna Graecia (in the 4th century, its population was 200,000), and its importance endured long after other Greek colonies had declined—it was not conquered by the Romans until the 3rd century BC. Ancient remains are sparse in today's Taranto, however; this is largely a modern, industrial city and a naval base that attracts little tourism. But its *Museo Nazionale* (National Museum; 1 Corso Umberto; phone: 99-432112), containing superb Greek statuary, pottery, and jewelry, is the second-most-prominent archaeological museum in southern Italy, after Naples. It's closed after 1:30 PM; admission charge.

Taranto does have a medieval city, which, as in Gallipoli, is on an island joined to the new city by a bridge. Both the Old and New Towns are sandwiched between an internal sea, the Mar Piccolo, and the larger Mar Grande, an extra scallop in the edge of the greater Gulf of Taranto. Given its special geography, it's hardly surprising that mussels, oysters, and other seafood are cultivated with great success. The city also is known for its waterside promenades and flowering parks, such as the Lungomare Vittorio Emanuele III along the Mar Grande and the *Villa Peripato,* with a terrace overlooking the Mar Piccolo (both in the New Town).

The *Duomo,* in the Old Town, built from the 10th to the 12th century, was redone again and again; its façade is Baroque, although traces of its original form remain in Byzantine-style mosaics and frescoes. In 1971, Gio Ponti, the late architect and urban developer, built another cathedral in the New Town. Since Taranto, like Bari, is a major port and attracts more than its share of thieves, don't leave anything valuable in your car, and don't carry much cash.

Several renowned *Holy Week* events take place in Taranto: On *Holy Thursday,* there is a procession of hooded penitents, and during *Good Friday's Procession of the Mysteries,* groups of statues depicting the Passion of Christ are paraded through the streets from church to church. The information office of the provincial tourist authority (*EPT*) is at 113 Corso Umberto (phone: 99-432392; fax: 99-432397).

Il Caffè Tastefully renovated, with a fashionable clientele, this is one of the best restaurant in town. The menu, which features international and local dishes, specializes in seafood. Closed Sunday dinner, Monday lunch, and two weeks in August. Reservations advised. Major credit cards accepted. 8 Via d'Aquino, Taranto (phone: 99-452-5097). Expensive.

Delfino This modern, air conditioned hostelry has 200 rooms—some with terraces overlooking the sea—a pool, a garden, and a commendable alfresco restaurant. 66 Viale Virgilio, Taranto (phone/fax: 99-3205). Expensive.

Milan Bar A casual *ristorante*/pizzeria in the heart of the New Town, it offers more than 15 delicious kinds of pizza. Specialties include *mitili* (mussel dishes; try them with spaghetti or stuffed and baked); *frittatas* (omelettes) made to your liking; and *fritto misto di mare* (lightly fried squid, octopus, cuttlefish, and shrimp). Don't leave without sampling the homemade gelato made with goat's milk. Closed Sundays and *Christmas* week. Reservations advised. No credit cards accepted. 49 Via Cesare Battisti, Taranto (phone: 99-362860). Moderate.

Plaza Offering 112 modern, air conditioned rooms, this hotel is conveniently located in the center of the New Town and around the corner from the bridge leading to the Old Town. 46 Via d'Aquino, Taranto (phone/fax: 99-490775). Moderate.

En Route from Taranto If time is short, pick up the autostrada (A14) to Bari, where connections can be made to various Italian cities. Otherwise take S7 to the turnoff for Castellaneta, and from there, A14 to Bari.

CASTELLANETA Hollywood buffs might not consider a visit to Puglia complete without a stop in this village, the birthplace of Rudolph Valentino (the house where he was born is at 114 Via Roma). Castellaneta is set dramatically high on a ravine, and its late-Gothic cathedral (in the center of the divided old quarter) was completely rebuilt in 18th-century Baroque style.

Basilicata and the Cilento

Basilicata is one of Italy's most wildly beautiful and mysterious areas. The smallest Italian region and one of the most ancient areas of human settlement in Europe, it forms the instep and ankle of Italy's boot, barely touching the Tyrhennian and Adriatic Seas at either end. In the Middle Ages, when Basilicata was known as Lucania, it also comprised much of southern Campania, including the Cilento Peninsula, which juts into the Tyrhennian Sea below Paestum.

Unlike most of Italy's south, the area largely has been spared the influence of the Mafia. As a result, rugged Basilicata has less crime and friendlier people, and at times it appears almost pristine when compared with other southern regions, such as Calabria. Tourism still is very much in its infancy, and many *lucani,* as the locals are called, continue to live their lives much as they did in the past. They also enjoy a beautiful and varied landscape, including some outstanding examples of Byzantine, Norman, and Baroque architecture—castles, churches, *sassi* (natural cave dwellings), and charming rustic farmsteads.

The Gulf of Policastro, on which the jewel-like town of Maratea is perched, arguably is one of Italy's finest and least spoiled coastlines. For more information, see *Italy's Best Beaches* in DIVERSIONS. The Cilento, although no longer part of Basilicata, is included here because of its proximity, fine beaches, and historical and cultural connections with the rest of the region.

Along the longer, flatter Ionian shore to the east, the impressive remains of the ancient Greek settlements of Heraclea (now Policoro) and Metapontum (now Metaponto), with houses, temples, and a sanctuary to the goddess Demeter, are a worthwhile stop for anyone interested in the distant past. Still protecting the land from erosion are the remains of the ancient forest of Policoro.

The inland scene is one of striking mountains, hills, deep gorges, lush meadows, clay ravines, lakes, rivers, fortified towns, and graceful, castellated homesteads called *masserie.* Wild nature reserves are common. In the Ionian hinterland the eerie town of Matera tells its prehistoric tale on the limestone uplands known as the Murge. The bizarre, lunar landscape of the *calanchi* (clay worn away by erosion) around Tursi and *argille* (as the locals refer to the stark terrain) farther inland will remind travelers of a semiarid desert. South of the Sinni Valley magnificent Monte Pollino, now principally a natural park, rises to over 7,600 feet. Farther north the Vulture region near Potenza—once brigand country—provides an alternative mountain holiday, complete with skiing in winter.

In the Middle Ages Lucania came to be called Basilicata, from *basilikos,* the Byzantine word for justice administrator. Several centuries later, in

1932, Mussolini sent the local government a telegram ordering that Basilicata once again be called Lucania. This was in keeping with the Fascist ideology of restoring Italy's regions to their ancient glory. In fact, Basilicata had no ancient glory—only a long history of sacrifice and submission. Always heavily taxed, during the Fascist years the peasant *lucani* were asked to dig still deeper. In 1947 the region returned to the name Basilicata.

Basilicata first came to Italy's attention in 1945 with the publication of the novel *Christ Stopped at Eboli*. Written by Carlo Levi, a medical school graduate and painter from Turin who had been exiled to Basilicata for his anti-Fascist views, it underlines the region's plight and celebrates the poignant humanity of its people. Steeped in realism, the book was a success in the salons of the north and drew attention to the area, sweeping away some national preconceptions about southern Italy. Unfortunately, however, negative images of the south still linger. And like most of the bottom of Italy's boot, Basilicata still is struggling, fairly unsuccessfully, to cling to the coattails of an ever-modernizing Europe.

Perhaps Levi, who grew to love Basilicata and to become its most famous adopted son (he is buried here), would have appreciated the irony of the region today—virtually untouched by mass tourism and big industry. One of the words most commonly used in Levi's book to describe the area is *incantevole* (enchanting, but eerily so). Basilicata's fascinating geological formations, such as Matera's unique *sassi*—many of which are occupied still—are much the same as they were 8,000 years ago. Human presence in Basilicata dates back some 300,000 years, making it one of the oldest populations in Europe. The original residents eventually integrated with settlers from Asia Minor who were versed in the working of copper. By 1,000 BC they had formed highly organized townships and trade links with the Mycenaeans. When the first Greek settlers arrived at Siris, near Policoro, two centuries later, they discovered a thriving community.

The *lucani,* warriors from northern Italy, arrived next, followed by the Romans, who used the region's Basento and Bradano River Valleys as a trade route to the Ionian Sea. Later, a large influx of settlers—Byzantines, Longobards, Normans, Swabians, and Angevins—left their mark.

Today it is not uncommon to find *lucani* who will tell you that Rome was responsible for the decline of Basilicata by allowing an important and sophisticated agricultural system, instituted nearly 3,000 years ago by the Greeks, to waste away. The Bourbons' rule of Naples from the mid-1700s also contributed to the region's difficulties—taxation reached an all-time high, attempted uprisings were common, and *brigantismo* (the term not only refers to highwaymen but also connotes a social phenomenon) was rampant. Social and economic conditions were so poor that it was not uncommon for the people to rob and often kill the *galantuomini* (gentlemen), whom they viewed as parasites. Eustachio Chit, called "Chitaridd," one of Basilicata's most celebrated turn-of-the-century *briganti,* was hunted for many years for the murders of dozens of people. After the police finally trapped and killed him, they sent his skull to Naples to be examined—to see "what made him tick."

Basilicata's winters are relatively mild; its summers, at times, unbearably hot. The best times to visit are September through November and May through July. In the spring (which comes early to Basilicata) the countryside is lush; in summer, however, it often is parched, though the barrenness has a beauty of its own.

This driving route begins at Maratea, the only town in Basilicata geared to tourism. From Naples take the A3 autostrada south. Exit at Lagonegro and take S585 to Maratea Castrocucco. Then head up the S18 coast road for 6 miles (10 km) to Maratea. Taking leave of Maratea and the Cilento—almost a lazy week's holiday in itself—head into the hills behind. From Lauria go east along the Sinni Valley, lying in the shadow of 7,620-foot Monte Pollino. The area is now a park, noted for its wild natural beauty and fauna—including wolves (who stay far from the main road). At either Francavilla or Senise, site of Lago di Monte Cotugno, a large artificial lake, detour to the hill town of San Paolo Albanese (settled by Albanians), or go directly to the Ionian Sea before heading north to Matera. North of Sant'Arcangelo are Aliano (Levi country) and Stigliano, center of the *argille* region. To the east is the *calanchi* district around Tursi. At the Ionian coast the road winds south to Policoro and north to Metaponto, with their Greek ruins, then veers inland to the Murge and Matera, via Ferrandina. The tour finishes at Matera.

The food of Basilicata takes its cue from its lingering peasant culture. Most meat dishes are made from pork, and salami is often spicy and red because of the addition of hot peppers—called *diavolicchio* (devilish). A favorite local dish, *capriata*, uses grains and beans grown in the region—barley, lentils, chick-peas, and beans—to produce a delicious vegetable stew. *Orecchiette*, small ear-shaped shells, reflecting the Apulian influence in much of Basilicata, is the most popular pasta. Meat often is cooked *in cartoccio* (in brown paper) to retain its moisture. Local cheeses include dried, hard ricotta, which often is very salty and used mainly for grating. Wine is predominantly red, full-bodied, strong, and almost always made from Apulian grapes.

For more information on the area, contact the *Assessorato Regionale al Turismo* (Via Anzio, Potenza 85100; phone: 971-332601; fax: 971-332630); the *Ufficio Informazioni* (4 Via Alianelli, Potenza 85100; phone: 971-21812); the *Ente Provinciale per il Turismo* (12 Via Cavour, Potenza 85100; phone: 971-411839; fax: 971-36196); or the *Azienda Autonoma Soggiorno e Turismo* in Maratea (see below).

Most of the hotels and restaurants in this area are open from *Easter* through September, although Maratea's tourist office (see below) can provide information about those open year-round. Maratea's accommodations can cost considerably more than those in other towns in Basilicata, but they still are quite inexpensive when compared with other resorts in Italy. In hotels rated as expensive, expect to pay $110 or more per night for a double room with breakfast; in those listed as moderate, from $55 to $100; and in inexpensive places, $50 or less. All hotels feature private baths unless otherwise indicated. Many seaside hotels encourage guests to take half board, though this rarely is obligatory. In an expensive restaurant expect to pay $50 or more for a dinner for two without wine; in a moderate one, $30 to $45; and in an inexpensive place, $30 or less. All restaurants are open for lunch and dinner unless otherwise noted. For each location hotels and restaurants are listed alphabetically by price category.

Note that some sites of interest in Basilicata close for a midday break, generally from noon or 1 PM to 2 or 3 PM; we suggest calling ahead to check exact hours.

MARATEA More than just a pretty resort, Maratea stretches along Basilicata's immaculate and tiny (barely 25 miles long) Tyrhennian coastline, with an explosion of emerald green waters, enchanting coves, sea caves, and strange and wonderful geological formations that date to the Pliocene Age. Maratea proper, a pristine and almost Greek-looking town hugging 2,000-foot Monte San Biagio, is set over the Gulf of Policastro, equidistant from the Calabrian and Campanian borders. The 70-foot-high statue of *Cristo Il Salvatore* (Christ the Redeemer), the guardian of the gulf, is perched on top of the mountain.

· Nestled below amid the lush profusion of an olive-green landscape, Maratea Porto, the town's port, is a winter haven for veteran sailors and beached fishing nets. In season it is filled with fishing vessels, and *caffè* tables spill onto the water's edge. There are hotels, restaurants, and bijou-like beaches in Maratea Porto, as well as among the coves that dot the coast from Castrocucco to Acquafredda. To the south, and near Calabria, cliffs and stalacmite caves—a snorkler's paradise—are the order of the day. To explore the many grottoes and secluded inlets, rent a small boat or join a group on a larger one. Most boats are available right on the beach; for more information, contact Maratea's tourist information office, the *Azienda Autonoma di Soggiorno e Turismo* (*AAST;* 32 Piazza Gesù, Santavenere Fiumicello; phone: 973-876908; fax: 973-876425), which is open daily. For port information, call 973-876050. For information on area campgrounds (which are open April through September), contact *Campeggio Maratea* (Castrocucco di Maratea; phone: 973-879097).

Thirty-five years ago, the area was virtually unknown. This anonymity ended in 1958, when Count Stefano Rivetti, an enterprising nobleman from the north, purchased one of the six old Spanish watchtowers (now a private residence) that line the coast. On an isolated point just north of the port he built the *Santavenere* hotel (see *Best en Route*), a hacienda-style resort, and started two textile firms nearby. Although "greater Maratea," as its collection of little resorts might be called, is now Basilicata's primary source of tourism, it still operates on a delightfully small scale. Even in high season little of the coast is invaded by bronzed bodies. Rather, it is largely populated by wild broom and rosemary bushes, pine, olive, fruit, and oak trees. Accordingly, prices are relatively low, the people friendly, and the food fresh.

Perched above on two levels, the town of Maratea is a cluster of red roofs, convents, churches, and a monastery with a fine, 16th-century courtyard. Explore the town, a haven of narrow alleyways lined with geraniums, wicker baskets, and copperwork for sale, or sit at the *caffè* tables in charming Piazza Buraglia. Atop Monte San Biagio is the *Santuario San Biagio,* an interesting medieval sanctuary that houses the remains of its namesake. One day a year, in the second week of May, those remains travel in a life-size silver reliquary to the lower town in a colorful procession replete with local shepherd bagpipers.

Maratea also boasts a fine cathedral (on Piazza del Duomo) whose campanile and tiled dome date from the Middle Ages. Inside is a notable 14th-century choir. In August the town is treated to a procession of collectors' antique cars and a *sagra del pesce,* a fish festival at which you can eat fresh local fish that is fried in giant pans down at the port.

Maratea is an ideal spot from which to explore some of the towns on the Cilento Peninsula, particularly Scario, Marina di Camerota, and Palinuro (see below). We recommend taking a boat to these villages, as the roads are difficult. You may also visit Capri by hydrofoil. For information on boats and hydrofoils, contact the *AAST* (see above).

BEST EN ROUTE

La Locanda delle Donne Monache In the *centro storico,* here are 29 rooms but no restaurant. 4 Via Carlo Mazzei, Maratea (phone: 973-877487; fax: 973-877687). Expensive.

Pianeta Maratea With 165 spotlessly clean rooms (10 of them suites), this modern complex offers all the usual amenities plus an excellent restaurant, a piano bar, a video disco, three pools, a beach, and three tennis courts. There also is a car park and patios with exceptional views. Open year-round. Santa Caterina, Maratea (phone: 973-876996; 800-223-5695; fax: 973-876385). Expensive.

Santavenere Basilicata's best has 44 tastefully decorated rooms and a dining room, set in a park on a private peninsula. For more details, see *Italy's Most Memorable Hostelries* in DIVERSIONS. Open year-round. Santavenere Fiumicello, Maratea (phone: 973-876910; fax: 973-877654). Expensive.

Taverna Rovita Small and full of character, this is the best restaurant in the region. The staff and owners put on nearly as good a show as does the kitchen. The fish crêpes are especially good, as are the desserts. Open daily. Reservations necessary. Major credit cards accepted. Via Rovita, *centro storico,* Maratea (phone: 973-876588). Expensive.

Za' Mariuccia Fish is the star of this family-run seaside establishment, and it's cooked the way the locals prefer—*alla griglia* (grilled with herbs and garlic). Closed November through April. Reservations advised in high season. Major credit cards accepted. Via Porto, Maratea Porto (phone: 973-876163). Expensive.

Bellavista Tables on the terrace here overlook the port. Specialties include *cavatelli alla pescatore* (pasta with seafood) and *spigola all'acqua pazza* (whitefish with tomato sauce). Open daily. Reservations advised. Major credit cards accepted. Via Profiti, Maratea Porto (phone: 973-876200). Moderate.

La Quercia Named after an old oak tree just outside the restaurant, this place is a favorite with locals because of its fine seafood. Closed mid-October to mid-April. Reservations advised. No credit cards accepted. On the coast road, Fiumicello, Maratea (phone: 973-876907). Moderate.

Villa Cheta Elite There are 17 rooms and a restaurant in this century-old, family-style villa. Guests have access to a delightful beach. Open April through September. Across the road from the entrance to the *Villa del Mare* (see below), at 24 Via Nazionale, Acquafredda, Maratea (phone: 973-878134/5; fax: 973-878135). Moderate.

Villa del Mare A delightful 75-room hillside hideaway, it offers fine views of the exquisite private cove below and a good restaurant. Open April through October. Via Nazionale, Acquafredda, Maratea (phone: 973-878007; fax: 973-878102). Moderate.

Il Piccolo Ranch Specialties served in this curious Italian log cabin include a variety of salami and fresh herbs and vegetables picked from the nearby hills. The antipasti are delicious, and owner Biagio Monterosso will top a pizza with almost anything—even wild asparagus. Open year-round. Reservations advised. No credit cards accepted. Near the *Pianeta Maratea* hotel in Santa Caterina, Maratea (phone: 973-870237). Moderate to inexpensive.

La Tana Many of the 20 comfortable rooms open onto the attractive garden, brimming with flowers and fruit trees. Each has a TV set and a telephone. An air conditioned restaurant, a bar, and a parking area round out the amenities. Open year-round. Contrada Castrocucco, Maratea (phone: 973-879000; fax: 973-871720). Inexpensive.

SCARIO With its picturesque marina and *lungomare* (boardwalk), this fishing village across the gulf from Maratea is worth a prolonged pause. Called L'Orecchio del Porco (The Pig's Ear) by the locals because of the port's shape, it was a simple fishermen's hamlet until the 1600s, when a church and an inn were built here. Set at the mouth of the verdant Bussento Valley, Scario's irregular coastline offers sandy beaches lined with caves and coves at every turn. The gaping-mouthed Grotta degli Uccelli (Bird's Grotto) is the most celebrated; another, the Grotta del Vitello, bears a prehistoric wall drawing of a calf. Many of the grottoes are reachable only by sea.

MARINA DI CAMEROTA The starting point of a lovely coast, this town is a pleasing blend of old and new. The area boasts some delightful bays, including a natural harbor, Porto Infreschi, that was used for fishing vessels until the 1700s.

PALINURO Watched over by the ancient *Castel della Molpa* and the Old Town of Centola, the marina of Palinuro sits next to the point of the same name and directly north of Marina di Camerota. Shaped like a great hook, it has beautiful beaches and coves, grottoes, towers, and a clear emerald sea. It's a beachcomber's and skin diver's haven, since important Paleolithic finds have been uncovered in many of its caves. A sandy beach, Spiaggia della Molpa, reached by climbing through olive groves, perhaps is the most remarkable. Strange prehistoric forms loom up at Scoglio del Coniglio (Rabbit Shoal) and at caves farther along, such as the Grotta delle Ossa (Grotto of Bones). Along the way is another magnificent beach, Buondormire.

Return to Maratea to enter the heartland of Basilicata.

BEST EN ROUTE

L'Approdo A clean, modest, and recently restored hotel set amid olive trees, it has 25 rooms (some with views of the gulf) and a restaurant. Open *Easter* through September. Via Rione Nuovo, Scario (phone: 974-986070 or 974-986513). Moderate.

Gabbiano On the beach are 37 air conditioned rooms, a pool, a restaurant, a bar, and parking. Open May through September. Corso Piscane, Palinuro (phone: 974-931155). Moderate.

Happy Village The best place to take advantage of the coast, this aptly named "tourist village," with its own quarter-mile of beachfront, has 230 beds in private *tukuls*—Polynesian-style huts—under olive trees. Each hut sleeps from two to six people. *Tukuls* with private baths are available, as is a restaurant (for hotel guests only) in a charming old villa on the premises. Open June through September. Marina di Camerota, on the coast road to Palinuro (phone: 974-932326). Moderate.

Saline Right on the beach, this establishment offers 51 rooms, each with a telephone, a TV set, and air conditioning. On the premises are tennis courts, a pool, a landscaped garden, and parking. Open mid-May through October. Via Saline, Palinuro (phone: 974-931112; fax: 974-931418). Moderate.

Baia delle Sirene Though this hotel with 72 air conditioned rooms isn't right on the beach (it's nearby), it has a pool, tennis courts, a restaurant, a bar, and parking. Via Sireni, Marina di Camerota (phone: 974-932122). Moderate to inexpensive.

La Conchiglia Modern yet cozy, this 24-room hotel with an attractive terrace and sea views is a stone's throw from the beach. The restaurant serves regional fare. Open *Easter* through September. Via Indipendenza, Palinuro (phone/fax: 974-931018). Inexpensive.

En Route from Maratea Take the unmarked road northeast 14 miles (22 km) to S19. Head north 2½ miles (4 km) to Lauria, stopping to investigate its *Collegio dell'Immacolata Concezione,* a small, 15th-century church with the remains of a fine cloister. From Lauria take S104 toward Senise, passing Latronico, a medieval village and thermal bath center in the Apennines, about 15½ miles (25 km) from Lauria. Stop off to see Latronico's early 18th-century *Chiesa Parrocchiale* before heading on to Episcopia. Shortly after, at Francavilla, a detour to the left, about 7 miles (11 km) inland, brings you to Chioramonte, an attractive town that has the remains of an early castle and walls, as well as some important palaces. An alternative route from Francavilla is to head south on S92 for about 8 miles (13 km) to San Paolo Albanese. Some 3,000 feet above sea level, San Paolo Albanese is a community of only 600 people whose origins date back to the 16th century, when Albanians migrated to the slopes of Monte Pollino. To this day significant traces of their language, religion, and brightly colored dress remain almost intact. The village, too, is almost as it existed 400 years ago.

In nearby San Costantino Albanese (also settled by Albanians) is the Byzantine-domed *Santuario della Santa Maria della Stella.* Inside is a nativity scene dating from 1699. The town celebrates an ancient custom on the second Sunday of May, when it burns elaborately constructed, life-size paper puppets, called *nusazit.* They depict a couple dressed in Albanian costume, together with two workers and a two-faced devil. The rite represents the sacredness of the family and of work and the danger of temptation. In mid-June in Terranova, farther up Monte Pollino (its peak borders Calabria), another ancient ritual takes place, with participants singing and dancing the tarantella around a felled tree.

Return to S104 and continue to Senise, following the shoreline of Lago di Monte Cotugno, an artificial lake. Turn left on S92 to S598, about 15½ miles (25 km) from Senise. Head west 5 miles (8 km) to Missanello, and then north on the small, unmarked roads up into the hills, 8 miles (13 km) to Aliano and another 12½ miles (20 km) toward Stigliano. This is Carlo Levi country, typified by the strange clay and rock foundations of the hills and ravines—the *argille* and *calanchi.* In Aliano visit Levi's house (where he was confined during the Fascist years), his tomb, and his collection of paintings. Continue to Stigliano, turning right just after the Sauro River.

Isola di Lauria This pleasant, air conditioned, 36-room hotel has a restaurant specializing in refined cooking—not a common occurrence in earthy Basilicata. Order the *risotto alla crema di crostacei* (risotto with a seafood cream sauce) and the *carne di maiale coperto in spezie* (pork smothered in herbs). There also are tennis courts. Open year-round. Piazza M. d'Ungheria, Lauria (phone: 973-823905; fax: 973-823962). Moderate.

Luna Rossa Genuine and very good mountain fare that has won acclaim down in the valley, including homemade pasta, spicy meat dishes, and excellent cheese. Closed Wednesdays. Reservations necessary, especially on weekends. No credit cards accepted. Via Marconi, Terranova di Pollino (phone: 973-932540). Inexpensive.

Ricciardi This hotel and restaurant are in the heart of mountainous Chioramonte, 7 miles (11 km) north of S104. All 38 well-decorated rooms have air conditioning; there's also a car park. Open year-round. 27 Via Calvario, Chioramonte (phone/fax: 973-571031). Inexpensive.

STIGLIANO Once a thriving mountain town, Stigliano acted as a fortress during the time of the Goths, and for centuries it was governed by the powerful Colonna family. In the 18th century it had a population of 7,000—the same as now—and briefly was the capital of the entire region. Stigliano has some excellent examples of art and architecture. Particularly fine is the interior of the *Chiesa Parrocchiale,* a cathedral with three naves and a wealth of ornate detail, especially the 16th-century polyptych, partly done by Simone da Firenze. The small *Chiesa di San Antonio* nearby has a splendid façade, the stone reworked in a diamond motif in 1763. Next to it is a bell tower, topped by an onion-shaped dome.

Trattoria Carmela Fornabaio The pasta is delicious, as is the traditional local fare, such as the spicy red salami, *lampascioni* (sweet baby onions), and tomatoes *sott'olio* (marinated in oil), stuffed with capers, parsley, and anchovies. The roast meat dishes are an added bonus. Closed Wednesdays. No reservations or credit cards accepted. 69 Via Cialdini, Stigliano (phone: 835-661437). Moderate to inexpensive.

En Route from Stigliano Proceed east on S103 about 29 miles (46 km) to S176. Turn left onto S176 and head 5 miles (8 km) north to Pisticci, a sun-baked town typical of the area for its characteristic tiered rows of houses. The *Chiesa Madre,* built on earlier ruins, dates to the 16th century. There also are the remains of a medieval castle. Return to S103 south; after 5 miles (8 km) turn left (southeast) onto S598 and drive 10½ miles (17 km) to reach the sea at Scanzano Ionico. Another worthwhile detour via S103 is to Tursi, 8 miles (13 km) inland, reached by continuing south from the junction of S103 and S598. Boasting its own bewitching *calanchi* nearby, the town is filled with caves that at one time were used as dwellings, and its notable churches include the *Rabatana* (its name comes from the Arabic word *rabad,* meaning town), which contains an early medieval crypt and frescoes. Nearby is the 11th- to 13th-century Norman cathedral of ancient Anglona, once part of one of the most impressive settlements in Basilicata and now reduced to rugged countryside after early invaders razed it to the ground. S103 from Stigliano toward the sea also passes a string of *masserie,* farmsteads fortified by nobles against invaders and, later on, by brigands; they provide an excellent example of vernacular architecture in Basilicata.

BEST EN ROUTE

Motel Agip Comfort, service, a pool, and a good restaurant come before warmth and charm at this 64-room hostelry, which is under new managenent. Open year-round. S407 at S176, Pisticci Inferiore (phone: 835-462007). Moderate.

THE METAPONTINO This coastal plain is an archaeological treasure trove (as well as an area that enjoys magnificent stretches of beach). The two principal sites are ancient Heraclea, at Policoro (about 2½ miles/4 km south of Scanzano on S106), and Metaponto (take S106 11 miles/18 km north of Scanzano).

Founded by Greeks in the 6th century BC, Heraclea became in less than 200 years the capital city for the entire area. By the Imperial Roman period it had already sunk into decline. Excavations have uncovered foundations of houses and one of the town's main roads, where kilns fired vases and votive statues. There also are remains of a temple and a sanctuary to Demeter, goddess of fertility. Heraclean finds are displayed in the *Museo Archeologico Nazionale* (Via Laveran, Metaponto Borgo; phone: 835-745327) near the sanctuary. It is closed after 1 PM; no admission charge. Also in Policoro stop off at the *Museo Nazionale della Siritide* (Via Colombo; phone: 835-972154), which houses a collection of 7th- to 5th-century BC antiquities from two nearby Greek colonies. It is closed Mondays and after 2 PM; admission charge.

Believed to be Magna Graecia's most magnificent city, ancient Metapontum was settled by Greeks from Sybaris, the city that gave meaning to the word "sybaritic," in the early 8th century BC. The town boasts a vast archaeological park and a theater dating from the 4th century BC. There are remains of four Greek temples, including the celebrated *Temple of Hera* (about 3 miles/5 km north of Metaponto), called the *Tavole Palatine* (Palatine Tables), from the 5th century BC. The remains—a partial floor and a dozen columns—mark the spot where Pythagoras taught mathematics. In later years knights from southern Italy assembled here before embarking on the Crusades. In Metaponto excavation finds are housed in the *Antiquario,* a museum near the *Tavole Palatine*. It's closed Sundays and Mondays, and Tuesdays through Saturdays for a midday break; no admission charge (phone: 835-745151).

Despite economic development programs, Metaponto's beaches remain untouched swaths of sand, sheltered by grassy dunes. A few concessions have been built, but they can be avoided altogether with ease.

Metaponto's useful tourist office (Viale delle Sirene; phone: 835-741933) has good maps of the area's archaeological sites. It's open daily from July through September; closed the rest of the year.

BEST EN ROUTE

Da Fifina Six miles (10 km) from Metaponto in Bernalda, this restaurant is considered the best in the area. The locals swear by the *pasta e fagioli* (pasta with beans) and the spaghetti *alle vongole veraci* (with clams). Closed Sundays. No reservations or credit cards accepted. Corso Umberto, Bernalda (phone: 835-743134). Moderate.

Kennedy All 33 large and lovely rooms at this seaside hotel have balconies; 23 have private baths. The service is quite good and there's restaurant, where full board is required in August. Viale Jonio, Lido di Metaponto, Bernalda (phone: 835-741832; phone/fax: 835-741960). Inexpensive.

Turismo Near the beach are 61 air conditioned rooms, a restaurant, and a bar. Full board required in August. Open April through September. 5 Viale delle Ninfe, Lido di Metaponto, Bernalda (phone: 835-741918; fax: 835-741917). Inexpensive.

En Route from the Metapontino Take S407 23 miles (37 km) to Ferrandina, a picturesque town of whitewashed dwellings. Turn right onto S7 and drive 19 miles (30 km) to Matera, passing the long, fish-shaped Lago di San Giuliano along the way. The lake is a wildlife reserve, where there is a *World Wildlife Fund* headquarters.

MATERA One of the most unusual towns in Italy, Matera has a particular form of dwelling, the *sasso*—a crude, whitewashed house whose inner rooms are prehistoric caves that gouge the town's northern flank. Often an entire family of eight would live in barely two rooms. The *sassi* have a long and fascinating history—from their use as practical dwellings in Paleolithic times and as a sanctuary for monks persecuted during the 9th century to their occupation by mystics and radicals during the late 1960s. In recent years the local government has restored many of the *sassi*, and an interesting mixture of artists, farmers, and idealists wishing to experience an ancient way of life has moved in.

Spiraling from top to bottom on two different rock faces are the Sasso Barisano and the Sasso Caveoso, which are separated by the Gravine, a vertiginous ravine dotted with whitewashed *chiese rupestre* (Greek-frescoed country cave churches). The churches were founded by Byzantine monks who settled here in the Middle Ages. Whether viewed from the Gravine or the Civita, the oldest part of town, the sight is unforgettable. The *sassi* amazed director and writer Pier Paolo Pasolini, who decided to film *The Gospel According to Matthew* in Matera, setting a trend for other filmmakers.

To best appreciate the *sassi* and *chiese rupestre,* go with a guide. Ask the tourist office (9 Via de Viti de Marco; phone: 835-221758 or 835-212488; fax: 835-333452) for a list of authorized guides. Two of the *chiese rupestre* worth visiting are the *Chiesa di Santa Lucia alla Malve* and the *Chiesa di Santa Maria d'Idrid*, both on Via Madonna della Virtù. Their beautiful Byzantine frescoes date from the 11th century.

The town also has some excellent examples of architecture dating from the Renaissance and Baroque periods, some important palazzi, and a number of fine churches. Most important is its Romanesque cathedral (on Piazza del Duomo), with its beautifully carved doorways and a fine rose window. It is perched on top of the ancient Civiltà rock—its interior incorporates part of a *sasso*. More elegant than its northern Italian contemporaries, the cathedral became more lavish through the years, from the original 13th-century construction to the magnificent 16th-century *Cappella dell'Annunziata* (Chapel of the Annunciation). It contains a fresco of the Madonna della Bruna, Matera's patron saint, which dates from the 12th century. The *Chiesa di San Giovanni Battista* (Church of St. John the Baptist; Via San Biagio) has an elaborate portal, but it is the graceful Gothic interior, with its high vaulting and elegant columns, that draws people here. Both churches are closed afternoons.

Every year at the end of June the Madonna is honored in one of the most famous festivals in the entire region—the *Festa di Santa Maria della Bruna*. As the sun sets tiny twinkling lights illuminate an effigy of the Madonna, drawn by mules in an elaborate cart and accompanied by townspeople dressed as medieval knights and clergy. After she is returned to the *Duomo,* the cart is torn to bits by the spectators who keep the pieces as relics. In summer Matera's beautiful outdoor theater in Piazza San Pietro Caveoso is the site of an arts festival, with nightly concerts, dance, and theater. The tourist office has the schedule of events, or pick one up outside the theater.

The *Museo Domenico Ridola* (Archaeological Museum; 24 Via Ridola; phone: 835-211239) houses important Greek objects that were found in the area, as well as examples from much earlier periods. The oldest completely intact oven in the world was found in a *sasso* in Matera. The museum is closed Mondays and after 2 PM; no admission charge.

Matera's cuisine includes *frittata di spaghetti* (well-spiced pasta fried in olive oil with anchovies, garlic, and eggs) and *pane di grano duro,* referred to jokingly as "eternal bread." Like the pasta, it is made with very hard wheat and keeps for weeks.

Trattoria Lucana Regional specialties such as *bocconcini alla Lucana* (mushrooms, olives, and tomato wrapped in thin meat slices) and *orecchiette alla materana* (small pasta with a vegetable sauce) are served here. Closed Sundays and September. Reservations advised. Major credit cards accepted. 48 Via Lucana, Matera (phone: 835-336117). Expensive to moderate.

Italia All 31 tastefully decorated rooms have views of the *sassi*. Great attention is paid to detail and comfort, and antiques fill the halls and public spaces. The hotel, which also has a restaurant, is built over caves, many of which now serve as party and meeting rooms. Open year-round. 5 Via Ridola, Matera (phone: 835-333561; fax: 835-330087). Moderate.

De Nicola This comfortable hotel has 83 large rooms, a fine restaurant, and a garage. Open year-round. 158 Via Nazionale, Matera (phone: 835-385111; fax: 835-385113). Moderate.

Il Terrazzino Perhaps the best way to soak in the hallowed atmosphere of the *sassi* at dusk is to sit on this restaurant's terrace and contemplate their ancient beginnings. Take a good look inside this eatery—this is what a modern *sasso* looks like. The pasta is homemade, the sauces delicious and simple, and the native bread excellent. Meat and fish are cooked in the traditional way. Closed Tuesdays. Reservations necessary for dining outside. No credit cards accepted. 7 Vico San Giuseppe, Matera (phone: 835-334119). Moderate.

Casino del Diavolo Good local fare and an attentive staff make this friendly trattoria a good place to stop. As everywhere in Basilicata (and Puglia as well), starters such as black olives and cheese or a dish made with sausage, hot and mild peppers, and tomatoes are de rigueur, and *lucani* serve them with pride. The roast meat is imaginatively prepared; the chef uses local herbs. Closed Tuesdays. Reservations advised on weekends. No credit cards accepted. Via Martella, Matera (phone: 835-261986). Inexpensive.

Calabria

Calabria, the southernmost portion of the Italian mainland—the "toe" of the Italian boot—once had an infamous reputation. For centuries, its mountains were home to bandits, its cities and villages prey to corrupt government and bloody personal feuds. The region still remains an economic backwater, overlooked by the broad sweep of industrialization that lost its momentum just south of Naples. But, until fairly recently, Calabria has also been neglected by the hordes of tourists that have made the rest of Italy one of Europe's star attractions. As a consequence, the air is clean, the richly forested mountains preserved, and the 450 miles of coastline some of the least developed along the Mediterranean. Government and tourism have intruded just enough in the last two decades or so to make Calabria a safe, hospitable place to visit.

The stretches of uncluttered sands, blessed with sunshine from April through October, are a temptation, but the "impressive and mystic" Calabria about which Stendhal wrote lies in the higher hinterlands. The Apennines, the chain of mountains that forms the backbone of the entire country, dominate Calabria. There are four main mountain groupings within the region, the Pollino, the Sila plateau, the Serre, and the Aspromonte—the last being the southernmost and the highest, touching 6,000 feet and blanketed by beech, pine, oak, chestnut, and ash.

Although three-quarters of Calabria is officially classified as "nonviable," historically the land has been the essential provider. And irrigation and water reclamation projects have immeasurably improved the lot of the farmer here during the past 30 years. In remote villages where the last remnants of a rapidly disappearing peasant culture can occasionally be found, rows of narrow terraces yield vegetables (eggplant, zucchini, peppers), fruits (melons, cherries, figs, and grapes for the area's wonderful wine), and grain. On the more fertile coastal plain are orange groves, almond trees, and rows of gnarled olive trees that look as if they date from the times when the ancient Greeks occupied this land.

Calabria's economic problems have been much greater than those of other regions of Italy. Despite government attempts since World War II to entice industry here, subsistence has been a struggle for its people, who are very different from the excitable, smiling image many foreigners have of southern Italians. Yet their misfortunes have done nothing to dampen their quiet dignity and the hospitality of which they are justly proud.

Thousands of years ago, the area that is now Calabria prospered as part of the expansion and surge of art and civilization known as Magna Graecia, but since that time it has been plagued by a succession of natural disasters and unhappy dominations. It is one of the most seismic zones in the Mediterranean, and earthquakes have consistently wiped out whole towns and most vestiges of the past. Slowly, dedicated archaeologists, backed by the Italian government, have begun to exhume fragments of Calabria's rich antiquity. Hardly a place exists that doesn't have its archaeological treasure, and the entire region is sometimes referred to as an open-air museum. Particularly exciting was the discovery of two 5th-century Greek statues—magnificent six-foot bronze warriors, trimmed with silver and copper—in coastal waters near Riace. (They are now on permanent display at the *Museo Nazionale* in Reggio di Calabria.) The remains of what might well be the oldest synagogue in Europe, thought to have been built during the Roman Empire, were found in the tiny town of Bova Marina.

When the Romans took control of this region, they created problems from which it has never fully recovered. In search of food and wood for ships and other domestic needs, they ravaged the forests of the high valley. Lack of protective trees meant accelerated erosion, which affects agriculture in some parts of Calabria to this day. In medieval times, Christianity developed along the internal routes carved out by the Romans. Around 476, when the region fell under Byzantine rule, there was a revival of Hellenic traditions. Some mountain villages still conserve Graecanic traditions and speak a language closely resembling Greek. When the Byzantine domination collapsed under the Norman penetration, Calabria enjoyed a long period of peace and tranquillity. Subsequent Angevin, Aragonese, and Spanish rule, however, marked the beginning of a long, painful period in Calabrian history. Essentially feudal and exploitive governments existed, even under the later Bourbons and Bonapartes, until Italian unity in 1861.

At first, political unity did little to alleviate the problems of the deep south. Thousands of years of neglect and continual wars and upheavals inhibited agricultural productivity. The poor Calabrian peasants could not compete with rich northern Italy, from which they were cut off by a vast mountain range. However, instead of trying to improve the productive state of the land and the social conditions of the peasants, government officials were intent on creating infrastructures mostly for military needs. Many peasants found the only solution to their problems in emigration: Between 1882 and 1902, more than 300,000 people left Calabria, most for North America.

In the first half of this century, a series of devastating earthquakes, one of which leveled Reggio, followed by World War I, a worldwide depression, and then World War II, precluded any aid for Calabria. Finally, in 1950, the *Cassa del Mezzogiorno,* an investment organization, was established to introduce industry to the south on a grand scale. One successful project was the building of the Autostrada del Sole, which connected Calabria with the rest of Italy and made the region accessible to tourists. This in turn helped to stabilize the economy, though it also marked the beginning of the abandonment of rural communities in favor of coastal towns and construction of tourist facilities. Many émigrés have returned home, believing that the development of their coastal resources for tourism is the key to future prosperity.

The region is divided into three provinces named after their capital cities: Cosenza, the inland section in the north; Catanzaro, farther south, near the Ionian coast; and Reggio di Calabria, at the tip of the toe, separated by only a narrow strait from Sicily.

If this is your first visit to Calabria, we suggest driving from central Italy. Although it's possible to fly to Lamezia Terme or Reggio di Calabria and rent a car there, the drive south from Salerno along the Autostrada del Sole (A3) is worth the time. Despite the increasing number of tourist resorts popping up indiscriminately along the coast, the 248-mile (397-km) drive from Salerno to Reggio can be breathtaking. An alternative to A3 is S18, which follows the coast more closely and is a little rougher and more winding than the newer autostrada.

Leave the autostrada at Lagonegro for Praia a Mare and follow S18 down the coast. After detouring inland to see Cosenza, drive farther east into the Sila Massif, or head directly south to Pizzo. From here, continue south along the Costa Viola (Violet Coast). This is a strip of small towns and sandy beaches lapped by a sea of violet and turquoise stretching from Gioia Tauro to Santa Trada Cannitello just north of the provincial capital, Reggio di Calabria. From Reggio, the region's most modern city, continue around the toe of the boot to the site of the ancient Greek city of Locri. From here it is a 15-minute drive up the mountain road to the medieval town of Gerace.

If you're not in a hurry to get to Sicily or want to proceed to Puglia instead, we recommend the following route up the instep of the boot: From Gerace, return to Locri and take the scenic drive along the coast as far as Monasterace Marina; then turn inland up to the religious sights at Stilo and Serra San Bruno. From here, proceed down the mountain road back to the coast. Continue north to Catanzaro and farther inland to Taverna for some interesting Baroque art and architecture. Return to the coast for a lovely (and, usually, lonely) stretch of the Ionian coast for more remnants of Magna Graecia at Capo Colonna and Crotone. Bear slightly inland to Byzantine monuments in and around Rossano and finally on to the evocative plain of Sibari, site of the notorious Greek colony of Sybaris. From Sibari, continue past more archaeological excavations at Metapontum in the region called Basilicata, and on to Taranto in Puglia. Alternatively, E844 connects easily to A3, which leads back to Cosenza or parts north.

Driving is difficult in Calabria, and distances between points of interest are quite long, so it's a good idea to carefully consult a topographical map before plotting the journey. In winter there is often snow on the roads; it's a good idea to ask if they are passable before setting off. For more information on the region, contact *Calabria Turismo* (61 Viale de Filippis, Catanzaro; phone: 961-773325; fax: 961-772690).

Hotels in Calabria have improved considerably over the past several years. There aren't many luxurious hotels, however, and those that do exist tend to be modern and impersonal. Expect to pay $110 or more per night for a double at an expensive hotel; from $65 to $100 at a moderate one; and $60 or less in an inexpensive place. All hotels feature private baths unless otherwise indicated. An attractive summer alternative to hotels is provided by Calabria's many holiday villages, which have the added advantage of being built close to the crystal-clear blue sea. There are no really expensive restaurants in Calabria, and all serve generous portions of southern Italian cooking. Expect to pay about $60 for a dinner for two at those restaurants categorized as moderate, and from $35 and $50 at those in the inexpensive category. Prices do not include drinks or tips. All restaurants are open for lunch and dinner unless otherwise noted. For each location, hotels and restaurants are listed alphabetically by price category.

Note that a few sites of interest in Calabria close for a midday break, usually from 1 PM to anywhere from 3 to 5 PM; we suggest calling ahead to check exact hours.

En Route from Salerno Exit the autostrada (A3) at Lagonegro, and take S18 33 miles (53 km) to Praia a Mare. The sandy beach here faces the Isola di Dino, a tiny island where legend says Ulysses landed long ago. This part of the coast has been most developed for tourism; for a more peaceful coastal town, continue another 17½ miles (28 km) on S18 to Diamante. Both towns provide a fine introduction to the province of Cosenza, with its wooded plains and rocky beaches.

En route to Diamante, detour to see the caves with Paleolithic drawings at Papasidero. At Scalea (about 6 miles/10 km south of Praia a Mare), turn off S18 onto S504 and travel 17½ miles (28 km) to Papasidero. This will be your first encounter with the winding roads so typical of the Calabrian inland. The route passes through forests, vineyards, and orchards, with frequent glimpses of the coast. In Papasidero, visit the ruins of the Byzantine castle and the 14th-century frescoes of the *Santuario della Santa Maria di Costantinopoli* and the *Grotta del Romito*. To get to the caves, continue along S504 toward the Lao River to the village of Montagna. From here, walk along a mule track for about 40 minutes toward the Lao Valley. In one of the caves is a Paleolithic drawing of two oxen; it is believed to be one of the oldest manifestations of art in Italy. Excavations inside the caves have revealed human skeletons—one with his breast pierced by a stone arrowhead.

Beyond Papasidero and Montagna, at the town of Mormanno (15½ miles/25 km from Papasidero on S504), those in a hurry can pick up A3 and speed 60 miles (96 km) down to Cosenza (after the visit, return to S18, the coast road, via S107, a fast, modern road that goes the 21 miles/34 km back up to Paola). Otherwise, retrace the path from Papasidero back to

S18 and continue the journey down to Diamante, about 8 miles (13 km) away, and a few more beach towns before turning inland to Cosenza.

BEST EN ROUTE

Garden Not only is there a refreshing garden here, but this 39-room hotel has a restaurant and a bar, beach access, and considerable hospitality. Via Roma, Praia a Mare (phone: 985-728281). Moderate.

Sant'Elena An excellent restaurant, a garden, and parking are the amenities at this comfortable, rustic 31-room hotel. Open year-round. Via Salviera, Mormanno (phone: 981-81052/3; fax: 981-81002). Moderate to inexpensive.

DIAMANTE In addition to a wide, yellow-sand beach, this pretty resort town has the ruins of a Roman mausoleum and a view of an ancient fortress on the nearby island of Cirella. Diamante is famous for its murals depicting the hardships of southern Italian life and the area's politics, painted on walls and houses throughout the town by contemporary artists, some internationally known.

BEST EN ROUTE

Ferretti From the terraces of this romantic, Mediterranean-style 45-room hotel, guests get a spectacular view and a suntan without even going down to the private beach. The hotel also has a pool, a tennis court, and an excellent restaurant, *La Pagoda,* which offers a delicious introduction to traditional Calabrian cooking. Open *Easter* through October. 4 Via Pastani, Diamante (phone: 985-81428/9; fax: 985-81114). Moderate.

La Ribalta Enzo Ritondele, the owner of this attractive restaurant on the beach, frequently arranges for musicians, poets, and traveling stage troupes to perform for diners. Arrive early to get a table—this place is popular. Closed Mondays. No reservations. No credit cards accepted. Corso Vittorio Emanuele, Diamante (no phone). Moderate.

Riviera Bleu Right on the sea's edge, this hotel's 60 rooms are simple but clean. There is a restaurant and a bar. Open *Easter* through October. Località Pastani, Diamante (phone/fax: 985-81363). Moderate.

En Route from Diamante The stretch of S18 from Diamante down through Belvedere, about 4½ miles (7 km), offers lovely views of mountain slopes covered with olive trees, where peasants can be seen at work in the fields. The colors are reminiscent of the rich greens and browns used in traditional glazes on Calabrian pottery. Beyond the pleasant beach town of Cetraro, another 12 miles (19 km) down the coast, turn off onto S283 at the sign for Terme Luigiane.

San Michele One of the few hostelries in Calabria awarded four stars by the *Touring Club Italiano,* this cliff-top 73-room hotel—a beautifully renovated old villa set in a park of grape vines, oleander, bougainvillea, and geraniums—is a few miles north of Cetraro. The estate produces a fine rosé and red wine for guests' consumption, along with 80% of its food, all organically grown. The villa itself offers a homey atmosphere mixed with turn-of-the-century elegance. Two charming farmhouses on the estate also provide a number of apartments. An elevator takes guests down to the "secret" beach below. The hotel has a pool and a fine restaurant, and summer visitors can listen to a concert while dining on the terrace. On the grounds is a nine-hole golf course. Open January through October. S18, Tirrena Superiore, Località Bosco, Cetraro (phone: 982-91012/3; fax: 982-91430). Expensive.

TERME LUIGIANE Just after the turn onto S533 near Guardia Piemontese are the *terme* (thermal baths) themselves, famous since ancient times for their alleged healing powers. They are named after the Bourbon Louis, Count of Acquila, who frequented the springs. The waters are said to be particularly good for arthritis, rheumatism, and respiratory and gynecological disorders and ear, nose, and throat ailments. Mud baths, massages, and post-surgical treatments can be had at the two well-equipped baths of San Francesco and Thermae Novae. Above, in the town of Guardia, locals still speak a French-Piedmont dialect that their ancestors brought with them over 600 years ago.

Delle Terme In addition to 128 modern rooms, a private beach, a pool, and tennis courts, this property is connected to the baths and provides physiotherapy and beauty treatments. There is also a restaurant and a bar. Open June through October. Viale Stazione, Guardia Piemontese, Terme Luigiane (phone: 982-94475; fax: 982-94478). Moderate.

Parco delle Rose Surrounded by mountains and not far from the sea, this small hotel has 50 comfortable rooms, a restaurant, a bar, a pool, and tennis. Open year-round. Via Pantano, Terme Luigiane (phone: 982-94090). Inexpensive.

En Route from Terme Luigiane S533 northeast offers excellent scenery, and the rural communities along the route provide a real flavor of peasant life in Calabria. Rejoin A3, about 24 miles (38 km) from Terme Luigiane, and drive 31 miles (50 km) south to Cosenza. Watch carefully for signs, and study a map beforehand; some crossroads can be confusing. Alternatively, proceed 9 miles (14 km) south on S18 to Paola.

PAOLA The most important commercial and agricultural center on the Tyrrhenian coast, Paola is famous for being the birthplace (in 1416) of San Francesco di Paola, the saint of humble charity who founded the Minim order of the Franciscan brotherhood. Every May, pilgrims come from all over southern Italy to pay tribute to the saint; ceremonies include a procession into the sea. The *Santuario di San Francesco* is on a hill behind the town, on the spot where the saint built a convent in 1435 to commemorate St. Francis of Assisi. Unwary motorists may accidentally pass the sanctuary—directional signs are unclear. The basilica has an awe-inspiring collection of cast-off crutches, splints, trusses, and other gruesome body cages strung from the ceiling or draped across the stone walls of the rooms below.

En Route from Paola Drive east, then south about 21 miles (34 km) on S107 to Cosenza. Inland, the road to Cosenza climbs through vineyards, orchards, and forests.

COSENZA The Old Town, dominated by its 12th-century Norman castle, is built on seven hills above the confluence of the Crati and Busento Rivers. To enter the castle, which is open by appointment only, contact one of the tourist offices. There's one at Piazza Rossi (phone: 984-30595, 984-390595, or 984-38441), which is closed weekends, and another at the train station (phone: 984-482620), which is closed Sundays and after 2 PM. The modern city sprawls north of the Busento . In the part of the river that divides the old from the new, according to legend, Alaric the Visigoth was buried with his treasure in AD 412. The waters were supposedly diverted for the burial and then restored to their natural course. For years, archaeological teams have searched the riverbed at various points but have failed to find any evidence to support the legend.

Cosenza was part of Magna Graecia and later part of the Roman Empire. The imperial road Via Pompilia passed through the town, linking Rome with Reggio Calabria. Cosenza was twice destroyed by the Saracens before it was conquered by the Norman Robert Guiscard in the 11th century. Under subsequent Aragonese, Angevin, and Spanish rule, it was the most important town in Calabria. Today it is an important commercial and agricultural center. The *Università di Calabria* (University of Calabria)—one of Italy's newest and most modern—is on the outskirts of the city.

For the visitor, the most interesting part of Cosenza is the Old Town, and the most romantic point of entry is by way of the road that skirts the castle and leads straight into Piazza XV Marzo, site of the *Museo Civico.* In it are some striking prehistoric bronze pieces—statues, medals, and hair ornaments. The museum is closed Sundays and after 1 PM; admission charge (phone: 984-73387). Next door is the *Teatro Rendano,* built in the 9th century and reconstructed after being destroyed in World War II. Fine opera is staged here from January through the spring (local groups put on drama and music performances the rest of the year). Corso Telesio leads from the square into the heart of the Old Town and passes the Gothic *Duomo,* which has its origins in the late Roman period and was rebuilt after the 1184 earthquake. It adjoins the archbishop's palace, which contains one of Calabria's most precious treasures—a bejeweled Byzantine reliquary cross, said to have been the gift of Frederick II. There are many other art treasures in the churches of old Cosenza. A visit to the *Chiesa di San Domenico* will reveal a splendid rose window.

BEST EN ROUTE

Executive Conveniently located at the Cosenza Nord exit of the A3, this 95-room place offers all the amenities of a luxury hotel, including a pool, a disco, an auditorium, and a garage. The restaurant is mediocre. Open year-round. A short drive into the center of town, at 59 Via Marconi, Rende (phone: 984-401010; fax: 984-402020). Expensive.

Centrale Centrally located near the station and well marked on the road into Cosenza are 48 rooms, a good restaurant, a bar, efficient service, and a garage. Open year-round. Via Macallè, at the corner of Corso Mazzini, Cosenza (phone: 984-73681/2; fax: 984-75750). Expensive to moderate.

La Calavrisella In its own garden, this popular, attractive restaurant offers traditional Calabrian cooking. Try *marille con melanzane* (pasta with a spicy blend of vegetables and meat) or *capretto alle frasche d'origano* (kid cooked with oregano). Other dishes include mushrooms, picked wild, stuffed, and even roasted, a Cosenza specialty. Closed Saturdays, Sunday dinner, and one week in August. Reservations unnecessary. Major credit cards accepted. 11/A Via Gerolamo de Rada, Cosenza (phone: 984-28012). Moderate.

Royal One of the best in town, it has 44 rooms, a restaurant, and a lounge. Open year-round. 24 Via Molinella, Cosenza (phone: 984-412461). Moderate.

Trattoria Peppino Hearty regional dishes, prepared with wonderful fresh mushrooms from the wild mountains of the Sila, are served here. Closed Sundays. No reservations. No credit cards accepted. Just outside the entrance to the Old Town, at 4 Piazza Crispi (phone: 984-73217). Inexpensive.

En Route from Cosenza It is possible to drive 53 miles (85 km) directly south to Pizzo via A3. But for spectacular views and villages rich in crafts, take a detour into the Sila Massif via S107 east to Camigliatello Silano, about 19½ miles (31 km) from Cosenza. The highway winds through a forest that becomes alpine, at which point it turns into a pleasant mountain road. The Sila Massif is a pristine mountain chain covered with virgin forest, lovely lakes, and flowing streams.

CAMIGLIATELLO SILANO Resembling an alpine fairyland, Camigliatello Silano is in fact a well-equipped, year-round resort town in the pine forests above Lake Cecita. The hiking is wonderful; one of the best hikes is the 3-mile trek up the Sila Massif's highest mountain, Monte Botte Donato, which commands excellent views of the Ionian and Tyrrhenian Seas. Its ski facilities are among the best in Calabria (optimum skiing is from *Christmas through March*); in the fall, before the season starts, the local slopes yield some of the best mushrooms in the region, celebrated each October in the *Sagra dei Funghi* (Mushroom Festival). Note that many hotels here require full board in August, December, and January.

BEST EN ROUTE

Sila Here are 32 rooms, all with telephone, TV set, and mini-bar. Also on the premises are a restaurant and a bar. Camigliatello Silano (phone: 984-578484/5/6/7; fax: 984-578286). Expensive.

Aquila & Edelweiss The restaurant at this modern, 40-room hotel serves several mushroom-based dishes and other specialties of the Sila, such as *trota* (mountain trout), *cinghiale* (wild boar), *caciocavallo* (a creamy cheese), and *butirro* (*caciocavallo* wrapped around creamery butter). 11 Viale Stazione, Camigliatello Silano (phone: 984-578044; fax: 984-578753). Expensive to moderate, hotel; moderate to inexpensive, restaurant.

Camigliatello The 38 well-appointed rooms, the restaurant, and the bar are heavily scented by the surrounding pines, making a stay here quite pleasant. Via Federici, Camigliatello Silano (phone: 984-578496/7; fax: 984-578628). Moderate.

Mancuso Full board is required in August and December at this 28-room hotel (26 have private baths). There's a restaurant and a bar. 55 Via del Turismo, Camigliatello Silano (phone: 984-578082). Inexpensive.

En Route from Camigliatello Silano Head northeast for 22 miles (35 km) on S177, which follows the shore of Lake Cecita, goes past Mt. Altare, and winds through the pines to Longobucco.

LONGOBUCCO Sitting strategically in its own valley beneath *Parco La Fossiata Nazionale* (La Fossiata National Park), this town dates from the Middle Ages. Its church, *Santa Maria Assunta* (which is flanked by a curious Baroque leaning bell tower), is located on the Piazza Santa Maria Assunta and contains a noteworthy wood sculpture of the Madonna and Child and objects made of silver from nearby mines. More works of the once-flourishing local silversmith's art are in the *Museo Parrochiale*, which is located next to *Santa Maria Assunta*. It's closed after 1 PM; no admission charge (no phone). Fine woodcarvings can be seen in the *Chiesa di Santa Maria Maddalena*. Crafts are still a mainstay of the community's economy, especially carpets and fabrics that the women of Longobucco and neighboring villages handweave into Oriental patterns. In August, the weavers gather in Longobucco to display and sell their wares.

En Route from Longobucco S177 winds slowly back down to S107. Proceed east on S107 about 17½ miles (28 km) to San Giovanni in Fiore.

SAN GIOVANNI IN FIORE In the 12th century, Gioacchino da Fiore founded an abbey here, and over the centuries the town grew up around it. The most interesting part of San Giovanni in Fiore is the lower, older section, where the restored abbey, the *Badia Florense,* is located, housing the notable *Museo Etnografico* (Ethnographic Museum). The museum is closed after 1:30 PM; no admission charge (no phone). Legend has it that Gioacchino also designed the characteristic black-and-white costumes and elaborate, plaited hair style still occasionally worn by the women, meant to represent the life and death of Christ. San Giovanni in Fiore also has a strong crafts tradition, primarily in goldsmithing and carpet weaving in the Armenian tradition.

BEST EN ROUTE

Florens A delectable array of specialties of the Sila—trout, game, and dairy products—is served in a homey atmosphere. Closed Wednesdays. No reservations. No credit cards accepted. Località Pirainella, San Giovanni in Fiore (phone: 984-992757). Moderate to inexpensive.

Dino's This comfortable 34-room getaway offers plenty of mountain air and a restaurant. Open year-round. 166-168 Viale della Repubblica, Località Pirainella, San Giovanni in Fiore (phone: 984-992370). Inexpensive.

En Route from San Giovanni in Fiore Take S107 west to the junction of S108 *bis,* where it hugs the north shore of Lake Arvo. As soon as you begin to see the lake on the left, look for the turnoff on the right for the mountain road that leads to the top of Botte Donato for spectacular views of the surrounding area. Then return to S108 *bis* and turn right along the lake to Lorica, about 17½ miles (28 km) from San Giovanni in Fiore.

LORICA The modern appearance of this ski village, panoramically situated in a beech and pine forest, is more than compensated for by a natural beauty that's profusely pine-scented. The local tourist office (*Pro Loco)* is on Via Nazionale (phone: 984-997069).

BEST EN ROUTE

Pesce Fresco This delightful trattoria is on the edge of the *Piana di S. Eufemia* (St. Eufemia Plain—a natural wildlife reserve), a must for travelers proceeding along the coast or descending from the mountains. Closed November through April. Reservations unnecessary. No credit cards accepted. Stay on S18, and exit at Gizzeria/Lamezia Terme (A3; phone: 968-51105). Moderate to inexpensive.

Lorica With a hundred rooms, this lodge is comfortable, modern, quiet, and romantic. Ask for a room with a view of Lake Arvo. No restaurant. Open mid-May to mid-October. 57 Viale Libertà, Lorica (phone: 984-537039). Inexpensive.

En Route from Lorica Take the winding scenic drive (S108 *bis*) back to Cosenza (almost 25 miles/40 km) along Lake Arvo, turning right on S178 at the junction before the village of Quaresima. Pick up A3 to Pizzo.

PIZZO Also called Pizzo Calabro, Pizzo is a picturesque fishing town that looks down from a cliff onto a beautiful sea with white sandy beaches. It is famous for the castle where Napoleon's brother-in-law Joachim Murat, ex-King of Naples, was imprisoned and shot in 1815, five days after he had landed in an attempt to recover his throne. Part of the castle is now used as a youth hostel. All that remains of the original structure is an archway and towers. Also be sure to visit the *Chiesetta di Piedigrotti* in a grotto facing the sea. Several of the church's small chapels are filled with lifelike figures at prayer, all carved from the rock of the cave.

BEST EN ROUTE

La Marinella A modern 36-room hostelry with sea views, telephones, and TVs, it has a reputation for superior service and good food in its restaurant. Open year-round. Via Prangi, Pizzo (phone: 963-264060; fax: 963-264084). Moderate.

La Medusa As popular with the locals as with visitors, this eatery is in the heart of Pizzo. Try *risotto ai gamberi* (rice with prawns) or the delicious stew-like fish soup. Closed Mondays from November through March. Reservations unnecessary. No credit cards accepted. Via Salomone, Pizzo (phone: 963-531203). Inexpensive.

Sonia At this comfortable, family-run hotel, 37 of the 47 rooms have private baths; there's also a restaurant. Open year-round. 110 Riviera Via Prangi, Pizzo (phone: 963-531315). Inexpensive.

En Route from Pizzo For the 6 miles (10 km) to Vibo Valentia, S18 winds around the hills; silver-gray olives and prickly-pear cacti tumble down the steep slopes. About 1¼ miles (2 km) north of Vibo, stop to see the remains of an ancient Greek temple and an imposing wall with a view of the Tyrrhenian coast.

VIBO VALENTIA As with most towns on the Calabrian coast, Vibo Valentia is divided into two—the hill town and the beach town, or marina. The hill town is dominated by a Norman castle; the marina has been developed so tourists can take advantage of its beautiful beaches. Now a large commercial city, most of Vibo is not particularly attractive, but its past is rich. It was always a strategic center for the possession of central Calabria, hosting Greeks, Romans, Byzantines, Normans, and Bourbons. It was an important intellectual center in the 18th century and a provincial capital under Murat. The small but interesting *Museo Archeologico Statale* in *Palazzo Gagliardi* (Piazza Garibaldi; phone: 963-43350) is worth a visit for its impressive collection of Greek pots and votive statues, relics of the 7th century BC. The museum is closed Mondays and after 1 PM; admission charge. The tourist office (*AAST*) is at 8 Piazza Diaz (phone: 963-42008).

BEST EN ROUTE

501 A modern 124-room hotel on the slope leading up to town, it has tennis courts and an excellent view of the Gulf of Tropea. At the main restaurant inside (open year-round), the emphasis is on fish, and the antipasti are free. Outside, diners can dawdle over puddings and local wines at the poolside dining spot (open summer only). 1 Via Nazionale, A3 turnoff for Vibo Valentia, Località Madonnella (phone: 963-43951 or 963-44560; fax: 963-43400). Hotel, expensive; restaurants, moderate.

L'Approdo People in the know come from nearby Tropea and Vibo Valentia to eat here, despite its location in the less-than-quaint port of Vibo Marina (5 miles/8 km from Vibo Valentia). The cooking is of an extremely high standard; try the *pesce spada affumicato* (smoked swordfish) and the delicious homemade *tagliatelle* with mussels and clams. Closed in winter. Reservations advised. No credit cards accepted. 22 Via Roma, Vibo Marina (phone: 963-240640). Moderate.

En Route from Vibo Valentia Follow S522 toward the coast for 31 miles (50 km) to Tropea.

TROPEA Crouched on a cliff above the sea, Tropea is one of the few old towns that has remained virtually intact in earthquake-prone Calabria; it is also one of the most picturesque fishing villages on this part of the coast. Many of its 15th- and 16th-century buildings are still standing, though the origins of the town date back even farther. Illuminated façades and statues of saints towering on the hills provide a striking silhouette against the night sky.

BEST EN ROUTE

Baia Paraelios in Parghelia About 2 miles (3 km) before Tropea, this is one of Calabria's most renowned holiday villages. There are 84 rooms in ochre-colored villas set in gardens of tumbling geraniums, olive trees, palms, and cacti. Book early, as this place is very popular in midsummer. Open April through September. Località Fornaci, Parghelia (phone: 963-600004 or 963-600300; fax: 963-600074). Expensive.

Pimm's Among the few restaurants in town, this eatery stands out. The kitchen concocts some excellent dishes, and the seafood and tasty starters are heavenly. Closed late autumn and winter. Reservations advised in summer. No credit cards accepted. Largo Migliarese, Tropea (phone: 963-666105). Moderate.

La Pineta Modern and comfortable, this 43-room seaside hotel caters to conventioneers and vacationers. There is a restaurant, a bar, tennis courts, and a parking area. Open late March to mid-October. 150 Via Marina, Tropea (phone: 963-61700 or 963-61777; fax: 963-62265). Moderate.

En Route from Tropea It's sensible to study directions in this area well before arriving. As the excellent Italian guidebook to Calabria *Incontro con la Calabria,* by Domenico Laruffa, points out, the access roads to Nicotera are "quite accidental." S522 winds along the coast for 25 miles (40 km) beyond Tropea to Nicotera, and the view is particularly stunning, passing lush fields of olives, wheat, and onions, for which the area is famous.

NICOTERA The Old Town clings to the hill above. Drive to the top, and if it's Sunday morning, join the market throng surveying the many food stalls stuffed with local sausage, pecorino cheese, fresh almonds, and the traditional honey bread—formed into animal shapes or musical instruments. Walk down into the old part of the town, and wander the winding little streets. An agricultural and fishing village, Nicotera is particularly famous for its granite, which adorns many of the town's buildings. Nicotera also is home to many artisans; a few miles down the road at Badia di Nicotera, master ceramist Giuseppe Cocciolo works in his *laboratorio* (Piazza Fontana; phone: 963-85323). He makes wonderful terra cotta masks that, according to tradition, ward off evil spirits.

BEST EN ROUTE

Miragolfo On the outskirts of town, the 68 rooms have balconies overlooking the sea in front and the countryside in back; there also is access to a private beach, a cozy restaurant, and a bar. Open year-round. 63 Via Corte, Nicotera (phone: 963-81470; fax: 963-81700). Moderate to inexpensive.

En Route from Nicotera S522 continues 19 miles (30 km) down the coast to Gioia Tauro.

GIOIA TAURO The first town on the Costa Viola is now an industrial port and canning center, but below it lies the ancient Metauria, a Greek colony of Locri. Olive trees on the Plain of Gioia are said to have been growing in this region since the time of Christ.

Il Buco Northern Italian dishes, primarily from Emilia, share the menu with local fare. Closed Mondays. Reservations unnecessary. No credit cards accepted. 115 Via Lo Moro, Gioia Tauro (phone: 966-51512). Moderate to inexpensive.

En Route from Gioia Tauro On the 5-mile (8-km) drive south on S18 to Palmi, the road suddenly opens out to the largest of Palmi's sandy beaches, La Tonnara, where the Costa Viola begins its stretch down to Reggio.

PALMI Lush subtropical plants and uncultivated flora—jasmine, bougainvillea, prickly pear, and bergamot—fill the air here with a sweet fragrance. The view from Mt. St. Elia, "the balcony over Tyrrhenia," just south of the city, includes Mt. Etna and Messina in Sicily, the Aeolian Islands, and the Calabrian coast as far north as Capo Vaticano.

The *Museo del Folklore* (Folklore Museum; no phone) is housed in the *Casa della Cultura,* a modern cultural center on the road leading out of Palmi to Mt. St. Elia. The museum has a wonderful collection of old and new terra cotta masks and water vessels, Greek-style ceramics from the Ionian coast, hand-carved wooden utensils from the Aspromonte Mountains, and examples of traditional costumes. The museum is closed Saturdays through Mondays, and for a long (1 to 5 PM) break; admission charge.

In summer, Palmi stages two of Calabria's most spectacular *feste.* On August 16, a hundred townspeople celebrate the feast day of Palmi's patron, St. Rocco, by donning cloaks and crowns made of thorns and parading through town. On the last Sunday in August, 200 local men drag the "Varia," an 80-foot votive "mountain" made of steel and papier-mâché, through the streets. Perched on top is a young girl, usually an orphan, chosen to represent the Virgin Mary.

To learn more about the ceramic pots and masks displayed at the *Museo del Folklore,* take a side trip to the little town of Seminara, less than 2 miles (3 km) southeast of Palmi. The artisans here make the traditional green and yellow pottery according to ancient methods that have been passed on from generation to generation. Their wares are sold in shops in the town's main piazza. Stop at 30 Corso Barlaam to see the work of master potter Il Mago (The Magician), as Paolo Condurso is called. His ceramics have been exhibited throughout Europe; even Picasso was enchanted by them.

BEST EN ROUTE

La Lampara This rustic restaurant serves excellent fish dishes, especially *involtini di pesce spada* (swordfish) in season. Try the excellent local wine. Closed November and December. Reservations unnecessary. No credit cards accepted. Lido Tonnara, Palmi vicinity (phone: 966-46332). Moderate to inexpensive.

La Margherita Specialties at this pizzeria are *pizza alla pioggia* and *la struncatura* (homemade whole wheat pasta in anchovy sauce). Open daily. Reservations unnecessary. No credit cards accepted. Across the road from the northern end of Lido Tonnara (no phone). Moderate to inexpensive.

Arcobaleno On the road between Palmi and the Taureana beach (about 4 miles/6 km north of the town proper), this 51-room hotel has a restaurant, a covered heated pool, and tennis courts. Open year-round. Via Provinciale Taureana, Palmi (phone: 966-46275 or 966-46315). Inexpensive.

La Pineta Pizza is served here under pine trees. Open daily. Reservations unnecessary. No credit cards accepted. Monte Sant'Elia (phone: 966-22926). Inexpensive.

En Route from Palmi About 10 miles (16 km) south, beyond the famous Zibibbo vineyards, is Bagnara Calabra, the swordfishing center of the Costa Viola.

BAGNARA CALABRA Between April and late July or August, when the *pesce spada* (swordfish) come to the coastal waters to spawn, life in Bagnara Calabra (or simply Bagnara) centers around their capture, sale, and preparation. This activity hasn't changed since the days of the early Greeks; fishermen still harpoon the swordfish by hand. While the men are at sea (for superstitious reasons, women are not allowed to go), the town operates under a matriarchy; when the men return with the catch, the women prepare the fish in a seemingly infinite variety of ways—most often grilled and then doused with *salmoriglio,* a tasty sauce of garlic, oregano, and olive oil. A *bagnarota* (woman of Bagnara) walking around with a *pesce spada* on her head is a typical sight. While in Bagnara, look for locally made glassware and *torrone* (nougat made with almonds and honey).

BEST EN ROUTE

Taverna Kerkyra Marika, the Greek woman who runs this restaurant, brought her favorite recipes for swordfish from Corfu. In addition to Greek fare, there are some pasta dishes. Closed Mondays, sometimes Tuesdays, mid-June to mid-July, and early November. Reservations unnecessary. No credit cards accepted. 217 Corso Vittorio Emanuele, Bagnara (phone: 966-372260). Moderate.

En Route from Bagnara Calabra Six miles (10 km) farther south is Scilla.

SCILLA The sailing here is treacherous, as Homer's sailors found in *The Odyssey,* when they survived the waters of the gulf only to die on the legendary rock of Scylla (Scilla in Italian) in the sea. These legends are based on real natural phenomena: High winds often break on the cliffs of the Calabrian coast, including the rock of Scilla, and strong alternating currents create whirlpools at six-hour intervals in the Strait of Messina.

Near La Chianalea, Scilla's picturesque fishermen's quarter, where houses and cottages literally descend into the sea, is an impressive medieval Aragonese castle, seemingly sculpted out of the rock of Scilla itself. Its ruins house a youth hostel—one of the best—and a disco. Locals claim that 400-year-old treasures once were walled up in a secret chamber of the castle. The castle, as well as the grand terrace of the main town square, is worth a visit. Now a favorite promenade for residents and visitors, the terrace overlooks the rooftops of the Old Town and the beautiful sandy Sirens Beach.

BEST EN ROUTE

Da Glauco Off the main road into La Chianalea is a sign for this restaurant. Ring the bell of Famiglia Pontillo, and go upstairs. It's a typical Scillan house-turned-restaurant, and its terrace overlooks the fishermen's houses, the port, and the sea. Extra-special dishes are the spicy tomatoes and pickled eggplant antipasto. Closed Sundays and Mondays. Reservations advised. No credit cards accepted. Via Chianalea, Scilla (phone: 965-46330). Moderate.

Ulisse A former stable has been tastefully converted into Scilla's smartest restaurant. Try the *tris dello chef* (three different kinds of homemade pasta) or *linguine al cartoccio* (a steaming plate of pasta with giant prawns, squid, mussels, and clams). Closed Mondays. Reservations advised in summer. Diners Club accepted. In the lower town at the end of the Lungomare, at 1 Via Omiccioli, Scilla (phone: 965-790190). Moderate.

Virtigine Alfresco dining affords one of the best views of the castle, either at sunset or when it is floodlit at night. With a cool drink in hand and light fare, there is hardly a better place in town. Open daily to midnight. No reservations. No credit cards accepted. 14 Piazza San Rocco, Scilla (no phone). Moderate.

Alla Pescatora When Peppino isn't making fishing boats, he's turning out mouthwatering *involtini di pesce spada* (swordfish rolls) and other coastal fare. Closed Tuesdays and mid-December through March. Reservations advised in summer. No credit cards accepted. On the sea at Marina Grande, 32 Lungomare Scilla, Scilla (phone: 965-754147). Moderate to inexpensive.

En Route from Scilla The Costa Viola ends with Santa Trada Cannitello, the peninsula's closest point (about 2 miles) to Sicily. Rejoin A3 here and continue to Reggio (see below). Or stay on S18 for Villa San Giovanni, 5½ miles (9 km) down the road from Scilla.

VILLA SAN GIOVANNI If the glimpses of Sicily are tempting, take one of the regular car ferries or a hydrofoil across the Strait of Messina. Similar transport to Messina also is available from Reggio, making a day trip to Taormina (only 31 miles/50 km from Messina) almost irresistible. At the gas station on A3, just before the turnoff for Villa San Giovanni, an information office has up-to-date schedule information.

BEST EN ROUTE

Albergo Piccolo While waiting for the ferry, have a meal at this family-run establishment in front of the docks. Try the *involtini di pesce spada,* the *saltimbocca al Piccolo Hotel* (thin slices of veal in a subtle, light sauce), or *risotto con funghi porcini* (rice with *porcini* mushrooms). The wine is good, as are the homemade sweets and ice cream. Open daily. Reservations advised in summer. No credit cards accepted. Piazza della Stazione, Villa San Giovanni (phone: 965-751410 or 965-751153). Inexpensive.

En Route from Villa San Giovanni About 9½ miles (15 km) farther is Reggio di Calabria.

REGGIO DI CALABRIA Founded in the 8th century BC by the Greeks, Reggio is one of the biggest cities in Calabria. It certainly had the most splendid past, particularly in the Greek, Roman, and Byzantine periods. Unfortunately, visitors will find few remains of ancient Rhegion, as the Greeks called it. Virtually no building dates before 1908, the year a massive earthquake devastated the entire area. Much of the city was rebuilt in a pleasant, turn-of-the-century style.

Like most southern Italian towns, Reggio was not designed with the automobile in mind, so it is difficult to pass through the narrow streets and impossible to park. Avoid spots marked "Zona Auto Rimozione"—they're tow-away zones, and the process of retrieving a towed car is quite complex.

Wander along the elegant and typically Mediterranean boardwalk, called the Lungomare Marina, with its central strip of grass, enormous fig trees, and majestic palms. At the north end of the Lungomare, turn right for Piazza de Nava, where the *Museo Nazionale* has an interesting collection of antiquities from archaeological excavations of the ancient towns of Magna Graecia—Sibari, Locri, Medma—and artifacts from later Roman civilizations. This museum is particularly well known for its *Bronzi,* the bronze warriors of Riace. These two stunning statues, both over six feet in height, thought to be the most interesting examples in existence of the great Greek Bronze Age, have become symbols of the city. The museum is closed Mondays after 1 PM; Sundays after 12:30 PM; and Tuesdays through Saturdays for a midday break; admission charge (phone: 965-812255).

An excellent selection of local arts and crafts is on display at the local government's *Centro di Documentazione per le Arti Popolari Calabresi* on Corso Garibaldi, the town's main thoroughfare and the best place for shopping. The tourist office is next door at No. 329 (phone: 965-892012); there is another one at the central train station (phone: 965-27120). Both have highly irregular hours, bearing no relation to those posted. Drop into the bar next to the tourist office to sample the famous *granita di caffè con panna e brioche* (coffee-flavored ice with cream and sweet pastry), a Calabrian summer specialty. People turn out in large numbers for their evening *passeggiata* along the waterfront and Corso Garibaldi. During the *Feste di Settembre* (September Festivals), concerts, exhibitions, and religious celebrations take place throughout the city. The biggest celebration is the *Festa della Madonna della Consolazione*, which is held from September 8 to 12.

From Reggio, you can take a ferry or hydrofoil to Messina in Sicily, just across the narrow strait, and to the Aeolian Islands (craft operate on a rotating schedule from mid-June to mid-September). Ferries also depart year-round to Syracuse in Sicily and then go on to Malta. Check with the *Italian State Railways* or *SNAV* at the pier for information.

BEST EN ROUTE

Ascioti Here are 26 rooms, with all the modern comforts (including television sets and telephones in the rooms) but no dining room. 79 Via San Francesco da Paola, Reggio di Calabria (phone: 965-97041/5; fax: 965-26063). Expensive.

Bonaccorso One of the finest restaurants in Calabria serves fine pasta and local specialties, as well as excellent traditional Italian dishes. Closed Fridays. Reservations advised. Major credit cards accepted. 5 Via N. Bixio, Reggio di Calabria (phone: 965-896048). Expensive.

Excelsior One of the links in the deluxe Excelsior chain, this is the best hotel in town. Right behind the *Museo Nazionale,* the hotel and its well-regarded restaurant display a traditional elegance. Its 92 rooms provide modern comforts. 66 Via Vittorio Veneto, Reggio di Calabria (phone: 965-25801; fax: 965-93084). Expensive.

Grand Albergo Miramare At one of the cleanest, most traditional hotels in town, with 92 attractively redecorated rooms. Don't be put off by the "dark"— the lights go on once you've hung the key on the hook above the switch! The relaxing restaurant turns out excellent food. Open year-round. 1 Via Fata Morgana, Reggio di Calabria (phone: 965-91881; fax: 965-91885). Expensive to moderate.

Palace Masoanri's Less elegant than its sister hotel the *Excelsior* (see above), it is nonetheless very comfortable, with 64 rooms and a restaurant. Open year-round. 95 Via Vittorio Veneto, Reggio di Calabria (phone: 965-26433; fax: 965-93084). Expensive to moderate.

Primavera Simple but comfortable, this 52-room hotel in suburban Pentimele overlooks the Strait of Messina. There's a restaurant. 177 Via Nazionale, Reggio di Calabria (phone: 965-44904 or 965-47081; fax: 965-47121). Expensive to moderate.

Baylik Sample traditional raw fish specialties of the Ionian Coast, dine on excellent Calabrian dishes, and enjoy beautiful sea views in this pleasant dining spot. Closed Thursdays and late July to mid-August. Reservations advised. Major credit cards accepted. 1 Via Leone, Reggio di Calabria (phone: 965-48624). Moderate.

Conti An elegant restaurant close to the *Museo Nazionale,* it serves traditional Calabrian dishes and is always adding new items to the menu. The handmade macaroni, swordfish in season, and pastries are particularly recommended. Closed Mondays, except from June through September. Reservations advised. Diners Club accepted. 2 Via Giulia, Reggio di Calabria (phone: 965-29043). Moderate.

Gambero Rosso Classic Calabrian dishes are served with art and tradition. Meat is cooked over a wood fire, and antipasti are served in infinite varieties. Try the *penne alla brigante* (spicy pasta with hot peppers and salami). Closed Wednesdays. Reservations advised. Major credit cards accepted. 34 Via Provinciale Gallina, Reggio di Calabria (phone: 965-682654). Inexpensive.

La Pignata Right off Corso Garibaldi is this restaurant with beautifully carved wood ceilings that serves excellent seafood and pizza, both with a good spicy sauce. Closed Wednesdays and July. No reservations. No credit cards accepted. 122 Via Tripepi, Reggio di Calabria (phone: 965-27841). Inexpensive.

Pizzeria Giardino Filled with Reggio's bejeweled after-theater crowd, this wonderful eatery near the marina is a beehive of activity into the late hours. The delicious pizza is served on brightly painted majolica platters; because of its size, you will want to share one. Closed Mondays. Reservations advised, but be prepared to wait anyway. No credit cards accepted. 8 Largo Colombo, Reggio di Calabria (phone: 965-28460). Inexpensive.

En Route from Reggio di Calabria Continue south on S106 along the Costa dei Gelsomini. On this gorgeous coastal route, long stretches of bright blue water, green fields, and an odd goatherd and shepherd are still visible, despite considerable urban development. Behind many of the little coastal towns are mountain villages bearing the same names. Because of their position and the difficulty of access, many have remained unchanged for centuries. The nearest and most accessible is Bova Marina, about 31 miles (50 km) from Reggio. The people here trace their ancestry back to Magna Graecia and speak a language similar to modern Greek. Each year in June or July, they host a festival with costumes and music for all members of Calabria's Graecanic community. The view from the Norman castle at the summit of the village is well worth the rather frightening trip up. At the nearby towns of Condofuri and Galliciano, reached by turning off at Condofuri Marina, a few miles west of Bova Marina, villagers not only speak Greek but make and play the famous *zampogne,* rustic bagpipes. Another 33 miles (53 km) along S106 are the remains of the Hellenic city of Locri Epizephyri, whose name was borrowed by modern Locri.

LOCRI The New City here is a lively commercial area, flat, modern, and little resembling its predecessor. Locri is noted for the manufacture of mattresses, bitumen, and garden ornaments. In times past, the town was famous as the kidnapping capital of Italy (though visitors are not likely targets).

Buried in an olive grove, the ruins of ancient Locri are spread out like a relief map among the grasses and shrubs. From the road the remains of a temple and a wall are visible. A little farther on, at Portigliola, are a Greek-Roman theater and a Doric temple. Beyond those is the celebrated sanctuary of Persephone, the center of ancient Locri's religious life. The area has not been fully excavated, but much of what has been found, including 37 bronze law tablets, is now in Reggio's *Museo Nazionale.* The small, modern antiquarium beside the ruins has clear plans and photos of the history and artistic development of the city, as well as bronzes and some pottery and votive statues. Local craftsmen still make terra cotta pots closely resembling some of those seen in the antiquarium. It is closed Mondays though Saturdays after 2 PM; closed Sundays after 1 PM; longer afternoon hours in summer; no admission charge (phone: 964-390023). Locri also has a terrific white sand beach and offers a variety of water sports, as well as tennis. The tourist office (1 Via Fume; phone: 964-29600) has information about Locri and Gerace (see below). It is closed Sundays in July and August; closed weekends and after 2 PM the rest of the year.

BEST EN ROUTE

Demaco The seaside rooms are preferred in this modern 28-room hotel just behind the train station. There is a garage and meeting rooms. Open year-round; restaurant open in summer only. 28 Via Lungomare, Locri (phone: 964-20247 or 964-21751). Inexpensive.

Trattoria Rocco Simone Rocco Simone used to work in the fields, but he now serves his wife's excellent cooking to anyone who drops in to his little trattoria behind the Greek theater. Although the atmosphere is far from luxurious, the food is outstanding. Take the left-hand turn for Moschetta, just before entering Locri from Reggio di Calabria, and follow the trattoria's signs for about 2½ miles (4 km). Closed Mondays and from late October to early November. Reservations unnecessary. No credit cards accepted. Piazza Contrada Moschetta, Locri (phone: 964-390005). Inexpensive.

Da Umberto Diners can sample small portions of local specialties at this eatery near the ruins. Closed Mondays. Reservations unnecessary. No credit cards accepted. Contrada Caruso (phone: 964-29794). Inexpensive.

En Route from Locri About 7½ miles (12 km) up S111, an excellent mountain road, is Gerace.

GERACE This picturesque medieval town boasts art treasures unequaled in the region. Its position has helped protect it from modern spoiling. Founded in the 9th century BC by Greek refugees from Saracen raids, it later became one of the strongest Byzantine fortresses in the south. Gerace's Norman-Gothic cathedral is the largest sacred building in Calabria. It was built in 1045 and later altered and restored, and its 26 supporting columns are believed to have come from the temples of ancient Locri. Gerace is timeless and well worth a detour to visit its churches and wander through its narrow streets. The *botteghe artigiane di vasai* (local potters' workshops) turn out amphora-type pots from local clay, using the methods their ancient predecessors.

BEST EN ROUTE

Fagiano Bianco If this lovely *cantina* is closed, you can enjoy the same food at the bar on Piazza Centrale, where a few tables are set outdoors in fine weather. The *antipasto della casa* and the wine are excellent. No credit cards accepted. Piazza Centrale, Gerace (no phone). Inexpensive.

En Route from Gerace Drive back down S111 to Locri. Rather than retrace the route back to Reggio di Calabria, head north on S106 toward Marina di Gioiosa Ionica, and pick up the SGC road for a less than 30-minute drive back to A3 at Rossarno.

Sicily (and the Aeolian Islands)

To many Americans, the mention of Sicily conjures up visions of black-clad elderly women, timeworn peasants, barefoot children, and ominous-looking Mafia dons. But this island, the largest in the Mediterranean (almost 10,000 square miles), possesses a rich natural beauty and a unique artistic patrimony that reflects its tumultuous history and curious mix of cultures. Centuries of occupation by invaders left a legacy of Baroque churches, Norman castles, and Moorish domes and arches. Sicily's spectacular Greek temples and amphitheaters are the best-preserved Hellenic sites outside Greece.

Located off the "toe" of the Italian peninsula, from which it is separated by the narrow Strait of Messina, Sicily has a remarkably varied landscape. Believed to be a natural continuation of the Apennine chain of mountains that runs down the Italian peninsula, the island is mountainous in the north and east, with a vast central plateau that slopes down to its fertile coastline. Mt. Etna, Europe's largest active volcano, dominates the eastern region.

Much of Sicily's history has been shaped by its position in the center of the Mediterranean, enabling successive waves of conquerors to possess it. Its name comes from its earliest inhabitants, the Siculi, an ancient tribe that occupied the western part of the island. Sicily was known to Phoenician traders as far back as the 10th century BC. Greek colonization, which began in the 8th century BC, brought a long period of growth, prosperity, and cultural development. Powerful city-states such as Syracuse, Agrigento, and Selinunte competed to construct the most spectacular Doric temples and theaters. In the 3rd century BC Rome took control of the island, and Sicily gradually declined. Subsequent invasions by Ostrogoths and Byzantines led to the Saracen conquest in AD 878. Under Arab domination, Sicily's influence in both trade and culture expanded. In 1072, the Norman King Roger I conquered the island. Norman rule eventually was replaced by Spanish and Bourbon domination, which ended when Sicily became part of the united Italy in 1860.

For decades, however, the Italian central government pursued a policy of benign neglect in Sicily, causing massive numbers of emigrants to leave in search of better economic opportunities. Today, the island—with a population of just over six million—is semi-autonomous, and there are some signs of social and economic progress. Sicily is an important agricultural center, producing—among other things—citrus fruit; tomatoes, eggplants, zucchini, and other vegetables; olive oil; and wine.

The Mafia continues to be powerful in Sicily, and, despite strong measures taken by the Italian government, Mafia-related deaths on the island remain a vicious fact. The Mafia influences many aspects of life in Sicily—many bars, hotels, stores, and restaurants regularly pay off some group or family in order to keep their doors open, and some new enterprises are controlled by them. Although the Mafia represents a social and economic problem, it would be misleading to assert that it colors every aspect of Sicilian life—or that it represents any special danger for the casual visitor. In general, the island's calm Mediterranean rhythm is extremely appealing and restful. Sicilians still savor simple pleasures—an unhurried *aperitivo,* a pre-dinner stroll, a pleasant visit to a favorite *caffè.*

Note that some sites of interest in Sicily close for a midday break, usually from 12:30 or 1 PM to 3 or 4 PM; we suggest calling ahead to check exact hours.

TOURIST INFORMATION

Spring and fall are the best times for a visit here. Summers can be hot and crowded, though the beaches are beautiful; winters are mild, with occasional rain.

As in the rest of Italy, most stores close for a three-hour lunch break, generally from 1 to 4 PM, and then reopen until 7:30 or 8 PM. Many churches close between noon and 4 PM; museums usually close at 2 PM and do not have regular afternoon hours. Many archaeological sites, for example, remain open "until one hour before sunset"—a time subject to interpretation. In general, expect to find variations in official hours. The hours listed here are subject to change; call ahead to confirm times.

Local tourist information offices, located throughout the island, will provide brochures on sights, hotels, and restaurants. Major tourist offices are in the following Sicilian cities: *Agrigento* (71-73 Via Empedocle; phone: 922-20391); *Catania* (5 Largo Paiesseillo; phone: 95-312124); *Cefalù* (77 Corso Ruggero; phone: 921-21050); *Enna* (6 Piazza N. Colajanni; phone: 935-26119); *Erice* (11 Viale Conte Pepoli; phone: 923-869388); *Lipari* (202 Corso Vittorio Emanuele; phone: 90-988-0095); *Messina* (45 Piazza Cairoli; phone: 90-293-3541); *Palermo* (34 Piazza Castelnuovo; phone: 91-583847); *Piazza Armerina* (15 Via Cavour; phone: 935-680201); *Sciacca* (84 Corso Vittorio Emanuele; phone: 925-21182); *Syracuse* (43 Via San Sebastiano; phone: 931-461477); and *Taormina* (*Palazzo Corvaja,* Piazza Santa Caterina; phone: 942-23243). Tourist offices are usually closed Sundays (except in high season); Saturdays after 2 PM; and weekdays for a short (2 to 4:30 PM) break.

GETTING AROUND

AIR Italian domestic airlines operate regular daily connecting flights from all major Italian cities to Palermo, Catania, and Trapani. In summer, there also are a few regularly scheduled direct flights to Sicily from abroad.

BUS Many cross-Sicily routes are covered by Sicilian bus companies, the largest of which are *AST (Azienda Siciliana Trasporti)* and *SAIS (Servizi Automobilistici Scelfo Ingegnere)*. There is regular bus service between Palermo and Catania (about two hours) and between most other Sicilian cities and towns. Buses are considerably faster than trains and only nominally more expensive.

CAR RENTAL The best way to see Sicily is by car. Most roads skirting the coast, where nearly all the important cities and sights are located, are good. Roads into the interior are winding and, therefore, slower in mountainous areas. Gas stations are located throughout the island; most close during the three-hour lunch break but tend to have self-service facilities with machines that take 10,000-lire notes. In every town at least one service station is required by law to stay open. The hotels will know which one.

Major car rental firms have offices in the principal Sicilian cities; some offer special low rates for non-Italian visitors, generally by the week. *Catania: Avis* (14 Via Federico De Roberto; phone: 95-536470; and at the airport; phone: 95-340500 or 95-578323); *Hertz* (45 Via Toselli; phone: 95-322560; and at the airport; phone: 95-341595). *Messina: Avis* (35 Via Vittorio Emanuele at Cortina del Porto; phone: 90-662679); *Hertz* (113 Via Vittorio Emanuele; phone: 90-363740); *InterRent* (498/A Viale Libertà; phone: 90-47852); *Maggiore* (46 Via T. Cannizzaro; phone: 90-675476). *Palermo: Avis* (28 Via Principe Scordia; phone: 91-333806; and at the airport; phone: 91-591684); *Budget* (120 Via Fisco Crispi; phone: 91-605-7160/1; and at the airport; phone: 91-591680); *Hertz* (7/E Via Messina; phone: 91-331668; and at the airport; phone: 91-591682); *Maggiore* (27-33 Via Agrigento; phone: 91-625-7848; and at the airport; phone: 91-591681).

FERRY *Ferrovie Italiane dello Stato (FS)* operates a car ferry across the Strait of Messina. The trip takes 20 minutes from Villa San Giovanni or Reggio Calabria. *Tirrenia* (2 Rione Sirignano, Naples; phone: 81-720-1111; and 41 Via Bissolati, Rome; phone: 6-474-2041), Italy's largest privately operated ferry service, offers daily and overnight service from Naples to Palermo and, less often, from Naples to Catania and Syracuse; make advance reservations. Two private companies, *Caronte* (phone: 90-45183) and *Tourist Ferry* (phone: 90-41415), offer runs across the strait. There is occasional service from Genoa, Livorno, and Cagliari (Sardinia) and to and from Tunis. Regular service operates between the Aeolian Islands and Milazzo, Messina, and Palermo in the summer (see *Aeolian Islands,* below).

GUIDED TOURS Local travel agencies can arrange five- to eight-day tours originating in Palermo, Catania, or Taormina.

TRAIN Along with direct trains from the mainland across the Strait of Messina, *FS* operates several Sicilian lines; the two main ones are *Palermo–Messina* and *Messina–Catania–Syracuse.* The fastest trains are generally the *rapido* express trains originating on the mainland; nevertheless, delays along the way are almost inevitable. Advance reservations are recommended. The *rapidi* require a *supplemento* (supplementary payment). Local trains are slow and crowded.

SPECIAL EVENTS

Colorful religious events take place during *Lent,* culminating in numerous *Easter* celebrations. *Carnevale* festivals at Acireale, Sciacca, and Termini Imerese usher in the *Lenten* season. At Prizzi, near Palermo, *Easter* revelers drink and frolic at the *Abballu delli Diavuli,* a festival in which costumed devils take over the city for a day until the Madonna and her angels arrive to drive them out. Residents of Piana degli Albanesi, also near Palermo, parade in Albanian Byzantine costume on *Easter Sunday.* Worshipers at Caltanissetta participate in six *Holy Week* processions that are basically unchanged from the Middle Ages, with groups of "living statues" and a Black Christ. The most moving *Easter* pageantry is at Trapani, where *I Misteri* (The Mysteries)—20 groups of statues depicting the crucial moments in Christ's life—wind through the Old City in a magnificent procession.

A Greek theater festival is held in Syracuse in May and June of even-numbered years (there are opera and ballet performances in odd-numbered years); tickets are available from the *Istituto Nazionale del Dramma Antico* (29 Corso Matteotti; phone: 931-65373). In odd-numbered years, the festival takes place in Segesta; obtain tickets from the *Azienda Provinciale per il Turismo* (*APT;* 1/A Piazza Saturno, Trapani; phone: 923-27077). Erice holds a program of theater, music, and dance each summer; contact the *Ufficio Informazioni* (11 Viale Conte Pepoli; phone: 923-869388). Erice also has a festival of Mediterranean folk music instruments in December (for details, see *Italy's Most Colorful Festas* in DIVERSIONS). For information on Palermo's *Festival delle Marionette* and Taormina's *Taormina Arte,* see the individual chapters in THE CITIES.

SPORTS AND FITNESS

DEEP-SEA FISHING The best angling, especially for tuna, is near the port of Milazzo and off the Aeolian Islands. With a little Italian and some inquiries at port *caffès,* an enterprising angler can probably find a boat and a fisherman/guide. Or contact the *Azienda Autonoma di Soggiorno e Turismo* in Lipari (see *Tourist Information*).

SKIING For information on skiing near Cefalù, see *Palermo* in THE CITIES. There are also runs on Mt. Etna's northeast slopes; from Linguaglossa, follow yellow signs marked Etna or Sci for ski runs in the midst of the nearby pine forest.

TENNIS Many hotels have courts or access to them. There are *Valtur* vacation villages in Brucoli, near Augusta, and another near Cefalù. For more information, see *Top Tennis* in DIVERSIONS.

WATER SPORTS Sicily has countless beautiful beaches for swimming. Many resort hotels have facilities (and larger cities have clubs and schools) for sailing, water skiing, scuba diving, and windsurfing. Contact the local *Azienda Autonoma di Soggiorno e Turismo (AAST)*.

FOOD AND WINE

Given the lushness of Sicilian fruits and vegetables and the rich-tasting local meat and fish, it is not surprising that the pleasures of the palate play such an important role in Sicilian life. Though Americans tend to confuse it with the garlic and tomato sauces of Naples, Sicilian cuisine stands apart from other Italian food in its noticeable Arab influence. The sweet-and-sour contrasts are all-important to Sicilian cooks, who frequently use raisins and pine nuts or almonds and who liberally spice their sweet desserts with cinnamon, sesame, almond, and pumpkin. Gastronomic traditions vary from city to city, so be sure to intersperse visits to local monuments with samplings from area restaurants and trattorie.

TOURING SICILY

Hotels on Sicily and in the Aeolian Islands are rated expensive if they charge $120 to $180 per night for a double room; moderate, from $60 to $120; and inexpensive, less than $60. All hotels feature private baths unless otherwise indicated. A dinner for two, including wine and tips, in a restaurant listed as expensive costs $75 or more; moderate, $50 to $75; and inexpensive, less than $50. Many small hotels, *pensioni,* and trattorie in small towns, especially inland, are well below this range. All restaurants are open for lunch and dinner unless otherwise noted. For each location, hotels and restaurants are listed alphabetically by price category.

MESSINA Located on the strait separating Sicily from the Italian mainland, Messina is the third-largest city in Sicily (pop. 271,000). Almost totally destroyed in the earthquake of 1908, in which 84,000 people (two-thirds of the residents) perished, Messina has been rebuilt with broad streets and low buildings. Called Zancle by the Greeks because of the sickle-shaped peninsula enclosing the port, Messina was a major settlement in ancient times. During the Middle Ages, it was an important departure point for the Crusades—a stronghold of the Plantagenets and a wintering place for Richard the Lion-Hearted and his troops. It was the birthplace of the Renaissance painter Antonello da Messina and the setting of Shakespeare's *Much Ado About Nothing.*

Because of various disasters over the centuries, few of the city's most important monuments have survived intact. But the *Fonte d'Orione* (Orion Fountain), first built in 1547, and the twice-destroyed *Duomo* (Cathedral)—both at Piazza del Duomo—have been restored along original lines. The *Museo Nazionale* (Viale della Libertà; phone: 90-353605) houses some ancient artworks and a good collection of Renaissance paintings. It is closed

Mondays; Tuesdays through Saturdays after 2 PM; and Sundays after 1 PM; admission charge.

BEST EN ROUTE

Jolly Hotel dello Stretto Centrally located, this hotel with 96 comfortable rooms overlooks the Strait of Messina. Its restaurant has a view of the strait. 126 Corso Garibaldi, Messina (phone: 90-383860; fax: 90-590-2526). Expensive.

Royal Palace In the center of town, this well-kept hotel offers excellent service, although the 106 rooms can be a bit noisy. There's parking and dining for hotel guests only. 224 Via Tommaso Cannizzaro, Messina (phone: 90-292-1161; fax: 90-292-1075). Expensive.

Sporting This refined seafood restaurant offers a vast selection of antipasti (the caponata is especially delicious) and a good assortment of fish and meat dishes. Try the *farfalle* (butterfly-shaped pasta) with vegetables and shellfish and the *bracioletta alla messinese* (meat stuffed with cheese, bread crumbs, pine nuts, and parsley). Closed Fridays and November. Reservations unnecessary. Major credit cards accepted. Lido del Tierreno-Mortelle, Messina (phone: 90-321009). Expensive.

Pippo Nunnari An airy place decorated with Sicilian artifacts, it made its reputation with excellent and original pasta dishes, such as *cannellini* with zucchini, and macaroni with ricotta, basil, eggplant, and tomato. The fresh fish, especially the swordfish, is delicious. Closed Mondays and the first two weeks of July. Reservations advised. Major credit cards accepted. 157 Via Ugo Bassi, Messina (phone: 90-293-8584). Expensive to moderate.

En Route from Messina It is a quick drive (about 30 miles/48 km) down the coast on either the autostrada (A18) or the state highway (S114) to Taormina, the beautiful and balmy cliffside resort that first put Sicily on the international tourist map.

TAORMINA Set on Monte Tauro within sight of both the blue Ionian Sea and majestic Mt. Etna, Taormina has been known since antiquity for its fine climate and calm beauty. For complete coverage, see *Taormina* in THE CITIES.

En Route from Taormina Both A18 and S114 continue south 31 miles (50 miles) to Catania. Just north of Acireale, a town of interesting Baroque architecture built on seven overlapping streams of lava, begins a stretch of rocky seacoast known as the Riviera dei Ciclopi (Coast of the Cyclops). This area is known for its charming bays, grottoes, and fishing villages. According to mythology, Polyphemus, the Cyclops, hurled the rock formations in the harbor at Aci Trezza after Ulysses blinded him by thrusting a burning stake into his eye. Aci Castello is dominated by an 11th-century black lava-rock castle.

Da Federico Try the sumptuous *zuppa di pesce* (fish soup) and other dishes from the sea at this eatery. Closed Mondays. No reservations. Major credit cards accepted. 115 Piazza Giovanni Verga, Aci Trezza (phone: 95-276364). Inexpensive.

CATANIA Sicily's second-largest city (pop. 400,000) and the capital of the eastern part of the island, this busy seaport has a long and tormented history of conquest. But even more calamitous were the forces of nature. Destroyed by a massive earthquake in 1169, the city was rebuilt, only to be razed again and again by earthquake or by eruption of its powerful, menacing neighbor, Mt. Etna (see below).

Modern Catania has a well-laid-out, spacious center, and many of its buildings are made of black lava rock. Some traces of the classical past remain—for instance, the Greco-Roman theater and a smaller odeon— but far more impressive are the medieval and Baroque palaces and churches that give the city its air of 18th-century well-being. At the center of the Old Town is Piazza del Duomo, in the middle of which stands a lava ele-phant–obelisk statue that has become the symbol of the city. The *Duomo— Chiesa di Sant'Agata*—was built by the Norman King Roger in 1090 and rebuilt after the 1693 quake. Its Baroque façade includes granite columns from the Greco-Roman theater. The *Chiesa di San Nicolò* (Piazza Dante) is the largest church in Sicily (ask the guard, who works irregular hours, to let you in). Also of note is the monumental Swabian *Castello Ursino* in Piazza Federico di Svevia; it houses the *Museo Civico* (Civic Museum; phone: 95-345830), which was closed at press time for restoration. The exceptional *Teatro Massimo Bellini* (Piazza Bellini; phone: 95-312020), with its opulent foyer, was built in 1890 by the Milanese architect Carlo Sada. The theater is open to the public Mondays, with a short (12:30 to 3 PM) closing, and when music performances are held.

The city's Baroque flavor is best expressed on Via dei Crociferi, which starts at Piazza San Francesco and is lined with palaces, churches, and monasteries. The 2-mile-long Via Etnea is the most important thorough-fare, running north and south through the city and on toward the volcano. Catania is also known for its lava-rock beaches stretching north to Aci Castello, where there are plenty of bathing spots and restaurants. (Note: Stay away from La Plaja and other beaches on the city's southern coast, which are havens for petty thieves.)

The life and landscape of eastern Sicily are dominated by Etna, the active volcano. To visit the volcano, leave Catania by Via Etnea, take the 8 AM bus from *Stazione Centrale* at Piazza Stazione, or hop the *Circumetnea* train, with almost hourly departures daily from Corso Italia. Organized day tours are offered in summer; for information, call *Ferrovia Circumetnea* (phone: 95-541250). From Nicolosi, the main town on the southern slope (about 10 miles/16 km from Catania), drive to the Sapienza refuge; from here, in good weather, visitors can make jeep or cable car excursions to the summit. The road leads around the mountain to other towns such as Zafferano and Linguaglossa in the midst of lovely pine woods. For more information on the volcano, see *Taormina* in THE CITIES.

BEST EN ROUTE

Central Palace A simple, comfortable, and quiet hostelry, unobtrusively tucked away, it has 107 modern rooms, most overlooking the hanging garden, and a restaurant. 218 Via Etnea, Catania (phone: 95-325344; fax: 95-715-8939). Expensive.

Costa Azzurra Outside town on the Gulf of Ognina, this dining spot serving good seafood and local wines has huge picture windows and a terrace overlooking the sea. Closed Mondays and August. Reservations advised. Major credit cards accepted. 4 Via de Cristofaro, Ognina (phone: 95-494920). Expensive.

Excelsior Once a grand style hotel, this property is now in need of a face-lift. Conveniently located in the heart of the commercial area, it has 163 comfortable rooms and a good restaurant. 39 Piazza Giovanni Verga, Catania (phone: 95-325733; fax: 95-537015). Expensive.

Grand Hotel Baia Verde Situated on a volcanic cliff right on the Catania Gulf, this airy hotel is 2½ miles (4 km) from the town center. There are 120 spacious rooms, many with terraces and sea views. Other facilities include a tennis court, a pool, a garden, and a restaurant with alfresco dining in summer. The hotel provides morning bus service into town. 8-10 Via Angelo Musco, Catania-Cannizzaro (phone: 95-491522; fax: 95-494464). Expensive.

Jolly Part of the well-known chain, it offers 159 comfortable rooms and excellent service in an ideal location near the elegant shopping district on Corso Italia. There's a dining room. 13 Piazza Trento, Catania (phone: 95-316933; fax: 95-316832). Expensive.

Al Poggio Only the freshest local ingredients are used and dishes are prepared with great care here. The many types of pasta served are creative and delicious, and there is a good assortment of baked and grilled fish. The extensive wine selection includes some of the best Italian whites. Closed Sunday dinner and Monday lunch. Reservations advised. Major credit cards accepted. 7 Via Paolo Gaifa, Catania (phone: 95-330016). Expensive.

La Siciliana A classic family-style restaurant, it offers traditional Catanese dishes such as rigatoni *alla norma* (with tomato, fresh basil, and fried eggplant) and Sicilian meat rolls. There is garden dining in summer. Closed Sunday dinner, Mondays, and two weeks in August. Reservations advised. Major credit cards accepted. 52 Viale Marco Polo, Catania (phone: 95-376400). Expensive.

Enzo 2 There is a vast choice of fresh fish prepared to order at this simple, family-run eatery. Try it with pasta in a light garlic and parsley sauce, or taste it delicately stewed. There is a good selection of local wines. Closed Mondays. Reservations advised. No credit cards accepted. 26 Via Malta, Catania (phone: 95-370878). Moderate.

Il Giardino d'Inverno A mixture of French and Italian fare is served at this lovely *caffè*/restaurant. Dessert choices include chocolate mousse and French pastries. Closed Mondays. Reservations advised. Major credit cards accepted. 34 Via Asilo Sant'Agata, Catania (phone: 95-532853). Moderate.

Nettuno Both an outdoor pool and a good restaurant are found at this hotel with 85 rooms. Out of town on the noisy coastal road, at 121 Viale Ruggero di Lauria, Catania (phone: 95-493533; fax: 95-498066). Moderate.

Pagano This central spot serves excellent pasta, fish, and wines in a pleasant setting. Try the pasta with octopus ink and black broccoli. Closed Saturdays and August. Reservations advised. Major credit cards accepted (37 Via De Roberto, Catania; phone: 95-537045). From June through August, a dinner-only branch of the restaurant, offering alfresco dining, operates on the coastal drive. Reservations necessary. Major credit cards accepted. *Filenz Club* (21 Lungomare Galatea, Acitrezza; phone: 95-711-6505). Moderate, both restaurants.

En Route from Catania South of Augusta, S114 passes several minor archaeological sites. Try to ignore the hideous petrochemical plants, which together form the largest refinery complex in Europe. Shortly after Faro, a dirt road leads to the few remains of Megara Hyblaea, a colony founded by Greeks from Megara in the 8th century BC. It crosses the Magnisi Peninsula site of the ancient port of Thapsos, where the Athenian fleet anchored before the siege of Syracuse in 415 BC. Finally, just before Syracuse stands the ruin of the 4th-century BC *Castello Eurialo* (Castle of Euryalus), Sicily's most complete Greek military fortification, where Archimedes is said to have burned invading Roman ships from the shore by using a complex system of mirrors. Syracuse is 36 miles (58 km) from Catania.

SYRACUSE Situated on the Ionian Sea in southeastern Sicily, Syracuse (Siracusa in Italian) is a small, sun-bleached provincial capital. But in ancient times it was the western capital of Magna Graecia and one of the greatest cities in the world. Founded in 734 BC by settlers from Corinth, Syracuse gradually grew to rival Athens in military and commercial importance. The Greek mathematician Archimedes and the poet Theocritus were both from Syracuse.

Many of the buildings from this ancient period have survived. Most are in the "archaeological zone," in the town's ancient *Parco Monumentale della*

Neapoli (Viale Rizzo). The Greek theater—in a natural, wooded bowl—is the largest and one of the best preserved in the Hellenic world; in late May and June of even-numbered years (as was the practice in ancient times), festivals of Greek tragedies are produced in this spectacular setting. In odd-numbered years, the theater hosts opera and ballet. The *Altar of Hieron II,* once used for religious sacrifices, is also the setting for concerts and ballets. The *Latomie del Paradiso* is a steep-walled quarry and onetime prison for 7,000 Athenians routed in battle in 413 BC that, with much of its roof collapsed, has been taken over by flourishing semitropical vegetation. In one corner of the quarry is the famous *Ear of Dionysius,* a huge artificial cavern with impressive acoustics. Legend has it that slaves worked in this cave, hewing stone, and that Dionysius eavesdropped on them through a crack in the ceiling. (The name was coined in 1586 by the painter Caravaggio, who was referring to the shape of the cave's entrance.) The sites are open daily; admission charge.

The city's *Museo Archeologico Nazionale* (Viale Teocrito; phone: 931-67629) occupies a huge, modern complex on the grounds of *Villa Landolina.* The impressive collection, beautifully presented, chronicles eastern Sicily's Greek past. Closed Mondays; the second and fourth Sundays of each month; and after 2 PM; admission charge.

The small offshore island of Ortygia, which is connected to "mainland" Syracuse by two bridges, is the site of the medieval Old Town. A network of narrow, intersecting crossways, Ortygia is one of the most charming places in Sicily. Its faded, balconied houses near the *Castello Maniace* (Piazza Federico di Svevia) appear unrelated to the 20th century. In the center of the island is Piazza del Duomo, where the city's cathedral—*Chiesa di Santa Maria del Piliero*—is located. The *Duomo* was built on the site of the Greek *Temple of Athena,* and its original columns still remain. It's open daily, with a long (noon to 4 PM) closing. Also in the square is the Baroque *Municipio* (City Hall). Nearby on the waterfront is the *Fonte Artusa* (Fountain of Arethusa), supposedly the spot where the nymph reemerged from the sea after hiding from her impetuous suitor, the river god Alpheus. It is now stocked with papyrus, ducks, and geese. You may want to visit the *Istituto di Papiro* (Institute of Papyrus; 66 Viale Teocrito, Syracuse; phone: 931-22100), which also houses a museum and gift shop. It is closed Sundays and for a short (1 to 3 PM) break; admission charge.

After sightseeing, stop by *Marciante* (39 Via della Maestranza; phone: 931-67303) for the best sweets in the area. For night owls, Syracuse is known for its after-dark entertainment. On Friday and Saturday evenings in summer, the under-30 set come from as far away as Catania to dance at the seaside disco *Tonnara* (Lungomare, in the Terra Uzza district) or at *Il Veleno* (Via Maestranza) in the historic center. For those interested in quieter socializing, stop at *The Pub* or *Troubador* in Piazza Archimede in the historic center.

Syracuse's coastline, especially to the south, is renowned for its beauty, clear waters, and mythological scenery. There are romantic coves and wide, sandy beaches.

BEST EN ROUTE

Jonico 'A Rutta è Ciauli Housed in a small, attractive villa in a garden overlooking the Ionian Sea, this restaurant offers warm-weather dining on a verandah. Try the spaghetti with anchovies or fresh tuna, Sicilian-style. Closed Tuesdays. Reservations advised. Major credit cards accepted. Best to take a taxi. 194 Riviera Dionisio il Grande, Syracuse (phone: 931-65540). Expensive.

Rossini Everything that comes out of the kitchen here is well prepared by Pasqualino Giudice, known throughout Italy for his creative culinary talent. The spaghetti *all siracusana* (with anchovies) is a real treat, as is the *farfalle in salsa di gamberoni* (butterfly-shaped pasta in shrimp sauce). Try the tuna, cooked to order, or the *polpetti affogati* (stewed meatballs). Closed Tuesdays. Reservations advised. Major credit cards accepted. 6 Via Savoia, Syracuse (phone: 931-24317). Expensive.

Arlecchino Traditional and family-style, with a wide variety of seafood specialties. Closed Sunday dinner, Mondays, and August. Reservations advised. Major credit cards accepted. 5 Via dei Tolomei, Syracuse (phone: 931-66386). Expensive to moderate.

Bellavista Although this small (45 rooms), family-run place is a bit out of the way, it is located in a picturesque spot. For those on a tight budget, this is a good value. There's a restaurant. 4 Via Diodoro Siculo, Syracuse (phone: 931-411355; fax: 931-37027). Moderate.

Don Camilio In the center of the Old Town, this attractive restaurant is noted for its fresh fish prepared according to local traditions. Specialties include *zuppa di pesce* (fish stew). Closed Sunday dinner and Mondays. Reservations advised. Major credit cards accepted. 96 Via Maestranza, Syracuse (phone: 931-67133). Moderate.

La Foglia Local artists dine and display their work in this appetizing vegetarian and fish place. Closed Tuesdays and July. Reservations unnecessary. Major credit cards accepted. 21 Via Capodieci, Syracuse (phone: 931-66233). Moderate.

Grand–Villa Politi Said to have been Winston Churchill's favorite, this 95-room hotel with a restaurant, a pool, and gardens has Old World charm. 2 Via Politi Laudien, Syracuse (phone: 931-412121; fax: 931-36061). Moderate.

Park Just outside the city, this hotel offers 155 rooms, a pool, tennis courts, and a private garden. 80 Via Filisto, Syracuse (phone: 931-32644; fax: 931-38096). Moderate.

Taverna Aretusa This attractive, rustic hideaway is cluttered with bric-a-brac. It serves fresh fish, excellent pasta, organically grown vegetables and fruits, and local wine. Closed Wednesdays and the first three weeks in November. No reservations. Visa accepted. 32 Via Santa Teresa, Syracuse (phone: 931-68720). Inexpensive.

Trattoria il Cenacolo Located in a lovely courtyard in Ortygia, this simple eatery offers both three-course meals and pizza. Closed Wednesdays. Reservations unnecessary. Major credit cards accepted. 9-10 Via del Consiglio Reginale, Syracuse (phone: 931-65099). Inexpensive.

Tutto Gelato e Tutto Pizza A lively spot near the *Fonte Aretusa* in Ortygia, it's great for pizza (served only at night) or wonderful ice cream. Closed Tuesdays. No reservations. No credit cards accepted. 12 Lungomare Alfeo, Syracuse (phone: 931-67756). Inexpensive.

En Route from Syracuse The area around Syracuse is dotted with archaeological sites. S124 leads to the *Pantalica* necropolis, about 25 miles (40 km) from Syracuse by way of *Floridia,* the largest and best-preserved prehistoric necropolis in Sicily. Rocky walls near the ruins of the ancient town of Hyblaea are honeycombed by 5,000 cave-tombs. The road continues to *Palazzolo Acreide* (it has fine buildings, a Greek theater, and sculptures, known as *santoni,* carved out of the nearby cliffs) and the remains of Akrai, a military colony founded by the Syracusans in 664 BC. Either head south 19 miles (30 km) on S287 to Noto from Akrai or proceed straight from Syracuse on S115 about 20 miles (32 km).

Several miles out of Syracuse, S115 crosses the Anapo and Ciane Rivers. The latter is famous for its source, 4 miles (6 km) inland, where papyrus, introduced by either Hieron II or the Arabs, grows in wild profusion. Papyrus is a local souvenir industry as well as an object of serious study, as attested to by the *Istituto di Papiro* in Syracuse (see above). Boat trips can be arranged from the marina, reached by following signs to Canicattini (best done from the center of Syracuse and along Via Necropoli del Fusco). The marina is equidistant from S124 and S115.

NOTO The second-largest town in Syracuse province features the best examples of Sicilian Baroque architecture. Noto's major monuments are located in three groups along the main street, Corso Vittorio Emanuele. Beyond the entrance to the town through the *Porta Reale,* the *corso* widens first into a square framed by the *Chiesa di San Francesco* (also called *L'Immacolata*), the *Chiesa di Santa Chiara,* and the *Convento di San Salvatore.* Next it leads into a square dominated by the *Municipio* (City Hall), the *Chiesa di San Nicola,* the *Chiesa di San Salvatore,* and the *Palazzo di Landolina di Sant'Alfano.* A third square contains the theater and the *Chiesa di San Domenico.* Antico Noto, 7 miles (11 km) northwest, is the site (with remains) of the ancient town; its abandonment in 1693, due to an earthquake, gave rise to the present Noto, a feat of harmonious town planning. Noto Marina, 4 miles (6 km) east of Noto, has lovely public beaches.

BEST EN ROUTE

Corrado Costanzo Stop in this typical *pasticceria* for mouth-watering marzipan, cannoli, and possibly the best ice cream you've ever tasted. The flavors most favored by Signor Corrado (known and written about the world over) and his customers are jasmine, rose petal, and mandarin, which tastes more authentic than the fruit itself. Closed Wednesdays and the first 10 days of September. No reservations. No credit cards. Behind the *Municipio* at 7-9 Via Silvio Spaventa, Noto (phone: 931-835243). Inexpensive.

Falconara Known for its pizza, this restaurant on the way to Noto Marina also serves all types of regional pasta, meat, and fish. Closed Tuesdays, except in summer. Reservations unnecessary. Visa accepted. Noto Marina (phone: 931-812122). Inexpensive.

En Route from Noto S115 leads through Rosolini and Ispica to Modica, 25 miles (40 km) away, and then on to Ragusa. The Cava d'Ispica, a deep chalk gorge whose walls are dotted with medieval cave dwellings and prehistoric tombs, can be reached by a turnoff after Ispica at the junction for Bettola del Capitano. Modica, built on two sides of a gorge, is noted for its medieval and Baroque monuments.

RAGUSA The outskirts of Ragusa are surrounded by huge chemical plants. But the old part of town, Ragusa Ibla—originally a Byzantine settlement and then an important Norman stronghold—is extremely picturesque. The New Town has a small but well-organized museum—the *Museo Archeologico* (Via Natalelli; no phone). It is closed Mondays; Tuesdays through Saturdays after 2 PM; and Sundays after 1 PM; admission charge.

BEST EN ROUTE

Villa Fortugno An old villa is the setting for this wonderful restaurant with a seasonal menu. Don't miss the *ravioli di ricotta al sugo di maiale* (cheese ravioli with a pork and tomato sauce) or the stuffed pork chops. Local and regional wines are available. Closed Mondays and August. Reservations advised. No credit cards accepted. On the state road south toward Marina di Ragusa, 2 miles (3 km) from town (phone: 932-28656). Expensive.

Rafael Ultramodern and clean, this 22-room hotel offers great value. Featured are every convenience for the business traveler, including in-room computers, fax machines, and room service. On the premises are a parking garage and three common terraces; across the street is a restaurant. 40 Corso Italia, Ragusa (phone: 932-654080; fax: 932-653418). Moderate to inexpensive.

En Route from Ragusa Head west 5½ miles (9 km) on S115 to S514. Go 22 miles (35 km) north, and then take S124 west 13 miles (21 km) to the Queen of the Hills—Caltagirone, one of the most flourishing communities in the Sicilian interior.

CALTAGIRONE Its position on three hillsides gives Caltagirone its winding streets and irregularly shaped piazze. For centuries it has been known as a center for pottery and ceramics. The lovely *Museo della Ceramica* (off Via Roma in the public garden; phone: 933-21680) exhibits pottery from prehistoric times through the 19th century. It's open daily; no admission charge. A huge staircase linking two levels of the town is lined with an extraordinary array of tiles. On the nights of July 24, 25, and 31 every year, this staircase becomes the stage for *La Luminaria*—the lighting of over 4,000 different colored oil lanterns. The lamps give off various images, similar to those used to decorate the ceramics for which the town is famous.

BEST EN ROUTE

Grand Hotel Villa San Mauro In this 92-room hostelry, which is comfortable but in need of refurbishing, are a garden, a pool, and a restaurant. 18 Via Portosalvo, Caltagirone (phone: 933-26500; fax: 933-31661). Moderate.

En Route from Caltagirone Twenty miles (32 km) northwest of Caltagirone on N124 and S117 *bis* is Piazza Armerina.

PIAZZA ARMERINA A medieval and Baroque jewel, this small town has an impressive *Duomo* with a fine 15th-century Gothic-Catalan campanile; it's closed for a long (1 to 4 PM) break. Piazza Armerina also is known for its colorful August 15 *Festa dell'Assunta* (Feast of the Assumption), during which the Byzantine *Madonna of Victory,* said to have been given by Pope Nicholas II to the Norman King Roger, is carried through the streets in medieval procession.

Four miles (6 km) south of town on Strada Provinciale 15 is the ruin of the 4th-century *Villa Romana del Casale* (a Roman imperial villa), possibly the most important Roman construction in Sicily. Note the mosaic floors running through most of the villa. For more information, see *Remarkable Ruins* in DIVERSIONS. The villa is open daily; admission charge (phone: 935-680036).

Nearby, past Aidone on S288, are the ruins of the ancient walled city of Morgantina. They bear traces of pre-Greek, Greek, and Roman civilizations. The *Museo Morgantina* in Aidone (easily reached by following the signs) has an excellent collection of artifacts excavated from Morgantina. It's closed after 1 PM; no admission charge.

Pepito Regional dishes prepared with imagination are offered at this family-run trattoria. Specialties include spaghetti *alla Pepito* (with mushrooms, eggplant, anchovies, and tomatoes) and *carne alla Pepito* (broiled veal with green peppers). Closed Tuesdays. Reservations unnecessary. Major credit cards accepted. 138 Via Roma, Piazza Armerina (phone: 935-685737). Inexpensive.

Al Ritrovo da Nunzio Here the *ragù* is as hearty as in days of old, and the charcoal-broiled lamb chops are delicious. Closed Fridays. Reservations advised. No credit cards accepted. On the way out of town toward Enna, S117 *bis,* Piazza Armerina (phone: 935-681890). Inexpensive.

Selene This hotel is reasonable for a stopover, though its 42 rooms are in need of modernization. There's a restaurant. Centrally located, at 30 Viale Generale Gaeta, Piazza Armerina (phone/fax: 935-682254). Inexpensive.

La Tavernetta Traditional Sicilian food is served in huge portions. The homemade fettuccine *alla norma* (with eggplant, basil, ricotta, and tomatoes) is excellent, as are the meat and fish. Closed Sundays and January. Reservations advised. No credit cards accepted. 14 Via Cavour, Piazza Armerina (phone: 935-685883). Inexpensive.

En Route from Piaza Armeria Take S117 *bis* north 15 miles (24 km) to S192; from there, head west for 9 miles (14 km) to Enna.

ENNA Its commanding position on a steep hill made Enna—called Castrogiovanni until changed by Mussolini in 1927—an impregnable stronghold in ancient times and earned it the nickname "the Belvedere of Sicily." The town is built on the site of ancient Henna, which, according to mythology, was the site of the rape of Persephone by Pluto. It became the center of the cult of Demeter, or Ceres, Persephone's mother. A fountain behind Piazza Vittorio Emanuele illustrates the legend.

An agricultural center today, Enna has several major monuments. The 14th-century *Duomo* (Piazza Duomo), founded by Eleonora, wife of Frederick II of Aragon, is a strange mixture of Gothic and Baroque, with interesting carved black alabaster columns in the nave. It is open daily, with a long (1 to 4 PM) break. The massive *Castello di Lombardia* at the end of Via Roma is one of the most important medieval castles in Sicily, although only six of the original 20 towers survive. The castle is closed Mondays; admission charge. On the other side of the Old City is the octagonal *Tower of Frederick II of Swabia.* Enter from the *Giardino Pubblico* (Public Garden); it's open daily, and there's no admission charge.

On a peak 4 miles (6 km) north of Enna (take Strada Provinciale 2 to S290), the red-hued medieval town of Calascibetta got its name from the

Arabs, who called it Kalat-Scibet. A walk around town is a stroll into the past. Calascibetta's belvedere commands splendid views.

BEST EN ROUTE

Ariston Stylishly discreet and run by the owners of the *Sicilia* hotel (see below), this restaurant excels in the preparation of local specialties, such as *agnello arrosto* (roast lamb) and homemade *cavatelli* (twisted pasta). Closed Sundays and the second half of August. Reservations unnecessary. No credit cards accepted. 365 Via Roma, *Galleria Bruno,* Enna (phone: 935-26038). Moderate.

Centrale Delicious Sicilian and Ennese specialties are served in a friendly atmosphere. Try the homemade ravioli, the vast assortment of appetizers, and stuffed homemade breads, followed by a mixed grill of lamb, beef, and pork. Closed Saturdays (except in summer) and the first two weeks of October. Reservations unnecessary. Major credit cards accepted. 9 Piazza VI di Dicembre, Enna (phone: 935-500963). Moderate to inexpensive.

Sicilia The only worthwhile place to stay in the town center is this comfortable hotel with 84 rooms and a restaurant. 5 Piazza Colajanni, Enna (phone: 935-500850; fax: 935-500488). Moderate to inexpensive.

La Fontana Near the center of town, this trattoria offers typical Sicilian fare such as risotto *all'Enna* (with tomatoes, mushrooms, black olives, and pecorino cheese), *cavatelli alla siciliana* (homemade pasta in a sauce of tomato, basil, eggplant, red pepper, and cheese), and grilled lamb. Closed Sundays and January. Major credit cards accepted. Reservations unnecessary. 6 Via Vulturno, Enna (phone: 935-25465). Inexpensive.

En Route from Enna About 23½ miles (38 km) southwest is Caltanissetta. The quickest route from Enna is via the A18 autostrada; S117 *bis* provides a scenic but mountainous alternative.

CALTANISSETTA This largely modern town was built on the site of the ancient city of Nissa. The *Duomo (Chiesa di Santa Maria la Nova e San Michele)* has two *campanili* and some interesting paintings inside. A street running alongside the *Duomo,* Via San Domenico, leads through an old quarter with narrow, winding streets. The *Museo Civico* (Civic Museum; 3 Via Colaianni; phone: 934-25936) has a small archaeological collection. It is closed Mondays and after 1 PM; admission charge.

BEST EN ROUTE

Cortese Modern, it offers an excellent *cavatelli al ragù* (homemade pasta in sauce) and *involtini* (veal rolls). Closed Mondays and August 10 to 20. No reservations. Visa accepted. 166 Viale Sicilia, Caltanissetta (phone: 934-31686). Moderate.

En Route from Caltanissetta S122, one of two routes to Agrigento, 36 miles (58 km) away, passes through picturesque towns like Naro, with its crenelated city walls and Baroque churches and convents, and Favara, a Norman town that grew up around the 1275 *Castello Chiaramonte,* which stands in Piazza Cavour.

AGRIGENTO In ancient times, Agrigento—known to the Greeks as Akragas—was one of the most prosperous cities in ancient Sicily. With its location in a vast natural amphitheater between the mountains and the sea, it probably was also one of the most beautiful. Modern Agrigento is overbuilt and unattractive, but the surviving Doric temples of the ancient city, the excellent archaeological museum, and parts of the old medieval and Baroque town make it an essential part of any Sicilian visit.

The ruins in the Valley of Temples are built in a more or less straight line running parallel to the sea. They are hauntingly beautiful at dawn, twilight, or at night, when they are illuminated by floodlights. The most intact is the *Temple of Concord,* built in 450 BC and possibly the best-preserved Greek temple in the world after the Theseion in Athens. Its 34 exterior columns are still standing. To the east is the imposing *Temple of Juno,* built 20 years later but with only 25 columns intact. To the west, separated by the 6th-century early Christian burial ground, stand the remains of the *Temple of Hercules,* built in 520 BC and the oldest monument here; it may originally have been as large as the *Parthenon* in Athens. Farther west and on the other side of the Via dei Templi, the road running through the archaeological zone, are the widely scattered remains of the mammoth *Temple of Olympian Jove,* whose roof was originally supported by 38 *telamoni* (stone giants). Stretched out on the ground is a reassembly of one of the giants. Of the *Temple of Castor and Pollux,* only the four columns of the northwest corner survive. The *Tomb of Theron* is believed to hold the remains of the Greek tyrant who once ruled Akragas. Other monuments include the *Temples of Aesculapius* and of *Vulcan.* There are also the remains of the ancient Hellenic-Roman quarter.

Across the road from the Hellenic-Roman quarter is the *Museo Archeologico* (Archaeological Museum; phone: 922-29008), whose collection includes vases and amphorae from the 6th to the 3rd century BC, some magnificent Attic pottery, early and later Bronze Age material, architectural fragments from the temples, and Greek and Roman sarcophagi, helmets, and other artifacts. It's open Mondays, Wednesdays, and Fridays from 9 AM to 1:30 PM; Tuesdays, Thursdays, and Saturdays from 9 AM to 5:30 PM; Sundays and holidays from 9 AM to 12:30 PM; no admission charge.

Next door is a 3rd-century BC *Ekklesiasterion* (Meeting Hall). Adjoining it is the 12th-century *Chiesa di San Nicolò,* with its Romanesque-Gothic façade and 15th- and 16th-century paintings and frescoes and the *Phaedra Sarcophagus*. The church is closed afternoons.

Agrigento's medieval Old Town also has appeal. Via Atenea, the main street, leads into the Salita Santo Spirito and on to the *Convento Cistercense* (Cistercian Convent), where the nuns still produce and sell *frutta della martorana* (marzipan fruits), *couscous dolci* (couscous sweets), and other confections. The church has a Gothic portal and 17th-century stucco decorations. A cloister and refectory hall house the public library. *Santa Maria dei Greci* is a small church built on the site of a Doric temple; it can be viewed on request to the custodian (though he is reportedly hard to find). Nearby is the 14th-century *Duomo* (open daily, with a long—noon to 5 PM—closing) and the *Teatro Luigi Pirandello* (Piazza Municipio), named after the Italian playwright, who was born in the simple village of Kaos at the edge of town. In the house where Pirandello was born (the clearly signposted *Casa Natale di Luigi Pirandello*), also in Kaos, is a museum with memorabilia pertaining to the playwright's life. It is open daily, with a short (12:30 to 2:30 PM) closing; no admission charge.

BEST EN ROUTE

Kalòs In the center of town, this establishment offers regional and Italian fare and a good selection of fresh fish. Specialties include macaroni with pistachio nuts, and spaghetti with shellfish. Closed Tuesdays. Reservations necessary. Major credit cards accepted. Piazza San Calogero, Agrigento (phone: 922-26389). Expensive.

Villa Athena A small, comfortable 18th-century villa, it's set amid the olive and almond trees surrounding the Valley of Temples. The hotel's terraces and balconies and many of its 40 rooms overlook the three principal temples. There is a pool and a good restaurant. 33 Via Valle dei Templi, Agrigento (phone: 922-596288; fax: 922-402180). Expensive.

Le Caprice Views over the Valley of the Temples and an unbeatable antipasto buffet with an emphasis on vegetables and fresh fish attract a large local following, especially at lunch. Try the fettuccine *all'aragosta* (in a tomato, garlic, parsley, and lobster sauce). Closed Fridays and the first two weeks of July. Reservations advised. Major credit cards accepted. 51 Via Panoramica dei Templi, Agrigento (phone: 922-26469). Expensive to moderate.

Kaos At the edge of town where Pirandello was born is this 105-room, air conditioned, seaside hotel housed in a beautifully restored patrician villa. It has lovely grounds with ponds, fountains, a pool, and tennis courts. The restaurant offers alfresco dining in summer. S115 toward Marsala, in Villaggio Pirandello (phone: 922-598622; fax: 922-598770). Moderate.

Villa Eos Right next to *Kaos* (see above), this clean, simply furnished, 23-room hotel is a tranquil spot with lovely views. On the grounds are a pool, a tennis court, and an alfresco restaurant. Contrada Cumbo, Villaggio Pirandello (phone: 922-597170; fax: 922-597188). Moderate.

Del Vigneto Set in a vineyard overlooking the temple area, this trattoria offers good, rustic, regional fare. Try the fresh fish. Closed Tuesdays and November. No reservations. Visa accepted. 11 Via Cavaleri Magazzeni, Agrigento (phone: 922-414319). Inexpensive.

En Route from Agrigento The coast road west (S115) to Sciacca—39 miles (63 km) away—passes a turnoff for the excavation site of *Eraclea Minoa,* a Minoan colony located in an isolated spot at the far point of a rocky cape. The site is open daily; no admission charge.

SCIACCA Known today for its thermal baths and its ceramics industry, this fishing village also has some interesting medieval monuments. An important trading center since the Roman era 2,000 years ago, Sciacca became a major harbor during Arab domination. Significant building and fortification took place under the Normans and Spaniards. Of particular note are the richly decorated 16th-century *Porta di San Salvatore,* the 14th-century *Chiesa di Santa Margherita,* and the 15th-century *Palazzo Steripinto.*

BEST EN ROUTE

Mirell Club Fresh fish is the specialty at this popular seashore restaurant. Try the linguine with fish sauce or the fettuccine with lobster sauce. Closed Tuesdays and the first two weeks of July. Reservations advised. Major credit cards accepted. 26 Via al Lido, Sciacca (phone: 925-23621). Moderate.

Grande Albergo Terme This pleasant, modern establishment is on the sea road just out of town, near one of the principal spas in the area. It offers 72 rooms and some spa services, including an outdoor heated spring-water pool. 1 Viale Nuove Terme, Sciacca (phone: 925-23133; fax: 925-21746). Moderate to inexpensive.

En Route from Sciacca Follow S115 for 25 miles (40 km) to Selinunte.

SELINUNTE The ancient town of Selinus was founded in 682 BC by settlers from Megara Hyblaea, a Greek colony near Syracuse. It was most prosperous and powerful in the 5th and 6th centuries BC, when most of its temples were built. Selinunte today is one of Sicily's most important archaeological sites. The disarray of the ruins—crumbled walls, toppled columns—is believed to have been caused more by earthquakes than by enemies.

Occupying three hills close to the sea, the ruins are divided into two distinct groups. The eastern group includes the remains of three large temples believed to have been dedicated to Hera, Athena, and Apollo. The western group, across a gorge (Gorgo di Cottone) that may have been one of the town's ancient harbors, includes the massive walls of the *Acropolis,* five more temples, and several lesser buildings. The now famous metopes (Doric temple carvings) excavated from this complex are housed in Palermo's *Museo Nazionale Archeologico.*

En Route from Selinunte S115 leads north to Castelvetrano and then west toward Marsala, 22 miles (35 km) away.

MARSALA The city that produces the sweet, musky wine of the same name was known to the Arabs as Mars-al-Allah (Harbor of God), and its history is closely linked with the sea. Both the town and its environs have a distinctly Arabic feel. Founded by refugees from the 8th-century BC Phoenician town of Motya, it was destroyed by the Syracusan tyrant Dionysius I and rebuilt by the Carthiginians in the 4th century BC as Lilybaeum. On the Capo Boeo headland, its remains include a Roman bath, a Punic-Roman necropolis, and 6th-century fortifications. Wine merchants who started businesses here during the 18th and 19th centuries brought a decidedly English influence; the city's Baroque cathedral (Piazza della Repubblica) is dedicated to St. Thomas of Canterbury. Garibaldi and his Thousand landed in Marsala in 1860 with the help of the British, commencing the movement for Italian unification.

The fortified wine bearing the city's name is enjoying a comeback after a decline in popularity. Of the marsala producers that can be visited, the best-known is *Florio,* which sprawls along the *lungomare,* just south of the port (1 Via Florio, Marsala; phone: 923-781111). It's closed August; weekends; and Fridays after 2 PM; no admission charge. It is always advisable to have your hotel or the tourist office (45 Via Garibaldi; phone: 923-714079) call first.

BEST EN ROUTE

Delfino An excellent seaside restaurant with alfresco dining, it specializes in shellfish salad, fish soup, grilled fish, and the house specialty, seafood couscous. Closed Tuesdays in winter. Reservations advised. Major credit cards accepted. About 3½ miles (6 km) from town, at 672 Via Lungomare Mediterraneo, Marsala (phone: 923-998188). Moderate.

Gnazziu u Pazzu Located in an old *baglio* (wine warehouse), this attractive restaurant offers well-prepared local fare, including fresh pasta, fish stew with tomatoes and pine nuts, and grilled lamb and goat. Closed Mondays. Reservations unnecessary. Major credit cards accepted. Lungomare Boeo, Marsala (phone: 923-712284). Moderate.

President With 68 rooms, this comfortable hotel offers a restaurant, a pool, and excellent service. 1 Via Nino Bixio, Marsala (phone: 923-999333; fax: 923-999115). Moderate.

En Route from Marsala S115 continues another 19 miles (30 km) to Trapani, a large city with only a few interesting monuments and churches clustered near the port. Trapani is the departure point for the three relatively unspoiled and undeveloped Egadi Islands, Favignana, Lévanzo, and Maréttimo, and for Pantelleria and Tunisia. Ferries leave regularly year-round from the maritime station. Above perches Erice, less than 9 miles (14 km) northeast of the city.

ERICE Ancient Eryx—founded, like nearby Segesta, by the Elymnians, another ancient tribe—was famous for its temple to the goddess of fertility, Venus Erycina. The town was mentioned in Virgil's *Aeneid*. Despite its mythological and ancient origins, Erice primarily bears the stamp of its Norman rulers. Its stone houses and fortified castles have retained, almost intact, a medieval aura. The streets are paved with stone blocks; the tiny balconies are filled with songbirds and flowerpots; and hidden behind austere doorways are charming courtyards that belong to another century. The lovely *Chiesa Matrice* is right at the entrance to town. Inside the town walls is the *Duomo* (Via Carvini), with an elaborate interior. It is open daily, with a long (12:30 to 4 PM) closing. At the top of the hill is a castle, built over what are believed to be remains of the *Temple of Venus*. Erice's mountain perch above the sea provides a number of impressive views, but the little town is often shrouded in fog, particularly in winter; try to visit in good weather and early in the day.

BEST EN ROUTE

Elimo Converted from an attractive palazzo, this 21-room hotel has an especially good location in the *centro storico* (historic district), plus on-premises dining. 23 Via Vittorio Emanuele, Erice (phone: 923-869377; fax: 923-869252). Moderate.

Ermione A bit drafty but otherwise pleasantly appointed, it has 38 rooms (ask for one facing the sea). In the noteworthy restaurant, the cook turns out excellent local dishes, including Trapani seafood couscous. On the outskirts of town, at 43 Pineta Comunale, Erice (phone: 923-869138; fax: 923-869587). Moderate.

Moderno This cozy, whitewashed 40-room hotel is ensconced in a 19th-century palazzo near the *Duomo,* and there's a tastefully renovated annex across the street. Some rooms are furnished with antiques; others have attractive bamboo furniture. In the main building is a pleasant restaurant. 63 Via Vittorio Emanuele, Erice (phone: 923-869300; fax: 923-869139). Moderate.

Taverna di Re Aceste The walls of this tavern are decorated with scenes from the *Aeneid* in which King Acestus, according to legend the first King of Erice, offers a funeral banquet to Aeneas to console him after the death of his father, Anchises. Try the pasta with Erice pesto, followed by grilled fish or meat. Closed Wednesdays and November. Reservations advised. Major credit cards accepted. Via Conte Pepoli, Erice (phone: 923-869084). Moderate.

En Route from Erice The seacoast route toward Palermo meanders around Capo San Vito (look in on the charming San Vito lo Capo resort, where many Trapani residents have summer homes) and runs along the coast to the lovely Golfo di Castellammare, rimmed with orange groves. From here pick up S113 at Alcamo. Alternatively, take S113 directly from Erice east to Segesta, about 12 miles (20 km) away.

SEGESTA Selinunte's ancient rival is believed to have been founded as long ago as the 12th century BC by the Elymni, a people possibly descended from Greek-Trojan stock. Although its *cavea* (semicircular seating area of the theater) apparently was never completed, Segesta's huge Doric temple is one of the most impressive ancient monuments outside Greece. For more information, see *Remarkable Ruins* in DIVERSIONS.

En Route from Segesta Take S113 northeast for about 15 miles (24 km) to Alcamo.

ALCAMO Named for the Arab fort *Alkamuk,* once situated on top of Mt. Bonifato, the town was rebuilt by Frederick II of Swabia in the 13th century. The 14th-century *Basilica di Santa Maria Assunta,* which has frescoes by Borremans, was restored in the 17th century; its campanile is the original.

BEST EN ROUTE

La Funtanazza On a hill overlooking Alcamo and the Golfo di Castellammare, this simple restaurant offers good local and traditional Italian dishes. There also are six guestrooms. Closed Tuesdays and September 10 to October 10. No reservations. No credit cards accepted. Four miles (6 km) out of Alcamo, in Località Monte Bonifato (phone: 924-25314). Inexpensive.

En Route from Alcamo About a half-hour's drive south of the junction of S113 and S186 is a small mountain village well worth visiting. Piana degli Albanesi is an Albanian community dating from the 15th century. On important holidays, such as *Easter* and *Epiphany* (January 6), the people dress in traditional costumes. Rejoin S186 and continue east; 5 miles (8 km) from Palermo is the small hilltop town of Monreale. Over the centuries, Monreale has grown up in the shadow of its magnificent cathedral, *Santa Maria la Nuova.* (For a complete discussion, see *Palermo* in THE CITIES.) The road out of Monreale leads directly into downtown Palermo.

PALERMO Sicily's capital contains few Greek vestiges, but it does have some of the island's most impressive Norman-Arab and Baroque monuments. Arab-style outdoor markets coexist with medieval churches and monasteries. For complete coverage, see *Palermo* in THE CITIES.

En Route from Palermo Take S113 east for 9 miles (14 km) to Bagheria.

BAGHERIA This small town originally was set in the midst of orange groves, but with the capital's expansion it has become almost a suburb. A few of its lovely 18th-century villas are open to the public. For example, the *Villa dei Principi di Cattolica* is a conspicuous landmark on the Palermo road; it now houses the local museum, which has a large collection of works by Renato Guttuso, a well-known 20th-century painter from Bagheria. It is closed Mondays; admission charge (phone: 91-905438). The *Villa Palagonia* (Piazza Garibaldi; phone: 91-934543) was built in 1715 by the Prince of Palagonia; an eccentric grandson later added dozens of statues of grotesque figures to the garden wall. The villa is open daily, with a midday closing; admission charge.

En Route from Bagheria Turn off onto the coastal road to Capo Zafferano, and follow the signs to Santa Flavia. Beyond the village of Aspra and the fishing enclaves of Sant'Elia and Porticello is Santa Flavia, home of the 17th-century *Villa Filangeri* and, nearby, the 18th-century *Villa Valdina,* which houses important paintings by Pietro Novelli. Continue on past Salunto, a tuna fishing village, rejoin S113 heading east from Bagheria, and, immediately thereafter, turn left for Solunto.

SOLUNTO In an isolated spot on the slopes of Mt. Catalfano overlooking the sea, Solus was an important 4th-century BC Greek settlement. Visitors enter the complex of ruins through a small museum that leads to an agora (marketplace), a gymnasium, and a large cistern, along with the remains of houses with important mosaics and murals. It is open daily; no admission charge.

En Route from Solunto About 13 miles (21 km) southeast on S113 is Termini Imerese, originally settled by inhabitants from the neighboring Greek towns of Thermae and Himera. Conquered by Carthage after the destruction of Himera by Hannibal in 409 BC, it later fell to Syracuse and eventually to Rome. The modern town has some ancient ruins and an antiquities museum.

Continuing eastward along the coast, if you turn south onto S120, after about 6 miles (10 km) will be the small hilltop town of Cerda, devoted to the cultivation of artichokes; in the town center, several trattorias serve entire meals of artichokes prepared in every conceivable way. Returning to the coast road, E1 passes near the ruins of Himera, founded by settlers of ancient Zancle (Messina) in 648 BC and destroyed two centuries later by Hannibal. The birthplace of the 7th-century BC poet Stesichorus, Himera was also the site of Carthage's defeat by Gelon of Syracuse. Excavations have unearthed a large Doric temple built in 480 BC to celebrate Gelon's victory. There are also three small 6th-century temples and a necropolis with 22 tombs.

Head east 19 miles (30 km) to Cefalù.

CEFALÙ This ancient Greek seaport now is known mostly for its lovely beaches and delicious seafood. Its *Duomo* (Piazza Duomo) is one of the most beautiful Norman cathedrals in Sicily. Built by Roger II in the 12th century, the *Duomo* stands against a massive cliff. Inside are an unusual triple apse and well-preserved Byzantine-style mosaics that rival those of Palermo and Monreale. The *Duomo* is open daily, with a long (noon to 3:30 PM) closing. The nearby *Palazzo Paraino* and *Palazzo Martino* contain fine examples of late Renaissance–style decoration. Also in the Old Town is the medieval public bathhouse, *Lavatoio Pubblico* (Via Vittorio Emanuele), originally an Arab bath and now a museum. It is open daily; no admission charge. The *Museo Mandralisca* (13 Via Mandralisca; phone: 921-21547) has an interesting collection of ancient coins and other artifacts and some Renaissance paintings, including the famous *Ignoto* by Antonello da Messina. The museum is open daily, with a long (12:30 to 3:30 PM) closing; admission charge. On the *rocca* (promontory) overlooking Cefalù are the ruins of a feudal castle, a 6th-century BC cistern, and an ancient temple said to be dedicated to the goddess Diana.

BEST EN ROUTE

La Brace A Cefalù side street is not the place a visitor would expect to find a restaurant with a wide range of well-prepared exotic foods, including everything from Chinese and Indonesian fare to a Sicilian menu and simple, delicious hamburgers. To accompany all this, try the red *secco* (dry) wine, made in the village, and conclude with a delectable chocolate mousse. Closed Mondays, December, and January. Reservations advised. Major credit cards accepted. 10 Via XXV Novembre, Cefalù (phone: 921-23570). Expensive to moderate.

Kalura One mile (1.6 km) east of Cefalù, this clean, pleasant establishment with 80 rooms (many with balconies and sea views) offers a restaurant, a bar, a beach, a pool, tennis, mini-golf, and a private park and gardens. Half board required July through September. Open year-round. 13 Via Vincenzo Cavallgro, Località Caldura, Cefalù (phone: 921-21354; fax: 921-23122). Expensive to moderate.

Osteria del Duomo In the main piazza facing the *Duomo,* this excellent *osteria* is a favorite among Italians who come for the seafood and *penne in barca* (a delicious pasta dish made with white sauce, clams, parsley, and caviar). Closed Mondays from October through May. Reservations advised. Major credit cards accepted. 5 Via Seminario, Cefalù (phone: 921-21838). Expensive to moderate.

Baia del Capitano On a bay 3 miles (5 km) west of Cefalù, this unpretentious white stucco hotel has 39 rooms, eight with terraces and most with lovely sea views. There are a lighted tennis court, a *bocce* court, a playground, a private beach, a pool, and a restaurant. Open year-round. Contrada Mazzaforno, Cefalù (phone: 921-20003; fax: 921-20163). Moderate.

Le Calette This very pleasant 51-room hostelry has a pool, a private beach, and a restaurant serving good local cuisine. It's a mile (1.6 km) east of Cefalù. Weekly excursions to the Aeolian Islands are offered from June 15 to September 15. Open May through September. Località Caldura, Cefalù (phone: 921-24144; fax: 921-23688). Moderate.

Paradiso Club All 41 rooms here have terraces; there also are 11 bungalows. Amenities include a restaurant with alfresco dining, a private beach, a tennis court, and a pool set in gardens; sailing, windsurfing, and scuba diving lessons are available. Half board required in August. Open year-round. 18-20 Via dei Mulini, Cefalù (phone: 921-23900; fax: 921-23990). Moderate.

Tourist On the shore road, this comfortable 46-room hostelry has a pool, access to the beach, and a restaurant. Open April through September. Lungomare G. Giardina, Cefalù (phone: 921-21750). Moderate.

En Route from Cefalù The 110-mile (176-km) drive to Messina is dotted with picturesque places. On the stretch of road leading from Cefalù to Santo Stefano di Camastro, a local pottery center, side roads lead inland to Castelbuono (a good starting point for a drive through the Madonie Mountains), Pollina, San Mauro Castelverde, and Tusa, all of which have interesting minor churches. S117 from Santo Stefano leads inland to the charming medieval town of Mistretta. S113 and A20 continue along the coast to Capo d'Orlando, from which S116 leads to Naso in the Nebrodi Mountains and on to the ruins of Tyndaris (Tindari), founded by refugees fleeing the Spartans. Twenty-seven miles (43 km) from Messina is Milazzo.

MILAZZO Ancient Mylae was founded by settlers from the Greek city-state of Zancle (Messina) in the 8th century BC. The second-largest harbor in Sicily, Milazzo is the choice point of departure for the Aeolian Islands. The town's most important monuments—the *Duomo Vecchio,* the castle, and the ancient city walls—are in the Città Alta (Upper City). Colorful folk processions are held on the second Tuesday after *Easter* and on the *Festa di Santo Stefano* (the first Sunday of September).

BEST EN ROUTE

Villa Marchese One of the most esteemed eateries in Sicily offers a wide variety of local fresh fish creatively prepared and exquisitely presented. For more information, see *The Best Restaurants of Italy* in DIVERSIONS. Closed Mondays and November. Reservations advised. Major credit cards accepted. Strada

Panoramica, Contrada Paradiso, Capo Milazzo (phone: 90-928-2514). Expensive.

Il Chiostro Sicilian dishes such as fresh fish and pasta with clams or sardines are the drawing card of this charming small restaurant high above the harbor. Closed Tuesdays in winter and two weeks in November. Reservations advised. No credit cards accepted. Piazza San Francesco, Milazzo (phone: 90-922-2001). Moderate.

Silvanetta Palace In this large, pleasant hotel are 90 nicely appointed rooms, many with balconies and harbor views. There also are tennis courts, a pool, a beach, and a restaurant. About a mile (1.6 km) out of town, toward Messina, at 1 Via Acqueviole, Milazzo (phone: 90-928-1633; fax: 90-922-2787). Moderate.

TOURING THE AEOLIAN ISLANDS

Off Sicily's northeastern coast, these islands are considered by many to be the most beautiful in Sicilian waters. They were named after Aeolus, the mythical god of the wind, who the ancients believed made his home in a cave here. There are seven major islands—Lipari, Vulcano, Salina, Panarea, Stromboli, Filicudi, and Alicudi—and numerous minor islets and outcroppings. Created by volcanic eruptions thousands of years ago in this deepest part of the Tyrrhenian Sea, they have a primitive, rocky beauty, softened here and there by such Mediterranean greenery as acanthus, broom, rosemary, wild fennel, and caper. The natural beauty of the islands, combined with the simple lifestyle of their inhabitants, has made them an attractive vacation spot. Cars, especially for non-residents, are discouraged on a few of the islands, most of which are small enough to maneuver on foot. Many of the most beautiful and secluded beaches and the best diving or fishing spots are accessible only by boat, which for the tourist means hiring a local fisherman on a daily or hourly basis. Not surprisingly, with fish and shellfish in abundance, there are some particularly fine restaurants on the larger islands and numerous pleasant, if simple, trattorie throughout the archipelago. Price ranges are slightly higher than those for Sicily (see *Touring Sicily*).

Although it is possible to get to the Aeolian Islands from other ports—there is overnight ferry service from Naples year-round and ferry and hydrofoil service from Naples, Palermo, Cefalù, Messina, Reggio Calabria, Vibo Valentia, and Maratea in summer—Milazzo is the major departure point. If you are traveling from the US, it is easiest to fly to Naples and take a ferry or hydrofoil from the port. There is year-round daily service from Milazzo to all of the islands; frequency increases in the summer. The seven islands also are connected to one another by ferry, hydrofoil, and private boat. Departure times vary according to season and weather; inquire about timetables locally, and, in summer, make reservations in advance. In Milazzo, book through *Agenzia N.G.E.* (26 Via dei Mille; phone: 90-928-4091; fax: 90-928-3415); on Lipari Island, through *Agenzia Eolian Tours* (Via Amendola; phone: 90-981-2193) or the *Azienda Autonoma di Soggiorno e Turismo delle Isole Eolie* (*AAST;* 202 Corso Vittorio Emanuele, Lipari; phone: 90-988-0095). Exchange your money before you go, as few banks on the islands offer this service.

LIPARI Ancient Meligunis (as Lipari used to be called) probably was settled in the 6th century BC, as indicated by traces found on the promontory overlooking the town of Lipari and the harbor. Artifacts found at the site are displayed at the island's small but well-known *Museo Archeologico* (Via Castello Lipari; phone: 90-988-0174), housed in a 16th-century Spanish castle that incorporates fragments of an ancient acropolis. It is closed Mondays through Saturdays after 2 PM; closed Sundays and holidays after 1 PM; no admission charge. Since Lipari, the largest of the Aeolian Islands, has good roads, it is possible to tour the entire island by rental car or vespa. Other towns include Terme San Calogero, the site of hot water springs and 19th-century baths (now closed); Acquacalda, with its pumice quarries; and Rocche Rosse and its obsidian beds. From the port in Lipari, it is possible to book day trips by boat around this island or to any of the others in the archipelago.

BEST EN ROUTE

Carasco There are 89 quiet, comfortable rooms at the island's best hotel. It was built beside the sea, so there are wonderful views, as well as a pool, private beach facilities, and a restaurant. Open April through September. Porto delle Genti, Lipari (phone: 90-981-1605; fax: 90-981-1828). Expensive.

Filippino At the foot of the castle, this well-known restaurant (the oldest in the islands) offers homemade macaroni, black risotto, fish soup, and Chinese-style lobster, plus good local wines such as Salina malvasia, which has made the nearby island of Salina famous. Several inexpensive rooms also are available. Closed Mondays from October through May, and November 10 to December 10. Reservations advised. Major credit cards accepted. Piazza Municipio, Lipari (phone: 90-988-0726). Expensive.

La Nassa The favorite among certain locals, this family-run restaurant is decorated in good taste, with attention to detail. Regional dishes emphasize freshly caught fish, local produce, and spices. Try the pasta *con pesce* (with sea urchin and eggplant) or the *zuppa di pesce* (fish soup). The excellent wine list includes some homemade vintages. Open April through October. Reservations advised. Major credit cards accepted. 36 Via Franza, Lipari (phone: 90-981-1319). Expensive to moderate.

Gattopardo Park An attractive 62-room holiday village five minutes from the sea, it was designed around an 18th-century villa and set among lush vegetation. The alfresco restaurant serves island specialties. It offers bus service to the beach at Cannetto, about 2 miles (3 km) away. The hotel is open year-round (a rarity!), but be sure to check ahead; the restaurant is closed November through February. Viale Diana, Lipari (phone: 90-981-1035; fax: 90-988-0207). Moderate.

Giardino sul Mare A short walk from the port and center of town and perched above the sea, this place has 46 rooms, most boasting terraces and sea views. There also is a pool, a scuba diving center, and a charming outdoor restaurant. Open *Easter* through September. 65 Via Maddalena, Lipari (phone: 90-981-1004; fax: 90-988-0150). Moderate.

E' Pulera In a lovely garden are secluded tables where hearty island-style meals are served. A piano bar offers local music every evening. Closed for lunch and from October through May. Reservations advised. Major credit cards accepted. 51 Via Diana, Lipari (phone: 90-981-1158). Moderate.

Al Pirata This eatery was literally dug out of the foundations of the *Chiesa di San Giuseppe,* with a terrace on the water. Local seafood, traditional fare, and pizza are served. Closed Mondays (except in summer) and November. Reservations advised. Major credit cards accepted. By the hydrofoil port, Salita San Giuseppe, Lipari (phone: 90-981-1796). Moderate to inexpensive.

VULCANO A short distance from Lipari, this is the most tourist-oriented of all the islands, largely because of its four volcanic craters, one of which, Vulcano della Fossa, is still slightly active. The crater's circumference of roughly 1,650 feet can be covered on foot in about an hour. Another seismic site is at Porto di Levante. Only a few yards from the sea lies a lake of thermal, mineral-rich mud, reportedly with vast healing powers.

BEST EN ROUTE

Arcipelago Built in an extraordinary setting, on ground "reclaimed" after an underwater eruption in the 2nd century BC, this hotel has 80 rooms, many with sea views, and a pool. Full board is preferred in high season. Open April through mid-October. Località Vulcanello, Vulcano (phone: 90-985-2002; fax: 90-985-2451). Moderate.

Lanterna Blu Country dishes such as *ricotta in fornata* (pasta with baked ricotta cheese) are the specialties in this characteristic trattoria. There is also an inexpensive pensione. Open year-round. Reservations advised. No credit cards accepted. 58 Via Lentia, Vulcano (phone: 90-985-2287, pensione; 90-985-2287, restaurant). Moderate.

Tony Maniaci Before trying the well-prepared pasta, rice dishes, and local catch at this family-run trattoria, start off the meal with lightly fried eggplant or steamed local tuna. Closed November through February. No reservations. No credit cards accepted. Località Gelso, Vulcano (phone: 90-985-2395, proprietor). Inexpensive.

SALINA On the other side of Lipari, Salina has only two visible volcanic craters but far more vegetation than the other islands. About two-thirds of this unspoiled island has been designated a wildlife preserve. It also has extensive vineyards that produce the excellent local malvasia wine. The rocky coastline has high cliffs and only a scattering of accessible beaches. Visitors can make the easy trek up to Mt. Fossa delle Felci, 1,900 feet, and admire the views; visit the picturesque village of Pollarta, located in the crater of an extinct volcano; or view the small salt lake in Lingua.

BEST EN ROUTE

Signum The best on the island, this charming family-run inn is set in a garden overlooking the sea. Furnished tastefully with antiques in simple Aeolian style, all 16 rooms have terraces with sea views. The restaurant features regional dishes. Open year-round. 15 Via Scalo, Loc. Malfa, Salina (phone: 90-984-4222; fax: 90-984-4102). Moderate.

L'Ariana This old colonial villa now is a quiet, intimate, antiques-filled hotel with 15 rooms and a fine restaurant on the sea. Hotel open year-round; restaurant closed November through February. 11 Via Rotabile, Località Rinella di Leni, Salina (phone: 90-980-9075; fax: 90-980-9250). Hotel, inexpensive; restaurant, moderate.

Delfino Typical island food can be had at this cozy, eight-room pensione on the sea. Open year-round. Via Marina Garibaldi, Località Lingua, Salina (phone: 90-984-3024). Inexpensive.

PANAREA Many Italians consider this, the smallest of the islands, to be the most beautiful—its cliffs of dark volcanic rock a dramatic background for the whitewashed fishing villages. There are few paved roads, but the food is excellent and the scenery breathtaking. The ancestors of today's Panareans settled here thousands of years ago. At Capo Milazzese lie the remains of a prehistoric village with 23 huts. The site is an hour's walk from the town of San Pietro or a short boat ride to Cala Junco. The sea floor here is a vast underwater platform, dotted with shoals and small islets. The largest of these, Basiluzzo, has rosemary and caper plants growing amid the traces of ancient Roman villas. Panarea is a favorite with scuba divers.

BEST EN ROUTE

La Raya Built into a hill, this quiet hotel is the best on the island. Each of the 38 rooms has an expansive terrace and spectacular sea view. Down the hill is a very good alfresco restaurant serving Sicilian fare and a disco (*the* night spot on the island). The architecture is North African—white and salmon walls and arches, reflective of the Egyptian owner's roots. Half board required from mid-July through August. Open May through October. Località San Pietro, Panarea (phone: 90-983013 or 90-983029; fax: 90-983103). Expensive.

Cincotta An excellent little hotel—25 of the 29 rooms overlook the sea—boasting a pool and a restaurant that serves homemade pastries and ice cream. Open *Easter* through September. Località San Pietro, Panarea (phone: 90-983014; fax: 90-983211). Moderate.

Lisca Bianca Here are 25 rooms, all with terraces; most have lovely views of the sea. Small villas are also available. There is a terrace bar. No restaurant, but a *rosticceria* (grill) serves light meals. Open from *Easter* through October. 1 Via Lani, Panarea (phone: 90-983004). Moderate.

La Piazza The most comfortable hotel on the island is surrounded by lovely gardens, with 30 rooms overlooking the sea, a pool, and a simple but good alfresco restaurant. Open April through October. Via San Pietro, Panarea (phone: 90-983154; fax: 90-983003). Moderate.

STROMBOLI Vulcan, the god of fire, is said to have made his home in the mountain here; hence the slow-burning fire of this constantly (though not violently) active volcano. In modern times, it gained short-lived notoriety when in 1949 it served as the trysting spot (and movie title) for the then scandalous liaison between Ingrid Bergman and Roberto Rossellini. The view from the slopes of the volcano is awesome. The ascent from Ficogrande, by foot, is strenuous in its final leg along precipitous pathways but well worth the trek. You must go with a guide. Contact Nino or Antonio (near the *Duomo;* phone: 90-986263 or 90-986211). Groups (minimum of 10 people) leave most afternoons for the seven-hour trip; if the group does not fill up, they drive a hard bargain, and you may be asked to pay extra. The crater emits plumes of volcanic ash and fumes of sulfurous gas. Private boats make trips at night to view the explosions, as well as around the island during the day. Inquire at the port. The Serra Vancori forms the summit. The remains of an ancient volcanic crater, it provides an excellent vantage point. All around the island, beaches of black volcanic sand border the cool, aqua sea.

BEST EN ROUTE

Note: A less expensive alternative to staying in a hotel on Stromboli is renting a room or a house from one of the locals. One choice is Umberto Palino (phone: 90-986026), who offers every type of accommodation, from a room to a villa on the beach.

Puntazzo Excellent fresh fish and pasta dishes, as well as wild rabbit, are the specialties here. A prodigious bar offers 300 labels from around the world.

Closed Mondays except in high season and mid-January to mid-March. Reservations advised. Major credit cards accepted. In Ginostra, on the opposite side of the island from Ficogrande; boat transportation is available, either by hydrofoil or private boat from Ficogrande (phone: 90-981-2464). Expensive.

Barbablu Open year-round, this trattoria serves regional fare and Venetian and local wines. Try the *pennette alla trapanese* (pasta with chopped fresh almonds, garlic, and tomatoes) and the gnocchi with tomatoes and basil. There also are four guestrooms. Closed January. Reservations advised. Major credit cards accepted. 15-17 Via Vittorio Emanuele, Stromboli (phone: 90-986118). Moderate.

La Sciara Quiet, it features 62 rooms, a saltwater pool, a beach, tennis courts, a restaurant, and a lovely park. Six small villas are also available for long- and short-term rental. Open April through October. Via Cincotta, Stromboli (phone: 90-986004; fax: 90-986284). Moderate.

La Sirenetta Park The best on the island, this hotel has sea views, a seawater pool, and wide black beach facilities near its renowned skin diving school. Windsurfing, sailboat, rowboat, and motorboat rentals are also available. All 43 rooms have terraces with seaviews; at press time, 15 guestrooms were being added. There is a very good alfresco restaurant, *La Tartana Club,* across the street. Open April through September. 33 Via Marina, Stromboli (phone: 90-986025; fax: 90-986124). Moderate.

Da Zurro This family-run restaurant, with an outdoor terrace overlooking the beach, serves raw fish antipasto and other nautical specialties caught daily by the Zurros. Closed December through *Easter.* Reservations advised. Major credit cards accepted. Near the port, at 18 Via Marina, Stromboli (phone: 90-98628). Moderate.

ALICUDI AND FILICUDI These two small islands in the western part of the archipelago are well off the tourist track and are a favorite with underwater sports enthusiasts. Not surprisingly, accommodations are scarce, and many who visit come in private boats.

BEST EN ROUTE

Ericusa The only hotel on Alicudi has just 12 rooms and a restaurant. Open June through September. Località Pirciato, Alicudi (phone: 90-988-9902 or 90-988-9910). Moderate to inexpensive.

La Canna With only eight rooms, each offering access to the common terrace, this pensione with a restaurant is beautifully situated above the port. Open year-round. 43 Via Rosa, Filicudi (phone: 90-988-9956; fax: 90-988-9966). Inexpensive.

Glossary

Useful Words
and Phrases

Unlike the French, who have a reputation for being snobbish and brusque if you don't speak their language perfectly, the Italians do not expect you to speak Italian—but are very flattered when you try. In many circumstances, you won't have to, because staffs at most hotels and tourist attractions, as well as at a fair number of restaurants, speak serviceable English, which they are eager to use. Off the beaten track, however, you will find at least a rudimentary knowledge of Italian very helpful. Don't be afraid of misplaced accents or misconjugated verbs—in most cases you will be understood.

You also might consider taking a course in Italian before you go. Language courses are offered at most adult education and community colleges. *Berlitz,* among others, has a series of teach-yourself language courses on audiocassette tapes, available from Macmillan Publishing Co. (100 Front St., Riverside, NJ 08075; phone: 800-257-5755).

The list below of commonly used words and phrases can help get you started.

Greetings and Everyday Expressions

Good morning! (also, Good day!)	*Buongiorno!*
Good afternoon/evening!	*Buona sera!*
Hello!	
(familiar)	*Ciao!*
(on the telephone)	*Pronto!*
How are you?	*Come sta?*
Pleased to meet you!	*Piacere!* or *Molto lieto/a!*
Good-bye!	*Arrivederci!*
(final)	*Addio!*
So long! (familiar)	*Ciao!*
Good night!	*Buona notte!*
Yes!	*Sì!*
No!	*No!*
Please!	*Per favore* or *per piacere!*
Thank you!	*Grazie!*
You're welcome!	*Prego!*
Excuse me!	
(I beg your pardon.)	*Mi scusi!*
(May I get by?; on a bus or in a crowd)	*Permesso!*

I don't speak Italian.	Non parlo italiano.
Do you speak English?	Parla inglese?
Is there someone there who speaks English?	C'è qualcuno che parla inglese?
I don't understand.	Non capisco.
Do you understand?	Capisce?

My name is . . .	Mi chiamo . . .
What is your name?	Come si chiama?
miss	signorina
madame	signora
mister	signor(e)

open	aperto
closed	chiuso
. . . for annual vacation	chiuso per ferie
. . . for weekly day of rest	chiuso per riposo settimanale
. . . for restoration	chiuso per restauro
Is there a strike?	C'è uno sciopero?
Until when?	Fino a quando?

entrance	entrata
exit	uscita
push	spingere
pull	tirare

today	oggi
tomorrow	domani
yesterday	ieri

Checking In

I would like. . .	Vorrei. . .
I have reserved. . .	Ho prenotato. . .
a single room	una camera singola
a double room	una camera doppia
a quiet room	una camera tranquilla
with private bath	con bagno privato
with private shower	con doccia privata
with a sea view	con vista sul mare
with air conditioning	con aria condizionata
with balcony	con balcone/terrazza
for one night	per una notte
for a few days	per qualche giorno
for a week	per una settimana

with full board	*con pensione completa*
with half board	*con mezza pensione*
Does the price include	*Il prezzo comprende*
breakfast	*la prima colazione*
service charge	*servizio*
taxes	*tasse*
May I pay with traveler's checks?	*Posso pagare con assegni (per) viaggiatori?*
Do you accept this credit card?	*Accettate questa carta di credito?*
What time is breakfast served?	*A che ora si serve la prima colazione?*
It doesn't work.	*Non funziona.*

Eating Out

ashtray	*un portacenere*
bottle	*una bottiglia*
chair	*una sedia*
cup	*una tazza*
fork	*una forchetta*
knife	*un coltello*
napkin	*un tovagliolo*
plate	*un piatto*
spoon	*un cucchiaio*
table	*una tavola*
hot cocoa	*una cioccolata calda*
coffee	*un caffè* or *un espresso*
coffee with milk	
(served in a bar with steamed milk)	*un cappuccino*
(usually served at breakfast or at a bar, with warm milk— more than is in a cappuccino)	*un caffè latte*
fruit juice	*un succo di frutta*
lemonade	*una limonata*
mineral water	*acqua minerale*
carbonated	*.gassata*
not carbonated	*non gassata*
orange juice	*la spremuta d'arancia*
orangeade	*un'aranciata*
tea	*un tè*
water	*acqua*

beer	*una birra*
red wine	*vino rosso*
rosé wine	*vino rosato*
white wine	*vino bianco*
cold	*freddo/a*
hot	*caldo/a*
sweet	*dolce*
(very) dry	*(molto) secco*
bacon	*la pancetta*
bread/rolls	*il pane*
butter	*il burro*
eggs	*le uova*
hard-boiled	*uova sode*
poached	*uova affogate/in camicia*
soft-boiled	*uova al latte*
scrambled	*uova strapazzate*
sunny-side up	*uova fritte all'occhio di bue*
honey	*il miele*
jam/marmalade	*la marmellata*
omelette	*la frittata*
pepper	*il pepe*
salt	*il sale*
sugar	*lo zucchero*
Waiter!	*Cameriere!*
I would like. . .	*Vorrei. . .*
a glass of	*un bicchiere di*
a bottle of	*una bottiglia di*
a half bottle of	*una mezza bottiglia di*
a carafe of	*una caraffa di*
a liter of	*un litro di*
a half liter of	*un mezzo litro di*
a quarter liter of	*un quarto di*
The check, please.	*Il conto, per favore.*
Is the service charge included?	*Il servizio è incluso?*

Shopping

bakery	*il panificio*
bookstore	*la libreria*
butcher shop	*la macelleria*
camera shop	*il negozio d'apparecchi fotografici*

delicatessen	*la salumeria/la pizzicheria*
department store	*il grande magazzino*
drugstore (for medicine)	*la farmacia*
grocery	*la drogheria/la pizzicheria*
jewelry store	*la gioielleria*
newsstand	*l'edicola/il giornalaio*
pastry shop	*la pasticceria*
perfume (and cosmetics) store	*la profumeria*
shoestore	*il negozio di scarpe*
supermarket	*il supermercato*
tobacconist	*il tabaccaio*
cheap	*a buon mercato*
expensive	*caro/a*
How much does it cost?	*Quanto costa?*
large	*grande*
larger	*più grande*
too large	*troppo grande*
small	*piccolo/a*
smaller	*più piccolo*
too small	*troppo piccolo*
long	*lungo/a*
short	*corto/a*
antique	*antico/a*
old	*vecchio/a*
new	*nuovo/a*
used	*usato/a*
handmade	*fatto/a a mano*
washable	*lavabile*
What is it made of?	*Di che cosa è fatto/a?*
camel's hair	*pelo di cammello*
cotton	*cotone*
corduroy	*velluto a coste*
lace	*pizzo*
leather	*pelle/cuoio*
linen	*lino*
silk	*seta*
suede	*pelle scamosciata*
synthetic material	*materiale sintetico*
wool	*lana*

brass	*ottone*
bronze	*bronzo*
copper	*rame*
gold	*oro*
gold plate	*placcato d'oro*
silver	*argento*
silver plate	*placcato d'argento*
stainless steel	*acciaio inossidabile*
wood	*legno*

Colors

beige	*beige*
black	*nero/a*
blue	*celeste* or *azzurro/a*
(navy)	*blu*
brown	*marrone*
gray	*grigio/a*
green	*verde*
orange	*arancione*
pink	*rosa*
purple	*viola*
red	*rosso/a*
white	*bianco/a*
yellow	*giallo/a*
dark	*scuro/a*
light	*chiaro/a*

Getting Around

north	*nord*
south	*sud*
east	*est*
west	*ovest*
right	*destra*
left	*sinistra*
straight ahead	*sempre diritto*
far	*lontano/a*
near	*vicino/a*
airport	*l'aeroporto*
bus stop	*la fermata dell'autobus*
gas station	*la stazione di rifornimento/ stazione per benzinaio*
subway	*la metropolitana*
train station	*la stazione ferroviaria*
travel agency	*l'agenzia di viaggi*

map	*una carta geografica*
one-way ticket	*un biglietto di sola andata*
round-trip ticket	*un biglietto di andata e ritorno*
first class	*prima classe*
second class	*seconda classe*
no smoking	*non fumare/divieto di fumare*
track	*il binario*

gasoline (generic reference or leaded gas)	*la benzina*
unleaded gas	*benzina verde* or *benzina senza piombo*
diesel gas	*diesel* or *gasolio*
tires	*le gomme/i pneumatici*
oil	*l'olio*

Fill it up, please. — *Faccia il pieno, per favore.*

Where is . . . ?	*Dov'è . . . ?*
Where are . . . ?	*Dove sono . . . ?*
How many kilometers are we from . . . ?	*A quanti chilometri siamo da . . . ?*
Does this bus go to . . . ?	*Quest'autobus va a . . . ?*
What time does it leave?	*A che ora parte?*

Danger	*Pericolo*
Dead End	*Strada Senza Uscita*
Detour	*Deviazione*
Do Not Enter	*Vietato l'Accesso*
Falling Rocks	*Caduta Massi*
Men Working	*Lavori in Corso*
No Parking	*Divieto di Sosta*
No Passing	*Divieto di Sorpasso*
One Way	*Senso Unico*
Pay Toll	*Pagamento Pedaggio*
Pedestrian Zone	*Zona Pedonale*
Reduce Speed	*Rallentare*
Ring Road	*Raccordo Anulare*
Stop	*Alt*
Use Headlights in Tunnel	*Accendere i Fari in Galleria*
Yield	*Dare la Precedenza*

Personal Items and Services

aspirin	*l'aspirina*
Band-Aids	*i cerotti*

barbershop	*il barbiere*
beauty shop	*l'estetista*
condom	*il preservativo/il profilattico*
dry cleaner	*la tintoria*
hairdresser	*il parucchiere*
laundromat	*la lavanderia automatica*
laundry	*la lavanderia*
post office	*l'ufficio postale*
sanitary napkins	*gli assorbenti igienici*
shampoo	*lo shampoo*
shaving cream	*la schiuma da barba*
shoemaker	*il calzolaio*
soap	*il sapone*
soap powder	*il sapone in polvere*
stamps	*i francobolli*
tampons	*gli assorbenti interni*
tissues	*i fazzoletti di carta*
toilet	*il bagno/il gabinetto/la toletta*
toilet paper	*la carta igienica*
toothbrush	*lo spazzolino da denti*
toothpaste	*il dentifricio*
Where is the men's/ladies' room?	*Dov'è il bagno?*
The door will say:	
for men	*Uomini* or *Signori*
for women	*Donne* or *Signore*
Is it occupied/free?	*E occupato/libero?*

Days of the Week

Monday	*lunedì*
Tuesday	*martedì*
Wednesday	*mercoledì*
Thursday	*giovedì*
Friday	*venerdì*
Saturday	*sabato*
Sunday	*domenica*

Months

January	*gennaio*
February	*febbraio*
March	*marzo*
April	*aprile*
May	*maggio*
June	*giugno*
July	*luglio*
August	*agosto*

September	*settembre*
October	*ottobre*
November	*novembre*
December	*dicembre*

Numbers

zero	*zero*
one	*uno*
two	*due*
three	*tre*
four	*quattro*
five	*cinque*
six	*sei*
seven	*sette*
eight	*otto*
nine	*nove*
ten	*dieci*
eleven	*undici*
twelve	*dodici*
thirteen	*tredici*
fourteen	*quattordici*
fifteen	*quindici*
sixteen	*sedici*
seventeen	*diciassette*
eighteen	*diciotto*
nineteen	*diciannove*
twenty	*venti*
thirty	*trenta*
forty	*quaranta*
fifty	*cinquanta*
sixty	*sessanta*
seventy	*settanta*
eighty	*ottanta*
ninety	*novanta*
one hundred	*cento*
1995	*mille novecento novantacinque*

WRITING RESERVATIONS LETTERS

Restaurant/Hotel Name
Street Address
Postal Code, City
Italy

Dear Sir:	*Caro Signore:*
I would like to reserve a table for (number of) people for lunch/dinner on (day and month), 1995, at (hour) o'clock.	*Vorrei prenotare per il pranzo/la cena un tavolo da* (number) *persone il* (day and month) *alle* (time using the 24-hour clock).
or	or
I would like to reserve a room for (number of) people for (number of) nights from (day and month) to (day and month), inclusive.	*Vorrei prenotare una camera per* (number) *persone per* (number) *notte dal* (day and month) *fino al* (day and month).
and	and
Please confirm the reservation as soon as possible.	*Prego confermare l'avenuta prenotazione al più presto possibile.*
Yours truly,	*Distinti saluti,*
(Signature))	(Signature)

(Print or type your name and address below your signature.)

Climate Chart

Average Temperatures (in °F)

	January	April	July	October
Bologna	30–41	50–64	68–86	54–68
Florence	36–48	46–66	64–86	52–68
Genoa	41–52	52–63	70–81	59–68
Milan	32–41	50–64	68–84	52–63
Naples	39–54	48–64	64–84	54–72
Palermo	46–61	52–68	70–86	61–77
Rome	41–52	50–66	68–86	55–72
Siena	37–45	46–61	64–82	54–59
Taormina	46–57	54–66	72–88	61–73
Trieste	37–45	50–63	68–82	55–64
Turin	28–39	46–64	66–84	48–63
Venice	34–43	50–63	66–81	52–66
Verona	32–43	48–64	63–84	50–64

Index